July 11–15, 2011
New York, NY, USA

Association for Computing Machinery

Advancing Computing as a Science & Profession

DEBS'11

Proceedings of the 5th ACM International Conference on

Distributed Event-Based Systems

Sponsored by:

ACM SIGMOD & ACM SIGSOFT

Supported by:

IBM & Manning Publications

**Association for
Computing Machinery**

Advancing Computing as a Science & Profession

The Association for Computing Machinery
2 Penn Plaza, Suite 701
New York, New York 10121-0701

ISBN: 978-1-4503-0905-9 (Digital)

ISBN: 978-1-4503-1390-2 (Print)

Additional copies may be ordered prepaid from:

ACM Order Department
PO Box 30777
New York, NY 10087-0777, USA

Phone: 1-800-342-6626 (USA and Canada)
+1-212-626-0500 (Global)
Fax: +1-212-944-1318
E-mail: acmhelp@acm.org
Hours of Operation: 8:30 am – 4:30 pm ET

Printed in the USA

Foreword

It is our great pleasure to welcome you to the *Fifth ACM Conference on Distributed Event Based Systems – DEBS'11*. This conference continues the tradition of its four predecessors, and the five editions of the DEBS workshops — each held in conjunction with other major conferences, until it became the flagship conference of an emerging community. This community has been established during recent years and consists of researchers and practitioners who come from the distributed computing area (the "pub/sub" community), the event processing area, various sub-communities of the database area (active databases, data stream management and temporal databases), business process management and programming languages. This community also held two Dagstuhl seminars, and several other shared activities.

The call for papers solicited research contributions in three major umbrella topics: (1) Models, Architectures and Paradigms; (2) Middleware Infrastructures for Event-Based Computing; and (3) Applications, Experiences, and Requirements. The call for contributions to the research track attracted 95 submissions from around the globe. The research program committee accepted 23 papers that cover a variety of topics related to programming paradigms, languages, tools, system considerations, user interfaces, optimization of performance and more. In addition the industry track program committee accepted 10 papers that relate to implementation within event processing platforms and to applications and experience reports.

The conference also includes four keynote talks provided by: Christopher Bird, Donald F. Ferguson, Johannes Gehrke, and Calton Pu, one invited talk by Edward Epstein, and five tutorials, as well as a PhD workshop, poster and demo session, a DEBS challenge session and the first DEBS "gong show".

We thank all our colleagues who volunteered to help with the organization and the program: the organization chairs: Buğra Gedik and Gabriela Jacques-Silva; the web chair: Darko Anicic, the track chairs: Nenad Stojanvic (demos, posters and DEBS challenge), Robert Berry and Mani Chandy (PhD workshop) and Adrian Paschke (tutorials). Thanks also to the ACM staff supporting the conference, and the ACM-Sheridan Processing service orchestrated by Lisa Tolles, for compiling these proceedings. We also thank IBM Research for hosting the conference, and ACM SIGMOD and SIGSOFT for sponsoring the conference.

Last but not least we thank all authors for their submissions, the program committee members and additional reviewers for reviewing the papers, and the conference participants.

We hope that you will find this program interesting and thought-provoking, and that the conference will provide you with a valuable opportunity to share ideas with other researchers and practitioners from institutions around the world.

Opher Etzion
DEBS'11 General Chair

Avigdor Gal and Stan Zdonik
DEBS'11 Research Track Program Chairs

Paul Vincent
DEBS'11 Industry Track Program Chair

David Eyers
DEBS'11 Proceedings Chair

Table of Contents

DEBS'11 Conference Organization ix

DEBS'11 Sponsors & Supporters xi

Keynote Address 1

- **Avoiding He Said/She Said Arguments in Distributed Event Handling Systems** .... n/a
  Christopher Bird *(Progress Software)*

Session 1: Implementation within Event Processing Platforms (Industry Track Session)
Session Chair: Paul Vincent *(TIBCO Software)*

- **A General Extension System for Event Processing Languages** 1
  Alexandre de Castro Alves *(Oracle Corporation)*

- **PRONTO – Support for Real-Time Decision Making** 11
  Pekka Kaarela, Mika Varjola *(Mattersoft Ltd)*, Lucas P. J. J. Noldus *(Noldus Information Technology BV)*,
  Alexander Artikis *(NCSR Demokritos)*

- **Capture Fields: Modularity in a Stream-Relational Event Processing Language** 15
  Naomi Seyfer, Richard Tibbetts, Nathaniel Mishkin *(StreamBase Systems Inc.)*

- **ARCADE – Abstraction and Realization of Complex Event Scenarios Using Dynamic Rule Creation** 23
  Ashish A. Kulkarni *(IBM India Pvt. Ltd.)*

- **Complex Events and Actions to Control Cyber-Physical Systems** 29
  Rüdiger Klein, Jingquan Xie, Andrij Usov *(Fraunhofer, IAIS)*

- **User-Oriented Rule Management for Event-Based Applications** 39
  Hannes Obweger, Josef Schiefer, Martin Suntinger, Peter Kepplinger *(UC4 Senactive Software GmbH)*,
  Szabolcs Rozsnyai *(IBM Thomas J. Watson Research Center)*

Keynote Address 2

- **Distributed Event Based Challenges for Systems and Applications Management** 49
  Donald Francis Ferguson *(CA Technologies, Inc.)*

Session 2: Event-driven Business Process Management
Session Chair: Nenad Stojanovic *(FZI, Karlsruhe)*

- **Business Artifacts with Guard-Stage-Milestone Lifecycles: Managing Artifact Interactions with Conditions and Events** 51
  Richard Hull *(IBM T.J. Watson Research Center)*, Elio Damaggio *(University of California, San Diego)*,
  Riccardo De Masellis *(University of Rome, La Sapienza)*, Fabiana Fournier *(IBM Haifa Research Lab)*,
  Manmohan Gupta *(IBM Global Business Services, India)*,
  Fenno (Terry) Heath, III, Stacy Hobson, Mark Linehan *(IBM T.J. Watson Research Center)*,
  Sridhar Maradugu *(Finsoft Consultants, Inc.)*,
  Anil Nigam, Piwadee (Noi) Sukaviriya, Roman Vaculin *(IBM T.J. Watson Research Center)*

- **Towards Context-Aware Adaptive Fault Tolerance in SOA Applications** 63
  Jonas Buys, Vincenzo De Florio, Chris Blondia *(University of Antwerp)*

- **Discovering Event Correlation Rules for Semi-Structured Business Processes** 75
  Szabolcs Rozsnyai, Aleksander Slominski, Geetika T. Lakshmanan *(IBM T.J. Watson Research Center)*

Keynote Address 3

- **Declarative Data-Driven Coordination** 87
  Johannes Gehrke *(Cornell University & Max Planck Institute for Software Systems)*

Session 3: Event Processing Modeling and Tools
Session Chair: Francois Bry *(LMU University, Munich)*

- **Rapid Detection of Rare Geospatial Events: Earthquake Warning Applications** 89
  Michael Olson, Annie Liu, Matthew Faulkner, K. Mani Chandy *(Caltech)*
- **Pattern Rewriting Framework for Event Processing Optimization** 101
  Ella Rabinovich, Opher Etzion *(IBM Haifa Research Labs)*,
  Avigdor Gal *(Technion – Israel Institute of Technology)*
- **Program Analysis for Event-Based Distributed Systems** 113
  K. R. Jayaram, Patrick Eugster *(Purdue University)*
- **Towards Proactive Event-Driven Computing** 125
  Yagil Engel, Opher Etzion *(IBM Research Israel)*
- **High-Performance Composite Event Monitoring System Supporting Large Numbers of
  Queries and Sources** 137
  SangJeong Lee, Youngki Lee, Byoungjip Kim *(Korea Advanced Institute of Science and Technology)*,
  Kasim Selçuk Candan *(Arizona State University)*, Yunseok Rhee *(Hankuk University of Foreign Studies)*,
  Junehwa Song *(Korea Advanced Institute of Science and Technology)*
- **Controlled English Language for Production and Event Processing Rules** 149
  Mark H. Linehan *(IBM T.J. Watson Research Center)*, Sylvain Dehors *(IBM La Gaude-Sophia Antipolis)*,
  Ella Rabinovich, Fabiana Fournier *(IBM Haifa Research Lab)*

Session 4: Pub/sub and Distributed Infrastructure
Session Chair: Antonio Carzaniga *(University of Lugano)*

- **Disclosure Control in Multi-Domain Publish/Subscribe Systems** 159
  Jatinder Singh *(University of Cambridge)*, David M. Eyers *(University of Otago)*,
  Jean Bacon *(University of Cambridge)*
- **Towards Vulnerability-Based Intrusion Detection with Event Processing** 171
  Amer Farroukh, Mohammad Sadoghi, Hans-Arno Jacobsen *(University of Toronto)*
- **High Performance Content-Based Matching Using GPUs** 183
  Alessandro Margara, Gianpaolo Cugola *(Politecnico di Milano)*
- **NIÑOS Take Five: The Management Infrastructure
  for Distributed Event-Driven Workflows** 195
  Siddarth Ganesan, Young Yoon, Hans-Arno Jacobsen *(University of Toronto)*
- **End-to-End Reliability for Best-Effort Content-Based Publish/Subscribe Networks** 207
  Amirhossein Malekpour, Antonio Carzaniga, Fernando Pedone, Giovanni Toffetti Carughi *(University of Lugano)*
- **Fine-Grained Parallel XML Filtering for Content-Based Publish/Subscribe Systems** 219
  Eberhard Grummt *(bbv Software Services AG)*

Keynote Address 4

- **A World of Opportunities: CPS, LOT, and Beyond** 229
  Calton Pu *(Georgia Institute of Technology)*

Session 5: Streaming Systems
Session Chair: Peter Pietzuch *(Imperial College)*

- **Fault Injection-Based Assessment of Partial Fault Tolerance
  in Stream Processing Applications** 231
  Gabriela Jacques-Silva *(University of Illinois at Urbana-Champaign & T.J. Watson Research Center)*,
  Buğra Gedik, Henrique Andrade, Kun-Lung Wu *(T.J. Watson Research Center)*,
  Ravishankar K. Iyer *(University of Illinois at Urbana-Champaign)*
- **Efficiently Correlating Complex Events Over Live and Archived Data Streams** 243
  Nihal Dindar, Peter M. Fischer, Merve Soner, Nesime Tatbul *(ETH Zurich)*
- **Space-Efficient Tracking of Persistent Items in a Massive Data Stream** 255
  Bibudh Lahiri *(Iowa State University)*, Jaideep Chandrashekar *(Intel Labs Berkeley)*,
  Srikanta Tirthapura *(Iowa State University)*

- **SpamWatcher: A Streaming Social Network Analytic on the IBM Wire-Speed Processor** 267
  Qiong Zou *(IBM Corporation, China Research Lab)*, Buğra Gedik *(IBM Corporation, T.J. Watson Research Center)*,
  Kun Wang *(IBM Corporation, China Research Lab)*

- **Complex Pattern Ranking (CPR): Evaluating Top-k Pattern Queries
  Over Event Streams** 279
  Xinxin Wang, K. Selçuk Candan *(Arizona State University)*, Junehwa Song *(Korea Advanced Institute of
  Science and Technology)*

- **Complex Event Pattern Detection Over Streams
  with Interval-Based Temporal Semantics** 291
  Ming Li *(Silicon Valley Laboratory, IBM Corporation)*, Murali Mani *(University of Michigan-Flint)*,
  Elke A. Rundensteiner *(Worcester Polytechnic Institute)*, Tao Lin *(Amitive)*

Session 6: Event Processing Applications – Experience Reports (Industry Track Session)
Session Chair: Alex Alves *(Oracle)*

- **An Intelligent Event-Driven Approach for Efficient Energy Consumption in Commercial
  Buildings: Smart Office Use Case** 303
  Nenad Stojanovic *(FZI, Research Center for Information Technology)*, Dejan Milenovic *(NovelTech)*,
  Yongchun Xu, Ljiljana Stojanovic, Darko Anicic, Rudi Studer *(FZI, Research Center for Information Technology)*

- **A Complex Event Processing Architecture for Energy and Operation Management:
  Industrial Experience Report** 313
  Jimi Y. C. Wen, Gu Yuan Lin, Today Sung, Minsiong Liang, Gary Tsai, Ming Whei Feng, Chien Ming Wu
  (Institute for Information Industry)

- **A Paradigm Comparison for Collecting TV Channel Statistics
  from High-Volume Channel Zap Events** 317
  Pål Evensen, Hein Meling *(University of Stavanger)*

- **Securely Disseminating RFID Events** 327
  Florian Kerschbaum *(SAP Research)*

Session 7: Middleware
Session Chair: Aniruddha Gokhale *(Vanderbilt University)*

- **Distributed Middleware Reliability and Fault Tolerance Support in System S** 335
  Rohit Wagle *(IBM T.J. Watson Research Center)*, Henrique Andrade *(Goldman Sachs)*,
  Kirsten Hildrum, Chitra Venkatramani, Michael Spicer *(IBM T.J. Watson Research Center)*

- **Scheduling for Real-Time Mobile MapReduce Systems** 347
  Adam J. Dou *(University of California, Riverside)*, Vana Kalogeraki *(Athens University of Economics and Business)*,
  Dimitrios Gunopulos *(University of Athens)*, Taneli Mielikäinen, Ville Tuulos *(Nokia Research Center)*

Tutorials

- **Processing Flows of Information: From Data Stream to Complex Event Processing** 359
  Alessandro Margara, Gianpaolo Cugola *(Politecnico di Milano)*

- **Event Processing Grand Challenges** 361
  Pedro Bizarro *(University of Coimbra)*, K. Mani Chandy *(California Institute of Technology)*,
  Nenad Stojanovic *(Karlsruhe Institute of Technology)*

- **Architectural and Functional Design Patterns for Event Processing** 363
  Paul Vincent *(TIBCO Software Inc.)*, Alexandre Alves *(Oracle Corporation)*, Catherine Moxey *(IBM)*,
  Adrian Paschke *(Freie Universität Berlin)*

- **Non Functional Properties of Event Processing** 365
  Opher Etzion, Ella Rabinovich, Inna Skarbovsky *(IBM Haifa Research)*

- **Hybrid Programming Abstraction for e-Science Workflows and Event Processing** 367
  Chathura Herath, Beth Plale *(Indiana University)*

DEBS Challenge

- **DEBS Challenge** 369
  Nenad Stojanovic *(FZI Karlsruhe)*

Demos

- **Demo: Distributed Event Processing for Activity Recognition** 371
  Visalakshmi Suresh, Paul Ezhilchelvan, Paul Watson, Cuong Pham, Dan Jackson, Patrick Olivier
  (Newcastle University)

- **Demo: fpga-ToPSS – Line-speed Event Processing on FPGAs** 373
  Mohammad Sadoghi, Harsh Singh, Hans-Arno Jacobsen *(University of Toronto)*

- **Demo: Complex Event Pattern Evolution Based on Real-Time Execution Statistics** 375
  Sinan Sen, Ruofeng Lin, Bijan Fahimi Shemrani *(FZI, Research Center for Information Technology)*

- **Demo: Altibase DSM: CTable for Pull-based Processing in SPE** 377
  Jaemyung Kim, Vladimir Verjovkin, Sergey A. Fedorov, Younghun Kim, Dae-Il Kim,
  Sungjin Kim *(Altibase Corporation)*, Sang-Won Lee *(Sungkyunkwan University)*

- **Demo: Efficient Energy Consumption in a Smart Office Based
  on Intelligent Complex Event Processing** 379
  Yongchun Xu, Ljiljana Stojanovic, Jun Ma, Darko Anicic *(FZI, Research Center for Information Technology)*

- **Demo: eQoSystem – Supporting Fluid Distributed Service-Oriented Workflows** 381
  Vinod Muthusamy, Young Yoon, Mohammad Sadoghi, Hans-Arno Jacobsen *(University of Toronto)*

- **Demo: A Scenario and Design Pattern Based Tool for Modeling and Evaluating
  Implementations of Event-based Reactive Systems** 383
  Vojislav D. Radonjic, Soheila Bashardoust, Jean-Pierre Corriveau, Dave Arnold *(Carleton University)*

Posters

- **Poster: Cost Analysis for Complex In-Network Event Processing in Heterogeneous
  Wireless Sensor Networks** 385
  Mumraiz Khan Kasi, Annika Hinze *(University of Waikato)*

- **Poster: Collaboration Pattern Assistant: An Event-Driven Tool for Supporting Pattern-
  Based Collaborations** 387
  Nikos Papageorgiou, Yiannis Verginadis *(National Technical University of Athens)*,
  Dimitris Apostolou *(University of Piraeus)*, Gregoris Mentzas *(National Technical University of Athens)*

- **Poster: SIP-Based QoS Support and Session Management for DDS-Based Distributed
  Real-time and Embedded Systems** 389
  Akram Hakiri, Pascal Berthou, Thierry Gayraud *(Université de Toulouse)*,
  Aniruddha Gokhale, Joe Hoffert, Douglas C. Schmidt *(Vanderbilt University)*

- **Poster: Representing Events in a Clinical Environment: A Case Study** 391
  Leendert W. M. Wienhofen, Andreas D. Landmark *(Norwegian University of Science and Technology)*

- **Poster: Efficient and Cost-Aware Operator Placement in Heterogeneous Stream-
  Processing Environments** 393
  Michael Daum, Frank Lauterwald, Philipp Baumgärtel, Niko Pollner, Klaus Meyer-Wegener
  (University of Erlangen-Nürnberg)

- **Poster: A Capacity Planning Framework for Event Brokers in Intelligent
  Transportation Cyber Physical Systems** 395
  Laura K. Poff, Mark P. McDonald, Aniruddha S. Gokhale *(Vanderbilt University)*

- **Poster: Towards an Adaptive Event Dissemination Middleware for MMVEs** 397
  Thomas Fischer, Johannes Held, Frank Lauterwald, Richard Lenz *(University of Erlangen-Nuremberg)*

- **Poster: DejaVu – A Complex Event Processing System for Pattern Matching
  Over Live and Historical Data Streams** 399
  Nihal Dindar, Peter M. Fischer, Nesime Tatbul *(ETH Zurich)*

- **Poster: Towards an Inexact Semantic Complex Event Processing Framework** 401
  Qunzhi Zhou, Yogesh Simmhan, Viktor Prasanna *(University of Southern California)*

- **Poster: Large-Scale, Situation-Driven and Quality-Aware Event Marketplace: The
  Concept, Challenges and Opportunities** 403
  Roland Stühmer, Nenad Stojanovic *(FZI Forschungszentrum Informatik)*

Author Index

Author Index 405

DEBS 2011 Conference Organization

General Chair: Opher Etzion *(IBM Research, Israel)*

Program Chairs – Research Track: Avigdor Gal *(Technion – Israel Institute of Technology, Israel)*
Stan Zdonik *(Brown University, USA)*

Program Chair – Industry Track: Paul Vincent *(TIBCO Software LTD, UK)*

Proceedings Chair: David Eyers *(University of Otago, NZ)*

Local Arrangements Chairs: Buğra Gedik *(IBM Research, USA)*
Gabriela Jacques-Silva *(IBM Research, USA)*

Tutorial Chair: Adrian Paschke *(FU Berlin, Germany)*

Demo and Poster Chair: Nenad Stojanvic *(FZI Karlsruhe, Germany)*

PhD Workshop Chairs: Robert Berry *(Aston University, UK)*
K. Mani Chandy *(Caltech, USA)*

Web Chair: Darko Anicic *(FZI Karlsruhe, Germany)*

Program Committee: Alia Abdelmoty *(Cardiff University, UK)*
Karl Aberer *(EPFL, Switzerland)*
Raman Adaikkalavan *(Indiana University South Bend, USA)*
Alex Alves *(Oracle Inc., USA)*
Henrique Andrade *(The Goldman Sachs Group, Inc., USA)*
Alexander Artikis *(NCSR "Demokritos," Greece)*
Jean Bacon *(University of Cambridge, UK)*
Umesh Bellur *(IIT Bombay, India)*
Francois Bry *(LMU München, Germany)*
Alejandro Buchmann *(TU Darmstadt, Germany)*
Antonio Carzaniga *(University of Lugano, Switzerland)*
Ugur Cetintemel *(Brown University, USA)*
Sharma Chakravarthy *(University of Texas at Arlington, USA)*
Badrish Chandramouli *(Microsoft Research, USA)*
Gregory Chockler *(IBM Research, Israel)*
Oscar Corcho *(Politecnica de Madrid, Spain)*
Gianpaolo Cugola *(Politecnico di Milano, Italy)*
Ernesto Damiani *(University of Milan, Italy)*
Schahram Dustdar *(TU Vienna, Austria)*
Alvaro A. A. Fernandes *(University of Manchester, UK)*
Ludger Fiege *(Siemens, Germany)*
Christof Fetzer *(University of Dresden, Germany)*
Michael Franklin *(UC Berkeley, USA)*
Buğra Gedik *(IBM Research, USA)*
Aniruddha Gokhale *(Vanderbilt University, USA)*

DEBS 2011 Sponsors & Supporters

Sponsors:

Supporters:

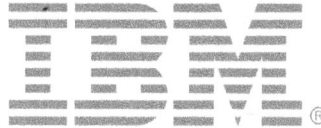

A General Extension System for Event Processing Languages

Alexandre de Castro Alves
Oracle Corporation
300 Oracle Parkway, Redwood Shores, CA USA
+1-650-607-0878

alex.alves@oracle.com

ABSTRACT

Event processing languages (EPLs) for Complex Event Processing (CEP) systems are descriptive in nature. This allows the authoring of event processing applications at a higher level of abstraction. However, they are less suitable for dealing with low-level tasks, such as String manipulation, and other programming-in-the-small problems. In addition, current EPL implementations lack the richness of other programming language libraries (e.g. Java), which have been built over several years of usage. We present an architecture whereby providers can integrate existing programming languages into CQL, our EPL language of choice, leveraging the advantages of other languages, while still retaining the expressiveness and conciseness of EPL. We also demonstrate how the architecture avoids the awkwardness of previous integration solutions, which generally were focused only at the function-level (e.g. User-Defined Functions, Java call-outs). Rather, the outlined solution is realized at the language level, through the extension of language implementation artifacts, such as type systems; thus resulting in a seamless, precise, and naturally blended environment for developing CEP applications. The architecture is based upon the concept of extension cartridges, which are modules that provide metadata describing the extensions. Finally, we show how these extension cartridges may be used in real-world CEP scenarios.

Categories and Subject Descriptors

D.3.3 [**Programming Languages**]: Language Contructs and Features – *abstract data types* --- *SQL, CQL, Java, Spatial*

General Terms: Languages

Keywords

CEP, CQL, JAVA, PROGRAMMING-IN-THE-SMALL

1. INTRODUCTION

In section two, we start by presenting the scenario of an event-processing application that interacts with general-purpose libraries to perform miscellaneous (programming-in-the-small) tasks. This

scenario helps us establish the requirements of the problem that we are addressing in this paper.

In section three, we present different known approaches that are being employed today for implementing the proposed scenario. We do so using Oracle CQL, however other EPL could have been used without loss of generality. We describe several disadvantages that these existing approaches have, and in light of these propose a new approach to solving the scenario, outlining its advantages.

In section four, we describe the architecture used to implement the new approach, which we denominate the *extensible language framework*.

In section five, we explain how the EPL and its extensions are used together seamlessly, following which in section six we describe the service provider interface for the extensible language framework itself.

In section seven, we provide the implementation of an industry use-case that makes use of the extensible language framework.

In section eight, we briefly elaborate on some of the details related to indexing and how they relate to the extensions.

Finally, in section nine, we conclude the paper, followed by discussing some of the related work in the area, and how it differs from the solution suggested in this paper.

2. SCENARIO

Consider a CEP application that is attempting to correlate sales of certain items to regional event news. For example, the result of a sport event may influence the sales of the winning team's merchandizes; or prolonged bad weather may increase the sales of weather-related items, such as umbrellas and raincoats. The goal of the CEP application is to determine which news events generate more sales, and which ones don't. Or, at a better instance, to quantify how much of a situation is needed to change the local spending behavior. For example, how many days of bad weather is needed to cause an increase on the average sales of umbrellas.

In this use-case, we can identify two sources of events, in other words, event streams. These are the *news* stream, and the *sales* stream. The news stream is unstructured in nature and is thus defined by a single *message* property of type *String*. The following event type defines the *sales* stream:

- item_description: String

- category: String

- location: String

- price: floating number

For our purpose, the *location* property specifies the city and state, comma-separated, where the item was sold. Following we have an instance of an event conforming to this type:

{item_description: "raincoat", category: "cloth", location: "San Francisco, CA", price: 10.5}

As stated previously, our object is to correlate a news event to a sales event. To achieve this, the first step is to define our window of interest. Let's set the window of time to 1 day using CQL:

```
SELECT * FROM
news [RANGE 24 HOURS],
sales [RANGE 24 HOURS]
WHERE …
```

Next, we need to define how the events will be correlated. To begin with, let's naively use the location to correlate the events. However, this presents itself as a problem: the news event does not have a *location* property that can be used for *joining*. One solution is to search for a String in the news message that represents the two-letter acronym of a state, and use this sub-string as the join criteria. For the String search, we are only interested on whole-words that are uppercase. For example, ", CA" should match, whereas "caveat" or "CATEGORY" should not.

This type of String search is easily done with regular expressions. For example, the following pattern matches any two-letter uppercase String separated by a blank space or punctuations:

"[.,;][A-Z][A-Z][.,;]"

Regular expressions is a common feature of most programming languages. For example, the following code fragment does exactly this using the Java programming language [16]:

```
Matcher matcher =
Pattern.compile("[.,; ][A-Z][A-Z][.,; ]").matcher(message);
if (matcher.find()) {
  System.out.println("Location = "
    + message.substring(matcher.start() + 1,
    matcher.end() - 1));
}
```

Moreover, Java and other commonly used programming languages today in the market are feature rich; they support a wide spectrum of libraries, ranging from regular expression matchers, XML parsers, message transport and socket implementations, date formatting and handling utilities, String manipulation tools, etc. These libraries are ideal for *programming-in-the-small* [20], that is, code that do simple tasks that contribute towards the overall program's objective, but is not part of the main program structure, design, or architecture.

Conversely, event-processing languages tend to focus on event processing-related verbs and subjects, such as the definition of the streaming window, as seen in Figure 1, and as such work at a higher level of abstraction, generally not being adequate for simple tasks and general-purpose code.

It is true that some EPL do have support for regular expressions, however this is generally in the form of a Boolean match, and wouldn't work in this scenario where the actual matched String (e.g. "CA") is needed.

As it can be concluded from the scenario, there is a need to be able to leverage these general-purpose libraries that are common today in the context of the EPLs. In the next section, we consider different ways to achieve this.

3. BLENDING LANGUAGES
Historically, the way used to invoke an external library is through the definition of user-defined functions (UDF).

3.1 User-Defined Functions
A UDF is a function defined by the application-writer that wraps some implementation code. In most cases, the implementation code must be authored using the platform's native language. For example, the CEP platform evaluated in this paper is implemented in Java; therefore a UDF in CQL is likewise implemented in Java, as demonstrated next:

```
create function statematcher(msg char) return char
as language java instance "javaMatcher"
```

This statement defines a function with the adequate signature and associates the Java instance "javaMatcher" as its implementation, which must provide a *Object execute(Object[] args)* method:

```
public class JavaMatcher implements SingleElementFunction
{
  private Pattern pattern;

  public JavaMatcher()
  {
    pattern = Pattern.compile("[.,; ][A-Z][A-Z][.,; ]");
  }

  @Override
  public Object execute(Object[] args) throws UDFException
  {
    String ret = null;
    String msg = (String) args[0];

    Matcher matcher =
      pattern.matcher(msg);

    if (matcher.find()) {
      ret = msg.substring(matcher.start() + 1,
        matcher.end() - 1);
    }

    return ret;
  }
}
```

This approach has the following disadvantages:

1. Every library usage must be wrapped by a UDF signature. This is counter-productive. Consider that the String class alone has over 50 public methods, which would have to be wrapped.

2. UDFs are by their very nature solely defined as functions, lacking the flexibility and abstraction provided by object-oriented types, containing constructors, methods, and fields.

3. It lacks a seamless integration between the hosting event-processing language and the implementation language of the UDF. For example, no support for casting, etc.

4. UDF is implemented using the platform's native programming language. For example, one would not be able to implement a UDF in C when running on a Java platform, without incurring the (productive) costs of

extending the platform itself (i.e. Java Native Interface - JNI).

An alternative approach to using UDF is to use the general-purpose library in the *action handler* of the EPL statement.

3.2 Action Handlers

The action handler of an EPL statement is the code *that is called back* when a *match* happens. This code is responsible for handling the matched event. For example, by sending the matched event to some external system through a messaging infrastructure.

In the CEP platform used, the action handler is implemented as Java objects outside of the declarative section that contains the specification of the CQL statements. In other words, one can visualize this CEP application as a graph of two nodes, the first node contains the CQL statements and defines the matching logic, the second node, which is downstream to the first node, contains the Java class that implements the action logic. The second node is trigged only when the first node finds a match. This graph of sorts is known as the event-processing network (EPN).

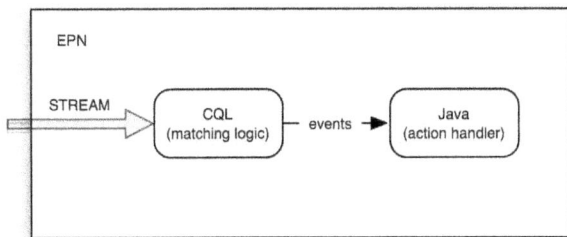

Figure 1. EPN containing Java code as an action handler

To implement our scenario using this approach, we would have to let the events pass-through and implement the matching logic in the Java code

SELECT * FROM news[RANGE 24 HOURS]

This is so because we would not be able to leverage the Java code directly in the WHERE clause. This is highly undesirable, as we would not be exploiting the declarative nature of the EPL.

For other EPLs, the action handler is coded as the right-hand-side in the EPL statement itself. In other words, the left-hand-side defines the match, and the right-hand-side defines the action. Nonetheless, in spite of the collocation of the matching and action logic, this approach is in essence similar to the previous approach employed where the action handler is part of a separate EPN node. This is so because there is still a clear delimitation between the matching and handler code, both in terms of the programming language used and the lifecycle of the entities involved. In other words, the action handles is still a separate code, implemented using a different language. This is demonstrated with the following example using a hypothetical event-processing language:

```
NEWS(message) AND SALES(location) :=
Matcher matcher =
  Pattern.compile("[.,; ][A-Z][A-Z][.,; ]").matcher(message);
  if (matcher.find()) { ... }
```

Although the action handler approach does not require a wrapping of the general-purpose libraries as the UDF approach does require, the action handler approach still yields several disadvantages, such as:

1. The EPL (i.e. matching logic) and the action handlers don't share context. This makes it hard to share parameters and results. For example, in our scenario, we would not be able to use the action handler logic directly within the WHERE clause of the CQL statement.

2. There is still no blending between the EPL and the action handler's programming languages. In other words, the user is clearly using two different languages, which entails on a less cohesive development environment.

What is needed is an approach that blends the languages, allowing the application writer to leverage both the declarative approach of the EPL together with the feature-rich libraries of other programming languages. In the next section, we propose a solution that addresses this.

3.3 Extensible Language Framework

Consider the following CQL statements that implements our scenario in question:

```
CREATE VIEW filtered_news(message, matcher) AS
SELECT message,
  Pattern.compile("[.,; ][A-Z][A-Z][.,; ]").matcher(message)
FROM news [RANGE 24 HOURS]

SELECT location, item_description, message
FROM filtered_news, sales[RANGE 24 HOURS]
WHERE matcher.find() = true AND
  news.message.substring(matcher.start() + 1,
  matcher.end() - 1) = sales.location
```

Let's investigate this in parts. We begin with the definition of a view that receives the news stream and generates a relation containing the last 24 hours of news messages and a matcher pattern object. The latter expression is the one that is subject of interest to us:

```
Pattern.compile("[.,; ][A-Z][A-Z][.,; ]").matcher(message)
```

This expression is invoking the static method *compile(String)* from the Java class *java.util.regex.Pattern*, following which it invokes the method *matcher(String)* on the object of the class *Pattern* that was returned from the *compile()* method. The return object from the method *matcher()* is stored as the attribute *matcher* of the generated relation represented by the view definition:

```
CREATE VIEW filtered_news(message, matcher)
```

Next, we use the *matcher* object to perform the join criteria between the *NEWS* stream and the *SALES* stream:

```
WHERE matcher.find() = true AND
  news.message.substring(matcher.start() + 1,
  matcher.end() - 1) = sales.location
```

In particular, we invoke several methods from the Java class *Matcher*, such as *find(), start(),* and *end()*. Note how the methods *start()* and *end()* need to be invoked on the same object that is being invoked the method *find()*, otherwise they will raise an illegal state exception. Next, we invoke the method *String.substring()*, using the return from the previous methods as arguments after evaluating a simple mathematical expression (e.g. + 1). The result from the *substring*() method is used as the join criteria together with the sales location.

Let's consider another example, where the user sends a message to an external system with the result. In this case, we are using the Java Message Service (JMS) [21] as the messaging infrastructure.

```
SELECT
  ApplicationTopicPublisher.getSingleton().
  publish(TextMessage(message))
...
```

In this case, we first invoke the constructor *TextMessage(String)* for the class *TextMessage*, passing to it the *message* attribute. Then we retrieve the singleton *TopicPublisher* object using the static method *ApplicationTopicPublisher.getSingleton()* and invoke its *publish()* method to send the message.

In the first example, we only used classes provided by the Java runtime environment, such as *String* and *Pattern*. In the second example, notice how we reference the class *ApplicationTopicPublisher*, which is being provided by the CEP application itself.

This set of examples show cases a tight integration between the EPL, which we denominate the *extensible language*, and the Java programming language, which we call the *extension language*. We shall call the overall approach here outlined as the *extensible language framework*.

All in all, the approach used in this section yields the following advantages:

1. No wrapping is needed to reference the general-purpose libraries. For example, the *Pattern* class is used directly.

2. There is a natural blending between the EPL and the language used to handle the general-purpose library. For example, the expression *"news.message.substring()"* nests the reference to a method (i.e. substring) of an attribute (i.e. message) of an stream (i.e. news).

3. Even though the examples restrict themselves to using Java as the extension language, the underlying architecture allows for any programming language to be used, and not just that of the hosting platform (as we shall see in the next section).

4. Types between the extensible and the extension languages are converted seamlessly, thus allowing the support for overloading, overriding and casting. In addition, one is able to use the extension language (e.g. Java) anywhere in the extensible language (e.g. EPL), including in the WHERE clause, thus possibly participating in a join criteria.

In the next section we explore the architecture used to implement this approach.

4. ARCHITECTURE

To be able to achieve a tight integration between the programming languages, they must share a common set of underlying concepts.

Upon close investigation of the examples provided in the previous section, one commonality that exists between both the extensible and extension language is that of attribute *types*. For example, the expression "matcher.find()" can be re-phrased as the invocation of an instance method on the complex type associated to the stream attribute *matcher*. Likewise, the expression "Pattern.compile(…)" is

indeed the invocation of an static method on the complex type *Pattern*. Furthermore, the expression "matcher.start() + 1" can be implemented as the conversion of the extension simple type *INT* (from the Java programming language) into the equivalent extensible native type *INTEGER* present in CQL.

In other words, all extension types have some mapping into the extensible language. However, this must be done in such a way that the extensible language does not need to know about any of the implementation details of the extension, but rather only needs to know enough to *make use of it*. Otherwise we would be duplicating the extension language within the extensible language.

In addition, the extension languages are handled as plug-ins of the extensible language. That is, the extensible language provides a registry, which must be used by any extension language that wishes to participate in the framework. This is similar to any other plug-in framework, such as the one provided by the OSGi service platform [19].

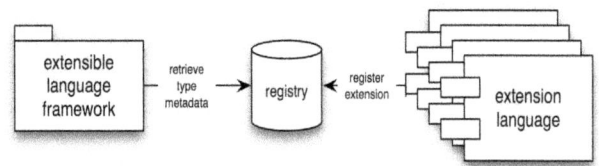

Figure 2 Plug-in architecture for extensible language framework

Let's look at the details of an example.

Consider the expression "Pattern.compile(…)". When the extensible language parses this expression, it breaks it into two identifiers, *Pattern* and *compile*. Next, it must find what kind of identifier the word "Pattern" represents. To do so, first it checks if there is any attribute named *Pattern* in any of the streams being used by the statement. If this check fails, the next check is to find if there is any type named *Pattern* in either the extensible language (e.g. CQL) or any of the plugged-in extension languages (e.g. Java). For this particular case, let's consider that the only extension language that has been plugged-in is the Java extension language. There is no type called *Pattern* in CQL, however the Java extension language does contain a type called *Pattern*, whose metadata is returned to the extensible language. Having retrieved the metadata for the identifier "Pattern" successfully, we can now move to the next identifier, the word "compile()". We know that "compile()" is a method invocation, because of the parentheses, likewise we know that it must be a member of the type represented by the previous identifier, because of the '.' operator. Hence, we check for the following conditions in the metadata returned for the identifier "Pattern":

- The metadata must be of a complex type (as opposed to a simple type).

- The metadata must contain a method whose name is "compile" and takes as parameter the type *String*.

If these conditions are met, the expression is found to be semantically correct. The final step is to handle the runtime invocation of an extension type. We do this by retrieving a function reference from the type's metadata for any of its members that are executable. For example, considering our previous case, the extensible language retrieves from the complex type *Pattern* a function reference that represents the execution of the method *compile()*. This function reference is then used later during the runtime processing of events by the CQL runtime environment. In other words, we use the concept of a function as the abstraction for a runtime executable component within our extensible language framework. This plays well, as a function is indeed the lowest denominator of other executable components, such as methods and constructors. For example, a method can be converted into a function whose first argument is the 'this' pointer for the method's object instance. In addition, functions are passable of being optimized in the query plan generated for the EPL (e.g. CQL) statements.

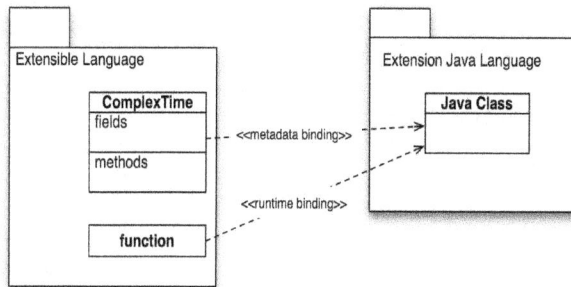

Figure 3 Extensible Language bindings to Java

Finally, it is noteworthy to highlight how the extensible language does not need to know any of the implementation details of the extension language. The extensible language framework only needs to know about the metadata of (complex) types, and how to generically invoke functions.

5. THE API

The extensible language framework described here has been implemented in Oracle CEP.

The implementation consists of changes to several modules of the CEP system, crossing several layers of the product, such as the following ones:

1. Parser module
2. Semantic Analyzer module
3. Registry module
4. Code Generation module
5. Runtime Code Executor module

However, from a user's perspective, the notable differences are modifications to the CQL language, or more precisely, to its grammar.

Specifically, the grammar is changed to support the following two concepts:

☐ Complex Types

☐ Links

These two important concepts are described next.

5.1 Complex Types

As it can be extrapolated from the Java based examples employed in the previous sections, the concept of an abstract type is a useful encapsulation mechanism for programming languages, one that is commonly materialized as *Classes* by object oriented languages. Therefore, to facilitate integration to popular languages, such as the Java programming language, we introduce support for complex types in CQL.

A complex type in CQL is a structured type made of the collection of other components. These components are called attributes (i.e. fields), and may be typed as either complex or simple. CQL supports the simple types one would generally expect, such as INT, BIGINT, BIGDECIMAL, FLOAT, DOUBLE, BYTE, STRING, BOOLEAN, as well as the perhaps less common (application) types of TIMESTAMP, INTERVAL, and XML.

The syntax for accessing a complex type's attribute is:

l-value '.' type-attribute-name

For example, consider the following expression:

SELECT S1.a1.f1 FROM S1

In this case, *S1.a1* is referencing to the attribute *a1* of the stream *S1*, which is of type complex. Next, *a1.f1* is referencing to the field *f1* of the object (l-value) represented by *a1*. As the identifier *S1* is optional in this query, the example can be re-arranged to:

SELECT a1.f1 FROM S1

Furthermore, a CQL complex type may also define methods and constructors for manipulating the objects of these types. The syntax for invoking methods and constructors is similar to that of most other object-oriented languages. Following up with the previous example, let's say that *S1.a1* is of type *java.lang.String*. In this case, the next example demonstrates how to invoke a method in the stream's attribute *a1*:

SELECT a1.f1.toString() FROM S1

Invoking a complex type's constructor creates a new stream attribute of the type, as in the following example:

SELECT java.lang.String("foo") as a1 FROM S1

That is, a new object of type *String* is created and associated as the value of the attribute "a1" of the output stream of the query.

Complex types can be used in any CQL clause that is able to handle stream attributes. In other words, complex types can be used not only as part of the *selection* list, but also in *where* predicates, *order by* lists, etc.

Next, we take a look at the concept of links.

5.2 Links

Types can be defined by metadata. For example, the metadata of the type *java.lang.String* says that the type is a class, containing the method *toString()*, amongst other methods and constructors.

Types are not the only construct that can be defined by metadata. For example, the native CQL function *'to_float(int): float'* is defined by a metadata that states that it takes a *int* argument, and returns a *float*. A function's metadata may even include the actual code to be executed when such function is invoked.

In the case of our extension framework, the metadata of the extensions need to be provided by the extension system itself and not by the native CEP implementation. For example, let's consider the Java class *String* used in the previous examples. When the Semantic Analyzer reaches the expression "f1.toString()", it needs to retrieve the type's metadata for the attribute *f1* and check if it contains the definition of a *toString()* method. In other words, the expression "f1.toString()" needs to be type checked appropriately.

However, who owns the definition of the Java type *String*? The native CEP implementation knows nothing of Java, or of any other programming language, it only knows of the native CQL types and functions.

It is the role of links to point to the location of the metadata of the extensions. A link is defined as an identifier used in combination with the '@' character and placed as a suffix of an extension's name. For example, the following expression informs the CEP system (i.e. the extensible framework) that the extension type *String* lives in the Java system:

> SELECT java.lang.String@java("foo") as a1 FROM S1

Other examples of expressions with links are:

> my-extension-function@@external-system("arguments")
> contain@spatial(shape1, shape2, dist)

In summary, a link ties an extension type or function to its metadata providing system. This metadata is retrieved by the Registry module and used by the Semantic Analyzer module to type check the expressions. Following, the Code Generation module uses the metadata to generate the proper instructions to be executed at runtime by the Runtime Code Executor module. This is described in Figure 4.

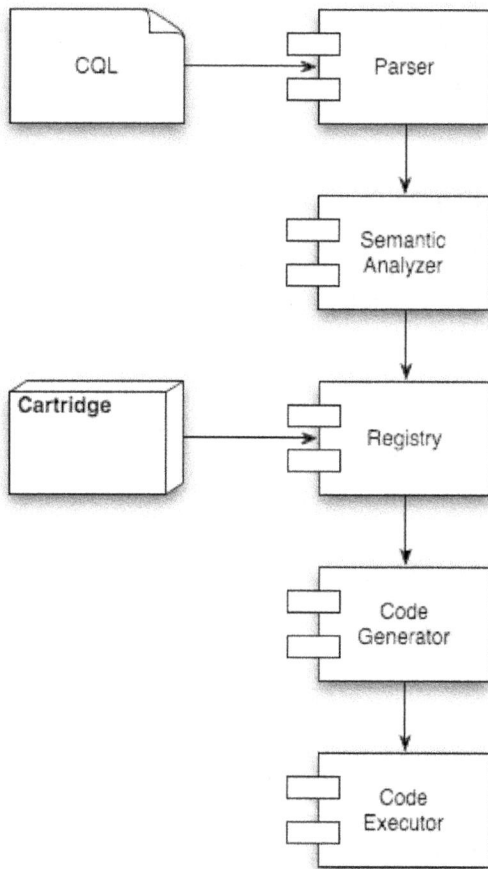

Figure 4 CEP layered modules and cartridge interaction

By default, if no link is specified, then the CEP system assumes that the Java extension module defines the extension. Therefore, the following two expressions are identical:

> SELECT java.lang.String("foo") as a1 FROM S1
> SELECT java.lang.String@java("foo") as a1 FROM S1

There is no need to specify the link if the l-value in question is already associated to a particular extension system. For example, in the expression "SELECT a1.toString() ...", there is no need to specify the location of *toString()* metadata, as it is clear that it is a method defined by the complex type of the attribute *a1*. However, if the l-value does not provide this information, then the specification of the link is mandatory. This is the case of the invocation of a static method.

Having understood how a user makes use of CQL language extensions, our next task is to understand how vendors can plug-in new extension systems. This is the subject of the next section.

6. THE SERVICE PROVIDER INTERFACE

As we have seen previously, the CEP system allows extension types and functions to be used in its EPL. The extension systems that provide the metadata for the extensions types and functions are called *CEP cartridges*.

CEP cartridges are registered in a global Cartridge Registry. The key used in this registry is the link name. For example, the literal "java" is used as the key for the Java CEP cartridge. This means that when an extension is used with the link "@java", the CEP system expects the Java CEP cartridge to provide the needed metadata for the extension in question.

Vendors may register their own CEP cartridges. All cartridges must implement the following (pseudo) interface:

```
Cartridge
{
    TypeLocator getTypeLocator();
    FunctionMetadataLocator getFunctionMetadaLocator();
    IndexInfoLocator getIndexInfoLocator();
    //...
}
```

As evident, the role of the cartridge is to locate the proper metadata for its extensions.

The *TypeLocator* interface is defined as:

```
TypeLocator
{
    Type getType(String extensionName);
    // ...
}
```

For example, to locate the definition of the extension type *java.lang.String*, the CEP system finds the cartridge for the implicit "java" link, and then invokes the method *TypeLocator.getType("java.lang.String")* of the Java cartridge.

The interface *Type* can be casted to *ComplexType*, which is defined as:

```
ComplexType
{
    MethodMetadata getMethod(String name,
                Type... params);
    AttributeMetadata getAttribute(String name);
    ConstructorMetadata getConstructor(String name,
    Type... params);
    //...
}
```

Next, let's drill down in the metadata of a method:

6

```
MethodMetadata
{
    Type[] getParameterTypes();
    Type getReturnType();
    Method getImplementation();
    //...
}
```

Finally, we need to define the implementation of the method itself:

```
Method
{
    Object invoke(Object target, Object [] args)
}
```

Although this may seem very similar to Java's reflection API, the reader should keep in mind that a CEP cartridge is working at a higher level of abstraction, therefore method metadata may be provided for non-Java types. For example, one may implement a Hadoop CEP cartridge, providing metadata for Hadoop's Bag (complex) type. In addition, a CEP cartridge also allows one to define non-Java concepts, such as function metadata, and as we shall see in following sections, extensible indexes.

At the time of writing, several CEP cartridges have been developed, some of which are provided by default in the Oracle CEP product:

☐ Java CEP cartridge: allows a CEP developer to seamlessly make use of Java code in CQL statements. The cartridge not only converts native types to Java, but also Java to native types, therefore allowing one to switch back and forward between Java and CQL.

☐ Spatial CEP cartridge: allows a CEP developer to make use of Spatial functions, such as contains, inside, etc; and Spatial types, such as Geometry, to implement location-enabled business intelligence solutions.

☐ JDBC CEP cartridge: allows a CEP developer to make use of SQL functions being provided by remote RDBMs.

Next, let's look into more details at the Java CEP cartridge.

6.1 The Java cartridge

The Java cartridge provides us with a great level of flexibility in the CEP applications, therefore allowing us to fulfill our programming-in-the-small scenarios.

However, to make it fully usable, three additional issues must be dealt with. First and foremost, we need to define how the Java CEP cartridge should load the Java classes being referenced in the CQL statements.

In the examples so far we have been using Java classes defined by the runtime library, such as *String*. These do not present any problems, as they are always present in Java's parent (root) class-loader. However, how should we handle classes defined by the CEP applications themselves? In Oracle CEP, a developer can deploy multiple CEP applications into the system, each defining their own set of CQL queries and Java classes. The Java classes can be used at different locations at the CEP application's EPN (Event Processing Network) [3]. It is even plausible that different applications may define the same Java Class (e.g. MyClass).

Therefore, the Java CEP cartridge provides two configurable options for loading the Java classes referenced in CQL:

1. Application-scoped class-space: In this option, the Java cartridge only loads classes defined by the CEP application that owns the CQL statements.

2. Server-scoped class-space: In this option, the Java cartridge considers all classes that are made public by all libraries and applications of the running CEP system.

In case of conflicts, a resolution is reached using the OSGi service platform [25], which is the underlying application server infrastructure being used by Oracle CEP. Additional details around how OSGi is being used are outside of the scope of this paper.

The second issue is that of usability. Java classes generally have long names, such as *java.util.regex.Pattern*, which tend to decrease readability of the programs. This is minimized in Java with the use of package imports, however CQL has no such feature.

To allow us to have shorter CQL statements, such as "SELECT Pattern.compile(...)" instead of "SELECT java.util.regex.Pattern.compile(...)", the Java CEP cartridge introspects the MANIFEST.MF file of the CEP applications and considers all OSGi Import-Package headers. For example, let's say an application includes the follow header:

    Import-Package: java.util.regex

Such application may omit the package name in the CQL query, therefore keeping it shorter: "SELECT Pattern.compile(...)". Again, the full details of OSGi wiring and its usage by the Java cartridge are outside of the scope of this paper.

Finally, it should be noted that the Java cartridge considers the full set of resolution rules as specified by the Java Specification Language (JSL), and therefore supports auto-boxing of the Java types. As an example, consider the following CQL expression:

    attribute.methodA(10)

Where *attribute* is of type *mypackage.MyType*, which defines the following overloaded methods:

    methodA(int)
    methodA(Integer)
    methodA(Object)
    methodA(long)

As the literal 10 is of the primitive type *int*, the order of precedence is:

    methodA(int)
    methodA(long)
    methodA(Integer)
    methodA(Object)

In the next section, let's take a look at a real world scenario that makes use of the Spatial CEP cartridge.

7. APPLICATION EXAMPLE

Consider an application that wishes to provide specialized marketing for a mobile subscriber. The application verifies the location of the subscriber and if within a certain distance of a particular shop, it notifies the subscriber with a discount or advertising message (e.g. SMS). The role of CEP in this application is to check if the location of the subscriber is within the distance of any registered shop.

To accomplish this scenario, the CEP application deals with two sources:

1. *LocationStream*: stream of events describing the current location of the subscriber in terms of longitude (*lng*) and latitude (*lat*) coordinates and the customer id (*custId*).

2. *ShopRelation*: a table of registered shops. A shop has two attributes, its *id*, and a *geometry* object representing its location as a polygon.

We assume that some form of location tracking adapter (i.e. GPS) generates the events as defined by the *LocationStream*. Next, we define a CQL view that converts the longitude and latitude coordinates to a Spatial cartridge type:

```
<view id="CustomerPositionStream">
    SELECT createPoint@spatial(
                lng, lat) as point, custId
    FROM LocationStream
</view>
```

The Spatial cartridge defines a *createPoint()* extension function, which takes as argument the coordinates and returns the Spatial extension *Point* type.

Next, we simply join the *CustomerPositionStream* with the *ShopRelation* applying the right predicate and temporal window:

```
SELECT
    loc.custId, shop.id
FROM
    CustomerPositionStream[NOW] AS loc,
    ShopRelation AS shop
WHERE
    contain@spatial(shop.geometry,
                loc.point, 2.0d) = true
```

This query outputs the customer and shop id for all customers within 2 miles of all registered shops considering the latest location of a customer.

In the next section, we discuss one important aspect of the spatial cartridge, which is that of extensible indexes.

8. EXTENSIBLE INDEXING

So far we have primarily dealt with extension types and extension functions. Another very useful extension is that needed for indexing operators. For example, consider the case of the Spatial CEP cartridge, and the previous query where the spatial *contain* function is employed:

```
SELECT … WHERE contain@spatial(geometry, point, d)
```

To improve the efficiency of the execution of the queries, it is common for indexing data structures to be used. However, the proper structured depends on the type of the operands and operators. For example, it would be advisable to hash functions when the operand is a String and the operation is *equals*.

In the case of the Spatial cartridge, the operands involved are generally that of geometry types, for which an appropriate indexing data structure is the R-Tree. However, the native CEP system does not provide such a structure, as it is not needed for its own native functions and operators. What we conclude is that we must also support the extension of the indexing data structures to be used by the appropriate extension functions. For example, the spatial *contain* function should index its relation operand with an R-Tree, essentially creating a minimum bounding rectangle (MBR) and improving the first pass filtering of checking if a point is within a geometry.

The full details of extensible indexing is being the scope of this paper, however it is here mentioned as it is an optional but yet very important aspect of CEP cartridge.

9. CONCLUSIONS

The extensible language framework allowed us to implement the scenario at hand in the most productive form, no additional implementation artifacts are needed, such as the creation of UDFs; furthermore there is a natural and efficient blending of languages.

The architecture employed to implement the extensible language framework provided a solution that is both flexible, as it allows different language bindings to co-exist, as well as scalable, as each language binding is optionally implemented in a separate physical plug-in or cartridge, which can be potentially distributed.

Three cartridges are described, namely the Java cartridge, the Spatial cartridge, and the JDBC cartridge. These cartridges allow a CEP developer to author complex applications, such a geotagging application, in a succinct and efficient manner. Furthermore, vendors may provide other CEP cartridges at will, thus validating the extensibility framework provided by the CEP cartridges infrastructure.

Further work is needed around the propagation of exceptions across the extension and the extensible languages.

10. RELATED WORK

In Esper [12], one can invoke Java methods directly from within its EPL, which is called EQL. This is done without the need of wrappings (e.g. UDFs). However, the integration between EQL and Java is still superficial, no constructors can be invoked, and there is no direct mapping between the native types and the Java types, hence features such as overloading and overriding are problematic. Furthermore, Java is the only supported extension language supported. If one desires to use a different programming language, then a different Esper product, implemented in a different platform, must be used.

Other CEP system implementations were investigated, and it was found that these tend to provide both mechanisms of UDFs (section 3.1) and action handlers (section 3.2). The UDFs are implemented using the platform's native language, generally being C++ and Java. The action handlers, which were sometimes called adapters, have both a co-located version using the platform's native language, as well as a remote version. The vendors provided SDKs in diverse languages (e.g. Python, Java) for the remote adapters.

11. ACKNOWLEDGMENTS

The Oracle CEP team.

12. REFERENCES

[1] Luckham, D. The Power of Events, An Introduction to Complex Event Processing in Distributed Enterprise Systems (2002).

[2] Arasu, A. and Babcock, B. and Babu, S. and Cieslewicz, J. and Datar, M. and Ito, K. and Motwani, R and Srivastava, U. and Widom, J. (2004) STREAM: The Stanford Data Stream Management System.

[3] Schulte, R., Bradely, A.: A Gartner Reference Architecture for Event Processing Networks, ID G00162454, 2009.

[4] Opher Etzion, EDA Conceptual Model (work in progress) – IBM, 3rd EPTS Event Processing Symposium, Orlando, September 2007

[5] Luckham, D. and Schulte, R. Event Processing Glossary – Version 1.1 (2008).

[6] A. Arasu, S. Babu, and J. Widom. The CQL Continuous Query Language: Semantic Foundations and Query Execution. Technical report, Stanford University, Oct. 2003. http://dbpubs.stanford.edu/pub/2003- 67.

[7] U. Srivastava and J. Widom. Flexible time management in data stream systems. In Proc. of the 23rd ACM SIGACT-SIGMOD-SIGART Symposium on Principles of Database Systems, June 2004.

[8] White, S., Alves, A., Rorke, D. WebLogic event server: a lightweight, modular application server for event processing. Proceedings of the second international conference on Distributed event-based systems (2008).

[9] Jain, N., Mishra, S., Srinivasan, A., Gehrke, J., Balakrishnan, H., Cetintemel, U., Cherniack, M., Tibbetts, R., Zdonik, S. Towards a streaming SQL standard. Proceedings of the VLDB Endowment (2008).

[10] Oracle CEP CQL Language Reference 11g Release 1. http://download.oracle.com/docs/cd/E12839_01/doc.1111/e12 048/toc.htm

[11] Oracle CEP IDE Developer's Guide for Eclipse. http://download.oracle.com/docs/cd/E12839_01/doc.1111/e14 301/toc.htm

[12] Esper for Java (version 3.3.0). http://esper.codehaus.org/esper/documentation/documentation. html

[13] Coral8 Engine Documentation. http://www.aleri.com/developers/documents/coral8

[14] Streambase and StreamSQL Documentation. http://streambase.com/developers-docs.htm

[15] Yuri Leontiev, M. Tamer Zsu, and Duane Szafron. 2002. On type systems for object-oriented database programming languages. ACM Computing Surveys (CSUR) Surveys Volume 34 Issue 4, December 2002.

[16] James Gosling , Bill Joy , Guy L. Steele, The Java Language Specification, Addison-Wesley Longman Publishing Co., Inc., Boston, MA, 1996.

[17] François Bourdoncle , Stephan Merz, Type checking higher-order polymorphic multi-methods, Proceedings of the 24th ACM SIGPLAN-SIGACT symposium on Principles of programming languages, p.302-315, January 15-17, 1997, Paris, France [doi>10.1145/263699.263743].

[18] Cardelli, L. 1989. Typeful programming. In Formal Description of Programming Concepts, E. J. Neuhold and M. Paul, Eds. IFIP State of the Art Reports Series. Springer-Verlag, New York. URL: http://www.luca.demon. co.uk/Bibliography.html.

[19] OSGi Service Platform Version 4. http://www.osgi.org/Specifications/HomePage

[20] Programming in the large and programming in the small. http://en.wikipedia.org/wiki/Programming_in_the_large_and_p rogramming_in_the_small

[21] Java Message Service. http://java.sun.com/products/jms/

[22] Oracle CEP Data Cartridge Documentation, . http://download.oracle.com/docs/cd/E14571_01/apirefs.1111/e 12048/datacartunder.htm#CCHCICHH

[23] Oracle CEP Java Cartridge Documentation, http://download.oracle.com/docs/cd/E14571_01/apirefs.1111/e 12048/datacartjava.htm#BGBEDIBC

[24] Oracle CEP Spatial Cartridge Documentation, http://download.oracle.com/docs/cd/E14571_01/apirefs.1111/e 12048/datacartspatial.htm#CHDBEAJA

[25] Alves, A. 2011. OSGi in Depth, Manning

PRONTO – Support for Real-time Decision Making

Pekka Kaarela, Mika Varjola
Mattersoft Ltd
Tampere
Finland
+358 10 322 5004
{pekka.kaarela,mika.varjola}@
mattersoft.fi

Lucas P.J.J. Noldus
Noldus Information Technology BV
Wageningen
The Netherlands
+31 317 473 300
l.noldus@noldus.nl

Alexander Artikis
NCSR Demokritos
Athens
Greece
+30 210 6503217
a.artikis@iit.demokritos.gr

ABSTRACT

For public transport authorities, the most important aspects for operations are passenger satisfaction and safety. Based on surveys, passengers regard punctuality as the most important aspect, which makes it an important factor of passenger satisfaction for the operators [10].

In the City of Helsinki, the public transport vehicles' movements and status are monitored through a real-time information system, which provides authorities information about punctuality of vehicles. Furthermore, the gathered information is used for route planning and scheduling.

Due to the existing information systems in Helsinki, the focus in operation planning has gradually moved from real-time timetables to other factors affecting passenger satisfaction and safety, aiming to find ways to further improve public transport operations.

The PRONTO research project focuses on two demonstration cases. One is emergency rescue operations in Dortmund, Germany. The other one is public transport in Helsinki, where the research focuses on developing methods for improving passengers' travel experience through monitoring and analyzing vehicle events in real-time. Through these methods, it is possible to further improve public transport punctuality and especially the driving style that would lead to improved passenger safety and satisfaction, as well as better vehicle endurance.

A variety of sensors and connections to existing systems have been implemented in order to provide the PRONTO system with valuable data about the both demonstration cases. This paper presents the activities and achievements so far of the public transport demonstration case.

Categories and Subject Descriptors

J.1 [**Computer Applications**]: Administrative Data Processing - *Business, Government*

General Terms

Management, Performance, Reliability, Human Factors.

Keywords

Complex Event Processing, City Transport Management.

1. INTRODUCTION

Due to the continuous traffic growth in many of the world's capital cities, there is a need to further improve public transport services and make them more attractive to passengers – while optimizing the use of available resources. This is also the case in the City of Helsinki in Finland, where the public transport authorities have been actively involved in improving especially real-time information services.

PRONTO[1] is an international research project, partially funded by European Commission. It was launched in March 2009. The project is due to last for three years and during this time, the main emphasis of the project is to investigate the impacts of event recognition on intelligent resource management (IRM). This is done by gathering data from various sources, analyzing it to extract useful information in the form of events and then delivering the resulting knowledge for decision making in emergency rescue operations and public transport.

In order to achieve this objective, PRONTO uses techniques and expertise from the areas of data fusion, information extraction, temporal representation and reasoning, machine learning and knowledge-based management systems.

PRONTO sets specific goals to its two main targets: real-time decision support for IRM in public transport and emergency rescue operations, both cases typically involving large volumes of various types of data.

2. PROJECT SCOPE

The PRONTO project has two demonstration cases and two test areas; city transport management in Helsinki, Finland, and emergency rescue operations in Dortmund, Germany [8]. The demonstration cases have their own specialties, but the common core is the same in both of them. This paper focuses on the city transport management demonstration case.

During the project a city transport management pilot is done in the City of Helsinki, Finland, where vehicles are equipped with computational units that send sensor information to a central server. The central server offers information about the current status of the transport system such as, for example, the location of the vehicles on a map, and the noise level, temperature, 3D acceleration of a vehicle.

The vehicles already have a mobile broadband connection, which makes it possible to send sensor data to the server in real time. That way the management can detect exceptions regarding the operations and even possible threats in the vehicle. Moreover, it is possible to effectively use this information in analyzing the need

---

[1] http://www.ict-pronto.org/.

for interaction with the driver or authorities in terms of stabilizing exceptional situations. In the pilot phase of the PRONTO project, scheduled to take place in late 2011, the aim is to detect various complex events that create a need for decision making.

In terms of city traffic management, the study emphasizes in detecting events that cause decreasing passenger safety, passenger satisfaction and vehicle endurance. These events will be analyzed in real-time. Moreover, the gathered information will also be used in post analysis.

3. SYSTEM ARCHITECTURE

Vehicles connected to the system transmit sensor data to a centralized server, as frequently as once per second. In the server, data is processed for detecting simple events when sensor data values change. Various types of simple events are used to derive and detect complex events that would be interesting from the user point of view. The data processing is done continuously and in

real-time. An interesting complex event concerns, for example, passenger comfort which is derived from cabin temperature and sound pressure level. Another interesting complex event concerns driving style, which is derived from vehicle acceleration changes.

The system receives information from vehicle sensors collecting following types of data: location, noise level, 3D-acceleration, technical vehicle data (for example, fuel consumption, engine temperature and engine revolutions) and departure information. The system also handles timetable and stop location data for monitoring the punctuality of the public transport operations.

Figure 1 presents a simplified view of the system architecture. The vehicles are equipped with sensors transmitting the data to the centralized server that takes care of the event detection. The system has real-time view for monitoring the detected complex events and a post analysis interface for a more detailed analysis of the events.

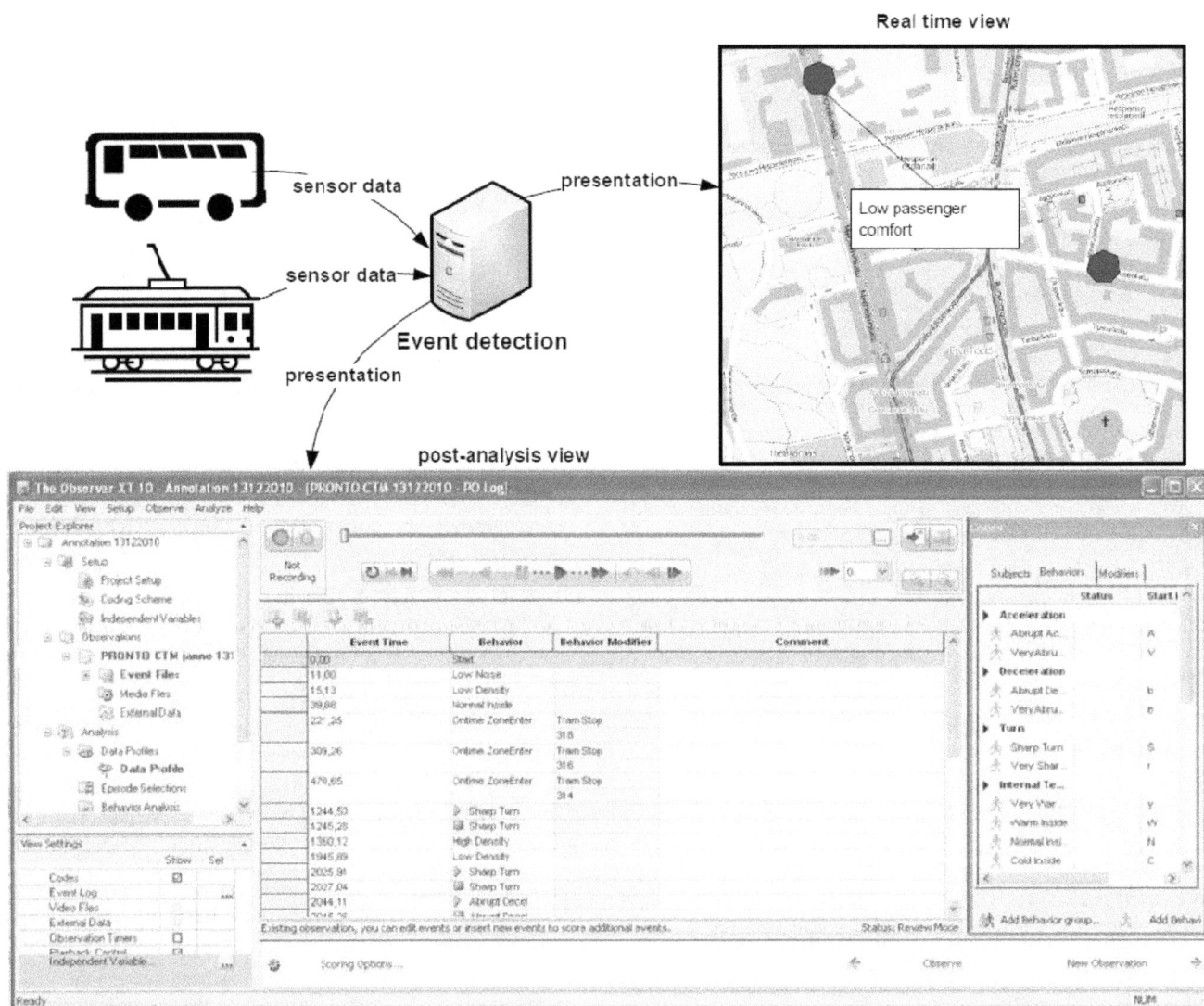

Figure 1. PRONTO system architecture[2]

---

[2] The system developed includes the use of The Observer XT, provided by Noldus Information Technology BV [6] and Mattersoft Live! system provided by Mattersoft Ltd [5], Map by OpenStreetMap [7].

4. USE CASES

The system has two use cases, real-time event detection and post analysis of driving.

4.1 Real-time event detection

In event detection, the most important aspect is to automatically detect and forecast events that require instant reaction. These types of events concern passenger and driver safety, as well as issues that significantly affect vehicle condition. Real-time information not only enables analyzing transportation in a wider perspective, but also demonstrates the system performance.

The system is capable of detecting exceptional changes in acceleration that can be a result of an accident, for example. Also changes in driving style that threaten passenger safety can easily be detected, and the driver can then be contacted in order to prevent accidents from occurring.

The system is also capable of detecting vehicles gathering up on a limited area. With this information it is possible to detect traffic jams or impassable obstacles in certain routes and thus detect the need for re-routing.

4.2 Post analysis

Typically passengers do not communicate with drivers about their driving. For operators, the feedback is given only when something exceptional has happened. However, feedback is an important way of driver guidance and training, and the system is capable of offering feedback and helping the drivers to develop a better driving style.

By following and giving feedback on driving style, the aim is to be capable of having an impact on passenger comfort, safety, vehicle endurance and fuel consumption.

Before, the driving style has been impossible to monitor on a wider scale with any other ways than observing it on the vehicle and collecting feedback. Thus, by automatically analyzing the driving style, driver training and guidance can be renewed completely.

Driving style follow-up and analysis enables realistic and equitable driver feedback. Also, several drivers' driving style can be compared to each other and the feedback given equivalently. With collected location data, the system is capable of pointing out where problems in driving style or operations have been and what have, or could have been the outcomes. On the other hand, the system points out skillful drivers according to their merits.

When renewing vehicles in Helsinki, it was noticed that intersections of tramlines are problematic for the vehicles, infrastructure and people living in the area. Because of this, the trams should drive in intersections with a limited speed. With an event-based approach, vehicles and drivers driving too fast in intersections can also be easily detected by the PRONTO system.

5. COMPLEX EVENT DETECTION MODULE

To perform complex event detection we developed a dialect of the Event Calculus (EC) [3]. EC is a logic programming language for representing and reasoning about events and their effects. (A recent overview of logic-based languages for complex event detection may be found in [2].)

The formal semantics of EC allows for validation and traceability of the effects of events. The declarative semantics of EC facilitates considerably the interaction between the complex event 'definition' developers and the users (city transport officials, in this case).

EC allows for the succinct and structured representation of all complex events of interest in city transport management. The availability of the full power of logic programming is one of the main attractions of employing EC as the temporal formalism. It allows event definitions to include not only complex temporal constraints - EC is at least as expressive as purely temporal reasoning systems proposed in the literature - but also complex atemporal constraints.

To perform real-time event detection we implemented a caching algorithm for our EC dialect. The performance of our EC dialect is summarized below. Details about our current empirical evaluation of the complex event detection process, as well as the implemented caching algorithm, may be found in [1].

During rush hour, at most 1050 vehicles operate at the same time in Helsinki, that is, 80% of the total number of available vehicles. It is estimated that no more than 21000 simple events are detected per minute on the 1050 operating vehicles. The user requirements can be met by running, in parallel, EC on four desktop processors. Using each processor, EC detects the complex events concerning one quarter of the operating vehicles - at most 263 vehicles. The complex event detection on each processor is performed in less than 100 milliseconds, taking into consideration the simple events detected in the last 10 seconds.

6. CONCLUSIONS AND FURTHER WORK

The PRONTO system brings unforeseen added value for public transportation management and especially to driver training. The driver can be given specific feedback more detailed than they have ever received. The system also points out event locations and ensures the feedback is not only equal, but also righteous.

The event-based architecture has enabled surprisingly fast the development of such features that were not originally on the requirement list. These features include, for example, vehicle chaining detection and fuel consumption monitoring.

The next phase in the project is to test event detection in order to ensure the credibility of information provided by the system, which is a major requirement for being able to utilize the system comprehensively.

Our logic programming approach to complex event detection has the advantage that machine learning techniques, such as abductive and inductive logic programming, can be directly employed in order to construct or refine complex event definitions in an automated way. We are currently developing such a machine learning technique that takes advantage of very large datasets, where available.

Finally, we are extending our Event Calculus dialect for reasoning under uncertainty in order to deal with noisy sensor information. To achieve this we are using two different technologies: a probabilistic logic programming framework [4], and Markov Logic Networks [9].

ACKNOWLEDGEMENTS

This work has been partially funded by EU, in the context of the PRONTO project (FP7-ICT 231738).

REFERENCES

1. Artikis A., Kukurikos A., Paliouras G., Karampiperis P. and Spyropoulos C. Final version of knowledge base of event definitions, and reasoning algorithms for event recognition. Deliverable 4.1.2 of EU-funded PRONTO project (FP7-ICT 231738). Available from the authors.

2. Artikis A., Paliouras G., Portet F. and Skarlatidis A. Logic-Based Representation, Reasoning and Machine Learning for Event Recognition, International Conference on Distributed Event-Based Systems (DEBS), pp. 282-293, ACM, 2010.

3. Artikis A., Sergot M. and Paliouras G. A Logic Programming Approach to Activity Recognition, ACM International Workshop on Events in Multimedia, 2010.

4. Kimmig A., Demoen B., De Raedt L., Santos Costa V., and Rocha R. On the Implementation of the Probabilistic Logic Programming Language ProbLog. Theory and Practice of Logic Programming, 2010.

5. Mattersoft Ltd: Mattersoft Live!, http://live.mattersoft.fi

6. Noldus Information Technology: The Observer XT, version 10.1. http://www.noldus.com/observer

7. OpenStreetMap: Map data © OpenStreetMap contributors, CC-BY-SA. http://www.openstreetmap.org

8. Pottebaum J., Artikis A., Marterer R., Paliouras G. and Koch R. Event definition for the application of event processing to intelligent resource management. International Conference on Information Systems for Crisis Response and Management (ISCRAM), 2011.

9. Richardson M. and Domingos P. Markov Logic Networks. Machine Learning 62(1-2), 2006.

10. Vanhanen K., Toiskallio K., Aalto P., Lehto H., Lehmuskoski V., Sihvola T., 2007. Factors affecting the total quality of public transport with a focus on local transport – partial report 3 (Finnish), *Ministry of transport and communications Finland.* http://www.lvm.fi/fileserver/LVM_66C_2007.pdf

Capture Fields

Modularity in a Stream-Relational Event Processing Langauge

Naomi Seyfer
StreamBase Systems
181 Spring St.
Lexington MA 02421
naomi@streambase.com

Richard Tibbetts
StreamBase Systems
181 Spring St.
Lexington MA 02421
tibbetts@streambase.com

Nathaniel Mishkin
StreamBase Systems
181 Spring St.
Lexington MA 02421
mishkin@aya.yale.edu

ABSTRACT

Complex Event Processing Platforms are a popular technology for developing real-time responsive information processing systems. Because these systems are domain-specific, the programming languages used to develop them are consumed by many different users, from domain experts to systems programmers, who want to build applications quickly and change them often. In many application domains, such as trading and system monitoring, data volumes and application constraints make performance critical. This leads to competing priorities between developer productivity and application performance. Support for modular components and component reuse is one area where this tradeoff is apparent.

The preexisting module system in the StreamBase Stream-SQL programming language was developed for performance, enabling whole program analysis and static typing. It suffered from limitations in error reporting and module reusability. We present newly developed extensions to the Stream-SQL module system which allow modules to be used in a variety of environments, hygienically preserving any information that must pass through unchanged. This approach preserves application performance and type-safety while improving reusability of modules and increasing error transparency, as measured by the average time taken to find and fix certain kinds of errors. We conclude that a stream-relational language like StreamSQL can have flexible and performant type-safe modules, and that programmers of all abilities benefit from this functionality.

Categories and Subject Descriptors

D.2.13 [**Software Engineering**]: Reusable Software—*reusable libraries*; D.3.3 [**Programming Languages**]: Language Constructs and Features—*modules, packages, polymorphism, data types and structures*

General Terms

Languages

1. BACKGROUND

1.1 StreamBase, an Event-Driven Relational Programming Language

StreamBase is a programming language for event processing in which a relational model is augmented with streams of events that may interact with the relations. A StreamBase application consists of a set of *tables*, a set of *streams*, and set of *operators* that define how the tables and streams interact with each other.

A *stream* in StreamBase is a named category of *events*. The *schema* of a stream defines the fields and types of events on a stream. An *event* consists of a single *tuple* (a collection of values associated with the field names and types as defined in the schema) associated with a particular stream. Within a given StreamBase module, events are ordered in time. An event can be caused by enqueueing a tuple onto an input stream, or by the output of an operator.

A *table* in StreamBase is a relation. The definition of a table consists of its name, its schema, and one or more indexes which will be used to search the table. When a StreamBase program is running, each table may contain any number of tuples.

A StreamBase *operator* has connections to a number of streams and/or tables, depending on the particular operator. Each operator consumes any events on its input streams, has read and/or write access to any tables connected to it, and may cause events to occur on any of its output streams. Examples of operators in StreamBase include:

map Takes one input stream and produces one output stream. For every event on the single input stream, produces an event on its output stream using an arbitrary expression for each field. A map's output schema need not be the same as its input schema.

filter Takes one input stream and produces any number of output streams, each of which is assigned a predicate. For every event on the input, emits the same tuple on the first output for which the predicate returns true.

read query Takes one input stream and connects to one table, and has one output stream. For each tuple on the input stream, outputs an event for each matching table row. A table row match is determined either by a range bound based on fields from the input tuple and the table columns, or by predicate.

insert query Takes one input stream and connects to one table, and has one output stream. For each event that occurs on the input stream, inserts the corresponding tuple into the table.

A StreamBase *module* is a collection of StreamBase streams, tables, and operators with certain streams and tables designated as `input` or `output`. A module is used by creating a *module reference* in an application. The module reference will instantiate a module with specific parameters. A module reference is a sort of user-defined operator whose definition is in the module being referred to. Each of the referenced module's input streams define the inputs to that operator and the referenced module's output streams define the outputs to that operator. Similarly, tables in the referenced modules can be accessed by queries in the referencing application. Modules may be nested within other modules to any depth.

A StreamBase *application* is a module intended to be run by itself. To run an application, it is loaded into the StreamBase server, which provides the StreamBase runtime environment. One instance of the StreamBase server may run multiple applications at any time.

StreamBase code is written in one of two dialects with nearly identical semantics. StreamBase EventFlow is a visual language, where programmers use an IDE to connect boxes representing operators with arrows representing streams and relations. StreamBase StreamSQL is a text-based language based on SQL. In this paper most example code will be provided in StreamSQL form.

1.2 Modularity Troubles

Modularity and abstraction are important in any high-level programming language. Large StreamBase programs are composed of dozens or even hundreds of modules, enabling code reuse, team development, separation of concerns, scalability, and good software architecture. In the course of heavy industrial use of the StreamBase module system, some problems have been identified, which are outlined in this section.

1.2.1 Flexible storage

StreamBase modules, while useful for promoting modularity and code reuse in StreamBase projects, lack certain desirable properties for polymorphic code reuse. In previous versions of StreamBase the programmer could choose one of two ways of incorporating a module at a reference site – either *strict* checking, or *loose* checking.

Using strict checking, each input stream connected to the module reference was required to have the exact same schema as the corresponding stream inside the module. On the other hand, loose schema mode overrode the stated schemas of each input stream and table in the module with the schema of the corresponding element in the outer application.

To see the problems with both of these approaches, consider a relatively trivial StreamBase module: a key-value store.

Listing 1: kvstore

```
create schema KeyValueSchema (k string, value string);
create schema KeySchema (k string);
create input stream TableInsert KeyValueSchema;
create input stream TableRead KeySchema;
create output stream ReadOut;
create table Store KeyValueSchema primary key(k);
insert into Store
    select * from TableInsert
    on duplicate key update
        Store.value = TableInsert.value;
select Store.* from Store, TableRead
    where TableRead.k == Store.k
    into ReadOut;
```

This module contains two input streams and one output stream. The TableInsert stream stores a key-value pair inside the module by inserting it into Store. The TableRead stream reads from Store the row that matches the given key, and outputs it onto the ReadOut stream. This is simpler than most modules used in actual systems written in StreamBase, but it is sufficient to explain our problem.

The module could be used as follows:

Listing 2: toplevel1

```
create schema KeyValueSchema (k string, value string);
create schema KeySchema (k string);
create input stream Insert KeyValueSchema;
create input stream Read KeySchema;
create output stream Out;
apply module kvstore
    from TableInsert=Insert, TableRead=Read
    into Out;
```

But what if you later decide that you'd like to store more than just the one value string? We'd like to store an integer in addition, associated with our key.

Listing 3: toplevel2

```
create schema KeyValueSchema
    (k string, value string, intfield int);
create schema KeySchema (k string);
create input stream Insert KeyValueSchema;
create input stream Read KeySchema;
create output stream Out;
apply module kvstore
    from TableInsert=Insert, TableRead=Read
    into Out;
```

Unfortunately, regardless of our type of schema checking, this results in an error. In strict mode, the extra field that we handed to our `kvstore` module doesn't match its input schema, so the program does not compile. In loose mode, the KeyValueSchema from `toplevel2` overrides the input schema of `TableInsert` on `kvstore`, but the insert statement attempts to insert all three fields from that input stream into the table, which only has two fields. Another error results.

We could rewrite the inner module to only insert the key and value fields, but this would still not get us closer to our goal — the table would only store the two fields, and our `intfield` integer field would be forever lost.

In more recent versions of StreamBase, programmers may take several routes to work around this limitation. They may have the inner module require the outer module to provide the table to insert things into, in which case the outer-module-provided table's schema will override the inner module's input table's schema. This creates extra responsibility for the users of the module, which will cause the module not to work if the setup of the provided table is wrong. They may also just make more than one version of the inner module, one for each schema they would like to use, creating an unmaintainable mass of copied-and-pasted code. Neither of these workarounds is satisfactory.

1.2.2 Name conflicts

Additionally, in loose schema checking mode, StreamBase modules suffer from the same set of name conflict problems that afflict all unhygienic macro systems. [4] For example, consider the following module that outputs every other input tuple:

Listing 4: everyother
```
create schema InSchema ();
create input stream In InSchema;
declare c long
    default 0
    update from (select c+1 from In);
select In.* as *, c as count
    from In
    => create stream Middle;
select * as *, except count
    from Middle
    where count%2 == 0
    => create output stream Out;
```

The input schema of this module, in loose schema mode, will be overwritten with whatever the outer module provides. Unfortunately, if that schema has a field named count, it will conflict with the count field used as an intermediate value inside the module, and the module will fail to typecheck.

Users may relatively easily avoid the name conflict problem by choosing names that are unlikely to conflict, but the fact that the problem exists at all indicates the StreamBase module system is ripe for some improvement.

1.2.3 Build-Time Performance

In loose schema checking mode, each use of a given Stream-Base module must be checked for type and name errors and compiled independently, because the module may or may not be valid with a given set of input schemas. We would like to be able to check a module once, and then use the result to avoid doing extra work for each further invocation of that module.

2. DESIGN GOALS

We would like a solution to these problems that allows users to write reusable, polymorphic code. Modules should be able to freely manipulate and store any input that is a legitimate subtype of their declared inputs. They should be able to output tuples of their input types, or other types based on their input types (as long as these derived types cause no field name conflicts *on the output streams*). The validity of such a module should be independent of any names used inside the module, though it may depend on names from the module that appear on the inputs and outputs.

Furthermore, we would like to provide all of the above in a way that requires minimal rewriting of code for our existing customers. Existing applications should require trivial or no changes to take advantage of the new features, and the style of writing new applications should remain similar.

3. CAPTURE FIELDS

3.1 Type Parameterization

In StreamBase, the type system is made up of tuple schemas. We consider a schema S to be a subtype of another schema T if S has at least every field in T, with matching names and types. S may also have additional fields not present in T.

Allowing modules to take in any subtype of their declared schema as inputs certainly helps our problem, but does not completely solve it. After all, the loose schema module reference mode already allows this. What we need is some way to *reference* the input types inside the module, and provide the module's caller some guarantees about what the output types will be, based on the input types. We need *type parameterization*.

We have come up with a new category of field type in StreamBase to act as a type parameter, a *capture type*, and a new way of including module references that is neither strict or loose. Each capture type is associated with a name, which is scoped to a module. Within a given module reference each use of a capture field with the same name binds to a particular set of fields. When an input stream or table has exactly one capture type in its schema, any fields present on the schema outside the module but not present in the inner declared schema become bound to that capture type. Any capture type of the same name must bind to the same fields, with the same types, otherwise the typechecker will raise an error. An input stream or table may not have more than one capture field in its schema; when it has no capture field, the schema will be checked strictly. In text, a capture type is represented with a leading at-sign; for example an input stream's schema might be declared as follows:

Listing 5: schema declaration fragment
```
create schema KeyValueSchema
    (k string, value string, extra @extraschema);
```

While the module is running, each input tuple's extra fields are "captured" into the value of the capture field inside the module. This field behaves, within the module, as an opaque field value. It may be stored to tables, included or excluded in map operations, or tested for nullity. Streams and tables within the module may be defined to have schemas that include capture types that are bound on inputs elsewhere. When a capture field is present on a module's output stream, the fields are "released" — the outer module sees the individual fields that were bound into the capture field. This allows programmers to successfully write the key-value store example. In fact, the only difference required to listing 1 is to use the schema declaration in listing 5.

The captured field values are fully opaque inside the module, which avoids the name conflict problem. Only if a name conflict persists to an output will it be considered an error. For example, a module that internally uses a field named count will not conflict with an input that has a count field, but a module that specifically outputs tuples that have the same schema as its input with an additional count field will remain an error.

4. IMPLEMENTATION

4.1 Calling Convention

StreamSQL source compiles to Java bytecode. Each module compiles to a Java class, and each operator within that module compiles to a method. At the end of the method for every operator, it calls the methods for each of the next operators in the flow. Events propagate in this way through a StreamSQL application, until all immediate effects of the initial event have been processed.

The StreamBase calling convention specifies that each schema in the application has a corresponding *data class*. The data class for a schema is a compiled Java class that has a field for each field in the schema, including nested fields. This allows the generated bytecode quick access to all fields in the tuple, no matter how nested, while allowing any operator that outputs the same set of values that occurred on its input to pass the data class through unchanged.

In production, StreamBase applications tend to have thirty to sixty fields in most of their streams' schemas — yet many modules in production systems tend to carry many or most of those fields through unchanged. We designed our implementation of capture fields to eliminate the need to copy these unchanged fields any time the inner module changes the other fields in the tuple, when the inner module passes them along in a capture field. To achieve this end, we pack the fields to be captured in their own data class on entry to the inner module. The data class of captured fields becomes the internal representation of the capture field's value, and can be passed through the inner module unchanged, without the inner module even caring what the concrete type of the data class is, only that it is descended from the runtime base data class.

On exit from the inner module, the outer module (already knowing the concrete type of the the capture field's data class) expands the capture field out to consist of normal schema fields again.

4.2 Improved Error Messages

The error messages produced by StreamBase for certain cases of an incorrectly applied module differ greatly between a module that uses loose schema matching and an equivalent module that uses capture fields. With loose schema matching, the error message is produced within the module itself, and is sometimes hard to locate — when the user looks at the module that produced the error, it is not apparent, because the error is only in the version of the module with schemas overridden. Using capture fields, this kind of error is always produced by the module call site. For example, the loose schema matching error message for a missing field that the module needs may be something like:

> In file InnerModuleName element InnerOperatorName parameter update-expression: the field "f" is not available from any stream

In contrast, the equivalent error with capture fields is:

> SchemaMismatchException: the schema for module input port Input is missing field "f", which is present in ModuleInputStream. Expected "(f int, whatever @W)", got "(g string, h string)"

The latter is much clearer about the actual problem, that the user failed to specify the correct input schema.

5. RESULTS

5.1 Case Study: Financial Trading Systems

The StreamBase Trading System Framework is a collection of EventFlow modules designed to support applications that manipulate multiple financial asset classes (equities, FX, derivatives, etc.). Some of the modules are logically insensitive to asset class. For example, we have a set of these "common modules" to support tracking the state of the *order book* (a list of offers to buy and sell some quantity of a security at a particular price) for a set of securities. The logic for doing this does not depend on the fact that, for example, a security "instrument" is defined in FX as a pair of currency names (e.g., {EUR, USD}), whereas in equities it is defined by a single string symbol name (GOOG).

5.1.1 Overall simplification

Prior to the changes described in this paper, writing these common modules required understanding the way in which the StreamBase language defines how the schemas of arcs and tables that are inputs to nested modules "override" the actual schemas defined in the module being connected to, and playing unintuitive tricks with that knowledge. For example, when a table is provided outside a common module (it is defined as a *placeholder table* in the module), the schema of the outside table overrides whatever schema the placeholder table was defined with. If a corresponding input schema was overridden in the exact right way (for example, by both happening to have the same schema for the Instrument sub-tuple), this allowed the ability to use the same common module to store a variety of instrument types.

This approach had several drawbacks:

- It reversed the intuitive dependency structure. A module with the responsibility of maintaining a table should export the table from within, not import it from without.

- Due to a limitation on allowed indexes on query tables (indexes can be on only top-level fields in the table's schema), it required that the schema of tables that hold incoming tuples include some of the tuples' fields twice — once for the purpose of indexing and once inside the sub-tuple field used to "capture" all the input fields. (Explicit enumeration of all the fields within the sub-tuple would render the module asset-class-specific.)

- Modules defined in this way are fragile and easy to break during development. Assumptions about which sub-tuples must be the same are implicit, and are easy to break. Errors due to this are cryptic and difficult to fix.

The addition of the captured fields language mechanism eliminates all of the above complexity. An asset-class-specific module can supply tables and input streams that have a superset of the schemas expected by the common modules. The common modules define their schemas in a way that captures the asset-class specific fields that they don't care about. For example, the schema that defines an FX instrument (FXInstrumentSchema) has two fields of type string (one for each currency in the pair), whereas the schema that defines a common instrument (AbstractInstrumentSchema) has no declared fields, but consists only of a field capture. The schemas of the input streams of a common module are defined using AbstractInstrumentSchema. When a common module is used by an FX module, the common module's input stream's schema ends up with all the FX-specific field in the captured portion of AbstractInstrumentSchema.

5.1.2 Specific task: Adding a custom field

A typical Foreign Exchange Trading System Framework deployment consists of the following modules:

Market Data Handler receives quote information from a venue

Top of Book Aggregator calculates the best quote at any given time for each instrument

Execution Strategies custom code to execute orders based on market conditions

Order State Manager keeps track of the state of pending and completed orders

Parent-Child Order Manager correlates requested orders (parent orders) with the actual orders made by the execution strategies in the market (child orders). Each parent order may spawn more than one child order, either sequentially or simultaneously.

Profit and Loss measures the minute-to-minute profit or loss broken down along various axes

Execution Handler sends orders to a venue; receives back order status updates

Consider the task of adding a custom `Counterparty` field to the schemas for both quotes (so as to see which counterparty is offering this price) and trades (to request or manage a trade with a particular counterparty). Assuming the native format of the venue supplies and uses this information, what changes are necessary to the trading system deployment to allow the Execution Strategies access to this information?

Without capture fields, all modules that store either quote or trade information to tables would need to be modified to take into account the adjusted schema. This includes every one of the above modules except the Profit and Loss module. With capture fields, only the modules that interact directly with the venue (Market Data Handler and Execution Handler) and the modules that will directly use the extra field (Execution Strategies) must be modified. Specifically, the Top of Book Aggregator, the Order State Manager, and the Parent-Child Order Manager may be used as-is. The additional field is captured in the capture fields, stored correctly, and is available to the Execution Strategies without any need to change the common framework modules.

5.2 Error Message Effectiveness

We did some preliminary work to gauge the relative effectiveness of typecheck error messages in similar situations, comparing capture fields with loose schema module calls. Four subjects were each presented with four situations in which they were asked to find and fix a typecheck error. Two of the situations involved a missing field, one using capture fields and one not; two of the situations involved a duplicated field, one using capture fields and one not. Two of the subjects were presented with the capture field scenarios first, and two with the loose schema matching scenarios first. We measured the time each person took to find and resolve the typecheck error in each scenario.

The users took an average of 52 seconds to resolve the missing field scenario with capture fields, and 51 seconds without. In the duplicated field scenario, users took an average of 83 seconds with capture fields, and 157 seconds without. Though the variance of our sample is too high to draw certain conclusions about the effectiveness of the error messages, the better performance of the capture fields duplicate-field scenario is encouraging.

5.3 Performance

To judge the performance difference between use of capture fields and the previous StreamBase behavior of overwriting the schemas inside the modules, we constructed a test application to model the work a production application would do, in a simpler way. Our test application consists of two modules. The first is an outer module that takes in a tuple, calls `nanotime()` to timestamp it, feeds it to an inner module, receives it back from the inner module, and calculates the elapsed time with another call to `nanotime()`. The inner module takes a tuple from the outer module, passes it through a series of ten map operators, and outputs the tuple back to the outer module. Each of the ten map operators adds one to a payload integer on the tuple. Five of the map operators additionally add a field to the tuple, and five of them remove the added fields. In keeping with the schema sizes most StreamBase users produce, the input schema to the application is a total of 51 fields wide — five nested tuples of ten fields each (one integer, one list of integers, one long, two doubles, and four strings), along with one "payload" integer. The input schema of the inner module declares only the payload integer, because that is the only piece of information the inner module manipulates. The latency measures we report are the in-application elapsed time as measured by our two calls to `nanotime()`.

All of the benchmarks we report here were run on a computer running Mac OS X 10.6.5 with a 2.8 GHz Intel Core 2 Duo processor and 8 GB RAM. The JVM was set to use 256 MB of heap space, and to use the concurrent mark-sweep garbage collector option.

Our tests compared a version of the inner app with capture fields enabled against a version of the inner app that did not enable capture fields, instead using our previous "loose schemas" behavior. We used the Java-embedded version of our runtime environment that we ship for writing tests to script our benchmarks. For each benchmark, we first warmed up the target application by passing 20,000 tuples through it and waiting three seconds. This ensures that the JVM has finished all the JIT compilation it is going to do, so our tests better portray the steady-state behavior of the application.

For the latency tests, we then input a series of 10,000 tuples, separated by about 1 ms each. We recorded the internal-application elapsed time for each of these tuples. We found capture fields to improve the mean latency by 40%, from 11.4 μs to 6.9 μs. Capture fields also improved the median latency from 11 μs to 6 μs, and the 99th percentile latency from 30 μs to 19 μs. We believe that this speedup is the result of copying fewer arguments from one function call to the next in the inner module's flow.

We also ran a throughput test, in which we enqueued and dequeued 30,000 tuples one at a time from each application as fast as the embedded server API would allow. The two applications performed very similarly in these tests: with capture fields we measured 13,918 tuples per second, and without capture fields we measured 14,038 tuples per second, a difference of about 0.85%.

There is no significant difference between the amounts of memory used in these cases. The per-tuple memory cost of a capture field is one pointer, no more expensive than a single additional integer field.

Capture Fields	Mean latency	Median latency	99th percentile latency	Throughput
Disabled	11.4 μs	11 μs	30 μs	14.038 tup/s
Enabled	6.9 μs	6 μs	19 μs	13,918 tup/s

We conclude that capture fields can provide a significant performance improvement over previous schema-overwriting behavior, especially when large portions of the input schema to a module are captured.

6. RELATED WORK

There exists extensive prior work on programming language design, modularity, and flexibility for reuse. While other languages have been able to address these issues, we believe StreamBase is unique in its support for message-orientation, static-typing, hygene, and performance optimization.

6.1 Object Oriented Inheritance

Object oriented languages generally accomplish reuse of a single code unit against multiple kinds of data through inheritance. The required functionality or data for an operation will be provided by a base class or interface, and clients of the code must pass in objects which implement the interface properly.

This technique requires additional layers of indirection, such as virtual method dispatch or heap-allocated objects, in order to cope with the variable sized data and potentially varying object layout. In languages with just in time (JIT) compilation such as Java, the cost of these indirections can be compiled out for monomorphic code blocks.[2] Other languages such as C++ support more efficient forms of abstraction through templating, discussed below.

In relational languages, such as the POSTGRES system [5] new datatypes can be added, and datatype inheritance structures can be created. While logic can be created that works on supertypes, there is no similar facility for parameterizing logic over types and operating opaquely on additional datafields. However, the POSTQUEL language did contain support for storing queries with data and automatically executing those queries. This facility introduces a lot of flexibility (and complexity).

6.2 Message Passing Systems

Languages with built in or popular message passing systems have a similar challenge to StreamBase. Erlang, a massively parallel language based around message passing, enjoys easy code reuse thanks to dynamic typing. [1] Modules and processes need not know the types of messages they expect or handle. Unfortunately this makes optimization and specialization of message passing difficult. [3]

Scala combines functional programming, strong typing and object-oriented data techniques. The Scala Actors model combines object orientation with a message passing oriented concurrency model.

6.3 Macro and Template Systems

Macro and template systems have similar flexibility to the system described in this paper. In fact, they often have far greater flexibility, lending them power but impacting usability, because it can be difficult to predict what a macro or template will do, and difficult to diagnose errors.

LISP macros are one such template system. In many versions of LISP and Scheme macros can be used hygienically, preventing naming collisions and namespace pollution.[4] In C++ templates generally introduce their own scopes to avoid namespace pollution. The system combines flexibility and transparency, enabling compiler optimization for performance.[6] However, errors often impact usability.

7. FUTURE WORK

Though capture fields address many requirements for flexibility of StreamSQL, we envision some additional improvements in the future.

Schema Inheritance Schema inheritance would allow users to define a schema "based on" another schema they have already defined. This would work together with capture fields by allowing users to take the schemas their portable modules were written to be compatible with, and adapt them to the users' own purposes easily and without duplication.

Separate Compilation Currently, modules are compiled once specifically for each call site. Capture fields allow us to compute the output schemas for a module reference site given only the type signature of the module, rather than by re-typechecking the entire module as if it had the schemas of the reference site. Capture fields also allow generated bytecode for module references to be agnostic to the types of the fields that the module does not use. Using capture fields, we expect we will be able to compile each module once for use at any call site.

Runtime Type Parameterization Currently, any capture fields in the top level application that is run are ignored. We may implement a way for users to specify the extra fields they would like to capture in each tuple for each of their top-level applications.

Downcasting in Extension Points An Extension Point, in StreamSQL, is similar to a module reference but may refer to more than one module, and may determine the modules it refers to in a configuration file rather than in source code. We may, in the future, be able to have a way for the contents of extension points to safely downcast capture fields back into non-opaque fields. This downcast would be checked when the application was loaded into the server. Upon exiting the extension point, the extra fields would be again encapsulated in a capture field.

8. CONCLUSION

In any programming language, modular abstraction is important. Flexibility is a key requirement to drive reuse of modules. In stream-relational languages, flexibility over the types of messages to be processed facilitates reuse. This flexibility can create challenges in error reporting and in efficiency, which need to be addressed.

We demonstrate that in stream-relational languages, both visual and textual, modular abstraction benefits from type parameterization, the ability to capture types from the inputs, and the ability to manipulate unexpected fields opaquely. The precision of manipulating these fields allows us to produce better error messages. These error messages are responsible for a qualitatively improved user experience, as well as quantitatively faster times to resolve errors and to adapt code to new requirements.

The system described not only improves development time flexibility and productivity, it also meets and exceeds the runtime performance of the previous generation system, by optimizing the handling of captured fields which are not accessed in the module.

We recommend that other implementers of stream-relational or message passing languages, particularly where static typing or runtime performance are a concern, consider adopting similar functionality. We also present possible future improvements to the systems described.

9. REFERENCES

[1] Joe Armstrong, Robert Virding, Claes Wikström, and Mike Williams. Concurrent programming in erlang, 1993.

[2] Timothy Cramer, Richard Friedman, Terrence Miller, David Seberger, Robert Wilson, and Mario Wolczko. Compiling java just in time. *IEEE Micro*, 17:36–43, May 1997.

[3] Erik Johansson, Mikael Pettersson, and Konstantinos Sagonas. A high performance erlang system. In *Proceedings of the 2nd ACM SIGPLAN international conference on Principles and practice of declarative programming*, PPDP '00, pages 32–43, New York, NY, USA, 2000. ACM.

[4] Eugene Kohlbecker, Daniel P. Friedman, Matthias Felleisen, and Bruce Duba. Hygienic macro expansion. In *Proceedings of the 1986 ACM conference on LISP and functional programming*, LFP '86, pages 151–161, New York, NY, USA, 1986. ACM.

[5] Michael Stonebraker and Lawrence A. Rowe. The design of postgres. In *Proceedings of the 1986 ACM SIGMOD international conference on Management of data*, SIGMOD '86, pages 340–355, New York, NY, USA, 1986. ACM.

[6] David Vandevoorde and Nicolai M. Josuttis. *C++ Templates*. Addison-Wesley Longman Publishing Co., Inc., Boston, MA, USA, 2002.

ARCADE - Abstraction and Realization of Complex Event Scenarios Using Dynamic Rule Creation

Ashish A Kulkarni
Solution Architect
IBM India Pvt. Ltd., EGL, Bangalore 560 071
+91-80-417 76582

ashiskul@in.ibm.com

ABSTRACT

This system capitalizes on the fact that the complex event scenarios in an industry are repetitive in nature. It abstracts these scenarios into reusable templates with configurable parameters. This is an advantage that the system brings over the existing Complex Event Processing tools. These tools provide the capability of defining complex event scenarios but not the ability to reuse them. This system defines Complex event scenario templates using a complex event processing tool. The job of a tooling expert ends here.

These templates are then consumed by a client application. They can be instantiated any number of time by passing the parameters resulting into Complex event scenario instances. These parameters are specific to that complex event scenario in the industrial context and do not require knowledge of any tool. This allows a Business user to effortlessly create these instances.

The system also maps these complex event scenario instances to their event sources thereby allowing dynamic subscription of these event sources. The system can be further enhanced to dynamically map the complex event scenario instances to business processes.

Categories and Subject Descriptors

H.3.4 [**Information Storage and Retrieval**]: Systems and Software – *Distributed systems*; H.4.2 [**Information Systems Applications**]: Types of Systems – Decision Support (e.g. MIS).

General Terms: Design, Theory.

Keywords

complex event processing, business event

1. INTRODUCTION

Before we proceed with the main discussion, it is imperative to understand the meaning of complex event processing. What follows is a set of definitions.

Event: Occurrence of something. For instance, withdrawal of money, temperature reading from a sensor, arrival of a car at an assembly line etc.

Event cloud: A set of events with no particular event relationship that might totally order the events. In other words, a partially ordered set of events.

Complex event: An event that is composed of or abstracts other events. Events participating in a complex event are related by either time, causality, abstraction, aggregation or any other relationships. For instance, withdrawal of money transaction exceeding Rs. 15,000 by the same user thrice in the last 15 minutes or temperature reading from a sensor going below 30 or above 50 degrees Celsius.

Event source: An entity that sends events. E.g. Sensor, Software application, event processing agent etc.

Event sink: An entity that receives events. E.g. event processing agent, person, business application etc.

Complex event processing (CEP): A technology to process multiple events from an event cloud and identify meaningful events. It uses techniques like event pattern detection, event correlation, and event relationships like causality, time, abstraction etc.

The concepts of events and event processing are not novel. Events are everywhere around us. Rising of sun in the morning, getting ready for office, stopping the car when the traffic signal light turns red, grabbing a sandwich when you are hungry are all examples of events that we experience everyday. We as humans have always been reacting to events. It is by events like these and others that we learn about opportunities and impending threats.

Yet most of the enterprise software systems did not make use of this fact until now. It is now that the systems driven by events and not by user requests are gaining importance. Events are also increasingly being recognized as the source of tracking business performance. They also provide a critical foresight of business opportunities and threats thus prompting enterprises to take proactive measures.

It is the rise of three important concepts - *Event Driven Architecture* (EDA), *Business Activity Monitoring* (BAM), and *Business Process Management* (BPM) - that has brought complex event processing into focus. EDA is a style of application architecture centered on an asynchronous push based communication model. Applications designed using EDA are easier to modify than traditional applications as business requirements change. BAM provides real-time access to critical business performance indicators to improve speed and effectiveness of business operations. BPM defines the actions to be taken in response to the information gathered through BAM dashboards. EDA is the underpinning architecture and BAM and BPM go hand-in-hand with CEP (see Figure 1). It is this dependence that has driven and will continue to drive the rising importance of complex event processing.

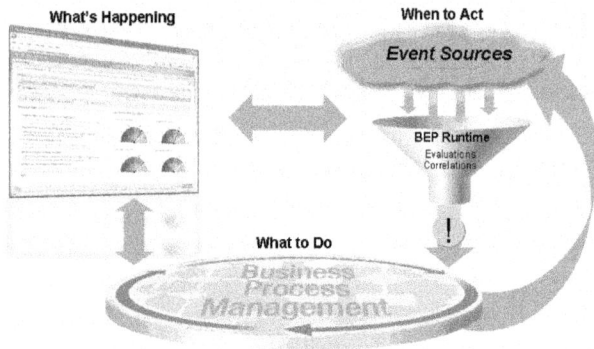

Figure 1. Know what's happening, when to act and what to do

2. INDUSTRY SCENARIOS

In this section we look at some of the industry scenarios that manifest as complex event processing use cases. We have chosen Chemical & Petroleum and Water management as samples but complex event processing finds applications in many other areas too. Algorithmic trading and fraud detection in finance, hospital monitoring, military surveillance, sensor networks using RFID and GPS, intrusion detection and denial of service as part of security, and air traffic control in airlines are a few examples.

The chemical and petroleum industry is facing a lot of challenges that are economical, environmental, and technical or operations related. There is overwhelming amounts of complex data from instrumented equipment. Need for near real time collaborative decision making, production costs, integrated operations, improved asset management are some of the main focus areas in this industry. RFID and sensors help in gathering various data points from the equipment. Continuous monitoring of this equipment for performance, and downtime is critical from operations perspective. This involves continuously monitoring the three phase flow of sediments (water, oil and gas) retrieved from reservoirs, calculation of gas to oil ratio (GOR) and comparing the well potential with actual output, detection of wells that are not performing properly, computing flow rates at multiple choke valves, identifying unacceptable drift during well performance monitoring.

Now let us look at a different case – that of water management. Water is increasingly becoming a scarce resource with no substitute. It is ridden with many issues mainly concerning ineffective usage, manual quality and quantity readings and close linkage with energy and carbon management as pumping water consumes power and generates greenhouse gases. In the water treatment facilities of the future, it will be imperative to apply advanced analytics to water quality in real time. Water quality analyzers collect many instrumented parameters like turbidity, conductivity, pH, chlorine residual, pressure, temperature, ammonia, oxidation - reduction potential and total organic carbon. It is desirable to monitor the pH variance for example and detect as it goes beyond acceptable thresholds. The input to such a system can even come from or the output can go to advanced analytics system, or to enterprise asset management systems, or real time control systems.

Based on these and other industry use cases, we came up with a bunch of complex event scenarios.

Scenario 1: Measurement value from equipment goes beyond the threshold.

Scenario 2: Measurement values from multiple equipment exceed their respective thresholds.

Scenario 3: At a given instant of time, 'n' out of 'm' equipment in a group are above their respective threshold values for certain period of time.

Scenario 4: The case of equipment going down: Absence of data for a certain period of time.

Scenario 5: Case of frozen equipment: In a realistic scenario, it is expected to have white noise around mean data points. Non existence of it or in other words a flat curve of values from equipment should raise an alarm.

Scenario 6: Case of bad equipment: The data values not meeting the expected quality is an indicator of the equipment going bad.

Scenario 7: The rate of rise or fall of data points over a period of time is higher than expected.

These complex event scenarios are representative of the use cases seen in the chemical & petroleum, automotive or other manufacturing industry and industries concerning water management or energy and utility in general.

In the world of integrated operations, there is also a strong driver to bridge the gap between business and IT. The business would like to continuously monitor their business operations, and be able to change what they are looking at with minimal or no intervention from their IT. They want to be able to do this at real time. It is like looking through the kaleidoscope at the different patterns by varying the mirror angle. Of course it is not always a pretty picture that the patterns show. Sometimes the patterns reveal interesting trends that might help the business to cross-sell especially true of product sales, retail, supply-chain and similar businesses. At other times, the event patterns disclose potentially harmful trends, faulty equipment or an equipment about to go down. And at yet other times, they aid in identifying frauds or their likelihood. By observing these events, the business can control its inventory, change its manufacturing process, raise an asset maintenance order, alert key stake holders or take other appropriate action. The ability to control and vary what they are looking at not only saves them IT services cost but lets them take immediate advantage of business opportunities and react to impending breakdowns and failures.

In the complex event scenarios that we identified above, we observed that the business was often interested in varying certain facets of the complex event scenario definition. Some wanted to monitor the pH of water against a threshold of 6.8 while others wanted to monitor it for a lesser threshold. Some wanted a level 1 alert on the temperature of a transmitter reaching certain value 1, a level 2 alert on the temperature breaching value 2 and be able to vary these thresholds on temporal and need basis.

3. COMPLEX EVENT PROCESSING TOOLS

Before event rules – simple or complex – can be detected, they have to be defined. Many complex event processing tools exist that allow definition of simple to complex rules. They differ in their definition language and require training and expertise to use them. We evaluated two complex event processing tools – IBM Active Middleware Technology (AMiT) and IBM Websphere Business Events (WBE).

For definition of complex event scenarios, AMiT requires definition of Situations and Lifespans. Being non intuitive for the business users, an IT intervention is indispensable. Every time a new complex event scenario has to be defined or an existing one updated, the business needs help from the tooling expert. This is more cumbersome when there are bound to be frequent updates to the event scenarios like when one is doing 'what-if' scenarios or predictive analysis. In the seven scenarios that we defined above, imagine if the user wants to change the temperature threshold from 80 degree Celsius to 85 degree Celsius; or say wants to define a new event scenario to monitor water pH exceeding 6.2. The tooling expert has to define the necessary lifespans, situations and other artifacts and then deploy the complex event definition to the complex event engine underlying the tooling. AMiT does provide support for reusing the situations and lifespans already defined. This eases the job of the tooling personnel. The person can create a new complex event definition by reusing the situations and lifespans. Still quite a bit of an effort and cannot be done by the business user.

WBE suffers from similar drawbacks. It provides two separate tools for IT analysts and business in an attempt to bridge the IT-business gap. The IT analysts use the WBE design tool to define the touchpoints, Events, Event objects, Intermediate objects, connectors and actions. The business users then use this partial definition to define the filters, and interaction sets representing the business rules. This is a big step forward in terms of ease of definition. However it still requires considerable amount of training and significant effort to modify things as simple as a temperature threshold.

Based on the study of industry scenarios around business events and available tools for complex event definition, we made the following key observations:

1. In the industry, new type of event scenario definition is an infrequent activity.

2. There is a frequent need to reuse the existing event scenarios and create new similar event scenarios.

3. It is also fairly common to update the complex event scenarios or remove them if they are no longer required.

4. The available complex event tools approach the problem of complex event definition from a technical domain. They do not capture the business domain of the event definition.

5. The existing tools therefore require trained personnel and significant effort to achieve the industry requirements around complex event definition.

We therefore felt the need of a system that presents the problem of complex event definition in a language that the business can understand. More importantly it should allow reuse of existing event definitions and dynamically create new ones with ease.

4. BUSINESS EVENT DEFINITION REUSE

A Business event is an event of interest to the business. It is realized by defining a complex event. A complex event can in turn contain other simple or complex events. There are other types of complex events too that are temporal in nature or get triggered in the absence of an event. The industry scenarios that we identified earlier are thus business events. We now define a new term and we call it a *Complex Event Template*.

A complex event template is a complex event definition with variables. We call these variables *Scenario parameters*. If we look at the scenarios again closely, we can identify these variables.

Here are the scenarios redefined this time in terms of their variables.

Scenario 1: Measurement value M_1 from equipment E_1 goes beyond the threshold T_1.

Scenario 2: Measurement values $[M_1, M_2, ..., M_n]$ from multiple equipment $[E_1, E_2, ..., E_n]$ exceed their respective thresholds $[T_1, T_2, ..., T_n]$.

Scenario 3 : At a given instant of time 't', 'n' out of 'm' equipment in a group $[E_1, E_2, ..., E_m]$ are above their respective threshold values $[T_1, T_2, ..., T_n]$ for certain period of time $t-t_0$ where $[E_1, E_2, ..., E_m]$ is a subset of all equipment $[E_1, E_2, ..., E_m, ..., E_n]$.

Scenario 4 : The case of equipment E_1 going down: Absence of data for a certain period of time $t-t_0$.

Scenario 5 : Case of frozen equipment E_1: In a realistic scenario, it is expected to have white noise around mean data points. Non existence of it or in other words a flat curve of values from equipment E_1 for duration $t-t_0$ should raise an alarm.

Scenario 6 : Case of bad equipment E_1: The data values not meeting the expected quality Q is an indicator of the equipment E_1 going bad.

Scenario 7 : The rate R of rise or fall of data points over a period of time $t-t_0$ is higher than expected T_r.

We use the existing complex event tools to define these complex event templates. Note that this is very different from defining the complex events themselves using the tooling. A complex event template is not a realization of a business event. It is just what the name suggests – a template – and at best can be treated as a new type of event scenario definition (Refer observation #1 in the previous section). Since such new types are not defined frequently, this IT intervention will be rare. Also, the definition of these event scenarios or the templates in our case is not trivial. It requires a complex language, tooling and runtime engine support. We use the existing tooling to achieve the complex event template definition.

Since we use the existing tooling, the method for definition of these templates is dependent on the language and features of that tool. Table 1 shows the complex event definition generated by a CEP tool. It defines a template rule set called "Track_average_temp_events" with a "monitoring_duration" parameter and an input complex event "avg_temp_sit" and a lifespan. It then defines the corresponding instance called "track_average_temp" with parameter values – monitoring_duration of 20000 and situation called avg_temp_sit.

Note that this was the result of a tooling engineer using the tool to define the complex event to realize a business event. The definition as can be seen contains all the necessary artifacts, the template, instances, situations, lifespans, parameters, and their values.

Next, we use the same tool to define the complex event template alone. It has semantically rich parameters with meaningful descriptions. Some of these like "monitoring_duration" are user defined and carry a description of "SParam" (for Scenario parameter). A business user provides a value later while creating an instance of this template. Others like "avg_temp_sit" are automatically populated by the system with the name of the instance. They carry a reference to the template in their descriptions.

Table 1. Complex event definition as generated by a CEP tool

```
<templateRuleSet name="Track_average_temp_events" updateDefinition="add">
        <identification createdBy="Administrator" createdOn="8/2/07"/>
        <parameterType defaultValue="20000" description=""
          name="monitoring_duration" xsi:type="integer"/>
        <parameterType defaultValue="report_avg_temperature"
          description=""
          name="avg_temp_sit" xsi:type="string"/>
        <lifespans>
            <lifespan      name="Track_average_temp_events"      updateDefini-
tion="add">
                <initiator>
                  <eventInitiator as="initiator"
                    correlate="ignore" name="$avg_temp_sit$" where=""/>
                </initiator>
                <terminator>
                  <expirationInterval timeInterval="$monitoring_duration$"/>
                </terminator>
            </lifespan>
        </lifespans>
</templateRuleSet>
<templateInstance name="track_average_temp"
templateName="Track_average_temp_events" updateDefinition="add">
        <identification createdBy="Administrator" createdOn="5/29/08"/>
        <parameter description=" " name="monitoring_duration"
                          type="integer"                      value="20000"
                      xsi:type="valueAttribute"/>
        <parameter description="ReportAverageTemperature:"
                name="avg_temp_sit"    type="string"     value="avg_temp_sit"
xsi:type="valueAttribute"/>
        <comment commentText=""/>
</templateInstance>
<situation certaintyThreshold="1" initialActivation="true" internal="false" life-
span="track_transmitter_by_id" name="avg_temp_sit" persistent="false" updateDe-
finition="add">
        <report          detectionMode="deferred"          repeatMode="once"
where="T1.average&gt;=0">
            <operandReport addToSum="false" as="T1"
                average="T1.Measurement" eventType="Transmitter8" max=""
                min="" override="false" partAvg="true" partMax="false"
                partMin="false" quantifier="each" retain="false"
                sampleMeasurementUnit="occurrences" sampleRate="1"
                          sum="" threshold=""/>
        </report>
        <situationAttribute      attributeName="avg_measurement"      expres-
sion="T1.average"/>
</situation>
```

What we achieved by modifying the definition is a complex event template defined in terms of meaningful variables (monitoring_duraion in this case). This is exactly what we desired when we redefined the business event scenarios at the beginning of this section. Again the method itself to come up with such templates will vary based on the underlying CEP tool and its features.

The template is persisted in a database for later use. The job of the tooling expert is limited to the template definition. We have reduced IT intervention. We also have a reusable template definition and have therefore removed all duplication. The template is

rich in business context. The variables like threshold, equipment, and monitoring duration are all business events specific and abstracted from the corresponding complex event realization.

Table 2. Modified definition as a reusable complex event template

```
<templateRuleSet name="Track_average_temp_events" updateDefinition="add">
        <identification createdBy="Administrator" createdOn="8/2/07"/>
        <parameterType defaultValue="20000" description="SParam"
          name="monitoring_duration" xsi:type="integer"/>
        <parameterType defaultValue="report_avg_temperature"
          description="ReportAverageTemperature:"
          name="avg_temp_sit" xsi:type="string"/>
        <lifespans>
            <lifespan      name="Track_average_temp_events"      updateDefini-
tion="add">
                <initiator>
                  <eventInitiator as="initiator"
                    correlate="ignore" name="$avg_temp_sit$" where=""/>
                </initiator>
                <terminator>
                  <expirationInterval timeInterval="$monitoring_duration$"/>
                </terminator>
            </lifespan>
        </lifespans>
</templateRuleSet>
```

4.1 Dynamic Realization

The complex event template is not a realization of the business event scenario. It is not complete until it is supplied with the values for its variables. We present the complex event template and its parameters to the user. The user then provides values for these parameters. These parameters as we discussed capture the business context of the business events and can therefore be populated by the user. We call the artifact resulting from the population of the parameter as *Scenario parameter instance*.

We use these scenario parameter instances and the complex event template to dynamically create the complex event definition. We call this the *Complex event instance*. It is the complex event Instance that realizes the business event scenario. Just like the complex event templates, the method to create these instances varies depending on the underlying CEP tool. For one of the CEP tools that we used, the method required creation of an XML instance for the XSD exposed by the tooling. In case of another CEP tool, the process involved sending certain events to the CEP runtime engine. Whatever the process, it requires no IT intervention. The user can now use the same complex event template, populate it with the parameter values, thereby creating as many instances as required. Looking back at our complex event templates, a user can create an instance of scenario 1 like so –

Measurement value 'temperature' from an equipment 'temperatureTransmitter' goes beyond the threshold '100'.

Another user can use the same template to define a different complex event instance –

Measurement value 'pH' from an equipment 'waterAcidity' goes beyond the threshold '6.5'.

Just like the templates, the complex event instances and their parameter instances are also persisted.

4.2 Lifecycle of templates and instances

The persistence of complex event templates and their instances enables us to define a lifecycle around these artifacts. The templates and their parameters are defined using the CEP tooling and exported to a database. We then define Create-Read-Update-Delete (CRUD) verbs on these artifacts. This makes it possible to present these in a client application. The users can use this application to look at the available complex event templates, their parameters and delete the templates if they are no longer needed.

Similar CRUD operations can be defined for the complex event instances and the corresponding scenario parameter instances. This lets users view the existing instances and update them. This was one of the requirements that we commonly saw in the industries that we worked with. Of course the users can also remove instances that have served their use. Another interesting use that we put this to was to remove the complex event instance from the CEP runtime but not from the persistent store. That way the instance is still available for later use. This also came up as one of the requirements where the users wanted to temporarily hide the business event that they were monitoring. We introduced the notion of *Activation* and *Deactivation* of complex event instances. Activation is the deployment of the complex event instance in the CEP runtime. It is only after activation that the runtime engine starts monitoring for the occurrence of the complex event. Deactivation is the removal of the instance from the runtime. It is still available in the store but is no longer being monitored by the engine.

4.3 Summary

The as-is approach to realizing business event had a lot of IT dependence, was time consuming and tedious (see Figure 2).

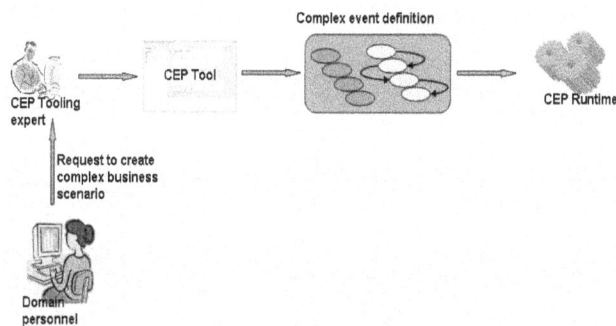

Figure 2. As-is approach to complex event definition

The approach that we discussed in this paper achieves the much needed separation of concerns. The notion of complex event templates and instances significantly limits the IT intervention, simplifies business event realization and allows their dynamic life cycle management (see Figure 3).

5. MEASUREMENT SUBSCRIPTION

A complex event definition is composed of a set of input events and a set of rules. The input event comes from an *Event Source*. If we look back at the business event scenario 1 that we identified, the measurement M_1 from equipment E_1 is the input event; equipment being the event source. The rule is to check if the measurement value exceeds the threshold. Similarly we can identify the measurements and rules for the other business event sce-

narios. Alternately we can also say that the scenario parameters are of two types- Measurement type and Rule type. This distinction is quite useful.

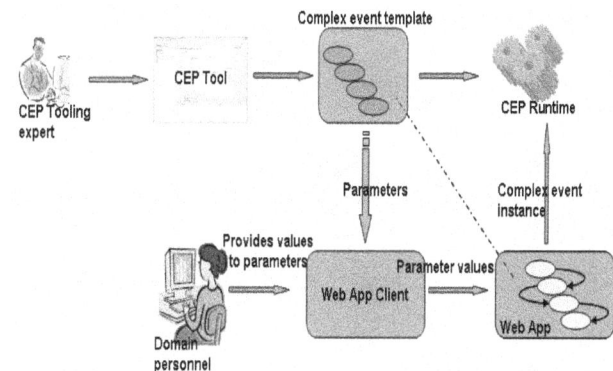

Figure 3. Modified approach using complex event templates and instances

This enables us to define a publication – subscription architecture for the measurement type parameters. When a new complex event instance is created and activated, we subscribe to the scenario parameter instances of the measurement type parameters. There is a corresponding publish model around the event source as well. Whenever the event source generates a measurement value, it is published for all the subscribing complex event instances to receive and act on it. There is also an intermediate step of *Event Adaptation*. Event adaptation involves creation of an event from the measurement value in a format expected by the underlying CEP runtime engine (see Figure 4).

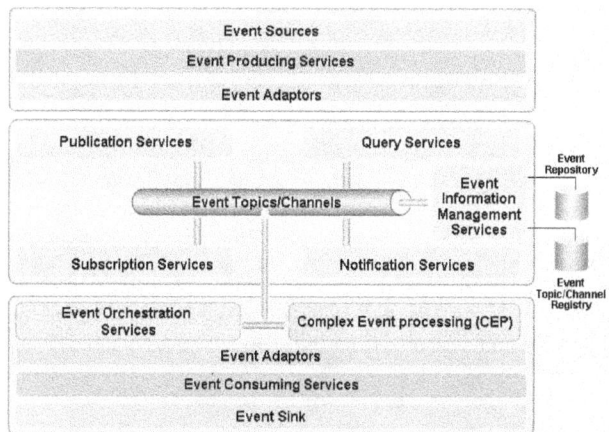

Figure 4. Publication – Subscription Architecture

The other important blocks in the figure are the *Event Information Management Services* that map to the CRUD operations around the complex event templates and instances. The *Query Services* allow querying for the complex event templates, instances, scenario parameters, parameter instances and other artifacts. *Event Orchestration Services* map to the CEP tooling for creating complex event templates, and the *Notification Services* enable notification when a complex event is detected. There is an adaptation before the *Event Sink* to transform the complex event in a format expected by the sink. Event sink is a consumer of the business event. The *Event Repository* maps to the persistent store that we discussed. Together with the *Event Topic/Channel Registry* it helps in maintaining the measurement subscriptions. The subscriptions are live as long as there is at least one complex event instance receiving events through that subscription. When all the instances subscribing to a measurement are deactivated, the subscription is no longer needed and can be removed.

Note that the measurement parameters are only a special case of the scenario parameters. Just like any other scenario parameter they can be updated during the lifecycle of the complex event instance with which they are associated. New measurement subscriptions might get created and the old subscriptions might get deleted during these updates.

6. FOR FURTHER RESEARCH
We now discuss a few topics that would be of interest and can be worked on over and above this work.

6.1 Search capability
An organization could potentially have thousands of business events of interest. As complex event templates and instances are created, they could soon grow to a large number. A search capability built around these artifacts would then be imperative. It would not only enable users to query for artifacts of interest but also avoid duplicity of these artifacts. The duplicity itself could be dealt as a separate problem though and ways for the system to identify duplicate instances be investigated.

The search could be based on various attributes of the complex event templates and instances. It could either be the names of these artifacts, their scenario parameters, or measurements that they subscribe to. One could even annotate these artifacts with extra attributes like tags and use that information for search. Whatever be the method, it should be based on the metadata. Making it dependent on the implementation would make it highly complex. For instance while one complex event template might be defined with a condition 'greater than threshold'; the same can also be implemented as 'not less than or equal to threshold'. Getting into the implementation details might make this feature more involved than the requirement demands.

6.2 Dynamic action mapping and invocation
Till now we only discussed about the definition of the business events and their realization using complex event templates and instances. We also discussed about subscription to input events from event sources. But what happens after a complex event processing engine detects the occurrence of a complex event? Say a threshold was breached or equipment went down. Someone should be intimated or a work order be raised for equipment re-

pair. CEP tools of today allow mapping of an *Action* to a complex event. Action as the term suggests is something that is done in response to the occurrence of a complex event. The action could be an email, SMS, a web service or a business process or an HTTP call. Here again there is a dependency on the tooling and an IT intervention is must. An oft seen requirement is to change the action on the fly. The action needs to be different for the same complex event based on time or user preference.

Thus there is a need for a dynamic complex event – action association. With such a capability, the users would no longer be tied to a particular action or require the services of an expert to change it.

7. ACKNOWLEDGMENTS
I would like to acknowledge Venkatesh Patil and Sarika Chandramohan who were involved along with me during the design of this system.

8. REFERENCES
[1] Adi, A., Botzer, D., Etzion, O. Semantic Event Model and its implication on Situation Detection. *IBM Research Laboratory in Haifa, Israel.*

[2] Adi, A., and Etzion, O. The Situation Manager Rule Language. *IBM Research Laboratory in Haifa, Israel.*

[3] Luckham, David C., and Frasca, Brian. 1998. Complex Event Processing in Distributed Systems. *Program Analysis and Verification Group Computer Systems Lab Stanford University.* August 18, 1998.

[4] Lundberg, Alan. 2006. Leverage Complex Event Processing to improve Operational Performance. *Business Intelligence Journal.* Vol. 11, No 1.

[5] webMethods, Inc. 2006. Business Activity Monitoring (BAM) The new face of BPM. June 2006. www.webMethods.com

[6] Zimmer Detlef, and Unland Rainer. The Formal Foundation of the Semantics of Complex Events in Active Database Management Systems. *Cooperative Computing & Communication Laboratory (Siemens Nixdorf Informationssysteme AG, Universitat Paderborn).*

Complex Events and Actions to Control Cyber-Physical Systems

Rüdiger Klein
Fraunhofer IAIS
Sankt Augustin 53757, Germany
+49 2241 14-2608
ruediger.klein@iais.fraunhofer.de

Jingquan Xie
Fraunhofer IAIS
Sankt Augustin 53757, Germany
+49 2241 14-2542
jingquan.xie@iais.fraunhofer.de

Andrij Usov
Fraunhofer IAIS
Sankt Augustin 53757, Germany
+49 2241 14-2551
andrij.usov@iais.fraunhofer.de

ABSTRACT

Cyber-Physical Systems (CPS) are controlled complex technical systems. On one hand they do exist and behave in the physical world with their dedicated physical and technical rules. On the other hand they are controlled according to certain policies – frequently by a "tandem" of control systems and human operators. Modern cars, aircrafts, power grids, production lines etc. are typical cyber-physical systems. The unprecedented technology development has enabled these systems to play an increasingly central role in modern societies. However, to ensure the reliability and effectiveness of CPS operations is always a challenging task since they are often heterogeneous, large-scale and very complex for conventional software systems. In this paper we propose a novel rule-based approach combining deductive and reactive rules to specify and describe CPS. Complex Event Processing (CEP) and Event-Condition-Action (ECA) rules are used to detect situations of interest in CPS and issuing (complex) control actions, respectively. This allows us to focus on the "what" of CPS control (situation detection, reaction specification) and leaves the "how" to a well defined event and action engine. Whereas events are treated in CPS much the same as in other fields actions are quite different because they happen in the real world. We describe an approach to CPS actions which takes these important particularities into account. Another important issue is the integration of physical models into event and action processing. Temporal aspects play a central role here. Our approach enables us to control CPSs under both normal and exceptional conditions in a flexible and efficient way. In order to illustrate the basic features and expressivities of the proposed approach we consider realistic industrial situations.

Categories and Subject Descriptors

D.2.11 [Software Architectures]: Domain-specific architectures, Languages, Pattern, Data abstraction

General Terms

Design, Reliability, Experimentation, Languages

Keywords

Cyber-Physical System, Complex Event Processing, Complex Actions, Event-Condition-Action Rules, System Control

1. INTRODUCTION

Cyber-Physical Systems (CPS) [16,17,21] are controlled complex technical systems like modern automobiles, aircrafts, power grids, production lines, etc. They exist as complex physical systems in the "real world" with their behaviour determined by physical and technical rules and embedded in a physical environment. They are *dynamic* systems with *changing* situations. *Control* is an essential part of these systems. Control influences the states of a cyber-physical system in a purposeful way according to certain criteria. The control system has to work adequately under *normal* and *exceptional* situations. The communication between the physical and the control system through sensors and actuators is an essential aspect of CPS.

Up to now CPS control systems are implemented with conventional software engineering techniques, i.e. with high-level imperative programming languages like C, C++ or Java, or even (partially) using low level assembler programming. The heterogeneity, large scale, complexity and intrinsically concurrency of cyber physical systems made the design of control system a challenging task. Such software tends to be difficult to implement, maintain, verify and validate.

In this paper we propose an innovative approach to CPS control. It is based on a combination of complex events and reactive rules. This adds another important layer of *abstraction* to CPS control systems clearly separating the "what" from the "how" of CPS control. Complex events allow the control system to process incoming sensor information into situation assessment. Reactive rules allow it to assign adequate reactions to these situations according to defined policies. Temporal issues of situations and reactions can be represented explicitly by complex events and reactive rules.

Neither complex events nor their combination with reactive rules are new. They are developed in a couple of fields like active databases, business process modeling, data stream computing, or RFID networks. Their usage in the context of cyber-physical systems is associated with a couple of challenges. Some of them will be addressed in this paper: the communication between the physical and the control system through events and actions under normal and exceptional conditions, the integration of models and simulations into event and action processing, and the role of forecast in decision making.

Our view on cyber-physical systems will be described in more detail in the following chapter. Related work will be outlined Chapter 3. The main issues of our approach will be described in Chapter 4, followed by an informal introduction of our event and action language in Chapter 5. In Chapter 6 we introduce the event and action processing machinery. In Chapter 7 a practical example will be given to illustrate the basic features and functionalities of the proposed approach: a simple elevator. In the end, section 8 concludes and summarizes future works.

2. CYBER-PHYSICAL SYSTEMS

The notion of cyber-physical systems was introduced recently [16,17]. It describes complex technical systems which are physical *and* computational systems. CPS research *as such* is still at its beginning though it can be based on a large amount of previous work in different areas. Recent progress in sensor and communication technology, the increased complexity of technical systems, and dramatically grown computational capabilities prepared the ground for a new generation of technical systems like modern cars with their sophisticated safety, control and driver assistance, new airplane generations, transport systems, industrial plants, critical infrastructures, etc. Previous generations of such systems were mainly *human* controlled mechanical/hydraulic systems with *some* control functionality based on embedded micro-processors and their hard-coded control logic.

We aim at a new generation of control systems for cyber-physical systems. These systems are complex, heterogeneous *systems of systems*. They show dynamic behaviour according to the rules of physics. *Temporal* aspects between events, states, and actions, interactions between sub-systems, and error handling are important issues. CPS are embedded in and influenced by more or less uncontrolled environments. They have to be controlled according to well defined policy rules under normal and under exceptional conditions. The control has to take the physical behaviour under these *differing* conditions explicitly into account. In modern CPS human operators frequently change their role into a kind of supervisor where the great majority of decisions is made automatically. Especially in order to manage exceptional and emergency situations operators need support by sophisticated IT systems.

Today, CPS control systems are implemented with classical software engineering. The complexity and heterogeneity of CPS in general, and the temporal aspects in particular, make it a challenge to design, implement, maintain, validate, and verify this software.

Programming is logic plus control [15]. Instead of classical software with its mixture of logic and control we propose an innovative approach to CPS control based on complex events and reactive rules. It adds a new layer of abstraction separating the "what" – the detection of events, the classification of states, the assignment of reactions to situations – from the "how": the processing of events and actions. The latter is done by an event and action *engine* with clearly defined semantics. This allows us to focus on the "what": the formulation of complex event patterns, of state definitions, and of reactive rules.

Compared with other application fields of CEP and ECA rules like active databases, BPM, RFID networks, etc. which are

basically IT systems we encounter a couple of important particularities for cyber-physical systems.

1) Communication: in CPS one of the main aspects is the communication between the physical system and the control system. The physical and the control system communicate through sensors which send event messages to the control system about the physical system's state and its changes, and through actuators which receive control commands from the control system to change the physical system's state. A standard complex event approach can be used in order to assess the physical system's situation. The control system has to process events from quite different sensors including their temporal, spatial, and other relationships and to relate them to complex events and states. Reactive rules are used to assign reactions to observed situations. Event messages from sensors are used to confirm (or deny) successful execution of action commands.

2) Normal and exceptional conditions: whereas IT systems are highly reliable physical systems show a significantly higher rate of failure or disturbance. This may result from external/environmental influences, from depending systems, or from component failures in the system itself. Sensors or communication lines may be broken sending erroneous event messages or losing them at all. Similar problems may occur with actuators or their communication links. Consequently it is important for the control system to keep track of action execution including temporal aspects. Also other components in the physical system may be disturbed or broken, or the environment may be in an unintended state and influence system operation other than intended. Both may result in exceptional system behavior and have to be managed adequately by the control system.

3) Model based: physical systems frequently do not provide all information describing their state to the control system. By reasons of practicality or costs only some data are transmitted through appropriate sensors. This may be sufficient for normal operation. The control system knows when a metro train left the platform and "knows" that typically after 2 min. the train will arrive in the next station. It does not know precisely where the train is in between – it can just estimate. In a case of fire in a complex metro station the system knows where the fire is but it does not know how the smoke propagates through the platforms, staircases, etc. This is especially true for the future which is important for decision making and where naturally no event messages are available. Both aspects – incomplete sensor information and forecast – are important reasons for model based event and action processing. The control system has to maintain a model of the CPS with all relevant kinds of information: spatial attributes and topological relations, material properties, technical systems with their characteristics and dependencies, etc. We need an integration of complex events and actions with model based information processing. This includes various kinds of numerical simulations needed to describe physical behaviour aspects (see Chapter 4.3). Our logic based event and action approach enables us to take all these issues of model based processing explicitly into account.

3. RELATED WORKS

Cyber-physical systems is an emerging research area. It adapts concepts from system control [11], from embedded systems [17], and from other areas. CEP and reactive rules did not yet play (to the best of our knowledge) a significant role in this field.

Complex Event Processing (CEP) [18] has its roots in different areas, for example in pattern detection in discrete event simulations [13], composite event detection in active database management systems [12] and temporal representation and reasoning in Artificial Intelligence [3].

A key issue in CEP is the effective and efficient detection of complex events within a given event stream with certain constraints. Until now this is also the hottest research area in CEP. Different approaches from both academia and industry have been proposed and some of them are even already commercially available. Up to now, there are four styles of query languages in CEP summarized in [10].

- Event algebra: Most of these languages come from the Active Database research, e.g. SNOOP [8].

- Data stream query: This style is widely used in industry commercial systems, e.g. the CQL language used in STREAM system [4]. The great advantage for this style is that it is very similar to standard SQL. Therefore, the learning curve is notably shorter.

- Production rules: This style of language is based on state changing of systems. It utilizes a fixpoint theory and works in a "match-act" manner through some forward-chaining algorithm like Rete. Typical languages are Drools (aka. JBoss Rules), ILOG JRules, etc.

- Logic based: In this category the most elaborated one is XChangeEQ [10].

The Event-Condition-Action (ECA) paradigm is mainly rooted in Active Database systems [20,22]. ECA rules and its variant production rules are widely used in both database systems as triggers [9] and expert systems [7]. Most of them are limited in database domain with transactions and rollback support. Since the Semantic Web [6] becomes more popular, ECA rules have gained more attentions as a general paradigm to specify reactivity on the Web [2,5].

Most CEP systems combine complex event detection and reaction, for example AMiT [1,19]. Although most of them have provided powerful language-level support for complex event detection a language-level support for executing (complex) actions is still missing. Currently most actions are implemented with high-level imperative programming languages like Java and the execution complexity is embedded in "hard-wired" software.

DEAL [14] as a new developing language for both complex event detection and action execution is a similar approach. A dedicated language is designed which is capable to specify complex events, complex actions and ECA rules in an integrated way.

4. OVERVIEW OF THE APPROACH

In Chapter 2 we outlined the three main issues to be considered in the context of event and action processing for cyber-physical systems: situation assessment and reactions, communication, and integration with model based simulations.

4.1 Situation assessment and reactions

Situation assessment is a key issue in CPS control. In contrast to other CEP applications where "complex events" means the combination of some sensor signals, of business events, or database transactions, in CPS situations are multi-faceted and complex. States play a central role in situation assessment: components and systems are functional, off, or broken; rooms have temperatures, pressures, ventilations; cars have positions, driving directions, and speed. States are properties of stateful objects providing a certain kind of persistency for situations. States may be discrete or continuous. The control system may maintain a set of abstract control states (like "abnormal operation mode", "emergency situation") in order to provide an abstract description level for related control actions. Every change of a state may be recognized by an associated sensor and trigger an event informing the control system about this change. The interpretation of events can depend on states. The interpretation of complex events and states can include temporal relations between contributing events and may also depend on "static" information like topological, spatial, or physical relations of involved entities.

Situations are complex patterns of states. The main challenge for CPS control is modeling: which aspects have to be taken into account, in which granularity and with what systematics. The application of actions, for instance, frequently depends on a normal or exceptional operation mode. But what is "normal"? Which conditions and states have to be considered for this decision?

The other main "ingredient" for CPS control are actions. Whereas in active databases actions describe database updates things are different in cyber-physical systems. Events are treated in CPS much similar to how they are treated in other event based systems. Actions are significantly different because they happen in the real world. Consequently, action treatment is in the focus of events and actions for CPS.

Primarily, actions describe intentional state changes the control system initiates in the physical system: a switch has to be turned on or off, the power level of an engine has to be increased, etc. Actions have two facets: they are messages sent by the control system to actuators in the physical system to be executed by the actuator in order to bring it into a new state. At the same time actions are stateful objects on their own, i.e., pieces of information the control system has to keep track of by checking their state of execution (see below). Successfully executed actions are used to update the internal model the control system maintains about its physical system.

Besides physical actions there may be also control actions which change internal states of the control system itself (like changing the operational mode from normal to exceptional). They are typically related to states in the physical system but do not have a direct correspondence there.

These actions which are directly executable are called atomic. They may be composed into complex actions. Complex actions can be seen as a kind of macros collecting more atomic actions into a useful procedure or workflow. Primarily, this is a matter of modeling adequacy and usability. Instead of using complex actions one may always describe control by a logically equivalent set of atomic actions. Nevertheless, it is important to see which logical and temporal relations are needed between actions. We consider mainly three: sequence, concurrency, and alternatives. Sequence means that a successor action can only be executed *after* the predecessor action has been executed successfully. This is mainly a logical relationship. Concurrency means both actions can be executed independent from any temporal or other constraints, and alternative means that at least (or exactly) one of them has to be executed successfully. This may be accompanied with preference constraints: do action-2 only if action-1 failed.

Temporal relations are, of course, very important: between events, state changes, and actions, and between actions. We may say that an action has to start immediately after an event happened, or that an action has to end together with another action. The approach suggested here allows us to formulate all relevant temporal relations precisely and explicitly.

Both states/situations and actions are related to each other in event condition action (ECA) rules. When an atomic or complex event happens matching the event part of an ECA rule and the pre-conditions are fulfilled then the associated atomic or complex action is initiated for execution. This does not guarantee that it can be executed (see below). Which actions are adequate in a certain situation (i.e., how to formulate the ECA rules) is a matter of complex domain knowledge.

4.2 Communication

As described above communication between the physical and the control system is an important aspect of CPS control. Events, states, and actions allow us to formulate the rules of communication in a clear and precise manner.

One way of communication (from the physical system and its sensors to the control system) goes through event messages sent from sensors and processed by the event engine in the control system. The other way goes through action messages sent from the control system to actuators in the physical system changing their states in a purposeful way. Both communication channels are connected through feedback loops: events are processed into complex events, states, and situation assessments and trigger – through ECA rules – appropriate actions. The execution of actions (or its denial) will result in new events: if an engine starts after receiving the corresponding command results in a confirmation event by the associated power state sensor. If it does not start the same sensor sends a failure signal, etc.

It is extremely important for the control system to keep track of action execution in the physical system. That's why we use actions in a dual way: as command *messages* sent from the control system to actuators, and as "stateful information objects" on their own maintained by the control system. If the message is just generated and sent this object is in state 'sent'. An event message may be received confirming the successful execution of this action or indicating its failure. Then the state of the action message is set to 'confirmed' or 'failed'. Additionally, we may specify time-out constraints for those cases where neither a confirming nor a denial event message are received after a certain while. Then the action is in state 'unknown'.

In active databases failed transactions can trigger roll-back operations. This is normally not appropriate for CPS: the action changed the physical state and can normally not just be undone. For failed and unknown actions appropriate reactions have to be specified – depending on *domain specific* rules. It's the advantage of our approach that the state of actions is explicitly available to the control system.

The state of complex actions is determined by the states of their constituents. This is an important aspect of the meaning of complex actions. If all constituents are in state 'sent' the complex action is in this state, too. If all are in state 'confirmed' then the complex action is confirmed, too. If one constituent action failed the complex action is in this state, too. If one is 'unknown' and none failed the complex action is 'unknown', too.

If actions are composed in a sequence the successor action can only be processed after the predecessor action has been confirmed. This is important for an adequate treatment of complex actions in CPS. The event and action engine will directly process events and actions in this way.

These action states are important to assess the situation in which the whole system is. It is important to provide appropriate rules for each of these situations.

4.3 Model Based Event and Action Processing

As outlined in Chapter 2 the control system has to maintain a model of the physical system containing *all relevant aspects* of this system. This has two main issues: first, those aspects of physical system behavior which can not be described on a logical level like aero or fluid dynamics, mechanical or electro-magnetic behavior have to be taken into account through appropriate means of description. Frequently, these will be numerical computations allowing us to simulate physical behavior. These simulations allow us to take physical effects into account for events as well as for actions. If we detect an event in the physical system at a certain point in time we can use simulations to determine what the situation will be after a certain time interval. Simulations help us to find out what the situation in the physical system is without being able to get this information directly from the physical system.

The second main issue of simulation is forecast. We are not only interested in how the system's situation will develop in the future – we also want to know how this development will be influenced by actions to be undertaken. Before the control system initiates an action it will frequently check if the resulting system development is in accordance with what is intended.

In is important to integrate event and action processing coherently with simulations. Simulation results are available by the event and action machinery in the same way information about the real system is available. On the other hand, the event and action machinery can initiate simulations based on all static, event, state, and action information it maintains.

5. CPS EVENT ACTION LANGUAGE

The following outlines the main elements of a language for complex events, states, actions, and reactive rules taking the special requirements for cyber-physical systems into account.

5.1 Events

Situation assessment is one of the main issues to control cyber-physical systems. For this purpose we have to deal with atomic events, complex events as patterns of (more) elementary events, and states and their changes.

Atomic events are the elementary happenings in the physical system which generate messages sent to the control system.

They are sent by different types of sensors as messages to the control system and indicate a certain state change in the physical system. They have a unique identity, they may have types like temperature event or switching event, they are related to sensors which have a position, a type, and other attributes, they may carry values like temperature or voltage, and they are of course characterised temporally by a begin and an end time[1]. We may assign confidentiality values, precision values and other kinds of information to them. The annotation is

$$e(Id, Type, X) \qquad \text{or simply}^2 \qquad e(X)$$

Atomic events provide basic information like "temperature at sensor s1 at 9:21 p.m. is 23°". Complex events allow us to deduce "condensed" information by combining different kinds of more elementary information from different sources including logical and temporal relations into a useful "pattern". We can combine different temperature events from different sensors at different times to see the propagation of a heat pattern through a sensor network. We can combine temperature events with video signals, etc. We can deduce complex events by definition rules from (more) atomic events, from states, and from logical and temporal constraints:

$$ce(X) :- e1(X), e2(X), \ldots, cond(X), temp(X).$$

with the usual meaning that a complex event is detected whenever its "ingredient events" are detected and the logical conditions $cond(X)$ and the temporal conditions $temp(X)$ are fulfilled. A complex event starts with its first ingredient, and it ends with the end of its last ingredient.

5.2 States

The other main element in our language are states. For CPS control the concept of states plays a central role in situation assessment. Different types of system components and subsystems of a CPS have different states, for instance, whether a switch is still functional, already off or even broken. Different types of components may have different possible states. Entities in a CPS may have discrete states (opMode = on, off, broken), or continuously changing states (like rooms have temperatures, pressures, etc.) For these attributes most important is their "dynamic" nature, i.e. their values change according to the time following the underlying rules of physics.

These states are related to "stateful objects", i.e., entities in the physical or the control system which may carry different states. These states can be freely defined according to the specific application domain. Their main issue is to provide a kind of *persistence* to the information the control system maintains about the physical system and about its own state of affairs. Every state has a starting point and an end point in time.

$$s(Obj, State, Value, X) \qquad \text{or simply} \qquad s(X)$$

State *changes* result in events. Though in some sense similar to complex event definitions which are deductive rules state rules apply *changes* to the information:

$$s(X) := ce(X), s1(X), cond(X), temp(X).$$

with the meaning that if the logical expression on the right is fulfilled the new state $s(X)$ holds overwriting the previous state of the same stateful object.

5.3 Atomic and Complex Actions

The third main element of our language are actions. They can be atomic or complex. Atomic actions change directly the state of objects either in the physical system or in the control system. They are characterised by a starting time and an end time, they have a unique identifier, a state they are going to change, a value, and maybe some other information.

$$a(Id, State, Value, X) \qquad \text{or simply} \qquad a(X)$$

Atomic actions can be commands sent to actuators in the physical system or simply control actions dedicated to stateful objects in the control system itself (like "switch overall operation mode from normal to exceptional"). In order to enable the control system to keep track of the execution state of actions in the physical system the physical actions are represented as stateful objects on their own maintained by the control system. The control system introduces a specific stateful object for each action sent to the physical system describing this action. They occur in four states:

- $a(X, 0)$ for actions just *sent* to the physical system;
- $a(X, +)$ for actions which have been *confirmed* by an appropriate event to be successfully executed;
- $a(X, -)$ for actions where *failure* of execution has been explicitly confirmed; and
- $a(X, ?)$ for actions where the control system after a certain specific delay (time out) did neither receive a confirmation nor a denial message (*unknown*).

At the beginning this action is in state $a(X, 0)$. If a confirmation event (defined in a corresponding rule – see below) occurs the state of the action object is set to 'confirmed': $a(X, +)$. In parallel, the corresponding state of the object in the physical system the control system maintains is set to the new state indicated by the action. If the failure event message is received the action state is set to $a(X, -)$. If after the time out neither the confirmation nor the failure message arrived the action state is set to $a(X, ?)$.

Actions can be composed into complex actions. Complex actions are just a kind of *macros* allowing us to formulate necessary domain specific relationships between actions. In principle, we can formulate a Turing complete programming language out of events, states, and actions (including ECA rules combining them – see below). For the purpose of this paper we restrict the language to the two most important kinds of compositions: concurrency and sequence[3].

Concurrency: $\qquad ca(X) == a_1(X) \mid a_2(X) \mid \ldots \mid a_n(X).$

Sequence: $\qquad ca(X) == a_1(X) \otimes a_2(X) \otimes \ldots \otimes a_n(X).$

---

[1] We focus on occurrence times here though other temporal aspects like detection time, processing time, etc. may be relevant, too.

[2] By space limitations we avoid to introduce a full formal syntax. We use a Prolog-style notation where ‚X' generally means a *vector* of logical variables and/or constants, and ‚,' means logical conjunction. All logical variables in rules are all-quantified over the whole rule.

[3] Alternative actions can easily be expressed as independent reactive rules, loops by combinations of conditions and recursive actions, etc.

with the meaning that the complex action ca(X) is a macro containing the concurrent actions $a_1(X)$, $a_2(X)$ till $a_n(X)$, or the sequence of actions $a_1(X)$ followed by $a_2(X)$ followed by the other actions till $a_n(X)$, respectively. Each action $a_i(X)$ in a complex action may be a complex action on its own composed of more atomic actions. Consequently, concurrent and sequential operation may be interwoven within a complex action. Additionally, we may formulate complex actions including logical and/or temporal conditions between involved atomic actions, for instance:

$$ca(X) == a_1(X) \otimes (cond_2(X), a_2(X)) \otimes \ldots \otimes (cond_n(X), a_n(X)).$$

Concurrent actions are an important aspect of CPS control. In a given situation frequently a "whole bunch" of actions has to be taken in order to react adequately. The same holds for sequences. The actions in a concurrent complex action or in a sequence of actions are related to each other in many different ways formulated as logical and/or temporal conditions.

Complex actions are treated by the control system in a way similar to atomic actions: the control system maintains a stateful object ca(X, S) for each complex action initiated which is in state S='sent' at the beginning and in one of the states 'confirmed', 'failed', or 'unknown' later. The state of complex actions is determined by the states of its involved actions (see Chapter 4.2).

The processing of complex sequential actions is related to the states of its constituents. An action in a sequence is only initiated after its predecessor action was successfully executed and the corresponding confirmation message was sent to the control system.

5.4 Event Condition Action Rules

The main issues of CPS control are to analyse and assess the situation in which the system is and to react adequately according to a defined policy. Which reactions are adequate in a given situation is an issue which needs domain specific knowledge. The approach introduced here is based on the assignment of reactions to situations in event condition action rules. Though understanding *why* a certain action is adequate in a given situation can not be provided in this approach it is still beneficial to know explicitly the '*what*'.

As usual event condition action rules combine events, states, and logical/temporal conditions with complex (or atomic) actions:

$$ce(X) \wedge cond(X) \rightarrow ca(X).$$

All logical variables are all-quantified over the rule, and there are no variables on the right hand side (the action part) which do not also occur on the left hand side (the event and condition part). The conditions 'cond(X)' can contain *states* allowing us to interpret events in a situation dependent way.

The meaning of ECA rules is as usual: whenever an (atomic or complex) event is detected the conditions will be checked, and if this is successful the corresponding action is initiated. Every event triggers an ECA rule just once, but it can trigger multiple rules.

As mentioned in the previous chapter complex actions are just macros for combinations of more elementary actions. We can replace every ECA rule containing a complex action by a logically equivalent set of ECA rules containing the constituent actions. This simplifies their treatment and allows us to give them clear semantics.

6. EVENT AND ACTION PROCESSING

The language introduced here with atomic and complex events, states, atomic and complex actions, and ECA rules allows us to formulate complex control systems for CPS. In order to guarantee that these systems work correctly it is important to describe the event and action processing machinery precisely. Here we provide an informal description[4].

The following main issues are to be solved:

- situation assessment with complex events and states;
- assignment of concrete actions to given situations, i.e., instantiation of actions in ECA rules; and
- processing of complex actions.

Complex events are defined through deductive rules. On the right hand side they contain logical expressions which can be processed as logical queries on the event data stream and the system model containing states and static information. A newly detected atomic event triggers all queries containing it on the right hand side. All complex events detected in this way trigger other complex event definitions which contain them on their right hand side. A single newly detected atomic event may generate a whole avalanche of new complex events.

State changes are treated much the same way – with one important difference. Whereas complex events are deductively inferred from the event data stream state change rules change the information available in the system. The previous state is "closed" (logically invalidated) and replaced by the newly derived state. The right hand side of a state rule is processed (as in complex event definition rules) as a query to the atomic and complex event stream including the other states and the static information. If this query succeeds the left hand side state change is executed on the state database.

ECA rules consist of two parts: the event/conditional part (LHS) can be used as a query to the event stream/state database and static data. For a given ECA rule it may succeed for none, for a single, or for multiple tuples of data binding the logical variables in the query and, consequently, in the action part of the rule on the right hand side. So, every tuple in the answer set initiates an action with corresponding parameters (variable bindings).

Every action generated in this way is initiated to be processed by the event and action machinery. A single event may trigger a set of (atomic and/or complex) actions to be processed in response to it. This set of actions is to be processed *concurrently*.

For each complex action within this set of concurrent actions the rules apply which have been outlined in the previous chapters. Actions in a sequence are only processed after the predecessor action has been successfully executed and the corresponding confirmation event has been detected and processed. If a failure occurred the following actions are suspended and the complex action as a whole is set to state 'failed'. No roll-back is applied because this is (frequently) not feasible in the physical world.

---

[4] A formal description will follow in a forthcoming paper.

Nevertheless, the system should contain rules which have to be applied in such cases.

In order to avoid conflicts between rules as much as possible we apply complex action decompositions combined with a "lazy evaluation" strategy: all ECA rules with complex actions are decomposed according to the approach outlined in Chapter 5.4 into rules only containing atomic actions, and are evaluated "independently". The corresponding atomic action is only processed if the conditions on the LHS of the decomposed ECA rule are evaluated to true.

This approach allows us to describe precisely how events, states, and actions work together in CPS control.

7. ELEVATOR EXAMPLE

In this section, as an illustration a small but practical cyber-physical system will be described and specified with our approach. This CPS is an elevator. We do not believe that elevators are good candidates for our approach. They are too small and too simple. Nevertheless, it allows us to describe our approach with some details. We have chosen it as our example because of its simplicity: most people know how an elevator works. We will go through all relevant aspects proposed in our approach for CPS control including definition of complex events, states propagation and complex actions, etc.

Up to now the control system of most elevators are implemented with classical software engineering based on microprocessors. In this example we will try to formulate a set of rules describing complex events, states, complex actions, and ECA rules. According to the specification of these rules, the proposed elevator system should be able to work under both normal and exceptional situations.

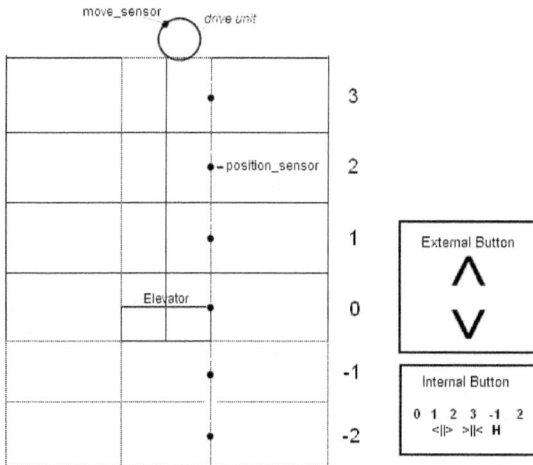

Figure 1 Schematic structure of the elevator system

The structure of our sample elevator is illustrated schematically in Figure 1. It has totally 6 floors: four of them are on top of the ground and two of them are underground. On each floor there is a sensor which observes the current position of the elevator. There are two buttons in front of the elevator door on each floor and the user can press one of them to say if he wants to go upstairs or downstairs (One sample of these two buttons are illustrated in Figure 1 on the top of the right side). There is a group of buttons inside the elevator. These buttons provide the interface for options like choosing the destination floor, closing

or opening the door, and calling for help (These buttons are illustrated in Figure 1 on the bottom of the right side). Additionally, we have a drive unit and a sensor measuring activities of this unit.

7.1 Elevator State and Event Definitions

For simplicity we have only chosen a couple of entities which can have states: an elevator and its doors.

States:

`position(A).`

a state saying that the elevator halts at the specified floor A.

`direction(B).`

the state describing the elevator's current moving direction (upstairs or downstairs)

`request(pos(A),dir(B)).`

indicates a state either as internal request to go to floor A or an external request from floor A with the direction B

`doorState(C).`

the elevator door is in state {open, closed, blocked}

Additionally, we have a drive unit with a sensor measuring the drive behaviour (see Figure 1).

Events: In our modeling context, there are a couple of sensors sending events about their measurements. These messages are the atomic events to be processed by the event engine.

`position_sensor(pos(A),status(F)).`

The status is one of {up, down, halt}. There is one position sensor on each floor. The sensor message informs the control system if the elevator moves up, down or stops at a certain floor.

`door_sensor(state(G)).`

with G∈{open, closed}. This sensor sends an event when the door of the elevator is open or closed.

`light_barrier(state(H)).`

with H∈{free, blocked}. This event says if there is something which prevents the door to close as normal.

`move_sensor(state(I)).`

I∈{up, down, halt}. This sensor event signals the current running directions of the elevator.

`internal_button(goal(A)).`

Pressing the internal button sends an event to the control system about the user's wish to halt at the goal A.

`external_button(pos(A),dir(B)).`

The external button pressed by a user sends an event to the control system informing it about the user's call of the elevator to this position.

7.2 Actions

Actions are messages sent by the control centre to the actuators with the goal to change their state.

`move_to(pos(A)).`

This is a complex action to move the elevator to the position A. It includes atomic actions like closing the doors and the direct move1 command which goes directly to the driving unit. The complete definition about this complex action is listed below.

`move(dir(B)).`

An atomic action moving the elevator in the given direction.

```
stop_at(pos(A)).
```

A complex action which lets the elevator move to the destination and stop there. More about the definition of this complex action see below.

```
stop(pos(A)).
```

The atomic action drives the elevator to stop at the corresponding floor.

```
change_dir(dir(B)).
```

This action changes the direction of the elevator movement after all requests in the previous direction have been processed and meanwhile there is another request in the opposite direction.

```
open_door.
```

The atomic action sent to the door actuator to open the door.

```
close_door.
```

A complex action which checks if the door can be closed (the light barrier is free)

```
close_door1.
```

The atomic action to close the door.

7.3 State rules

Events indicate a state transition in the physical system. Therefore the control system will try to update its model after an event has been detected, e.g. update the state according to events. In our approach every new state will be directly inserted into the database to indicate the state update.

Every "press event" of the external button produces a new request state:

```
request(pos(A),dir(B))
  := external_button(pos(A),dir(B)).
```

Every internal button event produces a new request state:

```
request(pos(A), _) :=
internal_button(pos(A)).
```

The state of the door is updated according to the event generated by the door sensor:

```
doorState(A)  := door_sensor(state(A)).
```

If the position sensor signals an event indicating that the elevator stopped at a position the position state is updated accordingly, then we have:

```
position(A) :=
position_sensor(pos(A), state(stopped)).
```

7.4 Complex Actions

The concept of complex actions has been introduced above. Here we give some examples of complex action definitions to illustrate our approach.

The stop_at action is a complex action consisting of a sequence of two atomic actions: the immediate stop command to the drive unit followed – if successful - by the open door command:

```
stop_at(position(A)) ==
  stop(position(A)) ⊗ open_door.
```

The move_to complex action is a sequence of three actions: close the doors, start moving into direction, and stop at destination.

```
move_to(position(A)) ==
  close:door ⊗
  (direction(dir(B)), move(dir(B))) ⊗
  stop_at(position(A)).
```

Each atomic action can only be processed after its immediate predecessor has successfully been executed.

7.5 ECA Rules

To enable a complete control of an elevator a couple of reactive rules will be needed. Here we just list several typical ECA rules to illustrate the features of the proposed approach.

First a complex event type ce1 will be defined to enable the situation assessment.

```
ce1(A,B,C):-
  request(goal(C),dir(D)) ∧
  position_sensor(pos(A), dir(B)).
```

Then an ECA rule can be written to assign reactions for this situation.

```
ce1(A,B,C)∧(A='up', A+1=C)  →  stop_at(C).
ce1(A,B,C)∧(A='down',A-1=C)  →  stop_at(C).
```

Similar to the ECA rules above, if control buttons are pressed certain actions should also be issued in the control system to affect the physical system.

Action confirmation: various complex actions are defined as sequence of atomic action. Before the elevator can move it has to close the door. The move_to action consists of three sequential actions: close_door, move, and stop_at. The close_door action needs confirmation by an event from the door sensor. This event changes the state of this action the control system maintains for it:

```
close_door1(+):=
door_sensor(state(closed)).
```

As soon as this state change happened two operations are performed by the control system: first, the state of the door in the model of the control system is changed to 'closed'. Second, the action confirmation enables the control system to execute the next action in this sequence: move. Etc.

8. CONCLUSION AND FUTURE WORKS

Cyber-physical systems are a new approach to complex, heterogeneous, controlled, technical systems. Today, control systems are based on traditional software which is hard to specify, implement, maintain, validate, and verify for such complex systems. As alternative we propose a new approach based on complex events, states, complex actions, and ECA rules. This provides another level of abstraction where we can concentrate on the 'what' of CPS control leaving the 'how' to a well specified event action machinery. Special emphasis is given in our approach to complex actions: in contrast to action based approaches dealing with information systems our actions are dedicated to changes in the physical world. This needs a specific approach how the control system maintains their state of execution. Communication between the physical and the control system is an essential issue here: through event messages sent from sensors and action commands send from the control system to actuators in the physical system. Physical models and simulations are fully integrated into event and action processing to take the dynamics of the physical system into account.

These innovations open a couple of important new opportunities for a next generation of CPS control. First, we separate modeling from processing. Models of control for normal and exceptional operation in CPS tend to be quite complex. We provide an abstract logic based description of all relevant issues: from atomic and complex events over states and actions to ECA rules for control. The logic based descriptions of events, states, situations, and actions provide a new level of abstraction. This can provide the basis for improved modeling support like validations and verifications. This will be one the main issues in our ongoing research. To provide adequate modeling support for such complex models of events and actions is another challenging research area.

The other main aspect is event and action processing. We outlined an informal approach to event and action processing which will be further elaborated into a formal one.

9. ACKNOWLEDGMENTS

The research introduced in this paper was partially funded by the EU FP7 project EMILI, Grant Nr.242438. The concepts introduced here were influenced by discussions with our project partners. Nevertheless, the authors take full responsibilities for all shortcomings of this paper.

10. REFERENCES

1. Adi, A. and Etzion, O. Amit - the situation manager. *The VLDB Journal The International Journal on Very Large Data Bases 13*, 2 (2004), 177-203.

2. Alferes, J.J. and May, W. Evolution and Reactivity for the Web. In N. Eisinger and J. Małuszyński, eds., *Reasoning Web*. Springer Berlin / Heidelberg, 2005, 134-172.

3. Allen, J.F. Maintaining knowledge about temporal intervals. *Communications of the ACM 26*, 11 (1983), 832-843.

4. Arasu, A., Babu, S., and Widom, J. The CQL continuous query language: semantic foundations and query execution. *The VLDB Jour. 15*, 2(2006), 121-142.

5. Behrends, E., Fritzen, O., May, W., and Schenk, F. Embedding Event Algebras and Process Algebras in a Framework for ECA Rules for the Semantic Web. *Fundamental Information 82*, 3 (2008), 237-263.

6. Berners-Lee, T., Hendler, J., and Lassila, O. The Semantic Web. *Scientific Amer. 284*, 5 (2001), 34-43.

7. Brownston, L., Farrell, R., Kant, E., and Martin, N. *Programming expert systems in OPS5: an introduction to rule-based programming*. Addison-Wesley Longman Publishing Co., Inc., Boston, MA, USA, 1985.

8. Chakravarthy, S., Krishnaprasad, V., Anwar, E., and Kim, S.-K. Composite Events for Active Databases: Semantics, Contexts and Detection. *Proceedings of the 20th International Conference on Very Large Data Bases*, Morgan Kaufmann Publ. (1994), 606-617.

9. Dayal, U. *Active Database Systems: Triggers and Rules for Advanced Database Processing*. Morgan Kaufmann Publishers Inc., San Francisco, CA, USA, 1994.

10. Eckert, M. Complex Event Processing with XChangeEQ: Language Design, Formal Semantics, and Incremental Evaluation for Querying Events. 2008, 301. http://edoc.ub.uni-muenchen.de/9405/.

11. Friedland, B. *Control System Design: An Introduction to State-Space Methods (Dover Books on Engineering)*. Dover Publications, Incorporated, 2005.

12. Gehani, N.H., Jagadish, H.V., and Shmueli, O. Composite Event Specification in Active Databases: Model & Implementation. (1992), 327-338.

13. Gennart, B.A. and Luckham, D.C. Validating discrete event simulations using event pattern mappings. *[1992] Proceedings 29th ACM/IEEE Design Automation Conference*, IEEE Comput. Soc. Press (1992), 414-419.

14. Hausmann, S., Brodt, S., and Bry, F. *EMILI Deliverable D4.3 DEAL – Concepts*. 2011.

15. Kowalski, R. Algorithm = logic + control. *Commun. ACM 22*, 7 (1979), 424-436.

16. Lee, E.A. Cyber Physical Systems: Design Challenges. *Proceedings of the 2008 11th IEEE Symposium on Object Oriented Real-Time Distributed Computing*, IEEE Computer Society (2008), 363-369.

17. Lee, E.A. and Seshia, S.A. *Introduction to Embedded Systems, A Cyber-Physical Systems Approach*. http://LeeSeshia.org, 2011.

18. Luckham, D. *The Power of Events: An Introduction to Complex Event Processing in Distributed Enterprise Systems*. Addison-Wesley Professional, 2002.

19. Magid, Y., Sharon, G., Arcushin, S., Ben-Harrush, I., and Rabinovich, E. Industry experience with the IBM Active Middleware Technology (AMiT) Complex Event Processing engine. *Proceedings of the Fourth ACM International Conference on Distributed Event-Based Systems - DEBS '10*, ACM Press (2010), 140.

20. Paton, N.W. and Díaz, O. Active database systems. *ACM Computing Surveys (CSUR) 31*, 1 (1999), 63-103.

21. Sha, L., Gopalakrishnan, S., Liu, X., and Wang, Q. Cyber-Physical Systems: A New Frontier. In *Machine Learning in Cyber Trust*. Springer US, 2009, 3-13.

22. Widom, J. and Ceri, S., eds. *Active Database Systems: Triggers and Rules for Advanced Database Processing (The Morgan Kaufmann Series in Data Management Systems)*. Morgan Kaufmann, 1995.

User-Oriented Rule Management for Event-Based Applications

Hannes Obweger, Josef Schiefer,
Martin Suntinger, Peter Kepplinger
UC4 Senactive Software GmbH
Prinz-Eugen-Straße 72, Vienna, Austria

{firstname.secondname}@uc4.com

Szabolcs Rozsnyai
IBM Thomas J. Watson Research Center
19 Skyline Drive, Hawthorne, New York

srozsny@us.ibm.com

ABSTRACT

Event-pattern rules are the foundation of Complex Event Processing (CEP) applications. Yet, despite the vast potential CEP offers for agile business applications, its practical relevance rises and falls with the manageability within the organizational framework conditions of an enterprise. In this paper we present a novel rule-management framework for the event-based system UC4 Decision. It caters to the needs of power users as well as business users: Power users model infrastructural rules based on visual decision graphs and a dedicated expression language. Business users compose rule logic in a simplified web interface from abstracted, configurable building blocks.

Categories and Subject Descriptors

C.2.4 [**Computer-Communication Networks**]:
Distributed Systems.

General Terms

Management, Design, Human Factors.

1. INTRODUCTION

Complex Event Processing (CEP) enables real-time monitoring of business incidents and automated, event-driven decision making. *Event-pattern rules* – which Luckham called "the foundation for applications of CEP" [14] – may be considered as decision logic in the form *"if situation x occurs in the event stream, then generate response y"*. For example, in the online-gambling domain, an exemplary rule could be defined as follows: "If a user shows suspicious betting behavior, then notify fraud department". In a broader sense, rules express the business logic to identify key activities occurring in the business environment from captured event data and the tactical actions to be taken in response.

Despite this definition, we observed that in many practical applications, event-pattern rules rather serve as multi-purpose toolkits to accomplish tasks at different granularities, being applied for the high-level business logic of an application, but also for the lower-level *(pre-)processing logic* required for integrating this business logic with underlying source systems. In particular, these tasks include (cf. [10][14]):

- Filtering – reducing the overall set of events to be processed by an event-processing agent to those events that are actually relevant for the given processing task, e.g., removing erroneous or incomplete data (processing logic).

- Transformation – conditional enrichment and/or adaptation of events, e.g., setting an event attribute a based on the value of another attribute b (processing logic).

- Aggregation – aggregating lower-level events to higher-level *complex events* based on semantic, temporal and sequential conditions; e.g., create a complex "Bet Finished" event from a sequence of related "Bet Placed", "Sports Event Ended", and "Bet Won" events (processing logic).

- Situation detection – triggering actions in the source systems in response to the occurrence of defined event situations, e.g., blocking an account in response to fraudulent betting behavior (business logic).

Depending on their particular function within an event-based system, event-pattern rules are associated with different user groups in an enterprise, each having specific skills, responsibilities and competences. Existing approaches to *rule management* for event-based applications – i.e., the overall set of tools and workflows provided for the creation, application and administration of event-pattern rules – tend to disregard the above-described diversity of event-pattern rules, though. This reflects in rule-management systems offering the level of control and expressiveness to cater to the needs of modeling sophisticated processing logic, but neglecting the needs of business users for simple management and control over the business logic. As a consequence, business users are either required to have extensive technical skills or rely on technical experts from the IT department to implement changes in the business logic (Figure 1a).

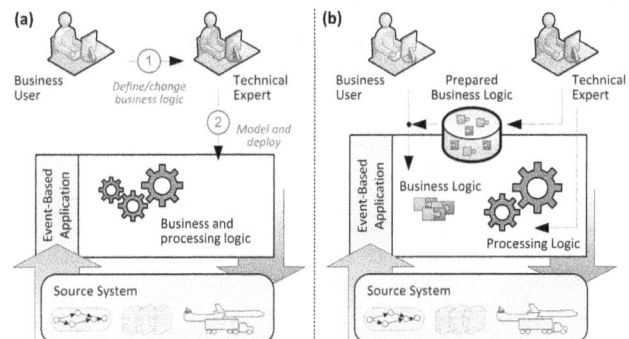

Figure 1. Comparison of rule-management workflows in existing systems (a) and the proposed approach (b).

In this paper, we present a novel approach towards rule management for the Complex Event Processing system *UC4 Decision*.[1] We propose a framework of tools and workflows for modeling processing logic and business logic based on a unified rule-evaluation model. Yet, comparing to other existing approaches the degree of control and complexity is adjusted to the needs and skills of the different user groups in an enterprise: Developers and technically-skilled domain experts model rules by means of visual decision graphs and a specific expression language yielding highest expressiveness. Business users combine and deploy rules from predefined building blocks of business logic in a simplified, wizard-based interface. The resulting change in the rule management workflow is depicted in Figure 1b.

We claim that such an approach eases the administration of business rules, facilitates authorization and security control for business critical rules and reduces the number of errors associated with rule modeling.

1.1 Conceptual Foundations

As a conceptual foundation for our approach to rule management, we propose a differentiation of event-pattern rules by the general function of a rule, into

    a. *infrastructural rules* and
    b. *Sense-and-Respond (S&R) rules*.

Both kinds of rules are equivalent regarding their basic semantics: In both cases, actions are triggered in response to detections of an event pattern in underlying streams of events. They differ, however, in the way they are created, applied and administrated in the proposed rule-management framework. Figure 2 shows the roles of infrastructural and S&R rules in an event-based application.

Infrastructural rules, on the one hand, include all rules that serve as an input for other parts of an event-based application, but not respond back to underlying source systems by themselves. Along with an event-type model, an event-service orchestration and possible mechanisms for aggregating event data, the collection of infrastructural rules of an event-based system may therefore be considered the *event-based infrastructure* for creating an event-based, near real-time abstraction of the source systems: All relevant real-world incidents and state changes are then accessible at a proper level of granularity, via accordingly pre-processed events and/or aggregated event data

Being part of a so-defined integration layer between the real-world business environment and the actual decision making, infrastructural rules are critical to the overall functioning and performance of an event-based application, and must operate in full accordance with the other elements of an event-based infrastructure. In the proposed model, we thus provide for infrastructural rules to be managed by technically-versed power users of a CEP framework: These so-called *system operators* model infrastructural rules in a single, comprehensive model (as so-called *rule definitions*) and directly apply them at the respective rule-execution units in an event-based application. The proposed workflow especially focuses on *efficiency*, *transparency* and *immediacy* and strives to minimize administrative overhead as would arise from a more abstracted approach.

---

[1] http://www.uc4.com/products/uc4-automation-platform/uc4decision.html

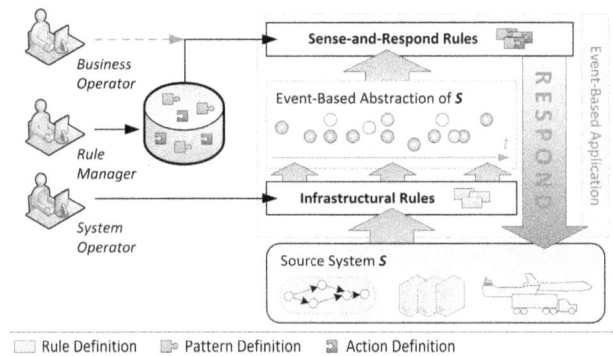

Figure 2. Infrastructural vs. Sense-and-Respond rules.

Sense-and-Respond (S&R) rules, on the other hand, include all rules that do not again serve as an input for other parts of an event-based application, but directly or indirectly respond back to the source system. Setting up on an up-and-running event-based infrastructure (including the *infrastructural rules* of an application), S&R rules therefore cover the actual decision making for supervising and steering an underlying business environment: S&R rules continuously monitor the given event-based abstraction for relevant business situations, and, in response to such situations, trigger respective actions in the source systems.

Eventually feeding back to underlying source systems, appropriately-defined S&R rules are critical to the correct operation of an observed business environment. However, creating and applying such rules "from scratch" would not only require the domain-specific expertise of customer-side representatives, but would also force these users to get acquainted with the diverse mechanisms for creating and applying such rule logic as part of an event-based application. We therefore propose a two-step workflow for managing S&R rules:

In the first step, we allow for technically adept and well-trained domain experts – so-called *rule managers* – to define a catalog of configurable, easy-to-use "building blocks" of a.), encapsulated pattern-detection logic (*pattern definitions*), and b.), encapsulated reaction logic (*action definitions*). These buildings blocks strictly abstract from underlying complexity; i.e., from an end-user point of view, the prepared catalog of event-processing logic appears as a collection of relevant business situations (e.g., "suspicious user behavior") and possible actions (e.g., "send an email to the fraud-prevention department").

In the second step, appropriately-configured buildings blocks are then assembled to concrete S&R rules in the form *"if event situation, then action(s)"* depending on the actual controlling requirements of the underlying business environment. The creation and maintenance of the concrete steering logic still requires domain-specific, detailed knowledge of the source system; however, it fully abstracts from the event-based foundations of an application. Also, due to S&R rules' "read-only" access to the underlying event stream of real-world incidents, they may be added, changed and removed without having users to consider any side-effects to other parts of the application. The process of instantiating concrete S&R logic from prepared building blocks is performed so-called *business operators*, which will usually be domain experts with little or no technical expertise.

Covering both processing logic and business logic, the overall process of creating a full-fledged, up-and-running event-based application can now be summarized as follows:

- *System operators* establish an *event-based infrastructure*, including all infrastructural rules of an application.
- *Rule managers* create a catalog of "building blocks" of encapsulated pattern-detection logic and reaction logic.
- *Business operators* assemble these building blocks to concrete Sense-and-Respond rules.

The remainder of this paper is structured as follows: In Section 2, we present related work. Section 3 gives a short introduction to the event-processing facilities of UC4 Decision, which serves as the basis for our approach. Section 4 and Section 5 discuss the proposed approaches to infrastructural rule management and sense-and-respond rule management in greater detail. Section 6 discusses the implementation of our framework with UC4 Decision. Section 7 concludes this paper and provides a short discussion of the experiences we made with the presented framework.

2. RELATED WORK

Since introduced to a wider community by David Luckham and his seminal work on "The Power of Events" [14], Complex Event Processing has inspired numerous projects of both academic (e.g. [1][3][7][17][21]) and commercial nature (cf. [11]) as well as in the Open Source community [9].

Albeit more and more end users are concerned with the setup and maintenance of event-based applications in their daily work, discussions on CEP have long focused on operational features such as expressiveness and performance (cf. [12]), and there is little work on rule management in event-based systems. Luckham [15] lists rule management as one of the challenges for future CEP systems. GRUVe [22] is a four-phase methodology for managing complex event patterns throughout their lifecycle. It primarily builds upon the reuse of existing event patterns, which is supported by a semantic event-pattern model. We agree with the authors that reuse is of paramount importance for efficient rule management. However, we believe that one common workflow for both business and power users will in many cases lead to restrictions for at least one group of users.

While little work addresses the broader issue of rule management, there is an active discussion on how to make CEP accessible to business users. Etzion and Niblett [10] see the development from programming-centred to semi-technical development tools as one of the emerging directions in event processing. Chandy and Schulte [5] identify the ability to "enable business users to tailor systems to their needs" as a major criterion for the relevance of an event-based system, arguing that a one-size-fits-all specification of events and responses doesn't work. Mismatches between the complexity of event-processing logic and the abilities of potential adopters have already inspired the definition of domain-specific reference models [4] and an approach to automated rule parameter prediction and correction [23]. We support business users with a tailored workflow, where fully-abstracted, configurable building blocks are assembled to rule instances. An alternative, less abstracted workflow is provided for power users.

The presented separation of event-pattern rules into infrastructural rules and Sense-and-Respond rules eventually results in a two-layered architecture for event-processing applications. Layered application models have a long history in CEP. Luckham [14] and Paschke and Vincent [16] discuss layered models for event-processing networks (EPNs). MavEStream [6] is a layered architecture that allows integrating continuous query processing and CEP. Kellner and Fiege [13] present the separation of two viewpoints in a CEP application, which facilities a business-oriented, top-down approach based on Key Performance Indicators (KPIs). The authors claim that with their approach "changes in situations to be detected can be handled without affecting the derivation of values for KPIs that are more stable". Similarly, our approach allows changing high-level business logic decoupled from low-level processing rules. Eckert and Bry [8] present XChange^{EQ}, a high-level event-processing language differentiating event-pattern rules based on their function within a CEP application into deductive rules and reactive rules. With slightly different syntaxes, the separation intends to make an application more clear. Similarly, we separate rules into infrastructural and S&R rules. Yet, in contrast to the described approaches, we explicitly associate the layers with different workflows and user groups. This provides not only a clear application structure, but also enables to tailor workflows and user interfaces to the according user groups and achieve a clear separation of concerns.

In the field of business rules, rule management is long recognized as an important component for practical deployments. Business Rule Management Systems (BRMSs) complement business rule engines with rule repositories and rule authoring tools. Most BRMSs aim to provide a rule syntax that is close to natural language. Domain-specific languages (DSLs) are an extension to general-purpose rule languages that can be defined by power users based on the requirements of a given business scenario. To our best knowledge, there is no event-processing language (EPL) in the CEP space that claims to converge to natural language. We believe that this is because of the increased complexity of event-pattern rules in comparison to business rules. Rule templates are partially defined rules with placeholders to be populated by business users. Allowing business users to instantiate arbitrarily complex rule logic, rule templates are particularly suitable for CEP, and have, for instance, been used with AMiT [2]. In our approach, we extend the concept of rule templates and provide templates not only for complete rules, but also for decoupled "building blocks" of rule logic. Such building blocks can then instantiated and assembled to concrete rules by business users.

3. ARCHITECTURAL BACKGROUND

UC4 Decision is a commercial CEP platform that is based on *Sense-and-Respond Infrastructure* (SARI) as originally proposed by Schiefer et al. [20] at DEBS'07. In the following, we give an overview to the general architecture and core event-processing facilities of UC4 Decision; our approach to user-oriented rule management as presented in Section 4 and 5 of this paper will set up on these concepts and extends them towards manageability for the different user groups within an enterprise. For more detailed discussions on UC4 Decision/SARI, its rule language, its approach to distributed event processing and data management, the interested reader may refer to related work [18][19][20].

The central concept of any UC4 Decision application is the *event-processing map*, a user-defined orchestration of *event adaptors* and *event services* as sketched in Figure 3. Event adaptors may be considered the actual interface to underlying source systems: Depending on their implementation, event adaptors translate real-

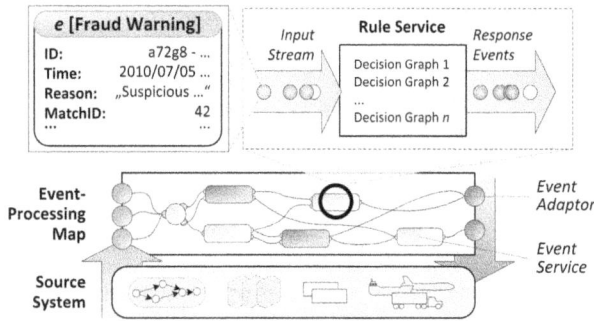

Figure 3. Sense-and-Respond Infrastructure.

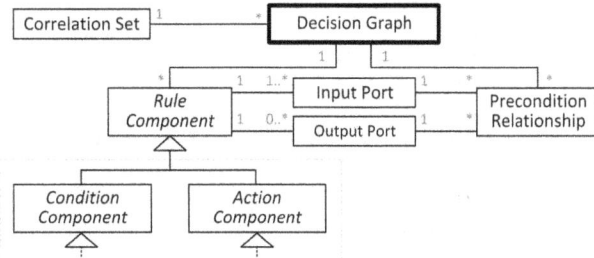

Figure 4. Decision graph meta-model.

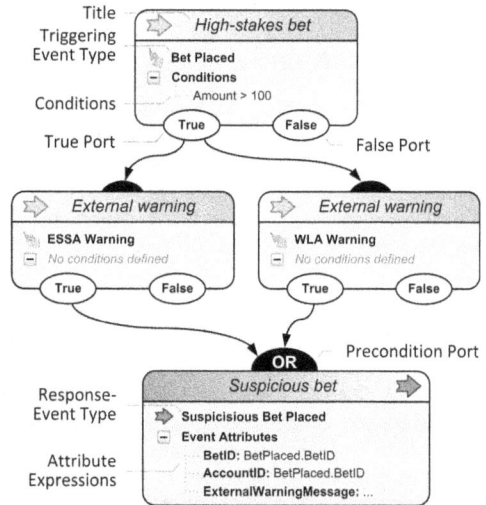

Figure 5. Exemplary decision graph.

world actions (such as a user *actually* placing a bet in an online gambling platform) into event representations of certain *event types*, and vice versa. As shown for an exemplary "Fraud Warning" event in Figure 3, events may further characterize signified real-world incidents through collections of *event attributes* as defined in their event type. *Event services* receive events from event adaptors or other event services, process them based on implementation-specific logic and respond back to the event processing map. Event services therewith cover the entire event processing of a Decision application; an event service could, for instance, pick from a stream of events those that are relevant in a certain context, publish events to a repository for later analysis, or serve as a hub. *Rule services* are special event services that allow evaluating sets of *decision graphs* on incoming event streams.

Decision graphs form the foundation of any pattern detection in UC4 Decision and will serve as a technical basis for both *infrastructural rules* and *S&R rules* as discussed in the remainder of this paper. A decision graph may be considered a directed, acyclic graph of easy-to-understand pieces of rule logic – so-called *rule components* – such as "the occurrence of an event of type T, with certain attribute values" or "the generation of a response event of type U". Predecessors in the decision graph are then considered as preconditions in the evaluation process: To activate a rule component, an event stream must conform to (at least) one valid path through the decision graph.

Figure 4 shows the meta-model for decision graphs. Depending on its implementation, each rule component has a collection of *input ports* and *output ports*: While former allow generally activating a rule component, latter represent possible results of the encapsulated logic. A precondition relationship associates an output port of a rule component c_i with an input port of another rule component c_j. In case of multiple predecessors, a binary *input-port operator* defines whether all, at least one, or exactly one precondition must be fulfilled in order to activate an input port.

Rule components may encapsulate a wide range of event-processing logic and make decision graphs a powerful and extensible toolkit for detecting event situations. Rule components may generally be separated into *condition components* and *action components*, respectively. Condition components allow modeling the certain characteristics of an event situation by evaluating user-defined expressions on the incoming event stream and activating their output ports depending on the result of that evaluation. *Event conditions*, for instance, evaluate a Boolean expression on each occurrence of a user-defined event type; output ports are available for "true" and "false". Action components typically serve as the end nodes of a decision graph and encapsulate reaction logic to be executed whenever an event stream conforms to the component's preconditions. *Response-event actions*, for instance, encapsulate the generation of a certain kind of response event, which is then published to the event processing map.

Figure 5 shows the rendering[2] of a simple decision graph from the fraud-detection domain, assembled from two event conditions and a response-event action. In the example, high-stake bets (with a bet amount greater than 100$) are transformed into "Suspicious Bet Placed" events whenever an external warning is retrieved from at least one of two global early-warning systems. Via its event attributes, the response event holds the concerned account and bet IDs as well as warning message. Note that correlation information – e.g., that all events must belong to the same sports event – is defined in a separate model; these so-called *correlation sets* [19] are referred by the decision-graph model. For accessing elements of the underlying event stream and performing calculations on these data, rule components use a tailored expression language, so-called *EA Expressions* [18]: In the above example, EA Expressions are used both for formulating a condition on the triggering "Bet Placed" event in the initial "High-stakes bet" component and for addressing event attributes of a preceding "Suspicious Bet Placed" event in the response-event action.

---

[2] Decision-graph renderings as shown in this paper have been optimized for readability.

Business entities eventually allow aggregating the state of durable entities in application-wide, typed data structures. A business-entity instance can be retrieved via a (possibly composite) key and updated and queried via an interface. UC4 Decision currently supports three basic kinds of business entities: *Scores* are numeric values that are typically used as counters. *Base entities* and *sets* allow establishing virtual representations of corresponding real-world structures. While base entities group collections of attributes, sets offer methods for adding and removing items and can then be queried for metrics such as the average sojourn time.

4. INFRASTRUCTURAL RULES

In Section 1, we have introduced the notion of *infrastructural rules* for all rules that prepare data for other parts of an application, but do not by themselves respond back to the underlying source system. In the following, we present our approach to *infrastructural rule management* and its realization as part of UC4 Decision's event-processing architecture. It is based on the idea of letting power users of an event-processing framework – so-called *system operators* – define infrastructural event-processing logic in a single, comprehensive model and directly place and enact this logic at respective parts of an event-based application.

We identified the following requirements for an approach to infrastructural rule management:

- *Expressiveness:* Rule-based event processing has proved useful for a wide range of infrastructural issues, including filtering, event enrichment, the creation of composite events and the maintenance of *business entities*. Infrastructural rules must be expressive enough to accomplish these tasks and establish an appropriate abstraction of underlying source systems.

- *Efficiency of use:* Infrastructural rules are created and applied by power users of a CEP framework. To facilitate the efficient creation of an event-based infrastructure, a framework shall therefore make infrastructural rule management as *immediate*, *clear* and *transparent* as possible, and focus on these aspects in preference to however-defined abstractions from underlying complexity. Infrastructural rule management shall furthermore minimize any overhead that may arise from administrating rules and their assignment to rule services.

- *Full and system-wide access:* Being part of the event-based infrastructure of an application, adding, changing or removing infrastructural rules is likely to affect calculations in other parts of the application. A framework shall therefore provide full and comprehensive access to an application, enabling users to efficiently investigate and handle possible side effects.

In the presented framework, system operators model infrastructural event-processing logic as application-wide *rule definitions*, in parallel and fully integrated with the other elements of an application's event-based infrastructure. Rule definitions may be considered as self-contained, fully-functional pieces of rule logic: Encapsulating event-processing logic of the form "if pattern, then action(s)" in an integrated model that is interpretable to UC4 Decision, rule definitions can directly and without further instantiation steps be applied to incoming event streams. For its enactment as part of a Decision application, system operators eventually assign a rule definition to one or more *rule services* across the event-processing map of an application. During run time, each rule service then evaluates an independent instance of the represented event-processing logic.

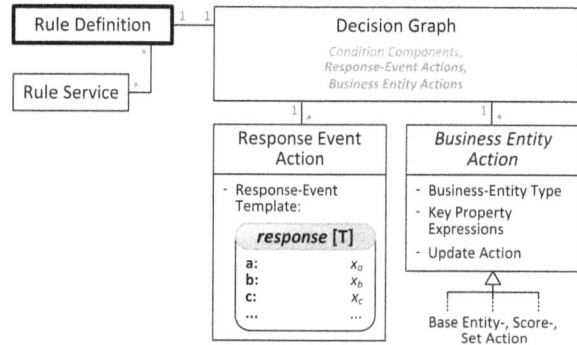

Figure 6. Rule definition meta-model.

UC4 Decision supports the described workflow through a comprehensive, power-user-oriented IDE for event-based applications; in *UC4 Decision Modeling Studio*, system operators are provided with tools to create and administrate event-processing map, rule definitions, event types and business entities.

Figure 6 shows the meta-model for rule definitions. The key element of any rule definition is a *reactive decision graph*, i.e., a decision graph that is assembled from condition components and one or more *action components*. UC4 Decision currently features four types of action components: *Response-event components* generate a response event based on a user-defined response-event template. The response-event template is defined by an event type T, and, for each event attribute $(i, t) \in T$, an expression on the underlying event stream returning a value of type t. *Base entity-*, *score-* and *set-action components* allow updating the different kinds of business entities in an application. In all cases, a rule component is defined by a business-entity type, and, for each key property of that type, an expression on the underlying event stream. On the identified business-entity instance, the rule component then invokes a user-defined update function; a rule component could, for instance, increment or reset a score.

A so-defined rule definition clearly implies a tight coupling of pattern-detection logic and response logic, preventing users from reusing rule logic in other contexts. Note, however, that infrastructural rules typically encompasses highly specific logic that is required exactly once in a system and makes sense only "as is". Decoupling the pattern-detection part and the reaction part of an infrastructural rule would therefore cause considerable effort not only for the actual decoupling, but also for the administration of the so-created sub-entities, for little or no gain. Also, using a single decision graph provides a comprehensive view on a rule; this simplifies the creation of complex rule logic and bug-fixing.

5. SENSE-AND-RESPOND RULES

In Section 1, we have introduced the notion of *Sense-and-Respond (S&R) rules* for all rules that do not prepare data for other parts of an application but directly or indirectly respond back to the source system. In the following, we discuss our proposed approach to *S&R rule management*. It is based on the idea of a.), *rule managers* preparing building blocks of pattern detection and reaction logic, and b.), *business operators* assembling these building blocks to concrete rules of the form "if pattern, then action(s)".

From the idea of easy to use building blocks, we derived the following requirements for an approach to S&R rule management:

- **Decoupling** of pattern-detection and reaction logic.
- **Reusability** of building blocks across different use cases, i.e., *configurability*.
- **Ease of use:** Performed by business users with limited technical expertise, the administration of S&R rules shall be *as simple and fail-safe as possible*, and fully abstract from the event-based foundations of decision making. Users shall neither have to care about the implementation of building blocks nor about the execution of concrete S&R rules as part of an application.
- **Hot deployment:** Given a running event-based infrastructure and a set of predefined building blocks, business operators shall be able to work autonomously, generally independent from other users or any kinds of temporal restrictions. As a consequence, an approach to S&R rule management shall support "hot deployment" of rules, i.e., to enact, change and remove rules without having to stop the entire system.
- **Security:** A rule-management framework shall enable rule managers to clearly define the competences of a given business operator, i.e., to define which building blocks are available to him or her for creating concrete S&R rules.

In the following, we discuss the key elements of our approach to S&R rule management. *Pattern definitions* and *action definitions* implement the concept of prepared building blocks of pattern detection and reaction logic. *Rule instances* represent concrete S&R rules assembled from these building blocks. *Rule spaces* group related building blocks and serve as a basis both for mapping S&R rule logic to rule services and user rights management.

5.1 Pattern Definitions

Encapsulating pattern-detection logic of a form that can be interpreted by UC4 Decision, pattern definitions represent the first category of easy-to-use "building blocks" in the proposed approach to S&R rule management. Together with their counterpart for reaction logic – so-called *action definitions* – pattern definitions form the base elements of any concrete S&R rule: Any rule is, eventually, based on the instantiation of a pattern definition; when an event situation matches the pattern, the associated reaction logic is triggered. In the proposed workflow, both kinds of building blocks are created by technically-versed domain experts – so-called *rule managers* – based on the general monitoring requirements of an enterprise. As with system operators, rule managers use the *Modeling Studio* for editing a Decision application; yet, in contrast to the former, rule managers are granted access to pattern and action definitions only.

Figure 7 and Table 1 show the meta-model for pattern definitions along with a concrete example. A pattern definition $p = (IN, OUT, d, t)$ is defined by a collection of *input parameters IN*, a collection of *output parameters OUT*, a *passive decision graph d* and a *textual representation t*. A decision graph is said to be passive if it does not contain any action component but is assembled from condition components and so-called *signals* only.

Input parameters allow configuring the pattern-detection logic of a pattern definition based on the specific use case in which it is used, without having to change and understand the encapsulated low-level pattern-detection logic. Within the decision graph of a pattern definition, input parameters may be used as typed placeholders in the various expressions of the used rule components; given an integer-typed parameter "Threshold", a condition on "Bet Placed" events could be defined as follows:

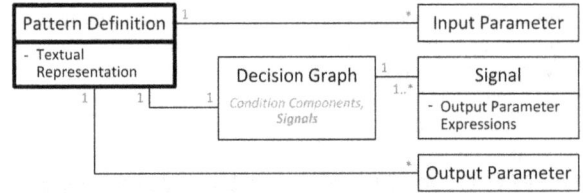

Figure 7. Pattern definition meta-model.

Table 1. Pattern definition example.

$$BetPlaced.Amount > \$Threshold$$

An input parameter $in = (i, t, validate)$ is defined by an identifier i, a data type t and an optional validator $validate: t \rightarrow \{0,1\}$. If specified, a validator allows further restricting the set of possible input-parameter values for in; given an input-parameter value $v: t$, $validate(v) = 1$ must hold.

Output parameters. In almost any use case, the action part of an event-pattern rule demands access to selected characteristics of the triggering event situation. The extraction of such data requires, however, detailed knowledge of the matched event sequence. Pattern definitions provide for an abstraction of the triggering event situation through the use of output parameters, which enable rule managers to specify those aspects of a triggering event situation that are supposed to be relevant when using the pattern definition in concrete S&R rules. To integrate the action part with the pattern part of a rule, business operators may then resort to a plain list of typed data fields. In the proposed model, an output parameter $out = (i, t)$ is defined by an identifier i and a data type t; the actual value of an output parameter is calculated in the various *signals* of the pattern definition's decision graph.

Signals. The actual event-processing logic of a pattern definition is defined as a decision graph, which allows evaluating instantiated pattern-detection logic on common rule services. The decision graph of a pattern definition is thereby required to be *passive*, which means that is must not contain any action components; instead, the specific actions to be taken in response are specified on the level of S&R rules, by *business operators*. A decision graph still requires, however, a dedicated class of rule components to signify the detection of a matching event situation. *Signals* are special action components that abstract from concrete reaction logic and simply notify the detection of an event situation to

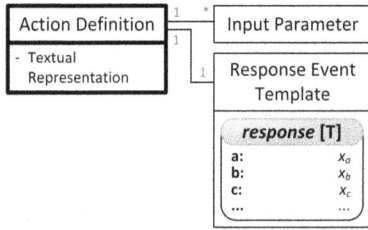

Figure 8. Action definition meta-model.

Table 2. Action definition example.

Input Parameters	ID	Type	Validation
	Text	String	-
	Priority	Integer	$1 \leq x \leq 5$
Textual Representation	(then) send alarm with text *Text* and priority *Priority* to fraud department		
Response-Event Template	**Response-Event Type:** com.example.common.Email		

Event Attribute ID	Type	Expression
To	String	"fraud@example.com"
Subject	String	"Alarm! Alarm!"
Text	String	"Alarm: " + $text
Priority	Integer	$priority
…	…	…

arbitrary signal listeners. A signal $s = (i, X_{OUT})$ is defined by an identifier i and a collection of *output-parameter expressions X_{OUT}* for all output parameters in OUT. When a signal is activated, these expressions are evaluated and concrete output-parameter values are calculated. By definition, the decision graph of a pattern definition must contain at least one signal.

Textual representation. Pattern definitions (as well as action definitions) are eventually provided to business operators in the form of a natural-language, textural representation t of the encapsulated event-processing logic, with placeholders for all input parameters. To facilitate a high-level, business-oriented approach to rule creation, the textual representation of a pattern definition would typically describe the real-world business situation that originally caused a matching event situation rather than the exact event sequence by itself; for instance, given a fraud pattern, one would speak of a "fraud attempt in league x" rather than a specific sequence of "Cash In", "Bet Placed" and "Cash Out" events. In Table 1 and 2, input parameters are shown in italic font.

5.2 Action Definitions

Action definitions encapsulate pieces of reaction logic and form the counterparts to above-described *pattern definitions* on the level of easy-to-use building blocks of business logic. In the presented rule-management framework, an action definition may thereby be considered as a blueprint for concrete *response events*; at run time, such response event then triggers the depicted real-world action in a downstream event service or the source system. For instance, an action "Email to fraud department" could encapsulate the generation of an event of type "Email", with the event attribute "Receiver" set to "fraud@example.com".

Figure 8 and Table 2 show the meta-model for action definitions along with a concrete example. An action definition $p = (IN, r, t)$ is defined by a collection of *input parameters IN*, a *response-event template r* and a *textual representation t*. As with pattern definitions, input parameters allow configuring the encapsulated event-processing logic depending on the specific context in which it is used. Within an action definition, an input parameter may now be used as a typed placeholder in the diverse event-attribute expressions of the response-event template; the concrete attribute values of a response event then depend on the input-parameter values as eventually specified in an S&R rule. The response-event template $r = (T, X)$ defines the general structure of an action definition's event representation. It is defined by an event type T and a collection of *event-attribute expressions X* for all event attributes in T. The textual representation t of an action definition would typically describe its ultimate result (as it would be visible to business operators) rather than its immediate, technical implications; for instance, an action definition that results in an event of type "Email" would be described as "sending an email".

5.3 Rule Instances

In the final step of the proposed workflow, pattern definitions and action definitions are eventually presented to *business operators,* which assemble these blocks to concrete event-processing logic of the form "if patterns, then action(s)". With both kinds of building blocks abstracting from underlying complexity through high-level, textual representations of the encapsulated event-processing logic, the process of assembling a S&R rule can thereby be presented to users as assembling a natural-language sentence of the form "if real-world situation, then real-world action(s)", from prepared clauses. Input parameters are seamlessly integrated into the textual representations and can successively be replaced by concrete values during the instantiation process.

For the creation and administration of S&R rules, UC4 Decision provides business operators with an easy-to-use, wizard-based web interface – the so-called *Web Control Center.* Figure 10 shows a screenshot from the Web Control Center's central rule-creation wizard: After choosing a pattern definition in the previous step of the wizard, the user may add action definitions to the rule instance by dragging the respective building blocks from a selection panel to the rule structure. Input parameters are rendered as links; on clicking a link, a popup dialog allows setting a constant value or an EA Expression in a type-safe editor.

Figure 9 shows the meta-model for rule instances. A rule instance $r = (p, X_p, B)$ is defined by a pattern definition p, a collection of *input parameter expressions X_p* for all input parameters of p and a collection of *bindings B*. Bindings are auxiliary constructs that associate the pattern definition with one or more action definitions; a binding $b = (a, X_a, C) \in B$ is defined by an action definition a, a collection of input-parameter expressions X_a for all input parameters of a and a collection of *conditions C*.

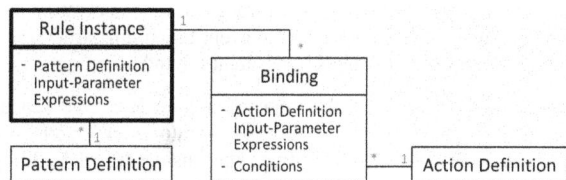

Figure 9. Rule instance meta-model.

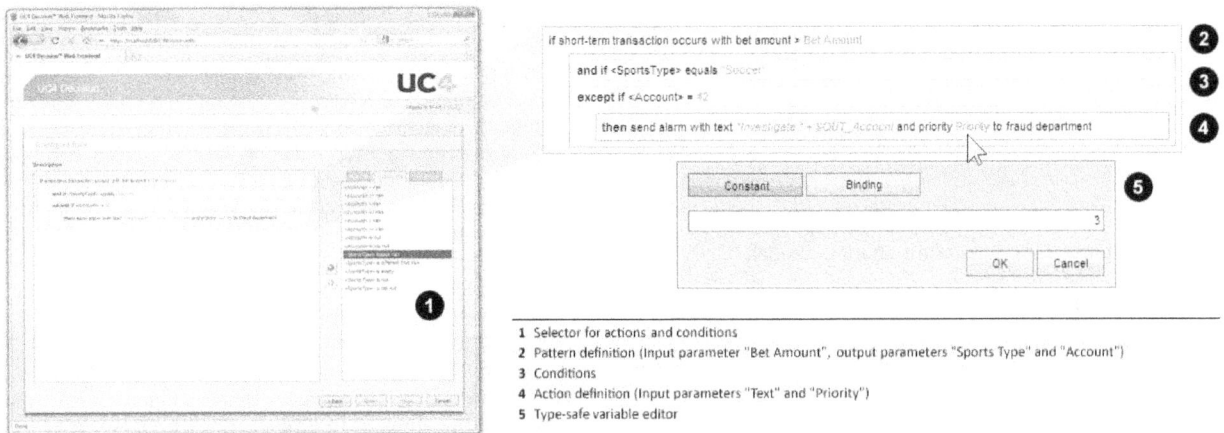

1 Selector for actions and conditions
2 Pattern definition (Input parameter "Bet Amount", output parameters "Sports Type" and "Account")
3 Conditions
4 Action definition (Input parameters "Text" and "Priority")
5 Type-safe variable editor

Figure 10. Creating Sense-and-Respond rules using *UC4 Decision Web Control Center*

Input parameter expressions define concrete values for the diverse input parameters of the rule's pattern definition and its action definitions, respectively. In case of action definitions, input parameter expressions may calculate such value from the output parameters of the pattern definition. This enables business operators to adapt reaction logic dynamically based on the triggering event-situation instance. Pattern-definition input-parameter expressions, by contrast, are necessarily constant.

Conditions provide a simple mechanism for business operators to further specify pattern-detection logic based on the characteristics of a triggering event situation, in a way that abstracts from the event-based foundations of decision making. A condition may basically be considered is a Boolean expression involving one or more output parameters of the pattern definition, which is evaluated whenever the pattern is detected. Only if all conditions of a binding evaluate to true, the associated action is executed. In the Web Control Center, meaningful conditions are generated based on the output parameters of the chosen pattern definition and can be added by "drag and drop" similar to action definitions.

It is essential to note that rule instances are not directly mapped to rule services; by contrast, such association is established *implicitly* – in a way that is transparent to business operators – through the concept of *rule spaces* as discussed in the next section.

5.4 Rule Spaces

Rules spaces group the pattern definitions and action definitions of a Decision application (both, in many-to-many relationships) based on the organizational tasks to which they belong; for instance, a rule space "Fraud Detection" could contain event-processing logic for detecting different kinds of fraudulent user behavior, notifying the fraud department, and blocking an account automatically. In this way structuring the overall S&R event-processing logic of an application, rule spaces play a crucial role for both the creation of S&R rules through business operators and the integration of S&R rules with the event-based infrastructure of an application, in a way that is transparent for end users.

Creating S&R rules: In the proposed architecture, rule spaces form the basic workspaces for business operators: Each S&R rule is created *within* a rule space, from the business-level building blocks of that rule space. With rule spaces grouping event-processing logic that makes sense concerning a certain organiza-

tional task, business operators are thereby confronted with task-relevant building blocks only, which facilitates a quick, secure and fail-safe rule creation process. Rule spaces eventually serve as the primary unit for user rights management as they can be assigned to business operators depending on their specific skills and functions within a company.

Executing S&R rules: Each rule space is assigned to a collection of *rule services*, which are then said to "host" the given rule space. During run time, all S&R rules that are created within a rule space are implicitly assigned to all hosting rule services; i.e., whenever a business operator creates a rule, this rule is automatically and transparently applied in appropriate parts of an underlying event-processing map. Accordingly, while the creation of a rule space and the grouping of building blocks is up to rule managers, the assignment of rule spaces to appropriately configured rule services lies in the responsibility of system operators. Both tasks are performed using the *Modeling Studio*.

In accordance with the overall role of S&R rules as sketched in Figure 2 – setting up on an event-based abstraction of underlying source systems – a rule space may now be considered as setting up on an event-based abstraction of a certain "aspect" of a business environment. Which parts of a source system actually belong to such aspect is defined by system operators, through the specific event-processing logic that precedes the concerned rule service(s) in the application's event-processing maps. Figure 11 illustrates the described role of rule spaces in UC4 Decision.

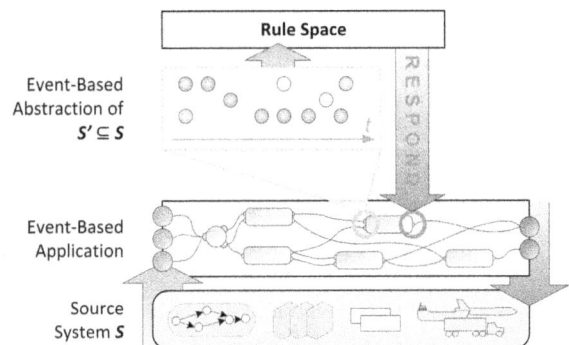

Figure 11. Rule spaces in a Decision application.

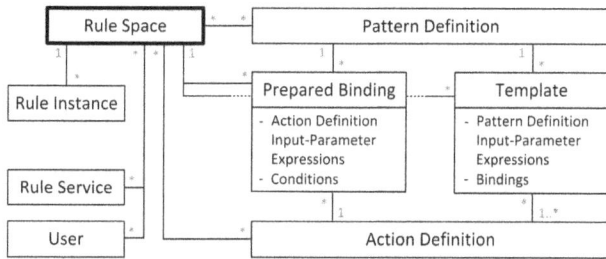

Figure 12. Rule space meta-model.

Figure 12 shows the meta-model for rules spaces. Besides associating pattern and action definitions, rule instances, rule services and authorized user accounts, rule spaces provide additional mechanisms for guiding the work of business operators through collections of *templates* and *prepared bindings*:

Templates are structurally equivalent to rule instances, however, may leave open input-parameter expressions for both the pattern and all action definitions. To create a rule from a template, a user simply defines the still missing input-parameter expressions, if any. Rule managers will typically provide templates for rule logic that is required frequently, with equal or similar configuration.

Prepared bindings enable rule managers to prepare associations between pattern and action definitions which are considered as meaningful and/or commonly requested in practical use cases. When creating a rule based on a pattern definition *p*, all prepared bindings for *p* are suggested to the business operator as being particularly suited in response to the given event situation; whether or not "non-prepared" action definitions are available depends on the specific authorizations of a business operator.

6. IMPLEMENTATION ARCHITECTURE

Over the past months, the presented approach to user-oriented rule management has been implemented as an extension to UC4 Decision's existing event processing and rule authorizing facilities. Figure 13 sketches the implementation architecture from a high-level perspective. On the data layer of the architecture, XML-based *application descriptions* define the static structure of the various Decision applications in an installation; among others, such definitions include an application's event-processing map, rule-, pattern- and action definitions, as well as its rule spaces. Each application description eventually refers to an *application database*, containing all data required during the execution of an application. Apart from active and historic event and correlation data, these include the present set of rule instances.

On the back-end layer, a collection of *executor nodes* is responsible for actually carrying out the event processing in a distributed execution environment. Infrastructural rules are retrieved from the application description during the deployment of an application. To support *hot deployment* of business logic, rule instances are retrieved from the application database at regular time intervals. For this purpose, each executor hosts a dedicated *rule-instance monitor*, which distributes updates to an application's rule services depending on the concerned rule spaces. Note that both infrastructural rules and S&R rules are, essentially, based on *decision graphs*, which allows using one and the same evaluation mechanism. While the separation between pattern detection and reaction logic in S&R rules requires some special handling, this has no relevant impact on overall event-processing performance.

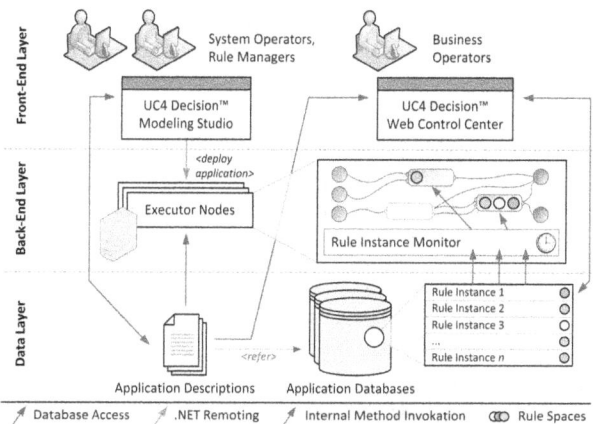

Figure 13. Implementation architecture.

On the front-end layer, tailored interfaces are provided to the different user groups of an application. *UC4 Decision Modeling Studio* is a .NET-based desktop application that provides power users with sophisticated facilities for creating and modeling Decision applications. Providing editors for rule-, pattern- and action definitions as well as rule spaces, the Modeling Studio is used by system operators as well as rule managers; while former are granted full access to an application, latter are authorized for creating and updating pattern- and action definitions only. Rule instances are eventually administrated via an easy-to-use, wizard-based *Web Control Center* as shown in Figure 10. While building blocks are retrieved from the application description, the interface does not provide any access to the event-based infrastructure of an application, which allows it to remain simple and focused on high-level decision-making. The Web Control Center has been implemented as an AJAX-based browser application using Google Web Toolkit (GWT).

7. CONCLUSION

Event-pattern rules of the form "if pattern, then action(s)" are a key element of Complex Event Processing (CEP) applications and showed to be useful for tasks across different conceptual layers of a systems: On the level of low-level *(pre-)processing and integration logic*, rules could be used to continuously filter, transform and aggregate events as emerging from the source system. On the level of high-level *business logic*, rules allow detecting exceptional business situations and triggering counteractions in near real time. We experienced that depending on their particular function in an application, rules are typically associated with different user groups within a company, each having its specific skills, competences and responsibilities. We thus claim that the potential of CEP for building agile business applications can only be unleashed if platforms become manageable and usable within the organizational framework conditions of an enterprise.

In this paper, we presented a novel rule-management framework for CEP applications that caters to the needs of technical-versed power users as well as business users. Technical experts model event-pattern rules in parallel and fully integrated with the others elements of an event-processing application. Business users assemble business logic from prepared, easy-to-use building blocks via a simplified, wizard-based web interface in a workflow that fully abstracts from underlying complexity.

Since implemented as part of UC4 Decision, the presented framework has successfully been set up at customers from different business domains. Experience from these projects confirmed that a separation into *infrastructural* and *Sense-and-Respond rule management* is particularly useful when the high-level business logic of an application shall be administrated by end users with restricted technical skills, and/or changes frequently. Here, significant efficiency enhancements could be achieved for both the customers' IT departments – which may now focus on maintaining the low-level processing logic of an application – and the involved domain experts, which may now administrate their rules by themselves, a straightforward and fail-safe manner.

Experience also showed, however, that in comparison to less flexible solutions that are based on *rule definitions* only, setting up a full-fledged rule-management system requires considerable additional efforts, e.g., for identifying event-processing logic that qualifies as a "building block", abstracting from such logic through input and output parameter, and defining and configuring rule spaces. Such efforts may not be justified in smaller installations or if all users have sufficient skills anyway. It is essential to note, though, that the proposed framework provides full support for both kinds of architectures; if a separate S&R layer is not rewarding, the entire functionality can just as well be implemented as part of the event-based infrastructure.

Resulting in applications that are inherently generic and adaptable to the current processing needs of an enterprise through S&R rules, existing projects eventually showed that our framework supports the definition of "standardized" CEP solutions, which can be offered to multiple customers with similar basic processing requirements and business environments. Customers can then benefit from the typical advantages of commercial off-the-shelf (COTS) software, including reduced costs, rapid deployment, well-tested and documented functionality, standardized updates, etc. Following from a large project from the workload automation domain, many of the created pattern and action definitions evolved into a so-called *solution template*, which by itself could be delivered to several other customers with minimum customer-specific adaptations, if any.

8. REFERENCES

[1] Abadi, D. J., Carney, D., Cetintemel, U., Cherniack, M., Convey, C., Lee, S., Stonebraker, M., Tatbul, N., and Zdonik, S. 2003. Aurora: A new model and architecture for data stream management. *VLDB Journal*, 12(2): 120–139.

[2] Adi, A., Botzer, D., Nechushtai, G., and Sharon, G. 2006. Complex Event Processing for financial services. In *Proceedings of the IEEE Services Computing Workshops (SCW'06)*. IEEE Computer Society, Washington, DC.

[3] Adi, A. and Etzion, O. 2004. AMIT – The situation manager. *VLDB Journal*, 13(2): 177–203.

[4] Ammon, R. v., Silberbauer, C., and Wolff, C. 2007. Domain specific reference models for event patterns. In *VIP Symposia on Internet related research with elements of M+I+T++*.

[5] Chandy, K. M. and Schulte W. R. 2010. *Event Processing: Designing IT Systems for Agile Companies*. McGraw-Hill, New York, NY.

[6] Chakravarthy, S. and Jiang, Q. C. 2009. *Stream Data Processing*. Springer, Berlin.

[7] Demers, A., Gehrke, J., Panda, B., Riedewald, M., Sharma, V., and White, W. 2007. Cayuga: A general purpose event monitoring system. In *Proceedings of the International Conference on Innovative Data Systems Research*, 412–422.

[8] Eckert, M. and Bry, F. 2010. Rule-based composite event queries: the language XChange^{EQ} and its semantics. *Knowledge and Information Systems*, Springer, London.

[9] Esper, http://esper.sourceforge.net

[10] Etzion, O. and Niblett, P. 2010. *Event Processing in Action*. Manning Publications, Stamfort, CT.

[11] Gualtieri, M. and Rymer, J.R. 2009. *The Forrester Wave™: Complex Event Processing (CEP) Platforms, Q3 2009*. Forrester Research, Cambridge, MA.

[12] Hinze, A., Sachs, K., and Buchmann, A. 2009. Event-based applications and enabling technologies. In *Proceedings of the Third ACM International Conference on Distributed Event-Based Systems (DEBS'09)*. ACM, New York, NY.

[13] Kellner, I. and Fiege, L. 2009. Viewpoints in complex event processing: industrial experience report. In *Proceedings of the Third ACM International Conference on Distributed Event-Based Systems (DEBS'09)*. ACM, New York, NY.

[14] Luckham, D. 2002. *The Power of Events*. Addison-Wesley, Boston, MA.

[15] Luckham, D. 2006. What's the Difference Between ESP and CEP? http://complexevents.com/?p=103

[16] Paschke, A. and Vincent, P. 2009. A reference architecture for Event Processing. In *Proceedings of the Third ACM International Conference on Distributed Event-Based Systems (DEBS'09)*. ACM, New York, NY.

[17] Paschke, A., Kozlenkov, A., and Boley, H. 2007. A homogenous reaction rules language for Complex Event Processing. In *Proceedings of the 2nd International Workshop on Event Drive Architecture and Event Processing Systems (EDA-PS'07)*

[18] Rozsnyai, S., Obweger, H., and Schiefer, J. 2008. Event access expressions: A business user language for analyzing event streams. In *Proceedings of the 25th International Conference on Advanced Information Networking and Applications (AINA'11). To be published.*

[19] Schiefer, J., Obweger, H., and Suntinger, M. 2009. Correlating Business Events for Event-Triggered Rules. In *RuleML'09*, 67–81. Springer, Berlin.

[20] Schiefer, J., Rozsnyai, S., Rauscher, C., and Saurer, G. 2007. Event-driven rules for sensing and responding to business situations. In *Proceedings of the International Conference on Distributed Event-Based System (DEBS'07)*, 198–205.

[21] Seiriö, M. and Berndtsson, M. 2005. Design and Implementation of an ECA Rule Markup Language. In *RuleML'05*, 98–112. Springer, Berlin.

[22] Sen, S. and Stojanovic, N. 2010. GRUVe: A methodology for Complex Event Processing life cycle management. In *International Conference on Advanced Information Systems Engineering (CAiSE'10)*. Springer, Berlin.

[23] Turchin, Y., Gal, A., and Wasserkrug, S. 2009. Tuning complex event processing rules using the prediction-correction paradigm. In *Proceedings of the Third ACM International Conference on Distributed Event-Based Systems (DEBS'09)*. ACM, New York, NY.

Distributed Event Based Challenges for Systems and Applications Management

Donald Francis Ferguson
CA Technologies, Inc.
New York, New York, USA
donald.ferguson@ca.com

Abstract

IT system and application management is critical to business use of IT systems. Distributed event processing is core to application and systems management, even for applications that are not "event driven." Emerging technology like virtualization and cloud computing significantly increase the central role of distributed event processing. IT systems and applications management introduces major challenges and requirements not typically seen in application centric event processing. This presentation provides an overview of IT system and application management use of distributed event processing, and the evolution for cloud computing. The presentation then provides an overview of current solutions and technology to the requirements. Finally, there will be a discussion of open issues and research challenges.

Categories & Subject Descriptors: D.0: Software [General].

General Terms: Design, Management, Performance, Reliability, Standardization

Keywords: Application Management; Systems Management

Business Artifacts with Guard-Stage-Milestone Lifecycles: Managing Artifact Interactions with Conditions and Events

Richard Hull[*1], Elio Damaggio[†2], Riccardo De Masellis[‡3], Fabiana Fournier[‡4],
Manmohan Gupta[5], Fenno (Terry) Heath III[1], Stacy Hobson[1], Mark Linehan[1],
Sridhar Maradugu[§6], Anil Nigam[1], Piwadee (Noi) Sukaviriya[1], Roman Vaculín[1]

[1]IBM T.J. Watson Research Center, USA
({hull,theath,stacypre,mlinehan,anigam,noi,vaculin}@us.ibm.com)
[2]University of California, San Diego (elio@cs.ucsd.edu)
[3]University of Rome, La Sapienza (demasellis@dis.uniroma1.it)
[4]IBM Haifa Research Lab, Israel (fabiana@il.ibm.com)
[5]IBM Global Business Services, India (manmohan.gupta@in.ibm.com)
[6]Finsoft Consultants, Inc., USA (sridhar1@us.ibm.com)

ABSTRACT

A promising approach to managing business operations is based on *business artifacts*, a.k.a. *business entities (with lifecycles)*. These are key conceptual entities that are central to guiding the operations of a business, and whose content changes as they move through those operations. An artifact type includes both an *information model* that captures all of the business-relevant data about entities of that type, and a *lifecycle model*, that specifies the possible ways an entity of that type might progress through the business. Two recent papers have introduced and studied the *Guard-Stage-Milestone* (*GSM*) meta-model for artifact lifecycles. GSM lifecycles are substantially more declarative than the finite state machine variants studied in most previous work, and support hierarchy and parallelism within a single artifact instance. This paper presents the formal operational semantics of GSM, with an emphasis on how interaction between artifact instances is supported. Such interactions are supported both through testing of conditions against the artifact instances, and through events stemming from changes in artifact instances. Building on a previous result for the single artifact instance case, a key result here shows the equivalence of three different formulations of the GSM semantics for artifact instance interaction. One formulation is based on incremental application of ECA-like rules, one is based on two mathematical properties, and one is based on the use of first-order logic formulas.

Categories and Subject Descriptors

D.2.2 [**Software Engineering**]: Design Tools and Techniques; H.4 [**Information Systems Applications**]: Office Automation—*Workflow management*

General Terms

Design, Theory, Verification

Keywords

Business Artifact, Business Entity with Lifecycle, Business Operations Management, Business Process Management, Case Management, Data-centric Workflow, Declarative Workflow, Event-Condition-Action Systems

1. INTRODUCTION

There is increasing interest in frameworks for specifying and deploying business operations and processes that combine both data and process as first-class citizens. One such approach is called Business Artifacts, or "Business Entities (with Lifecycles)"; this has been studied by a team at IBM Resarch for several years [18, 5, 17], and forms one of the underpinnings for the EU-funded Artifact-Centric Services Interoperation (ACSI) project [2]. Business artifacts are key conceptual entities that are central to the operation of part of a business and that change as they move through the business's operations. An artifact type includes both an *information model* that uses attribute/value pairs to capture, in either materialized or virtual form, all of the business-relevant data about entities of that type, and a *lifecycle model*, that specifies the possible ways that an entity of this type might progress through the business, and the ways that it will respond to events and invoke external services, including human activities. The IBM team has recently [12, 7] introduced a declarative approach to specifying artifact lifecycles, using the *Guard-Stage-Milestone* (GSM) lifecycle meta-model.[1] The current paper describes research on the formal specification and properties of an operational semantics for GSM, with an emphasis on (a) how GSM supports declarative specification of interaction

[*]This author partially supported by NSF grant IIS-0812578.

[†]Research by this author performed while visiting IBM Research, supported by NSF grant IIS-0812578.

[‡]The research leading to these results has received funding from the European Community's Seventh Framework Programme FP7/2007-2013 under grant agreement number 257593 (ACSI).

[§]Work by this author performed while an employee of IBM India.

[1]Following the tradition of UML and related frameworks, we use here the terms 'meta-model' and 'model' for concepts that the database and workflow research literature refer to as 'model' and 'schema', respectively.

between business artifacts, (b) how ECA-like rules are used to provide one of the three equivalent formulations of the GSM operational semantics, and (c) how results of [7] are generalized to the context of multiple artifact types and instances.

As described in [12], a core motivation of the research leading to GSM has been to create a meta-model for specifying business operations and processes that is based on intuitively natural constructs that correspond closely to how business-level stakeholders think about their business. GSM supports high-level and more details views of the operations, and supports a spectrum of styles for specifying the operations, from the highly "prescriptive" (as found in, e.g., BPMN) to the highly "descriptive" (as found in Adaptive Case Management systems). Importantly, GSM provides a natural, modular structuring for specifying the overall behavior and constraints of a model of business operations in terms of ECA-like rules.

There are four key elements in the GSM meta-model: (a) *Information Model* for artifacts, as in all variations of the artifact paradigm; (b) *Milestones*, which correspond to business-relevant operational objectives and are achieved (and possibly invalidated) based on triggering events and/or conditions over the information models of active artifact instances; (c) *Stages*, which correspond to clusters of activity intended to achieve milestones; and (d) *Guards*, which control when stages are activated. Both milestones and guards are controlled in a declarative manner, based on triggering events and/or conditions.

This paper is focused primarily on the *operational semantics* used by the GSM meta-model. This semantics is based on a variation of the Event-Condition-Action (ECA) rules paradigm, and is centered around *GSM Business steps* (or *B-steps*), which focus on what happens to a snapshot (i.e., description of all relevant aspects of a GSM system at a given moment of time) when a single incoming event is incorporated into it. In particular, the focus is on what stages are opened and closed, and what milestones are achieved (or invalidated) as a result of this incoming event. Intuitively, a B-step corresponds to the smallest unit of business-relevant change that can occur to a GSM system.

The semantics for B-steps has three equivalent formulations, each with their own value. These are:

Incremental: This corresponds roughly to the incremental application of the ECA-like rules, provides an intuitive way to describe the operational semantics of a GSM model, and provides a natural, direct approach for implementing GSM.

Fixpoint: This provides a concise "top-down" description of the effect of a single incoming event on an artifact snapshot. This is useful for developing alternative implementations for GSM, and optimizations of them; something especially important if highly scalable, distributed implementations are to be created.

Closed-form: This provides a characterization of snapshots and the effects of incoming events using an (extended) first-order logic formula. This permits the application of previously developed verification techniques to the GSM context. (The previous work, [3, 9, 6], assumed that services were performed in sequence, while in GSM services and other aspects may be running in parallel.)

This paper describes and motivates these three formulations of the semantics, and sketches the proof of their equivalence. Reference [7] provides a more rigorous presentation of these results, using an abstract version of GSM that permits a focus on the essential aspects of the meta-model. The current paper expands on those results in two specific ways: (1) Generalize from a single artifact type and single artifact instance to a context of multiple artifact types and instances, including the possibility of new artifact

instance creation in B-steps; and (2) Providing support for artifact instance interaction based on multi-instance conditions, and status-change events in one instance directly impacting another instance.

Although not a focus of the current paper, we note that in the GSM framework, it is generally assumed that *ad hoc* queries can be made against the family of currently active artifact instances; this follows a central philosphy of artifacts, namely, that the attribute data is business relevant and should be exposed (subject to appropriate access restrictions).

The GSM meta-model describe here is being implemented in the Barcelona prototype at IBM, a descendant of the Siena prototype [4]. Due to space limitations, the exposition here is brief with a focus on the intuitions, main concepts, and main results; more details are available in [13].

Organizationally, Section 2 gives an overview of the GSM meta-model through an example, including a discussion of how GSM supports declarative specification of interactions between business entities. Section 3 introduces some of the formalism used to specify GSM models. Section 4 introduces the ECA-like "Prerequisite-Antecedent-Consequent (PAC)" rules, and the "Polarized Dependency Graph (PDG)" which is used to define a well-formedness condition on GSM models, and to guide the application of the PAC rules. Section 5 presents the three formulations of the GSM operational semantics and their equivalence. Section 6 describes related work, and Section 7 offers brief conclusions.

2. MOTIVATING EXAMPLE

This section provides an informal introduction to GSM by describing how it can be used to model a Requisition and Procurement Orders (RPO) scenario.[2]

2.1 The Scenario

Briefly, in RPO a *Requisition Order* (or "Customer Order") is sent by a Customer to a Manufacturer. The Requisition Order has one or more *Line Items*, which are individually researched by the Manufacturer to determine which Supplier to buy it from. The Line Items are bundled into *Procurement Orders* which are sent to different Suppliers.

A Supplier can reject a Procurement Order at any time before completion and shipment to the Manufacturer. In this case, the Line Items of that order must be researched again, and bundled into new Procurement Orders.

We focus here on the management of the orders, from Customer to Manufacturer and from Manufacturer to Suppliers. (We do not consider assembly of the parts received from the Suppliers.) It is natural to model this scope of the Manufacturer's operations using three artifact types, as follows.

Requisition Order (RO): Each RO instance will manage the overall operation of a single Requisition Order (from a Customer to the Manufacturer), from initial receipt by the Manufacturer to delivery of the good(s) requested.

Line Item (LI): Each LI instance manages a single line item of a single requisition order. The main focus is to support the research for identifying which Supplier(s) to use, and to track the progress of the line item as it moves through research to being in a procurement order to arriving at the manufacturer.

Procurement Order (PO): Each PO instance manages a single procurement order (from the Manufacturer to a Supplier), from when

---

[2]The authors thank Joachim (Jim) Frank of IBM for first introducing them to a form of this problem scenario. We are using a simplified version of the scenario here.

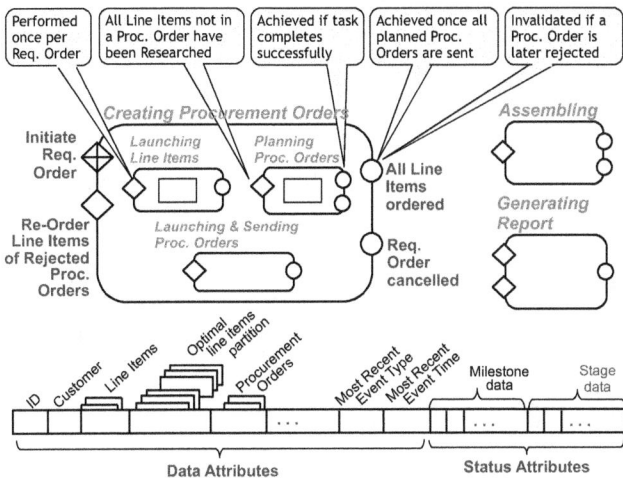

Figure 1: Sketch of artifact type for Requisition Order

it is initially sent to a supplier to the receipt of the goods or rejection by the supplier.

Due to space limitations, we do not consider error-handling in the scenario presented here. We note that typical error-handling will have business significance, and it can in general be modeled within the GSM framework.

2.2 Surrounding Framework for GSM Systems

In the general setting, an *Artifact Service Center (ASC)* is used to maintain a family of related artifact types and their associated instances. Speaking intuitively, the ASC acts as a container and supports conventional SOA interfaces (using both WSDL and REST) to interact with an (*external*) environment. The most significant part of the environment for the discussion here is its ability to support 2-way service calls, which may be short-lived (as with most automated activities) or long-lived (as with most human-performed activities). The environment can also send 1-way messages into the ASC, and can request that the ASC create new artifact instances.

GSM, as with most BPM, case management, and workflow systems, is intended to support the *management* of business-related activities, but not support the details of executing those activities. Thus, most of the "actual work" in connection with a GSM model is typically performed by actors in the environment. In particular, values of the data attributes are in general provided by human or automated agents that perform the tasks in a GSM model.

As noted in the Introduction, there are four primary components in the GSM meta-model, summarized here (further details given below).

Information model: Integrated view of all business-relevant information about an artifact instance as it moves through the business operations. In practice, this view might be materialized, virtual, or a hybrid.

Milestone: Business-relevant operational objective (at different levels of granularity) that can be achieved by an artifact instance. A milestone may be "achieved" (and become true when considered as a Boolean attribute) and may be "invalidated" (and become false when considered as a Boolean attribute).

Stage: Cluster of activity that might be performed for, with, and/or by an artifact instance, in order to achieve one of the milestones

owned by that stage. Each milestone corresponds to one alternative way that the stage might reach completion. A stage becomes "inactive" (or "closed") when one of its milestones is achieved. Intuitively, this is because the overall motivation for executing a stage is to achieve one of its milestones.

Guard: These are used to control whether a stage becomes "active" (or "open").

Also very important in the GSM model is the following notion.

Sentry: This consists of a triggering event type and/or a condition. Sentries are used as guards, to control when stages open, and to control when milestones are acheived or invalidated. The triggering events may be incoming or internal to the ASC, and both the internal events and the conditions may refer to the artifact instance under consideration, and to other artifact instances in the ASC.

2.3 Drill-down into the RO Artifact Type

Figure 1 illustrates the key components of the GSM meta-model through a sketch of the Requisition Order artifact type. This artifact type is centered around the information model, shown across the bottom. Here we see *Data Attributes*, which are intended to hold all business-relevant data about a given RO instance as it moves through the business. Speaking very loosely, these attributes are generally filled up from left to right, although they may be overwritten. The *Status Attributes* are also illustrated; these hold information about the current status and update time of all milestones (true or false) and all stages (open or closed).

The upper portion of Figure 1 illustrates parts of the *lifecycle model* of the RO artifact type. *Milestones* are shown as small circles associated with stages. Some of the sentries for the milestones are suggested in the call-out boxes of that figure. For example, one of the milestone achieving sentries of **All Line Items ordered** will become true if all of the planned PO's have been sent. In this case the milestone is said to be *achieved* at that moment, and also the milestone, considered as a Boolean attribute, is assigned the value *true*. Milestones may be *invalidated* or "compromised", and become false. As an example of invalidation, **All Line Items ordered** is invalidated if a Procurement Order is rejected, in which case the Line Items in that Procurement Order will have to be researched again and one or more new Procurement Orders will have to be generated.

The rounded-corner rectangles correspond to *stages*. (By construction, at most one milestone of a stage can be true at a time. Intuitively, each milestone of a stage corresponds to a distinct objective which might be achieved by the stage.) As illustrated by the stage **Creating Procurement Orders**, stages may be nested. Also illustrated are two *atomic* stages, namely **Launching Line Items** and **Planning Proc. Orders**. Both of these contain *tasks*, which in this case call services that exist outside of the ASC. involve activities that are modeled outside of the GSM model. There are three categories of task: to (a) invoke 2-way service call against the "environment", (b) send 1-way message to the environment (or to another artifact instance), and (c) send a 1-way message to the ASC calling for the creation of a new instance.

The diamond nodes are *guards*. If a guard for a currently closed stage S becomes true, and if there is a parent of S which is already open, then S becomes open. The guards shown in Figure 1 are labeled with names as a convenience; in the formal model these names are not accessible to the sentries. The diamonds with a cross are "bootstrapping" guards, which are used to indicate the conditions under which new artifact instances may be created.

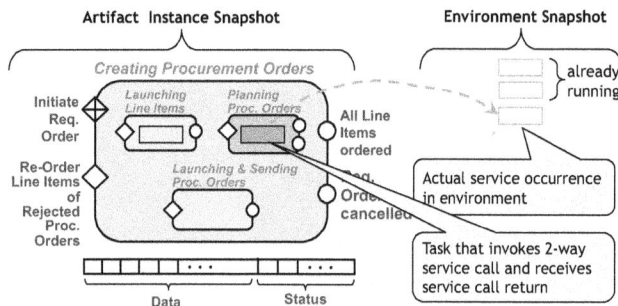

Figure 2: Invoking 2-way service calls that run in the environment

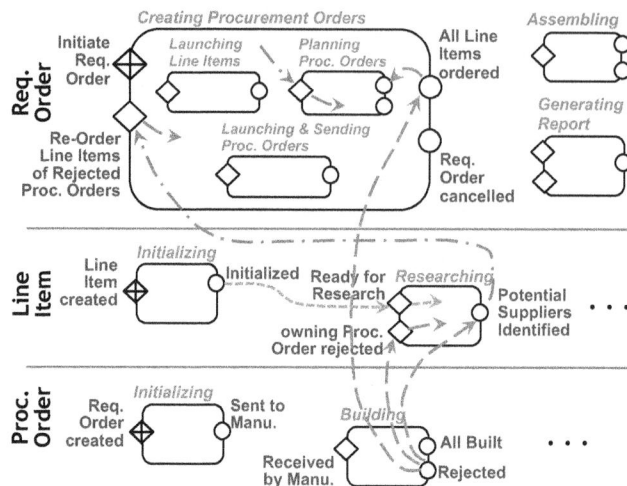

Figure 3: Interactions between artifact types

Two broad categories of events may be used in sentries: "incoming" and "internal". One form of *incoming event* corresponds to events that come from the environment *into* one or more artifact instances. There are three kinds of such event: (a) the return calls from 2-way service calls that were invoked by some artifact instance; (b) 1-way messages from the environment, and (c) requests from the environment that a new artifact instance be created. The second form of *incoming event* arises when one artifact instance generates a message intended for another artifact instance (or to create an artifact instance); in this case the ASC acts as an intermediary. Such events, when passed by the ASC to the target (or newly created) artifact instances, behave in much the same way as the first form of incoming event. There are three categories of artifact to artifact incoming events: (d) 1-way messages; (e) a request to create a new artifact instance, and (f) a return message to an artifact instance creation request, that holds the ID of the newly created artifact instance.

Internal events correspond to the changes in status of milestones (at the moment of being acheived or invalidated) and of stages (at the moment of being opened or closed).

2.4 Interaction with the Environment

Figure 2 illustrates at an intuitive level how 2-way service calls are invoked by artifact instances and run in the environment. The figure shows parts of one artifact instance snapshot that is part of the way through its execution. A stage is shown in (dark) green if it is currently open, and in (light) pink if it has run at least once and is currently closed. Assume that this is the snapshot that arises after the Requisition Order has been in existence for some time, after the initial Procurement Orders have been launched, after at least one of those orders has been rejected, and just when Planning Proc. Orders opens. As illustrated in the figure, there are two 2-way service call occurrences that are already running in the environment. The act of opening the Planning Proc. Orders stage leads to the invocation of an occurrence of the 2-way service specified by the task within that stage. Note that this service may be long-running (e.g., if it is performed by a human). This service may eventually terminate, in which case a service call return message will be sent from the environment back to the ASC, which will in turn "route" the message to the instance that called the service occurrence. This will have the effect of closing the stage occurrence of Planning Proc. Orders. Alternatively, a different milestone might be achieved with the effect of closing the stage occurrence (e.g., if a manager determines that the overall activity should be stopped). The service occurrence might continue to run, but the service call return would be ignored by the artifact instance that called it. In practical situations, the agent agent performing the service occur-

rence may be alerted that the service occurrence should be aborted. Also, in a practical setting, a richer style of interaction between an agent performing a service and the ASC might be supported.

2.5 Declarative Specification of Artifact Interactions

To conclude the discussion of the this example, we illustrate how the GSM constructs combine to permit the declarative specification of interactions between stages of a single artifact instance, and between related artifact instances.

A GSM Business step (B-step) corresponds to the incorporation of a single incoming event into a GSM system, including all implied achieving/invalidating of milestones and openings/closings of stages. Using informal diagramatic conventions, the colored, dashed lines in Figure 3 illustrate three possible B-steps.

For the first example, consider the two blue arrows (with short dashes) in the LI lifecycle. In this example, the milestone Initialized is triggered by an incoming event (e.g., that the automated process that checks certain validity conditions about the line item has completed). Also, suppose that the guard labeled Ready to Research has no condition, and has as event that the milestone Initialized has been achieved. In the notation used in the current paper, this is written as +l.Initialized (here l is the "context variable" for the type LI, and is used to refer to "self" in this case). In the B-step where milestone Initialized is achieved, the guard Ready to Research will become true and the stage Researching will be opened.

For the second example, consider the five green arrows (with long dashes) coming from the PO milestone Rejected. These correspond to kinds of actions that might occur in a B-step if some PO instance p achieves the milestone Rejected. In particular, the milestone All Line Items ordered for the RO instance that "owns" p, if it is currently true, will be invalidated. This corresponds to the intuition that there are now some LI instances that must be ordered from some other Supplier. Also, the milestone for successful completion of Planning Proc. Orders is invalidated whenever All Line Items ordered is invalidated. Turning to the impact on LI, for each LI instance l that is "owned" by p, the milestone Potential Suppliers identified for l, if true, is invalidated. Also, the guard owning Proc. Order rejected of the Researching stage is triggered, and this stage is re-opened.

For the third example, consider the four purple arrows (with long-short dashes), starting with the one that connects the Potential Suppliers identified milestone of LI with the guard Re-Order Line Items of Rejected Proc. Orders of Creating Procurement Orders in RO. That guard has no explicit triggering event, and its condition states, basically, "for each PO instance p that achieved Rejected, each LI instance "owned" by p has achieved Potential Suppliers identified". Speaking intuitively, if this condition becomes true, then each of the LI instances from a rejected PO has been researched, and so a new round of PO planning can be initiated. In particular, as suggested by the arrow from the guard to the interior of Creating Procurement Orders, if the guard becomes true then this stage will open. Furthermore, in this example the guard of substage Planning Proc. Orders will become true once its parent stage is open, and so the substage will also open.

When using a guard with no explicit triggering condition, it is important to ensure that the guard does not become true inappropriately. As a simple example, suppose that g is the guard of Launching Line Items in Figure 1, and the m is the milestone. In principle, the stage should open when the parent stage Creating Procurement Orders opens, and so g could be simply *true*. However, the intention is that the stage Launching Line Items should occur just once, and not repeatedly. This can be achieved here by using not p.m as the guard g. This device, of including the negations of milestones of a stage as conjuncts into a guard, is a useful pattern when using guards without triggering conditions.

2.6 Adding Flowchart Arrows to Lifecycle Models

We briefly mention that conditional flowchart arrows can be added as a formal part of a GSM lifecycle model. The specification of the most common kind of flowchart arrow arises when there is a guard g of form "**On** $+x.m$ **if** φ" where m is a milestone. This is essentially equivalent to having a flow arrow from the milestone m to guard g, where the arrow is annotated with the condition φ, meaning that the arrow should be traversed when the miletone is achieved but only if φ is true at that time. If desired, additional kinds of arrow can be incorporated, corresponding to different combinations of how one kind of status change (i.e., achieving or invalidating a milestone, opening or closing a stage) leads to another.

3. GSM META-MODEL

This section formally introduces the GSM meta-model. As such, there will be some redundancy with the informal introduction to GSM presented in Section 2. (Full definitions are provided in [13].)

3.1 Domain Types and Extended FOL

The artifact meta-model presented here supports the use of arbitrary scalar types, including Boolean, integer, etc. Two specialized types are **IncEVENT**, which ranges over the possible (names of) types of incoming events, and **TIMESTAMP**, which ranges over the "logical" timestamps corresponding to the times that B-steps are executed. Also, for each artifact type R we assume a set **ID**$_R$ of ID's for instances of type R.

The domains of all of these types are extended with the null value $\bot$. Collections of scalars, and collections of records of scalars are supported. Finally, the family of all *permitted* types for artifact attributes is denoted **TYPES**$_{permitted}$.

(In the practical GSM meta-model, arbitrarily deep nesting of the relation construct is permitted.)

In the formal GSM meta-model, we use an extension of First-Order Logic (FOL) that supports (i) multiple sorts; (ii) objects with structure record of scalars and collection of record of scalars; (iii)

the use of ordered pairs to represent values, where one coordinate holds a Boolean that indicates whether the value is $\bot$ or not; (iv) the "dot" notation to form path expressions (both into record types and to follow links based on artifact IDs); (v) a binary predicate $\in$ to test membership in a collection; and (vi) quantification over both collection types in artifact instances and over the full domain of currently active instances of an artifact type. It is well-known that expressions in this extended FOL can be transformed into equivalent expressions in classical FOL.

3.2 Artifact Types and GSM Models

This subsection introduces the notion of artifact type, which provides the structure for instances of business artifacts, and the notion of GSM model, which provides the structure for families of related business artifact types and their instances.

Definition: An *artifact type* has the form

$$(R, x, Att, Typ, Stg, Mst, Lcyc)$$

where the following hold:

- R is the *name* of the artifact type.
- x is a variable that ranges over the IDs of instances of R. This is called the *context variable* of R and is used in the logical formulas in *Lcyc*.
- *Att* is the set of attributes of this type. *Att* is partitioned into the set *Att*$_{data}$ of *data attributes* and *Att*$_{status}$ of *status attributes* (see below).
- *Typ* is the *type function* for the data attributes, i.e., *Typ*:*Att* $\to$ **TYPES**$_{permitted}$.
- *Stg* is the set of *stage names*, or simply, *stages*.
- *Mst* is the set of *milestone names*, or simply, *milestones*.
- *Lcyc* is the *lifecycle model* of this artifact type (defined below).

The set *Att*$_{data}$ must include an attribute *ID*, which holds the identifier of the artifact instance.

Additional restrictions are made so that events and their time of occurrence can be tested by sentries. In particular, *Att*$_{data}$ should include two attributes: *mostRecEventType*, which holds the type of the most recent incoming event that affected this artifact instance; and *mostRecEventTime*, which holds the logical timestamp of the processing of that most recent incoming event. For each milestone $m \in M$, there are two attributes in *Att*$_{status}$, namely: a Boolean *milestone status value* attribute, denoted simply as m, and a *milestone toggle time attribute*, denoted as $m^{mostRecentUpdate}$, which holds the most recent time that the status value changed. Analogously, for each stage $S \in Stg$, there are two attributes in *Att*$_{status}$: a Boolean *stage status value* attribute, denoted as *active*$_S$, and a *stage toggle time attribute*, denoted as *active*$_S^{mostRecentUpdate}$.

An artifact type $(R, x, Att, Typ, Stg, Mst, Lcyc)$ is often referred to using simply its name R. We use **ID**$_R$ to denote the type of IDs of artifact instances of R.

The structure of artifact type lifecycle models is defined next.

Definition: Let $(R, x, Att, Typ, Stg, Mst, Lcyc)$ be an artifact type. The lifecycle model *Lcyc* of R has structure

$$(Substages, Task, Owns, Guards, Ach, Inv)$$

and satisfies the following properties.

- *Substages* is a function from *Stg* to finite subsets of *Stg*, where the relation $\{(S, S') \mid S' \in Substages(S)\}$ creates a forest. The roots of this forest are called *top-level stages*, and the leaves are called *atomic stages*. A non-leaf node is called a *composite stage*.

- *Task* is a function from the atomic stages in *Stg* to *tasks* (defined in Subsection 3.4).

- *Owns* is a function from *Stg* to finite, non-empty subsets of *Mst*, such that $Owns(S) \cap Owns(S') = \emptyset$ for $S \neq S'$. A stage S *owns* a milestone m if $m \in Owns(S)$.

- *Guards* is a function from *Stg* to finite, non-empty sets of *sentries* (defined in Subsection 3.7). For $S \in Stg$, an element of $Guards(S)$ is called a *guard* for S.

- *Ach* is a function from *Mst* to finite, non-empty sets of sentries. For milestone m, each element of $Ach(m)$ is called an *achieving sentry* of m.

- *Inv* is a function from *Mst* to finite sets of sentries. For milestone m, each element of $Inv(m)$ is called an *invalidating sentry* of m.

If $S \in Substages(S')$, then S is a *child* of S' and S' is the *parent* of S. The notions of *descendant* and *ancestor* are defined in the natural manner.

We now have:

Definition: A *GSM model* is a set Γ of artifact types with form $(R_i, x_i, Att_i, Typ_i, Stg_i, Mst_i, Lcyc_i)$, $i \in [1..n]$, that satisfies the following:

- **Distinct type names:** The artifact type names R_i are pairwise distinct.

- **No dangling type references:** If an artifact type $\mathbf{ID}_B$ is used in the artifact type R_i for some $i \in [1..n]$, then $R = R_j$ for some (possibly distinct) $j \in [1..n]$.

As a convenience, we also assume that all of the context variables are distinct.

Let GSM model Γ be as above. As will be seen, the sentries of guards and milestones in one GSM type R_i of Γ may refer to the values of attributes in Att_j for type R_j for any $j \in [1..n]$, not just for $j = i$.

3.3 (Pre-)Snapshots and Instances

The notions of "snapshot" and "instance" for both artifact types and GSM models are now introduced. Structural aspects of these notions are captured using the auxiliary notion of "pre-snapshot". We shall use pre-snapshots to describe the incremental construction of a new GSM snapshot in a B-step.

Let Γ be a GSM model, and $(R, x, Att, Typ, Stg, Mst, Lcyc)$ be an artifact type in Γ. In this context, an artifact instance *pre-snapshot* of type R is an assignment σ from Att to values, such that for each $A \in Att$, $\sigma(A)$ has type $Typ(A)$. (Note that $\sigma(A)$ may be $\perp$ except for when $A = ID$.)

Let σ be an artifact instance pre-snapshot and let $\rho = \sigma(ID)$. If understood from the context, we sometimes use ρ to refer to the pre-snapshot σ. In this case, if A is an attribute of R, then $\rho.A$ is used to refer to the value of $\sigma(A)$. If attribute A has type $\mathbf{ID}_{R'}$ for some artifact type R' with attribute B, then $\rho.A.B$ refers to the B-value of the (pre-)instance identified by $\rho.A$. More generally, *path expressions* can be constructed that correspond to arbitrarily long chains of this kind of reference.

The relationship of stages and milestones is fundamental to the GSM meta-model. Core aspects of this relationship are captured in the following three *GSM Invariants*, which apply to artifact instance pre-snapshots. Let σ be an instance pre-snapshot of artifact type R with ID ρ. The GSM Invariants are specified as follows.

GSM-1: Milestones false for active stage. If stage S owns milestone m, and if $\rho.active_S = true$, then $\rho.m = false$.

GSM-2: No activity in closed stage. If stage S has substage S', and $\rho.active_S = false$, then $\rho.active_{S'} = false$.

GSM-3: Disjoint milestones. If stage S owns distinct milestones m and m', and $\rho.m = true$, then $\rho.m' = false$.

The third invariant stems from the intuition that milestones serve as alternative ways that a stage may be closed. This invariant is typically enforced in practice by syntactic properties of the milestone achieving sentries. The first two are enforced as part of the operational semantics below.

An artifact instance *snapshot* of type R is an instance pre-snapshot σ of type R that satisfies the three GSM Invariants.

An *artifact instance* of R is a sequence $\sigma_1, \ldots, \sigma_n$ of snapshots of type R such that $\sigma_1(ID) = \sigma_2(ID) = \cdots = \sigma_n(ID)$. Intuitively, an instance of R will correspond to a single conceptual entity that evolves as it moves through some business operations.

We now turn to GSM (pre-)snapshots and instances. A *pre-snapshot* of Γ is an assignment Σ that maps each type R of Γ to a set $\Sigma(R)$ of pre-snapshots of type R, and that satisfies the following structural properties:

- **Distinct ID's:** If σ and σ' are distinct artifact pre-instance snapshots occurring in the image of Σ, then $\sigma(ID) \neq \sigma'(ID)$.

- **No dangling references:** If an ID ρ of type $\mathbf{ID}_R$ occurs in the value of a non-ID attribute of some pre-snapshot in $\Sigma(R')$ for some R' in Γ, then there is a pre-snapshot σ in $\Sigma(R)$ such that $\sigma(ID) = \rho$.

Finally, a *snapshot* of Γ is a pre-snapshot Σ of Γ such that each artifact instance pre-snapshot in the image of Σ is an instance snapshot.

Let Γ be a GSM model and Σ a pre-snapshot of Γ. We now extend the function Σ to ID's and path expressions in the natural manner (e.g., $\Sigma(x. < path > .A[x/\rho])$) will evaluate to the value of attribute A for the artifact instance identified by the path $\rho.<path>$ when followed in (pre-)snapshot Σ).

In application, an *Artifact Service Center* (*ASC*) is used as a container for the set of artifact instances of the artifact types in Γ. The ASC can provide a variety of functionalities, including the relay of messages from an artifact instance out to the environment or to other artifact instances, and the relay of messages from the environment into the artifact instances.

3.4 Events and Tasks

As mentioned informally in Subsection 2.3, there are three kinds of *incoming* events (1-way message, 2-way service call return, and artifact instance creation request), and three kinds of *generated* events (1-way message, 2-way service call, and service call return for artifact instance creation request). These events are represented in the formalism as *messages* that have types, payload signatures, and a unique artifact type as target. For a *ground* event, the main part of the payload is a sequence $(A_1:c_1, \ldots, A_n:c_n)$ where, for each $i \in [1..n]$, A_i is a data attribute of the target type and c_i is a value of appropriate type. Depending on the message type there may also be payload attributes to help with correlation of service call returns. In practice, the message payloads may also include fault information.

Speaking informally, incoming events are received by the sentries associated with guards and milestones. Generated events are created by *tasks* contained in atomic stages. In particular, there are task types for generating 1-way messages (when invoked they wait for a "handshake" from the ASC indicating success or failure), generating 2-way service calls (when invoked they wait for the ASC to provide the service call return from the called service or a time-out

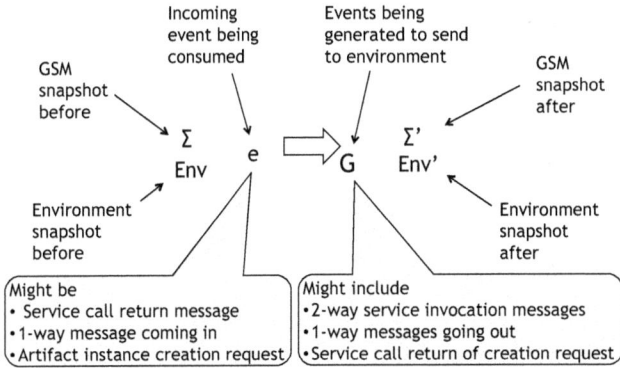

Figure 4: Illustration of a single GSM Business step (B-step)

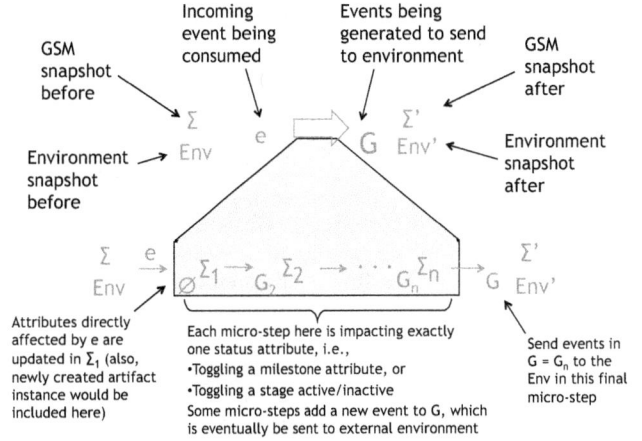

Figure 5: Incremental formulation of GSM semantics

message), and requesting the creations of a new artifact instance (which waits for a service call return with the ID of the newly created artifact instance).

3.5 The Immediate Effect of an Incoming Event

Let Σ be a snapshot, e a ground incoming event, and t a logical timestamp greater than all logical timestamps occurring in Σ. The ASC determines the set of artifact instances in Σ that are *directly affected* by e, using an event-specific query against the family of active artifact instances. For 2-way service call returns the correlation information in the message payload is used to identify the relevant artifact instance. 1-way messages might impact multiple artifact instances.

The *immediate effect* of e on Σ at time t, which is denoted as $ImmEffect(\Sigma, e, t)$, is the pre-snapshot that results from incorporating e into Σ, including

- Changing the values of the *mostRecEventType* and *mostRecEventTime* attributes of directly affected (or created) artifact instances, and

- Changing the values of data attributes of directly affected artifact instances (or initializing those data attributes in a newly created artifact instance), as indicated by the payload of e.

The immediate effect does not incorporate any changes to status attributes, nor cause any firing of guard or milestone sentries; this is addressed by the notion of B-step, presented next.

3.6 GSM Business Steps and Logical Timestamps

The operational semantics for GSM are focused on the notion of B-steps, which correspond to the impact of a single incoming event occurrence e at a logical timestamp t on a snapshot Σ of a GSM model Γ. This is illustrated in Figure 4. In this figure and the next, the "environment" is assumed to include data resulting from artifact-to-artifact messages that is held by the ASC. The semantics characterizes 5-tuples of the form $(\Sigma, e, t, \Sigma', Gen)$, where the following hold.

1. Σ is the *previous* snapshot.

2. e is a ground occurrence of an incoming event type associated with Γ.

3. t is a logical timestamp which is greater than all logical timestamps occurring in Σ.

4. Σ' is the *next* snapshot.

5. *Gen* is the set of ground *generated event occurrences*, all of whose types are outgoing event types associated with Γ.

To illustrate the notion of B-step, we describe key aspects of the incremental formulation of the operational semantics. In this case, Σ' is constructed in two phases (see Figure 5). The first is to incorporate e into Σ, by computing $ImmEffect(\Sigma, e, t)$. (If $ImmEffect(\Sigma, e, t) = \Sigma$ then the incoming event e is discarded and no B-step performed.) The second phase is to incorporate the effect of the guards, achieving sentries for milestones, invalidating sentries for milestones, and the first two GSM invariants. A family of ECA-like rules corresponding to these constructs is derived from Γ (Subsection 4.2). The second phase builds a sequence

$$\Sigma = \Sigma_0, \Sigma_1 = ImmEffect(\Sigma, e, t), \Sigma_2, \ldots, \Sigma_n = \Sigma'$$

of pre-snapshots, where each step in the computation, called a *micro-step*, corresponds to the application of one ECA-like rule, and where no ECA-like rule can be applied to Σ_n. (There are restrictions on the ordering of rule application, as detailed in Subsection 5.1.) Here Σ' corresponds to the result of the B-step. For each micro-step one also maintains a set G_j of *generated events*, which are sent to the environment at the termination of the B-step.

Although the creation of Σ' and *Gen* from Σ and e may take a non-empty interval of clock time, in the formal model we represent this as a single moment in time, called a *logical timestamp*. One can think of t as the clock time at the moment when the system began processing event e.

Each message in *Gen* is the result of opening an atomic stage with a message-generating task inside. The attributes of the message payloads are drawn from the data attributes of the artifact instance, which remain fixed once $ImmEffect(\Sigma, e, t)$ is computed. Thus, given the set of stages opened by a B-step it is straightforward to determine the set of messages that will be generated by that B-step. For this reason, the set *Gen* is not considered in the formalism below.

3.7 Sentries

Definition: An *event expression* for an artifact type R with context variable x is an expression $\xi(x)$ having one of the following forms.

- **Incoming event expression:** This includes expressions of the form $x.M$ (for 1-way message type M), $x.F^{return}$ (for service call return from F), and $x.create_R^{call}$ (which is a call to create an artifact instance of type R).

- **Internal event expression** (also known as **status change event expression**): This includes

  1. $+\tau.m$ and $-\tau.m$, where τ is a well-formed path expression of form $x.<path>$ with type $\textbf{ID}_{R'}$ for some artifact type R' in Γ, and where m is a milestone of type R'. Intuitively, an event occurrence of type $+\tau.m$ $[-\tau.m]$ arises whenever the milestone m of the instance identified by $x.<path>$ changes value from false to true [true to false, respectively].

  2. $+\tau.active_S$ and $-\tau.active_S$, where τ is a well-formed path expression of form $x.<path>$ with type $\textbf{ID}_{R'}$ for some artifact type R' in Γ, and where S is a stage name of type R'. Intuitively, an event occurrence of type $+\tau.active_S$ $[-\tau.active_S]$ arises whenever the stage S of the instance identified by $x.<path>$ changes value from closed to open [open to closed, respectively].

Definition: A *sentry* for artifact type R is an expression $\chi(x)$ having one of the following forms, where x is the context variable of R: "**on** $\xi(x)$ **if** $\varphi(x)$", "**on** $\xi(x)$", or "**if** $\varphi(x)$", and where the following hold.

(a) If $\xi(x)$ appears, then it is an event expression for R.

(b) If $\varphi(x)$ appears, then $\varphi(x)$ is a well-formed formula over the artifact types occurring in Γ that has exactly one free variable.

Expression $\xi(x)$, if it occurs, is called the *(triggering) event*. Expression $\varphi(x)$, if it occurs, is called the *condition*.

We now consider what it means for a pre-snapshot Σ to *satisfy* a sentry χ at time t, denoted $(t, \Sigma) \models \chi$. Satisfaction of a condition by Σ is straightforward, and not considered further. If χ involves an incoming event type E, the expression $\rho.E$ for artifact instance ρ is true if $\rho.currEventType = E$ and $\rho.currEventTime = t$. Similarly, if χ involves a status change event of form $\odot\rho.\tau.s$ (for polarity $\odot$, path expression τ, and status attribute s), the event expression is considered true if the value of $\rho.\tau.s$ matches the polarity $\odot$ and $\rho.\tau.s^{mostRecentUpdate} = t$.

4. PAC RULES AND POLARIZED DEPENDENCY GRAPHS

This section introduces two pillars of GSM. First is a family of ECA-like rules, called "Prerequisite-Antecedant-Consequent (PAC)" rules (Subsection 4.2). Second is the notion of "Polarized Dependency Graph (PDG)" (Subsection 4.3), which is used to define the well-formedness condition on GSM models, and to provide a form of stratification for the application of PAC rules.

4.1 Two intuitive principles

This subsection introduces and motivates two more-or-less equivalent intuitive "principles" that have guided the design of the GSM semantics. The first principle is phrased in terms of the incremental formulation of the GSM semantics, and the second is phrased in terms of the fixpoint formulation.

Toggle-once Principle. In a B-step (Σ, e, t, Σ'), if Σ' is constructed from (Σ, e, t) through the incremental application of PAC rules, then each status value attribute can change at most once during that construction.

Change Dominates Principle: In a B-step (Σ, e, t, Σ'), if the antecedents of two rules calling for opposite changes to a status value attribute $\rho.s$ of an artifact instance are both applicable to Σ', then the rule that changes the value of $\Sigma(\rho.s)$ dominates over the other rule, and $\Sigma'(\rho.s) \neq \Sigma(\rho.s)$.

A primary intuitive motivation behind these principles is that a B-step is intended to be a "unit of business-relevant change". In terms of the incremental semantics, this means that if a status value attribute changes during application of PAC rules, then that change should be visible (and incorporated into Σ'), rather than being hidden in the internal processing that computes Σ'. In terms of the Change Dominates Principle, this means that if there is a reason to change a status value attribute, then the change should be "documented" in one of the snapshots that is presented to the business, i.e., should be visible in between B-steps.

4.2 Prerequisite-Antecedent-Consequent Rules

All three formulations of the semantics for GSM are based on a variation of Event-Condition-Action (ECA) rules, called *Prerequisite-Antecedent-Consequent* rules, or *PAC* rules. Each such rule has three parts. The rules can be interpreted in two ways. The first is in the context of the incremental formulation, at a point where we have built up the sequence $\Sigma = \Sigma_0, ImmEffect((,\Sigma,,)e,t) = \Sigma_1, \ldots, \Sigma_i$. The other context is that of the fixpoint formulation, which focuses on the completed B-step (Σ, e, t, Σ'). We now give the intuition of the three components of the rules, in their grounded form, for both of these contexts.

Prerequisite: This part of the rule is considered relative to Σ in both contexts. It may be thought of as a prerequisite for determining whether the rule is relevant to (Σ, e, t).

Antecedent: This part of the rule is considered relative to Σ_i in the incremental formulation, and relative to Σ' in the fixpoint formulation. If the rule is relevant, then the antecedent can be thought of as the "if" part of a condition-action rule. As will be seen below, the antecedant will correspond to a sentry, and thus may include both a (first-order logic equivalent of a) triggering event and a condition.

Consequent: In the incremental formulation, if the rule is relevant, and if the antecedent is true in Σ_i, then the rule is considered to be *eligible*, and it may be *fired* to create Σ_{i+1} according to the consequent. In the fixpoint formulation, if the rule is relevant and Σ' satisfies the antecedent, then Σ' should also satisfy the result called for by the consequent.

For the fixpoint formulation, the reader may wonder why the antecedent is considered relative to Σ' rather than Σ. Intuitively, the focus is on creating Σ' to be the fixpoint, in the spirit of logic programming, of applying the PAC rules to $ImmEffect(\Sigma, e, t)$. In logic programming, the fixpoint itself satisfies all of the if-then rules, considered as first-order logic formulas. Similarly, in GSM the fixpoint Σ' satisfies the AC part of each PAC rule.

Figure 6 describes two sets of *abstract* PAC rules that may be associated with a GSM model Γ. Part (a) of the figure lists the templates for the set $\Gamma_{PACsimp}$ of *simplified PAC rules* for Γ. Part (b) lists the template PAC-4; the set Γ_{PAC} of *(enhanced) PAC rules* for Γ is the set of rules formed from $\Gamma_{PACsimp}$ by removing rules generated from PAC-4^{simp}, and adding all rules generated by PAC-4. Brief intuitions behind both sets of rules are now described.

First, consider the simplified PAC rules (Figure 6(a)). The first three kinds of rule are called *explicit*, and they correspond, respectively, to guards, to milestone achieving sentries, and to milestone invalidating sentries. The second three kinds of rule are called *invariant preserving*, because they focus on preserving the Invariants

	Basis	Prerequisite	Antecedent	Consequent
Explicit rules				
PAC-1	Guard: if **on** $E(x)$ **if** $\varphi(x)$ is a guard of S. (Include term $x.active_{S'}$ if S' is parent of S.)	$\neg x.active_S$	**on** $E(x)$ **if** $\varphi(x) \wedge x.active_{S'}$	$+x.active_S$
PAC-2	Milestone achiever: If S has milestone m and **on** $E(x)$ **if** $\varphi(x)$ is an achieving sentry for m.	$x.active_S$	**on** $E(x)$ **if** $\varphi(x)$	$+x.m$
PAC-3	Milestone invalidator: If S has milestone m and **on** $E(x)$ **if** $\varphi(x)$ is an invalidating sentry for m.	$x.m$	**on** $E(x)$ **if** $\varphi(x)$	$-x.m$
Invariant preserving rules				
PAC-4^{simp}	Opening stage invalidating milestone: If S has milestone m.	$x.m$	**on** $+ x.active_S$	$-x.m$
PAC-5	If S has milestone m.	$x.active_S$	**on** $+ x.m$	$-x.active_S$
PAC-6	If S is child stage of S'.	$x.active_S$	**on** $- x.active_{S'}$	$-x.active_S$

(a) PAC rules for Γ, "simplified" version

	Basis	Prerequisite	Antecedent	Consequent
PAC-4	Guard invalidating milestone: If S has milestone m and has guard **on** $E(x)$ **if** $\varphi(x)$ of S, where $E(x)$ is not $-x.m$, and where $\neg x.m$ does not occur as a top-level conjunct in $\varphi(x)$. (Include term $x.active_{S'}$ if S' is parent of S.)	$x.m$	**on** $E(x)$ **if** $\varphi(x) \wedge x.active_{S'}$	$-x.m$

(b) The "enhanced" rule template for PAC-4, which helps to maintain Invariant GSM-1.

Figure 6: Prerequisite-Antecedent-Consequent (PAC) rule templates associated with a GSM model Γ

GSM-1 and GSM-2. (Recall that Invariant GSM-3 is assumed to be maintained by properties of the milestones themselves.)

Consider PAC-1. The antecedent is basically the guard that the rule is derived from. If S is the child of S', then the conjunct $x.active_{S'}$ is added to the antecedent. The consequent corresponds to the intention of the guard to open stage S. In the incremental semantics leading to the computation of Σ' from (Σ, e, t), it is possible that both S' and S are closed in Σ, that some incremental step opens S', and that a subsequent incremental step opens S. In the final result Σ', both S and S' are open.

In general, the prerequisites are included to ensure that the Toggle-Once property is maintained.

We consider briefly PAC-4^{simp} and PAC-4, which are focused on Invariant GSM-1. PAC-4^{simp} follows the pattern and intuition of PAC-5 and PAC-6, and can be used in many situations. There are situations, however, in which it is desirable for a guard of a stage S to include as a condition that one or more of the milestones owned by S are currently not true. (This was illustrated in connection with stage Launching Line Items in Section 2.) In such cases, PAC-4^{simp} is needed so that the GSM model will still satisfy the well-formedness condition.

4.3 Stratification via Polarized Dependency Graphs

In the general case, the set of PAC rules of a GSM model Γ will involve a form of negation. As is well-known from logic programming and datalog, the presence of negation in rules can lead to non-intuitive outcomes. In the GSM operational semantics this will be avoided using an approach reminiscent of stratification as developed in those fields [1, 10]. In particular, the approach involves (i) requiring that a certain relation defined on the rules be acyclic,

and then (ii) requiring that the order of rule firing comply with that relation.

Let Γ be a GSM model. We construct the *polarized dependency graph* (PDG) of Γ, denoted $PDG(\Gamma)$, as follows. The set V_Γ of nodes for $PDG(\Gamma)$ contains the following for each artifact type R in Γ.

- For each milestone m of R, nodes $+R.m$ and $-R.m$
- For each stage S of R, nodes $+R.active_S$ and $-R.active_S$
- For each guard g of R, node $+R.g$

The set E_Γ of edges for $PDG(\Gamma)$ is based largely on the rules in Γ_{PAC}. In the following, R, R' range over not necessarily distinct artifact types in Γ; s, s' range over not necessarily distinct status attributes of those types; and "$\odot, \odot'$" correspond to polarities, that is, they range over $\{+, -\}$. Let x be the context variable for R. Also, in expression $\odot' \tau(x).s'$, $\tau(x)$ evaluates to ID's of type R'.

- Suppose that (π, α, γ) is a PAC rule in Γ_{PAC} having the form of PAC-2, PAC-3, PAC-5, or PAC-6.
- If α includes as a triggering event the expression $\odot' \tau(x).s'$ and γ is $\odot x.s$, then include edge $(\odot' R'.s', \odot R.s)$.
- If α includes in its condition an expression $\tau(x).s'$ and γ is $\odot x.s$, then include edges $(+R'.s', \odot R.s)$ and $(-R'.s', \odot R.s)$.
- Suppose that (π, α, γ) is a PAC rule in Γ_{PAC} having the form of PAC-1, that is created because of guard g for stage S in type R.
- If α includes as a triggering event the expression $\odot' \tau(x).s'$, then include edge $(\odot' R'.s', +R.g)$.
- If α includes in its condition an expression $\tau(x).s'$, then include edges $(+R'.s', +R.g)$ and $(-R'.s', +R.g)$.
- Suppose that (π, α, γ) is a PAC rule in Γ_{PAC} having the form of PAC-4, that is created because of guard g and milestone m for stage S in type R.

- If α includes as a triggering event the expression $\odot'\tau(x).s'$, then include edge $(\odot'R'.s', -R.m)$.
- If α includes in its condition an expression $\tau(x).s'$, then include edges $(+R'.s', -R.m)$ and $(-R'.s', -R.m)$.
- Finally, if g is a guard for stage S in type R, then include edge $(+R.g, +R.active_S)$.

Definition: A GSM model Γ is *well-formed* if $PDG(\Gamma)$ is acyclic.

The acyclicity of the PDG is used to guide the ordering of rule application in the incremental formulation. For example, if in the PDG there is an edge from $-R.m$ to $+R'.g$, this indicates that in the incremental formulation, all rules that might make $\rho.m$ false (for any ρ of type R) should be considered before any rule that might use $\rho'.g$ to open its stage (for any ρ' of type R').

In some cases it is helpful to use a more lenient notion of well-formed, that is based on the acyclicity of all of the *event-relativized* PDGs. For an event type E, the event-relativized PDG for Γ and E is constructed in the same manner as $PDG(\Gamma)$, except that a rule (π, α, γ) is not considered if π is an incoming event type different from E. (Although not considered here, the results of Section 5 hold for this more lenient notion of well-formed.)

5. THREE FORMULATIONS OF THE GSM OPERATIONAL SEMANTICS

This section describes the three formulations of the GSM operational semantics, and presents the equivalence theorem. The section also considers B-steps in series.

5.1 The Incremental Formulation

Assume that GSM model Γ is given, and let us focus on incorporating event e into snapshot Σ at time t. Recall from Subsection 3.6 and Figure 5 that the incremental formulation is based on the construction of a sequence

$$\Sigma = \Sigma_0, \Sigma_1 = ImmEffect(\Sigma, e, t), \Sigma_2, \ldots, \Sigma_n = \Sigma'$$

(where $\Sigma_1 \neq \Sigma$).

Given Σ_j, $j \geq 1$, a ground PAC rule (π, α, γ) is *applicable* to (or *eligible* to fire with) Σ_j if $\Sigma \models \pi$ and $\Sigma_j \models \alpha$. *Applying* (or *firing*) such a rule would yield a new pre-snapshot Σ_{j+1}, that is constructed from Σ_j by "applying" the effect called for by γ (that is, toggling exactly one status attribute of one artifact instance).

In the incremental formulation, the application of the ground PAC rules must *comply* with the ordering implied by $PDG(\Gamma)$, i.e., for each pair r, r' of ground rules with abstract actions $\odot R.s$ and $\odot'R'.s'$, respectively, if $\odot R.s < \odot'R'.s'$ then the rule r must be considered for firing before the rule r' is considered for firing.

LEMMA 5.1: *Suppose that (Σ, e, t) is a snapshot, ground event, and time greater than all times in Σ. Suppose further that $\Sigma_1 = ImmEffect(\Sigma, e, t)$. Then there is at least one snapshot Σ' obtained by firing the rules of Γ_{PAC} in an ordering that complies with $PDG(\Gamma)$, and where no more rules can be fired. Furthermore, if Σ' and Σ'' are constructed in this manner, then $\Sigma' = \Sigma''$.*

Proof (sketch): The existence of at least one Σ follows primarily from the facts that a change called for by one rule cannot be "undone" be another rule (mainly due to the prerequisites of the rules), and the fact that any sequence of rule firings will terminate (because there are only finitely many status attributes in a pre-snapshot). For uniqueness, assume that Σ' and Σ'' are different end results, and let $\odot\rho.s$ be a least ground status attribute that only one of Σ' or Σ''

changes, where ρ is of type R. Suppose without loss of generality that Σ' is the one where $\rho.s$ changes. Since Σ', Σ'' agree on all of the ground nodes that correspond to the abstract nodes preceding $\odot R.s$ in $PDG(\Gamma)$, the rule that triggered the change to $\odot\rho.s$ in Σ' is also applicable in Σ'', and could thus be fired there, yielding a contradiction. $\square$

Definition: A tuple (Σ, e, t, Σ') *satisfies* the incremental formulation of the GSM operational semantics if Σ' is the unique result of applying the PAC rules in appropriate order to $ImmEffect(\Sigma, e, t)$.

5.2 The Fixpoint Formulation

The fixpoint formulation for the GSM semantics is analogous to the one used in logic programming. In our context, we start with (Σ, e, t) and $ImmEffect(\Sigma, e, t)$ as before, and characterize snapshots Σ' that satisfy two key mathematical properties stemming from Γ_{PAC}.

Intuitively, the first property states that Σ' must comply with all of the demands of the PAC rules.

Definition: Given Γ and (Σ, e, t) as above, with non-trivial immediate effect, then snapshot Σ' is *compliant* with respect to Γ and (Σ, e, t) if

- Σ' and $ImmEffect(\Sigma, e, t)$ agree on all data attributes, and
- for each ground PAC rule (π, α, γ) of Γ_{PAC}, if $\Sigma \models \pi$ and $\Sigma' \models \alpha$, then $\Sigma' \models \gamma$.

Intuitively, the second property states that if a status attribute toggles between Σ and Σ', then that toggling must be "justified" by some ground PAC rule.

Definition: Given Γ and (Σ, e, t) as above, with non-trivial immediate effect, then snapshot Σ' is *inertial* with respect to Γ and (Σ, e, t) if the following holds for each artifact instance ID ρ in $\Sigma_1 = ImmEffect(\Sigma, e, t)$ having type R, and each status attribute s of type R: if $\Sigma_1(\rho.s) \neq \Sigma'(\rho.s)$ then there is some ground PAC rule (π, α, γ) of Γ_{PAC} such that: (a) $\Sigma_1 \models \pi$; (b) $\Sigma' \models \alpha$; and (c) the value of $\Sigma'(\rho.s)$ corresponds to the application of γ.

Definition: A tuple (Σ, e, t, Σ') *satisfies* the fixpoint formulation if Σ' is compliant and inertial with respect to Γ and (Σ, e, t).

5.3 The Closed-Form Formulation

The closed-form formulation of the GSM semantics is based on the observation that the properties of compliance and inertial can be captured in an extended FOL formula. The construction of the overall formula is reminiscent of constructions used for logic programming with negation, and in particular, when characterizing "negation as failure" [14].

The formula will work on structures of the form (Σ, e, t, Σ'). To express the formula over this structure, following the convention from verification theory, we use atomic formulas of the form $\varphi(x_1, \ldots, x_n)$ to range over Σ, and of form $\varphi(x_1', \ldots, x_n')$ to range over Σ'. Also, given a formula α involving un-primed variables, we use α' to denote the formula obtained from α by priming all of the variables (and thus making all of the atomic formulas relevant to Σ'.)

For a type R of Γ, status attribute s in R, and polarization $\odot$, let $Cnsq(\odot R.s)$ be the set of rules in Γ_{PAC} whose consequent is $\odot R.s$. Also, define $\psi_{+R.s}$ to be

$$((\neg R.s \wedge \bigvee_{(\pi, \alpha, +R.s) \in Cnsq(+R.s)} (\pi \wedge \alpha')) \rightarrow R.s') \wedge$$
$$((\neg R.s \wedge \bigwedge_{(\pi, \alpha, +R.s) \in Cnsq(+R.s)} \neg(\pi \wedge \alpha')) \rightarrow \neg R.s')$$

and define $\psi_{-R.s}$ to be

$$((R.s \wedge \bigvee_{(\pi,\alpha,-R.s)\in Cnsq(-R.s)} (\pi \wedge \alpha')) \rightarrow \neg R.s') \wedge$$
$$((R.s \wedge \bigwedge_{(\pi,\alpha,-R.s)\in Cnsq(-R.s)} \neg(\pi \wedge \alpha')) \rightarrow R.s')$$

Finally, the closed-form formula Ψ_Γ is defined as the conjunction of all of the formulas $\psi_{\odot R.s}$, along with a formula $\psi_{incorp\text{-}event}$ (not defined here) that states that the data attributes of Σ' match those of *ImmEffect*(Σ, e, t) (and that a new artifact instance has been created if e calls for that to happen).

Definition: A structure (Σ, e, t, Σ') *satisfies* the closed-form formulation of the GSM operational semantics if $(\Sigma, e, t, \Sigma') \models \Psi_\Gamma$.

5.4 The Equivalence Theorem

The equivalence of the three formulations of the GSM semantics holds for all GSM models Γ such that $PDG(\Gamma)$ is acyclic.

THEOREM 5.2: *Let Γ be a well-formed GSM model; Σ, Σ' two snapshots of Γ, e a ground incoming event, t a timestamp that is after all timestamps in Σ. Assume ImmEffect$(\Sigma, e, t) \neq \Sigma$. Then the following are equivalent.*

- (Σ, e, t, Σ') *satisfies the incremental formulation.*
- (Σ, e, t, Σ') *satisfies the fixpoint formulation.*
- (Σ, e, t, Σ') *satisfies the closed-form formulation.*

There is exactly one Σ' that satisfies these properties.

Proof (sketch): The second two formulations are equivalent because Ψ_Γ captures in extended FOL precisely the conditions of compliant and inertial. Let Σ' be constructed according to the incremental formulation. Note that the application of rules is monotonic, in the sense that in the sequence of rule firings, each rule applied makes a new change to the preceding pre-snapshot, and no change is "undone". Also, if a rule is fired, then all attributes in its antecedent cannot change after that rule firing. Finally, since no rule can be applied to Σ', we have the compliance property. For inertial, note that a status attribute is changed from Σ to Σ' only if there is a rule firing that changed it. For the opposite direction, given Σ' that is inertial and compliant, one can identify a ground rule that justifies each change between Σ and Σ'. Order these rules according to $PDG(\Gamma)$. Based on this, create a sequence of pre-snapshots that satisfies the incremental formulation. Uniqueness follows from Lemma 5.1. $\square$

5.5 B-steps in Series

This subsection briefly considers situations where it makes intuitive sense to consider a cluster of B-steps as a single unit. Recall that if an atomic stage contains a computational task (e.g., assigning one data attribute to equal another one), then this stage is opened in one B-step b_1 and is closed in some subsequent B-step b_2. Because the assignment is purely computational, it makes sense to have b_2 happen immediately after b_1. The same is true if B-step b_1 generates a message to the ASC intended for another artifact instance, or that calls for creation of an artifact instance, and b_2 processes that message. In practice, we define a *macro-B-step* to be a family of B-steps that starts with incorporation of an incoming event from the environment, and includes any subsequent B-steps stemming from automated actions within the BSC. Macro-B-steps are not guaranteed to terminate, nor to be unique. (We also note that in some corner cases, a change made by one B-step may be "undone" by another B-step in the same macro-B-step.)

6. RELATED WORK

The GSM approach draws on previous work on ECA systems (e.g., [16]), but develops a variant useful for data-centric management of business operations and processes.

There is a strong relationship between the business artifact paradigm and Case Management [21, 8, 22]. Both are data-centric, and support *ad hoc*, constrained styles for managing what activities should be performed and when. In both [21] and GSM, models are defined by adorning activities with a form of pre- and/or postconditions, and the operational semantics is based on ECA rules derived from them. GSM appears to be more general than [21], and incorporates an explicit milestone construct. The approaches of [21] and GSM may help to provide formal foundations for Case Management systems.

The AXML Artifact model [15] supports a declarative form of artifacts based on Active XML. The approach takes advantage of the hierarchical nature of the XML data representation used in Active XML. In contrast, GSM uses milestones and hierarchical stages that are guided by business considerations.

DecSerFlow [20] is a fully declarative business process language, in which the possible sequencings of activities are governed entirely by constraints expressed in a temporal logic. Condition-Response-Graph structures [11] support a family of intuitive constructs that are somewhat related to the GSM constructs, but with formal semantics defined using DecSerFlow. Neither system incorporates data with the prominence that GSM does. GSM does not attempt to support the level of declarativeness found in DecSerFlow, but instead relies on ECA-like rules and a fixpoint characterization.

There is a loose correspondence between the artifacts approach and proclets [19]. Both approaches focus on factoring business operations into components, each focused on a natural portion of the overall operations, and where communication between components is supported in some fashion. GSM places places more emphasis on data, and permits conditions against multiple artifact instances as a declarative form of communication between them.

7. CONCLUSIONS

This paper extends on-going work in the general area of event-driven, declarative, data-centric business process management. Building on two previous papers that introduce the Guard-Stage-Milestone (GSM) approach for specifying business artifact lifecycles, this paper describes how GSM supports the interaction between artifact instances in a declarative manner. The overall behavior of a GSM system is specified in terms of ECA-like rules. These rules are derived from the guards and milestones of stages, providing a natural modular structure for the rules. A precise operational semantics is given, and three formulations for that semantics are shown to be equivalent.

Research currently being pursued includes transactional properties, enabling stages to operate on members of a collection attribute, enabling a stage to operate on multiple artifact instances, and incorporating people and roles.

Acknowledgements

The authors thank the people in the extended Project ArtiFact team, the ACSI team, and several others. Most notable among these are: Diego Calvanese, David Cohn, Giuseppe De Giacomo, Nirmit Desai, Alin Deutsch, Amit Fisher, Nanjangud C. Narendra, Jianwen Su, John Vergo, and Victor Vianu.

8. REFERENCES

[1] K.R. Apt, H. Blair, and A. Walker. Towards a theory of declarative knowledge. In J. Minker, editor, *Foundations of Deductive Databases and Logic Programming*, pages 89–148. Morgan Kaufmann, Los Altos, CA, 1988.

[2] Artifact-centric service interoperation (ACSI) web site, 2011. `http:/acsi-project.eu/`.

[3] K. Bhattacharya, C. E. Gerede, R. Hull, R. Liu, and J. Su. Towards formal analysis of artifact-centric business process models. In *Proc. Int. Conf. on Business Process Management (BPM)*, pages 288–304, 2007.

[4] D. Cohn, P. Dhoolia, F.F. (Terry) Heath III, F. Pinel, and J. Vergo. Siena: From powerpoint to web app in 5 minutes. In *Intl. Conf. on Services Oriented Computing (ICSOC)*, 2008.

[5] D. Cohn and R. Hull. Business artifacts: A data-centric approach to modeling business operations and processes. *IEEE Data Eng. Bull.*, 32:3–9, 2009.

[6] E. Damaggio, A. Deutsch, and V. Vianu. Artifact systems with data dependencies and arithmetic constraints. In *Proc. Intl. Conf. on Database Theory (ICDT)*, 2011.

[7] E. Damaggio, R. Hull, and R. Vaculín. On the equivalence of incremental and fixpoint semantics for business artifacts with guard-stage-milestone lifecycles. In *Intl. Conf. Business Process Mgmt. (BPM)*, 2011. to appear.

[8] H. de Man. Case management: Cordys approach, February 2009. `http://www.bptrends.com/ deliver_file.cfm?fileType=publication&file Name=02-09-ART-BPTrends%20-%20Case%20 Management-DeMan%20-final.doc.pdf`.

[9] A. Deutsch, R. Hull, F. Patrizi, and V. Vianu. Automatic verification of data-centric business processes. In *Proc. Intl. Conf. on Database Theory (ICDT)*, 2009.

[10] A. Van Gelder. Negation as failure using tight derivations for general logic programs. In *IEEE Symp. on Logic Programming*, pages 127–139, 1986.

[11] T. Hildebrandt and R. R. Mukkamala. Distributed dynamic condition response structures. In *Pre-proceedings of Intl. Workshop on Programming Language Approaches to Concurrency and Communication Centric Software (PLACES 10)*, 2010.

[12] R. Hull et al. Introducing the guard-stage-milestone approach for specifying business entity lifecycles. In *Proc. of 7th Intl. Workshop on Web Services and Formal Methods (WS-FM 2010), Revised Selected Papers*, Lecture Notes in Computer Science. Springer, 2010.

[13] R. Hull et al. A formal introduction to business artifacts with guard-stage-milestone lifecycles, Version 0.8, May, 2011. Draft IBM Research internal report, available at `http://researcher.watson.ibm.com/researcher/ view_page.php?id=1710`.

[14] John. W. Lloyd. *Foundations of Logic Programming, 2nd Edition*. Springer, 1987.

[15] B. Marinoiu, S. Abiteboul, P. Bourhis, and A. Galland. AXART – Enabling collaborative work with AXML artifacts. *Proc. VLDB Endowment*, 3(2):1553–1556, Sept. 2010.

[16] D. R. McCarthy and U. Dayal. The architecture of an active data base management system. In *Proc. ACM SIGMOD Intl. Conf. on Mgmnt of Data (SIGMOD)*, pages 215–224. ACM Press, 1989.

[17] P. Nandi et al. Data4BPM, Part 1: Introducing Business Entities and the Business Entity Definition Language (BEDL), April 2010. `http://www.ibm.com/ developerworks/websphere/library/ techarticles/1004_nandi/1004_nandi.html`.

[18] A. Nigam and N. S. Caswell. Business artifacts: An approach to operational specification. *IBM Systems Journal*, 42(3):428–445, 2003.

[19] W. M. P. van der Aalst, P. Barthelmess, C.A. Ellis, and J. Wainer. Proclets: A framework for lightweight interacting workflow processes. *Int. J. Coop. Inf. Syst.*, 10(4):443–481, 2001.

[20] Wil M. P. van der Aalst and Maja Pesic. Decserflow: Towards a truly declarative service flow language. In *The Role of Business Processes in Service Oriented Architectures*, 2006.

[21] W.M.P. van der Aalst, M. Weske, and D. Grünbauer. Case handling: a new paradigm for business process support. *Data Knowl. Eng.*, 53(2):129–162, 2005.

[22] W.-D. Zhu et al. Advanced Case Management with IBM Case Manager. Published by IBM. Available at `http://www.redbooks.ibm.com/redpieces/ abstracts/sg247929.html?Open`.

Towards Context-Aware Adaptive Fault Tolerance in SOA Applications

Jonas Buys
Performance Analysis of
Telecommunication Systems
University of Antwerp
B-2020, Antwerp, Belgium
jonas.buys@ua.ac.be

Vincenzo De Florio
Performance Analysis of
Telecommunication Systems
University of Antwerp
B-2020, Antwerp, Belgium
vincenzo.deflorio@ua.ac.be

Chris Blondia
Performance Analysis of
Telecommunication Systems
University of Antwerp
B-2020, Antwerp, Belgium
chris.blondia@ua.ac.be

ABSTRACT

Software components are expected to exhibit highly dependable characteristics in mission-critical applications, particularly in the areas of reliability and timeliness. Redundancy-based fault-tolerant strategies have long been used as a means to avoid a disruption in the service provided by the system in spite of the occurrence of failures in the underlying components. Adopting these fault-tolerance strategies in highly dynamic distributed computing systems, in which components often suffer from long response times or temporary unavailability, does not necessarily result in the anticipated improvement in dependability.

In fact, as these dependability strategies are usually statically predefined and immutable, a change in the operational status (context) of any of the components involved may very well jeopardise the schemes' overall effectiveness. In this paper, a novel dependability strategy is introduced supporting advanced redundancy management, aiming to autonomously tune its internal configuration in view of changes in context. It is apparent from our preliminary experimentation that this strategy can effectively achieve an optimal trade-off between service reliability and performance-related factors such as timeliness and the degree of redundancy employed.

A prototypical service-oriented implementation of the proposed adaptive fault tolerant strategy is presented thereafter, leveraging WS-* specifications to gather and disseminate contextual information.

Categories and Subject Descriptors

C.2.4 [**Distributed Systems**]: Distributed applications; C.4 [**Performance of Systems**]: Fault tolerance; Reliability, availability, and serviceability; Measurement techniques; D.2.0 [**Software Engineering**]: Standards; D.2.8 [**Metrics**]: Performance measures

General Terms

Measurement, Reliability, Performance, Algorithms, Design

Keywords

dependability, service-oriented architecture (SOA), context-awareness, adaptive fault tolerance, quality of service (QoS), distance-to-failure (*dtof*), WS-* specifications

1. INTRODUCTION

There is a growing move to transform legacy distributed systems into service-oriented architectures (SOA), mainly driven by the prospects of interoperability, agility and legacy leverage. The widespread adherence to the service-oriented computing paradigm can be justified as it comprises the best practices in distributed computing of, roughly estimated, the past twenty years, and by the numerous standardisation initiatives backed by major industry consortia. Among the available technological solutions to SOA, XML-based web services, which have become the predominant implementation technology for encapsulating and deploying software components, are now being used in a diversity of application domains, ranging from enterprise software to embedded systems.

Business- and mission-critical applications are increasingly expected to exhibit highly dependable characteristics, particularly in the areas of availability and QoS-related factors such as timeliness. For this type of applications, a complete cessation or a subnormal performance of the service they provide, as well as late or invalid results, are likely to result in significant monetary penalties, environmental disaster or human injury. However, software components deployed within distributed computing systems may inherently suffer from long response times or temporary unavailability, the latter due to failures having occurred. Considering the compositional nature of many service-oriented applications, it is easily foreseeable that failures in the constituent components not properly dealt with can propagate and may subsequently perturb the service provided by the application. Moreover, each of the web services used within a given application introduces a potential point of failure.

There exist numerous web services (WS-*) specifications related to the dependability of XML-based web services, mainly in the areas of reliable messaging, transactional support and end-to-end-security [1]. Although rudimentary syntactical constructs for dealing with the previously described deficiencies have been provided in orchestration tools such as WS-BPEL, XML-based SOA does not, in itself, necessarily contribute to the construction of dependable web services.

Redundancy-based fault-tolerant strategies have long been used as a means to avoid disruptions in the service provided by the system in spite of failures having occurred or occurring in the underlying software components or hardware. Various approaches to achieve fault tolerance have appeared in the literature [2, 3, 4, 5]. Common to all these approaches is a certain amount of redundancy aiming to guarantee high availability and increased reliability of the functional service provided by the redundant system components. Deploying multiple instances of a particular software component in a distributed system has proved successful in improving the scalability, and may as well lower the risk of a complete system failure as the result of hardware failures [6, pp. 345–349].

It is however estimated that the vast majority of computer errors originate from software faults, estimations ranging from 60 up to 90 percent [7, 8]. Within distributed SOA applications, the bulk of the complexity is situated in the application layer, and there always remain design faults which eluded detection despite rigorous and extensive testing and debugging. Hence, traditional replication schemes, which were conceived to tolerate permanent hardware faults primarily and transient faults caused by external disturbances secondarily, do not offer sufficient protection for tolerating software faults (often referred to as design or specification faults) [3, 4].

Current software fault tolerant techniques attempt to leverage the experience of hardware redundancy schemes, and require diversity in the designs of redundant components in order to withstand design faults. The rationale is that redundantly deploying multiple functionally-equivalent but independently implemented software components will hopefully reduce the probability of a specific software fault affecting multiple implementations simultaneously, thereby keeping the system operational. This fundamental conjecture would guarantee that correlated failures do not translate into the immediate exhaustion of the available redundancy, as it would happen, e.g., by using identical replicas of the same software component [5, Chap. 8]. Replicating software would obviously incur replicating any residual dormant software fault.

The n-version programming (NVP) mechanism, a well proven design pattern for software fault tolerance, was first introduced in 1985 as "the independent generation of $n > 1$ functionally-equivalent programs from the same initial specification" [9]. An n-version module constitutes a fault-tolerant software unit — a client-transparent replication layer in which all n programs, called versions, receive a copy of the user input and are orchestrated to independently perform their computations in parallel. It depends on a generic decision algorithm to determine a result from the individual outputs of the versions employed within the unit. Many different types of decision algorithms have been developed, which are usually implemented as generic voters. Examples include, amongst others, majority, plurality and consensus voting [10][5, Chap. 4].

Regardless of the various controversies and debate to which design diversity has been subjected ever since its inception, the application of redundant implementations does have the potential to improve the reliability and scalability of software systems. It clearly brings with it some tangible impacts, the foremost of which are a significantly higher development cost and associated, increased infrastructural requirements. This additional investment could be justified for judiciously selected key components providing critical functions or with high reuse potential. Furthermore, even though the architectural complexity of the voting mechanism within an NVP module is of minimal magnitude compared to the complexity of the application logic, critics would state that it can become a single point of failure. This issue is traditionally overcome by conducting extensive testing to determine its reliability.

SOA systems exhibit highly dynamic characteristics, and changes in the operational status of web services, in particular their availability and response time, are likely to occur frequently. Conversely, classic fault-tolerant design patterns, including NVP, have traditionally been applied on an immutable set of resources (i.e. replicas), and are context-agnostic, i.e. they do not take account of changes in the operational status of any of the components contained within the redundancy scheme, which may jeopardise the effectiveness of the overall fault-tolerant unit.

Firstly, web services may often suffer from temporary unavailability. On the one hand, this may be the result of a failure, e.g. originating from the manifestation of a design fault or hardware malfunction. On the other hand the web service may become unreachable because of a network failure. The temporary unavailability of any specific web service comprised within a service-oriented application may cause the whole application to fail. Whereas such a point of failure may be addressed by applying, e.g. NVP with redundant web service implementations, such redundancy-based fault tolerance schemes will not necessarily result in an increase in availability. "Whether or not the availability is improved depends on the amount of redundancy employed and the availability of the software components used to construct the system" [4, 11]. From that point of view, it is therefore apparent that the effectiveness of any fault-tolerant redundancy scheme depends on how frequently its comprised resources become (temporarily) unavailable. Indeed, an NVP scheme, e.g. one based on majority voting, would fail to guarantee the availability of the service it seeks to provide if a majority of the resources employed have simultaneously become unavailable.

Secondly, the use of remotely deployed web service components may occasionally suffer from long response times, which is mainly to be attributed to any network latency as the result of message exchanges and, to a lesser extent, to excessive concurrency demands. For time-critical applications in which the timely availability of results is of paramount importance, any additional delay in the response time of a web service involved in an NVP scheme may impact the scheme's effectiveness to deliver an outcome within the imposed time constraints [12, 13].

There is thence an urgent need for adaptive software fault tolerant solutions, encompassing sophisticated context-aware redundancy management. The characteristic of context-awareness, referring to the fact that a redundancy scheme is aware of the environment (i.e. the context) in which it operates, is of considerable importance to support comprehensive redundancy management. Examples of contextual information include, but are not limited to, the amount of redundancy currently employed, the evolution of voting outcomes, and the operational status of each of the available resources such as dependability, load, execution time etc. Triggered by changes in the context, such adaptive fault tolerant strategies may autonomously tune the amount of redundancy or dynamically alter the selection of resources currently employed in the redundancy scheme so as to maintain the effectiveness of the dependability strategy, mitigating the adverse effect of employing inapt resources. In this paper, a novel dependability strategy is introduced supporting advanced context-aware redundancy management, aiming to autonomously and transparently tune its internal configuration. Designed to dynamically find the optimal redundancy configuration in order to preserve the intended dependability, the objective of this parameterised redundancy model is twofold.

Firstly, it is responsible for continuously monitoring any changes in the operational status of the available resources and other contextual information. Its purpose is to make sure that resources that may threaten the effectiveness of the overall redundancy scheme are excluded. It is noteworthy to mention that this resource selection procedure may target an optimal trade-off between dependability attributes as well as performance-related factors such as timeliness.

Secondly, the degree of redundancy employed is highly dependent on the current status of the context. On the one hand, in the absence of exceptional disturbances, the scheme should scale down its use of redundant resources so as to avoid unnecessary expenditure of resources. On the other hand, when the foreseen amount of redundancy is not enough to compensate for the currently experienced disturbances, it would be beneficial to dynamically revise that amount including additional resources — if available.

It is apparent from our preliminary experimentation that the proposed adaptive strategy enhances the overall effectiveness of proven fault-tolerance strategies, with little overhead incurred, attaining optimal performance, economical resource allocation notwithstanding.

The remainder of this paper is structured as follows: A set of application-agnostic context properties is presented in Sect. 2. Next, a property is introduced to capture the suitability of a particular software component within an NVP-based redundancy scheme with majority voting (NVP/MV). We then move on to elaborate on the internals of the proposed adaptive fault tolerance strategy in Sect. 4. A prototypical service-oriented implementation of this strategy is presented thereafter, leveraging established WS-* specifications. Furthermore, an illustrative example is given in Sect. 6 to clarify the measures and algorithm defined in the previous sections. Finally, related work is referred to in Sect. 7.

2. APPLICATION-AGNOSTIC CONTEXT PROPERTIES

The effectiveness of a fault-tolerant redundancy scheme such as NVP is largely determined by its redundancy configuration, i.e. the amount of redundancy used and, accordingly, a selection of functionally-equivalent software components. On the one hand, the amount of redundancy, in conjunction with the voting algorithm, controls how many simultaneously failing versions the NVP composite can tolerate whilst continuing to provide the user with

the expected service. For instance, an NVP/MV scheme can mask failures affecting the availability of up to a minority of its versions — a function of the amount of redundancy indeed. On the other hand, the dependability of any NVP composite is determined by the dependability of the versions employed in its redundancy scheme. As elucidated in [4, Sect. 4.3.3], the use of replicas of poor reliability can result in a system tolerant of faults but with poor reliability. Likewise, versions exhibiting low availability may result in a failure of the scheme when the amount of redundancy becomes insufficient to mask the ensuing failures. It is therefore of paramount importance to construct fault-tolerant systems using highly dependable software components.

Redundancy configurations of NVP schemes have traditionally been defined with a fixed amount of redundancy and an immutable set of versions. Having motivated the deficiencies of this approach in Sect. 1, this paper will introduce an adaptive NVP-based algorithm (A-NVP) in which the redundancy configuration is dynamically constructed in function of the context in which it operates. A context property will be introduced in Sect. 3 shortly, which will allow to obtain information regarding the reliability of a single version involved in an NVP/MV scheme.

Whether or not a particular version contributes to the success of a redundancy scheme may also depend on other aspects of a version's operational status. For instance, some mission-critical systems may require timely results. NVP voting schemes may be designed to return a reply within a guaranteed time slot. Any version failing to produce its response within the time constraints imposed by the voting system would translate in a performance failure and, as such, have a detrimental impact on the effectiveness of the redundancy configuration [2, 13]. The response time of a version will therefore also be considered as a context property in Sect. 4. Finally, another property of interest is the ability of the A-NVP scheme to optimally balance the load between the available resources. In order to achieve this, a context property to include in our focus shall be the number of pending requests, i.e. the number of requests currently being processed by a software component.

3. APPROXIMATING VERSION RELIABILITY IN NVP/MV

It was already pointed out that the dependability of any NVP composite is affected by the dependability of the components integrated within. Controversial opinions exist on whether it is meaningful to use probabilistic measures of dependability, most of which are based on an analogy of traditional hardware dependability, to evaluate the quality of software. In particular, many people have questioned the adequacy of software reliability to quantify the operational profile of a software system.

A first major objection that has frequently been put forth is that, in spite of the proliferation of software reliability models that have been developed since the early 1970s, only few of these models seem to be able to capture and quantify a satisfying amount of complexity without excessive limitations [15]. Failing to adequately quantify the reliability of a software component inhibits the application of commonly used analytical combinatorial techniques for reliability analysis of hardware redundancy schemes to equivalent schemes involving diversely designed functionally-equivalent software components [4, Chap. 4].

Moreover, it is hard to determine a quantitative approximation of the overall failure rate for a given software component. Apart from residual design faults, in SOA applications, the failure rate of a web service may be influenced as a consequence of a failure in the underlying deployment platform or hardware, in any required external web service or network connectivity failures [14, 13].

As an alternative to a probabilistic measure for the reliability of a software component, we now define a generic property to capture the suitability of a particular software component within an NVP/MV redundancy scheme.

3.1 Capturing the Effectiveness of the Current Redundancy Configuration

The distance-to-failure ($dtof$) metric, first introduced in [16], was meant to provide a quantitative estimation of how closely the currently allocated amount and selection of resources within an NVP/MV composite matched the observed disturbances — by shortcoming or excess. More specifically, $dtof$ can be used to deduce a measure of how well the currently employed redundancy configuration is capable of ensuring the availability of the composite's service.

We define the set V containing all functionally-equivalent versions available in the system. Let L be a set of monotonically increasing, strictly positive integer indices, such that each single voting round is uniquely identified. For a given round $l \in L$, the amount of redundancy used within the NVP/MV scheme is denoted as $n^{(l)} > 1$, such that the versions employed for round l are contained within $V^{(l)} \subseteq V$ and $n^{(l)} = |V^{(l)}|$. An indicator random variable $E^{(l)}(v)$ is defined for all $v \in V$

$$E^{(l)}(v) = \begin{cases} 0 & v \in V \setminus V^{(l)} & (1a) \\ 1 & v \in V^{(l)} & (1b) \end{cases}$$

and can be used to discriminate between idling versions and versions that are engaged in the current voting round l.

The essential part of any voting procedure is the construction of a partition $\wp^{(l)} = \{P_1, \ldots, P_{k^{(l)}}\} \cup P_F^{(l)}$ of the set of versions $V^{(l)}$. This partitioning procedure is heavily influenced by the disturbances that affected any of the versions involved during the voting round l. Throughout this paper, the notion of disturbance is used to denote the event of a single version struck by a failure perturbing the service it is expected to provide. We will now elaborate on several types of disturbances relevant to NVP/MV schemes and their effect on the generated partition. More specifically, disturbances will be categorised using the comprehensive list of failure classes for software components as presented in [2, Sect. 1.2.1].

A first category of disturbances comprises different types of failures resulting in the (temporary) unavailability of replicas. Having failed to obtain a response from these faulty versions, the voting algorithm will classify them in $P_F^{(l)}$. Examples include performance, omission and crash failures such as network connectivity failures, hardware malfunctions, design faults etc. [13].

Whereas it would be expected that functionally-equivalent versions sharing a common specification would return the same response when provided with identical input, discrepancies between their response values may arise due to response value failures [13]. The partition will subsequently hold equivalence classes $P_1 \ldots P_{k^{(l)}}$, such that each of these sets contains those versions which reported identical results[1]. Ideally, in a situation without disturbances of any kind, i.e. unanimous consensus, only one class P_1 would need to be created. Contrarily, dissenting versions require the creation of additional equivalence classes.

Let $P^{(l)}$ be the set in the generated partition $\wp^{(l)} \setminus P_F^{(l)}$ of largest cardinality and $c_{max}^{(l)} = |P^{(l)}|$. In other words, $c_{max}^{(l)}$ represents the largest consent found between the $n^{(l)}$ replicas at the end of voting round l. Then, in order for the majority voting procedure to be able to adjudicate the result of the scheme, there should be a consensus amongst an absolute majority of the $n^{(l)}$ versions, i.e. $c_{max}^{(l)} \geq M^{(l)}$. Conversely, if $c_{max}^{(l)} \leq m^{(l)}$, the voting procedure will not be able to determine a correct result.

$$M^{(l)} = \left\lceil \frac{n^{(l)} + 1}{2} \right\rceil \qquad (2)$$

$$m^{(l)} = \left\lfloor \frac{n^{(l)}}{2} \right\rfloor \qquad (3)$$

It logically follows from (2) and (3) that $M^{(l)} = m^{(l)} + 1$. Given these ancillary variables, the distance-to-failure for a specific voting round l is defined as

$$dtof^{(l)} = \begin{cases} 0 & c_{max}^{(l)} < M^{(l)} & (4a) \\ M^{(l)} - d^{(l)} & c_{max}^{(l)} \geq M^{(l)} \wedge n^{(l)} \text{ odd} & (4b) \\ m^{(l)} - d^{(l)} & c_{max}^{(l)} \geq M^{(l)} \wedge n^{(l)} \text{ even} & (4c) \end{cases}$$

where $d^{(l)}$ in (4b) and (4c) represents $n^{(l)} - c_{max}^{(l)}$, i.e. the number of versions that are either faulty or that returned a vote that differs from the majority, if any such majority exists[2]. If no majority can be found, $dtof$ returns 0. As can be easily seen, $dtof$ returns an integer in $[0, M^{(l)}]$ for any odd $n^{(l)}$ or in $[0, m^{(l)}]$ for any even $n^{(l)}$. This integer represents how close we were to failure at the end of voting round l. The maximum distance is reached when there is full consensus among the replicas, i.e. $\wp^{(l)} \setminus P^{(l)} = \emptyset$, therefore $V^{(l)} = P^{(l)}$ and accordingly $c_{max}^{(l)} = n^{(l)}$. Conversely, the larger the dissent, the smaller is the value returned by $dtof$, and the closer we are to the failure of the voting scheme. In other words, a large dissent (that is, small values for $dtof$) is interpreted as a symptom that the current redundancy configuration is not able to counterbalance the currently experienced disturbances. Figure 1 depicts some examples when the number of replicas is 7.

Intuitively, $dtof^{(l)} = 1$ corresponds to the existence of a consent between precisely $M^{(l)}$ versions, given that $n^{(l)}$ versions were involved during the current voting round l. Accordingly, for any $dtof^{(l)} > 0$, one can observe that

$$c_{max}^{(l)} = M^{(l)} + \left(dtof^{(l)} - 1 \right) \qquad (5)$$

---

[1] Note that in this paper, strict voting will be applied in view of the exchange of XML messages in SOA applications.

[2] For the sake of brevity, we say that the faulty versions in $P_F^{(l)}$ are in dissent with the responses returned by versions in $P_1 \ldots P_{k^{(l)}}$.

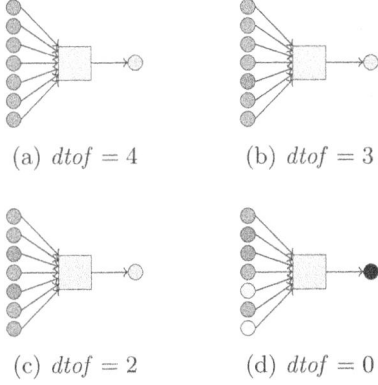

(a) $dtof = 4$ (b) $dtof = 3$

(c) $dtof = 2$ (d) $dtof = 0$

Figure 1: Distance-to-failure ($dtof$) in an NVP/MV scheme with $n = 7$ replicas. In (a), unanimous consensus is reached, which corresponds to the farthest "distance" to failure. For scenarios (b) and (c), more and more votes dissent from the majority (red and yellow circles) and correspondingly the distance shrinks. In (d), no majority can be found — thus, failure is reached.

In other words, $dtof^{(l)} - 1$ essentially quantifies how many versions there exist in excess of the mandatory $M^{(l)}$ versions that collectively constitute the majority for round l[3].

3.2 Quantifying the historical impact of a version on an NVP/MV scheme

Whereas the $dtof$ context property is a valuable metric for capturing the instantaneous impact of a given redundancy configuration on the effectiveness of an NVP/MV scheme, it fails to assess the impact of a particular version on the scheme over time. We therefore define a measure to quantify the historical and relative impact of any version $v \in V$ on the redundancy scheme — the normalised dissent :

$$D^{(l)}(v) = \begin{cases} 0 & \#rounds(v)=0 & \text{(6a)} \\ D^{(l-1)}(v)+p^{(l)}(v) & E^{(l)}(v)=1 \wedge dtof^{(l)}>0 \wedge v \notin P^{(l)} & \text{(6b)} \\ & E^{(l)}(v)=1 \wedge dtof^{(l)}=0 & \text{(6c)} \\ D^{(l-1)}(v) \times r^{(l)}(v) & E^{(l)}(v)=0 & \text{(6d)} \\ & E^{(l)}(v)=1 \wedge dtof^{(l)}>0 \wedge v \in P^{(l)} & \text{(6e)} \end{cases}$$

The number of voting rounds in which a version $v \in V$ was actively engaged, up until and including the current voting round l, is denoted by $\#rounds(v)$. The value of the normalised dissent is initialised to 0 — v. (6a). After that, it is updated at the end of each successive voting round for all versions $v \in V$.

The rationale is that a penalty $p^{(l)}(v) \in]0,1]$ is fined for any engaged version in dissent with the majority that resulted at the end of voting round l or when simply no majority was found, which corresponds respectively to (6b) and (6c). A version v that repeatedly failed to provide a

_____

[3] $P^{(l)}$ was previously used to denote the set of all versions in $V^{(l)}$ that contributed to the majority found at the end of round l. Let $P_M^{(l)} \subseteq P^{(l)}$ such that $|P_M^{(l)}| = M^{(l)}$. If $dtof^{(l)} = 1$, $P_M^{(l)} = P^{(l)}$. For $dtof^{(l)} > 1$, the majority is reconfirmed by $dtof^{(l)} - 1$ additional versions, i.e. $|P^{(l)} \setminus P_M^{(l)}| = dtof^{(l)} - 1$.

useful contribution to the voting procedure will therefore translate to a higher value $D^{(l)}(v)$. Inversely, a reward $r^{(l)}(v) \in]0,1[$ will weigh down previously accumulated penalties as they get older — v. (6d) and (6e). Both penalisation and reward mechanisms are presented in greater detail hereafter.

3.2.1 Acquiring Context Information

A substantial characteristic of both models is that the penalty addends and the reward factors they generate aim to capture the current context of the NVP/MV voting scheme. For a given voting round l during which a majority could be found, i.e. $dtof^{(l)} > 0$, let

$$w_e^{(l)} = 1 - \frac{dtof^{(l)} - 1}{n^{(l)} - M^{(l)}} \quad (7)$$

The above definition takes advantage of the $dtof$ metric as defined in (4) to acquire information on the effectiveness of the redundancy configuration employed during the voting round l. The fraction involved in (7) was designed so as to provide insight into the robustness of the redundancy configuration in face of the disturbances encountered. Specifically, the numerator can be regarded as the extent to which the majority is reconfirmed by $dtof^{(l)} - 1$ surplus replicas — cf. (5). This also expresses how many additional disturbances the redundancy configuration could have withstood during round l. Conversely, the denominator represents the maximum number of disturbances that the scheme can withstand, given the available amount of redundancy, $n^{(l)}$. As such, $w_e^{(l)}$ provides an estimation of how close a given redundancy configuration was to exhausting the available amount of redundancy whilst it tried to counterbalance the disturbances experienced during round l. Considering the premise that $dtof^{(l)} > 0$, it can be seen from (7) that $w_e^{(l)}$ is a real number contained within the interval $[0, 1]$. A critically low value $dtof^{(l)} = 1$, i.e. $w_e^{(l)} = 1$, represents a situation for which the majority was attained by only $M^{(l)}$ versions. During this voting round l, the available redundancy $n^{(l)}$ was completely exhausted to counterbalance the maximal number of disturbances the scheme could tolerate, i.e. $n^{(l)} - M^{(l)}$. If the scheme would have been subjected to additional disturbances affecting any of the versions $v \in P^{(l)}$, the scheme would have failed to reach a majority. Similarly, a value $w_e^{(l)} = 0$ corresponds to a voting round with full unanimity, i.e. $c_{max}^{(l)} = n^{(l)}$. Such additional consent contributes to the robustness of the scheme and its redundancy configuration, for it is resilient to withstand up to $n^{(l)} - M^{(l)}$ disturbances.

Furthermore, for $v \in V^{(l)}$, we define an ancillary function $c^{(l)}(v) = |P_j|$ for $P_j \in \wp^{(l)}$ such that $v \in P_j$, which allows to obtain the amount of versions that reported the same result as v at the end of round l. It can easily be seen that the range of this function is $[1, n^{(l)}]$.

3.2.2 Penalisation Mechanism

We now characterise the penalisation mechanism used in (6b) and (6c) for a subset of engaged versions $V^{(l)} \subseteq V$ — that is, a set of versions $v \in V^{(l)}$ for which $E^{(l)}(v) = 1$:

$$p^{(l)}(v) = \begin{cases} s^{(l)}(v) \times w_e^{(l)} & v \notin P_F^{(l)} \wedge dtof^{(l)} > 0 \quad (8\text{a}) \\[2mm] \dfrac{m^{(l)} - \left(c^{(l)}(v) - 1\right)}{m^{(l)}} & v \notin P_F^{(l)} \wedge dtof^{(l)} = 0 \quad (8\text{b}) \\[2mm] 1 & v \in P_F^{(l)} \quad (8\text{c}) \end{cases}$$

The penalty $p^{(l)}(v)$ inflicted by an engaged version $v \in V^{(l)}$ in dissent with the majority found at the end of round l is given by (8a). The idea behind the multiplier $w_e^{(l)}$ is that a replica disagreeing with the majority during round l should be penalised relatively to the detrimental impact it may have on the robustness of the currently selected redundancy configuration — cf. (7). The closer round l was to failure (that is, the closer to $dtof^{(l)} = 0$), the stronger the multiplier shall penalise the dissentient replica. The further away from failure, the less we penalise as the excess degree of consent enhances the robustness of the redundancy configuration such that it is capable of tolerating additional disturbances. Note how the above multiplier cannot evaluate to 0 for at least v is in dissent for round l, and therefore full consensus, i.e. the maximum value for $dtof^{(l)}$ as defined in (4), can never be reached — cf. (6b). The range of $w_e^{(l)}$, which was previously defined as $[0, 1]$ in (7), will therefore be confined to the interval $]0, 1]$.

The multiplicand $s^{(l)}(v)$ will then scale the intermediate penalty obtained using $w_e^{(l)}$ inversely proportional to the amount of consent between a minority of engaged versions, including v

$$s^{(l)}(v) = 1 - \frac{c^{(l)}(v)}{M^{(l)}} \qquad (9)$$

Indeed, any version v in dissent with the majority found is part of a minority equivalence class in $\wp^{(l)} \setminus \{P^{(l)}, P_F^{(l)}\}$. As the range of the previously defined function $c^{(l)}(v)$ will consequently narrow to $[1, m^{(l)}]$, one can observe from (9) that the values obtained for $s^{(l)}(v)$ lie in $]0, 1[$.

Having defined the maximum plurality that is not an absolute majority in (3), the penalty for any of the versions involved in voting round l for which no majority could be determined, can be found using (8b). A version v will be attributed the maximum penalty if its result is unique and in dissent with all the other versions, i.e. $c^{(l)}(v) = 1$. On the contrary, should there exist a minority of consentient active versions with cardinality equal to $m^{(l)}$, each of the versions would be penalised in the most gentle way. In other words, the more isolated the case, the heavier the penalty; the larger the cardinality of the minority to which a given version belongs, the less each of the versions that constitute the minority will be penalised.

Finally, faulty replicas that did not return a meaningful response are assigned the maximum penalty 1 – cf. (8c).

3.2.3 Reward Model

Whenever a version $v \in V^{(l)}$ produces a response that complies with the majority determined at the end of voting round l, a reward should compensate for any penalties that may have been imposed in previous voting rounds and consequently result in the gradual decline of the normalised dissent $D^{(l)}(v)$ — cf. (6e). Unlike the penalisation mechanism, which is only applicable to engaged versions, the reward model is also used for idle replicas that are not currently involved in the redundancy configuration for a given voting round l but that may have been used in previous voting rounds — cf. (6d).

Let $0 < k_2 < k_1 < k_{max} < 1$. We now define the reward factor $r^{(l)}(v)$ for a version $v \in V$ as:

$$r^{(l)}(v) = \begin{cases} k_1 + \left((k_{max} - k_1) \times w_i^{(l)}(v)\right) & E^{(l)}(v) = 0 \quad (10\text{a}) \\[2mm] k_2 + \left((k_1 - k_2) \times w_e^{(l)}\right) & E^{(l)}(v) = 1 \quad (10\text{b}) \end{cases}$$

For any version v, a smaller reward factor $r^{(l)}(v)$ will result in a steeper decline of its normalised dissent $D^{(l)}(v)$, whereas a larger factor would result in a more gradual decline. We now define $\#consent(v)$ as the number of those voting rounds which were accounted for in $\#rounds(v)$ for which v contributed to the majority. Consequently, $\#rounds(v) - \#consent(v)$ corresponds to those voting rounds in which v has been engaged, such that either v was in dissent with the majority, or no majority was found at all.

$$w_i^{(l)}(v) = \begin{cases} 0 & \#rounds(v) = 0 \quad (11\text{a}) \\[2mm] \dfrac{\#rounds(v) - \#consent(v)}{\#rounds(v)} & \#rounds(v) > 0 \quad (11\text{b}) \end{cases}$$

With $w_i^{(l)}(v)$ defined as a real number in $[0, 1]$, (10a) shows how the reward factor is determined for an idle version $v \in V \setminus V^{(l)}$ that is not involved in the current voting round l. It follows that $r^{(l)}(v)$ is contained within $[k_1, k_{max}]$. The upper endpoint of the range, k_{max}, is defined to be close to, but less than 1. This is motivated by the fact that, if k_{max} were equal to 1, a value $r^{(l)}(v) = 1$ would not be able to ensure that penalties accumulated during previous voting rounds are weighed down over time — cf. (6d) and (6e). The smallest reward $r^{(l)}(v)$ is equal to k_1 and corresponds to the case when v did not participate in any voting round so far, i.e. (11a), or when the replica contributed to the majority for every voting round it was previously engaged in, i.e. (11b) when $\#rounds(v) = \#consent(v)$. Larger reward values will be obtained for versions v, up to a maximum of k_{max}, proportional to the relative amount of voting rounds for which an engaged version v previously failed to support the voting scheme and was subsequently penalised, i.e. $w_i^{(l)}(v)$.

The reward procedure for engaged versions that were in consent with the outcome of the current voting round l is described in (10b). Having defined $w_e^{(l)}$ as a real number contained within the interval $[0, 1]$ in (7), it can be seen the range of $r^{(l)}(v)$ is delimited by $[k_2, k_1]$ for any version v engaged during round l. As it can be seen in (10b), larger values for $w_e^{(l)}$, i.e. $dtof^{(l)} - 1$ approaches 0, lead to a larger reward factor $r^{(l)}(v)$, up to the maximum value k_1. Contrariwise, more robust redundancy configurations translate into smaller values for $w_e^{(l)}$ and will be allotted smaller values for $r^{(l)}(v)$ accordingly. This allows to counterbalance and rectify a situation where v was undeservedly penalised in any preceding voting rounds it participated in, i.e. v did produce a correct result, but it was penalised because of an inadequate selection $V^{(l)}$.

As a final remark, we would like to point out that it was a deliberate design decision to define the reward model for idle versions in a separate range $[k_1, k_{max}]$, resulting in reward factors of comparatively greater magnitude, so as to ensure a more gradual decline in normalised dissent when compared to engaged replicas.

4. A NOVEL ADAPTIVE FAULT-TOLERANT STRATEGY

In this section, we introduce our adaptive NVP-based fault-tolerant strategy and elaborate on the advanced redundancy management it supports. Aiming to autonomously tune its internal configuration in view of changes in context, it was designed to dynamically find the optimal redundancy configuration. Our context-aware reformulation of the classical NVP/MV system structure encompasses two complementary parameterised models that jointly determine the redundancy configuration to be used throughout the next voting round l. During the first stage of this procedure, the redundancy dimensioning model, which will be explained shortly in Sect. 4.2, will select the appropriate degree of redundancy $n^{(l)}$ to be employed for a newly initiated voting round l in function of the disturbances experienced in previous voting rounds. Next, the replica selection model will establish which replicas $v \in V$ are most appropriate to constitute $V^{(l)}$. This second stage, which will be elaborated upon in Sect. 4.3, was designed to enrol those replicas targeting an optimal trade-off between the context properties introduced in Sect. 3.2 and 2, i.e. normalised dissent, response time and pending load, respectively.

4.1 Application-Specific Requirements

The optimal redundancy configuration is, however, not only determined by the quantitative assessment in terms of the context properties introduced in Sect. 2 and 3, but also by the characteristics of the application itself, or the environment in which it operates. For instance, some applications may be latency-sensitive, whereas others may operate in a resource-constrained environment. The A-NVP/MV algorithm was conceived to take these application-specific intricacies into account, in that the redundancy dimensioning and replica selection models can be configured by means of a set of user-defined parameters.

Our A-NVP/MV algorithm has been designed primarily to maximise the redundancy scheme's dependability, and secondarily, it may be configured to target other application objectives such as time constraints as well as load balancing. User-defined weights w_D, w_T and w_L for each of the three respective application objectives listed, can be used to configure the replica selection model such that it will engage the most appropriate replicas so as to maximise the overall effectiveness of the voting scheme. It is assumed that

$$\sum_{i \in \{D,T,L\}} w_i = 1 \qquad (12)$$

Furthermore, an optional user-defined parameter t_{max} represents the largest response time that the application can afford. A smaller value represents more stringent requirements on the scheme's response time, implicitly indicating that the application is more latency-sensitive. The t_{max} parameter is of particular interest as it is used to detect performance and omission failures: if a replica $v \in V^{(l)}$ failed to return its response to the NVP composite before the t_{max} time-out has lapsed since the execution of the voting procedure for round l was initiated, v will be classified in $P_F^{(l)}$ and penalised accordingly as described

in Sect. 3.2.2. Consequently, the response latency of the A-NVP composite is guaranteed not to exceed t_{max}. More specifically, if no absolute majority could be established before t_{max}, an exception will be issued to signal that consensus could not be found.

Finally, applications deployed in resource-constrained environments may benefit from the parameter n_{max} to set an upper bound on the number of replicas to be used in parallel, which may result in the utilisation of fewer computing and networking resources. This parameter may affect the degree of redundancy $n^{(l)}$ as determined by the redundancy dimensioning model, possibly at the expense of a significantly higher risk of failure of the voting scheme.

4.2 Redundancy Dimensioning Model

Given the set V of available functionally-equivalent versions in the system, our redundancy dimensioning model is responsible for autonomously adjusting the degree of redundancy employed such that it closely follows the evolution of the observed disturbances. In the absence of exceptional disturbances, the scheme should scale down its use of redundant replicas so as to avoid the unnecessary expenditure of resources. Contrarily, when the foreseen amount of redundancy is not enough to compensate for the currently experienced disturbances, it would be beneficial to dynamically revise that amount and enrol additional resources — if available.

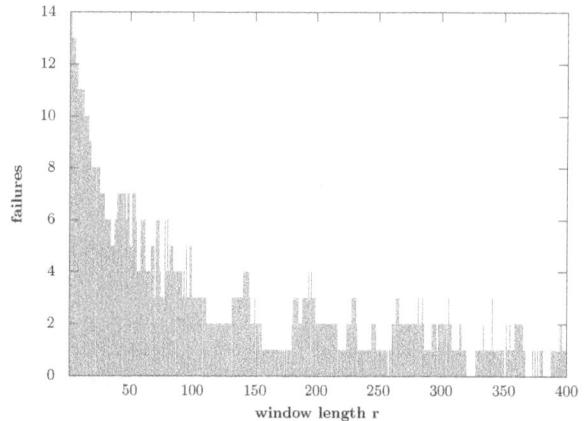

Figure 2: Number of voting scheme failures experienced while injecting faults in a simulation model for dynamically redundant data structures encompassing 10^7 rounds [16]. Abscissae represent how many consecutive voting rounds must have completed with $dtof^{(i)}_{i \in \{l-r,...,l-1\}} \geq 1$ before the employed degree of redundancy will be downshifted.

The redundancy dimensioning model is expected to determine $n^{(l)}$ upon initialisation of the voting round l, abiding the premise that $n^{(l)} \leq \min(|V|, n_{max})$. Note that the behaviour of the system is undefined when the optimal degree of redundancy as inferred by the model exceeds $n^{(l)}$. Depending on the application domain, the A-NVP scheme could simply report failure, or it could proceed with the suboptimal redundancy currently supported.

We will now briefly discuss a simplistic strategy that was originally published in [16], as a possible implementation for the redundancy dimensioning model. This strategy assumes a set V such that $|V| = 9$, and will only report an odd degree of redundancy, i.e. $n^{(l)} \in \{3, 5, 7, 9\}$. Moreover, the redundancy scheme is initialised such that it is capable of tolerating up to one failure, hence $n^{(0)} = 3$. If the voting scheme failed to find consensus amongst a majority of the replicas involved during the round $l-1$, the model will increase the number of redundant replicas to be used in the next voting round, to the extent that $n^{(l)} = n^{(l-1)} + 2$, provided that $n^{(l-1)} < |V|$. Conversely, when the scheme was able to produce an outcome for a certain amount r of consecutive voting rounds, which can be observed by values $dtof^{(i)}_{i \in \{l-r, \dots, l-1\}} \geq 1$, a lower degree of redundancy shall be used for the next voting round l, involving $n^{(l)} = \max(3, (n^{(l-1)} - 2))$ replicas. In other words, the model will maintain a sliding window so as to monitor the $dtof$ value obtained for the last r completed voting rounds.

As can be seen from Fig. 2, shorter window lengths may result in an incautious downscaling of the redundancy, which in itself might lead to failure of the voting scheme in subsequent voting rounds. The general trend shows that the redundancy scheme is less likely to fail due to the downscaling of the employed degree of redundancy for larger values of r, at the expense of postponing the relinquishment of excess redundancy. Unfortunately, even though the strategy is capable of scaling down the utilisation of system resources, it occasionally results in redundancy undershooting, even for relatively large values of r, as one may observe from the spikes in the graph shown above. It can be argued that the strategy, in its simplicity, does not take full account of the $dtof$ formalism as it was presented in Sect. 3.1. Had it been designed to consider, for instance, the actual amount of replicas that contributed to the majorities found during the last r voting rounds, it would have been able to determine to what extent the current level of redundancy could be decreased, and assess the risk of doing so — cf. (5) and (7).

4.3 Replica Selection Model

Having established the degree of redundancy $n^{(l)}$ to be employed throughout round l, the replica selection model will then determine a selection of versions $v \in V^{(l)}$ to be used by the redundancy scheme, such that $|V^{(l)}| = n^{(l)}$. The proposed model has been designed so as to achieve an optimal trade-off between dependability as well as performance-related objectives such as load balancing and timeliness, respectively represented as the w_D, w_L and w_T application-specific configuration parameters.

The suitability of a particular version $v \in V$ within an NVP/MV scheme can now be assessed quantitatively, leveraging the context properties introduced in Sect. 2 and 3. Let us now denote the last known values[4] of the normalised dissent, the number of pending requests and the average response time for a version $v \in V$ by $D(v)$, $L(v)$ and $T(v)$ respectively. If no such value was previously reported, all variables will hold the value 0. The process of determining

a trade-off between the different application objectives can now be facilitated by scaling the context properties, which were defined without any upper bounds, to the same range. We therefore define δ_D as the maximum value $D(v)$ for all versions $v \in V$. δ_L and δ_T are defined analogously as the maximum value of $L(v)$ and $T(v)$, respectively. Whereas $D(v)$, $L(v)$ and $T(v)$ are initialised to 0, the thresholds δ_D, δ_L and δ_T will be initialised to 1. Subsequently, the values for these context properties can now be scaled to a real number over the interval $[0, 1]$:

$$X_S(v) = \frac{\delta_X - X(v)}{\delta_X} \text{ for } v \in V \qquad (13)$$

where $X \in \{D, L, T\}$ stands for any of the three context properties normalised dissent, pending load and response time. Practically speaking, a larger value $X(v)$ for any of the three properties under consideration is representative of a worse impact of the replica v on the redundancy scheme. Accordingly, larger values of the scaled value $X_S(v)$ signal versions more suitable to support the redundancy scheme. After the context property values were scaled onto a common range $[0, 1]$, one can now determine the score $s(v)$ for each version $v \in V$ as follows:

$$s(v) = w_D \times D_S(v) + w_L \times L_S(v) + w_T \times T_S(v) \qquad (14)$$

The replica selection procedure is then reduced to a mere sorting problem, in which the versions are ranked by descending values of $s(v)$. At this stage, all information regarding the redundancy configuration is available, and the execution of the voting round l can proceed using the first $n^{(l)}$ versions.

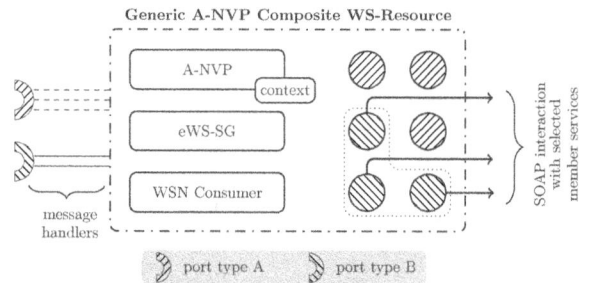

Figure 3: WSDM-enabled A-NVP WS-Resource aggregating several manageability capabilities. It can be seen from the message handlers that port type A exposes 3 operations and port type B exposes 2. All versions implementing port type A are assumed to be unreachable. When detected, the service group disables the corresponding message handlers.

Obviously, an important prerequisite to obtain an accurate resource selection $V^{(l)}$ is to have the required contextual information instantly available. As shown in Fig. 3, the A-NVP composite contains a context manager component that is responsible for continuously monitoring any changes in the operational status of the available resources, i.e. the context properties introduced in Sect. 2 and 3 for each of the functionally-equivalent versions $v \in V$ available in the system. When new information regarding one or more context properties is reported, the context manager will update its internal data structures accordingly, enforcing appropriate synchronisation

---

[4]The motivation for this weak definition is twofold. Firstly, the estimations of the pending load may be externally provided to the scheme and may therefore be subjected to delays. Secondly, even though the dependability metric $D^{(l)}(v)$ is harvested at the end of each voting round for versions $v \in V^{(l)}$, one cannot reasonably expect round $l-1$ to have completed by the time round l is initialised.

mechanisms so as to ensure data consistency. As such, any update of a context property $X(v)$ for a version v will instantaneously be reflected in the value of the corresponding δ_X. Property updates may account for internally deduced information, e.g. the $dtof$, normalised dissent and response time metrics, which are harvested by the A-NVP/MV scheme at the end of each voting round. Other metrics such as pending load may, however, be externally provided.

It was already pointed out in Sect. 4.1 that the optional user-defined parameter t_{max} is used to enable the detection of performance and omission failures. Whenever a replica v is detected to be affected by such a type of failure throughout the course of a voting round l, the stalled invocation request should promptly be abandoned, and a predefined internal failure message will be issued as the response message. Version v will consequently be classified in $P_F^{(l)}$, and penalised as described in Sect. 3.2.2, directly affecting the version's normalised dissent value.

The use of the t_{max} configuration parameter will also have repercussions on the $T(v)$ context property. As one can see in (14), if some context property value $X(v)$ for a specific replica v was not updated after its initialisation, i.e. $X(v) = 0$ and therefore $X_S(v) = 1$, the version is tacitly assumed to contribute to the success of the scheme in terms of the application objective associated with that property. We have therefore chosen to report t_{max} as the response time of versions that fail to return their response within the imposed time constraint, such that the system can guarantee that $T(v) \leq t_{max}$.

5. A-NVP WS-* SOA PROTOTYPE

In this section, we present a prototypical service-oriented implementation of the adaptive fault tolerant strategy as proposed in Sect. 4. The framework was conceived leveraging a set of ratified WS-* specifications, mainly capitalising on the features offered by the Web Services Resource Framework (WSRF), Web Services Distributed Management (WSDM) and WS-Notification (WSN) families of OASIS-published standards. Figure 4 shows a layered representation of the specifications relevant to our A-NVP implementation[5]. The framework was developed using the latest version of Apache MUSE to date, supplemented by our own implementation of the Management of Web Services (MOWS) specification[6].

A WSDM-enabled WS-Resource is essentially an aggregation of several manageability capabilities that are collectively exposed through a cohesive Web Services Description Language (WSDL) interface. A manageability capability defines a set of resource properties, operations,

---

[5]Due to space restrictions, introductory explanations of specific features of the specifications referred to cannot be provided. The reader may wish to consult www.oasis-open.org/committees/ for more information regarding the WSRF, WSDM and WSN specifications. Detailed information on W3C-driven specifications, particularly XML-related standards and first-generation WS-* standards such as WSDL, WS-Addressing and SOAP, may be retrieved from http://www.w3.org/TR/.

[6]For more information, refer to http://ws.apache.org/muse. The source code for the MOWS implementation is publicly available via http://pats.ua.ac.be/svn/muse.

events, metadata and other semantics supporting a particular management aspect of a WS-Resource service. Apart from a set of predefined foundational manageability capabilities, WSDM was designed for extensibility, allowing the development of domain-specific capabilities comprising customised manageability logic or that extend any of the foundational capabilities as appropriate. Having implemented the A-NVP composite as a WSDM-enabled web service, the core of its implementation consists of two capabilities, as can be observed in Fig. 3.

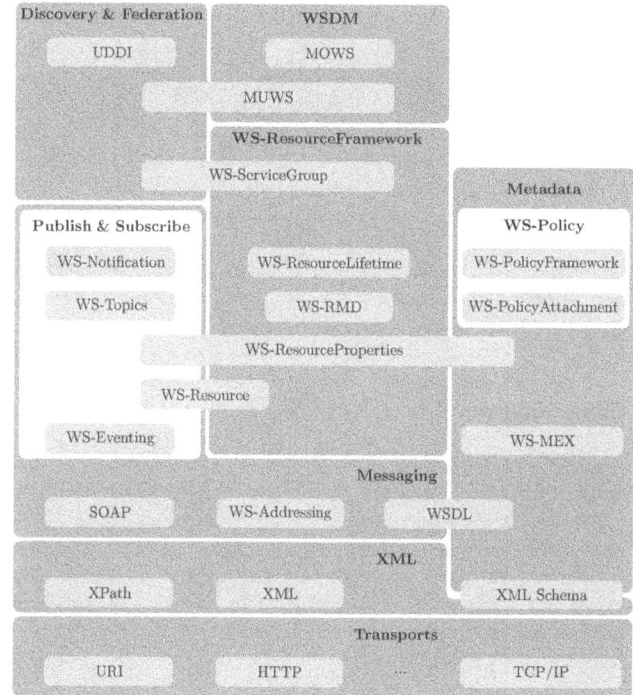

Figure 4: Layered overview of WS-* specifications illustrating WSRF and WSDM and their interdependencies relative to other industry standards.

5.1 Enhanced WS-ServiceGroup Capability

The composite A-NVP web service leverages the WS-ServiceGroup (WSSG) specification and the notion of membership content rules defined therein to manage federations of functionally-equivalent web services. The entries of the group represent locally or remotely hosted member web services, and membership content rules can be used to express constraints on the member services. Such rules can impose limitations on the WSDL port types that services in the service group must implement, as well as the resource properties the member services are expected to expose. The rationale behind the mandatory use of membership content rules is that web services implementing a common WSDL port type and exposing the same set of resource properties can be considered as functionally-equivalent.

We have crafted an enhanced WSSG capability supporting advanced replica management, including facilities to compensate for the occasional emerging and disappearing of web services in the system. A freshly discovered service may be added to the group as the result of an incoming Management Using Web Services (MUWS) advertisement notification, provided the reported service complies to the membership content rules. Upon addition of a replica member web service, its metadata will be validated, and the service group will automatically issue a WSN subscription request so as to be notified of changes in any additional mandatory resource properties that were declared in the membership content rules set on the service group — *cf.* Sect. 5.3. Conversely, the receipt of a WS-ResourceLifetime destruction event will trigger the removal of the member from the service group.

The A-NVP composite has been explicitly designed as a generic WSDM-enabled utility WS-Resource so as to support a diversity of applications, without the need to generate application-specific proxy classes at design time. When assembling the deployment artefact, the user is expected to supply the WSDL interface definitions containing the port type descriptions for admissible service group members. During the initialisation of the composite WS-Resource, the provided WSDL definitions will be inspected, and for each non-standardised, request-response operation declared within, a new message handler will be registered. Furthermore, the system will automatically initialise the membership content rules, given the port types that were found whilst scanning the user-supplied interface definitions. Note that the WSDL interface advertised for the A-NVP composite itself is predefined and exposes a single port type combining only the standardised operations defined for the WSSG and WSN Consumer capabilities.

Figure 3 shows how message handlers enable the A-NVP composite to accept application-specific SOAP request messages and hand these over to the A-NVP capability for execution. Should there remain no active member services in the group for a particular port type, the respective handlers will be disabled, such that they will dismiss any incoming SOAP request by reporting a WS-Addressing `ActionNotSupported` fault message.

5.2 Domain-Agnostic A-NVP Capability

Context information for any of the member web services within the federation is managed at operation level (Fig. 3). Specifically, for each operation for which a dynamic message handler was registered, the context manager provides adequate data structures for storing the values $D(v)$, $L(v)$, $T(v)$ and the respectively corresponding maxima δ_D, δ_L and δ_T as defined in Sect. 4.3, as well as the counters $\#rounds(v)$ and $\#consent(v)$ that were introduced in Sect. 3.2.3. Furthermore, application-specific configuration parameters can be specified for individual operations, thereby overriding the system defaults. One may do so by editing a deployment descriptor, in which a service operation can be uniquely identified by the service port type name and the WS-Addressing action URI.

The capability provides a single operation to accept NVP service requests. Upon invocation of the A-NVP composite, the system first determines the set of eligible functionally-equivalent member services in the service group, i.e. V. In order to do so, the payload of the incoming SOAP request as well as its WS-Addressing message headers are inspected so as to establish which of the registered port types exposes the targeted service operation. After acquiring all registered member services that implement the given port type, the capability proceeds by applying

the algorithm introduced in Sect. 4 so as to determine an adequate selection of versions $V^{(l)}$. Such selection is carried out referring to the context information pertaining to the targeted operation, as stored in the context manager. The SOAP request is then simultaneously forwarded to each of the selected versions. As soon as an absolute majority $M^{(l)}$ of the selected $n^{(l)}$ versions have returned their response, the voting scheme will determine and return the outcome of the current voting round l, without awaiting the remaining replicas to return. At the same time, the $n^{(l)} - M^{(l)}$ pending results will be collected after the response was sent to the client such that the *dtof* and normalised dissent can be computed at the end of the voting procedure and subsequently reported to the context manager.

It is noteworthy to point out that the voting procedure will assign any two versions to the same equivalence class of the partition $\wp^{(l)} \setminus P_F^{(l)}$ if the XML fragments enclosed within the body of their SOAP response messages are found to be syntactically equivalent, given the XSD schema definitions included in the WSDL interface. Special attention is paid to SOAP faults, however, which are typically used to convey error condition information when an exceptional situation occurs. In particular, one needs to clearly distinguish between application-specific and application-agnostic fault messages. Whereas the former type of fault messages are expected to carry domain-specific fault data and are processed like ordinary SOAP response messages, application-agnostic fault messages will directly be classified in $P_F^{(l)}$. Examples of this second category of messages include, e.g., standardised fault messages from various WS-* specifications, or SOAP faults reported for versions that were detected to be affected by performance or omission failures (*cf.* Sect. 4.1 and 4.3).

5.3 Externally Supplied Context Information

As pointed out in Sect. 4.3, the vast majority of the metrics and counters stored in the context manager is updated using information that was collected within the A-NVP composite itself, upon completion of a voting round. An exception to this approach though, is the number of pending requests $L(v)$, which needs to be supplied externally as it is conceivable that a member replica may concurrently be used by services other than the A-NVP composite. Specifically, we require any member web service to expose the metrics defined by the MOWS operation metrics manageability capability. As such, the resource property `OperationMetrics` is supposed to be included in the membership content rules of the A-NVP composite. Upon addition of a new member service, the enhanced service group capability will consequently issue a WSN subscription request in order to be notified for changes in the values of this resource property. Any valid value for the `OperationMetrics` resource property is defined to hold three direct XML child elements, i.c. `NumberOfRequests`, `NumberOfFailedRequests` and `NumberOfSuccessfulRequests`. Considering the non-negative integer values of these metrics, the context manager can easily determine the number of pending requests as `NumberOfRequests` − (`NumberOfFailedRequests`+`NumberOfSuccessfulRequests`). The estimation of the load on any of the registered member services is always a rough approximation, due to potential latency in the issuance and processing of the WSN notification messages.

6. EXPERIMENTS AND ANALYSIS

To illustrate the A-NVP strategy, we now present an example considering a set $V = \{A, B, C, D, E\}$ of 5 replicas, and a fixed amount of versions to be used $n^{(i)}_{i\in\{1,...,5\}} = 4$. A summary of the first 5 voting rounds has been given in Table 1 showing the disturbances the voting scheme encountered during each round.

l	$\wp^{(l)} \setminus P_F^{(l)}$	$P_F^{(l)}$	$dtof^{(l)}$	$w_e^{(l)}$
1	$\{A, E\}\ \{C\}$	$\{D\}$	0	-
2	$\{A, B, E\}$	$\{D\}$	1	1
3	$\{A, B, C, E\}$	$\emptyset$	2	0.5
4	$\{A, C\}\ \{B, E\}$	$\emptyset$	0	-
5	$\{A, B, E\}\ \{C\}$	$\emptyset$	1	1

Table 1: Overview of the disturbances and their impact on the voting procedure for the first 5 rounds of an A-NVP/MV composite. The displayed values have been computed at the end of round l.

It is assumed that the voting rounds do not overlap, that is, round $l + 1$ does not commence before round l has completed. The example displayed in Table 2 was constructed under the assumption that replica D was affected by a permanent fault, either because of a design fault, a broken network link or a malfunction of the underlying deployment platform. The reward model as defined in Sect. 3.2.3 was configured with parameters $k_1 = 0.85$, $k_2 = 0.75$ and $k_{max} = 0.95$. The example targets a trade-off between between dependability and timeliness, and does not consider load balancing, i.e. $w_D = 0.8$, $w_T = 0.2$ and $w_L = 0$. Moreover, the response times are assumed to be constant throughout the experiment such that $T(A) = T(C) = 10$, $T(B) = 12$ and $T(D) = T(E) = 8$, expressed in seconds. All values were computed using fixed decimal numbers with four significant digits. Table 2 illustrates how the normalised dissent $D^{(l)}(v)$ is updated at the end of each voting round l, the last column referring to the applicable formulae from Sect. 3.2.

We will now show how the replica selection model presented in Sect. 4.3 will select $V^{(3)} = \{A, B, C, E\}$. Considering $\delta_D = 2$ at the completion of round 2, the scaled normalised dissent is given by:

$$D_s(A) = D_s(E) = \frac{2 - 0.425}{2} = 0.7875$$

$$D_s(B) = \frac{2 - 0}{2} = 1$$

$$D_s(C) = \frac{2 - 0.95}{2} = 0.525$$

$$D_s(D) = \frac{2 - 2}{2} = 0 \qquad (15)$$

One can now observe from the calculations in (15) that version D has been found to perform the poorest in terms of reliability. Contrarily, $D_s(B)$ holds the maximum value 1, since B was not found to be previously affected by disturbances of any kind. Given $\delta_T = 12$ seconds, the normalisation of the aforementioned response times yields:

$$T_s(A) = T_s(C) = \frac{12 - 10}{12} = 0.1667$$

$$T_s(D) = T_s(E) = \frac{12 - 8}{12} = 0.3333$$

$$T_s(B) = \frac{12 - 12}{12} = 0 \qquad (16)$$

Since the configuration parameters for the replica selection model did not target load balancing, i.e. $w_L = 0$, one can now easily compute the score value for each of the replicas in V using (14):

$$s(B) = 0.8 \times 1 + 0.2 \times 0 = 0.8$$
$$s(E) = 0.8 \times 0.7875 + 0.2 \times 0.3333 = 0.6967$$
$$s(A) = 0.8 \times 0.7875 + 0.2 \times 0.1667 = 0.6633$$
$$s(C) = 0.8 \times 0.525 + 0.2 \times 0.1667 = 0.4533$$
$$s(D) = 0.8 \times 0 + 0.2 \times 0.3333 = 0.0667 \qquad (17)$$

The above score values have already been sorted in descending order. Given the fixed redundancy degree $n^{(3)} = 4$, we select the first 4 replicas from the above list, i.e. $V^{(3)} = \{B, E, A, C\}$, after which the scheme will invoke the selected versions and await their responses in order to complete the voting procedure. The faulty version D is excluded from $V^{(3)}$, due to the accumulation of the penalties that were added to its normalised dissent throughout the initial 2 voting rounds, as it can be seen from Tables 1 and 2d.

l	status	#rounds	#consent	$D^{(l)}$	$p^{(l)}$	$r^{(l)}$	
1	active	1	0	0.5000	0.5000	-	(8b)
2	active	2	1	0.4250	-	0.85	(10b)
3	active	3	2	0.3400	-	0.80	(10b)
4	active	4	2	0.8400	0.5000	-	(8b)
5	active	5	3	0.7140	-	0.85	(10b)

(a) Version A

l	status	#rounds	#consent	$D^{(l)}$	$p^{(l)}$	$r^{(l)}$	
1	idle	0	0	0	-	0.85	(10a)
2	active	1	1	0	-	0.85	(10b)
3	active	2	2	0	-	0.80	(10b)
4	active	3	2	0.5000	0.5000	-	(8b)
5	active	4	3	0.4250	-	0.85	(10b)

(b) Version B

l	status	#rounds	#consent	$D^{(l)}$	$p^{(l)}$	$r^{(l)}$	
1	active	1	0	1.0000	1.0000	-	(8b)
2	idle	1	0	0.9500	-	0.95	(10a)
3	active	2	1	0.7600	-	0.80	(10b)
4	active	3	1	1.2600	0.5000	-	(8b)
5	active	4	1	1.9267	0.6667	-	(8a)

(c) Version C

l	status	#rounds	#consent	$D^{(l)}$	$p^{(l)}$	$r^{(l)}$	
1	active	1	0	1.0000	1.0000	-	(8c)
2	active	2	0	2.0000	1.0000	-	(8c)
3	idle	2	0	1.9000	-	0.95	(10a)
4	idle	2	0	1.8050	-	0.95	(10a)
5	idle	2	0	1.7148	-	0.95	(10a)

(d) Version D

l	status	#rounds	#consent	$D^{(l)}$	$p^{(l)}$	$r^{(l)}$	
1	active	1	0	0.5000	0.5000	-	(8b)
2	active	2	1	0.4250	-	0.85	(10b)
3	active	3	2	0.3400	-	0.80	(10b)
4	active	4	2	0.8400	0.5000	-	(8b)
5	active	5	3	0.7140	-	0.85	(10b)

(e) Version E

Table 2: Evolution of the normalised dissent value.

7. RELATED WORK

A number of techniques for service reliability engineering have appeared in the recent literature. The approach presented in [14] aims to enhance the dependability of the system by combining multiple functionally-equivalent services. It defines three classic decision algorithms, which are named service operators, including majority voting. However, the described model requires manual orchestration of the versions, while acknowledging the need for dynamic redundancy configurations. An interesting contribution of [14] is the quantitative modelling of the reliability of a service request to evaluate the effectiveness of NVP-based service composites.

Applying NVP within SOA has been suggested in [17] as well, which also ranks the versions available in the system using a composite metric involving e.g. reliability and response time. Both [14] and [17] differ from our approach in that they work with given reliability estimates, whereas we use the *dtof* and normalised dissent $D^{(l)}(v)$ to capture all types of disturbances. Neither of the two papers referred to deal with the issue of redundancy dimensioning.

The dynamic parallel fault-tolerant selection algorithm described in [18] supports the automatic selection of the voting procedure in function of the system context. The redundancy configuration for the NVP scheme is determined by repeatedly predicting the response time of the versions and computing the dependability and execution time of the candidate configurations, which may incur a significant overhead as the number of replicas in the system increases.

8. CONCLUSION

In this paper, a novel dependability strategy was introduced supporting advanced redundancy management, aiming to autonomously tune its internal configuration in view of changes in context. Given a set of functionally-equivalent stateless web services, our A-NVP/MV strategy will dynamically select the most appropriate versions depending on the contextual information gathered during the runtime of the system. The principal contribution of this paper is the resource selection algorithm. We have defined two new metrics for capturing the reliability of a software component. The primary advantage of the distance-to-failure and normalised dissent metrics is that the dependability strategy need not rely on assumptions regarding the failure rates of software components. We have implemented the presented solution as a WSDM-enabled web service using the latest Apache MUSE distribution to date. As such, the adequacy of established WS-* specifications for fault-tolerant manageability purposes was illustrated.

As future work we plan to enhance the proposed algorithm to autonomously tune the degree of employed redundancy in function of the experienced disturbances. Furthermore, we are currently working on an evaluation of the performance overhead and efficiency of the selection algorithm.

9. REFERENCES

[1] Erl, T.: Service-Oriented Architecture: Concepts, Technology, and Design. Prentice Hall PTR, Upper Saddle River, NJ, USA (2005)

[2] De Florio, V.: Application-layer Fault-tolerance Protocols. IGI Global (2009)

[3] Dubrova, E.: Fault Tolerant Design: an Introduction (draft). Kluwer Academic Publishers (2002)

[4] Johnson, B.W.: Design and analysis of fault tolerant digital systems. Addison-Wesley Series in Electrical and Computer Engineering, Addison-Wesley Longman Publishing Co., Inc., Boston, MA, USA (1989)

[5] Diab, H.B., Zomaya, A.Y. (eds.): Dependable Computing Systems: Paradigms, Performance Issues, and Applications. Wiley Series on Parallel and Distributed Computing, Wiley-Interscience (2005)

[6] Erl, T.: SOA Design Patterns. Prentice Hall PTR, Upper Saddle River, NJ, USA (2008)

[7] Gray, J.; Siewiorek, D.P.: High-availability computer systems. Computer 24(9), pp. 39–48. (1991)

[8] Dependable Embedded Systems: Software Fault Tolerance, http://www.ece.cmu.edu/~koopman/des_s99/sw_fault_tolerance/

[9] Avizienis, A.: The n-version approach to fault-tolerant software. IEEE Transactions on Software Engineering SE-11(12), pp. 1491–1501 (1985)

[10] Lorczak, P., Caglayan, A., Eckhardt, D.: A theoretical investigation of generalized voters for redundant systems. In: IEEE Digest of Papers on the 19th International Symposium on Fault-Tolerant Computing (FTCS-19), pp. 444-451. IEEE Computer Society Press, New York (1989)

[11] De Florio, V., Deconinck, G., Lauwereins, R.: Software tool combining fault masking with user-defined recovery strategies. IEE Proceedings Software 145(6), pp. 203–211. IEEE Computer Society Press, New York (1998)

[12] Cardoso, J., Miller, J., Sheth, A., Arnold, J.: Modeling quality of service for workflows and web service processes. Technical report TR-02-002, LSDIS Lab, Computer Science Department, University of Georgia (2002)

[13] Cristian, F.: Understanding fault-tolerant distributed systems. Communications of the ACM 34(2), pp. 56–78 (1991)

[14] Götze, J., Müller, J., Müller, P.: Iterative service orchestration based on dependability attributes. In: Proceedings of the 34th Euromicro Conference on Software Engineering and Advanced Applications (SEAA2008), pp. 353–360. IEEE Computer Society Press, New York (2008)

[15] Lyu, M.R. (ed.): Handbook of software reliability engineering. McGraw-Hill, Inc., Hightstown, NJ, USA (1996)

[16] De Florio, V.: Software Assumptions Failure Tolerance: Role, Strategies, and Visions. In: Casimiro, A., de Lemos, R., Gacek, C. (eds.) Architecting Dependable Systems VII. LNCS, vol. 6420, pp. 249-272. Springer, Heidelberg (2010)

[17] Laranjeiro, N., Vieira, M.: Towards fault tolerance in web services compositions. In: Proceedings of the 2007 workshop on Engineering fault tolerant systems (EFTS '07). Association for Computing Machinery, Inc. (ACM), New York (2007)

[18] Zheng, Z., Lyu, M. R.: An adaptive QoS-aware fault tolerance strategy for web services. In: Empirical Software Engineering 2010(15), pp. 323–345 (2010)

Discovering Event Correlation Rules for Semi-Structured Business Processes

Szabolcs Rozsnyai
IBM T.J. Watson Research Center
19 Skyline Drive
Hawthorne NY 10532 USA

srozsny@us.ibm.com

Aleksander Slominski
IBM T.J. Watson Research Center
19 Skyline Drive
Hawthorne NY 10532 USA

aslom@us.ibm.com

Geetika T. Lakshmanan
IBM T.J. Watson Research Center
19 Skyline Drive
Hawthorne NY 10532 USA

gtlakshm@us.ibm.com

ABSTRACT

In this paper we describe an algorithm to discover event correlation rules from arbitrary data sources. Correlation rules can be useful for determining relationships between events in order to isolate instances of a running business process for the purposes of monitoring, discovery and other applications. We have implemented our algorithm and validate our approach on events generated by a simulator that implements a real-world inspired export compliance regulations scenario consisting of 24 activities and corresponding event types. This simulated scenario involves a wide range of heterogeneous systems (e.g. Order Management, Document Management, E-Mail, and Export Violation Detection Services) as well as workflow-supported human-driven interactions (Process Management System). Experimental results demonstrate that our algorithm achieves a high level of accuracy in the detection of correlation rules. This paper confirms that our algorithm is a step towards semi-automating the task of detecting correlations. We also demonstrate how correlation rules discovered by our algorithm can be used to create aggregation nodes that allow more efficient querying, filtering and analytics. The results in this paper encourage future directions such as distributed statistics calculation, and scalability in terms of handling massive data sets.

Categories and Subject Descriptors

H.3.4 [Systems and Software]: Distributed Systems, H.3.0 [Information Storage and Retrieval]: General, E.1 [Data Structures]: Data Structures

General Terms: Algorithms, Management, Performance

Keywords

Correlation discovery. Business Process Discovery, Complex Event Processing, Data Mining, Event Analysis

1. INTRODUCTION

Systems that support today's globally distributed, rapidly changing and agile businesses are steadily growing in size as well as complexity. They are becoming increasingly federated, loosely coupled, distributed and at the same time generating a huge number of events ranging from record entries representing business activities to more technical events at various levels of granularity.

Industries such as healthcare and insurance have witnessed an explosion in the growth of semi-structured business processes that has been fuelled by the advent of such systems. These business or scientific processes depart from the traditional kind of structured processes; their lifecycle is not fully driven by a formal process model. While an informal description of the process may be available, the execution of a semi-structured process is not completely controlled by a central entity (such as a workflow engine).

Monitoring such semi-structured business processes is useful because it enables a variety of business applications such as process discovery, analytics, verification and process improvement. Accomplishing this is an important research challenge. Such processes could be implemented on diverse event-driven architectures, where none of the components have to be aware of each other and the interactions are driven by events in an asynchronous fashion [10][16][17]. Creating a unified view of processes, also known in literature as composite business applications [9] is a difficult problem. Not every event contains a unified process instance identifier for creating an end-to-end view of the underlying processes. In certain scenarios, events are also transformed or aggregated during execution steps so that identifiers that relate events to process instances or to each other become extremely hard to track [18][19]. This is a key problem that arises when tracking process instances across various system and application layers. In fast changing environments where business processes are executed across a wide range of distributed systems it is difficult to trace process instances as the relationships of events must be explicitly known and defined. Furthermore, supposedly isolated process instances, a transport coordination process for example, can be related to other processes such as the order management and invoicing process. The attributes that bridge those distinct processes, however, can only be found in the events of isolated processes instances.

An important concept in event processing is event correlation which is linking event instances based on their payload values [1]. The first step towards isolating a process instance in the scenarios we are targeting involves correlation of events generated by heterogeneous and distributed systems. This allows one to isolate and track end-to-end instances of a given semi-structured business process. The problem of correlating events has been addressed in the past for the purposes of integrating large and complex data sources. In this area the task of matching schemas (relational database schemas for instance) for the purposes of tracking an end-to-end process instance has been identified as a very time-consuming and labor intensive process that requires tool-support and automation [1][4]. Consequently a significant amount of research effort has been devoted to information retrieval, knowledge representation, schema mapping and translation as well as integration [5]. Extensive work has also been conducted in the domain of data integration and exchange motivated by the requirements for processes such Extract Transform Load (ETL) processes in data warehousing. In data warehousing, an ETL process requires the extraction of data from various sources and the transformation of the data to match a corresponding target schema. Such data exchange scenarios require extensive knowledge about the semantics of data structures in order to convert messages from a source schema to a target schema. Existing work devoted to deriving relationships between data elements for the purposes of data exchange has a strong focus on foreign-key relationships and assumes relational data (i.e. normalized) [4][5][6][7]. Finding and defining relationships (correlations) in an arbitrary and non-normalized data space has thus far received little attention, and is the focus of our work.

In this paper we address the problem of automatically deriving correlations from arbitrary sources of data. A correlation, in the context of this work, is a set of rules that define which attribute(s) form a relationship between events. This type of correlation is to a certain extent comparable to foreign-key relationships known from the relational world. An important difference, however, is that we do not assume that events are grouped together in a normalized schema and nor do we assume that we have any information on meta-data that describes an event's attributes. In this paper we present a correlation discovery algorithm that is built upon some preliminary ideas presented in our recent workshop paper [1]. We describe the design and implementation of our correlation discovery algorithm and present a comprehensive evaluation of our algorithm's detection performance with respect to a real-world inspired order management and export compliance regulations scenario. We designed and implemented a simulator to implement this scenario. We also demonstrate the utility of our algorithm to create *aggregation nodes* that facilitate efficient calculation of composite level aggregate statistics. The discovered correlation rules produced by our algorithm can be used either during runtime to group related events together, such as events belonging to a process instance or to create a graph of relationships that enables querying and traversing relationship paths.

The first part of the paper (Section 2) defines and discusses certain terminologies that are essential for understanding the concepts and brings the contribution into a larger context to highlight the importance. In Section 3 we introduce the correlation discovery algorithm and explain the major concepts with simple examples. In Section 4 we introduce and discuss evaluation results. Finally, in Section 5 we put our solution in context with related work and in Section 6 we provide an outlook for the future work.

2. BACKGROUND AND TERMINOLOGY

In this section we define and discuss terminology that is essential for understanding the concepts described in this work. In addition we present correlation discovery in the context of event processing applications (Figure 2) and briefly discuss each layer to create a better understanding of the importance and usage of this paper's contribution in a broader context. Finally we discuss advanced correlation representations in order to highlight certain aspects of the correlation discovery.

2.1 Terminology

A *correlation* describes the relationship between two events and defines a collection of semantic rules to specify how certain events are related to each other. Correlations are defined through specifying correlating attributes between event types. The ability to define relationships between events is an important component in event processing applications such as event- driven rules [24]. Such applications allow the detection of business situations in order to trigger automatic responses such as early warnings to prevent damage, loss or excessive cost, and provide alerts to exploit time-critical business opportunities. Correlations are also an important aspect for event retrieval systems, pattern discovery and event mining [20]. The definition of a correlation between event types is called a *correlation rule*. For instance, the following expressions $A.x = B.y$ represents a correlation rule between the event types A and B over their attributes x and y. Single correlation rules are typically not capable of isolating specific patterns that are of interest. Therefore, it is necessary to combine several correlation rules in order to be able to define a correlation that includes all events that share a relationship in a certain context. The context might be, for example, the instance of a process, as demonstrated in the transportation process (illustrated in a example in Figure 1), that is executed across different systems and thus produces various events. If a user has enough knowledge about the underlying systems and events he or she can easily express the correlation rules as:

OrderReceived.OrderId = ShipmentCreated.OrderId,
ShipmentCreated.ShipmentId = TransportStarted.ShipmentId,
TransportStarted.TransportId = TransportEnded.TransportId,

This allows a correlation engine to isolate a desired process instance.

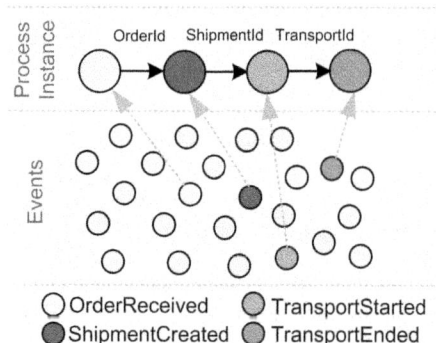

Figure 1: Tracking Correlation Rules for a Transportation Scenario

In the above example we isolate specific process instances. Events, however, might share all kinds of relationships that can be expressed. A user or component (e.g. a rule engine) might not always be interested in process instances, but in certain dimensions of events such as in the case of a correlation that groups all related events together if they have the same customer (orders placed by the same customer). Such a correlation would enable another component to continuously calculate the average order volume for instance. Correlation rules are defined on the basis of a user's objectives. Therefore a correlation discovery algorithm is a means for a user to group events via correlation rules in order to satisfy his or her objectives. Previous work [20] has separated correlations into two major groups – primal and bridged correlations. The *primal correlation* defines direct correlation relationships between event types and their attributes.

The *bridged correlation* extends this model by allowing the definition of correlations between several primal correlation. This type of correlation allows forming indirect relationships between events through defining bridging attributes between primal sets of correlations.

2.2 Conceptual Overview and Context

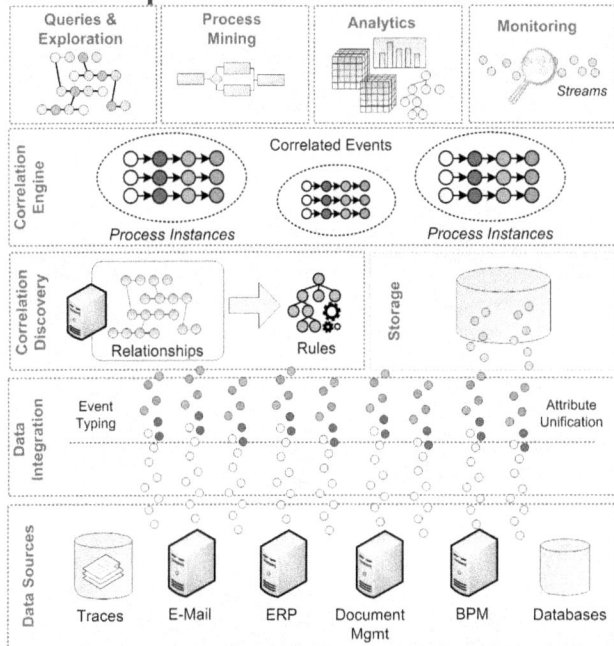

Figure 2: Correlation discovery and its applications

Figure 2 illustrates conceptually where a correlation discovery component would fit with respect to an end-to-end system serving different applications such as process mining, analytics, monitoring and querying. Next we describe each layer:

Data Sources. The bottom layer represents event processing source systems, producing a wide range of artifacts (events, records, logs, etc) from different domains at various levels of granularity.

Data Integration. The data sources produce events that represent activities or resources associated to processes and can be consumed by applications such as process analytics. Such events can be in different formats (XML, PDF, JSON, CSV, etc) and with various structures (XSD, column semantics of CSV files, etc). Furthermore, the data sources are constantly subject to change. Changes may occur when IT systems are replaced, when data structures are improved, errors are fixed or new components are introduced that add additional data. Connecting systems directly with the source is therefore rarely an alternative as every change is accompanied with large integration efforts. Therefore data integration creates an abstraction layer over those source events in order to have a stable representation which can be used by applications at higher layers. The advantage is that the abstracted layer does not change, but the data mapping and the extraction of the attributes from the source is altered.

Storage. Events extracted from various source systems can be either delegated to real-time event processing components or can be stored for further analysis following the *store everything, discover later* paradigm. The idea is that at the time the data is stored it is not necessarily known what a user is specifically going to look for in it. Therefore, it is important to store as much data as

possible in its original und unaltered form. This is particularly true for correlation discovery. At a later point in time a user may discover the importance of a specific group of events which had been of little interest in the past. Now such events can be analyzed by a correlation discovery algorithm to detect relationships between them for further use.

Correlation Discovery. The correlation discovery algorithm takes events from the storage component and determines correlations, by calculating a unique combination of statistics on attributes. The output of the correlation discovery algorithm are correlation rules that express how certain events are related to each other. Those correlations can either isolate process instances (e.g. an Order Process) or certain dimensions (by Customer, by Product).

Correlation Engine. A correlation engine uses the previously discovered and defined correlation rules during runtime to either group related events together or create a graph of relationships by connecting events through their shared dimensional relationships. A correlation engine might also apply the correlation rules on a storage system containing historical events to create a graph of relationships that then can be used later for analytical purposes.

Applications. Correlated events can have several applications. Events correlated at runtime might be used in monitoring applications or event-driven rules to detect exceptional situations and raise alerts. Another application is process mining. Process mining algorithms require historical traces of process instances from which they can derive a process model. Correlation rules can be applied to execution traces before applying a mining algorithm to isolate the process instances that are of interest. Correlated process execution instance traces can then be provided as input to the mining algorithms. Correlations can lead to graphs of relationships that can be utilized to speed up queries if events are stored. It would be possible to traverse through the graph of relations by accessing the various references that are represented by correlations. Correlations are particularly useful for features that require interaction, analysis and exploration of events.

2.3 Enabling Aggregation Nodes from Discovered Correlation Rules

The correlation discovery algorithm, described in detail in Section 3, generates a set of correlation rules that reflect valid correlations between events. The complete combination of rules do not always isolate process instances or specific dimensions of relationships between events such as for example grouping related events together if they have the same customer. The user must apply his or her domain knowledge and interest to group correlation rules so that a correlation engine is capable of creating a network of relationships that keeps track of correlated events for event processing purposes such as continuously calculating statistics, observing patterns and reacting to certain situations. Therefore, we introduce the concept of *aggregation nodes* to facilitate grouping correlation rules to represent certain aspects of an application that may be of interest to a user. Aggregation rules also enable efficient analytics and improve the ease of use and performance when querying, browsing and filtering events.

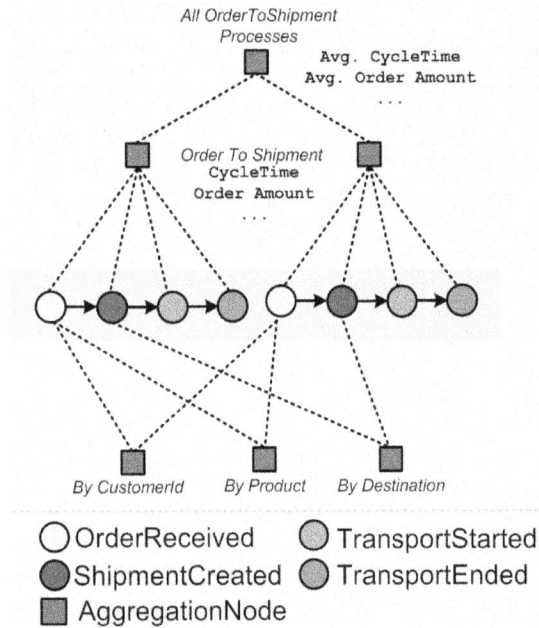

Figure 3: Aggregation Nodes for the Transportation Scenario

Figure 3 illustrates the data structure that can be applied to organize correlated events with such aggregation nodes. For clarity the middle layer in the figure shows the stream of events that are ordered. The events share a directed correlation.

OrderToShipment → *{OrderReceived.OrderId = ShipmentCreated.OrderId, ShipmentCreated.ShipmentId = TransportStarted.ShipmentId, TransportStarted.TransportId = TransportEnded.TransportId}*

The direction can be introduced by the correlation engine based either on chronological order or on another defined causal constraint. Each set of correlation rules gets an identifier assigned which can be used to generate an aggregation node such as the *OrderToShipment*. For every group of events that matches a group of correlation rules an aggregation node is created that references each event of the subset.

In the transportation example shown in Figure 3 there are two *OrderToShipment* aggregation nodes because there are two isolated groups of process instances. Such aggregation nodes can be used as a constraint in a query when the user wants to restrict the search space only to groups of correlated events that belong to the *OrderToShipment*. Aggregation nodes also help to create a logical grouping and enable easier querying when using the data in interactive visualizations as the related events already provide connections and do not need extra queries. Furthermore aggregation nodes can contain attributes that can contain calculated statistics of the lower level such as the *CycleTime* or the *OrderAmount* in the example shown.

By leveraging this concept of representing correlations, it is also possible to create higher level aggregations that include several lower level aggregation nodes. Statistics can be aggregated to provide information over all related events. For instance, in the above example the *All OrderToShipment Processes* aggregation node contains the average values (*Avg. CycleTime, Avg. Order Amount*) of all underlying processes. Dimensional information about events can be created by grouping the corresponding correlation rules, such as in the case for the aggregation nodes *By CustomerId, by Product* or *by Destination*. If the user queries for a particular customer the system could immediately retrieve the *By CustomerId* aggregation node, which could hold several key statistics (Total Orders, ...). By retrieving that aggregation node, references to all related orders and thus the order processes are maintained and can be immediately accessed.

3. CORRELATION DISCOVERY ALGORITHM

Our correlation discovery algorithm consists of three stages:

a) *Data Pre-Processing.* The first step of the correlation discovery process is to load and integrate the data into a data store (e.g. database, cloud storage, etc) that is then used to calculate statistics and determine correlation candidates.

b) *Statistics Calculation.* After the data has been loaded and integrated into the internal representation, various statistics, mainly on attribute values, are calculated and stored into a fast accessible data structure as illustrated in the table in Figure 4).

c) *Determining Correlation Candidates.* In the last step the correlation discovery algorithm determines correlation pairs with a certain confidence value based on the statistics calculated in the previous step.

In the following sections 3.1-3.3 we discuss each step in detail with respect to the transportation scenario introduced in this section.

3.1 Data Pre-Processing

The first step (Step 1 in Figure 5) is to infer a configuration setup for data integration and correlation discovery from data that may be present in sample execution traces or directly retrieved from other data sources.

Configuration requires specification of the:

a) *properties* (i.e. attributes) that should be extracted from the raw events, and

b) *attribute extraction algorithms* that should be applied to extract the events attributes.

For the purposes of simplicity the examples in this paper focus on data sources represented in XML. Nevertheless our proposed algorithm for detecting correlation identifiers is widely applicable to heterogeneous data sources and not limited to XML. The data sources specified as input are parsed and a *property definition* is created for each element and its attributes. A property is also referred to as an *alias* that is a representation of an extracted attribute of an event. Since we assume in this paper that sources are represented in XML, for each property a corresponding XPath expression is derived from the source structure that allows an extraction algorithm to extract the property each time an event is added to the storage.

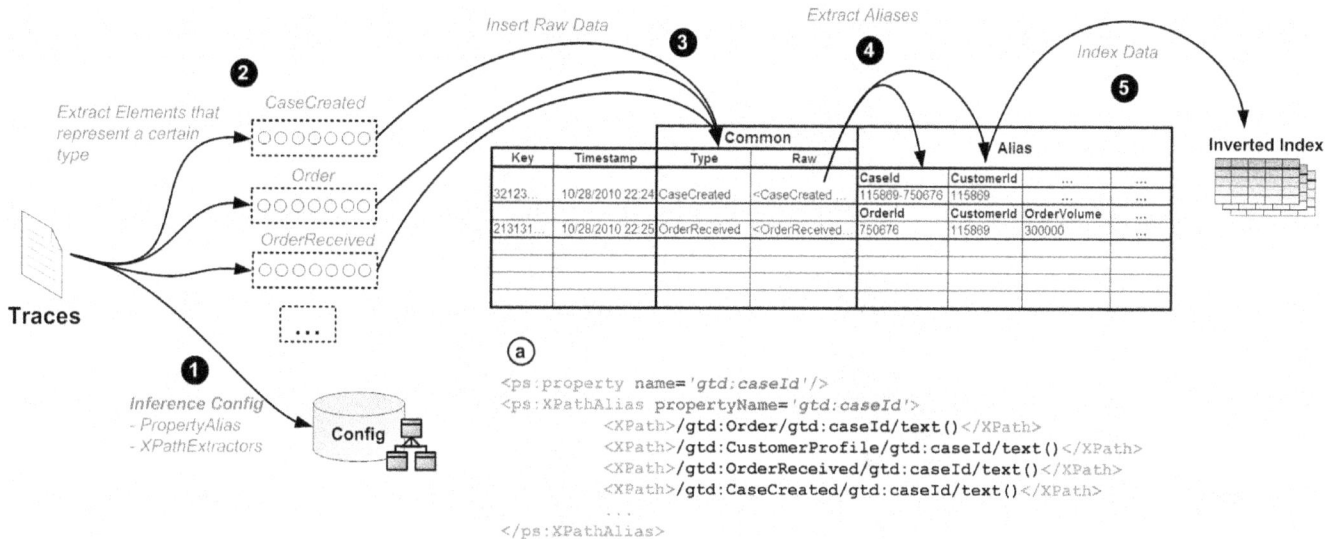

Figure 4: Data Pre-Processing

In situations where an XML element or an attribute is not unique and may exist as a child in other elements, their corresponding XPath expressions are grouped together as shown in the example (a) in Figure 4. The example (a) in Figure 4 shows a property definition named *gtd:caseId*. The element *ps:XPathAlias* refers to that property and defines a set of XPath expressions. After an event has been loaded into the data store as a record, the system is able to infer a configuration for it which consists of the *Property Aliases* and *XPath extractors*. Configuration allows automatic determination of the extraction algorithms which should be applied to extract the attributes of an event. In this example if the document is of a type *gtd:Order* then the *caseId* of the document is extracted and stored explicitly as an attribute.

In the next step (Step 2 in Figure 4), after the configuration has been generated, the raw event sources (such as event traces) or a sample set of them are loaded into data storage. The loading process is aware of the (semantic) *"type"* (e.g. it is an *Order*) of the data and flags data accordingly. In the example we depicted in Figure 1, the type is determined by the top-level XML element names such as *CaseCreated, OrderReceived*, etc. Other methods may be used to determine the type of an event. For instance by applying information known beforehand about the source or by more sophisticated methods of automatically discovering type characteristics. Regardless of the choice of method, events are separated into groups, clusters or types as the goal is to determine the relationships between those types or clusters of events.

We use HBase, an open source, non-relational, distributed database modelled after Google's BigTable. It consists of sorted key-value pairs where a key is a unique identifier and its value

spans an arbitrary number of immutable attributes (Step 3 in Figure 4). These attributes can be grouped together in *families* such as *Common, Alias* and *Graph*. Their structure is comparable to relational schemas with a major difference being that the attributes are schema-less. This means that there is neither a defined set of attributes nor a data type defined for those attributes [22]. For example a *CaseCreated* event may contain three attributes while an E-Mail may contain four completely different data types of attributes. This kind of data structure has many advantages in distributed cloud storage systems as tables are always sorted by their key and thus can be easily distributed horizontally over several machines. Applying MapReduce jobs (M/R) for analytical or query tasks over huge data sets can significantly boost performance. We intend to study the utilization of M/R jobs to speed up correlation discovery over large data sets in future work.

The raw event with its (semantic) type is inserted as-is into the *Common* family along with a unique identifier as the key. Based on the initial configuration that was created, the attributes are extracted and stored separately into the *Alias* family (Step 4 in Figure 4). The most important step is the indexing (Step 5 in Figure 4). Every extracted value of a raw event is stored into an inverted index. For each type and attribute a separate index table is created where the value of an attribute becomes the key and the value of the index table holds a list of references to the corresponding records where the key occurs. This enables the calculation of statistics that are needed for correlation discovery. A separate index for each attribute and type is created.

The next step is to compute statistics on the pre-processed data.

79

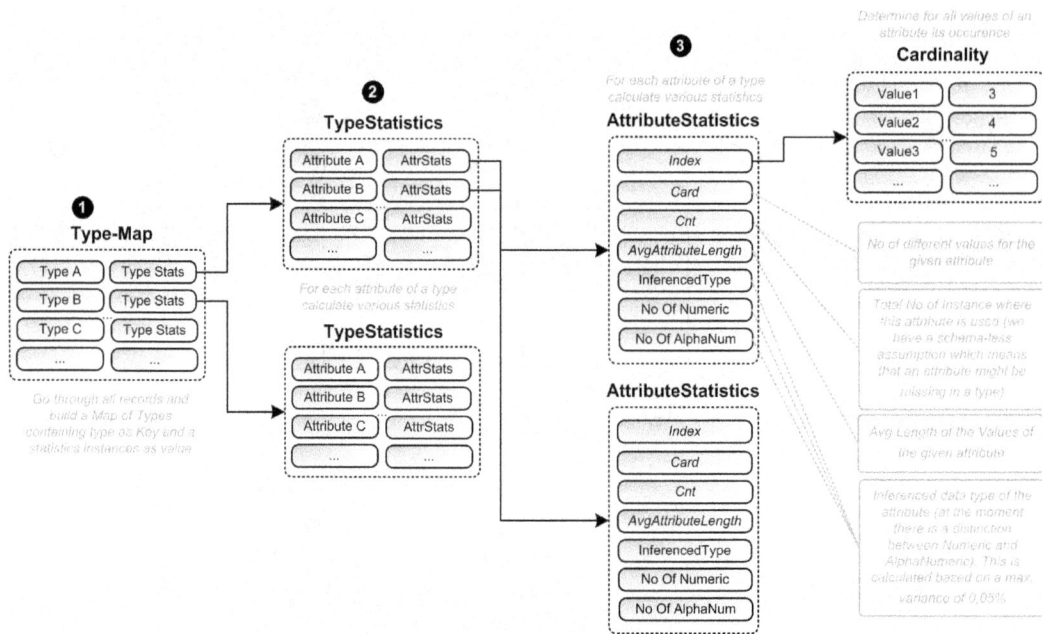

Figure 5: Type and Attribute Statistics

3.2 Statistics Calculation

After the raw events have been loaded and pre-processed the next step is to compute and store various statistics about the events. Figure 5 illustrates the data structure and lists the statistics that need to be calculated for each type and attribute in order to detect correlation candidates. For every event type a type-map *TypeStats* container (Step 1 in Figure 5) is created containing all attributes that ever occurred for that type including statistics, referred to as *TypeStats* (Step 2 in Figure 5), for each of those contained attributes. Each *TypeStat* contains the following calculated statistics (Step 3 in Figure 5):

- *Attribute Cardinality:* Based on the previously created inverted index, the *Attribute Cardinality* contains a map of each value and how often each of those values occur.

- *Card:* Determines the number of different values for the attribute (cardinality).

- *Cnt:* Represents the total number of instances in which the attribute occurs (count). As the data structure does not work on a defined schema it is possible that the attribute does not occur in every instance.

- *AvgAttributeLength:* Represents the average attribute length of the current attribute. This is an indicator about the potential uniqueness of a value. A long length value may signify that an attribute might be a unique identifier. Unique identifiers such as *OrderId* are potential attributes that occurs in other types and thus form a correlation. Long attribute lengths may also be misleading since a textual description may be very long and is unique but it is never used for correlating events.

- *InferencedType:* Defines the data type of an attribute. The data type of an attribute is an important characteristic of correlation discovery for the purposes of reducing the problem space of correlation candidates. The chances that a data type would correlate with another attribute given that the data type contains mostly alpha-numeric attributes are very low. We make a distinction between the numeric and alphanumeric attribute data types. This particular characteristic can, however, be

extended to significantly reduce the problem space. Time-stamps, for instance, could be filtered out of correlation candidates. The determination of the data type is made with a fault tolerance of 0.9 (e.g. min. 90% of the values must be numeric), and we refer to this as a parameter *Phi*. We support the following type of distinctions: Numeric or Alphanumeric, Timestamp/DateTime, Boolean and Descriptiontext.

- *NoOfNumeric:* Depending on the *InferencedType* this variable contains the number of values that are of numeric type.

- *NoOfAlphaNum:* Depending on the *InferencedType* this variable contains the number of values that are of type alpha-numeric.

3.2.1 Example

In this section we illustrate the calculation of the statistics by using a simple example. In the transportation scenario introduced earlier we distinguish between four different event types: *OrderReceived*, *ShipmentCreated*, *TransportStarted* and *TransportEnded*.

DateTime	OrderId	Product	Amount	DeliveryUntil	CustomerId
2011-01-01T09:35:52.50	166635	ProductA	10	2011-01-10T23:59:59.00	46546546
2011-01-01T09:40:54.50	166636	ProductB	2	2011-01-10T23:59:59.00	41231234
2011-01-01T09:41:51.30	166637	ProductC	1	2011-01-10T23:59:59.00	46123123
2011-01-01T09:43:32.50	166638	ProductD	7	2011-01-10T23:59:59.00	72123123
2011-01-01T09:43:42.50	166639	ProductA	2	2011-01-10T23:59:59.00	12312544

Figure 7: OrderReceived Events

Figure 7 shows a table representing *OrderReceived* event instances as rows and their attributes as columns. In the next section we explain the calculation of the statistics for the *Product* attribute.

Product_Index Value	Cardinality
ProductA	2
ProductB	1
ProductC	1
ProductD	1

Figure 8: Product Index

The attribute cardinality (named as *Index* in Figure 5) contains a map of each value and how often each of these values occur (Figure 8).

	DateTime	OrderId	Product	Amount	DeliveryUntil	CustomerId
Index	<<Map>>	<<Map>>	<<Map>>	<<Map>>	<<Map>>	<<Map>>
Card	5	5	4	4	1	5
Cnt	5	5	5	5	5	5
AvgAttributeLength	22	6	8	1.2	22	6
InferencedType	DateTime	Numeric	Alphanumeric	Numeric	DateTime	Numeric
NoOfNumeric	0	5	0	5	0	5
NoOfAlphaNumeric	0	0	5	0	0	0

Figure 9: OrderReceived statistics

Based on the index we can determine the cardinality (*Card*), which is four as we only have four different products occurring in our event instances. The *Cnt* for the Product attribute is in this case 5 as it occurs in every event. This might not always be the case. With the index we can determine the *AvgAttributeLength* for the Product. In this simple example the variance of the product names is zero and the *AvgAttributeLength* is 8. The type inference component also utilizes the index to determine the type (which is alphanumeric).

The next step is to compute correlation candidates on the basis of the computed statistics.

3.3 Determining Correlation Candidates

At this point data has been loaded into the storage and various statistics have been calculated for each type and attribute of events. This provides a foundation for determining the correlation candidates. The goal of the candidate matching algorithm is to utilize the statistics within certain boundaries (parameters) to present a result set containing pairs of potentially correlating attributes expressed by a *confidence score*. This has the advantage of allowing a user to specify approximate parameters and select desired candidates through a user interface. In a fully automated solution a system can select candidates with a very high confidence factor. The *confidence score* of correlation candidates is determined by the following three parameters with a default set of weights:

a) *Difference Set*. A difference set determines the difference between all permutations of pairs of all attribute candidates on their instance data and is assigned a weight of 60%.
b) *Difference between AvgAttributeLength*. The difference between the lengths of values of two correlation candidates is assigned a weight of 20%.
c) *LevenshteinDistance*. The Levenshtein distance between attribute names is assigned a weight of 20%

We determine the weights for each parameter experimentally. Now we explain the calculation of each of these parameters used for the overall confidence score calculation.

Difference Set. The first step in computing the confidence score is to compute the difference set of all permutations of pairs of all attribute candidates. To reduce the search space of candidates we apply an approach similar to [3][6][7][8], where we first want to determine *Highly Indexable Attributes* for each type and then *Mappable Attributes* to form pair candidates. A *Highly Indexable Attribute* is an attribute that is potentially unique for each instance of a type. This attribute is determined by the following equation:

$$IndexableAttributeSet := \{i \mid i \in Attributes \land (Card(i) / Cnt(i)) > Alpha \land AvgAttribtueLength(i) > Epsilon\}$$

Alpha is a threshold parameter that determines the minimum ratio (i.e. uniqueness) of *Card / Cnt* and thus allows a small deviation that can be caused for instance by duplicates. *Epsilon* is an additional parameter that defines the minimum average length of an attribute. The *Mappable Attribute* can be seen as a means to reduce the search space of potentially correlating attributes of a type. One approach is to set an upper threshold of how frequently a value of an attribute can occur. The assumption is that if it occurs more than x times it is unlikely that it is a correlation candidate. Our approach of reducing the search space is inspired from the relational data field. Consider for example an order relation that contains one unique key. Customer complaints are stored into a separate relation containing the order-key as a reference. We assume that that a complaint cannot occur more than 10 times for one order. The Mappable Attribute is defined as follows:

$$MappableAttributeSet := \{m \mid m \in Attributes \land Card(m) < Gamma\}$$

Gamma is a threshold parameter that can be set experimentally and customized to the application scenario based on knowledge of the events. This parameter bears the drawback of missing correlation candidates in some cases. For example, in a situation where a *Customer* has many *Orders* with a foreign-key relationship, it does not make sense to set a value for Gamma.

By determining all the *Indexable* and *Mappable Attributes* of all types the next step is to find candidates of pairs of attributes that potentially correlate with each other. Therefore a difference set $A \setminus B = \{x \mid x \in A \land x \notin B\}$ between all permutations of attribute candidates A and B is created where $A = IndexableAttributeSet$ and $B = MappableAttributeSet$. The size of $A \setminus B$ must be below a certain threshold in order to be taken into account:

$$|A \setminus B| <= DiffThreshold$$

Candidate pairs of the permutation mixes are excluded if they have a mismatch of data types based on the previously determined *InferencedType*. The *DiffThreshold* should be kept in a range between 80-90% for most cases depending on the domain. A difference, $|A \setminus B|$, can occur for instance if there are a lot of process instances that are not finished (i.e. do not contain all expected correlations) at the point when the algorithm is applied. This may also be true when using a subset of events as a sample set to discover correlations. Depending on the domain and the event sources, sampling can become a hard problem. If correlation discovery is applied on a subset representing one week's data, for instance, it would be successful in identifying lower-level events that occur frequently in short timeframes. This means that instances have a good likelihood of being discovered. On the other hand for long-lasting processes that span several weeks or months certain events might not be well represented in such a data sample. Therefore it is important to configure the *DiffThreshold* parameter based on knowledge of the scenario.

Difference between AvgAttributeLength. The second weighting factor for the confidence is the difference between the *AvgAttributeLength* of two correlation candidates. If the difference between attribute lengths has a strong variance it may indicate that they do not share significant relationships.

LevenshteinDistance. The last parameter that influences the computation of the confidence score is the Levenshtein distance between the names of two attributes. Attribute names from different sources might have the same or comparable names if they have the same meaning. For example, in one system the attribute that contains the identifier for an order is named *OrderId* and in the other it is named *order-id*.

3.3.1 Example

In the transportation example described in Section 3.2.1 we have determined the statistics for the *OrderReceived* event. Using the three steps described in the previous section we now show the determination of correlation candidates for the same example. To simplify the example for better understanding we focus on the *OrderReceived* and *ShipmentCreated* events.

	DateTime	OrderId	Product	Amount	DeliveryUntil	CustomerId
Index	<<Map>>	<<Map>>	<<Map>>	<<Map>>	<<Map>>	<<Map>>
Card	5 1	5 1	4 0.8	4 0.8	1 0.2	5 1
Cnt	5	5	5	5	5	5
AvgAttributeLength	22	6	8	1.2	22	6
InferencedType	DateTime	Numeric	Alphanumeric	Numeric	DateTime	Numeric
NoOfNumeric	0	5	0	5	0	5
NoOfAlphaNumeric	0	0	5	0	0	0

Figure 10: OrderReceived Indexables

In Figure 10 the ratio of *Card/Cnt* is 0.8 for the *Product* and *Amount* attributes, 0.2 for *DeliveryUntil* and 1 for the rest of the attributes as all of their attribute values are unique. The threshold *Alpha* = 0.9 and *Epsilon* = 5. Therefore, the highly indexable attributes are *DateTime, OrderId* and *CustomerId* based on the formula *Card/Cnt > Alpha ∧ AvgAttribtueLength > Epsilon.*

	DateTime	ShipmentId	OrderId	Carrier
Index	<<Map>>	<<Map>>	<<Map>>	<<Map>>
Card	5	5	5	3
Cnt	5	5	5	5
AvgAttributeLength	22	6	6	13.2
InferencedType	DateTime	Numeric	Numeric	Alphanumeric
NoOfNumeric	0	5	5	0
NoOfAlphaNumeric	0	0	0	5

Figure 11: ShipmentCreated Mappables

Figure 11 shows the statistics for *ShipmentCreated* events. In this domain it might be unlikely that a shipment has more than 10 orders. However this might cause problems in other domains or for certain relationships (one customer definitely has more than 10 orders). Therefore, we set *Gamma* = 10 and as *Card < Gamma* applies for all attribute they are all flagged as mappable attributes. Finally, the attributes *DateTime* are removed from the candidate list from both *OrderReceived* and *ShipmentCreated* as they are of type *DateTime* and thus they are not suitable for correlation pairs. This also applies for booleans and description texts. Now we have a pruned list of attributes that are potential correlation identifiers for each type and create a list of all permutations of possible correlation rules.

OrderReceived.OrderId = ShipmentCreated.ShipmentId
OrderReceived.OrderId = ShipmentCreated.OrderId
OrderReceived.CustomerId = ShipmentCreated.ShipmentId
OrderReceived.CustomerId = ShipmentCreated.OrderId
OrderReceived.CustomerId = ShipmentCreated.Carrier

Commutative rules are removed from this list. In this case every attribute within a pair has the same type. If attributes are not of the same type they are also excluded from the list and thus the difference set is not calculated (such as it is the case for *OrderReceived.OrderId = ShipmentCreated.Carrier*).

Based on this list, first we determine the *DifferenceSet* for all correlation rules. The remaining list contains only one correlation rule:

OrderReceived.OrderId = ShipmentCreated.OrderId

Then we determine the difference between the *AvgAttributeLengths* between the candidates and finally we calculate the *LevenshteinDistance*. The result is a table with all correlation rule candidates containing the previously determined weight. In this reduced case there is only one candidate where *DifferenceSet* = 0, *AvgAttributeLengths* = 0 and the *LevenshteinDistance* = 0. The confidence score is calculated based on the weights (*DifferenceSet* = 60%, *AvgAttributeLengths* = 20%, *LevenshteinDistance* = 20%) and is therefore 100% which means that *OrderReceived.OrderId = ShipmentCreated.OrderId* have a very significant correlation.

In the next section we discuss the result of implementing and testing our correlation discovery algorithm on a detailed order management scenario that contains the transportation scenario as a component of its implementation.

4. RESULTS AND EVALUATION

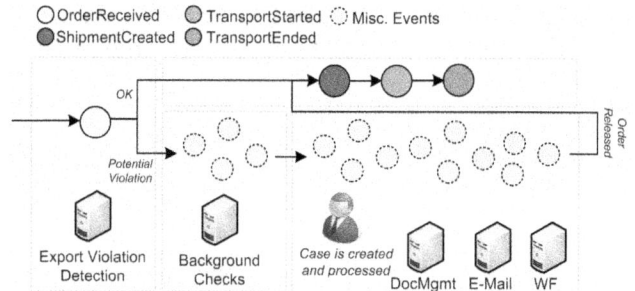

Figure 12: Order Management Scenario

For evaluating the detection accuracy of the correlation algorithm we implement a semi-structured case-oriented business process scenario relating to order management and export compliance regulations (illustrated in Figure 12). This scenario encompasses the transportations process that we introduced earlier in the paper and used to illustrate the concepts of the algorithm. The general idea of the scenario is that every order of a foreign customer has to be checked as to whether it violates certain export regulations. In the case of a clear export violation or inconsistencies the order is flagged, automated background checks are performed to collect information about the customer and the order and then a case is created. Before the order is finally declined or released, domain experts must perform some workflow driven investigation involving e-mail inquiries, site visits and also evidence gathering. This has to be done to ensure that decisions are made objectively and sufficient documentation is available for later justifications or audits (which is important for responsibly releasing an order). If a decision is made to release the order then the order-to-shipment process is continued as normal.

∧ Parameters

∨ Correlation Graph

RequestSiteVisit

CreateCase   AssignCase   BackgroundCheck   SendSurvey   ProfileCheck   ReviewRequest

RequestDenial

∨ Correlation Candidates

IndexableType	IndexableProp	MappableType	MappableType	Ind.Avg.Length	Map.Avg.Length	DataType	SetDiff	LevenstDiff	Confidence
RequestSiteVisit	gtd:caseId	CreateCase	gtd:caseId	13	13	VARCHAR	0%	0	100%
RequestSiteVisit	gtd:caseId	AssignCase	gtd:caseId	13	13	VARCHAR	0%	0	100%
RequestSiteVisit	gtd:caseId	BackgroundCheck	gtd:caseId	13	13	VARCHAR	0%	0	100%
RequestSiteVisit	gtd:caseId	SendSurvey	gtd:caseId	13	13	VARCHAR	0%	0	100%
RequestSiteVisit	gtd:caseId	ProfileCheck	gtd:caseId	13	13	VARCHAR	0%	0	100%
RequestSiteVisit	gtd:caseId	ReviewRequest	gtd:caseId	13	13	VARCHAR	0%	0	100%
RequestSiteVisit	gtd:caseId	UpdateCustomerPro	gtd:caseId	13	13	VARCHAR	0%	0	100%
RequestSiteVisit	gtd:caseId	RejectRequest	gtd:caseId	13	13	VARCHAR	0%	0	100%
RequestSiteVisit	gtd:caseId	WatchlistCheck	gtd:caseId	13	13	VARCHAR	0%	0	100%
RequestSiteVisit	gtd:caseId	ApproveRequest	gtd:caseId	13	13	VARCHAR	0%	0	100%
RequestSiteVisit	gtd:caseId	ReviewCase	gtd:caseId	13	13	VARCHAR	0%	0	100%
CreateCase	gtd:caseId	RequestDenial	gtd:caseId	13	13	VARCHAR	37%	0	62.2%

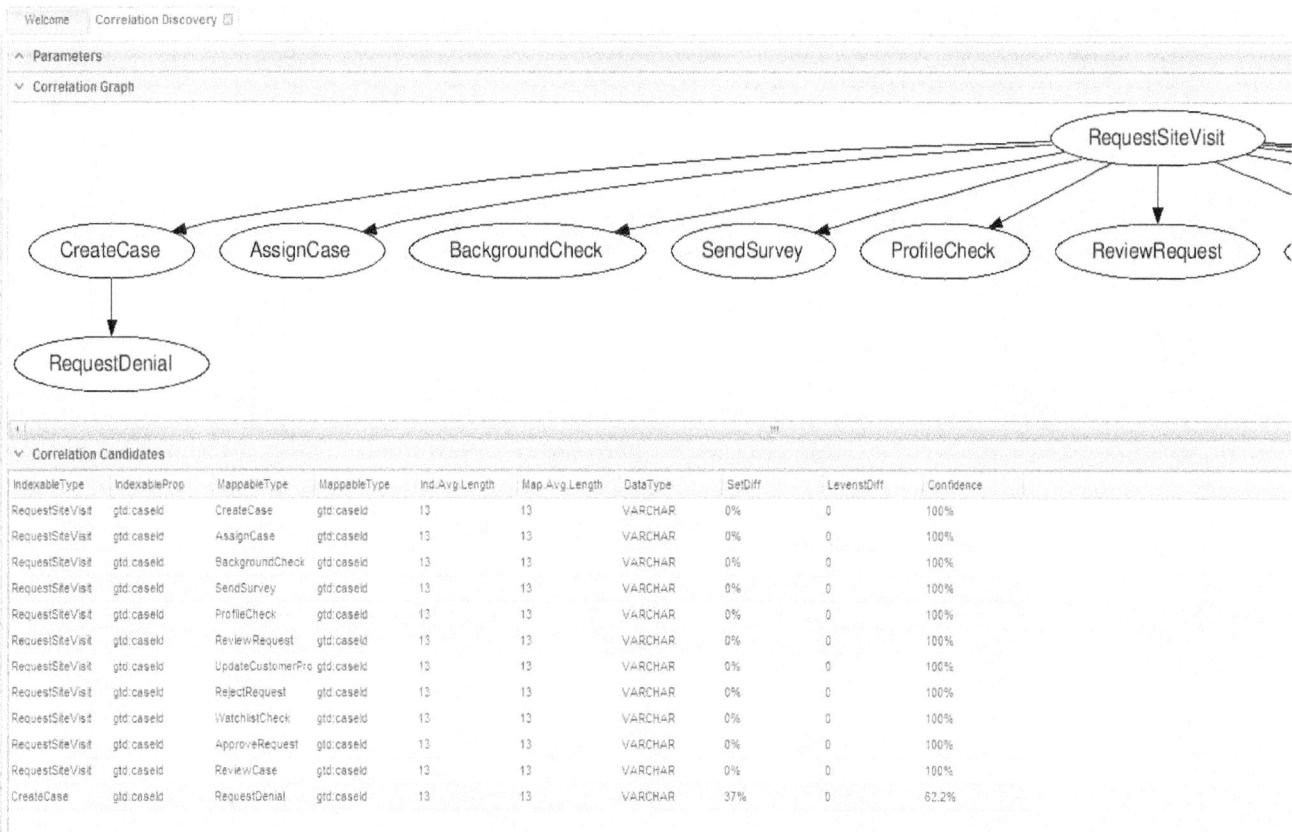

Figure 13: Correlation Discovery Example Screenshot

This scenario is particularly interesting for our purposes as it involves a wide range of heterogeneous systems (Order Management, Document Management, E-Mail, Export Violation Detection Services, …) as well as workflow-supported human-driven interactions (Process Management System). All of those systems generate a wide range of events at different granularity levels which makes it challenging to extract a set of correlation rules that can isolate process instances. The goal of our evaluation is to determine the precision of our proposed correlation algorithm in terms of its accuracy in determining correct correlations. To achieve this, we developed a tool that simulates events representing the processes and systems in the order management scenario and export compliance regulations. In our experiments we take 24 event types, consisting of altogether 95 attributes into account for correlation discovery. Normally, we determine the parameters based on experience and apply knowledge about the source data. We have made good empirical observations on different scenarios by applying the following parameter setup: Alpha = 0.95, Gamma = 1000, Epsilon = 5, Phi = 0.9 and DiffThreshold = 80.

In order to gain an understanding of the best parameter setup, we conduct an experiment and apply the correlation discovery algorithm with a large spectrum of parameter permutations. The following list presents the intervals of the parameters that have been tested:

- Alpha Range: 0.5 – 0.95 with steps increasing the parameter by 0.05

- Epsilon: 5 – 15 with steps increasing the parameter by 1

- Phi: 0.90 – 0.50 with steps increasing the parameter by 0.1

- DiffThreshold: 50 with steps increasing the parameter by 5

We left out the Gamma parameter for reasons described in Section 3.3 and set it to a high value. As a result of applying all permutations of the parameters we calculate a total of 1151349 correlation rule candidates for 4265 correlation sets. Among these 4265 sets we determine the threshold of parameters for the correlation set where all of the correlation rules have a confidence of 100%. In order to determine correlation candidates we remove transitive rules within a set. The resulting best configuration of parameters for this particular scenario is: Alpha = 0.95, Gamma=10000, Epsilon=6, Phi = 0.5, DiffThreshold=90.

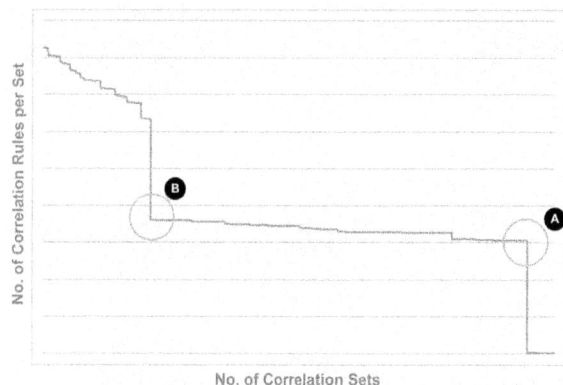

Figure 14: Number of correlation rules according to the number of correlation sets.

Figure 14 shows the distribution of the *number of correlation sets* (x-axis) against the *number of correlation rules per set* (y-axis) computed on the basis of the previously introduced range of permutations. The left side of the x-axis has the parameter combinations with the lowest selectivity and the right side shows the highest selectivity. Two interesting observations can be made from the graph: Point (A) shows a sharp break due to a very high *Epsilon* parameter. At that point *Epsilon=14* and filters out a large portion of correlation candidates as the majority of the potential correlation candidates have a lower minimum average length of their attributes (compare with Section 3.3). The second point of interest (B) in the chart shows a similar drastic change in the selectivity due to a major difference in the *DiffThreshold* settings. Basically a setting of *DiffThreshold > 90* has a high selectivity on the simulated scenario data.

We execute the correlation discovery algorithm with the best parameter setup computed above on simulated test data that contains 40 simulated cases. The algorithm detects a total of 464 correlation rules with one false positive and one undesired correlation rule. If the goal is to isolate a process instance then the precision of the algorithm is 99.56% (*No.of.RelevantCorrelationRules* / (*No.of. RelevantCorrelationRules + FalsePositives*) * 100). The execution time to calculate the correlation rule candidates for this scenario (total of 1.3MB process data) is on average 320ms on an Intel Core 2 Duo CPU (2.5Mhz) machine with 4GB RAM.

One example of incorrect correlation pairs is correlation over the attribute *orderVolume* that occurs in several events within a process instance. Avoiding this kind of false correlation rule is difficult as the attribute value has a certain length (over 6) that might indicate it is unique and the attribute occurs in several other events due to the same amount that has been ordered by various customers. The other exceptional correlation rule is the relationship between events via their *customerId*. This correlation is not technically false, but it conflicts with the goal to isolate process instances since a *customerId* forms relationships across independent process instances (orders of a particular customer).

Our experimental results demonstrate that the algorithm achieves good precision in extracting correlation sets. The algorithm extracts a large number of correlation rules that are correct but not all of the extracted correlation rules may be useful to isolate specific process aspects that are of interest to a user. For example, almost every event is correlated over an *orderId* and a *caseId*. However, one of them is enough to form a correlation that isolates a process instance. The large number of extracted correlation pairs can be reduced by removing transitive correlation rules (as done in the evaluation above). Another possibility is to apply graph reduction to reduce the number of correlation rules that isolate a process instance. In the particular example discussed above it is possible to reduce the number of correlation rules to 21. Figure 12 shows a screenshot of the correlation discovery user interface displaying an excerpt of the correlation rules discovered in our scenario and applies graph reduction to reduce complexity. The graph edges in the screenshot do not imply a direction. Nevertheless, for applying graph reduction we treat them as a direction. The arrow indicates which nodes contain a mappable attribute. Graph reduction may not be always desirable particularly if the rules are used to create a correlation graph between every related event.

Having implemented the correlation discovery algorithm, we leveraged discovered correlation rules to build aggregation nodes for the order management scenario. The resulting aggregation nodes demonstrate how they can be used to isolate process instances or specific dimensions of relationships between events to allow more efficient querying, filtering and analytics.

5. RELATED WORK

Some existing work addresses the problem of correlating events to create a historic view to explore and discover different aspects of business processes [20][21]. Process mining partly addresses the problem by analyzing logged execution data of process instances and generating a representation of a process model. Current work in the area of process mining and discovery such as [11] require clean pre-processed, chronologically ordered and correlated process instance traces [12][13]. The correlation specification in these papers is assumed to be conducted by a human having expert knowledge about the domain, the data sources and the applications involved.

The work by DePauw et al [8] is very relevant to our work and influenced the design of our correlation algorithm. Like DePauw et al. we also take the notion and determination of *Indexable* and *Mappable Paths* into account, but with the major purpose of reducing the problem space of candidate-pair permutations that need to be checked against each other for potential correlations. In our algorithm this step can be left out and instead every attribute of a type can be matched against every other attribute of the same type. As we store data for correlation discovery in a distributed data store, we can distribute statistics and matching calculations on several machines. This could allow us to significantly reduce the detection time depending on the cluster size and would not force one to make the trade off of reducing the problem space. This is the subject of our future work.

Our correlation algorithm also takes several other attribute-based statistics into account to improve the precision of the correlation candidate detection and also calculates a confidence score based on those statistics. Rostin et al. [14] take a machine learning approach to automatically discover foreign key constraints in relational databases. They compile and validate a list of the most selective rules for their purposes including rules such as (a) a foreign-key (FK) must have a good coverage of a primary key (PK), (b) the PK and FK column-names must have significant similarity, (c) the average length difference between the values of attributes should be as low as possible and (d) the value range of PKs should be only slightly outside the range of FKs. Their rules for detecting foreign key constraints share some similarities with our discovery algorithm with the difference that their rules are specific to their application. Therefore, from our point of view the weight confidence must be applied and be specified as parameters in order to adjust to changing data sources.

Research by Motahari Nezhad et. al. [23] is also relevant to our work. Their approach primarily takes instance based measures into account to determine the "interestingness" of correlation pairs (and groups of pairs). Similar to DePauw et. al. [8] they apply a basic ratio measure to prune correlation pairs up front. Their approach has a major advantage as instance characteristics are taken into account to significantly improve the result quality of the algorithm, particularly when the application domain is focused on process instance discovery. On the other hand it comes with a trade-off regarding the performance as it requires correlating a relatively large number of messages to form instances. Our approach, in contrast, focuses on determining correlation pairs based on computed statistics before correlating events as the goal is to produce correlation rules that can subsequently be applied to correlated events for further investigation.

The CORDS [6] tool makes use of statistical methods to discover correlations and soft functionalities between database columns to produce a dependency graph to improve the performance of query optimizers. Their approach of detecting correlation candidates is mainly based on the work of Haas and Brown [15] which generates pairing rules of tables and applies pruning rules, such as type and statistical constraints, to reduce the search space. A pairing rule in in the context of their work is a relationship between two attributes such as for example a join between two database tables over two attributes *(orders.orderID = deliveries.orderID)*.

In relational databases, data and its attributes are organized in tables (i.e. relations) to minimize redundancy in order to avoid undesired side-effects. For instance, inconsistencies can arise when applying operations (insertions, deletions). This process is commonly referred to as normalization. However, other modelling disciplines, such as Data Warehousing, apply de-normalized and redundant data structures in order to increase the query performance with the trade-off of lower insertion performance. In both cases, there is a detailed knowledge about the data available which is defined in a data schema. This means that there are defined relations with defined attributes and types (e.g. *integer*, *string*, *timestamp*, …). So for instance, a relation *Order* has a defined set of attributes such as an *orderId* as *Integer* or a *deliveryTime* as a *timestamp*. A key difference between our work and such other approaches is that our approach does not assume that events are grouped together in a normalized schema and nor does it have any information on meta-data that describes an event's attribute. Therefore there is no information available if an attribute is of a certain type and therefore the algorithm needs to inference these characteristics based on various attribute value statistics.

6. CONCLUSION AND FUTURE WORK
In this paper we address the problem of automatically deriving correlations from arbitrary data sources. The algorithm we present for correlation discovery is similar in principle to previous work that focuses on determining foreign-key relationships known from the relational world. A key difference, however, is that our correlation discovery algorithm does not rely on the assumption that the events are grouped together in a normalized schema and thus can deal with redundancies and does not have any information about meta-data that describes the event attributes.

We have implemented our correlation discovery algorithm and designed and implemented a simulator to validate the results. The simulator implements a semi-structured case-oriented business process scenario relating to export compliance regulations. Experimental results on events generated by the simulator indicate that our correlation discovery algorithm achieves good performance in terms of accuracy of generated correlation rules. This allows us to conclude that it is a promising tool for automatically discovering correlation rules.

The performance of our algorithm on very large data sets could be greatly improved by distributing the algorithm on multiple machines. The need for discovering correlation rules over large data sets arises for a variety of reasons. In domains where the algorithm needs to detect correlations between events, representing processes, it is not always possible to extract a small sample set of data. For instance, if a sample set of one week is sliced out for correlation discovery, certain events might be missing and chances that the right correlation rules are detected are low. The correct sample size for detecting the right set of correlation rules depends on the domain, the nature of the event producing systems and the processes. For example, in the case of the transportation scenario, we would expect that an end-to-end process would have a cycle-time of weeks. This means that a good sampling set would require more than a slice of a week.

Since the data storage of our system is based on a cloud infrastructure future work includes distributing the computation of statistics and analytics with the goal of operating on large sample sets delivering results in a reasonable amount of time. This would also enable the comparison of correlation rule changes over time. Slices of certain time-frames could be extracted to compute correlation rules for each of the corresponding time-intervals. Comparison of correlation rules from different time-frames could be used for instance to gain insight into process evolution.

Another avenue of future work could be the incorporation of semantic knowledge into the correlation discovery algorithm from an ontology space to bridge semantic gaps as Moser et al have done [25].

In order to achieve a fully automated correlation discovery system it is necessary to have a method for grouping or clustering source events. At the data staging step knowledge about the schema and the structure which introduces a type is required. The algorithm detects correlations between attributes of those types. In most cases this is naturally given by the source of the event or by some attribute. When a natural distinction is not possible, however, one needs to be able to create groups, clusters or types automatically without explicitly requiring humans to define ways to differentiate between them.

7. REFERENCES
[1] S. Rozsnyai, A. Slominski, and G. T. Lakshmanan. Automated Correlation Discovery for Semi-Structured Business Processes. DMA4SP 2011.

[2] R. S. Barga and H. Caituiro-Monge. Event correlation and pattern detection in CEDR. In Proc. Int. Workshop Reactivity on the Web, 2006.

[3] G. T. Lakshmanan, P. Keyser , and A. Slominski, F. Curbera, and R. Khalaf: A Business Centric End-to-End Monitoring Approach for Service Composites. IEEE SCC 2010: 409-416

[4] A. Halevy, A. Rajaraman, and J. Ordille. (2006). Data integration: the teenage years (p. 9-16). VLDB.

[5] E. Rahm, and P. A. Bernstein. (2001). A survey of approaches to automatic schema matching, 10(4), 334-350. Springer.

[6] I. Ilyas, V. Markl, and P. Haas, P. Brown. (2004). CORDS: Automatic discovery of correlations and soft functional dependencies.

[7] A. Rostin, O. Albrecht, F. Naumann, J. Bauckmann, and U. Leser. (2009). A Machine Learning Approach to Foreign Key Discovery, (WebDB).

[8] W. De Pauw, R. Hoch, and Y. Huang. (2007). Discovering Conversations in Web Services Using Semantic Correlation Analysis, (ICWS), 639-646. IEEE.

[9] G. Hohpe and B. Woolf, Enterprise Integration Patterns, Addison Wesley, 2004

[10] Niblett, P., Graham, S.: Events and Service-Oriented Architecture: The OASIS Web Services Notification Specifications. IBM Syst. J. 44(4). pp. 869--887. (2005)

[11] B. F. van Dongen and W. van der Aalst, "A meta model for process mining data", In Proc. of the CAiSE'05 Workshops, vol. 2, pp. 309–320, 2005.

[12] H. Gonzalez, J. Han, J. and X. Li, "Mining compressed commodity workflows from massive RFID data sets", CIKM '06: Proceedings of the 15th ACM International Conference on Information and Knowledge Management, ACM, pp. 162–171, 2006.

[13] G. Decker and J. Mendling, "Process instantiation", Data and Knowledge Engineering, 2009.

[14] A. Rostin, O. Albrecht, J. Bauckmann, F. Naumann, and U. Leser. A machine learning approach to foreign key discovery. In WebDB, 2009.

[15] P. J. Haas and P. G. Brown. BHUNT: Automatic discovery of fuzzy algebraic constraints in relational data. In Proc. 29th VLDB, pages 668–679. Morgan Kaufmann, 2003.

[16] Gregor Hohpe. Programming without a call stack - event-driven architectures. www.enterpriseintegrationpatterns.com/docs/EDA.pdf, 11 2007.

[17] Jean-Louis Marechaux. Combining service-oriented architecture and event-driven architecture using an enterprise service bus. http://www-128.ibm.com/developerworks/webservices/library/ws-soa-eda-esb/index.html, 112007.

[18] K. Gerke, J. Mendling, and K. Tarmyshov, "Case construction for mining supply chain processes", In W. Abramowicz, editor, Proc. of the Conf. on Business Information Systems, Springer, 2009.

[19] K. Gerke, A. Claus, and J. Mendling, "Process Mining of RFID-based Supply Chains", In Proc. IEEE CEC, 2009

[20] S. Rozsnyai, R. Vecera, J. Schiefer, and A. Schatten. „Event cloud - searching for correlated business events", In CEC/EEE, IEEE Computer Society, 409–420, 2007

[21] H. Roth, J. Schiefer, H. Obweger, S. Rozsnyai: "Event Data Warehousing for Complex Event Processing", In Proc RCIS, 2009.

[22] F. Chang, J. Dean, S. Ghemawat, W. C. Hsieh, D. A. Wallach, M. Burrows, T. Chandra, A. Fikes, and R. E. Gruber. Bigtable: A distributed storage system for structured data. In Proc. of the 7th OSDI, November 2006

[23] H. R. Motahari Nezhad, R. Saint-Paul, B. Benatallah, F. Casati, Event Correlation for Process Discovery from Web Service Interaction Logs, Accepted in VLDB Journal, August 2010.

[24] J. Schiefer, S. Rozsnyai, C. Rauscher, and G. Saurer. Event-driven rules for sensing and responding to business situations. In Proc. DEBS, pages 198–205. ACM, 2007.

[25] T. Moser, H. Roth, S. Rozsnyai, R. Mordinyi, and S. Biffl. Semantic Event Correlation Using Ontologies. In Proceedings of the Confederated International Conferences, CoopIS, DOA, IS, and ODBASE 2009.

Declarative Data-Driven Coordination

Johannes Gehrke

Department of Computer Science, Cornell University; Ithaca, NY, USA
and Max Planck Institute for Software Systems; Saarbruecken, Germany
johannes@cs.cornell.edu

Categories and Subject Descriptors

H.4 [**Information Systems Applications**]: Miscellaneous

General Terms

Languages

Abstract

There are many applications that require users to coordinate and communicate. Friends want to coordinate travel plans, students want to jointly enroll in the same set of courses, and busy professionals want to coordinate their schedules. These tasks are difficult to program using existing abstractions provided by database systems because in addition to the traditional ACID properties provided by the system they all require some type of *coordination* between users. This is fundamentally incompatible with isolation in the classical ACID properties of transactions.

In this talk, I will argue that it is time for the database and event processing communities to look beyond isolation towards principled and elegant abstractions that allow for communication and coordination between some notion of (suitably generalized) transactions. This new area of *declarative data-driven coordination* (D3C) is motivated by many novel applications and is full of challenging research problems.

I will start by surveying existing abstractions in database systems and explain why they are insufficient for D3C [2]. I will then describe *entangled queries*, a coordination language that extends SQL by constraints that allow for the coordinated choice of result tuples across queries originating from different users or applications, and I will discuss algorithms for evaluating entangled queries [1]. I will conclude with a set of research challenges for event processing in this new area.

Acknowledgments

This talk describes joint work with Christoph Koch and Milos Nikolic from EPFL and Gabriel Bender, Nitin Gupta, Lucja Kot, and Sudip Roy from Cornell University.

The research described in this talk has been supported by the NSF under Grants IIS-0534404, IIS-0911036, by a Google Research Award, and by the iAd Project funded by the Research Council of Norway. Any opinions, findings, conclusions or recommendations expressed in this paper are those of the authors and do not necessarily reflect the views of the sponsors.

Biographical Sketch

Johannes Gehrke is a Professor in the Department of Computer Science at Cornell University. Johannes' research interests are in the areas of database systems, data mining, and data privacy. Johannes received an NSF CAREER Award, an Arthur P. Sloan Fellowship, an IBM Faculty Award, an Humboldt Research Award, and the 2011 IEEE Computer Society Technical Achievement Award. He co-authored the undergraduate textbook Database Management Systems (McGrawHill (2002), currently in its third edition), used at universities all over the world. Johannes was Program co-Chair of SIGKDD 2004, VLDB 2007, and he is currently Program co-Chair of ICDE 2012.

Johannes is also an Adjunct Faculty Member at the University of Tromsø in Norway. From 2007 to 2008, he was Chief Scientist at FAST, A Microsoft Subsidiary. He is currently visiting the Max Planck Institute for Software Systems in Kaiserslautern and Saarbrücken in Germany.

1. REFERENCES

[1] N. Gupta, L. Kot, S. Roy, G. Bender, J. Gehrke, and C. Koch. Entangled queries: enabling declarative data-driven coordination. In *SIGMOD*, 2011.

[2] L. Kot, N. Gupta, S. Roy, J. Gehrke, and C. Koch. Beyond isolation: research opportunities in declarative data-driven coordination. *SIGMOD Record*, 39(1):27–32, 2010.

Rapid Detection of Rare Geospatial Events: Earthquake Warning Applications

Michael Olson
Caltech
molson@cs.caltech.edu

Annie Liu
Caltech
aliu@cs.caltech.edu

Matthew Faulkner
Caltech
mfaulk@caltech.edu

K. Mani Chandy
Caltech
mani@cs.caltech.edu

ABSTRACT

The paper presents theory, algorithms, measurements of experiments, and simulations for detecting rare geospatial events by analyzing streams of data from large numbers of heterogeneous sensors. The class of applications are rare events - such as events that occur at most once a month - and that have very high costs for tardy detection and for false positives. The theory is applied to an application that warns about the onset of shaking from earthquakes based on real-time data gathered from different types of sensors with varying sensitivities located at different points in a region. We present algorithms for detecting events in Cloud computing servers by exploiting the scalability of Cloud computers while working within the limits of state synchronization across different servers in the Cloud. Ordinary citizens manage sensors in the form of mobile phones and tablets as well as special-purpose stationary sensors; thus the geospatial distribution of sensors depends on population densities. The distribution of the locations of events may, however, be different from population distributions. We analyze the impact of population distributions (and hence sensor distributions as well) on the efficacy of event detection. Data from sensor measurements and from simulations of earthquakes validate the theory.

Categories and Subject Descriptors

C.2.1 [**Computer-Communication Networks**]: Network Architecture and Design; G.3 [**Probability and Statistics**]: Experimental Design

General Terms

Algorithms, Design, Experimentation

Keywords

seismology, paas, cloud, sensor networks

1. INTRODUCTION

A Grand Challenge.

A grand challenge for distributed event-based (DEB) systems is helping communities sense and respond to global calamities such as earthquakes, tsunamis, nuclear radiation, and fires [1]. DEB systems can help save many thousands of lives by rapid, accurate detection of events and dissemination of warnings to people and systems that must respond quickly. This paper presents theory, architecture, and early experience with one grand challenge: applications that help the community respond to earthquakes. Rapid detection of near-field earthquakes also helps in early warning of close offshore tsunamis.

Community-Based Event Detection.

We describe a DEB system in which the community, as a whole, helps to sense and respond to rapidly unfolding events. All members of a community are effected by earthquakes, tsunamis, nuclear reactor meltdowns, and fires. An effective DEB system must involve all members of the community as well as agencies charged with first response. Equipping ordinary citizens with sensors and enabling them to contribute data to a system has problems [2] — the data is likely to be noisy; the same type of sensor, operated by different people, may behave in very different ways; and open systems are also more open to spoofing and attacks. We explore problems of community-based DEB systems.

Detecting Events with Phones and Low-cost Sensors.

The recent trend towards smart phones and other Internet-enabled devices offers unique possibilities for decentralized event detection. Smart phones contain a rich suite of sensors, such as GPS, accelerometers, and cameras that can gather information about a variety of geospatial phenomena. Smart phones, tablets and laptops have accelerometers that are being used by our project and others [3, 4] to obtain seismic measurements.

Cellphone coverage is increasing dramatically in all parts of the world, including regions such as Haiti that suffer from devastating earthquakes and have populations with less disposable income. Further, the cost of MEMS accelerometers and other sensors continues to drop due to their mass-market use in video game systems. We speculate that smart phones will become less expensive and will be adopted in greater numbers in developing economies in the coming decades.

The widespread use of digital communication/computing devices and decreasing costs of sensors allows for the development of dense sensor networks where the sensors are owned and operated by individuals in the community. To capitalize on the pervasiveness of these sensors, systems must be prepared to deal with high sensor densities, and consequently, large numbers of distributed event publishers. The incoming events must be managed accurately and rapidly if the information generated is to be of use in mitigating the damaging effects of disasters.

Event-Based Systems in the Cloud.

Platform-as-a-Service (PaaS) cloud computing systems can be valuable components of DEB systems. An advantage of cloud computing systems is that they are distributed so that events such as earthquakes and tsunamis do not destroy the infrastructure. Just as importantly, cloud computing systems can be accessed by any point on the globe with Internet access. Some regions that have suffered devastating earthquakes — such as Haiti, Lima Peru, and Gujarat State in India — do not have dedicated seismic networks; however, they do have access to the Internet, and as a consequence can use cloud computing systems distributed around the globe for helping to respond to calamities. PaaS systems have limitations too, and this paper describes some of these limitations and how they can be overcome.

Our work focuses on how event detection with very large numbers of publishers can be performed on a distributed detection platform with the imposed architectural limitations described in Section 3. Specifically, we explore how limits on data access and synchronization imposed in the name of scalability affect the algorithms used to perform detection of ongoing events.

Geospatial-Temporal Analysis for Event Detection.

Responding to earthquakes requires analysis of data over multiple complex geospatial and temporal scales. For example, a rupture along the San Andreas fault, on the West Coast of the U.S., can travel hundreds of kilometers, but first responders need information about building damage at the block-by-block level. We present a data structure — the "geocell" — that is well suited to the range of spatial scales. Using the geocell, we present theory and experimental evidence for detecting events over large geospatial regions over time, and shows how events are detected over time series in a distributed manner.

Designs of Event-Based Cyber Physical Systems.

Event detection systems often focus on reliable in-order delivery of events from publishers to ensure that described events are detected. In this paper, we evaluate the use of unreliable sensors as event publishers and explore the process of event detection using out of order messages with no guarantee of delivery. The event publishers all possess different reliability characteristics, owing to differences in both the type of sensor and the environmental conditions in which each sensor is installed. The sensors used in the network are described in detail in Section 6, as well as how their reliability affects detection performance.

There is a design tradeoff between the amount of data that should be communicated and where data should be stored. For example, a cellphone can send raw accelerometer data continuously to cloud computing servers; this approach is

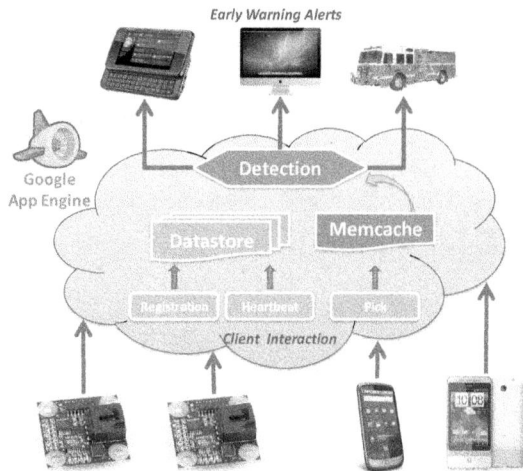

Figure 1: Overview of the CSN architecture.

not cost effective with over a million phones in a region such as Los Angeles. An alternate approach is for a phone to carry out simple event detection and send a short message when it detects an event. Seismologists refer to the detection of an event by a sensor as "picking" an event, and refer to the event data as a "pick." One of the many questions is what information should be sent to servers with each pick.

DEB systems that help respond to physical events such as earthquakes use models of the underlying physical environment — in our case, models and theories of seismological structures. The model of the physical environment is coupled with models of the cyber infrastructure to predict how a given system design will behave. In Section 7, we analyze of the combined cyber and physical layers.

2. COMMUNITY SEISMIC NETWORK

We are building an experimental seismic event detection platform that utilizes a large number of lower quality sensors rather than the small number of high quality sensors traditionally employed by organizations such as the USGS. To obtain the envisioned density of sensors, the CSN recruits volunteers in the community to host USB accelerometer devices in their homes or to contribute acceleration measurements from their existing smart phones. The goals of the Community Seismic Network (CSN) include measuring seismic events with finer spatial resolution than previously possible, and developing a low-cost alternative to traditional seismic networks, which have high capital costs for acquisition, deployment, and ongoing maintenance.

The CSN is designed to scale to an arbitrary number of community-owned sensors, yet still provide rapid detection of seismic events. It would not be practical to centrally process all the time series acceleration data gathered from the entire network, nor can we expect volunteers to dedicate a large fraction of their total bandwidth to reporting measurements. Instead, we adopt a model where each sensor is constrained to send fewer than a maximum number of simple event messages ("picks"), per day to an App Engine fusion center. These messages are brief, containing only the sensor's location, event time, and a few statistics such as the peak observed acceleration. The process of pick detection is discussed in Section 5. Due to privacy constraints, decen-

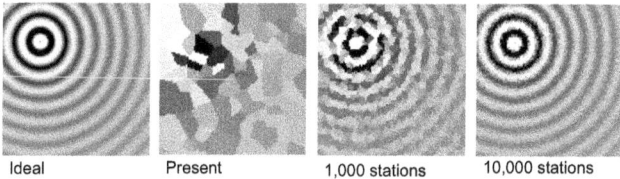

Figure 2: How sensor density affects the detection of seismic waves.

tralized algorithms with a trusted center may be preferred to distributed implementations, where phones are required to know the identity of other members of the network.

An overview of the CSN infrastructure is presented in Figure 1. A cloud server administers the network by performing registration of new sensors and processing periodic heartbeats from each sensor. Pick messages from the sensors are aggregated in the cloud to perform event detection. When an event is detected, alerts are issued to the community.

Dense Community Network.

There are several advantages to a dense community network. First, higher densities make the extrapolation of what regions experienced the most severe shaking simpler and more accurate. In sparse networks, determining the magnitude of shaking at points other than where sensors lie is complicated by subsurface properties. As you can see in Figure 2, a dense network makes visualizing the propagation path of an earthquake and the resulting shaking simpler. With a dense network, we propose to rapidly generate a block-by-block shakemap that can be delivered to first responders within a minute.

Second, community sensors owned by individuals working in the same building can be used to establish whether or not buildings have undergone deformations during an earthquake which cannot be visually ascertained. This type of community structural modeling will make working or living in otherwise unmonitored buildings safer.

Lastly, one of the advantages of relying on cheap sensors is that networks can quickly be deployed to recently shaken regions for data collection or regions which have heretofore been unable to deploy seismic network because of cost considerations. As the infrastructure for the network lies entirely in the cloud, sensors deployed in any country can rely on the existing infrastructure for detection. No new infrastructure will need to be acquired and maintained, rather, one central platform can be used to monitor activity in multiple geographies.

3. SYSTEM INFRASTRUCTURE

Rather than relying on a parallel hardware platform for streaming aggregation[5], our work focuses on the use of the often constrained environments imposed by Platform-as-a-Service (PaaS) providers for event aggregation. In this work, we focus specifically on Google's App Engine[6]. App Engine provides a robust, managed environment in which application logic can be deployed without concern for infrastructure acquisition or maintenance, but at the cost of full control. App Engine's platform dynamically allocates instances to serve incoming requests, implying that the number of available instances to handle requests will grow to match demand levels. For our purposes, a request is an arriving event, so

it follows that the architecture can be used to serve any level of traffic, both the drought of quiescent periods and the flood that occurs during seismic events, using the the same infrastructure and application logic.

However, App Engine's API and overall design impose a variety of limitations on deployed applications; the most important of these limitations as it concerns event processing are the following.

3.1 Synchronization limitation

Processes which manage requests are isolated from other concurrently running processes. No normal inter-process communication channels are available, and outbound requests are limited to HTTP calls. However, to establish whether or not an event is occurring, it is necessary for isolated requests to collate their information. The remaining methods of synchronization available to requests are the use of the volatile Memcache API, the slower but persistent Datastore API, and the Task Queue API.

Memcache's largest limitations for synchronization purposes are that it does not support transactions or synchronized access and that it only supports one atomic operation: increment. Mechanisms for rapid event detection must deal with this constraint of Memcache. More complex interactions can be built on top of the atomic increment operation, but complex interactions are made difficult by the lack of a guarantee that any particular request ever finishes. This characteristic is a direct result of the timeframe limitation discussed next.

The Datastore supports transactions, but with the limitation that affected or queried entities must exist within the same Entity Group. For performing consistent updates to a single entity, this is not constraining, but when operating across multiple affected entities, the limitation can pose problems for consistency. Entity Groups are defined by a tree describing ownership. Nodes that have the same root node belong to the same entity group and can be operated on within a transaction. If no parent is defined, the entity is a root node. A node can have any number of children, as can its own children.

This imposes limitations because groups can only have one write operation at a time. Large entity groups may result in poor performance because concurrent updates to multiple entities in the same group are not permitted. Designs of data structures for event detection must tradeoff concurrent updates against benefits of transactional integrity. High throughput applications are unlikely to make heavy use of entity groups because of the write speed limitations.

Task Queue jobs provide two additional synchronization mechanisms. First, jobs can be enqueued as part of a transaction. For instance, in order to circumvent the transactional limitations across entities, you could execute a transaction which modifies one entity and enqueues a job which modifies a second entity in another transaction. Given that enqueued jobs can be retried indefinitely, this mechanism ensures that multi-step transactions are executed correctly. Therefore, any transaction which can be broken down into a series of steps can be executed as a transactional update against a single entity and the enqueueing of a job to perform the next step in the transaction.

Second, the Task Queue creates tombstones for named jobs. Once a named job has been launched, no job by that same name can be launched for several days. The tombstone that the job leaves behind prevents any identical job from being executed. This means that multiple concurrently running requests could all make a call to create a job, such as a job to generate a complex event or send a notification, and that job would be executed exactly once. That makes named Task Queue jobs an ideal way to deal with the request isolation created by the App Engine framework.

3.2 Timeframe limitation

Requests that arrive to the system must operate within a roughly thirty-second timeline. Before requests hit the hard deadline, they receive a catchable DeadlineExceeded exception. If they have not wrapped up before the hard deadline arrives, then an uncatchable HardDeadlineExceeded exception is thrown which terminates the process. Prior work[7] indicates that factors outside of the developer's control can create a timeout even for functions which are not expected to exceed the allocated time. Therefore, it is quite possible for a HardDeadlineExceeded exception to be thrown anywhere in the code, including in the middle of a critical section. For this reason, developers must plan around the fact that their code could be interrupted at any point in its execution. Care must be taken that algorithms for event detection do not have single points of failure and are tolerant to losses of small amounts of information.

3.3 Query limitation

Several query limitations are imposed on Datastore queries. The most important limitation is that at most one property can have an inequality filter applied to it. This means, for instance, that you cannot apply an inequality filter on time as well as an on latitude, longitude, or other common event parameters. We discuss our solution to solving the problem of querying simultaneously by time and location in Section 4. Additionally, the nature of the Datastore makes traditional join-style queries impossible, but this limitation is circumventable by changing data models or data queries.

4. NUMERIC GEOCELLS FOR GEOSPATIAL QUERIES

Since queries on App Engine are limited to using inequality filters on only one property, a different method is needed for any form of geospatial queries. Our solution involves the use of 8-byte long objects to encode latitude and longitude pairs into a single number. This single number conveys a bounding box rather than a single point, but, at higher resolutions, the bounding box is small enough that it can be used to convey a single point with a high degree of accuracy. We define the resolution of a numeric geocell to be the number of bits used to encode the bounding box. A resolution 14 geocell uses 14 bits, 7 for latitude and 7 for longitude, to encode the resolution. A resolution 25 geocell uses 25 bits, 12 for latitude and 13 for longitude.

It's important to note that the ratio of the height to the width of a bounded area depends on the number of bits used to encode latitude and longitude. For even-numbered resolutions, an equivalent number of latitude and longitude bits are used. For odd numbered resolutions, one additional longitude bit is used. This permits bounding boxes with different aspect ratios. An odd numbered resolution at the equator creates a perfect square, while an even-numbered resolution creates a rectangle with a 2:1 ratio of height to width.

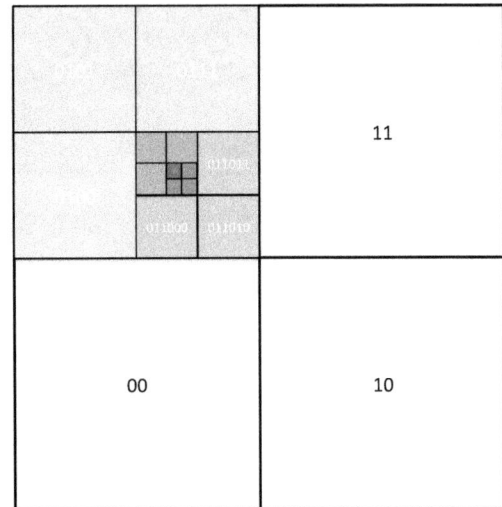

Figure 3: How bounding boxes divide the coordinate space.

Geocells are created using a latitude, longitude pair. This is done by dividing the world into a grid and starting with the (90°S, 180°W), (90°N, 180°E) bounding box, which describes the entire world. Each additional bit halves the longitude or latitude coordinate space. Odd numbered bits, counting from left to right in a bit string, convey information about the longitude, while even-numbered bits convey information about the latitude. After selecting an aspect ratio by choosing even or odd numbered resolutions, geocells are made larger or smaller in increments of 2. This means that each larger or smaller geocell selected will have the same aspect ratio as the previous geocell.

For this reason, each bit pair can be thought of as describing whether the initializing point lies in the northwest, northeast, southwest, or southeast quadrant of the current bounding box. Subsequent iterations use that quadrant as the new bounding box. To work a simple example, consider (34.14°N, 118.12°W). We first determine whether the desired point lies east or west of the mean longitude and then determine whether it lies north or south of the mean latitude. If the point lies east of the mean longitude, the longitude bit is set to 1, and if the point lies north of the mean latitude, the latitude bit is set to 1. In our example, the point lies in the northwest quadrant, yielding a bit pair of 01 for a resolution of 2. Iterating through the algorithm yields the following bits for a resolution of 28:

0100110110100000010000000101

For an illustration of how increasing resolution divides the coordinate space, see Figure 3. Because these representations are stored as fixed-size numbers, the resolution of the geocell must also be encoded. Otherwise, trailing zeros that are a result of a less than maximum resolution would be indistinguishable from trailing zeros that represent successive choices of southwest coordinates. Therefore, the last 6 bits of the long are used to encode the resolution. The other 58 bits are available for storing resolution information.

For space considerations, we also have an integer representation capable of storing resolutions from 1 to 27 using 4 bytes, as well as a URL-safe base64 string based implementation that uses a variable number of bytes to store resolutions from 1 to 58. The integer implementation uses 5 bits to store the resolution, and the remaining 27 bits are available for resolution information. The string based implementation always encodes the resolution in the final character, occupying 6 bits of information in 1 byte, while the remaining characters encode the resolution information.

Our analysis of geocell sizes at various resolutions led us to the conclusion that the most useful geocell sizes for event detection were resolutions 12 through 28. Resolution 29 ranges from 1.5 kilometers square to 0.65 kilometers square depending on the point on earth (see Limitations) and is too small to be useful for aggregation in all but the densest networks. Resolution 12 is quite large, encompassing anywhere from 84,000 square kilometers to 195,000 square kilometers. This resolution is still useful for aggregation of extremely rare events that may be spread out over a large region.

4.1 Comparison

Two similar open methods of hashing latitude and longitude pairs into simple strings have been previously proposed: GeoModel[8] and Geohash[9]. Our algorithm is capable of translating to and from representations in both systems. Numerous other systems exist; however, many are variations on a similar theme, and the earlier systems not designed for computer derivation each suffer from different shortcomings. The UTM[10] and MGRS[11] systems not only have a complicated derivation algorithm[12] but also suffer from exceptions to grid uniformity. The GARS[13] and GEOREF[14] system utilize an extremely small number of resolutions: 3 and 5, respectively. The NAC System[15] is proprietary and has different aims, such as being able to encode the altitude of a location.

GeoModel, Geohash, and our own system all bear similarity to the well known quad tree algorithm for storing data. All of these algorithms rely on dividing the plane into sections: quad tree algorithms divide the plane into quadrants, our own algorithm divides the plane into 2 sections per resolution while GeoModel and Geohash divide the plane into 16 and 32 sections respectively. While the algorithm for finding a storage point in a quad tree is the same, what the other algorithms actually compute is equivalent to the path to that storage point in a quad tree with a storage depth equal to the resolution. The focus of the quad tree method is on the in-memory storage of spatial datapoints, while the focus of the other algorithms is computing an effective hash for datapoints. The path serves at that hash.

Our numeric geocells have one key advantage over the Geohash and GeoModel algorithms: the numeric representation allows for the description of a broader range of resolutions. GeoModel and Geohash encode 4 and 5 bits of information per character, respectively, using the length of the character string to encode the resolution. Numeric geocells therefore have 4 to 5 times more expressive power in possible resolutions.

Resolution density has a strong impact on the number of cells required to cover a given region or the amount of extra area selected by the cells but not needed. When selecting cells to cover a region, it is possible that several smaller geocells could be compressed into one larger geocell. This can happen more often when more resolutions are available. For instance, 16 GeoModel cells and 32 Geohash cells compress into the next larger cell size, where only 4 numeric geocells

compress into the next larger numeric geocell (when maintaining aspect ratio). This comes at the expense of having to store more resolutions in order to perform the compression. Section 4.3 contains more information on the selection of geocells to query.

Space filling curves, such as the Hilbert curve, can provide similar advantages by using an algorithm to ascribe addresses to all the vertices in the curve. Whatever advantage these curves might have derives from their visitation pattern, which can yield better aggregation results for queries that rely on ranges. Our query model utilizes set membership testing for determining geographic locality, which means that we cannot derive a benefit from the visitation pattern of space filling curves. We rely on the simpler hash determination method used in quad trees instead.

4.2 Limitations

Because they rely on the latitude and longitude coordinate space, numeric geocells and similar algorithms all suffer from the problem that the bounded areas possess very different geometric properties depending on their location on Earth. The only matter of vital importance is the coordinate's latitude; points closer to the equator will have larger, more rectangular geocells while points farther from the equator will have smaller, more trapezoidal geocells.

Algorithms which rely on the geometry of the geocells, if applied globally, will not operate as expected. Instead, algorithms must be designed without taking specific geometries into account, or must be tailored to use specific resolutions depending on the point on earth. In the following table, we compare the size, in terms of area, of four different locations. The area is expressed as a ratio of the size to Jakarta, the site used with the largest geocells. Geocells of any resolution converge to this ratio between sizes beginning with resolution 16. The ratio of the height to the width is also included for both even and odd resolutions.

	Jakarta	Caltech	London	Reykjavik
A:Jakarta	1	0.83	0.63	0.44
H:W Even	1.99	1.66	1.24	0.87
H:W Odd	0.99	0.83	0.62	0.44

Finally, prefix matching with any of these algorithms suffer from poor boundary conditions. While geocells which share a common prefix are near each other, geocells which are near each other need not share a common prefix. In the worst case scenario, two adjacent geocells that are divided by either the equator, the Prime Meridian or the 180th Meridian will have no common prefix at all. For this reason, geocells are used exclusively for equality matching.

4.3 Queries

When querying for information from the Datastore or Memcache, geocells can be used to identify values or entities that lie within a given geographic area. A function of the numeric geocell library allows for the southwest and northeast coordinates of a given area, such as the viewable area of a map, to be given and returns a set of geocells which covers the provided area. Given that no combination of geocells is likely to exactly cover the map area, selecting a geocell set to cover a specified area is a compromise between the number of geocells returned and the amount of extraneous area covered.

With smaller geocells, less area that is not needed will be included in the returned geocells, however, more geocells

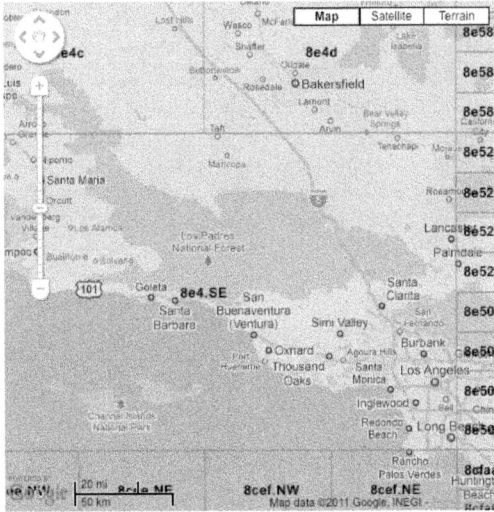

Figure 4: Combining geocells of multiple resolutions to cover an area.

will be required to cover the same geographical area. Larger geocells will require a smaller number of geocells in the set, but are more likely to include larger swaths of land that lie outside the target region. Balancing these two factors requires a careful choice of cost function which takes into account the cost of an individual query for a specific size, which depends on the network density.

With a low density, smaller numbers of queries across larger parcels of land are optimal as discarding the extraneous results is less costly than running larger numbers of queries. With very high sensor densities, too many extraneous results may be returned to make the extra land area an efficient alternative to a larger number of queries, and so reducing the size of the geocells to help limit the area covered is helpful.

Another feature of numeric geocells is that smaller cells can be easily combined to form larger cells. If an object stores the geocells that it exists within at multiple resolutions, then any of those resolutions can be used for determining whether or not it lies within a target geographical area. The algorithm for determining the set of geocells to query can then combine several smaller geocells into larger geocells, which allows larger geocells to be used in the interior of the map with smaller geocells along the exterior.

For instance, Figure 4 shows how smaller geocells can be combined into larger geocells of varying sizes. Importantly for our purposes, the determination of neighboring geocells is a simple and efficient algorithm. By using minor bit manipulations, it is possible to take a known geocell and return the geocell adjacent to it in any of the four cardinal directions. This means that if an event arrives at a known location, not only can the cell that the event belongs to be easily identified but also the neighboring cells. This factors in to our event detection methods, which are described next.

5. DECENTRALIZED DETECTION WITH COMMUNITY SENSORS

The CSN system performs decentralized detection of seismic events by allowing each individual sensor to generate picks of potential seismic events and then aggregating these pick messages by geocell in the cloud to determine if and where an event has occurred. The different algorithms used at the sensor and server levels are discussed next.

5.1 Sensor-side Picking Algorithms

Different sensor types are likely to experience different environmental and noise conditions, and so different picking algorithms may be best suited to particular sensor types. We studied two picking algorithms: the STA/LTA algorithm, designed for higher-quality sensors in relatively low-noise environments, and a density-based anomaly detection algorithm suited to handling the complex acceleration patterns experienced by a cell phone during normal daily use. These algorithms are described in detail in [16] and summarized here.

Event Detection using Averages: STA/LTA.

STA/LTA (Short Term Average over Long Term Average) computes the ratio between the amplitude of a short time window (STA) and the amplitude of a long time window (LTA) and decides to "pick" when the ratio reaches above a threshold. In our analysis, we used a short term window size $ST = 2.5$ s and a long term window size $LT = 10$ s. This simple algorithm can detect sudden changes in transients that may indicate the occurrence of an event in a low-noise environment. In an ideal situation where the sensors have fixed orientation, the signal on each axis can be used to derive the direction of the incoming wave. We do not assume consistent orientation here, but instead simply take the L2 norm of all three axes before computing the STA/LTA.

Anomaly Detection using Density Estimation.

Earthquakes are rare, complex natural phenomena, and consequently are difficult to model. Further, heterogeneous community sensors such as cell phones differ widely in quality and reliability due to varying hardware and software platforms, as well as differing environmental conditions. However, sensory data in the absence of earthquakes is plentiful, and can be used to accurately estimate a probability distribution over normal observations. This density estimate is then used to identify anomalies (observations assigned sufficiently low probability by the model) and transmit them as picks to the fusion center.

Phones frequently change their orientation, producing large changes in signal as the sensor rotates relative to gravity. This effect can be removed by automatically determining the phone's orientation. A decaying average is used to estimate the direction of gravity. The data is rotated to point the gravity component in the negative Z direction, and then the acceleration due to gravity is removed. While this process reliably orients the phone's Z axis, the other axes cannot be consistently oriented. Instead, the Euclidean norm $||X, Y||_2$ of the remaining components, which is invariant to rotations about the Z axis, is computed.

Processing accelerometer time series within the computational limits of smart phones requires a concise and informative representation of the raw data. A 3-axis Android accelerometer produces $\approx$ 50-100 samples per axis each second. The raw acceleration stream is broken into 1 second time windows, and a feature vector is computed to summarize the data in each window. The feature vector is formed by first computing a vector of statistics: 16 Fourier coefficients, the second moment, and the maximum absolute acceleration for both the Z axis and the Euclidean norm $||X, Y||_2$. The final feature vector is obtained by projecting these 36 statistics onto the top 16 principal components computed by PCA, and retaining the projection error as an additional feature. We arrived at this choice of feature vector by extensive cross validation on acceleration data gathered from volunteers' Android phones.

Our anomaly detection requires a density estimate and a probability threshold that separates normal data from anomalies. We use a Gaussian mixture model for density estimation. Model selection (number of Gaussians) and estimation can be computed offline, and uploaded to the phones. Due to the rarity of large earthquakes, nearly all anomalies detected by a phone will be false positives resulting from unusual day-to-day motions. We use this fact to both control the average number of messages sent by each phone and to bound the rate of false positives reported. Each phone uses online percentile estimation to learn a probability threshold that classifies a desired fraction of the data as anomalies. This fraction can be chosen according to bandwidth constraints and is precisely the sensor false positive rate.

5.2 Server-side Pick Aggregation

Picks generated by the sensors are sent to the App Engine server. These simple events are aggregated using the numeric geocells described in Section 4. However, a few factors complicate complex event association and detection.

First, the time of App Engine instances is not guaranteed to be synchronized with any degree of accuracy. This means that relative time determination within the network must be handled by clients if any guarantees about clock accuracy are to be made. This is currently done through the inclusion of an NTP client in the sensor software which determines the drift of the host computer to the network time at hourly intervals.

Second, requests may fail for a variety of reasons. We have previously estimated that as many as 1% of requests on App Engine will fail for reasons beyond the control of the developer. These kinds of errors include requests that wait too long to be served, hard deadline errors, and serious errors with the App Engine servers. In addition to these system errors, clients may go offline without notice due to a software error or something as simple as the host computer going to sleep.

These system conditions mean that the detection algorithm must be: insensitive to the reordering of arriving messages, which occurs by variations in processing or queueing time or by inconsistent determination of network time, and insensitive to the loss of small numbers of messages either due to client or server failures.

The server's job is to estimate complex events such as the occurrence of an earthquake from simple events that indicate an individual sensor has experienced seismic activity. This is done by estimating the frequency of arriving picks by allocating arriving picks to buckets. Buckets are created by rounding the pick arrival time to the nearest two seconds and appending the geocell to the long representation of the time. This gives a unique key with which a bucket is created that all arriving picks in the same time window and region will use to create estimates of the number of firing sensors at that point in time. For instance, an example bucket name would be '12e55d89260-4da040500000001c'.

This bucketing necessarily removes any ability to detect events based on arrival order, but permits event detection based on both arrival frequency and the content of arriving events. Whenever a pick arrives, the appropriate bucket name is calculated and the number of arriving events for that bucket is incremented. The number of active clients for location identified by the bucket's key is also retrieved, which makes it possible to determine the ratio of clients that have experienced a seismic event. For each arrival, the contents of the buckets of the current time window and the surrounding time windows are summed to help manage inconsistencies in arrival time and time of computation.

The sum of the arriving picks across a known time interval is then divided by the number of active clients to determine whether or not a specific geocell has exceeded a threshold level of activity to perform further computation. This is the first trigger which generates a complex event that a given geocell has activated. Activation of the geocell is managed by a Task Queue job which is created to proceed with further analysis. The job is named, which means that for any number of arriving picks in the same time window, only one job will be created per geocell per time window.

The execution of the named job involves probing the surrounding geocells to determine what other geocells have recently fired. The total number of sensors reporting seismic activity in any region for a given time window can be computed by calculating the bucket names under which those events would have been aggregated and summing their contents. The sequence of activation is then used to extrapolate what kind of event the network is experiencing. Of particular importance is the reliability of this detection, which is discussed in Section 6.

6. ESTIMATING SENSOR PERFORMANCE

A question we are trying to answer is: are inexpensive sensors capable of detecting seismic events? The CSN currently uses two types of sensors: the accelerometers in Google Android cell phones and 16-bit MEMS accelerometer USB sensors manufactured by Phidgets, Inc. Measurements from a variety of Android phones while at rest showed device noise with standard deviation of ≈ 0.08 m/s^2. Phidgets at rest showed device noise with standard deviation ≈ 0.003 m/s^2. For reference, earthquakes of Gutenberg-Richter magnitude 4 produce accelerations of approximately 0.12 m/s^2 close to the earthquake's point of origin. These numbers suggest that cell phone accelerometers should be sensitive enough to be able to detect large earthquakes.

Without waiting to observe several large earthquakes, we can only estimate the performance of each picking algorithm under several moderately large seismic scenarios. Detection performance on these simulated event recordings should provide a lower bound on sensor performance during larger events; this claim is experimentally validated in [16].

We obtain simulated acceleration time series recordings for both Phidget and Android sensors by combining historical earthquake recordings from the USGS Southern California Seismic Network (SCSN) with noise recordings from volunteers' Phidget and Android sensors. We collected a set of 54 SCSN records of magnitude M5-5.5 earthquakes from seismic stations between 0-100 km. The SCSN recordings are down-sampled to 50 samples per second to be comparable with low-end consumer accelerometers, and are then overlaid with Phidget or Android recordings from the volunteer data set in order to obtain a realistic noise profile.

6.1 Lower Bounds for Sensor Performance

Receiver Operating Characteristic (ROC) curves are used to gain insight into the performance of a binary classifier. The curve plots true positive rate (TPR) against false positive rate (FPR) for each possible decision threshold. ROC curves allow us to estimate the obtainable TPR of a sensor, given a constraint on its FPR, such as a limit on the average number of pick messages per day.

Using the data set of synthetic historical recordings, we can compute ROC curves for each sensor type, under a variety of seismic scenarios. From a data set of magnitude $M = 5 - 5.5$ earthquakes, we extract 5 sets of records, containing data from stations at varying distances away from the epicenter. The data sets correspond to distance ranges d in kilometers, $d = \{0 - 10, 20 - 30, 40 - 50, 70 - 80, 90 - 100\}$. Figure 5 illustrates the performance of the the STA/LTA algorithm (evaluated on synthetic records made with volunteers' Phidget data), and the anomaly detection algorithm (evaluated on synthetic records made with volunteers' Android data). These ROC curves demonstrate that the Phidgets - higher resolution sensors that are typically not subjected to user motion - obtain superior performance to the Android sensors at all distance ranges. The curves also reflect the $1/r^2$ decay rate of shaking intensity, where r is distance from the quake epicenter.

6.2 Geocell Detection Performance

From the ROC of a single sensor, we can analyze the collective behavior of a group of sensors. Consider a number of sensors occupying a relatively small geocell (e.g. several street blocks). Inside this cell, each sensor experiences similar seismic shaking during an event, and independent noise (such as motions caused by a cell phone's user) in the absence of an event. We can roughly say that all sensors within a cell have the same signal to noise ratio (SNR) and that their picks can be well approximated as independent, identically distributed binary random variables when conditioned on whether an event has occurred or not. By fixing the decision rule for each sensor, and a decision rule for cell-wide event detection, we can evaluate the event detection performance as a function of the number of sensors in the cell.

The sensor decision rules can be specified by constraining the maximum allowable rate of false positive picks. Here, we constrain the Phidget USB sensors to produce at most 1 false pick per hour, and constrain the Android sensors to at most 1 false pick per 5 minute interval. The cell-wide false positive rate is constrained to no more than 1 per year, on average. Figure 6(a) and Figure 6(b) show cell detection performance as a function of sensor density, generated from synthetic M5-5.5 records. These results indicate that a cell containing 30 Phidgets or 100 Androids could reliably detect a moderately large earthquake at a distance of 50km from the epicenter, and that the higher-quality Phidget sensors are capable of detecting the signal from up to 100km.

6.3 System-wide Detection

While sensors within several kilometers of each other are likely to experience similar shaking during an event and thus have similar SNR, sensors distributed across a city or other large region can be expected to behave quite differently. In Section 7, we evaluate how system-wide detection performance is impacted by aggregating picks using a grid of geocells.

7. EXPERIMENTS

In this section, we describe simulation results that study the detection performance of dense, heterogeneous seismic networks during several earthquake scenarios. To simplify the discussion, we restrict our focus on detection to a single subcontinental area, e.g. the Greater Los Angeles Area rather than the North hemisphere. This is reasonable, as one can identify a priori clusters of sensors in different geographic regions so that there is little correlation between clusters. We experimentally evaluate an event association algorithm which aggregates picks by geocell, and compare its performance against a baseline naive event association algorithm which aggregates all pick messages within the region.

7.1 Simulation Platform

An earthquake is a complex event that differs in every occurrence depending on where in the world it occurs. Simulators developed by seismologists often have a large number of input parameters. In comparison, this study focuses on capturing the behaviors of a large-scale network of noisy sensors. Without loss of generality, we assume a much simpler seismic model that includes a point source (i.e. the epicenter is a single point) which is isotropic (i.e. the wave travels in all directions with equal speed).

Based on the sensor characterizations described in Section 6, we can begin to study the detection performance of a total system with a given deployment of sensors. To aid these studies, we have developed a simulation platform that allows time series of sensor picks to be simulated, based on a set of specified sensor TPR,FPR operating points. These operating points can be chosen to maximize detection performance, while satisfying the per-sensor bandwidth constraints.

Given the location of each sensor in the network and the origin of a seismic event, the program computes the probability that each sensor picks during each time instance, and generates picks with those probabilities to produce a time series of pick messages. Figure 8 shows a snapshot of simulated detection of a M5.5 event. The snapshot is taken 20 seconds after the event occurs. For this simulation, the Phidget FPR is set at 1 pick per hour and the Android FPR is set to 1 pick every 5 minutes. The pick messages are timestamped after factoring in network delays. The counts of message arrived at the server in this specific simulation run is shown in Figure 6(c) as a function of time from the start of the event.

7.2 Naive Event Association

Section 5.2 describes a procedure for identifying if a single geocell contains a significant number of picks within a small interval of time. While the activation of one geocell could be used to generate system-wide alerts, such a policy neglects the physical laws governing how earthquakes spread.

In this section, we study the system level detection performance, starting with a simple event association algorithm.

At each time step, the system decides whether an event has occurred based on the pick messages it has received so

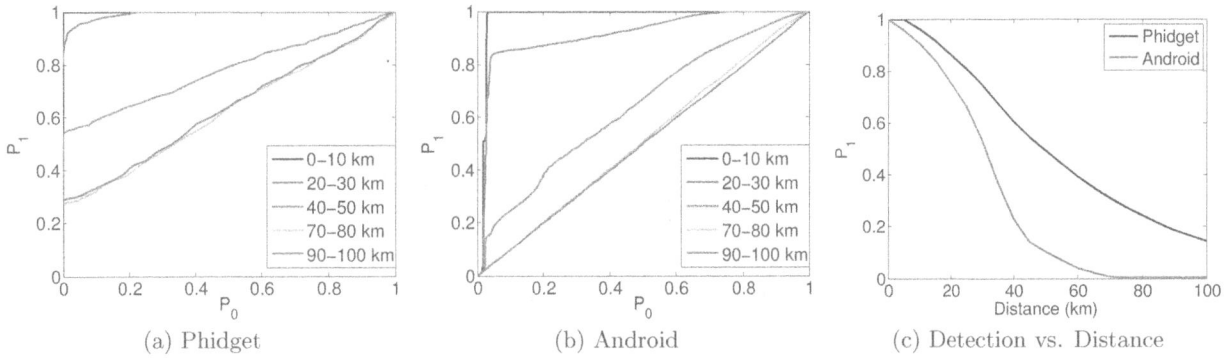

Figure 5: ROC curves for (a) Phidget and (b) Android. (c) Detection performance vs. distance from epicenter under the guarantee of at most 1 false message per hour for the Phidget and 1 false message every 5 minutes for the Androids.

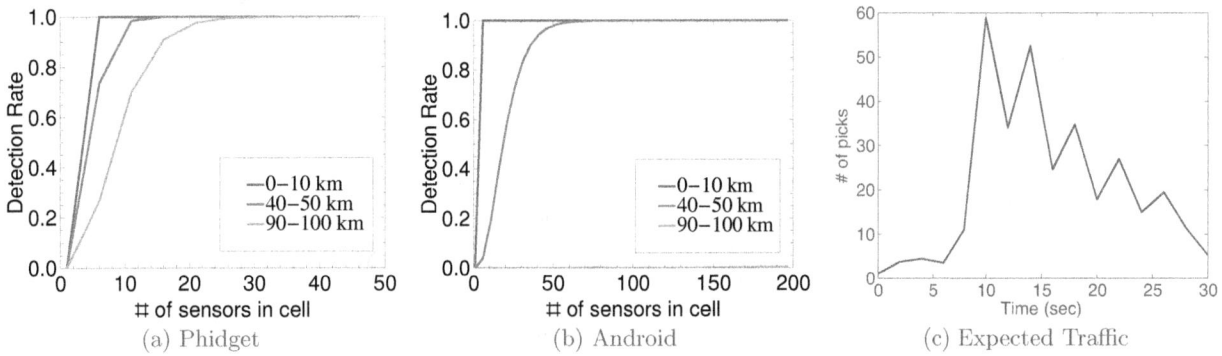

Figure 6: (a) Single cell of varying number of Phidgets observing 3 levels of seismic events of M5.5 and lower. (b) Single cell of varying number of Androids observing 3 levels of seismic events of M5.5 and lower. (c) Number of pick messages received by the system as a function of time since the event started.

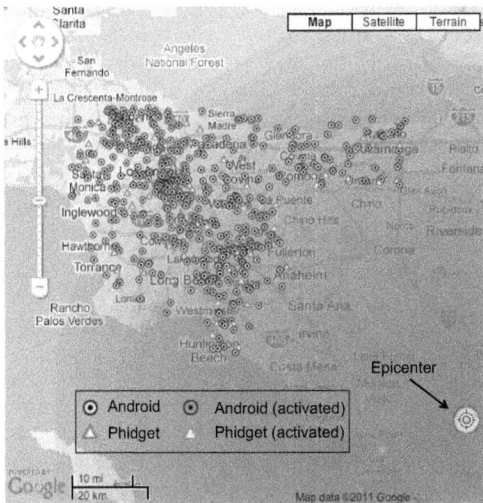

Figure 8: Snapshot of simulated detection of a M5.5 event 80 km outside the great Los Angeles area. There are 100 Phidgets and 1000 Androids distributed according to population density. The snapshot is taken 20 seconds after the event occurred.

far. One naive decision rule is to perform hypothesis testing on the aggregated pick counts in the past few seconds, that is, to compute the ratio of likelihood for the two hypothesis: 1) that there is an event ($p = p_1$), and 2) that there is no event ($p = p_0$). In other words, the naive decision rule performs the test

$$\frac{Binomial(k; n, p_1)}{Binomial(k; n, p_0)} \geq r$$

where n is the total number of sensors in the system, k is the number of picks observed in the past few seconds and r is the decision threshold chosen to satisfy a constraint on the system false positive rate. If the inequality holds, the system declares detection.

This algorithm is naive because it disregards the varying strengths of geospatial correlation between sensors as well as the pattern in which seismic waves travel. Depending on the distance and direction of the wave relative to the region of sensors, different number of sensors are affected at a given time. Therefore it may not be reasonable to consider measurements from all sensors equally at all times. We will present a different association algorithm that exploits these behaviors in the next section. Here we study the naive algorithm as a lower bound for the system level detection performance.

We collected 1000 sets of measurements from 2000 Androids and 20 Phidgets separately during a simulated M5.5

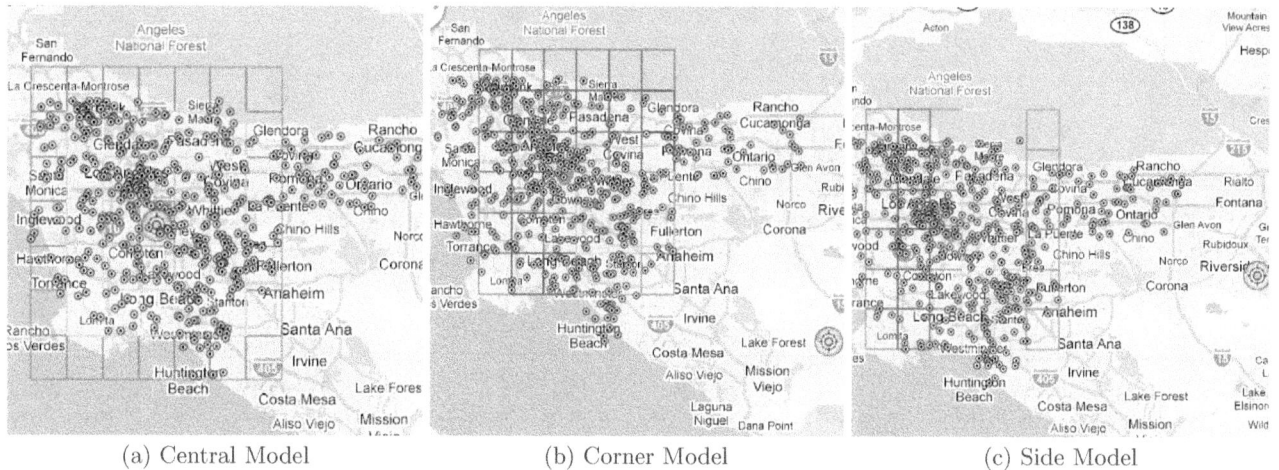

| (a) Central Model | (b) Corner Model | (c) Side Model |

Figure 7: Regions of different sizes and shapes are activated in different sequence for each of the three scenarios. The rainbow-colored rings indicate the order of activation. Red: first. Purple: last

event within 60 km of downtown Los Angeles. During a period of $T = 0 - 10$ seconds after the event occurs, we perform the naive association algorithm on each 2-second interval and compute the system level detection rate while maintaining the guarantee of at most 1 false alarm per year. The results are shown in Figure 9 as the lower bounds for the two types of sensors.

7.3 Geocell-based Regional Event Association

A seismic event can be very coarsely modeled as an isotropic point source event that travels in all directions at a constant speed. With this assumption in mind, we can break down the detection problem into a few case scenarios in terms of how the incoming waves come to contact with the identified cluster of sensors. By exploiting sensor co-activation patterns in these scenarios, one can design a more logical online event association algorithm. Figure 7 shows three such possible cases after we pre-gridded the area into geocells — (a) the epicenter is inside the cluster, (b) the epicenter is diagonally away from the cluster, and (c) the epicenter is on the side and away from the cluster. In each of these cases, regions of different sizes and shapes will be activated in different sequences during san event. While it is computationally nontrivial to partition a 2-dimensional space into arbitrary regions, the geocell library provides the tools to compute these regions efficiently. We can perform hypothesis testing in parallel for each possible regions to improve the system-wide detection performance.

We computed the system-wide detection performance for each of the scenarios illustrated in Figure 7 with either 20 Phidgets or 2000 Androids distributed according to the population density in the area. The regions in terms of activation sequence are identified a priori using the geocell library. A region consists of multiple nearby geocells. Each geocell is $\approx 10 \times 10$ km in size, which is approximately how far the shock wave travels in 2 seconds. Two seconds is also roughly the short-term integration window used in both STA/LTA and anomaly detection algorithm. We can thus safely assume that all sensors in the same region have the same SNR and model them as independently identically distributed random variables, following the analysis in Section

6.2. In each time step of 2 seconds, we perform hypothesis testing on each of the regions and compute the system-wide ROC curves.

Figure 9(a) shows an example of how ROC curves of 2000 Androids evolve in time for the corner case illustrated in Figure 7(b). We slice the surface of this figure at the false alarm rate of 1 per year and retrieve the detection rate as a function of time in Figure 9(b) and 9(c). The results are compared to the baseline results computed using the naive total association algorithm discussed in Section 7.2. These results clearly highlight the benefit of intelligent event association by locality. They also touch on the tradeoffs between delayed decision making and gain in detection confidence. In the case with 2000 Androids (Figure 9(b)), we can fire off alarm at T=2 second that allows us to give 10s of seconds of early warning to surrounding cities such as Santa Barbara or San Diego but with only 20% confidence. Or we can wait till T=10 second or after to fire the alarm with $\approx$ 100% confidence but give slower warnings.

While making the assumption of simple geometry about a highly complex event such as earthquake, this study serves as insights to the intelligent association choice based on geospatial relationship of the sensors and the event.

8. RELATED WORK

Seismic Networks.

The Quake Catcher Network[3] is closely related to CSN; QuakeCatcher shares the use of cheap MEMS accelerometers in USB devices and laptops, however, our system differs in its use of algorithms designed to execute efficiently on cloud computing systems and its incorporation of statistical algorithms for detecting rare events. The incorporation of mobile phones, which pose their own challenges distinct from those of USB devices, also distinguishes this work. The NetQuakes project[17] is related in its deployment of expensive stand-alone seismographs at the homes of community volunteers. The more expensive devices employed by NetQuakes make different tradeoffs between cost and accuracy than the sensors used by CSN.

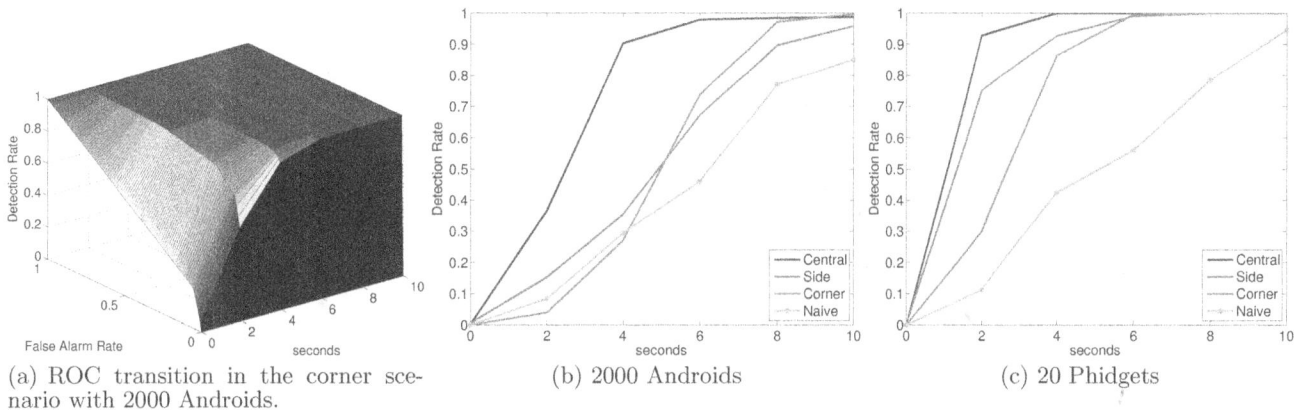

(a) ROC transition in the corner scenario with 2000 Androids.

(b) 2000 Androids

(c) 20 Phidgets

Figure 9: Detection of a M5.5 event with (b) 2000 Androids and (c) 20 Phidgets in the three scenarios described in Figure 7. This result guarantee at most 1 false alarm per year at the system-wide level. Results computed using the geocell-based association algorithm are compared to those using the naive algorithm.

Community and Participatory Sensing.

CSN is not alone in its use of sensors owned and operated by citizen scientists to aid in research. Some projects [18, 19] have incorporated mobile phones to monitor traffic and road conditions while others [20, 21] use community sensors for environmental monitoring by obtaining up-to-date measurements of the conditions participants are exposed to. Like CSN, these applications stand to be benefit from high sensor densities, but their aims of monitoring ongoing phenomena rather than detecting rare events makes them distinct.

Distributed and Decentralized Detection.

The classical hierarchical hypothesis testing approach has been analyzed by Tsitsiklis [22]. Chamberland et al. [23] study classical hierarchical hypothesis testing under bandwidth constraints. Their goal is to minimize the probability of error, under constraint on total network bandwidth. Martinic et al. [24] perform distributed detection on multihop networks by clustering nodes into cells, and comparing observations within a cell to a user-supplied "event signature." The communication requirements of these detection algorithms cannot be met in community sensing applications since sensors cannot communicate with neighbors due to privacy and security restrictions.

Anomaly Detection.

There has also been a great deal of research on anomaly detection in the statistics, machine learning, and complex-event processing communities. Yamanishi et al. [25] develop the SmartSifter approach that uses Gaussian or kernel mixture models to efficiently learn anomaly detection models in an online manner. Davy et al. [26] develop an online approach for anomaly detection using online Support Vector machines. One of their experiments is to detect anomalies in accelerometer recordings of industrial equipment. They use produce frequency-based (spectrogram) features, similar to the features we use. However, their approach assumes the centralized setting. Subramaniam et al. [27] develop an approach for online outlier detection in hierarchical sensor network topologies. This approach is not suitable for the community sensing communication model, where each

sensor has to make independent decisions. Onat et al. [28] develop a system for detecting anomalies based on sliding window statistics in mobile ad hoc networks (MANETs). However, their approach requires nodes to share observations with their neighbors, and so may not be suitable under the privacy constraints inherent in community sensing.

9. CONCLUSION

This paper presents results from an ongoing multi-year project carried out by researchers in geology, civil engineering, and computer science. We presented initial steps at meeting a grand challenge: building DEB systems that save thousands of lives by improving responses to disasters. The architecture, analysis of tradeoffs, and new theory presented in this paper were applied to the specific problem of responding to earthquakes. The results are, however, applicable to responses to many rapidly evolving crises.

The unfolding catastrophe due to the earthquake, tsunami, fires, and nuclear reactor explosions in Japan provides an immediate and stark example of information technology saving lives. The community, as a whole, participated in the response. This paper described how community-based event-detection systems, in which individual members of the community install and operate sensors and responders, can help society to deal with disasters collectively.

Important trends over the last five years include widespread use of cellphones and cloud computing services in all parts of the world. Even people in remote rural parts of developing economies use phones and cloud services such as those that provide weather information. This paper showed how these trends can be exploited to deploy event-based applications anywhere in the world, especially economically disadvantaged areas.

10. ACKNOWLEDGMENT

The authors would like to thank the following Caltech collaborators who are all working to make the Community Seismic Network a success: Prof. Robert Clayton and Prof. Jean-Paul Ampuero from the Seismo Lab; Prof. Tom Heaton, Dr. Monica Kohler, and Ming-Hei Cheng from Earthquake Engineering; Prof. Andreas Krause and Rishi Chandy from

Computer Science; Dr. Julian Bunn, Michael Aivazis, and Leif Strand from the Center for Advanced Computing Research.

This research is supported in part by the National Science Foundation Cyber-Physical Systems program.

11. REFERENCES

[1] K. M. Chandy, O. Etzion, and R. von Ammon, "10201 Executive Summary and Manifesto – Event Processing," in *Event Processing*, ser. Dagstuhl Seminar Proceedings, no. 10201. Dagstuhl, Germany: Schloss Dagstuhl - Leibniz-Zentrum fuer Informatik, Germany, 2011. [Online]. Available: http://drops.dagstuhl.de/opus/volltexte/2011/2985

[2] A. Campbell, S. Eisenman, N. Lane, E. Miluzzo, R. Peterson, H. Lu, X. Zheng, M. Musolesi, K. Fodor, and G.-S. Ahn, "The rise of people-centric sensing," *Internet Computing, IEEE*, vol. 12, no. 4, pp. 12 –21, 7-8 2008.

[3] E. Cochran and J. Lawrence, "The quake-catcher network: Citizen science expanding seismic horizons," *Seismological Research Letters*, vol. 80, p. 26, Jan 2009.

[4] (2011, 3) Measuring shaking intensity with mobile phones. [Online]. Available: http://ishakeberkeley.appspot.com/mission

[5] S. Schneidert, H. Andrade, B. Gedik, K.-L. Wu, and D. S. Nikolopoulos, "Evaluation of streaming aggregation on parallel hardware architectures," in *Proceedings of the Fourth ACM International Conference on Distributed Event-Based Systems*, ser. DEBS '10. New York, NY, USA: ACM, 2010, pp. 248–257.

[6] (2011, 3) Google app engine. [Online]. Available: http://code.google.com/appengine/

[7] M. Olson and K. M. Chandy, "Performance issues in cloud computing for cyber-physical applications," in *Proceedings of the 4th IEEE International Conference on Cloud Computing*. IEEE, 2011.

[8] S. S. Roman Nurik. (2011, 3) Geospatial queries with google app engine using geomodel. [Online]. Available: http://code.google.com/apis/maps/articles/geospatial.html

[9] geohash.org. (2011, 3) Geohash. [Online]. Available: http://en.wikipedia.org/wiki/Geohash

[10] *DMATM 8358.2 The Universal Grids: Universal Transverse Mercator (UTM) and Universal Polar Stereographic (UPS)*, Defense Mapping Agency, Fairfax, VA, 9 1989.

[11] *DMATM 8358.1 Datums, Ellipsoids, Grids, and Grid Reference Systems*, Defense Mapping Agency, Fairfax, VA, 9 1990.

[12] Locating a position using utm coordinates. [Online]. Available: http://en.wikipedia.org/wiki/Universal_Transverse_Mercator

[13] L. Nault, "Nga introduces global area reference system," *PathFinder*, 11 2006.

[14] (2011, 3) Georef. [Online]. Available: http://en.wikipedia.org/wiki/Georef

[15] N. G. P. Inc. (2011, 3) The natural area coding system. [Online]. Available: http://www.nacgeo.com/nacsite/documents/nac.asp

[16] M. Faulkner, M. Olson, R. Chandy, J. Krause, K. M. Chandy, and A. Krause, "The Next Big One: Detecting Earthquakes and Other Rare Events from Community-based Sensors," in *Proceedings of the 10th ACM/IEEE International Conference on Information Processing in Sensor Networks*. ACM, 2011.

[17] (2011, 3) Netquakes. [Online]. Available: http://earthquake.usgs.gov/monitoring/netquakes/

[18] R. Herring, A. Hofleitner, S. Amin, T. Nasr, A. Khalek, P. Abbeel, and A. Bayen, "Using mobile phones to forecast arterial traffic through statistical learning," *Submitted to Transportation Research Board*, 2009.

[19] A. Krause, E. Horvitz, A. Kansal, and F. Zhao, "Toward community sensing," in *Proceedings of the 7th international conference on Information processing in sensor networks*. IEEE Computer Society, 2008, pp. 481–492.

[20] M. Mun, S. Reddy, K. Shilton, N. Yau, J. Burke, D. Estrin, M. Hansen, E. Howard, R. West, and P. Boda, "Peir, the personal environmental impact report, as a platform for participatory sensing systems research," in *Proceedings of the 7th international conference on Mobile systems, applications, and services*. ACM, 2009, pp. 55–68.

[21] P. Völgyesi, A. Nádas, X. Koutsoukos, and Á. Lédeczi, "Air quality monitoring with sensormap," in *Proceedings of the 7th international conference on Information processing in sensor networks*. IEEE Computer Society, 2008, pp. 529–530.

[22] J. Tsitsiklis, "Decentralized detection by a large number of sensors," *Mathematics of Control, Signals, and Systems (MCSS)*, vol. 1, no. 2, pp. 167–182, 1988.

[23] J. Chamberland and V. Veeravalli, "Decentralized detection in sensor networks," *Signal Processing, IEEE Transactions on*, vol. 51, no. 2, pp. 407–416, 2003.

[24] F. Martincic and L. Schwiebert, "Distributed event detection in sensor networks," in *Systems and Networks Communications, 2006. ICSNC'06. International Conference on*. IEEE, 2006, p. 43.

[25] K. Yamanishi, J. Takeuchi, G. Williams, and P. Milne, "On-line unsupervised outlier detection using finite mixtures with discounting learning algorithms," *Data Mining and Knowledge Discovery*, vol. 8, no. 3, pp. 275–300, 2004.

[26] M. Davy, F. Desobry, A. Gretton, and C. Doncarli, "An online support vector machine for abnormal events detection," *Signal processing*, vol. 86, no. 8, pp. 2009–2025, 2006.

[27] S. Subramaniam, T. Palpanas, D. Papadopoulos, V. Kalogeraki, and D. Gunopulos, "Online outlier detection in sensor data using non-parametric models," in *Proceedings of the 32nd international conference on Very large data bases*. VLDB Endowment, 2006, pp. 187–198.

[28] I. Onat and A. Miri, "An intrusion detection system for wireless sensor networks," in *Wireless And Mobile Computing, Networking And Communications, 2005.(WiMob'2005), IEEE International Conference on*, vol. 3. IEEE, 2005, pp. 253–259.

Pattern Rewriting Framework for Event Processing Optimization

Ella Rabinovich
IBM Haifa Research Labs
Haifa 31905, Israel
ellak@il.ibm.com

Opher Etzion
IBM Haifa Research Labs
Haifa 31905, Israel
opher@il.ibm.com

Avigdor Gal
Technion – Israel Institute of
Technology, Haifa 32000, Israel
avigal@ie.technion.ac.il

ABSTRACT

A growing segment of event-based applications require both strict performance goals and support in the processing of complex event patterns. Event processing patterns have multiple complexity dimensions: the semantics of the language constructs (e.g., sequence) and the variety of semantic interpretations for each pattern (controlled by policies). We introduce in this paper a novel approach for pattern rewriting that aims at efficiently processing patterns which comprise all levels of complexity. We present a formal model for pattern rewriting and demonstrate its usage in a comprehensive set of rewriting techniques for complex pattern types, taking various semantic interpretations into account. A cost model is presented, balancing processing latency and event throughput according to user's preference. Pattern cost is then estimated using simulation-based techniques.

This work advances the state-of-the-art by analyzing complex event processing logic and by using explicit means to optimize elements that were considered "black box." Our empirical study yields encouraging results, with improvement gain of up to tenfold relative to the non optimized solutions that are used in the current state-of-the-art systems.

Categories and Subject Descriptors

H3.4. Systems and software (Performance evaluation), D3.3 Language constructs and features (Patterns).

General Terms

Algorithms, performance, experimentation.

Keywords

Event processing, event patterns, event processing optimization, simulation-based optimization, bi-objective goal function.

1. INTRODUCTION AND MOTIVATION

Rapid evolution of the use of event-based applications in enterprises poses high agility and scalability requirements for event processing systems. Such requirements call for performance optimization to achieve low latency and high throughput. Among the event-based systems there is a growing segment of applications that have (typically conflicting) requirements for both strict performance and processing of event patterns with an increased complexity level. As an example, an auditing

application may be used to verify a certification process that consists of multiple steps and needs to be finalized in the correct order and with an acceptable combination of completion status [24]; the complexity here stems from the quantity of steps in some workflows (>20) and the multiple assertions among events representing finalization of states. In the financial industry, an anti-money laundering system may monitor a continuous stream of customers' transactions for suspicious activities while looking for complex trends [23]. On the Internet, the variety of Web2.0 applications generate vast amount of real-time information that can be analyzed to infer social activities; again, using complex patterns.

Typical benchmark and optimization work in the event processing domain has been geared towards the simple functionality cases. Previous studies [1][14] indicate that there is a major performance degradation as application complexity increases (ratio of 1:90 for both latency and throughput between scenarios), thereby evidencing that optimization efforts comprise a great potential value for the high-end applications in the complexity scale.

The potential optimization value of pattern rewriting, along with rapid evolution of the complexity of event processing systems, stimulated our effort to develop a formal and methodical approach for event pattern rewriting, while considering the most complex cases of patterns and their various semantic interpretations. In this work, we provide a model and algorithms for complex event patterns rewriting as an optimization mechanism. The rewriting technique, underlying the core part of this work involves splitting a pattern or unifying several patterns by using patterns of the same type. We propose a formal model for rewriting of the two commonly used patterns, namely all and sequence, for (1) subsumption of the common logic, and (2) splitting a pattern into sub-patterns for parallel execution, where possible (e.g., multi-core platform). These techniques assist in reducing CPU consumption in the first case and improving a system throughput in the second.

We also propose a rewriting technique that provides a choice (realized by different pattern rewritings) between eager and lazy evaluation of the sequence pattern. We demonstrate that eager vs. lazy evaluation of the sequence pattern mirrors the latency vs. throughput tradeoff performance phenomenon. Driven by the possible pattern split alternatives, we generate a set of Pareto efficient solutions with respect to pattern performance indicators; this allows the system designer to select a favorable solution, by tuning a bi-objective performance goal function. Our empirical study produced encouraging results, demonstrating up to tenfold improvement in pattern latency, achieved by the rewritten version when compared to its original alternative.

Our approach advances the state-of-the-art in the domain of event processing optimization, by proposing enhanced solutions to complex patterns. Therefore, the contribution of this paper is twofold. First, we establish a methodical approach for event pattern rewriting. Second, we describe a framework for tuning the performance objectives of the <u>sequence</u> pattern, employing the pattern rewriting techniques, as a proof of usefulness of the rewriting approach.

The rest of the paper is structured as follows: Section 2 provides the background and sets the terminology used throughout the paper. In Section 3, we present the pattern rewriting model, formally proving pattern rewriting validity for one pattern and extending the discussion to additional cases. Section 4 describes in depth the idea of bi-objective optimization of the <u>sequence</u> pattern and Section 5 presents our empirical study. We discuss related work in Section 6 and conclusions in Section 7.

2. PRELIMINARIES

The terminology we use in this paper is based on the event processing model defined by Etzion and Niblett [5]. In this section we briefly overview the main constructs used in this work.

2.1 Event Processing Constructs

An *event* (e) is an occurrence within a particular system or domain; it is something that has happened, or is contemplated as having happened in that domain. An *event type* (E) is a specification for a set of events that share the same semantic intent and structure. Given an event *e*, we define its event type by *e.type*. An event type can represent an event arriving from a producer or an event produced by an event processing agent (see below). We denote such events as *raw* and *derived*, respectively.

An *event processing agent* (EPA) is a processing element that applies logic on a set of input events, to generate a set of output (derived) events. A *stateful event processing agent* maintains its internal state over successive invocations. For example, an EPA that performs aggregation of events over a time window is *stateful*, while an EPA that filters events by applying a predicate to a single event's attributes is considered *stateless*.

A *context* is a named specification of conditions that groups event instances so that they can be jointly processed. While there exist several context dimensions, in this work we refer to the temporal dimension, one of the most commonly used dimensions. A *temporal context* consists of one or more time intervals, possibly overlapping. Each time interval corresponds to a context partition, containing events that occur during that interval.

An *event processing network* (EPN) [11][19] is a conceptual model, describing the event processing flow execution. It consists of a collection of EPAs, producers, and consumers linked by event channels. An *event channel* is a processing element that receives events from one or more source elements (producer or EPA), makes routing decisions, and sends the input events unchanged to one or more target elements (EPA or consumer) in accordance with the routing decisions. A schematic presentation of an EPN, as presented by Moxey et al. [15], is illustrated in Figure 1. The EPN follows the event driven architecture where EPAs are communicating in asynchronous fashion by receiving and sending events. Although a channel can route several event types, in this work we assume that it is manifested as an edge in the graph, connecting a single source with a single sink carrying a single event type.

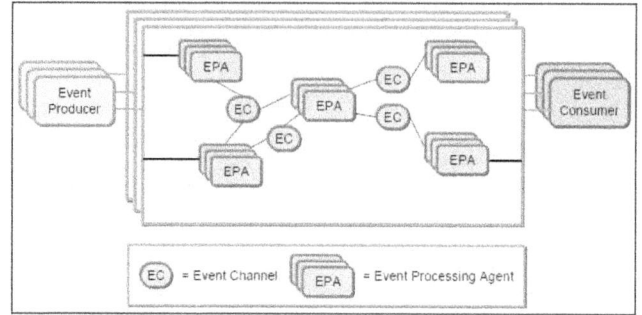

Figure 1: Schematic representation of EPN

2.2 Pattern Matching

Pattern matching (also known as pattern detection) is a type of EPA that enables the analysis of collections of events and the relationship between them. Informally, we say that a conditional combination of events matches a pattern if this combination satisfies the particular pattern definition. Pattern matching EPA examples are: <u>all</u>, <u>sequence</u>, <u>absence</u>, and <u>any</u>. Pattern matching EPAs are stateful, involving both detection of multiple event combinations and temporal semantics; thereby introducing the majority of performance optimization challenges.

A *relevant event types set* (RTS) of a pattern matching EPA is a list of event types to which a matching function is applied. Pattern *participant set* (PS) is a collection of event instances that occur within this pattern agent's context partition (time window). These events are instances of event types mentioned in the pattern's RTS. Pattern *matching set* (MS) is the output of pattern matching process; it is a subset of the *participant set*, satisfying a certain pattern definition.

A basic form of pattern *derived event* (DE) generation is a composition of all event instances in a matching set, denoted by Compose(MS). Pattern derivation can alternatively be performed by computing output event attributes as a function of event values in a matching set.

Figure 2 demonstrates the concept of a pattern matching EPA. Event instances in the PS comply with event types defined by RTS, and MS contains a subset of PS satisfying the pattern.

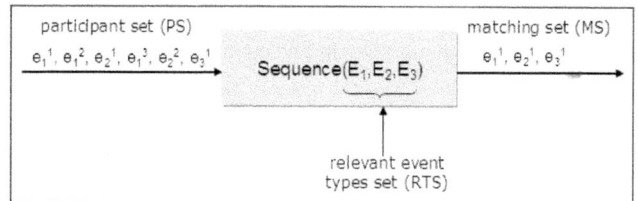

Figure 2: Pattern matching EPA

A *pattern assertion* (PA) is a condition that the matching set is required to meet for the pattern to be satisfied. Pattern assertion is a predicate, i.e., Boolean expression including variables (event attributes), mathematical (e.g., +, -, *, <, >, =) and logical (e.g., AND, OR, NOT) operators, and custom functions. We distinguish a pattern assertion that refers to a single event type (e.g., event *threshold condition* such as $E_1.price > 100$), from pattern assertion that encapsulates several event types (e.g., $E_1.price > E_2.price$), further denoted by *cross-event pattern assertion*.

Pattern *policies* (Policies) [1][5] are used to fine-tune and disambiguate pattern matching semantics. In this work we consider the following subset of pattern policies: *evaluation* policy determines when the matching sets are produced with possible values in {immediate, deferred}; *cardinality* policy determines how many matching sets are produced within a single context partition (e.g., time window) with possible values in {single, unrestricted}; *repeated type* policy handles multiple events of the same type, and has possible values in {first, last, override, every}; *consumption* policy determines the status of a participant event after it has been included in a matching set with possible values in {consume, reuse}. All policies are specified at the pattern level and *repeated type* and *consumption* policies can be overridden for specific event types.

2.3 Speculative Broker Scenario

We illustrate the basics of event processing, as demonstrated in sections 2.1 and 2.2 through a concrete use case.

Example 1:

A speculative broker is a broker who buys and immediately sells, with profit, the same stock at least three times within a ten minutes time window.

E_1: StockBuy event type with the following attributes: {transactionID, transactionTS, stockID, price, volume}

E_2: StockSell event type with the following attributes: {transactionID, transactionTS, stockID, price, volume}

Pattern: sequence(E_1^i, E_2^j, E_1^k, E_2^l, E_1^m, E_2^n), where the superscript numbers are used to distinguish among various instances of the same event type, such that $i<k<m$ and $j<l<n$.

Pattern assertion:

(E_1^i.stockID==E_2^j.stockID AND E_1^i.price<E_2^j.price) AND
(E_1^k.stockID==E_2^l.stockID AND E_1^k.price<E_2^l.price) AND
(E_1^m.stockID==E_2^n.stockID AND E_1^m.price<E_2^n.price)

Pattern policies:
evaluation: immediate
cardinality: single
repeated type: first
consumption: ---

Consider the ordered set of event instances along with the relevant attributes, as specified in Table 1. Events whose name starts with e1 and e2 are instances of E1 and E2 event types respectively.

The pattern matching set, and therefore the pattern derived event (Compose(MS)) will consist of a single matching set that contains the following event instances:

$<e_1^1, e_2^1, e_1^2, e_2^3, e_1^3, e_2^4>$

Note that a single matching set is reported due to the "single" cardinality policy; this policy allows disregarding the consumption mode, which is only relevant for multiple detections. The first instance is selected from within a sequence of events of the same type, e.g. e_2^1 is selected for the matching set from the existing $<e_2^1, e_2^2>$ instances, due to the "first" repeated type. The "immediate" evaluation policy forces the detection report upon the e_2^4 instance arrival, and not at the end of a ten minutes time window, as would be the case with the "deferred" mode.

Changing the cardinality policy to "unrestricted", repeated type policy to "last" and setting the consumption policy to "reuse" would produce two matching sets:

$<e_1^1, e_2^2, e_1^2, e_2^3, e_1^4, e_2^4>$ and $<e_1^2, e_2^3, e_1^4, e_2^4, e_1^5, e_2^5>$

Unlike the previous case, several matching sets are reported and the last event from all existing instances is selected for a matching set, e.g. e_2^2 from the possible $<e_2^1, e_2^2>$. Finally, the "reuse" consumption mode gives rise to a repetitive appearance of certain instances in multiple matching sets, e.g. e_1^4.

Table 1: Event sequence for speculative broker pattern

event name	transactionID	symbol	price	volume
e_1^1 (buy)	1110	ICO	160	50
e_2^1 (sell)	1145	ICO	175	25
e_2^2 (sell)	1177	ICO	175	25
e_1^2 (buy)	2011	CCHOF	200	75
e_2^3 (sell)	2014	CCHOF	207	75
e_1^3 (buy)	2175	WBD	170	40
e_1^4 (buy)	2200	WBD	170	25
e_2^4 (sell)	2201	WBD	177	65
e_1^5 (buy)	2210	ICO	160	50
e_2^5 (sell)	2245	ICO	175	50

3. PATTERN REWRITING MODEL

In this section we introduce the idea of event processing pattern rewriting (Section 3.1), along with the formal model that comprises the basis of our policy-based rewriting approach (sections 3.2 and 3.3). We prove rewriting validity for a representative pattern (Section 3.4) and extend the discussion to additional cases (Section 3.5).

3.1 Introduction to Pattern Rewriting

The idea of expression rewriting has been around for quite some time. Both unification and subsumption of logical assertions were introduced in the AI literature more than 30 years ago [16]. Some event processing related rewritings, such as extracting common sub-expression logic, were demonstrated in the SMILE project [21]. We now introduce an approach that aims at fitting the complexity of current event processing systems.

The rewriting technique, underlying the core part of this work involves either splitting a pattern or unifying several patterns by using patterns of the same type, as demonstrated in Figure 3. The <u>sequence</u> pattern at the top part of the figure (f1) is split into two successive <u>sequence</u> patterns (f2' and f2"), where DE is the derived event type produced by f2'; f2" monitors a series of DE, E3 and E4 instances, thus completing the sequence of E1, E2, E3 and E4, as required for detection of the original pattern.

Among the new and nontrivial challenges, posed by the event processing language expressiveness for pattern rewriting, are cross-event pattern assertions and pattern policies. Each aspect increases the complexity of the pattern rewriting procedure and requires a distinct analysis of rewriting alternatives, as well as an appropriate formal representation. The detailed exploration of these challenges is given in sections 3.3 and 3.4.

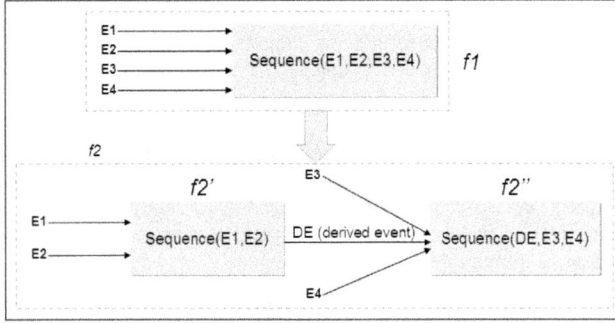

Figure 3: Pattern rewriting example

Another category of rewritings is inspired by the redundancy in event processing languages; i.e. there exist several alternatives for expressing the same logic. A simple example is the pattern sequence(E_1,E_2) that can be rewritten using all(E_1,E_2) and <u>filter</u> EPAs, while the <u>filter</u> EPA will filter the derived events that comply with E_1.timestamp<E_2.timestamp from all(E1,E2). A more complex example is the rewriting of all(E_1, E_2) into any(sequence(E_1,E_2),sequence(E_2,E_1)).

In this work we focus on the first category of rewriting by using patterns of the same type, proposing several rewriting alternatives, showing formally the rewriting correctness and demonstrating concrete usages.

3.2 Formal Definition of Pattern Detection

We employ the denotational semantics approach [20], which defines an event processing pattern as a function, mapping pattern's input into its output. The denotational approach provides natural and intuitive means for proving patterns' equivalence: we demonstrate that for the same input, two rewriting alternatives generate the same output. This formal evidence is a necessary and sufficient condition for a rewriting validity.

Due to space considerations, we refrain from the full-scale formal model of the observed pattern types and policies. We demonstrate the approach by modeling the <u>sequence</u> pattern with the policies: (1) evaluation="immediate", (2) cardinality="single" (3) repeated type="first" and (4) consumption="consume". RTS stands for relevant event types set, PA for pattern assertion, PS for participant set and MS for matching set.

We are given f(sequence, RTS, PA, Policies, PS) = MS, where

Policies = <immediate, unrestricted, first, consume>,

RTS = <E_1, E_2, E_3, ... E_N>, PS = <e_1, ..., e_M>, and

e.ts is the timestamp of event instance e.

We define an event collection EC to be a subsequence of PS. In what follows, events in an event collection of size N are enumerated as e_1, ..., e_N, regardless of their enumeration in PS.

The conformance of an event collection EC with relevant event types set RTS is computed as follows:

$$\text{Conforms(EC,RTS)} = \begin{cases} \text{true} & \text{if } (e_i.type = E_i) \wedge e_1.ts< ... <e_N.ts, \\ & \forall (1 \leq i \leq N) \\ \text{false} & \text{otherwise} \end{cases}$$

Definition 1: *A pattern assertion PA over PS is a function from the domain of subsequences of PS to {true, false}. PA(EC) is computed to be true if the assertion PA is satisfied by EC.*

We define a candidate matching sets CMS to be

CMS = {EC | Conforms(EC,RTS) $\wedge$ PA(EC)}.

We say that a candidate matching set CMS is valid if it is not empty (CMS != $\varnothing$). Validity is denoted using the indicator ValidMatch(CMS). It is worth noting that the "first" repeated type policy induces lexicographical order on all event combinations that are candidates for a matching set, yielding chronological ordering between event instances, i.e. e1 $\prec$ e2 iff e1.ts<e2.ts. Therefore, event collections ordering is defined using lexicographical order notation.

Definition 2: *For EC' = <e'_1, ..., e'_N>$\in$CMS and EC'' = <e''_1, ..., e''_N>$\in$CMS we say that EC' precedes EC'', denoted by EC' $\prec$ EC'' iff $\exists (1 \leq m \leq N)$ $\forall (i<m)$ ($e'_i.ts==e''_i.ts \wedge e'_m.ts < e''_m.ts$).*

Definition 3: *EC participants comply with the "first" repeated type if $\forall (EC' \in CMS)$, EC' != EC, EC $\prec$ EC'. We denote such compliance with an indicator First(EC).*

Definition 4 *Given a candidate matching set CMS, a pattern matching set is defined to be:*

MS = (EC$\in$CMS | First(EC)).

The defined model serves validation of the rewriting procedure by proving the equivalence of two pattern alternatives, as presented in Section 3.4.

Employing cross-event pattern assertion introduces one of the main difficulties when approaching pattern rewriting. This challenge and its solution are detailed in the following section.

3.3 Assertion-based Rewriting

Splitting of a single pattern into two patterns, as demonstrated in Figure 3, infers assertion partitioning into two groups: an assertion related to the first pattern (f2') participants and an assertion related to second pattern (f2'') participants. Such a partitioning gives rise to several assertion-related issues: (1) the direct connection of f2' (sequence(E_1,E_2)), with f2'' (sequence(DE,E_3,E_4)) automatically implies "AND" operator between the two assertion parts, since both assertions need to be satisfied by the final matching, and (2) since f2' and f2'' participant types do not overlap, the assertion is assumed to be *separable* (see below) into two independent parts, in terms of assertion variables.

We take the following steps to discover independent components in a pattern assertion, thus implying possible rewritings of the given pattern:

- Convert the pattern assertion expression into conjunctive normal form (CNF). Since CNF requires Boolean literals, each sub-expression (e.g., A.key>B.key) can be treated as a Boolean literal. The conversion to CNF is obtained by employing De Morgan laws [6].

- Identify independent participants' sub-groups in the newly created CNF assertion. This can be achieved by creating assertion variables dependency graph, where variables are represented by nodes and their *connections* by edges. Variable A is *connected* to variable B iff there exists a mathematical operator between them (e.g., A.key > B.key, A.key+B.key < 7) or variable A appears with variable B in the same OR clause.

Disconnected components in such a dependency graph induce partitioning of assertion variables into independent groups, thus creating independent patterns.

- Splitting an assertion into maximal number of independent partitions implies the finest granulation we can perform on the assertion expression; that is, the maximal split of the original pattern into interconnected sub-patterns.

As an example, consider the following pattern:

Example 2

sequence(A,B,C,D,E,F) with pattern assertion:
(A.key > B.key) AND (D.key > E.key) AND NOT
((E.key==F.key) AND (C.key==77))

Applying the above technique would result in the following steps:

Convert pattern assertion into CNF:

(A.key > B.key) AND (D.key > E.key) AND
(NOT(E.key==F.key) OR NOT(C.key==77))

Identify independent variables partitions, as depicted in Figure 4.

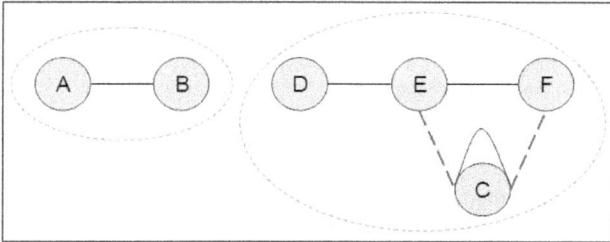

Figure 4: Disconnected components in assertion graph

Note that C is self-connected due to its comparison to constant and it is connected to E and F since they jointly appear in the same OR clause. The (interconnected) variables A and B are disconnected from the rest of the graph, thus creating two independent assertion variables parts. The pattern split induced by assertion partitioning generates two sub-patterns, as follows:

sequence(A,B) with pattern assertion:
(A.key > B.key)

followed by

sequence(C,D,E,F) with pattern assertion:
(D.key > E.key) AND (NOT (E.key==F.key) OR NOT
(C.key==77))

In a more laconic writing: sequence(A,B,sequence(C,D,E,F))

When considering the <u>sequence</u> pattern, variable partitioning should preserve events order as specified by the relevant event types set. Consider again the <u>sequence</u> pattern in Example 2: in case the pattern assertion was slightly modified to produce {A,F} and {B,D,E,C} independent variables sets, such a partitioning would have been sufficient for pattern of type <u>all</u>, but not for <u>sequence</u>, where events order is of importance.

Expression evaluation optimization was extensively investigated in other areas, including compilers optimization, CSP (Constraint Satisfaction Problems) and Production Rules [12]. Several known techniques (e.g., converting assertions to CNF, identification of graph disconnected components) are leveraged at the demonstrated algorithm to allow assertion-based pattern rewriting. In this work we restrict ourselves to pattern assertions that are

separable by "AND"; this can be extended to other connectors, such as "OR" and "XOR".

3.4 Patterns Equivalence Definition and Proof

Pattern assertion analysis is a fundamental step in the procedure of pattern rewriting. Pattern policies pose another nontrivial challenge of preserving the semantic interpretation of the pattern, while rewriting. We now present a formal proof of pattern rewriting equivalence for a basic set of policies and extend the discussion for more complex cases.

The formal definition introduced in Section 3.2 and assertion-based splitting techniques allow us to derive a formal justification for pattern rewriting, i.e. a proof that the original pattern is equivalent to the rewritten pattern in the sense that they produce an equivalent output to identical input. Complying with the query rewriting principle in database systems [3], we demonstrate that for the same input (pattern participant set), the original and the rewritten alternatives produce the same output (matching set).

When considering patterns we also need to refer to the temporal perspective, demonstrating that in the original and the rewritten alternative the equivalent output is produced at identical time points. Referring to absolute time points is not feasible for alternatives with different latencies, since execution of distinct rewritings may yield different absolute timestamps. Therefore, we consider two rewriting alternatives to be equivalent if they produce the same output in identical order, with respect to identical input events snapshot. The latter property can be viewed as temporal synchronization, thus satisfying the additional requirement introduced by patterns.

A split of a pattern into two consecutive patterns, as depicted in Figure 3, is defined as follows:

Definition 5 *(split):*

Given f1 of type <u>sequence</u>, a split of f1, denoted by f2, is a set (f2',f2"), such that:

f1(sequence, RTS, PA, Policies, PS) = MS1,

f2'(sequence, RTS', PA', Policies', PS') = MS2',

f2"(sequence, Compose(MS2').type ∪ RTS", PA", Policies", Compose(MS2') ∪ PS") = MS2" = MS2

RTS = RTS' ∪ RTS", PS = PS' ∪ PS",

Compose(MS) is a union of events composing all instances in MS,

CMS1 is a candidate matching set of f1,
CMS2' is a candidate matching set of f2',

PA can be separated at event type Ei, further denoted as "separable at i", PA' is pattern assertion of f2', PA" is pattern assertion of f2",

Policies is set of policies of f1, Policies' is set of policies of f2' and Policies" is set of policies of f2"

Using Definition 5 we now demonstrate the formal method for proving equivalence of patterns. We show that the <u>sequence</u> pattern with the following set of policies: (1) evaluation="immediate", (2) cardinality="single" and (3) repeated type="first", can be split into two <u>sequence</u> patterns. For the sake of conciseness we denote by ValidMatch(f) the application of ValidMatch to the outcome of f(pattern type, RTS, PA, Policies, PS), which is an MS.

Proposition1: *Given f1 and split f2=(f2',f2'') of f1, it holds that:*

1. ValidMatch(f2) → ValidMatch(f1)

2. ValidMatch(f1) → ValidMatch(f2)

3. MS1 = MS2

Proof:

1. ValidMatch(f2) → ValidMatch(f1):
the same as proving !ValidMatch(f1) → !ValidMatch(f2)

!ValidMatch(f1) → CMS = ∅ →

!∃(EC=<e₁, ..., eₙ>⊆PS | Conforms(EC,RTS) ∧ PA(EC)) →
(since the assertion is separable at i)

!∃(EC'=<e₁, ..., eᵢ>⊆PS') | Conforms(EC',RTS') ∧ PA'(EC')) OR

!∃(EC''=<eᵢ₊₁, ..., eₙ>⊆PS'' | Conforms(EC'',RTS'') ∧ PA''(EC''))→

CMS' = ∅ OR CMS'' = ∅

!ValidMatch(f2') OR !ValidMatch(f2'') →

!ValidMatch(f2)

□

2. ValidMatch(f1) → ValidMatch(f2):

We assume that Compose(MS1).ts = eᵢ.ts and pattern split temporal correctness is forced by implementation

ValidMatch(f1) → CMS != ∅

∃(EC=<e₁, ..., eₙ>⊆PS | Conforms(EC,RTS) ∧ PA(EC)) →
(since the assertion is separable at i)

∃(EC'=<e₁, ..., eᵢ>⊆PS' | Conforms(EC',RTS') ∧ PA'(EC')) ∧

∃(EC''=<eᵢ₊₁, ..., eₙ>⊆PS'' | Conforms(EC'',RTS'') ∧ PA''(EC'')) →

ValidMatch(f2') ∧ ValidMatch(f2'') ∧
Compose(MS1).ts<eᵢ₊₁.ts →

ValidMatch(f2)

□

3. MS1 = MS2

This is trivial for #1; for #2:

ValidMatch(f1) → CMS1 != ∅ →

MS1 = (EC=<e₁, ..., eₙ>∈CMS1 | First(EC)) →

MS1 = (EC'=<e₁, ..., eᵢ>∈CMS2' ∪ EC''=<eᵢ₊₁, ..., eₙ> | First(EC' ∪ EC'')) → (since the assertion is separable at i)

MS1 = (EC'=<e₁, ..., eᵢ>∈CMS2' | First(EC')) ∪ (EC''=<eᵢ₊₁, ..., eₙ> | First(EC'')) → (according to def. of MS)

MS1 = MS2' ∪ (EC''=<eᵢ₊₁, ..., eₙ> | First(EC'')) →

MS1 = MS2' ∪ EC'' *

PS_{f2''} = <Compose(MS¹_{f2'}), ..., Compose(MSᴷ_{f2'})> ∪ PS''

MS2 = (Compose(MS_{f2'}∈CMS2') ∪ EC_{f2''}=<eᵢ₊₁, ..., eₙ>) | First(Compose(MS_{f2'}) ∪ EC_{f2''}) →
(since the assertion is separable at i)

MS2 = (Compose(MS_{f2'}∈CMS2') | First(Compose(MS_{f2'})) ∪ (EC_{f2''}=<eᵢ₊₁, ..., eₙ> | First (EC_{f2''})) →

MS2 = (Compose(MS2') ∪ EC'') → Compose(H) = {h| h∈H}*

MS2 = (MS2' ∪ EC'') →*

MS2 = MS1

□

3.5 More Pattern Equivalences

While the equivalence demonstrated in the previous section is quite intuitive, other kinds of rewriting are more complex, requiring modification of pattern assertion and individual patterns policies to make the equivalence valid. In this section we show additional pattern rewritings. Due to space consideration, we refrain from presenting formal correctness statements.

We begin with the pattern sequence(E_1,E_2,E_3) comprising pattern assertion that is separable at E_3 and the following set of policies: (1) evaluation="immediate", (2) cardinality="single" and (3) repeated type="last". When rewritten into two patterns: sequence(sequence(E_1,E_2),E_3), the new pattern policies should change slightly to satisfy the desired equivalence. For event scenario <e_1^1, e_2^1, e_2^2, e_3^1>, f1 will report the <e_1^1, e_2^2, e_3^1> as the matching set. If we keep working with the same policies at the rewritten alternative, f2' will report <e_1^1, e_2^1> as a matching set and f2'' will attach the last e_3^1 event to this pair, eventually reporting <e_1^1, e_2^1, e_3^1>, which is incorrect. Figure 5 demonstrates the temporal fallacy of this example, leading to the undesired result. Due to the temporal decoupling between f2' and f2'', f2' will report its matching set "too early," ignoring instances that arrived after the first detection (due to the "single" cardinality policy, and "immediate" evaluation policy), thus losing synchronization with respect to the original pattern f1.

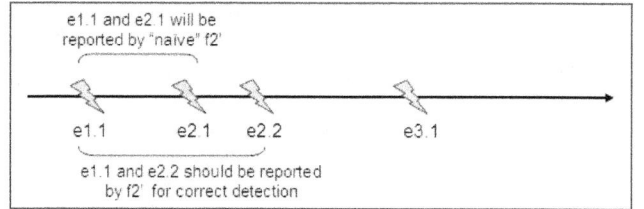

Figure 5: Temporal inconsistency keeping original policies

The solution for this undesired situation lies in modifying the pattern policies. Changing f2' cardinality policy to "unrestricted" (unbounded number of detections) and setting its consumption policy to "reuse" (keeping event instance for further detections after it was included in a matching set) will achieve the desired effect, resulting in equivalence of the original and the rewritten alternatives: f2' will produce two matching sets: <e_1^1, e_2^1> and <e_1^1, e_2^2>, and f2'' will consider the last derived event; therefore, upon e_3^1 arrival it will eventually emit <e_1^1, e_2^2, e_3^1>, as required.

The example above can be concluded by a summary of the original and the rewritten pattern alternatives, driven by pattern policies as demonstrated in Table 2. f1 refers to the original pattern, while f2' and f2'' refer to the rewritten first and second patterns, respectively.

Note that while the example refers to the <u>sequence</u> pattern, a theoretical analysis infers the same solution for a simpler case, the <u>all</u> pattern. This observation also holds for all further detailed rewritings, and its proof is similar to the demonstrated one up to the event ordering requirement removal.

106

Table 2: Pattern rewriting by policies modification (1)

Pattern type: sequence/all			
Policy	f1	f2'	f2"
Evaluation	immediate	immediate	immediate
Cardinality	single	unrestricted	single
Repeated Type	last	last	last
Consumption	-	reuse	-

Another nontrivial example involves the pattern sequence(E_1,E_2,E_3) such that the pattern assertion is separable at E_3, and the following set of policies (1) evaluation="immediate", (2) cardinality="unrestricted", (3) repeated type="override" and (4) consumption="consume". Again, we consider a split into two patterns sequence(sequence(E_1,E_2),E_3). Similarly to the previous example, we should assign the "reuse" consumption policy to f2'. However, while in the former example the entire processing was terminated after the first detection ("single" cardinality policy), in this case we are not limited to a single detection ("unrestricted" cardinality policy). This poses an additional difficulty: after any detection at f2", the entire matching set should be consumed, at odds with f2' consumption mode, which is "reuse". In order to prevent f2" from reporting "consumed" events over and over again, we would like to prevent the consumed events from arriving at f2", filtering them out on their way to f2". This can be achieved by assigning a filter EPA between f2' and f2" in the rewritten alternative, which filters in only relevant events, and filters out all the consumed events by querying an in-memory consumed events pool. This rewriting is schematically demonstrated in Figure 6.

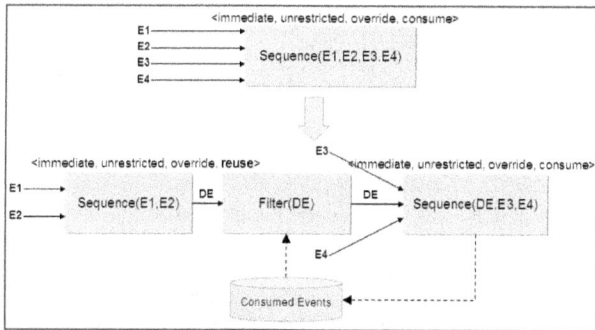

Figure 6: Pattern rewriting using filter EPA

A summary of the original and rewritten pattern alternatives in the example above is presented in Table 3.

Table 3: Pattern rewriting by policies modification (2)

Pattern type: sequence/all			
Policy	f1	f2'	f2"
Evaluation	immediate	immediate	immediate
Cardinality	unrestricted	unrestricted	unrestricted
Repeated Type	override	override	override
Consumption	consume	reuse	consume
filter between f2' and f2"			

The most complex case we have encountered is the one combining both "last" repeated type policy from the first example and "unrestricted" cardinality policy from the second one. Consider the following event instances collection: $<e_1^1, e_1^2, e_2^1, e_2^2, e_3^1, e_3^2>$. For consumption policy="consume", the original pattern will produce two matching sets: $<e_1^2, e_2^2, e_3^1>$ and $<e_1^1, e_2^1, e_3^2>$. Applying

previously mentioned rewriting techniques ("reuse" consumption policy and filter EPA) will be insufficient, producing the incorrect second matching set: $<e_1^2, e_2^2, e_3^1>$, $<e_1^2, e_2^1, e_3^2>$. Note that the pair $<e_1^1, e_2^1>$ required for the correct second detection was not derived by f2' at all. We need to force f2' to report all possible combinations, and then select the correct ones carefully upon f2" detection attempt. Such an effect can be achieved by using "every" repeated type policy at f2', instead of the original "last" policy.

A side effect of using "every" policy will cause redundant matching sets generation at f2' and their arrival to f2"; that is, for a given example, at the first detection point, the internal state of f2" will contain the $<e_1^2, e_2^1>$ derived event, that should not be used after the first detection, which consumes e_1^2. In order to get rid of derived events, already stored at f2" internal state, but (partially) consumed, we constrain f2" to include only instances not consumed yet at its matching sets, by extending f2" pattern assertion with validation check against a consumed events pool.

Figure 7 and Table 4 summarize the described observations:

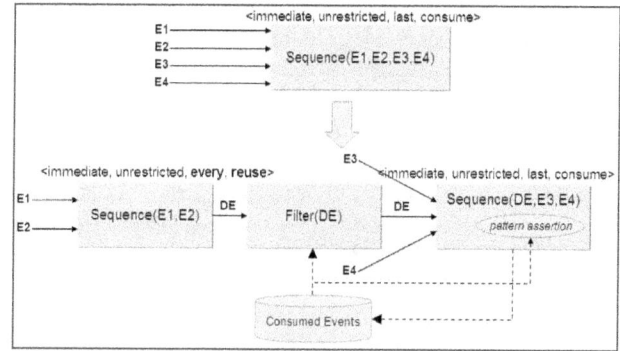

Figure 7: Pattern rewriting using extended pattern assertion

Table 4: Pattern rewriting by policies modification (3)

Pattern type: sequence/all			
Policy	f1	f2'	f2"
Evaluation	immediate	immediate	immediate
Cardinality	unrestricted	unrestricted	unrestricted
Repeated Type	last	each	last
Consumption	consume	reuse	consume
filter between f2' and f2"			
extended pattern assertion in f2"			

In order to complete the picture of pattern rewriting with respect to the most useful set of policies, we bring an additional mapping (Table 5), employing the already mentioned rewriting techniques. (the "reuse" consumption policy, filter and extended assertion).

Table 5: Pattern rewriting by policies modification (4)

Pattern type: sequence/all			
Policy	f1	f2'	f2"
Evaluation	immediate	immediate	immediate
Cardinality	unrestricted	unrestricted	unrestricted
Repeated Type	first	each	first
Consumption	consume	reuse	consume
filter between f2' and f2"			
extended pattern assertion in f2"			

Policies not covered here (e.g. "deferred" evaluation policy and "reuse" consumption policy), pose similar rewriting challenges, thus we omit them in this paper.

The mapping of policies, as presented in this section, provides a initial set of techniques for pattern rewriting. An individual fine tuning (e.g., forcing ascending lexicographical order for the "first" repeated type policy in f2") for some of the presented rewritings is required; this is achieved by further extending of the pattern assertion on top of the predefined policies-based rewriting schemes detailed in tables 2 to 5.

3.6 Summary

Although the pattern assertion analysis presented in Section 3.3 was mainly motivated by the desired pattern rewriting, it can be used as white-box pattern optimization technique. One can examine pattern assertion, in terms of its independent parts, and apply an optimized assertion evaluation upon pattern detection attempt. As an example, the pattern detection procedure can be discarded when identified that a certain (independent) assertion part can not be satisfied with respect to a pattern internal state; that instead of performing a naïve nested loop on all candidates, in order to find an event combination satisfying the entire assertion.

A trivial observation from the analysis presented in this section is that rewriting techniques are also valid for a simpler case, when there is no pattern assertion, i.e. the pattern assertion is "true". This kind of assertion can be observed as separable at any i for RTS=$<E_1$, ..., $E_N>$, thus inferring N-1 splitting alternatives.

In this section we have demonstrated rewriting techniques for the all and sequence patterns, splitting a single pattern into two consecutive patterns or unifying them. A formal definition and a proof were demonstrated for a representative case, evidencing rewriting logical validity and supporting our intuition of employing policies modification for rewriting.

4. BI-OBJECTIVE OPTIMIZATION OF SEQUENCE PATTERNS

In this section we discuss how the rewriting means gained by now are utilized to improve an application's performance according to predefined objectives. Section 4.1 defines various performance indicators of event processing systems, Section 4.2 identifies the tradeoff between these indicators and in sections 4.3 and 4.4 we discuss how pattern rewriting techniques can be leveraged to achieve the desired performance objectives.

4.1 Pattern Performance Objectives

Due to the rapid growth of event processing technology, large variety of application domains, and lack of standards [13], performance metrics are subject to various interpretations, often leading to incomparable product benchmarks. Among the most commonly used performance indicators are throughput and latency (response time), as well as scalability, security, correctness and other non-functional requirements.

When considering throughput and latency, various performance optimization goals exist, including max input/processing/output throughput, minmax latency, and minavg latency. The specific optimization goal function is typically derived from the application's requirements. For example, minmax latency should be employed by real-time systems that aim to provide an upper bound over the worst case performance, while minavg latency is a reasonable goal function for non real-time applications. Our work focuses on minavg latency and max input throughput performance functions, targeting what we believe are the most commonly used performance indicators in event processing applications.

Stimulated by the conceptual similarity of communication [10] and event processing networks, we define event processing application *processing throughput*, hereafter denoted by *throughput*, as an average rate of events the system can process. We use events per second (event/s) to measure throughput. Similarly to [2] and [13], we define a system *latency* as a delay between the last input event causing a certain scenario detection and the detection itself, resulting in derivation of an output event. An application's latency is usually measured in milliseconds (ms).

The throughput and latency of a single pattern detection EPA (which is a special case of an event processing network), are defined as the average rate of events that this EPA can process and the average delay from the detecting event arrival to pattern's detection, respectively. For instance, if E_4 is derived from the pattern matching of sequence(E_1,E_2,E_3), latency is the time interval between the detection time of E_3 (time it arrived to the system) and the detection time of E_4 (time it is derived by the system).

Performance tuning of pattern matching EPA is important when done as part of the entire application optimization; it becomes critical in systems where a pattern embodies entire path in an EPN, as well as in highly distributed systems, where a single pattern can be assigned to a processing node.

4.2 Performance Objectives Tradeoff

Throughput vs. latency tradeoff is a general phenomenon in performance oriented systems. We sometimes face a choice between doing eager and lazy evaluation, where eager evaluation performs computing when possible in anticipation that it will be used later, and lazy evaluation is done on demand. Recall that the latency of sequence(E_1, ..., E_N) is defined as a response time between E_N instance arrival and emission of the derived event, if detected. According to this definition, the eager evaluation choice biases towards low latency and reduced throughput, since the (occasionally redundant) pre-processing is done in advance. The lazy evaluation, however, biases towards high throughput and increased latency, since the necessary processing is only triggered by E_N arrival. Intuitively speaking, we observe that improved latency comes at the cost of decreased throughput.

Pattern rewriting offers natural means for tuning the throughput vs. latency tradeoff for the sequence pattern. Consider again the speculative broker scenario: maintaining the entire logic in a single pattern (sequence(E_1^i, E_2^j, E_1^k, E_2^l, E_1^m, E_2^n)) produces a solution with high throughput. However, splitting the pattern into two patterns (sequence(sequence(E_1^i, E_2^j, E_1^k, E_2^l), E_1^m, E_2^n)), leaving only a light processing delta for the last, potentially detecting event (E_2^n), produces a low latency oriented alternative.

While the two rewritings above serve two extremes, highest throughput and lowest latency respectively, there is a range of Pareto optimal solutions on the throughput vs. latency tradeoff spectrum, realized by additional rewriting alternatives; these solutions are discussed in Section 5.2. Constrained by pattern assertion decomposability, the only additional rewriting in our example is sequence(sequence(E_1^i, E_2^j), E_1^k, E_2^l, E_1^m, E_2^n).

4.3 Bi-objective Goal Function

Our model enables a system designer to define a bi-objective performance function that stems from the application's characteristics. This is done by assigning a scalar weight for each objective to be optimized, i.e. weight of α to pattern throughput (th) and a complementary weight of 1-α to its latency (lt). Striving to minimize latency and to maximize throughput, the general form of the bi-objective performance function is min $\alpha*lt+(1-\alpha)*(1/th)$. In addition to application requirements, the goal function is also affected by the application's properties. For example, for a pattern triggered by low-rate events we will rather focus on improving latency, adjusting the α weight accordingly.

Given a bi-objective performance function, a rewrite that optimizes this function is selected using an empirical simulation-based approach (see Section 4.4), given that the analytic approach poses challenges, including difficulty to estimate pattern internal state size and assertion satisfactory probability with respect to pattern internal state at a certain time point.

Application rewriting decisions can be done off line, therefore we can tolerate simulation-based optimization duration. In cases where the rewriting decision has time constraints, such as on-line ("hot") updates of an application definitions, a heuristic-based approach can be taken. While the heuristic approach discussion is beyond the scope of this paper, we discuss simulation-based techniques in details in the next section.

4.4 Simulation-based Optimization

Given a sequence pattern and a bi-objective goal function (g) of the form $g=\alpha*lt+(1-\alpha)*(1/th)$, simulation-based optimization empirically analyzes all rewriting alternatives and selects the one optimizing the goal function, i.e. gaining the minimal value for g.

Applying the described rewriting techniques on a given pattern, we generate a number of logically equivalent alternatives $A=\{A_1, \ldots A_K\}$ that are subject for analysis. Our goal is to select the rewriting alternative that minimizes the *expectation* (E) estimator of g, i.e. we aim to find $argmin_{Ai}(\hat{g})$, where $\hat{g}$ is the estimated Expectation of $\alpha*lt + (1-\alpha)*(1/th)$.

A close look at the presented goal function reveals anomaly that stems from its bi-objective character. In case both latency and throughput indicators have roughly the same scale and same relative importance, the function above will lead to a deceptive decision: it will constantly favor the latency part ($\alpha*lt$) over the throughput part ($(1-\alpha)*(1/th)$), due to the element of division in the latter one. A simple, yet satisfactory solution is to normalize both of them to the same order of magnitude.

Due to the lack of standard approaches to such normalization (to the best of our knowledge), we compute the throughput *coefficient* C by performing a series of latency and throughput estimations and multiply the right hand side of the goal function by it; intuitively speaking, we are adjusting both sides of the function g to the same scale. The final form of g therefore is

$$g = \alpha*lt + C*(1-\alpha)*(1/th)$$

and we aim to find $argmin_{Ai}(\hat{g})$.

For a set A of rewriting alternatives, expectation estimator and its 95% confidence interval are calculated for each $A_i \in A$ $1 \leq i \leq K$ by computing average and variance of N individual measurements:

$$\hat{g}_i = \frac{1}{N}\sum_{j=1}^{N} g_i^{\ j} \ , \ S_i^{\ 2} = \frac{1}{N-1}\sum_{j=1}^{N}(g_i^{\ j} - \hat{g}_i)^2$$

With sufficiently large number of measurements, e.g. N>120, the 95% confidence interval of $\hat{g}_i$ is calculated using the Central Limit Theorem, to be:

$$g_i \in \hat{g}_i \pm \frac{1.96 S_i}{\sqrt{N}}$$

After producing a set of estimators $\{\hat{g}_1, \ldots, \hat{g}_K\}$, the minimal one is selected, inducing the optimal rewriting alternative with respect to a given bi-objective goal function.

5. EVALUATION

Our evaluation has two main goals. Firstly, assessing the potential efficiency gains of pattern optimization; and secondly, providing empirical support for rewriting equivalence in addition to the theoretical background demonstrated in Section 3.

We conducted an empirical study for the sequence pattern, experimenting on a subset of pattern assertions, policies and relevant events sets. In our experiments we varied control parameters that impact performance the most. Among these parameters are event arrival rate (such as λ for Poisson distribution) and pattern assertion satisfaction probability for a randomly chosen attributes values. The latter can be tuned by varying the event attributes' domain size.

5.1 Experiment Setup

In our simulation framework event distribution types (e.g. Poisson or uniform), and arrival rates are configurable parameters. In addition, each pattern is examined within the temporal window (context) it is associated with, e.g. ten minutes window in the speculative broker scenario (Example 1).

Our framework assigns uniform distribution to event attribute values, i.e. each value in the domain has equal probability for random sampling. We use a uniform distribution of integer event attributes in [0,100] domain. Finally, the normalization coefficient C in the goal function was set to 3000 in all experiments.

The simulation was performed on a Lenovo T60 ThinkPad, with Intel Core 2 Duo 1.83-GHz processor, 2.00 GB memory, using Microsoft Windows XP operating system and Java 1.6.

5.2 Experiments

Extending the speculative broker scenario in Example 1, the following pattern was chosen for the basic experiment:

Pattern: sequence($E_1, E_2, E_3, E_4, E_5, E_6, E_7, E_8$),
s.t. each event type Ei has a single integer attribute ID

Pattern assertion:

E_1.ID==E_2.ID AND E_3.ID==E_4.ID AND
E_5.ID==E_6.ID AND E_7.ID==E_8.ID

Pattern policies:

evaluation:	immediate
cardinality:	unrestricted
repeated type:	---
consumption:	consume

Pattern context:	10 minutes (fixed window)

The system parameters were configured as follows:

All event types follow the Poisson distribution with average rate of 50 events per second ($\lambda(E1)=\ldots=\lambda(E8)=50$).

Pattern assertion analysis draws four possible rewritings:

sequence(E_1, E_2, E_3, E_4, E_5, E_6, E_7, E_8) denoted by 0:4
sequence(E_1, E_2, sequence(E_3, E_4, E_5, E_6, E_7, E_8)) denoted by 1:3
sequence(E_1, E_2, E_3, E_4, sequence(E_5, E_6, E_7, E_8)) denoted by 2:2
sequence(E_1, E_2, E_3, E_4, E_5, E_6, sequence(E_7, E_8)) denoted by 3:1

The simulation results are shown in Table 6.

Table 6: Simulation results

#	rwrt.	throughput (event/s)	latency (ms)
1.	0:4	113	134
2.	1:3	80	50
3.	2:2	104	30
4.	3:1	44	14

In this case the highest throughput is achieved at the unified alternative (0:4); that, along with the worst latency, demonstrate the approach of performing pattern computation in lazy evaluation, i.e. on arrival of the (potentially detecting) E_8 event instance. Another extreme is the 3:1 alternative where almost the entire computation is done in eager evaluation, thus favoring latency over throughput. The first rewriting (0:4) will be selected by assigning $\alpha=0$ at the goal function, attempting to minimize $g=C*(1/th)$, and the last one (3:1) by assigning $\alpha=1$, thus gaining minimum for $g=lt$.

An interesting observation from Table 6 is that rewriting #2 was outperformed by rewriting #3 both in terms of throughput and latency, i.e. alternative #3 strictly dominates alternative #2, thus excluding #2 from the efficient set of rewritings. The complete mapping of optimal rewriting alternatives by α and goal function values inferred by it is presented in Table 7. Note that complying with the observation above, the 1:3 rewriting alternative (#2) is never chosen as optimal solution.

Table 7: Mapping of optimal rewritings by goal functions

#	rwrt.	$\alpha-0$	$\alpha-1$	$\alpha-0.5$	$\alpha=.25$	$\alpha=.80$
1.	0:4	26.55	134	147.27	53.41	112.51
2.	1:3	37.50	50	43.75	40.63	45.77
3.	2:2	28.85	30	29.42	29.13	29.77
4.	3:1	68.18	14	41.09	54.64	24.84

While the latency metric behaves in an intuitive way, constantly decreasing as more emphasis is given to eager evaluation, the throughput is more difficult to predict. As opposed to latency, a rewriting throughput is affected by both sides of a split, as well as by seemingly contradictory factors: easily satisfiable pattern assertion increases pattern throughput due to the decrease in processing time of a potentially detecting event, however each such detection involves a generation of a derived event and an invocation of the consecutive pattern part. As a result pattern rewriting throughput behaves in a non-monotonic fashion; thus there is a set of Pareto optimal solutions, drawing rewrites favorable over others for the same value of α. A Pareto efficient set of solutions for this experiment is illustrated in Figure 8.

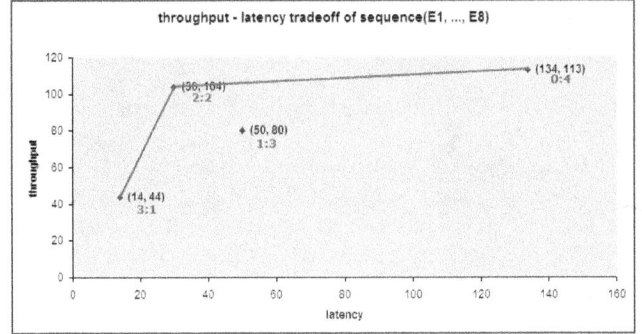

Figure 8: Pareto frontier for sequence(E1, …, E8)

Additional experiment was held on sequence with sixteen participating events (E_1, E_2, …, E_{16}) and an accordingly extended pattern assertion. A Pareto frontier generated by the simulation in this case is demonstrated in Figure 9.

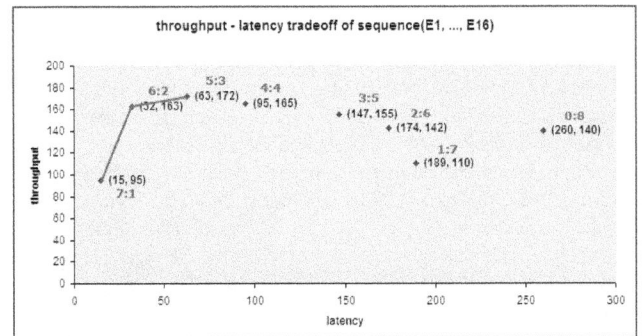

Figure 9: Pareto frontier for sequence(E1, …, E16)

An interesting observation from Figure 9 is that the initial pattern alternative (non-split pattern version – 0:8) is dominated by other alternatives with respect to both throughput and latency, making this most common implementation of sequence inferior to other alternatives. This observation remains sound when approaching rewriting of patterns with big relevant types set, making rewriting remarkably beneficial in these cases.

5.3 Sensitivity Analysis

Next we perform a sensitivity analysis of the goal function g in order to assess the relation between different parameters and the value of g. Such an analysis, yielding insights about the way various parameters impact the goal function, can serve as a basis for a heuristic approach for selection of a rewriting alternative.

We experimented with the 2:2 rewriting (alternative #3 in tables 6 to 7), varying event arrival rates and pattern assertion satisfaction probability. The schematic representation of this rewriting is depicted in Figure 10.

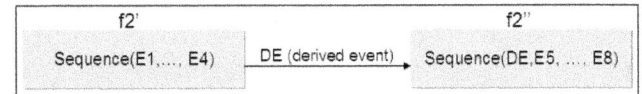

Figure 10: Experimental pattern rewriting

Experiment 1: Reducing f2' detecting event arrival rate, $\lambda(E_4)$: 50→25. The simulation results are presented in Table 8.

Table 8: Experiment 1 results

#	alt.	$\lambda(E_4)=50$		$\lambda(E_4)=25$	
		through.	latency	through.	latency
3.	2:2	104	30	134	26

While the latency remains nearly unchanged, the throughput improves. That can be explained by the reduced detection rate at f2', leading to reduced derived event generation rate and f2" invocation, which in turn results in a lower average processing time for each event instance; and thus, higher average throughput.

Experiment 2: Reducing f2" detecting event arrival rate, $\lambda(E_8)$: 50→25. Table 9 presents the simulation results.

Table 9: Experiment 2 results

#	alt.	$\lambda(E_8)=50$		$\lambda(E_8)=25$	
		through.	latency	through.	latency
3.	2:2	104	30	98	45

The reduced arrival rate of E8 gives rise to longer detection attempts at f2", since more $E_5, \ldots E_7$ candidates are accumulated upon E_8 arrival, resulting in a higher latency.

Experiment 3: Relaxing pattern assertion at f2' by reducing f2' event attributes domain: [0,100]→[0,10]; thus increasing assertion satisfactory probability. Simulation results are presented in Table 10.

Table 10: Experiment 3 results

#	alt.	A at $(E_1 \ldots E_4)$: [0,100]		A at $(E_1 \ldots E_4)$: [0,10]	
		through.	latency	through.	latency
3.	2:2	104	30	67	27

Comparing this experiment with Experiment 1, the increased detection rate at f2' causes more detections, generations of derived events and invocations of f2". This, in turn, results in higher time for handling a single event, yielding lower throughput.

Experiment 4: Relaxing pattern assertion at f2" by reducing f2" event attributes domain: [0,100]→[0,10]. Table 11 presents simulation results.

Table 11: Experiment 4 results

#	alt.	A at $(E_5 \ldots E_8)$: [0,100]		A at $(E_5 \ldots E_8)$: [0,10]	
		through.	latency	through.	latency
3.	2:2	104	30	127	11

Pattern assertion relaxation at f2" makes detection easier, and therefore the entire rewriting benefits. A quick detection naturally leads to an improved overall latency.

5.4 Discussion

Our experiments fit the intuition for extreme cases, demonstrating the lowest and highest latency biased results for the eager and the lazy evaluation respectively. Reasonable results, with respect to latency, are provided for other rewriting alternatives, lying in between the two extremes.

Performance indicators show that the rewriting that favors latency over throughput carries more than fourfold increase in latency, along with almost half the throughput, when compared to its throughput-oriented alternative; therefore both versions yield a performance benefit. Moreover, in a basic experiment (Table 6), almost tenfold

latency improvement was obtained (134 ms in 0:4 vs. 14 ms in 3:1). The Pareto frontier of goal function values points out alternatives unconditionally favorable over others, assisting in the choice of the desirable rewriting alternative.

Although the discussion on indicator tradeoffs and experiments were conducted on the sequence pattern, the entire approach can be extended to additional pattern types, e.g. all. The theoretical background presented in Section 3 remains sound for pattern of type all, and the empirical evaluation is easily extendable.

Commercial products present benchmarks with seemingly much higher throughput; however these benchmarks are typically conducted for simpler cases, e.g. stateless EPAs and simple patterns [1][14]. As noted in the introduction, experimental studies indicate that the performance indicators between simple and complex scenarios have ratio of 1:90 both in terms of latency and throughput. Our implementation in this work introduces results that are fairly comparable to commercial tools for high end cases in the complexity scale.

6. RELATED WORK

Various types of optimization techniques have been discussed in the event processing literature [8][9][22][25]. According to Etzion and Niblett [5], these optimizations are typically based on a single objective, optimizing either latency or throughput, and can be classified into three categories: (1) optimization related to application components assignment: partitioning, distribution, parallelism and load balancing; (2) optimization related to the coding of a specific component: code optimization and state management; (3) optimization related to the execution process: scheduling and routing optimizations. Our work falls into the second category. The idea of rewriting in event processing networks was suggested by Perrochon et al. [17] more than a decade ago. Perrochon mentions some performance oriented optimization techniques, such as compression (e.g., grouping two agents into a single one), common sub-expression elimination (e.g., extracting commonly used part into a separate agent) and reordering (e.g., pushing the filter to an early point of the event processing network). [17] offers an informal description of the techniques above, neither considering pattern assertion, nor pattern policies.

Simple cases of pattern rewriting for application optimization are discussed by Poul et al. [18]. The authors present an event processing language that facilitates rewriting of "next" (sequence) and "union" (any) patterns for optimized deployment of event processing system across multiple machines. Considering only a binary sequence pattern, their rewriting rationale is to minimize the rate of intermediate derived events generation given event arrival distribution and rate. The proposed model assumes a single set of policies, and does not employ pattern assertion.

Another work that mentions pattern rewriting is [2] where the authors present an approach for communication-efficient complex event detection over distributed sources. A multi-step detection plan for a complex event is generated on the basis of event frequency statistics, postponing the monitoring of high frequency events to later steps in the plan. Events relevant to each step are pulled from a distributed source, carrying a potential reduction in transmission cost. As an example, the "seq"(sequence) operator is rewritten into several consequent sequence sub-operators, and execution of each sub-operator is conditional upon the detection of earlier ones, eliminating the need for communication in some cases. While the authors proposed a cost-based model for n-ary event operators, pattern assertion and policies are not considered.

Several research efforts were devoted to the formal definition of event processing languages. Early works [17] only cover a subset of the language constructs with partial functionality (limited set of operators, no policies). Recent papers [4][7] present a more comprehensive approach, but still lack some language aspects (n-ary event operators, some policies, cross-event pattern assertions). One of the most mature works in this field is [1] by Adi et al., which we refined to better fit the purpose of this work.

7. CONCLUSION AND FUTURE WORK

A methodic approach for pattern rewriting, presented in this paper, serves as a step forward in rewriting-based optimization of event processing applications targeting systems with both pattern complexity and performance requirements. The ability to automatically rewrite certain application parts and thereby gain an optimized, yet logically equivalent alternative, exists in most declarative languages (e.g. database queries). This capacity is still missing from the event processing domain and is required to help making event processing systems more pervasive and mature.

The pragmatic impact of this work will be in deploying the proposed techniques within existing products, by automatically rewriting application patterns for subsuming common logic and splitting for parallel execution (where possible) in the deployment phase. Rewriting the sequence pattern can be employed as an advanced technique for bi-objective tuning of the performance indicators, thereby yielding an optimization value.

The potential value of pattern rewriting leaves much for further exploratory and practical activities. Our future plans include the investigation of additional rewritings and suggesting an algorithm for rewriting of an event processing network. In the context of the sequence pattern, we plan to continue exploring the heuristic-based approach for selection of the rewriting alternative, thus providing a solution for online rewriting decisions.

8. REFERENCES

[1] Adi A., Etzion O. Amit - the situation manager. The VLDB Journal — The International Journal on Very Large Data Bases. Volume 13 Issue 2, 2004.

[2] Akdere M., Cetintemel U., Tatbul N. Plan-based Complex Event Detection across Distributed Sources. In proceedings of the VLDB Endowment, Vol. 1. 2008.

[3] Calvanese D., Giacomo G., Lenzerini M., and Vardi M. What is Query Rewriting? In proceedings of the 7th International Workshop on Knowledge Representation meets Databases (KRDB), 2000.

[4] Cugola G., Margara A. TESLA: A Formally Defined Event Specification Language. In proceedings of DEBS 2010.

[5] Etzion O., Niblett P. Event Processing in Action, Manning Publications, 2010.

[6] Goodstein R.L. Boolean Algebra. Dover Pubns, 2007.

[7] Hinze A. and Voisard A. EVA: An EVent Algebra Supporting Adaptivity and Collaboration in Event Systems. ICSI Technical Report TR-09-006. International Computer Science Institute,

2009. http://www.icsi.berkeley.edu/cgi-bin/pubs/publication.pl?ID=002680.

[8] Khandekar R.et al. COLA: Optimizing Stream Processing Applications via Graph Partitioning, Middleware 2009.

[9] Lakshmanan G., Rabinovich Y., Etzion O. A stratified approach for supporting high throughput event processing applications. In proceedings of DEBS 2009.

[10] Leon-Garcia A., Widjaja I. Communication Networks: Fundamental Concepts and Key Architectures. Second edition. McGraw-Hill. 2004.

[11] Luckham, D. The Power of Events: An Introduction to Complex Event Processing in Distributed Enterprise Systems. Addison-Wesley, Boston, 2002.

[12] Maheshwari S. Optimize the performance of condition evaluation part of rule sets. http://drupal.org/node/761624.

[13] Mendes M., Bizarro P., Marques P. A Framework for Performance Evaluation of Complex Event Processing Systems. In proceedings of DEBS 2008.

[14] Mendes M., Bizarro P., Marques P. Benchmarking event processing systems: current state and future directions. WOSP/SIPEW 2010: 259-260.

[15] Moxey C. et al: A Conceptual model for Event Processing Systems, an IBM Redguide publication. http://www.redbooks.ibm.com/redpapers/pdfs/redp4642.pdf

[16] Nilsson N. Principles of artificial intelligence. Tioga, 1980.

[17] Perrochon L., Kasriel S. and Luckham D. Managing Event Processing Networks. Technical report CSL-TR-99-788, Stanford University Computer Systems Lab, 1999. ftp://reports.stanford.edu/pub/cstr/reports/csl/tr/99/788/CSL-TR-99-788.pdf.

[18] Poul N., Migliavacca M., Pietzuch P. Distributed Complex Event Processing with Query Rewriting. In proceedings of DEBS 2009.

[19] Sharon, G. and Etzion, O. Event Processing Networks: model and implementation. IBM System Journal, 2008, 47(2), pages 321-334.

[20] Stoy J. Denotational Semantics: The Scott-Strachey Approach to Programming Language Semantics. MIT Press, Cambridge, Massachusetts, 1977.

[21] Strom R., Dorai C., Buttner G., Li Y. SMILE: distributed middleware for event stream processing. In proceedings of the 6th international conference on Information processing in sensor networks, 2007.

[22] Tatbul N., Cetintemel U., Zdonik S. Staying FIT: Efficient Load Shedding Techniques for Distributed Stream Processing. In proceedings of VLDB 2007.

[23] FIU's (Financial Intelligence Units) in action. http://www.egmontgroup.org/library/download/21, page 80.

[24] W.M.P. van der Aalst, K.M. van Hee, J.M. van der Werf, and Verdonk M. Auditing 2.0: Using Process Mining to Support Tomorrow's Auditor. IEEE Computer, 43(3):90-93, 2010.

[25] Wolf J., Bansal N., Hildrum K., Parekh S., Rajan D., Wagle R., Wu K., Fleischer L. SODA: An Optimizing Scheduler for Large-Scale Stream-Based Distributed Computer Systems, Middleware 2008: 306-32.

Program Analysis for Event-based Distributed Systems *

K. R. Jayaram
Department of Computer Science
Purdue University
jayaram@purdue.edu

Patrick Eugster
Department of Computer Science
Purdue University
peugster@purdue.edu

ABSTRACT

Designing distributed applications around the idiom of events has several benefits including extensibility and scalability. To improve conciseness, safety, and efficiency of corresponding programs, several authors have recently proposed programming languages or language extensions with support for event-based programming.

The presence of a dedicated programming language and compilation process offers avenues for program analyses to further improve simplicity, safety, and expressiveness of distributed event-based software. This paper presents three program analyses specifically designed for event-based programs: *immutability analysis* avoids costly cloning of events in the presence of co-located handlers for same events; *guard analysis* allows for simple yet expressive subscriptions which can be further simplified and handled efficiently; *causality analysis* determines causal dependencies among events which are related, allowing unrelated events to be transferred independently for efficiency. We convey the benefits of our approach by empirically evaluating their performance benefits.

Categories and Subject Descriptors

D.1.3 [**Programming Techniques**]: Concurrent Programming—*Distributed Programming*; F.3.2 [**Logics and Meanings of Programs**]: Semantics of Programming Languages—*Program Analysis*; C.2.4 [**Computer-Communication Networks**]: Distributed Systems—*Distributed Applications*

General Terms

Languages, Performance

Keywords

event, distributed, correlation, language, program analysis

*This research is supported, in part, by the National Science Foundation (NSF) under grants #0644013 and #0834529, and by DARPA under grant #N11AP20014.

1. INTRODUCTION

Event-based design *decouples* system components thus improving extensibility and scalability of the software. More precisely, decoupling is achieved by using a dedicated runtime system that delivers events from *sources* (producers, publishers) to *sinks* (consumers, subscribers) which are not a priori aware of each other, yielding the following benefits:

Simplicity. Decoupling avoids name binding of components, yielding modules which are largely independent. Components can thus be developed, extended, or tested independently from each other. By the same token, new components can be deployed into a running application.

Efficiency. The use of a dedicated middleware system allows for communication to be performed efficiently and in a scalable manner by aggregating and sharing traffic among components where possible.

Event-based middleware systems include *message queues* (an event is consumed by one *of* many sinks) and *publish/subscribe* systems (an event is delivered to *all* sinks interested in it). Systems include research engines (e.g., Siena [10], JEDI [12], and PADRES [28]) or industrial solutions (e.g., Amazon's Simple Queue Service, ActiveMQ, or FioranoMQ), several of which provide both types of communication.

Programming solutions for event-based programming range from simple design patterns (observer design pattern) to language extensions capturing concurrency through asynchronous events (e.g., Ptolemy [35], Responders [11], Scala [20] following an Actor model) to even higher-level coordination and event correlation abstractions (e.g., SCHOOL [32], Cω[7] based on Join Calculus [16]). Language-based approaches have several well-known benefits [9]. First, by providing specific constructs and abstractions these approaches further improve the *simplicity* of programs. Second — and among the prime motivations for language design research in general — choosing the right abstraction can improve the *efficiency* of language implementations. Third, based on language constructs, the compiler can ensure static or dynamic *safety* properties, such as type conformance.

Program analysis offers many intriguing avenues to increase the efficiency and other aspects of distributed event-based applications, but remains underexploited. This is precisely the motivation for this paper. We present three program analyses yielding benefits in terms of simplicity, efficiency, as well as safety:

Immutability analysis: When an event is consumed multiple times by different handlers in a same process then the event and its attributes (representation) must be cloned in most cases to not hamper the decoupling nature of event-based interaction and pass-by-value semantics that are used to support it. Immutability analysis infers cases where attributes are not modified in any way (e.g., by assignment) by handlers or further down the line, such that expensive cloning can be avoided. This may have a cumulative effect as co-locating handlers of a same event allows for limiting the times an event is sent over the wire.

Guard analysis: Guards are the natural way to express subscriptions in event-based languages. Besides allowing for statically verifying compliance of subscriptions with the events they are expressed on, guards naturally capture advanced features such as *parametric subscriptions* [22, 25] which have been shown to benefit efficiency. In contrast to an API-based support for the subscriber-local variables underlying such subscriptions, programming language support allows for complex subscriptions, e.g., those involving arithmetic and multiple variables to be expressed, and for the compiler to automatically simplify these and infer the relevant parameters.

Causality analysis: Causal order between events, especially when these are broadcast, has traditionally been achieved by manually mapping events to "broadcast groups", implemented by means of appropriate protocols [37], to capture dependencies. This is not only tedious for programmers (groups may overlap) but unsafe as dependencies are easily overlooked. Pessimistically funneling all events — even those requiring no ordering with respect to others and each other — through a same group strongly hampers efficiency. Causality analysis infers all *possible* dependencies (for safety) from programs, and with hints from the programmer on independencies (for efficiency) allows for groups to be be created adequately and manipulated automatically by the runtime.

These analyses can implemented on top of event processing middleware API as well with some minor additional effort. For the sake of presentation simplicity, we present them however in the context of our EventJava language [15], which has been designed with emphasis on *genericity*, *extensibility* and *flexibility* to thwart the potential limitations of domain-specific programming languages. EventJava is an extension of the mainstream Java programming language, implemented with an extensible compiler. EventJava's runtime is implemented as a framework of substitutable components, accessible directly through API, which allows existing middleware systems to be plugged in.

In summary, this paper makes the following contributions:

1. We introduce a subset of (mostly) static program analyses tailored to event-based programming which we have devised for EventJava, namely *immutability analysis*, *guard analysis*, and *causality analysis*.

2. We illustrate the benefits of our approach through empirical evaluation of performance gains enabled by our analyses.

Roadmap. Section 2 introduces the EventJava framework. Sections 3-5 present our analyses. Section 6 demonstrates the performance benefits of our approach. Section 7 summarizes related work. Section 8 concludes with final remarks.

2. EVENTJAVA LANGUAGE FRAMEWORK

We present an overview of EventJava. EventJava combines (1) a design leveraging *core abstractions* for fundamental constituents of distributed event-based programming — event *representation*, *production*, *delineation*, *selection*, and *consumption* — and (2) an *open framework*-based implementation. For brevity, we focus on these core abstractions and omit other features or options.

2.1 Event Representation

An application event *type* is implicitly defined by declaring an *event method*, a special kind of asynchronous instance-level method. The formal arguments of an event method correspond to the (explicit) attributes of the event type. For example, quote(**long** time, String org, **float** price) represents the signature of stock quotes. An event method declaration is preceded by the **event** keyword, which makes the distinction between a regular, synchronous, method with **void** return type and an asynchronous event method. This is similar to *chorded* languages (e.g. signal in Join Java [23], async in Cω [7]; cf. Section 7). For instance, an interface Stock could simply declare a quote event:

```
interface Stock ... {
    event quote(long time, String org, float price);
}
```

The knowledge of event *types* in contrast to *structural conformance* [31] has several immediate performance benefits, as events of different types can be handled in parallel. On the other hand, static typing of events does not preclude the addition of new event types at runtime [3]. The small overhead incurred by such infrequent additions is largely outweighed by the gain on every event [24].

2.2 Event Production

Most languages and systems focus on either notifying events to individual parties (unicast) *or* to several parties (multicast). EventJava distinguishes these choices syntactically allowing for "generalized specialization".

2.2.1 Unicast (one-to-one)

In the simplest case, an event can be notified to a single object by invoking an event method on a single object. For example, a stock quote event can be notified to an instance s of Stock simply as s.quote(...). An event method invocation however decouples the invoker from any invokee (for any production mode) in time. Chorded languages focusing on concurrency mostly follow this unicast addressing scheme.

2.2.2 Multicast (one-to-many)

The alternative to unicast is multicast, corresponding to publish/subscribe-based systems and languages. For multicast we can distinguish several sub-cases:

a. all-*of*-many: In this case, all objects in an application which implement the event method will be notified. This is achieved by reusing the notation known from **static** methods: Stock.quote(...) dispatches the event to all objects conforming to Stock (including by subtype subsumption). The same kind of call can be made on any class C implementing Stock, limiting the event to all instances of C and its sub-classes. Note that "all" refers to the set of *addressed* objects. All-of-many represents a *potential* broadcast, as the delivery of the event to a particular object — with any production model chosen — will always be subject to any *guards* on that object as we will see shortly.

b. some-*of*-many: This second case corresponds to the explicit addressing of a *set* of objects, or in other terms, to an *explicit* multicast or *group* broadcast. Here, as in group communication scenarios, a group proxy can be used and specific libraries can be offered to select among different protocols for dissemination and membership management upon proxy instantiation.

c. one-*of*-many: As a special case of b. above, one-of-one ensures that an event is not delivered by more than one object. It can be achieved by means of specific proxies. This scenario is referred to as *point-to-point* in Java Message Specification parlance [40].

2.3 Event Delineation

By enabling reactions to *complex* events rather than only individual events, application components can be simplified and repetitive or spurious coordination, composition, and communication can be further avoided. We also refer to such complex events also simply as *patterns*. EventJava enables the delineation of such patterns in *time* and *space*.

2.3.1 Composition in time

Composition in time is supported in EventJava through event *windows* which are syntactically unified with arrays. As an example, we can declare a class Broker which composes streams of events over a window size of 4 as follows:

```
class Broker implements Stock ... {
    event quote[4](long time, String org, float price) {...}
}
```

The attributes of an individual event can be referred to by indexing. For example, quote[2].time represents the time value of the third instance of quote (indices start at 0 just like arrays). This syntax supports efficient implementations by making the number of instances explicit as opposed to other approaches which represent streams as specific types which functions can iterate over by fetching the "next" instance [8]. The syntax provides the best of a declarative correlation style which accounts for the popularity of SQL-derived languages for correlation, in a core imperative model. The time attribute here refers to physical time, and the assumption in this example is that the clocks of producers are synchronized. One therefore expects time to be monotonically increasing with an increasing index i for quote[i]. EventJava includes domain-specific aspects which allow event timestamps to be abstracted as a first-class *context* together with other *implicit* attributes, e.g., source information, credentials. Domain-specific aspects can be used to support other notions of time like vector clocks, when clocks of producers are not synchronized. These are discussed in detail in [21].

2.3.2 Composition in space

Composition in space refers to the ability of composing events of different types through *joins*. These are expressed by comma-separated lists of event method *headers*. For instance, a class Broker2 can combine quote with analyst forecast events as follows:

```
class Broker2 implements Stock ... {
    event quote[4](...), forecast(...) {...}
}
```

The method body, referred to simply as *reaction*, is thus "shared" among the different event method headers. Of course, the separation of time and space for composition is only an abstraction; events composed in space are not all generated at the exact same point in time. In practice composition occurs in a mixed time&space form. Overloading and overriding become more intricate in the presence of composition [15]. In this context, it is sufficient to know that EventJava does not allow an event method to appear in multiple patterns of same class.

2.4 Event Selection

EventJava separates the expression of *which* events are composed from *how* they are composed by the introduction of *guards*. We can extend the example above as follows:

```
class Broker3 implements Stock ... {
    event quote[4](long time, String org, float price),
        forecast(long time, String org, float price)
    when (forecast.price > quote[0].price &&
        quote[0].time > forecast.time &&
        forall k in [0..2] quote[k].time < quote[k+1].time &&
        forall i in [0..2] quote[i].price > quote[i+1].price &&
        forall j in [0..3] quote[j].org == forecast.org) {...}
}
```

to express a strategy consisting in reacting upon a four-fold decrease in the price of a stock following an analyst forecast (assuming synchronized clocks). A guard can use regular Java operators for boolean expressions, such as negation (!) or disjunction (||). The absence of a guard is interpreted as **when true**. Fully qualified notation (e.g., forecast.org) can be simplified by renaming arguments (e.g., using org1 in forecast). Compilation will yield an error message if ambiguity exists. There is no *implicit* matching on homonymous attributes across events. As we will elaborate on more in the context of our analyses, EventJava supports certain uses of local program variables within guards. These allow for *dynamic* subscriptions, preserving the potential for runtime adaptation of late binding of subscriptions (by expression through strings) while avoiding malformed subscriptions.

2.5 Event Consumption

Our design supports two different models of event consumption. The default is asynchronous consumption, which is typical with declarative event correlation patterns – namely that a reaction is triggered *as soon as* a matching set of events has been identified. In the Broker3 example above, asynchronous consumption entails that the reaction is triggered as soon as four quote events and one forecast event *matching* the guard are received. As an alternative to asynchronous consumption, EventJava provides the **queue** keyword as a "substitute" for **event**. More precisely, a comma-separated list of event methods can be preceded by **queue** instead of **event**, with otherwise identical syntax, meaning that matching of the events in the corresponding composition will only be triggered *explicitly* by using the **next** keyword at the beginning of a statement followed by the names of involved events (without attributes). A statement **next** quote, forecast; in any of the methods of Broker3 or its subclasses would trigger the matching. This allows for the separation of complex events and reactions, and their timing.

Alike chorded languages, EventJava supports as syntactic sugar the possibility of including at most one regular, synchronous, method into a complex event. A reaction for a complex event with return type can return a value to the corresponding method invocation via the **return** statement.

2.6 Implementation Framework

The EventJava compiler translates EventJava to standard Java, including calls to interfaces of a runtime framework with substitutable components (see Figure 1). In short, an event notification is passed to the communication *substrate* which takes care of remote communication including unicast and multicast. In the multicast case, the substrate delivers all the serialized event method invocations to the *dispatcher*, which determines the classes on which the methods were invoked and interacts with *multicast objects* (omitted for simplicity) for those classes. These objects pass the events to the sinks, from where they are passed to the *matcher* where they are typically added to an *event store* (e.g., a queue). The matcher is responsible for checking the stored events for completed patterns. The matcher may also apply a garbage collection policy or update/replace stored events.

Serializer, dispatcher and multicast objects represent type-specific code generated at compilation to avoid costly calls through Java reflection. The substrate, matcher, and handler components are defined as APIs. Multicast invocations typically lead to calls to a multicast method of the Substrate interface. The compiler also generates string-based subscription filters from guards. These follow a syntax extending that of *selectors* in JMS [40]. They can be used by a substrate to perform message filtering during propagation [10].

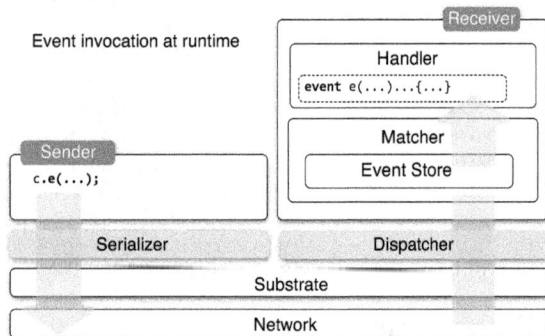

Figure 1: The EventJava runtime framework. Shaded portions represent application-specific components generated by the compiler.

3. IMMUTABILITY ANALYSIS

Immutability analysis avoids costly cloning of events in the presence of co-located handlers for the same event. Immutability analysis is the simplest of the proposed analyses and thus we present it first. It is related to different *pointer analyses* in programming languages.

3.1 Event Attribute Sharing

Like other systems, EventJava accepts Serializable types as event attributes and not only primitive types. While multicasting, such an attribute can be passed to several objects even in a same JVM, and such attributes can be used in reactions just like formal arguments of any method. Since serializability does not imply immutability, and we do not want to restrict the programmer to certain types yet want to avoid unwanted sharing of event attributes, attributes passed to multiple objects would have to be cloned. Yet cloning of objects can become expensive especially if the event attributes being cloned are complex (containing multiple fields and/or several levels of nesting), represent larger structures such as XML structures or image files, or have to be notified to a large number of co-located sinks. Consider, for simplicity below, the slight alteration of the stock trading example

```
class Broker4 ... {
    event ticker[4](long time, Quote q),
        forecast(long time, String org, float price)
    when (forecast.price > ticker[0].q.price &&
        forall i in [0..2] ticker[i].q.price > ticker[i+1].q.price
        && forall k in [0..2] ticker[k].time < ticker[k+1].time
        && ticker[0].time > forecast.time &&
        forall j in [0..3] ticker[j].q.org == forecast.org) {...}
}
```

where Quote is straightforwardly defined as follows:

```
class Quote implements Serializable {
    String org;
    float price;
    ...
}
```

We can have multiple instances of Broker4 in a same address space, or also co-locate these with instances of subclasses of Broker4 which for instance override the guard to implement other strategies. Unless we clone a *quote*'s q attribute for these different reactions/reacting objects, there can be implicit sharing of q.

The body of the reaction depicted in class Broker4, or in a subclass of it, could decide to *retain* certain Quotes to keep track of trends for later analysis or as integral part of correlation strategies. Then, nothing prevents a reaction from modifying any of the fields of q (e.g., q.price =q.price + provision) before say storing q in a collection, while another reaction stores the original q.

3.2 Pessimistic Static Analysis

To avoid unnecessary cloning, yet remain on the safe side to avoid "data races" through the manipulation of event attributes in reactions, we perform an *immutability analysis* on event method arguments. This analysis determines for serializable formal arguments whether they *might be* eventually modified through method invocations or direct assignment to any of their fields. If the analysis can not assert immutability (without inspecting the whole program), the EventJava compiler inserts code to clone matched events before they are used to dispatch the reaction.

4. GUARD ANALYSIS

Next we present the analysis of guards performed in EventJava. In fact this analysis consists in several sub-analyses which are aligned with the guard syntax.

4.1 Dynamic guards

Algorithmic stock trading — one of the classic showcases for publish/subscribe interaction — thrives on rapid adaptations in subscriptions, consisting mostly in adapting the range of permissible values for event attributes [39].

EventJava thus supports *parametric subscriptions* [22, 25], i.e, *dynamic* guards, by allowing for fields of consumer objects to be used in guards. In EventJava an example like the following looks like quite natural:

```
class Broker5 implements Stock ... {
    float targetPrice = ...;
    float thresholdFactor
    event quote(long time, String org, float price)
    when price < thresholdFactor*targetPrice {...}
}
```

Observe that thresholdFactor and targetPrice are not **final** and can thus change throughout the life-time of a Broker4 instance. Any updates to the local variables will take effect.

More precisely, EventJava allows fields of sink classes to be used in guards. By abuse of language but for brevity, we use the term *guard fields* to refer to such fields f (`this`.f). To exploit these fields, assignments have to be supported. This is achieved by a *guard analysis*, statically verifying restrictions on guard fields to ensure that updates to those fields *can be* tracked (without whole-program analysis), and inserting code for tracking actual updates. Of course fully exploiting them requires a corresponding middleware system, which registers for corresponding updates with the framework thus receiving selectors in an extended syntax including variable names. Without this, the updates are translated to issuing a new subscription and canceling the outdated one. As we will illustrate later, support for dynamic guards as enabled by our static analysis improves performance under subscription updates. Note that EventJava allows the evaluation of guard fields to be kept local, if desired, by "pinning" these fields through a modifier local in their declarations.

4.2 Completeness

Tracking all possible updates that affect fields is impossible in practice in the presence of nested types, recursion, and aliasing. EventJava thus imposes the following restrictions (enforced by the type system) on fields used in guards:

R1 Guard fields must be of primitive types.

R2 Guard fields must be **private** or **protected** fields.

These restrictions capture the two possible ways in which fields can be modified, namely by method invocations and assignments. More precisely, R1 ensures that when an object gains access to a field of a sink — for example such a field can be used as return value of a method — no method calls can be performed on the referenced object. Methods can namely have side-effects which could alter an invoked object. Tracking and instrumenting all possible places where method invocations could lead to such alterations can potentially require any class to be instrumented. Thanks to R2, the places where field assignments must be tracked are limited to sink classes and their subclasses.

4.3 Tracking Updates in Single-Field Guards

In this subsection, we consider dynamic guards where event attributes are compared to a single guard field. Even in single-field guards, to track updates, assignments to guards fields are instrumented such as to notify updates to the run-time infrastructure. Since guard fields can appear in several

guards for a given sink class, several update notifications might be generated by a single field assignment. In practice these can be combined into single notifications.

It is important to consider the possibility of concurrent updates to guard fields. To ensure that the order of updates is not permuted and that no relevant updates are lost, assignments to guard fields have to occur in mutual exclusion. Any sink class is thus added a *lock field* f Lock of type FIFOMutex for each of its guard fields f, to serve as a FIFO mutex, regrouping and protecting updates to f and engendered update(...) calls to the runtime infrastructure (substrate). Such calls in the case of the EventJava runtime infrastructure are made wait-free in that they simply "drop" the update into a buffer, which stores only the last yet unhandled update request for a given parameter. The default implementation for middleware systems which do not inherently support parametric subscriptions leads to a re-subscription – issuing a new subscription and unsubscribing the outdated one.

Instrumentation occurs on every **private** field used in a guard, and on every **protected** field declared by a sink class. The possibility of inheritance with protected fields makes it necessary to pessimistically instrument every modification of such fields declared by sink classes, even for fields which are never used in any guard – not even in respective subclasses. Inversely, if a sink class C has a super-class C' (possibly recursively) which is not subscribed to any events, then C' must be re-compiled if C uses any protected fields of C' in its guards.

4.4 Expressiveness

We would like guards to be as expressive as possible, without entailing much support in the substrate. We discuss extensions to the subscription grammar implemented by EventJava – an extension handled purely by program rewriting and then two extensions benefitting from runtime support.

4.4.1 Parameter expressions

Consider a navigation system that uses GPS sensors to display traffic density around the current location (i.e., GPS X and Y coordinates) of an automobile. This can be expressed in EventJava as follows (the fields constituting subscription parameters are italicized and underlined:

```
class TrafficMonitor {
    float myXPos, myYPos, myXRange, myYRange;
    TrafficMonitor(...) {... /* Init values */ }
    // Subscribe to events from (X, Y) s.t.
    // abs(myXPos - X) ≤ myXRange and abs(myYPos - Y)
            ≤ myYRange
    event trafficDensity(float vehiclesPerSec, float xPos,
            float yPos)
        when (xPos >= myXPos − myXRange &&
            xPos <= myXPos + myXRange &&
            yPos >= myYPos − myYRange &&
            yPos <= myYPos + myYRange) {
            ... // E.g., update navigation screen
    }
    public void setXPos(float newXPos) {
        myXPos = newXPos;
    }
}
```

Our earlier work [25] on parametric subscriptions does not directly support such *complex* expressions on variables

```
class TrafficMonitor{
    float myXPos, myYPos;
    float myXRange, myYRange;
    //Generated Variables
    float __gen1, __gen2, __gen3, __gen4;

    ...
    TrafficMonitor(...) {
        ... // Init values like myXPos, myYPos, myXRange...
        // Instrument the constructor accordingly
        __gen1 = myXPos − myXRange;
        __gen2 = myXPos + myXRange;
        __gen3 = myYPos − myYRange;
        __gen4 = myYPos − myYRange;
    }
    event trafficDensity(float vehiclesPerSec, float xPos,
        float yPos)
        when (xPos >= __gen1 && xPos <= __gen2 &&
            yPos >= __gen3 && yPos <= __gen4 ) {
            // E.g., update navigation system
    }
    public void setXPos(float newXPos) {
        myXPos = newXPos;
        // Instrument methods to reevaluate any generated
        //     variable
        // that could be affected by an assignment
        __gen1 = myXPos − myXRange;
        __gen2 = myXPos + myXRange;
        //Instrument methods to send update messages
        Substrate.update("__gen1", __gen1);
        Substrate.update("__gen2", __gen2);
    }
}
```

Figure 2: Translating expressions in guards to use single variables. Backlit portions are compiler-generated; *Emphasized* variables represent actual subscription parameters. Their use in guards is underlined.

in a subscription. EventJava can however easily deal with them by translation. To implement parametric subscriptions with expressions, i.e., comparing an event attribute to an expression containing possibly multiple constants and guard fields, the EventJava compiler simplifies these expressions by introducing *virtual* variables into the program which represent the values of high-level expressions. For example, the subscription in the TrafficMonitor class described above is translated as outlined in Figure 2. Backlit portions are compiler-generated. In this figure, *italicized* variables represent *actual* subscription parameters. Their use in guards is underlined. Locks are omitted for presentation simplicity.

In the TrafficMonitor example, each expression in the subscription is captured by a variable that the compiler introduces, e.g., __gen1 captures the value of the combined expression myXPos − myXRange. The compiler also generates code to initialize __gen1 after each of its components, i.e., myXPos and myXRange is initialized in constructors. Also, whenever the value of any component changes (as in setXPos(...)), the values of all generated variables depending on that component (e.g., myXPos) are recomputed and parameter update requests issued.

4.4.2 Attribute expressions

If a traffic monitor were interested in traffic density in a *circular* area of radius myRange, we would like to express this subscription in EventJava as outlined below:

```
class TrafficMonitor2 {
    float myXPos, myYPos;
    float myRange;

    ...
    // Subscribe to events from (X, Y) s.t.
    // ((myXPos - X)² + (myYPos - Y)²)^{1/2} ≤ myRange
    event trafficDensity(float vehiclesPerSec, float xPos,
        float yPos)
        when (EuclideanDistance(myXPos − xPos, myYPos −
            yPos) <= myRange) {
            ... // E.g., update navigation screen
    }

    static float EuclidianDistance(float xDist, float yDist) {
        return Math.sqrt((xDist ∗ xDist) + (yDist ∗ yDist));
    }
}
```

This example illustrates several things. First, the method EuclidianDistance is really only syntactic sugar as it is side-effect free (it is a "pure function") and can be supported without whole-program analysis by placing several syntactic restrictions on such methods. Equivalently, the expression constituting the return value can be inlined into the guard. Second, however, this expression compared to myRange contains several *attributes* as well as a nested pure function Math .sqrt part of the standard Java class libraries. While Event-Java's own substrate supports such attribute expressions as well as the use of standard pure functions, it generates code to interface also with substrates which do not support such expressive subscriptions through corresponding code for local evaluation of the euclidian distance. EventJava currently does not support comparisons of two expressions containing an arbitrary set of constants, attributes, and variables *on both sides of the comparison* because we have not yet encountered applications depending on them.

4.4.3 Switches

Another interesting scenario not captured above is that of a guard predicate based solely on local variables and constants, acting as a "switch" to repeatedly enable/disable a subscription. An example is the first predicate in the guard below:

```
class Broker6 {
    float threshold, balance, tradeLevel;
    event quote(long time, String org, float price)
        when (balance > tradeLevel + 5000 && price >
            threshold) ...
}
```

In fact, the EventJava compiler here will insert code to track updates to all involved variables, but will introduce a virtual boolean variable which simply represents the predicate value. We have extended our substrate to support such boolean variables.

4.4.4 EventJava Substrate

The default substrate for EventJava has three event dissemination modes – a group communication mode and two content-based publish/subscribe (CPS) modes. The group communication mode uses JGroups for the dissemination of events, while the CPS modes uses a CPS system with a broker overlay network, subscription summarization based on subsumption, and the Rete algorithm for matching events to subscriptions in a broker. The difference between the two CPS modes is in the support for expressive dynamic guards – the two modes will be referred to as CPS-Traditional and CPS-Dynamic in the rest of this paper. We will compare the performance of CPS-Traditional and CPS-Dynamic to gauge the benefits due to guard analysis. EventJava with CPS-Traditional uses re-subscriptions for updating guards.

5. CAUSALITY ANALYSIS

Several event processing systems or languages support correlation based on the order of *occurrence* of events. In EventJava, this can be expressed in a guard by writing $e < e'$ where $C.e$ and $C'.e'$ are two event types, declared by C and C' respectively, in the corresponding pattern.

5.1 Causal Dependencies

The order $<$ can be defined by a physical notion of time, or in the absence of synchronized clocks in asynchronous distributed systems, can be based on a logical notion of time such as *causality* [27]. Such a notion in the presence of multicast can be achieved by employing a *causal* order multicast substrate, employing dedicated protocols [37] to avoid jeopardizing safety and/or liveness in the presence of even a single failure. Two factors however complicate the bigger picture: First, these protocols induce a significant overhead compared to un-ordered approaches. Second, other than by the presence of order-based correlation with $<$ in guards, it is impossible in the general case to infer automatically from a program which types of events require causal order (or other ordering guarantees for that matter). The approach of pessimistically conveying every event of a given application through a same causal order multicast group will however lead to a severe bottleneck especially as the number of involved processes increases. At present, programmers thus must explicitly deal with setting up and managing multiple multicast groups, which can involve the same or overlapping sets of application components.

5.2 Local Static Analysis

EventJava thus relies only on programmers to indicate (1) event types whose instances need to be causally *ordered among each other* (which is impossible to infer in general as mentioned), and (2) event types whose respective instances are *causally independent* of each other. By analyzing EventJava programs, the compiler performs a static analysis to infer dependencies among types identified by (1) that are introduced through the program. This ensures safety in the sense of consistency. By reducing the dependencies by (2) a high-overhead pessimistic approach can be avoided. For simplicity we omit in the following subtyping at first. *Direct* dependencies are twofold and trivially inferred:

Direct consume-produce dependency: Any event type $C.e$ produced (e.g., $C.e(...)$) directly by a reaction to a pattern involving event type $C'.e'$ implies a consume-produce dependency between instances of $C'.e'$ and of $C.e$.

Direct consume-consume dependency: Any correlated events types $C.e$ and $C'.e'$ appearing in a pattern together (with

or without explicit correlation $<$) pessimistically may lead to dependencies among the instances of $C.e$ and of $C'.e'$.

Such consume-produce and consume-consume dependencies can however occur also *indirectly* and *transitively*: for instance, a reaction consuming instances of $C.e$ can through a chain of dependencies involving method invocations (control-flow dependencies) and writes/reads of fields (data-flow) contribute to the generation of an event of type $C'.e'$.

Our static analysis thus computes for every method $C.m$ and reaction to an event $C.e$ (in a pattern), $out(C.m)$ and $out(C.e)$ respectively, which contain the set of events generated, the set of methods invoked, as well as the set of fields written by $C.m$ or $C.e$ respectively. Further the analysis computes $in(C.m)$ and $in(C.e)$, which represent the set of fields read by $C.m$ or $C.e$ respectively.

5.3 Dynamic Closures

Upon loading a class, the runtime computes *locally* the *reflexive transitive closures* $out^+(......)$ of the above output sets for that class. The closure of $in(......)$ is not needed as the closure of $out(......)$ includes all chains of transitive field writes+reads. The same sets are updated for previously loaded classes.

Inheritance is taken into account when computing closures for methods and events. Assume a class C' which extends a class C. For every method m of C overridden by C', $out(C.m) \leftarrow out(C.m) \cup out(C'.m)$.

Now, two events $C.e$ and $C'.e'$ are dependent, noted $C.e \longrightarrow C'.e'$, iff they are directly dependent (see above) or

Indirect consume-produce dependency: there is an indirect consume-produce dependency between $C.e$ and $C'.e'$, i.e., $C'.e' \in out^+(C.e.)$, or

Indirect consume-consume dependency: there is an indirect consume-consume dependency between $C.e$ and $C'.e'$, i.e., there exists a field $C''.f \in (out^+(C.e) \cap out^+(C'.e'))$.

The symmetric binary relation $\longleftrightarrow$ denotes a dependency either way, i.e., $C.e \longleftrightarrow C'.e' \Leftrightarrow C.e \longrightarrow C'.e' \vee C'.e' \longrightarrow C.e$.

A programmer can specify independence $C.e$ `indep` $C'.e'$ to override our pessimistic program analysis. The $\longleftrightarrow_0$ relation is obtained from $\longleftrightarrow$ by removing pairs in `indep`. $\longleftrightarrow^+$ is the reflexive and transitive closure of $\longleftrightarrow_0$. Finally, $\longleftrightarrow^+$ gives rise to *dependency sets* $\bar{d}=d_1,...,d_q$ where $\{C.e, C'.e'\} \subseteq d \in \bar{d} \Leftrightarrow C.e \longleftrightarrow^+ C'.e'$

5.4 Runtime Support

Now that we know the local dependencies for every JVM component, we need to coordinate across components. This requires more dedicated runtime support described below.

5.4.1 Group membership

For simplicity we assume in the following a *distributed locking service* like Apache ZooKeeper[1], with a hierarchical name space.

- There is a node /groups/*sid* for every dependency set $d = \overline{C.e}$ (i.e., $d = C_1.e_1 \cdot ... \cdot C_n.e_n$) where *sid* is the concatenation of the event names $C_i.e_i$ (with a dedicated separation symbol) ordered lexically (we write

---

[1]http://hadoop.apache.org/zookeeper/

```
1: init
2:   d̄                              {dependency sets in service}
3:   d̄'                             {based on local dependency sets}
4:   d̄'' ← sets from reflexive and transitive closure of ⟷_g
       ∪ ⟷'_g on {C.e | C.e ∈ d_i ∨ C.e ∈ d'_i}

5: for all d''_i do
6:   d̄''' ← {d_j | d_j ⊆ d''_i}
7:   events ← {C.e | C.e ∈ d''_i}
8:   if |events| > |d'''_1| then
9:     sid ← sid(d''_i)
10:    create node /groups/sid with value gid(sid)
11:    create group gid(sid)
12:    for all d'''_k do
13:      merge gid(sid(d''_k)) to gid(sid)
14:      remove node /groups/sid(d'''_k)
15:    for all C.e ∈ events do
16:      if ∃ node /events/C.e then
17:        set value of node to sid(d''_i)
18:      else
19:        create node with value sid(d''_i)
```

Figure 3: Reconciling sets of causally dependent event types across nodes.

$sid = sid(d)$ for brevity). The value gid stored for the node is a group identifier and is given by the hash $hash(sid)$ of the sid of the dependency set. Note that a dependency set may contain only one event.

- There is a node /events/$C.e$ for every event $C.e$. The value stored for the node is the identifer sid of the respective dependency set.

A component has a local hashtable with $\langle C.e, gid \rangle$ entries, where gid is the group identifier for $C.e$.

5.4.2 Group operations

Every time a VM identifies a local change in its dependencies (upon loading of a set of classes), its first locks the node hierarchy. Next it reads all groups from the locking service $\overline{d}$, where each $d_i = \overline{C.e}$. Let $\longleftrightarrow_g$ and $\longleftrightarrow'_g$ represent the symmetric dependency relations (transitive and reflexive closures) underlying $\overline{d}$ and $\overline{d}'$ where the latter represents the local dependency sets.

Let d be the total set of event types across $\overline{d}$ and $\overline{d}'$. Then $\overline{d}''$ is the dependency set constructed from d and the relation $\longleftrightarrow_g \cup \longleftrightarrow'_g$ as described in Figure 3. The *merging* of two multicast groups (see Line 13) happens by having nodes of the two joined groups join the newly formed joint group (at Line 11) individually. To that end, specific merge messages are multicast within the two joined groups.

6. EVALUATION

This section empirically evaluates the benefits of the static analyses presented in the previous section in terms of performance.

6.1 Benefits of Immutability Analysis

To evaluate the benefits of our immutability analysis, we deploy a matcher that correlates events of several types on a single node. We assume that each event has 20 primitive attributes. The matcher correlates 100 event types across

# of attributes	# of sinks	% throughput decrease
10	20	3.6%
10	200	13.4%
10	100	42.3%
20	20	6.34%
20	200	15.5%
20	1000	66.7%

Table 1: Benefits of immutability analysis.

20 correlation patterns, and delivers events that match each of the patterns to a set of sinks. The throughput of the matcher is the number of matched events delivered per second. Table 1 demonstrates the decrease in throughput when matched events are cloned before being delivered to sinks. Table 1 clearly shows the effect, due to cloning, of (1) the number of attributes of events and (2) the number of sinks to which events have to be delivered on the throughput.

6.2 Benefits of Guard Analysis

In this section, we evaluate the benefits of expressive dynamic guards in EventJava.

6.2.1 Metrics

We use four metrics:

(a) **Delay:** Delay is the time period between an update and the reception of the first corresponding event. If a subscriber r_i changes its subscription Φ_i to Φ'_i at time t_0, and the first event method matching Φ'_i but not Φ_i is delivered at time t_1, then the delay at subscriber r_i is defined as t_1-t_0.

(b) **Throughput:** Throughput is the average number of useful events *delivered* by a subscriber per second. This throughput depends on the number of publishers, event production rates at each publisher, the selectivity of the subscriptions of the subscribers, and the rate at which each subscriber updates its subscriptions. Selectivity of a subscription is the probability that an event matches a subscription. A selectivity of 1.0 implies that a subscription is satisfied by every published event of the respective type and a selectivity of 0.0 implies that none do.

(c) **Spurious events:** The effect of inefficient updates might be offset if brokers are powerful dedicated servers or individual clients are only interested in few events to start with. Increased stress might otherwise manifest, especially on resource-constrained clients. To gauge this stress, we measure the amount of spurious events delivered by clients. If a subscriber r_i changes its subscription Φ_i to Φ'_i at time t_0, then spurious events are those matching Φ_i but not Φ'_i and received by the client *after* t_0 and filtered out locally to it.

(d) **Latency:** We use the term latency to refer to event dissemination latency: if an event e is produced at time t_1 and is received by a subscriber at time t_2, then the dissemination latency of that event is $t_2 - t_1$. Since we average over a number of runs with the same deployment for all scenarios and systems and the goal is not to measure *exact* latency but rather to gauge (relative) improvements, the clocks of publisher and subscribers

(a) Throughput

(b) Delay

(c) Latency

(d) Spurious events

(e) Benefits of causality analysis

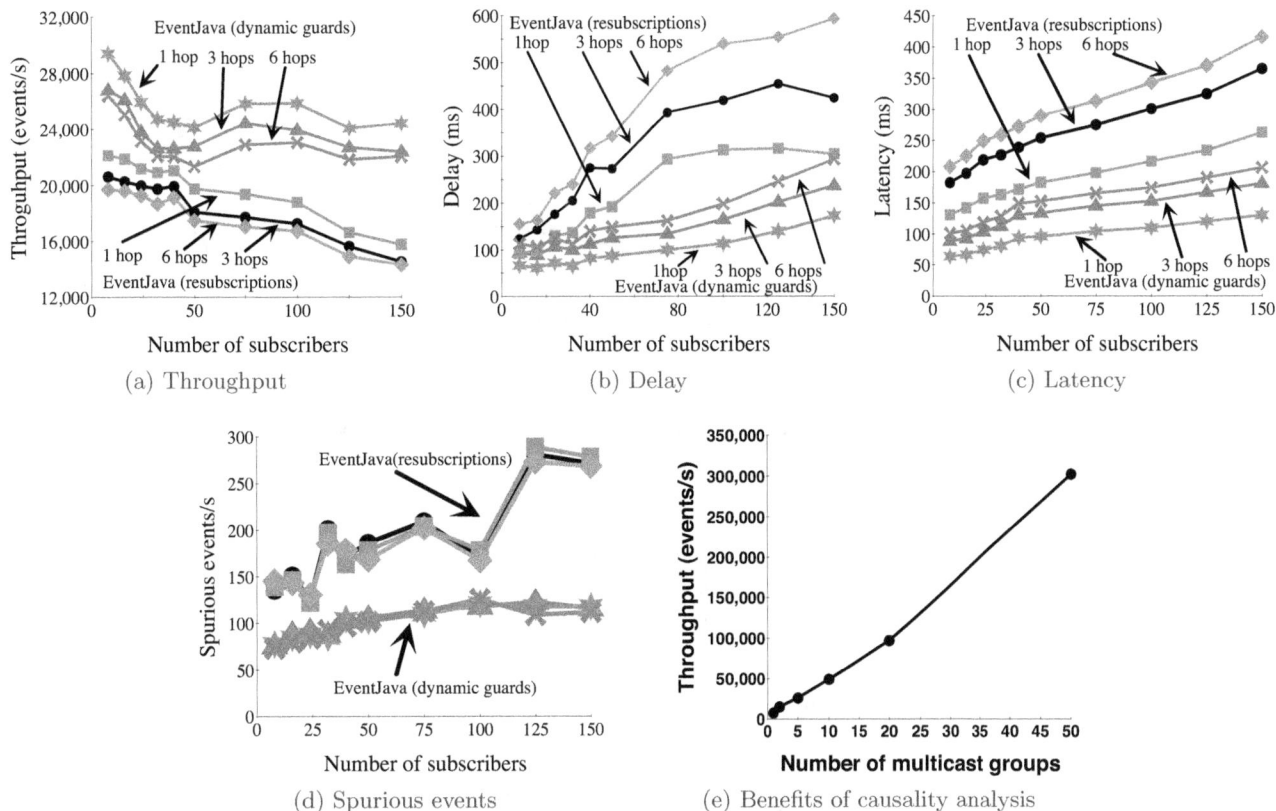

Figure 4: Benefits of various static analyses. Figures (a) to (d) compare the performance of EventJava with and without support for expressive dynamic guards. Figure (e) shows the benefits of causality analysis.

do not need to be perfectly synchronized. Nonetheless, and regardless of the fact that our routing algorithms described in this paper do not require or directly benefit from synchronized clocks, we ensured that clocks of publishers and subscribers were synchronized for the experiments that measured latency.

6.2.2 Benchmark for guard analysis

We first evaluate the benefits of guard analysis using an artificially generated workload of subscriptions. We use an overlay network of 25 brokers, 30 publishers and up to 150 subscribers. We used an even distribution of $<, \leq, >, \geq, ==$ in the subscriptions, each operator was used in 20% of subscriptions from each subscriber. The broker overlay used for evaluating guard analysis is an undirected acyclic graph. Subscribers are uniformly distributed all over the broker overlay, with maximum number of hops between a publisher and a subscriber being 6. We measure the average throughput, latency, delay and frequency of spurious events at all subscribers with the same number of hops away from any producer. At each subscriber, all the generated subscriptions compared event attributes to expressions on field variables. We did not use any single-field guards because the benefits of using single-field guards has already been exhaustively evaluated by [25]. 50% of the generated subscriptions at each subscriber used arithmetic expressions on variables, while the remaining 50% used functions from java.lang.Math.

All brokers were executed on dual core Intel Xeon 3.2GHz machines with 4GB RAM running Linux, with each machine executing exactly one broker. Subscribers were deployed on

eight core Intel Xeon 1.8GHz machine with 8GB RAM running Linux, with 8 subscribers deployed on each node (one subscriber per core), or on dual code Intel Xeon 3.2GHz machines with 4GB RAM running Linux with 4 subscribers per node. Publishers were deployed on dual core Intel Pentium 3GHz machines with 4GB RAM, with no more than 2 publishers per machine (one publisher per core). Deploying publishers, subscribers and brokers on different nodes ensured that all relevant communication (publisher-broker, broker-broker and subscriber-broker) was over a network, and in many cases across LANs. 10ms delays were added to each network link to simulate wide area network characteristics as is done in EmuLab [2].

6.2.3 Results

We assess the benefits of dynamic guards, which are facilitated by our guard analysis.

Figure 4(a) shows the difference in throughput between EventJava (with expressive dynamic guards) and EventJava with CPS-Traditional. Figure 4(a) shows that the different in throughput between the two versions of EventJava becomes more pronounced as the number of subscribers increases. Figure 4(a) also shows that the throughput is slightly higher when the number of hops decreases. The average throughput at subscribers located 1 hop away from the publishers is about 1%-4% higher than the average throughput at subscribers located 3 hops away. Similarly, the throughput at subscribers located 3 hops away from the publishers

[2] http://www.emulab.net

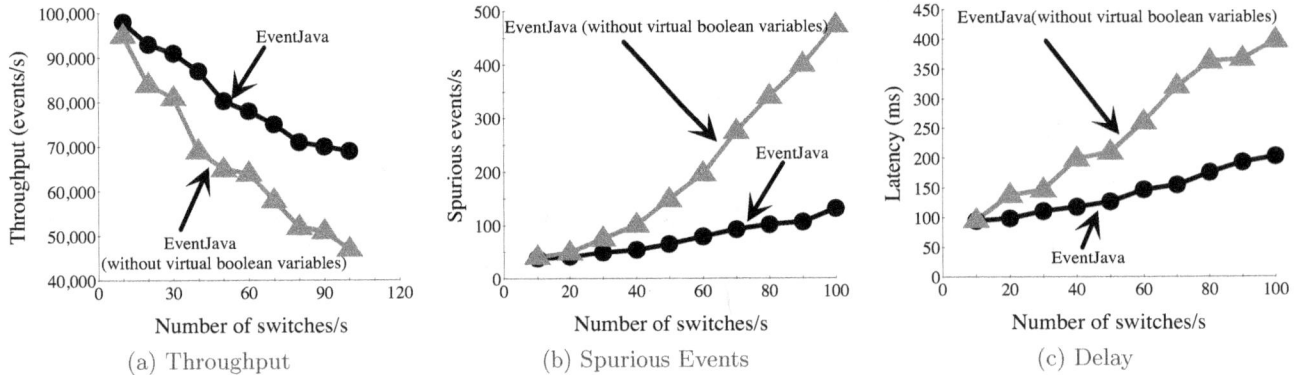

(a) Throughput   (b) Spurious Events   (c) Delay

Figure 5: EventJava with and without boolean guard variables.

is about 9%-12% higher than average throughput at subscribers located 6 hops away.

Figure 4(c) shows the difference in throughput between EventJava (with expressive dynamic guards) and EventJava with CPS-Traditional. Figure 4(c) shows that the difference in latency between the two versions of EventJava increases as the number of subscribers increases. As expected, the event dissemination latency increases as the number of hops increases. The average latency at 3 hops is approximately 28% higher than that at 1 hop, and the average latency at 6 hops is approximately 42% higher that that at 1 hop. A similar trend can be seen in update delay. Figure 4(c) shows that the average delay at 3 hops is approximately 32% higher than the delay at 1 hop, while the delay at 6 hops is approximately 49% higher than the delay at 1 hop.

Figure 4(d) shows that EventJava with resubscriptions receives spurious events at a higher frequency than EventJava with expressive dynamic guards, and this increases the number of subscribers increases. The differences between the average frequencies of spurious events when the distance between the producers and subscribers increases is statistically insignificant – this is because the edge broker immediately applies updates and unsubscriptions to its local data structures. Although the number of spurious events between brokers may increase when the number of hops between the producer and subscriber increases, they are filtered away at the edge broker, and hence the frequency of spurious events received by the subscriber doesn't depend on its distance from the producer.

6.2.4 *Virtual boolean variables*

Figure 5 shows the difference in throughput, number of spurious events and delay between two versions of EventJava – (a) with support in the matcher for boolean variables, and (b) without such support but by (un-)subscribing upon changes in the boolean value.

For this experiment, we used the algorithmic trading benchmark with 1000 event methods and 200 correlation patterns. We also extended our Rete-based matcher to perform distributed matching in a cluster. The matcher divides the correlation patterns uniformly into a n groups if there are n nodes in the cluster, such that each node correlates roughly the same number of event types. Consequently, this experiment doesn't depend on the overlay. We deployed our distributed matcher with and without support for boolean

variables on 20 nodes of a cluster of Amazon Elastic Cloud 2 (EC2) large instances (dual core with 7.5 GB memory). Figure 5 shows that the use of boolean variables improves throughput by up to 31.4%, reduces the number of spurious events by up to 3.5× and reduces delay by up to 2×.

6.3 Benefits of Causality Analysis

The objective of causality analysis is to identify as many clusters of events as possible which are not causally related to each other, based on their types. The consequence is that the entire set of application events can be divided into independent sets of events, and using one multicast group per set increases overall throughput. To assess the benefits of conveying unrelated events with independent causal multicast groups we created a varying number of such groups to multicast the same set of events of 500 event types.. To not over-accentuate any trends, we used a lightweight causal ordering protocol based on vector clocks stripped of parts of the actual fault tolerance mechanisms which could have lead to waiting time even in the absence of failures. That way the protocol is not destined upfront to be a bottleneck. Figure 4(e) demonstrates that throughput (of event transmission from source to sinks) increases almost linearly as the number of multicast groups used increases from 1 to 50.

7. RELATED WORK

We summarize related work on support for engineering distributed event-based applications.

7.1 Publish/Subscribe

The benefits of event-based design for distributed software has been long recognized. The path has been led by systems such as JEDI [12] or Siena [10]. Early work on the publish/subscribe architectural pattern [31] targeted enterprise application integration specifically, and thus advocated *self-describing* messages which avoid any agreement on event types or schemas. Much literature on subscription handling at event *brokers* similarly alluded to conformance models by side-stepping the issue of typing events (e.g. [2]) while most respective systems do implement stronger forms of typing. Self-describing messages/structural conformance provide much flexibility yet for many applications designed upfront around the idiom of events nowadays they incur an unnecessary overhead, and bear type safety issues [34]. These are shared by manipulation of SQL-like queries [42].

Several publish/subscribe systems have been extended for correlation (e.g., Gryphon [2], PADRES [28]).

7.2 Programming Languages and Models

Several programming languages support event-based programming. Rather than focusing on the underlying programming paradigms (e.g. objects, functional), we summarize these languages according to three dimensions $\langle k, m, n \rangle$ of expressiveness: 1. the maximum window sizes k for streams of individual event types (k-size windows), 2. the maximum number m of event types that can be correlated (m−way joins), and 3. the maximum number of event types n involved, transitively, in a guard (n−ary subscriptions). Typically, supporting only intra-event predicates in guards leads to 1-ary subscriptions. Obviously 3. is upper bound by 2. # represents the absence of a bound. We focus on correlation as return values are mostly a syntactic sugar, and the mechanisms for unicast or multicast are better understood currently than syntax and semantics of correlation.

Simple event handlers $\langle 1, 1, 0 \rangle$ — provided by most library-based event handlers, the observer design pattern, and simple languages like Ptolemy [35] — support reactions to single instances of multicast events, without guards. nesC [17] is a supports reactions to singleton events, but only for vertical (local, inter-module) interaction (and not horizontal, inter-process, interaction). Languages like CML [36] and Erlang [6] support only *staged* correlation where the occurrence of an event of a first type conditions the consumption of the second one etc. In CML, events are reified as function *evaluations* such as reads or writes on channels, which can be combined. Staged event matching imposes an order on how events are matched to a correlation pattern. This gives the programmer control over the exact matching semantics, but means implementing partial matching schemes repeatedly. In many cases, more advanced schemes expressed with staged matching can require "re-inserting" an event, which quickly complicates code.

Simple guarded event handlers $\langle 1, 1, 1 \rangle$ include languages inspired by the publish/subscribe paradigm. ECO (*events, constraints, objects*) [18] or Java$_{PS}$ [14] extend C++ and Java respectively. ECO introduces specific first-class constructs to reify events, while Java$_{PS}$ uses objects of specific serializable types. Actor-based languages or libraries supporting guards on *individual* messages such as Erlang [6] are similar yet with unicast.

Chorded languages $\langle 1, \#, 0 \rangle$ correspond to the Join Calculus [16] family. Examples are Join Java [23] or Polyphonic C# [7] – now Cω. Chorded languages provide a means to react to correlated asynchronous method invocations, without guards. The only multicast supported is a form of one-*of-many* where several patterns on a *same* object can compete for an event. While Cω is integrated with .NET remoting thus allowing for distributed interaction, most other languages focus on centralized, concurrent systems.

Guarded chorded languages $\langle 1, \#, \# \rangle$ are second generation chorded languages such as JErlang [33] with support for guards with conditions involving n-ary predicates but no streams. Scala Joins [19] represent a special, isolated, case of guarded chorded language supporting only 1-ary predicates on event attributes ($\langle 1, \#, 1 \rangle$). Other than that the features provided are as for the common chorded languages.

Generic correlation $\langle \#, \#, \# \rangle$ is to the best of our knowledge only supported by EventJava [15]. Several systems (e.g., Cayuga [13], Borealis [41], StreamBase [1]) implement all correlation features, with unicast. CQL [5] and Stream-SQL [1] are SQL derivations with comparable expressiveness. In our earlier work on EventJava[15], we formalize and proves guarantees (e.g., total order) in the presence of correlation. We exploit the language to generate code for efficient correlation of events [24].

Other related languages include the StreamIt [4] dataflow language for fine-grained highly parallel stream applications. While StreamIt programs can be parallelized automatically, the language is hardly suited for general purpose applications because of the lack of data types offered and the restricted programming model. StreamFlex [38] is a Java API for stream processing inspired by StreamIt but providing high-predictability implemented on top of a real-time virtual machine. StreamFlex provides *filters* and (unicast) *channels* with explicit pull-style consumption of events, leading to a similar staged matching model as CML.

7.3 Aspect-oriented Techniques

Several aspect-oriented programming languages have been proposed for distributed systems programming. As pointed out in [35], joinpoints of AspectJ [26]-like languages can be viewed as expressing *implicit* events as opposed to the explicit events of EventJava and related languages. AWED (*aspects with explicit distribution*) [29]) and DADO (*distributed aspects for distributed objects*) [43] are aspect languages supporting the remote monitoring of distributed applications with distributed pointcuts and advice. DJcutter [30] extends AspectJ with remote joinpoints and pointcuts. At the runtime level, DJcutter has a hardwired centralized aspect-server, which constitutes a bottleneck in a large distributed systems. Implementations of other systems are similarly fixed and lack scalability.

8. CONCLUSIONS

The full potential of the event idiom for programming complex distributed applications has yet to be discovered and exploited. In this paper we have presented a programming language framework guiding developers in writing correct and efficient complex event-based distributed applications without hampering flexibility in the use of existing middleware systems or adaptability of resulting software. We have presented several program (mostly) static program analyses implemented in EventJava, yielding benefits in simplicity, efficiency, and safety. It is straightforward to see that guard analysis eliminates the need for a programmer to *manually* (1)introduce variables to capture expressions on guard fields, (2)examine application code to identify any point at which a guard field's value changes. Causality analysis eliminates the need to manually identify direct and indirect produce-consume/consume-consume relationships between events, and handle dynamically loaded classes. Guard and causality analyses respectively guarantee that no update to a guard field or causal dependency between events is missed, because the compiler generates code to track updates, manage broadcast groups and handle dynamic class loading. We are currently refining the core abstractions of our language framework (e.g., reaction synchronization and threading) and extending their options (e.g., correlation with multiple return values). We are also in the process of designing further analyses.

9. REFERENCES

[1] www.streambase.com.

[2] M. Aguilera, R. Strom, D. Sturman, M. Astley, and T. Chandra. Matching Events in a Content-Based Subscription System. In *PODC '99*.

[3] H. Alavi, S. Gilbert, and R. Guerraoui. Extensible Encoding of Type Hierarchies. In *POPL '08*.

[4] S. P. Amarasinghe, M. I. Gordon, M. Karczmarek, J. Lin, D. Maze, R. M. Rabbah, and W. Thies. Language and Compiler Design for Streaming Applications. *International Journal of Parallel Programming*, 33(2-3), 2005.

[5] A. Arasu, S. Babu, and J. Widom. The CQL Continuous Query Language: Semantic Foundations and Query Execution. *The VLDB Journal*, 15(2), 2006.

[6] J. Armstrong, R. Virding, C. Wikström, and M. Williams. *Concurrent Programming in Erlang*. Prentice-Hall, 2nd edition, 1996.

[7] N. Benton, L. Cardelli, and C. Fournet. Modern Concurrency Abstractions for C#. *ACM TOPLAS*, 26(5), 2004.

[8] G. Bierman, E. Meijer, and W. Schulte. The Essence of Data Access in Cω. In *ECOOP'05*.

[9] J.-P. Briot, R. Guerraoui, and K. Löhr. Concurrency, Distribution and Parallelism in Object-Oriented Programming. *ACM Computing Surveys*, 30(3), 1998.

[10] A. Carzaniga, D. Rosenblum, and A. Wolf. Design and Evaluation of a Wide Area Event Notification Service. *ACM TOCS*, 19(3), 2001.

[11] B. Chin and T. D. Millstein. Responders: Language Support for Interactive Applications. In *ECOOP'06*.

[12] G. Cugola, E. D. Nitto, and A. Fuggetta. The JEDI Event-Based Infrastructure and Its Application to the Development of the OPSS WFMS. *IEEE TSE*, 27(9), 2001.

[13] A. Demers, J. Gehrke, M. Hong, M. Riedewald, and W. White. Towards Expressive Publish/Subscribe Systems. In *EDBT'06*.

[14] P. Eugster. Type-based Publish/Subscribe: Concepts and Experiences. *ACM TOPLAS*, 29(1), 2007.

[15] P. Eugster and K. Jayaram. EventJava: An Extension of Java for Event Correlation. In *ECOOP'09*.

[16] C. Fournet and C. Gonthier. The Reflexive Chemical Abstract Machine and the Join Calculus. In *POPL'96*.

[17] D. Gay, P. Levis, R. von Behren, M. Welsh, E. Brewer, and D. Culler. The *nesC* Language: A Holistic Approach to Networked Embedded Systems. In *PLDI'03*.

[18] M. Haahr, R. Meier, P. Nixon, V. Cahill, and E. Jul. Filtering and Scalability in the ECO Distributed Event Model. In *PDSE'00*.

[19] P. Haller and T. V. Cutsem. Implementing Joins using Extensible Pattern Matching. In *COORDINATION'09*.

[20] P. Haller and M. Odersky. Scala Actors: Unifying Thread-based and Event-based Programming. *Theoretical Computer Science*, 410(2-3), 2009.

[21] A. Holzer, L. Ziarek, K. R. Jayaram, and P. Eugster. Putting Events in Context: Aspects for Event-based Distributed Programming. In *AOSD'11*.

[22] Y. Huang and H. Garcia-Molina. Parameterized Subscriptions in Publish/Subscribe Systems. *Data Knowl. Eng.*, 60, 2007.

[23] S. V. Itzstein and D. Kearney. The Expression of Common Concurrency Patterns in Join Java. In *PDPTA'04*.

[24] K. R. Jayaram and P. Eugster. Scalable Efficient Composite Event Detection. In *COORDINATION'10*.

[25] K. R. Jayaram, C. Jayalath, and P. Eugster. Parametric Subscriptions for Content-based Publish/Subscribe Networks. In *Middleware'10*.

[26] G. Kiczales, E. Hilsdale, J. Hugunin, M. Kersten, J. Palm, and W. Griswold. An Overview of AspectJ. In *ECOOP'01*.

[27] L. Lamport. Time, Clocks, and the Ordering of Events in a Distributed System. *CACM*, 21(7), 1978.

[28] G. Li and H.-A. Jacobsen. Composite Subscriptions in Content-Based Publish/Subscribe Systems. In *Middleware '05*.

[29] L. Navarro, M. Südholt, W. Vanderperren, B. D. Fraine, and D. Suvée. Explicitly Distributed AOP using AWED. In *AOSD'06*.

[30] M. Nishizawa. Remote Pointcut: A Language Construct for Distributed AOP. In *AOSD '04*.

[31] B. Oki, M. Pfluegl, A. Siegel, and D. Skeen. The Information Bus - An Architecture for Extensible Distributed Systems. In *SOSP'93*.

[32] A. Petrounias and S. Eisenbach. Fairness for Chorded Languages. In *COORDINATION'09*.

[33] H. Plociniczak and S. Eisenbach. Jerlang: Erlang with Joins. In *COORDINATION'10*.

[34] D. Popescu. Impact Analysis for Event-based Components and Systems. In *ICSE'10 Doctoral Symposium*.

[35] H. Rajan and G. T. Leavens. Ptolemy: A Language with Quantified, Typed Events. In *ECOOP'08*.

[36] J. H. Reppy and Y. Xiao. Specialization of CML Message-passing Primitives. In *POPL'07*.

[37] A. Schiper, K. Birman, and P. Stephenson. Lightweight Causal and Atomic Group Multicast. *ACM TOCS*, 9, 1991.

[38] J. H. Spring, J. Privat, R. Guerraoui, and J. Vitek. Streamflex: High throughput Stream Programming in Java. In *OOPSLA'07*.

[39] J. Stokes. *How a stray mouse click choked the NYSE & cost a bank $150K*, 2010.

[40] Sun Microsystems Inc. *Java Message Service - Specification, version 1.1*, 2005.

[41] N. Tatbul, U. Çetintemel, and S. B. Zdonik. Staying FIT: Efficient Load Shedding Techniques for Distributed Stream Processing. In *VLDB'07*.

[42] Z. Tatlock, C. Tucker, D. Shuffelton, R. Jhala, and S. Lerner. Deep Typechecking and Refactoring. In *OOPSLA'08*.

[43] E. Wohlstadter, S. Jackson, and P. Devanbu. DADO: Enhancing Middleware to Support Crosscutting Features in Distributed, Heterogeneous Systems. In *ICSE '03*.

Towards Proactive Event-Driven Computing

Yagil Engel   Opher Etzion

IBM - Haifa Research Lab
Haifa, Israel
{yagile,opher}@il.ibm.com

ABSTRACT

Event driven architecture is a paradigm shift from traditional computing architectures which employ synchronous, request-response interactions. In this paper we introduce a conceptual architecture for what can be considered the next phase of that evolution: proactive event-driven computing. Proactivity refers to the ability to mitigate or eliminate undesired future events, or to identify and take advantage of future opportunities, by applying prediction and automated decision making technologies. We investigate an extension of the event processing conceptual model and architecture to rt proactive event-driven applications, and propose the main building blocks of a novel architecture. We first describe several extensions to the existing event processing functionality that is required to support proactivity; next, we extend the event processing agent model to include two more type of agents: predictive agents that may derive future uncertain events based on prediction models, and proactive agents that compute the best proactive action that should be taken. Those building blocks are demonstrated through a comprehensive scenario that deals with proactive decision making, ensuring timely delivery of critical material for a production plant.

Categories and Subject Descriptors

H.1.0 [**Information Systems**]: Models and Principles:General

General Terms

Design

Keywords

Proactive, Event Processing

1. INTRODUCTION

Event driven architectures and conceptual models that support them have evolved in the last several years, departing from the traditional computing architectures which employ synchronous, request-response interactions between client and servers. This is a paradigm shift in two senses: first, event driven architectures support applications that are reactive in nature, in which processing is triggered in

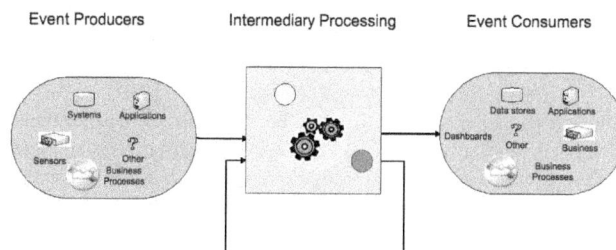

Figure 1: Components of Event-Driven Architecture.

response to events, contrary to traditional responsive applications, in which processing is done in response to an explicit request. Second, event driven architecture adhere to the decoupling principle, in which there are event producers, event consumers and event processing agents that are mutually independent. Figure 1 shows an illustration of such architecture [7].

We introduce a conceptual architecture for what can be considered as the next phase of the evolution: proactive event-driven computing. Proactivity refers to the ability to mitigate or eliminate undesired future events, or to identify and take advantage of future opportunities, by applying prediction and automated decision making technologies. Consider the three examples in Figure 2. A *responsive* application is the one where a student is querying the Web in order to get material needed for writing a school assignment; many consumer and enterprise applications are of the same type (e.g. getting quote from insurance company, querying a data warehouse for a summary of sales in a certain segment). A *reactive* application detects a traffic jam, either by a single camera observation (raw event), or by summing up the number of vehicles that enter a road segment within a certain time interval (a complex event), and reacts by changing a street light schedule. The third is an example of a *proactive* application: a technician is delayed at a customer's house, and because there is also a traffic jam, he is expected to miss the next scheduled customer he should visit; while this has not happened yet, we wish to eliminate this anticipated event, by rescheduling the planning of all the technician team.

Proactive applications have been developed in an ad-hoc manner for several years; in particular in the IT infrastructure and management domain. Some examples include proactive security systems [5], proactive routing in mobile ad-hoc wireless networks [14], proactive network management with failure handling [8], proactive SLA negotiation in service oriented systems [17], and proactive caching [13]. Observing the evolution from responsive to reactive computing, we note that reactive applications have been developed for many years in ad-hoc hard-coded sporadic fashions; however, the major breakthrough that turned event-driven application perva-

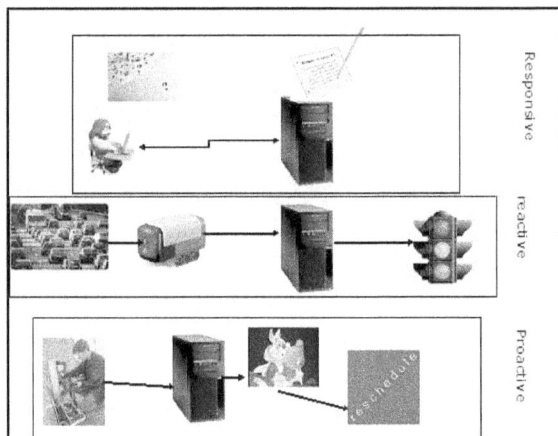

Figure 2: Evolution of computing paradigms.

sive and part of the main-stream computing was the development of models and tools to express and execute reactive systems in an easy way. A similar breakthrough is required in order to enable pervasive use of proactive computing, instead of ad-hoc, multiple models "gluing" employed today.

Several factors in today's computing infrastructure open the door for such a generic evolvement: (i) the growing availability of cheap and pervasive sensor technology, (ii) the spreading of broadband connectivity, pretty much anywhere, and (iii) the developments in predictive analytics technology. The latter highlights a different angle to this process. Analytics has evolved from being merely *descriptive* (understanding of historical data), to being *predictive* (providing forecasts of future behavior). The next step is *prescriptive analytics*, a term which stands for the use of data to prescribe the best course of action to realize the best outcome [24]. We can view the proactive idea as the event-driven variation of prescriptive analytics; reactive computing, coupled with predictive analytics, yields the ability to react to events *before* they occur, which is the essence of proactive event-driven computing.

After motivating the proactive event-driven paradigm using examples below, we introduce the conceptual model and architecture of proactive event-driven applications. In Section 2 we discuss the concepts and facilities of event driven architecture and event processing conceptual model, and provide essential background on the decision making models we employ; in Section 3 we overview our approach for proactive architecture, in Sections 4, 5, and 6 we drill down to explain the new architecture constructs: predictive agents and proactive agents, and in Section 7 we show a complete scenario modeled with the conceptual architecture we presented.

1.1 Example Scenarios

There are numerous examples for the applicability of proactive event-driven computing, ranging from instantaneous operational control, through financial markets, and to heavy industries. We begin with the following example scenarios, provided by IBM customers and business partners, in order to give a flavor of the type of problems we address.

EXAMPLE 1 ([3]). *A power company controls both the production of electric power, as well as its allocation to different geographic areas. This is a typical resource management setting: given a set of resources (power production in specific plants) and demands (coming from different geographic areas), the overall operational control problem is to manage and allocate resources to*

match demands. *The actions available to the power company correspond to increasing/decreasing production at various costs; for instance, the company can start up diesel generators which are approximately 10 times more expensive than the coal generators. In addition, the company can launch emergency fix to many or all of its coal generators; coal generators normally lose some of their production capacity over time, and are fixed according to a regular maintenance schedule. Finally, power companies can also affect consumption through particular pricing mechanisms with industrial consumers; the contract with these consumers defines the timing in which a price increase can be announced.*

The example above represents a typical enterprise operational control problem of resource management and allocation in face of uncertainty about resource availability and the demand for the enterprise's services. Two kinds of actions are typically available to the system: actions that change resource-allocation policy, and actions that affect the availability of resources for a certain period of time. In many cases events affecting production and demand can be forecasted in advance; for example, consumption is affected by weather conditions. Production is also affected by particular conditions: for example, severe weather conditions may harm coal generators and power lines; sun and wind affect renewable power production. These weather conditions can in turn be predicted rather accurately using various measurements. The role of the proactive application in this scenario would be: (i) detect those early measurements and predictive factors using standard event processing means (e.g., detect an event pattern that usually precedes a generator failure), (ii) generate event prediction, and (iii) alter the policy given the specific prediction (e.g., emergency fix of all generators).

EXAMPLE 2. *A chemical and petroleum (C&P) company operates various heavy machinery. The overall objective is to minimize maintenance costs while preventing damage to machines and ensuring maintenance is performed at convenient times. In recent years it becomes evident that following manufacturers' maintenance schedules is overly conservative; these schedules are designed for a worst case scenario, whereas in practice preventive maintenance should depend on the actual condition of the machine, which in turn depends on its usage and operation environment. The alternative is a* proactive maintenance approach: *track the machine condition using various indicators, and if a change in a machine condition is predicted, adapt the maintenance policy.*

The role of the proactive application in this scenario is similar in nature to the previous example: (i) detect events that can predict a change in machinery condition, (ii) forecast the specific change of condition, and (iii) change maintenance policy accordingly.

EXAMPLE 3. *Logistics scenarios of long distance shipping usually require complex planning, and involves high degree of uncertainty due to the dependency on several shipping companies, on traffic and weather conditions, customs procedures, insurance, and others. These factors often require a change of plans during the scenario execution. Currently, many freight providers use various software solutions for plan optimization; however, when the need for plan change arises, the online nature of the decision often leads to highly sub-optimal results. A proactive system can greatly enhance the online decision making in this domain; we illustrate that with a modeling example in Section 7.*

2. BACKGROUND AND RELATED WORK

We now provide background in several areas: conceptual modeling of *event processing (EP)*, uncertainty in event processing, and models for optimal decision making over time.

2.1 The conceptual model of event processing

The conceptual model of proactive event-driven applications is built as an incremental part over the existing work in event processing architectures, thus we briefly survey the concepts we are using. At the heart of this model is the notion of *event processing network (EPN)*; looking back at Figure 1, there is a layer of intermediary event processing that stands between the event producers and consumers. This layer is not monolithic, but rather consists of various types of processing elements called *event processing agents (EPA)*, each performing single type of processing. The notion of event processing network has been defined by Luckham [15] and refined by Etzion and Niblett [7] as a collection of event processing agents, producers, and consumers connected by a collection of channels. A channel is a processing element that receives events from one or more sources and routes them to one or more sinks. Event processing agents are further refined into types, as shown in Figure 3.

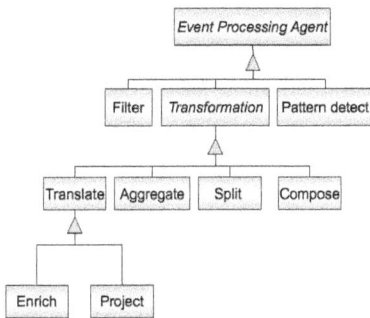

Figure 3: Event Processing Agent Types

The main types of event processing agents are as follows. *Filter* decides whether an event continues to flow in the system, based on satisfaction of an assertion; *transformation* derives events as function of input events in various ways (e.g. aggregation); and *pattern detection* derives events based on detection of patterns. In the logistic use case, an example for an event pattern is the scanning of all the items in a delivery, except one, in a location; this indicates a missing item. In the C&P scenario, an abnormal series of signals from a machine may indicate a failure.

2.2 Inexact event processing

Current models are based on the assumption that the events processed by an EPN based system are certain. However, in reality there are cases where event processing becomes inexact. Uncertainty can be on whether an event actually occurred, on the content within the event's payload, or on the matching between the situation that is to be detected, and the pattern that is used to detect this situation.

Inexactness may refer both to raw events and derived events; one of the reasons for inexactness is the propagation, i.e., an input event to an EPA is by itself an inexact derived event, thus the inexactness is propagated further. Several related studies have been conducted that have taken probabilistic approach. Among them were the investigation of probabilistic event propagation rules using Bayesian Networks [29]; application of probabilistic query techniques on stream events [23], and models for causal probabilistic networks using logic programming [27].

2.3 Markov Decision Processes

Our vision for proactive computing relies heavily on the solution of dynamic and uncertain decision problems. We provide background on the model we consider the most appropriate in this setting; this background is essential for understanding Sections 3.2 and 6.1.

A *Markov Decision Process (MDP)* is a quadruple $\langle \mathcal{S}, R, \mathcal{A}, T \rangle$, where $\mathcal{S}$ is the state space describing the world, and $R : \mathcal{S} \to \Re$ is the *reward function*, indicating a numeric value of being one time step in a given state. $\mathcal{A}$ is a set of actions, and $T : \mathcal{S} \times \mathcal{A} \times \mathcal{S} \to [0, 1]$ is a transition function with $T(s, \alpha, s')$ capturing the probability of achieving state s' by applying action α in state s; for each $(s, \alpha) \in \mathcal{S} \times \mathcal{A}$, $\sum_{s' \in \mathcal{S}} T(s, a, s') = 1$.

MDP models a sequence of decision points over time. A solution to an MDP is a *policy* $\pi : \mathcal{S} \to \mathcal{A}$, indicating the optimal action to perform at each state. During runtime, it is expected that at each time point the system observes its current state $s \in \mathcal{S}$ and executes $\pi(s)$. The criterion for optimality is measured by a *value function* $v_\pi : \mathcal{S} \to \Re$, which indicates the long-term value of performing the action $\pi(s)$ at state s. Long-term value can be measured in several ways; the most common model is *infinite-horizon accumulated discounted reward*. Infinite horizon indicates that the value is measured as if the process continues forever, however the discount factor $\gamma < 1$ indicates that future time steps worth less than the current time step; the reward at time $x + t$ in state s is worth $\gamma^t R(s)$ when we are at time x. The utility of a sequence of states $[s_0, s_1, s_2, \ldots]$ is therefore $\sum_{t=0}^{\infty} \gamma^t R(s_t)$. With $\gamma < 1$ this value is finite. However, when we are at state s_0 we do not know what is the sequence of future states, therefore the value $v(s_0)$ should indicate the expected utility from the future sequence. This can be calculated recursively using the *Bellman Equation*:

$$v(s) = R(s) + \gamma \max_{a \in A} \sum_{s' \in \mathcal{S}} T(s, a, s') v(s')$$

In words, the value of being at state s is the reward at the current state, plus the (discounted) expectation over the value of the next state. This equation inspires the common solution scheme for MDPs, called *value iteration*, in which the solution is calculated by iteratively going though all the states and updating their values according to the current values of their neighboring states. A second scheme, called *policy iteration*, is iteratively improving a given policy by solving a system of linear equations or by performing several value iteration steps. For more details on MDP and solution methods we refer to Boutilier et al. [2].

The typical drawback of the MDP model is that the space of real problems tends to be large. In fact, state spaces are usually constructed as the cartesian product of the domains of a set of variables $V = \{v_1, \ldots, v_n\}$, also called *state features*. Of course, this turns the size of the state space exponential in the number of its features. To overcome this difficulty, various methods were proposed to maintain a state space factored according to its features and perform solution algorithms directly on the factored space; when the state features are sufficiently decoupled this means that the number of actual states we consider is much smaller than the size of the cartesian products. We refer to Guestrin et al. [9] and subsequent works for more details.

Another practical caveat is associated with the discount factor. The discount factor is essential in ensuring that the utility of an infinite sequence of states is finite. However, in the business scenarios we consider, a discount factor is typically not that realistic. For example, an energy company will not consider a power outage next week less significant than a power outage this week. An alternative policy optimality criterion is to calculate *non-discounted average reward.* However when this is calculated over infinite time horizon, one needs to add a *bias function* towards the initial states; otherwise the result is independent of the current state and the value function becomes meaningless. We do not elaborate on this technical issue and refer to Mahadevan [16] for details.

3. APPROACH

We commence with a high-level description of our approach.

3.1 Overview

In this work we lay out our proposal for a proactive event-driven architecture. The design strives to achieve two requirements which are natural in operational systems: (i) *tractability* is essential for practicality of the solution, and (ii) *optimality*, which in this context refers to the optimal exploitation of information. The two modules of our proposed architecture represent these two types of requirements. On the one hand, current event-processing systems have capability to digest large amounts of online information while avoiding complex world models; they use rules in order to identify specific situations of interest. On the other hand, work in related fields such as Operational Research (OR) and Artificial Intelligence (AI) lays out decision management frameworks that employ a model of the relevant world; they encapsulate all relevant information available to the system and behave optimally given that information. We believe that these two extreme approaches fit naturally into a single architecture that enjoys the benefits of both; decision making should be done by a comprehensive (either model-based or not) system, which at least provides the means to exploit all available information in order to make a decision, whereas an event processing system can be used to reduce the complexity of the model by synthesizing the online data to specific bits of information which have direct effect on decisions.

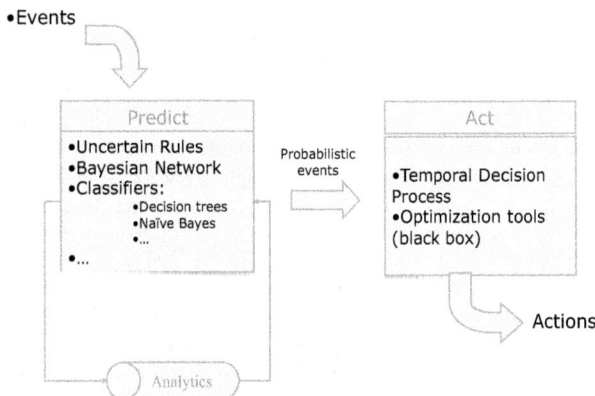

Figure 4: Architecture Overview

This is the motivation for our two modules architecture, depicted in Figure 4. The module *predict* is a predictive event processing system. It processes streams of incoming events, and sends derived events to the module *act*. The derived events can be predicted to occur in the future, and can be probabilistic, which means that the event processing system is not only capable of identifying current, certain situations, but also performs probabilistic and temporal reasoning. However, because the module *predict* does not need to take the actual decision, it does not require a world model but only specific predictive models which mostly output probabilistic future events based on (probabilistic) current and past events. In the energy scenario, the EP module will process all weather indicators, calendar events, and other factors that can affect consumption and production; based on these, it will generate specific timed predictions regarding expected variations in production, consumption, and power outages. The predictive models can be learned from data, using an analytics (sub) module, or built from expert knowledge. Similar to current event-processing systems [7], we envision the processing capability to be distributed through *event-processing agents*.

The second module, *act*, contains a decision making mechanism. It is initialized with a world model, and initially solved offline to obtain an optimal decision policy. *act* is triggered by events predictions provided by the module *predict*, and it is expected to incorporate the probabilistic information carried by the event predictions to optimize its actions. Those predictions potentially change the world model, in which case *act* incorporates the new information, solves the new model, and recommends changes in policy or specific actions.

The architecture implies several major leaps in comparison to current event processing architectures; the two which stand out are the introduction of model-based decision making module, and the predictive and temporal capabilities of the event processing agents. These and additional extensions are discussed in Section 4.

3.2 General Model

Let S denote the possible states of the world. S can be described by a set of numeric variables (or *features*) $V = \{v_1, \ldots, v_n\}$, with domains $d(v_1), \ldots, d(v_n)$, such that $S = \times_{i=1}^{n} d(v_i)$. Equivalently, we say that a state in S is an assignment to the vector $(v_1, \ldots, v_n)$. The decision maker incur cost, or reward, from being in a particular state. This is modeled via a reward function $R : S \to \Re$. The state of the world can change by two means; namely actions and events, both of which can be described in terms of their stochastic effect on the state of the world.

Such world dynamics is usually modeled as an MDP, in which the events are compiled into the transition function and captured by the stochastic effects of actions. Because our framework should facilitate exploitation of event information, we employ an *explicit event model* [2], which is a tuple $\langle S, V, R, \mathcal{A}, T, \mathcal{E}, T_e \rangle$, where R, $\mathcal{A}$, and T are reward function, actions, and transition model as in MDP. $\mathcal{E}$ is a set of possible distinct events, and $T_e : S \times \mathcal{E} \times S \to [0, 1]$ models the effect of each event on the world, where $T_e(s, e, s')$ denotes the probability that e occurs at s and results in the system moving to state s'. An explicit example of the model is provided for the sample logistics scenario in Section 7.

The events $\mathcal{E}$ are all random variables, for which we may or may not have a prior probability distribution. In addition, we consider the variables in V as random variables too, because in general their value is not deterministic. The decision maker can, however, affect the value of a subset of V through its actions A.

In the energy example, the set of random variables includes all the weather variables, variables whose value can predict weather (such as atmospheric pressure measurements), calendar events, etc. Decision variables are production, consumption, and power outages. The power company has actions such as activation of diesel generators or peak prices declaration; these have stochastic affect on production and consumption (respectively).

The system's input consists of event streams, which provide indication as for the values of any of the variables. In an observable world, we assume that any change of value of a variable either triggers an event which indicates the new value, or can be observed as a global state variable.

4. ENHANCING EP INFRASTRUCTURE

In this section we outline the first pillar in the evolution from event-processing to proactive event-driven computing, which is the extension of the current state-of-the-art in event processing.

4.1 Event Uncertainty and Time Intervals

Proactive systems rely on events, both raw and derived, that may exhibit uncertainties in several levels: meta-data uncertainty, inexactness of the event's occurrence time, and uncertain event derivation. We use probability as a measure for uncertainty; this can be replaced with other interpretations.

4.1.1 Meta-data support

Event meta-data should support uncertainty at two levels: The event level and the attribute level. Event uncertainty is represented by two attributes in the event's header: EventOccuranceProbability, which designates the probability that the event happens, and UncertainAttributeProbabilities which consists of a list of pairs <attribute-name, probability> for each attribute whose value's probability is less than 1. The defaults for the former is 1, and for the latter is an empty list, together making the regular event processing assumptions a default.

4.1.2 Inexact occurrence time

In the proactive framework, event occurrence time can be a result of probabilistic prediction, and hence be inexact. However, there are various known issues in the accuracy of occurrence time even in conventional systems, where occurrence time is the timestamp in which an event happened in reality, as reported by the event source. We address both cases by assuming that the event occurred somewhere within an interval, and the exact time point is unknown. There are several complications caused by supporting intervals:

Distribution over the interval: A simple approach is to assume that all time points within the interval have equal probability, approximating it to uniform distribution. In many cases a normal distribution (meaning that the event is more likely to occur around the center of the interval) can be more appropriate, and in yet other settings an exponential distribution (where the event is becoming more likely as more time passes) is the most applicable. We thus add to the event's header a possibility to designate the occurrence time in interval and the distribution function over that interval.

Pattern matching: When event time is uncertain, there are various ways to order sets of events, hence the detection of event sequences becomes problematic. This problem has been addressed in the literature; we refer in particular to Zhang et al. [31].

Context window: This problem is addressed in Section 4.2.

4.1.3 Support of assignment of inexactness

The probabilistic values for the events and attributes are provided by the source. When the source is an external event producer, it should provide the probabilities, either explicitly, or by the systems assigning defaults associated with this particular producer. When the source is an EPA deriving event, then the EPA functionality is extended to derive the event probability along with the time interval. We currently limit attribute uncertainty to be triggered only by external producers.

4.2 Future and Inexact Context

Recent work on the Event-Processing paradigm establishes the key role of the concept of *context* [7, 6]. The term context refers to several usages: (i) *temporal context* divides the stream of events into time slices, (ii) *segmentation context* divides the event stream according to some segmentation function, for example the value of a single attribute (e.g., customer id), or a condition over several attribute values, and (iii) *state context* allows an EPA to be active or not, depending on values of state variables. Of these, only the temporal context is sensitive to the changes introduced in Section 4.1. A temporal context is *opened* when the time window associated with the context begins, and *closes* when the time window ends. EPA instance is associated with a specific context; for example, an EPA that detects a sequence (e_1, e_2, e_3) during a working day is created per working day. In our architecture, temporal context should be able to support two novel functionalities:

Context for intervals Continuing the example, assume we encounter e_1 whose occurrence time is between 7am and 9am. Assuming a working day starts at 8am, the event could belong to either context windows; the event should therefore be duplicated; the probability of which it belongs to each of the windows is computed according to the distribution of e_1 occurrence time over the interval.

Future context Some existing event processing systems enable the assignment of occurrence time and hence may also derive future values; however, without the support of processing within future contexts, such system cannot take advantage of this information. A proactive system must process contexts that relate to *future windows at the present time*; but this requires careful implementation. A temporal context for a present time window is usually triggered by a calendar event; in our example a context will be opened every day at 8am and closed at 5pm. *Future contexts* should be opened for specific time windows in the future, only when there is a chance to detect a pattern during that context. In our example, a context should be opened for day x only after receiving a prediction that e_1 will occur in day x. Note that for other types of patterns the requirements may be different.

4.3 Proactive EPN

The network presented in Figure 5 is built on event-processing architecture laid out by Etzion and Niblett [7], and elaborates on the overview given in Figure 4. The *predict* module of Figure 4 is implemented through EPAs, which, as in standard event processing, receive their input (e_1, e_2) from event producers and generate derived events. The events are channelled to (predictive) EPAs.[1] EPAs analyze input event streams and potentially use predictive models to generate derived events (d_1, d_2, d_3), which can be at any time point or interval, and can indicate uncertainty via probability of occurrence. EPAs transfer events to other EPAs downstream, or to a novel building block, which is the *proactive agent (PRA)*.

The role of the PRA is to implement the *act* module from Figure 4; it derives optimal decision policy based on all the currently available information. A PRA receives events, potentially uncertain and in future time, updates its internal state, and sometimes performs an internal optimization process. If it decides that an action needs to be taken, it outputs action request or action recommendation (depends on the role of the system in the global operation). The actions (e.g., A_1) are sent to a specific type of event consumers called *actuators*.

Next, we describe several of the design decisions associated with the network in Figure 5.

Event Life Span: In current systems, derived events are retained as active in the system as long as they are processed by EPAs; when they are consumed, they can be "forgotten". In contrast, event predictions must be retained in the system until overridden by the real event it predicts. More explicitly, under the new architecture a derived event could represent an uncertain future event, and as such its information may change until the actual time it will occur or not.

---

[1] We ignore the function of *channels*, which remains similar to current architectures as described for example by Etzion and Niblett.

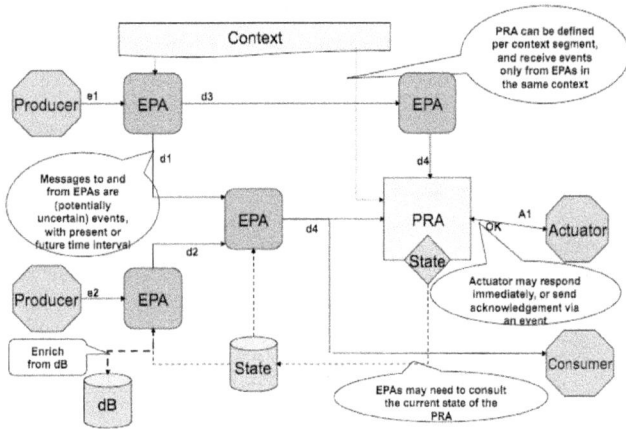

Figure 5: Proactive Event Processing Network

Most commonly, new information may indicate that its probability of occurrence changed, or that the expected time changed. This requires a new treatment of an event instance as an object which can be processed multiple times.

Response from actuators: Currently, an EP system may trigger action, but as a derived event the triggered action is again forgotten and the system is not expected to follow its execution. An acknowledgement can possibly be sent back as an event, but such an event is treated just like any other event. In our architecture the system activates external actuators, and must get feedback about: (i) whether or not an action was taken, (ii) when the action was taken, and (iii) what was the action's result and associated events. This is because *the result affects the world model on which the system operates*. For example, if our system decides to perform emergency generator fix, it should know what is the resulting capacity of the generators in order to update its production model. The feedback can be provided through events; we believe, however, that there is benefit in allowing direct request / response communication (as depicted with the "OK" response in Figure 5) between proactive agents and actuators; for example, to allow the proactive agent to suggest an alternative action, in the same timestep, in case its first recommendation cannot be executed.

Multiple Proactive Agents: The network allows using more than a single proactive agent; this will be useful in situation where the set of decision variables (see Section 6) can be partitioned into subsets, and A can be divided to (not necessarily disjoint) subsets $A^1, \ldots, A^m$ such that actions in A^i affect the variables in one subset, and does not affect the rest of the variables. For example, we might have several deliveries being shipped at the same time in close geographic locations, and assume they require different kinds of resources because they contain different type of goods. They are all affected from the same random variables, but the routing decisions in one do not affect the performance of the other hence the decision can be done independently.

State Variables: The communication between predictive agents and proactive agents is in one direction: predictive agents send events to proactive agents. However, proactive agents change the state variables V, which may be used as features in the EPAs' predictive models; this can be considered as means for the other direction of communication. Such situation comes up in the example scenario in Section 7.

Enrichment: As in standard event-processing, agents can enrich events with information from database. This is particularly

important in proactive applications, because the dynamic decision making done by the active module may rely on information (such as resource availability) which changes over time.

Extensions that should be made to the concepts of event and context are discussed in this section above; the evolvement of EPAs to become *predictive* is discussed in Section 5. Implementations of PRA are discussed in Section 6.

5. PREDICTIVE AGENTS

The predictive agent in our architecture is foremost an extension of the event-processing agent. We build on the capability to process (potentially large) streams of input events, and detect patterns that were predefined. The main difference is that the derived events that an agent generates may not be certain (i.e., indicate the probability of occurrence), and may have specific time interval in which it is expected to occur with the specified probability. Most of the patterns that EP agents handle today, and are used for detection of particular situations, are also applicable for detection of future events probabilistically; in many cases their operation is in fact similar to their function today. For example, a weather system today may process various weather indicators and generate *storm alerts*. If we also wish to know when the storm will occur, we will define various events such as "storm within an hour", "storm this afternoon", and so on. In the predictive EP framework, this capability will be inherent, along with the ability to specify the *probability* of the storm over a *time interval*.

As can be understood from the scenarios in Section 1.1, we envision a wide range of applications for proactive event-driven computing. Applications vary in the criticality of operations, in the available historical data, and in the available domain expertise; therefore an architecture should be flexible enough to accommodate various levels of comprehensiveness in its input. We thus propose several models for predictive agents: from simple rule-based agents, which basically enhance today's EP agents with probabilistic and temporal information, up to agents which incorporate an elaborate temporal probabilistic predictive model.

5.1 Rule-Based Predictive Agents

Event Processing Agents (EPAs) under standard EP paradigm turn a stream of input events into specific derived events. Simple EPAs detect a specific event and translate it into a derived event (which may for example represent an alert), and more complex agents perform pattern matching, which can become quite sophisticated, on the input stream and generate derived events when the pattern they seek is matched. A basic extension to this model is that derived events are generated with degree of uncertainty, which is part of the agent's definition. For example, a pattern matching agent may detect a sequence of events, of the form (e_1, e_2), and generate a derived event ϵ with probability p of occurrence.

In addition, the agent's derivation rule will include a time interval. Extending the previous example, we might have an agent whose derivation rule is *if the sequence (e_1, e_2) is detected, then event ϵ will occur in $5 - 10$ time step with probability p.* Formally, a *derivation rule* in the proactive architecture is a tuple $\rho = \langle \pi, \epsilon, p, t \rangle$, where π is an event pattern, $\epsilon \in \mathcal{E}$ is the derived event, which is expected to occur if π is encountered, p is a probability measurement, and t is a time interval in which ϵ is expected to occur with probability p. p can also be defined to indicate a probability distribution of the occurrence time of e over t.

A rule set can model some predictions very naturally. In particular, they are geared towards the detection of specific patterns, where we are merely interested in the occurrence or non-occurrence of the pattern and wish to avoid specifying a complete conditional probability distribution over the derived event. However, rules have limitation, as we consider next.

5.1.1 Partial Satisfaction of Rules

In many types of event patterns, arrival of some events immediately changes the probability that the rule will be satisfied. For example, if $\pi = (e_1, e_2)$, and e_1 occurs, the probability that π occurs usually increases. In the context of the proactive network, this should trigger a derived event with the new probability of ϵ. However, without additional information in the rule definition there is no way to determine what that probability is; this depends on the prior distributions over e_1 and e_2 which are not part of that definition. Because we do not have conditional probability information among the elements of a pattern, in order to trigger a probability update given partial satisfaction of π, one must define a rule for any partial pattern that should trigger such a derived event. In the example above, we will add a rule ρ' with $\pi' = e_1$, and p', t' indicating the probability and time interval that ϵ occurs if we just encountered e_1.

5.1.2 Probabilistic Pattern Matching

An event processing network facilitates layered handling of events in the sense that derived events from one agent can serve as input events to another agent. This emphasizes the following requirement: input events (those captured by the pattern π) can also be uncertain. The probability of events in π must of course affect p, the probability of the derived event ϵ. The computation of the probability of a pattern of probabilistic events is not trivial, in particular when events appear multiple times within a context and the pattern can have multiple overlapping matches. A comprehensive formalization of this setting is presented by Wasserkrug et al. [28, 29]. The problem of probabilistic pattern matching is similar to the problem of confidence computation for query results on uncertain databases with lineage, problem which has been studied by Sarma et al. [26].

5.2 Bayesian Agents

The two limitations above can be overcome through the use of *predicitve models*. Bayesian networks [21] (BN) is a powerful predictive model, allowing various levels of probabilistic reasoning. It consists of a *directed acyclic graph (DAG)*, whose nodes correspond to random variables, and in each node there is a *conditional probability table (CPT)*, which indicates the probability of each value of the variable represented by that node, given any combination of values of the variables represented by its parents in the graph. The set of edges of the graph represents the structure of probabilistic dependence between the random variables. Avoiding the technical details, we indicate that in general the less interdependent the random variables are, the graph becomes more sparse, the representation more compact, and the probabilistic reasoning algorithms perform faster. The most common type of query in BN is called *belief assessment*: given new information, called *evidence*, which is usually a certain assignment to a subset of the variables, we ask what is the probability of a given subset of variables (the *query variables*). The rest are *hidden* variables: we do not know their value, nor are we asked what is their probability.

In a predictive EPN, we can employ a BN which will have a single leaf, corresponding to a derived event, which is always the query variable. Incoming events serve as evidence. Each time a new relevant event comes in, it triggers a belief assessment query which is answered through a reasoning algorithm. There is rich literature on exact and approximate belief assessment (e.g., [21]). If the graphical structure corresponds to a *polytree* (i.e. there are no

indirected cycles), then even exact inference is proven to be polynomial [21].

To clarify, the use of BN we offer here is different than the automatically generated BN described in the context of rule based EP [28, 29], in which the BN serve as an algorithmic tool for probabilistic reasoning; this approach can be applied by rule based agents in the proactive system. Here we propose that a proactive system should have the knowledge representation capabilities of BN. BN can represent any probability distribution over the random variables, $V \cup E$. This means that we can model any expert or learned knowledge regarding the probabilistic relationship between random variables in the system, in order to generate event predictions. For example, in the energy scenario, a BN can serve as a predictive model over energy production, by expressing the complex probabilistic relationship between weather predictors and weather factors (e.g., how barometric pressure predicts rain and / or snow), within the weather factors (e.g., how wind changes the probability of snow), and between weather factors and production factors (e.g., condition of the generators, amount of renewable energy, etc.). A more explicit example is provided in Section 7.

With the use of BN, the support for uncertain input events is inherent. The information in CPTs of roots in the network is the prior distribution over the value of the corresponding random variable; if this information changes as a result of an uncertain input event, we update the CPT and perform belief assessment again. If the input event is not a root, its probability still overrides the conditional probability information held in its CPT, and again it triggers a belief assessment query. It is also very natural to consider partial patterns; the BN can be queried at any time, and respond according to the information it has at the moment, information which may include a part of a pattern that has been seen so far. A rule may still be more convenient to use when the probabilistic information is limited. For example, sequence patterns for which we do not have available explicit probabilities for each sequence element conditional on its predecessors.

5.2.1 Predictions with Time Stamps

In rule-based agents, a time interval is associated with each rule, specifying the delay with which we expect the rule head to occur after the rule body is matched. With Bayesian agents, which have a single leaf corresponding to its derived event, we can achieve a similar capability by attaching a time interval corresponding to the query. However, this will not provide the flexibility to condition those time interval on specific combinations of input event patterns and on specific attribute values. A more comprehensive solution is to enhance the graphical model with temporal information. We propose two existing approaches.

Discrete Time Models Dynamic Bayesian Networks (DBN) [19] allow reasoning over discrete time steps. A DBN includes two copies of the network, each corresponding to a time step, and arcs between time steps represents relationship between variables over time. In complex, real world systems, usage of DBN becomes problematic for various reasons, the most evident of which is that the granularity of the time steps depends on the shortest time between events. Reasoning algorithms are available for our temporal prediction purposes. However, in complex real world system (in particular when there are varying sizes of time steps) DBN reasoning can quickly become intractable.

Continuous Time Models *Continuous time Bayesian Networks (CTBN)* [20] represent temporal relationship between any two nodes in the Bayesian network using a *conditional intensity matrix*. In short, a temporal Markov process over the possible values of a random variable is represented using the parameter of an exponential distribution. When this transition depends on the values of other nodes (either the parents of the variable in the BN or not), then this parameter is specified as a function of the joint values of the nodes it depends on. The representation can also be adapted to other types of distributions, in particular Gaussian distribution, which is more suitable when there is a specific time frame in which an event is likely to occur, and the probability of occurrence is higher closer to the middle of the range.

5.3 Classifying Agents

As mentioned above, the main task a predictive model is facing is to assess the probability of occurrence of a specific event. The BN represents a comprehensive approach, that allows us to take all relevant information into account in order to come up with the most accurate probability estimation. Sometimes this accuracy cannot be achieved because there is not enough data or expert knowledge. A classifier, such as a *decision tree*, does not need to incorporate explicit probability measures. Therefore, training a classifier usually requires substantially less data than training a BN with a similar size. A classifier is a predictive model which, based on a set of input values (corresponding to the evidence), assesses to which of a given set of classes a case belongs. The input values can correspond to detected events, detected event patterns, and state variables. The *case* here is the derived event we care about. On the flip side, a classifier such as decision tree cannot provide the specific probability of the derived event, and it is not well suited to support uncertain input events.

5.4 Training predictive models

Unlike predictive rules, which allow domain experts to easily express specific knowledge of the relationship between current event patterns and future events, comprehensive predictive models are harder to populate with numeric probabilistic and temporal information directly from experts. As indicated in Figure 4, predictive models can be trained by an analytics software component, using historical data. There is rich literature on training predictive models, and the purpose of this section is merely to provide pointers to the works which are most relevant to the proactive architecture.

A framework for performing supervised learning in order to discover predictive patterns in data has been proposed by Han et al. [10]. The input is a set of past records, labeled according to he future event we wish to predict. The algorithm consists of four stages: (1) Partition data according to labels (2) Apply data mining methods to find frequent event patterns in each partition, (3) Define feature set which includes the frequent patterns as features, (4) Perform supervised learning to obtain a predictive model.

Step (2) is probably the most challenging one, and belongs to the realm of data mining. Our setting requires an algorithm which discovers patterns with explicit time stamps, and preferably one that finds the time delay between the predictive pattern and the predicted event, such as MINEPI [18]. Moreover, the EP framework makes common use of event patterns with specific assertions on attributes [7]. In particular, a pattern without the assertion may have no predictive power at all. For example, a series of three deposits to a single bank account within a week may indicate nothing, but a series of three deposits above a certain amount may indicate a case of money laundering, and hence predicts a transfer of funds abroad. A recent approach proposed by Hellerstein et al. [11] deals with multiatttribute event patterns.

Step (3) and (4) are typical machine learning tasks, and the specific algorithm used depends on the type of predictive model we are trying to learn. There is vast literature on learning Bayesian Networks (e.g., [4]), and on learning classifiers (e.g., [25]). Litera-

ture is thinner when it comes to learning temporal models; however there are several works (e.g., [30]) which deal explicitly with learning CTBN over event streams in practical settings. Another line of work which can be exploited deals with learning temporal causal relationships between time series events (e.g., [1]).

To summarize, the problem of training the predictive models in our framework is not a solved problem, but there is sufficient relevant literature on the topic to make it possible.

6. PROACTIVE AGENTS

A proactive agent dynamically computes optimal policy based on the current information it has available. In this section we elaborate on several candidate implementation approaches; as in the case of predictive agents, one solution does not fit all, and the right approach should be selected on a case by case basis, according to the characteristics of the system.

6.1 Decision Theoretic Agent

The problems in the scope of proactive event-driven computing are essentially those of operational control, which involve decision making under uncertainty and over time. The common approach in OR and AI is to model these settings as an MDP. Conceptually, the factored state space of the MDP could correspond to V, thus contain any possible combination of values of the variables $v_1, \ldots, v_n$. There are several problems with such approach: first, V includes all factors that can affect the decision, other directly or indirectly. For example, in the energy scenario, any measurement which contributes to weather predictions must be included. This implies that n will most likely be too large to allow any tractable reasoning algorithm. (ii) MDP contains a complete transition model over the state space; this implies in particular that we must have prior probability distribution over the set of events $\mathcal{E}$, because they potentially affect state transitions. In many cases this information is not available. (iii) Even if prior information is available, it becomes useless once we receive a prediction with updated probabilities of specific events in the near future; such a prediction changes the transition function and render the computed policy potentially suboptimal.

To overcome these difficulties, we exploit the following assumption, which is motivated by the scenarios of Section 1.1: our typical systems have a default work mode which is applicable *most* of the time. In our example scenarios, the petroleum company has a default maintenance policy, the power company has its usual consumption/production profile, and logistics scenarios usually progress according to the plan. We model this "normal" or "default" dynamics of the world as follows: Let $M^0 = \langle \mathcal{S}_d, V_d, R, A, T^0 \rangle$, where $V_d \subset V$, and $\mathcal{S}_d$ is the projection of $\mathcal{S}$ on V_d. This MDP is therefore a sub-MDP of the global model introduced in Section 3.2. The choice of V_d is part of the design of the system: these are the *decision variables*, and should minimally include any variable which can be affected by the actions in A. V_d includes additional variables if: (i) they are expected to change often, and (ii) we can obtain a prior probability distribution over their values and transitions. T^0 represents the transition probability over the state space $\mathcal{S}_d$.

Different events (e.g., heat-wave, equipment failure, or a major televised event) will have different effects on the dynamics of the system, and hence would change the transition function in different ways. Therefore, our MDP is more generally described as $M(E) = \langle \mathcal{S}_d, V_d, R, A, T(E) \rangle$, where $E \in dom(\mathcal{E})$.[2]

---

[2]We do not consider the question of how this mapping from $\mathcal{E}$ to MDPs is represented internally. A reasonable representation could be a Dynamic Bayesian Network (see [2]) in which the exogenous variable(s) appear in the first (pre-action) layer, but not in the post-action layer.

A basic assumption we make is that M^0 has been solved, possibly offline, using value or policy iteration. Therefore its optimal π^0 and v^0 are known. This reflects the typical case, in which a system has a default operation policy in use. As described in Section 3.1, a proactive agent receives input events from (predictive) event processing agents. These events can either be current, certain events, or future events. Current events affect values of variables in V_d, and hence trigger a change of state in M^0. Future events may also be uncertain, and they essentially change the transition function T^0. If the current MDP is $M(E)$, a future event e changes the MDP to $M(E \cup \{e\})$. When the time interval associated with e passes, or when e occurs and hence not expected to occur again, the MDP changes back; if at the time the MDP is $M(E)$ it changes to $M(E \setminus \{e\})$. In practice, based on the scenarios we examine above, we expect that future events which we care about will not occur very often; usually, after receiving prediction of event e, the system will return to its default mode M^0 before a new prediction e' is obtained. Hence operation will usually be according to M^0, with deviations of the form $M(\{e\})$.

Whenever a new future event is received by the PRA, the PRA decides whether the optimal policy should be recomputed, given the information that a new transition model will be in place for a given period of time. This decision, and the computation of a new policy given a prediction (*replanning*) are challenging problems, in particular because they are done in realtime, during system operation, and often the system must act before a new optimal policy is computed. The exploration of this problem and various solution methods are the topic of a parallel work [3].

6.1.1 Sampling Methods

Because exhaustive MDP solving is often intractable, rich literature exists on solutions that employ sampling methods instead of exhaustive search. Two directions are particularly promising: *Approximate Dynamic Programming (ADP)* [22] is a collection of methods that approximate a value function by iteratively running future trajectories. These methods are suitable for real time computation because they have the anytime property: the more iterations we perform the more accurate the results are. The second direction is to use AI search as a framework, and perform sampling in particular steps to avoid expansion of a large search tree. A work by Kearns et al. [12] employs such sampling in a search framework.

6.2 Black Box Optimization

Practical problems often involve a complex optimization problem. In many cases, these problems are too complex for an explicit modeling as an MDP. Moreover, in many domains (such as, for example, the logistics domain) there are existing, dedicated optimization tools which are not easily replaceable by a transparent MDP. An optimization engine can be integrated in our framework as follows: whenever the proactive agent gets future event predictions, it invokes the optimization engine with new parameters, and gets a new policy as output. If the optimization tool supports anytime computation, the proactive agent queries for the current result whenever it needs to perform an action.

7. EXAMPLE: CRITICIAL SHIPMENT

The general logistics setting is described in Section 1.1. We consider the following specific scenario: a customer in Valencia, Spain orders an air shipment of 1.5 tons of critical machinery parts from near Maastricht, The Netherlands. The shipment will be ready on 8am the next day, and should be unloaded in the customer's plant near Valencia by 8pm in order to be ready for the beginning of production early morning. Each loading of the goods on a carrier

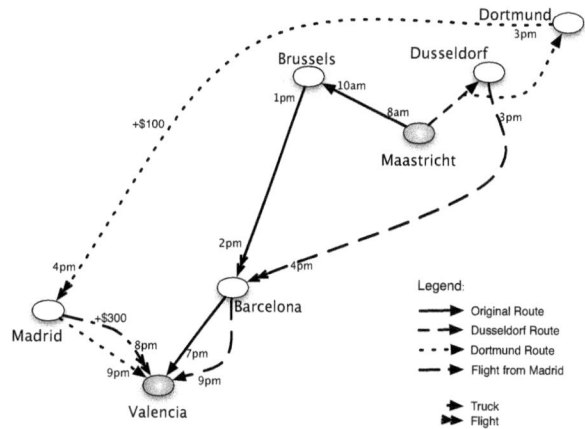

Figure 6: Routes from Maastricht to Valencia.

is expected to take one hour, and each unloading is expected to take one hour as well. In order to be admitted to a flight, the shipment should be ready at an airport warehouse two hours prior to departure. The transportation planner (either person or software) comes up with the cheapest scenario that allows arrival on time: the shipment will be picked up by the trucking company "Maas Trucks" from the plant near Maastricht, driven to Brussels Airport (about 1 hour), loaded on a (regular) flight departing at 1:00pm to Barcelona, arriving at 2pm, unloaded by 3pm and picked up by another trucking company, "Barca Trucks". The truck trip is expected to take three hours after one hour of loading, and hence unloading will be completed just on time in Valencia.

The contract specifies delay penalties: for up to two hours there is a penalty of $200/hour, but above three hours the delay will affect production hence the penalty increases to $600/hour. Delays can occur in several ways: (i) shipment not ready on time, (ii) traffic delays the arrival at Brussels, (iii) security controls at Brussels delay the loading on the flight, (iv) the flight is delayed, and (v) the trip within Spain takes longer due to traffic conditions.

In case one of the above occurs, the plan may change. Assume we realize ahead of time that we risk missing the 1pm flight from Brussels. Because the next flight is a connection which arrives in Barcelona only at 9pm, the best alternative is to drive the other way to Dusseldorf airport and load on the 3:00pm flight to Barcelona. In such case the pickup time at Barcelona Airport should change to 5:00pm (to avoid overpaying the trucking company) and a two hour delay in arrival to Valencia is expected. If we expect delayed departure, we risk getting into the more expensive 3rd hour delay, and we might prefer to drive an additional 50 minutes to Dortmund Airport. From Dortmund there are no flights to Barcelona, but there is a 3pm flight to Madrid, which costs $200 more. In such case a new pickup should be arranged with "Mad Trucks", at 5pm in Madrid, and the trip will still be expected to be completed with the mild two hours delay. Finally, we might also realize that the traffic conditions around Barcelona or Madrid will cause an additional delay. From Madrid, the system can overcome this problem by taking a connecting flight to Valencia, departing at 5:30pm, which will cost additional $600 (cargo transfer can be completed within the 90 minutes connection time). This flight lasts 30 minutes, and after the unloading in the airpot, and the loading on the truck, the cargo will be unloaded in destination by 9pm (driving time from the airport is negligible). There is no such option from Barcelona. The possible routes are described in Figure 6.

We now turn to the technical modeling of the system. The set of raw and derived events is as follows.

eLocation Change in the location of the shipment; for example, truck or flight departure / arrival (attribute: new location).

eBOL Bill of Lading is ready.

eUnload Shipment unloaded at current location.

eLoad Shipment loaded (attribute: specific truck or flight).

eBrusselsTraffic Severe traffic conditions on the way to Brussels (attribute: expected delay).

eSecurityAlert Security level in Europe upgraded.

eSecurityInspection The shipment is taken for a further security inspection (takes approx. 45 minutes).

eFlightDelay The flight from Dusseldorf to Barcelona is delayed (attribute: length of the delay).

eFlightMiss The shipment misses the flight from Brussels.

eSpainWeather Severe weather conditions in northern Spain.

eSpainTraffic Severe traffic conditions around Madrid and Barcelona (attribute: expected delay).

eConfirmation Booking confirmation (attribute: specific booking).

7.1 MDP Model

In this scenario the number of alternative routes is small enough to be specified in advance; in practice we may need to generate new routes dynamically from database. As a specific example, this scenario can be easily modified so that the time of a later flight from Brussels is not known in advance, but loaded from database when needed, through enrichment of the event *eFlightMiss*.

In logistics scenarios, we model the chosen route as *Homogeneous Markov Process* over a small set of states. The states represent foremost the location of the shipment along the route (with additional state variables specified below). A Markov Process represents the expectation that we move along the states at some rate, where the rate, also called *intensity* of transition is represented through a parameter q_{ij}, which is the parameter of the exponential distribution which represents the probability to move from state i to state j at a given time step. For example, if the expected travel time from Maastricht to Brussels is one hour, and our time step is 10 minutes, then for the transition from $i =$"to Brussels" to $j =$"at Brussels" we have $q_{ij} = \frac{1}{6}$, and then the expected number of time steps it will take to move from i to j is $\frac{1}{q_{ij}} = 6$. A Markov Process is a specification of MDP to a given policy, which is the chosen route. At any state the MDP specifies available actions: the "no action" option is to continue along the current policy, hence according to the specified transitions. There are additional actions in some of the states which let us change the route to another route (in our example, all of which are pre-specified). While the intensity parameters facilitate the computation of the expected time of a route, during execution a change of state only occurs when events indicate a change in the physical world.

Finally, predicted events in this domain indicate expected delay in some part of the trip; this is incorporated into the intensity parameter. When, for example, the event *eBrusselsTraffic* is received, along with an attribute which provides the expected delay d, the parameter of the transition from "to Brussels" to "at Brussels" changes from q to $\frac{1}{\frac{1}{q}+d}$ (unless we are already on the way to Brussels, in which case we have to reduce from q the time already spent on the way). When the delay event is not certain, but is expected with some probability p, the delay has to be weighted by p. We now define the specific building blocks of the MDP.

S **(state space) :** The complete set V_d of state variables is:

sLocation Current part of the trip. Possible values: all the specific locations (e.g., "at Maastricht", "at Dusseldorf"...), during truck trips (e.g., "to Dusseldorf", "Madrid to Valencia"), and during flights (e.g., "F. to Barcelona").

sLoad Load status: "off carrier", "on truck", "on aircraft", "flight transfer".

sPickup The currently booked pickup arrangement in Spain: "truck 3pm", "truck 5pm", "truck 10pm", "air".

sFlightArrival Current flight arrival time: "2pm", "4pm", "9pm".

The variable *sLoad* is required in order to determine whether rerouting is possible; for example, the shipment can be rerouted from Dusseldorf to Dortmund only before unloaded from the truck. The third variable (*sPickup*) is required for accurate modeling of the reward: the trucking company is paid from the time it is booked, even if the actual shipment arrives late; changes to the booking must be done at least two hours in advance. Finally, *sFlightArrival* allows to accurately model the time it takes to transition from (e.g.) *sLocation*="at Madrid" to *sLocation*="Madrid to Valencia" given the current value of *sPickup*. S is the cartesian product of the domains of these four variables.

R **(reward function):** defined over the state space according to the penalties and costs specified above and additional omitted details such as the trucking fee.

A **(actions):** The possible actions (except for "no action") are listed in Table 1. The conditions in the third column model restrictions of the environment; for example, changing pickup time can be done only before departure, to model the two hours lead time.

T **(transition function):** Table 1 shows the state which results from each action *if the action succeeds*; for example, if the action *aDortmund* succeeds, the truck will turn towards Dortmund, and the system's state will change so that *sLocation*="to Dortmund". However, a change of route requires several procedures: placing orders with air carriers, changing the order with trucking companies, etc. These actions can fail. The system learns about the results of the actions through event *eConfirmation*. If the rerouting fails, because for example there is no space on the flight from Dortmund or no available pickup truck in Madrid, then the system's state does not change as a result of the action. For the simplicity of presentation we avoid the specific probabilities of failures.

The transition function for "no action" is defined, as explained above, according to the time the phyisical state transition is expected to take. For example, when *sLocation*="at Brussels" and *sLoad*="on Truck", the expected transition time to *sLoad*="off carrier" is one hour. When *Location*="at Barcelona", however, the expected transition time of *sLoad* from "off carrier" to "on truck" depends on the difference between *sFlightArrival* and *SPickup*. For example, if *sFlightArrival*="4pm", but *SPickup*="truck 10pm", the expected transition time is 6 hours. This is a mechanism that prevents the MDP solver from proposing the action *acBarcaTruck10* unless we expect to arrive in Barcelona only at 9pm.

7.2 Event Processing Network

Standard event-processing agents are depicted as the smaller boxes in Figure 8. *aLOC* receives raw events from scanning items and GPS signals of carrier, and derives *eLocation*. *aBOL* detects sequence of events from supplier IT system to determine when *eBOL* should be generated. *aLOAD* translates item scans to *eLOAD* events, *aTRF* filters traffic alerts from traffic service and generates *eSpainTraffic* and *eBrusselsTraffic*, *aWEA* filters weather alerts to generate *eSpainWeather*, and finally *aCONF* receives booking confirmations from reservation system. Derived events are sent to the

action	description	in states	resulting states
acDusseldorf	Change to the Dusseldorf route	*Location* = "at Maastricht"	*Location*="to Dusseldorf"
acDortmund	Change to the Dortmund route	*Location* = "at Dusseldorf", *LoadSt* = "on carrier"	*Location* = "to Dortmund"
acMadridFly	Book flight Madrid - Valencia	*Location* ="to Dortmund" or "F. to Madrid"	*SPickup*="air"
acBarcaTruck10	Reschedule Barca Truck to 10pm	*Location* ="to Brussels" or "at Brussels"	*SPickup*="10pm"

Table 1: Actions available in the proactive agent MDP.

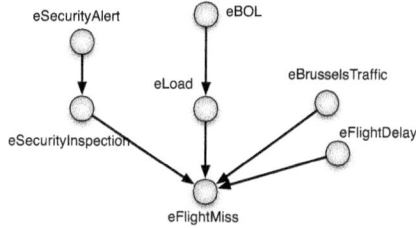

Figure 7: Graphical model of agent *aFlightMiss*.

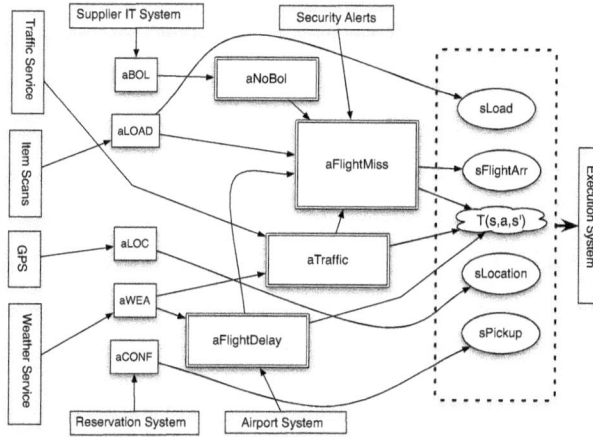

Figure 8: EPN for the critical shipment scenario

predictive agents (double-framed), or to the (dotted frame) PRA (note that in general predictive agents may receive input directly from producers). Certain events sent to the PRA affect state variables directly. For example, when the event *eUnload* is received, *sLoad* changes to "off carrier". When the event *eLocation* is received, its attribute indicates new value for the variable *sLocation*. If *eFlightMiss* is received, then *sFlightArrival*="9pm".

The following is the list of predictive EPAs, and the uncertain derived events they generate:

aFlightMiss (Bayesian) Forecasts the probability of missing the 1pm flight from Brussels (*eFlightMiss*). A graphical predictive model for this agent is shown in Figure 7.[3]

aTraffic (Rule) If *eSpainWeather* is received, then derive *eSpainTraffic* for interval 5pm-8pm, with specific probability.

aFlightDelay Either predict *eFlightDelay* from weather conditions, or receive it explicitly from airport system.

---

[3]Figure 7 provide the qualitative relationship between events, and avoids specific probabilistic data and temporal relationships.

7.3 Specific Scenario Execution

We describe a hypothetical execution of the scenario. The scenario starts when the shipment is prepared on Tuesday morning. When the event *eBOL* is not received by 8:30am, agent *aFlightMiss* predicts a 30 minutes delay in *eLoad*, leading to a higher probability that *eFlightMiss* will occur. In the terms of Section 6.1, where e is the event *eFlightMiss* with probability p, $M(\{e\})$ is an MDP which is similar to M^0, but indicates lower probability (higher q) to move from a state where *sLocation* = "at Brussels", to *sLocation*="F. to Barcelona". However, the probability of missing the flight is still relatively low (unloading can be done faster when needed) and replanning finds that current route is still optimal. The *eBOL* event arrives at 7:40 (before another replanning is triggered). At 8am the system is notified of a security alert at the airport, increasing the probability of security inspection, and in turn increasing the probability of *eFlightMiss* more. This time the replanning does result in changing the route to Dusseldorf. A *eLoad* event arrives at 8:15, and the truck departs towards Dusseldorf.

On the way, at 8:45 we get a *eSpainWeather* event with high probability, causing agent *aTraffic* to issue a *eSpainTraffic* event (for time 5pm-8pm) with high probability. Now the predicted MDP will have lower probability to transition from *sLocation*="Barcelona to Valencia" or "Madrid to Valencia" to *sLocation*="Valencia" (in other words, higher expected time on the way). The PRA receives the event and performs replanning, resulting with a new optimal policy. The new policy indicates that: (i) perform action *acMadridFly* immediately, and (ii) when *sLocation*="Dusseldorf", *sLoad*= "on carrier", and *sPickup*= "air", perform action *acDortmund*. The last condition ensures that the rerouting to Dortmund occurs only if we secured space on the flight from Madrid to Valencia.

In our example execution, the booking is confirmed and the location becomes "to Dortmund". The next event is *eLocation* in Dortmund. The rest of the events (unloading and loading on flight, departure and arrival in Madrid, loading and departing to Valencia, and so on) are received as expected, and the shipment is unloaded in its destination at 9pm. The result is that the shipment arrived with two hours delay, and hence $400 penalty is occurred, and we also pay an extra $800 for the two flights. However, without predictive and proactive capabilities the original scenario would have been executed, most likely resulting in missing the flight from Brussels and paying a much higher penalty.

We stress that this scenario is significantly simplified to fit into this paper. Typically, there will be more types of events we should consider, and many more transportation alternatives. In addition, the stream of incoming events will consist of a much larger number of specific raw events (for example, at each mile stone the truck reaches), and these streams will be synthesized by additional EPAs, resulting in the small number of significant events we consider here. We also note that specific scenarios will not be modeled from scratch each time; a system designer will create a domain-specific template, including the types of events, agents, and state variables that are used by the shipping company in its operations. For specific scenarios, the designer selects the appropriate agent types and supplies necessary parameters.

8. CONCLUSIONS

We introduce a high-level conceptual architecture for proactive event-driven computing. We present the major constructs of the architecture, some of which at a relatively abstract sense, leaving the door open for several means of implementation. We motivate proactive event-driven computing with real world applications, and provide a detailed, drilled-down example of the modeling of a specific scenario. Our approach brings together various existing models from several disciplines, leveraging them towards a framework which facilitates automation and efficiency improvement of a vast variety of practical problems in the realm of operational control.

This work raises several types of requirements for the realization of proactive event-driven computing. In general terms, the requirements can be divided according to: generalization of the event-processing methodology (Section 4), building of probabilistic event prediction capabilities (Section 5), and facilitating dynamic and intelligent optimization and decision making under uncertainty (Section 6). The weight of each particular requirements raised in each section vary according to specific domains; moreover, solutions to each requirement may also be domain-specific. Furthermore, future research should address several general difficulties raised in the paper: (i) the approach relies on the ability to adapt an existing policy quickly when an event prediction is received in real time. This policy adaptation must be done very fast and in an anytime manner, and thus must take advantage of the particular properties of this setting. A work in this direction was conducted in parallel [3]. (ii) The problem of modeling a specific scenario remains a key challenge; in particular, one must determine what should be the state variables and how they are updated by events. Most of this task remains manual in most of the state-space based applications; however, we believe that at least the task of determining V_d out of V can be automated based on the causality structure of the problem. (iii) The applicability, in particular in terms of performance, of temporal models such as CTBN to this kind of application should be verified.

9. REFERENCES

[1] A. Arnold, Y. Liu, and N. Abe. Temporal causal modeling with graphical granger methods. In *ACM SIGKDD*, 2007.

[2] C. Boutilier, T. Dean, and S. Hanks. Decision theoretic planning: Structural assumptions and computational leverage. *Journal of AI Research*, 11:1–94, 1999.

[3] Ronen Brafman, Carmel Domshlak, Yagil Engel, and Zohar Feldman. Planning for operational control systems with predictable exogenous events. In *AAAI, to appear*, 2011.

[4] D.M. Chickering, D. Heckerman, and C. Meek. A bayesian approach to learning bayesian networks with local structure. In *UAI*, 1997.

[5] S. Dolev, M. Kopeetsky, and A. Shamir. RFID authentication efficient proactive information security within computational security. *Theory of Computing Systems*, pages 1–18, 2011.

[6] O. Etzion, Y. Magid, E. Rabinovich, I. Skarbovsky, and N. Zolotorevsky. Context aware computing and its utilization in event-based systems. In *DEBS*, 2010.

[7] O. Etzion and P. Niblett. *Event Processing in Action*. Manning Publications, 2010.

[8] S. Fu and C.Z. Xu. Exploring event correlation for failure prediction in coalitions of clusters. In *ICS*, 2007.

[9] C. Guestrin, D. Koller, R. Parr, and S. Venkataraman. Efficient solution algorithms for factored MDPs. *Journal of Artificial Intelligence Research*, 19(1):399–468, 2003.

[10] J. Han, H. Cheng, D. Xin, and X. Yan. Frequent pattern mining: current status and future directions. *Data Mining and Knowledge Discovery*, 15(1):55–86, 2007.

[11] J.L. Hellerstein, S. Ma, and C.S. Perng. Discovering actionable patterns in event data. *IBM Systems Journal*, 41(3):475–493, 2010.

[12] Michael J. Kearns, Yishay Mansour, and Andrew Y. Ng. A sparse sampling algorithm for near-optimal planning in large markov decision processes. *Machine Learning*, 49(2-3):193–208, 2002.

[13] M. Kohler and R. Fies. Proactive caching-a framework for performance optimized access control evaluations. In *IEEE POLICY*, 2009.

[14] T. Kunz and R. Alhalimi. Energy-efficient proactive routing in MANET: Energy metrics accuracy. *Ad Hoc Networks*, 8(7):755–766, 2010.

[15] D.C. Luckham. *The power of events*. Addison-Wesley, 2002.

[16] S. Mahadevan. Average reward reinforcement learning: Foundations, algorithms, and empirical results. *Recent Advances in Reinforcement Learning*, pages 159–195, 1996.

[17] K. Mahbub and G. Spanoudakis. Proactive SLA negotiation for service based systems. In *6th World Congress on Services*, 2010.

[18] H. Mannila, H. Toivonen, and A. Inkeri Verkamo. Discovery of frequent episodes in event sequences. *Data Mining and Knowledge Discovery*, 1(3):259–289, 1997.

[19] AE Nicholson and JM Brady. Dynamic belief networks for discrete monitoring. *IEEE Transactions on Systems, Man and Cybernetics*, 24(11):1593–1610, 2002.

[20] U. Nodelman, C.R. Shelton, , and D. Koller. Continuous time bayesian networks. In *UAI*, 2002.

[21] J. Pearl. *Probabilistic reasoning in intelligent systems: networks of plausible inference*. Morgan Kaufmann, 1988.

[22] W.B. Powell. *Approximate Dynamic Programming: Solving the curses of dimensionality*. Wiley-Interscience, 2007.

[23] C. Ré, J. Letchner, M. Balazinksa, and D. Suciu. Event queries on correlated probabilistic streams. In *ACM SIGMOD*, 2008.

[24] A. Robinson, J. Levis, and G. Bennett. INFORMS news: INFORMS to officially join analytics movement. *INFORMS, OR/MS Today*, 37(5), 2010.

[25] S.J. Russell and P. Norvig. *Artificial intelligence: a modern approach*. Prentice hall, 2009

[26] D. Sarma, M. Theobald, and J. Widom. Exploiting lineage for confidence computation in uncertain and probabilistic databases. In *ICDE*, 2008.

[27] J. Vennekens, M. Denecker, and M. Bruynooghe. CP-logic: A language of causal probabilistic events and its relation to logic programming. *Theory and Practice of Logic Programming*, 9(03):245–308, 2009.

[28] S. Wasserkrug, A. Gal, and O. Etzion. A model for reasoning with uncertain rules in event composition. In *UAI*, 2005.

[29] S. Wasserkrug, A. Gal, O. Etzion, and Y. Turchin. Efficient processing of uncertain events in rule-based systems. *IEEE Transactions on Knowledge and Data Engineering*, 2010.

[30] J. Xu and C.R. Shelton. Intrusion detection using continuous time bayesian networks. *Journal of Artificial Intelligence Research*, 39:745–774, 2010.

[31] H. Zhang, Y. Diao, and N. Immerman. Recognizing patterns in streams with imprecise timestamps. *Proceedings of the VLDB Endowment*, 3(1), 2010.

High-Performance Composite Event Monitoring System Supporting Large Numbers of Queries and Sources

SangJeong Lee, Youngki Lee, Byoungjip Kim, K. Selçuk Candan[*],

Yunseok Rhee[§], Junehwa Song

Korea Advanced Institute of
Science and Technology
Computer Science Department

{peterlee, youngki, bjkim,
junesong}@nclab.kaist.ac.kr

[*]Arizona State University
School of Computing, Informatics,
and Decision Science Engineering

candan@asu.edu

[§]Hankuk University of Foreign Studies
School of Electronics and
Information Engineering

rheeys@hufs.ac.kr

ABSTRACT

This paper presents a novel data structure, called *Event-centric Composable Queue (ECQ)*, a basic building block of a new scalable composite event monitoring (CEM) framework, *SCEMon*. In particular, we focus on the scalability issues when large numbers of CEM queries and event sources exist in upcoming CEM environments. To address these challenges effectively, we take an *event-centric sharing approach* rather than dealing with queries and sources separately. ECQ is a shared queue, which stores incoming event instances of a primitive event class. ECQs are designed to facilitate efficient shared evaluations of multiple queries over very large volumes of event streams from numerous event sources. ECQs are composable and form a single shared network within which multiple queries are simultaneously evaluated. In this paper, we present efficient shared processing techniques operating on top of the proposed shared ECQ network. The performance evaluation shows that the proposed approach achieves a high level of scalability compared to conventional separate processing approaches in large-scale CEM environments.

Categories and Subject Descriptors

H.3.3 [**Information Storage and Retrieval**]: Information Search and Retrieval – *Information filtering*; H.2.4 [**Database Management**]: Systems – *Query processing*

General Terms: Algorithms, Performance, Design.

Keywords: Composite Event Monitoring, Scalable Processing, Event Streams.

1. INTRODUCTION

Efficient monitoring of composite events over large volumes of event streams is critical in many application domains, including product management [1], network monitoring [2], stock market analysis [3], and traffic monitoring [4]. In many applications, a multitude of composite event monitoring (CEM) queries are registered and all of them are simultaneously monitored by the system over the same event streams. Previous research in

composite event detection, however, has focused on optimizing the monitoring of *individual* queries [1][3][5]. We note that optimizing system resources "*separately*" for each query has inherent limitations when the system needs to deal with large numbers of simultaneous queries and event sources. Thus, we propose a novel scalable CEM framework that efficiently evaluates in a "*shared*" manner large numbers of CEM queries against input streams from numerous event sources.

Challenges. CEM frameworks are often confronted with the scalability challenges that arise from the presence of very large numbers of (a) simultaneous CEM queries and (b) event sources. For example, to identify effective advertising targets, a credit card company may want to identify card holders following certain purchasing event patterns of many diverse scenarios such as couple dating, sporting events, shopping sprees, travel, etc. Each of these cases would be represented as a multitude of CEM queries registered in the system and they all would be tracked simultaneously over the stream of credit card transaction events. In a metropolitan city, there often exist thousands of purchasing patterns of interest as well as millions of credit card holders.

A straightforward approach to process simultaneous CEM queries is to evaluate these individual queries separately [1][3][5]. Figure 1-(a) describes the approach using multiple CEM queries. In this setup, given a set of CEM queries, as many query processing plans need to be created and evaluated. Moreover, incoming event instances need to be delivered to the relevant plans and possibly stored in each plan for later query evaluation. It is obvious that such an approach would be extremely wasteful: Although there are common events engaged in multiple processing plans, their storage and computation cannot be shared effectively across different plans. Processing times would then increase with the number of queries and input rates. Moreover, the approach would require considerable storage space to hold incoming instances and intermediate states for each plan; this would make high-performance in-memory processing of large-scale CEMs difficult.

Recently, the researcher community started considering multiple event sources. Yet, effective approaches dealing with very large numbers of sources are elusive. Wu et al. showed that in non-deterministic finite automata (NFA) based CEMs, unnecessary state transitions can frequently occur when there are different event sources [1]. To tackle this challenge, they partition stacks of event instances for separate processing of individual sources. Note that there exist separate stacks partitioned for different sources in the processing plan of query Q_1 in Figure 1-(a). However, when the number of sources is very large, this implies that a large

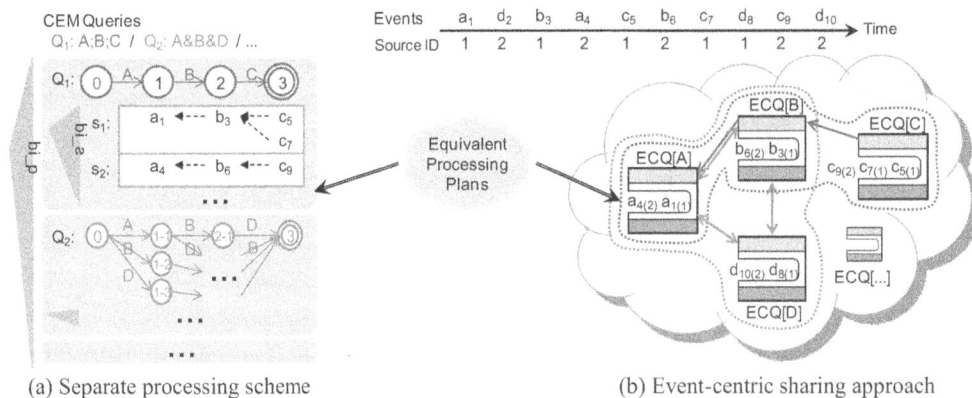

(a) Separate processing scheme (b) Event-centric sharing approach

Figure 1. "Separate processing" scheme vs. proposed "event-centric sharing" approach

number of separate stacks need to be created, resulting in severe storage and management overheads.

Proposed Solution. In this paper, we take an *event-centric sharing* approach to address the inefficiencies due to duplicated data structures and separate processing of conventional CEMs when supporting large numbers of queries and sources. Our approach is based on the idea that a primitive event, specified commonly in multiple queries, can be shared for efficient processing and storage. Moreover, all incoming instances of a given event class, regardless of their sources, can be stored and handled together within a shared storage, e.g. a queue. Based on the composition patterns of all registered CEM queries, these shared queues can form a single *shared network* in which processing and storage for each primitive event class are inherently shared by all relevant queries. For instance, Figure 1-(b) illustrates the key idea of the proposed approach; the queues are shared by two event sources as well as two CEM queries. The comprehensive discussion on Figure 1 will be given in Section 3.

Our Contributions. Based on the observations of shared processing opportunities, we develop a new scalable composite event monitoring (CEM) framework, *SCEMon*. SCEMon, in its core, is an automata-based architecture; but it consists of data structures and algorithms that are designed to maximize event and sub-pattern sharing across multiple queries as well as sources. The contributions of this paper can be summarized as follows:

- We explore the scalability problem arising in large-scale CEM environments. We investigate the performance of conventional separate processing schemes and explore inherent limitations when dealing with large numbers of queries and sources.

- We then propose a novel data structure, *event-centric composable queue (ECQ)*, that enables efficient shared processing of large numbers of simultaneous queries and event sources. An ECQ is a shared queue storing incoming event instances of a primitive event class. For each primitive event class, only a single ECQ is allocated and is shared by multiple CEM queries. ECQs are composed flexibly within a single shared network to support the diverse composition semantics of the queries. Each ECQ is also shared by all event sources. This design substantially reduces processing and storage overhead necessary to manipulate intermediate results for each query and event source separately.

- On top of this sharable data structure, we develop a suit of efficient shared processing techniques including *event instance*

sharing, *sub-pattern sharing*, and *partial matching block (PMB) reduction*. These techniques are brought together in SCEMon which localizes each instance manipulation on a corresponding ECQ and a few *adjacent* ECQs, and evaluates CEM queries incrementally with each subsequent event instance. SCEMon supports various types of composite event patterns such as sequence, conjunction and disjunction.

- We experimentally demonstrate that relying on the novel data structures and shared processing techniques, the scalability issues can be tackled effectively. The performance results of our extensive evaluation show the competitive performance of SCEMon against conventional CEM approaches.

The rest of the paper is organized as follows: Section 2 introduces related work. Section 3 discusses the proposed approach of SCEMon in comparison to conventional approaches. Section 4 presents the data structure of ECQ and Section 5 describes the shared processing techniques using ECQs. Section 6 gives the performance cost analysis. Section 7 discusses the experimental results for performance, and finally Section 8 concludes the paper.

2. RELATED WORK

Event monitoring systems have evolved and been expanded for diverse application domains, online transaction logs [8], built-in-sensor reporting in a building [9], RFID readings in a market [1] and stock trading [3]. The current approaches can be roughly classified into *automata*-based complex event management systems, such as SASE [1] and Cayuga [5], *Petri Net*-based systems like SAMOS [6], *event tree*-based systems, such as Sentinel [7] and ZStream [3], and *event graph*-based systems including InfoFilter [10].

There have been continuous research efforts to improve the performance of CEMs. SASE [1][11] extends non-deterministic finite automata (NFA) to deal with multiple event sources. Cayuga [5], also NFA-based, focuses on efficient predicate evaluation using indices along with automata transition. Recognizing that NFA-based CEMs are limited to sequential patterns due to the explicit state transitions of NFAs, ZStream [3] takes an event tree-based approach to support rich composition semantics such as concurrent events or negated events that should not occur. It provides the cost model for different composition patterns and the optimization technique to search for an optimal evaluation plan. Akdere et al. also develop the event graph-based CEM across distributed event nodes [2]. They generate multi-step event acquisition and processing plans that minimize event transmission costs. However, conventional CEMs have difficulties in dealing with large numbers of simultaneous queries and event sources together. Most of them treat multiple queries and sources separately; their main contributions are not to develop shared processing techniques, but to optimize individual processing plans per query and source. Such separate CEM processing may potentially limit the scalability required for massive processing.

Previous works on multi-query optimization, e.g., predicate indexing [5], sub-graph merging [10], and sub-event sharing [2] can be considered as efforts to address the problem. However, it is not straightforward to make the data structures of existing CEMs be shared effectively, since they are still founded on NFAs or event trees. A state in an NFA represents not only the current event class but also the history of state transitions with past event instances. Thus, the state can hardly be shared unless the state transitions to the state from the beginning are identical between different NFAs. Achieving performance benefits through sharing would be moderate due to the rare chance of sharing. Since an intermediate node in an event tree also designates partial compositions, it can be rarely shared among multiple queries.

3. COMPOSITE EVENT MONITORING

The CEM semantics and language we adopt in this paper are analogous to those used in other CEM systems [1][3][11]. Based on the basic CEM notation, we present a common approach of CEM processing and discuss the potential challenges in large-scale CEM environments. Then, we introduce our event-centric sharing approach dealing with such scalability challenges.

3.1 CEM Notation

We define **primitive events** as atomic occurrences of interest. More precisely, we represent an incoming event instance as a tuple $<src\_id, event\_class, start\_ts, end\_ts, attrs[]>$, where src_id refers to the identifier of the event source, $event\_class$ refers to the class that the instance belongs to, $start\_ts$ and end_ts refer to the start and end timestamps of the event instance respectively, and $attrs[]$ refers to the list of attribute values.

On receiving primitive events, **composite events** are detected from a collection of primitive and/or other composite events. CEM queries associate primitive or composite events together to form new composite events. The most frequently used composition type **sequence (A;B)** finds the instances of event B following the instances of event A within a specific time window. **Conjunction (A&B)**, i.e., concurrent events, denotes that event A and event B occur within a specified time window in any orders. **Disjunction (A|B)** means that either event A or event B occurs. This is simply a union of the two event classes and, in its most generic definition, no time constraints on the events are included.

The formal semantics of CEM queries with different patterns is given in Table 1. The PATTERN clause specifies the type of composition patterns such as sequence, conjunction, and disjunction. The WITH clause presents a list of the event classes that should occur to form the composite event. The WHERE clause imposes predicates on event attributes while the WITHIN clause describes the time window for the events.

Upon an input event instance, each CEM query can generate different results depending on a *selection mode*. It can generate at most one composite event instance which represents the most recent composition of participating events. This can be considered as a *recent* selection mode in active database among several different composition modes [8]. An *all* selection mode is also

Table 1. Formal semantics of CEM queries

Given event instance stream, $e\_strm = (e_1, e_2, ..., e_i, ...)$ – infinite series
Upon the arrival of $e_i = <src\_id, event\_class, start\_ts, end\_ts, attrs[]>$,
each query generates composite event instances, c's, satisfying the below conditions:

Pattern	Query Language	Monitoring Semantics
Sequence	**qry_seq:** PATTERN Sequence WITH $E_1, E_2, ..., E_n$ WHERE [symbol] WITHIN t_cond	$c = <src\_id, qry\_id=qry\_seq.id, start\_ts, end\_ts, (e_{M1}, e_{M2}, ..., e_{Mn})>$, where • $c.src\_id = e_i.src\_id = e_{Mj}.src\_id$ for all $1 \le j \le n$, • e_{Mj} is an instance of the event class E_j for all $1 \le j \le n$, • $e_{Mj-1}.end\_ts \le e_{Mj}.start\_ts$ for all $2 \le j \le n$, • $c.start\_ts = e_{M1}.start\_ts$, $c.end\_ts = e_{Mn}.end\_ts$, • $(c.end\_ts - c.start\_ts) \le qry\_seq.t\_cond$, • $e_{Mn} = e_i$, and • $\forall e_k \ni e_k.src\_id = e_i.src\_id$ and $c.start\_ts \le e_k.start\_ts \le e_k.end\_ts < c.end\_ts$.
Conjunction	**qry_cnj:** PATTERN Conjunction WITH $E_1, E_2, ..., E_n$ WHERE [symbol] WITHIN t_cond	$c = <src\_id, qry\_id=qry\_cnj.id, start\_ts, end\_ts, (e_{M1}, e_{M2}, ..., e_{Mn})>$, where • $c.src\_id = e_i.src\_id = e_{Mj}.src\_id$ for all $1 \le j \le n$, • e_{Mj} is an instance of the event class E_j for all $1 \le j \le n$, • $c.start\_ts = min(\{e_{Mj}.start\_ts\})$ for all $1 \le j \le n$, $c.end\_ts = e_i.end\_ts = max(\{e_{Mj}.end\_ts\})$ for all $1 \le j \le n$, • $(c.end\_ts - c.start\_ts) \le qry\_cnj.t\_cond$, and • $\forall e_k \ni e_k.src\_id = e_i.src\_id$ and $c.start\_ts \le e_k.start\_ts \le e_k.end\_ts < c.end\_ts$.
Disjunction	**qry_dsj:** PATTERN Disjunction WITH $E_1, E_2, ..., E_n$	$c = <src\_id, qry\_id=qry\_dsj.id, start\_ts, end\_ts, (e_i)>$, where • $c.src\_id = e_i.src\_id$, • e_i is an instance of the event class E_j for any $1 \le j \le n$, • $c.start\_ts = e_i.start\_ts$, and $c.end\_ts = e_i.end\_ts$

used frequently that generates all composite event instances satisfying the monitoring conditions. SCEMon can support the two modes; different output generation of SCEMon depending on different selection modes is discussed later in Section 5.1.

CEM queries can be used to specify diverse purchasing event patterns for credit card companies. CEM query 1 below presents an example of a sequential pattern.

CEM query 1. Sequential pattern

PATTERN	*Sequence*
WITH	*CNMA_A, RSTR_B, BAR_C*
WHERE	*[symbol]*
	$20 < CNMA_A.payment < $50 AND
	$80 < RSTR_B.payment < $120 AND
	BAR_C.payment < $50
WITHIN	*5 hours*

This query is intended to represent a particular purchasing event pattern potentially related to "dating", i.e., two seats purchased at a theater (CNMA_A), meals for two at a restaurant (RSTR_B), and some (but not too much) drinking at a bar (BAR_C). Note that [symbol] means the condition of matching source ids among incoming event instances.

CEM query 2. Conjunction pattern

PATTERN	*Conjunction*
WITH	*BRND_A, BRND_B, BRND_C*
WHERE	*[symbol]*
	BRND_A.payment + BRND_B.payment
	+ BRND_C.payment < $200
WITHIN	*1.5 hours*

CEM query 2 may represent a shopping pattern in an outlet mall. Since the shopping order does not matter here, the query uses the conjunction type. As discussed in [12], such queries can be handy for shop managers who would like to send coupons or advertisements to attract the customers who have not bought brand goods sufficiently.

These types of queries open the opportunity for credit card companies to advanced mobile advertising and business promotions based on credit card holders' purchasing patterns. A large number of CEM queries can be created in various ways over a given set of available purchasing event classes, and issued by third-party advertising agencies or business owners to target their own potential customers in mobile computing environments.

3.2 Query/Source-Separate Processing

A common approach to CEM processing involves developing separate processing plans for individual queries and dealing with individual sources separately in each plan; this is illustrated in Figure 1-(a) with multiple CEM queries, i.e., Q_1, Q_2, etc. Such an approach mostly takes full advantage of indices built over many queries and sources. Upon an input event instance, it would identify queries of interest (which involve an event class of the instance in their patterns) by using the query index. For each relevant query processing plan, it would *search* for the data structure designated to an event source of the instance, *evaluate* relevant composition transitions and *store* the instance and intermediate evaluation results into the data structure if necessary. Additionally, it would *delete* any obsolete stored instances from query plans for efficient memory management.

For example, upon an input event instance b_3 from source #1, the approach would identify Q_1 and Q_2 using the 'q_id' index and invoke the processing plans of Q_1 and Q_2 respectively. Each plan would be evaluated with b_3 and store it into the instance stacks responsible for the corresponding source respectively. Note that b_3 is stored twice in the stacks of s_1 in Q_1 and Q_2 plans. Later, it would be deleted from each plan if it is determined to be no more necessary for further processing.

In large-scale CEM environments, there may exist numerous CEM queries of interest for each input event instance since a large number of simultaneous queries are specified using a set of event classes. In such cases, the same *search*, *evaluate/store*, and *delete* operations may need to be invoked repeatedly many times and this may result in very huge processing overheads. Specifically, the processing cost is significantly influenced by the numbers of queries and sources. First, the processing overhead caused by search, evaluate/store, and delete operations are multiplied by the number of the evaluated query plans which would substantially increase with larger numbers of simultaneous queries. Second, when there are a large number of event sources, the costs of the individual operations can be significantly raised due to the severe management overhead of numerous separate data structures assigned for individual sources. Even with an index built on source ids, searching for the data structure of a specific event source mostly takes up $O(\log Ns)$ time[1], where Ns is the number of sources. Thus, "separate processing" schemes can hardly cope with large-scale CEM environments.

3.3 Event-centric Sharing Approach

In this paper, our goal is to develop an efficient shared processing approach that deals with such large numbers of simultaneous CEM queries and event sources. SCEMon takes advantage of a novel data structure, called ECQ, which manages all incoming instances of a primitive event class together regardless of queries and sources. SCEMon identifies a set of essential primitive event classes for all queries, constructs a single network of corresponding ECQs respectively taking each class in charge, and evaluates all the queries simultaneously in conjunction with the

constructed network. Figure 1-(b) illustrates the proposed event-centric sharing approach of SCEMon; it visualizes a shared ECQ network where four ECQs are composed into two *virtual* processing plans which are equivalent to the first two plans in Figure 1-(a). Note that, in this example, upon arrival of b_3 or b_6, Q_1 and Q_2 can be evaluated together by ECQ[B]. In essence, ECQ enables multiple sources to easily share the processing for their respective instances, and further enables multiple queries to aggressively share their common processing.

Our event-centric sharing approach is especially advantageous when there are many popular event classes of common interest specified in registered CEM queries. Let us consider the mobile advertising application discussed earlier and note that modern cities have many hot spots such as popular shopping complexes and multiplex cinemas. A large portion of CEM queries will involve such hot places, and primitive events happening in the places may trigger the evaluation of large numbers of simultaneous CEM queries. SCEMon is expected to be highly effective in such a scenario.

In addition, the proposed approach is highly beneficial in monitoring long term patterns, where the processing tends to rapidly increase the volume of intermediate evaluation results. For example, human activity patterns of interest often involve long-term processing for several hours or even days. Our sharing approach can substantially reduce the amount of the intermediate results, and thus makes the long-term processing more effective in terms of storage consumption as well as computation.

4. EVENT-CENTRIC COMPOSABLE QUEUE (ECQ)

As the basis of SCEMon, this section presents the data structure of ECQ, and constructs the shared network of ECQs developed for the efficient shared processing of SCEMon.

ECQ maintains three data structures *shared instance queue (SIQ)*, *composition link table (CLT)*, and *partial matching block (PMB)*. Figure 2 illustrates the state of a specific ECQ, denoted as ECQ_i, that deals with the k-th incoming event instance, e_k.

Shared Instance Queue (SIQ) manages the recent event instances for all event sources with regard to all event classes. It stores the event instances in the order of their arrivals. This single instance queue in an ECQ is shared by all relevant event sources. SIQ uses a hash table with *source_id* as its key to facilitate accesses to the recent instance e_k.

Composition Link Table (CLT) enables the construction of an integrated ECQ network that supports the shared processing of CEM queries. For ECQ_i, the corresponding CLT contains a set of composition links, one for each CEM query that ECQ_i participates in. Each link, denoted as $CLink(ECQ_i, Q_j)$, represents the association of ECQ_i with the other ECQs specified in the j-th CEM query, Q_j.

$CLink(ECQ_i, Q_j)$ is formally described as a 6-tuple *(query_id, type, t_cond, {ptr_ECQ}, flag, attr_cond)*, where *query_id, type, t_cond,* and *attr_cond* are the identifier, type, time constraint and attribute condition of Q_j, respectively[2].

{ptr_ECQ} and *flag* play critical roles in network construction:

---

[1] Due to the memory limit, the hash lookup with O(1) search time can hardly be used in practical main-memory systems. Memory-efficient tree-based hash tables could be used instead.

[2] We regard the query_id of Q_j as j for the convenience of explanation.

Composition Link Table

query_id	type	t_cond	ptr_ECQ	flag	attr_condi (CNF)
a	SEQ	t_x	{ptr_ECQ$_i$}	INIT	price>\$100
...	CNJ	...	{}	FINE	...
j	DSJ	...	{}	...	...

CLink(ECQ$_i$, Q$_j$)

Shared Instance Queue

Partial Matching Block

query_id	t_start	ptr_instance
a	t_1	{ptr_e$_p$}
j	...	...

query_id	t_start	ptr_instance
b	t_2	{ptr_e$_q$}
...	...	...

PMatch(e$_k$, Q$_j$)

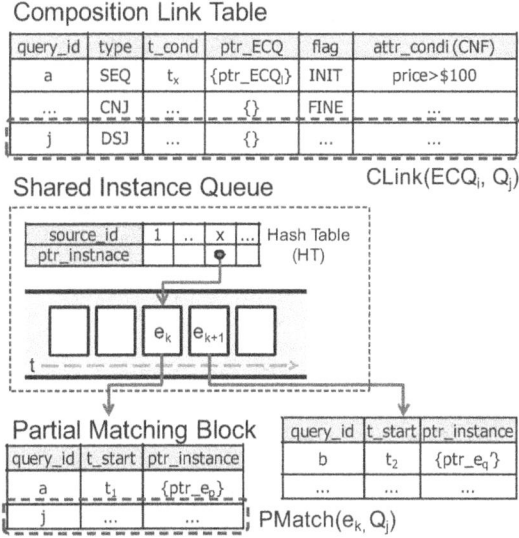

Figure 2. Data structure of ECQ

- *{ptr_ECQ}* contains the pointers to the other ECQs. The pointers facilitate tracing of the related ECQs in the network.
- *flag* marks the position of the ECQ$_i$ in the query; it can be INIT to indicate the first ECQ starting the composition, FINE to indicate the last ECQ finishing the composition.

Figure 1-(b) shows the composition link examples using the blue and red arrows for Q$_1$ and Q$_2$, respectively. For the sequence query Q$_1$, the CLink of ECQ[A], i.e., CLink(ECQ[A], Q$_1$), is (1, SEQ, t_1, {}, INIT, null), while that of ECQ[C] is (1, SEQ, t_1, {ptr_ECQ[B]}, FINE, null). For the conjunction query Q$_2$, CLink(ECQ[A], Q$_2$) is (2, CNJ, t_2, {ptr_ECQ[B], ptr_ECQ[D]}, INIT|FINE, null). Note that CLink(ECQ[A], Q$_2$) points to the other two ECQs and it is also marked as INIT and FINE since any ECQ in Q$_2$ can start and finish the conjunction composition.

Partial Matching Block (PMB) supports incremental evaluation of CEM queries. As shown in Figure 2, a block is allocated to each event instance e$_k$ to store the current states of partial matching in which e$_k$ participates. The block has a set of partial matching entries, one for each composition query. The block allows the incremental extension of partial matching until the matching becomes completed. PMatch(e$_k$, Q$_j$), if it exists, represents that the partial matching of the query Q$_j$ has been successfully extended by the instance e$_k$ at ECQ$_i$. PMatch(e$_k$, Q$_j$) is formally specified as a tuple *(query_id, t_start, {ptr_instance})*;

- *query_id* is the identifier of Q$_j$,
- *t_start* is the start time of the partial matching, and
- *{ptr_instance}* is a set of pointers to the precedent instances, stored in other ECQs, leading to the current partial matching.

For example, an input event instance b$_3$ in Figure 1-(b) would have two PMatch entries for Q$_1$ and Q$_2$. PMatch(b$_3$, Q$_1$) is (1, 1, {a$_{1(1)}$}) since the partial matching is initiated at time 1, i.e., the start time of a$_{1(1)}$, and the precedent instance is a$_{1(1)}$. On the other hand, PMatch(b$_3$, Q$_2$) is (2, 3, {}) since b$_3$ initiates a new partial matching of conjunction and no precedents are required.

When the matching is complete, the pointers are followed iteratively to obtain all the participating event instances. Intuitively, the CLT of the ECQ$_i$ for a primitive event class shows the schematic compositions in which ECQ$_i$ participates, while the

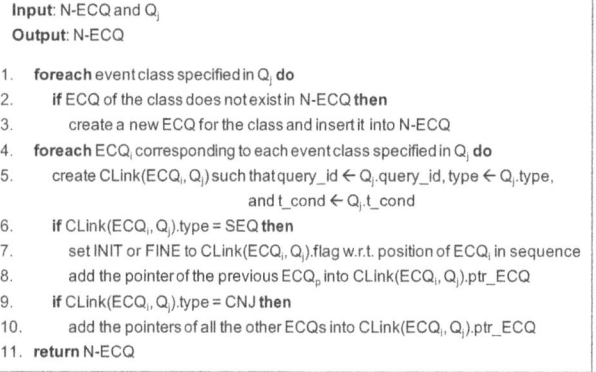

```
Input: N-ECQ and Q_j
Output: N-ECQ

1.   foreach event class specified in Q_j do
2.       if ECQ of the class does not exist in N-ECQ then
3.           create a new ECQ for the class and insert it into N-ECQ
4.   foreach ECQ_i corresponding to each event class specified in Q_j do
5.       create CLink(ECQ_i, Q_j) such that query_id ← Q_j.query_id, type ← Q_j.type,
                                                     and t_cond ← Q_j.t_cond
6.       if CLink(ECQ_i, Q_j).type = SEQ then
7.           set INIT or FINE to CLink(ECQ_i, Q_j).flag w.r.t. position of ECQ_i in sequence
8.           add the pointer of the previous ECQ_p into CLink(ECQ_i, Q_j).ptr_ECQ
9.       if CLink(ECQ_i, Q_j).type = CNJ then
10.          add the pointers of all the other ECQs into CLink(ECQ_i, Q_j).ptr_ECQ
11.  return N-ECQ
```

Figure 3. Algorithm for inserting a CEM query to SCEMon:
N-ECQ denotes the shared network of ECQs

PMB shows the status of current partial matching in which a specific instance e$_k$ of the primitive event class participates.

Given a set of CEM queries, SCEMon constructs a single network of ECQs. In the network, the ECQs of each query are networked with each other via composition links, or CLink's.

The algorithm for the network construction is presented in Figure 3. It is constructed by inserting a CEM query into the network as follows: For a new query, a new ECQ is instantiated for each primitive event specified in the WITH clause (Lines 1-3 in the figure). Some ECQs might not be created if they have already been defined in already registered queries. For the new query, the comprising ECQs are associated with each other by adding a CLink entry in their CLT (Line 5). For the sequence type, ECQs are linked sequentially; each CLink(ECQ$_i$, Q$_j$) points to the ECQ of the precedent activity, and the first and final ECQs are marked accordingly in the flag field (Lines 6-8). For the conjunction type, ECQs are linked and marked accordingly (Line 9-10).

Deleting a CEM query from SCEMon is straightforward. For each event class participating in the query, we remove the corresponding CLink entry in the corresponding ECQs. If the CLT becomes empty, the ECQ is deleted since it does not participate in any CEM queries.

5. SHARED PROCESSING TECHNIQUES

This section presents the shared processing algorithm running on top of the ECQ network. Then, the performance benefit for the proposed algorithm is discussed. We further develop advanced techniques available to improve the processing efficiency.

5.1 Shared Processing Algorithm with Instance Sharing

Upon arrival, each new event instance e$_k$ is dispatched to its corresponding ECQ, say ECQ$_i$. The evaluation process inside the ECQ$_i$ consists of two major phases: *test* and *insert*. The *test* phase evaluates whether e$_k$ could lead to a partial or complete matching for some CEM queries. The *insert* phase updates the data structures of ECQ$_i$ if a new composition happens.

5.1.1 Test Phase
ECQ$_i$ identifies the set of active queries associated with it in the CLT. For each CLink entry of the CLT, it may *probe* the other neighboring ECQs specified in {ptr_ECQ} of the entry for testing the extension of partial matching. The probing is based on the

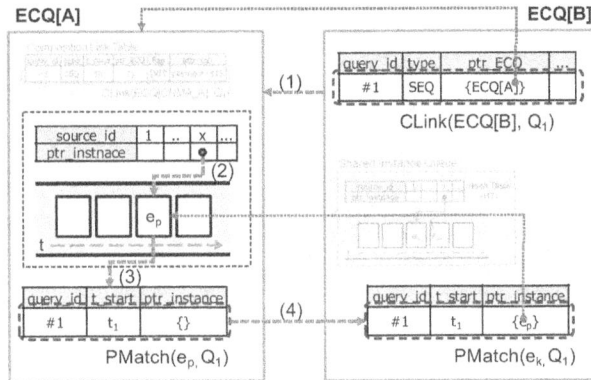

Figure 4. Processing flow of Probe function

source identifier of the incoming instance, i.e., e_k.source_id, and performed by looking at the target SIQ through the hash table. Probing is implemented as a single **Probe** function. Figure 4 illustrates the processing flow of the function using the two ECQs of the CEM query 1. Upon arrival of e_k in ECQ[B], the function looks up the recent event instance, e_p, of the same source with the incoming instance, e_k, in the target ECQ[A], i.e., e_p.source_id = e_k.source_id (Step (1) and (2) in the figure). It then finds from the PMB of e_p the existing partial matching entry for the query, PMatch(e_p, Q_1) (Step (3)). With PMatch(e_p, Q_1), the function tests if e_k can successfully extend the existing partial matching of Q_1. In detail, it is tested if the starting time of the partial composition, PMatch(e_p, Q_j).t_start, satisfies the time constraints of Q_j, i.e., Q_j.t_cond. If so, it returns the partial matching entry to designate the extension of the partial matching (Step (4)).

Using this Probe function, the test phase handles each composition pattern differently:

Sequences. The test phase deals with three different cases with respect to the position of ECQ_i in a sequence; *start*, *middle* and *end*. The pseudo code for the algorithm is presented in Figure 5. It first deals with the "*start*" case in which ECQ_i is marked as INIT in CLink(ECQ_i, Q_j). At ECQ_i, incoming e_k starts a new partial matching of Q_j; PMatch(e_k, Q_j) is created and the start time is set to the start time of e_k (Lines 1-3 in the figure). For the "*middle*" and "*end*" cases, the test phase probes the precedent ECQ, i.e., ECQ_p, in the sequence. If the Probe function confirms the extension of the partial matching, it creates a new entry PMatch(e_k, Q_j) for e_k (Lines 4-7). Especially for the "*end*" case that ECQ_i is marked as FINE in the CLink, if PMatch(e_k, Q_j) has been created already, the test phase completes the matching of Q_j with e_k and generates composite event instances as output by following the pointers in {ptr_instance} of PMatch entries (Lines 8-10). Finally, it returns the created PMatch(e_k, Q_j) to inform the insert phase of the status update (Line 11).

The output generation is different to support different selection modes, i.e., *recent* and *all*. For the recent selection mode, it follows the precedent instance pointers specified in {ptr_instance} of PMatch entries recursively to the initial matching ECQ and output a series of those instances in the form of a composite event instance. To support the all mode, every previous instance of the same source, stored in the same ECQ of the pointed instances, is harvested to compose output results as long as they satisfy the time conditions.

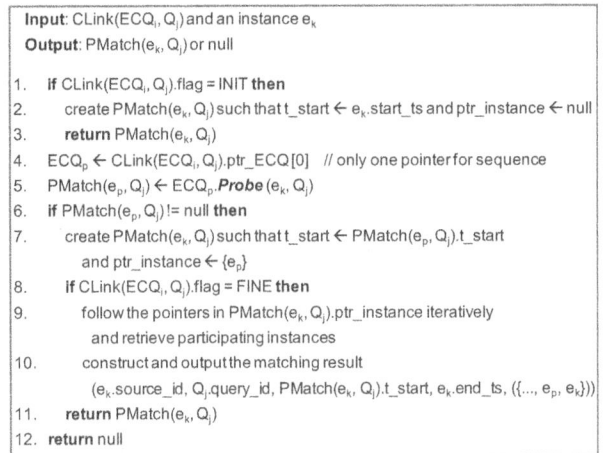

Figure 5. Algorithm for sequence in test phase

Conjunctions. Conjunction is similar to sequence except that all the incoming event instances can initiate a new matching and thus we need to probe all the other connected ECQs via the Probe function. As such, the proposed ECQ-based processing algorithm can easily support conjunction queries of simultaneous queries, compared to conventional automata-based CEMs.

Disjunctions. The evaluation of disjunction is straightforward: it simply generates union of its inputs. It does not need to look up other ECQs nor check time constraints. Thus, SCEMon does not create any PMatch entries, resulting in no insertion of instances.

5.1.2 Insert Phase

The insert phase updates ECQ_i, reflecting the dynamic composition status affected by the event instance e_k. That is, e_k as well as the PMatch entries, newly created in the test phase, are stored into ECQ_i. (1) First, the entries are added into the PMB of e_k. (2) Then, e_k is inserted into the SIQ. (3) Finally, the insertion updates the hash entry HT(e_k.source_id) so that it points to the newly added e_k in the queue. Note that, for an incoming e_k, insertion takes place *at most once* even for the case where e_k extends multiple partial matching.

For efficient memory management, SCEMon needs to delete any obsolete stored instances from ECQs. All the ECQs in the shared network are accessed periodically to remove old instances from each SIQ and update the corresponding hash table accordingly.

5.1.3 Correctness of Incremental Query Processing

Receiving event instances, SCEMon changes the state of the shared ECQ network. It computes the matching results for multiple queries incrementally, as if multiple query processing plans are evaluated independently. Let $e_k \in E_i$ denote an instance e_k of event class E_i (for all e_k, there is a single E_i such that $e_k \in E_i$). Also, let $E_i \in Q_j$ denote that E_i is a member event class of the CEM query Q_j. Then the following theorem holds:

Theorem 1. Correctness of Incremental Processing for Sequence: *For a sequence query Q_j with event classes E_1, E_2, ..., and E_n with time condition t_cond, if there exists PMatch(e_n, Q_j) such that $e_n \in E_n$, then there exists (e_1, e_2, ..., e_{n-1}) such that*

- *$e_1 \in E_1$, $e_2 \in E_2$, ..., $e_{n-1} \in E_{n-1}$,*
- *e_i.end_ts $\leq e_{i+1}$.start_ts, and*
  e_n.end_ts - e_1.start_ts $\leq Q_j$.t_cond for $1 \leq i \leq n-1$.

The complete matching result is given by (e_1, e_2, ..., e_{n-1}, e_n).

Proof.

By definition, if there exists PMatch(e_k, Q_j) such that $e_k \in E_1$, then PMatch(e_k, Q_j).t_start = e_k.start_ts.

By Lemma 1, if there exists PMatch(e_n, Q_j) such that $e_n \in E_n$, there exists PMatch(e_{n-1}, Q_j) such that $e_{n-1} \in E_{n-1}$, e_{n-1}.end_ts $\leq$ e_n.start_ts, (e_n.end_ts - PMatch(e_{n-1}, Q_j).t_start) $\leq Q_j$.t_cond. ...(1)

By induction, there exist PMatch(e_{n-2}, Q_j), ..., PMatch(e_2, Q_j), and PMatch(e_1, Q_j) such that $e_{n-2} \in E_{n-2}$, ..., $e_2 \in E_2$, $e_1 \in E_1$, and e_{n-2}.end_ts $\leq e_{n-1}$.start_ts, ..., e_1.end_ts $\leq e_2$.start_ts.

By definition, PMatch(e_{n-1}, Q_j).t_start = PMatch(e_{n-2}, Q_j).t_start = ... = PMatch(e_1, Q_j).t_start = e_1.start_ts.

Thus, (e_n.end_ts - e_1.start_ts) $\leq Q_j$.t_cond. (By equation (1))

$\therefore$ Corresponding (e_1, e_2, ..., e_{n-1}) exists.

End of Proof

Lemma 1.

For any $E_k \in Q_j$ where k > 1, if there exists PMatch(e_k, Q_j) such that $e_k \in E_k$, then there exists PMatch(e_{k-1}, Q_j) such that

- $e_{k-1} \in E_{k-1}$,
- e_{k-1}.end_ts $\leq e_k$.start_ts, and
- (e_k.end_ts - PMatch(e_{k-1}, Q_j).t_start) $\leq Q_j$.t_cond.

Proof.

There exists PMatch(e_k, Q_j) such that $e_k \in E_k$ for k > 1, if and only if there exists e_{k-1} such that

$e_{k-1} \in E_{k-1}$ ($\because E_{k-1} \in$ CLink(ECQ$_k$, Q_j).ptr_ECQ),

e_{k-1}.end_ts $\leq e_k$.start_ts ($\because e_{k-1}$ was already stored), and

(e_k.end_ts - PMatch(e_{k-1}, Q_j).t_start) $\leq Q_j$.t_cond.

$\therefore$ Corresponding PMatch(e_{k-1}, Q_j) exists.

End of Proof

For conjunction, the algorithm probes all participating ECQs to check where the matching is complete; for disjunction it probes none. Therefore, for these patterns, correctness follows trivially.

5.1.4 Shared Processing with Instance Sharing

The processing algorithm presented in this section is designed to inherently share incoming event instances by multiple CEM queries on top of the shared ECQ network. We note that the performance improvement of SCEMon is brought mainly at the insert phase; the algorithm stores a small number of instances in ECQs. The cost of the delete operation necessary to clean memory with obsolete instances is also reduced accordingly. Thus, the costs of insert and delete operations become constant regardless of the number of queries, resulting in significant performance improvement. Next, we discuss how to further optimize the processing of SCEMon by leveraging additional sharing and redundancy reduction opportunities.

5.2 Sub-Pattern Sharing

In the basic SCEMon discussed so far, individual queries are handled separately during the test phase since CLT maintains them separately. Thus, when different queries share a partial pattern, this pattern is tested multiple times (See Figure 1 for the example of a partial pattern, i.e., **A;B** and **A&B**, in our two example queries; here it is necessary to probe ECQ[A] twice for an input instance of ECQ[B]).

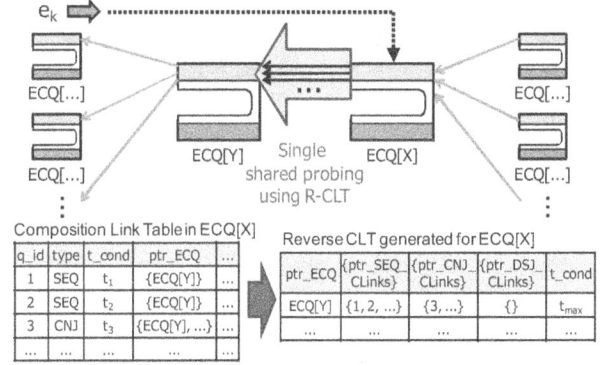

Figure 6. Sub-pattern sharing using R-CLT

Specifically, for a *binary* pattern formed by two adjoining ECQs, its former ECQ needs to be probed by the later ECQ multiple times. Thus, this redundant work can be eliminated substantially by sharing a probing result among different queries. The probing result can also be shared between the queries of different composition patterns, e.g., between sequence and conjunction queries. In addition, successive application of such binary pattern sharing can effectively support any longer sub-patterns. Note that such sub-pattern sharing opportunities, especially sharing of any binary patterns rather than longer sub-patterns, exist plentifully in large-scale CEM environments, for instance, monitoring population patterns in hot spots of a city.

Figure 6 illustrates the general case of the sub-pattern between two adjoining ECQs, i.e., ECQ[X] and ECQ[Y]. For a number of CEM queries, ECQ[Y] is specified to be probed by ECQ[X] multiple times in *any* positions of *any* composition patterns. Note that it is not identical to the case of prefix sharing techniques such as 'prefix-caching of automata states' in [16] and 'pre-fix state merging' in [17]. Unlike in previous work, instead of trying to reuse intermediate results matching entire common prefixes, we reuse partial processing results through probing as shown in the figure. Since common prefixes require complete matches from the beginning of the pattern, they are less frequently available than the partial results we are probing. Thus the proposed mechanism results in further savings by taking advantage of extended sub-pattern sharing opportunities.

5.2.1 Reverse CLT (R-CLT) and R-CLinks

To share a probing result among all relevant queries, we extend the CLT structure to include the information on the many diverse queries to share the probing result. For this purpose, we introduce a new table, called *Reverse CLT (R-CLT)*. **Reverse CLT (R-CLT)** is generated from CLT in each ECQ and contains a set of *Reverse CLinks (R-CLinks)*, which is formally defined as 5–tuple (*ptr_ECQ, {ptr_SEQ_CLinks}, {ptr_CNJ_CLinks}, {ptr_DSJ_CLinks}, t_cond*), where

- *ptr_ECQ* is a pointer to an ECQ that needs to be probed;
- the three sets, *{ptr_SEQ_CLinks}*, *{ptr_CNJ_CLinks}*, and *{ptr_DSJ_CLinks}*, contain the pointers of CLinks including the probed ECQ in the CLT, which correspond to sequence, conjunction, and disjunction queries respectively; and
- *t_cond* is the maximum value of the time conditions among the CLinks in {ptr_SEQ_CLinks} and {ptr_CNJ_CLinks}.

R-CLT is derived easily from CLT. (a) For each distinct ptr_ECQ specified in CLinks, an R-CLink entry is created. (b) Then, the corresponding CLinks are inserted into {ptr_SEQ_CLinks}, {ptr_CNJ_CLinks}, or {ptr_DSJ_CLinks}. (c) Finally, those CLinks which do not have any pointers to other ECQs, (i.e., CLinks of disjunction or CLinks flagged as INIT in sequence), are gathered into a special R-CLink whose ptr_ECQ is null.

When sub-pattern sharing is enabled, SCEMon enumerates R-CLT instead of CLT in the test phase. For each R-CLink in R-CLT, it probes the corresponding ECQ *only once* with the largest time condition. If the Probe function returns a precedent instance that satisfies the time condition, SCEMon evaluates the extension of partial matching for each CLink specified in the sets, {ptr_SEQ_CLinks} and {ptr_CNJ_CLinks}. If it returns null, then no further evaluation is needed. For those R-CLink's whose ptr_ECQ is null, it is not necessary to probe another ECQ; thus, SCEMon simply proceeds to the insert phase.

5.2.2 Shared Processing with Sub-Pattern Sharing

The cost of the Probe function is mainly caused by searching for a precedent instance of a specified event source stored in SIQ, especially with the presence of a large number of event sources. Thus, the reuse of precedent event instances once returned by the Probe function plays a critical role in sharing benefits. This sharing is highly beneficial when there exist a large number of the CEM queries that monitor some binary patterns of common interest frequently. The cost of the probe operation during the test phase can be reduced significantly as the degree of sub-pattern sharing among CEM queries. Even for the worst case, the cost is bounded by the number of primitive event classes (or the number of ECQs), not by the number of CEM queries.

5.3 PMB Reduction

SCEMon also shares among multiple queries the partial matching information of individual event instances. This is especially useful when those queries are triggered initially by common event instances. For those cases, the PMB size can be reduced by helping share the PMatch entries across queries.

Since SCEMon investigates each PMatch entry to evaluate the possible extension of partial matching of a corresponding query, the PMB size corresponding to an event instance can influence the processing cost. As the size of PMB increases, SCEMon needs to spend more time for accessing necessary PMatch entries.

Let Ps denote the selection probability, meaning how many subsequent instances extend the partial matching in sequence queries. If Ps is small enough, PMatch entries of initial matching for the sequence queries are dominant in PMB. We note that the PMatch entries of initial matching contain redundant information for the corresponding sequence queries: all the recorded PMatch.t_start's corresponding to the same start timestamp. Moreover, the PMatch.{ptr_instance} values are null. Thus, we can drop these entries from PMB and substitute the start timestamp of the event instance for the corresponding initial matching time. By doing this, we can reduce the size of PMB approximately as a factor of Ps. Consequently, we can reduce the evaluation cost of partial matching extensions during the test phase significantly for small values of Ps.

6. PERFORMANCE ANALYSIS

The processing cost of SCEMon mainly includes five components: the cost of searching for an ECQ (C_{ECQ}), the cost of probing other ECQs to search for precedent instances (C_{Probe}), the cost to evaluate the extension of partial matching ($C_{Evaluate}$), the

cost to insert an instance into an ECQ (C_{Insert}), and the cost to clean obsolete instances (C_{Clean}). Therefore, the cost CP is:

$$C_P = k_1 C_{ECQ} + k_2 C_{Probe} + k_3 C_{Evaluate} + k_4 C_{Insert} + k_5 C_{Clean}$$

The weights k_1 through k_5 are infrastructure-specific.

C_{ECQ} depends on the number of all ECQs, which is equal to the total number of primitive event classes, Npc. As long as a small number of primitive events are shared by a large number of CEM queries, the cost can be considered tiny compared to other terms.

C_{Probe} is a function of the average number of queries that an ECQ participates in (n_q), the average number of probing for a query (n_{pr}), and the unit cost of probing (c_{pr}).

- n_q can be computed as the degree of event class sharing D_S, ($Nq\ Nqec$) / Npc, where Nq is the number of queries, $Nqec$ is the average number of event classes used in a query, and Npc is the total number of primitive event classes used in SCEMon.
- n_{pr} is estimated differently for different composition types: it is approximately 1 for sequence, $Nqec$ for conjunction, 0 for disjunction.
- C_{pr} involves lookups to the index in the SIQ. This cost depends on the implementation of ECQ. In SCEMon, these lookups have logarithmic complexity $O(\log Ns)$ by using *STL:map* [13] for the index[3], where Ns is the number of event sources.

Hence, the term C_{Probe} is calculated as ($D_S\ n_{pr} \log Ns$), which is proportional to Nq and $\log Ns$. Yet, thanks to the sub-pattern sharing discussed in Section 5.2, this cost can be bounded by ($Npc\ n_{pr} \log Ns$) since n_q is at most the number of ECQs, i.e., Npc.

$C_{Evalute}$ is mainly dependent on the size of the PMB of a precedent instance, since it looks up the partial matching information for a query. The average size of PMB can be approximated to n_q, which is D_S. Therefore, $C_{Evaluate}$ can be computed as $O(\log D_S)$. According to Section 5.3, this cost can be reduced by the PMB reduction by a factor of Ps.

C_{Insert} is a function of the probability of insertions (p_{ins}) and the unit insertion cost (c_{ins}): $C_{Insert} = p_{ins}\ c_{ins}$. Since we use *STL:deque* and *STL:map* for the queue and the index in the SIQ, c_{ins} has the logarithmic complexity $O(\log Ns)$ for the insertions. The probability, p_{ins}, is between 0 and 1; our experiments in Section 7 showed that in practice most input event instances are inserted into some ECQ. Hence, taking a conservative approach, p_{ins} can be approximated as 1 for all composition types (except for disjunction, for which p_{ins} is approximated as 0 since we do not store event instances for disjunction). Note that C_{Insert} is not proportional to the number of CEM queries, Nq. This is because of the instance sharing technique presented in Section 5.1.

Finally, C_{Clean} is a sum of the cost to check all SIQs (c_{chk}) and the cost to delete obsolete instances in them (c_{del}).

- c_{chk} is estimated as the number of ECQs, i.e., Npc. Note that for the conventional separate processing scheme in Figure 1-(a), it is very large, i.e., ($Nq\ Ns$).
- c_{del} is proportional to the average number of stored instances and the unit cost of deletions. Due to the instance sharing, SCEMon stores incoming event instances at most once regardless of the number of queries. Thus, it is only proportional to Ns, not to Nq.

---

[3] Refer to http://www.cplusplus.com/reference/stl/ for the complexity of STL containers.

The storage cost of SCEMon, C_S, can be estimated as follows: Let the rate of input event instances incoming to SCEMon is (Ns r_e), where r_e is the average rate of event generation from a source. The length, T_W, of the time window for storing events is determined based on the time constraints of the registered CEM queries. Let c_s is the size of the memory consumed by each instance, then C_S can be calculated as (p_{ins} Ns r_e T_W c_s). As we discussed above, p_{ins} is 0 for disjunction and approximately 1 for all the other types with a large number of the queries. Note that, thanks to the ECQ sharing, C_S is proportional to Ns, but not to Nq.

7. PERFORMANCE EVALUATION

In this section, we evaluate the performance improvement of SCEMon over conventional separate processing (SP) schemes in large-scale CEM environments. The experiments were run on Intel Core 2 Quad Yorkfield Q9550 CPU (2.83GHz) and 8 GB RAM. The machine was running Debian Linux 2.6.18 64-bit.

Workloads. For the evaluation, we generate synthetic input event instances and CEM queries. Input event instances are generated randomly in the form of a tuple (*source_id*, *event_class*, *start_ts*, *end_ts*), as described in Section 3.1. CEM queries are generated based on the sequential query templates given below.

CEM query template

PATTERN	*Sequence*
WITH	*A, B, C*
WHERE	*[symbol]*
WITHIN	*[200-240] mins*

The primitive event classes in the WITH clause, i.e., A, B and C, are randomly selected among a given set of primitive event classes. The time condition in the WITHIN clause is also randomly specified in the value range. In this work, we focus on the efficient processing of composition patterns so that any additional predicate conditions in the WHERE clause are not included.

As default setting, we use 1K sequential queries and 1K event sources assuming 50 primitive event classes. Upon the start of experimental runs, queries are registered into the system. Also, generated event instances are loaded into the main memory and pulled into the system at the maximum rate it could accept.

Evaluation metrics. We measured the performance in terms of processing and storage costs. First, for the processing cost, we use the *unit processing time* as an evaluation metric; it is defined as $t_{elapsed}$ / N_{total_event}, where N_{total_event} is the total number of the input event instances, and $t_{elapsed}$ is the total elapsed processing time, not including time to deliver the output. Second, for the storage cost, we count the average number of event instances stored in ECQs; note that the amount of stored instances indicates the storage consumption in CEM processing. The number of the stored instances is counted before and after each memory cleaning, and the average is computed over 15 cleanings after warm-up.

Comparing techniques. For comparison, we have implemented a conventional SP scheme based on the work done by Wu et al. [1]. The SP scheme illustrated in Section 3.2 is implemented in C++ using STL [13]. The SP scheme is fairly implemented by performance comparisons with publically available CEM implementations, Cayuga [14] and Esper [15] (See Section 7.6 for the detailed discussion).

To closely investigate the effectiveness of the shared processing techniques employed in this work, we use three different SCEMon implementations: (1) with event instance sharing (Section 5.1), (2)

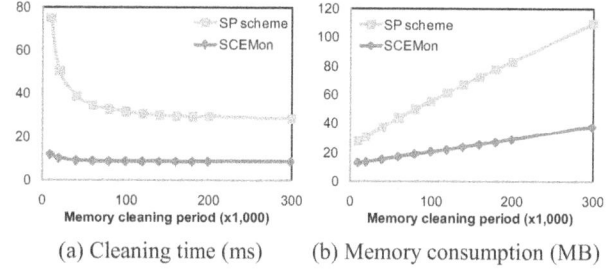

(a) Cleaning time (ms)   (b) Memory consumption (MB)

Figure 7. Effect of memory cleaning period (N_c)

with instance sharing and sub-pattern sharing (Section 5.2), (3) with instance sharing, sub-pattern sharing and PMB reduction (Section 5.3). For fair comparison, SCEMon is also implemented in C++ using STL [13].

Memory cleaning period. The system performs periodic cleaning, where it deletes obsolete instances older than the maximum time window of all relevant queries. Cleaning obsolete activity instances is critical for in-memory processing of CEM queries. It has significant impact on the processing as well as storage cost. It is especially important for the SP scheme since the memory space would quickly be exhausted due to the numerous per-object stacks.

We examine the effect of the cleaning on the processing and the storage cost. Figure 7 shows the results while we perform the cleaning every Nc updates of event instances. We observe that there exists a trade-off between the cleaning time and memory usage. The cleaning time of SCEMon is not much affected by the cleaning period. The time-ordered instances stored in shared ECQs make the cleaning process highly efficient since the number of the queues to be scanned is relatively small and the set of obsolete instances is easily identified. On the other hand, for the SP scheme, a huge number of the per-source stacks should be scanned to delete obsolete event instances as well as empty stacks. The figure presents that too frequent cleaning causes unnecessary scanning with rarely effective deletions, resulting in the excessive cleaning time. The figure also shows that it is hardly beneficial to defer cleaning beyond some extent, since the cleaning time decreases marginally. Meanwhile, deferred cleaning substantially increases the memory consumption to hold more obsolete instances and unused stacks. In the experiments below, we set the base cleaning period to 100K where the cleaning time starts to be saturated while the memory consumption increases linearly.

7.1 Processing Scalability

This section shows the scalability of the SP scheme and SCEMon in large-scale CEM environments. Figure 8 presents the unit processing time in microsecond.

Scalability with the number of queries (Nq). We increase the number of queries from 100 to 5K. As shown in Figure 8-(a), the unit processing times of the SP scheme drastically increase for larger Nq's compared to SCEMon. In contrast, the suit of shared processing techniques based on ECQs enables SCEMon to significantly reduce the processing time, especially at larger Nq's With 5K simultaneous queries, for instance, it shows about 32 times better performance than the SP scheme.

Scalability with the number of sources (Ns). Figure 8-(b) shows the performance with increasing the number of sources up to 5K. The result illustrates that the processing times of the SP scheme and SCEMon increase proportionally to (log Ns); note that X-axis

(a) Increasing Nq (b) Increasing Ns

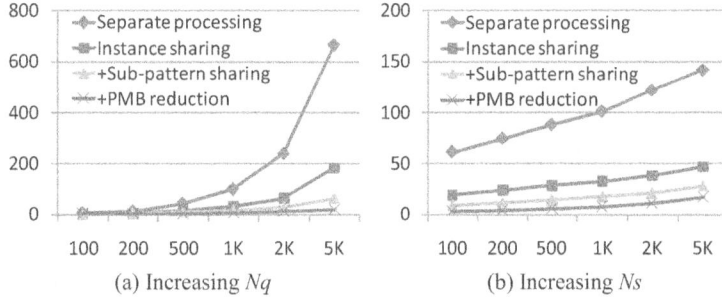

Figure 8. Unit processing times (μsec) of SP scheme vs. SCEMon

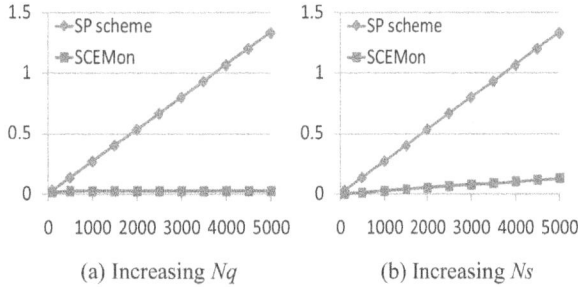

Figure 9. Performance breakdown of conventional SP scheme vs. SCEMon

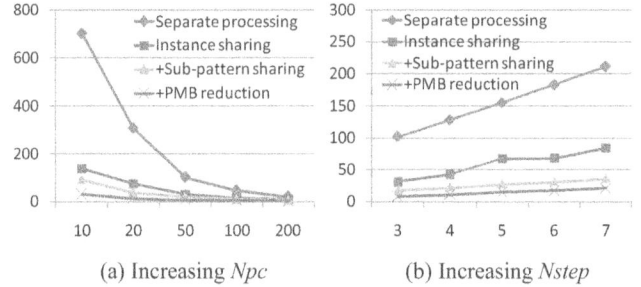

(a) Increasing Nq (b) Increasing Ns

Figure 10. Number of stored event instances (M)

(a) Increasing Npc (b) Increasing $Nstep$

Figure 11. Unit processing times (μsec)

of the graph has a logarithmic scale. Yet, it also shows that SCEMon deals with a large number of event sources much more efficiently than the SP scheme.

7.2 Effectiveness of SCEMon Techniques

In this section, we closely investigate where the significant performance gain comes from. Figure 9 shows the breakdowns on the unit processing times of the SP scheme and SCEMon in default setting, i.e., 1K queries and 1K sources. The figure shows that almost a half of the processing time in the SP scheme is spent to search for a proper data structure corresponding to a source of an incoming instance (labeled "*Source(SP)*") due to the overhead of managing many event sources. The time for deleting obsolete event instances in separate data structures ("*Clean*") takes the second place. Yet, the time for evaluating state transitions for individual instances ("*Evaluate*") is shown to be relatively small.

In SCEMon with the instance sharing, the times for storing incoming event instances and deleting obsolete instances ("*Insert*" and "*Clean*") are reduced significantly, compared to those of the SP scheme. The performance improvement conforms to our expectations and analysis we performed while designing the shared storage of ECQs. However, the times for probing other ECQs and evaluating the extension of partial matching ("*Probe(SCEMon)*" and "*Evaluate*") are not reduced sufficiently.

For SCEMon with additional sub-pattern sharing, the time for probing other ECQs ("*Probe(SCEMon)*") is reduced. This shows that the probing operation is optimized by using the R-CLT and happens only once for each target ECQ. Moreover, we simplify the probing operation by omitting the step for checking up the initial matching time in the PMB and defer it to the evaluation step. Thus, the time for evaluating the extension of partial matching ("*Evaluate*") increases slightly. This result also conforms to the analysis in Section 6.

Finally, for SCEMon with full sharing techniques, the time for evaluating the extension of partial matching ("*Evaluate*") is

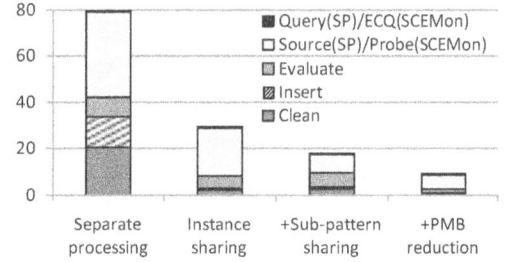

reduced, since the PMB reduction technique is designed to reduce the PMB access time during the evaluation. In addition, event instances stored in ECQs are associated with smaller PMBs, resulting in the time for deleting obsolete event instances ("*Clean*") is reduced accordingly.

7.3 Storage Scalability

We also evaluate the storage performance of SCEMon compared with the SP scheme. Figure 10-(a) shows the average number of event instances stored in the data structure as the number of queries (Nq) increases. The SP scheme stores event instances in each NFA separately and does not share them at all. This leads to the redundant storage consumption proportional to the number of queries. For SCEMon, however, the numbers of stored instances are saturated for larger Nq's. This is the result of instance sharing by which only a single copy of individual incoming instances is stored regardless of a multitude of simultaneous queries.

Figure 10-(b) demonstrates the remarkable storage efficiency of SCEMon over the SP scheme for large numbers of sources. In fact, the storage costs of SCEMon also increase linearly with the number of sources (Ns) due to the higher rates of incoming event instances for larger Ns's. However, SCEMon keeps the storage costs much lower, almost 10% in the setting, compared to the SP scheme by virtue of instance sharing.

7.4 Performance Characteristics of SCEMon with Other Attributes

We have also performed the performance evaluation of SCEMon and the SP scheme with varying numbers of primitive event classes and sequence steps in the template sequence query.

Performance with the number of primitive event classes (Npc). We investigate how the performance of SCEMon varies due to the degree of event class sharing. We change the number of primitive event classes from 10 to 200 so that an identical number of simultaneous queries share them in different levels of sharing.

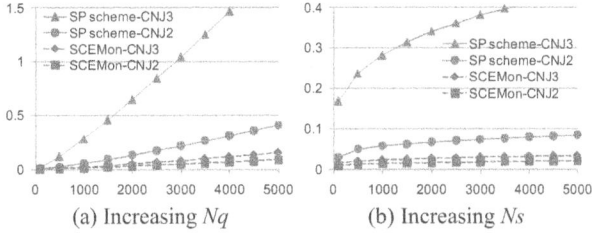

(a) Increasing Nq (b) Increasing Ns

Figure 12. Unit processing time (ms) with conjunction

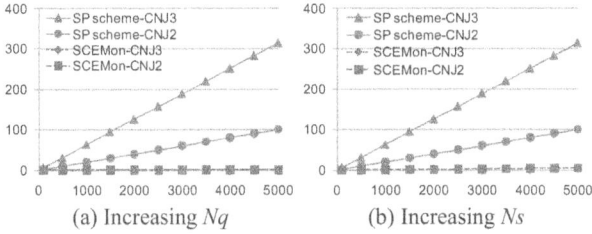

(a) Increasing Nq (b) Increasing Ns

Figure 13. Number of stored instances (M) with conjunction

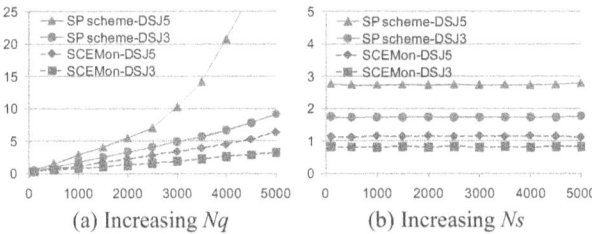

(a) Increasing Nq (b) Increasing Ns

Figure 14. Unit processing time (ms) with disjunction

(See Figure 11-(a).) When Npc is 10, i.e., we only use 10 primitive event classes in the setting, an event class should be shared by large numbers of simultaneous queries. On the other hand, when Npc is 200, the degree of sharing decreases. Due to the proposed event-centric sharing approach, the performance of SCEMon becomes much better than that of the SP scheme with smaller Npc's. As expected, with larger Npc's, the performance gap between the SP scheme and SCEMon gets smaller, but SCEMon still performs better than the SP scheme.

Performance with the number of sequence steps ($Nstep$). The number of sequence steps also influences the degree of event-class sharing, since each query can contain more numbers of primitive event classes with larger $Nstep$'s. Figure 11-(b) demonstrates that the unit processing times of the SP scheme and SCEMon increase as $Nstep$ increases, similar to the impact of increasing Nq. However, the impact is not as significant as that of increasing Nq, since a large portion of incoming event instances fails to extend partial matching and is discarded without any further evaluation.

7.5 Performance Evaluation with Conjunction and Disjunction

We have also evaluated the performance of SCEMon with conjunction and disjunction queries. Figure 12 and 13 show that SCEMon outperforms the SP scheme significantly for conjunction for increasing Nq's and Ns's. This is because the SP scheme instantiates all the permutated sequences of the participating event classes in an NFA, which results in a huge number of NFA states loaded in the system. Our results show the sharp increase in the processing cost for the conjunction queries of three event classes, i.e., CNJ3. On the other hand, Figure 14 shows the results of disjunction. As a larger number of NFAs are instantiated (see

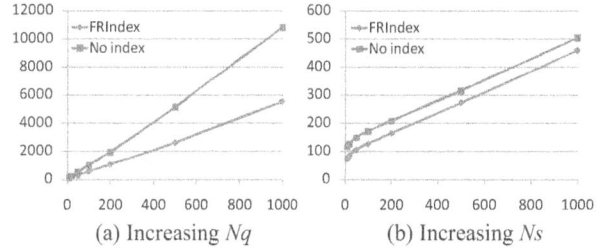

(a) Increasing Nq (b) Increasing Ns

Figure 15. Unit processing time of Cayuga: *FRIndex* **is a primary optimization technique suggested in Cayuga that provides optimized access to attributes among different queries. We have built the index on the event class ids so that the effectiveness of the index gets significant with increasing Nq.**

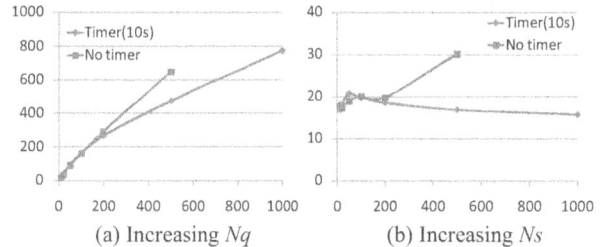

(a) Increasing Nq (b) Increasing Ns

Figure 16. Unit processing time of Esper: *Timer* **is a kind of stopwatch. If associated pattern expressions do not turn true within the specified time period, they are stopped and permanently false. The setting of no timer with 1000 sources causes out-of-memory exception.**

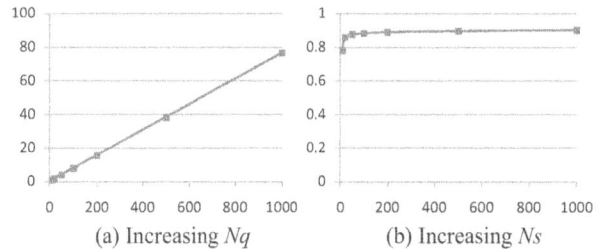

(a) Increasing Nq (b) Increasing Ns

Figure 17. Unit processing time of our SP scheme implementation

disjunction of five events, i.e., DSJ5, compared to DSJ3), the processing time of the SP scheme gets longer due to the lack of sharing. In Figure 14-(b), note that the processing cost of disjunction queries remains almost constant with a fixed number of queries. This is because the incoming event instances are not stored and looked up for disjunction at all.

7.6 Performance of Publically Available Implementations

To understand the performance of conventional SP schemes with large numbers of queries and sources, we have conducted the performance evaluation using publically available implementations. First, we retrieved the Cayuga implementation from [14] and ran it on a 32-bit Windows XP machine of Intel Core 2 CPU (2.13GHz) and 3.50GB RAM. The Linux configuration of the Cayuga implementation is not correctly supported so that we use Windows instead.

The evaluation shows that Cayuga is not efficient for large numbers of queries and sources. We measured the unit processing time in microsecond as we increase the number of queries (Nq) and the number of sources (Ns) from 10 to 1K respectively. (We used 10 as the default values of Nq and Ns in each experiment. It could not support 1K queries and 1K sources at the same time.) The results shown in Figure 15 demonstrate that the unit processing time of Cayuga increases linear proportionally to N_q and N_s. We further challenged Cayuga with larger scales and observed that the implementation consumes too much memory to run in the experimental setting.

Figure 16 presents the performance evaluation of another publically available CEM implementation, *Esper*. We retrieved the implementation from [15] and performed evaluation in the same setting as Cayuga. It shows better performance than Cayuga, yet the processing times are larger than those of our SP scheme implementation (See Figure 17 that presents the processing times of our implementation in the same setting). This is because ours is much specialized to the core processing of CEM while Cayuga and Esper are involved in additional processing such as dealing with XML input. Based on these results, we note that our implementation of conventional SP schemes is reasonable for fair comparison to SCEMon.

8. CONCLUSION and DISCUSSIONS

In this paper, we focused on the scalability issues when large numbers of CEM queries and event sources exist in upcoming CEM environments. To address these challenges effectively, we take an *event-centric sharing approach* rather than conventional query/source-separate processing approaches. ECQ is a novel data structure designed to facilitate efficient evaluations of multiple queries over very large volumes of event streams from numerous event sources. ECQs are composable to build a single shared network within which multiple queries are efficiently evaluated. We developed a set of the shared processing techniques on top of the ECQ network. Our evaluation showed that our approach outperforms the conventional approaches in large-scale CEM environments.

While we did not discuss it in this paper, SCEMon can easily support negation and Kleene closure; these require slight modifications in the *Probe* function. For negation, the condition testing, i.e., if any event instance exists and satisfies the time constraints, should be inversed; for Kleene closure, the Probe function checks the number of the stored precedent instances satisfying the time and value constraints in the SIQ. In addition, the test phases for sequence and conjunction also need to be modified. All ECQs designated to generate outputs need to look up the ECQs participating for negation and Kleene closure, before it generates output results. Since these modifications are straightforward, we do not present the algorithms in this paper.

Another aspect of CEM processing not discussed in this paper is nested query monitoring. A nested query consists of different patterns, e.g., a conjunction of sequences, a sequence of conjunctions and disjunctions, etc. Supporting such nested queries has been considered as an important issue in composite event processing research, yet rarely addressed. SCEMon can have virtual primitive event classes for individual composition patterns in nested queries. We register each pattern as a CEM query and define a virtual primitive event class (VPEC) for the results of the query. SCEMon feedbacks the results redefined as the instances of the VPEC as input. In other words, SCEMon constructs the shared network of ECQs that are responsible for real primitive event classes

and VPEC's. Treating nested patterns as primitive event classes, SCEMon can evaluate complicatedly nested queries effectively within the shared network of ECQs.

9. ACKNOWLEDGMENTS

This research was supported by Future-based Technology Development Program through the National Research Foundation of Korea (NRF) funded by the Ministry of Education, Science and Technology (2010-0020729).

10. REFERENCES

[1] Wu, E., Diao, Y. and Rizvi, S. 2006. High-performance complex event processing over streams. In Proc. of SIGMOD.

[2] Akdere, M., Çetintemel, U. and Tatbul, N. 2008. Plan-based Complex Event Detection across Distributed Sources. In Proc. of VLDB.

[3] Mei, Y. and Madden, S. 2009. ZStream: A Cost-based Query Processor for Adaptively Detecting Composite Events. In Proc. of SIGMOD.

[4] Yang, D., Rundensteiner , E. and Ward, M. 2009. A Shared Execution Strategy for Multiple Pattern Mining Requests over Streaming Data. In Proc. of VLDB.

[5] Demers, A., Gehrke, J., Panda, B., Riedewald, M., Sharma, V. and White, W. 2007. Cayuga: A general purpose event monitoring system. In Proc. of CIDR.

[6] Gatziu, S. and Dittrich, K. 1994. Events in an active object-oriented database, In Workshop on Rules in Database Systems.

[7] Chakravarthy, S., Krishnaprasad, V., Anwar, E. and Kim, S. 1994. Composite events for active databases: Semantics, contexts and detection. In Proc. of VLDB.

[8] Urban, S., Biswas, I. and Dietrich, S. 2006. Filtering features for a composite event definition language. In Proc. of SAINT.

[9] Hinze, A. 2003. Efficient filtering of composite events, In Proc. of BNCD.

[10] Elkhalifa, L., Adaikkalavan, R. and Chakravarthy, S. 2005. InfoFilter: A system for expressive pattern specification and detection over text streams. In Proc. of SAC.

[11] Agrawal, J., Diao, Y., Gyllstrom, D. and Immerman, N. 2008 Efficient pattern matching over event streams. In Proc. of SIGMOD.

[12] Ananthanarayanan, G., Haridasan, M., Mohomed, I., Terry, D. and Thekkath, C. 2009. StarTrack: A framework for enabling track-based applications. In Proc. of MobiSys.

[13] Standard Template Library, http://www.cplusplus.com/reference/stl/

[14] Cayuga source code, http://sourceforge.net/projects/cayuga/

[15] Esper official site, http://esper.codehaus.org

[16] Candan, K., Hsiung, W., Chen, S., Tatemura, J. and Agrawal, D. 2006. AFilter: Adaptable XML Filtering with Prefix-Caching and Suffix-Clustering. In Proc. of VLDB.

[17] Hong, M., Riedewald, M., Koch, C., Gehrke, J. and Demers, A. 2009. Rule-based multi-query optimization. In Proc. of EDBT.

Controlled English Language for Production and Event Processing Rules

Mark H. Linehan
IBM Watson Research Center
19 Skyline Drive
Hawthorne, NY 10598
+1 914 784 7002
mlinehan@us.ibm.com

Sylvain Dehors
IBM La Gaude-Sophia
Antipolis,
1167 Route de Saint Laurent
06610 La Gaude, France
+33 4 9296 8669
sylvain.dehors@fr.ibm.com

Ella Rabinovich
IBM Haifa Research Lab
Haifa 31905, Israel
+ 972 4 8296184
ellak@il.ibm.com

Fabiana Fournier
IBM Haifa Research Lab
Haifa 31905, Israel
+972 4 8296489
fabiana@il.ibm.com

ABSTRACT

In recent years, event processing has matured from an emerging technology to one with pervasive uses in various industries. There is a growing segment of applications comprising a diversity of rule types that are developed by high-level users, who have business logic and process expertise rather than software development skills.

Technical rule languages for business (production) rules systems differ from event processing rules because they target different execution modes. Corresponding differences exist in the respective rule languages employed to date. This paper describes an integrated rule language that supports both kinds of rules, thus enabling business applications that combine them. The integrated language targets non-technical "business users" who write rules that employ both production and event processing rule functions.

The language proposed here is a textual "controlled natural language" based on the Semantics of Business Vocabulary and Business Rules (SBVR) specification of the Object Management Group (OMG). We describe an implementation that uses an SBVR parser, and an SBVR "vocabulary" that defines the syntax and semantics for event processing rules. The parser treats business rule and event processing concepts indifferently, and can be extended to other language concepts by additional vocabularies. Knowledge of the event processing aspects is limited to a conversion utility that transforms rules written using this language to an event processing network.

Categories and Subject Descriptors

D.3.2 [**Programming Languages**]: Language Classification---Multiparadigm languages, Very high-level languages, Extensible languages, Constraint and logic languages, SBVR; C.2.4 [**Computer-Communication Networks**]: Distributed Systems---Event processing; I.2.4 [**Artificial Intelligence**]: Knowledge Representation Formalisms and Methods---Representation languages.

General Terms: Human Factors, Languages.

Keywords: Event processing language, complex event processing, controlled natural language, Structured English, Semantics of Business Vocabulary and Business Rules, SBVR.

1. INTRODUCTION AND MOTIVATION

In both academic work and industrial software, production business rules and event processing rules are generally treated as distinct technologies, with different rule languages, rule engines, and supporting tools. By "production rules", we mean declarative rules characterized by if-then expressions, often implemented in the well-known RETE algorithm. Such expressions may be represented as textual statements in an artificial or "natural language inspired" syntax, as decision tables, as decision trees, or in other formats. Typically, the consequent part of these rules either trigger actions or infer values for consideration by other rules.

The other class of rules that we consider in this paper, event processing rules, receive a stream of incoming events, and filter individual events (stateless processing) or recognize patterns among multiple events (stateful processing) and generate derived events. Our focus in this paper is on rules used for stateful event pattern recognition, sometimes called "complex event processing" rules. These rules have very complex forms, incorporating numerous aspects that we describe below in Section 3.1. As we describe in that section, these rules are usually modeled as event processing agents that are organized in an event processing network.

The distinction between these two kinds of rules is partially due to different heritages: production rule technology was originally developed in the 1970s, most notably in the OPS5 system of Forgy [7]. In the several decades since then, production rule systems have evolved into "business rule management systems" (BRMS) such as Tibco [24], IBM WebSphere ILOG JRules product [10] and many others. On the other hand, event processing rule systems are relatively recent, introduced particularly by Luckham [14] and Etzion and Niblett [5]. Commercial implementations are offered by Streambase [23], Microsoft [15], IBM [9] and other vendors.

Both BRMS and event-processing platforms externalize business rules so that it is easier to modify applications in which the rules change frequently or are shared among multiple applications. Both technologies can be used to support human decision making or to implement fully automated responses. In addition, business users are involved in specifying the logic for both types of engines. However, business rules engines are typically request-driven. An application program is working on a business transaction and needs to make a decision on how to proceed. The business rule engine swings into action to perform the computation and return the result to the application. By contrast, event processing engines are event-driven. They run continuously, processing events as they arrive.

In addition to the differences in form, function, and heritage that are very briefly outlined above, these two kinds of rules are usually employed for very different application scenarios. Production rules have found their greatest commercial success in declaratively capturing business rules, so that they can be managed more easily than rules implemented in procedural code. An example is computing discounts in e-commerce applications. Event processing rules, as implied by their name, are used to detect patterns as events arise. They are widely employed, for example, to recognize and respond to trading patterns in financial markets, and to provide control functions in automated systems.

Event processing and business rule processing can be used together to enable sophisticated, fast-responding business processes. The event processing technology performs continuous pattern matching on current event data as it arrives to implement descriptive analytics (understanding what is happening) and basic, implicit predictive analytics (understanding what will happen if nothing is done). When it detects a threat or opportunity situation, it invokes a rule engine to classify the data and determine an appropriate course of action (prescriptive analytics). The result may be decision support information and recommendations presented to a human user (for example, through a business dashboard) or it may be an automated response (for example, invoking a business process, service or other application system; or turn on a machine). The combination of event processing and rule-processing technology within one business process is likely to become more common in the future, as companies realize the business benefits of fast, event-driven action with intelligent rule-based decision making. The combination is most valuable when a continuous-intelligence application needs sophisticated business decisions on what to do with threat or opportunity situations it has detected [20].

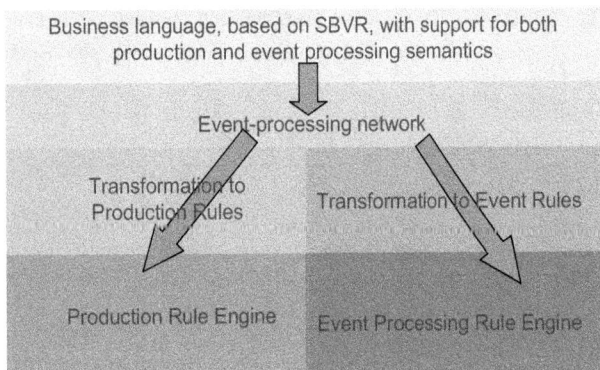

Figure 1: System Design

Although some systems that combine both production rules and event processing have been developed in the recent years (e.g. TIBCO [24], Drools [3]), in most cases, companies that use event processing and rule processing in concert, acquire the relevant technologies separately and then integrate them as part of the development process. For example, a financial services company that has bought an event-processing platform and tied it into a business rule engine to support capital markets trading application. In this work, we provide a pioneer unified business language with sufficient expressive power that addresses both kinds of rules and can be transparently translated into the implementation level.

Figure 1 summarizes the system that we built. In this paper, we address the top two levels of the figure: the business-oriented language that supports both production rule and event processing semantics, and a transformation that converts rules given in this business-oriented language to an Event Processing Network (EPN). We defer the discussion of the transformation of the EPN to runtime rule engines to another venue.

2. RELATED WORK

Event processing refers to an approach to software systems that is based on the idea of events, and that includes specific logic to filter, transform, or detect patterns in events as they occur [5]. Event processing is an emerging area and considerable research has been conducted during the last decade. A comprehensive introduction to event processing concepts and architecture can be found in [14] and [5]. In [14], Luckham introduces the Rapide™ event pattern language along with comprehensive use cases to illustrate the benefits of event processing systems. In [5], Etzion and Niblett describe how to use, design, and build event processing applications via a detailed example. The book also introduces the leading free and commercial tools available, along with several language implementations and many examples. A unified conceptual model of event-processing network for expressing the event-based interactions and event-processing specifications among components is offered in [21].

Commercial event processing became a viable market during the 2003 to 2005 time frame but the general industry awareness of EP platforms continues to expand, partly because of activities of the Event Processing Technical Society [6] and Object Management Group's new Event-Processing Community of Practice [16]. Revenue associated with EP platform products is growing faster than 30% per year [13]. Vendors include: Active Endpoints; Avaya; Axway; Decision-Zone; EsperTech; Event Zero; IBM; Informatica; InterSystems; Kx Systems; LG; McGraw Software; Microsoft; Oracle; Pegasystems; Progress Software; SAP; Software AG; StreamBase Systems; Systar; Tibco Software; Truviso; UC4 Software; Vitria; WestGlobal.

Previous work on production rules is quite extensive. Academic research as well as commercial products have been available for a number of years. Early production rule systems employed complex technical languages suitable for trained technical staff. In the last decade, the major actors (IBM WebSphere ILOG JRules, Blaze, Drools, Corticon) not only offered forward chaining rule execution, but also an authoring layer where users may write rules in more business friendly ways using decision tables, decision trees, or "controlled natural languages". The latter are structured versions of human languages, intended to be both meaningful to humans and have sufficient formal syntax and semantics to be automatable. Norbert Fuchs [8] and John Sowa [22] have explored the potential of controlled natural languages in some detail. This paper extends these ideas by including event processing rules.

A number of standardization activities have taken place around production rules and business rules. The RuleML initiative defines a family of Markup rule languages including production and "reaction" rules. It is a purely technical XML dialect for describing rules of different types.

W3C recommends the Rule Interchange Format (RIF) [25] for exchanging rules between systems. RIF defines description logic and production rules "dialects", but does not address event rules.

As an XML-based standard, W3C is not designed for direct human authoring.

The OMG supports two standards: *Production Rules Representation* (PRR, [17]) for the technical modeling of production rules, and *Semantics of Business Vocabulary and Business Rules* (SBVR, [18]) for modeling business rules in "Structured English" or other forms. PRR defines the structure of if-then rules, and delegates to OCL for formalizing expressions. SBVR specifies a metamodel for capturing the formal sense of human statements in terms of first-order logic, propositional logic, and modalities. This paper extensively builds on SBVR and discusses it in more detail in Section 4.

To date, there is no complex event processing standard. Vendors in this field use technical, proprietary, and non-interoperable languages.

Papers [1] and [2] by De Roover and Vanthienen discuss ways to implement SBVR business rules in part as event-condition-action (ECA) rules. However these rules are purely stateless, whereas this paper targets stateful event processing rules.

3. PRELIMINARIES

3.1 Event Processing Constructs

The terminology we use in this paper is based on the event processing language definition as presented by Etzion and Niblett in [5]. In this section we bring a brief overview of the main language constructs, fundamental for understanding the essence of the discussion below.

An *event type* is a specification for a set of event objects that have the same semantic intent and same structure; every event object is considered to be an instance of an event type. Event types can represent events arriving from a producer or events produced by an event processing agent (EPA). We denote such events as "raw" and "derived," respectively.

An *Event Processing Agent* (EPA) is a component that, given a set of input events, applies some logic for generating a set of output (derived) events. Possible EPA types are: filter, transformation, aggregation, pattern matching. We define a *stateful event processing agent* as an agent that maintains its internal state over successive invocations. For example, an EPA that performs aggregation of events over a time window is *stateful*, while an EPA that filters events by applying a predicate on the attributes of a single event is *stateless*.

There are three types of stateful EPAs:

1. Stateful filters that select the first m, the last m, or a random m of a set of events, where m is an integer.

2. Transformation EPAs that compute an aggregate (e.g. a total or an average) of a set of events, or combine several events.

3. Pattern matching EPAs that apply any of a variety of pattern matching rules. Examples include recognizing the presence or absence of a particular number of events of a specified event type, a sequence of events of specified types, events with a value that reach a minimum or maximum threshold, events that show movement in some spatial direction, etc.

A *context* is a named specification of conditions that groups event instances so that they can be processed in a related way. While there exist several context dimensions, in this work we refer to the three most commonly used dimensions: temporal, segmentation-oriented, and composite contexts. A *temporal context* consists of one or more time intervals, possibly overlapping. Each time interval corresponds to a context partition, which contains events that occur during that interval. This kind of context partition is often called a "time window".

A *segmentation-oriented context* is used to group event instances into context partitions based on the value of an attribute or collection of attributes in the instances themselves. As a simple example, consider an EPA that takes a single stream of input events, in which each event contains a customer identifier attribute. The value of this attribute can be used to group events so that there is a separate context partition for each customer. Each context partition contains only events related to that customer, so that the behavior of each customer can be tracked independently of the other customers.

A *composite context* combines two or more other contexts. Each composite context partition holds those events that meet the intersection of those other contexts. In the example used in this paper, a composite context combines a temporal context and a segmentation oriented context to select those events related to a single customer that occur within a time window.

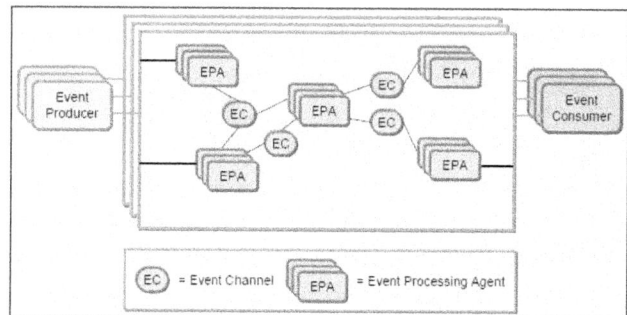

Figure 2: Schematic representation of EPN

An *Event Processing Network* (EPN) is a conceptual model, describing the event processing flow execution. It consists of a collection of event processing agents (EPAs), producers, and consumers linked by channels. The event processing network was first introduced in the field of modeling by Luckham in [14]. The conceptual model of EPN based on this idea was further elaborated by Sharon and Etzion in [21]. A schematic presentation of an EPN, including producers, consumers, EPAs and channels between them is demonstrated in Figure 2.

An EPN is event driven, thus EPAs communicate in asynchronous fashion by receiving and sending events. Although a channel can route several event types, in this paper we assume that a channel is manifested as an edge in the graph, connecting a single source with a single sink carrying a single event type.

3.2 Event Matching

A pattern matching agent (aka pattern detection) is a type of EPA that enables the analysis of collections of events and the relationship between them. Informally, we say that a combination of events matches a pattern if this combination satisfies the particular pattern definition. Pattern matching EPA examples are: all, sequence, absence and any.

A *pattern assertion* (PA) is a condition that a combination of events is required to meet for the pattern to be satisfied. Pattern assertion is a predicate, i.e. Boolean expression including variables (event attributes), mathematical (e.g. $+,-,*,<,>,=$) and logical (e.g. AND, OR, NOT) operators. We discriminate between *pattern assertion* referring to a single event type (e.g. A.price>100), aka event *threshold condition*, and assertion, encapsulating several event types (e.g. A.price>B.price), also denoted by *cross-event pattern assertion*.

As an example, consider the following synthetic scenario: sequence(A,B,C) where (1) A.price>B.price AND B.price>C.price; and (2) B.volume>100K. In this scenario we are looking for an ordered sequence of instances of types A, B and C respectively, with cross-event pattern assertion specified by (1) and event threshold condition specified by (2).

3.3 Business Rules Management Systems

A different style of pattern matching is used by business rule engines to identify specific patterns in a model (aka working memory) at a given point in time. The business rules are two-fold: a condition or pattern part that provides a match expression and an action or consequent part that indicates the functional implication of the match. A production rule engine maintains state in a single working memory, and matches the condition parts of rules against the instance data in the working memory, executing the consequent for each match. In contrast, an event processing engine maintains state in the context partitions mentioned above and performs stateful filtering, event pattern recognition, or transformations against the contents of the context partitions.

Business rules are combined to form complex decisions called rulesets. The rulesets are authored and managed in so called Business Rules Management Systems (BRMS) which synchronously processes input data when invoked by applications. BRMS are not sensitive to external events that may occur during the execution of a ruleset, unlike EPNs that asynchronously process events as they arrive.

3.4 Interactions among Event Processing and Business Rules

Applications requiring both event processing and business rules capabilities have developed to leverage advantages of these two fields. Stimulated by opportunities provided by such decision systems, some commercial and open source products (e.g. TIBCO [24], Drools [3]) have been developed to support both business rules and some event processing functions. We go beyond those systems by developing a "Structured English" language that address the combination of business and event processing rules.

Examples of possible interactions between event processing and business rules are: (1) EPA completion triggers a business rule (BR) execution, (2) BR completion (conditionally) triggers an EPA, (3) EPA uses a BR as part of its threshold condition or pattern assertion. We illustrate the second interaction example through a concrete use case in this paper, and extend the discussion to additional cases.

Consider the following use case: one of the indicators for money laundering detection is "frequent big cash deposits" for a certain account. Frequent big cash deposit is a financial pattern that is defined by "at least three big cash deposits to the same account within a month", while "big cash deposit" is not an absolute but rather customer-profile-related threshold. While there are several ways to model this pattern using event processing and business rules interactions, the most intuitive way to think of it is by a combination of a business rule responsible for deciding whether a transaction is a "big cash deposit", and an EPA that looks for three such transactions to the same account in a month. This feeds the output of the business rule into the EPA to evaluate whether a sequence of transactions should be recognized as a frequent big cash deposit. Figure 3 illustrates this scenario.

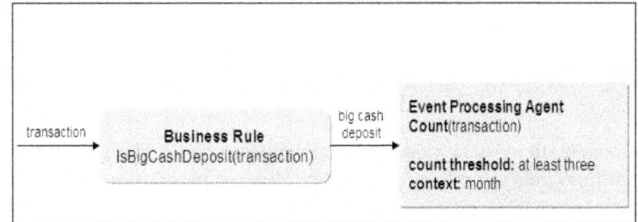

Figure 3: Frequent big cash deposits pattern

In addition to distinguishing "deposit" transactions from other transactions, and "cash" transaction from other payment forms, the business rule can evaluate the size of the deposit according to multiple customer related parameters: (1) customer's profile (Platinum, Gold), (2) customer's deposits average and standard deviation during the recent period, and (3) customer's employment. While such a sophisticated condition modeling and evaluation is not typical for event processing systems, BRMS are especially designed and optimized for this kind of task.

4. Design

From a technical point of view, event processing and business rules require quite different rule language forms. Our challenge is to hide this heterogeneity from our target "business user". We addressed this challenge by defining a common language that accommodates both kinds of rules.

We chose SBVR as the basis for this common language for several reasons. One is that SBVR can be extended with additional terms and semantics via what SBVR calls "business vocabularies". Although these vocabularies are normally used for business domain-specific concepts, they can also be used to add language features as required for event processing.

A second reason for choosing SBVR is that it defines a semantically rich knowledge representation metamodel that combines ontological concepts with first-order logic, modalities, and related ideas. We exploited many of these features of SBVR to address the requirements of event processing systems.

A third reason is the "Structured English" language suggested by the SBVR specification. "Structured English" is a controlled natural language intended to make SBVR statements understandable to business users. We aspire to the same goal, so building upon SBVR Structured English is a natural choice.

We chose not to describe SBVR in detail in this paper, since it is described adequately in sources such as [12] and [19]. We simply summarize SBVR as a specification that offers a very rich and extensible knowledge representation scheme.

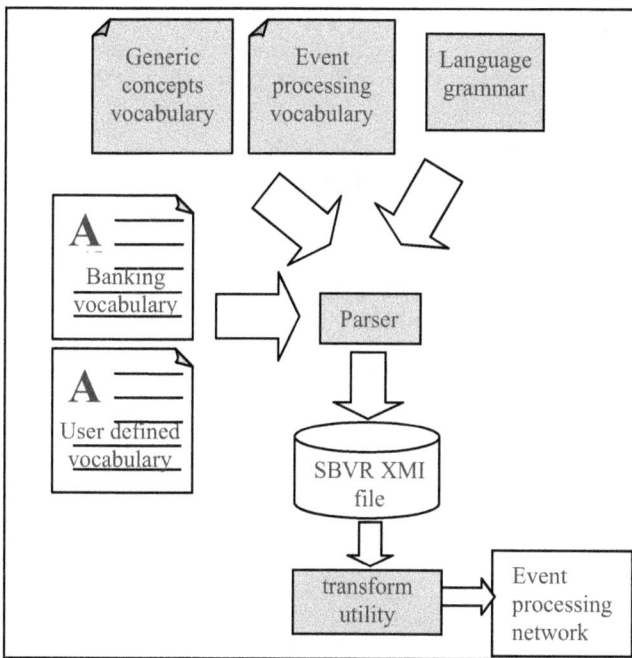

Figure 4: Detailed Design

Figure 4 shows the main elements of the tool we built. The predefined components are shown in light gray, while the parts specific to each tool usage are shown with white backgrounds.

The language grammar defines the basic syntax accepted by the parser and a set of fundamental SBVR concepts. The generic concepts and event processing vocabularies respectively contain additional SBVR concepts and a number of event processing concepts. These two vocabularies should be constant across many applications.

The primary contents of the vocabularies are noun concepts and verb concepts, each of which may have definitions and other properties. Noun concepts are the equivalent of UML classes or OWL classes, and use single- or multi-word terms such as 'derived event'. Verb concepts are equivalent to UML associations, and employ a combination of roles and verbs. Roles are references to noun concepts, while verbs are symbols that distinguish different verb concepts. For example, two verb concept 'customer *owns* account' and 'customer *opens* account' both mention the roles 'customer' and 'account' but use different verbs and presumably have different definitions (i.e. meanings). [1]

The banking vocabulary defines concepts specific to a particular industry domain, and the user-defined vocabulary adds concepts and rules of an application. Additional domain or application vocabularies can be added as desired.

The parser combines the input SBVR vocabularies and converts them to an XMI file in the format specified in the SBVR specification. The file contains the concepts, definitions, and rules of the input vocabularies in a form that is relatively easier to process than the original "Structured English". This file is input to a

transform utility that converts these inputs to the Event Processing Network form illustrated in Figure 4.

In the next sections, we discuss these components in detail: the SBVR parser, the generic and event processing vocabularies, the application vocabularies, the XMI file, and the transformation utility.

4.1 SBVR Parser

The parser shown in Figure 4 is a general-purpose controlled natural language parser that can be adapted to many different language syntaxes via a language grammar definition file. This grammar file is compiled into the parser and cannot be changed by regular users. The parser is based on the Earley parsing algorithm [4], which is well suited for this kind of language.

The language grammar file provides the initial core SBVR grammar used to start parsing the vocabularies. As the vocabularies are processed, their concepts dynamically extend the supported language. These concepts include both nouns and verbs ("fact types") that define the syntax and semantics of relationships between nouns. Users can add new concepts to the vocabularies, and immediately use them in other vocabulary elements or in rules. This enables users to extend the base SBVR grammar as compiled into the parser with additional language elements appropriate to their business domain.

Subsumption relationships can be defined in the vocabulary. For example, the language grammar file of Figure 4 defines the basic concept 'number' and the banking vocabulary file extends it to add a noun concept 'amount' using this syntax:

an amount.
{Definition: a number **that** is the sum of the funds transferred via a transaction}

This example defines a noun concept 'amount' that is a subtype of the builtin concept 'number'. The words after the keyword **'that'** are not recognized by the parser because they are not defined in any vocabulary or in the language grammar file. These words are treated as an informal text description of what differentiates an 'amount' from any other 'number'.

The following example defines a verb concept '*is less than*' that relates two instances of the builtin noun 'number'. The example also shows a "Synonymous Form" that gives an alternative syntax for the same relationship:

a number(1) *is less than* **a** number(2).
{Definition: the number(1) is mathematically less than the number(2)
Synonymous Form: a number(2) *is greater than* **a** number(1)}

The parser uses a typed grammar, thus applying subsumption relationships when matching concepts mentioned in rules against the roles of verb concepts. For example, in the rule "**It is obligatory that each** amount *is greater than* 0", the parser recognizes that an 'amount' is a kind of 'number', that the integer '0' is a 'number', and that "amount *is greater than* 0" is a use of the Synonymous Form shown above. By contrast, the parser would signal a parsing error for a rule such as "**It is obligatory that each** customer *is greater than* 0", presuming that a 'customer' is not a kind of 'number'.

SBVR specialists will recognize that the syntax shown above is an adaptation of the Structured English as used in the SBVR specification [18]. That document relies on text processing markups (paragraph formatting) to distinguish various parts of speech, such

---

[1] We adapt the usual SBVR styling conventions to this monochrome print format by underscoring nouns, italicizing verbs, and printing keywords as bold. Other text is uninterpreted by the parser.

as nouns versus verbs. This parser processes pure text, without any markups, as input. Since there is no paragraph formatting, we adapted the "Structured English" syntax to help the parser distinguish the various parts of speech. For example, we used braces to delimit the properties sections (Definitions, Synonymous Forms, etc.) of vocabulary entries. We also used indefinite articles such as "a" and "an" to introduce noun concepts vs verbs, and we used numbers in parentheses (as in "number(1)"), instead of subscripts, to differentiate verb roles that use the same concepts.

To provide modeling flexibility, SBVR permits definitions and other vocabulary components to mix vocabulary terms with undefined terms. For example, most of the words in a definition example given previously, "a `number` **that** `is the sum of funds transferred via a transaction`", are unrecognized by the parser. Such "partially formal" definitions are used in SBVR for ground concepts and to enable users to match their investment in vocabulary definitions to the value gained. We adapted the parser to tolerate such unrecognized text. We believe this parsing technology is quite innovative because it supports both parseable and non parseable text mixed in the same statements.

The design goal of the language grammar file is to support a minimal core set of SBVR concepts. Additional SBVR ideas are defined in the generic concepts vocabulary shown in Figure 4. Examples include SBVR's 'set', 'integer', and 'a number(1) *is less than* a number(2)'. This makes use of the capability to extend the parser through vocabularies.

We did find some need to extend SBVR's "Structured English" syntax to address requirements not considered in the SBVR specification. We describe these extensions below when we consider the event processing vocabulary in section 4.3.

The banking vocabulary shown in Figure 4 defines banking-specific concepts that may be reused in multiple banking applications. Examples are concepts such as 'customer', 'account', 'transaction', and 'customer *owns* account'. Partitioning the concepts into separate vocabularies, like this, enables modular reuse in multiple applications and minimizes conflicting uses of the same terms.

4.2 Event Processing Vocabulary

The event processing vocabulary of Figure 4 models the concepts of the recent *Event Processing in Action* book by Etzion and Niblett [5], which are summarized above in section 3.1.

We focus in this paper on pattern matching rules, which are the most sophisticated. We created a verb concept in the event processing vocabulary for defining derived events using pattern matching:

a `derived event` *matches* `events` *by applying* **an** `event pattern` *using* **a** `context`

This verb concept enables user-defined vocabularies to define events that are derived via patterns, as in this example:

a `frequent big cash deposit`.
{**Definition: a** `derived` `event` **that** *matches* {**a** `big cash deposit`} *by applying* **a** `frequent match` *using* **a** `frequent deposits in account context`}

The definition uses the previous verb concept to mean that frequent big cash deposits are a kind of derived event that is derived from a sequence of big cash deposits when they match a pattern called 'frequent match' and are grouped in a context called 'frequent deposits in account context'. The intent is that the runtime event processing engine should recognize frequent big cash deposits according to the definition.

Given this definition, one could further use the concept 'frequent big cash deposit' in other definitions or in rules. For example, one could write a business rule '**Each** frequent big cash deposit **must** *be reported to* **a** regulatory agency' using an additional verb concept such as 'event *is reported to* regulatory agency'. This would mean that the reporting should happen each time a frequent big cash deposit is recognized.

The definition of frequent big cash deposit given above references an event type called 'big cash deposit', which is based on banking vocabulary concepts:

a `big cash deposit`.
{**Definition: a** `deposit` **that the** `form` *of* **the** `deposit` *is* `cash` **and the** `amount` *of* **the** `transaction` *is greater than* `10,000`}

This definition is *fully formal*, meaning that each concept employed in the definition is defined in a vocabulary. In particular, 'deposit' is another defined concept, 'cash' is defined as a constant and one of the potential values of 'form'. The verb '*of*' relates 'form' and 'amount' as properties of 'deposit' and 'transaction', respectively.

A fully formal definition like this gives a classification rule that a production engine can use to distinguish (in this case) big cash deposits from other deposits. The example given here is much simplified for purposes of this paper; in the real use case, the deposit amount is compared with a threshold that depends upon complex characteristics of the deposit receiver.

The frequent big cash deposits definition shown above also depends upon two other concepts: 'frequent match' and 'frequent deposits in account context'. We discuss each of these next. Frequent match is an example of an event pattern, defined as:

a `frequent match`.
{**Definition: a** `threshold pattern` **that** *tests whether* **the** `count` *of* **the** `participant events` *of* **the** `derived event` *of* **the** `frequent match` *is greater than* `3`.}

This fully formal definition specifies that a 'frequent match' is a kind of 'threshold pattern' that is recognized when a Boolean expression 'the count *of* **the** participant events *of* **the** derived event *of* **the** frequent match *is greater than* 3' is satisfied. Any Boolean expression can be used after '*tests whether*', with the restriction that the expression can only refer to attributes of the threshold pattern. In this case, the reference 'participant events' is defined elsewhere as the actual events that participate in the derived event's context, which in this example is called 'frequent deposits in account context'.

The definition given above employs a verb concept 'an event pattern *tests* a boolean formula' and a definition of 'threshold pattern' as 'an event **that** *tests* a boolean formula'. All the various event pattern types are modeled in the event processing vocabulary using pairs of noun concepts that name the pattern and verb concepts that specify the elements of the event pattern. Whenever a pattern permits an arbitrary expression, the verb concept incorporates 'boolean formula' to indicate that to the parser. The parser then matches any boolean

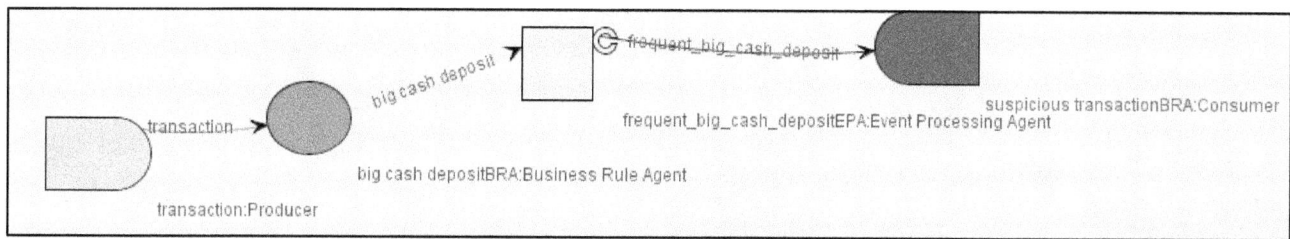

Figure 5: Event Processing Network

expression to the appropriate role of the verb concept. This demonstrates the flexibility of the parsing method.

The definition of 'frequent big cash deposit' also depends upon a context defined like this:

```
a frequent deposits in account context.
{Definition: a composite context that
composes {a same account context, a frequent
deposit period}}
```

The definition of 'frequent deposits in account context' specifies that we are interested in events that are in the intersection of two other contexts:

```
a same account context.
{Definition: a segmentation context that
segments a big cash deposit by {a receiver of
the big cash deposit}}
```

```
a frequent deposit period.
{Definition: a sliding fixed interval context
that starts after 1 day for 10 days}
```

These define 'same account context' as a segmentation context that organizes big cash deposits by their receiver, and 'frequent deposit period' as a 'sliding fixed interval context' that partitions events into 10-day time windows. They depend upon event processing vocabulary definitions of noun and verb concepts similar to those for event patterns.

For the example above, we chose to focus upon stateful event pattern recognition. We also defined several concepts to enable stateful event filtering and stateful event transformation:

```
a derived event filters events by applying a
stateful filter using a context.
a filtered event.
{Definition: a derived event that filters
events by applying a stateful filter using a
context}
```

```
a derived event transforms events by applying
a stateful transformation using a context.
a transformed event.
{Definition: a derived event that transforms
events by applying a stateful transformation
using a context}
```

These concepts exhibit the pattern we described above of having a noun concept paired with (and exploiting in its definition) a verb concept.

4.3 SBVR Extensions
We extended the core SBVR semantics in several ways via our "generic concepts vocabulary". We added the concept "list" as an

ordered version of SBVR's "set" because some event streams and some event patterns have an implicit order that has semantic meaning. We also added a subset of the date and time concepts specified in [11] because they are fundamental to events and temporal contexts.

We required additional support in the parser for some of these concepts. Most obviously, we implemented direct support for dates and time literals in the parser, so that values such as "2:00 pm" can be given in rules.

More subtly, we needed a way to specify that a role of a verb concept is filled by a boolean formula, not just a noun. For example, in the verb concept described above, 'an event pattern *tests* a boolean formula', the role 'boolean formula' can be filled by any boolean expression, not just a boolean noun concept or literal. The parser provides special support for this usage.

Although SBVR defines 'set', it's Structured English syntax does not provide a way to include literal set values in statements, as required when defining the event types that participate in derived events and the contexts that make up a composite context. For example, in the definition of 'frequent deposits in account context' given above, the syntax "{a same account context, a frequent deposit period}" specifies a list of event types. In the definition of a verb concept, we "tell" the parser that a set or list is expected for a role name by giving the role name in plural. For example, that definition relies upon the verb concept "a composite context *composes* member contexts", where "member contexts" (given in plural) indicates that literals should be supplied in uses of the verb concept.

Our event processing vocabulary has several verb concepts with three or four roles. "A derived event *matches* events *by applying* an event pattern *using* a context", given above, is an example of a verb concept with four roles. We extended the grammar language that drives the parser so that it could handle verb concepts with this many roles.

We devised these parser features in a generic way, so that they can apply to other domains. The parser itself has no special knowledge of event processing, any more than it does about, for example, the banking domain. It just parses vocabulary definitions and rules according to the concepts defined in the event processing vocabulary. The parser generates an internal parse tree that is then converted to the XMI file shown in Figure 4.

4.4 Parse Tree and XMI file
The parse tree developed by the parser associates the lexical components of parsed statements with the corresponding aspects of the vocabularies and the language grammar. To take a simple example, the definition of 'Silver Customer' as "a customer that *owns* at least one account" is converted into a tree that is simplified here:

```
concept: Silver Customer
```

```
definition:
    customer owns account
        each customer
        at least one account
```

The indented lines shown in this example are intended to illustrate the nodes in the parse tree. The format is like a reverse polish notation in that the operators are entered first in the tree, and their operands second. Note that quantifiers are embedded within the tree. Although not shown in this example, the parser, and the tree, do not collect together multiple uses of the same quantifier. What the tree does do is identify the verbs mentioned in a statement, and resolve the nouns of the statement against the roles of the verb concepts.

The next step in the process is the conversion of the parse tree to what SBVR calls "logical formulations", which are equivalent to first-order logic expressions. The key change from the parse tree is the collection of like quantifiers. The definition part of the example given above is converted to an internal form that is equivalent to:

$$\forall\ c: customer,\ \exists\ a: account,\ owns(c, a)$$

The logical formulations are written into the XMI file in the interchange format specified in clause 15.3 of the SBVR specification [18]. This format is used both because it is a standard and because it enables independence between the parser and the transformation utility of Figure 4.

4.5 Conversion from SBVR to Event Processing Network

The transformation utility is a batch program that reads the XMI file and converts it to a high-level event processing application definition represented by an Event Processing Network (EPN). It operates in several phases.

In the first step, the utility processes the XMI file and collects information about the noun concepts in all the vocabularies. It classifies each noun according to whether it is an event, or a derived event. It builds an internal data structure that captures the subsumption ("is a"), property ("has a"), and derivation relationships among the noun concepts. It does this by recognizing uses of event processing verb concepts such as "**a** derived event *matches* events *by applying* **an** event_pattern *using* **a** context."

In a second step, the utility analyzes the internal data structure, determines which noun concepts are not referenced anywhere, and avoids placing them in the EPN. This supports general-purpose domain vocabularies that may contain concepts that are unused in any particular event processing application. By omitting these unused concepts, the size and complexity of the generated EPN can be minimized without placing undue constraints on human users of the vocabularies.

In a third step, the utility generates EPA nodes in the EPN for each derived event, and produces business rule nodes for each event that is a subtype of another event. These nodes represent the event processing required to recognize the derived events, and the production rules required to distinguish event subtypes from their supertypes. The 'big cash deposit' example is a type of 'deposit' event, so it requires production rule handling and has a business rule node. The 'frequent big cash deposits' example is derived from other events using event processing that is represented by an EPA node.

Events that are not subtypes of other events are marked as "raw" events arriving from sources external to the EPN. They are generated from "producer" (source) nodes of the EPN. In the example given here, transactions are raw events. Events that are not sources for any other event are consumed by entities outside the EPN. These external entities are modeled as "consumer" (target) nodes in the EPN.

Once the EPN nodes are generated, the utility produces the links ("channels") that connect the nodes. Each channel represents the outputs from one node and the inputs to another, realized by events or business objects. Since 'big cash deposit' is a type of 'transaction', a channel conveys transaction events from a producer node to the business rule node that recognizes big cash deposits. Similarly, a link transmits big cash deposits from that business rule node to an event processing node that recognizes frequent big cash deposits. In effect, the EPN links represent the dependencies among the events described using the event processing vocabulary.

Figure 5 shows the EPN generated for the simple "frequent big cash deposit' example. The symbol on the left is a producer node that generates transactions. These transactions are passed to a business rule agent that determines whether each is a big cash deposit and forwards them to an Event Processing Agent This EPA recognizes frequent big cash deposits and passes them along to a consumer agent that treats them as suspicious transactions.

The example shown here is quite simple. Real applications may be much more complex, involving several dozens of nodes of both business rule and event processing types.

5. Discussion and Conclusion

In this work we explored a unified business language with sufficient expressive power to address both production and event processing rules. The proposed language integrates these two very different rule types and at the same time targets a non-technical class of users. We demonstrated that SBVR can be extended to address the heterogenous requirements of both kinds of rules. Our attempt to introduce a unified controlled natural language for business and event processing rules is a first step towards increasing the intelligence of complex rule-based systems, thus improving the person-system interaction.

In our approach, event processing agents (EPAs) are defined as SBVR noun concepts, such as 'frequent big cash deposit'. Reifying the concepts this way permits users to name their key concepts, enabling reuse by name across multiple language statements.

Our extensions to the SBVR metamodel and "Structured English" language seemed to fit well with existing features of SBVR. Some of these ideas, such as lists and generic support for "boolean formulae", might be useful contributions to the SBVR specification. The date and time aspects are already being considered for a possible OMG specification in [11].

We believe that our experience with the SBVR-to-EPN conversion supports an argument that the SBVR knowledge representation format can support other algorithms applied jointly to both kinds of rules. We are thinking particularly of static analysis and theorem proving algorithms applied to unified models that include both production and event processing rules.

We found that the format of the SBVR-specified XMI file shown in Figure 4 was complex, far from compact, and resulted in an inefficient model. We would consider using a proprietary format if we had to start again.

The event processing architecture described in Etzion and Niblett [5] is very rich, and requires a correspondingly full-featured language. We did not implement all features of that architecture. In particular, we did not address what Etzion and Niblett call "pattern policies", which are used to disambiguate the semantic interpretation of pattern matching. We are confident that we could smoothly extend the language as needed given more time.

The main disadvantage of this framework resides in the complexity of a language that tries to address all the possible event processing features. Although the language can utilize design features such as parallel construction of similar verbs and consistent use of nouns, it cannot avoid the fact that users are faced with a large set of functions to understand.

Although "Structured English" is attractive as a way to support business users, we believe that the sentence-oriented form should be complemented with the kind of diagram shown in Figure 5. The event processing network diagram visualizes the dependency relationships among event types, thus providing a complementary way to understand the entire application. As the size and complexity of a rule-driven application increases, such diagrams become absolutely necessary to manage the complexity.

We believe that such diagrams complement, rather than replace, concept-oriented vocabularies such those used with SBVR. Concepts and EPN diagrams represent two modes of thinking about events and event processing. Conceptualizing event types, using names such as 'frequent big cash deposit', helps business users understand and talk about them and supports integration of events with business rule systems. Event processing network (EPN) diagrams help people understand how these complex events are derived from other events. Offering just one of these ways of visualizing the rules denies use of the other mode of understanding them.

Business rules management systems and event processing platforms are complementary concepts. Commercial applications that combine production and event processing rules will become more pervasive in the near future, as companies realize the business benefits of fast, event-driven action combined with intelligent rule-based decision making. One of the main challenges faced by these emerging applications is providing a common, intuitive, and understandable platform for rule specifications. We believe that this work is a significant milestone towards achieving this goal.

6. REFERENCES

[1] De Roover, W. and Vanthienen, J. *A Transformation from SBVR Business Rules into Event Coordinated Rules by means of SBVR Patterns.* http://www.citt-online.com/downloads/edbpmucep2010_submission_4.pdf

[2] De Roover, W. and Vanthienen, J. *Unified Patterns to transform business rules into an event coordination mechanism.* edBPM 2010, 4th International Workshop on Event-Driven Business Process Management, Hoboken NJ, September 2010.

[3] Drools – Business Logic Integration Platform.

[4] Earley, J. *An efficient context-free parsing algorithm,* Communications of the Association for Computing Machinery, **13**:2:94-102, 1970.

[5] Etzion O., Niblett P. *Event Processing in Action*, Manning Publications, 2010.

[6] Event Processing Technical Society. See http://www.ep-ts.com

[7] Forgy, C., *OPS5 User's Manual*, Technical Report CMU-CS-81-135, Carnegie Mellon University, 1981.

[8] Fuchs, N. and Schwitter, R. *Attempto Controlled English* (ACE), CLAW 96, First International Workshop on Controlled Language Applications, University of Leuven, Belgium, March 1996.

[9] IBM WebSphere Business Events. See http://www.ibm.com/software/integration/wbe/.

[10] IBM WebSphere ILOG JRules. See www.ilog.com/rules.

[11] Linehan, M. et. al., *Date-Time Vocabulary* submission to the Object Management Group, forthcoming.

[12] Linehan, M. *SBVR Use Cases*. In: Bassiliades, N., Governatori, G., Paschke, A. (eds.) RuleML 2008. LNCS, vol. 5321, pp. 128–196. Springer, Heidelberg.

[13] Logan, D. and Knox, R. E. *Hype Cycle for Enterprise Information Management*, 2010. Gartner report number: G00200503. (2010)

[14] Luckham, D. *The Rapide pattern language. In The Power of Events: An Introduction to Complex Event Processing in Distributed Enterprise Systems.* Addison-Wesley, Boston, 2002, chapter 8.

[15] Microsoft StreamInsight. http://msdn.microsoft.com/en-us/library/ee362541.aspx

[16] Object Management Group (OMG) Event-Processing Community of Practice. See http://www.omg.org/marketing/omg-cop.htm

[17] Object Management Group (OMG). Production Rules Representation (PRR). (2009). http://www.omg.org/spec/PRR/1.0/

[18] Object Management Group (OMG), *Semantics of Business Vocabulary and Business Rules Specification*, Version 1.0. 2007, http://www.omg.org/spec/SBVR/1.0/

[19] Ross, R. ed. *SBVR Insider* section of the BRCommunity website, http://www.brcommunity.com/sbvr.php.

[20] Schulte, W. R. and Sinur, J. *Rule Engines and Event Processing.* Gartner report number: G00208509. (2010).

[21] Sharon, G. and Etzion, O. *Event Processing Networks: model and implementation.* IBM System Journal, 2008, 47(2), pages 321-334.

[22] Sowa, J. *Common Logic Controlled English*, 24 February 2004. http://www.jfsowa.com/clce/specs.htm

[23] Streambase. http://www.streambase.com/

[24] TIBCO. http://www.tibco.com/

[25] World-Wide Web Consortium (W3C). *Rule Interchange Format* (RIF). 2010. http://www.w3.org/standards/techs/rif#w3c_all

Disclosure Control in Multi-Domain Publish/Subscribe Systems

Jatinder Singh
Computer Laboratory
University of Cambridge, UK
jatinder.singh@cl.cam.ac.uk

David M. Eyers
Dept. of Computer Science
University of Otago, NZ
dme@cs.otago.ac.nz

Jean Bacon
Computer Laboratory
University of Cambridge, UK
jean.bacon@cl.cam.ac.uk

ABSTRACT

Publish/subscribe is an effective paradigm for event dissemination over wide-area systems. However, there is tension between the convenience of open information delivery, and the need to protect data from unauthorised access. Publish/subscribe security models tend to focus on protecting the client API, or encrypting events and managing disclosure through key distribution. However, some application environments require more stringent, fine-grained controls governing precisely the data disclosed and transmitted given particular circumstances. In this paper, we present Interaction Control, a policy model that overlays context-aware, point-to-point (hop-level) controls onto a publish/subscribe network. The approach is unique as it allows granular control over i) the construction of the dissemination network, and ii) the information flows *within the network*. Interaction Control was designed considering legal obligations, to enable those responsible for information to transmit data on a *need-to-know* basis. Security policies set the bounds for communication, enforced only where necessary at specific points of the publish/subscribe process, to provide control while retaining the efficiency benefits of the paradigm. We present implementation details and results showing that any security overheads must be considered with respect to the overall network load.

Categories and Subject Descriptors

C.2.0 [**Computer-Communication Networks**]: General—*security and protection*; C.2.4 [**Computer-Communication Networks**]: Distributed Systems—*distributed applications*

General Terms

Security, Design, Legal Aspects

Keywords

publish/subscribe, security, information flow control, access control, policy enforcement, data governance

1 Introduction

Publish/subscribe (pub/sub) is an effective paradigm for wide-area event distribution, in which *events* encapsulate self-contained data updates. *Clients* (information producers and consumers) are *decoupled*: producers produce (publish) events and consumers register their interest in (subscribe to) information they wish to receive. Pub/sub is *push-based*, where clients communicate through the pub/sub middleware. Routing is *information centric*, delivering relevant—based on the type, topic and/or content—events from producers to consumers as they occur. The paradigm is efficient and scalable, exploiting commonalities between client preferences to avoid redundant transmissions.

Client decoupling favours anonymous communication: the consumers are unaware of the information producers' identities/addresses/locations, and *vice-versa*. Such information could be encapsulated in the event itself, but even then the producer has no control over who receives their publications. The paradigm often includes the use of *brokers*—routing entities that interconnect to provide the pub/sub service. Clients communicate through brokers, where brokers inspect events (at varying degrees) to make routing decisions.

For some applications it may be enough to simply secure access to the entire pub/sub service, e.g. those services where clients register to subsequently receive information. This is typically sufficient for the financial services (stock quote) scenarios common to pub/sub research. However, there exist other application environments with more stringent security requirements that require wide-area notification services. Generally, pub/sub lacks the means to control the data released to a (particular) consumer. Often security concerns are context-dependent, in that the appropriate constraints for a transmission depends on the circumstances. Further, when considering wide-area services, such as at a national-level, events will flow between and through various domains of administrative control. Infrastructure (brokers) will be managed by different entities that co-operate to provide communication services. The security requirements can, and in practice will, often differ depending on the domains involved in a particular delivery operation.

This paper addresses these concerns through the presentation and evaluation of *Interaction Control* (IC), an approach that essentially overlays a *point-to-point* (i.e. hop by hop) security model onto a pub/sub network to enable precise control over connections and the information transmitted. It is novel in that it allows context-aware control *within* a broker network, at hop-level granularity, to account for notions of responsibility and the naturally varying levels of trust between components in a wide-area network. It enables security policy to be enforced at specific points of the pub/sub process and in specific circumstances, to facilitate control while retaining the efficiency benefits and delivery semantics (e.g. clients specifying their interests) of the paradigm.

IC was developed as part of our work concerning infrastructure for supporting healthcare services. We begin with a brief overview of the data governance requirements of England's *National Health Service* (NHS). We then detail IC, describing the policy rules that control broker-broker and broker-client connections, and that filter and transform information as it flows throughout the network. Next we describe our IC implementation, where controls are integrated into a pub/sub database system to facilitate policy enforcement, context management, event storage and audit. We present results indicating that despite the local (broker) overheads of policy enforcement, restrictions can actually improve the overall efficiency of a particular workload. We then conclude with discussion and areas for further research.

2 Healthcare Information

This work stems from our research into middleware for supporting federated national-level health services.[1] Healthcare is an interesting environment for the investigation of security issues, as information must be shared, yet protected.

The care process is highly collaborative, involving the sharing of health information between professionals from various health service providers, as well as with other supporting institutions, such as government and insurance companies. However, personal health data is highly sensitive, and remains so over time. Confidentiality underpins the carer-patient relationship. Those who handle personal health data as part of the care process are **legally responsible** for maintaining its confidentiality, which includes service providers that manage and maintain the technical infrastructure for their service [15]. In England, information may only be shared if patients have given consent, subject to certain exceptions. In many situations, privacy concerns *user* anonymity. Healthcare differs in that although patient data must remain confidential, system users are generally medical professionals, whose actions (send/query/receive) must be visible for reasons of accountability.

2.1 Information Sharing Protocols

For an organisation to meet its data management responsibilities, information is best shared on a *need-to-know* basis [16, 15]: disclosing only that information required given the circumstances. Appropriate disclosure is often context-dependent, e.g. access restrictions may be relaxed in emergency situations.

A national-level health service consists of a number of providers, whose information requirements differ depending on the particular service(s) they provide. For instance, a pharmacist requires different information from a pathologist, or an insurance agency. Often a health incident will be relevant to several professionals in several organisations, e.g. it may involve ordering medication, specialist testing and organising home care. A provider will have an understanding of the reasons for dealing with another provider, and thus the general information that the other party requires.

Health institutions define an *information sharing protocol* that describes precisely the data that may be shared

in the particular circumstances [7]. It is designed to suit local practice and procedure, but must also account for patient consent, and other legal/general practice requirements. The protocol facilitates explanation of the data shared for a course of treatment [26], which is useful for obtaining consent. Patients tend to trust their physicians to act as their information gatekeepers [3], meaning a prudent information sharing protocol will often meet patients' confidentiality expectations. However, the general protocol must be qualified by any patient-specific disclosure preferences.

2.2 Domains

We define a *domain* as a unit governed by independent administrative policy that provides particular services [1]. Clearly, domains exist in many application environments. A domain naturally maps to an organisation (a legal entity), or any body that is responsible for its own procedures, defines its own policies and manages its own infrastructure. Health service examples include a hospital, surgery, pathology laboratory or insurance company. A domain hosts a number of *entities*, such as doctors, nurses, software, accountants and managers, often through service/employment contracts. As part of its operations, a domain collects, stores and forwards information relevant to the service it provides. Each domain must appropriately share information with entities in the local environment, and with other domains. It follows that a domain is responsible for the information it handles.

We assume that a domain has control over its local communication infrastructure (brokers), and defines its local policy in accordance with that imposed by higher-level domains, global directives and legislation.

2.3 Sharing Infrastructure

Healthcare is a data-driven environment and thus suits push-based communication. This is not only to notify and alert in situations of concern (e.g. emergencies), but also to ensure that the numerous parties/domains involved in the care process are kept aware of the current situation and operate on the latest representation of state. Unlike much work supporting healthcare, we do not focus on the patient record, but instead consider the streams/dataflows (events) necessary to support the health service. These flows represent patient data, the actions of practitioners, support services such as billing, inventory and insurance, governmental information requirements, etc. Indeed, an event-based messaging middleware is considered an integral component of technical healthcare infrastructure.[2]

2.4 Threat Model: Security & Responsibility

Security research is usually presented along with a defined *threat model* that describes adversaries, system attacks and the proposed countermeasures. In our case, we address concerns that are orthogonal—and complementary—to those of specific security mechanisms: we are concerned with providing the means for users of the system to meet their responsibilities. We consider control *only* as it pertains to pub/sub (cf. more general, non-middleware security approaches) because our interests concern transmission within information-centric networks. Pub/sub generally deals with open information delivery; our work considers controlling dissemination in pub/sub by allowing definition of the bounds for

---

[1]We describe healthcare from the English NHS perspective.

[2]For instance, see the NHS *Transaction Messaging Service (TMS)* and the *TMS Event Service (TES)* at http://www.connectingforhealth.nhs.uk.

communication. Domains are autonomous, and co-operate with entities and other domains by sharing information, but this does not imply mutual, absolute trust. Clearly, it is wholly inappropriate to allow one to access any information they desire. Here security is realised by domains controlling the data they transmit, in line with their legal and social responsibilities. There must be the means to allow sharing on a *need-to-know* basis. This is a technology directed at realising the controls required by law, rather than simply the mechanisms that enforce access control, for example.

In this model, responsibility is associated with data. Each recipient becomes duly obliged to protect the information that they receive. The responsibility for transmission passes with the data itself; a domain meets its data management obligations by passing information to a connected entity/ domain in accordance with (sound) local policy. It is not responsible for the recipient's shortcomings if the disclosure was appropriate. Indeed, such a responsibility model tends to exist in any environment where separate administrative domains interact. Of course, this assumes that a domain has some concept of why it communicates with another entity/domain: the information exchange fits within some premeditated arrangement. This, however, is not unreasonable given the existence of sharing protocols in healthcare, and more generally, workflows in other application areas. We use healthcare as a real-world illustration where the responsibility model is overt, and legally imposed. Security is realised by a domain sharing information in line with its sharing protocol, qualified by any patient consent preferences.

IC enables these sorts of governance regimes to be built into middleware, by allowing policy to be defined in brokers for enforcement in particular circumstances at specific points of the pub/sub process. Middleware enforcement means security policy is consistently applied across applications/clients. Assuming a domain controls its technical infrastructure (a NHS goal [6]), IC allows a domain to define policy to set the bounds for communication, ensuring that data leaves *its* broker network—transferred to clients, or brokers in remote domains—only when appropriate.

3 Related Work

This work aims to enable those responsible for information to manage their communications, through explicit control over the information channels and event flows in a pub/sub system. We found that the literature in the area of pub/sub security addresses different concerns from those described.

Much research considers the use of encryption in pub/ sub services, where events are encrypted and then transmitted throughout the network. Some transmissions may be to parties that are unauthorised to access the underlying data. However, access to event content is managed through an additional step of distributing encryption keys: keys are only provided to those who are authorised to access event data. Approaches differ in whether the broker network is trusted, i.e. whether the brokers have access to event content [25, 18], and how keys are generated and shared [17, 13]. The liberal transmission of encrypted events throughout a pub/sub network, where key allocations control security, is unsuitable where information is perpetually sensitive. This is because a compromised key, or broken encryption scheme[3] at *any* time

in the future risks the inappropriate disclosure of a history of prior events. Such an approach runs against the described notions of control and responsibility. It follows that events, even if encrypted, should only flow to those authorised to receive that data. Further, encryption-based mechanisms impose key-management overheads, and tend not to easily deal with situations where access policy is context sensitive.

Other work concerns the enforcement of restrictions at the edges of a broker network. The delivery of events to a client can be controlled by restricting and/or validating subscription filters [14, 30]. These operate on event type/content. Access control mechanisms, such as *Role-Based Access Control* (RBAC) [2] and *Access Control Lists* [30] can protect access to the pub/sub API. These are described in the context of a single administrative domain, though [2] suggests that a *web-of-trust* can govern broker access to event types. Such approaches are limited in their flexibility. The responsibility model (§2) requires the possibility to govern *all* communications and connections, not just with clients (at the edge of the broker network), but also with other brokers— particularly where components reside in another administrative domain. Further, context-aware controls—considering more than just event type/content—are required to allow for more granular security policy. For example, the time of day, (client) location and situation's severity can be relevant to whether particular information should be disclosed.

A *scope* [11, 12] is a grouping structure that bundles sets of pub/sub brokers and clients, constraining the visibility of events to its members. A scope sets the boundaries for transmission, allowing control over the propagation of events to other scopes. A scope aligns well to the concept of domains. However, there are situations where different levels of visibility are required for members of the same scope/domain. Thus, it is necessary to enable control over the communication to *each* principal, regardless of domain structure.

Wun and Jacobsen [29] describe a generic policy framework that couples what are essentially *Event-Condition-Action* (ECA) rules with pub/sub operations. As the framework aims to be open and expressive, it addresses different concerns to those of a security infrastructure. For instance policy actions are not semantically defined, in that an action can undertake any (possible) function. This brings flexibility, though for security the functionality of policy actions should be defined to provide certainty, facilitate correctness and aid conflict resolution. Wun and Jacobsen describe policies for unstructured pub/sub overlays, where policy may be defined by clients, attached to events, advertisements and subscriptions to be enforced as they flow through the network. However, this is unsuitable in an environment of responsibility between federated co-operative domains, as it complicates policy combination and precludes separate notions of trust and accountability. Enforcement in [29] occurs with particular pub/sub operations, the authors concentrating on *post-matching* enforcement, where actions are executed after a filter match to avoid the overheads of separately evaluating policy conditions. However, this is inappropriate in certain security contexts, e.g. where a policy executed on delivery could circumvent a subscription filter (§5.1). For proper control, actions need not be coupled to pub/sub operations, but should be enforced where necessary.

The focus of IC differs from that of other pub/sub security approaches in that it brings about security by controlled disclosure, where those responsible for data meet their obli-

---

[3]For instance, we have seen increases in computing power cause encryption methods to be disregarded; e.g. 56-bit DES keys: `http://www.rsa.com/rsalabs/node.asp?id=2100`.

gations by setting granular, *contextually-sensitive* bounds for pub/sub communication. IC is unique in that it explicitly addresses pub/sub security by enabling specific control over *all* connections (topology construction) and event flows in a pub/sub network, including those between brokers. As a broker enforces local policy against its direct connections, issues of trust remain at the application-level. Our previous publications regarding IC present our initial work with respect to enforcement [24] and the controls as they apply to events [22, 23]. Here we present the whole, mature model, describing for the first time how the governance mechanisms apply in a *distributed* broker network, how broker interconnections are controlled, the management of requests and some engineering specifics including overhead analysis.

4 Interaction Control: Rules

The goal of *Interaction Control* (IC) is to provide the mechanism for realising a need-to-know, local responsibility model in a pub/sub middleware. This involves giving a broker, managed by a domain with a certain responsibility, the ability to govern all transmissions—including events, advertisements and subscriptions—to directly connected clients and brokers. Control is achieved through a policy model that enforces rules at specific points of the pub/sub process. Each broker maintains a set of rules to enforce on its direct connections.[4] Here we describe the specifics of these rules.

Background and Assumptions Like much pub/sub work, we consider application-layer routing. *Transport-layer security* [9] protects lower-layers of the stack.

We describe IC for *type-based pub/sub*, where each event conforms to a particular type, from the set of types τ. Each type $t \in \tau$ consists of a name and a particular set of attributes of specific data types. Events flow through a *channel*, which is a unidirectional, typed (logical) communication path between a broker and a connected client/broker. A number of channels can exist within a connection.

Clients communicate with brokers, where brokers interconnect to form the distributed pub/sub service. The only assumption of trust is that a client entrusts its local (directly-connected) broker to operate on its behalf. An event dissemination tree is built by brokers propagating advertisements and subscriptions [28], similar to the popular advertisement forwarding approach of Siena [4]. Also like Siena, we assume that brokers hold a particular position in the network topology—that *links* (broker interconnections) exist for a reason, to share particular information with specific brokers. This is in line with the notions of domain knowledge, co-operation and responsibility as described in §2. Note that this does not entail that brokers are continually connected; instead, the *possible* connections between brokers are pre-authorised (discussed later). In IC the connections themselves are dynamic, in the sense that a broker may connect/disconnect from another.

Broker Context Disclosure policy is encoded in rules defined for (particular) brokers. A broker enforces policy against its direct connections in accordance with its local ruleset. IC rules are context-sensitive, where context encapsulates anything accessible by the enforcing broker. Thus, "context" is implementation specific. Rules reference con-

text using sets of *predicates*, which a broker evaluates as part of the enforcement process. *Credential predicates* assert characteristics about a principal, including their unique identifier, group memberships, qualifications, roles or certificates that they hold. Such predicates define the class of users to which a rule applies. *Environmental predicates* refer to other aspects of context, such as system type, workflow state or patient status (e.g. stable, critical). See [22] for more details regarding IC predicates.

A *permission attribute* consists of an attribute name and type, the value for which a client must include with their advertisement/subscription. Rule predicates can reference the values of the permission attributes supplied in the request. This supplements broker-accessible context to allow computations with data outside the system, e.g. requiring the inclusion of a `patient_id` enables rules to verify a treating relationship between the subscriber and patient.

4.1 Authorisation Rules

Authorisation rules specify when to authorise the establishment of connections and event-channels between components. There are two types of authorisation rule:

Connection Authorisation *Principal authorisation rules* govern the connection of a principal (client/broker) to a broker. We define $\mathcal{C}$ to be the complete set of credential predicates. Each rule refers to a set of credential predicates $C \subseteq \mathcal{C}$ of the remote principal. This brings flexibility, in that a rule can apply to a specific principal by referencing its unique `id`; or to sets of principals, e.g. by referencing a role such as `doctor`, thus avoiding a separate rule for each. The rules apply equally to connecting brokers as they do to clients. These rules are simple as they merely concern connection, other rules govern channel establishment and transmission.

Request Authorisation An advertisement or subscription can be characterised as a *request*. A client issues a request to a broker to publish (through an advertisement) or subscribe to information. If authorised, a channel is established for the (directional) flow of events of the specified type.

Request authorisation rules define the circumstances in which channel establishment is allowed. Each such rule can be represented as a tuple of the form: $(rt, t, C, E) \in RT \times \tau \times \mathbb{P}(\mathcal{C}) \times \mathbb{P}(\mathcal{E})$. The set of *request types* is defined as $RT = \{\texttt{advertisement}, \texttt{subscription}\}$ and is used to indicate whether the rule applies to advertisement or subscription requests. The event type that this rule refers to is t. We use $\mathbb{P}$ to mean power-set: the set of all subsets. The target of the rule is defined by the set of credential predicates ($C \subseteq \mathcal{C}$) that are matched against those held by the requesting client. A set of environmental predicates ($E \subseteq \mathcal{E}$) further refine the circumstances in which the rule applies. To enable evaluation, a client must supply the permission attributes required by the rule's predicates.

Channels are durative, and persist until the channel is closed. Authorisation depends on context, thus a change in state can affect rule applicability. As such, the environmental predicates of an authorisation rule can be defined as *monitored*, causing re-evaluation of the request should the value(s) change. For example, a rule might authorise a doctor to subscribe to data while on duty in a ward: $C = \{\texttt{doctor}\}, E = \{\texttt{onDuty}(user)\}$. If the $\texttt{onDuty}(user)$ predicate is monitored, the request will be re-evaluated when the doctor ends his shift, in this case closing the channel.[5] As

---

[4]Disclosure policy is encoded in rules distributed to specific brokers to effect appropriate disclosure. A domain may have a number of brokers, but may define different rules for each, depending on the particular broker's role—e.g. in §7.1.

---

[5]Assuming that no other rule authorises the channel.

credentials represent the intrinsic characteristics of a principal, credential predicates are implicitly monitored as they define the rule's target(s). For example, if a doctor is struck-off, it is important that his access rights are reconsidered.

Request authorisation rules control access to event types by ensuring the legitimacy of event channels. Such rules are useful as they avoid the (potentially expensive) evaluation of authorisation conditions on each access attempt (event). Once a channel is established, individual events are controlled through imposed conditions and transformations.

4.2 Event Controls

The following two rules control the propagation of events through an event channel.

Imposed Conditions restrict the tranmission of events through a channel. They are similar to subscription filters, except that they are specified by policy rather than the subscriber. For example, a filter can ensure that details of a condition are not sent to a particular doctor.

An imposed condition rule r is a tuple: $(rt, t, C, E, R, h) \in IP \times \tau \times \mathbb{P}(C) \times \mathbb{P}(\mathcal{E}) \times \mathbb{P}(\mathcal{R}) \times H$. The rule restriction predicates $R \subseteq \mathcal{R}$ act to filter the event. These are evaluated in the context of an event instance, thus they may reference attributes of the event type. Also specified are a subset of credential predicates from C, an event type (from τ) and an interaction point $IP = \{\texttt{publication}, \texttt{subscription}\}$ that defines the target channel type for the imposed conditions.

Restriction filters may encode sensitive information. For instance, the restriction $\texttt{Treatment} \neq \texttt{HIV}$ might exist to prevent a particular patient's information from flowing to one of their doctors. Revealing this restriction to the doctor suggests that the patient could be HIV positive. Each rule selects from the set $H = \{\top, \bot\}$ as to whether the imposed conditions are disclosed to the client or not. If hidden, the filters are imposed silently: publications appear to be accepted but are ignored, while subscribers have events filtered without their knowledge of the restriction.

Event Transformations These transformation rules alter an event. They can enrich, degrade or produce new events that are related to the original event in some application-specific manner. While typically considered for interoperability [27, 11], from a security perspective transformations allow more than binary (permit/deny) access control, as event data can be tailored to the situation. Further, middleware transformations avoid clients publishing multiple instances of a semantically similar event with differing levels of visibility (see §7.2). An example transformation might obfuscate location data for a remotely monitored patient, save in emergency situations. In §7 we describe a transformation rule to effect data segmentation regarding prescriptions.

A transformation rule r is a tuple: $(ip, t, C, G, f, t', c) \in IP \times \tau \times \mathbb{P}(C) \times \mathbb{P}(\mathcal{G}) \times F \times \tau \times D$ where t, ip and C perform the same previously discussed function of relating the rule to the relevant channels. $G \subseteq \mathbb{P}(\mathcal{G})$ is the set of predicates that define when the transformation is performed. G is evaluated in the context of the event—if G holds, the transformation applies.[6] The transform occurs through the function $f : \tau \to \tau \in F$, which takes an event of type t and returns an event of type t': an altered event of the same or another type.

For flexibility, the $c \in D = \{\top, \bot\}$ tuple element allows each rule to specify whether or not it is *consumable*. Consumable functions prevent the original event from propa-

gating further—only the result from the function proceeds to the next stage of the pub/sub process. Non-consumable transformations allow all events to proceed.

4.3 Broker Controls

As mentioned, brokers interconnect to form a distributed dissemination network. An event dissemination tree is built by the brokers propagating advertisements and subscriptions [28], similar to the advertisement forwarding approach of Siena [4]. A broker connects to another via a *link*, which (logically) differs from a client connection as brokers only forward requests through links. Principal authorisation rules authorise links, meaning that rules can apply to classes of brokers, avoiding the enumeration of every broker combination. This better suits the scale of national-level services.

A broker maintains a set of policies to control the flow of information to *directly connected* principals. IC does not distinguish between events and requests received from clients and those from brokers that may be forwarding on behalf of others. Instead, an event received through a link is treated as a publication from the adjacent (remote) broker, and an advertisement or subscription received through a link is characterised as a request issued by the adjacent broker. IC rules are defined for, and enforced against, brokers just as they are for clients—subject to the same policies and enforcement processes. In this way, IC is a *point-to-point* security model since a rule *only* concerns interactions with the next hop. This is in line with the described model of responsibility, giving each domain *local control* over the transmissions of their brokers. Rules are defined to only restrict flows when necessary, concerning certain transmissions in particular circumstances. In this way, rules set the bounds for transmission. Requests and events are able to flow freely to allow wide-scale distribution, subject to the (necessary) constraints imposed by intermediate brokers (domains).

4.4 Request Forwarding and Processing

If a broker authorises a request and creates a channel, the request is forwarded to other brokers to establish the dissemination network. This requires control.

The mechanisms for controlling request propagation are similar to those for events, where requests can be transformed and filtered before transmission to the adjacent broker. The rules relevant to a broker depend on its position in the network infrastructure. Such restrictions are defined by administrators, who have specific knowledge/concerns of (local) network topology. Forwarding restrictions set the *general* boundaries for interaction.

Request Filters Conditions can be imposed on links to filter the requests forwarded to a broker. This is to protect any sensitive data related to what is on offer; e.g. filters can ensure that advertisements are forwarded only to brokers authorised to subscribe to the type, or that subscriptions are forwarded only to brokers in domains with a treating relationship to the patient who is the subject of the request.

The rules take the form $(rt, t, C, R_r) \in RT \times \tau \times \mathbb{P}(C) \times \mathbb{P}(\mathcal{R})$. They are defined for a particular request type (rt), advertisement/subscription, and event type (t). The set of credential predicates (C) refers to that of the remote broker. The restrictions (R_r) are evaluated in the context of a request pertaining to an event type, *not* in the context of the event itself; thus the filter predicates reference *request content*, along with other aspects of environmental state.

---

[6]This is subject to conflict resolution definitions—see §5.

Request Transformation rules allow a request to be tailored specifically to a remote broker. The rules facilitate interoperability, e.g. translating an identifier from a local system to a shared NHS ID, and controlled disclosure, e.g. anonymising identifiers or removing any sensitive information contained within the request.

Request transformation rules alter a request before propagation to an adjacent broker. A request transformation rule is a tuple of the form $(rt, t, \varsigma, G_r, f) \in RT \times \tau \times S \times \mathbb{P}(\mathcal{G}) \times F$ defined for a particular request type rt. The rule's guarding predicates (G_r) are evaluated in the context of the request. The transformation function f takes a request and returns a modified one. Request transformations implicitly consume (i.e. replace) the incoming request tuple. The rules are defined for a particular link, specified by ς, which identifies the principal authorisation rule authorising the connection to the adjacent broker. Events convey information, and thus it may be appropriate to transform and transmit a number of events. Request transformations, however, are enforced on (request) propagation to govern the establishment of channels with a particular broker. Thus only a single transformation function may be defined for an event type and link.

4.5 Rule Fragmentation

We do *not* encapsulate all restrictions—authorisations, restriction filters and transformations—into a single rule structure. Instead, rules are defined independently to allow a many-to-many relationship between the rules. This brings flexibility as it enables different sets of rules to apply in different circumstances. Further, it removes the need to re-author existing rules to deal with specific requests, e.g. we avoid modifying all rules concerning an event type when introducing a filter for an individual patient.

5 Interaction Control: Enforcement

Each IC broker maintains a set of rules that it enforces at particular points of the messaging process. In this section we describe enforcement. Given that IC rules are context sensitive, several can apply at an enforcement point. We begin by detailing the general process of enforcement. We then discuss the application of multiple rules, and methods for resolving conflict.

5.1 Event Flow Enforcement

A broker enforces its policies as an event passes through a particular enforcement point. A broker's processing of an event is illustrated in Fig. 1.

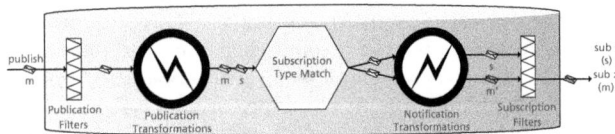

Figure 1: A broker's enforcement process for the publication of the event m.

A publication first is validated against any conditions imposed on the publication channel. If the filters are satisfied, the event is subjected to the relevant publication transformations. In this example, one transform applies that takes event m and produces s, an event of a different type. As

it does not consume the original event, both events move to the delivery phase. Note the output of a transformation function moves to the next stage of processing (see §5.3).

Delivery involves moving a copy of the event through each active notification (subscription) channel for its type. In this example, there exists one subscription for each type. The events are subjected to the notification transforms applicable to the subscriber in the circumstances. Here, a transformation function exists for sub 2 that consumes event m, returning a modified version m'. There is no transformation defined for s, so it passes through unperturbed. The final stage involves evaluating the event against the subscription (and imposed) filters. Only event m' is delivered, as s fails to satisfy sub 1's filter.

Subscription filters act as a barrier to prevent certain information from leaving the broker. IC involves a two-phase subscription matching process. First, the events are matched against active subscriptions considering only the event type; filter predicates are applied *after* the notification transformations. This prevents notification transformations from circumventing any filter restrictions.[7]

5.2 Request Enforcement

A connection must exist before requests and events can be transmitted. A broker will allow a connection if the request is authorised by a principal authorisation rule. On receipt of an advertisement request, the broker determines whether a request authorisation rule permits the request in the circumstances. If so, the channel is established. The advertisement is then forwarded to each adjacent broker after the execution of any request transformation, subject to validation against any advertisement filters defined for the link and event type. The request is only forwarded to those brokers that have not already received a similar advertisement.[8]

The process is similar for subscription requests. After the establishment of the subscription channel, the subscription request is forwarded to the adjacent brokers that advertise the event type, subject to any subscription transformation functions or filters defined for the advertising brokers.

5.3 Multiple Rules

As rules are context sensitive, it is possible that several rules (of the same type) apply at an enforcement point. An authorisation rule must hold to authorise a connection or the establishment of a channel. The rule's monitored conditions and the principal's credential allocations are monitored to trigger re-evaluation should values change. A number of imposed condition rules may apply at an enforcement point. The filter predicates of all relevant imposed condition rules are evaluated in conjunction, along with any client specified (e.g. subscription) filters. As request transformations are connected to (link) authorisation rules, only one request transformation applies per link.

In the appropriate context, a number of event transformation rules might apply to an event. In this situation, the transformation functions are executed in parallel, in that each function takes as input (a copy of) the original event, the output of which moves to the next stage of processing. An output event is not subject to further transforma-

---

[7] As opposed to the *post-matching* [29] application of policy.
[8] Our implementation only permits a broker to forward an advertisement to those that have the possibility of subscribing to the event type, as defined by its authorisation rules.

tion functions at the same enforcement point. This avoids complex transformation loops that can be difficult to reason about, particularly when the output is of the same type. An event transformation function is executed only once per event at an enforcement point, regardless of the number of policies causing the function to execute. This is to avoid duplicates resulting from multiple function invocations. The original (input) event will not propagate if any (applied) transformation is consumable.

5.4 Policy Conflict

Often it is appropriate that multiple policies apply at an enforcement point, however there will be situations in which policies *conflict*, in that they are incompatible. A common example of conflict concerns specialisation or exception, e.g. where a rule concerning a specific patient should override that for patients generally. It is argued that application-level conflict resolution is often better addressed by careful policy (re)authoring, rather than automated resolution [5]. We do not attempt to resolve conflicts automatically, as doing so in a complex environment such as healthcare is difficult and dangerous. Instead, we provide the tools for policy authors to detect possible conflicts, which they can ignore, redefine the policy-set, or specify a runtime resolution strategy. This is practicable given that IC policies are local to a broker, maintained by a single administrative domain.

Conflict Detection The first step in dealing with policy conflict is to determine the rules that have the potential to conflict. This is necessary given the declarative nature of our rules. Rule predicates can be statically compared with others to detect the situations in which multiple rules simultaneously apply. It is then for the policy author to decide whether the rules in fact conflict.

If rules *statically* overlap, then they all necessarily apply in certain conditions. Otherwise, it is some coincidental set of circumstances that causes the rules to apply. This is termed *dynamic* conflict, as there is the potential for the rules to apply depending on context. Such classification highlights the potential seriousness of a conflict, as statically conflicting rules are directed at similar targets. Other considerations can assist policy analysis, e.g. two notification transformations with the same output type may indicate a policy error, as the subscriber may be misled by receiving several (similar) events of the same type. There may also be other application/domain-specific considerations relevant to ranking a conflict, such as rules authored by the inexperienced.

Conflict Resolution An obvious method for handling conflict is to 'author-out' any issues by redefining the policy set. This involves detecting and presenting potential conflicts to a policy administrator who deals with resolution. There are strong arguments that this is preferable to automated strategies [5, 19]. However, re-definition may be inappropriate for certain classes of conflict, e.g. if the conflicts occur infrequently, or only in particular situations. As such, our model provides for the definition of constraints—ordering, overriding and explicit declarations of incompatibility—that instruct the system on how to enforce the policies at runtime. The constraints are defined as separate entities that refer specifically to the rules involved in the conflict. This provides certainty and visibility as to how the rules are combined. The enforcement process is depicted in Fig. 2.

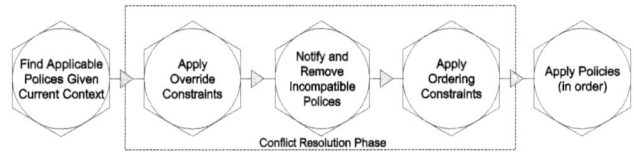

Figure 2: The process of policy enforcement.

6 IC-Database Integration

Our implementation integrates IC into *PostgreSQL-PS* [10, 28]: an extended PostgreSQL[9] database system that includes type-based pub/sub functionality. Databases are an integral component of large-scale infrastructure. A coupled database-messaging infrastructure has advantages over separate systems: a single interface and common type system, simplified replication, transactional delivery and improved performance (see [10] for discussion). Such an environment is particularly attractive for implementing IC functionality. An integrated pub/sub-database system enables IC predicates access to a rich representation of state: anything accessible from the broker, including event details, stored data, type schemata and stored procedures (that may call external services, e.g. shared credential services [22]). This provides much contextual information on which to base disclosure decisions. Persistence is facilitated, important not only for maintaining current (business/workflow) state, but also because the transfer of sensitive information often requires audit. Further, we can leverage existing database functionality, such as transactions, stored procedures and active rules to realise IC functionality and manage contextual change.

PostgreSQL-PS takes an advertisement-based approach to routing, where each database instance is a pub/sub broker. The filter model is highly expressive, allowing predicates to reference anything accessible by the query engine of the database-broker (subject to permissions). A store-and-forward approach is used for reliable delivery. We represent policy in the same format as events, so that rules may be defined using the same messaging infrastructure.

6.1 Hook Rules

We implement IC as a data control layer that operates above the pub/sub-database system. IC interacts with the pub/sub system through *hook rules* [24], which are active (ECA) rules, somewhat like triggers, that execute at specific points of the pub/sub process. Hook rules are distinct from IC rules, in that they are used to support the implementation of IC functionality.[10] A hook rule provides a *callback* mechanism, which we use so that the pub/sub layer executes a function in the appropriate circumstances to effect some data control operation(s). Hook rules are transformational: here a data structure containing relevant data/state is passed to a function in the data control layer, the output of which is returned to the pub/sub layer on which processing continues. Hook rules may be conditional, defined with (SQL) predicates that must hold for the rule to be enforced. Table 1 provides an overview of the hook rules used to realise IC and Fig. 3 illustrates their points of enforcement.

---

[9] http://www.postgresql.org

[10] There is not always a direct, *one-to-one* mapping between hook rules and IC rules. This is because hook rules are distinct, merely providing the callback (ECA) functionality for realising IC.

Table 1: Hook rule types and their associated description.

Rule Type	Input/Output	Purpose
CONNECTION VALIDATOR	Connection Details	Validates and authorises a connection. Establishes advertisement forwarding restrictions for brokers.
REQUEST VALIDATOR	Request	Authorises and processes the incoming request.
LINK ADV PROCESSOR	Advertisement	Executed when an advertisement is received through a link. Establishes subscription forwarding restrictions.
REQUEST TRANSFORM	Request	Modifies the request for delivery to a specific broker.
RESOLVE TRANSFORMS	Applicable Rules	Resolves any conflicts between applicable transformations at an interaction point.
EVENT TRANSFORM	Event	Executes the transformation function on the event.

The *validator* hooks use a function to determine whether the request/connection is authorised by any rules (after conflict resolution). For an authorised request, the *request validator* function loads the appropriate imposed conditions as channel filters, and creates the *event transform* hooks relevant to the newly created channel. Given that the applicable event transformations (hooks) are determined at runtime—evaluated in the context of an event—separate conflict resolution (*resolve transform*) hooks are required. The *request validator* function also creates the active rules to cause request re-evaluation on a change in monitored condition.

The advertisement restrictions relevant to a remote broker are loaded on link (connection) establishment by the *connection validator*. This is because advertisements are forwarded immediately after connection, or on receipt from another broker. Subscription forwarding restrictions, however, are loaded in response to the receipt of an advertisement from a broker. This is enabled by the *link adv processor* hook.

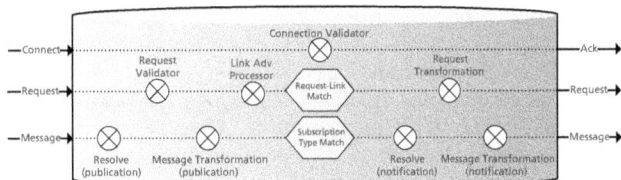

Figure 3: Hook rule enforcement points.

6.2 Audit

An IC implementation should facilitate audit by each broker recording data surrounding the operations that it undertakes. Such information is important as it provides *evidence* that one is meeting their data management responsibilities. In this way, audit brings about accountability. This information can also help to identify system or higher-level (organisational) issues, and may assist in discovering policy errors.

The database-broker environment greatly simplifies the implementation of audit processes. We use triggers to record in dedicated (unmodifiable) tables the details of pub/sub and IC operations including: request processing, connection/link state, event receipt/delivery, and the transformations and filters applied. This includes recording information of the applicable policies and those enforced (including details of conflict resolution), the clients/brokers involved and details of changes in context. Internal identifiers are assigned to processes to enable tracking of flows throughout the system, i.e. from receipt of an event to delivery (of it and its derivatives) to a number of clients. As audit data is persisted in tables, it can be queried using existing SQL constructs, and archived/managed in a similar manner to other data.

Audit may also be active, where the existing infrastructure is used to raise alerts (create new events) in particular situations; for example, to inform of a processing exceptions, policy incompatibilities or some higher-level concern.

7 Case Study: A Prescribing Scenario

In this section, we describe the use of IC in a scenario based on real-world health requirements. The focus of IC is to allow broker policy to set the boundaries for controlled dissemination. This is in contrast to other pub/sub security approaches, which rather than being tied to application-level semantics, focus on providing specific security mechanisms (see §3): security enforced at network edges ignores intermediaries, encryption-based schemes are inflexible and raise accountability concerns. Existing systems do not aim to provide a unified link between application concerns and granular, contextually-aware controls over connection/link establishment, event filtration and security transformations.

The enforcement of security policy necessarily imposes a processing overhead. However, any such overhead should be considered alongside whether it offers savings in data transmission and/or processing throughout the network. In this section, we apply IC to a prescribing scenario, presenting the rules necessary for restricting the data-flows of scenarios based on real-world requirements and to demonstrate that IC can in fact improve net performance of a pub/sub system.

Prescriptions are an integral part of care provision. Here we present two different implementations of a prescribing scenario, one from the perspective of a single *Surgery* broker that supports local and homecare services, the other considering a distributed broker network of a *Hospital*. Both have much the same restrictions. The dataflows of this scenario are presented in Fig. 4. This scenario, although simple, illustrates the need to control data flows to parties involved in the care process.

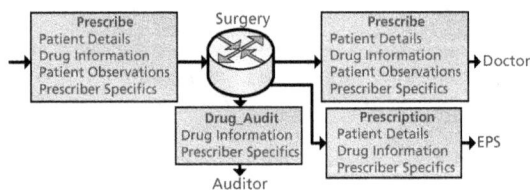

Figure 4: Data flows for `prescribe` events.

In providing care, nurses record symptoms and notes concerning patients' well being, and may also prescribe medication, though only for drugs within their competence [8]. As part of treatment, a nurse might publish a `prescribe` event[11] that encapsulates all data concerning a prescribing

---

[11] The notion of event-driven workflow is well established in the NHS, see §2.3.

incident, including the reasons for the medications. This information requires storage in the provider's care database(s), and must be transmitted to other domains for audit and dispensing purposes. Doctors access information from their surgery. A doctor may request notification of when drugs are prescribed for some patients, as this may indicate a situation of concern. An authorisation rule allows a doctor to subscribe to `prescribe` events for patients that they treat:[12]

(`subscription`, `prescribe`, {`doctor`}, {`treatsPatient(user`
, `att.patientid`)}) $\in RT \times \tau \times \mathbb{P}(\mathcal{C}) \times \mathbb{P}(\mathcal{E})$.[13]

Prescriptions must flow to the *Electronic Prescription Service* (EPS), a domain that operates as a clearing-house, assisting pharmacies in dispensing and reimbursement. The EPS requires prescription information, but *not* the reasons (notes or observations) for the medication. A transformation rule converts all `prescribe` events into a `prescription`, which involves copying relevant details from the `prescribe` events, and augmenting them with extra patient information, such as the patient's address and date-of-birth, and their surgery and/or hospital details. The rule is defined as: (`publication`, `prescribe`, $\emptyset$, $\emptyset$, `toPrescription`, `prescription`, $\bot$) $\in IP \times \tau \times \mathbb{P}(\mathcal{C}) \times \mathbb{P}(\mathcal{G}) \times F \times \tau \times D$, where an empty predicate set is interpreted as a need to always apply the rule. An authorisation rule allows the EPS to subscribe to all `prescription` events.

The auditor must be informed when certain 'controlled drugs' are prescribed. The audit is prescriber focused, thus the auditor will only receive patient details in exceptional circumstances. To balance confidentiality with the duty to inform the auditor, a `drug_audit` event is created through a transformation function that removes sensitive information by filtering various fields from prescriptions for controlled drugs. However, when a prescriber is under suspicion, the auditor may receive their `prescribe` events to provide detailed information to assist the investigation. This is because it is in the interests of public safety to ensure that the prescriber is acting appropriately. This transmission occurs in line with patient consent, which might be obtained when providing care, or perhaps in reference to the individual investigation. This is enforced by an imposed condition rule: (`subscription`, `prescribe`, {`auditor`}, {`auditConsent(msg.patientid`)}, {`investigating(msg.prescriberid`)}, $\bot$) $\in IP \times \tau \times \mathbb{P}(\mathcal{C}) \times \mathbb{P}(\mathcal{E}) \times \mathbb{P}(\mathcal{R}) \times H$.

7.1 Distributed Scenario

We extend the scenario to a distributed environment, where the hospital (an administrative domain) must also control the dataflows throughout its own broker network. Fig. 5 depicts the topology, where a number of nurses are assigned to work the wards. Each *ward* has its own broker. The *central* (ward) broker manages all ward information, receiving (subscribing to) all events from the wards. The hospital *dispenser* acts as the local pharmacy, and thus is responsible for distributing information to the EPS, and forwarding audit events for controlled drugs. The *local trust* broker (exclusively) manages the information flows to local health institutions. Here there are two *surgeries* who have doctors subscribing to information on their patients, as well as

the regional *auditor* who receives all `drug_audit` events and the `prescribe` events issued by nurses under investigation. The hospital is responsible for sending the appropriate patient information to the surgeries, who must then pass on the information to the relevant doctors. For both examples, the appropriate principal and request authorisation rules are defined to enable the described connections and data flows.

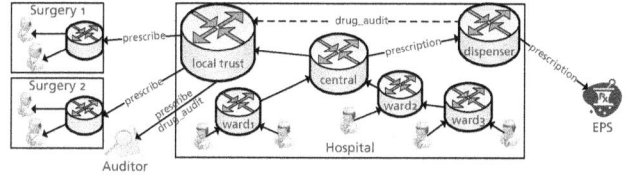

Figure 5: The distributed prescribing environment.

7.2 Experimental Setup

Each broker consisted of an integrated IC-PostgreSQL-PS instance running on its own Intel Core 2 Duo 2.4Ghz CPU machine with 2GiB of RAM. The clients were distributed amongst a number of machines on a different subnet from the brokers. We present the mean values over 10 trials. The environment contains 1,000 active patient records, where four doctors manage 250 patients each. Five nurses attend to the patients, raising `prescribe` events for the drugs they prescribe. Each doctor subscribes to `prescribe` events pertaining to the top 25 (10%) most critically ill patients that they treat. In the trials, the event size is fixed for each event type, as in practice many attributes are fixed length identifiers that refer to treatments, drugs and patients.

The workload involves each nurse publishing 1,000 events, 200 of which concern patients to which doctors are subscribed.[14] All of the `prescribe` events are transformed into `prescriptions`, and those for controlled medications into a `drug_audit` event. The auditor receives all `prescribe` messages published by the single nurse that is under investigation (all patients have consented). To better gauge the processing overheads of IC, it is necessary to compare that to an implementation of *vanilla* pub/sub; i.e. one lacking restriction functionality.[15] Without IC, the publishers become the sole source of information, who must deal with confidentiality concerns by publishing separate events for each level of visibility. This involves publishing two or three events for each prescription: `prescribe` relevant for the doctors/surgery/hospital/auditor, `prescription` as relevant for the EPS, and if the drug is controlled, a `drug_audit` event. We implement the vanilla pub/sub scenario using the same database-broker infrastructure,[16] to ensure that the information is reliably recorded, audited, processed and delivered. However, the vanilla implementation is unrestricted— i.e. without any IC rules. To enable comparison we assume

---

[12]For want of space, we only present only the most pertinent rules to serve as examples. The complete set of rules governing this scenario can be found in [20].

[13]Note that `att` refers to permission attribute values, `msg` to event content, and `user` to the client's unique idenitifer.

[14]In practice prescriptions occur relatively infrequently, i.e. in the order of tens per day. However, a large number of publications were used in this scenario to provide a *general* indication of performance, accounting for database optimisations such as write buffers and caching, and to ensure that nurses publish simultaneously to interleave processing.

[15]To reiterate, we do not compare IC to other pub/sub systems as we are unaware of any that provide a complete set of comparable controls. Instead, here the comparison is to illustrate that the overheads of policy enforcement must be considered with respect to overall system performance.

[16]Note that [10] compares the performance of (vanilla) PostgreSQL-PS to other pub/sub implementations.

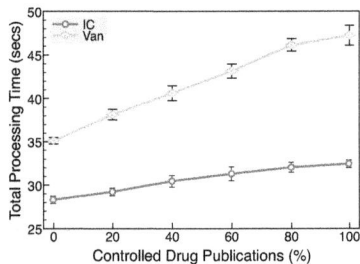

(a) Workload processing comparison

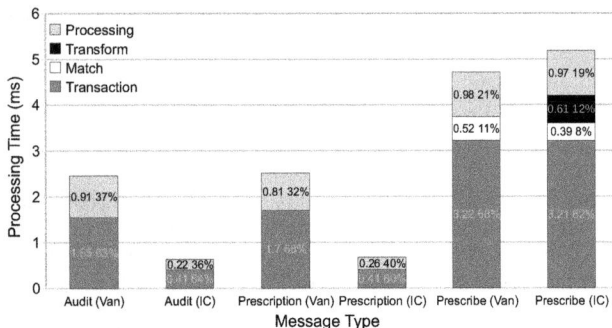

(b) Processing time per event type

Figure 6: Single broker performance results.

that the vanilla subscribers are honest and cooperative, issuing filters in line with the restrictions otherwise required by the scenario.

7.3 Single-Broker Comparison

Prescriptions for controlled drugs require more processing to create and deliver `drug_audit` events. Therefore, this scenario consisted of five workloads, each with a different percentage of controlled drug prescriptions. Fig. 6(a) shows that the overall processing time for the vanilla implementation is significantly greater than that of the IC model for each workload. This is because the vanilla approach involves a broker receiving 2–3 times the number of publications to account for varying levels of data visibility, where each publication is subject to all event processing operations.

To give a clearer indication of the overheads, Fig. 6(b) presents a breakdown of processing time per event type. Transactions are necessary for reliable processing of events; however, transactions also impose an overhead. Here, the transactional overheads (begin/commit) of event processing outweigh those imposed by the transformations.

The figure also shows that the `drug_audit` and `prescription` events for the IC approach involve a significantly lower processing time than their vanilla counterparts, due to the fact that the transformed events are subject to fewer messaging operations. The *match* category refers to the time the query engine spends in evaluating subscription filters. This is negligible where a subscription is filterless (i.e. match all), as for `prescription` and `drug_audit` subscriptions.

`Prescribe` events take greater processing effort as they are subject to more subscriptions, and thus involve more processing and transactions. The IC approach is slower at processing a single `prescribe` event due to the overheads imposed by the transformations; however, the difference is comparatively small with respect to the overall processing time for the event type. Considering the total processing time for a prescription *incident*, i.e. accounting for all infor-

mation flows for the action of prescribing, the IC implementation is shown to be more efficient, taking 6.48ms compared to 9.82ms for the vanilla approach.

7.4 Distributed Broker Scenario

Again, we compare a vanilla and IC implementation, however there is a slight variation in the routing paths between the approaches.[17] As the dispenser is responsible for all pharmaceutical data, a transformation enables the central ward to pass the prescription events to the dispenser, who forwards them to the EPS service. The dispenser is also responsible for producing the audit events. In the vanilla approach the routing paths are determined solely by (unrestricted) advertisement/subscription propagation. This means that `drug_audit` events are produced by the nurses (publishers) rather than the dispenser, and thus flow directly from the central broker to the local trust broker for distribution to the auditor. This experiment uses the same workload, except the number of controlled drugs publications is fixed at 40%. The nurse in Ward3 is under investigation.

We observed that for the workload, IC resulted in a ~36% reduction in events transmitted, and ~33% reduction in processing time. To show the effects of distribution, Fig. 7 presents a breakdown of processing for each broker in the topology. Each IC broker incurs equal, or significantly less overhead than its vanilla counterpart, except for the dispenser whose auditing responsibilities require additional operations in the IC implementation.

Generally, pub/sub models aim to reduce multiplicative event fan-out by pushing subscriptions as close to the publisher as possible. Similarly, transformations can improve distribution by routing a single copy of an event as far as possible before transforming it as relevant to the subscriber. This is reflected in Fig. 7(d),[18] where the prescription and audit events resulting from a transformation travel only one hop, as opposed to the vanilla implementation where events travel the whole path from the publisher to the subscriber. The other subfigures show that this reduces the event count, byte count and processing time. Where transformations do not impact on propagation, i.e. in the delivery of `prescribe` events, the results are similar for both approaches.

7.5 Scenario Discussion

As IC involves policy enforcement and event processing, it is useful to consider its overheads. Although our focus is on security rather than performance, this section demonstrates that the overheads brought by enforcing security policies should be considered with respect to the overall savings (in transmission/processing) throughout the infrastructure.

We observe that a significant proportion of processing time relates to transactions. We argue that transactions are necessary in an implementation because sensitive information is typically important, and thus must be reliably stored, audited, processed and delivered. It follows that transactional and storage overhead is likely to be incurred regardless of the implementation. In this scenario, transformation functions, despite involving queries on stored data, did not greatly impact overall performance as the operations were comparatively less expensive than the transactions.

---

[17]This is indicated in Fig. 5 by the dashed line for the `drug_audit` event.

[18]The bars in Fig. 7(d) represent the mean, and the error-bars the maximum and minimum hops travelled.

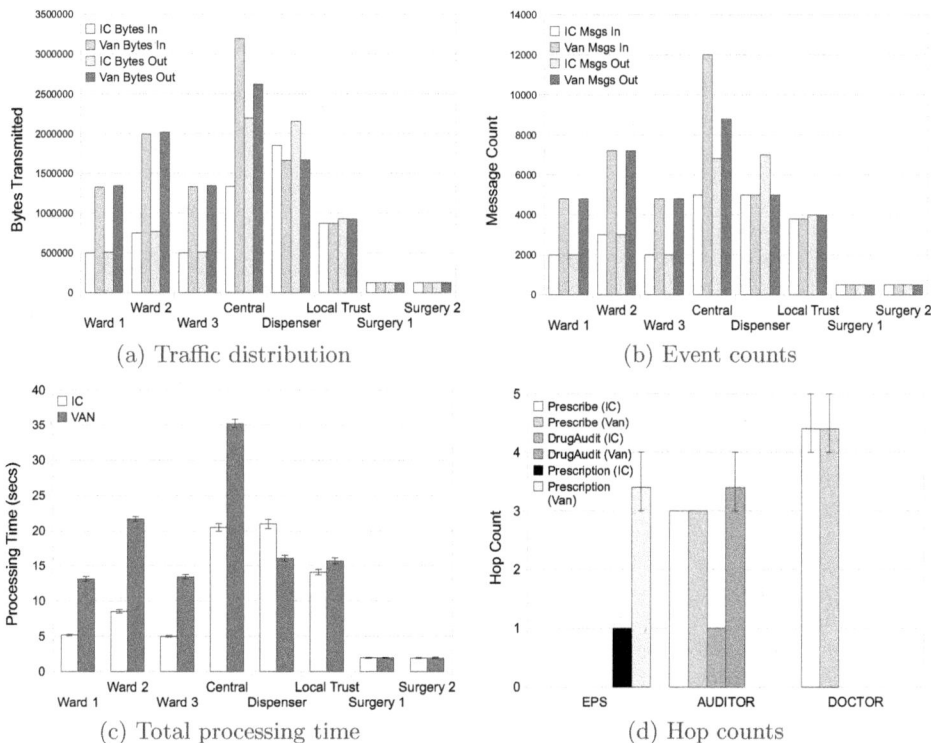

(a) Traffic distribution

(b) Event counts

(c) Total processing time

(d) Hop counts

Figure 7: Performance of the IC and Vanilla implementations in the distributed scenario.

Intuitively, processing overheads can be reduced given that restrictions and transformations can limit information flows, thereby reducing event fan-out. This, of course, depends on the nature of the scenario; clearly, the results will vary depending on the complexity of the operations (e.g. transformation functions), and the representation of context. These are application-level concerns, where performance characteristics depend on the specific requirements of the scenario and the implementation environment. That said, our experiments indicate the scalability of IC, where policy enforcement does not necessarily degrade performance, but in certain circumstances improves efficiency, particularly when considering the overall workload (net performance).

Although a vanilla implementation is unrestricted, and thus useful for performance comparisons as it avoids policy overheads, it is important to remember the differences regarding security. A vanilla approach assumes that clients are trusted i) to publish events with the appropriate level(s) of visibility for all potential recipients, and ii) to (only) subscribe to information for which they are authorised. Information is routed through the brokers in an uncontrolled manner, thus brokers are also trusted to behave appropriately. This is unsuitable in situations where data is sensitive, as even without malice, there are negligence and curiosity concerns. Further, the vanilla approach is insufficient even in an environment of overarching responsibility, as accountability is diminished. As described, other pub/sub security models lack a comparable set of controls, meaning that they would address only a subset of these issues.

8 Concluding Remarks

IC rules concern transmission (only) to the next hop. This is because a broker is not qualified to make decisions regarding the event flows of other brokers, especially those in other domains. To do so is impractical, as it requires information of the local processes, context and policies of each broker along the dissemination path. Further, enforcing disclosure policy at the subscriber's broker fails to protect inter-broker communications, while enforcing at the publisher's broker in the worst cases causes a separate event to be routed for each subscription. Aside from policy management and scalability concerns, such approaches complicate notions of responsibility and accountability.

Typically in practice, databases form an essential component of large-scale infrastructure. In addition to the fact that sensitive information not only requires transmission, but also storage and audit,[19] we have integrated IC into a database system to show that such controls can both operate with, and leverage from, technology already commonplace.

Local control underpins the model of responsibility. If domains manage their technical infrastructure, it seems reasonable to couple the control mechanisms with the data they protect. General pub/sub is by itself inappropriate for environments where information is sensitive, thus some security-related overheads will be imposed regardless of the implementation. As future work, we hope that gathering further experience in real deployments will allow us to make quantified statements of scalability: data is required concerning the number of clients, event types and policy rules, event load, rule complexity, connection churn, and other variables and constraints. Of course, this is a moving target. That said, although simple, our case study based on real-world requirements indicates that an IC implementation is possible by extending existing technology, and that the model can encapsulate the data flow requirements of real

---

[19]See [21] for a discussion of security issues concerning the replay of historical events.

care processes. While policy enforcement necessarily introduces overheads, we have shown that these must be considered with respect to any savings in overall network activity.

IC essentially overlays a point-to-point security model over a distributed pub/sub service. This is a direct product of the responsibility model (local-control). Domains process and share information for a particular purpose, meaning that connections and the associated security constraints form naturally. A domain maintains a sharing policy that it implemets within the brokers it controls. In this way, a broker's policy store merely reflects a domain's trust and security concerns. Local enforcement can lead to *Chinese-Whispers* effects, where an event/request changes or is filtered as it moves through the network. This is the result of the responsibility model. *End-to-end* concerns could arise if policy is incorrectly formulated (at the high-level) or specified (at the system-level); though clearly policy issues will affect any approach that enforces application-level considerations. IC rules enable the definition of the *boundaries* for communication, allowing events to flow freely where authorised. The purpose of IC is to allow the advantages of a scalable, push-based, subscription-oriented distribution paradigm safely in environments of sensitive information, by allowing security constraints to be imposed where necessary.

Ultimately, information protection is not just a technical issue. There are legal requirements and social pressures regarding the use and management of sensitive information. Technical infrastructure must facilitate data sharing, storage and protection, in line with higher-level concerns. IC is designed specifically for environments of federated policy, where those active in the environment are responsible for the information they access, generate and manage. It is novel in that it brings the notion of local-control to the pub/sub middleware, so that those responsible for information encode rules in their brokers to restrict data flows where necessary. The model is unique as it enables control in situations where wide-area notification services are required across administrative boundaries and/or where security policy dictates that data visibility must vary between clients and/or network components (brokers). It is not a security *panacea*—indeed, it is unlikely such a thing exists—but instead provides a mechanism for control, giving those managing data the ability to meet their data sharing and protection obligations. Local control and responsibility brings accountability, which is necessary for the protection of sensitive information.

Acknowledgments

The authors acknowledge the Technology Strategy Board (TS/H000062/1) and EPSRC (RG55622) for their support.

9   References

[1] J. Bacon, D. M. Eyers, J. Singh, and P. R. Pietzuch. Access control in publish/subscribe systems. In *DEBS '08*, pages 23–34. ACM, 2008.

[2] A. Belokosztolszki, D. M. Eyers, P. R. Pietzuch, J. Bacon, and K. Moody. Role-based access control for publish/subscribe middleware architectures. In *DEBS '03*, pages 1–8. ACM, 2003.

[3] Bolton Research Group. Patients' knowledge and expectations of confidentiality in primary health care: a quantitative study. *British Journal of General Practice*, 50:901–902, 2000.

[4] A. Carzaniga, D. S. Rosenblum, and A. L. Wolf. Design and Evaluation of a Wide-Area Event Notification Service. *ACM Transactions on Computer Systems*, 19(3):332–383, 2001.

[5] R. Chadha. A cautionary note about policy conflict resolution. In *MILCOM*, pages 1–8. IEEE, 2006.

[6] L. Darzi. *High quality care for all: NHS Next Stage Review*. Department of Health, 2008.

[7] Department of Health. Confidentiality: NHS Code of Practice, 2003.

[8] Department of Health. Safer management of Controlled Drugs, 2007.

[9] T. Dierks and C. Allen. *The TLS Protocol (RFC 2246)*. Internet Engineering Task Force (IETF), 1999.

[10] D. M. Eyers, L. Vargas, J. Singh, K. Moody, and J. Bacon. Relational database support for event-based middleware functionality. In *DEBS '10*, pages 160–171. ACM, 2010.

[11] L. Fiege. *Visibility in Event-Based Systems*. PhD thesis, TU Darmstadt, 2004.

[12] L. Fiege, A. Zeidler, A. Buchmann, R. Kilian-Kehr, and G. Muehl. Security aspects in publish/subscribe systems. In *DEBS '04*, pages 44–49. IEEE, 2004.

[13] H. Khurana. Scalable security and accounting services for content-based publish/subscribe systems. In *SAC '05*, pages 801–807. ACM, 2005.

[14] Z. Miklós. Towards an access control mechanism for wide-area publish/subscribe systems. In *ICDCSW '02*, pages 516–524. IEEE, 2002.

[15] NHS Care Record Development Board. The care record guarantee—our guarantee for NHS Care Records in England, 2009.

[16] NHS Information Authority. Share with Care! People's views on consent confidentiality of patient information, 2002.

[17] L. Opyrchal and A. Prakash. Secure distribution of events in content-based publish subscribe systems. In *SSYM'01*, pages 21–21. USENIX, 2001.

[18] L. I. Pesonen, D. M. Eyers, and J. Bacon. Access control in decentralised publish/subscribe systems. *Journal of Networks*, 2(2):57–67, 2007.

[19] C.-C. Shu, E. Y. Yang, and A. E. Arenas. Detecting conflicts in ABAC policies with rule-reduction and binary-search techniques. In *Policy '09*, pages 182–185. IEEE, 2009.

[20] J. Singh. *Controlling the dissemination and disclosure of healthcare events*. PhD thesis, University of Cambridge, 2010.

[21] J. Singh, D. M. Eyers, and J. Bacon. Controlling historical information dissemination in publish/subscribe. In *MidSec '08*, pages 34–39. ACM, 2008.

[22] J. Singh, D. M. Eyers, and J. Bacon. Credential management in event-driven healthcare systems. In *Middleware '08 Companion*, pages 48–53. ACM, 2008.

[23] J. Singh, L. Vargas, and J. Bacon. A model for controlling data flow in distributed healthcare environments. In *Pervasive Health '08*, pages 188–191. IEEE, 2008.

[24] J. Singh, L. Vargas, J. Bacon, and K. Moody. Policy-Based Information Sharing in Publish/Subscribe Middleware. In *Policy '08*, pages 137–144. IEEE, 2008.

[25] M. Srivatsa and L. Liu. Secure event dissemination in publish-subscribe networks. In *ICDCS '07*, page 22. IEEE, 2007.

[26] M. A. Stone, S. A. Redsell, J. T. Ling, and A. D. Hay. Sharing patient data: competing demands of privacy, trust and research in primary care. *British Journal of General Practice*, 55:783–789, 2005.

[27] D. Sturman, G. Banavar, and R. Strom. Reflection in the Gryphon message brokering system. In *Reflection Workshop, OOPSLA '08*, 2008.

[28] L. Vargas, J. Bacon, and K. Moody. Event-Driven Database Information Sharing. In *BNCOD '08*, pages 113–125. Springer, 2008.

[29] A. Wun and H.-A. Jacobsen. A policy management framework for content-based publish/subscribe. In *Middleware '07*, pages 368–388. Springer, 2007.

[30] Y. Zhao and D. C. Sturman. Dynamic access control in a content-based publish/subscribe system with delivery guarantees. In *ICDCS '06*, pages 60–68. IEEE, 2006.

Towards Vulnerability-Based Intrusion Detection with Event Processing

Amer Farroukh, Mohammad Sadoghi, and Hans-Arno Jacobsen
Middleware Systems Research Group
Department of Electrical and Computer Engineering
University of Toronto, Toronto, Canada
amer.farroukh@utoronto.ca, mo@cs.toronto.edu, jacobsen@eecg.toronto.edu

ABSTRACT

Computer systems continue to be breached despite substantial investments in defense mechanisms to stop attacks from propagating. The accuracy of current intrusion detection systems (IDSes) is hindered by the limited capability of regular expressions (REs) to express the exact vulnerability. Recent advances have proposed vulnerability-based IDSes that parse traffic and retrieve protocol semantics to describe the vulnerability. Such a description of attacks is analogous to subscriptions that specify events of interest in event processing systems. However, the matching engine of state-of-the-art IDSes lacks efficient matching algorithms that can process many signatures simultaneously. In this work, we place event processing in the core of the IDS and propose novel algorithms to efficiently match vulnerability signatures. Also, we are among the first to detect complex attacks such as the Conficker worm which requires correlating multiple protocol data units (MPDUs) while maintaining a small memory footprint. Finally, we show that our algorithms are resilient to attacks through extensive testing of the IDS under different workloads. Our approach incurs negligible overhead when processing clean traffic and is faster than existing systems.

Categories and Subject Descriptors

H.3.3 [**Information Search and Retrieval**]: Information filtering

General Terms

Algorithms, Design, Performance, Security

Keywords

Vulnerability Signature, Intrusion Detection, Signature Matching, Deep Packet Inspection, and Complex Event Processing

1. INTRODUCTION

The current defensive mechanism in the IT world consists of an intrusion detection system (IDS) that examines traffic for malicious content and raises alerts for any suspicious activity [19, 18, 1, 15]. Alerts are then forwarded to an event processing routine which correlates and prioritizes them and notifies the network administrator. However, such systems have severely failed to detect sophisticated attacks that require deep content inspection and state maintenance [6]. According to the Cyber Secure Institute, the economic loss due to the Conficker worm tallied up to $9.1 billion as it infected more than 10 million hosts in 2008 [2]. The currently deployed IDSes have failed to stop the propagation of this attack which raises the need for more sophisticated detection mechanisms that parse and analyze traffic beyond the network layer.

Event processing systems, on the other hand, can match events accurately through deep content inspection of structured event predicates [10, 14, 3, 12]. However, the functionality of such systems in the security domain has been limited to event correlation of alerts generated by the intrusion detection system (IDS) [27]. The accuracy and speed of current IDSes [19, 18, 1, 15] can be significantly improved by using event processing techniques that can parse and analyze traffic beyond the network layer and detect more sophisticated attacks which require correlation between multiple protocol data units (MPDUs) [10, 31, 16, 12]. To illustrate the need for deep content inspection and state maintenance, we describe the Conficker worm in more detail below.

Example: Conficker exploits a server service vulnerability in the Windows system (MS08-067) by sending a specially crafted WINRPC request that overflows the server buffer [2]. A successful attack results in remote code execution in which the attacker takes full control over the infected machine. We model the vulnerability signature for Conficker in Figure 1. The signature requires correlation of different single protocol data units (PDUs).

A single PDU signature is composed of a Boolean formula of predicates. Each predicate holds an attribute-value-matcher triplet and predicates are combined using operators such as AND (&) or OR (||). The BIND PDU consists of three predicates while the REQUEST PDU consists of four predicates. Each predicate has an attribute name (rpc_ver), a value (3), and a matcher (=). As field values can vary in type, different matchers must be used for each predicate. The UUID field requires a string matcher while the PathName field requires length checking as well as regular expression (RE) matching.

Moreover, the RPC version (rpc_ver,rpc_ver_minor) and interface ID (UUID) must be matched in the BIND PDU; the server acknowledgement (Accept) must be detected in

```
(BIND || ALTER_CONTEXT):
rpc_ver=3 & rpc_ver_minor=0 &
UUID="4b324fc8-1670-01d3-1278-5a47bf6ee188"

-> (BIND_ACK || ALTER_CONTEXT_RESPONSE):
rpc_ver=3 & rpc_ver_minor=0 &
result[UUID] = Accept

-> REQUEST:
rpc_ver=3 & rpc_ver_minor=0 & opnum=0x1f &
strlen(stub.PathName)> 256  &
matchRE(stub.PathName, "/^\x05\x00\x00")
```

Figure 1: MPDU Signature of Conficker Worm.

the BIND_ACK PDU; and the malicious code is passed as part of the REQUEST PDU to overflow the 256 byte buffer. To identify the PDU sequence, the NEXT ($\Rightarrow$) operator ensures that a client is successfully bound to the server interface before issuing a request (BIND $\Rightarrow$ BIND_ACK $\Rightarrow$ REQUEST). The OR (||) operator is essential to stop attackers from eluding detection as the same attack can be carried out using an ALTER_CONTEXT PDU to change the interface binding number [6].

Our extensive study of the Conficker worm has shown that regular expressions are not sufficient to detect such attacks. The signature language must be expressive enough to model the exact vulnerability which requires arbitrary matchers such as length checking, ranges, and regular expressions. As a result, the predicate matching phase must be completely isolated from the signature matching phase to support arbitrary matchers. Moreover, the IDS should support the AND, OR, and NEXT operators to correlate different protocol data units (PDUs) and detect such sophisticated attacks which require state maintenance. However, the signature language used in current IDSes [19, 18, 1] models one version of the attack as it cannot express the exact vulnerability exploited by the Conficker worm.

To elude detection by the IDS, attackers craft polymorphic variants of the attack in which the byte code used is different while maintaining the same malicious functionality [7]. Current IDSes [19, 18, 1] fail to detect polymorphic attacks due to the limited capability of regular expressions to express the exact vulnerability [24]. Recently, researchers have proposed vulnerability-based signatures to enhance the accuracy of the IDS [29]. A vulnerability-based signature is a set of predicates and each predicate consists of an attribute-value pair which is similar to the event processing language of subscriptions and events. Despite the similarity of language between intrusion detection and event processing domains, we list some of the differences which impose some challenges as well as create opportunities for enhancing performance.

First, event processing systems aim to support millions of users that can subscribe or unsubscribe at any time [11] while rules in an IDS are in the order of a few thousands, and they are precompiled at boot-time [19]. Second, the protocol specification in IDSes determines the order of fields, which can be exploited to accelerate parsing as irrelevant fields can be skipped [24]. However, predicates in event processing systems exhibit no specific order, and all predicates must be parsed to match the event [10]. Third, the norm in event processing is high number of matches as users often subscribe to events that occur frequently [14]. On the

other hand, the matching engine of IDSes must be optimized for the non-matching case (attack-free) since normal traffic constitutes the vast majority of Internet traffic [28]. Forth, publishers and subscribers are disjoint in event processing applications while clients and servers are grouped into connections in IDSes [18]. An IDS must handle thousands of connections simultaneously as it protects the whole network backbone [19]. As a result, memory footprint is a crucial factor when handling large number of connections separately [15]. Each connection requires a separate memory slot for partial matches; thus, matching algorithms must be optimized for speed and memory.

Given the differences between the two domains, the signature language must be expressive enough to support multiple data types and express the exact vulnerability. The rpc_ver in the Conficker example (Figure 1) requires integer matching while the PathName requires RE matching and length checking. As a result, the IDS must support arbitrary matching dimensions that can handle a more expressive signature language such as string length checking or regular expressions which are not commonly supported in event processing applications. These matching dimensions include exact matching of numbers, range checking, exact string matching, string length checking, and regular expression matching. More matching dimensions can be augmented to the IDS as the signature language evolves to cover emerging attacks. The message fields are evaluated against the individual predicate matchers and the results of all matchers are aggregated using AND, OR, and other operators. As modularity of individual matchers and the overall matching algorithm is vital for the functionality of IDSes, we investigate matching algorithms that exhibit this distinction and study their applicability in this domain [12, 31]. We examine algorithms that can support arbitrary matchers where predicate matching is isolated from signature matching as is the case for the counting algorithm [31]. Moreover, to detect complex attacks, such as the Conficker worm, we present our Memory Conscious Network (MCN) which correlates signatures matched by different PDUs to detect MPDU attacks. Our contributions are summarized as follows:

1. We present two novel algorithms, Access Predicate Pruning (APP) and Early Elimination (EE), which efficiently match single PDU signatures while maintaining a small memory footprint. Our algorithms reduce the matching time by pruning partial matches of signatures that will eventually not be matched. (Section 4)

2. We are among the first to support MPDU matching in IDSes through our Memory Conscious Network (MCN) that uses bit encoding to minimize memory and correlate messages within a single connection or across multiple connections. (Section 5)

3. We integrate our algorithms into state-of-the-art IDS, and we show that our proposed solutions are resilient to attacks by providing thorough evaluations for different traffic types ranging from normal traffic to extreme attack scenarios for average to large rule sets. (Section 6)

2. RELATED WORK

In this section, we describe the limitations of signatures used in current IDSes, discuss the matching algorithms used in the IDS domain, and survey event processing algorithms. We also provide an overview of the candidate selection algorithm [15] which serves as the baseline for our evaluation.

Current IDS Capabilities: The field of signature matching mainly focuses on three types of signatures: strings, regular expressions (REs), and vulnerability-based signatures [4, 19, 26, 25, 7, 24]. Despite continuous efforts to enhance the performance of the matching engine in current IDSes, the accuracy of such systems is hindered by the limited capabilities of regular expressions to represent all attacks as they incur a high number of false positives and false negatives. Such signatures are attack driven where a rule can only detect a single type of attack. Current IDSes such as Cisco [1], Snort [19] and Bro [18] use a combination of strings and REs to describe attacks in the signature database. The most widely used multi-pattern string matching algorithms in IDSes [19] are Aho-Corasick [4] and Wu-Manber [30] which scale much better when compared to single pattern matching algorithms that search for each pattern individually [13]. Regular expression (RE) signatures can be represented in deterministic finite automaton (DFA) [26] or non-deterministic finite automaton (NFA) [9]. Smith *et al.* [25] propose a combination of DFA and NFA called extended finite automaton (XFA) where a finite memory is manipulated by instructions attached to states and edges to track dependencies. An XFA is both memory-efficient and time-efficient. String matching algorithms and RE expression matching are orthogonal to our work as we focus on matching many vulnerability-based signatures simultaneously while supporting any type of predicates.

Vulnerability-based Signature Matching: Researchers have recently devoted many efforts on vulnerability-based signatures for IDSes [7, 24, 15, 29]. Wang *et al.* [29] first introduced vulnerability-driven signatures and several efforts focused on automatic generation of such signatures to match all polymorphic and metamorphic variants of an attack [7]. Schear *et al.* [24] present an architecture for integrating parsing and matching of vulnerability signatures. However, the complexity of manually modifying the parser specifications and the explicit maintenance of the protocol state machine by the signature author renders their system infeasible to support large numbers of vulnerability signatures. Netshield [15] researchers have proposed a framework for parsing and matching vulnerability-based signatures. They present the candidate selection algorithm to match many signatures simultaneously.

Candidate Selection (CS) Algorithm: The state-of-the-art algorithm for matching vulnerability signatures in IDSes is the candidate selection (CS) algorithm [15]. Matching is performed in a two-step fashion where predicates are first evaluated then forwarded to the CS algorithm which accumulates the results from the individual matchers [15] and outputs the matched signatures. The field order of the protocol specification is exploited to combine rules into blocks (RBs), decide the matcher order, and minimize matching time. At runtime, for every iteration RB_i, field matched, the results returned by individual matchers are merged as follows: $S_i = S_{i-1} \oplus A_i + B_i$ where S_i is the candidate list (CandList) of the current iteration and S_{i-1} is the CandList of the previous iteration. A_i is the set of candidates from RB_1 to RB_{i-1}, while B_i is the list of rules whose predicates are matched in the current RB_i. The operator $\oplus$ reduces the number of partial matches after every iteration but is

expensive to perform due to traversal of A_i and S_i lists as shown in Section 6. For more details, refer to [15].

The main network monitoring applications in event processing are Gigascope [8] which is a stream database for network monitoring and SNIF [17] which is a live stream matching framework that trades off accuracy for speed. In this work, we target algorithms that can support arbitrary matchers, rather than SQL queries, and can accurately match signatures [12, 31, 3, 10, 5, 20, 21]. Those algorithms fall under one of two categories: two-phase and single phase algorithms.

Two-phase algorithms such as counting [31] and GPX-Matcher [20] evaluate predicates in the first phase and match subscriptions in the second phase. Fabret *et al.* [10] use access predicates to group signatures based on common predicates and control access to subscription clusters. At runtime, all access predicates are scanned and the corresponding clusters are evaluated only if the access predicate is matched. Given the nature of the IDS matching problem in which arbitrary matchers must be supported with expressive operations such as regular expression matching and string length checking, two-phase algorithms best suit IDSes. The counting algorithm presented in [31] is the only algorithm that can support arbitrary matchers since phases 1 and 2 are completely distinct. The index structure of signatures and the abstract representation of predicate matches as counters allow for supporting arbitrary predicate matchers, such as regular expressions, substring matching, and Boolean expressions, which are essential to evaluate vulnerability-based signatures. Other algorithms, such as propagation [10], are domain specific and can only address specific types of predicates. The tight coupling between the algorithm and the predicate type renders such algorithms ineffective in the intrusion detection domain which requires supporting complex types such as regular expressions.

In single phase algorithms, typically novel tree organizations are used to match subscriptions [3, 21]; predicates are evaluated in internal nodes while leaf nodes represent subscriptions. These algorithms are fine-tuned for efficient event processing but are are not optimized for space. Similarly, Rete [12] is another well-known algorithm; however, Rete [12] also trades off space for matching efficiency and matching expressiveness. Guoli *et al.* [14] proposed an extended and improved version of the Rete algorithm to support composite event processing in publish/subscribe systems. Given the memory constraint of the IDS which is susceptible to memory-explosion attacks, we present our Memory Conscious Network (MCN) that optimizes for efficiency as well as memory footprint to support multiple protocol data unit (MPDU) matching which requires correlation between different packet flows and connections.

Hardware Support for Matching Given the large number of signatures (subscriptions) and the wire-speed processing requirements, Sadoghi *et al.* [22, 23] proposed the use of Field-programmable gate arrays (FPGAs) to further accelerate the matching engine (based on propagation [10] algorithm) in order to meet such stringent requirements.

3. SYSTEM ARCHITECTURE

We integrated our matching engine and MPDU algorithm into the open-source Netshield IDS [15] as shown in Figure 2. Packets are first reassembled to form connections and then forwarded to the appropriate protocol parser. Once a pro-

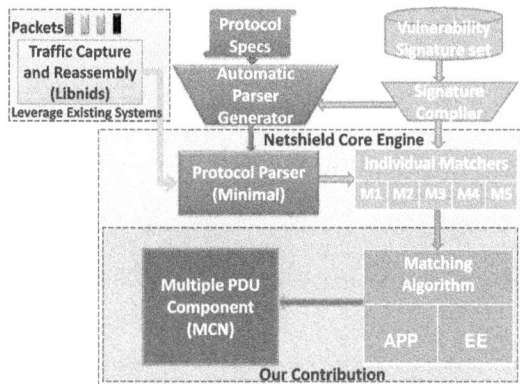

Figure 2: System Architecture.

tocol field is parsed, the corresponding matcher is invoked. Netshield supports five matching dimensions: exact matching and range checking of numbers using a binary search tree, exact string matching using a trie, string length checking using a binary search tree, and regular expression matching using a combined DFA. More matching dimensions can be easily supported if needed by the signature language. The results of the individual matchers are simultaneously sent to the core matching engine. We replace the CS algorithm of Netshield [15] with our own algorithms, Access Predicate Pruning (APP) and Early Elimination (EE), to reduce matching time. These algorithms accumulate the results of the partial matches produced by the individual matchers and indicate whether a whole signature is matched. The final component of the system is our own extension to the architecture to support MPDU matching. The MPDU signatures are compiled to build our Memory Conscious Network (MCN) that matches signatures efficiently. Our system can run in two different modes, simple signatures and MPDU signatures, based on the needed functionality of the IDS.

4. ACCESS PREDICATE ALGORITHMS

This section describes two novel algorithms that are used to accumulate partial matches from individual matchers and match a single PDU signature. We first present Access Predicate Pruning (APP) which minimizes the number of partial matches. Next, we present our Early Elimination (EE) algorithm that uses a two-list scanning technique to discard partial matches. Finally, we describe the data structures used for both algorithms and discuss their time and space complexities.

4.1 Access Predicate Pruning (APP)

Normal Internet traffic can cause partial matches of signatures where some predicates are satisfied, but no one signature is fully matched. For example, the signature $S_1:P_1\&P_2\&P_3$ where P_2 and P_3 are often matched but not P_1 incurs unnecessary overhead of processing partial matches as S_1 is never matched (P_1 is never satisfied). To reduce the overhead of processing a large partial matches list, we introduce the notion of access predicates to prune signatures that would not eventually be matched. Our definition of an access predicate is distinguished from earlier definitions [11] by maintaining a single access predicate per signature rather than per cluster [10]. Also, we push the access predicate distinction into the individual matchers to reduce runtime processing and to eliminate the expensive scan of all cluster access predicates as is the case for [10, 11]. Our approach ex-

ploits the pruning effect of access predicates used in [10] and supports arbitrary matchers as is the case for the counting algorithm [31].

The data structure for Access Predicate Pruning (APP) is shown in Figure 3, where signatures are controlled by an access predicate, and each signature has an initial counter that stores the number of predicates it holds including the access predicate. For example, signature S_1 has AP_1 as its access predicate and an initial counter of value three as it has two more predicates P_1 and P_2. In the pre-computation phase, the data structure is built and counters are initialized.

As shown in Figure 3, the individual matchers maintain two lists: an access predicate list and a predicate list. To reduce computation and save overhead, the access predicate distinction is pushed into the individual matchers. For example, consider a tree-based structure for string matching where predicates are evaluated at leaf nodes. If the predicate $user="admin"$ is an access predicate for signature S_1 but not for signatures S_2 and S_3, the predicate leaf node outputs the sets $\{S_1\}$ and $\{S_2, S_3\}$ instead of a single set $\{S_1, S_2, S_3\}$. At run time, each predicate is forwarded to the appropriate individual matcher based on its type. The individual matchers evaluate the predicate and output two lists that are processed by the APP algorithm.

The APP algorithm maintains a list of partial matches that counts the number of predicates matched by a single message for each signature. Elements of the access predicate list are added to the partial matches list without further processing since their access predicate is satisfied as per the individual matcher. However, elements of the predicate list in Figure 3 are discarded if their access predicates have not been satisfied. Signature pruning based on access predicates reduces the partial matches list which is evaluated at the end of the message after all its relevant fields have been parsed. If the number of predicates matched for each signature in the partial matches list is equal to its total number of predicates, the signature is output as a match. Consequently, access predicates play a significant role in minimizing partial matches, and we next discuss the selectivity of access predicates.

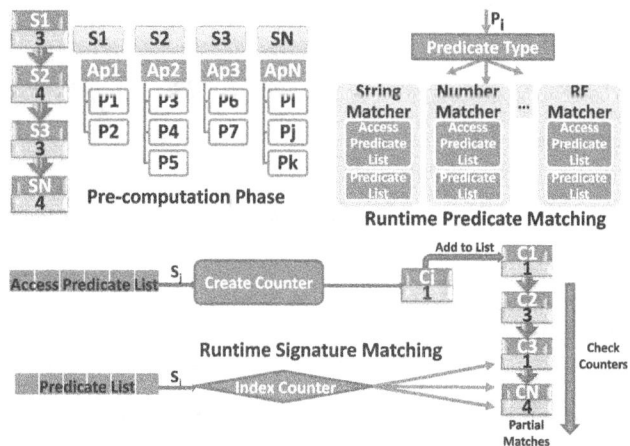

Figure 3: Access Predicate Pruning Data Structure.

Access Predicates: Consider the following signature which has three predicates: $(HTTP\_RequestLine.uri.path.$ $filename == "shtml.dll"$ & $len(HTTP\_Headers["Content$ $-Length"]) > 50$ & $HTTP\_Headers["Accept-Language"]$ $= "en-us")$. $Accept - Language = "en - us"$ is a poor choice of an access predicate as most HTTP requests satisfy this condition (significant amount of web sites support the English language). However, filename is a distinguishing factor of the signature as each signature usually protects one vulnerable filename (there is usually a single bug per web page). Filename is a selective access predicate that is rarely satisfied which reduces the number of partial matches. Moreover, we also exploit the selectivity of the individual matchers. For example, the string matcher is more selective than the RE matcher as $filename == "shtml.dll"$ matches only one file while $matchRE(filename, "*.dll")$ matches any file with a dll extension.

Since parsing and matching are intertwined and message fields have a pre-defined order, predicates whose fields appear first in a message are preferred as access predicates. Consider the following three predicates P_1, P_2, and P_3 whose fields have the same order in the protocol specification. P_2 cannot be an access predicate since P_1 is evaluated before P_2. When P_1 is matched, APP will not include the signature in the partial matches list since its access predicate P_2 is not yet satisfied. As the second field of the message is parsed and P_2 is matched, the signature is added to the partial matches list but is never fully matched since P_1 was discarded earlier. To match the signature correctly, P_1 must be the access predicate. However, if P_1 (method="GET") is not selective while P_2 (filename="shtml.dll") is, the matcher allows for buffering P_1 and processing P_2 first; thus, P_2 can be selected as the access predicate. While buffering fields can enhance access predicate selectivity and reduce partial matches, only a few fields that are small in size, 4 bytes or less, can be buffered due to memory constraints of the IDS which must support thousands of connections simultaneously. Nevertheless, some fields in the protocol specification do not exhibit any specific order and any of them can be elected as an access predicate. Next, we discuss the APP algorithm in more detail.

APP Algorithm: Each signature has a counter associated with the number of predicates to be satisfied for it to be matched. These counters are called initial_counters and are precompiled from the signature database before runtime processing as shown in Algorithm 1.

At run time, the individual matchers output two sets per matched predicate: AP_List (list of signatures which have this predicate as an access predicate) and P_List (list of signatures which have this predicate as a regular predicate). The Prune() function in Algorithm 1 adds the AP_List to the CandList as the access predicate is the first predicate in the signature; thus, any signature in the AP_List cannot have been previously present in the CandList and the pertaining runtime_counters are set to one. Moreover, for every signature in the P_List, if the runtime_counter is greater than zero (access predicate of this signature has already been satisfied), the runtime_counter is incremented. Otherwise, the signature is discarded.

At the end of all iterations (i.e., the whole message is parsed), for every signature in the CandList, CheckCounter() is invoked and the signature is matched if its runtime_counter and its initial_counter are equal. Moreover, counters of the CandList are reset to zero and the CandList is discarded to process a new message.

APP Complexity: For each predicate matched, APP adds counters for elements in the AP_List and checks the access predicate condition for elements in the P_List. At the

---

Algorithm 1 Access Predicate Pruning (APP)

Function Prune()
  for $Matcher_i$ in $AllMatchers_i$ **do**
    Match $Matcher_i$ and get AP_List_i, P_List_i
    for $SigID$ in AP_List_i **do**
      Add $SigID$ to CandList
      Increment $runtime\_counter[SigID]$
    for $SigID$ in P_List_i **do**
      if $(runtime\_counter[SigID] > 0)$ **then**
        Increment $runtime\_counter[SigID]$

Function CheckCounters()
  for $SigID$ in CandList **do**
    if $(runtime\_counter[SigID] = initial\_counter[SigID])$ **then**
      $SigID$ is matched

Function ResetCounters()
  for $SigID$ in CandList **do**
    $runtime\_counter[SigID] \leftarrow 0$
  Empty CandList

---

end of the message, APP evaluates and resets the counters of its CandList. Thus, the time complexity of APP is O(AP_List + P_List) for each predicated evaluated plus O(CandList) for the final scan of counters pertaining to the CandList. The APP algorithm reduces the size of the CandList as only signatures whose access predicates are satisfied (less likely to be) are included in the CandList. As a result, the final scan at the end of the message is fast as only a few partial matches, rather than the whole signature set, are considered. The runtime memory of APP is determined by the size of the CandList whose counters are maintained in memory.

4.2 Early Elimination (EE)

The APP algorithm significantly reduces the size of partial matches but requires traversal of both lists output by the individual matchers: the access predicate list and the predicate list. However, the average size of the access predicate list is significantly smaller than the predicate list since access predicates are less likely to be satisfied. The access predicate list represents signatures whose access predicates have been satisfied and whose other predicates can potentially be matched. As only a few elements in the predicate list are potential matches (their access predicates have already been satisfied), we introduce the Early Elimination (EE) algorithm that selectively scans signatures in the predicate list and discards others.

Access predicates in the EE algorithm have a more effective role in which they not only reduce the number of partial matches, but also improve matching time by truncating the predicate list to be scanned. As only elements in the partial matches list have their access predicates satisfied, we use the partial matches list to control access to the predicate list. The intuition behind the EE algorithm is scanning both lists simultaneously as long as there are elements in the partial matches list that can potentially match elements in the predicate list. All other elements are discarded when the assumption no longer holds.

Figure 4 gives an overview of the EE algorithm and its signature structure. Signatures are controlled by access predicates and a counter is maintained to keep track of the total number of predicates per signature. The signature IDs, however, are generated in a way that maintains order in which

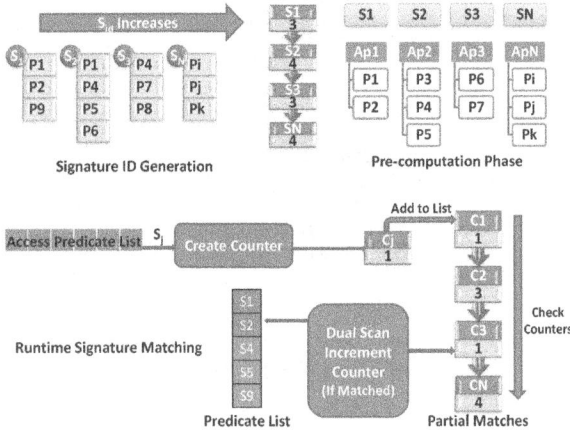

Figure 4: Early Elimination Data Structure.

signatures with smaller predicate IDs have smaller signature IDs. For example, the ID of the first signature (S_1) is less than the ID of the third signature (S_3) since the smallest predicate ID in S_1 is P_1 while it is P_4 in S_3. Also, the ID of the first signature (S_1) is less than the ID of the second signature (S_2) since the second smallest predicate ID in S_1 is P_2 while it is P_4 in S_2. Maintaining signature order during the compilation step of the algorithm is essential for early elimination of signatures based on their IDs.

At run time, the predicate list and the partial matches list are scanned simultaneously and the algorithm terminates as soon as all elements of either list have been scanned. In case an element is found in both lists (access predicate has been previously satisfied), the corresponding counter is incremented. Moreover, elements in the access predicate list are added to the partial matches list since their access predicates have been satisfied as per the nature of the list. At the end of the message, counters of the partial matches list are checked to find a match and are then reset.

EE Algorithm: The predicte list (P_List) and the access predicate list (AP_List) produced by the individual matchers are processed in the following fashion specified in Algorithm 2. The EarlyEliminate() function uses the partial matches list, CandList, to index the P_List. If the signature ID of an element in the P_List is equal to the signature ID of an element in the CandList, the signature runtime_counter is incremented. If the signature ID of an element in the P_List is greater than the signature ID of an element in CandList, the next element in the CandList is considered and vice versa. The scanning stops when all elements of either list have been scanned. Finally, the AP_List is simply added to the CandList and the corresponding runtime_counters are set to one.

At the end of the message, a final scan is performed on all counters in the CandList and a signature is matched if its runtime_counter is equal to its initial_counter. Moreover, runtime_counters are reset and the CandList is discarded.

EE complexity: The time complexity of the EE algorithm is dependent on the size of the partial matches list (CandList). For each predicate evaluated, a counter is created for every signature in the access predicate list. Also, the partial matches list and the predicate list (P_List) are scanned simultaneously until all elements of either list are scanned. At the end of the message, a final scan is required to check all counters in the CandList. Thus, the worst time of EE is O({P_List + CandList} + AP_List) in addition to the

---

Algorithm 2 Early Elimination (EE)

Function EarlyElimination()
  for $Matcher_i$ in $AllMatchers_i$ **do**
    Match $Matcher_i$ and get AP_List_i, P_List_i
    $j \leftarrow 0$, $k \leftarrow 0$
    if (P_List_i and $CandList$ are not empty) **then**
      loop
        if ($P\_List_i[j] > CandList[k]$) **then**
          Increment k
          if (k = $|CandList|$) **then**
            break
        else
          if ($P\_List_i[j] < CandList[k]$) **then**
            Increment j
            if (j = $|P\_List_i|$)) **then**
              break
          else
            Increment $runtime\_counter[CandList[k]]$, j, k
            if ((j = $|P\_List_i|$)OR(k = $|CandList|$)) **then**
              break
    for $SigID$ in AP_List_i **do**
      Add $SigID$ to $CandList$
      Increment $runtime\_counter[SigID]$

Function CheckCounters()
  for $SigID$ in $CandList$ **do**
    if ($runtime\_counter[SigID] = initial\_counter[SigID]$) **then**
      $SigID$ is matched

Function ResetCounters()
  for $SigID$ in $CandList$ **do**
    $runtime\_counter[SigID] \leftarrow 0$
  Empty $CandList$

---

final scan cost of O(CandList). The advantage of the EE algorithm is evident in the case where no access predicates are matched; i.e., the AP_List is empty and no elements are added to the CandList; thus, the P_List is simply ignored. Therefore, on average, the time for EE per predicate evaluated is O(min{P_List + CandList} + AP_List).

The memory footprint of EE is determined by the number of partial matches in the CandList. A single counter for each element in the CandList must be maintained in memory to keep track of the number of matched predicates per signature. These counters are evaluated at the end of the message to find a match.

5. MEMORY CONSCIOUS NETWORK

In our Memory Conscious Network (MCN), signatures are compiled into a list of connected nodes to maintain partial state between different PDUs. While the Rete [12] algorithm requires maintaining the actual PDU message (partial match data) as part of its nodes, we present a novel technique of bit encoding to represent partial matches and minimize the memory footprint. Each MPDU signature is composed of a set of single PDU signatures that hold some semantic relation between each other. The network is composed of a set of nodes where a node can hold a single PDU or represent a relation between two PDUs. Figure 6 shows an example of a MCN in which a circle represents a single PDU signature and a square represents a relation between two PDUs. For instance, the left square holds an OR relation between S_1 and S_2 and the node is satisfied if S_1 or S_2 is matched. Nodes in the network are designed to exploit sharing among MPDU signatures in which shared predicates are evaluated only once. As $(S_1 \& S_2)$ is a common predicate for S_4 and S_6, the AND condition is evaluated only once in node JN_3. The key concept of MCN is to exploit the network design to evaluate common predicates only once, thus improving performance.

The network is traversed as follows: When a single PDU is matched, the appropriate signature node is accessed and all join nodes connected to it are traversed. The condition in each join node is evaluated, and when it is satisfied, MPDU signatures associated with this node are output and all nodes connected to its output links are traversed. Network propagation ends when the condition in a join node is not satisfied or the node has no output links.

The condition in a join node represents a relation between two PDUs in a MPDU signature. A relation is expressed using one of the following operators : AND ($\&$), OR ($||$), and NEXT ($\Rightarrow$). Most signatures require conjunction of predicates as is evident in this example (PDU1: $HTTP\_RequestLine.uri.filename == "shtml.dll"$ & PDU2: $len(HTTP\_Headers["Content - Length"]) >= 100$). Moreover, there might be multiple ways of triggering the vulnerability as is the case for the WINRPC protocol. The attacker can bind to an interface using a BIND PDU or an ALTER_CONTEXT PDU, thus the need for the OR operator. Nevertheless, sequence is crucial in MPDU attacks in which the attacker must be bound to an interface before launching a WINRPC attack which can be detected by the NEXT operator. A vulnerable webpage that requires the user to be logged in before exploiting the vulnerability is another example for the NEXT operator (PDU1: $user\ logs\ in \Rightarrow$ PDU2: $server\ authenticates\ user \Rightarrow$ PDU3: $user\ launches\ an\ attack$).

To detect MPDU attacks such as the login example, the Memory Conscious Network (MCN) is composed of two types of nodes: signature nodes and join nodes. A signature node holds a unique ID and has output links to a set of join nodes. A join node, however, has a unique join node ID and has output links to other join nodes. It combines two input nodes using one of the three operators ($\&$, $||$, $\Rightarrow$). It also holds a list of MPDU signatures which are matched when it is satisfied.

Figure 5 shows the data structure used for each type of node. An AND join node requires two state bits to maintain the state of left and right hand input nodes accordingly. An AND node can be accessed through its left or right input link. If the AND node is reached through its left input link, for example, the left bit is set to one (left side is matched). Consequently, the other bit, the right bit, is checked and if it is one (right side was matched earlier), the AND condition evaluates to true and the MPDU signatures associated with this node are output. Finally, when the AND condition of the join node is satisfied, all nodes connected to its output links are traversed.

An OR join node has a similar structure but no state bits are required. An OR condition is satisfied when either of the sides is matched and it acts as a forwarder. When the OR node is accessed from either side (left or right side is matched), the corresponding MPDU signatures are output and all nodes connected to its output links are traversed. A NEXT join node requires a single state bit to track sequence. The structure of the NEXT node dictates that the left side must be matched first and then the right side for the condition to be satisfied. When the NEXT node is accessed from

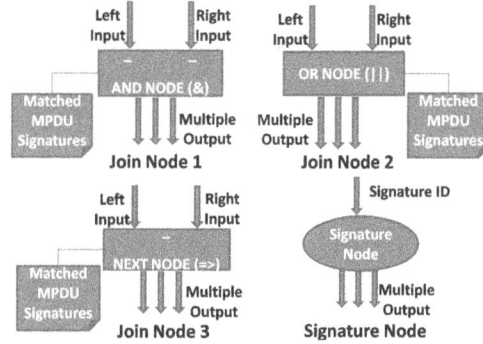

Figure 5: MCN Node Data Structure.

its left input link, the bit is set to one and the right side is ready to be matched. When the node is accessed through its right input link, the bit value is checked. If it is one (left side is already matched), the condition evaluates to true, MPDU signatures corresponding to this node are output, and all nodes connected to its output links are traversed. Otherwise, the condition evaluates to false as the left side was not previously matched, thus no further traversal of join nodes that are connected to the NEXT node output links.

Finally, a signature node has only one input which is the ID of the single PDU signature. The signature nodes are used to index join nodes with no condition to be evaluated.

MCN Consumption Policy: In the IDS domain, all attacks must be detected; thus, signatures must not be consumed once matched. In Figure 6, S_7 is output twice although S_3 came in once. We first run through the example, then explain the different consumption policies. When S_1 is matched, join nodes JN_1, JN_5, and JN_2 are traversed. JN_1 is an OR node which acts as a forwarder to JN_4. As a result, JN_4 which is an AND node, is accessed through its left side and the left bit is set to one. JN_5 is also an AND node and its left bit is set to one. Finally, the state bit of JN_2 is set to one as it is a NEXT node, and it is accessed through its left input link.

When S_3 is matched, JN_4 is accessed first and its right bit is flipped to one. As a result, both bits of JN_4 are set to one and the AND condition evaluates to true; thus, S_7 is matched. Next, the right bit of JN_3 is set to one.

When S_2 is matched, join nodes JN_1, JN_2, and JN_3 are accessed. The OR Node, JN_1, acts as a forwarder and since both bits of JN_4 have been previously set to one, S_7 is output once again. Next, JN_2 is accessed through its right link and since the state bit is one (S_1 previously matched), the condition evaluates to true and S_5 is matched. Finally, the left bit of JN_3 is set to one and the AND condition is satisfied as S_3 has been previously matched. As a result, S_4 is output as a match and JN_5 is accessed through its right input link. As both bits of JN_5 are set to one, S_6 is matched.

After S_7 was matched in the bottom left AND join node (JN_4), the bits of the JN_4 were not reset and any further occurrence of S_1, S_2, or S_3 can trigger the match of S_7 as the AND condition has already been satisfied. This notion of no-consumption policy is crucial to correlate all attack requests and to flag any MPDU combination that can trigger an attack. Nonetheless, a consume-once policy can be used in which join node bits are reset when the node is satisfied. For example, when S_7 is matched, both bits of JN_4 are reset to zero. When S_2 is matched, only the left bit of JN_4 will be set to one; thus, the AND condition is not satisfied. This

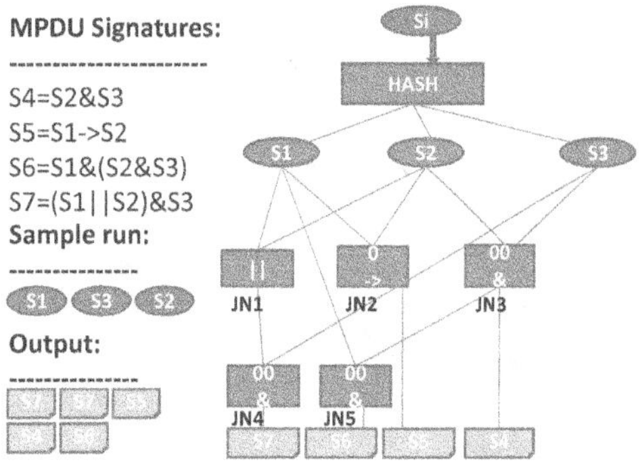

MPDU Signatures:

S4=S2&S3
S5=S1->S2
S6=S1&(S2&S3)
S7=(S1||S2)&S3
Sample run:

Output:

Figure 6: Memory Conscious Network Example.

policy will ensure that S_7 will be matched once as S_3 occurs only once. However, we adopt the first policy as it can detect larger number of attacks.

Consumption Policy Analysis: The no-consumption policy can result in deep network propagation as bits are not reset when the join node condition is satisfied. Once a condition is satisfied, it is always evaluated to be true which increases the average traversal depth of a signature match. Despite the disadvantage of longer traversal, no-consumption policy has a better attack coverage as all possible PDU combinations are considered. However, the consume-once policy has a shorter traversal path as once a join node condition is satisfied, the state bits are reset to zero. Future access to the same join node does not result in a match since the condition is evaluated again. The consume-once policy shortens the traversal path but incurs the overhead of resetting the state bits when a join condition is satisfied. Also, it detects only one MPDU combination for the attack. Consider a sample run of S_2, S_3, and S_2 for the same network given in Figure 6 and consume-one policy is used. S_4 is matched once since only the $\{S_2, S_3\}$ combination is detected. However, the no-consumption policy considers S_3 twice and can detect both combinations $\{S_2, S_3\}$ and $\{S_3, S_2\}$; as a result, S_4 is matched twice.

MCN Modes of Operation: The scheme described above can detect attacks within one connection or across multiple connections. Distributed denials of service (DDoS) attacks require examining multiple connections to correlate PDUs from different clients [18]. However, other attacks, such as Conficker, require isolation between connections [15]. Consider a login scenario in which an attacker first logs in to the server and then launches the attack. If attacker A is successfully logged in to the server and attacker B launches the attack, correlating the two PDUs can result in a false positive as attacker B is not logged in to the server and his request will eventually be denied.

Per-connection correlation is supported by maintaining separate join node bits per connection. The MCN network is shared among all connections but only the state bits are local to the connection being processed. To correlate attacks across multiple connections, join node bits are defined globally and are shared by all connections.

MCN Algorithm: The MPDU component is added on top of the single PDU matcher and the MPDU signature set is compiled to build the MPDU network. Each MPDU signature is composed of several single PDU signatures and every two PDU signatures are combined into one node using parenthesis to incorporate precedence. Algorithm 3 depicts the steps taken to evaluate a node. A signature node simply

triggers the evaluation of all join nodes without any processing. A join node, however, checks the corresponding bits based on its operator type and once its conditions are satisfied, it outputs all MPDU signatures associated with it and triggers further evaluation of all join nodes connected to its output links. As we adopt a no-consumption policy, the state bits are not reset when the join condition is satisfied.

Algorithm 3 Memory Conscious Network (MCN)

Function SignatureNodeEvaluation()
  for *link* in *AllOutputLinks* **do**
    call *JoinNodeEvaluation(SignatureNodeID)* of *link*

Function JoinNodeEvaluation(ID)
  if AND Operator **then**
    $bit[ID] \leftarrow 1$
    if both bits are set to 1 **then**
      All corresponding signatures are matched
    else
      return
  else
    if NEXT Operator **then**
      if ID is the first signature in the sequence **then**
        $bit[ID] \leftarrow 1$, return
      if bit[first signature] $= 1$ **then**
        All corresponding signatures are matched
      else
        return
  else
    if OR Operator **then**
      All corresponding signatures are matched
  for *link* in *AllOutputLinks* **do**
    call *JoinNodeEvaluation(JoinNodeID)* of *link*

MCN Complexity: The total memory used by our algorithm to maintain state is proportional to the number of operators in the MPDU signature set which is equal to $O((AND\_Nodes * 2 + NEXT\_Nodes)/8)$ bytes since the AND operator requires two bits, the NEXT operator requires one bit, and the OR operator requires no bits. When processing 100 MPDU signatures, this number is in the order of twenty bytes per connection which is feasible to support given the memory capacity of nowadays servers (4+ GB) and it is significantly smaller than the memory requirement of the basic Rete algorithm which requires storing matched PDUs (approximately 1500 bytes per PDU) in the join nodes. A typical IDS can handle thousands of simultaneous connections where MCN consumes only few MB for all connections. The memory footprint of MCN is significantly smaller when compared to the memory capacity of current servers (4+ GB) or the requirement of the Rete algorithm (hundreds of MB).

The time complexity is determined by the depth of the network traversed. When a single PDU signature is matched, the ID is hashed to index the appropriate signature node. Next, all output links of the signature nodes are traversed and any join node whose condition is satisfied can trigger further evaluation of its output join nodes. The ID hash is $O(1)$ while the join node time complexity is $O(links * Nodes\_Traversed)$.

6. EXPERIMENTS

We first evaluate the proposed matching algorithms over the HTTP protocol when processing a wide range of traffic and compare them to other existing techniques [15, 31].

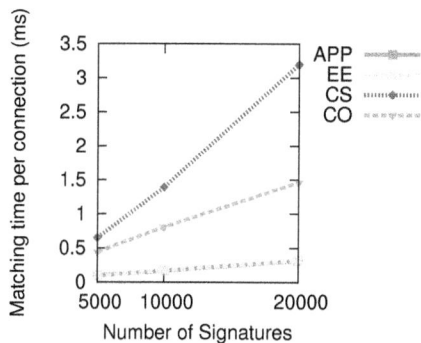

Figure 7: 600 HTTP Attacks Scenario

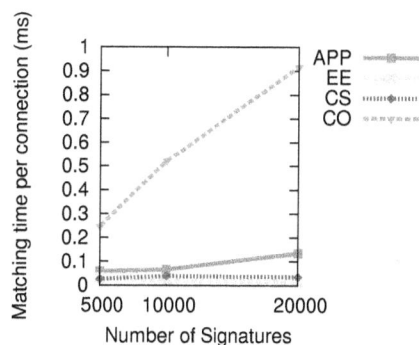

Figure 8: 600 HTTP Partial Attacks Scenario

Next, we study the matching time of the MPDU algorithm which was designed to detect more sophisticated attacks such as the Conficker worm. All algorithms are implemented in C++ and are integrated into the Netshield framework [15].

6.1 APP and EE Evaluation

We expose the matching engine of the IDS to different workloads to extensively study its performance. Given the largest available vulnerability-based signature set of 794 HTTP signatures [15], we generate new signatures by appending and truncating predicates to extend our database to 20,000 signatures and measure the scalability of the system. Moreover, we evaluate the IDS performance when processing normal traffic (attack-free), attacks, partial attacks, and well-known traffic such as the DARPA data set[28].

Attack Resiliency: To model the system behavior under stress attacks, we launch 600 HTTP attacks and vary the number of signatures from 1,000 to 20,000. Figure 7 shows degradation in performance of the CS algorithm due to the expensive calculation of the candidate selection list (S_i) and the previous rule blocks list (A_i) at every iteration. Since there is a match of one of the signatures, R_1 for example, S_i will always include R_1 for every iteration i and A_i will sometimes include R_1 whenever one of the predicates of R_1 is matched. The expensive operation, $\oplus$, of scanning A_i for every element in S_i hinders performance as R_1 will be carried forward all the way to the end. Furthermore, the CO algorithm requires evaluation of all runtime_counters only once at the end of the message but scanning all counters still hinders its performance since most of the counters are not modified and thus must not be checked.

The other algorithms (APP and EE) maintain a candidate list and only runtime_counters in this list are evaluated at the end of the message. As R_1 is carried forward across iterations, one time evaluation at the end of the message rather than for every iteration, as is the case for the CS algorithm, yields better performance and allows for matching more signatures. As the run time evaluation of APP and EE is determined by the number of partial matches and not the total number of signatures, they gracefully scale without exhausting the matcher as the number of signatures reaches 20,000. Under heavy-load attacks, the CS algorithm exhausts the matching engine and does not scale well as the matching time increases from $500\mu s$ to over 3 ms when going from 1,000 to 20,000 signatures. Our proposed algorithms exhibit 6-fold improvement over the CS algorithm when processing 20,000 signatures for the given traffic.

Partial Attacks: Normal traffic can still result in partial matches where no signature is matched but some of its predicates are. For example, the method field in the HTTP

header is a non-selective predicate and will result in a high number of partial matches as significant number of signatures can have $HTTP\_RequestLine.method == "GET"$ as a predicate. Moreover, an attacker can exhaust the IDS and force it to drop packets by sending requests that result in a high number of partial matches without sending a full attack and thus will not be detected. Algorithmic attacks [9] that induce worst-case behavior on the IDS is an example of such attacks and it is crucial to study how the proposed algorithms behave.

Figure 8 shows the performance of the matching algorithms when processing 600 HTTP partial attacks against 1,000 to 20,000 signatures. The access predicates in this experiment are not matched while other predicates in the system are matched. The CO algorithm is not affected by the type of experiment run as it always performs the same steps regardless of the number of matches thus it behaves poorly in this case as well. However, the APP algorithm only increments counters of signatures whose access predicates have already been matched which reduces the size of the candidate list (zero in this case) and results in smaller matching time.

Despite the access predicate list (AP_List) being empty, the APP algorithm must still scan the predicate list (P_List) at every iteration to check if the runtime_counter of any of its signatures is greater than zero (i.e., access predicate is already matched). The EE algorithm scans the P_List and the candidate list simultaneously and stops when all elements of either list are scanned. The AP_List is always empty thus the candidate list is also empty and the EE algorithm does not scan the P_List which results in faster matching time. The CS algorithm exhibits a similar behavior as the candidate selection list (S_i) is always empty since no access predicate is matched and the current rule block list (B_i) is always empty. Since the candidate list (S_i) is empty, the previous rule block list (A_i) will not be scanned although A_i has many elements which improves the matching performance. The scenario described in this experiment is essential to the performance of the IDS as partial matches are the common trend in normal traffic and attackers tend to use this technique to overload the IDS. The EE algorithm behaves extremely well in this case where it requires less than 20 μs to match 20,000 signatures, thus not affected by such attacks.

Netshield HTTP Signatures: Netshield researchers have converted snort signatures (973 HTTP signatures in version 11/2007) into 794 vulnerability-based signatures [15]. This is the largest publicly available dataset for vulnerability-based signatures which we use to evaluate our algorithms under different scenarios: clean traffic, attacks, and partial attacks. We also study the effect of access predicate selectivity on the matching time of APP and EE. Figure 9 shows that the CO algorithm behaves poorly for all workloads due to the expensive operation of evaluating all runtime_counters for every message processed.

To model clean traffic, we capture a HTTP trace of the Middleware Systems Research Group (MSRG) lab at the University of Toronto where users are accessing legitimate websites with an average connection size of 28KB. All other algorithms incur negligible overhead when processing clean traffic as no matches occur resulting in an empty candidate list and no runtime_counters are evaluated.

The APP and EE algorithms outperform the CS algorithm when the IDS is under attack as shown in Figure 9. The CS algorithm requires calculation of the candidate list (S_i), the previous rule blocks list (A_i), and the current rule block list (B_i) at every iteration. When the system is under attack, the candidate list (S_i) will include at least one element which must be checked against all elements in A_i for every iteration i. The other algorithms maintain a candidate list whose runtime_counters are checked only once at the end of the message; thus, outperforming the CS algorithm and conforming with the results of the attack resiliency experiment discussed previously.

The third histogram in Figure 9 shows the matching time of all algorithms when no full attacks are launched but only partial matches occur as is the case in the partial attacks experiment. The access predicates are not matched but some of the regular predicates are matched. As mentioned earlier, partial matches can occur in regular traffic and an attacker can force partial matches to exhaust the IDS and later launch the real attack. The EE algorithm performs best in this case as the candidate list is empty (no access predicates matched) and thus the predicate list (P_List) is not scanned. The APP algorithm has a slower matching time as the predicate list (P_List) must be scanned despite the candidate list being empty. In the CS algorithm, although the candidate list (S_i) and the current rule block list (B_i) are empty, the elements in the previous rule blocks list (A_i) are scanned to check if the $field_i$ holds a don't care value. Scanning the previous rule blocks list (A_i) is analogous to scanning the (P_List) in the APP algorithm, and thus the two algorithms exhibit similar performance.

The forth histogram in Figure 9 shows the effect of having selective access predicates on the performance of the access predicate aware algorithms. To quantify the selectivity of access predicates, we study a different case of partial matches where some of the access predicates are matched as well as other regular predicates without resulting in a full signature match. This experiment shows the importance of the choice of access predicates in which more selective access predicates result in a better matching time. Since some of the access predicates are matched, the current rule block list (B_i) and consequently the candidate list (S_i) in the CS algorithm are not empty. Moreover, as other regular predicates are matched, the previous rule blocks list (A_i) is not empty as well which explains the slower performance of the CS algorithm in Figure 9. As access predicates are not selective (traffic matches access predicates), the APP and EE algorithms exhibit a comparable behavior since access predicates are matched and candidate lists of both algorithms are similar. The EE algorithm requires scanning the predicate list (P_List) and the candidate list simultaneously. Since the access predicates are not entirely selective, the candidate list

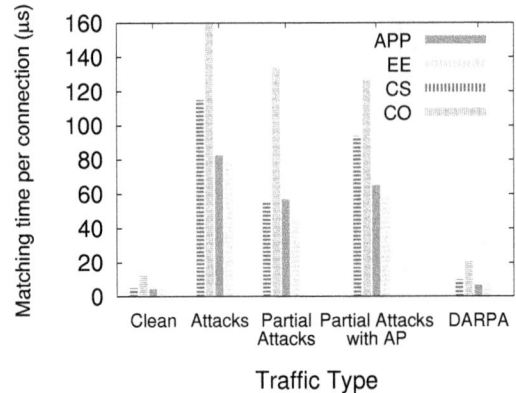

Figure 9: Netshield 794 HTTP Signature Set

is not empty and some elements of the predicate list (P_List) must be traversed, which explains the slower performance of the EE algorithm in this case when compared to the previous histogram where no access predicates are matched.

We finally test our algorithms against the most common benchmark, MIT 1998 intrusion detection data set (DARPA) [28], which is mainly composed of normal traffic with some intervals of attacks and partial attacks [15, 28]. The last histogram in Figure 9 indicates the poor performance of the CO algorithm due to the evaluation of all runtime_counters which is independent of traffic. All other proposed algorithms take on average $5\mu s$ to process one connection while the CS algorithm averages around $9\mu s$ per connection.

As shown in this experiment, the selectivity of access predicates is crucial to the performance of our proposed access predicate aware algorithms (APP and EE). Access predicates guard other predicates in the signature and control admittance of signatures to the candidate list. As a result, maintaining the size of the candidate list as small as possible, which is determined by the selectivity of the access predicates, yields the best performance.

6.2 MCN Evaluation

As there is no prior work to compare our MCN implementation to, we implement a sequential algorithm that loops over all MPDU signatures and matches them one at a time as a baseline for our evaluation. We use the Netshield 794 HTTP signature set to generate 1,000 MPDU signatures as today, no MPDU signature set exits. Given the nature of current attacks and the lack of MPDU signatures, we believe that MPDU signatures will constitute no more than 10% of the total number of single PDU signatures. We base our assumption on the Conficker worm signature which drove us to support MPDU signatures. Conficker exploits a vulnerability in the stateful WINRPC protocol for which 3,519 Snort (RE-based) signatures exist [19]. Those signatures are translated into only 45 vulnerability-based signatures which constitutes 1.3% of RE-based signatures [15]. Given the small number of WINRPC vulnerability signatures (45) and the significant reduction of the signature set when the signature language is more expressive, we believe that 10% is a reasonable value for a transition from single PDU to MPDU signatures. However, we also test our MCN algorithm against larger MPDU signature sets to measure scalability.

First, we devise two sets of experiments in which we study the effect of increasing the number of attacks on matching

Table 1: MPDU Workload Specification

MPDU Signatures (100)	High-Clustering		Low-Clustering	
Algorithm	Sequential	MCN	Sequential	MCN
Signature Nodes	290	72	490	234
AND Nodes	80	58	180	114
NEXT Nodes	85	68	185	115
OR Nodes	30	20	30	5
Memory per connection (bytes)	31	24	69	44

time and show the efficiency of our MCN implementation when MPDU signatures exhibit high level of sharing single PDU signatures. Table 1 shows the specification used for both experiments for 100 MPDU signatures with an average of 4 predicates per signature (4 single PDU signatures per one MPDU signature). We use the high-clustering signatures for attack resiliency testing and we compare the two signature sets in the second experiment. Finally, we vary the number of signatures from 100 to 1,000 and show that our MCN algorithm scales better than the sequential scan.

Attack Resiliency: The high-clustering workload specified in Table 1 is used in this experiment in which 100 MPDU signatures are built from 72 unique single PDU signatures. This workload exhibits high sharing of single PDU signatures to create 100 MPDU signatures since the sequential algorithm requires 290 signature nodes while MCN requires only 72 signature nodes. As our MPDU algorithm can detect attacks within one connection or across multiple connections, we differentiate the two cases in Figure 10 by suffixing the algorithm name with G. Correlating attacks across multiple connections requires maintaining global state bits that are accessed by different connections, which explains the G suffix in the algorithm name. However, the algorithm with no G suffix only correlates PDUs within one connection and a separate set of state bits is maintained per connection.

Figure 10 shows the average matching time per connection as we increase the percentage of attacks ranging from clean traffic to full attack scenario. An attack is carried out by sending a PDU that matches one of the simple HTTP signatures, thus matching a predicate in the MPDU signature set. The attacks are launched as follows: An attack is chosen at random from a set of malicious requests and for every connection, 1.5 attacks are launched on average. For example, 33% attack means that one in every three connections is malicious while the other two connections carry clean traffic that matches no signatures (single or multiple PDU). The sequential algorithm results in a linear increase in matching time as the number of attacks increases, reaching $250\mu s$ when fully under attack. The poor performance of the sequential algorithm is expected as it does not exploit sharing of predicates and each signature is evaluated separately. The sequential algorithm is a baseline for our evaluation as no other MPDU solutions exist.

In the case of clean traffic (0% attack), there is no overhead for any of the algorithms as no processing is required since no single PDU signatures are matched. The MPDU algorithm in our architecture is added on top of the single PDU matching block and is only invoked when a single PDU signature has been successfully matched which is not the case for the clean traffic (0% attack). As the percentage of attacks increases from 30 to 100, our MPDU implementation requires less than $25\mu s$ per connection and is 10 times faster than the sequential algorithm. To maintain partial state of the current MPDU signature set, 24 bytes are needed for MCN while the sequential algorithm requires 29% more bytes as is evident in Table 1. Figure 10 shows

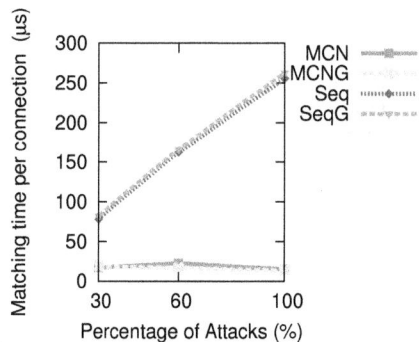

Figure 10: Attack Resiliency (100 MPDU Sigs).

no significant difference between the global and normal case of either algorithm. Correlating messages across different connections can result in more state transitions, while isolating connections requires resetting state bits for every new flow. On average 1.5 attacks are launched per malicious connection which results in about 3 state transitions for the global case. Moreover, isolating connections requires similar overhead to reset 24 or 31 bytes which explains the similar performance of the two implementations.

Clustering Effect: Our MCN implementation clusters common predicates among different signatures to speed up matching. To validate the efficiency of such clustering, we use two sets of 100 MPDU signatures that are built from 72 and 234 distinct single PDU signatures, respectively. The network size of the low-clustering signature set is significantly larger since the number of nodes increases as more distinct single PDU signatures are used which limits the amount of sharing between MPDU signatures. For each connection, we launch 15 attacks that trigger significant number of state transitions (partial matches of MPDU signatures).

Figure 11 shows about $7\mu s$ increase in the average matching time between the two signature sets when matching is carried out within one connection. The partial state bit number doubles between the two sets, which explains the increase in matching time due to the overhead of resetting 44 bytes for the low-clustering case. When matching is performed across connections (global matching), the matching time still increases as more nodes are traversed for a given attack since attacks from multiple connections are correlated. For the high-clustering workload, the global version performs worse than the per-connection version since a single match results in about 5 state transitions which takes longer than resetting 24 bytes for the other version.

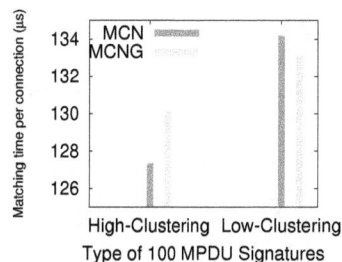

Figure 11: MCN Clustering Effect

Also, the low-clustering workload favors the global version as the number of state transitions decreases to one as few predicates are shared while the per-connection version struggles to maintain low matching time due to the overhead of resetting 44 bytes for each new connection.

Scalability: To ensure the scalability of our MCN al-

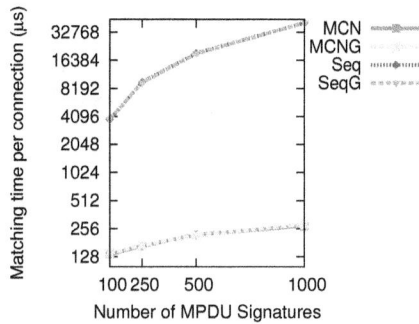

Figure 12: MCN Scalability

gorithm, we vary the number of MPDU signatures from 100 to 1000 signatures and launch multiple single PDU attacks. Figure 12 shows that the sequential algorithm behaves poorly as it requires 4ms and 40ms per connection when processing 100 and 1,000 MPDU signatures, respectively. The sequential algorithm is directly proportional to the number of MPDU signatures as a ten-time increase in signatures results in a ten-time increase in matching time. However, our MCN algorithm scales well as the average matching time per connection only increases by a factor of two when going from 100 to 1,000 MPDU signatures. As shown in Figure 12, MCN is 29 times faster than the sequential algorithm when processing 100 MPDU signatures and scales five times more.

7. CONCLUSION

To achieve acceptable coverage of attacks, the intrusion detection system (IDS) must support different matching dimensions and correlate multiple data protocol units (MPDUs). In this work, we presented two algorithms for single PDU matching: Access Predicate Pruning (APP) and Early Elimination (EE). Both algorithms incur negligible overhead when processing clean traffic and exhibit 6-fold improvement over the candidate selection (CS) algorithm when processing 20,000 signatures against heavy-attack traffic. As far as we are aware, this work represents one of the first efforts to support MPDU matching of vulnerability-based signatures in IDSes. We also presented our Memory Conscious Network (MCN) which exploits bit encoding to represent state transitions while maintaining a small memory footprint. Our solution scales five times more when compared to the sequential scan and is 29 times faster when processing 100 MPDU signatures.

8. REFERENCES

[1] Cisco IOS Intrusion Prevention System Deployment Guide, 2010.
[2] Conficker's estimated economic cost? $9.1 billion. Cyber Secure Institute. http://www.zdnet.com, 2009.
[3] M. K. Aguilera, R. E. Strom, D. C. Sturman, M. Astley, and T. D. Chandra. Matching events in a content-based subscription system. In *PODC '99*.
[4] A. V. Aho and M. J. Corasick. Efficient string matching: an aid to bibliographic search. *CACM '75*.
[5] G. Ashayer, H. K. Y. Leung, and H.-A. Jacobsen. Predicate matching and subscription matching in publish/subscribe systems. ICDCSW'02.
[6] R. Bidou. IPS Shortcomings. http://www.blackhat.com/presentations/bh-usa-06/BH-US-06-Bidou.pdf.
[7] D. Brumley, J. Newsome, D. Song, H. Wang, and S. Jha. Towards automatic generation of vulnerability-based signatures. In *SP '06*.
[8] C. Cranor, T. Johnson, O. Spataschek, and V. Shkapenyuk. Gigascope: a stream database for network applications. In *SIGMOD '03*.
[9] S. A. Crosby and D. S. Wallach. Denial of service via algorithmic complexity attacks. In *SSYM '03*.
[10] F. Fabret, H.-A. Jacobsen, F. Llirbat, J. Pereira, K. A. Ross, and D. Shasha. Filtering algorithms and implementation for very fast publish/subscribe systems. In *SIGMOD '01*.
[11] A. Farroukh, E. Ferzli, N. Tajuddin, and H.-A. Jacobsen. Parallel event processing for content-based publish/subscribe systems. In *DEBS '09*.
[12] C. L. Forgy. Rete: a fast algorithm for the many pattern/many object pattern match problem. *Artificial Intelligence '82*.
[13] D. E. Knuth, J. James H. Morris, and V. R. Pratt. Fast pattern matching in strings. *SICOMP '77*.
[14] G. Li and H.-A. Jacobsen. Composite subscriptions in content-based publish/subscribe systems. In *Middleware '05*.
[15] Z. Li, G. Xia, Y. Tang, Y. He, Y. Chen, B. Liu, J. West, and J. Spadaro. Netshield: Massive semantics-based vulnerability signature matching for high-speed networks. In *SIGCOMM '10*.
[16] M. R. N. Mendes, P. Bizarro, and P. Marques. A framework for performance evaluation of complex event processing systems. In *DEBS '08*.
[17] A. Mukherji, E. A. Rundensteiner, D. C. Brown, and V. Raghavan. Snif tool: sniffing for patterns in continuous streams. In *CIKM '08*.
[18] V. Paxson. Bro: a system for detecting network intruders in real-time. In *SSYM'98*.
[19] M. Roesch. Snort - lightweight intrusion detection for networks. In *LISA '99*.
[20] M. Sadoghi, I. Burcea, and H.-A. Jacobsen. GPX-Matcher: a generic boolean predicate-based XPath expression matcher. In *EDBT'11*.
[21] M. Sadoghi and H.-A. Jacobsen. BE-Tree: An index structure to efficiently match boolean expressions over high-dimensional discrete space. In *SIGMOD'11*.
[22] M. Sadoghi, M. Labrecque, H. Singh, W. Shum, and H.-A. Jacobsen. Efficient event processing through reconfigurable hardware for algorithmic trading. In *VLDB '10*.
[23] M. Sadoghi, H. Singh, and H.-A. Jacobsen. Towards highly parallel event processing through reconfigurable hardware. In *DaMoN'11*.
[24] N. Schear, D. R. Albrecht, and N. Borisov. High-speed matching of vulnerability signatures. In *RAID '08*.
[25] R. Smith, C. Estan, S. Jha, and I. Siahaan. Fast signature matching using extended finite automaton (XFA). In *ICISS '08*.
[26] R. Sommer and V. Paxson. Enhancing byte-level network intrusion detection signatures with context. In *CCS '03*.
[27] R. Sommer and V. Paxson. Outside the closed world: On using machine learning for network intrusion detection. In *SP '10*.
[28] C. Thomas, V. Sharma, and N. Balakrishnan. Usefulness of DARPA dataset for intrusion detection system evaluation. In *SPIE '08*.
[29] H. J. Wang, C. Guo, D. R. Simon, and A. Zugenmaier. Shield: vulnerability-driven network filters for preventing known vulnerability exploits. In *SIGCOMM '04*.
[30] S. Wu and U. Manber. A fast algorithm for multi-pattern searching. Technical report, University of Arizona, 1994.
[31] T. W. Yan and H. García-Molina. Index structures for selective dissemination of information under the boolean model. *TODS '94*.

High Performance Content-Based Matching Using GPUs

Alessandro Margara
Dip. di Elettronica e Informazione
Politecnico di Milano, Italy
margara@elet.polimi.it

Gianpaolo Cugola
Dip. di Elettronica e Informazione
Politecnico di Milano, Italy
cugola@elet.polimi.it

ABSTRACT

Matching incoming event notifications against received subscriptions is a fundamental part of every publish-subscribe infrastructure. In the case of content-based systems this is a fairly complex and time consuming task, whose performance impacts that of the entire system. In the past, several algorithms have been proposed for efficient content-based event matching. While they differ in most aspects, they have in common the fact of being conceived to run on conventional, sequential hardware. On the other hand, modern Graphical Processing Units (GPUs) offer off-the-shelf, highly parallel hardware, at a reasonable cost. Unfortunately, GPUs introduce a totally new model of computation, which requires algorithms to be fully re-designed. In this paper, we describe a new content-based matching algorithm designed to run efficiently on CUDA, a widespread architecture for general purpose programming on GPUs. A detailed comparison with SFF, the matching algorithm of Siena, known for its efficiency, demonstrates how the use of GPUs can bring impressive speedups in content-based matching. At the same time, this analysis demonstrates the peculiar aspects of CUDA programming that mostly impact performance.

Categories and Subject Descriptors

D.1.3 [**Programming Techniques**]: Concurrent Programming—*Parallel programming*; H.3.4 [**Information Storage and Retrieval**]: Systems and Software—*Distributed systems, Performance evaluation (efficiency and effectiveness)*

General Terms

Algorithms, Measurement, Performance

1. INTRODUCTION

Distributed event-based applications [24] are becoming more and more popular. They usually leverage a *publish-subscribe* infrastructure, which enables distributed compo-nents to *subscribe* to the *event notifications* (or "events", for simplicity) they are interested to receive, and to *publish* those they want to spread around.

The core functionality realized by a publish-subscribe infrastructure is *matching* (sometimes also referred as "forwarding"), i.e., the action of filtering each incoming event notification e against the received subscriptions to decide the components interested in e. This is a non trivial activity, especially for a *content-based* publish-subscribe infrastructure, in which subscriptions filter event notifications based on their content [13]. In such systems, the matching component may easily become the bottleneck of the publish-subscribe infrastructure. On the other hand, in several event-based applications, the performance of the publish-subscribe infrastructure may be a key factor. As an example, in financial applications for high-frequency trading [17], a faster processing of incoming event notifications may produce a significant advantage over competitors. Similarly, in intrusion detection systems [22], the ability to timely process the huge number of event notifications that results from observing the operation of a large network is fundamental to detect possible attacks, reacting to them before they could compromise the network.

This aspect has been clearly identified in the past and several algorithms have been proposed for efficient content-based event matching [14, 10, 2, 5]. While these algorithms differ in most aspects, they have one fundamental thing in common: they were designed to run on conventional, sequential hardware. This is reasonable, since standard computers are equipped with sequential CPUs, or, at most, with multi-core CPUs, which allow a limited number of processes to be executed in parallel. On the other hand, the importance of graphics in most application domains pushed industry into producing ad-hoc Graphical Processing Units (GPUs) to relieve the main CPU from the (complex) calculations required for graphics.

What is important here is that this hardware is strongly parallel and may operate in a way (largely) independent from the main CPU. A modern but medium level GPU, like those equipping most computers today, allows hundreds of operations to be performed in parallel, leaving the CPU free to execute other jobs. Moreover, several vendors have recently started offering toolkits to leverage the power of GPUs for general purpose programming. Unfortunately, they introduce a totally new model of computation, which requires algorithms to be fully re-designed. In particular, modern GPUs offer hundreds of processing cores, but they can be used simultaneously only to perform data parallel computations. Moreover, GPUs usually have no direct access to the main memory and they do not offer hardware managed caches; two aspects that make memory management a critical factor to be carefully considered.

In this paper we present CCM[1] – *CUDA Content-based Matcher* – a new content-based matching algorithm designed to run efficiently on GPUs that implement the CUDA architecture [11], and we evaluate its performance, comparing it against SFF [10], the matching component of Siena [7], usually considered among the most efficient solution for content-based matching. Our study demonstrates how the use of GPUs can bring impressive speedups in content-based matching, leaving the main CPU free to focus on the remaining aspects of publish-subscribe, like managing the networking connections with clients and (de)serializing of data. By carefully analyzing how CCM performs under different workloads, we also identify the peculiar aspects of GPU programming that mostly impact performance.

The remainder of the paper is organized as follow: Section 2 offers an overview of the CUDA architecture and programming model, focusing on the aspects more relevant for our purpose. Section 3 introduces the data model and the terminology we use in the rest of the paper. Section 4 describes CCM and how we implemented it on CUDA. The performance of CCM in comparison with SFF is discussed in Section 5, while Section 6 presents related work. Finally, Section 7 provides some conclusive remarks and describes future work.

2. GPU PROGRAMMING WITH CUDA

CUDA is a general purpose parallel computing architecture introduced by Nvidia in November 2006. It offers a new parallel programming model and instruction set for general purpose programming on GPUs.

Since parallel programming is a complex task, industry is currently devoting much effort in trying to simplify it. The most promising result in this area is OpenCL [29], a library that supports heterogeneous platforms, including several multicore CPUs and GPUs. However, the idea of abstracting very different architectures under the same API has a negative impact on performance: different architectures are better at different tasks and a common API cannot hide that. For this reason, although OpenCL supports the CUDA architecture, we decided to implement our algorithms in CUDA C [28], a dialect of C explicitly devoted to program GPUs that implement the CUDA architecture.

In this section we introduce the main concepts of the CUDA programming model and CUDA C, and we briefly present some aspects of the hardware implementation that play a primary role when it comes to optimize algorithms for high performance on the CUDA architecture.

2.1 Programming Model

The CUDA programming model is intended to help developers in writing software that leverages the increasing number of processor cores offered by modern GPUs. At its foundation are three key abstractions:

Hierarchical organization of thread groups. The programmer is guided in partitioning a problem into coarse sub-problems to be solved independently in parallel by *blocks* of threads, while each sub-problem must be decomposed into finer pieces to be solved cooperatively in parallel by all threads within a block. This decomposition allows the algorithm to easily scale with the number of available processor cores, since each block of threads can be scheduled on any of them, in any order, concurrently or sequentially.

Shared memories. CUDA threads may access data from multiple memory spaces during their execution: each thread has a *private local memory* for automatic variables; each block has a *shared memory* visible to all threads in the same block; finally, all threads have access to the same *global memory*.

Barrier synchronization. Thread blocks are required to execute independently, while threads within a block can cooperate by sharing data through shared memory and by synchronizing their execution to coordinate memory access. In particular, developers may specify synchronization points that act as barriers at which all threads in the block must wait before any is allowed to proceed [27, 3].

The CUDA programming model assumes that CUDA threads execute on a physically separate *device* (the GPU), which operates as a coprocessor to a *host* (the CPU) running a C/C++ program. To start a new computation on a CUDA device, the programmer has to define and call a function, called *kernel*, which defines a single flow of execution. When a kernel k is called, the programmer specifies the number of threads per block and the number of blocks that must execute it. Inside the kernel it is possible to access two special variables provided by the CUDA runtime: the *threadId* and the *blockId*, which together allow to uniquely identify each thread among those executing the kernel. Conditional statements involving these variables are the only way for a programmer to differentiate the execution flows of different threads.

The CUDA programming model assumes that both the host and the device maintain their own separate memory spaces. Therefore, before invoking a kernel, it is necessary to explicitly allocate memory on the device and to copy there the information needed to execute the kernel. Similarly, when a kernel execution completes, it is necessary to copy results back to the host memory and to deallocate the device memory.

2.2 Hardware Implementation

The CUDA architecture is built around a scalable array of multi-threaded *Streaming Multiprocessors* (*SMs*). When a CUDA program on the host CPU invokes a kernel k, the blocks executing k are enumerated and distributed to the available SMs. All threads belonging to the same block execute on the same SM, thus exploiting fast SRAM to implement the shared memory. Multiple blocks may execute concurrently on the same SM as well. As blocks terminate new blocks are launched on freed SMs.

Each SM creates, manages, schedules, and executes threads in groups of parallel threads called *warps*. Individual threads composing a warp start together but they have their own instruction pointer and local state and are therefore free to branch and execute independently. When a SM is given one or more blocks to execute, it partitions them into warps that get scheduled by a warp scheduler for execution.

All threads in a warp execute one common instruction at a time. This introduces an issue that must be carefully taken into account when designing a kernel: full efficiency

---

[1]CCM is currently available for download from http://cudamatcher.sf.net

is realized only when all the threads in a warp agree on their execution path. If threads in the same warp diverge via a data-dependent conditional branch, the warp serially executes each branch path taken, disabling threads that are not on that path, and when all paths complete, the threads converge back to the same execution path.

Inside a single SM, instructions are pipelined but, differently from modern CPU cores, they are executed in order, without branch prediction or speculative execution. To maximize the utilization of its computational units, each SM is able to maintain the execution context of several warps on-chip, so that switching from one execution context to another has no cost. At each instruction issue time, a warp scheduler selects a warp that has threads ready to execute (not waiting on a synchronization barrier or for data from the global memory) and issues the next instruction to them.

To give a more precise idea of the capabilities of a modern GPU supporting CUDA, we provide some details of the Nvidia GTX 460 [18] card we used for our tests. The GTX 460 includes 7 SMs, which can handle up to 48 warps of 32 threads each (for a maximum of 1536 threads). Each block may access a maximum amount of 48KB of shared memory implemented directly on-chip within each SM. Furthermore, the GTX 460 offers 1GB of GDDR5 memory as global memory. This information must be carefully taken into account when programming a kernel: shared memory must be used as much as possible, since it may hide the higher latency introduced by access to global memory. However, shared memory has a limited size, which significantly impacts the design of algorithms by constraining the amount of data that can be shared by the threads in each block.

3. EVENTS AND PREDICATES

Before going into the details of our matching algorithm we introduce the models of events and subscriptions we assume in this paper. To be as general as possible we assume a very common model among event-based systems [10].

For our purposes, an *event notification*, or simply *event*, is represented as a set of *attributes*, i.e., $\langle name, value \rangle$ pairs. Values are typed: in our algorithm we consider both numerical values and strings. As an example, $e_1 = [\langle area, \text{``}area1\text{''} \rangle, \langle temp, 25 \rangle, \langle wind, 15 \rangle]$ is an event that an environmental monitoring component could publish to notify the rest of the system about the current temperature and wind speed in the area it monitors.

The interests of components are modeled through *predicates*, each being a disjunction of *filters*, which, in turn, are conjunctions of elementary *constraints* on the values of single attributes. As an example, $f_1 = (area = \text{``}area1\text{''} \wedge temp > 30)$ is a filter composed of two constraints, while $p_1 = [(area = \text{``}area1\text{''} \wedge temp > 30) \vee (area = \text{``}area2\text{''} \wedge wind > 20)]$ is a predicate composed of two filters.

A filter f *matches* an event notification e if all constraints in f are satisfied by the attributes of e. Similarly, a predicate matches e if at least one of its filters matches e. In the examples above, predicate p_1 matches event e_1.

Given these definitions, the problem of content-based matching can be stated in the most general terms as follow: given a set of *interfaces*, each one exposing a predicate, and an event e, find the set of interfaces e should be delivered to, i.e., the set of interfaces that expose a predicate matching e.

In a centralized publish-subscribe infrastructure, it is the *dispatcher* which implements this function, by collecting pred-

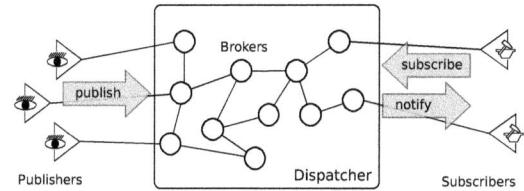

Figure 1: A typical publish-subscribe infrastructure

icates that express the interests of subscribers (each connected to a different "interface") and forwarding incoming event notifications on the basis of such interests. In a distributed publish-subscribe infrastructure the dispatcher is composed of several *brokers*, each one implementing the content-based matching function above to forward events to its neighbors (other brokers or the subscribers directly connected to it).

4. CUDA CONTENT-BASED MATCHER

The *CUDA Content-based Matcher (CCM)* algorithm we designed is composed of two phases: a *constraint selection* phase and a *constraint evaluation and counting* phase. When an event enters the engine, the first phase is used to select, for each attribute a of the event, all the constraints having the same name as a. These constraints are evaluated in the second phase, using the value of a. In particular, we keep a counter of satisfied constraints for each filter stored by the system: when a constraint c is satisfied, we increase the counter associated to the filter c belongs to. A filter matches an event when all its constraints are satisfied, i.e., when the associated counter is equal to the number of its constraints. If a filter matches an event so does the predicate it belongs to. Accordingly, the event can be forwarded to the interface exposing it.

As already mentioned in Section 2, using a GPU that implements the CUDA architecture may provide significant computational speedups, but requires the developer to carefully design the algorithm and the data structures to maximize parallelism, exploit programmable caches, and minimize the amount of information that has to be transferred from the main memory to the GPU memory and back. The rest of this section focuses on these aspects, while describing the design and implementation of CCM in details.

4.1 Data Structures

Figure 2 shows the data structures we create and use during processing. Almost all of them are permanently stored into the GPU memory, to minimize the need for CPU-to-GPU communication during event processing.

In Figure 2a we see the data structures containing information about constraints. The GPU stores table **Constraints**, which groups existing constraints into multiple rows, one for each name. Each element of such table stores information about a single constraint: in particular its operator (**Op**), its type (**Type**), its value (**Val**), and an identifier of the filter it belongs to (**FilterId**). Moreover, since different rows may include a different number of constraints, the GPU also stores a vector **SizeC** with the actual size of each row. Finally, table **Constraints** is coupled with map **Names** ($\langle name, rowId \rangle$), stored by the CPU, which associates each attribute name with the corresponding row in **Constraints**.

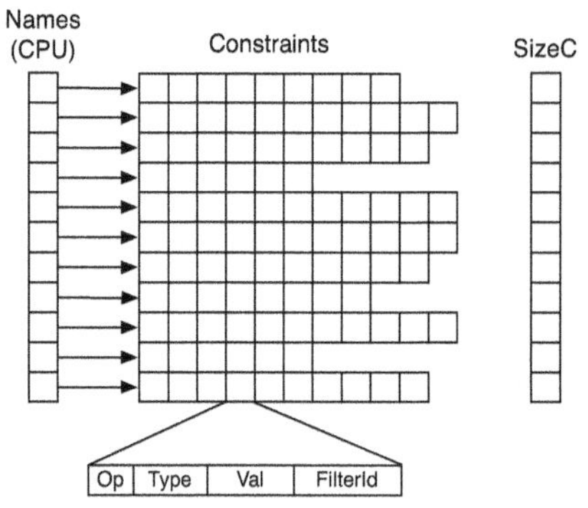

(a) Constraints

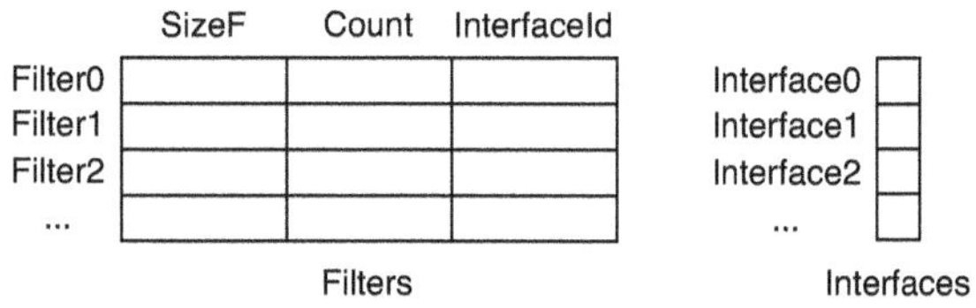

(b) Filters and Interfaces

Figure 2: Data structures

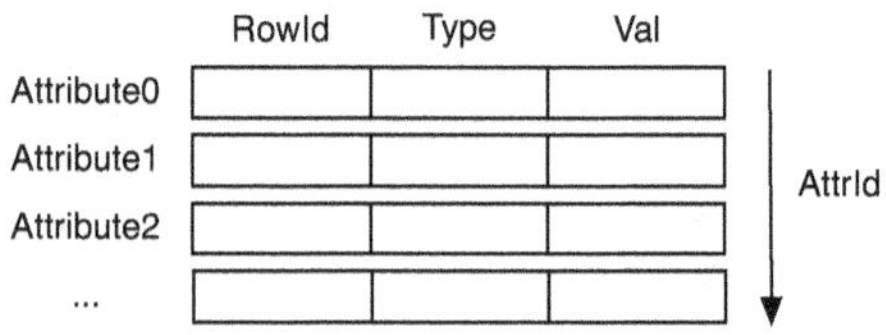

Figure 3: Input data

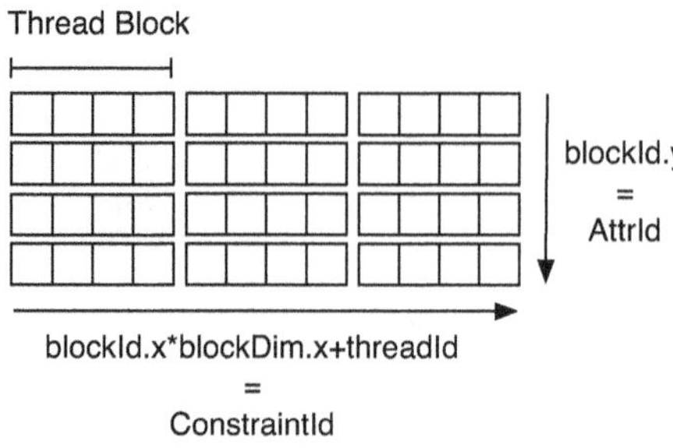

Figure 4: Organization of blocks and threads

Figure 2b shows the data structures containing information about filters and interfaces. Each row of table `Filters` represents a different filter and stores its size (`SizeF`), i.e., the number of constraints it is composed of, the number of currently satisfied constraints (`Count`), and the interface it belongs to (`InterfaceId`), i.e., the interface whose associated predicate includes this filter. As we will discuss in more details later, `Count` is set to zero before processing an event, and it is updated by different threads in parallel during processing.

Finally, `Interfaces` is a vector of bytes, with each position representing a different interface. As for `Count`, it is set to zero before processing an event e and it is updated during processing. A value of one in position x means that the event under processing must be forwarded through interface x. Accordingly, the content of vector `Interfaces` represents the result of the matching process, which has to be copied from the GPU memory to the CPU memory when the event under consideration has been processed.

4.2 Parallel Evaluation of Constraints

When a new event e enters the engine, the CPU uses the information included in e together with map `Names` to build table `Input` in Figure 3. It stores, for each attribute a in e, the id of the row in `Constraints` associated to the name of a (`RowId`), the type of a (`Type`), and its value (`Val`). This information is subsequently transferred to the GPU memory to match e against relevant constraints. Notice that, in

principle, we could avoid this phase, transferring the whole content of e to the GPU and letting it find the relevant constraints (those having the same names of e's attributes), using parallel threads. However, some preliminary experiments we performed show that the computational effort required to select constraints on the CPU using a STL map is negligible (less than 1% of the overall processing time); on the other hand, this selection can potentially filter out a huge number of constraints, thus making the subsequent evaluation on the GPU much faster.

After building table `Input` and transferring it to the GPU memory, the CPU launches a new kernel, with thousands of threads working in parallel, each one evaluating a single attribute a of e against a single constraint among those relevant for a in table `Constraints`.

As we mentioned in Section 2, at kernel launch time the developer must specify the number of blocks executing the kernel and the number of threads composing each block. Both numbers can be in one, two, or three dimensions. Figure 4 shows our organization of threads and blocks. It shows an example in which each block is composed of only 4 threads, but in real cases 256 or 512 threads per block are common choices. We organize all threads inside a block over a single dimension (x axis), whereas blocks are organized in two dimensions. The y axis is mapped to event attributes, i.e., to rows of table `Input` in Figure 3. The x axis, instead, is mapped to set of constraints. Indeed, since the number of constraints with the same name of a given attribute may exceed the maximum number of threads per block, we allocate multiple blocks along the x axis.

All threads part of the same kernel execute the same function, whose pseudo-code is presented in Algorithm 1. The only difference between threads are the values of the blockId and threadId variables, initialized by the CUDA runtime.

Using these values, each thread determines its x and y coordinates in the bi-dimensional space presented in Figure 4. More specifically, the value of y is directly given by the y value of blockId, while the value of x is computed as blockId.x·blockDim.x+threadId, where blockDim.x is the x size of each block.

At this point each thread reads the data it requires from tables `Input` and `Constraints`. Since all threads in the same block share the same attribute, i.e., the same element in table `Input`, we copy such element from the global memory to the block shared memory once for all. More specifically, the command at line 3 defines a variable shInput in shared memory, which the first thread of each block (the one having threadId equal to 0) sets to the appropriate value taken from table `Input`. All other threads wait until the copy is

Algorithm 1 Constraint Evaluation Kernel

```
1:  x = blockId.x·blockDim.x+threadId
2:  y = blockId.y
3:  _shared_ shInput
4:  if threadId==0 then
5:      shInput = input[y]
6:  end if
7:  _syncthreads()
8:  rowId = shInput.RowId
9:  if x ≥ SizeC[rowId] then
10:     return
11: end if
12: constraint = Constraints[x][rowId]
13: type = shInput.Type
14: val = shInput.Val
15: if ! sat(constraint, val, type) then
16:     return
17: end if
18: filterId = constraint.FilterId
19: count = atomicInc(Filters[filterId].Count)
20: if count+1==Filters[filterId].SizeF then
21:     interfaceId = Filters[filterId].InterfaceId
22:     Interfaces[interfaceId] = 1
23: end if
```

finished by invoking the _syncthreads() command in line 7. Our experiments show that this optimization w.r.t. the straightforward approach of letting each thread access table `Input` (which is stored into the slower global memory) separately, increases performance by 2-3%.

Once this initial phase has completed, each thread uses the `RowId` information copied into the shInput structure to determine the row of table `Constraints` it has to process (each thread will process a different element of such row). Notice that different rows may have different lengths: we instantiate the number of blocks (and consequently the number of threads) to cover the longest among them. Accordingly, in most cases we have too many threads. We check this possibility at line 9, immediately stopping unrequired threads. This is a common practice in GPU programming, e.g., see [32]. We will analyze its implication on performance in Section 5.

In line 12 each thread reads the constraint it has to process from table `Constraints` in global memory to the thread's local memory (i.e., hardware registers, if they are large enough), thus making future accesses faster. Also notice that our organization of memory allows threads having contiguous identifiers to access contiguous regions of the global memory. This is particularly important when designing an algorithm for CUDA, since it allows the hardware to combine different read/write operations into a reduced number of memory-wide accesses, thus increasing performance.

In lines 13 and 14 each thread reads the type and value of the attribute it has to process and uses them to evaluate the constraint it is responsible for (in line 15[2]). If the constraint is not satisfied the thread immediately returns, otherwise it extracts the identifier of the filter the constraint belongs to and updates the value of field `Count` in table `Filters`. Notice that different threads may try to update the same

---

[2]We omit for simplicity the pseudo code of the sat function that checks whether a constraint is satisfied by an attribute.

counter concurrently. To avoid clashes, we exploit a special atomicInc operation offered by CUDA, which atomically reads the value of a 32bit integer from the global memory, increases it, and returns the old value.

In line 20 each thread checks whether the filter is satisfied, i.e., if the current number of satisfied constraints (old count plus one) equals the number of constraints in the filter. Notice that at most one thread for each filter can positively evaluate this condition. If the filter is satisfied, the thread extracts the identifier of the interface the filter belongs to and sets the corresponding position in vector `Interfaces` to 1. It is possible that multiple threads access the same position of `Interfaces` concurrently; however, since they are all writing the same value, no conflict arises.

As we mentioned in Section 2, CUDA provides better performance when threads belonging to the same warp inside a block follow the same execution path. After table `Input` is read in line 5 and all unrequired threads have been stopped in line 10, Algorithm 1 has two conditional branches where the execution path of different threads may potentially diverge. The first one, in line 15, evaluates a single attribute against a constraint, while the second one, in line 20, checks whether all the constraints in a filter have been satisfied before setting the relevant interface to 1. The threads that follow the positive branch in line 20 are those that process the last matching constraint of a filter. Unfortunately, we cannot control the warps these threads belong to, since this depends from the content of the event under evaluation and from the scheduling of threads. Accordingly, there is nothing we can do to force threads on the same warp to follow the same branch.

On the contrary, we can increase the probability of following the same execution path within function sat in line 15 by grouping constraints in table `Constraints` according to their type, operator, and value. This way we increase the chance that threads in the same warp, having contiguous identifiers, process constraints with the same type and operator, thus following the same execution path into sat. Our experiments, however, show that such type of grouping of constraints provides only a very marginal performance improvement and only under specific conditions. On the other hand, it makes creation of data structures (i.e., table `Constraints` that needs to be ordered) much slower. We will come back to this issue in Section 5.

4.3 Reducing Memory Transfers

To correctly process an event, we first need to reset field `Count` associated with each filter and vector `Interfaces`. In a preliminary implementation, we let the CPU perform these operations through the cudaMemset command, which allows to set all bytes of a memory region on the GPU to a common value (0 in our case). Although optimized, the cudaMemset command introduces a relevant overhead, since it involves a communication between the CPU and the GPU over the (slow) PCI-E bus.

On the other hand, since the CUDA architecture executes blocks in non deterministic order and does not allow inter-blocks communication, we could not straightforwardly reset data structures within our kernel. Indeed, assuming a subset of threads is used to reset data immediately after launch, we cannot know in advance whether they are executed immediately, or if other threads (in other blocks) get executed before.

To overcome this problem, we decided to duplicate data structures `Count` and `Interfaces`. When processing an event we use one copy of these data structures and we reset the other using different threads in parallel, while we reverse the role of the two copies at the next event. Notice that in doing so we take care of writing adjacent memory blocks from contiguous threads: this minimizes the overhead introduced by this reset operation. Through this trick we avoid using the cudaMemset operation and do everything within the single kernel that also executes the matching algorithm. This way the interactions between CPU and GPU memory are reduced to the minimum: indeed, we only need to copy the event content to the GPU (filling table `Input`) to start processing and to copy vector `Interfaces` when computation is finished. In Section 5 we will analyze the cost of these operations in details, measuring the benefits of this approach.

5. EVALUATION

Our evaluation had three main goals: first of all, we wanted to compare CCM with a state of the art algorithm running on the CPU, to understand the real benefits of CUDA. Second, since the performance of a matching algorithm are influenced by a large number of parameters, we wanted to explore the parameter space as broadly as possible, to isolate the aspects that make the use of the GPU more profitable. Third, we wanted to profile our code to better understand the aspects of CUDA that mostly impact performance.

To fulfill the first goal, we decided to compare CCM with SFF [10] version 1.9.4, the matching algorithm used inside the Siena event notification middleware [7]. Similarly to CCM, SFF is a counting algorithm, which runs over the attributes of the event under consideration, counting the constraints they satisfy until one or more filters have been entirely matched. When a filter f is matched, the algorithm marks the related interface, purges all the constraints and filters exposed by that interface, and continues until all interfaces are marked or all attributes have been processed. The set of marked interfaces represents the output of SFF. To maximize performance under a sequential hardware like a traditional CPU, SFF builds a complex, strongly indexed data structure, which puts together the predicates (decomposed into their constituent constraints) received by subscribers. A smart use of hashing functions and pruning techniques, allows SFF to obtain state-of-the-art performance under a very broad range of workloads.

To compare CCM against SFF we defined a default scenario, whose parameters are listed in Table 1, and used it as a starting point to build a number of different experiments, by changing such parameters one by one and measuring how this impacts the performance of the two algorithms. In our tests we focus on the time to process a single event (i.e., latency). In particular, we let each algorithm process 1000 events, one by one, and we calculate the average processing time. To avoid any bias, we repeat each test 10 times, using different seeds to randomly generate subscriptions and events, and we plot the average value measured[3].

Tests were executed on a AMD Phenom II machine, with 6 cores running at 2.8GHz, and 8GB of DDR3 Ram. The GPU was a Nvidia GTX 460 with 1GB of GDDR5 Ram. We used

[3]The 95% confidence interval of this average is always below 1% of the measured value, so we omit it from the plots.

Number of events	1000
Attributes per event, min-max	3-5
Number of interfaces	10
Constraints per filter, min-max	3-5
Filters per interface, min-max	22500-27500
Number of names	100
Distribution of names	Uniform
Numerical/string constraints (%)	50/50
Numerical operators	$=(25\%)$, $!=(25\%)$, $>(25\%)$, $<(25\%)$
String operators	$=(25\%)$, $!=(25\%)$, $subString(25\%)$, $prefix(25\%)$,
Number of values	100

Table 1: Parameters in the default scenario

	CCM	SFF
Processing time in the default scenario	0.144ms	1.035ms
Subscriptions deployment time in the default scenario	527.5ms	992.28ms
Data structure size in the default scenario	33.9MB GPU Ram	42.4MB CPU Ram
Processing time with a Zipf distribution for names	2.06ms	14.68ms

Table 2: Analysis of CCM

the CUDA runtime 3.1 for 64 bit Linux. It is worth mentioning that nowadays the GTX 460 is a low level graphic card with a limited cost (less than 160$ in March 2011). Nvidia currently offers much better graphic cards, and also cards (TESLA GPUs) explicitly conceived for high performance computing, with a higher number of cores, and up to 6GB of memory, having higher bandwidth and speed.

Default Scenario. Table 2 (first row) shows the processing times measured by the two algorithms in the default scenario. This is a relatively easy-to-manage scenario. It includes one million constraints on the average, which is not a big number for large scale applications. Under this load, SFF exhibits a processing time that is slightly above 1ms. On the other hand, our CCM algorithm requires less than 0.15ms to process an event (with a potential throughput of more than 6000 events/s), providing a speedup of 7.19x.

Deployment of Subscriptions. Besides measuring processing time, we were also interested in studying the time required to create the data structures used during event evaluation. Indeed, they need to be generated at run-time, when new subscriptions are deployed on the engine. Even if it is common to assume that the number of publishing largely exceeds the number of subscribing/unsubscribing in any event-based application, this time has also to be considered when measuring the performance of a matching algorithm.

Table 2 (second row) shows the average time required by SFF and CCM to create their data structures. CCM requires 527.5ms: this time includes allocating memory on the GPU, building the data structures (part on the CPU and part on the GPU), and copying them from the CPU to the GPU memory. On the contrary, SFF has only to build the data structures in main memory: however, to attain its perfor-

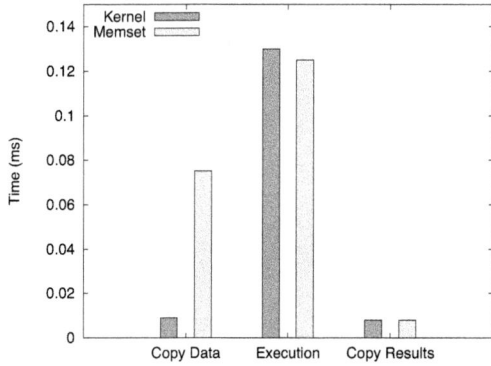

Figure 5: An Analysis of CCM Processing Times

mance under sequential hardware, SFF needs more complex structures, which need more time to be built (around 1s). This is true in all scenarios, where the advantage of CCM w.r.t. SFF was at least as large as the one we reported here (i.e., twice as fast). For space reasons we do not report the exact times we measured in the other scenarios, while we prefer to focus on the event matching time.

The complexity of the data structures used by SFF also reflects on their size. As shown in Table 2 (third row), CCM requires less memory to store data structure: the default scenario occupies 33.9MB of the GPU memory and the maximum occupancy we measured in our tests was below 200MB. Since GPUs nowadays have at least 1GB of Ram, contrary to what happens in many cases, GPU memory occupancy is not a problem for CCM. It is worth mentioning, however, that beside the data structures allocated for processing, the use of the CUDA toolkit introduces a fixed overhead of about 140MB of main (CPU) memory.

An Analysis of CCM Processing Times. Figure 5 analyzes the cost of the different operations performed by CCM during the matching process in the default scenario. In particular, it splits processing time into three parts: the time required to copy data from the CPU to the GPU memory (which also includes the time needed to build table `Input` matching STL map `Names` on the CPU), the time required to execute the kernel, and the time used to copy results back to the main memory. We compare two different versions of our algorithm: as described in Section 4.3, `Memset` resets field `Count` and vector `Interfaces` invoking the cudaMemset command twice, before kernel starts; on the contrary, `Kernel` resets data structures directly inside the kernel code (this is the version we will use in the remainder of this section).

First of all, we observe that in both cases the cost of executing the kernel dominates the others. If we compare the two versions of CCM, we notice how the kernel's execution time is higher when data structures are reset inside the kernel but by a very low margin (moving from 0.125ms to 0.13ms). On the other hand, the cudaMemset operation is quite inefficient and by not invoking it we strongly reduce the time to execute the first step of the algorithm (from 0.075ms to 0.009ms), thus making the `Kernel` version about 30% faster. In the `Kernel` version, which we will use in the remainder of this section, the cost for moving data back and forth over the (slow) PCI-E bus represents about 8% of the overall matching time, meaning that we are exploiting the

computational power of the GPU while introducing a relatively small overhead.

Distribution of Names. As we said in Section 4, our algorithm creates and launches a number of threads that depends from the size of the longest row in `Constraints` among those selected by the names appearing in the incoming event. As we observed in Section 4, in presence of rows with very different sizes, the number of unrequired threads may be relevant. To investigate the impact of this aspect, we changed the distribution of names for both constraints and attributes, moving from the uniform distribution adopted in the default scenario to a Zipf distribution.

Table 2 (fourth row) shows the results we obtained. First of all we notice how both algorithms significantly increase their matching time w.r.t. the default scenario. Indeed, both algorithms use names to reduce the number of constraints to process, and this pre-filtering becomes less effective with a Zipf distribution. What is most important for us, is that the speedup of CCM against SFF remains unchanged. This means that launching a higher number of unrequired threads does not influence the advantage of CCM over SFF.

As we mentioned in Section 4, during our experiments we investigated the benefits of ordering constraints according to their type, operator, and value, thus increasing the probability that threads of the same warp follow a common execution path inside the function sat. In the general case, this approach does not significantly decrease the processing time of events, while it has a very negative impact on the cost of deploying subscriptions. Accordingly, we decided not using it. However, when using a Zipf distribution, a large number of constraints, with their types, operators, and values, share a very limited set of names. In this particular case ordering constraints introduces a visible speedup moving the overall processing time from 2.06ms to 1.92ms. We can conclude that the idea of ordering constraints is worth in all those cases when the number of constraints with the same name grows above a few hundred thousands (in the Zipf case we have 500.000 constraints with the most common name, on average)

Number of Attributes. Figure 6 shows how performance changes with the size of events (i.e., the average number of attributes). In particular, Figure 6a shows the processing time of the two algorithms. Both of them exhibit higher matching times with a higher number of attributes. Indeed, increasing the number of attributes in the incoming events also increases the work that need to be performed, since each of them has to be compared with the stored constraints. However, SFF performs all these evaluations sequentially, while CCM launches several blocks of threads to perform them in parallel. This explains why the processing time increases faster in SFF, making the advantage of CCM larger with a high number of attributes. This is evident if we consider the speedup, plotted in Figure 6b: with 9 attributes per event, CCM is ten times faster than SFF.

Number of Constraints per Filter. Figure 7 shows how performance changes with the average number of constraints in each filter. Increasing such number, while keeping a fixed number of filters, increases the overall number of constraints deployed in the engine, and thus the complexity of the matching process. This is demonstrated by Figure 7a. As in the previous case, the possibility to process constraints in parallel advantages our algorithm: both CCM and SFF

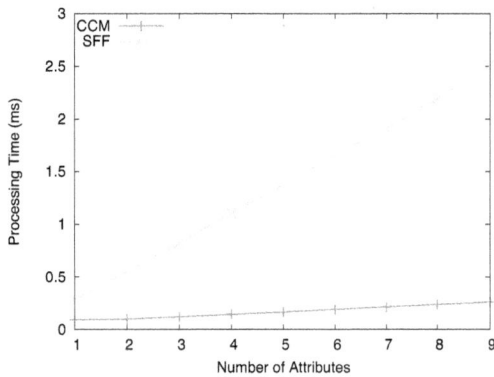

(a) Event Processing Time

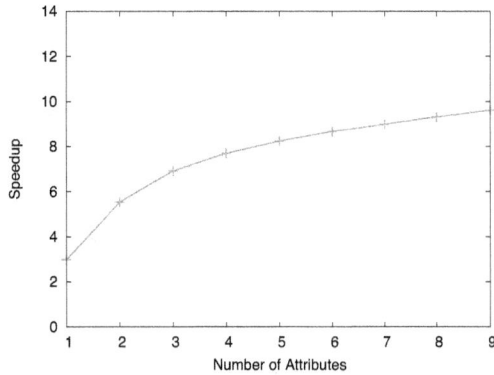

(b) Speedup

Figure 6: Number of Attributes

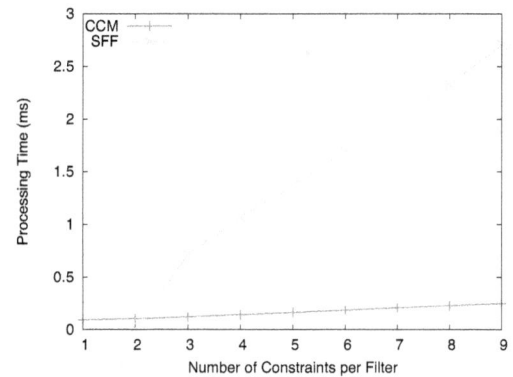

(a) Event Processing Time

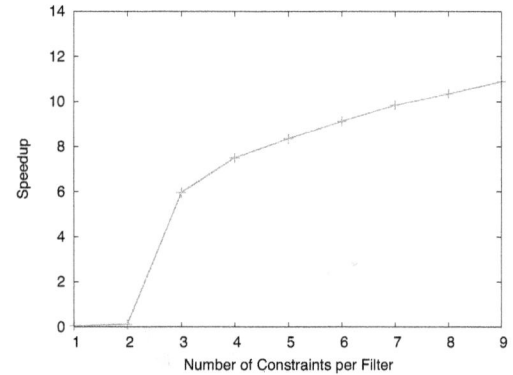

(b) Speedup

Figure 7: Number of Constraints per Filter

show a linear trend in processing time, but CCM times grow much slower than those of SFF. The speedup (see Figure 7b) overcomes 10x with 9 constraints per filter.

Notice that with one or two constraints per filter SFF performs better than CCM. Indeed, a lower number of constraints per filter results in a greater chance to match filters. With one or two constraints per filter we are in a very special (and unrealistic) case in which the chance to find a matching filter for a given interface is very high, such that at the end all events are relevant for all interfaces. The pruning techniques of SFF work at their best in this case, while CCM always process all constraints, albeit in parallel.

Number of Filters per Interface. Figure 8 shows how performance changes with the number of filters defined for each interface. As in the scenario above, increasing such number also increases the overall number of constraints, and thus the complexity of matching. Accordingly both algorithms show higher processing times (see Figure 8a) with CCM suffering less when the scenario becomes more complex. The speedup overcomes 13x with 250000 filters per interface, i.e., 10 millions of constraints (Figure 8b). Notice how the growth of the speedup curve decreases with the number of filters: indeed, a large number of filters increases the number of matching interfaces, allowing SFF to frequently exploit the pruning optimizations described above.

Also observe how a small number of filters favors SFF, which with less than 1000 filters performs better than CCM. Indeed, the latter pays a fixed fee to copy data from/to the

GPU memory and to launch the kernel. In a situation in which the computational complexity is very low, this fee accounts for a large fraction of the total cost. On the other hand, under such circumstances the matching is very fast, with both algorithm registering an average processing time below 0.05ms, which makes the advantages of SFF less relevant in practice.

Number of Interfaces. Another important aspect that significantly influences the behavior of a content-based matching algorithm is the number of interfaces. In Figure 9 we analyze its impact on SFF and CCM, moving from 10 to 100 interfaces. Notice that 100 interfaces can be a common value in real applications, in which several clients are served by a common event dispatcher that performs the matching process for all of them.

As in the previous experiments, increasing the number of interfaces also increases the number of constraints, and thus the complexity of matching. Accordingly, both algorithms show higher processing times as the number of interfaces grows (Figure 9a). Also in this case, the speedup of CCM increases with the complexity of processing (Figure 9b), moving from 7x to more than 13x.

Number of Names. Both SFF and CCM use the attribute names in the incoming event to perform a preliminary selection of the constraints to evaluate. Accordingly, the total number of possible names used inside constraints and attributes represent a key performance indicator.

Figure 10a shows how the processing time of the two algorithms changes with the number of names for attributes and

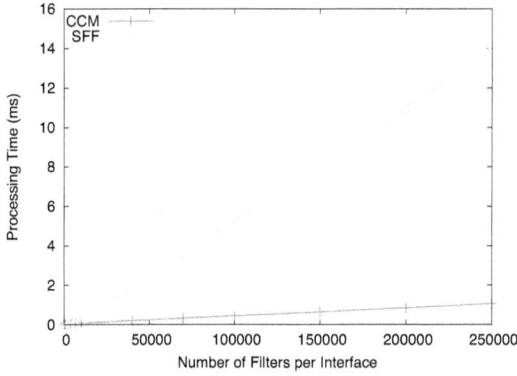
(a) Event Processing Time

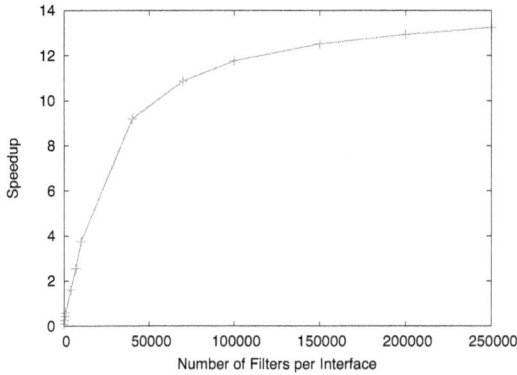
(b) Speedup

Figure 8: Number of Filters per Interface

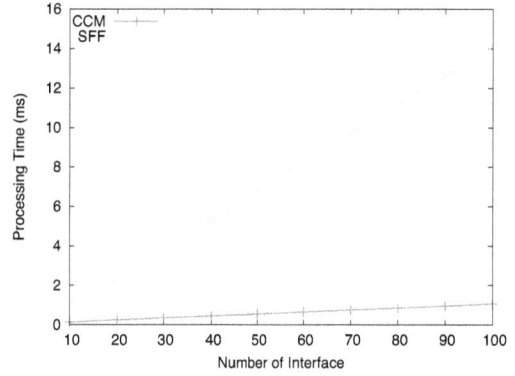
(a) Event Processing Time

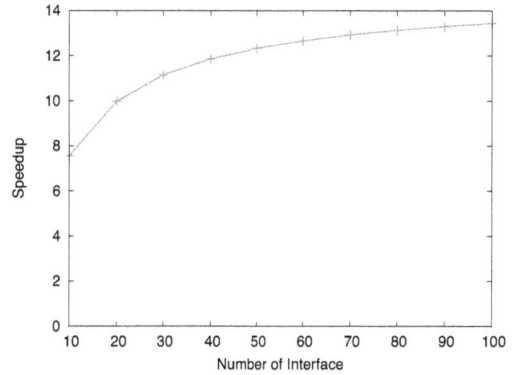
(b) Speedup

Figure 9: Number of Interfaces

constraints. Notice that increasing the number of names allows the "constraint selection" phase (performed on the CPU even by CCM – see Section 4), to discard a higher number of constraints. Accordingly, the cost of the "constraint evaluation and counting" phase (the more expensive in terms of computation and also the one that CCM performs on the GPU) decreases. This is demonstrated by Figure 10a where both algorithms perform better when the number of names increases, especially when moving from 10 to 100 names. After this threshold times tend to stabilize. This fact can be explained by observing that over a certain number of names the "constraint evaluation and counting" phase becomes so simple that the processing time does not decrease much.

If we look at the speedup (Figure 10b) we observe two different regions. When moving from 10 to 30 names the speedup of CCM increases. Indeed, with few names the probability for a filter to match an event is very high and this allows SFF to leverage its pruning techniques. This benefit vanishes when moving from 10 to 30 names. After 30 names the speedup decreases. Indeed, as we already noticed, increasing the number of names drops the complexity of the "constraint evaluation and counting" phase, which CCM performs in parallel on the GPU. Moreover, this phase has a minimal fixed cost for CCM (the cost of copying data from/to the GPU memory and launching the kernel).

Finally, we observe that even with a high number of names (1000) CCM outperforms SFF, with a 2x speedup on our reference hardware. This result is obtained with a uniform distribution of names. A Zipf distribution, considered

more representative of several real-case scenarios [15], would strongly favor CCM, as shown in Table 2 (fourth row). Indeed, in such scenario, most constraints would refer to a few attribute names, those also present in most events. In other terms, the results obtained with a Zipf distribution of a large number of names are similar to those obtained with a uniform distribution of much less names.

Type of Constraints. Finally, Figure 11 shows how performance changes when changing the type of constraints. In particular, we measured the processing time when changing the percentage of constraints involving numerical values (the remaining involve strings).

At a first look, the behavior registered in Figure 11a is counter intuitive, since apparently matching numerical values is more expensive than matching strings. On the other hand, we notice that the chances a numerical constraint matches an event are higher than those of a string constraint. On the average, about 1% of interfaces are selected when all constraints are on strings, and about 7% when all constraints are numerical. This means that a larger number of operations have to be performed in the latter case, increasing counters and checking if all constraint of a filter have been matched; while the low chance of matching strings means that a few comparisons on characters are enough to discover that the constraint does not matches. This has a very limited impact on CCM, where all such operations are performed in parallel, while it decreases the performance of SFF. Accordingly, as shown in Figure 11b, the speedup of

191

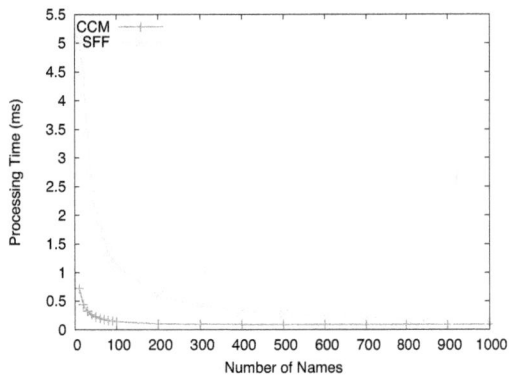

(a) Event Processing Time

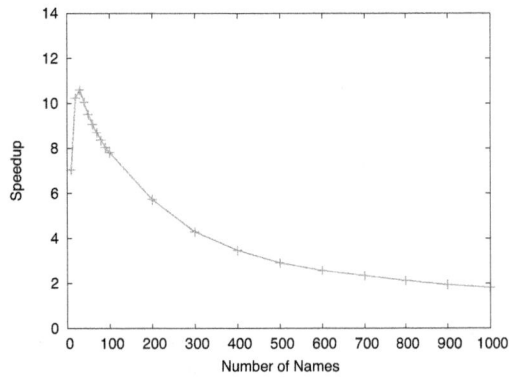

(b) Speedup

Figure 10: Number of Different Names

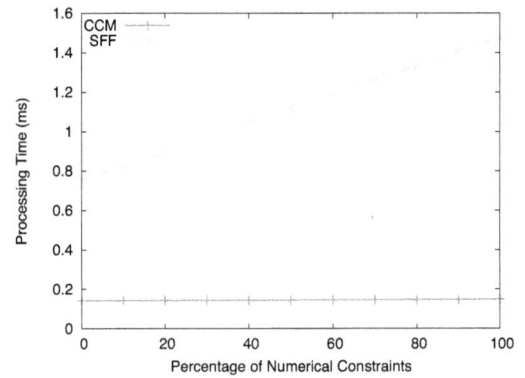

(a) Event Processing Time

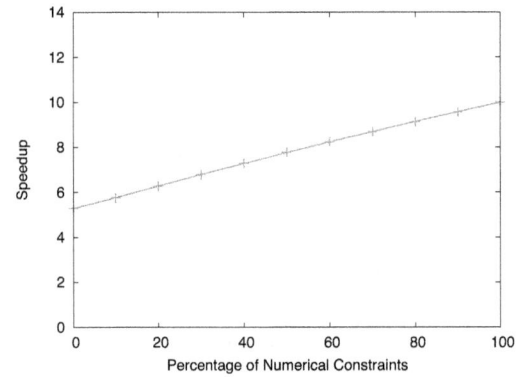

(b) Speedup

Figure 11: Type of Constraints

CCM increases linearly with the number of numerical constraints deployed.

Final Considerations. Our experience and the results presented so far allow us to draw some general conclusions about CUDA programming in general and content-based matching on CUDA in particular.

First of all we may observe how programming CUDA is (relatively) easy, while attaining good performance is (very) hard. Memory accesses and transfers tend to dominate over processing (especially in our case) and must be carefully managed (see the case of the initial cudaMemset operation), while having thousands of threads, even if they are created to be immediately destroyed, has a minimal impact.

Also, we observed the presence of a fixed cost to pay to launch the kernel, which makes (relatively) simple problems not worth being demanded to the GPU (see the case of simple filters with 1-2 constraints). Fortunately, at least for our problem, it is possible to determine if we are in one such cases or not before starting processing. In practical terms, we leverage this characteristics by implementing a translator from Siena events and subscriptions to those managed by our matching engine. This way the two engines, SFF and CCM, can be both integrated into Siena (and any similar publish-subscribe middleware) to postpone at run-time the decision if activating CCM from the very beginning or letting SFF solve the matching problem until enough subscriptions are collected that justify using CCM.

Focusing on the specific problem we addressed, we notice how using a GPU may provide impressive speedup w.r.t.

using a CPU, with the additional, fundamental advantage, of leaving the CPU free to focus on those jobs (like I/O) that do not fit GPU programming. Moreover, this speedup grows with the scale of the problem to solve.

A final consideration we can do is related with the availability of multicore CPUs. To the best of our knowledge, all existing matching algorithms are sequential, and consequently they do not leverage multicore hardware. On the other hand, an event-based infrastructure collects events from multiple sources and could, in principle, match them in parallel, using multiple cores. This promises to increase throughput in traditional systems (those using CPUs to perform matching) but the same promise holds for systems using GPUs. In fact, the new version of CUDA, currently under beta test, fully supports multiple kernels launched by different CPU threads in parallel. Moreover, it is possible to add more GPUs operating in parallel, to further improve performance.

6. RELATED WORK

The last years have seen the development of a large number of content-based publish-subscribe systems [26, 4, 13, 25, 12] first exploiting a centralized dispatcher, then moving to distributed solutions for improved scalability. Despite their differences, they all share the problem of matching event notifications against subscriptions.

Two main categories of matching algorithms can be found in the literature: *counting* algorithms [14, 10] and *tree-based* algorithms [2, 5]. A counting algorithm maintains a counter for each filter to record the number of constraints satisfied by the current event. Both SFF and CCM belong to this category. A tree-based algorithm organizes subscriptions into a rooted search tree. Inner nodes represent an evaluation test; nodes at the same level evaluates constraints with the same name; leaves represent the received predicates. Given an event, the search tree is traversed from the root down. At every node, the value of an attribute is tested, and the satisfied branches are followed until the fully satisfied predicates (and corresponding interfaces) are reached at the leaves.

To the best of our knowledge, no existing work has demonstrated the superiority of one of the two approaches. Moreover, SFF, which we used as a term of comparison in Section 5, is usually cited among the most efficient matching algorithms.

Despite the efforts described above, content-based matching is still considered to be a complex and time consuming task [9]. To overcome this limitation, researchers have explored two directions: on the one hand they proposed to distribute matching among multiple brokers, exploiting covering relationships between subscriptions to reduce the amount of work performed at each node [8]. On the other hand, they moved to probabilistic matching algorithms, trying to increase the performance of the matching process, while possibly introducing evaluation errors in the form of false positives [6, 20]. The issue of distributing the event dispatcher is orthogonal w.r.t. the matching algorithm. Indeed, brokers have to perform the same kind of matching we analyzed here. Accordingly, CCM can be profitably used in distributed scenarios, contributing to further improve performance. At the same time, some of the ideas behind CCM can be leveraged to port probabilistic algorithms inside GPUs. Indeed, probabilistic matching usually involves encoding events and subscriptions as Bloom filters of pre-defined length, thus reducing the matching process to a comparison of bit vectors: a strongly data parallel process, which perfectly fits CUDA. We plan to explore this topic in the future.

Recently, a few works have addressed the problem of parallelizing the matching process, using ad-hoc (FPGA) hardware [33], or multi-core CPUs [16]. While the first approach has limited applicability, since it requires ad-hoc hardware, we plan to compare, and possibly combine, the use of multicore CPUs with GPUs in the future.

The adoption of GPUs for general purpose programming is relatively recent and was first enabled in late 2006 when Nvidia released the first version of CUDA [11]. Since then, commodity graphics hardware has become a cost-effective parallel platform to solve many general problems, including problems coming from linear algebra [21], image processing, computer vision, signal processing [31], and graphs algorithms [19]. For an extensive survey on the application of GPU for general purpose computation the reader may refer to [30]. To the best of our knowledge, our work is the first one that explores the possibility of using GPUs to implement a content-based matching algorithm.

7. CONCLUSIONS

In this paper we presented a new content-based matching algorithm designed to run on GPUs implementing the CUDA architecture. We compared it with SFF, the matching algorithm of Siena, well known for its efficiency. Results demonstrate the benefits of GPUs in a wide spectrum of sce-

narios, showing speedups from 7x to 13x in most of them, especially the most challenging ones. This reflects the difference in processing power of the two platforms, as acknowledged by Intel itself [23]. Moreover, delegating to the GPU all the effort required for the matching process potentially brings other advantages to the whole system, by leaving the main CPU free to perform other tasks.

In our analysis we observed how the main overhead in using GPUs to perform content-based matching has to do with the need of transferring data between the main and GPU memory through the (relatively) slow PCI-E bus. Our algorithm reduces these memory transfers to the minimum making it convenient also in small scenarios.

Notice that our algorithm was presented here focusing on the case of content-based publish-subscribe systems, but the problem of matching is more general than this. Indeed, as observed by others [10, 13], several applications can directly benefit from a content-based matching service. They include intrusion detection systems and firewalls, which need to classify packets as they flow on the network; intentional naming systems [1], which realize a form of content-based routing; distributed data sharing systems, which need to forward queries to the appropriate servers; and service discovery systems, which need to match service descriptions against service queries.

Finally, in this paper we focused on exact matching, i.e., on an algorithm that does not produce false positives, since this makes our solution amenable to be straightforwardly integrated in most systems that require content-based matching. On the other hand, we plan to explore probabilistic, inexact matching as well, which we believe could receive great advantages if implemented on a GPU, using techniques similar to those we adopted in CCM.

Acknowledgment

This work was partially supported by the European Commission, Programme IDEAS-ERC, Project 227977-SMScom; and by the Italian Gov. under the project PRIN D-ASAP.

8. REFERENCES

[1] W. Adjie-Winoto, E. Schwartz, H. Balakrishnan, and J. Lilley. The design and implementation of an intentional naming system. In *Proc. of the 17th Symp. on Operating Syst. Principles (SOSP99)*, pages 186–201. ACM Press, Dec 1999.

[2] M. K. Aguilera, R. E. Strom, D. C. Sturman, M. Astley, and T. D. Chandra. Matching events in a content-based subscription system. In *Proc. of the 8th Symp. on Principles of distributed computing*, PODC '99, pages 53–61, New York, NY, USA, 1999. ACM.

[3] T. S. Axelrod. Effects of synchronization barriers on multiprocessor performance. *Parallel Comput.*, 3:129–140, May 1986.

[4] R. Baldoni and A. Virgillito. Distributed event routing in publish/subscribe communication systems: a survey. Technical report, DIS, Università di Roma "La Sapienza", 2005.

[5] A. Campailla, S. Chaki, E. Clarke, S. Jha, and H. Veith. Efficient filtering in publish-subscribe systems using binary decision diagrams. In *Proc. of the 23rd Intl. Conf. on Software Engineering*, ICSE

'01, pages 443–452, Washington, DC, USA, 2001. IEEE Computer Society.

[6] A. Carzaniga and C. P. Hall. Content-based communication: a research agenda. In *SEM '06: Proceedings of the 6th Intl. Workshop on Software engineering and middleware*, Portland, Oregon, USA, Nov. 2006. Invited Paper.

[7] A. Carzaniga, D. S. Rosenblum, and A. L. Wolf. Achieving scalability and expressiveness in an internet-scale event notification service. In *Proc. of the 9th Symp. on Principles of Distributed Computing*, pages 219–227, Portland, Oregon, July 2000.

[8] A. Carzaniga, M. J. Rutherford, and A. L. Wolf. A routing scheme for content-based networking. In *Proceedings of IEEE INFOCOM 2004*, Hong Kong, China, Mar. 2004.

[9] A. Carzaniga and A. L. Wolf. Content-based networking: A new communication infrastructure. In *NSF Workshop on an Infrastructure for Mobile and Wireless Systems*, number 2538 in Lecture Notes in Computer Science, pages 59–68, Scottsdale, Arizona, Oct. 2001. Springer-Verlag.

[10] A. Carzaniga and A. L. Wolf. Forwarding in a content-based network. In *Proc. of ACM SIGCOMM 2003*, pages 163–174, Karlsruhe, Germany, Aug. 2003.

[11] CUDA. http://www.nvidia.com/object/cuda_home_new.html, 2011. Visited Jan. 2011.

[12] G. Cugola and G. Picco. REDS: A Reconfigurable Dispatching System. In *Proc. of the 6th Int. Workshop on Softw. Eng. and Middleware. (SEM06)*, pages 9—16, Portland, nov 2006. ACM Press.

[13] P. T. Eugster, P. A. Felber, R. Guerraoui, and A.-M. Kermarrec. The many faces of publish/subscribe. *ACM Comput. Surv.*, 35:114–131, June 2003.

[14] F. Fabret, H. A. Jacobsen, F. Llirbat, J. Pereira, K. A. Ross, and D. Shasha. Filtering algorithms and implementation for very fast publish/subscribe systems. In *Proc. of the 2001 SIGMOD Intl. Conf. on Management of data*, SIGMOD '01, pages 115–126, New York, NY, USA, 2001. ACM.

[15] M. Faloutsos, P. Faloutsos, and C. Faloutsos. On power-law relationships of the internet topology. *SIGCOMM Comput. Commun. Rev.*, 29:251–262, August 1999.

[16] A. Farroukh, E. Ferzli, N. Tajuddin, and H.-A. Jacobsen. Parallel event processing for content-based publish/subscribe systems. In *Proc. of the 3rd Intl. Conf. on Distributed Event-Based Systems*, DEBS '09, pages 8:1–8:4, New York, NY, USA, 2009. ACM.

[17] L. Fiege, G. Mühl, and A. P. Buchmann. An architectural framework for electronic commerce applications. In *GI Jahrestagung (2)*, pages 928–938, 2001.

[18] Nvidia GeForce GTX 460. http://www.nvidia.com/object/product-geforce-gtx-460-us.html, 2011. Visited Jan 2011.

[19] P. Harish and P. J. Narayanan. Accelerating large graph algorithms on the gpu using cuda. In *Proc. of the 14th Intl. Conf. on High Performance Computing,*

HiPC'07, pages 197–208, Berlin, Heidelberg, 2007. Springer-Verlag.

[20] Z. Jerzak and C. Fetzer. Bloom filter based routing for content-based publish/subscribe. In *Proc. of the 2nd Intl. Conf. on Distributed Event-Based Systems*, DEBS '08, pages 71–81, New York, NY, USA, 2008. ACM.

[21] J. Krüger and R. Westermann. Linear algebra operators for gpu implementation of numerical algorithms. In *ACM SIGGRAPH 2005 Courses*, SIGGRAPH '05, New York, NY, USA, 2005. ACM.

[22] C. KrÃijgel, T. Toth, and C. Kerer. Decentralized event correlation for intrusion detection. In K. Kim, editor, *Information Security and Cryptology, ICISC*, volume 2288, pages 59–95. Springer Berlin / Heidelberg, 2002.

[23] V. W. Lee, C. Kim, J. Chhugani, M. Deisher, D. Kim, A. D. Nguyen, N. Satish, M. Smelyanskiy, S. Chennupaty, P. Hammarlund, R. Singhal, and P. Dubey. Debunking the 100x gpu vs. cpu myth: an evaluation of throughput computing on cpu and gpu. In *Proc. of the 37th Intl. Symp. on Computer Architecture*, ISCA '10, pages 451–460, New York, NY, USA, 2010. ACM.

[24] D. C. Luckham. *The Power of Events: An Introduction to Complex Event Processing in Distributed Enterprise Systems*. Addison-Wesley Longman Publishing Co., Inc., Boston, MA, USA, 2001.

[25] G. Mühl, L. Fiege, F. Gartner, and A. Buchmann. Evaluating advanced routing algorithms for content-based publish/subscribe systems. In *Proc. of the 10th Intl. Symp. on Modeling, Analysis, and Simulation of Comput. and Telecom. Syst. (MASCOTS02)*, 2002.

[26] G. Mühl, L. Fiege, and P. Pietzuch. *Distributed Event-Based Systems*. Springer, 2006.

[27] J. Nickolls, I. Buck, M. Garland, and K. Skadron. Scalable parallel programming with cuda. *Queue*, 6:40–53, March 2008.

[28] *Nvidia CUDA C Programming Guide*, 2010.

[29] OpenCL. http://www.khronos.org/opencl, 2011.

[30] J. Owens, D. Luebke, N. Govindaraju, M. Harris, J. Kruger, A. Lefohn, and T. Purcell. A Survey of General–Purpose Computations on Graphics Hardware. *Computer Graphics*, Volume 26, 2007.

[31] J. D. Owens, S. Sengupta, and D. Horn. Assessment of graphic processing units (gpus) for department of defense (dod) digital signal processing (dsp) applications. Technical report, Department of Electrical and Computer Engineering, University of California,, 2005.

[32] S. Schneidert, H. Andrade, B. Gedik, K.-L. Wu, and D. S. Nikolopoulos. Evaluation of streaming aggregation on parallel hardware architectures. In *Proc. of the 4th Intl. Conf. on Distributed Event-Based Systems*, DEBS '10, pages 248–257, New York, NY, USA, 2010. ACM.

[33] K. H. Tsoi, I. Papagiannis, M. Migliavacca, W. Luk, and P. Pietzuch. Accelerating publish/subscribe matching on reconfigurable supercomputing platforms. In *Many-Core and Reconfigurable Supercomputing Conference (MRSC)*, Rome, Italy, 03/2010 2010.

NIÑOS Take Five: The Management Infrastructure for Distributed Event-Driven Workflows

Siddharth Ganesan, Young Yoon, and Hans-Arno Jacobsen
{sid, yoon}@msrg.utoronto.ca, jacobsen@eecg.utoronto.ca
Department of Electrical and Computer Engineering
University of Toronto
Toronto, Ontario, Canada

ABSTRACT

Many workflows are inherently distributed over large-scale enterprise networks. These workflows involve many collaborating partners that interact in an autonomous and event-driven manner. Managing these workflows in an efficient and reliable manner is a challenging task. In this paper, we propose and evaluate the design for a distributed workflow management system that runs according to a set of protocols which utilize a content-based publish/subscribe messaging substrate. The novel features of our framework include elastic management of resources and flexible re-location of management entities to ensure cost-effective and low-latency management operations. Our experimental evaluation shows that the distributed and event-driven approach scales and maintains constant response time for varying management workloads. The average response time for management operations was reduced by 25% using our elastic management cluster approach compared to a fixed management cluster. Management requests were processed up to 10 times faster.

Categories and Subject Descriptors

H.4 [**Information Systems Applications**]: Miscellaneous

General Terms

Algorithms, Design, Experimentation, Management, Performance

1. INTRODUCTION

Many applications require interactions among collaborating partners that operate in different remote locations. For example, complex inter-departmental interactions (as shown in Figure 1) reported to us by an anonymous global electronics company, are not uncommon in the real world. Also, as part of recent initiatives focused on developing smart grids, companies such as Omicron [4] offer distributed control systems that enable interoperation among transmission towers based on the IEC standard protocol set [3]. Such interactions and interoperations can be defined as a workflow whose decomposed tasks can be deployed among the collaborating partners in a decentralized and event-driven runtime framework [26, 48, 34, 40, 49]. In general, the distributed interaction in a collaborative application is referred to as *distributed workflow* or *service choreography* [36].

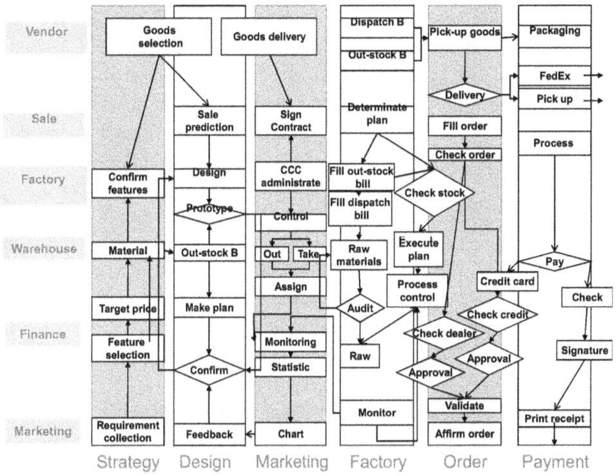

Figure 1: A sketch of a distributed workflow example from a global electronics manufacturing company.

Much research has focused on the development of distributed workflow concepts, including, but not limited to, standardization of the languages for describing interactions such as WS-CDL [43] and for the coordination of interactions such as WS-Coordination [44]; approaches for verification of workflow specifications [14, 18, 21, 29, 39, 11]; entire runtime frameworks [26, 48, 34, 40, 49]; and reliable decomposition techniques [15, 10, 33, 23].

However, related approaches lack insight into the issues involved in the reliable and efficient management of distributed and event-driven workflows, even though the management of these workflows is imperative for a number of reasons. For example, the timely and safe runtime control over workflows such as pause and resume is necessary for immediate handling of any anomalous situations. Discovery of the workflow status is also a critical feature for administrators to check the conformance of the workflow to its specification. While most commercially available centralized workflow processing systems [2, 5, 6, 9] support administrative functions, distributed workflow processing systems often lack equivalent functionality.

The management of distributed workflows is challenging in many respects. First, distributed workflows can typically scale to hundreds of collaborating partners and thousands of concurrent instances, which may generate large management workloads. Hence, management clients may have to issue thousands of status update

DEBS'11, July 11–15, 2011, New York, New York, USA.

inquiries for the purpose of proactively monitoring for failures. Second, the management workload can dynamically change over time and space. For example, in a smart grid, a sudden spike in the power usage may trigger events that are sent to the back-up power generators to produce additional energy. These events will result in a temporary increase in the management workload. Third, interference can occur amongst concurrent management operations which may result in costly damages. Suppose, two management operations of updating a variable associated with some running workflow instance are issued from two different sources. Not processing the operations in order, when they are planned to be executed in sequence, is a violation of the management logic. Lastly, management operations on distributed workflows are sensitive to network delays, as workflow tasks are dispersed across geographically remote locations. The network delays, for example, can hamper the timely discovery or the halting of an anomalous task.

A centralized management system is not sufficient to effectively meet the aforementioned challenges. Centralized management systems have scaling limits when handling large-scale distributed workflows (like the ones shown in Figure 1). They are vulnerable due to the single-point of failure they represent. Also, there can be cases where a single centralized management entity is not desired at all. For example, in a B2B scenario, delegating management functions to one of the collaborating partners or an external provider, may not be desirable for all interacting partners; rather a fully decentralized management approach, where each partner manages its part of the workflow would be a desirable scenario. Even for the workflows within a single business domain, multiple distributed management entities are necessary, if autonomous and localized control over the tasks at different remote locations is required.

In this paper, we introduce a novel *distributed* management system that conforms to a set of administrative operations, known as *Interface-5*, defined as part of the reference model suggested by the Workflow Management Coalition [45]. We further extend the semantics of Interface-5 to account for the concurrent nature of distributed workflows. That is, concurrent management operations can *interfere* with each other and cause semantically conflicting behavior [27]. For example, suppose there are two concurrent management operations to be executed in order. One is to skip a halted task and trigger the task following the halted task. The other succeeding management operation is to resume the halted task. If the operation of resuming the halted task takes place before the skip operation, then the two operations violate the management semantics. In order to avoid this violation, the skip operation should not be interfered with. We articulate this notion of interference in the management context and devise techniques to prevent interference. The techniques include basic in-order processing of management requests and isolating a batch of management operations based on scheduling constraints.

In addition, our distributed management system is built as part of a management infrastructure consisting of agents that form an elastic cluster, such that the agents can adaptively join or leave the cluster to relieve or consolidate the management workload. Also, the agents can flexibly relocate close to the remote task that requires frequent management operations, so that overall response time of management operations is kept minimal. These features are implemented on top of a content-based publish/subscribe broker overlay [20] as an event-driven messaging substrate. The brokers in this model decouple agents as publishers and subscribers in space and time, thus showing that the publish/subscribe paradigm is well-suited as a large-scale distributed workflow management system.

The rest of the paper is organized as follows: Section 2 reviews the key management operations and explains the challenges behind

executing management operations; Section 3 presents the design of the distributed architecture of the management systems and covers implementation details; Section 4 evaluates the feasibility of our approach based on key empirical results derived from our experiment; Section 5 puts our work in the context of existing workflow management systems and Section 6 concludes.

2. MANAGEMENT ACTIONS

This section reviews the primitive workflow management operations proposed by the Workflow Management Coalition specified in Interface-5 [45]. Based on this specification, we introduce *composite operations* that enable the isolated execution of concurrently running primitive operations. We also review the use of the publish/subscribe paradigm for the execution of workflows. Finally, we discuss various corner cases in the executing of management operations specific to distributed workflows.

2.1 Primitive operations

The typical primitive management operations in Interface-5 [45] are summarized in Table 2.1. The operations are applicable to particular runtime instances of an entire workflow, or to individual tasks the workflow is comprised of.

Type	Example
Workflow supervision	Pause, resume, jump, skip an instance or individual tasks. Terminate a workflow or instance. Assign or update attributes in a workflow.
User management	Establish, delete, suspend or amend privileges or roles of users or workgroups.
Audit management	Query, print, start new or delete an audit trail or event log for monitoring purposes.
Resource control	Set, unset or modify concurrency levels of an entire workflow instance or its individual tasks. Interrogate resource control data such as counts, thresholds, usage parameters.
Workflow status function	Open & close a workflow or task query with optionally set filter criteria.

Table 1: List of primitive management operations.

These primitive operations are executed based on the administrative needs. In order to understand how the primitive operations should be executed in a distributed environment, we first review how distributed workflows are processed in a publish/subscribe-based execution systems.

2.2 Distributed Workflow Execution

Our primary focus is on NIÑOS, a publish/subscribe-based distributed workflow execution system that offers concurrent and autonomous execution of tasks deployed across geographically distributed locations [26].

Figure 2 shows the distributed workflow execution architecture where *task agents* (TA) are deployed to the PADRES [20] broker network as both publishers and subscribers. A workflow is first *deployed* by having TAs exchange advertisement and subscription messages that are in the form of conjunctions over Boolean predicates or composite subscriptions. Unlike subscriptions, also referred to as *atomic subscriptions*, a composite subscription is used to correlate publications over time[1]. A composite subscription is

---

[1] A composite subscription is not related to a composite management operation introduced above.

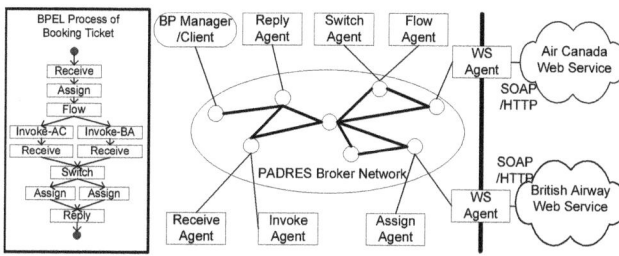

Figure 2: Distributed workflow execution architecture [26].

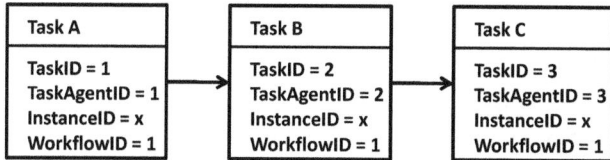

Figure 3: A sample distributed workflow.

needed to express the dependency of a successor task on two or more predecessor tasks, for example.

For example, suppose a sample sequential workflow with an identifier (ID) of "1" is given as shown in Figure 3. During the deployment phase, the TA for Task A advertises the following message.

[class, eq, TASK_STATUS],[workflow, eq, "1"], [taskName, eq, "Task A"],[IID, isPresent],[status, isPresent] [2]

The TA for Task B subscribes to the completion event (SUCCESS) of Task A by issuing the following subscription message.

[class, eq, TASK_STATUS],[workflow, eq, "1"], [taskName, eq, "Task A"],[IID, isPresent], [status, eq, "SUCCESS"].

Once the deployment is completed, the workflow is ready for execution. Workflows can be triggered from anywhere by publishing messages subscribed to by the task in the workflow. For example, the TA for Task A publishes the following message upon successful completion of Task A.

[class, TASK_STATUS], [workflow, "1"], [taskName, "Task A"], [IID, "1"], [status, "SUCCESS"].

Then, TaskAgent2, receives the publication and triggers the execution of Task B.

2.3 Management mechanisms

Assuming the coordination of workflows according to the aforementioned publish/subscribe-based coordination paradigm, we now look into the mechanisms required for executing the primitive management operations listed above. The primitive operations can be classified into three main categories: (1) Workflow modification, (2) discovery and (3) variable update. The discovery operations focus on monitoring the status of workflows, while the modification operations manipulate the workflow and its attributes at runtime. Variable update operations assist users in modifying the data associated with workflows. We select representative operations

---

[2] eq is the equal operator on string attributes. The complete description of the PADRES publish/subscribe syntax is available in http://www.msrg.utoronto.ca/projects/padres/docs/dev_guide.

from each category and explain how they are realized in the publish/subscribe system and how they work around corner cases that arise in an event-driven and distributed environment.

2.3.1 Modification operation: Pause/resume

To pause a particular running instance of a workflow, issuing a message to unadvertise/unsubscribe the completion event for the instance comes to mind. But, note that, during the deployment phase, the TAs do not advertise/subscribe to the value of an instance identifier (IID) of a workflow. The TAs, instead, advertise/subscribe to all IIDs of a workflow by specifying the following predicate, [IID,isPresent]. This is to avoid the re-deployment of the tasks when a new instance is triggered.

Therefore, a two-phase execution of the pause operation can be considered. First TAs unadvertise/unsubscribe to the events produced by the workflow, W. Then, TAs re-advertise/re-subscribe to exclude the instance that should be paused by using the not equal operator (neq) in the predicate such as, [IID,neq,<instance ID>]. However, during the first phase, instances other than <instance ID> are going to be disrupted as unadvertisement/unsubscription cause the completion events to be dropped, unless the TAs are synchronized amongst themselves through some coordination mechanism. Even given that coordination would be enforced, the approach of removing and reissuing advertisement and subscription messages is still not desirable, since the unadvertisement and unsubscriptions messages have to traverse through the network, and it can be expensive to delete and insert advertisements and subscriptions at the brokers on which TAs run.

A simpler and more cost-effective approach is to apply the pause mechanism on the broker event queues, as shown in Figure 4. After the pause request is received, each TA holds any events with the ID of the instance that has to be paused on a separate wait queue. A resume operation is symmetric to the pause operation such that TAs flush the wait queue that contains the paused events upon receiving the resume request. An unintended outcome can occur due

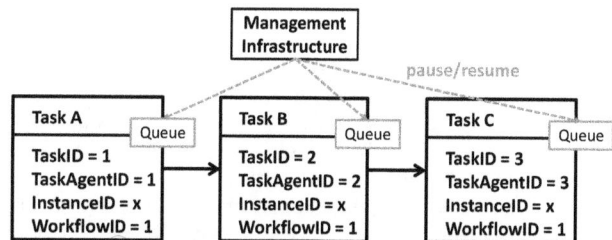

Figure 4: Execution of pause/resume operations.

to propagation delays. For example, given the sample workflow in Figure 3, assume that a pause operation of an instance at Task B. This command can fail, if the instance completes execution before the pause command actually reaches the TA running Task B. A few ways to solve this problem include: (1) Querying the status of the workflow just before pausing; (2) pausing a more distant task which has a lower chance of completing before the command reaches it. For instance, Task C can be paused instead of Task B, when Task A is currently being executed; (3) broadcasting the pause operation to all the TAs responsible for that instance or workflow and performing that operation at the earliest possible opportunity.

2.3.2 Modification operation: Skip

A running instance of a workflow, can skip over a task. For example, in Figure 5, Task B is to be skipped and then Task C is to be triggered instead upon the completion of Task A. The skip operation is performed as follows: (1) the TA for Task B halts the task of instance I by simply ignoring the completion event of instance I from the TA for Task A; (2) the TA for Task A newly advertises a completion event for instance I; (3) the TA for Task C subscribes to the event the TA for Task A publishes.

Note that the TA for Task B is still subscribed for the completion event coming from the TA for Task A. Thus, the events keep getting delivered unnecessarily to the TA for Task B, which may generate unnecessary messages. In order to prevent this, the TA for Task B, can unsubscribe to the completion events from the TA for Task A, and then re-subscribe to the completion events from the instances of the workflow W except the instance I using the not equal operation in the predicate as introduced in the previous section. This entails the risk of dropping the messages for instances other than I. To prevent the message drops, the TA for Task A must hold the completion events during the preparation of the skip operation. The overhead of the synchronization in this case is acceptable as the synchronization is applicable only to the TAs for the to-be-skipped (Task B) and skipping (Task A) tasks.

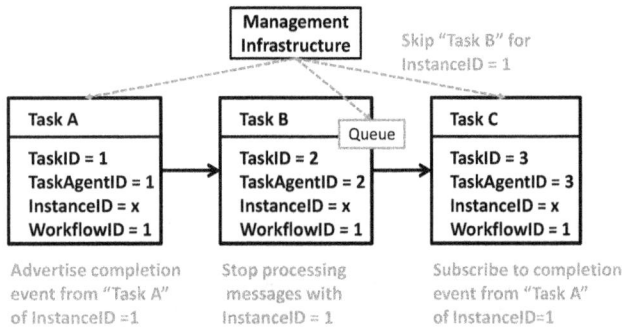

Figure 5: Execution of skip operations

2.3.3 Discovery

Each TA is responsible for the information regarding the instances it is currently executing or pausing. Information about completed instances are handled by the TA responsible for the final task of the workflow. Alternatively, a logically centralized service could be used to store and deliver all this information.

Discovery operations do not create concurrency issues with other management operations. However, there is a possibility that queries relating to concurrently executing workflow instances are ignored in the de-centralized case. Revisit the sample workflow in Figure 3, assume that Task A has completed and execution transitions to Task B for instance x. During this transition time, suppose a query for concurrently executing instances is issued to all TAs. While, execution transitions, both the TA for Task A and the TA for Task B do not include instance x in the query response. This is because, from the perspective of both TAs during the transition time, there is no concurrently executing task for the queried instance (instance x). To handle this concurrency problem, the TAs keep ownership of task instances until the succeeding TA takes ownership upon receipt of the trigger message.

2.3.4 Variable updates

This class of operations can support accessing or modifying variables and attributes associated with workflow instances and entire workflows. For example, user management operations and certain resource control operations such as set, unset, and modify of concurrency levels can be performed through variable updates. This

class of operations is discussed in detail by Li *et al.* in the context of the NIÑOS architecture [26].

2.4 Composite Operations

So far, we have looked into the mechanism for the execution of primitive operations. Primitive operations are issued by multiple management clients concurrently. For example, suppose two management clients (Client 1 and Client 2) issue operations on a workflow instance (l=1), as shown in Figure 6(a). The operations can be interleaved depending on the order in which they are requested. However, this can be unsafe as the operations may semantically conflict with each other. Suppose one client issues *"pause instance - amend privilege of a user - resume instance"* operations, while another client issues *"fetch instance status - resume"* that are executed between the *"pause instance"* and *"amend privilege"* operations. In such a case the user whose privilege was supposed to be amended can continue to execute a task of the workflow instance without properly updated privileges. To prevent such interference amongst multiple clients, we introduce *composite operations* in this section.

The management client may want a sequence of primitive operations on a set of instances to be executed as a batch, such that the batch does not interfere with operations issued by other management clients. We refer to a batch of primitive operations as a *composite operation*. The *interference* is more precisely defined in Definition 1.

Definition 1. A primitive or composite management operation that is applied to a set of instances $\mathbb{I}_1$, *interferes* with another management operation that is applied to a set of instance $\mathbb{I}_2$, if $\mathbb{I}_1 \cap \mathbb{I}_2 \neq \phi$.

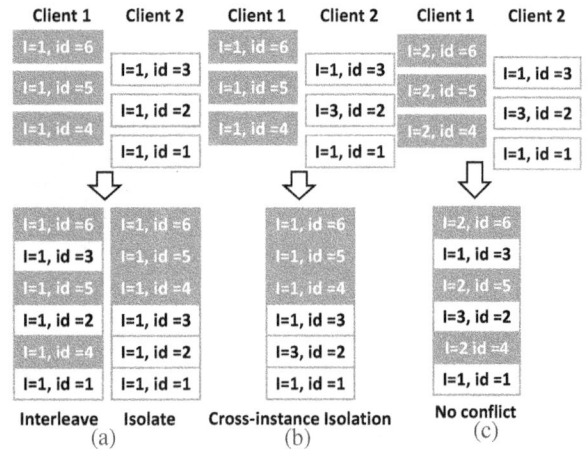

Figure 6: Example of isolation through composite operations.

Figure 6 illustrates isolation of concurrent management operations through the enforcement of composite operations. In Figure 6(a), suppose each client issues three management operations on the same workflow instance (l=1). In order to avoid that operations from the two clients interleave, the operations issued by Client 2 are blocked until all operations by Client 1 are completed. The operations by Client 1 are executed in a batch and they are not *interfered* with the operations of Client 2. Note that, as Definition 1 specifies, the composite operations can be applied across many instances as well. In such a case, if the set of instances intersects between two management operations, one of the management operations has to be blocked. For example, as shown in Figure 6(b), Client 2 is blocked, because Client 2 has two management oper-

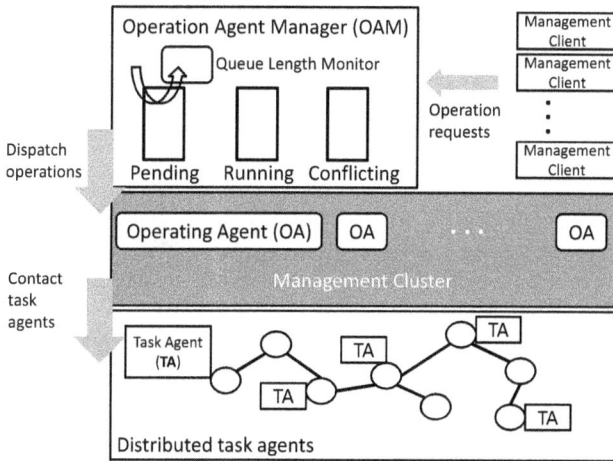

Figure 7: Architecture of the management cluster of OAs managed by an OAM.

ations (id=1 and id=3) on the workflow instance, I=1, which can intersect with the management operations of Client 1 (id=4, id=5 and id=6). However, if there is no set of instances that intersect between two management operations, then the two management operations can run fully concurrently. For instance, as shown in Figure 6(c), Client 1 and Client 2 issue management operations that do not overlap on a set of instances, therefore there is no concern for a conflict.

Composite operations trade off degraded concurrency for a conflict-free execution of management operations through isolation. A composite operation is similar in spirit to a transaction. However, at least for now, our composite operations do not support atomicity, consistency and durability, which is subject to future work.

In the following section, we discuss the distributed architecture of the management infrastructure.

3. MANAGEMENT INFRASTRUCTURE

In the previous section, we presented the mechanism of executing management operations over distributed workflows. A centralized management entity could interact with the TAs to issue management requests. However, a centralized approach may not scale and suffer from a single-point failure. Instead, we develop an event-driven and distributed management infrastructure where the management agents flexibly join, leave and move in an on-demand fashion.

3.1 Architecture

Our management infrastructure is built on top of the publish/subscribe-based workflow execution system described in Section 2.2. The management infrastructure consists of three main entities: Operation agents (OA), operation agent managers (OAM) and management clients (MC). The OA is responsible for dispatching management requests directly to the TAs (task agents). OAs form an elastic cluster managed by the OAM that distributes management requests from the MC amongst the available OAs. By default an OA cluster is provisioned for a single workflow, and the OAM keeps the mapping between the OA cluster and the associated workflows. OAs can also be clustered flexibly by the type of operation they perform. There can be multiple OAM-OA clusters in the entire system. Figure 7 shows the interactions among the different entities in more detail. The underlying communication substrate is the PADRES publish/subscribe system that allows all entities to be loosely-coupled

and benefit from location transparency [20]. The detailed specification of the publish/subscribe messages that are exchanged among the entities are available in the online appendix [22].

3.2 Scheduling of management operations

We provide the mechanism of processing the management request made concurrently by the MCs.

Primitive operations: Here, we explain how the primitive operations are scheduled. First, upon receipt of the management request for a particular instance I from some MC, the OAM checks if any previously issued management operation on I is still running by checking the list of running instances (*Running*) and pending operations (*Pending*) that are kept by the OAM. If there is already a management operation running or pending for I, then the current management operation is enqueued in the *Conflicting* queue (Algorithm 1:1-2), otherwise, the management operation is assigned to an OA that is available (Algorithm 1:5).

Algorithm 1: dispatch(op)

1 **if** *runningList contains op.instanceID || pendingQueue contains op.instanceID* **then**
2   conflictQueue.enqueue(op);
3 **else**
4   **if** *an OA is available* **then**
5   runningList.add (op.instanceID);
6   **else**
7   pendingQueue.enueue(op);

Algorithm 2: fetchNextOp

1 **for** $op \in conflictQueue$ **do**
2   **if** $\neg$ *(pendingQueue contains op.instanceID || runningList contains op.instanceID)* **then**
3   **if** *op is first for instanceID* **then**
4   conflictQueue.dequeue(op);
5   pendingQueue.enqueue(op);
6 opPending = pendingQueue.dequeue;
7 runningList.add(opPending.instanceID);

If there are no OAs available, a management operation will be put in the *Pending* queue as long as the operation does not conflict with the operation currently running or pending (Algorithm 1:7).

When, an OA becomes available the OAM first scans through the *Conflicting* queue to identify the first operation of any instance that does not conflict with the operations pending or running. The operation that does not conflict with any existing operations are enqueued in the *Pending* queue. Then, the OAM dequeues an operation from the *Pending* queue and assigns it to an available OA. The OAM fetches the earliest operation from either the *Pending* or *Conflicting* queue (Algorithm 2). This scheduling mechanism satisfies the following property.

Property 1. *Cross-client ordering of concurrent operations on an instance*: Suppose a pair of management operations, m_0 and m_1, for a given instance I are issued by two different clients. If the operations are received by an OAM, where m_0 is received before m_1, then the OAM must block m_1 until m_0 completes its execution.

Property 1 ensures that an operation on a particular instance is mutually and exclusively executed by a single OA in order to prevent out-of-order processing of concurrent operations through parallel OAs. An OA has time-outs on each operation to prevent infinite waits and consequently suffer from deadlocks. However, a high degree of concurrency can still be achieved if operations on different instances are issued concurrently.

Note that not all management operations have to be scheduled to be executed by an OA. For example, concurrent queries for workflow state, *i.e.*, discovery requests, do not have to be synchronized. Also, concurrency among variable update requests is already handled through the use of *variable agents* in NIÑOS[26]. For data stored in attached historic data stores (i.e., databases), databases themselves provide concurrency solutions which can be leveraged by a TA. Hence, an MC can contact variable agents, TAs or database service agents directly for these management operations. However, even these operations can be a part of composite operations which have to be scheduled through the OAM as explained in the following section.

If the same operation repeats itself either in the *Pending* queue or *Running* list, then only one of these operations will be executed to eliminate duplicates[3]. For example, if two management clients send commands to turn on the same device simultaneously, then only one of these commands is executed.

Composite operations: In case a batch of operations on multiple instances has to be executed without interruption, a composite operation can be used as explained in Section 2.4. Scheduling of composite operations is as follows. All primitive operations in a composite operation are issued by an MC in sequence. Each operation in the sequence is tagged with a composite operation ID. The operation is executed one at a time based on the availability of the OAs, while the other operations are put in the *Pending* queue. Once the last operation in the composite operation completes, the composite operation ID is removed from the *Running* list. Any other primitive or composite operations issued by other MCs are put in the *Conflicting* queue if they conflict with the previously submitted composite operations. Otherwise, they are put in the *Pending* queue. This scheduling mechanism for the composite operations satisfies the following property.

Property 2.*Per client and per instance set isolation:* Let a composite operation, m_0, in the sequence of primitive operations, p_0, $p_1, \ldots, p_i$, executed on a set of instances, $\mathbb{I}_0$, of a workflow, then any primitive or composite operations on $\mathbb{I}_1$ following p_0, such that $\mathbb{I}_0 \cap \mathbb{I}_1 \neq \phi$, is blocked until m_0 completes its execution. Each primitive operation in the composite operation also executes sequentially.

Property 2 ensures isolation and operation ordering of a composite operation by locking the instance set, $\mathbb{I}_0 \cup \mathbb{I}_1$. This degrades the level of concurrency.

A stronger isolation level applies for the case when the composite operation consists of a sequence of primitive operations on the set of instances across different workflows as stated in Property 3.

Property 3.*Per client and cross workflow isolation:* Let a composite operation, m_0, in the sequence of primitive operations, p_0, $p_1, \ldots, p_i$, execute on a set of different workflows, $\mathbb{W}_0$, then any primitive or composite operation on $\mathbb{W}_1$ following p_0, such that $\mathbb{W}_0 \cap \mathbb{W}_1 \neq \phi$, is blocked until m_0 completes its execution. Each primitive operation in the composite operation also executes sequentially.

Property 3 can be easily supported by having a single OAM handle multiple workflows. However, provisioning a single OAM for all the workflows in the system limits the scalability of the management infrastructure. Thus, multiple OAMs can be assigned to a subset of the workflows, and the OAMs can coordinate themselves to enforce isolation.

3.3 Deployment and dynamic migration

The communication channels among OAM, OAs and TAs are set at deployment time by using subscriptions and advertisements. Each TA subscribes to management operation command messages from OAs, and advertises management operation command response messages to the OAs.

On the other hand, OAs subscribe to management operation command response messages and advertise management operation command messages. The *status* attribute in the corresponding subscription or advertisement has three possible values: *completed*, *paused* and *in progress*. OAs and OAM exchange subscriptions and advertisements, via the *OpControlLogic* message class to set up the management control logic [22].

One of the challenges in building a distributed management infrastructure mentioned in Section 1 is caused by network delays inherent to the distributed character of the architecture. The response time of management operations can be sensitive to the location of the OAs that interact with the TAs. To address this challenge, we deploy the OAs and the OAM in a location on the underlying publish/subscribe-based messaging systems where the average distance between the OAM and the TAs is minimal. Given n TAs, the average distance between OAM and TAs is formulated as follows:

$$\frac{\sum_i^n (d(OAM, TA_i) + d(OA_j, OAM))}{n}, \quad (3.1)$$

where d(x,y) denotes the distance between x, y measured in message substrate overlay hop counts. Alternatively, other metrics could be used. OAs can be initially co-located with the OAM or placed in adjacent locations. This is a static approach that cannot account for the dynamic management workloads that can be skewed towards particular TAs over some period. To address varying workloads over time, OAM and OAs can be dynamically migrated towards the TAs that experience heavy traffic, so that overall latency in executing the management operations can be further reduced. Dynamic migration is based on the metric in Equation 3.2 which adapts Equation 3.1 to include the workload information:

$$\frac{\sum_{i,j}^{n,m} (w \times d(TA_i, OA_j) + d(OA_j, OAM))}{n}, \quad (3.2)$$

where w is the workload of TA_i that is measured as the number of management operations that are executed. The OAM maintains this information which is made available at deployment time. At deployment time, not only OAMs but also OAs are migrated to the new location through the movement protocol developed by Hu *et al.* [24]. The static approach in Equation 3.1 assumes that the workload is uniform, thus w is 1. The transactional concerns of the message delivery during the movement are atomicity, consistency, and isolation properties which are supported through the movement protocol. Hu *et al.* empirically proved the scalability of the protocol as it yielded constant average movement latency under 5 seconds in terms of topology size and the number of clients to move. Therefore, the movement protocol can be used to enforce service level agreement (SLA) [32]. In Section 4, we show the benefit of the dynamic migration in the management infrastructure.

3.4 Elastic management cluster

We assume that a pool of resources in form of a cloud, for example, is available throughout the enterprise network, which allows our management infrastructure to flexibly allocate OAs to handle high loads, or consolidate load during periods of low utilization of the existing OAs. A feedback loop is built to the OAM that monitors the queue length and determines the need for changing the management capacity through allocation or consolidation. We reassert the need of the publish/subscribe substrate, since dynamically joining OAs can seamlessly integrate themselves to the management cluster by simply issuing the set of advertisements and subscriptions to talk to the OAM whose location is transparent to the OAs.

4. EVALUATION

This section presents the experimental evaluation of our management infrastructure and the management mechanisms itself. The management infrastructure has been implemented on top of the open source PADRES[4] content-based publish/subscribe system. The management infrastructure was evaluated on a Dell PowerEdge 2900 with two quad-core 3.00 GHz processors and 16GB of RAM.

An acyclic and connected publish/subscribe broker overlay was constructed to enable asynchronous communication among the management entities. Five TAs were deployed to the overlay to process sequential workflow instances. Up to 12 OAs were utilized in a dynamically growing and shrinking management cluster managed by a single OAM. Management operations were issued at varying frequencies as high as 10 messages per second.

Given this evaluation setting, we conducted the following experiments: we profiled the performance of modification and discovery operations to assess the overhead of the management cluster; we analyzed the effect of an elastic management cluster; we observed the performance trade-off between isolation and concurrency by varying the number of conflicts in the management workload; and finally we demonstrated the effects of dynamic migration and an elastic management cluster.

4.1 Execution latency of primitive operations

This experiment evaluates the latency of executing two types of primitive operations: Workflow modification and discovery. The average, minimum and maximum execution latencies were measured by an MC that first initiates the management operations. The number of OAs was fixed at 5; all of which were managed by a single OAM. As shown in Figure 8, the management cluster was deployed to a overlay of PADRES brokers (n1, n2 and n3). The management cluster was placed on the location where the distance (Formula 3.1) between the OAM and each of the 5 TAs was constant, so that the effect of the network delay is controlled. Management operations were issued at a rate of at most 2 messages per second to emulate the actions of a human administrator. As shown in Figure 9, on average, a workflow modification operation such as pause, resume and skip took approximately 60 ms, while a discovery operation took approximately 10 ms. The 50 ms execution latency gap between the two different types of operations represents the overhead of the management cluster, since modification operations are processed through a management cluster of an OAM and OAs, while discovery operations directly communicate with the TAs as explained in Section 2. The execution latency for both categories of management operations remained constant during the experiment. This is because the management cluster was not saturated due to sufficient capacity (5 OAs). The elasticity of

[4]Available for download at http://padres.msrg.org.

our management cluster to handle overloads is demonstrated in the following experiment.

We also observe that the execution latency for any type of management operation can increase, if the TAs are overloaded. For example, if a TA is involved in a workflow that goes through frequent iterations, then, the TA may not promptly respond to the request from the management cluster or MCs. As optimization, management operations can be processed at a higher priority at the publish/subscribe brokers, so that more critical management operations can be delivered to the TAs more quickly.

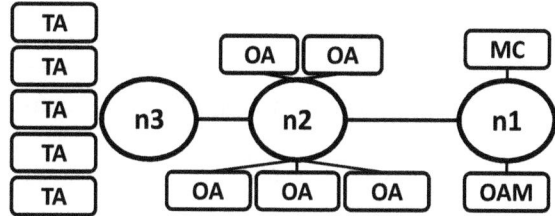

Figure 8: The topology for evaluating execution latency of primitive operations.

4.2 Effect of elastic management cluster

The effectiveness of a management cluster is measured by two parameters: The execution latency and the overhead of running the cluster. A more effective approach has both lower latency and lower overhead when faced with varying workloads. Execution latency is measured for different frequencies of incoming requests by using the management client (MC). The amount of resources used is measured by the size of the cluster, more specifically, by the number of OAs present in the management cluster. To evaluate both parameters, we compared two different clusters: one with an elastic cluster and the other with a fixed number (4) of OAs. The other settings were the same as in Section 4.1. As shown in Figure 10, the MC constantly tried to saturate the OAM with modification requests at increasing frequencies. This in turn increased the queue lengths within the OAM. So, the OAM grew the management cluster (by adding an OA) and kept the response time nearly constant. For any given management request frequency, the elastic management cluster had a better average execution latency of 45 ms when compared to 60 ms of the static management cluster (as observed in Figure 9). The MC sent a batch of 20 requests for every frequency. The duration represents the time interval in which all the requests of a given batch were completed.

4.3 Trade-off between isolation and concurrency

To evaluate the trade-off between isolation and concurrency, a key scheduling constraint, the number of conflicts to resolve, was modified while keeping the number of management requests per second constant. Given the same setting as the experiment in Section 4.1, the MC increased concurrency by issuing modification requests to more workflow instances so that the chance of interference, as defined in Definition 1, was reduced.

Figure 11 shows a sharp drop in execution latency at a concurrency level of 2. After which there is a gradual decrease from 58 ms at concurrency level 2 to 50 ms at concurrency level 10. The benefit of increased concurrency is reduced because the parallelism is bounded by the fixed number of OAs in the cluster, and each OA can process only one management request at a time. To let the management infrastructure scale and exhibit higher speedup, we have

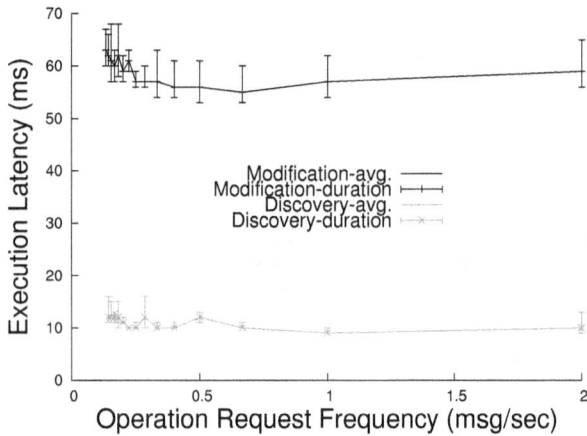

Figure 9: Execution latency trend of different primitive operations.

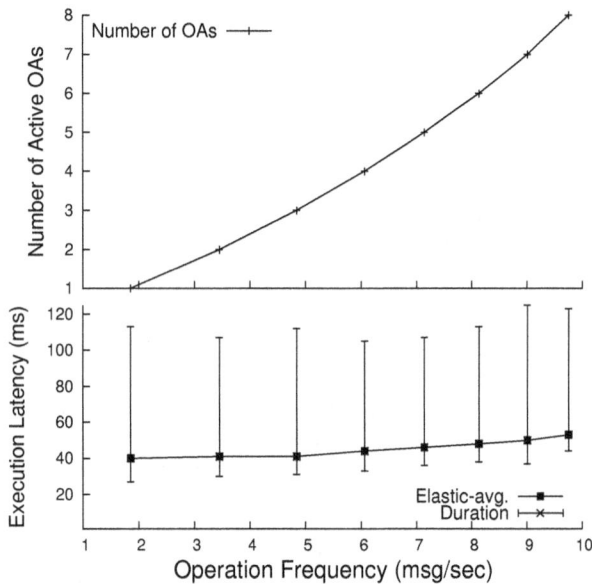

Figure 10: The effect of an elastic management cluster.

already demonstrated the growing and shrinking of the management cluster in Section 4.2.

4.4 Effect of dynamic migration

To highlight the benefit of dynamic migration, we moved the management entities along a flat publish/subscribe broker overlay to systematically vary the average distance from the OAM to TAs, as shown in Figure 12. OAs and OAM are connected to an edge broker (e.g., n19, n20). The locations of MC and TAs are fixed. When the load is uniformly random, (i.e., $w = 1$ in Equation 3.2), n9 would be the optimal location for all OAs and the OAM.

Two comparison runs for randomized requests with varying frequency were performed and their execution latencies were measured. One of the two runs had a random placement of the management cluster. This was emulated by using uniformly randomized delays (between 20 ms to 70 ms) in each OA and OAM. This was to emulate their offset from the optimal deployment position. In the other run, the cluster had dynamic migration and the entire cluster

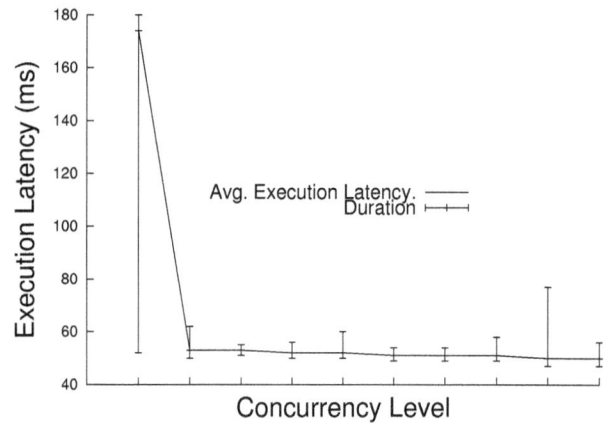

Figure 11: The effect of isolation on performance.

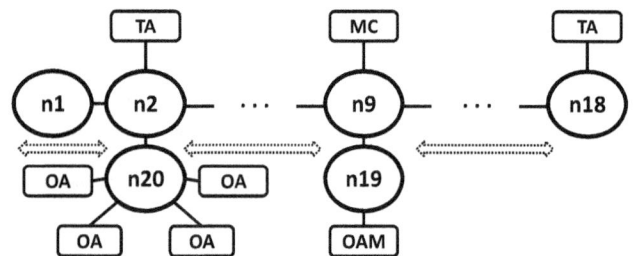

Figure 12: The dynamic migration experiment setting.

was attached to broker n9, so there were no additional emulated delays.

In Figure 13, when dynamic migration feature was enabled the execution latency was approximately 10 times lower than the execution latency with random deployment.

5. RELATED WORK

In this section, we put our work in the context of workflow management systems, distributed workflow processing systems, and management system from other domains that adopt publish/subscribe-style processing.

Workflow management systems: Notable commercial workflow management systems are IBM WebSphere MQ Workflow [2], Oracle Business Process Management [5], Sage ERP X3 [6], Symantec Workflow [9] and SAP Netweaver [7]. These products offer process change functions and real-time monitoring/analysis of process instances. The management is done in a centralized fashion and does not support distributed management and execution of workflows.

Event-driven monitoring approaches for the distributed Web services are found in [47, 28, 25, 38]. These approaches express policies and requirements in the event calculus, so that inconsistent events can be detected. For assessing performance interference, Taiani *et al.* provide a black-box approach for profiling concurrent and composite applications on grid [41]. These systems are focused mostly on discovery and monitoring features. Our approach goes beyond supporting discovery and monitoring operations; we aim at supporting the full pallet of workflow execution management, especially targeting distributed workflows.

Several existing management systems focus on ensuring isolation and consistency for transactional Web services in a workflow.

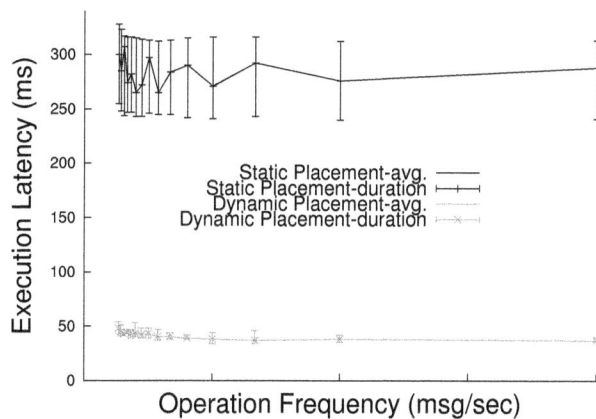

Figure 13: The effect of dynamic migration.

Choi *et al.* developed a management system that detects and fixes inconsistent states in loosely coupled Web services [17]. Paul *et al.* [35] and Puustjarvi *et al.* [37] focus on ensuring isolation properties in Web service transactions while maintaining acceptable levels of service and a high degree of concurrency. Alrifai *et al.* [13] introduce an extension to the Web service transaction protocol to ensure consistency of data when independent business transactions access data concurrently under relaxed transactional properties. These approaches focus on the reliable execution of transactional Web services, which is an orthogonal concern to the problem we address. In this paper, we focus on enabling different levels of isolation for executing concurrent management operations.

Distributed workflow processing systems: Distributed workflow processing has been studied to address scalability, fault resilience, and enterprise-wide workflow management [12, 46, 31]. Alonso *et al.* present a detailed design of a distributed workflow management system [12]. Muth *et al.* [31] describe a behavior preserving transformation of a centralized activity chart, representing a workflow, into an equivalent partitioned one. The transformation is realized in the MENTOR system [46]. The objective of this work is to enable the parallel execution of the partitioned flow, while minimizing synchronization messages, and to analytically prove certain properties of the partitioned flow [31]. Another parallelization approach is based on control flow and data flow analysis that are used to parallelize the business process so that the highest possible concurrency can be achieved [33]. Casati *et al.* present an approach to integrate an existing business processes into a larger workflow [16]. They defined event points in business processes where events can be received or sent using a centralized publish/subscribe model. The interaction of existing business processes is synchronized by event communication. These approaches focus on the processing a workflow according to a specification in a distributed environment; they often runtime re-configuration and control capabilities.

Li *et al.* [26] propose a workflow processing approach operating in a distributed environment, which partially addresses runtime management. In [26], activities in a business process are decoupled and are executed by activity agents, which are publish/subscribe clients, and the communication between agents is performed in a content-based publish/subscribe broker overlay network. Basic workflow supervisory functions such as pause and resume are supported, but at a coarse-grained level, *i.e.*, pausing or resuming entire activity agents. In this work, we extended the management capa-

bility in [26] to support a much more finer-grained level of control over individual tasks and workflow instances, also operating across different workflows.

Publish/Subscribe-based management systems: There is a proven track record for the successful adoption of publish/subscribe systems in supporting distributed applications with monitoring and control capabilities. Mukherjee *et al.*, for example, used a publish/subscribe system to monitor and detect intrusions [30]. Tock *et al.* built a stock-market monitoring system [42]. Fawcett *et al.* employed publish/subscribe to detect changes to a business activity [19]. For the distributed orchestration of interoperable electric devices, IEC 61850 specifies protocols such as the Generic Substation Event (GSE), which are used for real-time transfer of event data [3]. GSE is a publish/subscribe-based communication platform adopted by companies such as ABB and Siemens [1, 8]. The event-driven monitoring and control by means of a publish/subscribe system in the above listed approaches enables the asynchronous and scalable management of applications, properties directly founded in the publish/subscribe-based realizations.

6. CONCLUSIONS

We presented and evaluated an approach for the fine-grained management of event-driven and distributed workflows. Our approach employs a publish/subscribe messaging substrate that supports location transparency and asynchronous communication among all management entities and task agents. The management entities can flexibly join or leave the management infrastructure depending on the management workload. In addition, management entities can migrate to locations to reduce overall latency of management operations.

The experimental evaluation shows that our distributed and event-driven approach scales and maintains constant execution latency for varying management workloads. Also, the average execution latency was reduced by 25% using our elastic management cluster approach. The execution latency with dynamic migration enabled was substantially lower than without migration.

7. ACKNOWLEDGEMENT

This research was supported by IBM's Center for Advanced Studies and Bell Canada's Bell University Laboratories R&D program, and the Natural Sciences and Engineering Research Council of Canada. We would also like to thank our colleagues including Vinod Muthusamy and Chunyang Ye for providing valuable feedback on this manuscript.

8. REFERENCES

[1] ABB control systems. http://www.abb.com/product/us/9AAC910002.aspx.

[2] IBM WebSphere MQ workflow. http://www-01.ibm.com/software/integration/wmqwf/features/.

[3] IEC 61850. http://www.iec.ch/.

[4] Omicron GOOSE configuration. http://www.omicron.at/en/products/pro/communication-protocols/iec-61850/goose-configuration/.

[5] Oracle business process management. http://www.oracle.com/us/technologies/bpm/index.html.

[6] Sage ERP X3. http://www.sageerpx3.com/.

[7] SAP Netweaver business process management. http://www.sap.com/platform/netweaver/index.epx.

[8] SPPA-E3000 operational improvement and integration. http://www.energy.siemens.com/fi/en/automation/power-generation/operational-improvement-integration.htm.

[9] Symantec Workflow.
http://www.symantec.com/connect/workflow.

[10] W. M. P. d. Aalst and T. Basten. Inheritance of workflows: an approach to tackling problems related to change. *Theoretical Computer Science*, 270(1-2):125–203, 2002.

[11] W. M. P. v. d. Aalst, M. Dumas, C. Ouyang, A. Rozinat, and E. Verbeek. Conformance checking of service behavior. *ACM ToIT*, 8(3):1–30, 2008.

[12] G. Alonso, D. Agrawal, A. E. Abbadi, C. Mohan, R. Gunthor, and M. Kamath. Exotica/FMQM: A persistent message-based architecture for distributed workflow management. In *IFIP*, 1995.

[13] M. Alrifai, P. Dolog, and W. Nejdl. Transactions concurrency control in web service environment. In *ECWS*, 2006.

[14] R. Alur, K. Etessami, and M. Yannakakis. Realizability and verification of msc graphs. *Theoretical Computer Science*, 331(1):97–114, 2005.

[15] M. Broy, I. H. Krüger, and M. Meisinger. A formal model of services. *ACM ToSM*, 16(1):5, 2007.

[16] F. Casati and A. Discenza. Modeling and managing interactions among business processes. *Journal of Systems Integration*, 10(2):145–168, Apr. 2001.

[17] S. Choi, H. Kim, H. Jang, J. Kim, S. M. Kim, J. Song, and Y.-J. Lee. A framework for ensuring consistency of web services transactions. *Information and Software Technology*, 50:684–696, 2008.

[18] G. Decker, A. Barros, F. M. Kraft, and N. Lohmann. Non-desynchronizable service choreographies. In *ICSOC*, 2008.

[19] T. Fawcett et al. Activity monitoring: Noticing interesting changes in behavior. In *SIGKDD*, 1999.

[20] E. Fidler et al. Distributed publish/subscribe for workflow management. In *ICFI*, 2005.

[21] X. Fu, T. Bultan, and J. Su. Synchronizability of conversations among web services. *IEEE ToSE*, 31(12):1042–1055, 2005.

[22] S. Ganesan, Y. Yoon, and H.-A. Jacobsen. Pub/Sub implementation of the management infrastructure protocols. Technical report, March 2011.

[23] H. Giese, S. Burmester, W. Schäfer, and O. Oberschelp. Modular design and verification of component-based mechatronic systems with online-reconfiguration. In *FSE*, 2004.

[24] S. Hu, V. Muthusamy, G. Li, and H.-A. Jacobsen. Transactional mobility in distributed content-based publish/subscribe systems. In *ICDCS*, 2009.

[25] S. Kulvatunyou, J. Durand, J. Woo, and H. BenMalek. Governing web services using event-driven monitoring. In *IEEE EDOC*, 2007.

[26] G. Li, V. Muthusamy, and H.-A. Jacobsen. A distributed service-oriented architecture for business process execution. *ACM TWeb*, 4(1):1–33, 2010.

[27] L. T. Ly, S. Rinderle, and P. Dadam. Integration and verification of semantic constraints in adaptive process management systems. *Data Knowl. Eng.*, 64(1):3–23, 2008.

[28] K. Mahbub and G. Spanoudakis. Run-time monitoring of requirements for systems composed of web-services: Initial implementation and evaluation experience. In *ICWS*, 2005.

[29] M. Montali, M. Pesic, W. M. P. v. d. Aalst, F. Chesani, P. Mello, and S. Storari. Declarative specification and verification of service choreographiess. *ACM TWeb*, 4(1):1–62, 2010.

[30] B. Mukherjee et al. Network intrusion detection. *IEEE Network*, 1994.

[31] P. Muth, D. Wodtke, J. Weisenfels, A. K. Dittrich, and G. Weikum. From centralized workflow specification to distributed workflow execution. *Journal of Intelligent Information Systems*, 10(2):159–184, 1998.

[32] V. Muthusamy, H.-A. Jacobsen, T. Chau, A. Chan, and P. Coulthard. SLA-driven business process management in soa. In *CASCON*, 2009.

[33] M. G. Nanda, S. Chandra, and V. Sarkar. Decentralizing execution of composite web services. In *OOPSLA*, 2004.

[34] S. Overbeek, B. Klievink, and M. Janssen. A flexible, event-driven, service-oriented architecture for orchestrating service delivery. *IEEE Intelligent Systems*, 24(5):31–41, 2009.

[35] D. Paul, F. Henskens, and M. Hannaford. Isolation and web services transactions. *ICPDCAT*, 2007.

[36] C. Peltz. Web services orchestration and choreography. *Computer*, 36(10):46–52, 2003.

[37] J. Puustjarvi. Concurrency control in web service orchestration. In *CIT*, 2008.

[38] M. Rouached, O. Perrin, and C. Godart. A contract-based approach for monitoring collaborative web services using commitments in the event calculus. In *WISE*. 2005.

[39] G. Salaün and T. Bultan. Realizability of choreographies using process algebra encodings. In *IFM*, 2009.

[40] S. Tai, T. A. Mikalsen, and I. Rouvellou. Using message-oriented middleware for reliable web services messaging. In *WES*, 2003.

[41] F. Taiani, M. Hiltunen, and R. Schlichting. The impact of web service integration on grid performance. In *HPDC*, 2005.

[42] Y. Tock et al. Hierarchical clustering of message flows in a multicast data dissemination system. In *PDCS*, 2005.

[43] W3C. Web services choreography description language version 1.0, 2005. http://www.w3.org/TR/ws-cdl-10.

[44] W3C. Web services coordination, 2007. http://docs.oasis-open.org/ws-tx/wscoor/.

[45] WFMC. The workflow reference model, 1995. http://www.wfmc.org/reference-model.html.

[46] D. Wodtke, J. Weißenfels, G. Weikum, and A. K. Dittrich. The mentor project: Steps toward enterprise-wide workflow management. In *ICDE*, 1996.

[47] Z. Wu, Y. Liu, and L. Wang. Dynamic policy conflict analysis in operational intensive trust services for cross-domain federations. *ICIAS*, 2009.

[48] Y. Yoon, C. Ye, and H.-A. Jacobsen. A distributed framework for reliable and efficient service choreographies. In *WWW*, 2011.

[49] S. Zaplata, K. Hamann, K. Kottke, and W. Lamersdorf. Flexible execution of distributed business processes based on process instance migration. *Journal of Systems Integration (JSI)*, 1(3):3–16, 7 2010.

End-to-End Reliability for Best-Effort Content-Based Publish/Subscribe Networks

Amirhossein Malekpour
University of Lugano
Lugano, Switzerland
malekpoa@usi.ch

Antonio Carzaniga
University of Lugano
Lugano, Switzerland
antonio.carzaniga@usi.ch

Fernando Pedone
University of Lugano
Lugano, Switzerland
fernando.pedone@usi.ch

Giovanni Toffetti Carughi
University of Lugano
Lugano, Switzerland
toffettg@usi.ch

ABSTRACT

When it comes to reliability, there are two main categories of distributed publish/subscribe systems: reliable systems and best-effort systems. The former gives the highest priority to guaranteed and ordered delivery while the latter aims for high throughput and low delays. We propose a method to improve the delivery guarantees of the basic unreliable service offered by a best-effort publish/subscribe system. This method does not require any modification to the system's protocols or broker software, and instead simply uses the system's publish/subscribe API. The method is based on a technique, similar to reliable multicast, that enables subscribers to cooperatively recover lost messages. We experimentally demonstrate the effectiveness and performance of our recovery scheme in the presence of frequent message losses, and show that it enables subscribers to recover more than 70% of lost messages with minimum negative effects on the overall network performance.

Categories and Subject Descriptors

C.2.4 [**Computer Systems Organization**]: Computer-Communication Networks—*Distributed Systems*

General Terms

Reliability,Performance

Keywords

Content-based networking, publish/subscribe

1. INTRODUCTION

Message oriented middleware, and in particular content-based publish/subscribe systems, have a wide range of applications in enterprise environments, in areas such as process

Permission to make digital or hard copies of all or part of this work for personal or classroom use is granted without fee provided that copies are not made or distributed for profit or commercial advantage and that copies bear this notice and the full citation on the first page. To copy otherwise, to republish, to post on servers or to redistribute to lists, requires prior specific permission and/or a fee.
DEBS'11, July 11–15, 2011, New York, New York, USA.
Copyright 2011 ACM 978-1-4503-0423-8/11/07 ...$10.00.

control, work-flow, asset management, and system management. These applications usually have stringent requirements in terms of delivery guarantees, so to support such applications, system architects opt for publish/subscribe systems that provide guaranteed delivery. Various forms of reliability have been studied, along with various methods to achieve them [1, 2, 16, 8, 11]. However, in this paper we refer primarily to a form of reliable delivery also known as *message persistence* in such standards as the Java Messaging Service specification. According to this delivery mode, the service must guarantee not to loose messages due to failures of message brokers.

Persistent messages are clearly a desirable feature for applications, but they also have a cost in terms of lower throughput and greater end-to-end delay. In fact, in order to offer such higher delivery guarantees, the publish/subscribe system (distributed or not) must implement a store-and-forward mechanism whereby each broker must log each message onto a persistent storage before accepting the message for delivery from a client or from another broker, and such a commitment to deliver must also be confirmed to the sender.

On the contrary, systems in the "best-effort" class [10, 3, 6, 17] do not offer guaranteed delivery but instead try to maximize throughput and reduce end-to-end delay. So, typically, these systems do not log messages to a persistent storage, nor do they implement any mechanism to guarantee message ordering. Acknowledgment messages are not used and no explicit congestion control mechanism is in place. The advantage of these systems is that they allow for more streamlined message processing, with simpler protocols and with broker designs closer to those of network routers. Still, despite their better performance and simplicity, the unreliable nature of best-effort systems seems to limit their deployment significantly, especially in critical application domains.

Our goal in this work is to reduce the dichotomy between the reliable but more involved store-and-forward architecture, and the unreliable but streamlined best-effort architecture. In other words, our goal is to obtain a combination of the best features of both types of service. More specifically, we take a best-effort network as a basis for a content-based publish/subscribe service, and on top of that we design an end-to-end, probabilistic reliable service. The protocol is end-to-end in the sense that it requires no changes in the internal structure of the broker network or its protocols, and relies only on the participation of clients (though, the same technique we propose can be easily extended to take advantage of in-network caches). The resulting service is probabilistic in nature, in the sense that it can not guarantee delivery in an absolute sense, and in fact it probably would not achieve the same reliability as schemes that use stable storage within the network. Nevertheless, as we show experimentally, in practice the service can reduce message losses significantly, and with only minimal compromises in terms of throughput.

Our design is modeled after Scalable Reliable Multicast (SRM) [9]. Very briefly, SRM works as follows: a receiver that detects a message loss (using sequence numbers) tries to recover a copy of that message from other group members by multicasting a request to the group. SRM also uses an adaptive timer to reduce the number of duplicate requests and replies, and to cope with the effects of such duplicates.

However, SRM is not directly applicable to content-based publish/subscribe because messages are not explicitly addressed to a group, and therefore because it is not immediately clear how to address a request for a lost message. In fact, for the same reason, it is not even clear how to *detect* a message loss. This is because there is no clearly identifiable stream of messages other than what is published by a single source, and gaps in such a stream are very often due to the legitimate filtering of the content-based selection. In other words, simple sequence numbers do not allow a receiver to distinguish a lost message from a message that was legitimately filtered out by the receiver's subscriptions.

The protocol we propose addresses these two fundamental issues using a synthetic publication record that is attached to messages and that allows receivers to detect message losses and also to request the corresponding missing messages. We also extend SRM with a simple scheme for better cache management. We implemented and tested this protocol within a best-effort content-based publish/subscribe system. Our experiments show that the protocol is capable of recovering from a large number of messages losses in networks of different size and with different dynamics.

In Section 2 we first set the context of our work by discussing best-effort publish/subscribe networks and reliable IP multicast, and then present the problem we address and give an overview of the reliability protocol we propose as a solution. In Section 3 we detail the reliability protocol and its implementation. Section 4 presents the experimental evaluation and in Section 5 we review related research. Finally in Section 6 we offer some concluding remarks.

2. CONTEXT AND PRELIMINARIES

In order to put our end-to-end reliability protocol in the proper context, we briefly review best-effort content-based networks and the analogous reliability protocols for IP multicast. We also give a high-level summary of our solution.

2.1 Best-Effort Content-Based Networks

A best-effort content-based network is essentially a distributed publish/subscribe system architected as a datagram network, where routers act as event dispatchers. The addressing in this network is "content-based" in the sense that messages (publications) are addressed implicitly by their content and by the predicates (subscriptions) matching that content posed by receiver hosts. The communication service provided by the network is "best effort" in the sense that messages are treated as datagrams in an IP network, and therefore may be lost due to link instability and congestion in routers. A best-effort content-based network may be built as an overlay on top of an unreliable transport protocol like UDP, or on reliable TCP connections. There are also publish/subscribe systems that directly work atop IP multicast to disseminate events to large sets of subscribers [14]. However, regardless of the nature of the overlay or network underlay, congestion and errors in routers can still render the network unreliable. On the positive side, the goal of the best-effort design is to minimize the amount of state maintained within the network and reduce processing at each router, thereby promoting efficiency and scalability.

In this paper we assume a very common content-based publish/subscribe interface in which messages are at least in part structured as sets of *attributes*, and can be selected by subscriptions predicated upon the values of those attributes. In particular, the term *constraint* refers to a condition on the value of an attribute, the term *filter* denotes a logical conjunction of constraints (sometimes called a subscription) and the term *predicate* denotes a logical disjunction of filters (i.e., a set of subscriptions).

2.2 Reliable IP Multicast

A best-effort content-based network offers a service that is similar in nature to IP multicast. Since our goal is to improve the reliability of a best-effort content-based network, and specifically since we propose to do that with a pure end-to-end solution, we model our solution after the existing end-to-end reliability protocols developed for IP multicast. As we will discuss later, such protocols are not immediately applicable to a content-based addressing because of its greater expressiveness. Nevertheless, we review such protocols here and in particular we focus on Scalable Reliable Multicast (SRM) [9] as a basis for our reliability protocol.

In the context of IP networks, a number of reliability mechanisms have been proposed in the form of additions to the standard IP multicast. Among the most notable ones, Scalable Reliable Multicast (SRM) [9] and Reliable Multicast Transport Protocol (RMTP) [12] provide reliability without reliance on the routing infrastructure (i.e., "end-to-end") while Pragmatic General Multicast (PGM) [18] proposes additional functionalities to routers in order to provide reliability. In the terminology of these protocols, a *request* is a (broadcast or multicast) message whose function and meaning is similar to that of a negative acknowledgment (NACK), which is to request a missing message. The term *repair* refers to a reply (to a request) that carries the missing message. We use these terms with the same semantics in the rest of the paper.

We chose SRM as a basis for our reliability protocol for two reasons. First, SRM makes limited assumptions about the application logic, and second, it only relies upon a basic multicast service to recover lost messages without requiring any addition or modification to the underlying multicast service. Since in the paper we often refer to SRM semantics and internals, we now give a cursory description of how SRM achieves end-to-end reliability. For a detailed description we refer the reader to the original paper by Floyd et al. [9].

SRM is a general-purpose reliability protocol designed for large scale applications that use IP multicast. To be generic, SRM does not make any particular assumption about the formats and sizes of application-level messages. Thus, message loss detection is not embedded in the protocol but is instead assumed to be part of the application logic. Once the application detects the loss of a message within a group, it multicasts a *request* to the same group. Other applications in the same group that received (and cached) the message respond by multicasting a *repair* to the group. In order to reduce duplicate requests and repairs for the same message, nodes hold their requests and repairs for an initially random delay. A node holding a request would then progressively back off by doubling the delay every time it receives a request for the same message. A node holding a repair would simply cancel the repair upon receiving the same repair.

The random delays are chosen uniformly in the interval $[C_1 d_{s,a}, (C_1 + C_2) d_{s,a}]$ for request and $[D_1 d_{s,a}, (D_1 + D_2) d_{s,a}]$ for repair messages where $d_{s,a}$ is the average message trip-time from the multicast source to the node and C_1, C_2, D_1 and D_2 are adjustable parameters. The protocol has an algorithm for automatic tuning of these parameters so that the likelihood of duplicates and the time to recover lost messages are lowered to a minimum.

2.3 Problem and Overview of the Solution

To extend the simple idea of cooperative message recovery to content-based networks, we must overcome two main technical problems. The first problem is to enable receivers to *detect* message losses. For some applications, specifically when messages are channeled into identifiable streams and subscribers receive all messages in a stream, this can be easily done by marking each message within its stream with a sequence number. In this case, a gap in the sequence numbers indicates a message loss. However, such streams do not exist in a content-based publish/subscribe network, where messages are delivered only if they match the interests of subscribers, and where such interests may partially overlap. In other words, with partially overlapping receivers' interests, it is impossible to assign sequence numbers to messages so as to obtain continuous sequences for all receivers. Therefore, in practice, a receiver can not distinguish a message that was lost from a message that was not delivered because it does not match the receiver's interests.

We address this problem by adding some information to each message that allows a receiver to determine, with some probability, if any of the latest publications of the sender that were not received was in fact of interest for the receiver. This information, which we call the *publication record*, consists of a set of Bloom filters, each encoding one of the sender's most recent publications. We discuss this encoding below.

The second problem is to *recover* a lost message that was determined to be of interest. As in SRM, we propose a cooperative recovery scheme whereby a lost message is recovered from some other application in the network that might have received and cached the message. In SRM a receiver would multicast a request for a lost message to the same multicast group to which the message was sent, which conveniently identifies all potential caches from which the message might be recovered. Unfortunately, in a content-based publish/subscribe network it is not as easy for a receiver to address other receivers of a given message. One way to reach potential caches is to send a request to *all* caches, which can be done by having all caching applications subscribe for a generic "request" message. However, that solution might incur an unacceptable overhead for caching applications and

for the network in general, especially in situations where the network is already congested.

We address this second problem using the same publication record attached to messages. A receiver that receives a Bloom filter B_m from the publication record of a message m', and therefore determines that m was of interest, creates a request message that includes B_m. This request is intended for other applications interested in the same message m that are willing to serve as caches for lost messages, and therefore that would subscribe for request messages that match B_m.

The publication record, and in particular the encoding of messages into Bloom filters, is such that a subscription S can be evaluated against the Bloom filter B_m representing message m (without the original content of the message). This is what allows a receiver to verify that a message identified by a Bloom filter B in the publication record matches one of the receiver's subscriptions. So, our idea is to express this matching condition between a Bloom filter B and a receiver subscription S within another subscription. This is possible thanks to the structure of the Bloom filters that encode the message content, which we discuss below in Section 3.1.

Lastly, an application that has a cached copy of a lost message and that receives a request for a repair must somehow deliver that message to the requesting application. This can be done in a straightforward way through a direct (unicast) connection, or also through the publish/subscribe API by effectively republishing the message for the requesting receiver. Each of these solutions has advantages and disadvantages that we discuss below.

3. END-TO-END LOSS RECOVERY

3.1 Message Loss Detection

As stated in the previous section, in a content-based publish/subscribe network, where subscriptions can express partially overlapping interests, conventional sequence numbers are not sufficient to detect message losses. To remedy this problem we augment messages (publications) with an encoded summary of the latest publications of the same sender. This summary, which we call the sender's *publication record*, may allow a receiver to determine that a particular message that was not received was in fact lost.

A publication record is attached to a message m_k by its source s and consists of R entries representing the previous R messages $m_{k-1}, m_{k-2}, \ldots, m_{k-R}$ published by s. Each entry B_i is a Bloom filter obtained by encoding message m_{k-i} using the encoding scheme developed by Carzaniga et al. [4]. The encoding works as follows: first, a message m is mapped into a set of "categories" or "tags." For example, a message that contains the attributes (event=disk-failure, cause=overheating, priority=high) might be associated with tags "disk-failure," "overheating," and "high-priority." Then the set of tags is simply represented as a Bloom filter. In addition to defining sets of tags for messages, the encoding scheme also defines tags for subscriptions with the intended semantics that, if a message m matches a subscription S, then the tags associated with m are a *superset* of the tags associated with S. Carzaniga et al. describe one such encoding that is quite simple but that also incurs some false positives [4]. For the purpose of this paper we adopt the same encoding. In summary, a subscription S is encoded as a Bloom filter B_S (representing a set of tags) and a message

m is encoded as a Bloom filter B_m (representing a set of tags), and if m matches S then $B_m \supseteq B_S$ (where a Bloom filter B is interpreted as a set of bits).

When a subscriber receives a message m_k that carries a publication record $\langle B_1, \ldots B_R \rangle$ the subscriber checks whether it has received messages $m_{k-1}, \ldots, m_{k-R}$ from the same publisher. Then, for each message m_i that was not received, the subscriber checks whether the B_i entry in the publication record matches any of its subscriptions S. That is, the subscriber checks whether there is one of its subscriptions S such that $B_i \supseteq B_S$. (Of course, the subscriber does not have to recompute the encoding of its subscriptions for each message.) If one such subscription is found for B_i, then the subscriber concludes that message m_{k-i} was lost and may decide to try to recover the message.

3.2 Routing Requests

A subscriber may try to recover a lost message by requesting a copy of that message from other applications that received and cached the message. The problem is then to address such a request so as to reach all and only the receivers that might have cached a copy of the lost message.

We propose to transmit the request through the same publish/subscribe system, by constructing a special request message and by having receivers subscribe for those requests for messages that they might have received. So, an application with subscription S that is willing to cache messages for other applications must subscribe for requests for messages matching S. For example, a simplistic way to do that for a subscriber interested in, say, {news=sport, team=Yankees} would be to subscribe for a request message {reliability-message=request, news=sport, team=Yankees}. However, this simplistic approach does not work. For one thing, the second subscription is useless, since the first one would already match all corresponding request messages. More importantly, a subscription for a request that repeats the same constraints as a normal subscription would not work, because a receiver trying to recover a missing message may not be able to fill in the relevant attributes.

Consider in fact the following scenario. Application Alice subscribes for {team=Yankees} while application Bob subscribes for {news=sport}. Now, suppose Alice receives message m ={news=sport, team=Yankees} while the same message is lost on the way to Bob. Also suppose that Bob receives a following message m' ={news=sport, team=Mets} carrying a publication record that allows Bob to detect the loss of m. At this point, Bob can determine that the missing message m matches its own subscription {news=sport} and therefore might issue a request {reliability-message=request, news=sport}. However, that request would not reach Alice. In order for such a request to reach all potential caches, Bob would have to fill in all the attributes of m in the request. In other words, Bob would have to know m completely in order to issue an effective request to recover m.

We propose to overcome this problem by once again relying on the information contained in the publication record. In the scenario we just described, Bob does not know the content of the missing message m, but he does know its encoding B_m. Therefore, Bob could include B_m in a request message such that Alice could subscribe for it using an encoding of its own subscription. For example, suppose that Alice's subscription would be encoded in a Bloom filter B_A whose 1-bits are at positions 7 and 15 (all other

bits are zero). Then, Alice could subscribe for {reliability-message=request, b7=true, b15=true} effectively representing B_A by means of attributes each representing one of the 1-bits in B_A. Notice that what matters is the *presence* of such attributes, not their value. Now, Bob could do the same by composing his request for m using the encoding B_m he finds in the publication record. And since the encoding is such that a message m matching a subscription S would be encoded by a Bloom filter B_m whose 1-bits are a *superset* of the subscription's Bloom filter B_S, Alice would have to receive that request.

With the ability to detect lost messages and to route requests to all potential caches for those messages, the recovery process proceeds in a similar fashion as in SRM. We illustrate this process through a an example. Consider a subscriber A that has an active subscription and suppose that A is willing to provide repairs for all the events matching that subscription. To do that, A encodes the subscription and issues a second subscription using the 1-bit attributes as described above. As subscribers intending to participate in the recovery mechanism, B and C also initially issue an additional subscription to receive matching repair requests. As we will detail below, this is done to suppress duplicate requests.

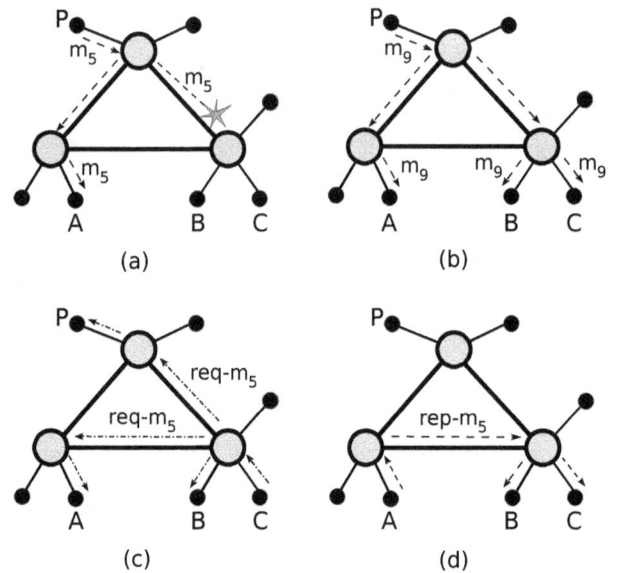

Figure 1: Message m_5 is lost before reaching B and C (a); having received m_9 (b), C publishes a request for m_5 (d); A replies with a repair (d).

Now, assume that later, a publisher P publishes an event m_5 matching A's subscription. The message is received by A but due to a temporary failure it is not received by B and C whose subscriptions also match m_5 (see Figure 1a). Later, P publishes another message m_9 that is received by B and C (because it matches their subscriptions). This message carries the publication record of P that includes the Bloom-filter encoding of m_5. Using that data, both B and C realize that they have missed m_5 (see Figure 1b).

The detection of a message loss triggers the recovery mechanism at B and C. Thus, B and C issue repair requests, but in doing that, they try to suppress duplicate requests. The two nodes start to count down from a randomly generated timer (discussed in Section 2.2). Assume that C picks the earlier timeout between the two. Once C's timer expires, C publishes a request for m_5 by including the 1-bit attributes corresponding to the Bloom-filter encoding of m_5 as well as a unique message id for m_5 (source plus sequence number) that is also part of the publication record. This request is received by both B and A because it matches their request subscriptions (see Figure 1c). Upon receiving the request, B, which has a timer running on an identical request, reacts by delaying its own request by doubling its timer value.

A instead reacts by searching its message cache for a message with the given id, and when it finds it, publishes a repair message consisting of the original message m_5 with an additional attribute that indicates that it is a repair (and therefore a duplicate publication). The repair message reaches both B and C (see Figure 1d), at which point B cancels its pending request and both B and C deliver m_5.

Thanks to the expressiveness of content-based networking, this request routing technique allows for fine grained control over the request messages and their receivers. On the one hand, it allows clients to precisely describe request message they are willing to reply to, if any. On the other hand, it also allows for the implementation of special policies for the distribution of request messages, for example to confine request and repair messages within a single administrative domain. It is also easy to use this recovery protocol with designated cache nodes distributed in strategic points over the network that take on the responsibility of providing repairs, as suggested in RMTP [12] for reliable IP multicast.

3.3 Sending Repairs

As explained in the example of Figure 1, a caching subscriber can respond to a request by re-publishing a message and by flagging that publication as a repair. Alternatively, the cache may send the repair directly to the requesting node through a unicast connection. Re-publishing is advantageous when the same message is requested by several receivers—something that might happen with overlapping subscriptions and non-local faults. Conversely, a unicast reply may be a better option when no other receivers requested the same message, and when that message would reach many receivers that already received the original copy. There may also be security and authenticity issues with the repair messages that are provided by caching nodes. This can be seen as a general trust and security management problem in the context of publish/subscribe systems, which is out of the scope of this paper.

3.4 Message Cache

An important parameter that is not discussed in the original paper on SRM by Floyd et al. [9] is the amount of memory a caching node (generally, a subscriber) has to allocate to its message cache. The cache should be allocated and managed so as to obtain a high cache-hit ratio while also avoiding unnecessary caching and therefore saving memory resources. In this section we elaborate on this issue.

On the one hand, for performance reasons we would like to have nodes maintain the message cache in main memory, within the limits of their memory constraints. On the other hand, it is also desirable to limit memory usage to a minimum. Therefore, nodes need to know when to drop some of the messages from their cache. The best strategy depends on various parameters, such as end-to-end message

Symbol	Meaning
λ	Publication rate
C_1, C_2	SRM request timers
P_m	Match probability
$d_{P,B}$	Trip time between requester and publisher
$d_{B,A}$	Trip time between requester and caching node
K	Cache size

Table 1: Parameters used in the calculation of the cache size.

delivery delay, sender publication rate, match probability, and timer parameters of the requesting nodes. A message cache of constant size is oblivious to such network dynamics and may sometime lead to memory waste and other times to cache misses. Instead, we seek an adaptive cache that would perform well under variable network conditions. In particular, we formulate an approximation for the optimum cache size focusing on the most common scenario.

We consider the message cache as a ring buffer with dynamic size, and we consider the problem of finding the optimum size of this ring buffer based on the parameters summarized in Table 3.4. (Indeed, our implementation uses a ring buffer for its message cache.) For this formulation we assume that message losses occur in bursts of S messages per second, where $1 \leq S < \lambda P_m$. We further assume that request messages are not lost.

Consider a publisher Z that publishes a message m_i. This message has two intended receivers: A that receives m_i and B that incurs a message loss and does not receive m_i. To find a lower bound for the size K of the message cache at A, we assume that A is closer to the publisher while B is farther away from the publisher in terms of end-to-end delay. Thus, on average, it takes $d_{Z,B} + \frac{1}{\lambda P_m} + \varepsilon$ time units for B to receive m_j, the next (relevant) message from Z, and detect the loss of m_i by investigating the publication record attached to m_j. We neglect ε, the small processing time of m_j. Therefore, the request message from B will be received by A after an expected delay of $(C_1 + \frac{C_2}{2})d_{Z,B} + d_{B,A}$ time units. Consequently, in order to be able to provide a repair for the lost message m_i, A has to store m_i in its ring buffer for at least $d_{Z,B} + \frac{1}{\lambda P_m} + (C_1 + \frac{C_2}{2})d_{Z,B} + d_{B,A}$ time units.

The minimal caching time we just computed determines, together with the arrival rate at A, determines a minimal cache size. Since A receives messages from the publisher with an expected inter-arrival time of $\frac{1}{\lambda P_m}$, and hence must overwrite m_i in its ring buffer approximately after $\frac{K}{\lambda P_m}$ time units. Thus, in order for A to be able to provide repair for m_i, the request must arrive at A before A overwrites m_i in its ring buffer. So we have:

$$d_{Z,B} + \frac{1}{\lambda P_m} + (C_1 + \frac{C_2}{2})d_{Z,B} + d_{B,A} \leq \frac{K}{\lambda P_m}$$

solving the inequality, we find a lower bound for the cache size K:

$$K > \lambda P_m[(C_1 + \frac{C_2}{2} + 1)d_{Z,B} + d_{B,A}]$$

The parameters of the above formula vary over time, and therefore must be continuously estimated. Each caching

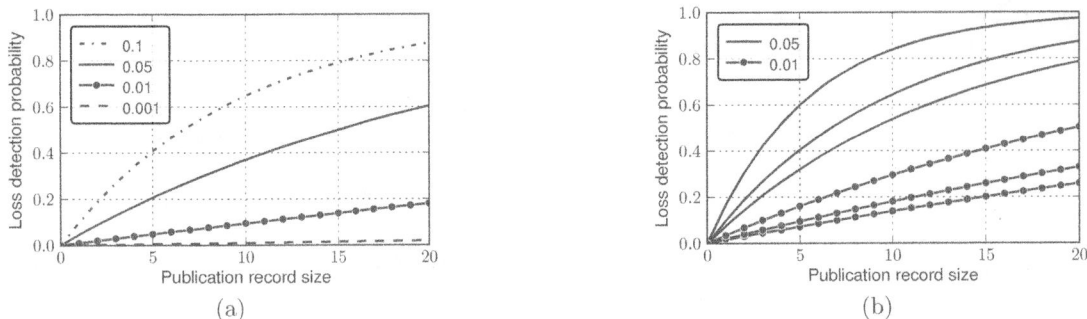

Figure 2: Probability of loss detection for (a) different sizes of publication record and match probability, (b) different sizes of publication record, match probability and different number of nodes sharing a loss (2, 3, 5 from bottom to top in each line category).

node A, can directly measure λP_m which equals the reception rate from the publisher Z at A. The value of $(C_1 + \frac{C_2}{2})d_{Z,B})$ is not measurable by A and therefore is included in each request message sent by B. The auto-tuning algorithm in SRM works in a way that the requesting node is likely to be the closest node to the point of failure. Thus, the requesting node for a given publisher is likely to often be the same node. Thus, this value is averaged over received requests for message of the publisher Z with the assumption that requests are coming from the same node or nodes at the same distance from the publisher. Finally, the value of $d_{B,A}$ is easily found by the simple method described by Floyd et al. in [9].

Algorithm 1 Adjust cache size

---
if closets_repair_provider = True **then**
    $a \leftarrow ((C_1 + \frac{C_2}{2} + 1)d_{Z,B} + d_{B,A})\lambda P_m + 1$
    $b \leftarrow 0$
    if $HitRatio < H$ **then**
        $b \leftarrow 1.1K$
    $c \leftarrow max(a, b)$
else
    $c \leftarrow 0.9K$
if $K_{min} \leq c \leq K_{max}$ **then**
    $K \leftarrow c$

Another consideration is that based on SRM semantics, via auto-adjustable timer parameters, the node that provides repair messages is usually the closest node (in terms of end-to-end delay) to the point of message loss, which is in fact a method to minimize recovery time. Therefore, it is better to have this node handle caching more aggressively and other nodes gradually reduce their cache size, since they are not actively involved in providing repairs for messages coming from that specific publisher. Moreover, given that the above formulation gives a lower bound for K, caching nodes also need to monitor their average hit ratio, which is updated upon reception of each request, and if this ratio is below a preconfigured value, increase their cache size. Algorithm 1 shows this procedure, which a caching node executes periodically. H is a preconfigured hit ratio and K_{min} and K_{max} are minimum and maximum allowed cache size, respectively, and are configurable parameters. This algorithm is quick to increase the cache size as a reaction to sudden spikes in publication rate λ, and instead reacts with a gradual increase (10%) of the cache size when the network is

stable but the hit ratio is lower than the configured level H. The algorithm is also rather conservative when it comes to reducing cache size, since we would like to avoid dropping cache entries too early as a result of abrupt changes in the network dynamics.

3.5 Discussion

The effectiveness of the proposed recovery protocol is primarily influenced by the effectiveness of the loss detection. Obviously, the publication record carried by each message must be limited in size due to practical limitations and also to limit traffic overhead. This is in fact, where the probabilistic nature of our recovery protocol stems from.

We now discuss the impact of publication-record size on the probability of loss detection. Considering a subscriber S and a publisher P whose publication matches S's subscriptions with probability P_{match}, the probability that S detects the loss of a message sent by P depends on the message loss probability P_{loss} on the path from P to S, the matching probability P_{match}, and the size R of the publication record. Simply put, if each message carries a publication record of size R, then the loss of a message m will not be detected by its intended receiver if none of the R messages published after m are received by that receiver. So, the probability of loss detection is:

$$1 - (1 - P_{match} + P_{match}P_{loss})^R \qquad (1)$$

Figure 2a shows the probability of loss detection for different sizes of publication record and different match probabilities for a loss probability of 0.01. As the figure suggests, when the match probability is 0.001 (i.e., out of every 1000 publications, only one message is expected to match the subscriber's interests) the loss detection mechanism is very inefficient. With 5% matching probability, a publication record of size 10 makes the loss-detection possible with a probability of 0.4. At a first glance, Figure 2a might suggest that this loss detection mechanism would limit the applicability of our recovery mechanism. While this is true for applications with very low match probability, note that Figure 2a demonstrates the worst case where there is only one intended receiver for the lost message. In other words, when a message loss is shared among multiple receivers, it is sufficient that only one of them detects the loss. This happens when subscribers have overlapping subscriptions.

As an example, let us consider a case of Figure 2a where

a node n has a match probability of 0.01. Let us also assume that there are k other nodes ($k = 1, 2, 4$ in Figure 2b) with the same matching probability as n and we also assume that all these nodes' subscriptions have a 50% overlap with n's subscriptions. That is, any message that matches n's subscription will match all of the other nodes' subscriptions with a probability of 0.5. Figure 2b (the three bottom lines) shows the growth of the loss-detection probability (the probability that at least on node detects a shared loss) with the growth of the publication-record size. The three top lines correspond to the case where nodes have a match probability of 0.05 and the rest of the scenario is similar. Notice that the growth of loss-detection probability with the size of publication record is faster for larger values of k.

Another consideration about this loss-detection mechanism is that if the publication rate (number of publications per time unit) is relatively low, detection of a message loss will be *late*, especially for subscribers with low match probability. This problem can be alleviated by periodic soft-state messages sent by the publisher. Such messages only serve the purpose of enhancing the loss detection on the receiver side. Receivers whose match probability is too low can subscribe for soft-state messages for faster and more successful loss detection.

Another way to mitigate the limitation of the proposed loss-detection mechanism is to maximize the number of messages that can be summarized into a publication record of a given size. Currently, we are investigating the *temporal locality* of events. That is, when two or more consecutive events sent out by a publisher have overlapping attribute/value pairs. We plan to exploit temporal locality to enhance the encoding scheme to allow for compression that is, merging the encoded format of a few similar events in a single Bloom filter. This might further increase the likelihood of a false positive however, we believe that the overall bandwidth usage will be improved with this compression mechanism. Entries of a publication record can be further compressed using compressed Bloom filters [13] to reduce space usage and bandwidth overhead.

4. EXPERIMENTAL EVALUATION

In this section we evaluate the performance of the recovery protocol with a focus on effectiveness and cost. More specifically, we are interested in measuring how many lost messages are recovered and how long it takes to recover them. Another practical question we explore is how much extra traffic is generated by the recovery protocol and what is the user-tangible impact on the ordinary traffic.

We note that the performance of the recovery protocol depends significantly on the choice of topology, workload, and message-loss probability. Our choice for these experimental settings does not aim to demonstrate the best-case performance of our protocol, but rather intends to examine its effectiveness under stress, in the presence of frequent message losses, and with conservatively chosen workloads that do not necessarily contribute to increase the effectiveness of the recovery protocol.

4.1 Experimental Setup and Workload

We implemented the recovery protocol as a pluggable module which integrates into any publish/subscribe application and protocol that provides a common publish/subscribe API. In particular, the publication record and other metadata re-

quired by the recovery protocol is attached to messages as an array of bytes treated by brokers as application payload not subject to the matching process. Most implementations of the Java Messaging Service (JMS) are capable of carrying an opaque payload and hence clients using such systems can take advantage of the recovery protocol when the system runs in best-effort mode. For the experiments presented in this section we used a recent implementation of the Siena publish/subscribe system that implements a best-effort content-based communication system [4].

Our experiment testbed is a cluster of Dell PowerEdge with two dual-core 2GHz AMD Opteron processors and 4GB of main memory running Linux with a 2.6.32 kernel. Connectivity is through an isolated high-throughput Gigabit Ethernet switch. Broker software, client and recovery protocol are implemented in Java and run on the 64-bit open-JDK VM. Each physical machine hosts an broker that serves 5 instances of the client (as their home broker) running on the same machine. To simulate a wide area network, we used the Linux traffic control tools to apply delay and message loss on all inter-broker and links. Each link's delay d_i, is randomly chosen in the range of $[25, 75]$ milliseconds, which also continuously varies during the execution in the range of $[d_i - 5, d_i + 5]$ milliseconds. This variation of ± 5 milliseconds is typical of the Internet, based on different Internet measurements.[1]

We present the results for two sets of experiments with two different network topologies and workloads. The first topology is composed of 12 brokers with a diameter of 5 broker-hops in which out of the total of 60 clients, 6 nodes are publishers and 54 are subscribers. Then to probe scalability of the recovery protocol, the second experiment involves a larger topology of 46 brokers with a diameter of 11 broker-hops. Among the total of 230 clients, 10 are publishers and the rest are subscribers.

Using the Linux traffic control tools, we apply a link-level message loss probability of 0.01 to all inter-broker links (i.e., each link loses approximately one message out of each 100 messages). This loss probability is rather large because for a network of diameter 11 it sums to unrealistically large likelihoods of message loss for some endpoints. For example, for a sender and a receiver 11 broker-hops apart, the probability of message loss is as large as 0.1. This is a deliberate choice to stress-test the recovery protocol under very frequent message losses.

In both experiments, we use synthetic workloads with varying publication rates that simulate sudden short-term spikes in publication rate of publishers, to simulate bursty traffic that causes queuing delays. In these experiments, all the nodes participate in the recovery process. That is, they all volunteer to provide repair for messages that they receive. As shown in Section 3.1, two crucial factors in the loss detection and hence in the effectiveness of the recovery protocol are the matching probability and the number of receivers for a message. To be conservative in our evaluation, we choose workloads that exhibit low subscription/publication match probability (the probability that a message matches a node's subscription) and a low number of receiver per message. Figure 3 characterizes the two workloads for the 12-broker and 46-broker experiments. As Figure 3a shows, in both work-

---

[1]For example see measurements by RIPE Network Coordination Centre (RIPE) available at
http://www.ripe.net/data-tools/stats/ttm/ttm-data

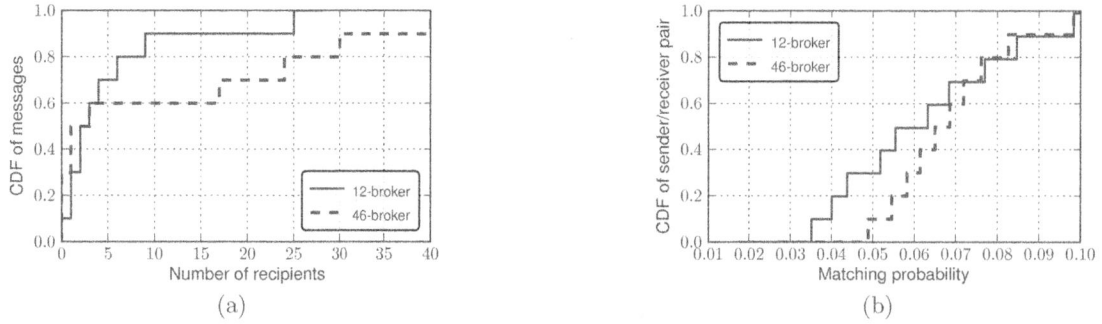

Figure 3: (a) Number of receivers for cumulative distribution of messages. (b) Match probability for cumulative distribution of subscriber/publisher pairs.

loads 50% of the messages have at most two receivers. Figure 3b plots the subscription/publication match probability for each pair of subscriber and publisher. In both workloads, 80% of the pairs have a match probability of less than 0.08 while the maximum match probability is not higher than 0.1.

Figure 4, plots the aggregate publication and delivery rates without the recovery protocol during the course of the experiments, which runs for a total of 5 minutes. The rapid changes in delivery rate is due to spikes in publication rates.

4.2 Recovery Effectiveness

First we look at the number of false negatives (that is, the number of messages that were not delivered to their intended receivers) with and without the recovery protocol. One determining factor in the effectiveness of the protocol is the size of the publication record. Figure 5 illustrates the effectiveness of the recovery protocol with different publication-record sizes. The y-axis shows the total number of false negatives (message losses) and zero on the x-axis represents the case where no recovery protocol is in place. The decrease in the number of false negatives is more pronounced in the 46-broker network while it is slower in the 12-broker network. Indeed, in the 12-broker experiment, growing the publication record size from 1 to 10 only halves the number of false negatives while in the 46-broker networks the false negatives are reduces by a factor of 3, approximately.

Our calculation of the probability of message loss detection by Equation 1 as well as Figure 2a explain this result, which is mostly due to the characteristics of the workload, i.e., small matching probability and small subscriber/message, which hinder a more effective loss detection in the 12-broker network. Furthermore, our experiments with smaller message loss probabilities showed that the exponential effect of publication record size on the recovery effectiveness is more substantial when message loss probability is smaller, which is also explained by Equation 1. For instance, in the 46-broker network when loss probability is 0.001, the recovery protocol with a publication record size of 10 reduces the number of false negatives by more than 8 times.

We now examine the network dynamics and the corresponding protocol behavior over time. To do that, we focus on the experiments with the best effectiveness results, that is, with a publication record of size 10. We choose this case because a larger size for the publication record generates larger amounts of network traffic and hence by studying this case we gain a better understanding of its impact on the network.

We begin our probe by looking at the aggregate rate of false negatives with and without the recovery protocol during runtime, shown in Figure 6. The reduction in the false negatives that is almost a factor of two for the 12-broker and a factor of three for the 46-broker network is persistent during the whole course of the experiment. So, at a high level, the recovery protocol does not show any pathological behavior during the experiment.

We now proceed to examine another aspect of the recovery effectiveness, namely the time it takes to recover a lost message. Figure 7 shows the end-to-end delay of the original (non-repair) messages as well as the repair messages. Note that the delay of repair messages is in fact the time difference between their publication by the original publisher and their delivery to the indented receiver as a repair. Figure 7 also plots the request/repair delay, which is the time difference between multicast of the first request for a certain message and the first repair for that message. An interesting observation is that the request/repair delay in both networks is relatively small: for 80% of the messages in 12-broker and 46-broker networks, this delay is below 200 and 350 milliseconds, respectively, while the total time to recover missing messages is considerably larger. This means that a large part of the recovery delay is due to "late" loss detection, which is a result of low matching probability and/or low publication rate. This is not surprising, since the publication rate of each publisher varies between 20 and 500 messages per second in the 12-broker, and between 20 and 250 messages per second in the 46-broker networks, and hence, with a match probability of 0.05, it might take up to 1 second to detect a message loss.

Also, note that our choice of large message loss probability causes many of the requests to be lost and so, some requests must be reissued for a second or a third time, each time after a timeout. In fact, in other experiments with 46-broker network when we applied smaller link loss probabilities, we observed that the request/repair delays were almost 50% smaller, which in turn resulted in smaller recovery times.

4.3 Performance and Network Overhead

We now turn our attention to the operating costs of the recovery protocol. In particular, We consider two measures: network usage and the overall impact on the receivers in terms of the extra delivery delay that the original messages incur. The extra network load is caused by the publication record attached to each message as well as the traffic of request and repair messages. In our workload all messages

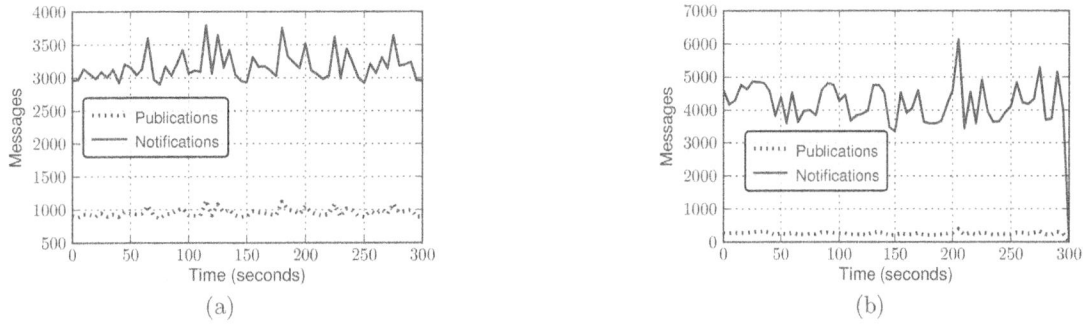

Figure 4: Aggregate publication and notification rates in (a) 12-broker and (b) 46-broker networks.

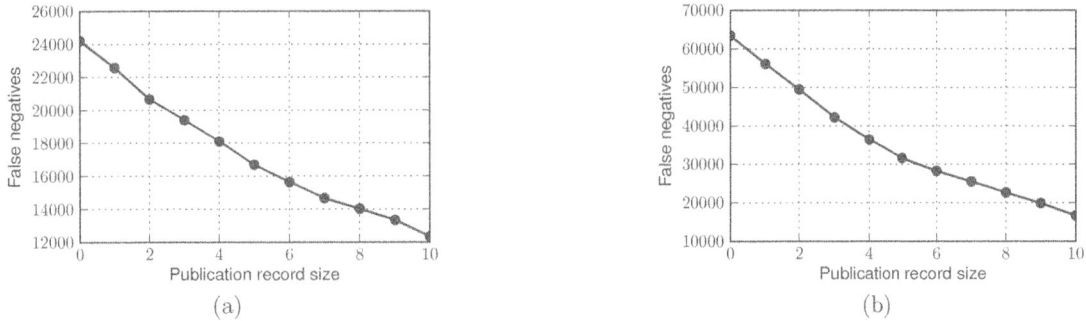

Figure 5: Impact of publication-record size on the effectiveness of the recovery protocol in (a) 12-broker and (b) 46-broker networks.

have 10 attributes and to produce each entry of a publication record we encoded a message in a Bloom filter of size 256 bits. Thus, a message with a publication record of size 10 carries 320 bytes of extra information. We deliberately used this large number of attributes and large-size Bloom filters to examine the negative effects of the recovery scheme in a rather extreme case. In reality though, where messages usually have smaller number of attributes, Bloom filters of size 128 or 64 would suffice and cause less network overhead.

Figure 8 illustrates the aggregate rate of request and repair messages during the experiment as well as the aggregate rate of publications to be used as a reference measure. Ideally, for each lost message there must be only one request and one repair message. However, in many cases request and repair messages are also lost, which is indeed the reason why in Figure 8 the number of requests is more than the number of repairs. Interestingly, we observed that in both networks the multicast suppression mechanism built in SRM works favorably well. More specifically, in the 12-broker network more than 90% of the request and 80% of the repair messages were not duplicated while in the 46-broker network these values were 80% and 70%, respectively. This larger duplicate number in the 46-broker network is due to the network's greater diameter, which is twice the diameter of the 12-broker network. A higher diameter has a slight affect on SRM's multicast suppression mechanism, but more importantly leads to more frequent losses of request/repair messages.

In effect, the overall and user-visible overhead is the change in the delivery delay of the messages when the recovery protocol is active and causes extra network traffic. Figure 9 shows the end-to-end delivery delay for cumulative distribu-

tion of messages with and without the recovery scheme. As the diagram suggests, the recovery protocol shifts the plot of end-to-end delay without recovery to the right, which implies a constant increase in the end-to-end delivery delay of all messages. Nevertheless, given the minimum and maximum values of end-to-end delay without recovery, an increase of 25 milliseconds in delay is not prohibitively large, since the dominant network traffic is the ordinary publication traffic and so, request/repair messages do not cause tangible impact on the overall network performance.

4.4 Adaptive Cache

We now examine the performance of the adaptive message cache by measuring the hit rate and the size of message cache in the network. A cache hit occurs when a request for a message is sent out and at least one of the nodes that received the request, is able to provide a repair. Thus, considering the whole network as a single cache, we define hit ratio as the ratio between total number of cache hits to the total number of requests.

In our experiment we assigned values of 5 and 300 to K_{min} and K_{max}, respectively, with an initial cache size of K_{min}. The the target hit ratio H (see Algorithm 1) was set to 1. Figure 10 plots the changes in hit ratio during the experiment. In both networks, the hit ratio grows rapidly in the first few seconds of the experiment and then does not exhibit large changes during the rest of the experiment despite the continuous oscillation of the publication rates.

The effectiveness of the adaptive cache is further demonstrated by Figure 11, which shows the minimum, mean, and maximum cache size among all the network nodes during the experiment. Despite the high hit ratio, the amount of mem-

215

(a)   (b)

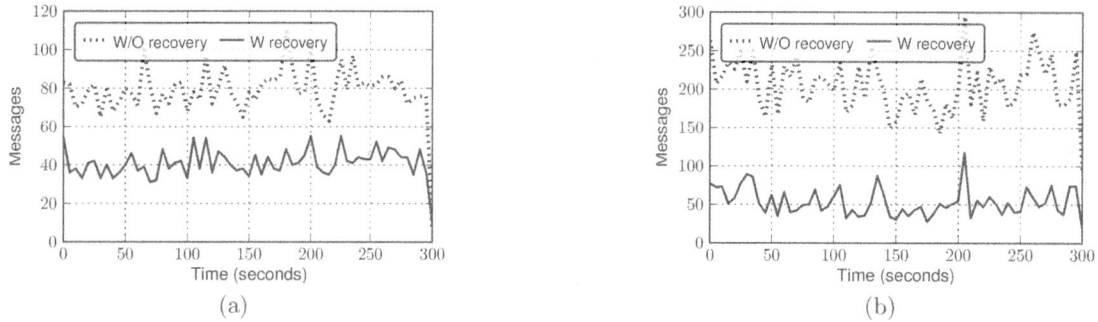

Figure 6: (a) Changes in the aggregate rate of false negatives (message loss) with and without the recovery protocol, for (a) 12-broker and (b) 46-broker networks.

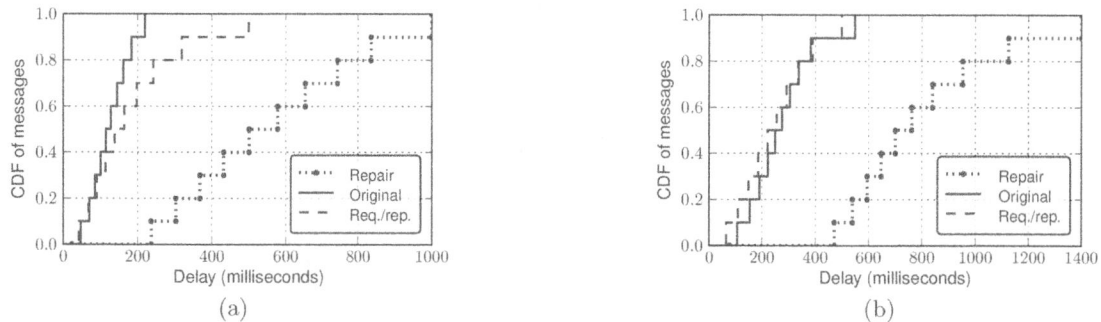

(a)   (b)

Figure 7: Cumulative distribution of the end-to-end delay for original and repair messages and request/repair delay for (a) 12-broker and (b) 46-broker networks.

ory used for caching was a small. This is because most of the nodes keep their cache size to a minimum (as evidenced by small value of the mean cache size). In turn, this is because the adaptive cache mechanism causes the nodes that do not actively participate in providing repair messages to reduce their cache size. On the other hand, nodes that are actively providing repairs adjust their cache size to accommodate changes in publication rate and improve hit ratio.

5. RELATED WORK

As we mentioned in Section 1, prominent implementations of publish/subscribe systems have taken two different approaches concerning reliable delivery. Systems in the first category strive to ensure that all subscribers receive all published messages that match their subscriptions [1, 2, 16, 8, 11]. Guaranteed delivery and service availability are provided by replication of brokers and logging of messages onto durable storage. Moreover, reception of messages by the intermediate brokers and the final recipients are acknowledged at each hop. These are known as *store and forward* systems. The main problem of the store and forward design is that it induces high delivery delays. Additionally, when the publication rate is high, logging messages onto disk might contribute to congestion.

In the second category there are *best effort* systems [10, 3, 6, 17]. These systems treat messages as datagrams in a network, and therefore do not store messages onto disk, nor they require any acknowledgment when transmitting messages from broker to broker or from a broker to a client. The advantage of the best-effort design is its simplicity and therefore its ability to scale in terms of throughput.

The idea of reliable message delivery in a publish/subscribe system without support from the broker network has been previously proposed in the work by Ostrowski and Birman[15]. The authors briefly mention the possibility of combining reliable multicast protocols like SRM and RMTP with an unreliable publish/subscribe protocol. However, the proposed general approach is limited to topic-based publish/subscribe systems. Even so, this work lacks a precise and concrete plan on how it can be implemented.

Costa et al. [5] and Esposito et al. [7] propose using epidemic and peer-to-peer techniques to provide reliability in publish/subscribe networks. Similar to our protocol, the work by Costa et al. [5] provides reliability in probabilistic terms. We believe that the work presented here is more generic and easier to implement and deploy.

6. FINAL REMARKS

The goal of this paper is to enhance the reliability of best-effort publish/subscribe systems with a minimum reduction in the high throughput and end-to-end delivery delay that such systems offer. Towards this end, we develop an end-to-end method that effectively considers the broker network as a black box. In essence, our solution consists of two components. The first is a message-loss detection mechanism; the second is a routing scheme to deliver request messages to nodes that volunteer to provide repairs. Both mechanisms are built on top of a standard publish/subscribe API, and therefore neither requires any modification to the broker network. Also, both mechanisms are based on a synthetic publication record attached to messages and in turn based on a space-efficient encoding of messages and subscriptions into

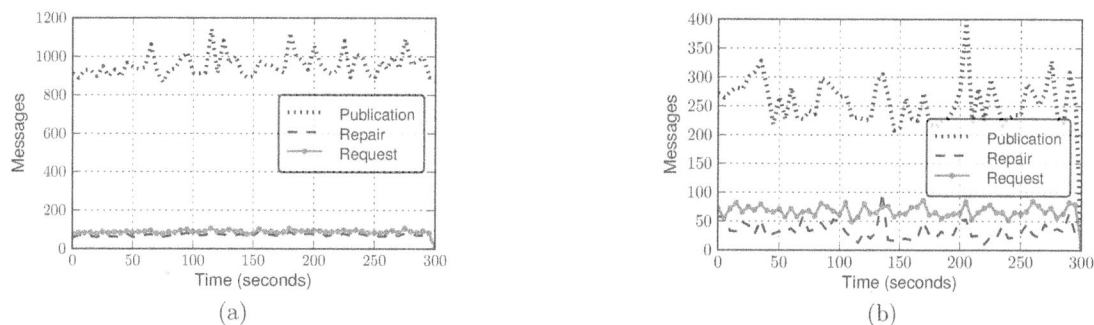

Figure 8: (a) Aggregate publication rate, request, and repair messages during the experiment for (a) 12-broker and (b) 46-broker networks.

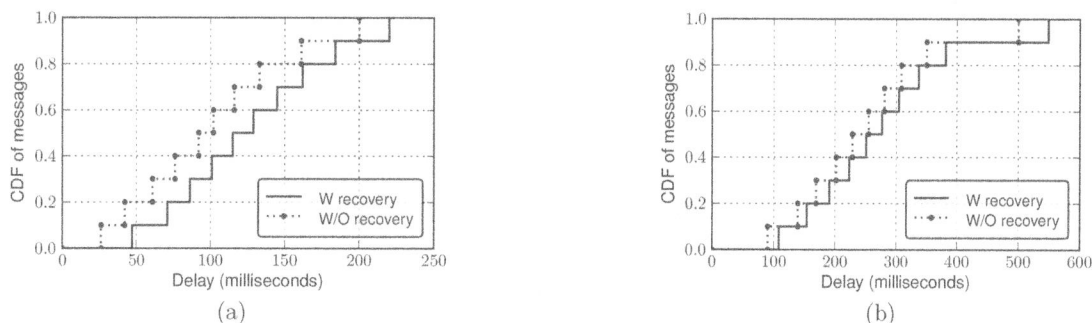

Figure 9: Delivery delay with and without the recovery protocol in (a) 12-broker and (b) 46-broker networks.

Boom filters. Through experimental evaluation, we show that this end-to-end reliability method is effective in recovering lost messages even in the presence of highly unstable network conditions and low link reliability.

We believe that best-effort content-based systems, thanks to their good performance and relatively simple architecture, have great potentials to emerge as a general-purpose communication paradigm integrated into the network fabric. Similar to IP networks, we believe that higher level guarantees, like message ordering and reliable delivery, ought to be built atop the basic service offered by the broker network, by involving the clients and potentially other dedicated network components in the process. Indeed, this work is a part of a project whose aim is to devise a *transport protocol* for best-effort content-based networking.

Acknowledgments

This work was supported in part by the Swiss National Science Foundation under grant number 200020-120188/1.

7. REFERENCES

[1] S. Bhola, R. E. Strom, S. Bagchi, Y. Zhao, and J. S. Auerbach. Exactly-once delivery in a content-based publish-subscribe system. In *DSN '02: Proceedings of the 2002 International Conference on Dependable Systems and Networks*, pages 7–16, Washington, DC, USA, 2002. IEEE Computer Society.

[2] S. Bhola, Y. Zhao, and J. Auerbach. Scalably supporting durable subscriptions in a publish/subscribe system. In *In proceeding of the international conference on dependable systems and networks (DSN 2003)*, pages 57–66, 2003.

[3] A. Carzaniga, D. S. Rosenblum, and A. L. Wolf. Design and evaluation of a wide-area event notification service. *ACM Trans. Comput. Syst.*, 19(3):332–383, 2001.

[4] A. Carzaniga, G. Toffetti Carughi, C. Hall, and A. L. Wolf. Practical high-throughput content-based routing using unicast state and probabilistic encodings. Technical Report 2009/06, Faculty of Informatics, University of Lugano, Aug. 2009.

[5] P. Costa, M. Migliavacca, G. P. Picco, and G. Cugola. Introducing reliability in content-based publish-subscribe through epidemic algorithms. In *Proceedings of the 2nd international workshop on Distributed event-based systems*, DEBS '03, pages 1–8, New York, NY, USA, 2003. ACM.

[6] G. Cugola, E. Di Nitto, and A. Fuggetta. The jedi event-based infrastructure and its application to the development of the opss wfms. *IEEE Trans. Softw. Eng.*, 27(9):827–850, 2001.

[7] C. Esposito, D. Cotroneo, and A. Gokhale. Reliable publish/subscribe middleware for time-sensitive internet-scale applications. In *Proceedings of the Third ACM International Conference on Distributed Event-Based Systems*, DEBS '09, pages 16:1–16:12, New York, NY, USA, 2009. ACM.

[8] E. Fidler, H. A. Jacobsen, G. Li, and S. Mankovski. The padres distributed publish/subscribe system. In *In 8th International Conference on Feature Interactions in Telecommunications and Software Systems*, pages 12–30, 2005.

[9] S. Floyd, V. Jacobson, C.-G. Liu, S. McCanne, and L. Zhang. A reliable multicast framework for

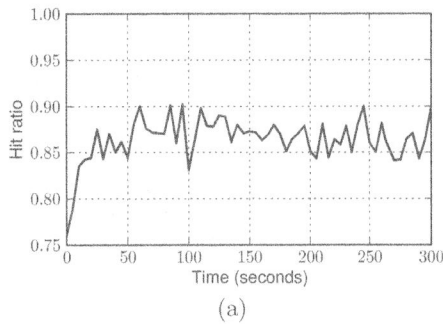

(a)

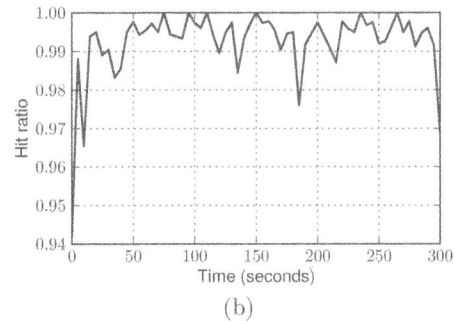

(b)

Figure 10: Changes in the cache hit ratio in (a) 12-broker and (b) 46-broker networks.

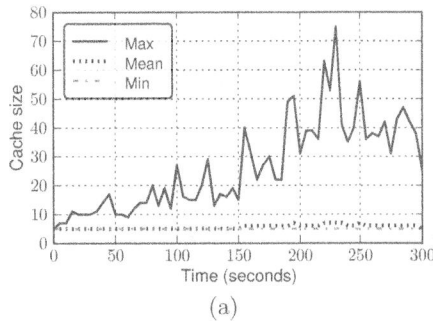

(a)

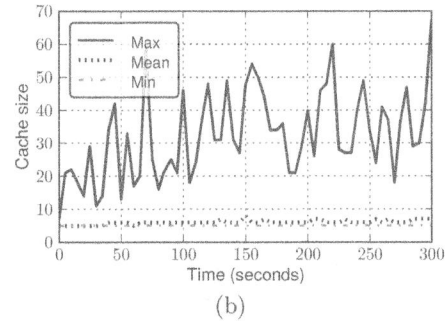

(b)

Figure 11: Changes in the minimum, mean, and maximum cache size of all nodes in (a) 12-broker and (b) 46-broker networks

light-weight sessions and application level framing. *IEEE/ACM Trans. Netw.*, 5(6):784–803, 1997.

[10] P. Jokela, A. Zahemszky, C. E. Rothenberg, S. Arianfar, and P. Nikander. LIPSIN: Line Speed Publish/Subscribe Inter-networking. In *SIGCOMM '09: Proceedings of the ACM SIGCOMM 2009 conference on Data communication*, pages 195–206, New York, NY, USA, 2009. ACM.

[11] R. S. Kazemzadeh and H.-A. Jacobsen. Reliable and highly available distributed publish/subscribe service. In *SRDS '09: Proceedings of the 2009 28th IEEE International Symposium on Reliable Distributed Systems*, pages 41–50, Washington, DC, USA, 2009. IEEE Computer Society.

[12] J. C. Lin and J. L. Sanjoy. Rmtp: A reliable multicast transport protocol. In *IEEE Journal on Selected Areas in Communications*, pages 1414–1424, 1996.

[13] M. Mitzenmacher. Compressed bloom filters. In *Proceedings of the twentieth annual ACM symposium on Principles of distributed computing*, PODC '01, pages 144–150, New York, NY, USA, 2001. ACM.

[14] L. Opyrchal, M. Astley, J. Auerbach, G. Banavar, R. Strom, and D. Sturman. Exploiting ip multicast in content-based publish-subscribe systems. In *IFIP/ACM International Conference on Distributed systems platforms*, Middleware '00, pages 185–207, Secaucus, NJ, USA, 2000. Springer-Verlag New York, Inc.

[15] K. Ostrowski and K. Birman. Extensible web services architecture for notification in large-scale systems. In *ICWS '06: Proceedings of the IEEE International Conference on Web Services*, pages 383–392, Washington, DC, USA, 2006. IEEE Computer Society.

[16] P. R. Pietzuch and J. Bacon. Hermes: A distributed event-based middleware architecture. In *ICDCSW '02: Proceedings of the 22nd International Conference on Distributed Computing Systems*, pages 611–618, Washington, DC, USA, 2002. IEEE Computer Society.

[17] A. C. Snoeren, K. Conley, and D. K. Gifford. Mesh-based content routing using xml. *SIGOPS Oper. Syst. Rev.*, 35(5):160–173, 2001.

[18] T. Speakman, J. Crowcroft, J. Gemmell, D. Farinacci, S. Lin, D. Leshchiner, M. Luby, T. Montgomery, L. Rizzo, A. Tweedly, N. Bhaskar, R. Edmonstone, R. Sumanasekera, and L. Vicisano. Pgm reliable transport protocol specification, 2001.

Fine-grained Parallel XML Filtering for Content-based Publish/Subscribe Systems

Eberhard Grummt
bbv Software Services AG
Blumenrain 10,CH-6002 Lucerne, Switzerland
eg@grummt.org

ABSTRACT

Current XML-based publish/subscribe systems only support coarse-grained message filtering: a message is either forwarded to a subscriber in its entirety or not at all. Fine-grained filtering of message elements is not supported. Such filtering capabilities can be used by subscribers to further detail their subscriptions or by message brokers to enforce fine-grained access control policies. This paper presents an XML filtering engine that enables fine-grained, parallel filtering of XML streams. It uses a novel subscription model based on the concept of nested filters and supports the efficient evaluation of constraints on node sets. We detail the data structures and algorithms used by the system to evaluate filters while parsing an XML stream and to reconstruct client-specific message versions. Experimental results show that the system can efficiently handle thousands of subscriptions and scales well with the number of active parallel filtering threads.

Categories and Subject Descriptors

H.4 [**Information Systems Applications**]: Miscellaneous

General Terms

Algorithms, Design

Keywords

XML Filtering, Publish/Subscribe, Event Matching, Complex Event Processing

1. INTRODUCTION

Asynchronous messaging plays an increasingly important role in enterprise application integration scenarios. Instead of directly linking multiple applications, a messaging system can be introduced to mediate and unify communication between them. Many existing messaging systems support the publish/subscribe paradigm, a many-to-many communication model. Message producers (publishers) can pass

messages to such a system, which in turn notifies all message consumers (subscribers) of all the messages they are interested in. The way such interests (subscriptions) can be specified by consumers is an important characteristic of any publish/subscribe system. Roughly, one can distinguish between type-based, topic-based, and content-based subscription models. Content-based subscription models are considered the most flexible approach because message consumers can specify conditions on any of the message attributes. One can furthermore differentiate between the expressiveness of different content-based subscription models. This is directly related to a second important aspect of publish/subscribe systems: its range of supported message data structures. A system might support unstructured text, key/value pairs, or complex nested data structures. In enterprise application integration scenarios, XML is usually a natural choice to represent the messages exchanged between different systems. A messaging system needs to correlate every incoming message against all registered subscriptions. This process is called *matching* or *filtering*. Existing XML-based publish/subscribe systems only provide coarse-grained message filtering capabilities. Messages are either sent to a subscriber in their entirety or not at all. *Fine-grained* filtering, i.e. the filtering of the message content itself, is not supported. Such filtering capabilities enable subscribers to formulate very detailed interests. More importantly, they are a prerequisite for a messaging system to support fine-grained access control policies. In this paper, we introduce a flexible content-based subscription model that enables fine-grained, client-specific filtering of XML messages. It is based on the concept of nested filters and supports constraints on element or attribute sets. We furthermore present an efficient streaming XML message filtering system that is based on this subscription model and supports parallel filtering of input streams.

The remainder of this paper is structured as follows. In Section 2, we present our XML subscription model. Section 3 introduces the filtering data structures that are the basis for our filtering approach which is described in Section 4. In Section 5, we give an overview of related work. We discuss our prototypical implementation and present performance evaluation results in Section 6. A summary and conclusions are given in Section 7.

2. SUBSCRIPTION MODEL

Regarding its basic structures, our subscription model is in line with common existing approaches. Put simply, a subscription is a disjunction of filters, which are conjunctions of predicates. The key differences are that filters refer to spe-

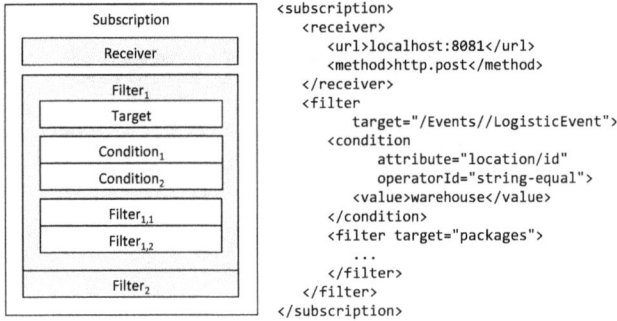

Figure 1: Subscription Format and example

```
<subscription>
    <receiver>
        <url>localhost:8081</url>
        <method>http.post</method>
    </receiver>
    <filter
        target="/Events//LogisticEvent">
        <condition
            attribute="location/id"
            operatorId="string-equal">
            <value>warehouse</value>
        </condition>
        <filter target="packages">
            ...
        </filter>
    </filter>
</subscription>
```

cific targets (XML node sets), can be nested, and predicates can have quantifiers (because message attributes can have multiple values).

A *Subscription* consists of a *Receiver* and a non-empty list of *Filters*. A Receiver specifies the network address, protocol, and other properties of the respective subscriber. A Filter contains a *Target*, a list of *Conditions*, and a list of other Filters (so Filters can be nested arbitrarily). A Target of a top-level Filter specifies which XML elements a subscriber wishes to be notified about, telling the system where actual "messages" can be found in the XML input stream. A Target of a nested Filter specifies which nested XML elements should be filtered. A Condition specifies a further constraint and consists of a *Quantifier* ("any" or "all" for existential or universal quantification), an *attribute name*, an *operator identifier*, and a literal *value*. Please note that an "attribute name" can refer to an XML attribute, but also to an XML element. To avoid confusion, we explicitly use the term "XML attribute" whenever we do not refer to message attributes in the broader sense. To specify Targets and attribute names in Conditions, we use a simplified XPath syntax that only supports child ("/"), descendent ("//"), XML attribute ("@"), and wildcard ("*") expressions. Fig. 1 illustrates the Subscription data structure and gives an XML example.

The semantics of a Subscription are as follows. If a "message" (an XML element identified by a top-level Filter's Target) matches at least one Filter of a Subscription, it is sent to the respective Receiver. An element e matches a Filter f if e matches f's Target and e fulfills all of f's Conditions. An element e matches a Target if the Target's XPath expression selects e. In this case, we say e is *filtered* (or *processed*) by f. An element e fulfills a Condition c if e contains the attribute specified by c and the operator specified by c applied to the attribute's values and the value specified by c evaluates to true for all of the attribute's values (if c's quantifier is "all") or for at least one of the attribute's values (if c's quantifier is "any"). Therefore, similar to many existing systems, the logical expressions in our subscriptions are in disjunctive normal form: a subscription contains a disjunction of filters, each of which being a conjunction of conditions (also called *predicates* in other systems). If an element e has matched ("passed") a Filter that contains a nested Filter f_n, then f_n is applied to e's child elements that match f_n's Target. Again, multiple Filters are combined disjunctively. Child elements not matching any nested Filter's Target are not filtered. So the default behavior is that an element that passed a Filter contains all its child elements.

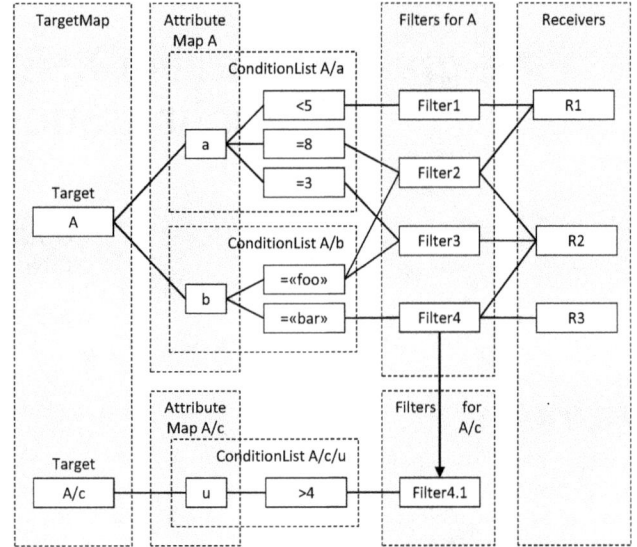

Figure 2: Filtering Network example

3. FILTERING DATA STRUCTURES

All subscriptions are integrated into a data structure called *Filter Network* that allows for their efficient, parallel evaluation against incoming XML streams. It is based on ideas of the content-based Forwarding Table presented by Carzaniga et al. [5] From a high-level perspective, our Filter Network consists of the following elements:

- The *Target Map* contains information about all existing Targets. It is used to determine relevant XML elements (elements that contain "messages" or other elements that need to be processed/filtered) while parsing the XML input stream. The Target Map links Targets to Attribute Maps.

- An *Attribute Map* links attribute to Condition Lists.

- A *Condition List* contains all Conditions that refer to the same attribute name.

- Every *Condition* is linked to all the *Filters* in which it is contained.

- Every top-level Filter is linked a number of *Receivers*.

- *Nested Filters* are inserted into the network just like top-level Filters. They do not have direct links to Receivers, but to their respective parent Filter.

Fig. 2 illustrates these concepts. Please note that starting in this section, we use terms already introduced in the subscription model to refer to some of the system's data structures.

Logically, Filter Networks can be nested. If for example an XML element passed a Filter that contains nested Filters, the process of filtering its child elements is basically sending these elements to the Filter Network defined by the nested Filters. However technically, our system does the fine-grained filtering *while* parsing the input XML. Whether a given element passed a given Filter or not can only be determined *after* the element and all of its child elements have been parsed completely. This is why all nested Filters are evaluated in parallel and the filtering results are attached to the individual elements.

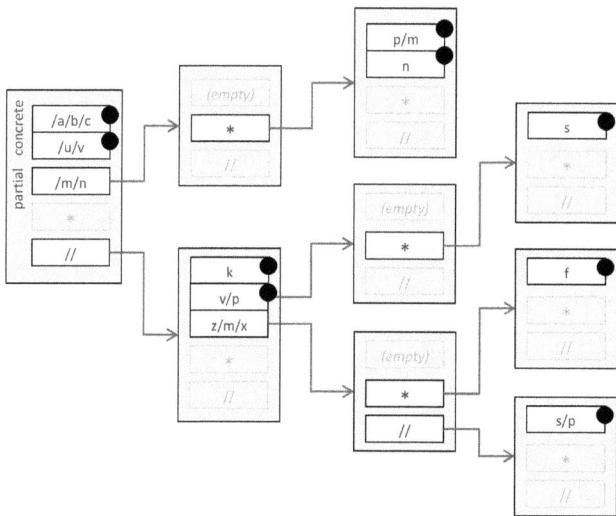

Figure 3: Target Map example

3.1 Target Map

Each target expression (such as `/Events//LogisticEvent`) is integrated into a data structure called Target Map. It enables fast matching of incoming XML elements to Targets and uses the following data structure:

```
TargetMap {
  HashMap<String, Target> concreteTargets
  NestedTargetMap root
}
```

`concreteTargets` is a hash map that maps every concrete target expression (i.e. the ones that do not contain "*" or "//") to the respective Target (see below). Other (non-concrete) target expressions are integrated into `root`, which is a Nested Target Map that has the following structure:

```
NestedTargetMap {
  Target target
  HashMap<String, NestedTargetMap> partialTargets
  NestedTargetMap childTargets
  NestedTargetMap decendantTargets
}
```

Target expressions starting with "*" or "//" are integrated into `childTargets` or `decendantTargets`, respectively. Other expressions (containing, but not starting with "*" or "//") are split and their left ("absolute") parts (the left-hand side until the first occurrence of "*" or "//") are inserted as keys in `partialTargets`. The respective values are new Nested Target Maps that represent the right parts of the expressions. A Nested Target Map can refer to a Target, but also to other Nested Target Maps. Just as the Target Map, it contains `childTargets` and *decendantTargets*. Fig. 3 gives an example of a Target Map (black dots indicate Targets). It represents the following XPath expressions:
/a/b/c, /u/v, /m/n/*/p/m, /m/n/*/n, //k, //v/p, //v/p/*/s, //z/m/x/*/f, and //z/m/x//s/p

3.2 Target and Attribute Map

A Target contains an Attribute Map which is used to identify XML elements and XML attributes in the input stream that are relevant for Conditions. It is structured just like a Target Map, but instead of Targets, it ultimately points to Condition Lists. An Attribute Map basically maps XPath expressions to Condition Lists, just as a Target Map maps such expressions to Targets.

3.3 Condition List

A Condition List is a container for all Conditions that refer to one attribute (for example `/head/@timestamp`) inside a Target (for example `/messages/weathermessage`). Depending on their operators, Conditions are further grouped inside a Condition List to speed up their evaluation. For example, all Conditions using the `string-equal` operator can be put into a hash map that maps the Condition's values directly to the Filters they belong to. Conditions using the `integer-greater-than` or `integer-less-than` operator can be put in lists that are sorted by the values.

3.4 Counting Filter and Receiver

Filters can contain links to the Receivers they belong to, as well as links to Nested Filters. Each Filter stores the number of its Conditions. It also holds a counter for the number of Conditions that have been fulfilled by the message (or element) that is being processed.

4. FILTERING PROCESS

The basic filtering process consists of the following steps: *Target Matching*, *Condition Matching*, *Filter Matching*, and *Message Reconstruction*.

4.1 Target Matching

Each opening element in the XML input stream is evaluated against the Target Map to determine if it is an element of interest. At any time, the concrete absolute Path p of the element currently being processed is known. In the simplest case, a Target can be found by successfully looking up p in the hash map `TargetMap.concreteTargets`. In other cases, we try to find matching hash map entries in the currently active Nested Target Maps' `partialTargets`. A Nested Target Map is "currently active" if it can, given p, potentially lead to Targets. We maintain a stack of currently active Nested Target Maps, adding Nested Target Maps when matching opening XML elements are parsed and removing them when the respective closing elements are encountered. If not empty, the "*"-Nested Target Map (`childTargets`) of a currently active Nested Target Map is added to the stack regardless of the type of the opening element. Likewise, a "//"-Nested Target Map (`decendantTargets`), if not empty, is added to the stack. It "moves up" to the top with each subsequent opening element. It is removed when the element that initially caused it to be put onto the stack is closed. When an element matches a Target, this element and all subsequent XML elements and attributes are stored in a temporary buffer called `Output Message Buffer` until the matching closing element is encountered. The latter triggers the Receiver-specific Message Reconstruction based on the Output Message Buffer's content (see Section 4.4).

4.2 Condition Matching

When a Target of a top-level Filter has been matched by an opening XML element (for example `AlarmEvent`), its child elements are evaluated against the Conditions that are linked to this Target. For each child element, the Target's

Attribute Map is used to determine suitable Condition Lists. The mapping of the element's (and its XML attributes') XPath expressions to Condition Lists in the Attribute Map works just like the mapping to Targets in the Target Map. If one or more matching Condition Lists have been found for the current element, all of the Conditions they contain are evaluated against the element's (or its attributes') values. This is done in an operator and type specific way. Sorting and indexing strategies to speed up condition evaluation are out of the scope of this paper. When a Condition (ignoring its quantifier) is fulfilled by an element, it is *hit*. Hitting a Condition tells it to inform all of the Filters it belongs to. The Filters then increase their counter of fulfilled conditions. However, the Condition's quantifier needs special attention. If it equals "ANY", then it is sufficient if one element in the current filtering context fulfills the Condition – we can hit the Condition whenever we encounter such an element. If the quantifier equals "ALL", then *all* of the elements in the current Filtering Context that match the Condition's attribute name must be fulfilled. A *Filtering Context* is a concrete element which has been matched by a Target and has not been closed yet. It is used by the Target's subordinate Condition Lists in various ways. To illustrate this concept, consider the following example. There is a top-level Filter and its Target expression is `EventList/AlarmEvent`. It has a Condition List with one Condition with quantifier=`ALL`, attribute=`alarmCodes/code`, operator=`string-match`, and value=`"*100"`. This means that every element e matching the XPath expression
`alarmCodes/code` in an `EventList/AlarmEvent` must fulfill the expression `string-match(e,"*100")` in order to match the Filter. Now the following XML is parsed:

```
1  <EventList>
2    <AlarmEvent @id="1">
3      <alarmCodes>
4        <code>2100</code>
5        <code>3100</code>
6      </alarmCodes>
7      <alarmCodes>
8        <code>4999</code>
9        <code>5100</code>
10     </alarmCodes>
11   </AlarmEvent>
12   <AlarmEvent @id="2">...</AlarmEvent>
13 </EventList>
```

When the parser reaches line 2, the Target is matched by the element `<AlarmEvent @id="1">`. This element becomes the Filtering Context for all Condition Lists / Conditions / Filters linked to the Target. (We added the XML attribute `id` to stress that a Filtering Context is always an individual element, not an XPath expression that refers to a set of elements.) One usage of the Filtering Context is to determine if certain counters and lists need to be reset. One such counter is `attributeOccCount` ("Occ" for occurrence) which counts the number of times an attribute (XML element or XML attribute) has been found within the current context. It is reset whenever a new context if found. This behavior is reflected in lines 1 to 5 in Algorithm 1. In the example, if an `alarmCodes/code` element is encountered in the context of `<AlarmEvent @id="2">` occurrence counter is set to 1, the new context is remembered in `lastContext`, and the list `watchConds` is cleared. `lastContext`, `attributeOccCount`

and `watchConds` exist in each individual Condition List (like instance variables in object-oriented programming). `watchConds` is a "watchlist" that holds Conditions that need to be fulfilled by *every* subsequent occurrence of an element. It is used to support the universal ("ALL") quantifier. If a fulfilled Condition c has this quantifier (line 17), we check if the current element is the first occurrence of its kind (line 18). Only in this case we have a chance that *all* of these elements (in the current context) will be fulfilled. To keep track of that, c is added to the list `watchConds` (line 19). Because we do not know how many times the element will occur, we hit Condition c. All Conditions in `watchConds` are checked against every subsequent occurrence of relevant elements (line 9 to 14). If one element fails to fulfill a Condition in `watchConds`, the whole Condition (with its universal quantifier) is not fulfilled. In this case, we remove c from `watchConds` (line 11) and *unhit* it (line 12). "unhitting" means the reverse of hit: the respective Condition informs all linked Filters that one Condition less is fulfilled. Obviously, unhit is never called without having called hit before.

Input: Element *element*, Element *context*

```
1  if context ≠ lastContext then
2      attributeOccCount = 1
3      lastContext = context
4      watchConds.clear()
5  end
6  else
7      attributeOccCount = attributeOccCount + 1
8  end
9  foreach Condition c ∈ watchConds do
10     if ¬c.isFulfilled(element) then
11         watchConds.remove(c)
12         c.unhit(element, context)
13     end
14 end
15 fulfilledConditions = getFulfilledConditions(element)
16 foreach Condition c ∈ fulfilledConditions do
17     if c.quantifier == "ALL" then
18         if attributeOccCount == 1 then
19             watchConds.add(c)
20             c.hit(element, context)
21         end
22     end
23     else
24         c.hit(context)
25     end
26 end
```

Algorithm 1: ConditionList.match

In our example, when line 4 of the input is parsed, the Condition List for `EventList/AlarmEvent/alarmCodes/code` is called to process the element. Because the context changed from something else (e.g. `null`) to `<AlarmEvent @id="1">`, the initialization block starting at line 1 is executed. The call to `getFulfilledConditions` returns our single Condition c because code's value 2100 matches `"*100"`. c's quantifier is "ALL" and `<code>` occured for the first time, so c is added to `watchConds` and is hit. When the XML's 5th line is parsed, `attributeOccCount` is increased (line 7) and our stored Condition in `watchConds` is checked (line 10). Because the second code element also fulfills it, nothing needs to be done. Because `attributeOccCount` is not equal to 1 (line 18), nothing else happens. When line 8 of the XML is parsed, the expression in line 10 of the algorithm is fulfilled, so our Condition is removed from `watchConds` and unhit. When the XML's 9th line is parsed, nothing happens because `watchConds` is empty and `attributeOccCount` is not equal to 1. The element `<AlarmEvent @id="1">` does therefore not match the example Filter.

When the closing element (`</AlarmEvent>`) is encountered, *Message Reconstruction* takes place if any top-level Filters were fulfilled. When the next opening `AlarmEvent` element is parsed, the filtering process described above starts with the context set to `<AlarmEvent @id="2">`. Note the situation would be different if the Filter's Target expression was `EventList/AlarmEvent/alarmCodes`. In this case, the first `alarmCodes` element would pass the Filter, while the second would not.

Input: Element *element*, Element *context*
1 **if** $context \neq lastContext$ **then**
2   **foreach** *Filter* $f \in filters$ **do**
3   f.hit(*context*)
4   **if** f.*isFulfilled(context)* **then**
5   *fulfilledFilters*.add(f)
6   *element*.addFilter(f)
7   **end**
8   **end**
9     $lastContext = context$
10 **end**

Algorithm 2: Condition.hit

Algorithm 2 shows how the `hit` method of a Condition works. Each Condition maintains a `lastContext` variable, just like a Condition List. Filters that are linked to a Condition should not be incremented more than once when the same Condition is fulfilled by multiple elements in the same filtering context. This is why Filters are hit only the first time a Condition is hit in a given context. If one of the hit Filters is fulfilled now, it is added to the list `fulfilledFilters`. In addition, the fulfilled Filter is added to the element itself, so each element has a list of Filters that it matched. The elements that have been parsed are stored in memory as long as the closing element of the opening element that matched the top-level Filter has not been parsed yet. The elements' lists of fulfilled Filters are used for the Message Reconstruction (see Section 4.4). Algorithm 3 shows the corresponding Condition.unhit algorithm, which undoes the effects of hit.

Input: Element *element*, Element *context*
1 **foreach** *Filter* $f \in filters$ **do**
2   **if** f.*isFulfilled(context)* **then**
3   *fulfilledFilters*.remove(f)
4   *element*.removeFilter(f)
5   **end**
6   f.unhit(*context*)
7 **end**

Algorithm 3: Condition.unhit

4.3 Filter Matching

The `hit` and `unhit` methods of a Filter are very similar to its Condition counterparts. `Filter.unhit` just decrements the counter for fulfilled Conditions. Algorithm 4 shows how `Filter.unhit` works. If a Filter is hit for the first time in a filtering context, its counter for fulfilled Conditions is set to 1 and the context is remembered. Otherwise, the counter for fulfilled Conditions (`numFulfdConditions`) is simply increased. Note that a Filter can be hit by different Conditions (referring to the same attribute or not) in the same context.

Input: Element *context*
1 **if** $context \neq lastContext$ **then**
2     $numFulfdConditions = 1$
3     $lastContext = context$
4 **end**
5 **else**
6     $numFulfdConditions = numFulfdConditions + 1$
7 **end**
8 **return** false

Algorithm 4: Filter.hit

A Filter is fulfilled if its number of fulfilled Conditions equals its total number of Conditions. For performance reasons, we do not reset every filter's counter to zero after certain closing XML elements have been parsed. Instead, we reset it on the first hit in a filtering context (cmp. algorithm 4, line 1). This fact is reflected in `isFulfilled`, where we require that the Filter has been hit in the filtering context.

Input: Element *context*
1 **if** $context == lastContext$ **then**
2   **return** $numConditions == numFulfdConditions$
3 **end**
4 **return** false

Algorithm 5: Filter.isFulfilled

4.4 Message Reconstruction

Whenever a closing XML element is encountered that matches a top-level Target, a complete message has been parsed and the respective Receivers can be notified. In previous publish/subscribe systems, the whole, unchanged message would have been transmitted to these Receivers. Because our system supports fine-grained message filtering, the reconstruction of different, Receiver-specific versions of the message is necessary.

Let $F = f_1, f_2, \ldots, f_n$ be the set of top-level Filters that are associated with a Receiver r and matched an element m ("m" for message). A version of m (called m') is sent to r if F is not empty. (That is, if r is associated with at least one top-level Filter that was matched by the message.) Let m_c be a child element of m. It is included in m' if: a) at least one Filter $f_k \in F$ did *not* contain a nested Filter that targeted m's type, or b) at least one Filter $f_l \in F$ did contain a nested Filter that targeted m's type *and* f_l was matched by m. These cases reflect two basic rules introduced in Section 2: an element that passed a Filter contains all its child elements unless they have been filtered by a nested Filter, and Filters associated with one Receiver are combined disjunctively. The latter also applies to nested Filters, but only if their parent Filters are matched. So if an element m matched two associated Filters f_1 and f_2, and they both contained nested Filters targeting m's child element m_c, then m_c would be included in the result if at least one of the nested Filters was matched by m_c. If f_1 did not

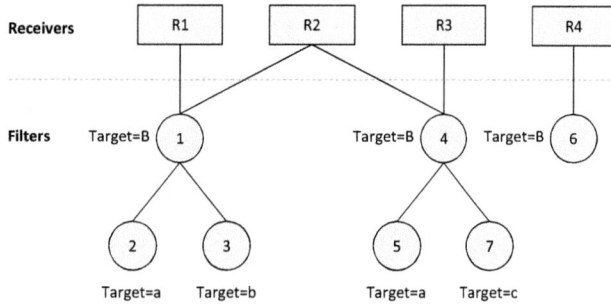

Figure 4: Example Receivers, Filters and results

Table 1: Example Filter Fulfillment Table

element	filtered by	fulfilled	w. rel.	inherit f.
B_1	1, 4, 6	1	1	–
a_1	2, 5	2	2	–
a_2	2, 5	5	–	–
b_1	3	3	3	–
b_2	3	–	–	–
c_1	7	–	–	1
B_2	1, 4, 6	4, 6	4, 6	–
a_3	2, 5	2, 5	2, 5	6
b_3	3	–	–	4, 6
c_2	7	7	7	6
d_1	–	–	–	6, 7
B_3	1, 4, 6	1, 4, 6	1, 4, 6	–
a_4	2, 5	2	2	6
a_5	2, 5	5	5	6
a_6	2, 5	–	–	6

Table 2: Resulting XML documents

original	R1	R2	R3	R4
B_1	B_1	B_1		
a_1	a_1	a_1		
a_2				
b_1	b_1	b_1		
b_2				
c_1	c_1	c_1		
B_2	B_2	B_2	B_2	B_2
a_3		a_3	a_3	a_3
b_3		b_3	b_3	b_3
c_2		c_2	c_2	c_2
d_1		d_1	d_1	d_1
B_3	B_3	B_3	B_3	B_3
a_4	a_4	a_4		a_4
a_5		a_5	a_5	a_5
a_6				a_6

contain a nested Filter targeting m_c, then m_c would be included no matter if f_2 did contain a nested Filter targeting m_c or not.

Practically, we achieve the message reconstruction by applying a counting algorithm to each individual XML element in the Output Message Buffer. For each element, we maintain four lists: *filtered by*, *fulfilled*, *fulfilled with relationship*, and *inherit from*. Each list contains references to Filters that have different logical relationships to the respective element e. *filtered by* contains all Filters whose Targets matched e. (Please note that in our implementation, we don't actually copy all the Filter references but only the Target references.) *fulfilled* contains the subset of the Filters in *filtered by* that e actually fulfilled/matched. *fulfilled with relationships* contains the subset of the Filters in *fulfilled* that are both fulfilled by e and whose respective parent Filters were also fulfilled by e's parent element. (In other words, all opening elements leading to e have matched a Filter in one Filter hierarchy.) During the Condition and Filter matching described in Section 4.2 and 4.3, we cannot verify this property. To make this clearer, consider the following XML:

```
1 <A>
2   <a>10</a>
3   <a>15</a>
4   <a>20</a>
5   <b>false</b>
6 </A>
```

If there is a nested Filter f_n that filters a elements, we will evaluate its Conditions even though later on we might recognize that the enclosing A element did not pass f_n's parent filter f. This is because we cannot know whether A will pass f until we have finished parsing all of A's child elements. And once we have parsed these child elements, it will be too late to evaluate their Conditions because of the streaming XML processing approach. So *fulfilled with relationship* is a sufficient filtering criteria, while *filtered by* and *fulfilled* together with the filter hierarchies only provide the necessary information to derive it. The last list attached to each element is *inherit from*. It contains all Filters in the columns *fulfilled with relationship* and *inherit from* of the element's parent element, but without those Filters that contain a nested Filter that filtered the element. By default, an element inherits fulfillment from the Filters that were fulfilled by its parent element. This is why the element's parent's *fulfilled with relationship*-list is considered. Because inheritance can span multiple levels, the element's parent's *inherit from*-list is considered as well. But if there is a nested Filter

that targets an element, the result of this Filter overrides the default inheritance (otherwise nested Filters would not have any effect at all).

Table 1 gives an example of a Fulfillment Table for an XML document consisting of three top-level B elements, each containing one or more a, b, or c elements. One c element also contains a d element. To distinguish individual elements, we used an index notation – the Filters are simply identified by numbers. Fig. 4 shows the example's Filter hierarchy and the Filter's association to Receivers. Filters 1, 4, and 6 all target B elements. Filter 1 contains Filter 2, targeting a elements, and Filter 3, targeting b elements. Filter 4 contains Filter 5, targeting a elements, and Filter 7, targeting c elements. Filter 1 is associated with Receiver $R1$ and $R2$, Filter 4 with $R2$ and $R3$, and Filter 6 is associated with $R4$. Please note that the Filters' Conditions and the XML elements' values have been omitted. This is why the values in column *fulfilled* cannot be derived from the information given in the example. It is given that B_1 fulfilled Filter 1, but not Filter 4 or 6, and that B_2 fulfilled Filter 4 and 6, but not Filter 1, and so on. Also shown in Fig. 4 are the resulting filtered messages to be sent to the respective Receivers. a_2 fulfilled Filter 5, but because its parent element did not fulfill Filter 4, a_2 is not sent to $R2$

or R_3. c_1 was filtered by Filter 5, but did not fulfill it. Still it is sent to R_1 and R_2 because it inherited fulfillment from Filter 1. It did not inherit fulfillment from Filter 4 because this Filter does contain a nested Filter targeting c elements, so the default inheritance behavior is overridden.

5. RELATED WORK

Carzaniga and Wolf [5], in the context of their influential SIENA system [4], propose data structures and algorithms for efficient content-based filtering of flat messages (key/value pairs). Their main data structure is the *Fast Forwarding Table* which stores constraints and filters in a redundancy-reduced way. Constraints are grouped by attribute and linked to the filters they belong to, which in turn are linked to the respective interfaces (message receivers). An extended counting algorithm based on earlier work [17, 11] is used to determine matching filters. We build on the work of Carzaniga and Wolf by extending the Fast Forwarding Table approach to support XML messages and nested filters. We also extend the counting algorithm to support quantifiers in constraints and use it to enable fine-grained filtering of individual message elements. Publish/subscribe systems supporting XML messages include XTreeNet [12], ONYX [10], and Sonnet [19]. Their filtering engines are based on automaton- or index-oriented approaches.

XFilter [1] is an early automaton-based XML filtering engine that uses finite state machines to detect incoming XML elements that match the XPath expressions of a filter constraint. Each XPath expression is represented by its own finite state machine, so similarities between expressions cannot be exploited. YFilter [9, 8] overcomes this drawback by representing all XPath expressions in one single nondeterministic finite automaton. Our Target Map data structure can be considered a representation of such a nondeterministic finite automaton where all Nested Target Maps are states, Nested Target Maps on top of the stack are active states, and Nested Target Maps with a non-empty Target are accepting states. However, we do not keep one "state" for each location step of an XPath expression but treat expression parts that do not contain * or // as a whole. Our `concreteTargets` hash map is a shortcut for simple XPath expressions. Moro et al. [15] present approaches to limit the number of queries that need to be evaluated against an incoming XML document. For path matching, the authors use a state machine as in YFilter; however they represent path queries in a reversed order. They employ bottom-up evaluation of XML documents to trigger fewer states of the state machine. Index-Filter [3] employs a preprocessing step that indexes input XML documents. The index used to efficiently derive structural relationships between XML elements during the actual matching step. It was shown to provide performance advantages over YFilter when the XML documents are relatively large and the number of queries relatively small. XTrie [6] identifies sub-strings that are shared by multiple XPath expressions and indexes them in order to speed up the matching process.

Ashayer et al. [2] pioneered the use of relational databases to perform efficient predicate and subscription matching in publish/subscribe systems. Their approach is suited for scenarios where the number of different event attributes and attribute values is known and relatively small. Tian et al. [16] and Zhao et al. [18] extend the idea of using relational database operators to filter XML documents. Other work

in the area of XML-based content-based routing focuses on distribution aspects. For example, Miliaraki et al. [13, 14] explore the use of distributed hash tables to distribute the matching process to different machines in a network. They build on YFilter's automaton approach, constructing distributed nondeterministic finite automata. Chan and Ni [7] present an approach that lets subsequent routing nodes in a distributed content-based routing system reuse XML matching information, thus reducing the parsing overhead of these nodes.

To the best of our knowledge, the problems of fine-grained filtering of XML documents against large numbers of subscriptions and the resulting necessity for client-specific message reconstruction have not been addressed before.

6. EVALUATION

To demonstrate their feasibility, we implemented a prototypical software system that follows the approaches presented in this paper. Furthermore, we conducted performance measurements to quantify their efficiency.

6.1 Implementation

Our system prototype was implemented in Java 6. For XML processing, we used the Sun Java Streaming XML Parser together with StAX (Streaming API for XML). Fig. 5 illustrates the system's main architectural components. Message *Senders* can send XML documents to the system. The *Thread Manager* dispatches sender requests to individual filtering threads. In Fig. 5, three filtering threads are shown. Each filtering thread has an *Input Buffer* which stores the incoming XML data. A thread's *StAX parser*

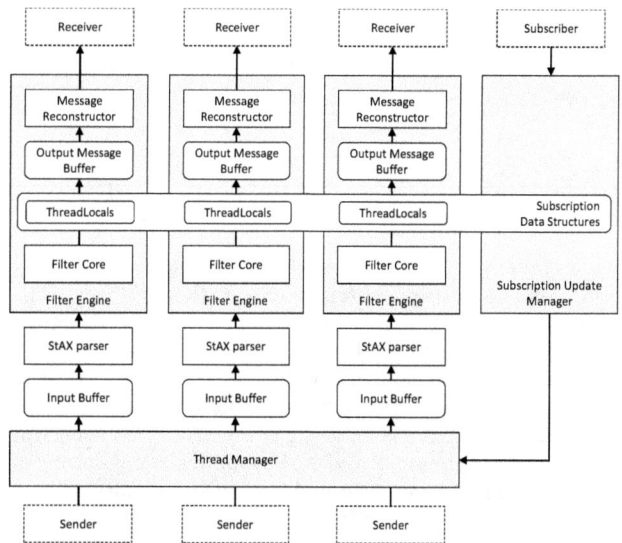

Figure 5: Prototype Architecture

processes this XML data element by element and sends respective events (*opening element*, *element data*, or *closing element*) to the actual *Filter Engine* using a simple interface. This way, the parser technology can be exchanged easily. At the heart of the Filter Engine is the *Filter Core*, which performs the process described in Section 4 of this paper. It shares the main Subscription, Filter, and Condition data structures with all other filtering threads. All counters, information about current contexts, and Condition watchlists are stored in *ThreadLocal* variables, so each thread can have its own state. XML elements that have been evaluated against the Subscription base are stored in the thread's *Output Message Buffer*. When processing of a message (element matching a top-level Filter) has finished, the client-specific versions of this message are built by the *Message Reconstructor* and are sent to the respective *Receivers*. The *Subscription Update Manager* handles the insertion and deletion of Subscriptions. It receives update requests and places them into an internal queue. To process one or more items from the queue, the Subscription Update Manager sends all filtering threads a pause request (via the *Thread Manager*, which has access to all current threads). After receiving a pause request, each filtering thread finishes its current filtering task and afterwards acknowledges the Thread Manager that it has paused. When all filtering threads are paused, the Subscription Manager is allowed to modify the subscription data structures. When this is done, the Thread Manager is informed that the filtering threads can continue processing elements from their input buffers. It is important that the subscription data is not modified while a thread performs filtering because it might lead to inconsistent results – Receivers might receive messages they did not subscribe to or might not receive message they did subscribe to.

6.2 Performance Analysis

Table 3: Performance analysis parameters

	m1	m2	m3	m4	m5	m6
n	10	10	10	10	10	10
a	5	3	10	3	5	3
a_n	3	3	10	3	3	3
v_a	500	100,000	100	1,000	500	1,000
c	2	1	5	3	2	3
r	100	100	100	100	100	100
s	x	x	x	x	50,000	50,000
t	8	8	8	8	x	x

We evaluated the run time behavior of our prototype under different subscription setups and XML workloads. The hardware was a standard PC equipped with 8 GB RAM and an Intel Core i7 CPU running at 2.8 GHz. We used Windows 7 running a Java HotSpot 64-Bit Server VM. The filtering performance (throughput in messages per second) was measured using the following approach. First, subscription sets of varying size and XML workloads consisting of 50,000 messages were generated into main memory. Then, we measured the time it took to process the XML ten times and calculated the throughput accordingly. Each Subscription contained exactly one Filter with exactly one nested Filter. The following parameters were varied:
number of message types (n), number of attributes (a), number of nested attributes per attribute (a_n), number of possible values per attribute (v_a), number of conditions (c), number of receivers (r), number of subscriptions (s), and number of threads (t) Table 3 shows the parameter values of the different test scenarios.

Figure 6 shows the throughput depending on the number of subscriptions in the four scenarios m1 to m4. The throughput varied from 2,597 events/second (large messages

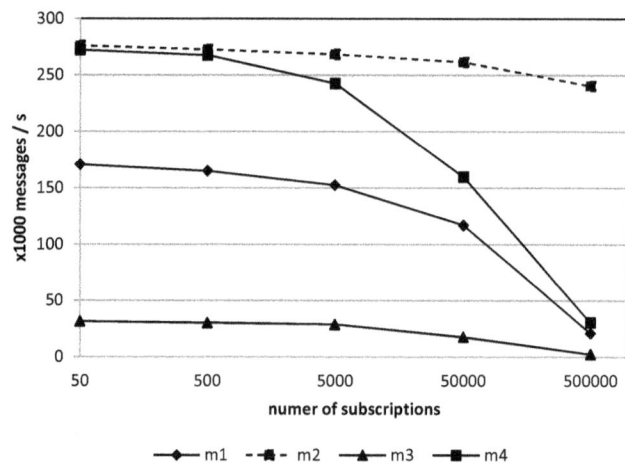

Figure 6: Performance analysis 1

with 10 * 10 attributes and 500,000 complex subscriptions) to 276,013 events/second (small messages with 3*3 attributes and 50 subscriptions). The message size turned out to have a bigger performance impact than the number of subscriptions or their complexity. Figure 7 shows the throughput depending on the number of active filtering threads in the two scenarios m5 and m6. As expected, the filtering performance increased with the number of threads that made use of the multi-core processors' parallelization capabilities. However, it did not increase linearly with the number of threads due to scheduling overhead. The per-core filtering performance ranged from 30,000 per core when only one thread was used to 15,000 per core when eight cores were used. Using more than eight threads (the processor's number of cores) did not further increase the filtering performance.

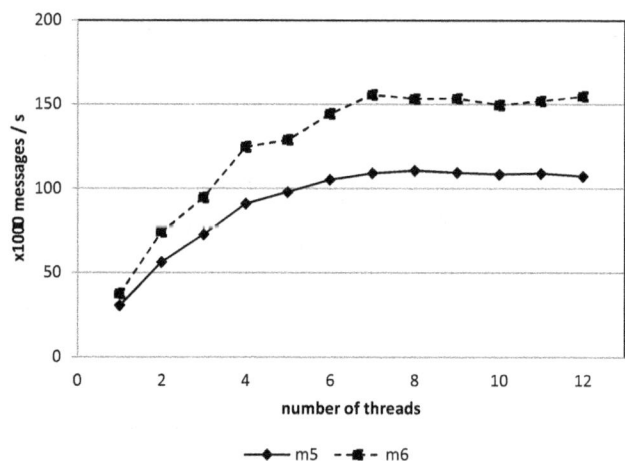

Figure 7: Performance analysis 2

7. SUMMARY AND FUTURE WORK

In this paper, we presented a new XML message filtering engine for content-based publish/subscribe systems. Using an XML-based subscription syntax, subscribers can specify filter criteria on XML elements and attributes. A novel aspect is that Filters can be nested, which allows for arbitrarily fine-grained filtering of nested XML elements. We showed how Filters can be evaluated efficiently against streams of XML elements. To find XML elements of interest, we use lookups in nested hash maps that are created from the Filter's Target and the Condition's attribute expressions. To evaluate Conditions and Filters, we use an extended counting algorithm. Furthermore, we presented an efficient way to evaluate Filter conditions that contain the universal quantifier against XML node sets. We described an approach to efficiently reconstruct different receiver-specific versions of a message using lists of Filter references attached to the XML message's individual elements. We also presented a prototypical implementation of our system which is built to support multi-threading from the ground up. Using performance measurements, we showed the viability and scalability of our approaches. For the future, we plan to focus on integrating the filtering engine in an actual publish/subscribe system that supports content-based routing. As a main use case for fine-grained message filtering, we want to investigate how access control at the XML element level can be included in such a system. Central questions are how access control policies can be described in terms of filters and how these filters can be logically combined with the subscriptions' filters. As a use case, we investigate the exchange of sensor-based business process event data with business partners that are not supposed to see certain message details. With a flexible and secure publish/subscribe infrastructure for XML messages at hand, business partners can perform inter-company event correlation in order to optimize their processes. We argue that message *filtering* should be clearly separated from message *correlation*, which is the task of Complex Event Processing (CEP) Engines. CEP Engines can however benefit by pre-filtered input streams. Another possible direction is to extend the core filtering engine to support conditions that not only correlate XML element or attribute values with constants, but with other element or attribute values from the same input stream. This would mean that conditions could not easily be evaluated *while* parsing the XML anymore because conditions could refer to values that have not been parsed yet.

8. ACKNOWLEDGEMENTS

Parts of the research presented in this paper were done at SAP Research, Dresden, funded by the German Federal Ministry of Education and Research under research grant 01IA08006 ("ADiWa"). The author would like to thank Volker Suschke and Marco Geissler for fruitful discussions and their contributions to an early version of our prototype.

9. REFERENCES

[1] M. Altinel and M. J. Franklin. Efficient filtering of xml documents for selective dissemination of information. In *Proceedings of the 26th International Conference on Very Large Data Bases*, VLDB '00, pages 53–64, San Francisco, CA, USA, 2000. Morgan Kaufmann Publishers Inc.

[2] G. Ashayer, H. K. Y. Leung, and H.-A. Jacobsen. Predicate matching and subscription matching in publish/subscribe systems. In *Proceedings of the 22nd International Conference on Distributed Computing Systems*, ICDCSW '02, pages 539–548, Washington, DC, USA, 2002. IEEE Computer Society.

[3] N. Bruno, L. Gravano, N. Koudas, and D. Srivastava. Navigation- vs. index-based xml multi-query processing. In *Proceedings of ICDE*, pages 139–150, 2003.

[4] A. Carzaniga and A. L. Wolf. Fast forwarding for content-based networking. Technical Report CU-CS-922-01, Department of Computer Science, University of Colorado, Nov. 2001.

[5] A. Carzaniga and A. L. Wolf. Forwarding in a content-based network. In *Proceedings of ACM SIGCOMM 2003*, pages 163–174, Karlsruhe, Germany, Aug. 2003.

[6] C.-Y. Chan, P. Felber, M. Garofalakis, and R. Rastogi. Efficient filtering of xml documents with xpath expressions. *The VLDB Journal*, 11:354–379, December 2002.

[7] C. Y. Chan and Y. Ni. Efficient xml data dissemination with piggybacking. In *Proceedings of the 2007 ACM SIGMOD international conference on Management of data*, SIGMOD '07, pages 737–748, New York, NY, USA, 2007. ACM.

[8] Y. Diao, M. Altinel, M. J. Franklin, H. Zhang, and P. Fischer. Path sharing and predicate evaluation for high-performance xml filtering. *ACM TRANS. DATABASE SYST*, 28:2003, 2003.

[9] Y. Diao and M. J. Franklin. High-performance xml filtering: An overview of yfilter. *IEEE Data Engineering Bulletin*, 26:41–48, 2003.

[10] Y. Diao, S. Rizvi, and M. J. Franklin. Towards an internet-scale xml dissemination service. In *Proceedings of the Thirtieth international conference on Very large data bases - Volume 30*, VLDB '04, pages 612–623. VLDB Endowment, 2004.

[11] F. Fabret, H. A. Jacobsen, F. Llirbat, J. Pereira, K. A. Ross, and D. Shasha. Filtering algorithms and implementation for very fast publish/subscribe systems. In *Proceedings of the 2001 ACM SIGMOD international conference on Management of data*, SIGMOD '01, pages 115–126, New York, NY, USA, 2001. ACM.

[12] W. Fenner, M. Rabinovich, K. K. Ramakrishnan, D. Srivastava, and Y. Zhang. Xtreenet: Scalable overlay networks for xml content dissemination and querying (synopsis). In *Proceedings of the 10th International Workshop on Web Content Caching and Distribution*, pages 41–46, Washington, DC, USA, 2005. IEEE Computer Society.

[13] I. Miliaraki, Z. Kaoudi, and M. Koubarakis. Xml data dissemination using automata on top of structured overlay networks. In *Proceeding of the 17th international conference on World Wide Web*, WWW '08, pages 865–874, New York, NY, USA, 2008. ACM.

[14] I. Miliaraki and M. Koubarakis. Distributed structural and value xml filtering. In *Proceedings of the Fourth ACM International Conference on Distributed Event-Based Systems*, DEBS '10, pages 2–13, New York, NY, USA, 2010. ACM.

[15] M. M. Moro, P. Bakalov, and V. J. Tsotras. Early profile pruning on xml-aware publish-subscribe systems. In *Proceedings of the 33rd international conference on Very large data bases*, VLDB '07, pages 866–877. VLDB Endowment, 2007.

[16] F. Tian, B. Reinwald, H. Pirahesh, T. Mayr, and J. Myllymaki. Implementing a scalable xml publish/subscribe system using relational database systems. In *Proceedings of the 2004 ACM SIGMOD international conference on Management of data*, SIGMOD '04, pages 479–490, New York, NY, USA, 2004. ACM.

[17] T. W. Yan and H. García-Molina. Index structures for selective dissemination of information under the boolean model. *ACM Trans. Database Syst.*, 19:332–364, June 1994.

[18] J. Zhao, D. Yang, J. Gao, and T. Wang. An xml publish/subscribe algorithm implemented by relational operators. In *Proceedings of the joint 9th Asia-Pacific web and 8th international conference on web-age information management conference on Advances in data and web management*, APWeb/WAIM'07, pages 305–316, Berlin, Heidelberg, 2007. Springer-Verlag.

[19] A. Zhou, W. Qian, X. Gong, and M. Zhou. Sonnet: an efficient distributed content-based dissemination broker. In *Proceedings of the 2007 ACM SIGMOD international conference on Management of data*, SIGMOD '07, pages 1094–1096, New York, NY, USA, 2007. ACM.

A World of Opportunities: CPS, IOT, and Beyond

Calton Pu
School of Computer Science
Georgia Institute of Technology, Atlanta, GA, USA
(calton.pu@cc.gatech.edu)

Abstract

The continuous evolution of computing and networking technologies (e.g., Moore's Law) is creating a new world populated by many sensors on physical and social environments. This emerging new world goes much further than the original visions of ubiquitous computing and World Wide Web. Aspects of this new world have received various names such as Cyber Physical Systems (CPS) and Internet of Things (IOT). CPS links many physical sensor data to detailed simulation models running on large data centers. IOT brings together many appliances, making much more environmental data available and supporting control of these appliances. CPS/IOT applications are many, including personalized healthcare, intelligent transportation, smart grid, sustainable environment, and disaster recovery as representative examples. These CPS/IOT applications are motivated and strongly pushed by significant new social, economic, and human benefits. At the same time, these applications are also mission-critical with serious quality of service requirements such as real-time performance, continuous availability, high security and privacy.

We will argue that the traditional process-oriented programming languages and software architectures should be augmented by distributed event-based facilities and abstractions for the construction of large scale distributed CPS/IOT applications. In addition to the focus on performance, we anticipate that other quality of service dimensions such as availability, reliability, security, and privacy will become important concerns in the research on distributed event-based systems. We will discuss research opportunities and challenges that bring the distributed event-based systems technology to CPS/IOT applications.

Categories & Subject Descriptors: **E.0:** Data (general), H.3.4: Data management (systems and software).

General Terms: Experimentation

Bio

Calton Pu was born in Taiwan and grew up in Brazil. He received his PhD from University of Washington in 1986 and served on the faculty of Columbia University and Oregon Graduate Institute. Currently, he is holding the position of Professor and John P. Imlay, Jr. Chair in Software in the College of Computing, Georgia Institute of Technology. He has worked on several projects in systems and database research. His contributions to systems research include program specialization and software feedback. His contributions to database research include extended transaction models and their implementation. His recent research has focused on automated system management in clouds (Elba project) and document quality, including spam processing. He has collaborated extensively with scientists and industry researchers. He has published more than 70 journal papers and book chapters, 200 conferences and referred workshop papers.

Fault Injection-based Assessment of Partial Fault Tolerance in Stream Processing Applications

Gabriela Jacques-Silva†♠, Buğra Gedik♠, Henrique Andrade♠*,
Kun-Lung Wu♠, Ravishankar K. Iyer†

†Coordinated Science Laboratory
University of Illinois at Urbana-Champaign
1308 W. Main St., Urbana, IL
rkiyer@illinois.edu

♠Thomas J. Watson Research Center
IBM Research
19 Skyline Dr., Hawthorne, NY
{g.jacques,bgedik,klwu}@us.ibm.com

ABSTRACT

This paper describes an experimental methodology used to evaluate the effectiveness of partial fault tolerance (PFT) techniques in data stream processing applications. Without a clear understanding of the impact of faults on the quality of the application output, applying PFT techniques in practice is not viable. We assess the impact of PFT by injecting faults into a synthetic financial engineering application running on top of IBM's stream processing middleware, System S. The application output quality degradation is evaluated via an application-specific output score function. In addition, we propose four metrics that are aimed at assessing the impact of faults in different stream operators of the application flow graph with respect to *predictability* and *availability*. These metrics help the developer to decide where in the application he should place redundant resources. We show that PFT is indeed viable, which opens the way for considerably reducing the resource consumption when compared to fully consistent replicas.

Categories and Subject Descriptors

D.2.5 [**Software Engineering**]: Testing and Debugging—*Error handling and recovery*; H.2.4 [**Database Management**]: Systems—*Distributed databases*

General Terms

Reliability, experimentation

1. INTRODUCTION

Stream processing applications *continuously analyze* the heterogeneous incoming data and perform a variety of computations over generally incomplete information [5]. High availability is a key requirement of stream processing systems [25], since they process continuous live data. Typically,

---

*Currently employed by Goldman Sachs.
Email: henrique.c.m.andrade@gmail.com

streaming applications are designed by assembling *stream operators* as data flow graphs, which can be distributed over a set of nodes to achieve high performance and scalability [12]. A fault in a computing node or in a stream operator can result in massive data loss due to the typical high data rates of incoming streams.

Although many fault tolerance techniques for stream computing [13, 16, 19] provide guarantees that no data is lost or any inconsistency exists (e.g., duplicate delivery of the same data item, which we refer to as data duplication), these methods usually cause significant degradation in performance. Aiming at reducing such performance overhead, partial fault tolerance (PFT) techniques [4, 17, 21, 23, 30] have been proposed. These techniques assume that data loss and data duplicates are acceptable under faulty conditions. The rationale is that many streaming applications tolerate data imprecision by design, and, as a result, can still achieve correctness without using stringent fault tolerance methods.

While all of the above techniques require a careful evaluation to assess the fault tolerance achieved and the resulting performance degradation, this is especially true for methods that provide PFT. Hence, the use of PFT is not viable without a clear understanding of the impact of faults on the application output.

This paper describes a fault injection-based [14] experimental methodology to evaluate the effectiveness of PFT techniques in streaming applications. Our first goal is *to assess the impact of PFT on the output of an application.* We use a fault injector to mimic the effect of a fault in the application when a specific PFT mechanism is in place. To the best of our knowledge, we are the first to describe a thorough fault injection experiment that evaluates PFT techniques in a streaming application. Our second goal is *to characterize how each stream operator used by the application behaves under failures,* so the developer can decide if the PFT technique in place is adequate for the target operator. We characterize each operator by calculating *four evaluation metrics* over the application output generated during the injection trials. In addition, the metrics can be used to identify which operators are most *critical* to the application output quality. Prioritizing most critical operators when protecting an application with PFT methods leads to lower resource utilization while maintaining output quality.

Analyzing the impact of faults in streaming applications has many challenges that are not addressed by traditional fault injection methodologies [8, 14, 20, 29]. Streaming applications can tolerate approximate results and be non-deterministic. In addition, these applications produce results continually, requiring a careful analysis of the output to estimate the fault impact. We address these issues by (i) defining an *output score function* (OSF) to measure the application output quality and compare it with the output under faults, and (ii) using the OSF over limited sections of the output to compute our proposed evaluation metrics.

Our fault injection experiment target is a simplified financial engineering application running on top of IBM's stream processing middleware, System S [1, 12]. We considered a bursty data loss fault model, which emulates the crash of a stream operator. Our results show the following: (i) the impact on the application output quality varies widely for faults in different stream operators, demonstrating that operator sensitivity to faults is an important differentiator in deploying PFT; (ii) the tested application provided some surprising results; specifically, one stream operator with high selectivity turned out to be the least critical in terms of quality degradation when subjected to data loss. This indicates that PFT can be a powerful technique to maintain the accuracy of the results and preserve computing resources by replicating only parts of the application.

2. PARTIAL FAULT TOLERANCE

Several researchers [4, 15, 17, 21, 22, 23, 30] have described PFT techniques that are applicable to stream processing applications. While many leverage the partial and often strategic employment of fault tolerance techniques to lower the performance loss, no technique can guarantee *perfect* application output under faulty conditions. Different PFT mechanisms have different *effects* on the *input/output stream* of the failed operator and, as a result, on the application output. Hence there is a need to conduct experiments to understand the behavior of streaming applications under faults.

One particular technique [17] is based on a stream operator checkpoint mechanism that leverages code generation to automatically provide specialized state serialization methods depending on the stream operator type. When an operator fails, its upstream operators do not buffer outgoing tuples[1] unless they are required to produce a semantically correct result after a fault. Checkpointing [17] results in *bursty tuple loss* on the operator *input stream*.

Another example of PFT is to employ *free running replicas*, as proposed by Murty and Welsh [21]. This technique does not enforce determinism among the stream operator replicas, resulting in different effects on the operator *output stream*, such as *tuple reordering*, *duplication*, *loss*, and *value divergence*.

S4 [22], the open-source distributed stream processing middleware from Yahoo!, provides fault tolerance by restarting an operator from scratch once a failure is detected. The state of the operator is rebuilt by processing new incoming stream data items. This approach is similar to the strategy defined in [15] as gap recovery. Both techniques lead to *bursty tuple loss* on the occurrence of failures.

To evaluate how applications behave under PFT techniques, it is critical to understand the *effect* of faults on input/output stream of the operator. Note that we are not concerned with the specific mechanism used by the stream processing middleware to detect a fault in a stream operator (e.g., heartbeats) and to restart the operator. Nevertheless, these detection and recovery times are important to determine the duration of the fault effect.

3. EVALUATION METHODOLOGY

The experimental methodology uses fault injection to characterize the output quality of a streaming application in the presence of faults while a specific PFT mechanism is in use. We assume that a fault detector and a fault tolerance mechanism are already in place and have been validated. We also assume that a stream operator fails by crashing in a fail-stop manner (i.e., without producing corrupted results) [6]. The selected fault model is broad because operator failures could be due to several distinct and indirect causes: a node failure (e.g., operating system kernel crash), a transient software fault (e.g., race condition), or a transient hardware fault (e.g., a memory bit flip that causes a process crash).

Characterizing the error behavior of streaming applications presents many challenges. Traditional fault injection methodologies evaluate the behavior of an application by checking its output after the injection of a fault [20, 29]. A deterministic application can be checked for correct behavior under faults by comparing the output of the faulty run to the output of the fault-free run (also called the *golden run*) [8]. In streaming applications, checking the *correct behavior* cannot be done by a simple bit-by-bit comparison of the faulty and fault-free outputs. Such applications are often non-deterministic[2], and are typically able to tolerate imprecise results.

To understand how a fault affects the application output, we compute an application-specific *output score function* (OSF). The OSF is calculated over a set of tuples of the output of the application, and is applied for the faulty and the golden output. Figure 1 shows two samples of streaming application outputs [1, 28]. Figure 1(a) shows a sample output of our target financial application described in Section 6.1. The output contains the *ticker* symbol of a company in the stock market and the projected *financial gain* obtained by buying a stock at a specific time. In this case, the OSF is a summation of the *financial gain* (i.e., 101.10). Figure 1(b) shows a sample output of a chip manufacturing application [28]. The output contains the *predicted wafer yield* of a manufacturing process, and a *prediction error*, indicating the extent to which the prediction deviates from the ground truth. In this case, the OSF is the *prediction error* average (i.e., 0.06). The result of the defined OSF over the application output data must have little variation (i.e., within error thresholds) when considering different non-faulty execution trials of a non-deterministic application.

To assess the *quality* of the output under faults, we define a *quality score* (QS), which is the *ratio* of the average OSF calculated over the faulty output (i.e., the application output produced in the presence of an operator fault) by the average OSF calculated over the golden output. This ratio estimates the fractional deviation of the faulty result and the correct result. The OSF average is obtained by executing the application multiple times with the same configuration (e.g., same injected fault). The average accounts

---

[1] A tuple is the basic unit of data in a stream.

[2] A source of non-determinism is the multiplexing of multiple streams, where the relative order of tuple arrival to an operator is arbitrary.

Ticker	Financial gain		Predicted wafer yield	Prediction error
IBM	41.66		95	0.06
BAC	30.56		98	0.02
TWX	28.88		92	0.10
	(a)		(b)	

Figure 1: Examples of output for a financial (a) and a chip manufacturing (b) application. The OSF is applied over the application result (e.g., financial gain or prediction error values).

for the stochastic deviations on output caused by the application non-determinism. The average OSF and the QS are the basis for the proposed evaluation metrics. In addition, our metrics consider that stream operators can fail at different execution times, and that the time to detect and repair from such failure can vary. Figure 2 illustrates a possible failure scenario. Different execution times are represented in our methodology by the injection of faults into operators at different *stream offsets* from the beginning of the input stream. Different detection and repair times are represented by the injection of faults with different *outage durations*. We do not make assumptions about the operator failure probability distribution.

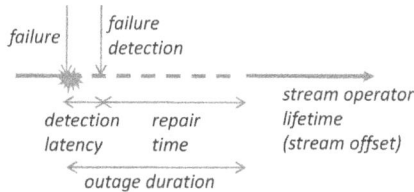

Figure 2: Timeline of a stream operator failure. The failure is detected after an average detection latency, and the detector triggers a repair procedure. The outage duration comprises the time to detect the failure and the repair time.

Our evaluation metrics characterize each operator in the following terms. (i) The *outage duration impact*, defined as the correlation coefficient between the outage duration and the QS computed over the part of the output stream affected by the fault. If the correlation coefficient is high, there is a direct quality improvement by applying techniques with lower recovery time for the target operator. (ii) The *data dependency*, defined as the standard deviation and analysis of variance (ANOVA) test of the QS obtained under faults injected into different stream offsets. A high standard deviation and rejected ANOVA test indicates that the impact of the fault on the quality is dependent on the specific data affected by the fault. (iii) The *recovery time*, defined as the P percentile of the QS observations over time that fall outside an error *threshold*. A high value for this metric indicates that the application takes a long time to stabilize and to start producing correct results again. (iv) The *quality impact*, defined as the sum of squares of the difference between the faulty QS and the golden QS evaluated over time. A high sum value indicates that answers produced by the application under faults are far away from the correct result. More details on the computation of each metric can be found in Section 5.2.

Our experimental methodology comprises the following steps:

1. *Choose a fault model according to the in place PFT technique* – the fault model is selected in correspondence to a recovery technique used to restore the operator upon a fault. In our experiments, we consider a *bursty tuple loss* model.

2. *Optimize fault injection target operators* – conditioned on the chosen fault model, only certain operators must be selected and subjected to fault injection. For example, operators that are not sensitive to the selected fault model do not need to be selected as an experimentation target.

3. *Use the actual expected data rate from stream sources to realistically model the effect of a fault* – for example, the knowledge of the real data input rate allows quantifying how much data is dropped when a fault occurs.

4. *Inject faults at different stream offsets and with distinct outage durations* – injecting faults at different stream offsets mimics random fault arrival times during the operator execution. Different outage durations mimics variations on the detection and recovery times;

5. *Evaluate the experimentation results* – based on the OSF function, each operator is characterized using the proposed metrics. These metrics can quantify the relative sensitivity of the operators to faults, and use it as a basis to compare different fault tolerance techniques.

4. FAULT INJECTION FRAMEWORK

To assess the impact of PFT, we built a fault injection framework to emulate the effect of these techniques on the input/output streams of a target stream operator. Currently, the framework supports a bursty tuple loss fault model, but it can be extended to include other fault models (e.g., tuple duplication). Bursty tuple loss can emulate the following situations: (i) a stateless operator crashes and restarts, and no in-flight tuples are saved; (ii) a stateful operator crashes and restores its state from a checkpoint upon restart, and no in-flight tuples are saved. The checkpoint preserves the operator state immediately before the occurrence of the fault; (iii) a stateful/stateless operator crashes and performs a failover to a replica. The operator has only one input stream and the backup replica is operating at approximately the same pace as the primary replica. In addition, injecting bursty tuple loss in the source operator can emulate faults affecting the real stream source (e.g., sensors) and data drop due to bursty data arrival and limited input buffer size. Emulating operator crashes by manipulating its input/output streams allows us to better control the fault injection experiment. Dropping approximately the same set of tuples in each experiment trial helps us to reduce the variation on the OSF result of different experiment trials.

4.1 Emulating Faulty Behavior

Our fault injection framework is designed to work seamlessly with SPADE (Stream Processing Application Declarative Engine) [12], the declarative stream processing language that is part of System S. SPADE offers language extensibility by allowing the implementation of *User-defined Built-in Operators* (UBOPs). When a developer identifies a general-purpose operation, he can describe it as a new type of stream operator, effectively extending the SPADE language.

Our framework uses UBOPs to extend the language with stream operators that mimic the faulty behavior of an operator when using a specific PFT technique. Figure 3 shows how the framework operates. First, it receives as input a SPADE application, a target operator, a fault model, and its injection parameters. Based on the target operator and the fault model, the framework modifies the SPADE program to embed a *fault injection operator* (FIOP) in specific positions in the data flow graph. For example, to emulate tuple loss at the *input ports* of an operator, all the operators connected to these input ports are re-routed to send their output streams to the FIOP. The FIOP is connected to the target operator. Based on the new flow graph, the framework generates multiple SPADE programs, each of them with a FIOP configured with a different fault injection parameter. After the compilation, the application is ready for fault injection runs.

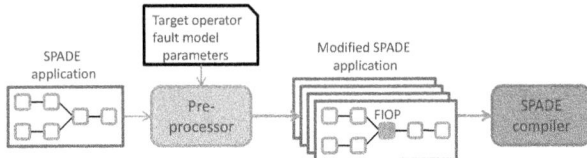

Figure 3: Fault injection framework changes the original application dataflow graph to include a fault injection operator (FIOP). The modified application is re-compiled and then executed with the fault injection parameters.

Figure 4 depicts how the injection occurs at runtime. The figure shows the injection of the *bursty tuple loss* fault model into the input port of operator OP2. In this example, OP1 sends tuples containing a stock symbol and a price to OP2. After the graph pre-processing, OP1 connects to the FIOP, which connects to OP2. The FIOP is placed right before the target operator and receives the following parameters: (i) the *outage duration*, specified in terms of the number of tuples to be dropped, and (ii) the *stream offset*, specified in terms of the number of tuples processed by the operator up until the fault. In Figure 4, the FIOP triggers a fault after it processes the stock symbol IBM at price USD 123.24. The duration of the fault is 2 tuples, leading the FIOP to drop the tuples with stock symbol YHOO and GOOG. After the FIOP drops the specified number of tuples, its operation goes back to normal, i.e., forwarding tuples received by OP1 to OP2.

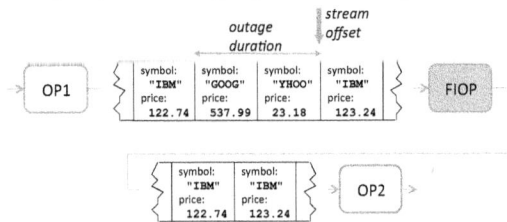

Figure 4: FIOP emulates a bursty tuple loss model by dropping tuples received after a specified *stream offset* and during a configured *outage duration*.

As described earlier in this Section, our framework does not actually crash and restart an operator during the injection. Even though the operator continues to run, it does not send or receive any new tuples for the time corresponding to the fault detection and recovery. As a result, its internal state (if any) remains unchanged.

4.2 Placing Injection Operators

To understand how the application behaves under faults,

in the worst case we may need to inject faults in all operators. However, streaming applications can have a substantially large number of operators. To reduce the number of required fault injection targets when evaluating a target application, the framework pre-analyzes the data flow graph. It selects as injection targets only those operators in which the injected fault results in a behavior that is different than a fault injected into another operator in the graph. An operator not chosen as fault injection target is assumed to have the same behavior as its upstream operator.

For the bursty tuple loss fault model, the inspection starts by selecting all *source operators* as injection targets. Injecting faults into the source mimics a fault affecting the stream feed originated outside the stream processing middleware (e.g., the raw sensor data feed), or the source operator itself.

From each source operator, the analysis continues to all downstream operators by doing a breadth-first traversal, until the *sink* is reached. A bursty tuple loss operator is placed in the data flow graph immediately before a chosen target operator. The framework selects an operator as a target if its position in the data flow graph meets one of the following properties:

1. *An upstream operator produces more than one output stream* – a common pattern in streaming applications is for one operator to have its outputs consumed by more than one operator downstream. As illustrated by Figure 5(a), both OP2 and OP3 consume the stream produced by OP1. If OP1 fails, part of its input stream is lost, affecting both OP2 and OP3. If OP2 fails, OP1 can continue to send data to OP3, but all data sent to OP2, while it is offline, is lost. These two different scenarios can impact the application output in different ways. Therefore, both scenarios must be emulated when evaluating the application behavior under faults.

2. *The operator consumes more than one input stream* – stream operators can consume outputs produced by more than one upstream operator. One such example is the *join* operator, which correlates events coming from two different streams. This is shown in Figure 5(b), where OP1 and OP2 send data to OP3. If OP1 fails, OP3 stops receiving data from one of its input ports, but it continues to process data coming from OP2. If OP3 fails, data sent by both OP1 and OP2 are lost. Since these two scenarios represent two different error modes, both of them should be emulated during the fault injection experiments.

3. *The upstream operator is stateful* – a stream operator can either be stateful or stateless. For example, an operator that filters a stream based on the attributes of the current tuple does not keep any state related to previously processed tuples. Figure 5(c) shows a data flow graph where a stateless operator OP1 sends data to a stateful operator OP2, which sends data to OP3. If OP1 fails, it loses input data from its upstream operator while it is offline. As a result, OP2 also does not receive input data during the time OP1 is offline and does not update its internal state. If OP2 fails, the behavior is analogous to a fault in OP1. OP2 loses its input data and does not update its internal state while it is recovering. However, the error behavior changes when OP3 fails. OP3 loses the input data, but OP2 still updates its internal state. Once OP3 is back up, OP2 is ready to send up-to-date information and does not spend any time rebuilding its internal state. These scenarios have different impact on the application output, and both must be evaluated.

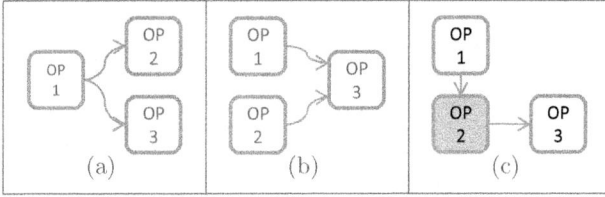

Figure 5: Placement rules for bursty tuple loss FIOPs consider the number of inputs and outputs of each operator, and if the operator is either stateless or stateful.

5. EVALUATING THE FAULT INJECTION OUTCOME

As mentioned in Section 3, we evaluate a fault injection outcome based on an application-specific *output score function* (OSF). The OSF characterizes how the application performs, and it can be computed independently of which stream operator failed. Next sections describe how we handle the continuous output of streaming applications and how we use the OSF to compute each of our metrics.

5.1 Handling Continuous Output

Stream processing applications typically produce output results continuously. If the output is not carefully analyzed, variations in the output due to the application non-determinism can be confused with the effects of a fault. This can lead to an overestimation of the faulty effect. We minimize this problem by limiting which segments of the continuous output stream are analyzed for estimating the faulty outcome. For example, results produced before the fault occurrence are ignored when computing the metric. In addition, results produced after the application started to produce output within error thresholds when compared to the golden run are also ignored.

Continuous output can also mask the effects of faults. For example, an application can manifest a fault by missing x alerts and misdetecting y alerts. When applying globally an OSF that considers the total number of detected alerts, the misdetected alerts compensate for the missed ones. This can erroneously lead the developer to think that the fault had low impact on the application output. We minimize this problem by computing the OSF over *local sections* of the output stream rather than once over the complete output set. The last two metrics described in Section 5.2 use a local OSF computation.

5.2 Evaluation Metrics

Table 1 summarizes our evaluation metrics. The first two metrics indicate the *predictability* of the stream operator behavior under faults. An operator that does not have predictable behavior under faults is not a good target for applying the PFT mechanism under test, because if such operator fails in the field, the application outcome is unknown. The last two metrics are related to system *availability*, and allow the assessment of which operators are more critical for the application to preserve output quality under faults.

Outage duration impact

By computing the *correlation coefficient between outage duration and quality score* (C^{oq}) we can assess the impact of the outage duration (Figure 2). If the QS and the outage

Metric	Operator characteristic	Definition
C^{oq}	Outage duration impact	Correlation coefficient between outage duration and quality score
D^{oq}	Data dependency	Standard deviation and analysis of variance test of the quality score for different stream offsets
R^{lq}	Recovery time	P percentile of local quality scores outside a threshold value
I^{lq}	Quality impact	Sum of squared errors of local quality score

Table 1: Summary of evaluation metrics

duration are highly correlated (i.e., the correlation coefficient is close to 1 or -1), the developer can use off-the-shelf curve fitting methods to find a function that describes the quality loss in relation to a certain outage. We can then feed this function with outage parameters extracted from real failures in the field and evaluate the risk (in terms of quality degradation) of using the evaluated PFT technique. If such behavior poses unacceptable risk to the application, this operator should be protected against faults.

The C^{oq} metric can be computed in the following way. A fault injection experiment for a single operator injects faults at m different stream offsets using n different outage durations. Each stream offset is referred to as SO_i, where $i \in [1..m]$, and each outage duration is referred to as OD_j, where $j \in [1..n]$. For each SO_i and OD_j, there are p repetitions, where each one generates an output stream with only a single section affected by the injected fault. Such section is estimated based on the SO_i and the maximum OD_j value. The OSF for the affected section of the stream is referred to as $FO_{i,j,k}$, where $k \in [1..p]$.

The average output score function $\overline{OSF_{i,j}}$ for each OD_j and a particular SO_i is computed as

$$\overline{OSF_{i,j}} = \frac{\sum_{k=1}^{p} FO_{i,j,k}}{p} \quad (1)$$

The OSF for the golden run is calculated over the section of the output stream affected by the fault with maximum OD_j value[3]. The golden run is executed q times, where each execution generates one $GO_{i,l}$, where $l \in [1..q]$. The *quality score* is referred to as $QS_{i,j}$ and is computed as

$$\overline{QS_{i,j}} = \frac{\overline{OSF_{i,j}}}{(\sum_{l=1}^{q} GO_{i,l})/q} \quad (2)$$

After this step, a particular SO_i has n OD_j values associated with it and their corresponding $\overline{QS_{i,j}}$ results. With these two sets of data, we compute the Spearman's rank correlation coefficient, which assesses if two sets of values have a monotonic relationship [24]. This step results in associating a correlation coefficient CC_i with each SO_i. Correlation coefficients have bounds [-1..1].

The operator C^{oq} is then calculated as

$$C^{oq} = \frac{\sum_{i=1}^{m} CC_i}{m}. \quad (3)$$

Data dependency

The D^{oq} metric is the *standard deviation (σ^q) and analysis of variance test (A^q) of the quality score for different stream*

---

[3]The index j is omitted in all formulas using a single fixed value of OD_j.

offsets. This metric evaluates how the *same fault* (i.e., the same fault model and outage duration) affects the output quality when injected at different stream offsets (Figure 2). A high variability in the application output quality under the same fault indicates *data dependency*, i.e., the impact on the output depends on the data being affected by the fault. An operator with a high σ^q and a rejected ANOVA test [27] is not a good candidate for PFT, since the result of a fault in the field is highly unpredictable. An operator with a low σ^q and an accepted ANOVA test indicates that the fault has a similar impact in output quality, independent of where the fault was injected.

To compute D^{oq}, we first calculate σ^q, similarly to the C^{oq} metric. The difference is that we choose the same fixed OD_j value for each SO_i, instead of considering all OD_j values. As before, we compute the $\overline{QS_i}$ for each SO_i.

The σ^q is calculated with the standard deviation formula, using the $\overline{QS_i}$ of each stream offset SO_i as data samples.

The analysis of variance A^q is a one-way ANOVA hypothesis test. This test assesses if there is a statistically significant difference between the observed means of different groups, where each group is obtained under a distinct condition [27]. For the D^{oq} metric, the test decides whether the changes in the stream offset of the injected fault affect the fault's impact on the application QS. If H_0 (null hypothesis) is *accepted*, it means that the target operator is not data dependent. A *rejected* H_0 indicates the opposite. Equation 4 shows the parameters for invoking the ANOVA test that returns an *accept* or *reject* value.

$$A^q = ANOVA((QS_{1,1}, ..., QS_{1,k}); ...; (QS_{i,1}, ..., QS_{i,k})), \tag{4}$$

where $QS_{i,k} = FO_{i,k}/((\sum_{l=1}^{q} GO_{i,l})/q)$. D^{oq} is the tuple (σ^q, A^q).

Recovery time

The R^{lq} metric is the *P percentile of quality scores outside a threshold value*. This metric estimates how long it takes for the application to recover and to start producing *normal* outputs after the occurrence of a fault. The larger the value of this metric, the larger is the impact of an operator failure on the application availability. This metric assesses the deviation of the application output quality *locally*, i.e., by computing the OSF over different intervals of the output stream (e.g., all tuples produced during a 1 second interval). For this metric, an OSF data point is considered *normal* when the difference between the faulty OSF and the golden OSF is less than a certain *threshold* (e.g., faulty OSF is less than 3% away from the golden OSF). Any difference greater than the threshold is considered to be an *erroneous* output. Our metric considers the coverage of $P\%$ of the erroneous output as it can provide enough accuracy in evaluating the recovery time of the application. In our experiments, we considered a P of 90%.

To compute R^{lq}, we choose the same single outage duration OD_j for all stream offsets SO_i. Each experiment trial k generates one output stream, which is divided in s sections. For each section, we compute the local OSF referred to as $LO_{i,k,t}$, where $t \in [1..s]$. The average of $LO_{i,k,t}$ over each experiment trial is referred to as $\overline{LO_{i,t}}$, and is computed similarly to Equation 1. A similar procedure is followed for each of the q trials of the golden run. The OSF for each section of the golden output stream is referred to as $GLO_{i,l,t}$.

$\overline{GLO_{i,t}}$ refers to the average of $GLO_{i,l,t}$ over each trial, and is calculated similarly to Equation 1.

In the next step, we build an *error array* based on $\overline{LO_{i,t}}$ and $\overline{GLO_{i,t}}$, with t starting at S_{begin}, where S_{begin} is the first section of the output stream produced by the golden run after the fault injection point. Each position of the array is referred to as $EQ_{i,u}$, where $u \in [1..s - S_{begin}]$, and is computed as

$$EQ_{i,u} = \frac{|\overline{LO_{i,t}} - \overline{GLO_{i,t}}|}{\overline{GLO_{i,t}}}. \tag{5}$$

For each position u in the *error array*, we compute the number of error values that are greater than the established *threshold* up until and including u^{th} error value $EQ_{i,u}$. This is denoted by $NE_{i,u}$ and is represented formally as

$$NE_{i,u} = \sum_{v=1}^{u} \mathbf{1}[EQ_{i,v} > threshold]. \tag{6}$$

Then, we compute the *index* R_i^{lq} where $P\%$ of the erroneous QS observations fall. That is:

$$R_i^{lq} = min \ u \ s.t. \ NE_{i,u} \geq p * NE_{i,s-S_{begin}} \tag{7}$$

The final step is to obtain the maximum index for all stream offsets SO_i, that is $R^{lq} = max_i \ R_i^{lq}$. Picking the maximum allows the assessment of the risk by considering the worst case manifested during experimentation.

Figure 6 shows an example of the R^{lq} metric. The line with a circle marker shows the QS values of the faulty run in relation to the golden run (square marker) for each section of the output stream. The dashed line shows the allowed error *threshold*. The R^{lq} metric covers 90% (P) of the data points that lie outside the threshold values (S13) after the fault is injected, showing an approximation of how long the application output takes to stabilize after a fault.

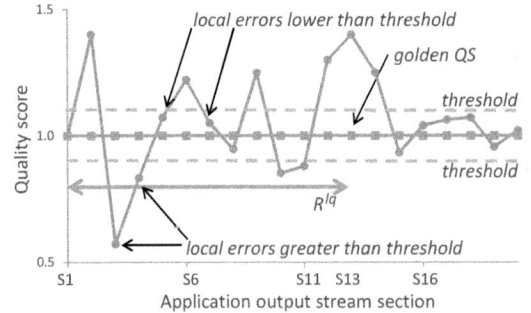

Figure 6: R^{lq} **metric considers the number of local QS observations that fall outside a specified error threshold when compared to the golden run.**

Quality impact

The I^{lq} metric is the *sum of squared errors (SSE) of local quality score*, which allows us to compare the fault impact of different operators on the application output quality. Similar to the R^{lq}, we consider local OSF values that are outside of a *threshold* tolerance. The *magnitude of the fault impact* is obtained by summing the squares of all local errors throughout the application execution after the injection up until the chosen P percentile of the R^{lq} metric.

The computation of this metric is similar to the R^{lq} computation. Instead of applying Equation 6, we calculate the

SSE of a single SO_i (referred to as I_i^{lq}) as

$$I_i^{lq} = \sum_{v=0}^{R_i^{lq}} (EQ_{i,v})^2 [EQ_{i,v} > threshold].\qquad(8)$$

I^{lq} is then $max_i \, I_i^{lq}$.

6. EXPERIMENTAL EVALUATION

Our experiment target is a simplified application from the finance engineering domain called *Bargain Discovery* [1]. In our experiments, we assume the following: (i) a stream operator crash is *always* detected, (ii) all stateful operators of the application are being checkpointed [17], and (iii) an operator restores its state to the state immediately before the fault occurrence.

6.1 Target Application

The target application processes stock *trades* and *quotes*, and outputs information on all stocks in which there is a *potential money gain* on buying the stock at a given time. Figure 7 shows the Bargain Discovery flow graph.

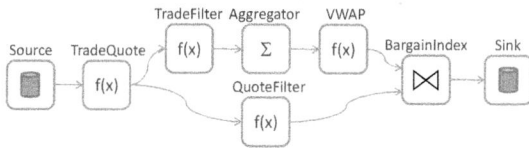

Figure 7: Stream operator graph of the Bargain Discovery application. One path processes only stock *trades*, while the other path processes only stock *quotes*. The streams are later correlated to decide if a given stock quote has a low price compared to its price history.

The application has one *source* operator, which reads trades and quotes events from a file[4]. Each entry in the file corresponds to a real event from the stock market. Each entry (tuple) contains a *ticker*, which is the symbol that identifies a company on an exchange. The *type* indicates the action taken by an investor. A *trade* action means an investor bought a certain number (*volume*) of shares at a specific *price*. A *quote* indicates an investor wants to sell a number (*ask size*) of stocks at a certain price (*ask price*).

The processing logic starts with the *TradeQuote* operator, which reduces the size of the tuple. Two different operators consume the output stream of *TradeQuote*, generating two branches in the application flow graph.

The first branch of the flow graph starts with *TradeFilter*, which filters all tuples of type *trade*. The *Aggregator* consumes all trades and sums up the *total volume* and *total price* for the 5 *most recent* trades of a given stock symbol. The operator generates a new sum every time a new trade of the corresponding symbol is processed on the input stream. The *VWAP* operator processes the *Aggregator* output stream and generates a tuple with the moving average price of a given stock symbol. The second branch of the flow graph has only the *QuoteFilter* operator, which outputs only tuples with type *quote*.

The processing logic finishes with the *BargainIndex*, which correlates the output streams of *VWAP* and *QuoteFilter*.

---

[4]In a real application deployment, data arrives as a continuous stream.

For every incoming *quote* tuple, it checks what is the most recent moving average stock price for the given ticker symbol. The operator estimates the potential money gain by multiplying the *ask size* by the difference between the moving average and the *ask price*. All outputs produced by the *BargainIndex* are stored into a file by the *Sink* operator.

For the purpose of fault injection, we modified the application input file by adding a *primary key* for each entry of the file. This key follows a strict ascending order. The application propagates this key until the *Sink*. With such key, we can precisely identify segments of the faulty output stream and match them with the equivalent segment of the *golden run*'s output stream. This allows an accurate comparison between the application OSF with and without faults.

6.2 Experiment Parameters

The input stream used in our experiments consists of real market trades and quotes transactions from December 2005. We limited the number of processed trades and quotes to 5 million events. This dataset has the following characteristics: (i) the average event rate is 500 tuples/second, with peak rate of 2200 tuples/second; and (ii) *quote* transactions account for 80% of input stream events.

For this experiment, we chose 6 different outage durations. They are specified in seconds and have the following values: 0.5, 1, 2, 4, 8 and 16. The value 0.5 second was estimated by measuring how long it takes the System S runtime to detect a crashed process and restore it to its normal operation. The value 16 seconds is the time that the System S runtime takes to detect that a node has failed and to migrate a stream operator to a different machine. As described in Section 4, the FIOP that emulates the bursty tuple loss fault model expects as parameter the outage duration specified in terms of the number of tuples. Each of the outage duration values was converted to the number of tuples that would be lost due to the fault using both the average and peak input rate we observed in our dataset. The average and peak input rates are converted according to the processing rates of each operator. We used System S built-in instrumentation features [11] to obtain the processing rates of each operator.

The chosen stream offset trigger values are the following: 0.5, 1.5, 2.5, 3.5, and 4.5 million. Similar to the outage duration, we approximate the offset trigger based on the number of tuples processed by each operator.

Due to the application non-determinism, the golden run was executed 300 times. Each outage duration and stream offset combination was executed 5 times, totaling 300 fault injections per operator. The target operators for this application are *Source*, *TradeFilter*, *QuoteFilter*, *VWAP*, and *BargainIndex*. They are highlighted in Figure 7 and were chosen based on the optimization criteria described in Section 4.2. All experiments ran on a single node with Linux operating system, 4 Intel Xeon 3GHz processors, and 8GB of RAM. The experiments ran on a single node to reduce the effects of non-determinism on the application output.

Output Score Function. We defined the OSF of the application as the total sum of the financial gain. This application can misbehave in two ways: (i) underestimating the OSF (QS below 1), i.e., the application fails to indicate opportunities for buying profitable stocks; and (ii) overestimating the OSF (QS above 1), i.e., the application is estimating that certain stocks are more profitable than they are in reality. This can lead a trader to make wrong decisions.

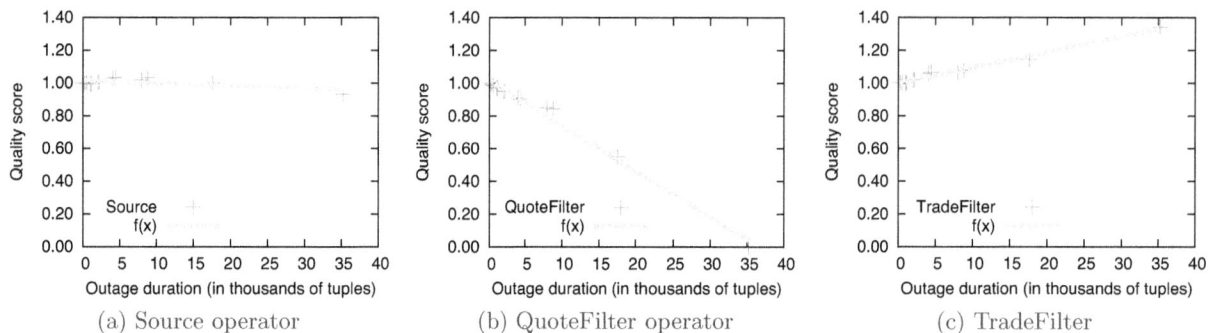

(a) Source operator	(b) QuoteFilter operator	(c) TradeFilter

Figure 8: Quality score for fault injection trials with stream offset 1.5 million tuples and different outage durations for operators Source, QuoteFilter, and TradeFilter. Figure 8(a) shows that the QS underestimations overcomes the overestimations when the Source operator is offline for a long period of time. Figure 8(b) shows that the longer the outage duration, the more the QS decreases. Figure 8(c) indicates that the longer the outage of the TradeFilter operator, the more the application overestimates the trading financial gain.

6.3 Results

Outage duration impact.

The C^{oq} metric assesses if the outage duration caused by a fault in an operator directly impacts the application output quality. As described in Section 5.2, this metric considers only the section of the output stream that is directly affected by the fault. In the Bargain Discovery, we estimate the affected output stream by identifying all trades that were lost due to the injected fault and all trades that were correlated with a moving average that was miscalculated due to the injected fault. For example, when the fault injection target is the *Source* operator, the downstream operators lose both *trade* and *quote* tuples. In this case, the affected segment of the output stream considers both the dropped quotes and the quotes correlated with miscalculated moving averages. However, when the fault injection target is the *QuoteFilter*, the affected segment of the output stream consists only of the dropped quotes. Note that this analysis is application-specific, and should be customized for each application, if a precise estimate of the affected output stream is desired.

Table 2 shows the C^{oq} result for all target operators. Note that the QS result is highly correlated with the outage duration when faults are injected into *TradeFilter*, *QuoteFilter*, and *VWAP*.

Operator	C^{oq}	D^{oq}	R^{lq}	I^{lq}
Source	-0.38	(0.21,R)	340	21.23
TradeFilter	0.97	(0.76,R)	340	48.70
QuoteFilter	-1.00	(0.00,A)	6	6.00
VWAP	0.99	(0.14,R)	73	30.87
BargainIndex	-0.69	(0.08,A)	43	7.89

Table 2: Operator metrics results for Bargain Discovery application

Figure 8 illustrates how the *quality score* (QS) varies under different outages for three operators. The x axis is the outage duration and the y axis is the QS result. The function $f(x)$ is the result of least-squares fitting of a linear function.

For the *Source* (Figure 8(a)) there is an OSF overestimation when the outage duration is small (less than 5000 tuples), and an OSF underestimation when the outage duration increases (greater than 15000 tuples). When a fault affects the *Source*, both trades and quotes are lost. When

data loss is small, not as many quotes are dropped, resulting in many correlations with a miscalculated moving average. When the data loss is big, the financial loss due to not correlating quotes for a long time is greater than the overestimation due to miscalculated averages.

Figure 8(b) shows the high correlation between QS and outage duration for the *QuoteFilter* operator. Note that the QS is 0.00 at the maximum injected outage duration. The QS is 0.00 because the C_{oq} metric considers only the affected output stream under the maximum outage duration for its computation. When we inject a fault into *QuoteFilter* with the maximum outage duration, the *BargainIndex* does not perform correlations with any quote tuple, and, as a result, the application does not produce any output during the outage period.

Figure 8(c) shows the QS values for the *TradeFilter* operator. When this operator fails, the operator that maintains the most recent trades stops adjusting the moving averages based on new trade values. This can lead to the evaluation of a non-profitable stock as profitable (case 1) and vice versa (case 2). In our dataset, the magnitude of case 1 was always greater than case 2. This indicates that the financial loss for buying non-profitable stocks is greater than the financial loss incurred because purchase opportunities were missed.

Data dependency. Table 2 shows the D^{oq} metric results. A stands for an accepted A^q, and R stands for a rejected A^q. The operator with the greatest σ^q is *TradeFilter*, and the one with the lowest σ^q is *QuoteFilter*. The only operators with an accepted ANOVA test (i.e., low QS variability under faults) with $\alpha = 0.05$ are *QuoteFilter* and *BargainIndex*. Figure 9 shows the QS result (y axis) for all injected stream offsets (x axis) under the maximum outage duration. The QS for *QuoteFilter* is 0.00 independently of which stream offset the fault is injected into. This is because *BargainIndex* cannot do any stream correlation when *QuoteFilter* fails. For *TradeFilter*, the lowest QS is 1.34 and the greatest is 3.35. This represents a considerable variation, which indicates that effect of a fault on the QS depends to a great degree on what data the outage affects.

Recovery time. The R^{lq} estimates how long the application takes to produce output below an error threshold once an operator fails. For the target application, we consider a threshold of 3% away from the OSF of the golden run. We computed the local OSF values considering the primary key

238

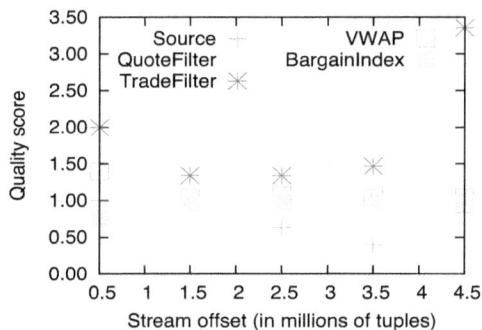

Figure 9: Quality score for different stream offsets under maximum outage duration. The impact of a failure in the TradeFilter operator on the application QS is highly data dependent, while the impact of a failure in QuoteFilter is independent of the data affected by the fault.

of the resulting tuple. All tuples with key values falling into an interval of 5000 units are grouped into one stream section (e.g., tuples with keys between 5000 and 10000). This approximates to one local observation at every 2.2 seconds when the input stream is producing tuples at its peak rate. Table 2 shows the R^{lq} for all target operators for an outage duration of 16 seconds under peak rate. Figures 10 and 11 show the R^{lq} value as vectors. The displayed value is the R^{lq} for the injected stream offset, and not the maximum value among all injected stream offsets.

The operators with highest recovery time are *Source* and *TradeFilter*. These two operators have the same R^{lq} value because during the injection trials the same exact set of tuples were dropped with respect to the *Aggregator*. Additionally, they have the highest R^{lq} because they both affect the state of the *Aggregator*, which maintains the history of the recent trades. Once new tuples are processed, the *Aggregator* updates its internal state, producing moving average estimations with fresh data. As seen in Figure 10 and 11, the QS result stabilizes as more tuples are processed.

The *VWAP* and *BargainIndex* operators (Table 2) have smaller R^{lq} values. When they fail, the state they affect downstream is quicker to rebuild in comparison to the *Source* and the *TradeFilter*. Once *BargainIndex* recovers from its checkpoint, its internal state contains outdated moving averages. However, it immediately starts receiving correct moving average values, allowing correct correlations with new incoming quotes. *QuoteFilter* has a small recovery time because it does not affect the state of operators downstream.

Quality Impact. The I^{lq} evaluates the magnitude of the impact on the application output when an operator fails. The outage duration, error threshold, and interval of sections of the output stream are the same ones used by the R^{lq} metric. Table 2 shows the I^{lq} values for an outage duration of 16 seconds under peak rate. Our results reveal that a fault in *TradeFilter* affects the application output the most, while a fault in *QuoteFilter* has the lowest impact.

Figure 10 shows the QS result (y axis) for every section of the output stream (x axis) for 3 target operators. The x axis starts at section 300, which corresponds to the injection stream offset after 1.5 million tuples have been processed. Figure 10(a) shows the QS for the *Source* operator. After the fault injection there are no tuples present in the output stream, leading to 100% underestimation of the OSF when

compared to the golden run. Once the operator resumes sending tuples, the application overestimates its results up to 59% percent. Figure 10(b) shows the QS observations for the *QuoteFilter* operator. The *QuoteFilter* has a low I^{lq} because it only affects the output during the outage period. When faults are injected into the *VWAP* operator (Figure 10(c)), the application produces high overestimates (up to 113% greater than the golden run OSF). This is because a fault in *VWAP* affects the *BargainIndex* state. As a result, the application continues to correlate new quotes with outdated moving average values. Note that when *VWAP* fails, the history of recent trades maintained by *Aggregator* is kept up-to-date. As a result, once *VWAP* recovers, it can immediately send up-to-date values downstream.

Figure 11 shows the QS for the *TradeFilter* when subjected to faults at stream offset after 3.5 million tuples have been processed and with different outage durations. Our experiments show that as the outage duration increases, the peak OSF overestimate for a certain stream offset and the I^{lq} increase. When the outage lasts 2 seconds (Figure 11(a)), the maximum overestimate is 7% and the I^{lq} is 0.25. For an outage of 8 seconds (Figure 11(b)), the maximum overestimate is 72% and the I^{lq} is 12.85. The peak overestimate for an outage duration of 16 seconds (Figure 11(c)) is 144% and the I^{lq} is 48.70. Our results show that even though the *TradeFilter* and *Source* are losing the same set of tuples under a injected fault with the same outage duration, the QS deviation is higher when the fault is injected into the *TradeFilter*. When *TradeFilter* fails, the *Source* continues to send new data, and the *BargainIndex* continues to correlate quotes with an obsolete moving average value. When the *Source* fails, the application stops the correlation of any data during the outage duration, resulting in errors with lower magnitude.

6.4 Discussion

Our results show the following regarding the Bargain Discovery application:

1. Influence of operator output stream on the state of the downstream flow graph determines the criticality of the operator – the total state size (in bytes) of operators downstream of a failed operator determines how long the application takes to fully rebuild its state and for how long the application produces erroneous results. As a result, operators with greater influence on the downstream state are more critical to maintain the application output quality. For example, the *TradeFilter* is the most critical operator with respect to bursty tuple loss, both in terms of the quality impact and recovery time, making it a top priority for protection against bursty tuple loss. Even though the *TradeFilter* operator is a stateless filter, it directly affects the stateful *Aggregator* and *BargainIndex* downstream. Another example is *QuoteFilter*, which is the least critical operator with respect to bursty tuple loss. This operator has low impact on application output quality, short recovery time, and very predictable behavior under faults ($A^q = accept$ and $\sigma = 0.00$). Although *BargainIndex* is stateful and consumes data from *QuoteFilter*, the *BargainIndex* does not keep internal state related to *QuoteFilter*'s output stream.

2. Checkpoint is not adequate to protect operators when faults have a long outage duration - our results show that checkpointing [17] provides good protection against faults with short outage duration (e.g., *TradeFilter* and *Aggrega-*

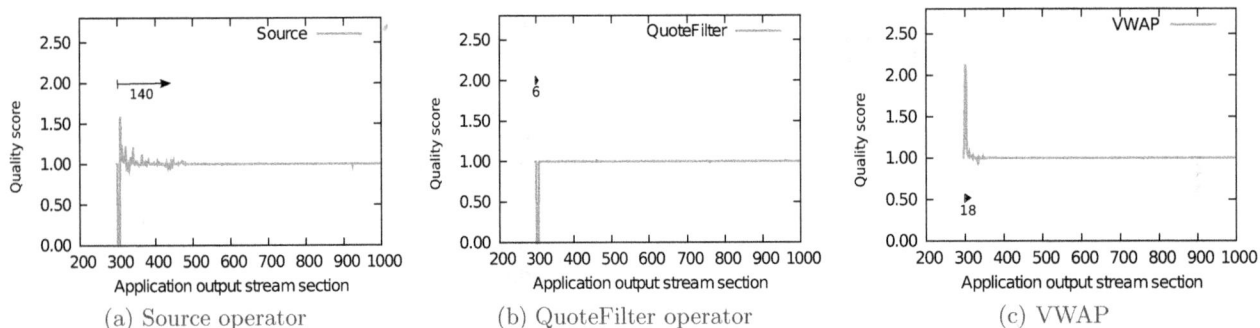

(a) Source operator

(b) QuoteFilter operator

(c) VWAP

Figure 10: Quality score for each section of the output stream with stream offset 1.5 million tuples and outage duration of 16 seconds under peak rate. Vector shows the value of the R^{lq} metric for each operator. Figure 10(a) shows that *Source* operator has a high R^{lq} value, while Figure 10(b) shows that the application quickly recovers from a failure in the *QuoteFilter* operator. Figure 10(c) shows that a *VWAP* failure has a short R^{lq} when compared to *Source*, but it generates QS observations with higher values.

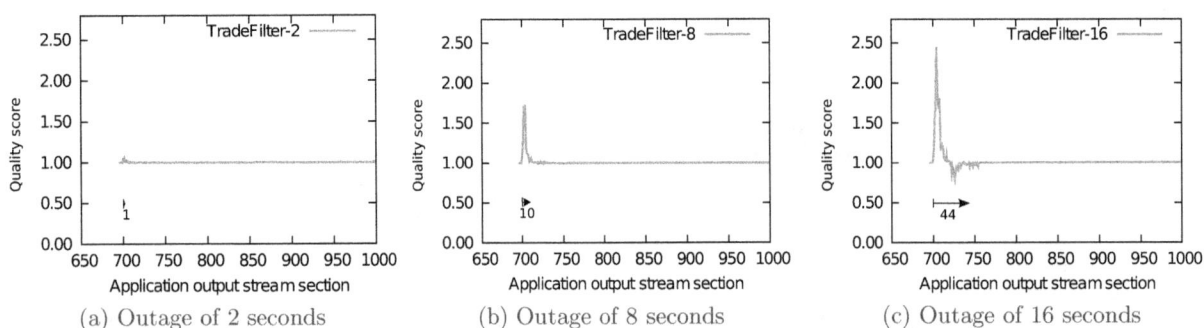

(a) Outage of 2 seconds

(b) Outage of 8 seconds

(c) Outage of 16 seconds

Figure 11: Local QS observations of the output stream with stream offset of 3.5 million tuples and different outage durations under peak rate for TradeFilter operator. I^{lq} and R^{lq} values increase as the outage duration increases.

tor in Figure 11(b)), but is not enough for faults with long recovery time.

3. Position in the flow graph is not an adequate heuristic for deciding operator criticality - although other researches [4, 21] suggest that the position in the flow graph can be used to deploy PFT, our study indicates that the position on the flow graph, and the type of operator alone are not adequate heuristics to characterize operator criticality. Although *QuoteFilter* and *TradeFilter* have both similar position in the flow graph and the same operator type, they have very distinct behavior under faults.

4. The proposed metrics can be used to reconfigure the application fault tolerance and to observe a measurable improvement in application output quality - based on our experimental results, we can improve the fault tolerance of the application by applying, for example, a technique with lower recovery time, such as *high availability groups* [17]. This technique maintains active replicas of operator groups of the application flow graph. Once an operator in the *active* group fails, the *backup* group becomes active. The failover time from one replica to the other is at most 2 seconds in System S. Our experiments show that by replicating a group of critical operators, such as the *TradeFilter*, *Aggregator* and *VWAP* (shown in Figure 12), we can see an improvement on the output quality of the application under faults. When either *TradeFilter*, *Aggregator*, or *VWAP* fails, the R^{lq} is 2 and the I^{lq} is 2. This is a significant improvement when compared to the previous values (I^{lq} of 48.70 and R^{lq} of

340). Under faults in the *Source* and the *TradeQuote*, the new I^{lq} is 1.05 and the R^{lq} is 39, in contrast to an I^{lq} of 21.23 and R^{lq} of 340 obtained in our previous tests. For other operators, such as the *QuoteFilter*, the metrics show that a simple restart is enough to maintain good application output quality. This has a big positive impact on resource utilization for our target application, given that *QuoteFilter* has an input selectivity of 80%, as described in Section 6.2.

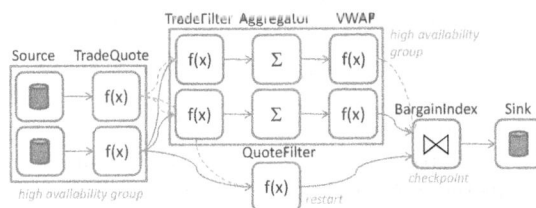

Figure 12: Fault tolerance reconfiguration of Bargain Discovery considers that operators with high metric values should be replicated, resulting in improved output quality on the occurrence of failures.

An important factor in deriving our conclusions was the OSF definition, which closely follows the semantics of our application. Our experimental methodology, together with a well-defined OSF, enabled us to make informed decisions with respect to fault tolerance, since we can evaluate the cost associated with the applied fault tolerance technique and the benefits such protection yields. Our results with the Bargain

Discovery application have also demonstrated robustness to different choices of OSF. We tested both *average financial gain* and *number of produced tuples* as OSFs, and the relative criticality of operators in terms of I^{lq} and R^{lq} were similar to the one obtained by the *total sum of financial gain*.

7. EXPERIMENTAL METHODOLOGY LIMITATIONS

Injecting faults into a streaming application and evaluating its results has many challenges, mainly imposed by the possible non-determinism of the application and its tolerance to approximate results. In this paper, we described an experimental methodology we used to evaluate the impact of PFT techniques on the output of a financial engineering application. We envision that our experimental methodology can be further generalized to be applicable to other streaming applications. In this section, we discuss some of the limitations of our current approach which should be studied in order to generalize the proposed methodology.

1. Application-specific quality metric - our basis to compare a faulty and a golden run is via an application-specific OSF. The OSF approximates the behavior of the application output and it copes with the non-determinism of the application output. For some applications, it may be hard to define an OSF. As a result, generic OSFs (e.g., number of tuples) can be investigated as an alternative for such cases.

2. Concurrent failures - our experiments assumed that operators fail independently. However, depending on the physical deployment of the application, multiple operators may fail together (e.g., if they reside in the same process [12] or run on the same node). We plan to investigate the emulation of such failures by considering the co-located operators as a single operator with a more complex internal logic.

3. Number of required injection trials for applications with large number of operators - our methodology injects faults in *each* operator considering different *outage durations* and *stream offsets*. In addition, if the application is non-deterministic, we execute the same injection configuration multiple times. This can result in a high number of experimental trials if the application has a large number of operators. In Section 4.2, we describe an optimization step based on the properties of the operator graph to help reducing the number of target operators. Considering co-located operators as a single operator can also reduce the number of required experiments.

8. RELATED WORK

Many fault tolerance techniques for streaming applications consider that no data can be dropped or duplicated [13, 16, 19], which depends upon the implementation of expensive buffer management and consistency protocols. These techniques do not evaluate the application output quality when faults occur, since they assume that the application produces the same output despite the occurrence of faults. Balazinska et al. [3] propose to produce *tentative* (lower precision) results during the occurrence of faults. The evaluation of this technique was based on the number of tentative tuples produced during faults, but there was no evaluation with respect to their impact on the output quality.

Previous literature on PFT techniques [4, 17, 21, 23, 30] do not describe how to systematically evaluate the impact of faults on the application output quality. Bansal et al. [4]

assume that the importance of each component in a streaming application can be described as a linear combination of importance of the inputs it is consuming. Our experiments show that this is not the case for our target application. Our earlier work [17] relies on the application designer to specify which components need to be fault-tolerant, while in this technique we inject faults to understand the application behavior under faults. Murty and Welsh [21] and Pietzuch [23] do not evaluate their proposed fault tolerance methods with respect to effects on the quality of an application's results. Zhu et al. [30] assess the output quality of their proposed fault tolerance method in terms of a Sum of Squared Errors. We propose three other evaluation metrics.

There is vast research on evaluating fault tolerant systems with fault injection methods [8, 14, 29]. Streaming applications have unique characteristics, such as non-determinism, and continuous data processing despite the occurrence of faults. This brings up additional challenges to the evaluation methodology, which cannot be attacked with the techniques described in the literature.

Model-based dependability evaluation techniques [18] are complementary to fault injection experimentation. One use of model-based approaches is to understand the impact of faults on the application availability under a given failure distribution. Fault injection assumes that a fault that can happen on a real installation has occurred in the system, independent of its frequency.

Our work is related to research in load shedding of streaming applications, where the stream processing middleware can drop data once it detects that the system is operating over its capacity. Tatbul et al. [26] study the problem of using application semantics to drop tuples via a loss-tolerance graph. This graph can only have stream operators of specific types. Babcock et al. [2] proposes an accuracy metric similar to our QS. We propose four different metrics which are based on the QS. Previous work [9] considers the operator type to establish a specific quality metric. Our methodology uses a quality metric that is application-specific, but that is independent of the types of operators used by the application.

Condie et al. [7] evaluate the accuracy of applications running on top of a MapReduce implementation that supports continuous queries. The characteristics of their target applications are distinct from ours. Although their target application is implemented as a continuous query, it has a final *exact* and *deterministic* answer (e.g., number of page views). Our scenario is more complex, since our application is non-deterministic and *every* tuple produced is a true independent outcome of the application, and not a value that gets adjusted over time.

Fiscato et al. [10] propose a model for streaming applications with quality metrics based on the importance of a tuple. The importance of tuples produced by an operator depends on the importance of its input tuples. Tuples coming from the same base stream are assumed to be equally important. In our experiments, this does not hold true. Specifically, although *QuoteFilter* and *TradeFilter* output streams are derived from the same input stream, they show very different behavior under faults.

9. CONCLUSION

Partial fault tolerance techniques aim at decreasing their impact on performance of streaming applications by allowing the application to lose and duplicate data when faults occur. In this paper, we described a fault injection methodology used to evaluate the impact of using PFT techniques on the output of a streaming application. Our results show that PFT can lead to better resource consumption, and that fault injection can be used to learn how to selectively deploy fault tolerance techniques in the application processing graph. In addition, our experiments indicate that some heuristics proposed by previous research [4, 21] on partial fault tolerance may not be the best option to maintain application output quality under faults.

As future work, we plan to evaluate other streaming applications to further generalize our experimental methodology and evaluation metrics. We believe there is a need for more fault injection experiments on stream processing applications, so that our insights and the body of knowledge with respect to the behavior of streaming applications under faults can be broadened.

10. REFERENCES

[1] H. Andrade, B. Gedik, K.-L. Wu, and P. Yu. Scale-up strategies for processing high-rate data streams in System S. In *ICDE*, 2009.

[2] B. Babcock, M. Datar, and R. Motwani. Load shedding for aggregation queries over data streams. In *ICDE*, 2004.

[3] M. Balazinska, H. Balakrishnan, S. R. Madden, and M. Stonebraker. Fault-tolerance in the Borealis distributed stream processing system. *ACM Transactions on Database Systems*, 33(1):1–44, 2008.

[4] N. Bansal, R. Bhagwan, N. Jain, Y. Park, D. Turaga, and C. Venkatramani. Towards optimal resource allocation in partial-fault tolerant applications. In *INFOCOM*, 2008.

[5] D. Carney, U. Çetintemel, M. Cherniack, C. Convey, S. Lee, G. Seidman, M. Stonebraker, N. Tatbul, and S. Zdonik. Monitoring streams: a new class of data management applications. In *VLDB*, 2002.

[6] S. Chandra and P. Chen. How fail-stop are faulty programs? In *FTCS*, June 1998.

[7] T. Condie, N. Conway, P. Alvaro, J. Hellerstein, K. Elmeleegy, and R. Sears. MapReduce online. In *NSDI*, 2010.

[8] D. Costa, T. Rilho, and H. Madeira. Joint evaluation of performance and robustness of a COTS DBMS through fault-injection. In *DSN*, 2000.

[9] A. Das, J. Gehrke, and M. Riedewald. Approximate join processing over data streams. In *SIGMOD*, 2003.

[10] M. Fiscato, Q. H. Vu, and P. Pietzuch. A quality-centric data model for distributed stream management systems. In *QDB*, 2009.

[11] B. Gedik, H. Andrade, and K.-L. Wu. A code generation approach to optimizing high-performance distributed data stream processing. In *CIKM*, 2009.

[12] B. Gedik, H. Andrade, K.-L. Wu, P. S. Yu, and M. Doo. SPADE: the System S declarative stream processing engine. In *SIGMOD*, 2008.

[13] Y. Gu, Z. Zhang, F. Ye, H. Yang, M. Kim, H. Lei, and Z. Liu. An empirical study of high availability in stream processing systems. In *Middleware'09*, 2009.

[14] M.-C. Hsueh, T. K. Tsai, and R. K. Iyer. Fault injection techniques and tools. *IEEE Computer*, 30(4):75–82, 1997.

[15] J.-H. Hwang, M. Balazinska, A. Rasin, U. Çetintemel, M. Stonebraker, and S. Zdonik. High-Availability Algorithms for Distributed Stream Processing. In *ICDE 2005*, 2005.

[16] J.-H. Hwang, U. Çetintemel, and S. B. Zdonik. Fast and highly-available stream processing over wide area networks. In *ICDE*, 2008.

[17] G. Jacques-Silva, B. Gedik, H. Andrade, and K.-L. Wu. Language level checkpointing support for stream processing applications. In *DSN*, 2009.

[18] G. Jacques-Silva, Z. Kalbarczyk, B. Gedik, H. Andrade, K.-L. Wu, and R. K. Iyer. Modeling stream processing applications for dependability evaluation. In *DSN*, 2011.

[19] Y. Kwon, M. Balazinska, and A. Greenberg. Fault-tolerant Stream Processing Using a Distributed, Replicated File System. In *VLDB*, 2008.

[20] H. Madeira, D. Costa, and M. Vieira. On the emulation of software faults by software fault injection. In *DSN*, 2000.

[21] R. N. Murty and M. Welsh. Towards a dependable architecture for Internet-scale sensing. In *HOTDEP*, 2006.

[22] L. Neumeyer, B. Robbins, A. Nair, and A. Kesari. S4: Distributed stream computing platform. In *KDCloud*, 2010.

[23] P. Pietzuch. Challenges in dependable Internet-scale stream processing. In *WDDDM*, 2008.

[24] C. E. Spearman. The proof and measurement of association between two things. *The American Journal of Psychology*, 14:72–101, 1904.

[25] M. Stonebraker, U. Çetintemel, and S. Zdonik. The 8 requirements of real-time stream processing. *ACM SIGMOD Record*, 34(4):42–47, 2005.

[26] N. Tatbul, U. Çetintemel, S. Zdonik, M. Cherniack, and M. Stonebraker. Load shedding in a data stream manager. In *VLDB*, 2003.

[27] K. S. Trivedi. *Probability and statistics with reliability, queuing and computer science applications.* John Wiley and Sons Ltd., Chichester, UK, 2002.

[28] D. S. Turaga, O. Verscheure, J. Wong, L. Amini, G. Yocum, E. Begle, and B. Pfeifer. Online FDC control limit tuning with yield prediction using incremental decision tree learning. In *Sematech AEC/APC*, 2007.

[29] K. Whisnant, R. K. Iyer, Z. Kalbarczyk, P. H. J. III, D. A. Rennels, and R. R. Some. The effects of an armor-based sift environment on the performance and dependability of user applications. *IEEE Transactions on Software Engineering*, 30(4):257–277, 2004.

[30] Q. Zhu, L. Chen, and G. Agrawal. Supporting fault-tolerance in streaming Grid applications. In *IPDPS*, 2008.

Efficiently Correlating Complex Events over Live and Archived Data Streams

Nihal Dindar, Peter M. Fischer, Merve Soner, Nesime Tatbul
Systems Group, ETH Zurich, Switzerland
{dindarn, peter.fischer, msoner, tatbul}@inf.ethz.ch

ABSTRACT

Correlating complex events over live and archived data streams, which we call Pattern Correlation Queries (PCQs), provides many benefits for domains which need real-time forecasting of events or identification of causal dependencies, while handling data at high rates and in massive amounts, like in financial or medical settings. Existing work has focused either on complex event processing over a single type of stream source (i.e., either live or archived), or on simple stream correlation queries (e.g., live events trigerring a database lookup). In this paper, we specifically focus on recency-based PCQs and provide clear, useful, and optimizable semantics for them. PCQs raise a number of challenges in optimizing data management and query processing, which we address in the setting of the DejaVu complex event processing system. More specifically, we propose three complementary optimizations including recent input buffering, query result caching, and join source ordering. Furthermore, we capture the relevant query processing tradeoffs in a cost model. An extensive performance study on synthetic and real-life data sets not only validates this cost model, but also shows that our optimizations are very effective, achieving more than two orders magnitude throughput improvement and much better scalability compared to a conventional approach.

Categories and Subject Descriptors

H.2.4 [**Database Management**]: Systems - Query Processing

General Terms

Performance, Languages, Theory

Keywords

Complex Event Processing, Pattern Matching, Data Streams, Stream Correlation, Stream Archiving

1. INTRODUCTION

Complex Event Processing (CEP) has proven to be a key technology for analyzing complex relationships over high volumes of

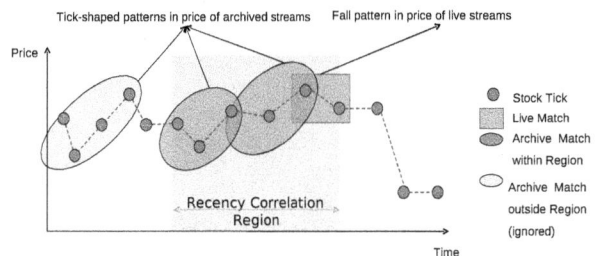

Figure 1: Financial use case: Whenever a price fall is detected on live, find all "tick-shaped" patterns on recent archive.

data in a wide range of application domains reaching from financial trading to health care. Complex events are typically expressed by means of patterns that declaratively specify the event sequences to be matched over a given data set.

Early CEP research primarily focused on pattern matching techniques over real-time event streams (e.g., Cayuga [13], SASE+ [10], ZStream [21]). More recently, there has been an increasing interest in archiving streams, not only for regulatory or reliability reasons, but also for supporting longer-term data analysis [16]. The presence of a stream archive enables a new class of CEP applications which can correlate patterns matched over live and archived event streams. Such correlations form the basis for forecasting or predicting future event occurrences (e.g., algorithmic trading in finance, or travel time estimation/route planning in intelligent transportation systems), as well as for identifying causal relationships among complex events across multiple time scales (e.g., medical diagnosis in health care [3, 4]).

We will present a motivating use case from the financial domain, which we will also use as a running example throughout the paper.

1.1 Running Example

In algorithmic trading, market data reports such as price quotes or bids [20] are evaluated using various heuristics to automatically predict the most profitable stocks to trade based on. We can model each individual report as an event and the trading algorithms as pattern matching queries over these events. Patterns are typically defined as regular expressions. Analysis in finance industry includes among others increase/decrease/stability of stock prices. As a concrete example, consider a simple query (used by e.g., a day trader), which does the following: Upon detecting a fall in the current price of stock X on the live report stream, look for a "tick"-shaped pattern for X within a recent archive, where a fall in price was followed by a rise in price that went beyond than the starting price of the fall (see Figure 1). Such an observation might indicate stocks that could bring profits in the near future. The high-rate live

```
        SELECT symbolL, initPriceL, minPriceL,
               initPriceA, maxPriceA
        FROM StockLive MATCH_RECOGNIZE(
            PARTITION BY symbol
            MEASURES  A.symbol AS symbolL,
                      A.price AS initPriceL,
                      LAST(B.price)AS minPriceL
            ONE ROW PER MATCH
            AFTER MATCH SKIP TO NEXT ROW
            INCREMENTAL MATCH
            PATTERN (A B+)
            DEFINE /* A matches any row */
                   B AS (B.price < PREV (B.price))
        ),
        StockArchive MATCH_RECOGNIZE(
            PARTITION BY symbol
            MEASURES  A.symbol AS symbolA,
                      A.price AS initPriceA,
                      LAST(D.price) AS maxPriceA
            ONE ROW PER MATCH
            AFTER MATCH SKIP TO NEXT ROW
            MAXIMAL MATCH
            PATTERN (A B+ C* D+)
            DEFINE /* A matches any row */
                   B AS (B.price < PREV(B.price))
                   C AS (C.price >= PREV(C.price)
                         AND C.price <= A.price)
                   D AS (D.price > PREV(D.price)
                         AND D.price > A.price)
        )
        WHERE symbol_a = symbol_l
        RECENCY = 7 seconds;
```

Fall in stock price — braces grouping the first MATCH_RECOGNIZE clause.

Tick-shaped in stock price — braces grouping the second MATCH_RECOGNIZE clause.

Correlation of live and archive patterns — annotation for the WHERE / RECENCY lines.

Figure 2: Financial use case: PCQ

stream and the high-volume archived stream, as well as the need for low-latency results for catching momentary trading opportunities to make profits, render this use case a highly challenging one.

This use case requires evaluating complex events over live (fall) and archived streams ("tick"-shaped), and correlating them based on a recency criteria. Price fall for a specific stock (live pattern) can be expressed as an event of that stock (A) followed by another event of the same stock (B), where $B.price < A.price$. Contiguous fall in price can be expressed with a regular expression as AB^+. Fall in price followed by a rise in price ("tick"-shaped archive pattern) can be expressed in a similar way. This query is expressed more concretely in Figure 2, based on the SQL syntax extended with a MATCH_RECOGNIZE clause for pattern matching over row sequences [25]. The first MATCH_RECOGNIZE clause utilizes the live stream (StockLive), capturing the price fall. The second one works on the archive stream (StockArchive), expressing a "tick" by a decrease and then an increase to a higher price than at the beginning. Finally, the two are correlated with an equality on the stock symbol and a recency criterion of 7 seconds.

1.2 Challenges

Correlating complex events over live and archived streams poses a number of technical challenges:

- First, the semantics for such queries should be cleanly defined. In general, correlations are based on some notion of similarity [11, 24], related to factors such as the structure of the data (e.g., temporal recency, spatial proximity) or application semantics (e.g., contextual similarity). A clean semantics is important not only in terms of usefulness and clarity

for the user, but also for the optimizations that it enables in evaluation of such queries.

- Second, the size of the stream archive will quickly grow, while depending on the correlation criteria, not all of it will be relevant to answer a given query. On the other hand, it may not always be possible to pre-fetch this relevant portion of the archive due to the live component in the query. As a result, a dynamic yet low-cost method is needed for selective archive access.

- Third, the system should scale well with potentially high live stream rates. In particular, CEP on high-volume stream archive should be able to keep up with CEP on high-rate live stream arrival.

- Last but not least, the whole problem becomes more difficult to handle due to the complexity of pattern matching queries involving variable processing window sizes and slides on both live and archive sources, some of which will result in non-match, not contributing to the result despite costing processing power. This makes both the cost and selectivity of live-archive pattern correlation queries more difficult to track.

1.3 Contributions and Outline

In this paper, we provide the following contributions to address the above listed challenges:

- a **formal definition** of pattern correlation queries (PCQs) with correlation criteria based on the notion of temporal recency (e.g., happened at most n time units before), providing a composable, useful, and optimizable semantics;

- a **set of algorithms and optimizations** for processing PCQs in storage- and computation-efficient ways in the context of the DejaVu CEP engine [15], focusing on recent input buffering, query result caching, and join source ordering optimizations;

- a **cost model** capturing the relevant trade-offs and cost factors in query processing for PCQs; and

- extensive **experimental evaluation** on synthetic and real-life data sets (NYSE TAQ data set [6]), validating our cost model and showing orders of magnitude benefits in throughput over a conventional approach.

The outline of rest of this paper is as follows: In the next section, we present how we model the semantics of recency-based pattern correlation queries (PCQs) in detail. In Section 3, we discuss the state of the art for processing PCQs in existing CEP systems (algorithm and its complexity analysis), and provide two possible baseline algorithms that suggest obvious improvements over the state of the art. Section 4 provides a detailed description of our techniques for further optimizing PCQs over the baselines. We present the results of our experimental performance evaluation in Section 5. Related work is summarized in Section 6, and we conclude the paper in Section 7 with a brief discussion of potential avenues for future work.

2. MODELING PCQ

In this section, we formally define the semantics of pattern correlation queries. Our formal semantics is based on three essential design goals:

1. *Total order of input streams:* Pattern matching queries over data sequences require establishing a total order among their elements.

2. *Total order of output streams:* For full query composability, it is also desirable to maintain the total order on output streams that result from pattern matching queries, including pattern correlation queries. This is especially challenging in the case of PCQs, as these queries involve two input sequences, one being the archive relative to the other. Thus, the correlations should be allowed only between pairs of events where one has happened before the other (e.g., an event should not be in the archive of itself, or two events should not be in the archive of each other at the same time). In this case, simply following the total order on the two input sources is not sufficient. Furthermore, a total order of the output resulting from PCQs also needs to be defined explicitly.

3. *Usefulness and clarity:* Pattern correlation queries should provide the necessary semantics for expressing a class of queries that are useful in real-life applications. Furthermore, users should be able to be grasp and apply these semantics.

We will gradually establish our semantics to meet these goals, beginning with a number of fundamental concepts (such as event streams, happened-before relation, recency correlation, etc.).

PCQs operate over live and archived streams of tuples, each representing an event. We distinguish between primitive and complex events. Primitive events happen at a specific point in time, whereas complex events are composed of a sequence of other events (primitive or complex) that happen within a time period. To model this, each tuple is assigned a start timestamp (t_s) and an end timestamp (t_e). Primitive events have identical t_s and t_e values, whereas complex events take on the minimum t_s and the maximum t_e of the events that contributed to their occurrence. Furthermore, to achieve total order on input streams (i.e., design goal #1), we assume that tuples have unique (t_s, t_e) values and they appear ordered in a stream (we show this order with $\prec$), primarily by their t_s values, then with their t_e values if a tie needs to be broken (e.g., $(1,4) \prec (2,3)$ and $(1,2) \prec (1,3)$). More formally:

Definition 1 (Time Domain) *The time domain $\mathbb{T}$ is a discrete, linearly ordered, countably infinite set of time instants $t \in \mathbb{T}$. We assume that $\mathbb{T}$ is bounded in the past, but not necessarily in the future.*

Definition 2 (Event) *An event $e \langle t_s, t_e, v \rangle$ consists of a relational tuple v conforming to a schema $\mathbb{S}$, with a start time value $t_s \in \mathbb{T}$, and an end time value $t_e \in \mathbb{T}$, where $t_e \geq t_s$. We use the notation $e.t_s$, $e.t_e$ to denote the start and end time value of an event e, respectively.*

Definition 3 (Primitive Event) *An event e is a primitive event if $e.t_s = e.t_e$.*

Definition 4 (Complex Event) *An event e is a complex event if $e.t_s \neq e.t_e$.*

Definition 5 (Stream) *A stream S is a totally ordered, countably infinite sequence of events such that:*

$$\forall e_i, e_j \in S, e_i \prec e_j, \text{iff } e_i.t_s < e_j.t_s$$
$$\vee (e_i.t_s = e_j.t_s \wedge e_i.t_e < e_j.t_e)$$

Establishing a total order on outputs of PCQs (i.e., design goal #2) requires the definition of a happened-before relation between two complex events. In the following, we will first define this relation, and then build the recency correlation definition on top.

Definition 6 (Happened-before Relation ($\rightarrow$)) *Given a pair of events $e_i, e_j \in S$, $e_i \rightarrow e_j$, if $e_i.t_e < e_j.t_e$ and $e_i.t_s < e_j.t_s$, Happened-before is:*

- *transitive:* $\forall e_1, e_2, e_3, if e_1 \rightarrow e_2 and e_2 \rightarrow e_3, then e_1 \rightarrow e_3$.
- *irreflexive:* $\forall e_1, e_1 \nrightarrow e_1$.
- *antisymmetric:* $\forall e_1, e_2, if e_1 \rightarrow e_2, then e_2 \nrightarrow e_1$.

Definition 7 (Archive of a Stream) *Archive of a stream S at time t (denoted as S_a^t) consists of all events $e \in S$ where $e.t_e < t$. Archive of a stream S as of an event $e \in S$ (denoted as S_a^e) contains all events $e_i \in S$ for which $e_i \rightarrow e$.*

Based on the above, S_a^e cannot contain e itself or any other event $e_j \in S$ which has not happened before e (i.e., $e_j \nrightarrow e$).

For PCQs, we take temporal recency as the main correlation criteria. In this case, two events are correlated if they are within a specified temporal distance from each other, which we call "recency correlation distance". More formally:

Definition 8 (Recency Correlation) *For a given stream S and a recency correlation distance of P, any event $e \in S$ has recency correlation with the following set of events*

$$recent(e, P) = \{\forall e_i \in S \text{ where } e_i \rightarrow e \text{ (i.e., } e_i \in S_a^e) \text{ and } e.t_e - e_i.t_s \leq P\}$$

The above definition ensures that for a given live event $e_l \in S$, if an archive event $e_a \in S_a^{e_l}$ has recency correlation with e_l, then all other archive events $e_i \in S_a^{e_l}$ for which $e_a \rightarrow e_i$ must also have recency correlation with e_l. This follows from the transitive property of the happened-before relation.

Recency-based PCQs join live events with archive events based on the recency correlation distance specified in the query, as we define next.

Definition 9 (Recency-based PCQ) *A recency-based PCQ $Q(S_a, p_a, S_l, p_l, P, q)$ takes six parameters: Archived and live data stream sources (S_a and S_l, respectively), patterns to be matched over these sources (p_a and p_l, respectively), a recency correlation distance (P), and a join predicate (q). For a given set of p_l matches over S_l as M_l and p_a matches over S_a as M_a, the recency-based PCQ's result will be as follows:*

$$M_a \bowtie_{P,q} M_l = \{\forall e_l \in M_l, \forall e_a \in M_a(e_l \bowtie_q e_a), \text{ where } e_a \in recent(e_l, P)\}$$

If a live event e_l joins with an archive event e_a to produce an output event e_o, then $e_o.t_s = e_a.t_s$ and $e_o.t_e = e_l.t_e$. Please note that, the total order for PCQ outputs (i.e., design goal #2) is guaranteed when: (i) all e_l's have unique t_e values, and (ii) all e_a's have unique t_s values. (i) is assured by the INCREMENTAL match mode in MATCH-RECOGNIZE for the live pattern specifications. In some sense, this is natural, as INCREMENTAL was specifically designed to be used with live data sources [25]. (ii) is guaranteed using the MAXIMAL match mode in MATCH-RECOGNIZE for the archive pattern specifications.

Definition 10 (Incremental Match) *Given a set with all possible match results for a pattern P as M, the incremental match mode reports only sets of the longest matches ending with each event (i.e., each match has a unique t_e). Results of incremental match mode pattern search M_i can be defined more formally as follows:*

$$\forall m, n \in M_i, m.t_e = n.t_e \text{ iff } m.t_s = n.t_s$$

Definition 11 (Maximal Match) *Given a set of all possible match results for pattern P as M, the maximal match mode reports only sets of the longest matches starting with each event (i.e., each match has a unique t_s). Results of maximal match mode pattern search M_x can be defined more formally as follows:*

$$\forall m, n \in M_x, m.t_s = n.t_s \; iff \; m.t_e = n.t_e$$

As a result of Definitions 9-11, output events that result from joins between live and archive events always get unique pairs of (t_s, t_e) values, maintaining the total order property given in Definition 5.

With the above PCQ semantics, our last design goal is also met, as the user has to only specify the recency correlation distance in time units, without worrying about total order requirements on input and output streams. This is quite intuitive as the three properties of the happened-before relation guarantees the expected semantics.

3. PROCESSING PCQ

In the previous section, we have established the formal semantics of recency-based PCQs. The next step is now to investigate algorithms that can perform this correlation in an efficient manner. In addition, these algorithms should integrate well with typical CEP/data stream processing environments, as to leverage existing standards, operations, and optimizations as much as possible. There are a few considerations on complexity and cost when evaluating these algorithms: Pattern computation is an expensive operation, involving many computations and a significant amount of state [18]. Nearly all of the existing pattern matching algorithms (e.g., [10]) need to "touch" all possibly relevant tuples at least once, thus raising the bar for efficient data management and indexing.

In this section, we will present three basic approaches for implementing PCQs, while investigating further optimizations in the next section:

1. Expressing recency-based correlation with the means of existing CEP or stream processing environments, in particular window-based joins followed by pattern processing.

2. Eagerly performing pattern processing on live and archive streams first, followed by a pattern-aware correlation operator which understands pattern output structure and recency.

3. Lazily performing the second-side (i.e., archive-side) of the pattern processing, driven by the pattern correlation operator and the need for these pattern instances.

As we will see throughout this section, (3) is the most promising.

3.1 State of the Art

Correlating two streams is a well-researched problem for which many approaches have been proposed (e.g., [23]). Most of these differ in their specific approach and semantics, but share a common idea: The possibly infinite stream on both sides is partitioned into a succession of finite subsequences, typically sliding windows. The contents of the windows on each side are joined/correlated to find matching data items. Once the join over this pair of windows is complete, the windows are advanced to handle newly arriving data items.

The policies how to exactly advance the windows are the main differentiator for these joins, but again there is similarity: Most approaches use item counts or timestamps as the underlying concepts. Precisely these concepts have a strong impedance mismatch with pattern correlation: Patterns could start/end with almost any arbitrary item, not just the next item or the item with the next higher timestamp.

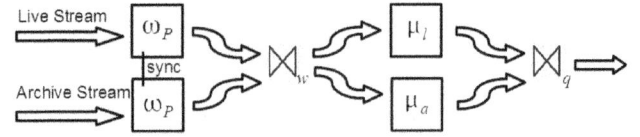

Figure 3: PCQ state of the art: Window correlation first

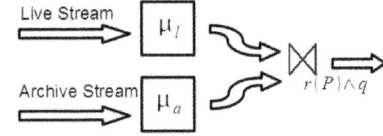

Figure 4: PCQ Pattern First

Despite the similarity of recency regions with sliding windows, only a very rough translation is therefore possible. We show this in Figure 3: Live and archive matches for a given recency region happen in a window with the same size as this recency region (ω_P). By placing such windows on live and archive streams and joining them on size/time ($\bowtie_W$), we can create the recency regions, on which we execute both patterns (μ_l and μ_a). Given the "advancing" mismatch, these windows can only slide by one item/timestamp value, while the pattern matches need to be computed anew for each window. As a result, the effort to compute all correlated matches for N items with a recency region of size P is $(N-1) * P * (c_l + c_a)$, where c_l and c_a are the cost to process a live/archive item on a pattern (see Table 2). While recency could provide significant savings in PCQ computation, using state of the art approaches to express it actually incurs an additional overhead.

3.2 Eager Pattern Processing

There are several ways to overcome the efficiency problems incurred by the semantic mismatch of using state of the art window-based stream correlation methods with PCQ. One approach would incorporate more and more pattern processing knowledge into window correlation in order to overcome the mismatch. Since this would lead to increased code complexity and runtime overhead in a CEP system, we are pursuing a different approach, which is shown in Figure 4: We first execute pattern matching on both live and archive streams on all input elements (μ_l and μ_a). On the pattern matching output, we use a special correlation operator that expresses the recency correlation logic ($\bowtie_{r(P) \wedge q}$, where $r(P)$ denotes a special recency correlation predicate that captures the recency correlation distance P). With this approach, we can ensure a complexity of $N * (c_l + c_a)$ for all pattern computation, since each pattern instance of both streams is computed exactly once, saving the factor P compared to the state of the art approach.

3.3 Lazy Pattern Processing

Eager Pattern Processing has the disadvantage that it needs to compute all patterns present in the data, even though they might never contribute to the result of a correlation. We therefore introduce a third option which has the potential to combine the best aspects of the previous ones: Compute all patterns on one side (e.g., live), but just the necessary patterns on the other side (e.g., archive). The data flow (as shown in Figure 4) does not change compared to the eager version, but there is a significant potential for cost savings. The baseline approach presented in this section can compute recency-based PCQ without additional memory overhead (other than pattern computation itself), but re-introduces some of the additional work of the state of the art approach. In the next

Input (t_s,p)	Live (t_s,t_e,p_{li},p_{lm})	Archive (t_s,t_e,p_{ai},p_{am})	Result $(t_s,t_e,p_{li},p_{lm},p_{ai},p_{am})$
(02:00,10)			
(02:01,6)	(02:00,02:01,10,6)		
(02:02,6)			
(02:03,5)	(02:02,02:03,6,5)		
(02:04,7)			
(02:05,6)	(02:04,02:05,7,6)	(02:02,02:04,6,7)	(02:02,02:05,7,6,6,7)
(02:06,11)			
(02:07,8)	(02:04,02:06,7,11)	(02:02,02:04,6,7) (02:04,02:06,7,11)	(02:02,02:07,11,8,6,7)
(02:08,8)			
(02:09,3)	(02:08,02:09,8,3)	(02:02,02:04,6,7) (02:04,02:06,7,11)	(02:02,02:09,8,3,6,7) (02:04,02:07,11,8,7,11) (02:04,02:09,8,3,7,11)
(02:10,3)			

Table 1: Lazy pattern matching - Baseline

Name	Description
N	total number of input tuples
c_l	average cost of live pattern processing per tuple (time)
c_a	average cost of archive pattern processing per tuple (time)
c_j	average cost of join per result (time)
M_l	total number of live matches
M_a	total number of archive matches
M_j	total number of join results
P_l	average number of input tuples inside the recency region of a live match
P_a	average number of input tuples inside the recency region of an archive match
c_l'	average cost of live pattern processing per tuple over recency region (time)
c_a'	average cost of archive pattern processing per tuple over recency region (time)
$\triangle_l$	average difference between two consecutive recency regions of live matches (# tuples)
$\triangle_a$	average difference between two consecutive recency regions of archive matches (# tuples)

Table 2: Workload cost factors for PCQs

section, we will study optimizations that reduce this additional cost by using additional memory.

A direct implementation of lazy pattern processing results in the following join algorithm, where L is the live source, A is the archive source, P is the recency region size, and q is the join predicate in the WHERE clause:

```
Hybrid_Loop_Join_PCQ(DStream L, DArchive A,
                     int P, Predicate q)
{
  FOR EACH match m_l over L
    FOR EACH match m_a over A[m_l.t_e-P,m_l.e-1]
        WHERE m_a.t_s < m_l.t_s
          AND m_a.t_s >= m_l.t_e-P
          AND m_a.t_e < m_l.t_e
      IF q(m_l, m_a) THEN
        append (m_l, m_a) to the result
}
```

Table 1 shows the execution of this algorithm on data from the running example of Figure 1. The first column (**Input**) shows the incoming simple events, each carrying a timestamp t_s and a price p. To clarify the presentation, we only show a single timestamp (start and end are the same) and have omitted the symbol information. The next two columns (**Live** and **Archive**) show the complex events produced as matches from the respective pattern specifications. The start (t_s) and end (t_e) timestamps are shown explicitly, since the computed complex events now cover a time period. Following the query specification in Figure 2, we show the initial price for each pattern: p_{li} and p_{ai}. Furthermore, the live events contain the minimum price (p_{lm}), and the archive events contain the maximum price (p_{am}). In the last column (**Result**), we show how the live and archive events are correlated to form the complete PCQ result.

Given the execution strategy of this lazy algorithm, we compute live events continuously in the outer loop. They are produced when the complete matching input is available. In this example, we have 5 matches of the live pattern (fall) in total showing up at 02:01, 02:03, ..., 02:09, each also covering the previous simple event. Based on these live matches, we can determine the recency region and compute the archive matches as required. Archive ("tick") events are produced at 02:05, 02:07, 02:09, when requested for the related live patterns. Their timestamps, however, correspond to the contributing simple events (such as 02:02 to 02:04). As one can see, archive pattern matches are computed several times due to the overlapping recency regions. When correlating live and archive events, the generated events are ordered first by start time and then by end time, as specified in Definition 5. The start time is determined by the archive match (following Definition 7), while processing occurs in live event order. We therefore need to sort archive/live match combinations, which incurs delays until the remaining live matches

for an archive match have been handled. This can be seen in particular on result (02:02,02:09,8,3,6,7) and (02:04,02:07,11,8,7,11). The latter would have been already available with the arrival of the input tuple (02:07,8), but needs to go after the former, which is only available at the arrival of the input tuple (02:09,3).

When categorizing this join algorithm one can say that it is a hybrid between a nested-loop join (when P is large) and a sort-merge join (when $P << |A|$), since the matches in both streams are generated in an ordered fashion, and the recency region is also advancing monotonically. Other join types are not applicable for the following reasons: Hash joins only work for equi-joins, and band-joins [14] are typically designed to establish the order we already get for free from our processing model. The main step keeping us from an optimal join execution is the overlap among recency regions, for which we introduce the result cache in Section 4.3. Another small overhead is incurred by having to sort result events according to their start time, while the current algorithm produces them by end time. This overhead is fairly small, however, and sorting is not needed when changing the join order (Section 4.4).

From this algorithm, we can formulate a basic cost formula consisting of three main parts: (i) cost of the outer pattern processing, (ii) cost of the inner pattern processing, and (iii) cost of joining the results.

$$Cost_{proc} = N * c_l + M_l * P_l * c_a' + M_j * c_j \qquad (1)$$

As shown in Table 2, we assume a constant average cost for processing a tuple in the first stream (c_l), in the active region of the second stream (c_a') and in the join (c_j). The number of items processed in the second pattern depends on the selectivity of the first pattern (M_l) and the average number of tuples inside the recency region of a live match (P_l). $M_l * P_l$ can become larger than N if there are many live matches and/or a large recency region, so that the cost could exceed that of eager pattern processing. The optimizations in the next section will show methods to overcome this problem. The number of actual join results (M_j) or the cost of computing each of them (c_j) does not depend on the join/pattern processing order and can be treated as a constant in this work.

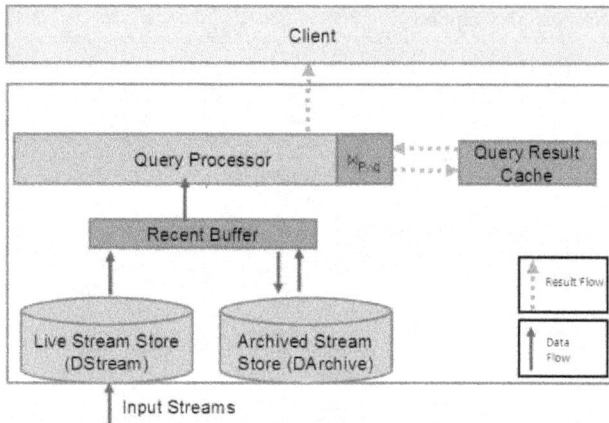

Figure 5: DejaVu CEP system architecture

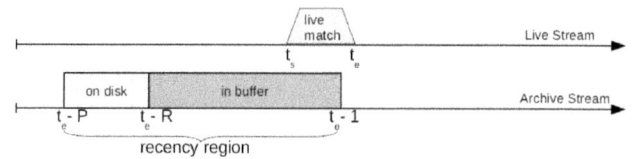

Figure 6: Recent Buffer

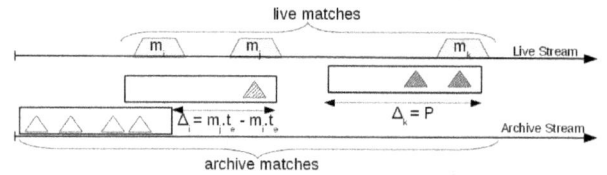

Figure 7: Query Result Cache

4. OPTIMIZING PCQ

As seen in the previous section, we need to address two main challenges in order to optimize recency-based PCQ: (i) managing and accessing the data efficiently, in particular creating a good working set from the archive, and (ii) efficiently processing the individual patterns and the correlations between them.

In this section, we will present three main optimization ideas (input buffering, query result caching, and join source ordering), that target these two challenges. We will also extend our cost model along the way, which helps us to analyze the impact of our proposed techniques.

We have studied and implemented our optimization techniques within the setting of the DejaVu CEP system. Therefore, we will first give a quick overview of DejaVu, before we dive into the details of our optimization techniques.

4.1 System Setting

DejaVu is a CEP system that integrates declarative pattern matching over live and archived streams of events [15]. DejaVu is built on top of MySQL [5] and implements a core subset of MATCH-RECOGNIZE [25].

Figure 5 shows the high-level architecture of DejaVu, including the three main extensions (colored in dark) that we have added for supporting and optimizing PCQs: (i) Recent Buffer, (ii) Query Result Cache, and (iii) PCQ operators. DejaVu's Live Stream Store (DStream) accepts live events into the system and feeds them to the Query Processor as they arrive, whereas its Archived Stream Store (DArchive) persists live events for long-term access. A fundamental design decision behind DejaVu was to route the live data to be archived through the Query Processor instead of directly storing it in a DArchive. As we will show, this approach not only enables important optimizations such as changing the order of join sources, but also simplifies working set maintenance.

4.2 Recent Input Buffering

To address our first challenge of managing and accessing the archive data during PCQ processing efficiently, we introduced the *Recent Buffer*. It is an in-memory data structure that mediates between the live and archived event stores (i.e., DStream as well as DArchive in DejaVu). By caching the most recent stream tuples, it provides the "hottest" subset of the DArchive with the same access costs and paths as for the DStream, thereby avoiding costly disk reads on recently archived data. Furthermore, it provides the means to perform bulk inserts into the DArchive.

Figure 6 depicts the structure of the *Recent Buffer*. P and R represent the recency region size (determined by the value of recency correlation distance defined in Section 2) and the *Recent Buffer* capacity, respectively. If $R \geq P$, then all the necessary tuples are stored in the *Recent Buffer*. If not, the *Recent Buffer* will only store the most recent R tuples. In such a case, the first portion of the recency region will be read from the disk by using a B+tree index on the start time values of the tuples.

The contents of the *Recent Buffer* need to be maintained as new inputs arrive into the DStream and as live matches are processed. The access properties of the patterns in our model (sequential scans, results only moving forward), and the recency region of size P lead to the following *Recent Buffer* maintenance approach: When there is a completed live match from time t_s to t_e, the region from the end of the match (i.e., $[t_e - P, t_e)$) needs to be considered for archive processing (see Definition 8). On the other hand, if no live match has been found yet and we are currently processing a tuple $T(t_s, t_e)$, we generally need to consider the region back from this tuple (i.e., $[T.t_e - P - 1, T.t_e]$), since a live match might be completed with the next arriving tuple. If a previous match m was found, however, we know that the next match will not end before $m.t_e$ (based on the INCREMENTAL mode discussion provided in Section 2). Therefore, we can take the maximum start points of these expected recency regions, ensuring that we never need more than P entries in the *Recent Buffer*. Given these properties, the *Recent Buffer* is implemented as a set of in-memory FIFO stores, with a separate one for each partition (specified with the PARTITION BY clause) in the query.

In addition to providing efficient memory management, our recent input buffering mechanism also facilitates our query optimization techniques, which we present next.

4.3 Query Result Caching

One important potential bottleneck of our baseline PCQ algorithm in Section 3 is the re-computation of pattern matching queries over the archived stream, because it leads to $\mathcal{O}(P_l * M_l)$ complexity.

One way to overcome this problem is based on the observation that the recency region of a live match intersects with the recency regions of other live matches, so that an archive match could be used by multiple live matches. This scenario resembles materialized views in traditional databases, where the access to the materialized results is faster than recomputing the view [17]. Figure 7 illustrates the relationship among such recency regions and the effect of using the *Query Result Cache* for different overlap scenarios. On the top lane, we see three live matches m_i, m_j, and m_k,

Live tuple (t_s,p)	Recent Buffer (t_s,p)	Query Result Cache (t_s,t_s,p_{ai},p_{am})	Result ($t_s,t_e,p_{li},p_{lm},p_{ai},p_{am}$)
	...		
(02:04,7)	(02:00,10) ... (02:04,7)		
(02:05,6)	(02:03,5) ... (02:05,6)	(02:02,02:04,6,7)	(02:02,02:05,7,6,6,7)
(02:06,11)	(02:03,5) ... (02:06,11)	(02:02,02:04,6,7)	
(02:07,8)	(02:05,6) ... (02:07,8)	(02:02,02:04,6,7) (02:04,02:06,7,11)	(02:02,02:07,11,8,6,7)
(02:08,8)	(02:05,6) ... (02:08, 8)	(02:02,02:04,6,7) (02:04,02:06,7,11)	
(02:09,3)	(02:05,6) ... (02:09,3)	(02:02,02:04,6,7) (02:04,02:06,7,11)	(02:02,02:09,8,3,6,7) (02:04,02:07,11,8,7,11) (02:04,02:09,8,3,7,11)
(02:10,3)	(02:05,6) ... (02:10,3)	(02:04,02:06,7,11)	

Table 3: Lazy Live First with Query Result Cache

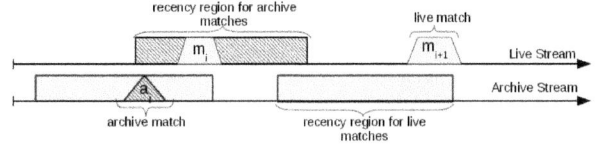

Figure 8: Join Source Ordering & Selectivities

(yellow tetragon) each spanning a recency region on the archive side (hollow rectangles) with archive matches (triangles). The recency regions of m_i and m_j overlap, making the effective distance $\triangle_j$ smaller than P_l and allow the reuse of the last archive match of m_i for m_j. In turn, $\triangle_k$ is equal to P_l, since there is no recency region overlap.

We can now adapt Equation (1) to only cover the computation of archive matches that have not been previously computed, covering a smaller portion of the recency region $\triangle_l$. Since cache retrieval is very cheap compared to pattern computation, we do not include it in our cost formula:

$$Cost_{proc} = N * c_l + M_l * Min(P_l, \triangle_l) * c_a' + M_j * c_j \qquad (2)$$

Since we are only targeting the correlation of pattern queries, we do not need to burden ourselves with the overhead of general view maintenance [17], but can use a much simpler approach instead: The underlying data sources are append-only, and the recency regions advance monotonically. Therefore, a FIFO-based data structure is sufficient. In addition, the pattern correlation (Section 2) demands that there is only one pattern starting per time unit in the recency region; therefore, the maximum size of the *Query Result Cache* has a linear correlation with the size of the recency region.

Similar to the *Recent Buffer*, the *Query Result Cache* is also implemented as a set of stores, one for each partition in the query. According to our measurements and analysis, we expect the number of *Query Result Cache* entries to be much smaller than the number of *Recent Buffer* entries, since a complex event pattern can easily aggregate dozens or more input tuples. Nonetheless, using both of these data structures is still beneficial, since the *Recent Buffer* speeds up the computation of archive results at their first access, and can be shrunk to just the $\triangle_l$ regions. Furthermore, both can share a memory pool, since the *Query Result Cache* needs most capacity when there is matching, whereas the *Recent Buffer* needs most memory when not matching.

Table 3 illustrates the contents of the Recent Buffer and Query Result Cache for a snapshot of the execution trace of our running day trader example when our baseline algorithm (i.e., Lazy *Live First*) is enhanced with a *Query Result Cache*. The results show the expected behavior: *Query Result Cache* entries are added when they are computed on demand (e.g., live match (02:02,02:04,6,7) at input (02:05,6)) and stay in the cache until no recency region can

cover them any more (e.g., at (02:10,3)). The *Recent Buffer* is now only needed for input items which are not covered by the *Query Result Cache*, so it only needs to start one item after the start of the most recent *Query Result Cache* entry (e.g., (02:03,5) at (02:05,6), when the archive match starts at 02:02).

4.4 Join Source Ordering

Traditional relational query optimization approaches have established several ways to optimize join queries with expensive predicates or nested subexpressions [19]. Yet, most of these approaches are not applicable to our problem, since they assume that the expensive operations can be freely moved around through the query plan. This is not possible in our case, since attributes of the patterns are used in the join.

Nonetheless, we can still exploit the opportunities for changing the order of join sources in our hybrid loop join algorithm, when the selectivity of live and archive patterns differs. This way, using the less selective partner on the outer side will also reduce the overall workload, as fewer recency regions will need to be inspected. A second factor comes from the observation that pattern queries have significant variances in their cost depending on their input data, e.g., when the number of match candidates varies greatly. This effect is amplified by the correlation operations we are performing, since the recency regions will change when changing the join order. In this case, changing the recency region might help skip the processing of the hot spots. Figure 8 gives an example of such a tradeoff: The upper lane with tetragons shows the live matches, the lower with triangles shows the archive matches. Rectangles shaded in the same way as the matches show the respective recency regions, where the archive recency regions is constructed in a forward manner. As one can see, *Live First* would compute two live matches and accordingly two recency regions, whereas *Archive First* would just compute a single archive match, and accordingly a single recency region.

As a result, our cost formula will have two variants:

$$Cost_{proc\_live\_first} = N * c_l + M_l * Min(P_l, \triangle_l) * c_a' + M_j * c_j \qquad (3)$$

$$Cost_{proc\_archive\_first} = N * c_a + M_a * Min(P_a, \triangle_a) * c_l' + M_j * c_j \qquad (4)$$

The above equations are conceptually symmetric, but they capture the different cost and selectivity distributions.

Since recency by itself is not symmetric, several design decisions were made so data source re-ordering would work efficiently: Our recency correlation function (Definition 8) covers the region from start of archive match to end of live match, and does not allow any part to exceed this range. Therefore, we can also easily process forward from an archive match to discover the relevant live matches. The recency regions actually processed will now be slightly different (starting from an archive match forward), but the same set of combined events will be produced. What will change, however, is the order in which the results are computed: Since archive matches drive the "outer loop", we will receive combined events ordered by their start time, not their end time (as in *Live First*). This is actually an advantage, since we can avoid reordering to achieve the desired start time ordering. The *Recent Buffer* can now be attached to the first data source of the join.

Input Tuple (t_s,p)	Recent Buffer (t_s,p)	Query Result Cache (t_s,t_e,p_{li},p_{lm})	Result $(t_s,t_e,p_{li},p_{lm},p_{ai},p_{am})$
...			
(02:03,5)	(02:03,5)		
(02:04,7)	(02:03,5) (02:04,7)		
(02:05,6)	(02:03,5) ... (02:05,6)	(02:04,02:05,7,6)	(02:02,02:05,7,6,6,7)
...			
(02:07,8)	(02:03,5) ... (02:07,8)	(02:04,02:05,7,6) (02:06,02:07,11,8)	(02:02,02:07,11,8,6,7)
(02:09,3)	(02:03,5) ... (02:09,3)	(02:04,02:05,7,6) (02:06,02:07,11,8) (02:08,02:09,8,3)	(02:02,02:09,8,3,6,7) (02:04,02:07,11,8,7,11) (02:04,02:09,8,3,7,11)
(02:10,3)	(02:07,8) ... (02:10,3)	(02:06,02:07,11,8) (02:08,02:09,8,3)	

Table 4: Lazy Archive First with Query Result Cache

Table 4 illustrates the contents of the Recent Buffer and Query Result Cache for a snapshot of the execution trace of our running day trader example when the order of the join sources in our baseline algorithm are swapped (i.e., Lazy Archive First) is addition to using a *Query Result Cache*. The *Query Result Cache* now contains live matches which are collected while performing forward processing starting from the archive matches. They stay in the cache until archive processing overtakes them (e.g., at (02:10,3)). The *Recent Buffer* is also filled in a forward fashion, covering the start of the current archive match until the current data item. In contrast to *Live First* processing, restarting the archive computation after the previous starting point (e.g., (02:03,5) for the archive match from (02:02,6)) requires keeping the full recent region, not just the difference.

5. PERFORMANCE EVALUATION

5.1 Experimental Setup

DejaVu is built as an extension of MySQL-6.0.3-alpha, modifying its query parser, optimizer, run-time and storage engine. All experiments were executed on an Intel Xeon X3360 (2.8Ghz) with 8 GB RAM and a single 1 TB S-ATA disk, running Redhat Enterprise 5.4 64bit; the stock GCC 4.2.4 at optimization level -O2 was used for compilation, following the default setting for MySQL.

In order to evaluate the effectiveness of our optimization techniques and understand the factors in our cost model, we performed experiments in three directions:

- maintenance and access of archive data (recent buffer)
- query processing parameters (query result cache + join order)
- verification of our results on a real-life data set (NYSE TAQ)

We ran two variants of the financial query presented in Section 1.1. Both employ complex and costly patterns on the live and the archive clauses:

- *Q1* looks for a fall pattern on the live stream and correlates it with a "tick"-shaped pattern on the archive stream (see Figure 1 and Section 1.1).
- *Q2* also looks for a fall pattern on live stream but correlates it with a rise pattern on the archive stream. This query is used to model workloads where live and archive patterns are anti-correlated.

Workload variance in our setups comes from the input streams, which we adapt according to the parameters discussed in Section

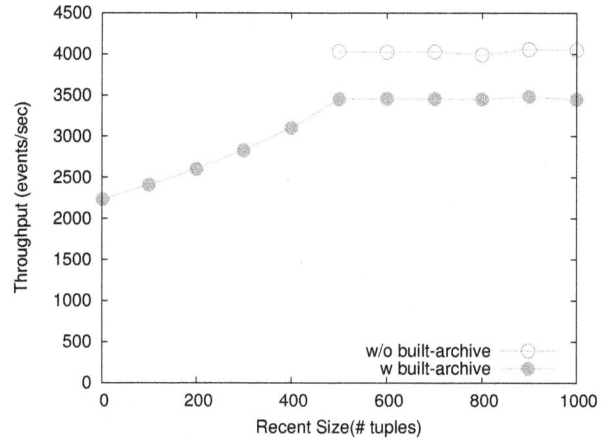

Figure 9: Archive storage and Recent Buffer, Q1, P_l=500

4. We use a single input data stream with schema (t_{start}, t_{end}, *symbol*, *price*) and one tuple recorded at every time unit. This stream is pre-generated and pushed completely into the live store, from where it is pulled by DejaVu for query processing and archiving.

In our study, we focus on overall throughput, since it is most indicative of the processing cost. More specifically, throughput is defined as the number of input tuples processed per second, and compute it by dividing the total number input tuples by the total query processing time.

5.2 Evaluation of Recent Input Buffering

The first part of our analysis focuses on the overhead of storage management, both from creating the archive and reading data out of it. Figure 9 shows (i) the impact of different recent buffer sizes when an archive is maintained, and (ii) the gain in throughput when not building an archive. Query processing is done in a naive way (i.e., live-first, no query result cache); we will study query processing parameters in the next section. Figure 9 verifies that, to avoid having to read from disk when performing archive pattern processing, the recent buffer should be at least as big as the recency region size (P_l), in this case 500 tuples (and cannot be smaller than this when "w/o built-archive"). If a smaller recent buffer is used (due to, e.g., limited memory), the performance degrades proportionally to the available buffer size, accounting for the tuples having to be fetched from the portion of the archive that is on disk. In this case, since fetching can by done using an index scan and the cache replacement policy of the recent buffer always discards the oldest tuples, we still achieve a throughput value better than 2500 tuples/second. Archive building causes a more-or-less constant overhead; it can only be avoided if the recent buffer is large enough to cover the recency region completely. Overall, archive reading is clearly a bottleneck when doing naive query execution. On the other hand, the focus of this work is not to optimize stream archiving, but to optimize query processing for PCQs that utilize an underlying stream archive. By introducing an in-memory recent buffer component into our architecture, we support the query processor in accessing the more recent archive data faster. We therefore run the rest of our experiments with a sufficiently big recent buffer.

5.3 Evaluation of Query Processing

The main part of our performance study focuses on query processing, as it has the most profound impact on throughput and a larger set of parameters to explore. We vary the input data to stress

P_l		10	50	100	200	300	400	500	600	700	800	900	1000
No Result Cache	Max Recent Items	10	50	100	200	300	400	500	600	700	800	900	1000
Query Result Cache	Max Recent Items	10	49	49	49	49	49	49	49	49	49	49	49
	Max Cache Entries	0	1	3	7	11	15	19	23	27	31	35	39

Table 5: Item count for Recent Buffer and Query Result Cache, varying P_l (Figure 10)

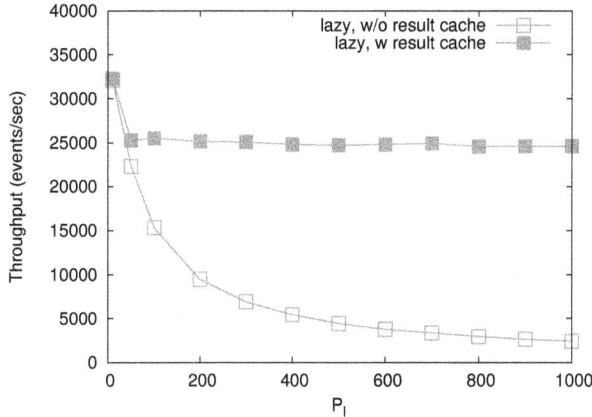

Figure 10: Varying P_l; Q1; fixed M_l, $\triangle_l$, and c'_a

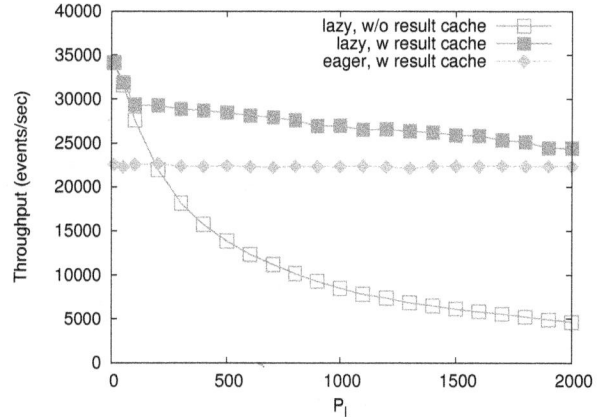

Figure 11: Varying P_l; Q1; fixed M_l, $\triangle_l$, and c'_a

particular cost factors, in particular investigating the impact of the recency region size, the presence of the query result cache, and join source ordering.

Figure 10 illustrates the performance impact of varying the size of the archive correlation region, which is the core of our correlation model. As predicted by the cost model, we see a quadratic cost increase (and accordingly a throughput decrease) as soon as the recency region size is large enough to actually produce archive pattern matches. Hence, we need to recompute all these matches for every live match (similar to a nested-loop join). Using the result cache, we can reduce this cost, since each of these matches only needs to be computed once. Therefore, the cost is now proportional to the number of results, which results in a linear throughput decrease (similar to a hash join).

We also measured the maximum utilization of both the recent buffer and the result cache, to see the required capacity. The results are shown in Table 5: When no result cache is used, the recent buffer usage is as big as P_l, since we always have to keep the full recency region available. When a result cache is used, this changes significantly, since the recent buffer is used only when "sliding" between live matches. In our test dataset, it is dominated by the difference between live matches, which is 49 tuples. The number of entries in the result cache is linear to the size of P_l, since our model ensures distinct starting points for the matches (Section 2). Furthermore, it is often much smaller than the number of input tuples, since a pattern clause consumes many input tuples to produce a single output tuple.

As a result, the total memory consumption is linear to P_l, ensuring good scalability for higher values of P_l.

5.3.1 Lazy vs. Eager Pattern Processing

Figure 11 compares the throughput of the system, when different processing strategies are used. As explained in Section 3, the *Eager* strategy computes both live and archive patterns over the whole dataset, which makes its performance independent of the recency correlation distance (P_l). This can be attributed to the observation that the join between live and archive matches is significantly

cheaper than the pattern processing itself. Due to the independence from P_l, the throughput of the *Eager* strategy stays constant with varying recency correlation values. As the figure shows, the *Eager* strategy performs better than *Lazy w/o result cache* since the latter has quadratic cost on the archive side (as the cost formula from Section 3 and 4 predicts). On the other hand, *Lazy with result cache* outperforms *Eager* for small P_l values since it can skip unneeded parts on the archive side, whereas *Eager* needs to compute patterns on these. As P_l increases and the gaps on the archive side shrink, the cost of *Lazy with result cache* converges with *Eager*, since both need to perform the same workload. Yet as the cost model predicts, *Eager* never actually outperforms *Lazy with result cache* in terms of throughput. Given this result, we have focused on the *Lazy* strategy for our remaining experiments.

5.3.2 Query Result Cache Sensitivity

The effectiveness of the query result cache depends on two factors: The overlap between the consecutive recency regions and the cost of archive processing. As Figure 12a shows, a decreasing overlap $\triangle_l$ (i.e., the distance between two consecutive recency regions) entails a decrease in throughput, due to the lower cache utilization. When $\triangle_l$ is as big as P_l (and thus no overlap exists), cache and no-cache performance converges, showing that there is no performance overhead in employing an unused cache. This can be explained by the very small cost of a maintaining and probing an in-memory queue compared to pattern matching operations.

Since the query result cache eliminates the cost of recomputing the pattern on the second data source, its benefit becomes more pronounced the more expensive the second pattern query is. Figure 12b illustrates this trend by comparing the relative throughput gain $((TP_{cache} - TP_{nocache})/TP_{nocache})$ of the cache-based approach when modifying the cost of archive processing (c'_a).

As a result of our query result cache experiments, we can clearly see that a result cache should be used whenever there is no extreme memory shortage. It enables significant performance gains on appropriate workloads, does not carry a measurable performance overhead in the worst case, and has very modest memory consumption.

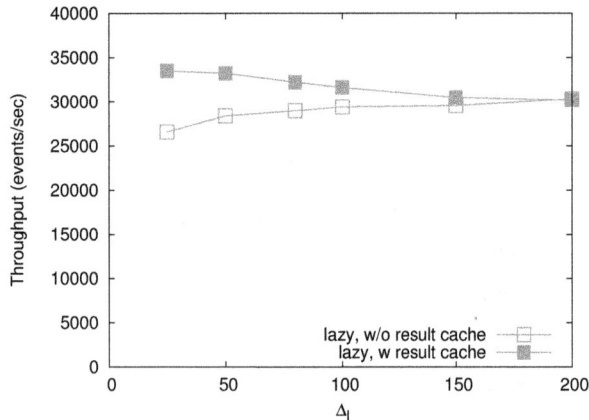

(a) Varying $\triangle_l$; Q1; fixed M_l, $P_l = 200$, and c_a' (b) Varying c_a'; Q1; fixed M_l, $\triangle_l = 80$, and $P_l = 200$

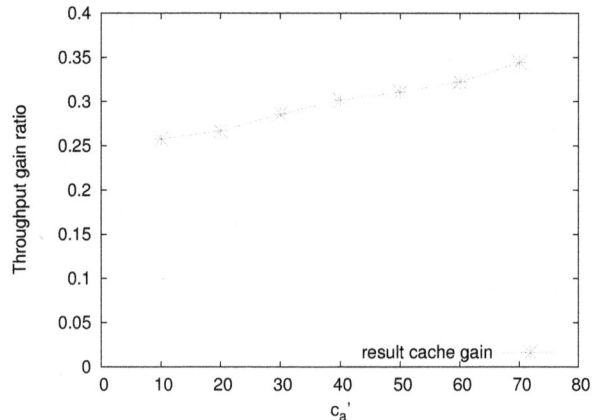

Figure 12: Impact of Query Result Cache when $\triangle_l$ or c_a' is varied

5.3.3 Evaluation of Join Source Ordering

As outlined in Section 4.4, changing the join order is beneficial if there is a significant selectivity or cost difference between the two join inputs. If such a difference exists, the more selective/less costly input is best used as the outer loop. In our case, there is a potential for optimization even if the two join partners have the same overall selectivity: The correlation of live and archive matches can create "empty" regions or "hotspots", which can then be skipped.

The join order experiments are performed in both workloads where the result cache is beneficial, as well as in workloads where it is not. Doing both yields additional insight, since join order and result cache can have competing effects: Join order works best in bringing the most selective join partner to the outer loop, whereas result caching reduces the cost of the inner loop.

We used *Q2* in these experiments, since the archive pattern of *Q1* contains the live pattern, thus fixing both the selectivity and cost ratios: There is a fall pattern instance (live) inside every "tick"-shaped (fall followed by increase) pattern (*Q1* archive) instance, which prohibits varying relative cost and selectivities among the two sources. Section 5.4 shows the results of running *Q1* in both join orders on our real-life data set, showing that our results for *Q2* also apply for *Q1* on a realistic data set.

In the first set of the experiments, the cost of recency region processing is the same for live- and *Archive First* processing ($c_l' = c_a'$), and the cost of first pattern processing is set to a value that is proportional to the number of the first pattern matches ($c_l \propto M_l$ and $c_a \propto M_a$). Hence, according to our cost formula, the total processing cost depends on the selectivity of archive and live matches (M_l and M_a).

We varied the match ratio in the first experiment (see Figure 13a). Let us first discuss the case where the workload does not benefit from a result cache (empty square and triangle in the graph). If there is no difference in the selectivity of live and archive matches, the performance is the same. When there is a selectivity difference, then the pattern which is less likely to be matched should be processed first.

When the workload is amenable for result cache usage (filled square and triangle in Figure 13a), the trend is similar to the one in the *without result cache* scenario, but the relative benefits are smaller. Although the cost for the first pattern stays the same, pro-

cessing the second pattern becomes cheaper, since the result cache eliminates the quadratic overhead.

In the second set of experiments, we keep the selectivity of both patterns at the same level ($M_l = M_a$), but change the correlations between the recency regions and thus introduce variance in the "local" cost. In other words, changing the join order might help to skip the computationally expensive areas in the stream. As a result, the average cost of processing a tuple over the whole stream is much lower than processing it in the recency region.

Figure 13b shows our results. If the result cache is not effective (empty square and triangle in Figure 13b), the performance of the system increases when the less costly recency region is preferred. On the other hand, when a result cache is actually applicable, it leads to a significant cost reduction in processing the second data source, so that the join order has almost no impact (filled square and triangle in Figure 13b). Archive-first processing always performs slightly better than life-first, since it can access the recent buffer more efficiently, it can benefit from forward processing in the pattern, and does not need to re-order the final results.

These experiments clearly demonstrate the benefits of join ordering in PCQs. The performance factors are orthogonal, so we expect to see even better results when there is a skew in both selectivity and cost/correlation.

5.4 Results on Real-Life Data

Our experiments so far have been performed on synthetic data which was geared towards evaluating the cost model factors. In order to understand how relevant our optimizations are in real-world workloads, we took several days of stock-market data from NYSE (January 26 to 31, 2006), and selected the most heavily traded stock (Exxon Mobile, symbol XOM). We again ran *Q1*, and extended P_l to cover the equivalent of several hours. As Figure 14 shows, the total throughput is somewhat lower than for the synthetic data (Figure 10), whereas the benefit of result caching is even more pronounced on larger P_l, giving a factor of 54 performance gain for P_l=500 between the baseline approach (*Live First without cache*) and the best method (*Archive First with Cache*).

Although the actual numbers are different, we see the same trend regarding the benefit of result caching. The main reason behind the different throughput numbers is that real life data is more likely to produce matches than synthetic data. This means more recency

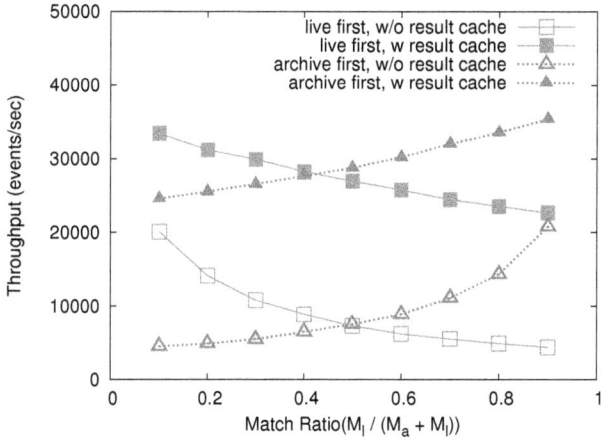

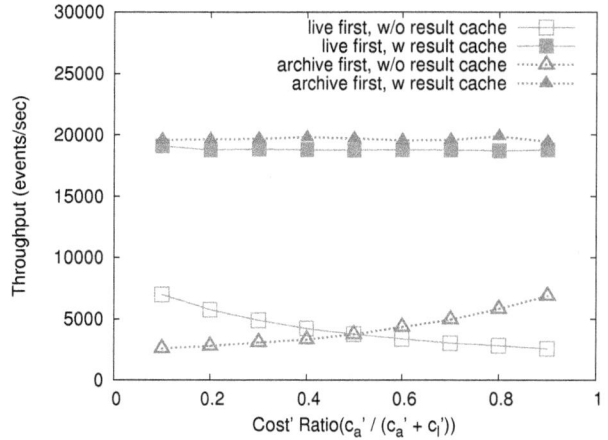

(a) Varying selectivity; Q2; $c_l'=c_a'$, $c_l \propto M_l$, $c_a \propto M_a$, $P_l = P_a = 500$

(b) Varying cost ratio; Q2; $c_l << c_a'$, $c_a << c_l'$, $M_l = M_a$, $P_l = P_a = 500$

Figure 13: Impact of Join Source Ordering when match selectivities or recency region processing cost is varied

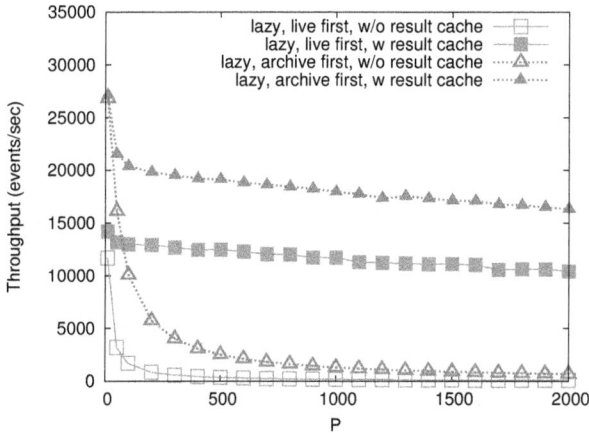

Figure 14: Real-life data, Q1, varying P, Lazy Live First & Lazy Archive First, with or without Query Result Cache

regions overlap more and more matches in the recency regions. Another important observation regarding the real life experiment is that *Archive First* processing achieves a better throughput. The reason behind it is that the archive pattern is more selective than the live pattern. As a reminder, each "tick"-shaped pattern instance includes at least one fall pattern instance, and "tick"-shaped pattern is less likely to be matched than a fall pattern. Here, the selectiviy difference dominates the join source ordering decision and makes *Archive First* with result cache the winner strategy.

5.5 Discussion

In our experiments, we have studied the impact of the different processing approaches and optimizations on throughput, both on synthetic and real-life data. The results lead to several clear conclusions: *Eager* is nearly always outperformed by *Lazy with Result Cache*, in the best case it manages to perform equally well. Therefore, there is little motivation to use *Eager* when focusing on throughput. Among the optimizations, using a result cache is always useful when there is at least some free memory available, as

it significantly speeds up processing when overlaps exists yet has extremely low overhead when none exists. In addition, memory requirements are low and well-bounded. In a similar fashion, a recent input buffer should be used whenever there is enough memory, since it significantly reduces the cost of archive access. The usefulness of join order depends on a skew in selectivity or correlation among the two inputs. If such a skew exists, it also provides measurable benefits. To sum up, all the optimizations we have investigated provide significant benefits, sometimes improving results by an order of magnitude or more.

6. RELATED WORK

There are several CEP engines (e.g., Cayuga [13], SASE [10], ZStream [21]) that propose languages and processing techniques for efficient pattern matching over live streams, but none of them supports stream archiving or pattern correlation queries. On the other hand, the DataDepot stream warehousing system [16] has been designed to automate the ingestion of streaming data from a variety of sources, as well as to maintain complex materialized views over them, but it does not provide any facilities for PCQs.

The need for combining the processing of live and historical events has also been recognized by previous work (e.g., Moirae [11], TelegraphCQ [12, 22], NiagaraST/Latte [24]), and they mostly tackle the efficient archive access problem. Moirae [11] prioritizes the processing of the recent historical data and produces approximate results by using multi-level storage, recent event materialization, and context similarity metrics. TelegraphCQ proposes an overload-sensitive disk access method where multiple samples of a stream archive are created and are selectively accessed depending on the input rates [12], and a bitmap-based indexing technique for efficiently querying live and historical stream data [22]. NiagaraST/Latte demonstrates how hybrid queries can be used for travel time estimation in intelligent transportation systems [24]. The focus is on window-based hybrid queries (no pattern matching) and on efficient archive access based on different similarity notions. Our recency-based correlation criteria falls under Latte's structural similarity notion.

Typical commercial SPEs also support hybrid continuous queries (e.g., [1], [8], [9]), where for every new item on the stream, a database query needs to be executed. We generalize this to finding correlated archive pattern matches for every new pattern match on the stream. As such, we face the additional challenges of variable processing window sizes on live and archive, variable archive scope due to variable slide on live, and more complex window computations.

Last but not least, Oracle CEP [7] and ESPER [2] also provide a basic implementation for MATCH-RECOGNIZE, though with some limitations that render their use not feasible for processing PCQs. More specifically, application-time based processing of MATCH-RECOGNIZE is not currently supported in Oracle CEP engine, whereas ESPER does not support joins across MATCH-RECOGNIZE clauses.

7. CONCLUSIONS AND FUTURE WORK

In this work, we have investigated the problem of efficiently correlating complex events over live and archived data streams, which we call Pattern Correlation Queries (PCQs). Applications for PCQs span various domains (such as financial or medical), which need real-time forecasting of events or identification of causal dependencies, while handling data at high rates and in massive amounts. In the paper, we first defined the formal semantics for recency-based PCQs, paying attention to usefulness, clarity, composability, and optimizability. After studying the state of the art and possible baseline algorithms for implementing PCQs according to their complexity, we have proposed three optimizations for efficient data management and query processing, including recent input buffering, query result caching, and join source ordering. An extensive performance study on synthetic and real-life data sets not only validates our cost model, but also shows that our optimizations are very effective, achieving more than two orders magnitude throughput improvements and much better scalability compared to a straightforward implementation.

In terms of future work, we plan to pursue additional optimizations such as result cache value indexing for further join optimizations and exploiting similarity of patterns to reduce matching cost. We also consider investigating how other performance criteria, such as response time, are affected by our design decisions and which optimizations are needed if they become more relevant. Another important direction to study is how other correlation criteria such as context similarity or temporal periodicity would work with our architecture and optimizations. We think that the role of the recent buffer will be reduced, whereas result caching will become even more important.

Acknowledgments.
We would like to thank Patrick Lau for his contribution in the development of DejaVu engine. This work has been supported in part by the Swiss NSF ProDoc PDFMP2-122971/1 grant.

8. REFERENCES

[1] Coral8, Inc. http://www.coral8.com/.
[2] ESPER. http://esper.codehaus.org/.
[3] MEDAN - Competence Center for Medical Data Warehousing and Analysis. http://www.inf.unibz.it/dis/projects/medan/index.html.
[4] Medical Use case. http://www.mamashealth.com/Bloodpressure.asp.
[5] MySQL. http://www.mysql.com/.
[6] NYSE Data Solutions. http://www.nyxdata.com/nysedata/.
[7] Oracle CEP. http://www.oracle.com/technetwork/middleware/complex-event-processing/index.html/.
[8] StreamBase Systems, Inc. http://www.streambase.com/.
[9] Truviso, Inc. http://www.truviso.com/.
[10] J. Agrawal, Y. Diao, D. Gyllstrom, and N. Immerman. Efficient Pattern Matching over Event Streams. In *ACM SIGMOD Conference*, Vancouver, Canada, June 2008.
[11] M. Balazinska, Y. Kwon, N. Kuchta, and D. Lee. Moirae: History-Enhanced Monitoring. In *CIDR Conference*, Asilomar, CA, January 2007.
[12] S. Chandrasekaran and M. Franklin. Remembrance of Streams Past: Overload-Sensitive Management of Archived Streams. In *VLDB Conference*, Toronto, Canada, August 2004.
[13] A. Demers, J. Gehrke, B. Panda, M. Riedewald, V. Sharma, and W. White. Cayuga: A General Purpose Event Monitoring System. In *CIDR Conference*, Asilomar, CA, January 2007.
[14] D. J. DeWitt, J. F. Naughton, and D. A. Schneider. An Evaluation of Non-Equijoin Algorithms. In *VLDB Conference*, Barcelona, Spain, September 1991.
[15] N. Dindar, B. Güç, P. Lau, A. Özal, M. Soner, and N. Tatbul. DejaVu: Declarative Pattern Matching over Live and Archived Streams of Events (Demo). In *ACM SIGMOD Conference*, Providence, RI, June 2009.
[16] L. Golab, T. Johnson, J. S. Seidel, and V. Shkapenyuk. Stream Warehousing with DataDepot. In *ACM SIGMOD Conference*, Providence, RI, June 2009.
[17] A. Gupta and I. S. Mumick. Maintenance of Materialized Views: Problems, Techniques, and Applications. *IEEE Data Engineering Bulletin*, 18(2), 1995.
[18] D. Gyllstrom, J. Agrawal, Y. Diao, and N. Immerman. On Supporting Kleene Closure over Event Streams. In *IEEE ICDE Conference*, Cancun, Mexico, April 2008.
[19] J. M. Hellerstein. Optimization Techniques for Queries with Expensive Methods. *ACM TODS Journal*, 23(2), June 1998.
[20] A. Lerner and D. Shasha. The Virtues and Challenges of Ad Hoc + Streams Querying in Finance. *IEEE Data Engineering Bulletin*, 26(1), March 2003.
[21] Y. Mei and S. Madden. ZStream: A Cost-based Query Processor for Adaptively Detecting Composite Events. In *ACM SIGMOD Conference*, Providence, RI, June 2009.
[22] F. Reiss, K. Stockinger, K. Wu, A. Shoshani, and J. M. Hellerstein. Enabling Real-Time Querying of Live and Historical Stream Data. In *SSDBM Conference*, Banff, Canada, July 2007.
[23] J. Teubner and R. Müller. How Soccer Players Would Do Stream Joins. In *SIGMOD*, 2011.
[24] K. Tufte, J. Li, D. Maier, V. Papadimos, R. L. Bertini, and J. Rucker. Travel Time Estimation using NiagaraST and Latte. In *ACM SIGMOD Conference*, Beijing, China, June 2007.
[25] F. Zemke, A. Witkowski, M. Cherniack, and L. Colby. Pattern Matching in Sequences of Rows. Technical Report ANSI Standard Proposal, July 2007.

Space-efficient Tracking of Persistent Items in a Massive Data Stream

Bibudh Lahiri
Dept. of ECE
Iowa State University
Ames, IA, USA 50011
bibudh@iastate.edu[*]

Jaideep Chandrashekar
Intel Labs Berkeley
2150 Shattuck Ave
Berkeley, CA, USA 94704
jaideep.chandrashekar@intel.com

Srikanta Tirthapura
Dept. of ECE
Iowa State University
Ames, IA, USA 50011
snt@iastate.edu [*]

ABSTRACT

Motivated by scenarios in network anomaly detection, we consider the problem of detecting persistent items in a data stream, which are items that occur "regularly" in the stream. In contrast with heavy-hitters, persistent items do not necessarily contribute significantly to the volume of a stream, and may escape detection by traditional volume-based anomaly detectors.

We first show that any online algorithm that tracks persistent items exactly must necessarily use a large workspace, and is infeasible to run on a traffic monitoring node. In light of this lower bound, we introduce an approximate formulation of the problem and present a small-space algorithm to approximately track persistent items over a large data stream. Our experiments on a real traffic dataset shows that in typical cases, the algorithm achieves a physical space compression of 5x-7x, while incurring very few false positives ($< 1\%$) and false negatives ($< 4\%$). To our knowledge, this is the first systematic study of the problem of detecting persistent items in a data stream, and our work can help detect anomalies that are temporal, rather than volume based.

Categories and Subject Descriptors

C.2.3 [**Computer-Communication Networks**]: Network Management, Network Monitoring

General Terms

Algorithms, Theory

---
[*]The work of Lahiri and Tirthapura was supported in part by the National Science Foundation through awards 0834743, 0831903.

1. INTRODUCTION

We consider the problem of identifying *persistent* items in a large data stream. This problem has particular relevance while mining various network streams, such as the traffic at a gateway router, connections to a web service, etc. Consider a stream of elements of the form (d, t) where d is an item identifier, and t is a timeslot during which the item arrived. Multiple items can arrive in the same timeslot, and the same item may arrive multiple times within a time slot. Suppose the total number of timeslots in the stream is n. The persistence of an item d is defined to be the number of distinct timeslots in which d was observed. The persistence of any item is an integer between 0 and n (inclusive). An item is said to be α-persistent, for some constant $0 < \alpha \leq 1$, if its persistence is at least αn. Given a user-defined α, the problem is to output the set of α-persistent items in the stream. Persistent items exhibit a repeated and regular pattern of arrival, and are significant items in the stream for many applications.

Giroire *et al.* [18] monitored traffic from an end-host to detect communication across botnet channels. They observed that very persistent destinations were likely to belong to one of two classes: either they were malicious hosts associated with a botnet, or they were frequently visited benign hosts. It was also observed that the latter set of hosts could be identified easily and assembled into a "whitelist" of known good destinations. They found that tracking persistent items in the network stream, followed by filtering out items contained in the whitelist, resulted in reliable identification of botnet traffic.

In general, persistent items are often associated with specific anomalies in the context of network streams: periodic connections to an online advertisement in a pay-per-click revenue model [36] is an indicator of click fraud [41], repeated (failed) connections observed in the stream is indicative of a failed or unreachable web service [20]; botnets periodically "phone home" to their bot controllers [18]; attackers regularly scan for open ports on which vulnerable applications are usually deployed [33]. While the narrative in this paper draws from applications in the network monitoring space, it appears that the general problem of detecting persistent items in a data stream is broadly applicable in other data monitoring applications. For example, persistent use of gathering techniques such as telephone interception or satellite imaging might indicate an "Advanced Persistent Threat" (APT) [34] for a target group, e.g., a government.

The persistent items in a stream could be very different from the frequently occurring items ("heavy-hitters") in a stream. An item is called a ϕ-heavy hitter if it contributes to at least a ϕ fraction of the entire volume of the stream. There is a large body of literature on heavy-hitter identification [28, 26, 14, 12, 8, 11, 13]. A persistent item need not be a heavy hitter. For example, the item may appear only once in each time slot and may not contribute significantly to the stream volume. Such "stealthy" behavior was indeed observed in botnet traffic detection [18]; the highly persistent destinations which were not contained in the whitelist did not contribute in any meaningful way to the traffic volume. In fact, the traffic to these destinations was stealthy and very low volume, perhaps by design to evade detection by traditional volume-based detectors. Conversely, a heavy-hitter need not be a persistent item either – for example, an item may occur a number of times in the stream, but all its occurrences maybe within only a couple of timeslots. Such an item will have a low persistence. Clearly, the set of persistent items in a stream can be very different from the set of heavy-hitters in the stream; their intersection can very well be empty.

There seems to be no easy reduction from the problem of identifying persistent items to the problem of identifying heavy-hitters. For example, one could attempt to devise a "filter" that eliminated duplicate occurrences of an item within a time slot, and then apply a traditional heavy-hitter algorithm on the resulting "filtered" stream. But this approach does not work in small space, because such a "filter" would itself take space proportional to the number of distinct items that appeared within the timeslot, and this number maybe very large, especially for the type of network traffic streams that we are interested in.

Prior work in Giroire *et al.* [18] used the following method to track persistent items in a stream of network traffic. For each distinct item in the stream, their method maintained (1)The number of timeslots in which the item has appeared in the stream so far, and (2)Whether or not the item has appeared in the current timeslot. This allowed them to exactly compute the number of timeslots that each item has appeared in, and hence exactly identify the set of persistent items. However, the space taken by this scheme is proportional to the number of distinct items in the stream. The stream could have a very large number of distinct items (for example, IP sources, or destinations), and the memory overhead may render this infeasible on a typical network monitor or a router. Thus the challenge is to identify the persistent items in a stream using a small workspace, and minimal processing per element. Further, all tracking must be done online, and the system does not have the luxury of making multiple passes through the data.

1.1 Contributions

In this work, we present the first small-space approximation algorithm for identifying persistent items in a data stream, and an evaluation of the algorithm. Our contributions are as follows.

Space Lower Bound: We first consider the problem of exactly tracking all α-persistent items in a stream, for some user-defined $\alpha \in (0, 1)$. For this problem, we show that *any* algorithm that solves it must use $\Omega(|D| \log n\alpha)$ space, where $|D|$ is the number of distinct items in the stream, and n is the total number of slots, *even when the number of persistent items is much smaller than* $|D|$.

Approximate Tracking of Persistent Items: In light of the above lower bound, we define an approximate version of the problem. We are given two parameters, α - the threshold for persistence, and $\epsilon < \alpha$, an approximation (or "uncertainty") parameter. The task is to report a set of items with the following properties: every item that is α-persistent is reported, and no item with persistence less than $(\alpha - \epsilon)$ is reported. We also formulate this problem for a "sliding window" of the most recently observed items of the stream.

Small Space Algorithm: For the above problem of approximate tracking of persistent items, we present a randomized algorithm that can approximately track the α-persistent items using space that is typically much smaller than the number of distinct items in the stream. The expected space complexity of the algorithm is $O\left(\frac{P}{\epsilon n}\right)$, where P is the sum of the persistence values of all items in the stream, and n is the total number of timeslots. The algorithm has a small probability of a false negative (i.e. an α-persistent item is missed). This probability can be made arbitrarily small, at the cost of additional space. Note that any algorithm will need space that is at least as large as the size of the output, i.e., the number of α-persistent items in the stream. The worst case scenario is when every item is α-persistent, forcing the algorithm to use space proportional to the number of distinct items! Fortunately, this situation does not seem to occur in practice and only a fraction of items are very persistent, and this helps our algorithm considerably. We also prove that if persistence of different items in a stream follow a power law distribution, then the space taken by our algorithm is $O(\frac{1}{\epsilon})$.

Sliding Windows: In most network monitoring applications, the data set of interest is not the entire traffic stream, but only a window of the recent past (say the last n timeslots into the past). For instance, Giroire *et al* [18] used this *sliding window* model in their work on botnet traffic detection. Though the size of the data set has decreased somewhat, when compared with the fixed window case, maintaining statistics over a sliding window is still a hard problem, since the data contained within a sliding window is often too large to be stored completely within the memory of the stream processor. When compared with the fixed window version, there is an additional complication in that there are elements that expire from the window as time moves forward. We present an extension to our fixed window algorithm to handle the sliding window model. The expected space cost of our sliding window algorithm is within a factor of two of the fixed window algorithm.

Experimental Evaluation: We evaluate our algorithm against a large, real world network traffic trace collected from an Internet backbone link. On this trace, our small space algorithm uses upto 85% *less* space than the naive algorithm and typically incurs a false positive rate of less than 1% and a false negative rate of less than 4%. We also see that false positive rate never exceeds 3% for any parameter setting, while the false negative rate stays below 5% for all but the most aggressive thresholds for persistence.

2. PROBLEM STATEMENT

Consider a world where time is divided into timeslots (or slots) that are numbered $1, 2, \ldots$. Let S be a stream of elements of the form $S = \langle (d_1, t_1), (d_2, t_2), \ldots \rangle$. Here each stream element is a tuple (d_i, t_i), where d_i is an item identifier (IP address, hostname, etc), and t_i is the time slot during which the element arrived. It is assumed that the t_is are in non-decreasing order. All elements that have the same values of t_i are said to be in the same timeslot. Clearly, a timeslot consists of elements that form a contiguous subsequence of the observed stream. The duration of a timeslot depends on the application on hand. In the botnet detection application [18], the duration of a timeslot was chosen to be between 1 hour and 24 hours, primarily because these were suspected to be the possible lengths of time between successive connections from the (infected) client to malicious destinations, for the botnets that they considered. Since then, there have been other botnet attacks that work on a much smaller timescale (see Section 4 for a discussion). In an eventual solution to botnet attack detection, we may need to consider running the algorithm simultaneously with different timeslot durations, to monitor multiple types of attacks. For a different application such as monitoring telephone calls, the length of timeslot is likely to be longer, since the user is likely to use the channel less frequently.

We define a window S_ℓ^r to consist of all stream elements (d_i, t_i) whose timeslots are in the range $[\ell, r]$, i.e. $S_\ell^r = \{(d_i, t_i) \in S | \ell \leq t_i \leq r\}$. The size of window S_ℓ^r is defined as $r - \ell + 1$, i.e. the number of timeslots it encompasses. For a given window we define the persistence of an item in that window as follows:

Definition 1. The persistence of an item d over a window S_ℓ^r, denoted $p_d(\ell, r)$, is defined as the number of distinct slots in $\{\ell, \ell + 1, \ldots, r\}$ that d appeared in.

$$p_d(\ell, r) = |\{t|((d, t) \in S) \wedge (\ell \leq t \leq r)\}|$$

Definition 2. An item d is said to be α-persistent in window S_ℓ^r if $p_d(\ell, r) \geq \alpha(r - \ell + 1)$. In other words, d must have occurred in at least an α fraction of all slots within the window.

We state two versions of the problem, the first version for a fixed window, and the second version for a sliding window. In practice, the sliding window version is more useful.

PROBLEM 1. **Identifying Persistent Items Over a Fixed Window:** *Devise a space-efficient algorithm that takes as input a prespecified window $W = S_1^n$ and a persistence threshold α, and at the end of observing the stream, returns the set of all items that are α-persistent. In other words, the algorithm will report every item that is α-persistent in W and will not report any item that is not α-persistent.*

A straightforward algorithm for this problem would track every distinct item in the stream, and for each distinct item, count the number of slots (from 0 to $n - 1$) during which the item appeared. For a single item, its persistence can be tracked in a constant number of bytes (assuming that the item identifier and slot number can be stored in constant space), by maintaining a counter for the number of timeslots the item has appeared in so far, in addition to one bit of state for whether or not the item has appeared in the current timeslot. The total space consumed by the naive algorithm is of the order of the number of distinct items in the stream. In general, this would be a large number and the space overhead may make it infeasible for this algorithm to be deployed within a network router.

Space Lower Bound for Exact Tracking: In fact, we can show that any algorithm that solves the above problem

exactly must require $\Omega(m)$ space in the worst case, where m is the number of distinct items in the input. Importantly, $\Omega(m)$ space is needed even if the number of persistent items is much smaller than m.

LEMMA 2.1. *Any algorithm that can exactly solve Problem 1 must use $\Omega(m \log(n\alpha + 1))$ bits of space in the worst case, where m is the number of distinct items in the input.*

PROOF. Without loss of generality, suppose that the m distinct items that appear in the stream are labeled $1, 2, 3, \ldots, m$. Consider the state of the stream after observing $k = n - (\alpha n)$ timeslots. Let n_i denote the number of timeslots among $1, 2, \ldots, k$ during which item i has appeared. Consider the vector $u = \langle n_1, n_2, \ldots, n_m \rangle$. Consider the following set V of possible assignments to u, where each component in u is chosen from the range $0, 1, 2, \ldots, \alpha n$. The size of V is $(1 + n\alpha)^m$. We now claim that any algorithm that solves Problem 1 must distinguish between two distinct vectors V, and hence must have a different state of its memory for two input streams that result in different assignments to u.

We use proof by contradiction. Suppose the above was not true, and there were two input streams A and B which, at the end of k slots, resulted in vectors $v_A, v_B \in V$ respectively. $v_A \neq v_B$ but the states of the algorithm's memory were the same after observing the two inputs. Now, v_A and v_B must differ in at least one coordinate. Without loss of generality, suppose they differed in coordinate 1, so $n_1(A) \neq n_1(B)$, and without loss of generality suppose $n_1(A) < n_1(B)$. Consider the rest of the stream, from slot $n - n\alpha$ onwards. Suppose these slots had $n\alpha - n_1(B)$ slots in which item 1 occurred. Clearly, appending this stream to stream A results in a stream with n slots where the persistence of item 1 is $n_1(A) + (n\alpha - n_1(B)) = n\alpha - (n_1(B) - n_1(A)) < n\alpha$, and appending this same stream to stream B results in a stream with n slots where the persistence of item 1 is $n\alpha$. Thus, item 1 must be reported as α-persistent in the latter case, and not in the former case. But this is not possible, since the algorithm has the same memory state for both A and B, and sees the same substream henceforth, leading to a contradiction.

To distinguish between any two vectors in V, the algorithm needs at least $\log |V|$ bits of memory. Since the size of V is $(n\alpha + 1)^m$, the lower bound is $\Omega(m \log(n\alpha+1))$ bits. □

In the network monitoring scenario, for example, the theoretical number of distinct items that can be observed at an internet gateway is 2^{32} (IP addresses are 32 bits long), which would require $4GB$ of memory or higher. In practice however, the space requirement is likely to be smaller. On a sample traffic trace collected over a backbone link, we observed 885 million packets in a 180 minute trace, which had about a million distinct destination IP addresses.

In light of the above lower bound on the space cost of exact tracking of persistent items, we define a relaxed version of the problem. Here, in addition to the persistence threshold α, the user provides two additional parameters, $\epsilon \in [0, 1]$, an "uncertainty parameter", and $\delta \in [0, 1]$, an error probability.

PROBLEM 2. **Approximately Identifying Persistent Items over a Fixed Window:** *Given a fixed window $W = S_1^n$, persistence threshold α, approximation parameter ϵ, and error probability δ, devise a small space algorithm that returns a set of items with the following properties.*

A. *All Persistent Items are reported. If $p_d(1,n) > \alpha$, then d is returned as being persistent with a probability at least $1 - \delta$.*

B. *Items that are far from persistent should not be reported. If $p_d(1,n) < (\alpha - \epsilon) \cdot n$, then d is not reported, with probability at least $1 - \delta$.*

Sliding Windows. The sliding window version of the problem requires that we continuously monitor the window of the n most recent timeslots in the stream.

PROBLEM 3. **Approximately identifying Persistent Elements over a Sliding Window:** *The problem of approximately tracking persistent items over a sliding window is the same as the above Problem 2, except that the window of interest, W, is the set of the n most recent timeslots in the stream, and changes continuously with time.*

We note that the sliding window makes the problem more challenging than the one for a fixed window. The fixed window version is a special case of the sliding window, where the window is equal to the entire stream. The space lower bound for fixed window obviously applies to the sliding window version, hence it is also necessary to consider an approximate version of the problem for sliding windows, if we are to achieve a small space solution.

3. AN ALGORITHM FOR APPROXIMATE TRACKING OF PERSISTENT ITEMS

We present algorithms for approximate tracking of persistent items in a stream. We first present the algorithm for tracking persistent items over a fixed window, followed by a proof of correctness and analysis of complexity. We then present the algorithm for sliding window.

3.1 Fixed Window

Intuition. The goal is to track the persistence of as few items in the stream as possible, and hence minimize the workspace used by the algorithm. Ideally, we track (and hence, use space for) only the α-persistent items in the stream, and not the rest. But this is impossible, since we do not know in advance which items are α-persistent.

The strategy is to set up a hash-based "filter". Each stream element is sent through this filter, and if it is selected by the filter, then the corresponding item's persistence is tracked in future timeslots. The filter behaves in such a way that if the same item reappears in the same timeslot, then its chances of being selected by the filter are not enhanced, but if the same item reappears in different time slots, then its chances of passing the filter get progressively better. For achieving the above, the filter for an item is carefully selected to be dependent on the output of a hash function whose inputs are both the item identifier as well as the timeslot within which it appeared. Let us denote this hash function by h, and for item d arriving in slot t, the item passes through the filter if $h(d,t) < \tau$, for some preselected threshold τ. The value of τ is small enough that an item with a small value of persistence is not likely to cross this filter; in particular, transient items which only occur in a constant number of timeslots will almost certainly not make it. Note that if the same item d reappears in the same timeslot t, then the hash output $h(d,t)$ is the same as before,

hence the probability of the item passing the filter does not increase.

After an item has passed the filter, the persistence of this item in the remaining time slots is tracked exactly, since this requires only a constant amount of additional space (per item). Finally, the persistence of an item is estimated as the number of slots that it has appeared in since it started being tracked (this is known exactly), plus an estimate of the number of slots it had to appear in before we started tracking it. An item is returned as α-persistent if its estimated persistence is greater than a threshold T (decided by the analysis). Note that there maybe items which are being tracked because they passed the filter, but are not returned as α-persistent, since the estimate of their persistence did not exceed T.

The higher the threshold τ, the greater is the accuracy in our estimate of the persistence, but this comes at the cost of higher memory consumption since more items will now pass the filter. Setting the value of τ gives us a way to tradeoff accuracy versus space.

Formal Description. Let $D(S)$ denote the set of distinct items in the stream S, and suppose that the timeslots of interest are $0, 1, \ldots, n-1$. The stream processor tracks only a subset of $D(S)$, and maintains a data structure that we call a "sketch", which summarizes the stream elements seen so far. Let S denote the sketch data structure maintained by the algorithm.

S is a set of tuples of the form (d, n_d, t_d), where d is an item that has appeared in the stream, n_d is the number of slots in which d has appeared, since we started tracking it. t_d is the most recent time slot during which d has appeared. For each item d, if d is being tracked, then there is one tuple of the form $(d, \cdot, \cdot)$ belonging in S, and otherwise, there is no such tuple in S. For each item d, there can never be more than one tuple of the form $(d, \cdot, \cdot)$ in S at a time. We say $d \in S$ to mean "there is a tuple $(d, \cdot, \cdot)$ belonging to S." Similarly, we say $d \notin S$.

The inputs to the algorithm are the persistence threshold α, the total number of slots n, approximation parameter ϵ, and error probability δ. The algorithm selects a hash function $h(d,t)$ where d is an item, and t is the time slot number. It is assumed that $h(d,t)$ is a uniform random real number in $(0,1)$, and that the outputs of h on different inputs are mutually independent; when presented with the same input (d,t), the hash function returns the same output. We note that it is possible to work with weaker assumptions of hash functions whose range is a finite set of integers, but we assume the current model for simplicity and ease of exposition.

Before any stream element arrives, Algorithm 1 Sketch-Initialize is invoked to initialize the data structures. When a stream element (d,t) arrives, Algorithm 2 is invoked to update the S data structure. When there is a query for persistent items in the stream, Algorithm 3 Detect-Persistent-Items is called to process the query and will return a list of all items deemed persistent.

Algorithm 1: Sketch-Initialize($m, \alpha, \epsilon, \delta$)

Input: Size of domain m; Total number of slots n; persistence threshold α; parameter ϵ; error probability δ

Initialize the hash function $h : ([1, m] \times [1, n]) \to (0, 1)$;
$\mathcal{S} \leftarrow \phi$; $\tau \leftarrow \frac{2}{\epsilon n}$; $T \leftarrow \alpha n - \frac{\epsilon n}{2}$

Algorithm 2: Sketch-Update(d, t)

Input: d is an item; t is the time slot of arrival
if $d \in \mathcal{S}$ **then**
    if $t_d < t$ **then**
        /* d appeared in a new slot   */
        $n_d \leftarrow n_d + 1$; $t_d \leftarrow t$;
else
    if $h(d, t) < \tau$ **then**
        /* Start tracking item d from now onwards
        */
        $\mathcal{S} \leftarrow \mathcal{S} \cup (d, 1, t)$;

3.1.1 Analysis of the Fixed Window Algorithm

We present the proof of correctness and analysis of space complexity. Consider an item d, with absolute persistence $p_d = p_d(1, n)$. For parameter q, $0 < q \leq 1$, let $G(q)$ denote the geometric random variable with parameter q, i.e., the number of Bernoulli trials till a success (including the trial when the success occurred), where the different trials are all independent, and the success probability is q in each trial.

For each item d that appeared in the stream, there are two possibilities: (1) either d is tracked by the algorithm from some time slot t onwards, or (2) d is not tracked by the algorithm, because none of the tuples (d, t) were selected by the filter. In each distinct slot where d appears, the probability of d being sampled onto the sketch is τ.

Consider $G(\tau)$, a geometric random variable with a parameter τ. If $G(\tau) > p_d$, then this will lead to case (2) above, and d will fail to make it into the sketch $\mathcal{S}$. On the other hand, if $G(\tau) \leq p_d$, this will lead to case (1), and d will be inserted into the sketch at some timeslot in Algorithm 2, and the counter $n_d = p_d - G(\tau) + 1$.

LEMMA 3.1. **False Negative:** *If an item d has $p_d \geq \alpha n$, then the probability that this item will not be reported as α-persistent by Algorithm 3 is no more than e^{-2}.*

PROOF. From Algorithm 3, the item will be not reported if $\hat{p_d} < T$, i.e., $n_d + \frac{1}{\tau} < T$. Using $\tau = \frac{2}{\epsilon n}$ and $T = \alpha n - \frac{\epsilon n}{2}$, we get:

Algorithm 3: Detect-Persistent-Items

---

foreach *tuple* $(d, n_d, t_d) \in \mathcal{S}$ **do**
    $\hat{p_d} \leftarrow n_d + \frac{1}{\tau}$
    if $\hat{p_d} \geq T$ **then**
        Report d as a persistent item

$$
\begin{aligned}
\Pr[\text{False Negative}] \quad &= \quad \Pr[p_d - G(\tau) + 1 + \frac{1}{\tau} < T] \\
&= \quad \Pr[G(\tau) > 1 + \frac{1}{\tau} + p_d - T] \\
&= \quad \Pr[G(\tau) > 1 + \frac{1}{\tau} + \frac{\epsilon n}{2} \\
&\qquad\qquad\qquad + (p_d - \alpha n)] \\
&\leq \quad \Pr[G(\tau) > \frac{2}{\tau}]
\end{aligned}
$$

In the last step, we have used the fact $p_d \geq \alpha n$. Using the fact $\Pr[G(p) > t] = (1 - p)^t$, we get

$$
\Pr[\text{False Negative}] \leq (1 - \tau)^{\frac{2}{\tau}} \leq e^{-2}
$$

In the last step, we have used the inequality $1 - x \leq e^{-x}$. $\square$

LEMMA 3.2. **Items that are far from persistent are not reported:** *If an item d has $p_d < (\alpha - \epsilon)n$, then d will not be reported by Algorithm 3 as a α-persistent item.*

PROOF. For such an item, the value of n_d at the end of observation is $n_d = p_d - G(\tau) + 1$. Let f denote the probability that d is reported as α-persistent. We have:

$$
\begin{aligned}
f \quad &= \quad \Pr[n_d + \frac{1}{\tau} \geq T] \\
&= \quad \Pr[p_d - G(\tau) + 1 + \frac{1}{\tau} \geq \alpha n - \frac{1}{\tau}] \\
&= \quad \Pr[G(\tau) \leq (p_d - \alpha n) + 1 + \frac{2}{\tau}] \\
&= \quad \Pr[G(\tau) \leq p_d - (\alpha - \epsilon)n + 1] \\
&\leq \quad \Pr[G(\tau) \leq 0] = 0
\end{aligned}
$$

$\square$

LEMMA 3.3. *The expected space taken by the $\mathcal{S}$ is $O(\frac{1}{\epsilon n} \sum_{d \in D(S)} p_d)$, where $D(S)$ is the set of all distinct items in stream S. We assume that storing a tuple (d, n_d, t_d) takes a constant amount of space.*

PROOF. The space taken by $\mathcal{S}$ is a random variable, since the decision of whether or not to allocate space to an item is a randomized decision. For item d, let random variable Z_d be defined as follows. $Z_d = 1$ if the algorithm tracks d, i.e $d \in \mathcal{S}$, and $Z_d = 0$ otherwise.

Let $Z = \sum_{d \in D(S)} Z_d$. If we assume that the space required for storing a single tuple $(d, \cdot, \cdot)$ in $\mathcal{S}$ is a constant number of bytes, say c, then the space used by $\mathcal{S}$ is cZ bytes. Now, for the random variable Z, by linearity of expectation, we get:

$$
E[Z] = E[\sum_{d \in D(S)} Z_d] = \sum_{d \in D(S)} E[Z_d] = \sum_{d \in D(S)} \Pr[Z_d = 1] \tag{1}
$$

$$
\Pr[Z_d = 0] = (1 - \tau)^{p_d} \tag{2}
$$

Using Taylor's expansion,

$$
\begin{aligned}
e^{-2\tau} \quad &\leq \quad 1 - 2\tau + 4\tau^2/2 \\
&\leq \quad 1 - 2\tau + \tau \text{(assuming } \tau \leq 1/2) \leq 1 - \tau
\end{aligned}
$$

Using in Equation 2, we get:

$$
\Pr[Z_d = 0] \geq (e^{-2\tau})^{p_d} = e^{-2\tau p_d}
$$

Thus,

$$\begin{aligned}
\Pr[Z_d = 1] &= 1 - \Pr[Z_d = 0] \le (1 - e^{-2\tau p_d}) \\
&\le (1 - (1 - 2\tau p_d))(\text{using } e^{-x} > 1 - x) \\
&= 2\tau p_d
\end{aligned}$$

Using in Equation 1, we get:

$$E[Z] \le \sum_{d \in D(S)} 2\tau p_d = 2\tau \sum_{d \in D(S)} p_d = \frac{4}{\epsilon n} \sum_{d \in D(S)} p_d$$

□

Discussion: The expression for the space complexity shows that the expected space required for an item d is proportional to p_d/n. Note that p_d can range from 1 till n, but in a typical stream, the persistence of most items can be expected to be small, with only a few items having a large persistence. Thus, in the typical case, for example, with a Zipfian distribution of packet frequencies and persistence, the space taken by the sketch will be much smaller than the number of distinct items in the input.

Space Complexity for Specific Distributions. Let $P = \sum_{d \in D(S)} p_d$ denote the sum of the persistence values of all items in the stream. We now show that if the persistence values of the different items followed a Zipfian distribution, then $P = O(n)$, leading to a constant space complexity, independent of the number of distinct items in the input.

LEMMA 3.4. *If the persistence of different items in $D(S)$ followed a Zipfian distribution, then the space complexity of the sketch is $O(\frac{1}{\epsilon})$.*

PROOF. Let ρ_k be the persistence of the kth most persistent item for $k \in 1, 2, ..., |D(S)|$. With a Zipfian distribution, $\rho_k = \frac{c}{k^\beta}$, for some $c > 0$ and $\beta > 1$. Since the persistence of an item is bounded by n, $\rho_1 = c \le n$. Let $\zeta(\cdot)$ be the Reimann Zeta function.

$$\sum_{d \in D(S)} p_d = \sum_{k \le |D(S)|} \frac{c}{k^\beta} \le c \sum_{k=1}^{\infty} \frac{1}{k^\beta} = c\zeta(\beta) \le n\zeta(\beta)$$

Thus, we have $E[Z] \le \frac{4}{\epsilon n} n\zeta(\beta) = \frac{4\zeta(\beta)}{\epsilon}$

By the Maclaurin-Cauchy test, we know for $\beta > 1$, the series represented by $\zeta(\beta)$ converges, and is usually a small constant, which proves the lemma. For example, if $\beta = 1.5$, then $\zeta(1.5) = 2.6$. For this case, we get: $\sum_{d \in D(S)} p_d \le 2.6n$, and thus, from Lemma 3.3, $E[Z] < \frac{11}{\epsilon}$. □

THEOREM 3.1. *The above algorithms 2 and 3 can be used in an algorithm for tracking persistent items in a fixed window with the following properties:*

A. *Each α-persistent item d is reported with probability at least $1 - \delta$.*

B. *No item d such that $p_d < (\alpha - \epsilon)n$ is reported.*

C. *The space complexity of the algorithm is $O(\frac{P \log(1/\delta)}{\epsilon n})$, where $P = \sum_{d \in D(S)} p_d$.*

D. *The processing time per stream element is $O(\log \frac{1}{\delta})$.*

PROOF. Algorithms 2 and 3 achieve most of the above properties. From Lemma 3.1, we get that the probability of a persistent item not being reported is no more than e^{-2}. The only task is to now bring down the probability of a false negative to δ.

To achieve this, we run $(1/2) \log \frac{1}{\delta}$ instances of Algorithm 2 in parallel, and return the union of the items reported by all the instances. For an item that is persistent, it is not reported only if it is missed by every instance. The probability that this happens is no more than $(e^{-2})^{(1/2) \log \frac{1}{\delta}}$, which is δ. For an item d whose persistence is less than $(\alpha - \epsilon)n$, from Lemma 3.2, we see that the item is not returned by any instance, and hence will not be present in aggregated result, proving property B.

Property C follows from Lemma 3.3, adding a multiplying factor of $O(\log \frac{1}{\delta})$. For the time complexity (property D), we note that Algorithm 2 can be made to run in constant expected time if the sketch S is organized as a hash table with the item identifier as the key. □

3.2 Sliding Window

In this setting, we are interested only in the substream elements that belong to the n most recent time slots. If c is the current timeslot, then the window of interest is S_{c-n+1}^c. Note that n here does not represent the number of timeslots in the stream, but the number of timeslots in the window. We now present an algorithm solving Problem 3, and the intuition for the sliding window algorithm is as follows.

Suppose we started a new fixed window data structure for each new timeslot. This would suffice, since any sliding window query in the future will be covered by one of these fixed window data structures. For now, suppose that S_t was the fixed window data structure that we start from time t onwards (this will serve the window S_t^{t+n-1}). At first glance, it seems like this would be too much space, since the cost would be n times the space for a single fixed window data structure.

The space can be reduced through the following observations: (1) when we start a fixed window data structure at a particular timeslot t, say, only a few of the items (approximately a τ fraction of the items) that arrive in timeslot t will be selected into this data structure; (2) for those items d that were not selected into S_t in timeslot t, the tuple for d in S_t can be shared with the tuple for d in S_{t+1}; (3) further, when the current timeslot is t, we can afford to discard S_r for $r \le (t-n)$, since these data structures will never be used in a future query.

Thus, the sketch used by our algorithm at time c is effectively $\cup_{i=c-n+1}^c S_i$, where S_i is the fixed window sketch starting at timeslot i. Through observation (2), we reduce the space by having a single tuple for d in $S_i, S_{i+1}, \ldots, S_j$ such that j is the first timeslot in $i, i+1, \ldots, j$ where d was selected into the sketch.

The formal description of the algorithm for the Sliding Window model is presented in Algorithms 4, 5, 6, and 7. The sketch S is a set of tuples of the form $(d, t, n_{d,t}, t_{d,t})$, where d is an item identifier, t is the time slot when this tuple was created, $n_{d,t}$ is the number of time slots since t when d has reappeared, and $t_{d,t}$ is some state that we maintain to eliminate counting reoccurrences of d within the same time slot. In the following discussion, we say "(d, t) belongs in the sketch", or "$(d, t) \in S$", if there is a 4-tuple of the form

$(d, t, \cdot, \cdot)$ in the sketch. In our sketch, for any item d and time slot t, there can be at most one tuple of the form $(d, t, \cdot, \cdot)$.

Algorithm 4: Sliding-Window-Sketch-Initialize $(m, n, N, \alpha, \epsilon, \delta)$

Input: Size of domain m; window size n; maximum number of slots N; persistence threshold α; parameter ϵ; error probability δ

Initialize the hash function $h : ([1, m] \times [1, N]) \to (0, 1)$;
$\mathcal{S} \leftarrow \phi; \tau \leftarrow \frac{2}{\epsilon n}; T \leftarrow (\alpha - \frac{\epsilon}{2})n$

Algorithm 5: Sliding-Window-Sketch-Update(d, t)

Input: d is an item; t is the time slot of arrival
if $(d, t) \in \mathcal{S}$ **then**
    ⌞ return
// Consider starting a new tuple, tracking d
    from slot t onwards.
if $h(d, t) < \tau$ **then**
    ⌞ $\mathcal{S} \leftarrow \mathcal{S} \cup (d, t, 1, t)$
foreach t' such that $(d, t') \in \mathcal{S}$ **do**
    Let $(d, t', n_{d,t'}, t_{d,t'})$ be the tuple corresponding to (d, t')
    // Incorporate (d, t) into this tuple if not
      been done yet
    if $t_{d,t'} < t$ **then**
        // d has not been seen in slot t by this
          tuple
        ⌞ $n_{d,t'} \leftarrow n_{d,t'} + 1$; $t_{d,t'} \leftarrow t$

During the initialization phase of the algorithm, $\mathcal{S}$ is initialized to empty, τ to $\frac{2}{\epsilon n}$, and T to $\alpha n - \frac{\epsilon n}{2}$. When we want to add an element (d, t) to the sketch, there are two possible cases. First, if there is an entry in the sketch of the form $(d, t, \cdot, \cdot)$, then this element can be safely ignored, since the same combination of item and time slot has been observed earlier. Otherwise, if (d, t) hashes to an appropriately small value (less than τ), then a new entry is created for tracking d, starting from time t onwards, that will serve to answer queries on certain windows that include t within them. Simultaneously, (d, t) is used to update each of the tuples in $\mathcal{S}$ that track d. Whenever time advances, and the window slides forward from t to $t + 1$, all entries $(d, t', \cdot, \cdot)$ in $\mathcal{S}$ such that $t' \leq (t - n)$ are discarded, because stream windows of current and future interest will not be served by this entry. Let $p_d^t = p_d(t - n + 1, t)$ denote the persistence of d over the window $[t - n + 1, t]$.

Algorithm 6: Actions taken when time slot changes from $c - 1$ to c

---

// Discard old items
Discard items $(d, t, \cdot, \cdot) \in \mathcal{S}$ where $t \leq (c - n)$

3.2.1 Correctness and Complexity

For a pair (d, t) where d is an item identifier and t is a time slot, (d, t) is said to be stored in $\mathcal{S}$ at time c if there exists a tuple $(d, t, \cdot, \cdot)$ in $\mathcal{S}$ at time c.

Algorithm 7: Sliding-Window-Detect-Persistent-Items(c)

Input: c is the current time slot. The window of interest is $[c - n + 1, c]$.
Let $\mathcal{S}_{cur}$ be all tuples $(d, t', n_{d,t'}, t_{d,t'})$ in $\mathcal{S}$ such that both the following conditions are true: (A) $t' \geq (c - n + 1)$ and (B) There is no t'' such that $(d, t'') \in \mathcal{S}$ and $(c - n + 1) \leq t'' < t'$.
foreach tuple $(d, \cdot, n_d, t_d) \in \mathcal{S}_{cur}$ **do**
    $\hat{p_d^c} \leftarrow n_d + \frac{1}{\tau}$
    if $\hat{p_d^c} \geq T$ **then**
    ⌞ Report d as a persistent item in the window

LEMMA 3.5. **Items that are far from persistent in the window are not reported:** *At time c, if an item d has $p_d^c < (\alpha - \epsilon)$, then d will not be reported as persistent in the window in Algorithm 7.*

PROOF. Consider such an item d, where $p_d^c < (\alpha - \epsilon n)$. We analyze the instances when d was processed by Algorithm 5. If d was never stored in the sketch from time $c - n + 1$ onwards, then there will not exist a tuple $(d, t', \cdot, \cdot)$ in $\mathcal{S}$ at time c, and d will not be reported by Algorithm 7.

Suppose at time c, there existed a tuple (d, t', n_d, t_d) in $\mathcal{S}$, such that $t' \geq (c - n + 1)$. This tuple was inserted into the sketch at time t'. From Algorithm 5, it can be seen that n_d is equal to the number of occurrences of d in time slots $t', t' + 1, t' + 2, \ldots, c$. This number cannot be more than p_d^c, and hence $n_d \leq p_d^c < (\alpha - \epsilon)n$.

In Algorithm 7, for item d, it must be true that:

$$\hat{p_d^c} = n_d + \frac{1}{\tau} < (\alpha - \epsilon)n + \frac{\epsilon n}{2} = (\alpha n) - \frac{\epsilon n}{2} = T$$

Since $\hat{p_d^c} < T$, d will not be reported as persistent. □

LEMMA 3.6. **Sliding Window False Negative:** *At time c, if an item d has $p_d^c \geq \alpha n$, then the probability that this item will not be reported as α-persistent in the current window by Algorithm 7 is no more than e^{-2}.*

PROOF. Suppose that d was sampled into the sketch later than time $(c - n)$, i.e., there exists a tuple $(d, t, n_d, \cdot)$ such that $t > (c - n)$. In such a case, Algorithm 7 selects the tuple (d, t', n_d, t_d) such that (A) $t' > (c - n)$ and (B) there is no tuple $(d, t'', \cdot, \cdot)$ in $\mathcal{S}$ such that $t'' < t'$. Thus, it follows that from time $c - n + 1$ onwards (inclusive), d was not selected into the sketch till time t'. The number of times that d needs to occur in slots $c - n + 1, c - n + 2, \ldots$ till it is sampled into $\mathcal{S}$ is $G(\tau)$ (the geometric random variable with parameter τ). The counter n_d keeps track of the number of times d occurred in different time slots starting from slot t' (inclusive). Since d occurred in the window in a total of p_d^c distinct slots, $n_d = p_d^c - G(\tau) + 1$.

$$\Pr[\text{False Negative}] = \Pr[p_d^c - G(\tau) + 1 + \frac{1}{\tau} < T]$$

In the proof of Lemma 3.1, it is shown that the above probability is no more than e^{-2} if $p_d^c \geq \alpha n$, and the lemma follows. □

3.3 Space Complexity

The following result is useful for the space complexity.

LEMMA 3.7. *A tuple (d,t) is stored in $\mathcal{S}$ at time c if and only if the following conditions are true:*

A. $t > (c - n)$

B. $h(d,t) < \tau$

PROOF. Suppose (d,t) is stored in $\mathcal{S}$ at time c. From Algorithm 6, it is clear that $t > (c-n)$, since otherwise (d,t) would have been discarded from the sketch. This proves condition A. Also, in Algorithm 5, if $h(d,t) \geq \tau$, then (d,t) would never have been inserted into the sketch. Thus, it must be true that $h(d,t) < \tau$, proving condition B.

Now, suppose that both A and B were true. Then, it is clear that in Algorithm 5, (d,t) will be inserted into the sketch when it first appears. Further, this tuple will never be discarded from the sketch in Algorithm 6 since our current time slot c satisfies $c < (t + n)$. □

LEMMA 3.8. **Space Complexity:** *Let Z_c denote the number of tuples in $\mathcal{S}$ at time c, and D denote the set of all distinct items that appeared during time slots $c - n + 1$ till c. Then,*

$$E[Z_c] = \frac{2}{\epsilon n} \sum_{d \in D} p_d^c$$

PROOF. First, it can be verified that in Algorithm 5, if the same tuple (d,t) occurs multiple times, then the effect on the sketch is the same as if (d,t) occurred only once in the stream. Thus we can ignore repeated arrivals of the same tuple (d,t).

For each tuple (d,t) that arrived, let random variable $Z_{d,t}^c$ be defined as follows. $Z_{d,t}^c$ is 1 if tuple (d,t) is stored in $\mathcal{S}$ at time c. Let $D(S)$ denote the set of all distinct tuples (d,t) in the stream so far.

We have

$$Z_c = \sum_{(d,t) \in D(S)} Z_{d,t}^c$$

From Lemma 3.7, we have that $Z_{d,t}^c = 0$ if $t \leq (c - n)$. Thus, we can rewrite the above as:

$$Z_c = \sum_{\{(d,t) \mid t > (c-n)\}} Z_{d,t}^c \qquad (3)$$

To compute the expectation of Z_c, we use linearity of expectation:

$$E[Z_c] = E\left[\sum_{\{(d,t) \mid t > (c-n)\}} Z_{d,t}^c \right] = \sum_{\{(d,t) \mid t > (c-n)\}} E\left[Z_{d,t}^c \right]$$

For a tuple (d,t) such that $t > (c - n)$, $Z_{d,t}^c$ is equal to 1 if it was sampled into the sketch at time t i.e., if $h(d,t) < \tau$. The probability of this event is $\tau = \frac{2}{\epsilon n}$. Let D denote the set of all distinct items that appeared in the stream during a timeslot i such that $(c - n) < i \leq c$.

$$E[Z_c] = \sum_{\{(d,t) \mid t > (c-n)\}} \tau = \sum_{d \in D} (p_d^c \cdot \tau) = \frac{2}{\epsilon n} \sum_{d \in D} p_d^c$$

□

4. EVALUATION

We evaluated our small space algorithm and contrasted its performance with that of a naive (exact) algorithm, by running the two algorithms on a real world traffic trace dataset. The trace used is a collection of 885 million packets collected during a 3 hour period from a large Internet backbone link (source: CAIDA [5]). The data consists of timestamped packet headers, with the source and destination addresses, in addition to other attributes. From this packet header trace, we extracted a sequence of (destination IP address, timestamp) pairs which forms the input data stream. We divided the entire trace into slots of 30 seconds (to obtain a trace of 360 slots). The sliding window length was set to 100 slots.

There is no obvious choice on what should be a suitable duration of the timeslot, since prior research has shown that the delay between successive botnet-related communications to the same destination can range from a few minutes to a few days. A duration of a few minutes is reasonable, since many botnets have multiple events occurring within this time frame. For example, Li *et al* [25] observed periodic botnet-related events about every half an hour. Rajab *et al* [31] reported that the average "staying time" for bots that they monitored was about 25 minutes, and 90% of them lasted less than 50 minutes. Over a 24-hour window, the BRAT project [35] reported probes by 8 fast-flux botnets which showed periodicity, the periods being in the range of 1-10 minutes. Porras *et al* [30] showed that for iKeeB, the iPhone-based botnet, a compromised iPhone runs a shell script once every 5 minutes. We finally decided on a duration of 30 seconds so that our 3 hour trace led to a sufficient number of slots – this helped us evaluate the scalability of our algorithm with increasing number of timeslots. With the above setting of parameters, we had a reasonably large number of timeslots (360) as well as a large number of packets per timeslot (more than 2 million, on average).

The algorithms were implemented in C++ using the STL extensions. For the hash functions used in the small space algorithm (Algorithm 5), we used an endian-neutral implementation of the *Murmur Hash* algorithm [3], which is generally considered to generate high quality hash outputs.

We obtained the ground truth about the persistence of individual items (IP addresses) by running the naive algorithm over the input data stream. In the process, we discovered that a large fraction of the windows do not contain many persistent items. On such windows, our algorithm will run in a space-efficient manner, but we did not consider these windows since there would not be enough data for a fair comparison. Thus, to simplify the presentation, we focus on 11 specific "query" windows: $[1, 100], [26, 125], [51, 150], \ldots, [251, 350]$. We use window $[a, b]$ to denote the window of all timeslots starting from a till b (both endpoints included).

First, we found that the cumulative distribution of the (relative) persistence values in the dataset was highly skewed, for every query window that we tried. We present the CDF of persistence for three out of the 11 query windows: $[1, 100]$, $[101, 200]$ and $[201, 300]$ in Figure 1, but all the 11 query windows showed similar pattern. For example, in the $[101, 200]$ window, more than 50% IP addresses occur in 1 slot only, and 95% of the IP addresses occur in 20 or less slots. This confirms the utility of an algorithm like ours, which requires less space when items have lower average persistence.

Metrics: The following metrics were used. For parameter α, an item that is not α-persistent is called "transient".
The **False Negative Rate (FNR)** is defined as the ratio of the number of items that were α-persistent, but were not reported by the small space algorithm, to the total number of α-persistent items in the window.
The **False Positive Rate (FPR)** is defined as the ratio of the number of transient items that were reported as persistent by the algorithm, to the total number of transient items.
The **Space Compression (SC)** is defined as the ratio of the number of tuples stored by the naive algorithm to the number of tuples stored by the small space algorithm.
The **Physical Space Compression (PSC)** is defined as the maximum resident set size of the naive algorithm to that of the small-space algorithm.

The notion of Space Compression (SC) is a logical one, and for the sliding window version of the problem (Problem 3), we were interested in the number of tuples of the form $(d, t, \cdot, \cdot)$, as referred to in algorithms 5 to 7. In the actual implementation, we maintained a single array for each distinct item d, rather than creating a separate entry for each unique pair (d, t). All the entries in the array were initialized to 0. The t'-th entry in the array indicates $n_{d,t'}$ - in how many distinct slots d has appeared since its appearance in slot t'. When d appears in slot t', the t'-th entry is initialized to 1 only if $h(d, t') < \tau$. Note that $t_{d,t'}$ - the last timeslot d has appeared in since its appearance in t', does not depend on t', and hence we maintained a single copy of this variable. We found that this implementation was faster in practice than an alternate implemenatation where we actually created and maintained a different tuple for each distinct slot t' the item d appeared in.

For computing the Physical Space Compression (PSC), for each combination of α and ϵ, we actually created a new process so that the resident set is created afresh. We expect the Physical Space Compression for (α, ϵ') to be higher than that for (α, ϵ) when $\epsilon' > \epsilon$ (because τ is lower for ϵ'), but we found that because of the way memory allocation algorithms work, if the algorithm runs first for (α, ϵ) and then for (α, ϵ') (using the same process), then, the memory allocated for (α, ϵ) is enough to accomodate the algorithm for (α, ϵ'), and the space-saving due to (α, ϵ') does not get reflected.

Note that both the numerator and the denominator of each metric depend on the query window $[c - n + 1, c]$ (n is the window length). To measure the ratios, we ran the small-space algorithm on the 11 query windows defined previously and in each window, recorded all the items that were marked as persistent by the algorithm. The only source of randomness in each run is the output of the Murmur Hash function and we ran each simulation thrice using different seeds (we saw very minor variation in the results when different seeds were used.) Thus, for each parameter setting we had 11×3 data points, and in each we recorded the false positives, the false negatives, and the number of tuples that were tracked. The ratios computed (by comparing to the naive algorithm) are then averaged across all the runs.

Observations:
For every value of α, the **False Negative Rate** (Figure 2(a)) increases as ϵ increases, which is expected. However, although Lemma 3.6 bounds the False Negative Rate to $\frac{1}{e^2} = 13\%$, the algorithm performed much better in practice - we found that even for $\alpha = 0.3$ and $\epsilon = 0.21$, the FNR was

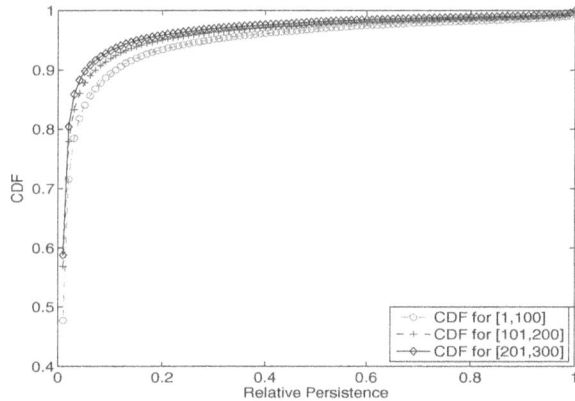

Figure 1: CDF of persistence values from 3 windows

as low as 2%. Note that $\frac{\epsilon}{\alpha}$ is a relative measure of error tolerance in α, which in this case is as high as 70%. Even the highest FNR we ever got was less than 10%. This was for the highest setting of α ($\alpha = 0.9$) - the number of false negatives for this were higher than for the other settings, for similar values of ϵ. One possible reason is that for $\alpha = 0.9$, the items that were 0.9-persistent had absolute persistence very close to $0.9n$. Whereas, many of the items that were 0.3-persistent had persistence values that were much larger than 0.3. Items that have persistence values close to the threshold, but higher than it, have a greater chance of not being reported. Hence, the false negative ratio for $\alpha = 0.9$ are a little higher.

The **False Positive Rate**, similar to the False Negative Rate, shows (Figure 2(b)) an increasing trend as ϵ increases. The maximum FPR was 2.69% (for $\alpha = 0.3$ and $\epsilon = 0.21$). Moreover, Figure 2(b) shows that for same value of ϵ, the FPR is lower for higher values of α. The possible reason is that when α is very high (e.g. 0.9), most items have (absolute) persistence much lower than αn (as is evident from the CDF in Figure 1), hence are very unlikely to cross the threshold T in Algorithm 7.

The **Space Compression** increases *linearly* with ϵ (Figure 2(c)), and we found the Space Compression is close to $\frac{1}{\tau} = \frac{\epsilon n}{2}$, for all values of α. This is expected since the naive algorithm creates a new tuple for an item everytime it appears in a different slot - where the small-space algorithm creates a tuple with probability τ only. For $\alpha = 0.9$, with $\epsilon = 0.63$, the logical space compression was as high as 32. For higher values of α, we could achieve better Space Compression as the tolerance ϵ could be made higher while keeping the false positives and the false negatives small enough. Like its logical counterpart, the **Physical Space Compression** also increases with ϵ (Figure 2(d)), and for each distinct value of α, the Physical Space Compression grows almost linearly with ϵ. For higher values of α, we could achieve better Space Compression as the tolerance ϵ could be made higher. While the size of our dataset was 58GB, the maximum resident set size of the naive algorithm went upto 3GB (at the query window [251,350]), whereas for typical parameters like $\alpha = 0.5$ and $\epsilon = 0.35$, the small-space algorithm took less than $\frac{1}{5}^{th}$ (600 MB) memory (on average) compared to the naive algorithm.

(a) Variation of FNR with α and ϵ

(b) Variation of FPR with α and ϵ

(c) Variation of SC with α and ϵ

(d) Variation of PSC with α and ϵ

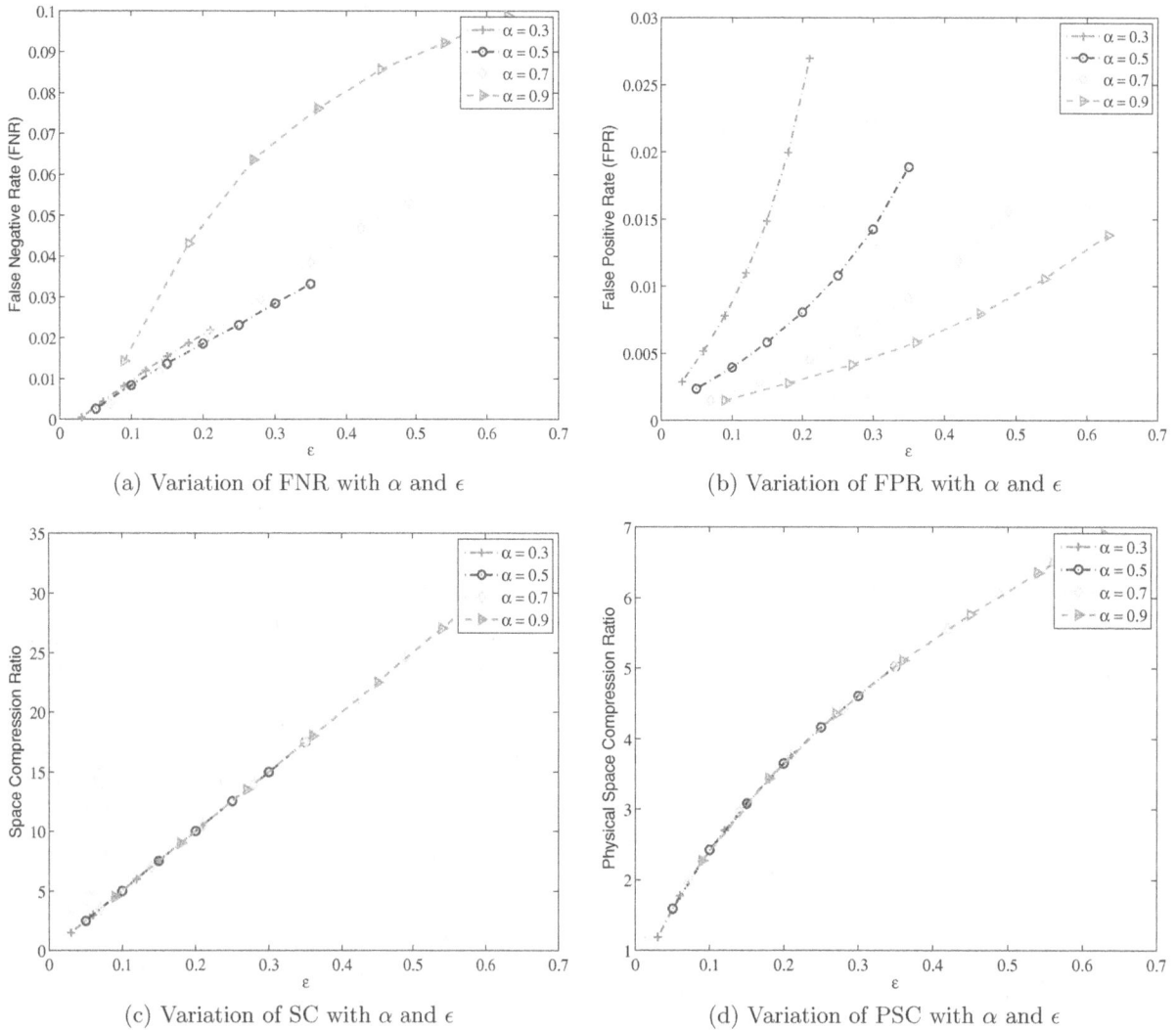

Figure 2: Trade-off between accuracy and space for the small-space algorithm over sliding windows. Each point in each plot is an average from 33 data points - 3 runs over 11 query windows each. Note that the Y-axis is different for each plot. Also, for each value of α, the values of ϵ range from 0.1α to 0.7α.

5. RELATED WORK

A large body of literature on network anomaly detection has focused on detecting volume-based anomalies, i.e., tracking IPs which send or receive an unusually large volume of traffic over an interval of time. While volume-based anomaly detection is relevant for Denial-of-Service type attacks like SYN flood [37], UDP flood [38], Ping flood or P2P attacks, there are many "stealthy" attacks [16], which can bypass the radar by never sending traffic in large volume, yet remaining active over long windows in time, and probing the target network/host once in a while. For example, port scans [33] look for open ports on remote hosts that have applications with known vulnerabilities deployed on those ports; bots installed on compromised hosts in a botnet keep on communicating with the C&C server, etc. Our work differs from these in that persistent items may not result in large volumes of traffic and may escape detection by a volume-based system.

It is interesting to compare how algorithmic techniques

for identifying heavy-hitters (or "frequent items") may work for the problem of identifying persistent items. Broadly, the techniques in the literature can be classified into "counter-based", "quantile algorithms", "sketches", or "random sampling-based" (see [10]). Counter-based techniques such as the Misra-Gries algorithm [28], and the "Space-Saving" algorithm [27] rely on maintaining per-item counters for counting the number of occurrences of each item that has been currently identified as being frequent; these counters are occasionally decremented to ensure that the space taken by the data structure is small. The difficulty in using this technique for our problem is that it is not easy to ensure that re-occurrences of the same item within a timeslot have no effect on the system state. For example, in the Misra-Gries algorithm, if there is a decrement of the counters between two occurrences of an item within the same timeslot, it seems hard to ensure that the second occurrence has no effect on the system state, especially given that the increment due to the first occurrence may have disappeared from the system (due to the decrement). The same argument is true for Lossy Counting too [26]. Quantile-based algorithms such as Greenwald and Khanna, or [19], the q-digest [32] view the space of all items as being a bijection with the set of integers, and associate counts with different ranges in this space of all items. In the q-digest algorithm, there are no decrements to these counters, so one may use "distinct counters" such as those by Flajolet-Martin [15], or Gibbons and Tirthapura [17], or Kane *et al.* [22], instead of regular counters. Such an approach based on maintaining distinct counters would not only be more complex than our approach, but also likely have a greater space complexity, since maintaining distinct counters with a relative error of ϵ requires $\Omega(1/\epsilon^2)$ space [21]. The sketch approach, such as count-sketch [7] or count-min sketch [13] also maintains multiple counters, each of which is the sum of many random variables. Replacing each such counter with a distinct counter leads to its own set of difficulties, one of which is the space complexity of distinct counting, explained above, and the other being the fact that each distinct counter is only approximate (exact distinct counting necessarily requires large space [2]), while the analyses in [7] and [13] rely on the different counters in the data structure being exact.

Finally, our algorithm is inspired by the random sampling approaches based on the "sample and count" scheme of Alon *et al.* [2, 1] and the "sticky sampling" algorithm of Manku and Motwani [26]. Both these algorithms use the following idea: "sample a random element in the stream, and track reoccurrences of this element exactly". In these works, the idea was applied to a different context than ours – sample and count was applied to track the size of a self-join in limited storage, and sticky sampling was used in the identification of heavy hitters using limited space. Our algorithm has the following technical differences when compared with the above works. The sampling of an item is done using a hash function that is based on the item identifier and the timeslot in which it arrived in. This hash-based sampling avoids giving greater sampling probability to an item if it occurs multiple times within the same timeslot. Further, reoccurrences are tracked in such a way that we do not overcount if the same item appears again in the same timeslot. In addition, we show how to handle sliding windows using nearly the same space, while the above works do not address the context of sliding windows. A distinguishing aspect of our work on sliding windows is that while the extension to sliding windows often requires asymptotically greater space than for the infinite window case (for example, see Arasu and Manku [4]), in our case the space complexity increases only by a factor of two.

Persistence is exploited to detect botnet traffic in [18], using an algorithm that tracked the state of every distinct item that arrived within the sliding window. Hence the memory used is of the order of the number of distinct items times the window size, which is potentially very high. In contrast, our algorithm tracks persistent items using much smaller space, while giving up some accuracy.

There has been much work in estimating various properties of the frequency distribution of stream items, including the frequency moments of a stream [2, 40, 22], heavy-hitters [26, 14, 13, 24], heavy-distinct-hitters [39] and the entropy [23, 6, 29]. Unlike the set of persistent items, all the above properties depend only on the frequency distribution of items in the stream – they are unaffected by re-ordering of

the stream elements, or by changing the times at which the elements arrive. In contrast, the set of persistent items in a stream is affected by the time and order in which elements arrive.

In a recent work on a temporal property of stream elements, Chen *et al* [9] addressed the problem of tracking long-duration flows from network streams. They identified flows for which the difference of timestamps between the first and the last packet in the flow exceed some threshold d. A flow might continue for a long duration and yet the total number of bytes sent in the flow may not be high enough to be detected by the heavy-hitter algorithms; whereas some other flow of shorter duration might qualify as a heavy-hitter because it sends many more bytes. Clearly, a long-lived flow is not necessarily persistent.

6. CONCLUSION

We formulated the problem of detecting *persistent* items in a data stream. Our lower bound result shows that an exact algorithm for the problem, which reports *all* persistent items, would need a prohibitively high memory, and is therefore impractical. Subsequently, we presented an approximate formulation of the problem that explores a tradeoff between space accuracy in identifying persistent elements. Allocating more memory leads to more accurate answers and this allows operators to tune their systems appropriately depending on the amount of resources available.

By running simulations of both the naive (exact) and small space algorithms on a real traffic dataset, we demonstrate that our algorithm works very well in practice: it uses upto 85% *less* space than the naive (exact) algorithm and incurs a false positive rate (and false negative rate) of less than 1% (and 4% respectively). We also see that false positive rate never exceeds 3% for any parameter setting, while the false negative rate stays below 5% for all but the most aggressive thresholds for persistence. The empirical false positive and false negative rates are much better than the analytical bounds: in the traffic dataset that we evaluated (and we suspect in most real world data), the distribution of persistent elements is quite skewed, which works to the advantage of the algorithm that we describe in this paper.

7. REFERENCES

[1] N. Alon, P. B. Gibbons, Y. Matias, and M. Szegedy. Tracking join and self-join sizes in limited storage. *J. Comput. Syst. Sci.*, 64(3):719–747, 2002.

[2] N. Alon, Y. Matias, and M. Szegedy. The space complexity of approximating the frequency moments. *Journal of Computer and System Sciences*, 58(1), 1999.

[3] A. Appleby. Murmurhash 2.0. http://sites.google.com/site/murmurhash/.

[4] A. Arasu and G. Manku. Approximate counts and quantiles over sliding windows. In *Proc. ACM Symposium on Principles of Database Systems (PODS)*, pages 286–296, 2004.

[5] CAIDA. OC48 traces dataset. https://data.caida.org/datasets/oc48/oc48-original/20020814/5min/.

[6] A. Chakrabarti, K. D. Ba, and S. Muthukrishnan. Estimating entropy and entropy norm on data streams. In *STACS*, 2006.

[7] M. Charikar, K. Chen, and M. Farach-Colton. Finding frequent items in data streams. In *ICALP*, pages 693–703, 2002.

[8] M. Charikar, K. Chen, and M. Farach-Colton. Finding frequent items in data streams. *Theoretical Computer Science*, 312(1), 2004.

[9] A. Chen, Y. Jin, and J. Cao. Tracking long duration flows in network traffic. In *INFOCOM*, 2010.

[10] G. Cormode and M. Hadjieleftheriou. Finding frequent items in data streams. *PVLDB*, 1(2):1530–1541, 2008.

[11] G. Cormode, F. Korn, S. Muthukrishnan, and D. Srivastava. Diamond in the rough: Finding hierarchical heavy hitters in multi-dimensional data. In *SIGMOD*, 2004.

[12] G. Cormode and S. Muthukrishnan. What's hot and what's not: tracking most frequent items dynamically. In *PODS*, 2003.

[13] G. Cormode and S. Muthukrishnan. An improved data stream summary: the count-min sketch and its applications. *Journal of Algorithms*, 55(1), 2005.

[14] C. Estan and G. Varghese. New directions in traffic measurement and accounting: Focusing on the elephants, ignoring the mice. *ACM Trans. on Computer Systems*, 21(3), 2003.

[15] P. Flajolet and G. N. Martin. Probabilistic counting algorithms for data base applications. *Journal of Computer and System Sciences*, 31:182–209, 1985.

[16] Y. Gao, Y. Zhao, R. Schweller, S. Venkataraman, Y. Chen, D. Song, and M.-Y. Kao. Detecting stealthy attacks using online histograms. In *International Workshop on Quality of Service*, 2007.

[17] P. Gibbons and S. Tirthapura. Estimating simple functions on the union of data streams. In *Proc. ACM Symp. on Parallel Algorithms and Architectures (SPAA)*, pages 281–291, 2001.

[18] F. Giroire, J. Chandrashekar, N. Taft, E. Schooler, and D. Papagiannaki. Exploiting temporal persistence to detect covert botnet channels. In *RAID*. 2009.

[19] M. Greenwald and S. Khanna. Space efficient online computation of quantile summaries. In *Proc. ACM International Conference on Management of Data (SIGMOD)*, pages 58–66, 2001.

[20] S. Guha, J. Chandrashekar, N. Taft, and K. Papagiannaki. How healthy are today's enterprise networks? In *IMC*, 2008.

[21] P. Indyk and D. Woodruff. Tight lower bounds for the distinct elements problem. In *Proc. 44th IEEE Symp. on Foundations of Computer Science (FOCS)*, page 283, 2003.

[22] D. M. Kane, J. Nelson, and D. P. Woodruff. An optimal algorithm for the distinct elements problem. In *PODS*, 2010.

[23] A. Lall, V. Sekar, M. Ogihara, J. Xu, and H. Zhang. Data streaming algorithms for estimating entropy of network traffic. In *SIGMETRICS/Performance*, 2006.

[24] L.-K. Lee and H. F. Ting. A simpler and more efficient deterministic scheme for finding frequent items over sliding windows. In *PODS*, pages 290–297, 2006.

[25] Z. Li, A. Goyal, Y. Chen, and V. Paxson. Automating analysis of large-scale botnet probing events. In *ASIACCS*, pages 11–22, 2009.

[26] G. S. Manku and R. Motwani. Approximate frequency counts over data streams. In *VLDB*, 2002.

[27] A. Metwally, D. Agrawal, and A. E. Abbadi. Efficient computation of frequent and top-k elements in data streams. In *ICDT*, pages 398–412, 2005.

[28] J. Misra and D. Gries. Finding repeated elements. *Science of Computer Programming*, 2(2), 1982.

[29] G. Nychis, V. Sekar, D. G. Andersen, H. Kim, and H. Zhang. An empirical evaluation of entropy-based traffic anomaly detection. In *IMC*, 2008.

[30] P. Porras, H. Saidi, and V. Yegneswaran. An Analysis of the iKeeB (duh) iPhone botnet (worm). `http://mtc.sri.com/iPhone/`.

[31] M. A. Rajab, J. Zarfoss, F. Monrose, and A. Terzis. A multifaceted approach to understanding the botnet phenomenon. In *Internet Measurement Conference*, pages 41–52, 2006.

[32] N. Shrivastava, C. Buragohain, D. Agrawal, and S. Suri. Medians and beyond: new aggregation techniques for sensor networks. In *SenSys*, pages 239–249, 2004.

[33] S. Staniford, J. A. Hoagland, and J. M. McAlerney. Practical automated detection of stealthy portscans. volume 10. 2002.

[34] Advanced Persistent Threat. `http://www.usenix.org/event/lisa09/tech/slides/daly.pdf`.

[35] Botnet Reporting and Termination. `http://spamtrackers.eu/wiki/index.php/Botnet_Reporting`.

[36] Google AdWords. `http://www.google.com/ads/adwords2/`.

[37] CERT advisory CA-1996-21 TCP SYN flooding and IP spoofing attacks. `http://www.cert.org/advisories/CA-1996-21.html`.

[38] CERT advisory CA-1996-01 UDP port denial-of-service attack. `http://www.cert.org/advisories/CA-1996-01.html`.

[39] S. Venkataraman, D. X. Song, P. B. Gibbons, and A. Blum. New streaming algorithms for fast detection of superspreaders. In *NDSS*, 2005.

[40] D. P. Woodruff. Optimal space lower bounds for all frequency moments. In *SODA*, 2004.

[41] L. Zhang and Y. Guan. Detecting click fraud in pay-per-click streams of online advertising networks. In *ICDCS*, 2008.

SpamWatcher: A Streaming Social Network Analytic on the IBM Wire-speed Processor

Qiong Zou
IBM Corporation
China Research Lab
qiongzou@cn.ibm.com

Buğra Gedik
IBM Corporation
T. J Watson Research Center
bgedik@us.ibm.com

Kun Wang
IBM Corporation
China Research Lab
wangkun@cn.ibm.com

ABSTRACT

The proliferation of mobile devices, coupled with continuous connectivity, has resulted in a world where massive amounts of data is being produced, on a daily basis, as a result of online interactions between people. These interactions are often captured as relationships in a social network graph, by service providers such as mobile carriers or social web applications. Social network analysis is becoming a common technique for extracting business intelligence from social network graphs in order to improve customer experience and provide better service. Some applications in this domain require processing massive data flows with high-throughput and low-latency, in order to deliver timely results. SpamWatcher is a streaming social network analysis application that fits this description. It is used for real-time filtering of short messages in mobile communications, with the goal of preventing spam. The ever increasing volume of mobile users and rates of messages make real-time detection of spam a challenging problem with respect to performance and scalability. In this paper, we present a solution for the SpamWatcher application using the IBM wire-speed processor - a system-on-a-chip with specialized co-processors and integrated network I/O. This solution goes beyond the state-of-the-art by (*i*) using a novel implementation technique that takes advantage of the pattern matching accelerator to minimize the latency of spam detection, and (*ii*) employing hardware primitives to reduce the overhead caused by thread synchronization in order to achieve good scalability with respect to number of cores used. Furthermore, the solution is implemented on System S - a commercial-grade stream processing middleware. We evaluate our approach using real-world data sets and experimentally demonstrate the substantial performance improvements it achieves compared to previously published results.

Categories and Subject Descriptors

C.3 [**Computer Systems Organization**]: Special-purpose and application based systems

General Terms

Algorithms

Keywords

stream processing, social network analytic, pattern matching accelerator

1. INTRODUCTION

With the fast growing popularity of social network applications in our society, *social network analysis* has emerged as a key technology that provides better social networking services. This is achieved through automated discovery of relationships within the social network and using this insight to provide value-added services, such as friend discovery, personalized advertisements, and spam filtering to name a few.

Social networks are used to capture and represent the relationships between members of social systems at all scales, from interpersonal to international. Using *graph*s is a typical methodology to represent social networks, where nodes of the graph connote people and edges connote their relationships, such as short messages, mobile calls, and email exchanges.

SpamWatcher, developed by our team and a China telecom operator, is a typical application based on social network analysis [6]. Short messaging is a popular service provided by cell phone companies worldwide. With the sharp increase in the number of mobile phone users, in particular, in emerging economies such as China[1], *spam* has become a concern for service providers and users alike. SpamWatcher aims to filter out spam messages using social network analysis technology.

SpamWatcher is continuous in nature, in the sense that external sources (cell phones) drive the computation (spam detection) by generating a stream of events (short messages). Our recent work [29] has demonstrated that SpamWatcher exhibits good performance when implemented using a distributed stream processing platform. However, when volumes and rates increase, a natural slowdown occurs even in a parallel implementation, as memory accesses become the bottleneck and synchronisation overhead grows.

In this paper, we tackle the performance and scalability problems of SpamWatcher with a new computational approach for social network analysis. This approach originates from the *wire-speed processor* (*WSP*) project, which is an advanced chip development project led by IBM Research and the IBM Systems and Technology Group [12]. The WSP represents a generic processor architecture in which processing cores, hardware accelerators, and I/O functions are closely coupled in a system-on-a-chip. The unique

---

[1]In 2009, the number of cell phone users in China reached 650 million [29].

hardware features of the WSP that are leveraged by our solution are the *pattern matching accelerator* and the `waitrsv` primitive. The former provides hardware acceleration for running regular expression queries, whereas the latter provides an efficient way to synchronize application-level threads.

Taking advantage of the pattern matching accelerator of the WSP, we develop a novel algorithm for the *clustering coefficient* computation, which is the main bottleneck operation in SpamWatcher. This new algorithm significantly improves the performance of spam detection (up to 3x compared to state-of-the-art), as we illustrate using real-world data sets. Using the `waitrsv` primitive, we reduce the overhead of synchronization in the multi-threaded parallel implementation of SpamWatcher. This results in good scalability as the number of threads increase, and significantly outperforms synchronization based on POSIX threads or spin-wait loops, especially when all the hardware threads in the WSP are put into use.

As we show later in this paper, employing our new approach leads to substantial performance improvements over the original implementation reported in our recent work [29]. Moreover, our new approach provides the means for a natural scale-out with the addition of more computational resources. In particular, our contributions are:

- Techniques for using new hardware features of the WSP to solve problems in social network analysis. In particular, the use of the pattern matching accelerator to compute clustering coefficients efficiently, and the use of the `waitrsv` primitive to reduce thread synchronization costs in parallel graph analysis.

- An extensive experimental evaluation on a real-world application called SpamWatcher, using real-world social network graphs. This experimental study compares the performance of our techniques to previously published results and shows vast improvements in the range of 2-3 times higher throughput and lower latency.

The rest of this paper is organized as follows. Section 2 gives an overview of the SpamWatcher application. Section 3 describes the underlying technologies used, namely IBM *System S* and IBM WSP. Section 4 gives a high-level architecture of SpamWatcher implemented as a stream processing application. Section 5 describes algorithms for clustering coefficient computation, including our novel algorithms that utilize the pattern matching hardware engine. Section 6 describes the use of the `waitrsv` primitive for efficient parallelization of the computation. Section 7 presents our experimental study. Section 8 discusses related work and Section 9 concludes the paper.

2. SPAMWATCHER PROBLEM OVERVIEW

Traditional anti-spam methods, such as scanning the message content for keywords or allocating a pre-defined quota on the number of short messages sent per person, usually do not provide satisfactory results, as they have obvious accuracy and usability shortcomings. Detecting spam based on social network analysis [6] is a promising direction, which does not suffer from these shortcomings. However, unlike the traditional approaches, social network analysis requires frequent access to the social network graph to perform the necessary analysis to determine if a given message is spam or not. With the ever increasing number of mobile users and devices, and the volume of message communication, accurate and resource efficient detection of spam messages using social network analysis techniques becomes a major challenge. SpamWatcher is designed to address this challenge.

The basic social network analysis approach we employ in SpamWatcher for detecting spam messages is based on techniques described earlier in the literature [6]. In what follows, we give a brief description of this approach, which serves as the basis for our hardware-assisted detection algorithm and parallelization strategy that are described later.

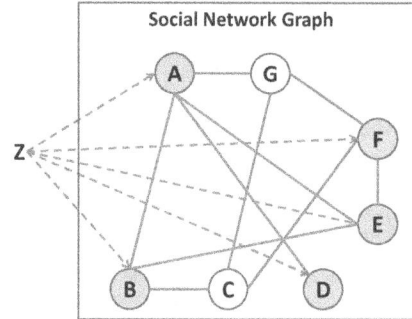

Figure 1: Sample computation of clustering coefficient: The relationships of A,B,C,D,E,F, and G constructs a social network graph. An edge between E and F means they have a connection. $CC_z = \frac{3+2+1+3+1}{5\times(5-1)} = 0.5$.

In essence, the application distinguishes spam from regular messages according to personal relationships between callers and callees as represented by a social network graph. In this graph, a vertex v_i denotes a mobile phone user and an edge $e_{i,j}$ between v_i and another vertex v_j (representing another user) indicates that the two users i and j *know* each other, as they have called one another in the past. The basic assumption behind such a model is that spam messages are usually sent out to a large number of randomly selected targets.

For a given message, clustering coefficient is a measure of how connected a target user of the message is with the set of all target users of the message. If this measure is high, then it implies that the message is sent to a set of users that know each other for the most part, and thus is not a spam message. To define this more formally, let z be a message and t_z be the set of users that are targets of this message. To compute clustering coefficient for message z, denoted by CC_z, we first look at each user $v \in t_z$ in the taget set of the message z and then compute the fraction of the users in the target set $t_z - \{v\}$ that are also in the set of v's neighbors, denoted by e_v. This measure is given by $|e_v \cap t_z|/(|t_z| - 1)$ for $v \in t_z$. After averaging over all target users, we get:

$$CC_z = \sum_{v \in t_z} \frac{|e_v \cap t_z|}{|t_z|.(|t_z| - 1)}$$

Given a social network graph augmented with a vertex representing the message z and edges connecting this vertex to the vertices in the target user set t_z, the numerator of the above equation is equal to the number of *closed triplets* around the central vertex that represents the message z. A closed triplet simply represents an edge between two vertices in the target user set t_z. This edge forms a triangle when connected with the vertex that represents the message z. In summary, in order to compute CC_z, we need to count the number of triangles formed by the vertex that represents z and two vertices from the target user set t_z of the message z, where the latter two are neighbors in the social network graph. Figure 1 shows a sample social network graph and how CC_z is computed.

There exist two general categories of algorithms for counting closed triplets: exact counting [1, 7, 18] and approximating counting [24, 4]. In this paper, we concentrate on exact counting of clustering coefficient. The fastest exact counting methods use matrix-matrix multiplication [7] and therefore have an overall time complexity of $O(n^{2.371})$, where n is the number of target users of the message. This is the state of the art complexity for matrix multiplication [9]. However, the space complexity is $O(n^2)$ and thus these algorithms are not used in practice due to their high memory requirements. Listing algorithms are preferred in practice for large graphs due to their modest memory requirements. *Edge-iterator* is a representative listing algorithm and Schank [27] has shown that edge-iterator performs better on large-scale graphs compared to other alternatives. As a result, we use edge-iterator as the basic algorithm in our work. The details about this algorithm are given in Section 5.1.

In a typical configuration, the SpamWatcher application manages a social network graph with several tens of millions of vertices. An important aspect of this dataset is that the social network evolves slowly. Thus, accurately scoring incoming messages does not require updating the graph in a streaming fashion. Instead, the social network graph can be updated offline, using a batch process. In contrast, counting the number of closed triplets accurately is a key ingredient in our clustering coefficient computation that needs to be performed on a per-message basis. Interestingly, based on our profiling runs, we have established that the queries for assessing inter-user connectivity in social network graphs (used for the closed triplet counting) account for approximately 90% of the total execution time in determining whether a message is legitimate or not, when the edge-iterator algorithm is used.

3. BACKGROUND

This section briefly describes the fundamental technologies used in the present work: the WSP and its specific hardware features utilized by our work; the System S stream processing middleware, and its programming language, *SPL*. Our aim here is to provide enough information for the reader to understand how we architected our framework (which we describe in Section 4), as opposed to being comprehensive. The detailed coverage of these technologies can be found elsewhere [12, 15].

3.1 WSP Overview

The WSP is built based on a heterogeneous architecture that integrates multiple general purpose cores with several domain-specific accelerators and I/O functions, in a system-on-a-chip. It includes four distinct complexes: the processor compute complex, the accelerator complex, the interconnect complex, and the network I/O complex. In this paper, we focus on the former two, which facilitate efficient implementation of our SpamWatcher application. For others, we refer the reader to [12].

The accelerator complex is composed of a set of special-purpose co-processors that are frequently used in many application domains. The WSP contains 4 such accelerators, namely: *pattern matching*, *compression / decompression*, *cryptography*, and *XML* accelerators. These accelerators are significantly more power efficient than general purpose processors [11] and will exceed the performance of highly-tuned software alternatives running on general-purpose processors. Among these hardware accelerators, our work makes use of the *pattern matching* engine.

The processor compute complex is composed of a large set of multi-threaded cores that provide high performance per watt and are optimized for parallel processing. There are 16 PowerPC cores, referred to as A2 cores, operating at 1.8 GHz. Each A2 core has 4 simultaneous threads of execution [21].

Besides these two complexes, wait reservation is another technology we employ in our solution. The `waitrsv` primitive allows a thread to wait on a previously established reservation and wake up when that reservation is lost. We use `waitrsv` in a manner similar to `monitor/mwait` [3], as a more efficient way to perform fine-grained synchronization.

3.2 System S and SPL

Emerging streaming workloads and applications gave rise to new data management architectures as well as new principles for application development and evaluation. Several academic and commercial frameworks have been put in place for supporting these workloads [22, 28].

System S [2, 20, 30] is a stream processing middleware from IBM Research, which supports the execution of multiple streaming applications on a set of compute nodes, simultaneously. System S applications take the form of dataflow processing graphs. A flow graph consists of a set of PEs (processing elements, i.e., execution containers for the application logic stated as a collection of operators) connected by streams, where each stream has a fixed schema and carries a series of tuples. The *operators* hosted by PEs implement stream analytics and can be distributed on several compute nodes. System S provides a multiplicity of services, such as fault tolerance mechanisms [19], scheduling and placement mechanisms [14], distributed job management, storage services, and security.

SPL [15, 16] is the programming language of System S. The SPL tooling includes a rapid application development environment, as well as visualization and debugging tools [8, 13]. The language can be used to compose parallel and distributed stream processing applications, in the form of operator-based dataflow graphs. The language makes available several operator toolkits, including a *stream relational* toolkit that implements relational algebra operations in the streaming context; an *edge adapter* toolkit comprising operators for ingesting data from external sources as well as publishing results to external consumers, such as network sockets, databases, file systems, as well as to proprietary middleware platforms. A distinctive feature of the SPL is its extensibility. New type-generic, configurable, and reusable operators can be added, enabling third parties to create application or domain-specific toolkits of operators.

4. ARCHITECTURE OF A STREAMING SOLUTION

In this section, we describe the high-level architecture of SpamWatcher as a stream processing application.

4.1 SpamWatcher on System S

Figure 2 shows a high-level view of SpamWatcher running on System S. The application receives, as input, a stream of short message events. Each event represents a short message that was sent from a number P_0 to a set of target numbers $\{P_1, \ldots, P_n\}$. For each event, the clustering coefficient is computed and compared against a threshold to detect if the short message involved is a spam message or not. If the clustering coefficient is smaller than or equal to a predefined threshold L, then the telecom operator will be informed that P_0 is a spam message sender and should be blacklisted. If not, then the message is considered as clean, and is forwarded to the list of users in its target set.

Our previous work [32] has shown that SpamWatcher can be implemented effectively as a streaming application. On the one hand, it follows the streaming paradigm as the computation performed is triggered by an external and continuous data source; on the other

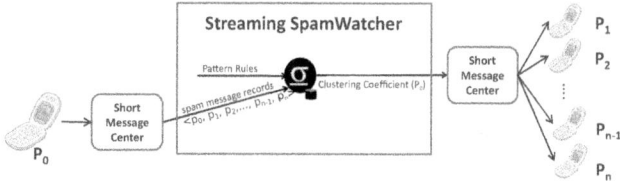

Figure 2: Architecture.

```
2    ClusteringCoefficient(input)
3    {
4      onTuple input:
5      {
6        mutable int32 tmp;
7        pmeHandle = get_pme_handle(pattern_file);
8        search_pme(pmeHandle, input, tmp);
9      }
10     output result: cc=tmp;
11   }
```

hand, the datasets can be partitioned and distributed across multiple backend servers or processing cores. We discuss the partition and distribution aspects of the problem in detail, in Section 6. In summary, System S provides a platform on which SpamWatcher can be effectively deployed as a distributed stream processing application.

4.2 Using WSP's Hardware on System S

As we mentioned earlier, clustering coefficient computation is the most time consuming component of the SpamWatcher application. To address this, we propose to accelerate this computation using the pattern matching engine (PME) on the WSP. In the rest of this section, we outline the main steps involved in accessing the PME from within an SPL application.

Before pattern matching can be performed using the PME, there are 3 preparation steps that have to be performed first:

1) Express the patterns which will be used for the match, as regular expressions.

2) Compile the regular expressions into a binary file. As part of the compilation, the patterns are organized into BART-based Finite State Machines as described in [31].

3) Load the pattern binary into the PME.

Once these steps are performed, data can be matched against the patterns. The compilation (step 2) takes a significant amount of time and cannot be executed too often. On the other hand, the overhead brought by the loading (step 3) is proportional to the size of the compiled pattern. As we will discuss in detail in Section 5.2, the algorithm we develop for the clustering coefficient computation relies on representing the social network graph as a pattern. Even though the compilation of patterns is a very expensive operation at this scale, it does not prevent us from utilizing the PME for the clustering coefficient computation. This is because the social network graph used by the SpamWatcher application is slow changing and does not need to be updated in real-time.

Listing 1 gives the SPL pseucode for performing pattern matching using the PME. The WSP provides C language APIs for using the PME and we have wrapped these APIs as SPL native functions to expose them within the streaming application. The `get_pme_handle` function call, shown in line 7, is used to load a binary pattern file, whose path it takes as a parameter. We assume that the binary pattern file was created by compiling the regular expression of interest, using the WSP's regular expression compiler. The function returns a handle, which can be used in a future `search_pme` function call to perform a match, as shown in line 8. The latter function takes as a parameter, in addition to the handle, an input string that will be matched against the pattern. The function returns (in an out-parameter) the number of matches that were found (`tmp` variable in the example).

Listing 1: Pseudo-code for PME usage in SPL

```
1   stream <int32 cc> result =
```

5. CLUSTERING COEFFICIENT COMPUTATION

In this section we describe the PME-assisted pattern matching algorithms we developed for the clustering coefficient computation. We also describe the basic algorithm that will serve as a baseline for our performance study in Section 7.

5.1 Base Algorithm without the PME

Section 2 gave an overview of common clustering coefficient computation algorithms. Among these algorithms, edge-iterator is effective with respect to both memory and performance and thus we use it as our baseline. Algorithm 1 gives the pseudo-code. The basic idea is to count the closed triplets around the vertex z that represents the source of the message. Lines 2 and 3 are used to get one edge $\langle u, w \rangle$ where $u \in t_z$ (u is in the target user set of z) and $w \in e_u$ (w is amongst the neighbors of u) in G; and line 4 checks whether $\langle z, u, w \rangle$ forms a closed triplet. This check can be implemented in different ways. A brute-force method simply iterates over every element in t_z to determine if $w \in t_z$, yielding a total running time complexity of $O(d.n^2)$, where n is the size of the target user set of the message, i.e. $n = |t_z|$, and d is the average degree of a vertex in the graph. For the messages that are likely to be spam, n is often much larger than d. Given this property, building a hash table out of t_z can reduce the cost of the $w \in t_z$ checking to $O(1)$. This brings the overall algorithmic complexity to $O(d.n)$.

Algorithm 1 Basic algorithm without PME

1: $CC_z \leftarrow 0$
2: **for** $u \in t_z$ **do**
3:   **for** $w \in e_u$ **do**
4:     **if** $w \in t_z$ **then**
5:       $CC_z \leftarrow CC_z + 1$
6:     **end if**
7:   **end for**
8: **end for**
9: $CC_z \leftarrow CC_z/(|t_z|.(|t_z| - 1))$

5.2 Advanced Algorithms with the PME

Section 4.2 described the main steps involved in using the PME. In this section, we describe two algorithms that employ the PME. Both of these algorithms work by converting the graph into patterns and performing regular expression matches on these patterns to count the number of closed triplets. In the following sections, we describe the *DirectSearch* and *PrefixGuidedSearch* algorithms we have developed using this idea to compute the clustering coefficient with PME acceleration. As part of this, we cover both the pattern representation of the graph and the input strings used with these patterns.

5.2.1 DirectSearch

In this algorithm, we map the adjacency list representation of the graph to a pattern by converting each adjacency list into a regular expression. For a vertex u, that is connected to vertices $e_u = \{v_1, v_2, \ldots, v_n\}$, its associated regular expression is given by: $v_1|v_2|\ldots|v_n$. We refer to this regular expression as the *rule* for the vertex u. The graph given earlier in Figure 1 can be represented as shown below:

```
Rule A: B|D|E|G
Rule B: A|C|E
Rule C: B|F|G
Rule D: A
Rule E: A|B|F
Rule F: C|E|G
Rule G: A|C|F
```

Algorithm 2 gives the pseudo-code for DirectSearch. The main idea is to load the set of vertex rules corresponding to the target user set t_z and then perform a search with the resulting pattern on the string representation of t_z as the input string. Each match represents a closed triplet. For instance, a match w from the rule of u represents a closed triplet $\langle z, u, w \rangle$. To see this, consider the example given in Figure 1. The input string will be ABDEF and for the rule of B, there will be 2 matches: A and E (as these are in the input string). These two represent 2 of the closed triplets: ZB**A** and ZB**E**.

The main advantage of this algorithm is that, the counting of the closed triplets is done using a single match via the PME, where the input string is the target user set and the pattern is the set of regular expressions representing the rules of the vertices in the target user set. This step is performed by the search_pme call in line 6. The major disadvantage of the algorithm is that, the set of rules that constitute the pattern is dependent on the target user set, which will be different for each message. As shown in lines 1- 3, the rules for the vertices are retrieved using the pattern_of call and are added to the pattern via the get_pme_handle (for the first one) and add_pme_file (for all others) calls. While each rule is already pre-compiled into a regular expression in an offline step, loading them into the PME has non-negligible cost. Assuming that the size of each compiled rule is $O(d)$, the loading part has a computational cost of $O(d.n)$ and the search part has cost $O(n)$. In short, the computational complexity of this algorithm is still $O(d.n)$, but part of the computation is accelerated by the hardware.

Algorithm 2 DirectSearch Algorithm

Require: $t_z = \{v_1, \ldots, v_n\}$
1: $handle \leftarrow get\_pme\_handle(pattern\_of(v_1))$
2: **for** $i \in [2..n]$ **do**
3: $\quad add\_pme\_file(handle, pattern\_of(v_i))$
4: **end for**
5: $input \leftarrow stringify(t_z)$
6: $CC_z \leftarrow search\_pme(handle, input)$
7: $CC_z \leftarrow CC_z/(n.(n-1))$

5.2.2 PrefixGuidedSearch

In this algorithm, we improve upon the DirectSearch algorithm by avoiding the individual loads of vertex rules for each message. Instead, we create a single pattern that combines the rules of all vertices and load it once into the PME. All input strings are searched using this same pattern. The main challenge in achieving this is to avoid the activation of rules for vertices that are not in the target

user set of the current message. In order to achieve this, we update the vertex rules to include a *rule prefix* that incorporates the vertex itself into the regular expression. Accordingly, we update the search string to include a *selector prefix* that identifies the vertex rules that need to be active.

As an example, again consider Figure 1. We extend the input string ABDEF into ABDEF#ABDEF. The first part, that is the rule prefix, indicates the set of vertices whose rules should be active; and the second part indicates the set of vertices we are looking for in the adjacency lists of the vertices in the target user set. To understand how the rules are modified to work with this new input string, let us consider the rules for B and G as examples. Note that the rule for B should be active, whereas the rule for G should be inactive, since the former is in the selector prefix, but the latter is not.

```
Rule B: B[^#]*#[^#]*(A|C|E)
Rule G: G[^#]*#[^#]*(A|C|F)
```

If you look at the rule prefixes, that is B[^#]*# for rule of B and G[^#]*# for rule of G, it is easy to see that they will only match an input string whose selector prefix includes the rule vertex. For instance, B[^#]*# will match ABDEF# but G[^#]*# won't. This will turn off the rule for vertex G, while enabling the one for B. The second part of a rule simply includes the adjacency list of the rule vertex, as in the DirectSearch algorithm. The second parts of the rules are matched against the second part of the input string, in order to count the number of neighbors of the active rule vertex that are also in the target user set, thus forming a closed triplet. Concretely, matching ABDEF#ABDEF (the input string) against B[^#]*#[^#]*(A|C|E) (the rule of vertex B) will yield 2 matches: BDEF#**A** and BDEF#ABD**E**, corresponding to the closed triplets: ZB**A** and ZB**E**.

The complete set of rules for the graph in Figure 1 is given as follows:

```
Rule A: A[^#]*#[^#]*(B|D|E|G)
Rule B: B[^#]*#[^#]*(A|C|E)
Rule C: C[^#]*#[^#]*(B|F|G)
Rule D: D[^#]*#[^#]*A
Rule E: E[^#]*#[^#]*(A|B|F)
Rule F: F[^#]*#[^#]*(C|E|G)
Rule G: G[^#]*#[^#]*(A|C|F)
```

Algorithm 3 gives the pseudo-code for PrefixGuidedSearch. Note that the algorithm does not involve loading rules on a per-message basis. Instead, the set of all vertex rules are compiled off-line and are loaded into the PME once. For each message, the input string is constructed by simply appending the string representation fot the target user set to itself, with the # character separating the two parts. A single search is made using the search_pme call. As a result, the computational complexity of this algorithm is $O(n)$.

Algorithm 3 PrefixGuidedSearch Algorithm

Require: $handle$: global variable representing the pre-compiled pattern
1: $input \leftarrow stringify(t_z) + \text{``\#''} + stringify(t_z)$
2: $CC_z \leftarrow search\_pme(handle, input)$
3: $CC_z \leftarrow CC_z/(|t_z|.(|t_z|-1))$

---

6. MULTI-THREADED IMPLEMENTATION

We have introduced different algorithms to compute clustering coefficient in Section 5. In this section, we describe how to parallelize these algorithms, including the data partitioning scheme used for the graph, the distribution mechanism used for the queries, and the synchronization techniques used for combining the results.

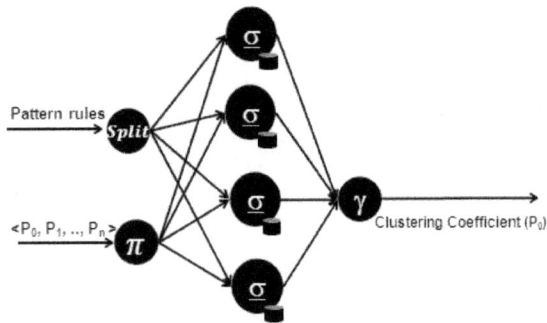

Figure 3: Execution flow after partitioning (using $N = 4$ partitions).

6.1 Parallelization Strategy

To increase the available parallelism, we partition the data set and replicate the queries to these partitions. Figure 3 shows the application flow graph after parallelization is applied. The partitioning of the graph is achieved by applying the *split* operator on the vertices. For the edge-iterator algorithm, this will result in distributing the adjacency lists amongst the partitions, whereas for the PME-based algorithms it will result in distributing the vertex rules. This data partitioning step is performed when the graph is first loaded. The queries are routed to all partitions using the π operator, and are processed by each partition thread using the σ operator, and finally the result is aggregated using the γ operator. The aggregation of results require the processing step for each partition to complete, thus a barrier synchronisation step is involved.

Overall, the effectiveness of our load balancing scheme depends on how well the split operator spreads the data set. If the subsets of query vertices that apply to each partition are uniformly sized, better load balancing will be achieved. We use a hand-tuned hash function [32] to implement the split operator in order to minimize skew.

6.2 Algorithmic Scalability

It is easy to see that the edge-iterator algorithm will scale linearly with the number of partitions, as the outer most loop will only iterate over the set of query vertices that belong to the current partition. However, the scalability of the PME-based algorithms is not as obvious. For the DirectSearch algorithm, the input string used for the pattern matching has to be the same independent of the number of partitions used. For the PrefixGuidedSearch algorithm, the selector prefix part of the input string can contain only the vertices that belong to the current partition. However, the remaining part of the input string does not change and thus the overall size of the input string is still proportional to the number of vertices in the query. This is problematic at first, as we have mentioned in Section 5 that the cost of the regular expression matching via the PME depends on the size of the input string only.

There are two important characteristics of the PME that makes the DirectSearch and the PrefixGuidedSearch algorithms scale. First, the PME supports executing pattern searches concurrently using multiple threads. Up to 16 concurrent searches are supported. Second, the cost of doing a pattern match via the PME depends on the number of *context*s needed to store the pattern, in addition to the size of the input string. The PME has up to 1024 contexts. While for small patterns (taking at most 1 context) the cost of the matching

solely depends on the size of the input string, when the patterns get large the matching (the `search_pme` call) is performed by doing a regular expression search (`regex_search` call) on each context in the partition, in a linear fashion. For a large pattern that takes up all the contexts, a single threaded implementation will result in making 1024 `regex_search` calls to process a query, whereas a multi-threaded implementation that uses $N \leq 16$ partitions will run $1024/N$ such searches on each one of the N threads.

6.3 Basic Synchronization

The basic version of our multithreaded implementation uses the Pthreads library for synchronization. NPTL implementation of Pthreads on Linux relies on futexes for synchronisation – a mechanism provided by the Linux kernel as a building block for fast users-pace locking. In this implementation, a thread that waits on a condition variable (via `pthread_cond_wait`) makes a futex system call with a `FUTEX_WAIT` argument, which causes the thread to be suspended and descheduled. When the worker notifies the blocked thread (via `pthread_cond_signal`), a futex system call with a `FUTEX_WAKE` argument is made, which casuses the waiting thread to be awakened and rescheduled.

When the number of threads is small, the overhead brought by synchronization can be ignored. However, with the increasing number of threads, it becomes a significant factor when compared to the time spent on computation. Figure 4 breaks down the execution time of the edge-iterator algorithm: the time spent on synchronization and the time spent on computation. The figure shows that the overhead of synchronization is around 4% for 48 threads and 28% for 64 threads. For PME-based algorithms that are faster than the edge-iterator algorithm, as it will be shown in Section 7.2, this cost is even more pronounced.

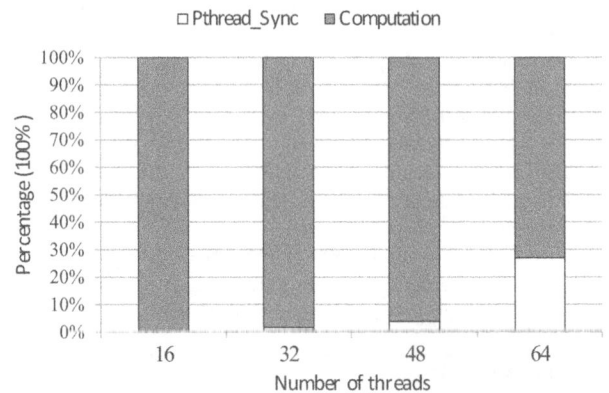

Figure 4: Execution time break down: the time spent on pthread synchronization vs. the time spent on computation

6.4 Synchronization with Waitrsv

IBM WSP introduced a new hardware instruction called `wait`. It enables a logical processor to enter into an performance-optimized state while waiting for a single store to a given address. This address can be set-up by the `lwarx` primitive, on any PowerPC core [25]. Different from the `monitor` / `mwait` instructions provided by Intel's Prescott core [17] at privilege level 0, these two instructions are available at the user-level. The `wait` and `lwarx` primitives are used together to create the `waitrsv` primitive on the WSP, which enables programmers to synchronize application-level threads on hyper-threaded cores.

In particular, the `lwarx` primitive atomically performs a read and sets the reservation on an address, which notifies the monitoring hardware to detect stores to this address. On the other hand, the `wait` primitive puts the processor into the low power state until a store on the monitored address, or a timer interrupt happens. It is architecturally similar to executing `nop` instructions while waiting for a store to the address set up by `lwarx` or a timer interrupt. However, when other threads are available for execution on a hyper-threaded core, the processor can execute those threads, without stalling. When used together, these two primitives provide an application-level synchronization mechanism that avoids the overhead of OS-level scheduling when compared to the futex-based synchronization primitives of the Pthreads library.

Listing 2: `waitrsv` primitive usage

```
1   void waitrsv(void* pbuffer) {
2     uint32_t val;
3     asm volatile(
4     loop:
5       // load and make reservation
6       lwarx %0, 0, %1
7       // exit if the value is non-zero
8       cmp %0, 0
9       bne exit
10      // make the thread reliquish resources
11      // and sleep until reservation is lost
12    wait
13      b loop
14    exit:
15      : "=&r" (val)
16      : "r" (pbuffer));
17  }
```

Listing 2 shows the implementation of the `waitrsv` primitive in our application, which sets up a reservation and waits for it to be cleared. As mentioned earlier, the wait could unblock due to events other than a write to the monitored address, such as an interrupt. As a result, we compare the current value of the monitored address against the original value, in order to determine if the exit from the wait resulted from a write or a different event. If it was due to an interrupt, then the wait must be executed again. However, the thread does not automatically go back into wait state after the interrupt is serviced. Thus, we repeat the reservation setup step via `lwarx`, before re-issuing the `wait`.

Listing 3: Pseucode for CC thread

```
1   void Transmitter_Thread() {
2     while(1) {
3       Recv(buf);
4       Write(Transmitter_CC, buf);
5     }
6   }
7   void CC_Thread() {
8     while(1) {
9       waitrsv(Transmitter_CC);
10      CC = PrefixGuidedSearch(Transmitter_CC,
11              pmeHandle);
12      Write(CC_Aggregate, CC);
13    }
14  }
```

Listing 3 gives the pseudo-code of the thread synchronization used in our implementation of the SpamWatcher application, based on the `waitrsv` primitive. Here, CC computation thread represents σ operator and *transmitter* thread means π operator. When the transmitter thread receives a query, it will write it into the memory areas shared with the CC computation threads (line 4). Once a CC computation thread detects the memory change via `waitrsv`, it starts the regular expression search using the PME (line 11).

Once complete, it puts the result into the memory are shared with the *aggregation* thread (line 12) (aggregation thread represents γ operator). While not shown here for brevity, the aggregation thread uses the `waitrsv` primitive to implement barrier synchronization, in order to wait for all CC threads to complete their work.

6.5 Performance of Synchronisation

Here, we provide a brief performance comparison of the synchronization primitives used. For this comparison, we use the IBM Mambo full-system simulator [5] in order to show fine-grained results. A partitioning setup with $N = 4$ is used for this comparison, as shown in Figure 3.

We measure the following quantities:

- T_{wakeup}: the time between the notification of the CC thread and the moment that it is actually awakened.

- T_{notify}: the time transmitter thread spends in invoking the appropriate notification primitive.

Table 1: Cost of wakeup and notify (in cycles).

primitive	T_{wakeup}	T_{notify}
Pthreads	92472	55917
waitrsv	181	3276

Table 1 presents the results from the evaluation of implementations with Pthreads and `waitrsv`, given in processor cycles. As shown, Pthreads implementation suffers from high wakeup and notification times, due to the long kernel control paths involved for both rescheduling and notifying the waiting thread. For `waitrsv`, the wakeup and notify are both very efficient, the former taking 0.2% of the cycles taken by the Pthreads alternative.

7. EXPERIMENTS

SpamWatcher is a streaming application that implements a real-time social network analytic, and thus it has stringent requirements on both throughput and latency. In this paper we have demonstrated techniques to improve the performance and scalability of SpamWatcher by leveraging the unique hardware features on the WSP. In this section we assess the effectiveness of our techniques, considering two key performance metrics: *query latency* and *query throughput*.

Query latency is important because it gives an indication of how long it takes for a query engine, in this case either using original algorithm or the equivalent algorithm with WSP's hardware, to compute the query results on behalf of the front-end application. Query throughput is important because, ultimately, the goal is to scale up the original application to accommodate higher worloads demanded by a production deployment. In other words, as the load increases (e.g., as more mobile phone users are added by the telecom provider using the SpamWatcher application) and as more computational resources are made available to the application, ideally, the goal is to keep the number of queries answered per unit of time constant.

Our study was conducted using a real WSP chip which consists of 16 embedded 64-bit PowerPC cores running at 1.8 GHz and a set of accelerator units, including one for pattern matching. Each core consists of 4 concurrent hardware threads that feed a single-issue in-order pipeline. Each group of 4 cores share a 2 MB L2 cache. The operating system is RedHat Enterprise 4.0 with 16 GB memory installed.

We use the three algorithms descried earlier for computing clustering coefficient, namely: *i*) edge-iterator algorithm, as a baseline, *ii*) DirectSearch, as the naive algorithm with hardware acceleration, and *iii*) PrefixGuidedSearch, as the advanced algorithm with hardware acceleration. Furthermore, we evaluate the multithreaded versions of these algorithms with both Pthreads and `waitrsv`-based synchronization.

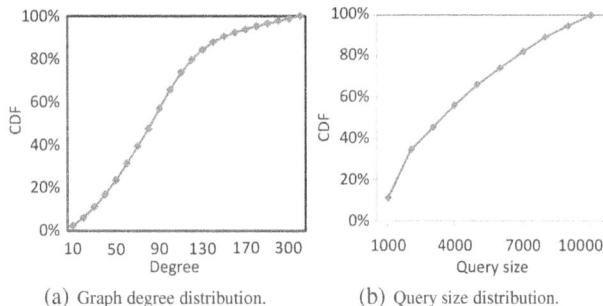

(a) Graph degree distribution.　　(b) Query size distribution.

Figure 5: Distribution for graph degree and query size

We use a real-world dataset for the social network graph, with sizes ranging from 128 MB (mobile users of a town scale) to 8 GB (mobile users of a province scale). The dataset has been anonymized, where mobile users are represented by unique ids, in place of their phone numbers. We used a query workload that was generated by randomizing the application traces we had from earlier field deployment. Figure 5 plots the degree distribution of the graph and the size distribution of the queries for our workload. We set the spam detection threshold L to be 0.15, which is an empirical value determined by the telecom operator.

7.1 Evaluation of clustering coefficient Algorithms

Our first set of experiments consider the clustering coefficient computation from the standpoint of its sensitivity to the query length and dataset size. For this purpose, we use single-threaded implementations of the three algorithms.

Figure 6 plots the average query latency (execution time for a query) as a function of the query length (number of target users of a message). As anticipated, all three algorithms scale linearly with increased query length. We observe that the PrefixGuidedSearch algorithm clearly outperforms the other two algorithms, providing

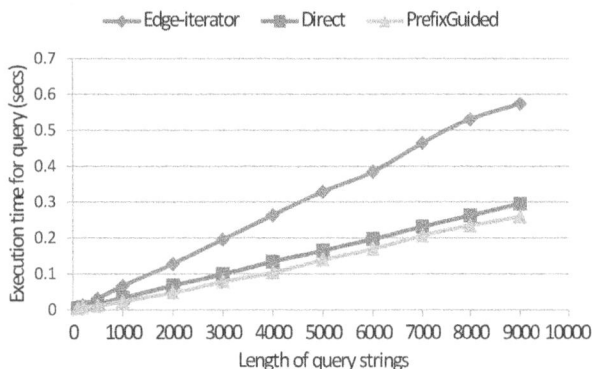

Figure 6: Latency of clustering coefficient computation vs. query length, with 1GB dataset, on a single thread.

1.1-fold speedup over DirectSearch and 1.6-fold to 3-fold speedup over the edge-iterator algorithm.

Figure 7 plots the average query throughput for varying dataset sizes (social network graphs of varying sizes). As expected, all algorithms exhibited a decrease in throughput as the dataset increases in size. Not surprisingly, the edge-iterator algorithm gives the lowest throughput. The pattern matching engine on the WSP and the algorithms that take advantage of it show a great deal of improvement in performance. We observe an average of 1.5-fold speedup for the DirectSearch algorithm and 3-fold speedup for the PrefixGuidedSearch algorithm. For the PrefixGuidedSearch algorithm, we only show results for dataset sizes less than or equal to 1 GB due to the current limitations of the PME compiler. This limitation is actively being worked on, and will be addressed in the future.

Figure 8 plots the average query latency for varying dataset sizes. We observe that the latency increases with increased dataset size. This is because of the increased cost of memory accesses. The DirectSearch algorithm provides a 2-fold speedup over the baseline edge-iterator algorithm, whereas the PrefixGuidedSearch algorithm provides a speedup of 3-fold. This improvement in performance can be attributed to the hardware acceleration in general. The PrefixGuidedSearch algorithm performs better than other alternatives, as it takes advantage of the PME without incurring the overhead of continuous pattern loading. This is unlike the DirectSearch algorithm, which, while being simpler with respect to the structure of the input string and the graph pattern, is hindered by the need for loading the relevant pattern rules, on a per-query basis.

7.2 Evaluation of Multithreaded Implementation

We now look at the clustering coefficient computation algorithms from the standpoint of their sensitivity to distributed execution as increasing the number of threads and dataset partitions. In these experiments, each data partition is hosted on a different thread and we apply the distribution and partition techniques described in Section 6.1. Again, we examine the impact on throughput and latency.

Figure 9 plots the speed-up in throughput relative to the single-threaded case, as a function of the number of threads used. We see that all configurations behave reasonably well, scaling almost linearly with the number of threads from 1 to 16. Nevertheless, for the edge-iterator and DirectSearch algorithms implemented with Pthreads (as described in Section 6.3), the scalability decreases sharply when the number of threads increase from 16 to 64. As we have seen in Figure 4, the overhead brought by thread synchronization increases as the number of threads grows, and it reaches to 28% when there are 64 threads. The DirectSearch algorithm, when implemented with the `waitrsv` primitive (as described in Section 6.4), scales better than other two configurations and achieves improvements up to 21% with 64 threads when compared to the Pthreads implementation.

Figure 10 plots the speed-up in latency (execution time) relative to the single-threaded case, as a function of the number of threads used. We can see that the results are similar to those for the throughput and our implementation which uses the `waitrsv` primitive scales the best. It provides improvements up to 38% with 64 threads, when compared to the Pthreads based alternative.

The results for PrefixGuidedSearch with `waitrsv` are similar to those for DirectSearch and are not shown for brevity. We show how PrefixGuidedSearch scales with the number of threads shortly.

7.3 Beyond the clustering coefficient Computation

All the previous experiments focused on executing the cluster-

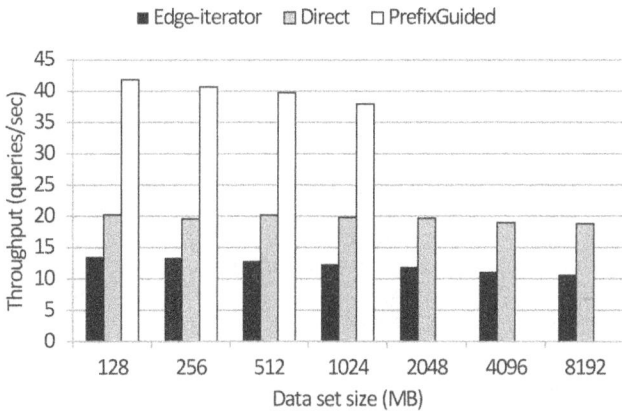

Figure 7: Throughput vs. data set size for bottleneck clustering coefficient computation, on a single thread.

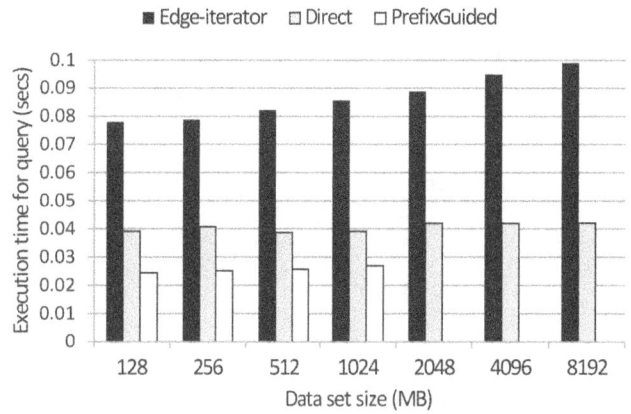

Figure 8: Latency vs. data set size for bottleneck clustering coefficient computation, on a single thread.

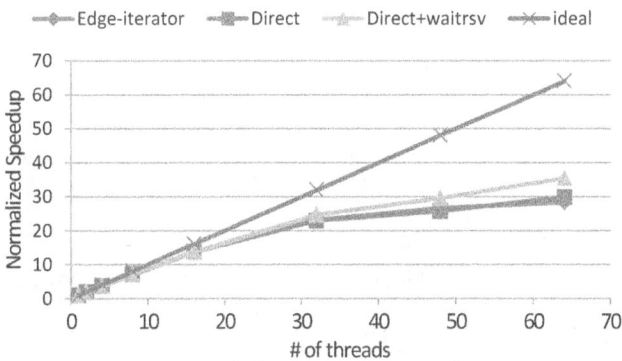

Figure 9: Throughput vs. number of threads used for clustering coefficient computation, with 8GB dataset.

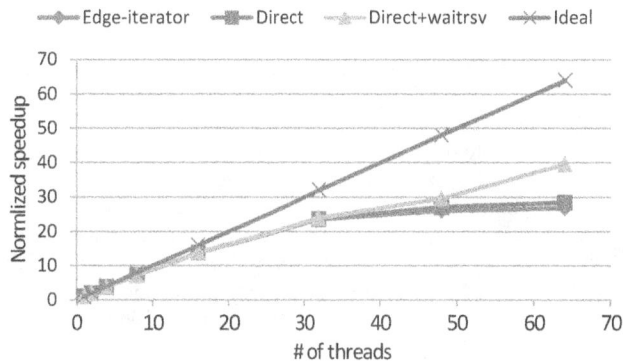

Figure 10: Latency vs. number of threads used for clustering coefficient computation, with 8GB dataset.

ing coefficient computation in isolation. In the experiments depicted by Figure 11, we implement both PrefixGuidedSearch and DirectSearch algorithms with `waitrsv` primitive, run the full application and measure the throughput. The intention is to assess the effectiveness of our algorithms in accelerating the end-to-end SpamWatcher application, as computational resources are scaled to handle additional load. As it can be observed from the figure, PrefixGuidedSearch-`waitrsv` performs the best over the other two and the speedup is the highest with 64 threads. We observe an average of 1.6-fold speedup over DirectSearch-`waitrsv` and 3.4-fold speedup over edge-iterator-pthread. The results are generally consistent with those seen in Figure 9. This is because the bottleneck clustering coefficient computation accounts for the bulk of SpamWatcher's computational budget. For this reason, we omit the latency results as they are very similar to what we have reported in Figure 11.

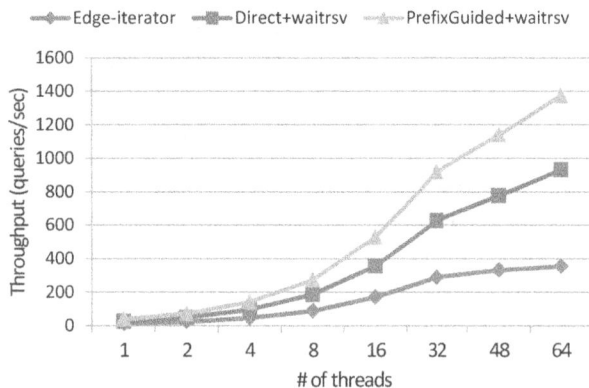

Figure 11: Throughput vs. number of threads used for the entire application, with 1GB dataset.

7.4 Discussion

Our empirical evaluation shows that our solution, which employed the pattern matching accelerator and the hardware synchronization primitives on the WSP, is a practical alternative for improving the performance and scalability of streaming social network analytics. Although these results are very encouraging, we have additional work items that need to be addressed before adopting this solution as a general framework for building scalable, real-time social network analytics. Our pattern matching compiler still has considerable room for improvement, such as supporting larger datasets (ideally we should be able to compile a pattern as long as the resulting binary fits into the available space provided by the PME). Furthermore, we consider our pattern matching libraries as not being at production-level yet. For example, improvements will have to be made with respect to the performance of loading pattern rules. Once these improvements are complete, additional performance gains are expected from our PME-enhanced clustering coefficient computation algorithms.

8. RELATED WORK

The first area of related work is clustering coefficient computation, which is the most important operation in SpamWatcher. Exact counting and approximate counting are two general categories of algorithms used for computing clustering coefficient. We have discussed the exact algorithms in Section 2, and later demonstrated that our hardware accelerated PrefixGuidedSearch algorithm outperforms the state-of-the art algorithms used for clustering coeffi-

cient computation. Approaches relying on one-pass algorithms [10] or approximate results [26, 24, 4] also exist. These algorithms deal with graphs that are too large to fit in main-memory. Our work focuses on parallel, in-memory algorithms due to the real-time requirements of SpamWatcher.

The second technique highlighted in our work is the thread synchronization mechanism. With the proliferation of cheap multi-threading architectures, thread-level parallelism becomes a key factor in achieving performance. In this regard, a critical issue is to decide the granularity of thread-level parallelism to be used. In this work, we focus on fine-grained parallelism due to the low-latency requirements of SpamWatcher. In this area, Kawano et al. [23] proposed a fine-grained parallel method which uses hardware primitives to implement highly efficient task scheduling. Our technique is about thread synchronization mechanisms and the most relevant work was done by Anastopoulos et al. [3]. The main difference from our work is that the `waitrsv` primitive provided by WSP is for user-level applications, while the `monitor`/`mwait` primitives described in [3] are at privilege level 0.

9. CONCLUDING REMARKS

In this work we have described a solution for a streaming social network analysis application – SpamWatcher, which requires processing massive data flows with high-throughput and low-latency. The SpamWatcher application faces major challenges with respect to performance and scalability due to increasing volume of mobile users and rates of messages. We have developed a scalable and high-performance solution using a commercial-grade stream processing middle-ware – System S. Our solution takes advantage of specialized co-processors and hardware primitives on the IBM WSP – a system-on-a-chip. This enabled us to scale-up the real-time detection of spam, while maintaining low latencies.

As part of our work, we have developed a novel implementation technique which leverages pattern matching accelerator to minimize the latency of spam detection. Furthermore, we have employed hardware primitives to reduce the overhead brought by thread synchronization. We have experimentally demonstrated, using real data-sets for the SpamWatcher application, that our solution results in substantial performance and scalability improvements.

We believe that the ideas proposed in this paper are applicable to other problems in the area of real-time social network analysis. The combination of a streaming application architecture and algorithm design that utilizes hardware acceleration leads to good performance and can be used to tackle performance bottlenecks in real-time social network analysis applications.

10. REFERENCES

[1] N. Alon, R. Yuster, and U. Zwick. Finding and counting given length cycles (extended abstract). In *ESA '94: Proceedings of the Second Annual European Symposium on Algorithms*, pages 354–364, London, UK, 1994. Springer-Verlag.

[2] L. Amini, H. Andrade, R. Bhagwan, F. Eskesen, R. King, P. Selo, Y. Park, and C. Venkatramani. SPC: A distributed, scalable platform for data mining. In *Proceedings of the Workshop on Data Mining Standards, Services and Platforms, DM-SSP*, 2006.

[3] N. Anastopoulos and N. Koziris. Facilitating efficient synchronization of asymmetric threads on hyper-threaded processors. In *Proceedings of the IPDPS Conference, IPDPS*, 2008.

[4] L. Becchetti, P. Boldi, C. Castillo, and A. Gionis. Efficient algorithms for large-scale local triangle counting. *ACM Trans. Knowl. Discov. Data*, 4(3):1–28, 2010.

[5] P. Bohrer, J. Peterson, M. Elnozahy, R. Rajamony, A. Gheith, R. Rockhold, C. Lefurgy, H. Shafi, T. Nakra, R. Simpson, E. Speight, K. Sudeep, E. Van Hensbergen, and L. Zhang. Mambo: a full system simulator for the powerpc architecture. *SIGMETRICS Perform. Eval. Rev.*, 31(4):8–12, 2004.

[6] P. O. Boykin and V. P. Roychowdhury. Leveraging social networks to fight spam. *Computer*, 38(4):61–68, 2005.

[7] D. Coppersmith and S. Winograd. Matrix multiplication via arithmetic progressions. In *STOC '87: Proceedings of the nineteenth annual ACM symposium on Theory of computing*, pages 1–6, New York, NY, USA, 1987. ACM.

[8] W. De Pauw and H. Andrade. Visualizing large-scale streaming applications. *Information Visualization*, 8(2), 2009.

[9] J. Dean and S. Ghemawat. MapReduce: simplified data processing on large clusters. In *OSDI'04: Proceedings of the 6th conference on Symposium on Opearting Systems Design & Implementation*, pages 10–10, Berkeley, CA, USA, 2004. USENIX Association.

[10] D. Ediger, K. Jiang, J. Riedy, and D. Bader. Massive streaming data analytics: A case study with clustering coefficients. In *Parallel Distributed Processing, Workshops and Phd Forum (IPDPSW), 2010 IEEE International Symposium on*, pages 1 –8, April 2010.

[11] K. Fan, M. Kudlur, G. Dasika, and S. mahlke. Bridging the computation gap between programmable processors and hardwired accelerators. In *Proceedings of the 2009 High Performance Computer Architecture (HPCA 2009)*, 2009.

[12] H. Franke, J. Xenidis, C. Basso, B. M. . Bass, S. S. Woodward, J. D. Brown, and C. L. Johnson. Introduction to the wire-speed processor and architecture. *JRD IBM Journal of Research and Development*, 54, 2010.

[13] B. Gedik, H. Andrade, A. Frenkiel, W. De Pauw, M. Pfeifer, P. Allen, N. Cohen, and K.-L. Wu. Debugging tools and strategies for distributed stream processing applications. *Software: Practice and Experience*, 39(16), 2009.

[14] B. Gedik, H. Andrade, and K.-L. Wu. A code generation approach to optimizing high-performance distributed data stream processing. In *Proceedings of the 2009 Conference on Information and Knowledge Management (CIKM 2009)*, 2009.

[15] B. Gedik, H. Andrade, K.-L. Wu, P. S. Yu, and M. Doo. SPADE: The System S declarative stream processing engine. In *Proceedings of the ACM International Conference on Management of Data (SIGMOD 2008)*, 2008.

[16] M. Hirzel, H. Andrade, B. Gedik, V. Kumar, G. Losa, M. Mendell, H. Nasgaard, R. Soulé, and K.-L. Wu. Spade – language specification. Technical Report RC24987, IBM Research, 2009.

[17] Intel 64 and ia-32 architectures software developer manual vol. 3a: System programming guide, part 1. *http://www.intel.com/products/processor*.

[18] A. Itai and M. Rodeh. Finding a minimum circuit in a graph. In *STOC '77: Proceedings of the ninth annual ACM symposium on Theory of computing*, pages 1–10, New York, NY, USA, 1977. ACM.

[19] G. Jacques-Silva, B. Gedik, H. Andrade, and K.-L. Wu. Language level checkpointing support for stream processing applications. In *Proocedings of the 2009 International Conference on Dependable Systems and Networks (DSN 2009)*, 2009.

[20] N. Jain, L. Amini, H. Andrade, R. King, Y. Park, P. Selo, and C. Venkatramani. Design, implementation, and evaluation of the linear road benchmark on the stream processing core. In *Proceedings of the International Conference on Management of Data (SIGMOD 2006)*, 2006.

[21] R. Kalla, B. SinHaroy, and J. Tendler. A smt implementation in power5. In *Hot Chips*, 2003.

[22] R. Kallman, H. Kimura, J. Natkins, A. Pavlo, A. Rasin, S. Zdonik, E. P. C. Jones, S. Madden, M. Stonebraker, Y. Zhang, J. Hugg, and D. J. Abadi. H-store: a high-performance, distributed main memory transaction processing system. *Proc. VLDB Endow.*, 1(2):1496–1499, 2008.

[23] T. Kawano, S. Kusakabe, R.-I. Taniguchi, and M. Amamiya. Fine-grain multi-thread processor architecture for massively parallel processing. *High-Performance Computer Architecture, International Symposium on*, 0:308, 1995.

[24] Z. Liu, C. Wang, Q. Zou, and H. Wang. Clustering coefficient queries on massive dynamic social networks. In *Conference on Web-Age Information Management (WAIM)*, 2010.

[25] Powerpc user instruction set architecture, book i. *http://www.ibm.com/developerworks/systems/library*.

[26] T. Schank and D. Wagner. Approximating clustering coefficient and transitivity. *Journal of Graph Algorithms and Applications*, 9:2005, 2005.

[27] T. Schank and D. Wagner. Finding, counting, and listing all triangles in large graphs, an experimental study. In *Workshop on Experimental and Efficient Algorithms (WEA)*, 2005.

[28] M. Stonebraker, S. Madden, D. J. Abadi, S. Harizopoulos, N. Hachem, and P. Helland. The end of an architectural era: (it's time for a complete rewrite). In *VLDB '07: Proceedings of the 33rd international conference on Very large data bases*, pages 1150–1160. VLDB Endowment, 2007.

[29] L. Weitao. China's mobile phone users hit 650 million. *http://www.chinadaily.com.cn/bizchina/2009-03/06/content_7547876.htm*, 2009.

[30] K.-L. Wu, P. S. Yu, B. Gedik, K. W. Hildrum, C. C. Aggarwal, E. Bouillet, W. Fan, D. A. George, X. Gu, G. Luo, and H. Wang. Challenges and experience in prototyping a multi-modal stream analytic and monitoring application on System S. In *Proceedings of the Very Large Data Bases Conference (VLDB 2007)*, 2007.

[31] F. Yu, Z. Chen, Y. Diao, T. V. Lakshman, and R. H. Katz. Fast and memory-efficient regular expression matching for deep packet inspection. In *ANCS'06*, pages 93–102, 2006.

[32] Q. Zou, H. Wang, R. Soule, M. Hirzel, H. Andrade, B. Gedik, and K.-L. Wu. From a stream of relational queries to distributed stream processing. In *Proceedings of the Very Large Data Bases Conference (VLDB 2010)*, 2010.

Complex Pattern Ranking (CPR): Evaluating Top-k Pattern Queries over Event Streams [*]

Xinxin Wang
School of CIDSE
Arizona State University
Tempe, AZ 85281, USA
xinxin.wang.1@asu.edu

K. Selçuk Candan
School of CIDSE
Arizona State University
Tempe, AZ 85281, USA
candan@asu.edu

Junehwa Song
Dept. of Computer Science,
KAIST
Daejeon, Korea
junesong@nclab.kaist.ac.kr

ABSTRACT

Most existing approaches to complex event processing over streaming data rely on the assumption that the matches to the queries are rare and that the goal of the system is to identify these few matches within the incoming deluge of data. In many applications, such as user credit card purchase pattern monitoring, however the matches to the user queries are in fact plentiful and the system has to efficiently sift through these many matches to locate only the few *most preferable* matches. In this paper, we propose a complex pattern ranking (CPR) framework for specifying top-k pattern queries over streaming data, present new algorithms to support top-k pattern queries in data streaming environments, and verify the effectiveness and efficiency of the proposed algorithms. The algorithms we develop identify top-k matching results satisfying both patterns and additional criteria. To support real-time processing of the data streams, instead of computing top-k results from scratch for each time window, we maintain top-k results dynamically as new events come and old ones expire. We also develop new top-k join execution strategies that are able to adapt to the changing situations (e.g., sorted and random access costs, join rates) without having to assume *a priori* presence of distributed stream statistics. Experiments show significant improvements over existing approaches.

Categories and Subject Descriptors

H.2.4 [**Information Systems**]: Database management—*Query Processing*

General Terms

Design, Algorithms, Language

Keywords

Complex event processing, pattern ranking, topk query

[*]Supported by Korea Research Foundation grant "A Framework for Real-time Context Monitoring in Sensor-rich Personal Mobile Environments."

SEQ	$S_1 = A; B; C$
WITH	A=(purchases in Brand-A),
	B=(purchases in Brand-B),
	C=(purchases in Brand-C)
WITHIN	10 hours
WHERE	A.CCID = B.CCID AND B.CCID = C.CCID
PREF	MAX[$S_1.exp = A.exp + B.exp + C.exp$] AND
	MIN[$S_1.t = C.t - A.t$]
SEQ	$S_2 = D; E$
WITH	D=(purchases in Brand-D),
	E=(purchases in Brand-E)
WITHIN	8 hours
WHERE	D.CCID = E.CCID
PREF	MAX[$S_2.exp = D.exp + E.exp$]
PATTERN	P_1 & P_2
WITH	P_1 = (sequence pattern S_1),
	P_2 = (sequence pattern S_2)
WITHIN	10 hours
WHERE	S_1.A.CCID = S_2.D.CCID
PREF	MAX[$S_1.exp+S_2.exp$] AND MIN[$S_1.t$]
RETURN	10

Figure 1: An example shopping pattern query on credit card purchasing data

1. INTRODUCTION

Complex event processing systems usually deal with the examination of interesting event patterns that occur within data arriving in the form of a stream. This problem is also known as the *pattern matching* problem: given a pattern of interest (represented in different forms under different models), the system needs to discover all matching event instances of the query within the stream.

Most existing approaches to complex event processing (e.g., [25, 7, 17, 9]) rely on the assumption that the matches to the pattern queries are rare and that the goal of the system is to identify these rare matches within the incoming deluge of data. In many applications, such as credit card purchase pattern monitoring, however the matches to the user queries are in fact plentiful and the system has to efficiently sift through these many matches to locate only the few *most preferable* matches.

Figure 1 presents a sample query for an application tracking shoppers for expensive brand goods. In this example, the input is a stream of credit card purchase transactions. The query aims to identify the heavy brand shoppers: more specifically, the query seeks individuals who purchase three goods from brand-A, brand-B, and brand-C in sequence within 10 hours and meanwhile two other goods from brand-D and brand-E within 8 hours; among all the matches, we are interested in identifying 10 matches with the highest overall shopping expenditure and the smallest shopping span between purchase of brand-A and brand-C.

Despite extensive work in complex event processing (see Section 2), there has been very limited previous work that focuses on challenges that involve processing such top-k pattern queries over data streams. Many works, such as [5, 13, 14], assume that the tuples to be ranked or aggregated arrive in the stream that are already materialized in the form of sensor readings or documents. We on the other hand focus on *pattern matches*: the patterns to be ranked need to be discovered on the fly and we want to avoid the cost of enumerating all pattern matches.

1.1 Contributions

In this paper we propose a *complex pattern ranking (CPR)* framework for specifying top-k pattern queries over streaming data, present new algorithms to support top-k pattern queries in data streaming environments and verify the effectiveness and efficiency of the proposed algorithms. The proposed framework lets the user specify pattern queries including user specified preference functions on event attributes. The algorithms we develop identify top-k matching results satisfying both the pattern query and additional criteria. The following is the list of our salient contributions:

- We present a language for top-k complex event processing and pattern ranking over data streams.
- We show that top-k sequence pattern matching problem can be posed in the form of a shortest path problem on so called *stratified stream graphs*. We propose a novel stratified-graph based k-shortest path algorithm (k-SSP) that leverages the stratified nature of the data graphs to locate best sequence match results quickly and incrementally. We then extend the algorithm to handle dynamically evolving data graphs without wasting resources for redundant re-computations as data graph evolves over time (k-DSSP).
- We propose an adaptive join scheduling strategy for TA and NRA top-k join processing algorithms [11] to combine multiple sequence pattern match results (potentially coming from different distributed streams). The proposed strategy is designed to tackle run-time variations in the data streams (e.g., variations in sorted and random access costs, join rates) without having to assume *a priori* presence of reliable data statistics (which are often impossible to assume in data streams). In particular, when dealing with a top-k join query with varying costs for sorted- and random-accesses for different data queues, the proposed *waste avoiding boundary selection (WABS)* approach adapts and re-schedules access orders to minimize the overall join cost.
- We experimentally evaluate the algorithms and compare against existing solutions under various scenarios.

1.2 Organization of the Paper

The paper is organized as follows: In the next section, we present the related work. In Section 3.1, we define the top-k pattern matching problem and in Section 3.2, we provide an overview of the overall system. Then in the following two sections, two core algorithms and the corresponding modules of the proposed system are described in detail. In Section 6, we experimentally evaluate the algorithms and the system. In Section 7, we conclude the paper.

2. RELATED WORK

2.1 Complex Event Processing

Early work on complex event processing were motivated by the limitations of DBMSs to scale to the performance requirements of publish/subscribe applications [9]. One of the earliest complex event processing works is SASE [25], which combines a series of optimization strategies to deal with classic sequence pattern queries on large scale of stream data. SASE includes plan based query monitoring and takes advantage of an extended NFA scheme to handle multiple queries at the same time. Later improvements on this work include [1, 26]. [7] presents Cayuga, another general purpose event monitoring system. Similar to the SASE, Cayuga focuses on pattern monitoring over large data sets and provides an automata-based pattern matching engine. The query language syntax used in Cayuga is similar to relational database query languages and, compared to SASE, is able to express more general queries.

These two automata-based works have been followed by many other approaches to large scale pattern matching. For instance, in [17], a petri-net based query model is proposed. Recent work in complex event processing also focused on out-of-order and uncertain events. proposed a K-Slack algorithm with K-delayed purging; i.e.,an out-of-order event is discarded if it is beyond a K boundary. [21] also deals with out-of-order events but proposes a stack-based mechanism to manage the events. Instead of focusing on patterns, [5, 13, 14] focus on ranking and aggregation of tuples in the input stream. [23] considers uncertainties that exist in timestamps and event attributes and focus on efficient evaluation of aggregates and joins under accuracy requirements.

In this paper, we note that most existing mechanisms (including the automata based approaches) are suitable for scenarios where one needs to retrieve all matches to the user's query. For top-k queries, where only a select few matches are required, these approaches would be highly inefficient due to their need to first retrieving all matches. Therefore, we present k shortest paths and top-k join based scheme which can handle top-k CEP queries efficiently, without enumerating all matches.

2.2 Top-k Join Processing

Ranked join algorithms, including [10, 11] and others, rely on weight-sorted input streams for pruning unpromising matches when identifying top matches to the users query. In one of the earlier works, Fagin [10] proposed an algorithm, known commonly as the FA, which assumes the availability of both the sorted and random accesses to the data. FA considers data from the sources in (progressively) descending order of desirability and, with the help of random accesses, enumerates top-k join results without having to access all the data from these sources. Later improvements to FA include the threshold algorithm (TA), which pro-actively schedules random accesses when they are cheap, and the no-random access algorithm (NRA), which is applicable when random-accesses are either unavailable or extremely costly [11].

Among these and other variants to the top-k join processing problem, a key challenge is to identify an appropriate *schedule* which states in which order the incoming data queues will be considered and how sorted and random accesses will be alternated. [12] attempts to leverage a greedy gradient based heuristic for reaching the threshold condition earlier. [3] assumes a priori knowledge of the distribution for each join queue and predicts the potential costs and rewards for expanding each queue. [24] addresses scenarios where different predicates have different costs. The algorithm collects statistics and picks an appropriate schedule in the runtime. In contrast, in this paper, we focus on situations (common in distributes scenarios) where reliable statistics about incoming streams are hard to obtain and that access costs and join rates can change over time.

2.3 k Shortest Paths

In this paper, we rely on graph-based techniques to enumerate sequence patterns. The k-shortest paths problem dates back to early 1950s. Early solutions include Yen's algorithm [18], which is known to have a computational complexity of $O(kn^3)$, where n is the number of vertices. Later works by Lawler [20] and Katoh et $al.$ [19] improved the basic Yen's algorithm, but the worse case complexity stays $O(kn^3)$. A recent improvement on Yen's approach can be found in [15]. Another approach to the k-shortest paths, differing significantly from Yen's work, with worst running complexity of $O(m+nlog(n)+klog(k))$, where m is the number of edges, has been proposed by Eppstein in [8] and a lazy version of this algorithm has been presented in [16]. While approaches similar to Yen's work on undirected graphs, Eppstein's algorithm works on directed graphs. Secondly, while Yen's algorithm returns only simple paths, Eppstein's algorithm can also identify paths with repeated nodes. However, while Yen's algorithm can work incrementally, Eppstein's approach is unable to obtain k-shortest paths in an incremental manner. Other approaches to this problem includes [2], an A-* search based approach that is able to deal with situations where only partial graphs can be loaded into the main memory. This also has the same worst case complexity as Eppstein's algorithm and, similarly, is not incremental.

In this paper, we propose k shortest paths algorithms that leverage the stratified nature of the data graphs that need to be considered during CEP processing for improved efficiency and that incrementally maintain the list of top-k shortest paths in the presence of dynamically evolving graphs.

3. OVERVIEW OF CPR

3.1 Notation and Query Language

As is common in complex event processing literature, we use **E** to represent event classes and **e** for event instances belonging to event class, E. Each event class, E, has certain associated attributes (**E.A**) and different event instances may have different values for these attributes. The timestamp, **t**, represents arrival time associated to each event instance.

Then we define a sequence pattern (**SEQ**) as follows:

SEQ	S_i
WITH	Event classes
WITHIN	Window constraints
WHERE	Additional constraints
PREF	Preference specification

Where, a sequence pattern (S_i) consists of a series of event classes defined in the "WITH" clause. In the "WITHIN" clause, we define the window constraint for S_i and only consider event instances within the window as valid. In addition to these patterns, users can specify predicates on the attributes of involved events; we refer to these as **addi-**

PATTERN	Sequence/Conjunction/Disjunction
WITH	Sequence Patterns (SEQs)
WITHIN	Window constraints
WHERE	Additional constraints
PREF	Preference specification
RETURN	Number of results to be returned

Figure 2: Top-k query pattern

tional constraints. The user can also provide a **preference specification** stating how the sequence matches should be ranked, where a sequence match is the combination of event instances that satisfy the sequence pattern.

For complex pattern queries, we consider three patterns over different sequence pattern: **Sequence,** $(S_i ; S_j)_w$, means all event instances of a sequence match of S_i occur before the ones of S_j within a time window w. **Disjunction,** $(S_i \parallel S_j)_w$, means a sequence match of either S_i or S_j occurs within w. **Conjunction,** $(S_i \& S_j)_w$, means sequence matches of both S_i and S_j must occur within w. Even more complex patterns can be constructed by replacing S_i and S_j above with other patterns.

The overall structure of a query statement is given in Figure 2. The "PATTERN" clause includes the pattern specification statements on sequences specified in the "WITH" clause. Similar to the sequence pattern, the "WITHIN" clause also defines the "window" within which we consider sequence matches as valid. Note that the "window" defined here provides a further constraint for each "window" defined by a sequence query. If one sequence query has a current window w_i beyond the overall window w, we only consider the part w_i overlapping with w as valid. In the "WHERE" part, additional constraints on attributes of events cross different sequence patterns are provided. The preference specification is provided within a "PREF" clause, which decides how scores from different sequence patterns are merged. The "RETURN" clause specifies the number of target results. An example was provided in Figure 1.

3.2 Architectural Overview

We propose to tackle the problem of top-k pattern detection over data streams by splitting it into two sub-problems:

- *Top-k sequence detection and maintenance:* The first problem we tackle in this paper is to detect and maintain top-k sequence matches. Unlike existing approaches to pattern detection, in this paper, we propose a graph-based approach. In particular, we show that given a sequence pattern, events in the current window can be modeled as a *stratified graph*. We then develop efficient k shortest path algorithms for the detection and incremental maintenance of top-k sequences over stratified graphs. The proposed approach enables us to focus on top-k matches directly without enumerating all results and then ranking them.

- *Top-k complex pattern detection and maintenance:* As we mentioned earlier, complex patterns can be seen as combinations of simpler sequence patterns. Therefore, top-k complex patterns can be enumerated by joining matches for sequence patterns. The challenge, of course, is to perform this combination efficiently and obtain top-k complex pattern matches without having to enumerate too many matches for the constituting simple sequence patterns.

As can be seen in Figure 3, our CPR framework consists of three modules: (a) an *event processing module (EPM)*, (b)

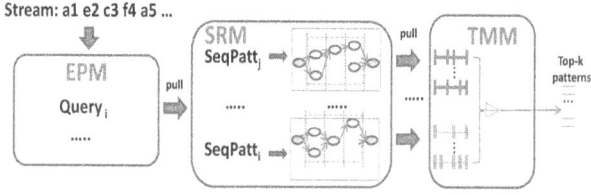

Figure 3: Architectural overview of CPR framework

(a) Sequence pattern   (b) Input stream

(c) Stratified stream graph

Figure 4: Stratified graph example

a *sequence ranking module (SRM)*, and (c) a *top-k merge module (TMM)*. EPM handles query registration and event dispatching. In *SRM*, we have one data structure for each sequence pattern in the query. *SRM* exposes access interfaces for sorted and random accesses for the next *TMM* module that combines partial results it pulls from its input queues into complex pattern rankings.

Since the costs of sorted access and random accesses to different pattern queues can be drastically different (and may depend on the incoming data), it is the responsibility of *TMM* to decide in which order the partial results will be pulled from the input queues and when random accesses (as opposed to sorted accesses) will be scheduled. The *SRM* module operates on an *on-demand* basis and *incrementally* produces additional sequence matches (in decreasing order of preference) as requested by *TMM*.

The output of the system is the list of top-k matches to the CEP query within the current window, ordered by the preference function, and maintained current as the stream evolves. When the time window moves, the top-k results are updated incrementally: this involves incremental updates to the sequence matches by *SRM* and incremental updates to the top-k merged matches by the *TMM*.

Example: Let us reconsider the query in Figure 1, where we have two sequence queries S_1 and S_2. The first sequence query S_1 can be considered as two sub sequence queries $s_{1,1}$ and $s_{1,2}$, where $s_{1,1}$ queries "A;B;C" sequence with Max[A.exp+B.exp+C.exp] and "A.CCID" = "B.CCID" = "C.CCID". $s_{1,2}$ ranks "A;C" sequence with "A.CCID" = "C.CCID" based on [$C.t - A.t$]. The "WINDOW" constraint for both of them stays the same as in S_1. Together in $s_{1,1}$ and $s_{1,2}$, we seek to find instances of the sequence "A;B;C" with the highest total purchase expense and the shortest time span between A and C. In S_2, we simply look for sequence matches of "D;E" with highest total purchase expense. Overall, we try to find the person that has highest expenditure sum over "A;B;C" and "D;E", and the shortest time span over purchase of "A" and "C". Suppose the events in current window are "a1 d2 b3 e4 a5 c6 e7 c8". *EPM* picks events "a1 b3 a5 c6 c8" and forwards them to *SRM* in the form of a stream. Simultaneously, *EPM* also picks "a1 a5 c6 c8" and forwards them to another instance of *SRM* as a different stream. *SRM* enumerates "A;B;C" sequence matches in decreasing order of total expenditure and makes these available to *TMM*. The second instance of *SRM* enumerates the "A" and "C" pairs in decreasing order of span and makes these available to *TMM*. For S_2, similarly, *EPM* picks "d2 e4 e7" to another *SRM* instance, where matches are presented in decreasing order of total expenditure by *SRM*. Finally, *TMM* performs rank-joins on the "A;B;C" and "A;C" sequence matches based on the IDs of "A" and "C" events, simultaneously rank-joins on the "A;B;C" or "A;C" with matches of "D;E" based on the IDs of "A" and "D" to identify the top results best satisfying both the overall

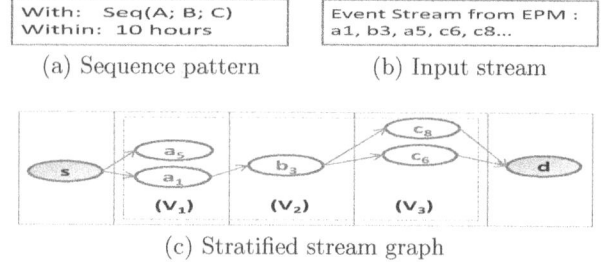

preference requirements. Since the overall preference specification in Figure 1 includes an "AND" operator, in this case *TMM* will use an appropriate score merge function (such as "min" [10]) that can represent fuzzy conjunction.

4. SEQUENCE RANKING

In this section, we propose a graph-based approach to discover highly ranked sequences within an input stream. This algorithm forms the core of the sequence ranking module (SRM) and operates when the preference function is *linear*[1]. When the preference function is non-linear, the enumeration process is handled directly by the top-k join module.

4.1 Stratifie Stream Graph

Given a sequence pattern, S, and a finite stream window, *str*, we represent the input pattern and the data in the stream, in the form of a *stratified graph*.

DEFINITION 1 (STRATIFIED GRAPH). *An acyclic directed graph $G(V, E)$ is a p-stratified graph if the set of vertices V can be partitioned into p non-overlapping sets, V_1 through V_p, such that the vertices in partition (or stratum) V_i have incoming edges only from the vertices in V_{i-1} and have outgoing edges to only those vertices in V_{i+1}.*

The stratified graph is constructed as follows: Firstly, for each event type in the sequence pattern, we initialize a set (or stratum) of vertices. Then, for each event instance in the input data stream, we create one new vertex for each corresponding event type in the sequence pattern and insert these vertices into the corresponding vertex strata. Then, for each pair of event instances in strata V_i and V_{i+1}, we check if they satisfy the same order in the data stream and if so, we add a directed edge from the vertex in stratum V_i to the vertex in V_{i+1}. We also create two dummy vertices, "start vertex" and "end vertex" denoted as s and d, such that s points to all vertices in strata V_1 and d is pointed by all vertices in strata V_p.[2] Figure 4 (a) shows an example.

THEOREM 1. *Let S be a sequence pattern and let str be a finite data stream (e.g., constrained by a window). There exists a stratified graph, $G_{S,str}$, that corresponds to the pattern S and the stream str.*

The proof follows trivially from the construction process.

---

[1] In fact, any *monoid* function would be admissible. For simplicity, in this paper, we only consider linear preference functions for sequence ranking by SRM.

[2] Our constructed stratified graph is similar to the stack based match buffer in automata based approach (e.g. SASE[1]), which enables our algorithms described below to be easily extended for existing approaches.

4.2 Preference Function and Vertex Weights

In a given stratified stream graph, each vertex corresponds to an event instance and these event instances can have associated attribute values. Given a *linear* preference function, $f()$, on these attribute values, we can then encode the contribution of each event-attribute to the preference function in the form of vertex weights: Let e_i of type E_j be an event instance in vertex stratum V_j and let the contribution of E_j to the *linear preference* function, $f()$, be $(c \times E_j.a_k)$ for attribute, a_k. Then,

- if we seek to minimize $f()$, we annotate the vertex corresponding to e_i with weight $(c \times e_i.a_k)$;
- if, on the other hand, we seek to maximize $f()$, we annotate the vertex weight $(-c \times e_i.a_k)$;

For example, in the query given in Figure 1, we want to find a sequence with the *largest* total expenditure. Thus, each event instance, e_i, will be annotated with $-e_i.exp$.

THEOREM 2   (RANKED SEQUENCE ENUMERATION).
Given a stratified graph, $G(V,E)$, whose vertices are weighted according to a linear *preference function, $f()$, (a) each sequence match corresponds to a path from the special node $s \in V$ to the node $d \in V$; and (b) the smaller the overall weight of the path is, the better its rank with respect to the target preference function and the given maximization/minimization criterion.*

The proof of the theorem follows from the associativity of the linear preference functions and acyclicity of the stratified stream graphs. This theorem enables us to reformulate the ranked sequence enumeration problem in the form of the ranked shortest path enumeration (or k-shortest path, KSP) problem over the given weighted stratified stream graph. While there are a number of solutions to the KSP problem, including Yen's [18, 6] and Eppstein's [8, 16] algorithms, a straight-forward adoption of existing algorithms KSP algorithms is not appropriate for ranked sequence enumeration over data streams: (a) firstly, existing KSP algorithms are not designed to take advantage of the stratified and vertex-weighted nature of the stream graphs; (b) secondly (and more importantly). Therefore, we first develop a KSP algorithm that leverages the stratified nature of the stream graphs and then discuss how to extend this algorithm to dynamically evolving graphs.

4.3 Stratified K-Shortest Path Algorithm

In this subsection, we develop an efficient k-shortest path algorithm for *static* stratified graphs. We note that stratified stream graphs are (a) acyclic and directed, (b) edges exist only between neighboring strata, (c) (assuming that events are indexed such that the earlier an event, the lower its in-stratum index) if there exists an edge between vertex pair from $v_{i,j}$, (i.e. vertex v_i in stratum V_j), to vertex $v_{i',j+1}$, (i.e. vertex v_i' in stratum V_{j+1}), there exist edges between all pairs $v_{m,j}$, and $v_{i',j+1}$, $1 \le m \le i$, and (d) the graph is vertex-weighted (as opposed to edge weighted).

We leverage the stratified nature of the input graph to construct a **pattern query array** (PQ-Array) data structure[3]: For each stratum, V_j, we create an array A_j; then, for each vertex, $v_{i,j} \in V_j$ (i.e. the ith vertex of V_j), we insert a triple $\langle minWeight, hPtr, vPtr \rangle$ into A_j:

[3]Note that PQ-Array data structure is reminiscent of the *pathstack* [4] used in XML path matching, though it is structured, constructed, and used differently.

```
Algorithm: Stratified-Shortest-Path
Input:
    PQ-Array; v_s /* v_s is the vertex where the shortest path starts
    */;
Output:
    the shortest-path p from v_s to end vertex d
Procedure:
    V_1 = {v_s}
    hPtr(v_s) = s
    for each stratum V_j (j= 2,3,...,|V|) do
        for each vertex v_{i,j} in stratum V_j do
            v_p = hPtr(v_{i,j});
            w_p = weight(v_{i,j}) + minWeight(v_p); /*smallest sum path
            with v_{i,j} */
            w_c = minWeight(v_{i-1,j}); /*smallest sum path without
            v_{i,j}*/
            if w_p ≤ w_c then
                minWeight(v_{i,j}) = w_p;
                vPtr(v_{i,j}) = v_{i,j};
            else
                minWeight(v_{i,j}) = w_c;
                v_c = vPtr(v_{i-1,j});
                vPtr(v_{i,j}) = v_c;
            end if
        end for
    end for
    find the best path p by following hPtr and vPtr from the end
    event d to start event s;
    return p;
```

Figure 5: Stratified shortest path algorithm (SSP)

- *minWeight* stores the best known total vertex weight (i.e. shortest path weight) from s to $v_{i,j}$;
- *hPtr* points (*horizontally*) to the latest vertex in the previous stratum that has an edge to $v_{i,j}$; and
- *vPtr* points (*vertically*) to the vertex that is *before or identical to* $v_{i,j}$ in stratum V_j and has the smallest *minWeight*. If two events before or identical to $v_{i,j}$ have the same smallest *minWeight*, then *vPtr* points to the later event.

Initially, for each vertex, *minWeight* is set to ∞ and *vPtr* is set to *null* ($\perp$). The start tuple, s, has both its *hPtr* and *vPtr* as $\perp$ and its *minWeight* is set to 0.

4.3.1 Shortest Path on a Stratified Graph

We first develop an algorithm for finding the *shortest* path from a given vertex v_s to the end vertex d in a stratified graph (Figure 5); this is later used as a sub-module in the k-shortest paths algorithm. The stratified shortest path algorithm uses dynamic programming on the *PQ-Array* data structure. The algorithm works by finding the shortest sub-path from s to the current stratum at each iteration and processing the next stratum in the following iteration. Once the algorithm completes, we can enumerate the shortest path by moving backwards among the strata: this is achieved by following *hPtr* from one stratum to the previous one and then following the *vPtr* within the current stratum (to locate the vertex on the shortest path in the current stratum). Note that the use of two pointers to track backwards (as opposed to only one) leverages the properties of the stratified stream graphs to enable the algorithm to compute in $O(|v|)$ time and, as we will see later, enables efficient dynamic updates on the graph.

Proof Sketch for the Correctness of SSP First, for each vertex $v_{i,j}$ in stratum V_j, we compute two values w_p and w_c. w_p stores the total weight of the shortest sub-path from s to $v_{i,j}$ and w_c stores the total weight of shortest sub-path from s to any $v_{m,j}$ where $m < i$. Then we use the smallest of w_p and w_c as *minWeight* and update the *vPtr* as itself or as v_m,

Algorithm: k-Stratified-Shortest-Path
Input:
PQ-Array; k;
Output:
k shortest paths
Procedure:
p = Stratified-Shortest-Path(PQ-Array, s) ; /*shortest path from s*/
put p into the k shortest paths list $\mathcal{L}$;
while not k results yet **do**
  get the last added path p_{last} from the $\mathcal{L}$
  for the jth vertex v_j in p_{last} **do**
    restore the original PQ-Array;
    weight(v_{j+1}) = ∞;
    for each path p_i, $i = 1, 2, ..., |\mathcal{L}| - 1$ in l **do**
      if p_i shares the same sub-path $p_{sub,1}$ from start vertex s to v_j (excluding v_j) with p_{last} **then**
        set the weight of next vertex of v_j in p_i as ∞;
      end if
    end for
    $p_{sub,2}$ = Stratified-Shortest-Path(PQ-Array', v_j); /* shortest path from v_j to the end */
    combine $p_{sub,1}$ and $p_{sub,2}$ to obtain p'
    insert the combined path p' into candidate heap $\mathcal{H}_{cand}$;
  end for
  remove top from $\mathcal{H}_{cand}$ and insert it to $\mathcal{L}$
end while
return $\mathcal{L}$

Figure 6: k stratified shortest path algorithm (k-SSP)

correspondingly. *vPtr* points to the latest vertex $v_{i',j}$ ($i' \leq i$) in V_j that provides the shortest path weight until stratum V_j. An inductive proof over the strata can show that this ensures that the overall shortest path weight corresponds to the *minWeight* of the end vertex d. To enumerate the shortest path itself, the algorithm follows the *hPtr* and *vPtr* backwards from d until it reaches s. Since the *hPtr* links each event to a relevant event in the previous stratum and since *vPtr* links to the latest event with the highest score (which occurs earlier than the event of interest) in that stratum, an inductive proof that iterates over the strata can show that this provides the shortest path.

Complexity of SSP: The SSP algorithm works in $O(|v|)$ time, because each vertex is considered only once and for each vertex only one incoming edge is investigated

4.3.2 k Shortest Paths on a Stratifie Graph

Once the shortest path in the stratified stream graph is found, we locate the k shortest paths incrementally (Figure 6): to find the ith shortest path, we use the previously discovered $(i-1)$ shortest paths (denoted as $paths_{cur}$). We create a min-heap to store potential candidates for the ith shortest path. For each vertex v of the $(i-1)$th shortest path (denoted as $path_{last}$), we check if there is a path $p \in paths_{cur}$ sharing the sub-path from the start event, s, to current vertex, v. If so, we set the value of the vertex following v on p to ∞. After this resetting of the vertex value, we re-apply the shortest path algorithm described above to find the shortest path p_{sub} from v in this revised stratified graph, combine p_{sub} with the sub path from s to v in $path_{last}$, and store it in the candidate heap. After this, we pick the path with the smallest value from the candidate heap and mark it as the ith shortest path. This process continues until we find all required k shortest paths; the algorithm completes in $O((sk)^2 + |v|sk)$, where $|v|$ is the number of vertices (i.e., events in the current window), s is the number of strata (i.e., the sequence pattern length), and k is the number of shortest paths required. Note that the complexity of the algorithm is significantly lower than that of conventional KSP algorithms (see Section 2) for small k and s.

Algorithm:
k-Dynamic-Stratified-Shortest-Path
Input:
PQ-Array, k, $\mathcal{L}$, $\mathcal{E}_{old}$, $\mathcal{E}_{new}$ /* $\mathcal{L}$ is the list of existing k shortest paths, $\mathcal{E}_{old}$ denotes the set of expired events, and $\mathcal{E}$ denotes the set of new events */
Output:
updated k shortest paths $\mathcal{L}$
Procedure:
1. update PQ-Array to PQ-Array$'$ by removing out-dated events;
2. remove paths with out-dated event from existing k shortest paths list $\mathcal{L}$;
3. complete $\mathcal{L}$ by calling *k-Stratified-Shortest-Path(PQ-Array', k)* in the PQ-Array' for r next shortest paths, where r equals to the number of removed paths;
4. move remaining k shortest paths from $\mathcal{L}$ into a temp list $\mathcal{L}_{old}$
5. set weights of each non-expired vertex v in the last stratum of PQ-Array' as ∞;
6.
for each vertex $v_{i,j}$ corresponding to a new event ordered by time **do**
  insert $v_{i,j}$ into stratum V_j;
  $hPtr(v_{i,j}) = v_{l,j-1}$ /*$v_{l,j-1}$ is the latest vertex in stratum V_j*/
end for
7.find k shortest paths in the new PQ-Array" by calling *Stratified-Shortest-Paths(PQ-Array$''$, k)* and put them into list $\mathcal{L}_{new}$ /*PQ-Array$''$ denotes the updated PQ-Array after inserting new events*/
8. pull the k shortest paths from $\mathcal{L}_{old}$ and $\mathcal{L}_{new}$ and put into $\mathcal{L}$.
9. restore weights of vertices previously set as ∞ in the last stratum
return $\mathcal{L}$

Figure 7: k Dynamic Stratified Shortest Paths algorithm (k-DSSP)

Proof Sketch for the Correctness of k-SSP: To prove the correctness of *k-Stratified-Shortest-Paths* algorithm, we first assert that the mth shortest path p_m must coincide with the $(m-1)^{th}$ shortest path p_{m-1} until some j^{th} vertex, $j = 1, 2, ...s$, where s is the number of strata. When $j = 1$, it means two paths only coincide in the start vertex, which is trivial since the start vertex is a dummy vertex. Suppose p_m and p_{m-1} coincide until the jth vertex. The algorithm sets the weight of the next vertex of all top $(m-1)$ paths that share first j^{th} vertex with p_m as ∞. This ensures that no new discovered shortest path will be the same as the previous $(m-1)$ shortest paths from the $(j+1)^{th}$ vertex. The algorithm considers all vertices in p_{m-1} (except the last dummy end vertex) and, for each case, it identifies a candidate shortest path (maintaining at most k candidates). The initial assertion ensures that the mth shortest path will be among the candidates that have been enumerated.

Complexity of k-SSP: When we compute the mth shortest path p_m, we need to investigate the graph for each vertex v in the $(m-1)^{th}$ path p_{m-1} and find the shortest path from v in it. Since this includes setting values for each of the previous shortest paths in their first i vertices coinciding with p_{m-1} and performing a shortest path search, the worst case time complexity of this step is $O(sm + |v|)$, which is $O(sk + |v|)$. Since each vertex in each of the s strata of the $(m-1)^{th}$ shortest path needs to be considered, this step takes $O((sk + |v|)s)$ time. Then, computing k results takes in the worst case $O((sk + |v|)sk)$ or $O((sk)^2 + |v|sk)$ time.

4.4 k-Shortest Paths on Dynamic Graphs

The algorithm described above leverages the stratified nature of the stream graphs to significantly reduce the cost of shortest path enumeration. However, when used naively, it would need to recompute paths from scratch each time the window shifts over the data stream. It is easy to see that this would be wasteful since, with high likelihood, many of the top-k paths may need to be kept even after the shift.

The algorithm for keeping the top-k pattern matches up-to-date as the *PQ-Array* data structure changes over time is shown in Figure 7. Suppose we already have k results for the current window. When the window shifts, some of the events, $\mathcal{E}_{old}$, will expire and some new events new events $\mathcal{E}_{new}$ will need to be considered.

We first consider the expired events. The first step of the algorithm updates the PQ-Array data structure appropriately. In the second step, any path that contains any event in $\mathcal{E}_{old}$ is dropped from the set, $paths_{cur}$, of current top-k paths. Let us assume that there remains $k' \leq k$ paths in $paths_{cur}$. Before we consider newly arriving events, we rerun the previously described k stratified shortest paths algorithm to discover $(k - k')$ new shortest paths.

We next consider the new events in the window. First we update the PQ-Array data structure with the new events. We then identify new candidate shortest paths by constraining the new paths to pass through at least one of the new events in the window. The final result is obtained by combining all the candidate paths to select the k shortest ones.

The worst case complexity of the algorithm is $O((sk)^2 + |v|sk)$ as before; however, as the experiments in Section 6 show, the worst case rarely happens.

Proof Sketch for the Correctness of k-DSSP: First, in Steps 1 and 2 of k-DSSP, we simply remove vertices corresponding to outdated events from the PQ-Array and outdated paths from the current k-shortest paths list $\mathcal{L}$. Now PQ-Array becomes PQ-Array'. In Step 3, we locate new shortest paths in the remaining set of vertices (i.e. PQ-Array') to increase the number of candidate shortest paths back to k. The remaining steps update the candidate set based on the new events in the window: The process (and the proof) are similar to k-SSP. The key to its correctness and efficiency are Steps 5 and 6. In Step 5, the algorithm temporarily sets the weights of all remaining vertices in the last stratum V_s of PQ-Array' to ∞. We observe that any remaining vertex v in V_s cannot be part of a new path, since all new vertices are later than v in terms of their corresponding timestamps. Other remaining vertices, on the other hand, can be part of new paths and, thus, we need to further consider them. Step 5 ensures that each of the new discovered paths will go through at least one new event in the last stratum. Since in Steps 1 through 3 we have found all k shortest paths going through one of the current vertices in V_s, we now only need to search for paths with at least one new added event. Step 6 revises the PQ-Array. Since new coming events are ordered by time, we can insert event one by one into PQ-Array in their time order. Each time we insert one event $v_{i,j}$ (i.e. the ith vertex in stratum V_j), we set its $hPtr$ as the current last vertex $v_{l,j-1}$ in its previous stratum V_{j-1}, since events inserted later into V_{j-1} will have no edge to $v_{i,j}$. Once the k-SSP algorithm is executed on the revised PQ-Array data structure, due to the careful placement of ∞ weights, the newly discovered shortest paths are guaranteed to go through at least one new event, ensuring that no paths are redundantly discovered. Finally in Step 9, we restore the weight of each vertex whose weight was temporarily set as ∞ in Step 5. This is because some of the previous paths containing such a vertex but not in the ear-

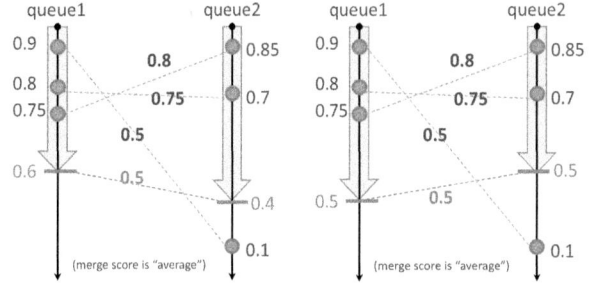

Figure 8: Two alternative termination *boundaries* that provide the same threshold (0.5) needed to commit top-3 candidates

lier top-k shortest paths list are now possible to be in top-k after the update of PQ-Array. By restoring the weights in Step 9, we ensure that those paths can still be considered.

Complexity of k-DSSP: Since the revision of the PQ-Array data structure takes only $O(|v|)$ time, the worst case complexity of k-DSSP is similar to that of k-SSP.

5. TOP-K MERGE MODULE (TMM)

When a complex query pattern includes combinations of multiple sequence patterns or when we need to deal with non-linear preference functions, the top-k merge module (*TMM*) is used for producing and ranking combined results. As mentioned earlier, as the window moves, *TMM* incrementally updates to the top-k merged matches[4]. Since disjunction can be handled by picking the highest scoring entries from the input queues, in this section, we focus on conjunctive patterns which require top-k joins.

5.1 Thresholds, Boundaries, and Scheduling

As discussed in Section 2, there are many top-k join algorithms, differing in the way the sorted and random accesses are scheduled and how the stopping condition is sought. The TA algorithm [22], for example, maintains the lower bound, lb, of the candidate results discovered so far and also computes an upper bound, ub, on the best value of the undiscovered objects; i.e., a *threshold* that the value of lb has to pass to declare the candidate objects as the top ones. When $lb \geq ub$, TA stops and returns the results found so far. NRA algorithm [11] also works similarly, but unlike TA which aggressively schedules random accesses to keep the lower bound as high as possible, the NRA algorithm does not schedule any random accesses. Consequently, the lb and ub cross later than in TA. In other words, NRA trades-off random accesses for sorted accesses as a scheduling strategy.

Even when TA or NRA is selected a priori, there is still room for improving the number of accesses to the input queues. The difficulty in both cases is that there can be different ways to reach the termination *boundary* (where the lower bound of seen and upper bound of unseen objects cross – Figure 8). Thus, the goal of any scheduling strategy would be to access the queues in an order in which the stopping condition is reached as early as possible. This requires the ability, at any given point in time, to *predict* the distance – in terms of execution time– to the termination condition for each alternative access option. [11] relies on a round-robin based strategy that does not give preference to any of the in-

---
[4]Due to space constraints, we only present the operation of *TMM* in a single window. However, experiments in Section 6 also shows the impact of the incremental operation of *TMM*.

```
Algorithm:
Waste-Avoiding-Boundary-Selection
Input:
    data queues, dq; k;
Output:
    Top-k results R;
Procedure:
    apply existing approach (e.g. round-robin) to find the top-2 re-
    sults and put top-2 results into R
    if k > 2 then
        while i <= k − 1 do
            for each alternative termination boundary, β*_{i−1} among the
            newly discovered data entries between boundaries β_{i−1} and
            β_i do
                /*lb_{i−1} is the score of β_{i−1}*/
                if score(β*_{i−1}) ≤ lb_{i−1} && cost(β*_{i−1}) < minCost then
                    minCost = cost(β*_{i−1}); /*initially, minCost = ∞*/
                    for h = 1, 2, . . . , |q| do
                        a_h = access-ratio(β*_{i−1},h); /*access-ratio(β*_{i−1},h) is
                        the overall ratio of accesses to queue q_h according to
                        β*_{i−1}*/
                    end for
                end if
            end for
            while TRUE do
                ∀ h = 1, 2, . . . , |q|, schedule a_h accesses to q_h
                /*let u be the number of results found*/
                put the new u results into R;
                i = i+u;
                if u > 0 then
                    break;
                end if
            end while
        end while
    end if
    return R
```

Figure 9: Waste-Avoiding Boundary Selection
Strategy (WABS)

put queues. [12] attempts to reach the termination condition
by always accessing to the data queue that has the steep-
est current core gradient. This, however, fails to account
for the differences in the sorted and random access costs
for different input queues. [24] addresses situations where
different queues have different costs by collecting statistics
and picking an optimized schedule in the runtime. The algorithm, however, needs statistics that can properly represent
the whole data set (obtained through sampling of the whole
data set), and as we will see in the experiments, when joining set of sequences that have not even been enumerated,
effective samples are not always available.

5.2 Waste-Avoiding Boundary Selection

When searching for the kth best result after the $(k−1)^{th}$ is
located, the ideal strategy would be the one that requires the
least amount of time to locate the next termination boundary. We refer to this as the *waste-avoiding* strategy and
the corresponding boundary as the *waste-avoiding boundary*.
Prior work tries to predict the score gradient, data/score
distribution, join selectivity, and/or access costs to seek the
waste-avoiding boundary. These are neither trivial tasks,
nor (as the experiments in Section 6.4 show) work very well
for combining dynamically generated sequences. In this paper, we propose to tackle this difficulty by a *continuously
adaptive boundary targeting* strategy which relies on the following simple assumption: *"the best scheduling strategy to
locate the termination boundary for the $(i+1)^{th}$ result will
have changed less drastically since the $(i−1)^{th}$ result than
since the $(i−j)^{th}$ result, for $j > 1$"*. This implies that we
can reduce the waste in the search for the $(i+1)^{th}$ boundary
if we could find the best strategy for the $(i−1)^{th}$ boundary

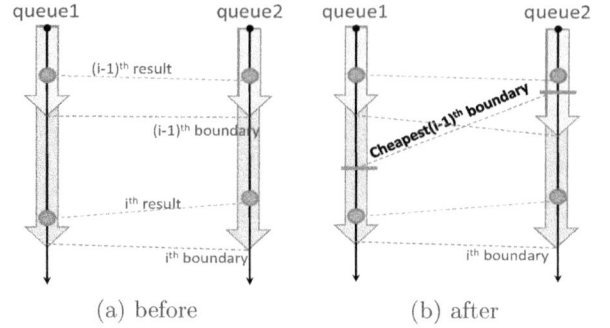

(a) before   (b) after

Figure 10: Revision of the $(i−1)^{th}$ boundary

in the light of the most recent inputs (possibly revising any
boundary found earlier) and use this to guide the search.

We provide the pseudo-code for the *waste-avoiding boundary selection (WABS)* strategy in Figure 9. In a given window, the strategy proceeds stepwise seeking the stopping
conditions for 1st, 2nd, . . . , and k^{th} results incrementally.
The strategy is revised between each consecutive pair of results. Let σ_i denote the access strategy (i.e., access ratios
for each queue) used for identifying the boundary β_i, for
the ith result, with combined score, lb_i. The boundaries for
the first two results are sought using an existing technique,
such as round-robin or gradient-based approaches. Let us
assume that we already have reached the ith ($i \geq 2$) boundary and we are seeking the boundary for the $(i+1)^{th}$ result
(Figure 10(a)). In order to revise the access strategy for
this boundary, we search for alternative ways to achieve the
boundary $\beta_{i−1}$ (the boundary for the $(i−1)^{th}$ result) also
taking into account the data entries accessed between the
enumeration of $(i−1)^{th}$ and i^{th} results.

We achieve this by considering newly discovered data entries (in increasing order of score) and see if they would lead
to a boundary combination with score $\leq lb_{i−1}$ with all the
data entries discovered so far. For each alternative combination whose overall score is $\leq lb_{i−1}$, we assess (based on
the actual access times that have been observed) how long
it would have taken the algorithm to reach to that particular combination of entries and locate the *cheapest* boundary
among all alternatives (Figure 10(b)). Once located, we use
the relative ratios of entries in each queue for this boundary
combination as the revised access strategy, $\sigma'_{i−1}$.

Since it represents the most locally-informed and least
wasteful boundary decision available, WABS then uses strategy $\sigma'_{i−1}$ to seek the threshold for the next result (i.e., as the
strategy σ_{i+1}). Let us assume that there are m queues and
between the $(i−1)^{th}$ and i^{th} results, Δ_j data entries are
accessed on the jth queue. The cost of strategy adaptation depends on the sizes of Δ_j and how far one has to go
back to discover a combination with threshold $\tau_{i−1}$. As we
will see in the experiments section, the cost of this process
is smaller than other techniques and, especially within the
context of complex event processing, negligible with respect
to the gains in access time.

6. EXPERIMENTS

In this section, we evaluate the proposed top-k complex pattern ranking framework and the underlying algorithms. We describe two sets of experiments: first, we evaluate the algorithms underlying the sequence ranking module (SRM). Second, we assess the effectiveness of the waste-

Parameters for the top-k sequence match experiments	
k	number of results to be returned
ref	relative event frequency
sl	sequence length
ws	window size
step	window shift length
Additional parameters for top-k joins on sensor data	
mf	merge function
rss	relative sensor selectivity
q	number of input queues
qp	query pattern

Table 1: Experiment parameters

Sequence queries used for the top-k sequence match experiments	
S1: sequence with ref=1X	EG EH EN
S2: sequence with ref=10X	EG EH EO
S3: sequence with ref=89X	EG EH EJ
S4: sequence with length 2	EG EH
S5: sequence with length 3	EG EH EJ
S6: sequence with length 4	EG EH EJ EI
Sequence queries used for top-k joins on sensor data	
S7	EG EH EJ
S8	EK EL EM
S9	EI EN EO
S10	EG EH
S11	EJ EK EL EM

Table 2: Sequence patterns used in the experiments

avoiding boundary selection strategy underlying the top-k merge module (TMM).

6.1 Data Set Specificatio

For the experiments in this Section, we use the **"Intel Berkeley Research lab**[5]**"** data set containing $\sim$ 2.3 million sensor readings with the following schema:

date:yyyy-mm-dd	time:hh:mm:ss.xxx	epoch:int	moteid:int
temperature:real	humidity:real	light:real	voltage:real

Here, *epoch* is an integer corresponding to a time stamp obtained approximately every 30 seconds and is monotonically increasing. There are readings with the same *epoch*, but with different *moteid*; the *epoch* attribute uniquely determines the *epoch* and *time*. *Temperature* is in degrees Celsius. *Humidity* is temperature corrected relative humidity, ranging between 0-100. *Light* is in Lux and *Voltage* in volts. Also, we have the 2D location information corresponding to each *moteid*. In particular, we use each sensor's distance from the point, $(0,0)$, as an additional attribute value.

In our evaluation scenarios, we focus on the following three attributes: *epoch*, *moteid*, and *temperature*. We also consider the location information associated to the sensor. We convert *epoch*s to unique timestamps by randomly perturbing the *epoch* values. For each temperature reading, we compute the temperature change from the previous reading on the same *moteid* and split the overall range (from -150 to 160) evenly into following subranges, each corresponding to a different event class:

EA: [-160, -140)	EB: [-140,-120)	EC: [-120, -100)
ED: [-100, -80)	EE: [-80,-60)	EF: [-60, -40)
EG: [-40, -20)	EH: [-20, 0)	EI: [0]
EJ: (0, 20)	EK: (20,40)	EL: (40, 60)
EM: (60, 80)	EN: (80,100)	EO: (100, 120)
EP: (120, 140)	EQ: (140,160]	

6.2 Setup

Table 1 lists the key experiment parameters. While most parameters are self-explanatory, the relative event frequency (ref) and relative sensor selectivity (rss) require explanations: (a) ref is proportional to the frequency of the last event class in the sequence pattern (we experimented with three event class with frequencies $1 \times f_{base}$, $10 \times f_{base}$, and $89 \times f_{base}$, where f_{base} is $\sim 3 \times 10^{-3}$); (b) rss is proportional to the join likelihood of the sequences in the input queues to the top-k join module (rss = 1 corresponds to the case where sequences match if the sensors that generate them are within id range +/- 1; in rss=0.1 and rss=0.01, the join conditions are 10 times and 100 times more strict, respectively).

In addition , we introduce two synthetic event classes: *ESTART* and *EEND* to represent the start and end event.

---

[5] Available at: http://db.csail.mit.edu/labdata/labdata.html

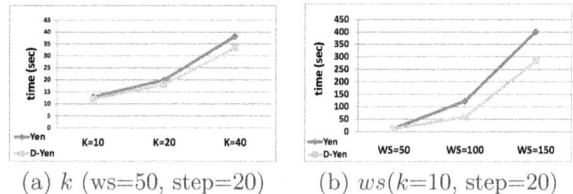

(a) k (ws=50, step=20) (b) $ws(k=10, \text{step}=20)$

Figure 11: Performance of the original Yen's algorithm vs. D-Yen over dynamically evolving graphs

Sequence patterns used in the experiments are listed in Table 2. For sequence matching experiments, we pick sequences with varying relative occurrences in the last event class (i.e. S1, S2 and S3). To evaluate the effects of sequence length, we choose three sequence (i.e. S4, S5, S6) with different lengths varying only the last event classes. For sequences used in top-k joins, we choose S7, S8, S9 shown in Table 2. For the experiments in which we evaluate the effects of divergent sequence lengths in the join, we used S10 (lenght=2) and S11 (length=4), also shown in Table 2

Experiments were run on a Windows XP box with Intel dual-core CPU @2.33GHz and 1.95GB RAM.

6.3 Evaluation of Top-k Sequence Enumeration on Dynamic Stratifie Graphs

We compare our k stratified shortest path algorithm against the following schemes: (a) *Enum-All*, an exhaustive algorithm which enumerates all matches before picking the top-k; (b)*D-Yen*, an incremental version of Yen's algorithm [6] based on the code available at *http://code.google.com/p/k-shortest-paths/* modified to eliminate redundant work in dynamically evolving graphs. To implement D-Yen, we follow an approach similar to the k dynamic stratified shortest path algorithm shown in Figure 7; we essentially replace the calls to the k stratified shortest paths algorithm with calls to Yen's k shortest paths algorithm. Figure 11 verifies under various parameter settings that our modification of the Yen's algorithm is indeed working more efficiently in the case of dynamically evolving graphs than a naive application of the Yen's algorithm. Here we do not consider Eppstein's non-incremental algorithm [8] which cannot be used to supply *TMM* with on-demand sequence matches.

In Figure 12, we compare the time costs of processing top-k sequence matches (for patterns of length 3 – the scoring of the events is based on the distance of the sensors from a given point in space). As can be seen here, the proposed approach outperforms both exhaustive and incremental Yen approaches by almost 3 orders of magnitude.

Figure 13(a) shows that the proposed algorithm scales well

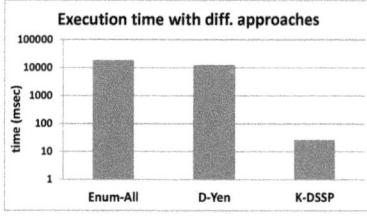

Figure 12: Comparison of top-k sequence matching approaches (k=10, sl=3, ws=50, step=20, ref=89)

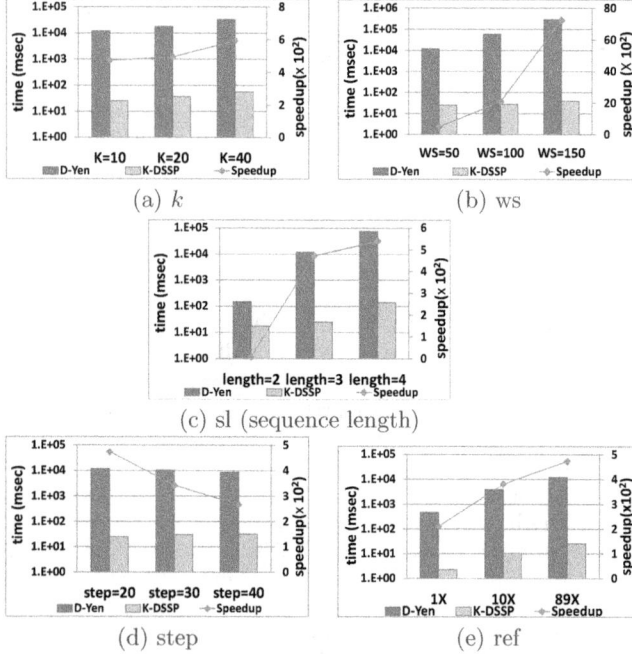

(a) k

(b) ws

(c) sl (sequence length)

(d) step

(e) ref

Figure 13: Comparisons of *D-Yen* and *k-DSSP* for different parameter settings (Default: k=10, sl=3, ws=50, step=20, ref = 89X)

as k increases from 10 to 40 and the difference between the incremental Yen's and the proposed approach gets larger when k increases. Figure 13(b) shows that, for larger window sizes, the event graph tends to be denser which results in more time to enumerate the top-k results. The *speedup* provided by the proposed approach also increases as the amount of needed work increases. This is also confirmed in Figure 13(c) which varies the target sequence length. Figure 13(d) evaluates the impact of the window shift size: A larger step implies a bigger change in the stratified graph and less of the top-k results remain in the next window. As expected, the speedup lowers, but the proposed algorithm remains > 100× faster. Finally, Figure 13(e) compares three sequence queries which differ only in the frequencies of the last event class. As before, the speedup increases with the graph complexity.

6.4 Evaluation of Waste-Avoiding Top-k Joins

In this section, we evaluate the proposed waste-avoiding boundary selection strategy (WABS) underlying the top-k join component by comparing it to round-robin, gradient-based (Güntzer [12]), and statistics-based (Hwang [24]) strategies. For the latter, statistics are collected based on data that has already been seen. In this section, we report experiments with the sensor data used above. When joining sequences on sensor IDs, random accesses (to fetch the

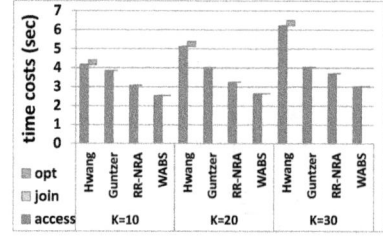

Figure 14: Different top-k join strategies (mf=avg, rss=1, q=2, ws=step=100, qp=[S7;S8])

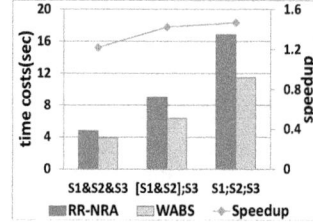

Figure 16: Performance evaluation on three-sequence join queries on sensor data (k=20, rss=0.01, mf=avg, q=3, sl=3 , ws=step=100)

best matching sequence with the given sensor ID in a given queue) are very expensive. Thus experiments in this section use NRA. Additional TA-based experiments on synthetic data, with more diverse parameter settings and random accesses, are included later in Section 6.4.1.

The key experiment parameters are listed in Table 1. Queries involve sequence patterns and their combinations. For example, the pattern qp = {[S7&S8];S9} would state that (a) sequences S7, S8 and S9 (all generated by the same sensor mote) should occur in the same window and (b) both S7 and S8 must occur before S9. Unless specified otherwise, we consider sequence patterns each with three event classes.

Also, in this section, we first consider the impact of the waste-avoidance strategies assuming that the *TMM* recomputes matches from scratch at each iteration. At the end of this section, we also investigate the impact of the fully incremental operation of *TMM*.

Figure 14 shows that the proposed WABS strategy performs the best among the alternatives for different k. Curiously, the gradient-based and statistics-based scheduling strategies perform worse than round-robin, indicating that they in fact lead to misleading or out-of-date plans. Therefore, in the rest of the experiments, we compare WABS directly to the round-robin strategy.

Figure 15 compares the WABS strategy against the round-robin strategy for two-queue top-k joins under different settings. Figure 15(a) shows that the more restrictive the join condition is the higher the speedup provided by WABS: this is because more work needs to be done to identify the k results and WABS helps prune redundant work. This is confirmed in Figure 15(b), where a more restrictive temporal order constraint ([S7;S8]), and in Figure 15(c), where a harder to commit merge function (*min*), provide larger speedups. Figure 15(d) shows that when there is a marked difference between the complexities (thus enumeration costs) of the sequence patterns being combined, WABS is able to identify and leverage this difference to boost the speedup it provides.

Figure 16 compares the results for more complex queries combining three sequence patterns. This figure also con-

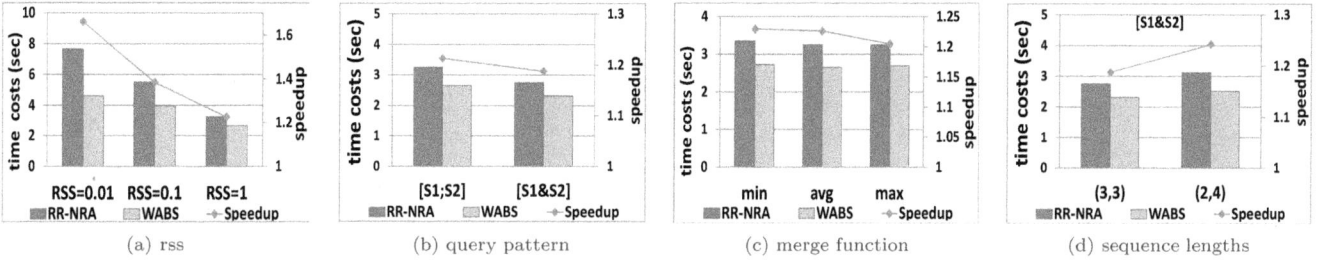

(a) rss   (b) query pattern   (c) merge function   (d) sequence lengths

Figure 15: Performance evaluation on two-sequence join queries on sensor data (Default: k=20, mf=avg, rss=1, q=2, ws=step=100, qp=[S7;S8], sl = 3 for both queues)

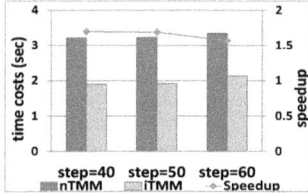

Figure 17: Incremental TMM ($iTMM$) vs. non-incremental TMM ($nTMM$)(k=20, rss=1, mf=avg, q=2, q=[S7;S8], sl=3, ws=100)

Parameters for top-k join experiments on synthetic data	
k	Top results to be returned
mf	merge function
rjs	relative join selectiviy
q	number of queues to be joined
dist.	uniform, normal or zipfian
cost ratio	$(cs_1 : \ldots : cs_i, cr_1 : \ldots : cs_i)$, for the ith queue

Table 3: Experiment parameters

firms the observation that the speedups provided by WABS increases as the pattern becomes more restrictive and, consequently, as it becomes harder for the NRA to identify the target k matches to the query.

Finally, Figure 17 provides a sample result showing the performance gain of the fully incremental version of TMM ($iTMM$), which reuses prior join computations when the window moves, over the non-incremental version ($nTMM$), which recomputes top-k matches from scratch for each window[6]. As can be seen in this figure, incremental TMM provides significant amounts of savings ($>1.5\times$ speedups) under different window update frequencies (i.e. step size). Since a smaller *step* enables more of the previous matches to remain in the window, as expected it provides higher "speedups". Since we did not discuss the implementation of iTMM in this paper due to space constraints, a more detailed study of iTMM vs nTMM is beyond the scope of this paper.

6.4.1 Discussion of Synthetic Data Experiments

As described earlier, however, an important limitation of joining sequences (as opposed to events) is that random accesses to the different queues are expensive to enumerate and thus experiments in that section applied WABS and NRA. In this section, we evaluate WABS using synthetic data; this provides more diverse parameter settings, including different value distributions a well as random accesses. Thus, this also enables us to evaluate WABS strategy in the case of TA-based top-k joins.

For each experiment reported in this section, we gener-

[6]Note that, both iTMM and nTMM leverage incremental computation of the shortest paths on the stratified graph; their difference is in the computation of the join process.

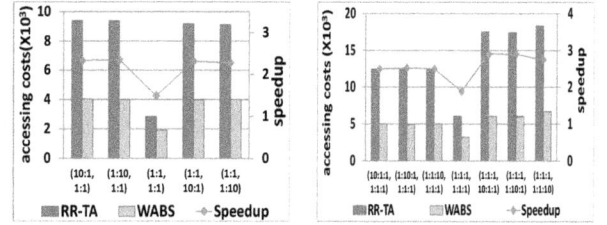

(a) two-queue join   (b) three-queue join

Figure 18: Comparison for varying access cost scenarios (Default: k=50, mf=min, rjs=1, uniform)

ate five sets of data and report the average performance. Each queue has 10K inputs and each input has a unique ID occurring once in one queue. Table 3 lists the experiment parameters used in this section. As before, k is the target number of results, mf denotes the merge function, and q denotes the number of queues. The other parameters are described below:

- **rjs** denotes the *relative join selectivity* of each queue. To be specific, when rjs=1, each entry in a given queue joins with exactly one other entry (the one with the same ID) on the other queues. When rjs=0.1, however, one of ten times entries with the same ID can be joined. Similarly, when rjs=0.01, one of one hundred times entries with the same ID can be joined. The later two cases provide 10 and 100 times more strict relative join selectivity than the case rjs=1.

- **dist** indicates the distribution of the scores in each queue. Queues are assumed to be independent.

- **cost ratio** indicates the relative access costs for different queues. For example, $(\alpha_1 : \alpha_2, \beta_1 : \beta_2)$ means the sorted access to the first queue has a cost of α_1 units and random access to it has a cost of β_1 unit; in contrast for the second queue, sorted and random accesses have α_2 and β_2 unit costs, respectively.

Figures 18(a) and (b) compares the top-k performance, under different cost ratio scenarios, for two and three queues, respectively. As can be seen, the WABS strategy is able to adjust to the differences in access cost ratios and provides the best speedups ($\sim 3\times$) as the complexity of the top-k join increases (e.g., when the number of input queues increase or when the cost asymmetry among the queues is high). Interestingly, even in the cases where the access costs are symmetric, WABS is able to provide up to $2\times$ gains.

Figure 19 studies the speedup provided by WABS strategy as for different parameters. Figure 19(a) through (c) show that, as was the case for the experiments on sensor data, the WABS provides ever increasing speedups as the top-k problem gets harder: in Figure 19(a) higher speedup

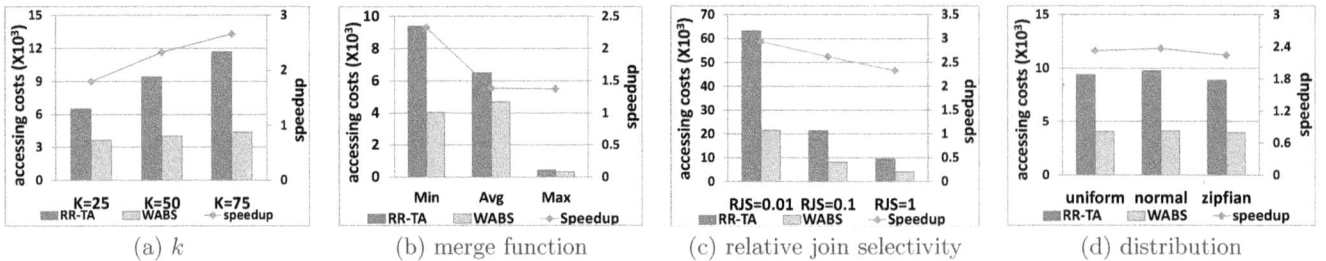

| (a) k | (b) merge function | (c) relative join selectivity | (d) distribution |

Figure 19: Performance comparison for varying parameter setting on synthetic data (Default: $k=50$, q =2 , mf=min, rjs=1, dist=uniform, cost ratio=[10:1, 1:1])

is observed for larger k, in Figure 19(b) higher speedup is observed for the *min* merge function (which in general requires more accesses than other merge functions), and in Figure 19(c) higher speedup is observed for $rjs = 0.01$, which is the case where it is hardest to locate inputs that satisfy the join condition.

Finally, Figure 19(d) studies the speedup provided by WABS strategy as for different score distributions. While, the speedups are similar, there are some noticeable differences. As expected, Zipfian distribution, in which there are less high scoring inputs is able to complete with least number of accesses, therefore the speedup is the lowest ($\sim 2.25\times$); in contrast, the normal distribution where there are a large number of mediocre (close to the mean) scores takes the most number of accesses and, consequently, the speedup is the largest ($\sim 2.35\times$) among the three distributions.

7. CONCLUSIONS

In this paper, we introduced the problem of top-k pattern evaluation over event streams and introduced a complex pattern ranking (CPR) framework. In order to efficiently identify the top sequence matches, we proposed a graph-based sequence enumeration strategy. We have first shown that events in a given window can be organized into what we refer to a *stratified stream graph* and that the best matches can be identified within this graph using a novel k-shortest path algorithm. We have also shown that within a streaming environment data changes in shifting windows can be captured as dynamic evolutions of stratified graphs and that shortest paths can be maintained without having to re-enumerate all shortest paths for each window shift. Experiments show that the proposed algorithms provide > 100× gains in execution times over alternatives. We next showed that in streaming environments top-k joins for combining sequence matches into complex patterns require new strategies that can adapt effectively (and cheaply) the changes. We proposed a waste-avoiding boundary selection strategy (WABS) for scheduling accesses to the input queues. Experiment results on the Intel-Berkeley sensor data showed that the proposed strategy can reduce the amount of work needed to enumerate top-k complex patterns using an NRA-based strategy up to 60%. TA-based experiments on synthetic data showed up to 3× speedups when the access costs are highly asymmetric.

8. ACKNOWLEDGMENTS

We thank Sangjeong Lee at KAIST for his invaluable feedback on the algorithms and the manuscript.

9. REFERENCES

[1] J. Agrawal, Y. Diao, D. Gyllstrom, and N. Immerman. Efficient pattern matching over event streams. In *SIGMOD*, 2008.

[2] H. Aljazzar and S. Leue. K * : A directed on-the-fly algorithm for finding the k shortest paths. Technical report, Univ. of Konstanz, 2008.

[3] H. Bast, D. Majumdar, R. Schenkel, M. Theobald, and G. Weikum. Io-top-k: Index-access optimized top-k query processing. In *VLDB*, pages 475–486, 2006.

[4] N. Bruno, N. Koudas, and D. Srivastava. Holistic twig joins: optimal XML pattern matching. In *SIGMOD*, 2002.

[5] G. Das, D. Gunopulos, N. Koudas, and N. Sarkas. Ad-hoc top-k query answering for data streams. In *VLDB*, 2007.

[6] E. de Queiros Vieira Martins, E. Queir, V. Martins, M. Margarida, and M. M. B. Pascoal. A new implementation of yen's ranking loopless paths algorithm. *4OR*, 2000.

[7] A. Demers, J. Gehrke, and P. Biswanath. Cayuga: A general purpose event monitoring system. In *CIDR*, 2007.

[8] D. Eppstein. Finding the k shortest paths. In *Proc. 35th Symp. Foundations of Computer Science*, pages 154–165. 1994.

[9] F. Fabret, H. A. Jacobsen, F. Llirbat, J. ao Pereira, J. A. Pereira, K. A. Ross, and D. Shasha. Filtering algorithms and implementation for very fast publish/subscribe systems. In *SIGMOD*, pages 115–126, 2001.

[10] R. Fagin. Combining fuzzy information from multiple systems . In *J. Comput. System Sci*, pages 216–226, 1996.

[11] R. Fagin. Combining fuzzy information: an overview. *SIGMOD Record*, 31:2002, 2002.

[12] U. Gützer, W.-T. Balke, and W. Kießing. Towards efficient multi-feature queries in heterogeneous environments. In *ITCC*, pages 622–628, 2001.

[13] P. Haghani, S. Michel, and K. Aberer. Evaluating top-k queries over incomplete data streams. In *CIKM*, pages 877–886, 2009.

[14] P. Haghani, S. Michel, and K. Aberer. The gist of everything new: personalized top-k processing over web 2.0 streams. In *CIKM 2010*. 2010.

[15] J. Hershberger, M. Maxel, and S. Suri. Finding the k shortest simple paths: A new algorithm and its implementation. *ACM Trans. Algorithms*, November 2007.

[16] V. M. Jiménez and A. Marzal. A lazy version of eppstein's shortest paths algorithm. In *WEA*, pages 179–190, 2003.

[17] X. Jin, X. Lee, N. Kong, and B. Yan. Efficient complex event processing over rfid data stream. In *ICIS*, 2008.

[18] J.Y.Yen. Finding the k shortest loopless paths in a network. *Managemen Science*, 17:712–716, 1971.

[19] M. H. Katoh N, Lbaraki T. An efficient algorithm for k shortest simple paths. *Networks*, page 411, 1982.

[20] E. Lawler. A procedure for computing the k best solutions to discrete optimisation problems and its application to the shortest path problem. *Management science*, page 401, 1972.

[21] M. Li, M. Liu, L. Ding, E. A. Rundensteiner, and M. Mani. Event stream processing with out-of-order data arrival. *Distributed Computing Systems Workshops*, 0:67, 2007.

[22] S. Nepal and M. Ramakrishna. Query processing issues in image(multimedia) databases. In *ICDE*, pages 22–29, 1999.

[23] T. Tran, L. Peng, B. Li, Y. Diao, and A. Liu. Pods: a new model and processing algorithms for uncertain data streams. In *SIGMOD*, 2010.

[24] S. won Hwang and K. C. chuan Chang. Optimizing top-k queries for middleware access: A unified cost-based approach. *ACM Trans. Database Syst.*, 32, March 2007.

[25] E. Wu, Y. Diao, and S. Rizvi. High-performance complex event processing over streams. In *SIGMOD*, pages 407–418, 2006.

[26] H. Zhang, Y. Diao, and N. Immerman. Recognizing patterns in streams with imprecise timestamps. *PVLDB*, 3(1):244–255, 2010.

Complex Event Pattern Detection over Streams with Interval-Based Temporal Semantics

Ming Li
Silicon Valley Laboratory
IBM Corporation
San Jose CA, USA
mingli3@us.ibm.com

Murali Mani
Dept. of CSEP
University of Michigan-Flint
Flint MI, USA
mmani@umflint.edu

Elke A. Rundensteiner
Dept. of Computer Science
Worcester Polytechnic Institute
Worcester MA, USA
rundenst@cs.wpi.edu

Tao Lin
Research and Development
Amitive
Redwood City CA, USA
taolin2004@gmail.com

ABSTRACT

In this work, we study the event pattern matching mechanism over streams with interval-based temporal semantics. An expressive language to represent the required temporal patterns among streaming interval events is introduced and the corresponding temporal operator ISEQ is designed. For further improving the interval event processing performance, a punctuation-aware stream processing strategy is provided. Experimental studies illustrate that the proposed techniques bring significant performance improvement in both memory and CPU usage with little overhead.

Categories and Subject Descriptors

H.2.4 [**Database Manager**]: Query Processing

General Terms

Algorithms, Design

1. INTRODUCTION

Event stream processing (ESP) [3] [8] [23] [14] [7] [2] [13] [15] has become increasingly important in modern applications, ranging from supply chain management to real-time intrusion detection. Existing ESP systems have focused on detecting temporal patterns from instantaneous events, that is, events with no duration. Under such a model, an event instance can only be happening *"before"*, *"after"* or *"at the same time as"* another event instance. However, such sequential patterns are inadequate to express the complex

temporal relations in some real-world application domains such as medicine, finance, logistics and meteorology, where events usually have durations and the durations could play important roles.

For example, an ESP system can be monitoring the events generated by the warehouse of a supermarket. Based on the temperature values sent by the readers, temperature fluctuations as event instances captured using interval semantics are generated and sent to the ESP system. We assume three different types of intervals: HIGH, MEDIUM and LOW. Besides that, the duration of an item staying in the warehouse is extracted and sent to the ESP system as an interval event instance after the item leaves the warehouse, which is denoted as STAY. The pattern of a HIGH interval event contains a STAY interval event means that the duration of an item staying in the warehouse is with a high temperature the whole time. We can use such pattern to indicate that the quality of this item might not be good.

Event instances happen instantaneously at a time point are called events with point-based temporal semantics (*point events* in short) and event instances occurs over a time interval are called events with interval-based temporal semantics (*interval events* in short). For an interval event e, we use $e.ts$ and $e.te$ to denote its start time and end time timestamps, which are called the *endpoints* of e.

According to the classification scheme introduced by Allen [4], there are 13 temporal relations between any two interval events: *"before"*, *"after"*, *"during"*, *"contain"*, *"meet"*, *"met by"*, *"overlap"*, *"overlapped by"*, *"start"*, *"started by"*, *"finish"*, *"finished by"* and *"equal"*. *Table 1* shows the detail of all these 13 temporal relations. Some of them are mirror relations. For example, *"overlap"* and *"overlapped by"* are mirror relations since *"a overlaps b"* can be represented as *"b is overlapped by a"*.

Relations between interval events can be expressed in terms of their endpoints, which is equivalent to the disjunction of relations given in Allen's classification above [22]. Given two interval events, if the order of all four endpoints of these two intervals are fixed, their temporal relation is one from the 13 relations given by [4]. While the order of endpoints are not fully fixed, relation between interval events can be even more flexible. Obviously, temporal relations among events in such interval-based scenario are more sophisticated than the sim-

Temporal Relation	Temporal Algebra
e before e'	$(e.te < e'.ts)$
e after e'	$(e.ts > e'.te)$
e during e'	$(e.ts > e'.ts) \wedge (e.te < e'.te)$
e contain e'	$(e.ts < e'.ts) \wedge (e.te > e'.te)$
e meet e'	$(e.te = e'.ts)$
e met by e'	$(e.ts = e'.te)$
e overlap e'	$(e.ts < e'.ts) \wedge (e.te > e'.ts) \wedge (e.te < e'.te)$
e overlapped by e'	$(e.ts > e'.ts) \wedge (e.ts < e'.te) \wedge (e.te > e'.te)$
e start e'	$(e.ts = e'.ts) \wedge (e.te < e'.te)$
e started by e'	$(e.ts = e'.ts) \wedge (e.te > e'.te)$
e finish e'	$(e.ts > e'.ts) \wedge (e.te = e'.te)$
e finished by e'	$(e.ts < e'.ts) \wedge (e.te = e'.te)$
e equal e'	$(e.ts = e'.ts) \wedge (e.te = e'.te)$

Table 1: Temporal Relations between Two Intervals

ple sequential relations in the point-based scenario. Thus, the query semantics and evaluation mechanisms used for detecting temporal patterns over streams with point events are not sufficient for pattern detection over interval streams.

Previous research on pattern detection over event streams mainly focused on extracting temporal patterns from point-based event data. For example, [23] proposes *sequence scan and construction* for implementing the SEQ operator. However it handles the *"before"* / *"after"* temporal relation only on point events. Even though in [3] [8] [7] the events are defined based on the interval model, only the *"before"* / *"after"* is supported. The data mining community studied discovering patterns over interval events [10] [19] [24]. [10] uses a hierarchical representation that extends Allen's interval algebra [4] for modeling complex event patterns over intervals. However, this representation is lossy as the exact relationships among the events cannot be fully recovered. [24] [19] devises a lossless representation to overcome the drawbacks of [10]. Based on their proposed representation, they design corresponding mining algorithms for pattern discovery over interval events. [19] also examines how the discovered temporal patterns can be utilized in classification to differentiate closely related classes thus building an interval-based classifier. However, these works mainly focus on pattern discovering algorithms instead of pattern detection algorithms. Besides that, they do not consider streaming input with window constraints.

Contributions. In this work, we study query processing over event streams with interval-based temporal semantics. The contributions include:

- We investigate an expressive language to represent the required temporal patterns among streaming interval events and design the corresponding temporal operator ISEQ.
- We study the physical implementation of ISEQ, focusing on its event buffering, result construction and state purge operations. Optimization utilizing the input order constraint of the interval events is provided and the ISEQ-incorporated query execution strategy is designed.
- For further improving the evaluation performance, we provide a mechanism to embed the Şinterval begin punctuationṪ (indicating the start of an upstream interval) to the event stream. Based on that, we provide the strategy for punctuation-aware interval event stream processing, which can greatly reduce the run-time memory and CPU footprint.

- We conduct experimental studies to demonstrate the efficiency of our proposed techniques in interval event stream handling.

Roadmap. The rest of the paper is organized as follows. *Section 2* proposes an evaluation mechanism for detecting temporal pattern over event streams with interval-based temporal semantics. Strategy of using punctuation for optimizing the interval stream processing framework is discussed in *Section 3*. Experimental results are presented in *Section 4*. The related work is given in *Section 5*, followed by conclusions in *Section 6*.

2. PATTERN DETECTION OVER INTERVAL EVENT STREAMS

2.1 Interval Event Query Model

An interval event e can be represented as two separated point events using its two endpoints, namely start endpoint and termination endpoint [22] [20]. We assume a data model in which an interval event is an atomic unit semantically. Thus an interval event is fully composed after it is completed. By then the event instance is ready to be sent to the ESP system. As discussed in *Section 1*, we use $e.ts$ and $e.te$ to denote the start time and end time timestamps of an interval event. As a simplified representation, we use a pair of numbers adjacent to e as $e_{t1|t2}$.

In the following discussion we assume that events' timestamps are globally ordered, reflecting the ordered semantics [15] of the physical events. In case of disordered event arrival, the mechanism introduced in [15] can be applied after some further adjustments and it will not affect the correctness of the basic approach introduced in this work. Each event is assigned a timestamp from a discrete ordered time domain. Such timestamps are assigned by a separate mechanism before events enter the event processing system and they reflect the true order of the occurrences of these events. For an ordered interval-based event stream, the event receiving order at the ESP system is the same as the order of the end time of the event instances.

Complex event pattern detection languages are studied in a number of existing works [3] [23] [7] [6]. In this work we adopt the query language defined in [3] [23] with supported set of event composite operators *SEQ*, *AND*, *OR* and *SELECT*, which specify a set of temporal and logical relations among events. For fully supporting event processing over interval streams, the query algebra and evaluation corresponding to detecting temporal relations among events need to be adjusted. The logical operators (i.e., AND / OR), which detect patterns with logical relations, apparently do not need to be adjusted for interval handling since they are independent from the temporal semantics [16] [17]. The pattern selection operator SELECT, which performs value-based predicate checking, needs special adjustment only if it is associated with negation patterns. However that can be simply avoided by pushdown of the SELECT operator [23]. Thus in this work, our main focus is on the event sequence operator SEQ.

A point event can be treated as an interval event with the same start time and end time timestamps. So the SEQ operator designed in [23] [3] for sequential pattern matching handles only the "*before*" / "*after*" temporal relation. Because of the transitive property of the "*before*" / "*after*" relation, this basic two-arguments operator can be extended to handle sequence with three or more event as $SEQ(E1, E2, E3, ...)$, which indicates that an $E1$ event is followed by an $E2$ and the $E2$ event is followed by an $E3$ event, and so on. For example, $SEQ(A, B, C)$ detects a sequential event patterns $<a, b, c>$ where a is an event instance of type A, b is an event instance of type B, c is an event instance of type C, a *before* b and also b *before* c.

As we have pointed out in *Section 1*, besides the simple sequential relations, additional temporal relations can be defined between interval events since that intervals could have overlapping portion. We consider an *interval temporal relation* to be a relation among two or more interval events. Since the relations between interval events can be expressed in terms of relations between the event endpoints, we divide interval temporal relation into two different categories, namely, *closed endpoint relations* and *open endpoint relations*.

An interval temporal relation where the order of all endpoints of the events are fixed is called a *closed endpoint relation*, which falls into the categories given by [4]'s classification. We refer to these temporal relations as *Allen-based relations*. An interval temporal relation where the order of all endpoints of the events are not fully fixed is called an *open endpoint relation*. Real-world applications might have customized requirement on interval pattern detection where open endpoint relations are needed to be defined. For example, we can define temporal relation R as "intervals of type $E1$ starts before intervals of type $E2$". The temporal algebra of such pattern is as $E1.ts < E2.ts$, where temporal relation is only given on the start endpoints. We can see that such temporal relation is the disjunction of several closed endpoint relations. Again take the temporal relation R defined above as an example. It is equivalent to the disjunction of several closed endpoint relations as $(E1$ *before* $E2) \vee (E1$ *meets* $E2) \vee (E1$ *overlaps* $E2) \vee (E1$ *finished by* $E2) \vee (E1$ *contains* $E2)$.

To express temporal relation between two intervals (referred to as *primitive temporal relation*), the simple SEQ operator becomes insufficient because it only considers "*before*" / "*after*" as temporal relations over point events. One approach to define a primitive temporal relation is simply using the 13 Allen-based relations and their disjunction using the syntax Rel[*list of Allen-based relations*]$(E1, E2)$, where *Rel* is a temporal operator defined by a list of Allen-based relations. For example, Rel[*overlap*](A, B) represents the *overlap* relation in Allen's model. Rel[*before, meet, overlap, finished by, contain*](A, B) represents an open endpoint temporal relation which is the disjunction of five different Allen-based relations.

While the expressiveness of such relation representation is no longer sufficient if it is extended to represent temporal relation among three or more intervals (referred to as *composite temporal relation*. as Rel[*list of Allen-based relations*]$(E1, E2, E3, ..., Em)$. One reason is that some temporal relation might not satisfy the transitive property, such as *overlap*. Take relation Rel[*overlap*](A, B, C) as an example. Given three interval event instances a of type A, b of type B and c of type C, "a *overlap* b and b *overlap* c" cannot infer "a *overlap* c" because that *overlap* relation does

not have the transitive property. This representation cannot express the pattern such as "*A overlaps B, B overlaps C and A overlaps C*". Another reason is that a composite relation might contain more than one temporal relations, such as a composite relation R defined as "*A contains B and B overlaps C*".

A *hierarchical representation* [10] is proposed to encode composite relations. Similarly, we can extend our previously defined operator syntax to represent a composite relation with multiple temporal relations as $\text{Rel}_n(...\text{Rel}_2(\text{Rel}_1[list\ of\ Allen\text{-}based\ relations](E1, E2), E3), ..., Em)$. It can express composite relation such as "*A contains B*, which as a composite event, *overlaps C*". However, such representation is still not expressive enough as it lacks the ability to represent pair-wise relations among events. Thus, this approach still cannot express temporal relations such as "*A contains B and B overlaps C*".

We introduce the endpoint-based encoding mechanism to represent temporal relations among interval events, following the work in [16] [17], where an endpoint sequence representation for intervals is studied. The basic idea is to express a relation using the conjunction of *temporal restriction*, which restricts the temporal relation to $<$, $<=$, $=$, $>$ and $>=$ between two interval endpoints. Such conjunction representation is called a *temporal restriction list* (*TList* in short). TList is with the syntax as "TList ::= TList∧TList | $I_1^* < I_2^*$ | $I_1^* <= I_2^*$" | $I_1^* = I_2^*$", where I_1^* and I_2^* define two event endpoints.

Example 1. Consider temporal relations $R1$: "A starts earlier than B, B starts earlier than C" and $R2$: "A overlaps B, B overlaps C". They are represented through TLists as "$(A.ts < B.ts) \wedge (B.ts < C.ts)$" and "$(A.ts < B.ts) \wedge (B.ts < A.te) \wedge (A.te < B.te) \wedge (B.ts < C.ts) \wedge (C.ts < B.te) \wedge (B.te < C.te)$" respectively.

As discussed earlier, primitive temporal relations between two intervals can be expressed using the 13 Allen-based relations and their disjunction. Thus the same expressibility of a TList can be achieved by conjunctions of such Allen-based representation between pair-wise intervals among the given composite pattern. For example, the temporal relation $R1$ given in *Example 1* above can be expressed through Allen-based relations as "$((A$ *before* $B) \vee (A$ *meets* $B) \vee (A$ *overlaps* $B) \vee (A$ *finished by* $B) \vee (A$ *contains* $B)) \wedge ((B$ *before* $C) \vee (B$ *meets* $C) \vee (B$ *overlaps* $C) \vee (B$ *finished by* $C) \vee (B$ *contains* $C))$". However, the endpoint-based approach utilized by TList has the advantage of simplicity in use and it is closer to business rules of the real-world applications [16] [17].

Please note that if there exists any conflicts in a TList, such as $(ep1 > ep2) \wedge (ep1 < ep2)$ where $ep1$ and $ep2$ are two event endpoints, the TList becomes invalid. We assume a validating process thus all the TLists in this work are considered valid. Also, a TList representation can be simplified using the transitive property of the $<$, $<=$, $=$, $>$ and $>=$ relations. For example, TList for $R1$ in *Example 1* can also be represented as "$A.ts < B.ts < C.ts$".

Using the TList, the EVENT clause of our query language for intervals is with the syntax as "EVENT *ISEQ* [TList]$(E1, E2, E3, ..., Em; W)$", where ISEQ is the temporal operator with the following semantics:

$$ISEQ[TList](E1, E2, ..., Em; W)[H] =$$
$$\{< e1\ e2\ ...\ em > \mid (TList(e1, e2, ..., em)) \wedge$$
$$(< e1\ e2\ ...\ em > \in E1[H] \times E2[H]... \times Em[H]) \wedge$$
$$(max(ei.te)_{i \in \{1,...,m\}} - min(ej.ts)_{j \in \{1,...,m\}} < W)\}. \tag{1}$$

In the ISEQ operator given above, $\{E1, E2, ..., Em\}$ is the set of event types defined in ISEQ and the TList defines the endpoint relation among the instances. An occurrence number will be attached to distinguish multiple occurrences of the same event type. In most event processing scenarios, it is assumed that the input to the system is a potentially infinite stream which contains all events that might be of interest [23]. Such real-time input is referred to as an *event trace*, which is denoted as H above. For an event trace H and an event type E, $E[H]$ denotes the set of all the event instances of E in H. Given E and E' defined in ISEQ, maximum four different temporal restrictions could be defined: *(1)* $E.ts\ Rel_1\ E'.ts$, *(2)* $E.ts\ Rel_1\ E'.te$, *(3)* $E.te\ Rel_1\ E'.ts$ and *(4)* $E.te\ Rel_1\ E'.te$. Rel_1 to Rel_4 are among possible point-based temporal relations $<$, $<=$, $=$, $>$ and $>=$ ('$>$' is the mirror relation of '$<$' and '$>=$' is the mirror relation of '$<=$'). For any given E in ISEQ, $E.ts <= E.te$ is always a required temporal restriction in the TList. We adopt the reasoning framework on the endpoint-based temporal representation studied in [16] [17]. It introduces an algorithm with exponential complexity which can be used to infer the temporal relation between two endpoints based on a given set of temporal restrictions.

In a traditional point-based event query algebra, the window constraint specification is expressed as the time window parameter, used for restricting the duration length among events in the temporal pattern. In [23], the window expression gives the time window argument W, which specifies the maximum time duration between the occurrences of the first and last events in the event temporal pattern. We follow the operator pushdown approach in [23] to handle the window-based filtering in ISEQ, which uses the window size W to control the maximum span of the result composite, defined as $max(ei.end)_{i \in \{1,2,...,m\}}$ - $min(ej.start)_{j \in \{1,2,...,m\}}$.

2.2 ISEQ Operator

The physical implementation of ISEQ has three core operations listed below:

Event Buffering. A newly received event instance is kept in the operator state of ISEQ if it is necessary. Given a newly received interval event e of type E which is among the set of expected events $\{E1, E2, ..., Em\}$, e needs to be buffered into a stack structure referred to as the *instance stack* if and only if it is possible to form result tuples using e together with some other received interval or future coming intervals. So, if E is with a given or inferred temporal restriction as $E.te > E'.te$ and no event instance of E' is currently buffered, the condition that requires an instance to be buffered is not satisfied thus e can be discarded directly (referred to as *on-the-fly dropping*). For other cases, e is added to the corresponding stack for buffering unless its interval length is larger than the window size.

Result Construction. The result construction is performed on the fly triggered by newly arrived tuples to ISEQ. Given a newly received and buffered interval event e of type E among expected event types, new results could possibly be constructed if and only if e might be contained by a result composite event consisting of currently received instances. So, if E is not with a given or inferred temporal restriction as $E.te < ep$, $E.te = ep$ or $E.te <= ep$, where ep is another interval endpoint, e could then possibly contribute in forming new result sequences consisting of the current buffered intervals. So the result construction condition is satisfied thus the construction process triggered by e can be called. The process uses a multi-join algorithm based on the attribute constraints on the interval endpoints defined by TList. In the join process, the values of event endpoints (both the start and termination endpoint) are used if the endpoints are associated with some temporal restrictions or with the window constraint.

Operator State Purge. Window constraints can be utilized in ISEQ to avoid unnecessary event buffering. It provides opportunity to purge events from the ISEQ operator dynamically when the event has fallen out of the sliding window. The latter is important in stream processing where runtime data structures need to be pruned to avoid memory depletion. Memory footprint is reduced due to such pruning. In addition, if the checking overhead is kept to be small, CPU footprint can also be reduced because of the saving on buffering-related operators and result construction Furthermore, similar to pushing down the window constraint into SEQ operator in [23], if the purge at ISEQ is conducted on a timely fashion, the checking on window constraint could be skipped thus the corresponding computation for window-based filtering is avoided in the result construction phase. Given a buffered interval event e of type E among expected event types, e can be safely purged from the buffer if and only if it is no longer contributing in forming new result sequences. So, if the termination endpoint associated with E is in given or inferred "$>$" temporal restrictions with all the endpoints in the pattern except itself, the purge condition is satisfied and the event instance e can be purged from the buffer once the result construction process triggered by e (if any) is completely finished. A window based purge named *cascading purge* could be performed: if E is with a given or inferred temporal restriction as $E.te > E'.te$ and the stack for E' events is empty, all the E events can be safely removed. The process can go on following the chain of such temporal restrictions on the interval termination endpoints. While a fine-grained duration constraint [16] [17] defined in ISEQ, it can be utilized to further avoid unnecessary event buffering. The basic idea is checking the window constraint dynamically while a new interval instance e of type E is received. For a buffered interval ei of Ei with a duration restriction as $Ej.te - Ei.ts(te) < W$, if $e.te - ei.ts(te) > W$, ei can be purged from the operator state of ISEQ. The correctness of this window-based purging mechanism is shown as follows. By the arrival of e, we can know any future interval e' satisfies $e.te < e'.te$. Thus, any future Ej instance ej will satisfy $ej.te - ei.ts(te) > W$. So, e is guaranteed to no longer contribute in forming further results.

An optimization can be brought into this process. Remember that we assume the input interval stream is ordered and the event receiving order at the ESP system is the same

Algorithm 1 Basic ISEQ Operations

```
 1: Procedure: ISEQOperation
 2: Input:
 3: (1) event Query EVENT ISEQ[TList](E1, E2, ..., Em; W),
 4: (2) newly received event e (under event type E)
 5: Output:
 6: matched result sequences triggered by the input event instance
 7:
 8: compute the inferred temporal restrictions
 9: form the DAG G representing the temporal restrictions
10: compute the indexing scheme
11: if CLOCK updates then
12:     perform window-based purge
13:     perform corresponding cascading purge
14: end if
15: checkState = true
16: if E is among E1, E2, ..., Em then
17:     if e.te - e.ts < W then
18:         if temporal restriction E.te > E'.te exists then
19:             if no event instance of E' is currently buffered then
20:                 checkState = false
21:             end if
22:         end if
23:         if CheckState then
24:             buffer e into the corresponding AIS stack if indexing is
                applied on E
25:             if E is not with any temporal restriction as E.te < ep,
                E.te = ep or E.te <= ep in G, where ep is a vertex in
                G and ep ≠ E.te then
26:                 produce event sequences containing e (if any)
27:             end if
28:             if G covers all the endpoints in the pattern and E is
                with a temporal restriction as E.te > ep for any ep ∈ G
                and ep ≠ E.te then
29:                 purge e
30:             end if
31:         end if
32:     end if
33: end if
```

as the order of the end time of the event instances. Such order semantics of the input intervals can be utilized to reduce the join computation in the result construction of ISEQ. This is similar to the idea of using a runtime stack nondeterministic finite automaton (NFA) for pattern retrieval on point events [23]. The optimization is for avoiding the multijoin on the longest path of termination endpoints linked through temporal restrictions. Let N denote the length of the path. Then the number of states in the NFA equals N+1 (including the starting state). The data structure *Active Instance Stacks* (AIS) associates a stack with each state of the NFA storing the events that trigger the NFA transition to this state. For each instance in the stack, an extra field *most Recent Instance in the Previous stack* (RIP) records the nearest instance in terms of time sequence in the stack of the previous state to facilitate sequence result construction. When the newly inserted event is an instance of the final stack then AIS computes sequence results. With the AIS states, the construction is simply done by a depth first search in the AIS stacks that is rooted at this instance and contains all the virtual edges reachable from this root. Each root-to-leaf path in the AIS stacks corresponds to the whole or a portion of a matched event sequence, which will be constructed through the rest of the multi-join process. With such AIS data structure, a more sophisticated cascading purge named *cascading AIS purge* could be performed: once an event instance is purged from the AIS stack, events whose RIP field pointing to this event can also be purged.

Algorithm 1 depicts the key ISEQ operations described above. Upon the arrival of a new interval event, buffering

decision is made and possible result sequences are produced at the earliest moment. Window-based and cascading purge are performed triggering by the CLOCK updates *Line 11*. The CLOCK value equals to the largest end time timestamp seen from the received intervals. The given and inferred temporal restrictions are managed as a DAG structure [12], with the edges marked as either ">", ">=" or "=". Corresponding construction for applying the AIS data structure is given in *Line 10* and *24*. In addition to that, specific AIS-incorporated computation (*Line 13* and *26*) are plugged in for utilizing the indexing structure.

Example 2. Consider event pattern query $Q = ISEQ[A.ts < B.te < C.te < D.te](A, B, C, D)$ and interval event trace $H = "b_{3|6}, d_{6|10}, b_{9|11}, c_{4|12}, a_{7|14}, d_{9|15}, a_{8|16}"$ (shown in *Figure 1*). Interval instance $d_{6|10}$ will be discarded upon arrival through the on-the-fly dropping since no C events are currently buffered and between C and D there is a temporal restriction defined as $C.te < D.te$. While $d_{9|15}$ arrives, the result construction is triggered to produce a result sequence $<a_{7|14} \; b_{9|11} \; c_{4|12} \; d_{9|15}>$. While $a_{8|16}$ arrives, the construction process is triggered again, producing another result sequence $<a_{8|16} \; b_{9|11} \; c_{4|12} \; d_{9|15}>$. Assuming the window size W equals to 30 and we further receive interval $e_{20|35}$, $b_{3|6}$ and $c_{4|12}$ can then be safely purged from the operator state.

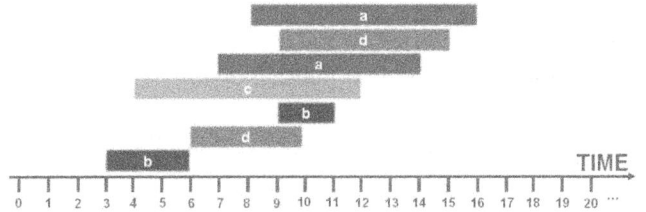

Figure 1: Interval Event Input Example

2.3 Query Execution Strategy

Algorithm 2 sketches the query execution strategy for a long running process of interval event pattern detection. The monitoring process is stopped when the event trace is terminated. Corresponding CPU and buffer resources are released on the fly. During the monitoring process, each received event triggers data buffering, result construction and operator state purge following *Algorithm 1* given in *Section 2.2*.

Algorithm 2 Execution Strategy

```
 1: Procedure: IntervalProcessingExecutionStrategy
 2: Input: real-time evolving interval sequence seq as "e1, e2,
    e3 ..." by the order of their termination endpoint, with the End
    of Stream (EOS) message arriving at the very end if input ter-
    mination is indicated
 3: Output: matched result sequences
 4:
 5: var e ← pull(seq) /* fetching instance from sequence queue */
 6: while e ≠ EOS do
 7:     process e:
 8:     perform necessary data buffering and state purge, construct
        new results if possible based on Algorithm 1
 9:     e ← pull(seq)
10: end while
11: terminate the pattern monitor for the current event trace
```

3. TOWARDS EFFICIENT INTERVAL PROCESSING

In many ESP applications, interval events are actually extracted from the raw primitive point events (such as the RFID sensor readings) by business intelligence (referred to as BI) middlewares [9] [18] and then passed to the downstream ESP systems. Consider the previous example given in *Section 1* where an ESP system is used to monitor the events generated by warehouses of a supermarket. Based on the temperature values sent by the temperature readers, temperature fluctuations, *HIGH*, *MEDIUM* and *LOW*, as the interval events are generated and sent to the ESP system. In real-world applications, such temperature fluctuation intervals are actually extracted by the middleware systems which receives the actual readings from the temperature sensors. Assume the *HIGH* temperature is above 100F, the *MEDIUM* temperature is within the range of (50F, 100] and the *LOW* temperature is 50F or lower. We also assume the sensor reads temperature every two seconds and reports the following reading: 01:00:00PM - 55F; 01:00:02PM - 70F; 01:00:04PM - 95F; 01:00:06PM - 80F; 01:00:08PM - 110F; 01:00:10PM - 120F; 01:00:12PM - 90F; 01:00:14PM - 60F; 01:00:16PM - 30F... The interval streams generated will be: "*MEDIUM* 01:00:00PM - 01:00:08PM, *HIGH* 01:00:08PM - 01:00:12PM, *MEDIUM* 01:00:12PM - 01:00:16PM ...". Assume we are having another two interval events, *WET* and *DRY*, to represent the humidity of the environment generated under a similar sensor layer as the one used for the temperature readings. By such context, a practical event query can be looking for the pattern of *HIGH* overlaps *DRY*. Such corner changes which trigger new intervals are called *critical state changes*. These critical state changes (as the begin and end of an interval) are captured by the BI middlewares and then composed into interval events and passed to the downstream ESP systems once the interval is fully formed. Thus, under the above application structure, the information of the "interval start" is actually known to the BI middlewares at real-time. A mechanism to improve the efficiency of interval stream processing is to embed the *interval begin punctuations* defined below into the input interval event streams.

Interval Begin Punctuation (IBP). IBP indicates the initialization of an interval instance. At the moment an interval event e starts, its corresponding IBP will be created and sent. It has associated a metadata schema as $ibp_e = <e.id, e.ts>$, where $e.id$ is the ID value of e, assigned automatically by the EPS. The ID value is unique among the events in the stream. Given an IBP p, its timestamp $p.t$ equals to $e.ts$.

In the discussion in *Section 2.1*, a data model in which an interval event is an atomic unit semantically is assumed. Thus an interval event is fully composed after it is completed and then it is sent to the ESP system. Applying IBPs does not require the change of this model. However, the IBP information can be used for effective interval event processing. The interval event sender (i.e., the BI middlewares as shown in the warehouse example) should have the mechanism to encode an unique ID to the interval events. The ESP system receives interval event streams mixed together with IBPs. Remember that we assume order for the input

interval stream. Under such model which interleaves IBPs with interval event instances, the order of receiving events and IBPs at the ESP system is the same as the order of their end time timestamps. Note that since IBPs are point-based data, the time stamp of an IBP equals to its end time timestamp.

An IBP-aware interval event processing approach can be utilized to reduce the runtime memory and CPU footprint for temporal pattern detection over interval event streams. The key operations of an IBP-incorporated ISEQ operator is given as below.

Event Buffering. The event buffering conditions in the basic ISEQ stays. However, the IBP information is also hold in the AIS for the events being indexed. We will have further discussion on this in the result construction. With the IBP information being available, additional on-the-fly event dropping becomes possible, as follows. Given a newly received IBP of E interval e, which is among the set of expected events $\{E1, E2, ..., Em\}$, if $E.ts$ is among the indexed start endpoints (referred to as the IBP of E being indexed) and *(1)* the AIS stack pointed by the AIS stack of ibp_e is empty, or *(2)* E is with a given or inferred temporal restriction as $E.ts > E'.te$ and no events of E' is currently buffered, the received IBP can be dropped without buffering. Given a newly received interval instance e of type E which is among the set of expected events $\{E1, E2, ..., Em\}$, if *(1)* the IBP of E is required to be indexed and no IBP entry corresponding to e is currently buffered, or *(2)* E is with a given or inferred temporal restriction as $E.te > E'.ts$, the IBP of E' is required to be indexed and no IBPs of E' is currently buffered, or *(3)* E is with a given or inferred temporal restriction as $E.te > E'.te$ and no events of E' is currently buffered, the condition that requires e to be buffered is not satisfied thus e can be discarded directly without buffering.

Result Construction. As discussed earlier, the result construction is performed on the fly triggered by newly arrived tuples to ISEQ. Given a newly received and buffered interval event e of type E among expected event types, new results could possibly be constructed if and only if e might be contained by a result composite event consisting of currently received instances. The conditions for result construction triggering in the basic ISEQ stays for the IBP-incorporated ISEQ. So, if E is not with a given or inferred temporal restriction as $E.te < ep$, $E.te = ep$ or $E.te <= ep$, where ep is another interval endpoint, e could then possibly contribute in forming new result sequences consisting of the current buffered intervals. So the result construction condition is satisfied thus the construction process triggered by e can be called. For the part without AIS indexing, the process uses a multi-join algorithm based on the attribute constraints on the interval endpoints defined by TList is applied to construct possible composite events. In the join process, the value of event endpoints (both the start and termination endpoints) are used if the endpoint is associated with some temporal restriction or with the window constraint. The AIS stack is brought into the multi-join process for the indexed temporal restrictions to avoid the joins on a path of event endpoints (both the start and termination endpoints) linked through temporal restrictions using not only the interval termination but also the IBPs. This is different than the AIS-based approach in the basic ISEQ, where the IBPs are not available. The path with the most join avoidance will be selected, which is the longest path in the DAG formed by the temporal restriction, and it is not counted as one join if an edge is formed by one single event type. For event types with only indexed termination endpoints, the AIS structure remains the same as the basic ISEQ operator. For event types with only indexed IBPs, a corresponding AIS stack at first holds the IBPs and later is filled with the corresponding full instances. Similar to SEQ, the RIP pointers can be applied to the stacks consisting of the IBP entries. If the path includes both the start and termination endpoints of an event type, two different AIS stacks will be applied and they both link to a shared structure (referred to as the *full edge stack*) holding the event instance. The construction on the indexed path remains as a simple depth first search in the AIS stacks that is rooted at this instance and contains all the virtual edges reachable from this root. Each root-to-leaf path in the AIS stacks corresponds to the whole or a portion of a matched sequence constructed through the multi-join process.

Operator State Purge. The conditions for operator state purging in the basic ISEQ stays for the IBP-incorporated ISEQ. So, if the termination endpoint associated with E is in given or inferred ">" temporal restrictions with all the endpoints in the pattern except the ones from E itself, the purge condition is satisfied and the event instance e can be purged from the buffer once the result construction process triggered by e (if any) is completely finished. However, more purging opportunities become possible with the IBP being available: the window-based purge and the corresponding cascading purge can be simply extended to cover the IBPs kept in the AIS stacks. The benefits of doing so is that it can lead to further on-the-fly dropping since there could be fewer IBPs kept in the indexes after the purge.

Algorithm 3 depicts the corresponding operations given above. We can see that upon the arrival of a new interval event and an event IBP, buffering decision is made and possible result sequences are produced at the earliest moment. Similar to the basic ISEQ, upon the arrival of new interval events, corresponding construction and operator state purge are triggered to performed. The query execution strategy based on ISEQ given in *Algorithm 2* stays the same for the IBP-incorporated ISEQ.

Example 3. Again consider the scenario given in *Example 2*. Interval event $b_{3|6}$ can be discarded without buffering, since we can guarantee that no future arrival of A could have a start time smaller than $b_{3|6}$'s end time by the fact that no IBPs of A is met before the arrival of $b_{3|6}$. Similarly, interval $b_{9|11}$ is required to be buffered, indicated by the IBP of $a_{7|14}$.

As mentioned earlier for the IBP-based solution, in many ESP applications, event intervals are actually extracted from the raw primitive point-based events (such as the RFID sensor readings) by BI middlewares and then passed to the downstream ESP systems. Following such application structure, the low level physical devices (i.e., the sensor network) with enough computing power would actually be able to capture these critical state changes. Such mechanism of pushing down the computation of interval event abstraction to the low level sensor network can greatly improve the efficiency and scalability for ESP applications with intense computing ability on the physical level devices. This is because

---

Algorithm 3 IBP-Incorporated ISEQ Operations

```
 1: Procedure: PunctuationAwareISEQOperation
 2: Input:
 3: (1) event Query EVENT ISEQ[TList](E1, E2, ..., Em; W),
 4: (2) newly received event IBP ibp_e / event instance e (under event
        type E)
 5: Output: matched result sequences triggered by the input event
        instance
 6:
 7: same as Line 8 to 14 in Algorithm 1
 8: if E is among E1, E2, ..., Em then
 9:    on the arrival of ibp_e:
10:    checkState = true
11:    if the IBP of E is required to be indexed then
12:       if the AIS stack pointed by the AIS stack of ibp_e is empty
          then
13:          checkState = false
14:       end if
15:       if E is with a given or inferred temporal restriction as E.ts
          > E'.te && checkState && no events of E' is currently
          buffered then
16:          checkState=false
17:       end if
18:    end if
19:    if checkState then
20:       buffer ibp_e into the corresponding AIS stack by the append
          semantics
21:    end if
22:    on the arrival of e instance:
23:    checkState = true
24:    startFlag, endFlag = false
25:    if e.te - e.ts < W then
26:       if the IBP of E is required to be indexed then
27:          startFlag = true
28:          if no IBP entry corresponding to e is currently buffered
             then
29:             checkState = false
30:          end if
31:       end if
32:       if the full instance of E is required to be indexed then
33:          endFlag = true
34:       end if
35:       if checkState && E is with a given or inferred temporal
          restriction as E.te > E'.ts && the IBP of E' is indexed
          and no IBP of E' is currently buffered then
36:          checkState = false
37:       end if
38:       if checkState && E is with a given or inferred temporal
          restriction as E.te > E'.te && no event instance of E' is
          currently buffered then
39:          checkState = false
40:       end if
41:       if checkState then
42:          if startFlag && !endFlag then
43:             insert e into the corresponding AIS entry based on
                the event ID
44:          else
45:             if !startFlag && endFlag then
46:                buffer e into the corresponding AIS stack by the
                   append semantics
47:             else
48:                if startFlag && endFlag then
49:                   buffer e into the full edge stack and buffer e's
                      reference into the corresponding AIS stack by the
                      append semantics, update existing AIS
50:                else
51:                   buffer e into the corresponding instance stack
52:                end if
53:             end if
54:          end if
55:          if E is not with any temporal restriction as E.te < ep,
             E.te = ep or E.te <= ep in G, where ep is a vertex in
             G and ep ≠ E.te then
56:             produce event sequences containing e (if any)
57:          end if
58:          if G covers all the endpoints in the pattern and E is
             with a temporal restriction as E.te > ep for any ep ∈ G
             and ep ≠ E.te then
                purge e
59:          end if
60:       end if
61:    end if
62: end if
```

that the computation of interval event abstraction happens much closer to the information source thus the cost of data transportation is avoided.

4. PERFORMANCE EVALUATION

4.1 System Implementation

The system architecture for incorporating the proposed interval event handling into an ESP system structure is shown in *Figure 2*. The ESP system receives events through an *Input Adapter*, which connects to different kinds of data sources, such as system transaction datalogs, supply chain RFID readings, stock market data and e-commerce online transaction data. The ESP connects to two different output sockets, one is the *Result Monitor*, which consists within the *ESP Console*, the other is the *Output Adapter*, which relays output sequences to downstream receivers, such as different operational applications, spreadsheets, BI tools and BI dashboards. The ESP console also includes the *Query Register* for defining customized pattern monitor requirements. The *Plan Generator* parses and translates a given event query into an execution plan. The *Execution Engine*, which constructs results on the fly, is the key component of the ESP system. The definition and implementation of the query operators are contained by the *Operator Containers*, which includes the *Libraries* of the *Logical and Physical Operators*. The proposed ISEQ operator is incorporated into the corresponding operator library containers. While the input is point events (seen as interval events each with the same start time and end time timestamps) and the AIS indexing is applied, the ISEQ operator behaves in the same way as a regular sequence operator. Thus, it can be treated as an extended SEQ operator.

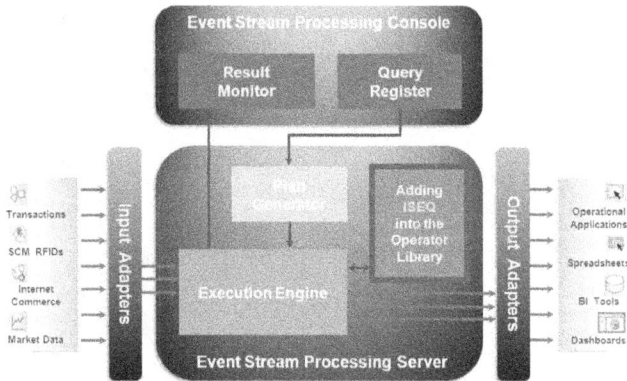

Figure 2: System Architecture

4.2 Experimental Setting

Experiments are run on two Pentium 4 3.0GHz machines, both with 1.98G of RAM. One machine sends the event stream to the second machine. From *Section 4.3* to *4.6* we are going to study the performance of the proposed interval event stream processing techniques on a 2G generated data input, which contains 20 different event types with uniform distribution.

Name	Description
100t-0s	100% termination endpoint
90t-10s	90% terminationendpoint and 10% start endpoint
80t-20s	80% termination endpoint and 20% start endpoint
70t-30s	70% termination endpoint and 30% start endpoint
60t-40s	60% termination endpoint and 40% start endpoint
50t-50s	50% termination endpoint and 50% start endpoint
40t-60s	40% termination endpoint and 60% start endpoint
30t-70s	30% termination endpoint and 70% start endpoint
20t-80s	20% termination endpoint and 80% start endpoint
10t-90s	10% termination endpoint and 90% start endpoint
0t-100s	100% start endpoint indexing

Table 2: Indexing % in Different Query Types

Totally four sets of experiments are run to test the effects of various factors: *(1)* the indexing percentage that controls the indexable endpoints and endpoints types (either start or termination); *(2)* the query length that controls the number of interval patterns in the ISEQ operator; *(3)* the average interval length that controls the average span of the interval events with the normal distribution and *(4)* the event density that controls the number of events within one sliding window with the normal distribution. The applied queries are with the template as "EVENT *ISEQ*[TList]$(A, B, ...; W)$", where the TList defines the endpoint temporal restrictions among the event patterns. Performances of *(1)* the basic ISEQ without AIS indexing (referred to as *naive ISEQ*) approach, *(2)* the basic ISEQ with AIS indexing (referred to as *basic indexing*) approach and *(3)* the IBP-incorporated ISEQ (referred to as *IBP-incorporated*) approach are measured respectively. Experimental results are given in *Section 4.3* to *4.6* below.

4.3 Varying Query Types

This set of experiments varies the percentage of indexable endpoints as well as the indexable endpoints types in the given query. The indexable endpoints will contribute to the AIS construction for the basic ISEQ with AIS indexing approach and the IBP-incorporated ISEQ approach. Ten different combinations are covered by the experiments, which is shown in *Table 2*. The query length is fixed as 10. The average interval length is fixed as W/10 (W is the sliding window size, which is fixed as 30 seconds for all queries) with the event density as 200 events per window. Results are shown in *Figure 3* and *4*. The property of the input event data such as the average interval length and event density greatly affects the performance, which will be studied later in *Section 4.5* and *4.6*.

Memory Consumption (*Figure 3*). X axis here shows the ten groups of queries categorized by indexing scheme discussed earlier (*Table 2*) and Y axis shows the accumulative memory consumption for each query. With the cascading AIS purge, the basic indexing approach and the IBP-incorporated approach both have less memory footprint than the naive ISEQ approach except the case with no termination endpoint indexing for the basic indexing approach. However it only shows a slight gain (less than 5% for the case with the most gain) under the given setting. With a smaller window, which can be achieved by increasing the average interval length or decreasing the event density, more memory footprint can be avoided. This will be further dis-

298

cussed in *Section 4.5* and *4.6*. Addition to that, for the basic indexing approach, the gain on memory consumption is affected by the percentage of indexable termination endpoints in the query.

CPU Performance (*Figure 4*). X axis still shows the ten different indexing scheme and Y axis shows the execution time for each query. We can see that the IBP-incorporated approach in all cases outperform the naive ISEQ approach. This is because that it has indexing support for all the query categories due to the IBP utilization. In most cases the basic indexing approach outperforms the naive ISEQ approach: with a higher percentage of the termination indexing, more CPU computation could be avoided in terms of result sequences construction using the costly multi-join algorithm. For example, in the best case (i.e., the query with 100% indexable termination endpoint patterns), execution with the basic indexing approach reduce the execution time of the plan with naive ISEQ by 60%. However, while the percentage of indexable termination endpoints is not high in the given query, the basic indexing approach has poor performance because the overheads on index construction and maintenance. The overhead ranges from 3% to 12% in the query categories of *20t-80s*, *10t-90s* and *0t-100s*. The overhead increases while decreasing the portion of indexable termination endpoints in the query. We can also observe that the basic indexing approach does not perform as well as the IBP-incorporated approach. This is due to the cost avoidance using the IBP information in the IBP-incorporated approach is not applicable for the basic indexing approach.

4.4 Varying Query Length

This set of experiments studies how varying the relative query length affects the interval stream processing cost. The query length is varied from 2 to 18. For example, among them a sequence query with length 6 (i.e., $ISEQ[A.ts < B.ts < C.ts < D.te < E.te < F.te](A, B, C, D, E, F)$) is run. The *50t-50s* indexing profile is applied to all the queries in this set of experiments. The average interval length is fixed as W/10 with the event density as 200 events per window, which stays the same as *Section 4.3*. Experimental results are shown in *Figure 5* and *6* and analysis is given as follows.

Memory Consumption (*Figure 5*). X axis here represents the query length and Y axis shows the accumulative memory consumption for each query. We can see that the ratio of memory consumption saving (the slight saving on memory footprint discussed earlier in *Section 4.3*) stays relatively steady for the index-applied approaches while the query length increases, since the interval events among different types are with uniform distribution.

CPU Performance (*Figure 6*). X axis still represents the query length and Y axis shows the execution time for each query. A query with a longer length requires much more CPU resources for the result construction than the naive ISEQ approach. Thus we can see that the ratio of CPU gain increases sharply for the index-applied approaches while the query length increases. Similar observation can be found in the comparison between the two index-applied approaches. The ratio of the IBP-incorporated approach's CPU gain over the basic indexing approach increases steadily while the query length increases, from 45% to 66%.

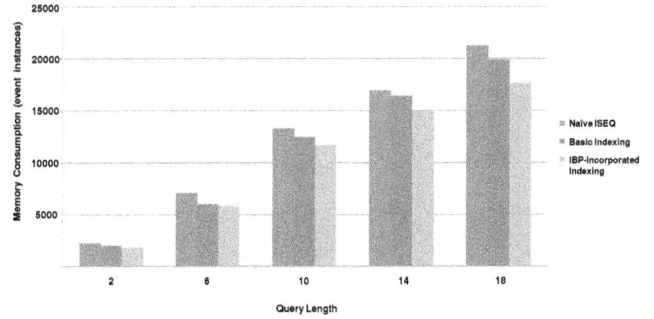

Figure 5: Varying Query Length (I)

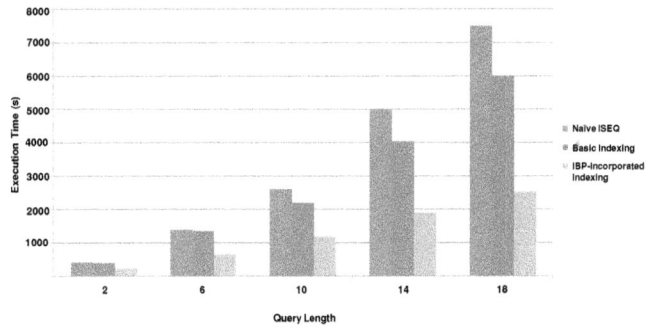

Figure 6: Varying Query Length (II)

4.5 Varying Average Interval Length

Since the input event stream is infinite, consistent performance over time can only be achieved by actively maintaining the data structures incrementally based on the given window constraint of the query [2]. Thus the size and density of the interval events both affect the cost of buffer consumption and the result construction since they both affect the amounts of active instances kept in the operator state. We next study the effect of interval size by varying it from W/100 to W/5. Similar to the earlier settings, the *50t-50s* indexing profile is applied to all the queries in this set of experiments. The event density is set to 200 events per window and the query length is set to 10. Experimental results are shown in *Figure 7* and *8* and analysis is given as follows.

Memory Consumption (*Figure 7*). X axis here represents the interval length and Y axis shows the accumulative memory consumption for each query. We can see that with larger intervals (thus relatively smaller sliding window size in terms of holding how many complete interval events), more memory footprint can be avoided for the IBP-incorporated approach. The ratio of the memory consumption gain scales with the average interval length. This is because that more intervals can be discarded directly through the on-the-fly dropping and more cascading AIS purge can be applied while intervals become easier to fall out of the sliding window. Similar observation can be found while comparing the basic indexing approach and the naive ISEQ approach.

CPU Performance (*Figure 8*). X axis still represents the interval length and Y axis shows the execution time for each

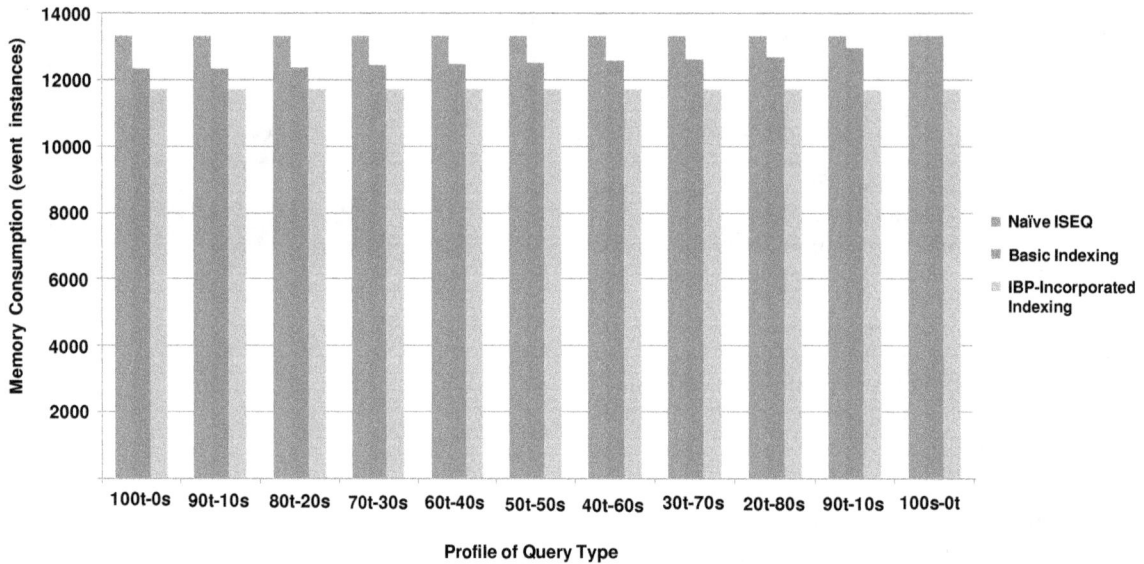

Figure 3: Varying Query Types (I)

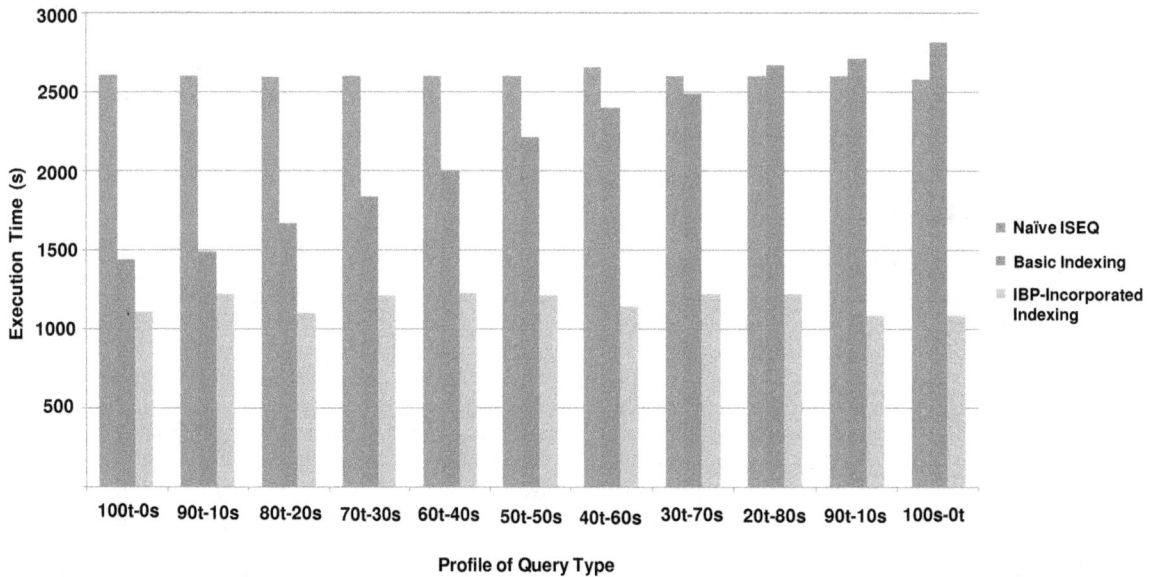

Figure 4: Varying Query Types (II)

query. Similar to the observation on the memory consumption, we can see that with larger intervals, more CPU cost can be avoided for both index-applied approaches, with a gain ratio in proportion to the interval length.

4.6 Varying Event Density

As the discussion in *Section 4.5*, the size and density of the interval events both affect the cost of buffer consumption and the result construction. In this set of experiments we study the effect of event density by varying it from 50 events per window to 800 events per window. Note that for intervals we consider the event center (the middle point of the

interval) as its representation. Similar to the earlier settings, the *50t-50s* indexing profile is applied to all the queries in this set of experiments. The average interval length is given as W/20 and the query length is set to 10. Experimental results are shown in *Figure 9* and *10* and analysis is given as follows.

Memory Consumption (*Figure 9*). X axis here represents the interval length and Y axis shows the accumulative memory consumption for each query. We can see that with more sparse input (thus relatively smaller sliding window size in terms of covering how many interval event centers), more memory footprint can be avoided for the IBP-incorporated approach. The ratio of the memory consump-

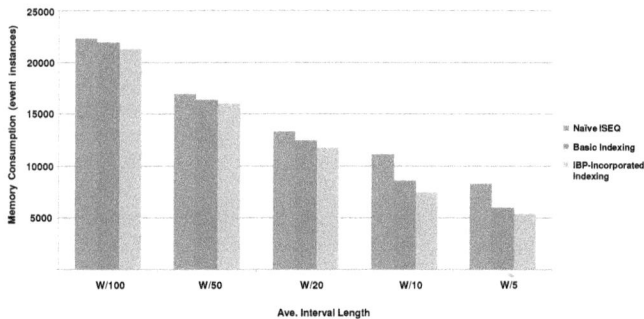

Figure 7: Varying Average Interval Length (I)

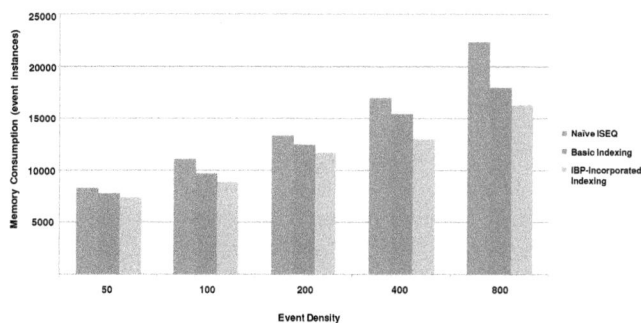

Figure 9: Varying Event Density (I)

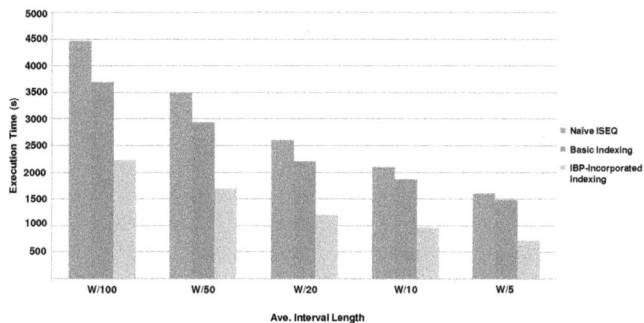

Figure 8: Varying Average Interval Length (II)

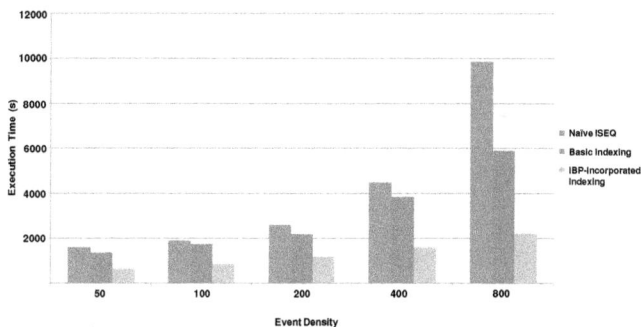

Figure 10: Varying Event Density (II)

tion gain is in inverse proportion to the event density. This is because that with a more sparser input data set, less data will be hold by the operator since the state purge. Similar observation can be found while comparing the basic indexing approach and the naive ISEQ approach.

CPU Performance (*Figure 10*). X axis still represents the interval length and Y axis shows the execution time for each query. Similar to the observation on the memory consumption, we can see that with more sparse input, more CPU cost can be avoided for both index-applied approaches. However, the ratio is no longer just in inverse proportion to the event density when the input becomes very dense. We can see that the CPU cost increases sharply for the naive ISEQ approach comparing with the index-applied approaches while the query density jumps from 200 to 400 and from 400 to 800. Similar observation can be found for the comparison between the two index-applied approaches. This is because that with larger operator state, the result construction for the patterns without indexing becomes more and more inefficient.

4.7 Conclusions of the Experimental Studies

Above experimental results reveal that the proposed interval event stream processing framework is practical in three senses: *(1)* interval streams are handled correctly by the proposed framework with expected query results; *(2)* the index-applied approaches outperform the naive ISEQ approach in most cases and *(3)* the IBP-incorporated outperforms the approach with the basic indexing.

5. RELATED WORK

Event-specific ESP technology, which has an event-specific system design and evaluation mechanism, is shown to be superior to generic stream processing solutions [1] [5] [11] [21] because it is being specifically designed for handling pattern queries over streaming event. In [23], the authors propose an expressive yet easy-to-understand language to support pattern queries on such sequential streams and propose customized algebra operators for the efficient processing of such pattern queries with sliding windows. [3] uses a plan-based technique to perform streaming complex event detection across distributed sources. These researches on event pattern detection over event streams mainly focused on extracting temporal patterns from point-based event data [23]. Even though in [3] [8] [7] the events are defined based on the interval model. However, only the "*before*" / "*after*" temporal relation is supported, which simplifies the interval-based temporal model to the point-based temporal model by overlooking the patterns where events as intervals can overlap with each other. [25] studied sequence pattern detection for point events with imprecise timestamps, where an event could occur somewhere within a time interval with uniform distribution. Instead our model considers interval events occurring over the entire time range. The data mining community studied discovering patterns over interval events [10] [19] [24]. [10] uses a hierarchical representation that extends Allen's interval algebra [4] for modeling complex event patterns over intervals. However, this representation is lossy as the exact relationships among the events cannot be fully recovered. [24] [19] devise a lossless representation to overcome the drawbacks of [10]. Based on their proposed representation, they propose corresponding mining algorithms for pattern discovering over interval events. [24] proposes the TPrefixSpan algorithm to mine the new temporal patterns from interval events. The completeness and accuracy of the results are also proven. Their experimental results show that the efficiency and scalability of the TPrefixSpan algorithm are satisfactory. An efficient algorithm called IEMiner is designed by [19] to discover frequent temporal patterns from interval events. The algorithm employs two optimization techniques to reduce the search space and remove unpromising candidates. [19] also examines how the discovered temporal patterns can be utilized in classification to differentiate closely related classes thus building an interval-based classifier called IEClassifier. Even though our endpoint representation is also lossless as in these works, we cannot adapt their algorithms because they mainly focus on pattern discovering algorithms instead of pattern detection algorithms. Besides that, they do not consider streaming input with window constraints.

6. CONCLUSIONS

Existing ESP systems have focused on detecting temporal patterns from instantaneous events, that is, events with no duration. However, such sequential patterns are inadequate to express the complex temporal relations in domains such as medical, multimedia, meteorology and finance where the durations of events could play an important role. Due to the differences between the temporal patterns over interval events and point events, the query semantics and evaluation mechanisms used for pattern detection over point events is not sufficient for pattern detection over interval events. An expressive language to represent the required temporal patterns among streaming interval events and corresponding evaluation mechanism for such event temporal queries is needed. In this work, we provide a framework to support interval event stream processing: (1) we introduce an expressive language to represent the required temporal patterns among streaming interval events; (2) we design the corresponding temporal operator ISEQ; (3) for further improving the event processing performance, we provide a mechanism to embed the "interval begin punctuation" into the interval stream and study the corresponding punctuation-aware interval processing; (4) we conduct experimental studies to validate our proposed approach.

7. REFERENCES

[1] D. Abadi, D. Carney, U. Cetintemel, M. Cherniack, C. Convey, S. Lee, M. Stonebraker, N. Tatbul, and S. Zdonik. Aurora: A new model and architecture for data stream management. *VLDB Journal*, 12(2):120–139, August 2003.

[2] J. Agrawal, Y. Diao, D. Gyllstrom, and N. Immerman. Efficient pattern matching over event streams. In *SIGMOD*, pages 147–160, 2008.

[3] M. Akdere, U. Cetintemel, and N. Tatbul. Plan-based complex event detection across distributed sources. *PVLDB*, 1(1):66–77, 2008.

[4] J. F. Allen. Maintaining knowledge about temporal intervals. *Commun. ACM*, 26(11):832–843, 1983.

[5] S. Babu and J. Widom. Continuous queries over data streams. *SIGMOD Record*, 30(3):109–120, 2001.

[6] G. Cugola and A. Margara. Tesla: a formally defined event specification language. In *DEBS*, pages 50–61, 2010.

[7] A. J. Demers, J. Gehrke, B. Panda, M. Riedewald, V. Sharma, and W. M. White. Cayuga: A general purpose event monitoring system. In *CIDR*, pages 412–422, 2007.

[8] L. Ding, S. Chen, E. A. Rundensteiner, J. Tatemura, W.-P. Hsiung, and K. S. Candan. Runtime semantic query optimization for event stream processing. In *ICDE*, pages 676–685, 2008.

[9] D. M. Eyers, L. Vargas, J. Singh, K. Moody, and J. Bacon. Relational database support for event-based middleware functionality. In *DEBS*, pages 160–171, 2010.

[10] P. Kam and A. W. Fu. Discovering temporal patterns for interval-based events. In *DaWaK*, pages 317–326, 2000.

[11] J. Kang, J. F. Naughton, and S. D. Viglas. Evaluating window joins over unbounded streams. In *ICDE*, pages 341–352, March 2003.

[12] D. Kozen. Automata and computability. In *W.H.Freeman and Company, New York*, 2003.

[13] M. Li, M. Mani, E. A. Rundensteiner, and T. Lin. Constraint-aware complex event pattern detection over streams. In *DASFAA*, pages 199–215, 2010.

[14] M. Li, M. Mani, E. A. Rundensteiner, D. Wang, and T. Lin. Interval event stream processing. In *DEBS*, 2009.

[15] M. Liu, M. Li, D. Golovnya, E. A. Rundensteiner, and K. T. Claypool. Sequence pattern query processing over out-of-order event streams. In *ICDE*, pages 784–795, 2009.

[16] B. Nebel and H.-J. Burckert. Reasoning about temporal relations: A maximal tractable subclass of allen's interval algebra. In *AAAI*, pages 356–361, 1994.

[17] B. Nebel and H.-J. Burckert. Reasoning about temporal relations: A maximal tractable subclass of allen's interval algebra. *J. ACM*, 42(1):43–66, 1995.

[18] A. Paschke and P. Vincent. A reference architecture for event processing. In *DEBS*, 2009.

[19] D. Patel, W. Hsu, and M. Lee. Mining relationships among interval-based events for classification. In *SIGMOD*, pages 393–404, 2008.

[20] G. Rosu and S. Bensalem. Allen linear (interval) temporal logic - translation to ltl and monitor synthesis. In *CAV*, pages 263–277, 2006.

[21] E. A. Rundensteiner, L. Ding, T. Sutherland, Y. Zhu, B. Pielech, and N. Mehta. Cape: Continuous query engine with heterogeneous-grained adaptivity. In *VLDB*, pages 1353–1356, 2004.

[22] D. Toman. Point vs. interval-based query languages for temporal databases. In *PODS*, pages 58–67, 1996.

[23] E. Wu, Y. Diao, and S. Rizvi. High-performance complex event processing over streams. In *SIGMOD*, pages 407–418, 2006.

[24] S. Wu and Y. Chen. Mining nonambiguous temporal patterns for interval-based events. *IEEE Trans. Knowl. Data Eng.*, 19(6):742–758, 2007.

[25] H. Zhang, Y. Diao, and N. Immerman. Recognizing patterns in streams with imprecise timestamps. *PVLDB*, 3(1):244–255, 2010.

An Intelligent Event-driven Approach for Efficient Energy Consumption in Commercial Buildings: Smart Office Use Case

Nenad Stojanovic
FZI, Research Center for
Information Technology

Haid-und-Neu-Str. 10-14,
76131 Karlsruhe, Germany

nstojano@fzi.de

Dejan Milenovic
NovelTech
Kummrütistrasse 103
8810 Horgen Swiss
Dejan.Milenovic@noveltech.ch

Yongchun Xu
FZI, Research Center for
Information Technology

Haid-und-Neu-Str. 10-14,
76131 Karlsruhe, Germany

xu@fzi.de

Ljiljana Stojanovic
FZI, Research Center for
Information Technology

Haid-und-Neu-Str. 10-14,
76131 Karlsruhe, Germany

stojanov@fzi.de

Darko Anicic
FZI, Research Center for Information
Technology

Haid-und-Neu-Str. 10-14,
76131 Karlsruhe, Germany

danicic@fzi.de

Rudi Studer
FZI, Research Center for
Information Technology

Haid-und-Neu-Str. 10-14,
76131 Karlsruhe, Germany

studer@fzi.de

ABSTRACT

In this paper we present a use case related to the intelligent processing of events coming from the conventional ("cheap") sensors in order to support better energy consumption in commercial buildings. The approach has been implemented using our iCEP framework and deployed in the office space of a real working environment. This research is a kind of the proof of the concept for a new technology that the industry partner would like to exploit.

The results are very encouraging: smart decisions for the efficient usage of energy can be made by the intelligent processing of "cheap" sensor events.

Categories and Subject Descriptors

H.3.4 [Information Systems]: SYSTEMS AND SOFTWARE – information networks.

General Terms

Design, Management, Experimentation, Performance, Economics.

Keywords

Energy Efficiency, Intelligent Complex Event Processing, Smart Office

1. INTRODUCTION

Energy efficiency in commercial buildings (office space) is a hard problem: none is interested in active supporting it (who does pay indeed), so that some methods for the automatic enforcing better

energy consumption have been introduced. Usually, there are some "simple" methods to switch some electric devices on or off based on the current occupancy. For example, if the space around a lamp is inactive for more than ten minutes that lamp will be automatically switched off. This context is based on time interval or other simple conditions, which capture only a part of the real situations that the system should react on. For example, the situation that someone, who was sitting on a desk, is leaving the office, cannot be captured precisely with the traditional sensor equipment (too many false positive, which means the situations are false detected because of unexpected conditions.). Another limitation is that the existing solutions are static, i.e. based on the set of predefined rules, which introduces the problem of maintaining such a rule set (changing the rules based on the changes in the office layout or preferences of employees).

On the other hand, real situations when an energy efficiency system should react on are more sophisticated (complex) and changeable due to the dynamicity in the daily usage of an office space. For example, in an office with more than five people it is difficult to assume that none will be moving for ten minutes. Obviously, not only the information that can be obtained from sensors, but also a kind of reasoning about this information (using domain knowledge) is needed to describe these situation of interests. For example, detecting the situation leaving the office, from above, requires reasoning about the movements of a person from her/his desk till the door, which is quite demanding in the case that the office has more than three desks. To put it in a more clear form: just collecting information from sensors placed from the desk till the door is not enough for a precise detection that only one person walked that trajectory: what is needed is real-time logic reasoning about different sensors that are sensing in the same time from different positions in order to detect that a person who left the desk just walked to the next desk and that colleague left the room. Additionally, it is difficult to assume that there are fixed/predefined patterns of behavior that would lead to switching on/off light. On the opposite, it is to be expected that the behavior patterns should be monitored continuously in order to dismiss old/useless patterns and propose new ones.

Obviously, due to the progress in the development of sensor technologies, there are some systems (e.g. based on the video observation or body heat detection) that can be used for a more precise detection of the above mentioned situations of interests, but the goal of this research is to exploit the usage of the conventional ("cheap") sensors (contact-, moving-, light barrier-sensors) for this task for two reasons:

- high price may stop many customer,
- portable, easily upgradable equipment that can be installed and maintained easily in many environments

The main idea of this research is to exploit full potential of intelligent complex event processing in the detection of real-time occupancy situations in an office environment, based on the events that are coming from traditional sensors. In other words, the vision is to enable precise occupancy detection by intelligent processing of "cheap" signals (events).

Although event-based approaches have been applied in some of the scenarios for energy efficiency[1], all of them are focused on the predefined set of situations that should be discovered (in the traditional way) in real time based on the events coming from various sensors. Although these approaches can change the set of patterns to be detected, none of them, to the best knowledge of authors, is taking into account:

a) the situational awareness based on the domain knowledge and real-time events
   - in order to describe complex situations in a flexible way
b) the dynamicity of the patterns to be detected
   - in order to enable continual adaptation of the system to new situations

In this paper we present a novel approach for achieving energy efficiency that exploits real-time situational awareness in office spaces based on the use of Complex Event Processing and Semantic Technologies.

The approach has been developed in the cooperation with a small engineering company that provides sensor-based solutions and does consulting in the energy domain and whose goal is the commercialization of the solution.

The main idea is to enable a semantic-based description of the situations of interests (i.e. energy consumption patterns) and perform reasoning about those situations in real-time. The approach leverages on our work in the domain of intelligent Complex Event Processing (iCEP)[2], especially complex event reasoning, that combines a very efficient in-memory processing (on the fly) of a huge amount of streaming data and the reasoning (on the fly) using available domain knowledge and semantic complex event pattern modeling. The approach assumes the existence of the domain knowledge represented in the form of an ontology (so called domain ontology). This knowledge is required for the reasoning process described above.

The approach has been implemented using the iCEP framework and deployed in the real office work space. In the paper we present main findings from the validation experiments which are very encouraging: our current system is able to detect precisely

about 80% of leaving the office situations. Rest of 20% of situations is mainly related to some unexpected behavior that could be resolved/modeled if needed (it would take into account some rather specific situations). We present also some experimental data about savings in the energy consumptions that can be achieved in real working environments (about 30% of the energy consumption for lighting, by using low cost equipment – total costs of the sensors and actuators for an office for six people is about 300EUR). This leads to the conclusion that the proposed approach can be provided as a low-cost energy efficiency solution that will pay off very fast after introduction.

Another conclusion is that intelligent CEP is a very powerful means for different application scenarios that require "more" complex event processing, especially better understanding of the meaning of low-level events. Indeed, the main advantage of our approach is that by using the "intelligence" (domain knowledge) we can do abstraction from atomic events (like a sensor is "on"), through real-world objects activities (like the door is open), to the so called "situations of interests" (like that someone left her/his desk and went out the room). However, a higher error rate (especially false negative cases) requires a very careful treatment of the intuitive constraints (like if someone moves around a lamp don't switch it off although such an event for switching it off has been detected) that should be modeled in a generalized way in the event detection process itself. We rely on the event reasoning capabilities of our ETALIS CEP engine [2].

Additionally, our current system is able to learn improvements in the detection process (mainly by providing suggestions for the placement of new sensors in order to update some proposed complex event patterns).

The paper is structured in the following way: In the second section we give more details about our Energy Efficiency use case, from the real-time consumption point of view. In the third section we outline the architecture of our solution. In section four we describe some evaluation details, whereas section five elaborates briefly on the related work. In section six we give some concluding remarks.

2. ENERGY EFFICIENCY IN OFFICES: STATE OF THE ART AND REQUIREMENTS ANALYSIS

With energy prices on the rise and the strong push for restrictions on carbon emissions, office managers must focus on minimizing energy consumption in order to keep their business ventures competitive. However, as mentioned in the introduction, saving energy in an office is a hard task. For example, while according to Logicalis[3], 94% of workers surveyed turn their lights off at home, only 66% thought about doing the same at work. Turning off all lights is often ignored in offices, whose lights continue to shine even after everyone has gone home. On the other hand, many of the energy saving activities can be automated, like "whenever workers leave a room, the lights should be turned off" (see more examples in the Evaluation section).

There are several approaches which are dealing with the automation of this process, which are usually taking into account the following factors for the lighting issues:

- Control of the user's presence in an office, as a necessary condition to turn on the light;

---

[1] An example: A. Vijayaraghavan a D. Dornfeld, Automated energy monitoring of machine tools, CIRP Annals - Manufacturing Technology 59 (2010) 21–24

[2] See iCEP.fzi.de

[3] http://www.energysavingsecrets.co.uk/HowToRunAnEnergyEfficientOffice.html

- Regulation of the artificial light, in relation to the natural light level;

- Possibility of a manual regulation of the light, forcing the automatic regulation, in order to better meet the user's needs.

Therefore, the automation of the energy saving process is related to an efficient sensing of the current situation in an office and reacting in particular situations. The best examples are the so-called occupancy controls that limit the operation of the lighting system based on the actual use of the space. Unlike scheduling controls, they do not operate by a pre-established time schedule. Instead, the system senses when the space is occupied and turns the lights on. When the system senses that there has been no activity in the space, it assumes the space is unoccupied and turns the lights off. To prevent the system from turning the lights off while the space is still occupied but there is very little activity, a time delay typically ranging from 1 to 15 minutes can be programmed into the controls.

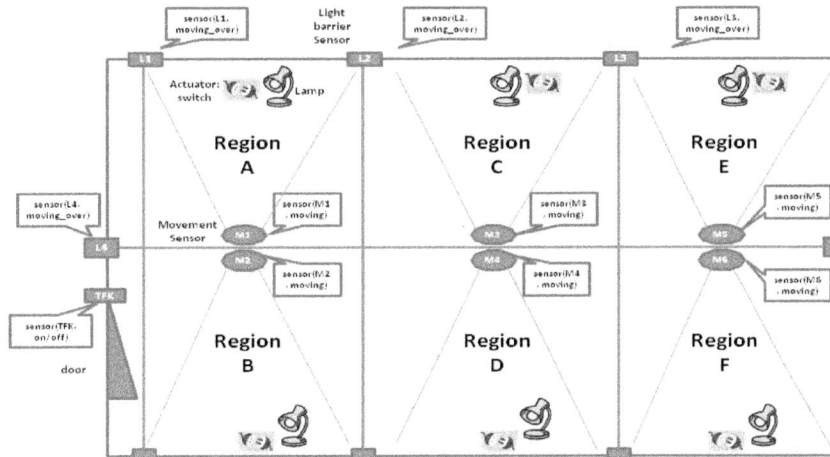

Figure 1: The distribution of sensors in a smart office. There are three types of sensors: 1) contact sensors (TFK - attached to the door), 2) moving sensors (M1 – M6) and Light barrier sensors (L1-L4)

Moreover, the need for more intelligent occupancy control has been reported in many analyses. For example, an analyses[4] in shows that intelligent control can increase the savings in the energy consumption for about 25% comparing to using standard occupancy sensors[5].

What is the main problem in current systems: lighting controls technology is not flexible (in terms of defining situations of non-occupancy) and leads to a high number of false-offs.

Let us consider the way how current control mechanisms work nowadays in a so called open office[6]:

• Requires first morning occupant to initiate Lights ON

• Permanent ON status during working hours

•Standard occupancy control during evening non-working hours

• Short time delays during late night guard walk through

The problem is that these systems have a set of predefined modus they can operate in. They can be even more sophisticated that the rules presented above, but the main limitation is that they are movement- and not situation-based. For example, state of the art system will detect the movement of a person in an office and try to react on it, e.g. if it is a first person coming in the morning, the lights will be switched on. The pattern can be even more complex, but the focus remains the same: detect movements and react on it.

Even the most sophisticated passive infrared sensors[7] that detect the heat given off by the human body that moves works on the level of a person movement.

However, in more complex, but realistic settings, such an approach demonstrates huge limitations: not only the movement, but a whole sequence of movements is relevant for detecting a situation when the occupancy of an office has been changed. Let us consider the situation depicted in Figure 1.

There is an office space with six desks with separated lighting. The task is to control the lighting of each desk by switching off/on corresponding lamp when a person (who works in the office) is leaving/entering the office. Obviously, leaving/entering the office is a complex situation in such an environment and can be detected only if the signals from different sensors (including the existence of infrared sensors) are combined in an intelligent way. In other words, the lighting control system should react on particular combinations of events generated by available sensors. For example, a combination describing that a person is leaving the region F cloud be (cf. Figure 1):

If sequence (InRegionF, InRegionD, InRegionB,OpenDoor)[8]
Then SwitchOff(LampF)   (1)

This means that a person started moving in region F, than continues through region D and B and opens the doorE. Note that there are several combinations of sensor events that describe the selected situation: leaving the room, like

If sequence (RegionF, RegionE, RegionC, RegionA, OpenDoor)
Then SwitchOff(LampF)   (2)

---

[4] http://www.objectvideo.com/objects/pdf/solutions/intelligent_bldg_automation.pdf

[5] On the other hand, standard occupancy sensors can save up to 70% of the energy consumption

[6] Example taken from: http://www.sensorswitch.com/nLight.aspx

[7] http://www.sensorswitch.com/companyoverview.aspx#_PassiveInfrared

[8] Due to the simplicity in the explanation time window is omitted

There are two problems in supporting this approach by existing control systems:

1) they can encode only simple combination (if at all) of sensor data,
2) they cannot deal with the general knowledge about the space and persons (e.g. they don't know the notion of the "neighbour regions" in an office) that can help in avoiding false positive cases (false offs)

For example, by defining the knowledge that if somebody is moving in a region, then the light in that region cannot be switched´off, we can avoid situations that although the patterns that a person is living a region has been detected, the system will not switch off the light if a movement in that region is detected in that moment.

Other important disadvantages of existing systems are:

1) the energy saving patterns are "hard-coded", which means that all patterns must be explicitly defined in order to be taken into account;

2) there is no abstraction in the pattern definition, so that any kind of generalization is excluded;
3) patterns are "static", so that any kind of changes in the initial setting cannot be realized easily.

In the following section we present an approach based on the intelligent complex event processing that satisfies these requirements.

Figure 2 shows the conceptual architecture of the combination of sensor system and iCEP system. On the left side is the sensor system containing sensors and actuators. On the right side is the iCEP system, which can process the sensor information in real time.

3. iCEP APPROACH FOR THE ENERGY EFFICIENCY

In the nutshell of the approach is the combination of a sensor system and our intelligent complex event processing (iCEP) system, as presented in Figure 2.

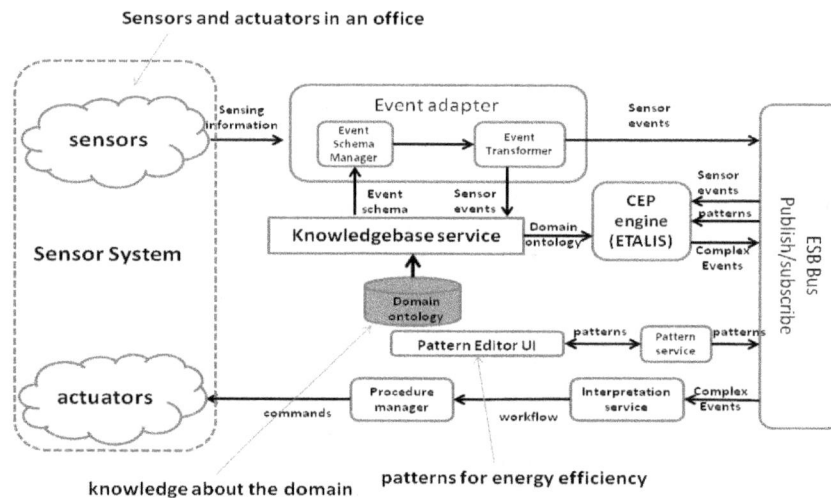

Figure 2: The conceptual architecture of the iCEP approach system for energy efficiency

Event adapter transforms the received sensing information to sensor events according to the event schema, which describes the event format that can be recognized by CEP engine. It has two sub components: **event schema manager** and **event transformer. Event schema manager** manages the event schema and sends the corresponding schema to **event transformer,** when the sensing information is received from sensors. **Event transformer** transforms the Sensing information to sensor events.

Knowledgebase service manages the all knowledgebase, which are used in our system, such as Domain Ontology. Domain ontology models the background knowledge of the use cases.

CEP engine (ETALIS) is the core of the iCEP system. ETALIS[9] is based on a declarative semantics, grounded in Logic Programming. Complex events are derived from simpler events by means of deductive rules. Due to its root in logic, ETALIS engine also supports reasoning about events, context (domain knowledge) and real-time complex situations. ETALIS loads the domain ontology and does reasoning in the domain ontology to achieve intelligent Complex Event Processing (iCEP).

ESB Bus is Enterprise Service Bus, such as Petals[10]. ESB uses publish/subscribe mechanism to transmit the data, i.e. events and patterns among other components. We use ESB in order to enable consumption of complex events by different services, like the visualization that is not presented in Figure 2.

Pattern Editor UI provides a graphic editor environment to users. **Pattern service** manages all defined patterns and sends them to the **CEP engine**.

Interpretation service interprets the results of the complex event processing and then **Procedure manager** sends the commands to the actuators.

In the rest of this section we describe how this architecture fulfills the requirements given in the previous section.

3.1. ETALIS
ETALIS Language for Events [2] is a logic-based formalism for Complex Event Processing (CEP) and Stream Reasoning. It uses SWI-Prolog Semantic Web Library to represent RDF/XML ontology as a set of Prolog rules and facts. ETALIS is an open-

---

[9] http://code.google.com/p/etalis/

[10] http://petals.ow2.org/

source implementation of the language. The language and a corresponding implementation are based on a novel event processing strategy which detects complex events by maintaining the intermediate states. Every time an atomic event (relevant w.r.t. the set of monitored events) occurs, the system updates the internal state of complex events. Essentially, this internal state encodes what atomic events are still missing for the completion a certain complex event. Complex events are detected as soon as the last event required for their detection has occurred. Descriptions telling which occurrence of an event furthers drive the detection of complex events (including the relationships between complex events and events they consist of) are given by deductive rules. Consequently, detection of complex events then amounts to an inference problem.

Event processing formalisms based on deductive or logic rules [4, 5, 6] have been attracting considerable attention as they feature formal, declarative semantics. Declarative semantics of a CEP system prescribe what the system needs to detect, i.e., a user does not need to worry how that will be detected. In this respect declarative semantics guarantees predictability and repeatability of results produced by a CEP system. Moreover, CEP systems based on deductive rules can process not only events, but also any additional background knowledge relevant with respect to the detection of complex situations in real-time. Hence a rule-based approach enables a high abstraction level and a uniform framework for programming realizing knowledge-based CEP applications (i.e., specification of complex event patterns, contextual knowledge, and their interaction). Such applications can be further supported by machine learning (more specifically data mining) tools, to automate the construction and refinement of event patterns (see [7]). Although the machine learning support per se is out of scope of this paper, we want to emphasize the importance of the formal, rule-based semantics which can further enable automated construction of both, event patterns (queries) and the background knowledge. These features are beyond capabilities of existing DSMS approaches [8, 9, 10], and this is one of reasons why ETALIS follows a logic rule-based approach for event processing.

In the following, we identify a number of benefits of the ETALIS event processing model, realized via deductive rules: First, a rule-based formalism (like the one we present in this paper) is expressive enough and convenient to represent diverse complex event patterns. Second, a formal deductive procedure guarantees the correctness of the entire event processing. Unlike reactive rules (production rules and ECA rules), declarative rules are free of side-effects; the order in which rules are evaluated is irrelevant. Third, although it is outside the scope of this paper, a deductive rule representation of complex events may further help in the verification of complex event patterns defined by a user (e.g., by discovering patterns that can never be detected due to inconsistency problems). Further on, ETALIS can also express responses on complex events (as complex actions), and reason about them in the same formalism [11]. Fourth, by maintaining the state of changes, the ETALIS event model is also capable of handling queries over the entire space (i.e. answering queries that span over multiple ongoing detections of complex events). Ultimately, the proposed event model allows for reasoning over events, their relationships, entire state, and possible contextual knowledge available for a particular domain (application). Reasoning in the ETALIS event model can be further exploited to find ways to reach a given aim, which is a task that requires some intelligence. For example, an application or a service needs to reach a stable or known (desired) state. To achieve this, the system has to have a capability to reason about, or to asses states (in a changing environment). Another example is to just "track and trace" the state of any entity at any time (in order to be able to "sense and respond" in a proactive way).

Technically, ETALIS approach is based on the decomposition of complex event patterns into intermediate patterns (i.e. goals). The status of achieved goals is materialized as first class citizens of a fact base. These materialized goals show the progress toward completion of one or more complete event patterns. Such goals are automatically asserted by rules as relevant events occur. They can persist over a period of time "waiting" in order to support detection of a more complex goal or complete pattern. Important characteristics of these goals are that they are asserted only if they are used later on (to support a more complex goal or an event pattern), that goals are all unique, and persist as long as they remain relevant (after that they can be deleted). Goals are asserted by rules which are executed in the backward chaining mode. The notable property of these rules is that they are event-driven. Hence, although the rules are executed backwards, overall they exhibit a forward chaining behavior. For more information, an interested reader is referred to [2].

3.2. Modeling domain knowledge

Using complex event processing (CEP) in a sensor system can improve the performance of the sensor system, especially in real-time requested or high data volume situation. By using patterns, users can define or change the event processing procedure without changing the hardware or software of the system. But it is not so easy for most users to define patterns, especially in the sensor system. The difficulty of the pattern definition can hurt the enthusiasm of users.

The most received events in the system are sent by sensors, which are associated with some real world entities. But normally the events contain only the identity of the sensor and the measured values and no information about the associated real world entities. Hence, the users must distinctly know the associations between the sensors and the real world entities, while the users define the patterns. This can be a too stringent requirement for most of users. Furthermore, because of large amount of the sensors the identity of the sensor is commonly a sequence of digits or letters, e.g. "15484112", "STK5125412" or "ADFBC78A", which is difficult to remember and can be easily mixed up. The measured value of an event is also a challenge: the meaning of the sensed value is not understood by every user, who wants to define the patterns.

Our intelligent complex event processing (iCEP) system uses domain ontology that models the background knowledge to solve the above problem. As shown in the Figure 3 the information of sensors, actuators and associated real world entities are modeled in the Domain ontology. *Sensor* **class** models the sensors, which are used in the system. Each sensor has several *states* according to different measured sensor values. *Actuator* **class** models the actuators of the system, such as a radio controlled switch. The functions of the actuators are described in **class** *Process*. The *Object* **class** refers to the real world entities, e.g. door, lamp and etc. Each object has several *statuses,* which describe the behaviors of the real world entities. Some of these statuses can be detected by *Sensor* with the special *State*, defined by **object property** *detectedWithState;* the others are controlled by *Actuator* by using related *Process*, defined by **object property** *controlledByProcess.* The associations between the sensors (or actuators) and real world entities are also described in the domain ontology by using **object property** *locatedIn.*

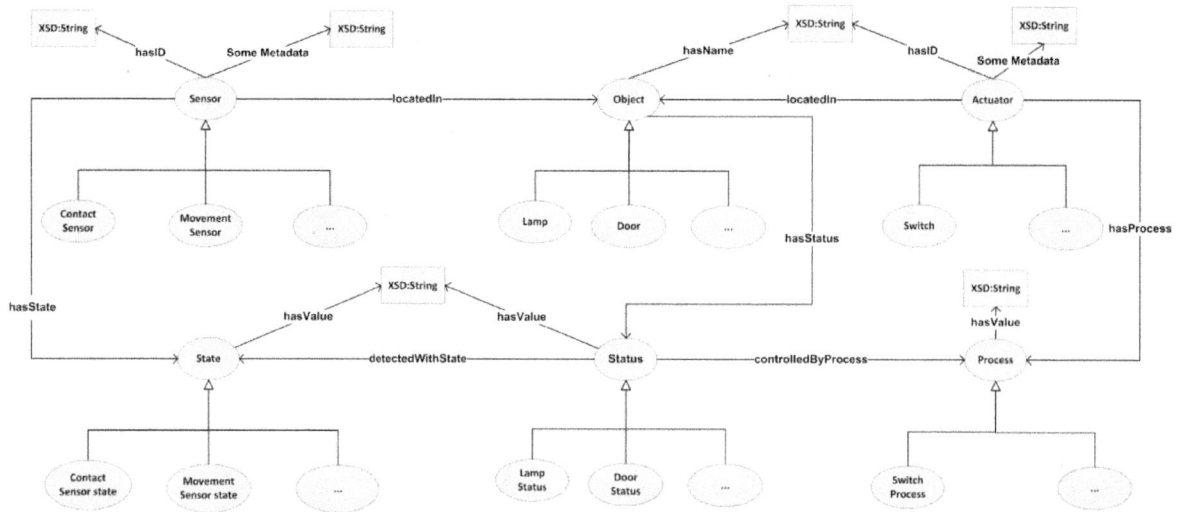

Figure 3: Domain Ontology

Since the background knowledge can be used during the event processing, pattern definition can be simpler and enable the users, who doesn't know much about sensors, defining the patterns easily.

In our iCEP system the events can be divided into two groups. The first event group is **sensor/actuator event** that is created by sensors or will be sent to actuators. The events of this type contain the sensor (or actuator) ID and the measured values (or process command for actuator), which can be difficult to grasp without special knowledge, such as *sensor ("1234453", "05H")*.

The second event group is **RWE Status event (real world entity event),** which presents the status of the real world entities. In the patterns RWE Status event can be used to describe the status of a certain real world entity, e.g. status ("front door", "open"), which can be easily understood by most users. Furthermore taking advantage of background knowledge in the domain ontology **RWE Status event** can also be used to describe the status of a kind of real world entities, which have the same character, such as status(X, "open") where (rdfs_individual_of(X, 'cep:Door')[11]), which means a door is opened. In this way we call it *universal RWE Status event.*

The patterns used in iCEP system can also be categorized into two types. The first pattern type is called a **transformation pattern**. We use transformation patterns to transform **sensor/actuator event** to **RWE Status event** or reversely. The transformation pattern should be defined by the user, who knows not only the sensor system but also the association between the sensors (actuators) and the real world entities. The following pattern is a simple example of the transformation pattern:

status(A, B) <- sensor(X, Y)[12]// transform sensor event to RWE event

WHERE

(rdfs_individual_of(Sensor, 'cep:Sensor'),	// **Sensor** is a sensor
rdf(Sensor, 'cep:hasID', X)[13],	// **Sensor** has ID **X**
rdf(State, 'cep:hasValue', Y),	// **Stats** has Value **Y**
rdfs_individual_of(State, 'cep:State'),	// **State** is a state
rdf(Sensor, 'cep:hasState', State),	// **Sensor** has a state **State**
rdf(Sensor, 'cep:locatedIn', A),	// **Sensor** is located in **A**
rdfs_individual_of(A, 'cep:Object'),	// **A** is an Object
rdf(A, 'cep:hasStatus', B),	// **A** has status **B**
rdf(B, 'cep:detectedWithState', State),	// **B** can be detected by **State**
rdfs_individual_of(B, 'cep:Status')).	// **B** is a status

3.3. Modeling complex situations

Complex situation are modeled using so called **procedure patterns**. These patterns are used to describe the workflows of the system, i.e., which status of the real world entity must be achieved when the conditions (the statuses of itself or other real world entities) are met. The procedure patterns consist of only **RWE Status events.**

The **procedure pattern** can be defined in two ways. Firstly users can use **RWE Status events** describing the status of certain real world entities to define the **procedure patterns**. Because the **RWE Status events** describing the status of certain real world entities are easy to understand, most users are able to create the patterns. The following pattern is a simple example of the procedure pattern:

status("lamp of Office 1", "on") <- status("door of office 1", "open") seq status("Desk 1", "used").

---

[11] **rdfs_individual_of**(*?Resource, ?Class*) is a function in SWI-Prolog Semantic Web Library. It tests whether the *Resource* is an individual of *class*. It returns true if *Resource* is an individual of *Class*. This implies *Resource* has an rdf:type property that refers to *Class* or a sub-class thereof. Can be used to test, generate classes *Resource* belongs to or generate individuals described by *Class*.

[12] All examples are provided in ETALIS language, see [2]

---

[13] **rdf**(*?Subject, ?Predicate, ?Object*) is a function in SWI-Prolog Semantic Web Library . It is an Elementary query for triples. Subject and Predicate are atoms representing the fully qualified URL of the resource. Object is either an atom representing a resource or literal (Value) if the object is a literal value.

This pattern describes a workflow: if the door of office 1 is opened and then the desk 1 is used, which means someone comes into the office 1 and works at desk 1, the lamp of office 1 will be switched on. This pattern defines only workflow for office 1.

In the second way users can use **universal RWE Status events** in the patterns. Such as:

status(Z, "on") <- status(X, "open") seq status(Y, "used")

WHERE

(rdfs_individual_of(W, 'cep:Office'),	// *W* is an office
rdfs_individual_of(X, 'cep:Door'),	// *X* is a door
rdfs_individual_of(Y, 'cep:Desk'),	// *Y* is a desk
rdfs_individual_of(Z, 'cep:Lamp'),	// *Z* is a lamp
rdf(W, 'cep:hasFacilities', X),	// *W* has door *X*
rdf(W, 'cep:hasFacilities', Y),	// *W* has desk *Y*
rdf(W, 'cep:hasFacilities', Z)).	// *W* has lamp *Z*

This pattern has the same function as the above pattern, but it defines the workflow not only for office 1 but also for all other offices, which are modeled in the domain ontology. We call such a pattern **general procedure pattern.** It can define the workflow for all similar situations and is easy to maintain, although it is not very simple for most users.

3.4. Reasoning with patterns

As already mentioned, one of the main advantages of our approach is the possibility to define the situations of interests in a declarative way and reason about them based on the incoming sensor data.

In order to illustrate the abstractions introduced by ETALIS, we present here a very illustrative example for the occupancy control based on the office context presented in Figure 1.

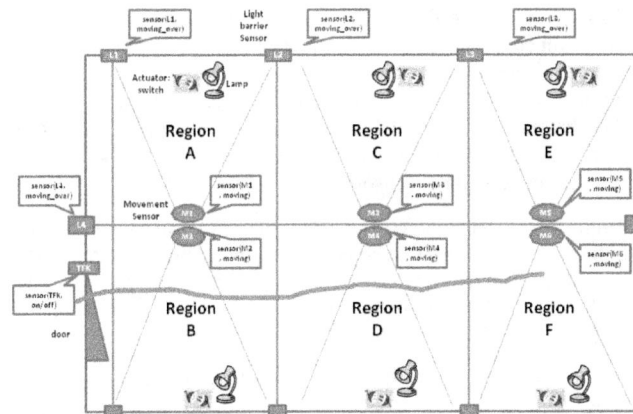

Figure 4: A possible path from the office desk to the door: a situation that can lead to switching off the lamp at the desk in the Region F

In the traditional approaches, the situation of interests:

"a person left the room and her/his desk lamp should be switched off within 5 sec"

must be described by using one rule for each possible situation. An example is illustrated in Figure 4: a person left the room by traversing from Region F, through Region D and B till the door.

Therefore, traditional approaches must cover all possible "evacuation" paths which is a tedious and error prone process. The situation is even worse when we consider that the distribution of objects in the office can be changed – the whole set of rules must be rewritten.

On the other hand, in our approach there is only one logic-based statement that covers all requested situations, by describing them declaratively:

Namespace: cep: http://www.icep.fzi.de/cepsensor.owl#

Pattern.event:

door_open <- status('cep:door', 'cep:door_opened').

status(A, B) <- sensor(X, Y)

WHERE

(rdfs_individual_of(Sensor, 'cep:Sensor'),	// *Sensor* is a sensor
rdf(Sensor, 'cep:hasID', X),	// the ID of *Sensor* is X
rdf(State, 'cep:hasValue', Y),	// the value of *State* is Y
rdfs_individual_of(State, 'cep:State'),	// *State* is a state
rdf(Sensor, 'cep:hasState', State),	// *Sensor* has a state *State*
rdf(Sensor, 'cep:locatedIn', A),	// *Sensor* is located in *A*
rdfs_individual_of(A, 'cep:Object'),	// *A* is an Object
rdf(A, 'cep:hasStatus', B),	// *A* has status *B*
rdf(B, 'cep:detectedWithState', State),	// status *B* is detected by *State*
rdfs_individual_of(B, 'cep:Status')).	// *B* is Status

movement(Loc1,Loc2) <- status(Loc1, 'cep:movementInRegion') SEQ status(Bord, 'cep:moveover') SEQ status(Loc2, 'cep:movementInRegion')

WHERE

(rdfs_individual_of(Loc1, 'cep:Region'),	// *Loc1* is a region
rdfs_individual_of(Loc2, 'cep:Region'),	// *Loc2* is a region
rdfs_individual_of(Bord, 'cep:Borderline'),	// *Bord* is a borderline
rdf(Loc1, 'cep:hasNeighbor', Loc2),	// *Loc1* is neighbour of *Loc2*
rdf(Loc1, 'cep:hasBorderline', Bord),	// *Loc1* has borderline *Bord*
rdf(Loc2, 'cep:hasBorderline', Bord))2sec.	// *Loc2* has borderline *Bord*

comment: this statement detects the situation that a person has changed the region, if within 2 sec the movement sensor and light barrier sensor for a Region has been activated

movement(Loc1,Loc3) <- movement(Loc1,Loc2) SEQ movement(Loc2,Loc3) .

movement(Loc, 'cep:door') <- (movement(Loc, 'cep:regionB') SEQ status(Bord, 'cep:moveover')) 2sec.

comment: this statement is the most crucial one: by introducing recursive rules we are able to describe all possible paths which are containing succeeding regions

SwitchOff(Loc) <- (movement(Loc, 'cep:door') SEQ door_open)5sec.

comment: this statement detects the situation that a person has left the room (after a sequence of traversing between regions) and that after 5 sec the light at the starting location should be switched off

The main advantages of the proposed approach are from the point of view of deploying it in real environment by using non-specialized personal:

- It separates the real world entity level from the sensor/actuator level
- It is easy to add new sensors or actuators and new associations between the sensor/actuator and real world entities by modifying the domain ontology.
- Transformation patterns don't need to be changed by adding new sensors/ actuators or changing the association between the sensors and real world entities, if there is no change in the ontology and event format.
- Procedure patterns are easy to understand and can be defined by most of users.
- General procedure patterns reduce the pattern definition overhead
- General procedure patterns simplify the maintenance of patterns.

4. EVALUATION

The presented approach has been developed as a part of the framework for Energy efficiency designed by an innovative SME, one of authors is with. The approach has been tested in a real office environment and in this section we present the most important results.

The use case is based on simulating occupancy control situations that limit the operation of the lighting system based on the actual use of the space. In other words, if there is a situation that leads to possibly saving energy, being recognized in a way specified in Section 3.4, the corresponding lighting source should be either dimmed or switched off. In order to make the test realistic we have implemented the set of energy consumption patterns developed for a Building Energy Challenge[14].

We have modeled all these patterns using ETALIS language and the Information model (ontologies) mentioned in Section 3. There were 35 ETALIS procedure patterns (understandable for non-specialized users) as described in Section 3.3. The setting of the sensors was very similar to that presented in Figure 1.

In the evaluation we used ELV FS20 sensor systems including FS20 PIRI-2 motion sensor, FS20 IR light barrier sensor, FS20 TFK contact sensor and FS20 ST-3 radio electrical socket. The motion sensor and the light barrier sensor have a minimal send time interval of 8 seconds, which means they can only send a single value every 8 seconds. In the case of a high activity frequency, the sensors can't detect all activities.

We performed two general types of tests:
A. Completeness of modeling situations using ETALIS language
B. Energy savings using the proposed approach

For *test A* we performed two tests:

1) the coverage of the situations from the Building Energy Challenge with the ETALIS rules in a declarative way

---

14 A contest regarding energy consumption between several office buildings within a company, see: http://www.artist-embedded.org/docs/Events/2010/GREEMBED/
0_GREEMBED_Papers/IntUBE 20- 20GREEMBED.pdf

Results:

- each relevant situation has been described with one ETALIS statement. For the manual method (describing each individual rule without any generalization as ETALIS can do) about 250 rules would be used. It is obvious that the rule maintenance in our case is much more easier
- ETALIS experts must be involved in the process of generating new statements. Especially error prone is the syntax of the language. We are anyway working on the editor for the ETALIS language that might resolve this problem (in a way)

2) The precision of the detection process

Result:

- In the specialized test that ran within ten days in the office environment we experienced 903 situations that belong to the list of defined energy consumption patterns. Using ETALIS engine we detected 734 situations (more that 80%). There were 42 situations which hadn't been detected since there was an error in sensors readings. ETALIS currently supports some types of the advanced detection, like out-of-order detection or event retraction that might help in such situations. However, in this experiment we didn't use them
- There were 135 situations that ETALIS couldn't recognize since the setting of sensors was not sufficient to recognize them due to various reasons we describe in *test B*

In the context of *test B* we performed an experiment in order to measure savings in the energy consumption. We have measured the power saving time in the period of one month on in an office with six work places. We find this setting as a very common one. As already explained, our declarative approach doesn't depend on the number of sensors and the size of the room. We performed several changes in the layout of the room (position of sensors) but without the need to change the complex event patterns. Therefore, the abstraction provided by our language is correct: interesting situations are defined on the level of objects, independently from the current position of sensors.

Table 1 presents the results from this experiment. In the last column we present the average value of measurements and in the rest of the columns the values for four particular days (1st, 10th, 20th and 30th) in order to illustrate how theses consumption values varied.

Power saving time represents the time when some electric devices were switched off because of the situation that the corresponding person (related to that device) had left the room.

We are quite satisfied with the general result of the experiment: the proposed approach leads to significant reductions in the energy consumption. We didn't encounter any example of the false positive.

The only problem we have faced is the rather huge error rate, whereas an error represents the number of situations that hadn't been detected by using currently deployed patterns (false negative). In the following we give an explanation (i.e. interfere factors) of these situations.

310

Table 1: The results from the experiment

	1st day	10th day	20th day	30th day	average
Power saving time:	33089s	19548s	58133s	42152s	**38255s**
Total time:	109199s	103665s	124676s	117021s	**111354s**
Proportion:	30.3%	18.9%	46.6%	36%	**34.3%**
Error:	12	13	18	10	**13**
Total times of switch:	67	56	59	56	**62**
Error rate	17.9%	23.2%	30.5%	17.9%	**18.3%**

The first interfere factor is the precision of the sensors. In the evaluation we used ELV FS20 sensor systems including FS20 PIRI-2 motion sensor, FS20 IR light barrier sensor, FS20 TFK contact sensor and FS20 ST-3 radio electrical socket. The motion sensor and the light barrier sensor has have a minimal send time interval of 8 seconds, which means it they can only send a single value every 8 seconds. In the case of a high activity frequency, the sensors can't detect all activities. Furthermore, the sensors can't detect some situations such as two people come into the office together. In this situation - the sensors are not able to recognize the number of the people and only one lamp will be switched on. To overcome this factor, we can use more sensors and the better sensors to increase the precision of the event detection.

The second interfere factor is unanticipated activity in the office. For example, one a user forgets to close the door after coming into the office. Then when another user leaves the office, he doesn't need to open the door, which is a necessary event according to the pattern. In this situation, the lamp will also not be switched off. Similarly, a visitor has visited the office, when he leaves the office, one lamp in the office will be wrongly switched off. This factor problem can be overcome by installing automatic door closing device and using new sensor technologies (such as RFID) to recognize the identity of the user such as RFID.

The third interfere factor is results from the fact that the pattern definition doesn't match the character of a user. In the pattern we have defined that the movement event and door open event must happen within 5 seconds to trigger the switch off event. If one a user is accustomed to do something else costing more than 5 seconds before he opens the door, then his lamp will not be switched off. The problem can be solved by doing some study on the characters of the users before defining the patterns.

Modeling the above mentioned situations will be one of the subjects of the further work.

Discussion: As we already stated in the introduction, these results are very encouraging: our approach can be used for precise modeling of about 80% of relevant situations that results in a saving of about 30% of average energy consumption in an office space with separated lighting system for each work place. Rest of 20% could be modeled by using more sensors or more complicated patterns. This procedure can be applied in some specific, customized use cases where the precision of the detection is a very important factor.

On the other side the sensor equipment we have used is very cheap: about 300EUR for the presented testing environment. It leads to the conclusion that such a solution will pay off in a short period of time. Obviously the business model for the provider of this solution would be offering services for modeling and maintaining situations, including modeling of domain ontology. By taking into account that the maintenance of this approach

(pattern management) can also be supported by the iCEP framework the total costs is still quite low.

In this paper we don't tackle the problem of false positive situations, i.e. switching on/off the lights in wrong situations. Very briefly, except some trivial design errors we faced at the beginning of experiments, this problem didn't disturb the participants in the experiment significantly (informal interviews). Since we have been focused on the energy saving, we performed only analyses related to that issue. However, false positive are the subjects of the test we are about to perform.

5. RELATED WORK

In this section we present only the related work regarding the current lighting control systems. Related work to our approach for complex event processing can be found in [2].

Current lighting and climate control systems often rely on building regulation maximum occupancy numbers for maintaining proper lighting and temperatures. However, in many situations, there are rooms that are used infrequently, and may be lighted, heated or cooled needlessly. Having knowledge regarding occupancy and being able to accurately predict usage patterns may allow significant energy-savings.

In [13], the authors reported on the deployment of a wireless camera sensor network for collecting data regarding occupancy in a large multi-function building. They constructed multivariate Gaussian and agent based models for predicting user mobility patterns in buildings.

In [14], the authors identified that the majority of this energy waste occurs during the weekdays, not during the weeknights or over the weekends. They showed that this pattern of energy waste is particularly suited to be controlled by occupancy sensors, which not only prevent runaway operation after typical business hours, but also capture savings during the business day.

An analysis of the impact of the new trends in energy efficient lighting design practices on human comfort and productivity in the modern IT offices is given in [14].

In [15], the authors presented the design and implementation of a presence sensor platform that can be used for accurate occupancy detection at the level of individual offices. The presence sensor is low-cost, wireless, and incrementally deployable within existing buildings.

An examination of different types of buildings and their energy use is given in [16]. The authors discussed opportunities available to improve energy efficient operation through various strategies from lighting to computing.

As a conclusion, there are many approaches for the lighting control, but none of them is using a more declarative approach that would enable efficient real-time situation detection.

6. CONCLUSION

In this paper we presented a novel approach for achieving energy efficiency in commercial buildings (especially sensor-enabled offices) based on the application of intelligent complex event processing and semantic technologies. In the nutshell of the approach is an efficient method for realizing real-time situational awareness that helps in recognizing the situations where a more efficient energy consumption is possible and reaction on those opportunities promptly. Semantics allows a proper contextualization of the sensor data (its abstract interpretation).

Complex event processing enables the efficient real-time processing of sensor data and its logic-based nature supports a declarative definition of the situations of interests.

The approach has been implemented using the iCEP framework and deployed in the real office work space. In the paper we present main findings from the validation experiments which are very encouraging: our current system is able to detect precisely about 80% of leaving the office situations. Rest of 20% of situations is mainly related to some unexpected behaviour that could be resolved/modeled if needed (it would take into account some rather specific situations). We present also some experimental data about savings in the energy consumptions that can be achieved in real working environments (about 30% of the energy consumption for lighting, by using low cost equipment – total costs of the sensors and actuators for an office for six people is about 300EUR). This leads to the conclusion that the proposed approach can be provided as a low-cost energy efficiency solution that will pay off very fast after introduction.

Another conclusion is that intelligent CEP is a very powerful means for different application scenarios that require "more" complex event processing, especially better understanding of the meaning of low-level events. One of the main advantages is the usage of the domain knowledge (ontology) that enables a very efficient abstraction from atomic events (like a sensor is "on"), though real-world objects activities (like the door is open), to the so called "situations of interests" (like that someone left her/his desk and went out the room).

Additionally, our current system is able to learn improvements in the detection process (mainly by providing suggestions for the placement of new sensors in order to update some proposed complex event patterns).

Future work will be related to modeling a more comprehensive set of patterns for representing more complex situations as described in the Evaluation section. Additionally, new tests for false positive cases have been planned

REFERENCES

[1] K. Thirunarayan, C. Henson, and A. Sheth, Situation Awareness via Abductive Reasoning for Semantic Sensor Data: A Preliminary Report , in Proceedings of the 2009 International Symposium on Collaborative Technologies and Systems (CTS 2009), Baltimore, MD, May 18-22, 2009.

[2] D. Anicic, P. Fodor, S. Rudolph, R. Stuehmer, N. Stojanovic, and R. Studer. A rule-based language for complex event processing and reasoning. In Proceedings of the 4th International Conference on Web Reasoning and Rule Systems (RR 2010), pages 42–57, 2010.

[3] M., Deepak: SNOOP: An Event Specification Language For Active Database Systems. Master Thesis, University of Florida, 1991

[4] D. Carney, U. Cetintemel, M. Cherniack, C. Convey, S. Lee, G. Seidman, M. Stonebraker, N. Tatbul, and S. Zdonik. Monitoring streams: a new class of data management applications. In VLDB '02: Proceedings of the 28th international conference on Very Large Data Bases. VLDB Endowment, 2002.

[5] Ray. Nonmonotonic abductive inductive learning. In Journal of Applied Logic, 2008.

[6] C. Gutierrez, C. A. Hurtado, and A. A. Vaisman. Introducing time into rdf. In the IEEE Transactions on Knowledge and Data Engineering, 19(2):207–218, 2007.

[7] E. Ryvkina, A. S. Maskey, M. Cherniack, and S. Zdonik. Revision processing in a stream processing engine: A high-level design. In Proc. Int. Conf. on Data Eng. (ICDE). Atlanta, GA, USA, 2006.

[8] J. Agrawal, Y. Diao, D. Gyllstrom, and N. Immerman. Efficient pattern matching over event streams. In Proceedings of the 28th ACM SIGMOD Conference, pages 147–160, 2008.

[9] R. S. Barga, J. Goldstein, M. H. Ali, and M. Hong. Consistent streaming through time: A vision for event stream processing. In Proceedings of the 3rd Biennial Conference on Innovative Data Systems Research (CIDR'07), pages 363–374, 2007.

[10] A. Arasu, S. Babu, and J. Widom. The cql continuous query language: semantic foundations and query execution. VLDB Journal, 15(2):121–142, 2006.

[11] D. Anicic and N. Stojanovic. Expressive logical framework for reasoning about complex events and situations. In Intelligent Event Processing - AAAI Spring Symposium 2009. Stanford University, California, 2009.

[12] Recommendation from the French Construction code for construction and housing

[13] http://www.legifrance.gouv.fr/affichCodeArticle.do;jsessioni d=87AE72FAE86DC9CF56B8673C1B88F9AD.tpdjo08v_2? cidTexte=LEGITEXT000006074096&idArticle=LEGIARTI 000006896264&dateTexte=20090619&categorieLien=id

[14] V. L. Erickson et al., Energy Efficient Building Environment Control Strategies Using Real-time Occupancy Measurements, in Proceedings of the First ACM Workshop on Embedded Sensing Systems for Energy-Efficiency in Buildings, pages 19--24, 2009.

[15] B. von Neida et al., An analysis of the energy and cost savings potential of occupancy sensors for commercial lighting systems, http://www.lrc.rpi.edu/resources/pdf/dorene1.pdf

[16] R. Walawalkar et al, Effect of Efficient Lighting on Ergonomic Aspects in Modern IT Offices, http://www.walawalkar.com/info/Publications/Papers/ EE&Ergonomics.pdf

[17] Y. Agarwal et al., Occupancy-driven energy management for smart building automation, in Proceedings of the 2nd ACM Workshop on Embedded Sensing Systems for Energy-Efficiency in Building, 2010

A Complex Event Processing Architecture for Energy and Operation Management

Industrial Experience Report

Jimi Y. C. Wen   Gu Yuan Lin   Today Sung

Minsiong Liang   Gary Tsai   Ming Whei Feng

Networks and Multimedia Institute, Institute for Information Industry, Taipei, Taiwan
{jimi, guyuan, today, minsiong, garytsai, mfeng } @nmi.iii.org.tw

ABSTRACT

In this report, we share our experience in developing a complex event processing architecture that bridges sensors networks to an energy management system used in the context of chain convenient stores. We analyze event data in real-time to generate immediate and predictive appliance/operation insights and enable instant response defined by simple business rules. For intuitive rule management, preprocessed events should be used in many cases instead of raw events collected from sensor network. We illustrate practical energy and operation management rules based on preprocessed events such as forecasted and classified events in addition to raw events.

Categories and Subject Descriptors

H.2.8 [**Database Management**]: Database Applications—*Data Mining, Prediction*; H.3.5 [**Information Storage and Retrieval**]: On-line Information Services—*Commercial services, Web-based services*; H.4.2 [**Information Systems Applications**]: Types of Systems—*Decision support*; I.5.1 [**Pattern Recognition**]: Models—*Statistical*; I.5.4 [**Pattern Recognition**]: Applications—*Signal Processing*; J.1 [**Administrative Data Processing**]: [Business]

General Terms

Algorithm, Performance, Design, Languages

1. INTRODUCTION

In this report, we share our experience in developing a complex event processing architecture that bridges sensors networks to an energy management system used in the context of chain convenient stores. Complex event processing (CEP) is the analysis of event data in real-time to generate

immediate insight and enable instant response to changing conditions [6]. Sensors networks (SN) are an important type of event data in the context of an EMS and SNs weave a picture of store operation from energy consumption. Continuous streams of sensor readings can be tapped and fed into analytical algorithms in real time for predictive analytics (PA) and generate alerts for possible response actions [11]. Integrating PA into CEP architectures opens a wide range of possibilities in several proactive computing application where the response action should be triggered earlier in anticipation before the occurrence event.

We differentiate three types concepts of events in our CEP architecture and discuss their role in the context of the EMS: I) *Raw events*: frequently updated time stamped (FUTS) data energy consumption data. This first type of events deal with interfacing the database with the CEP platform and event producer such as sensors and other FUTS data sources. II).(a) *Preprocessed event-forecasted*: the likelihood of the events forecasted using mathematical methods, when the maximum energy consumption is above given thresholds, based on *Raw events*. II).(b) *Preprocessed event-classified*: a derived event using artificial intelligence methods (AI) by classifying *Raw events* into store operation events. These second type of events deal with intelligent domain-specific data analysis, where the forecasting or classification algorithm can be packaged as configurable computational plugins and used in the higher level rule language. III) *Derived event*: a higher level event defined by declarative rules on raw or previously preprocessed events. The third type of events represents the event-condition of event-condition-action (ECA) rules, which is particularly suited to event-driven monitoring and control of, energy consumption and store operation.

We illustrate the effectiveness of our CEP architecture in the context of minimizing the maximum contracted demand (MCD [10]) contracts in large-scale chain convenience stores and monitoring the store's standard operating procedure (SOP) management. For effective and intuitive rule management in the application context, derived events are often needed, i.e., writing practical applications based raw events or sensor level data, would increase the complexity in the rule management. It is better to balance the '*C*' in CEP in both the event condition and the processing of data for more intuitive and powerful application development.

2. APPLICATION OBJECTIVES

Our CEP platform is implemented and experimented with the application objective of monitoring store operation with energy-econ-awareness.

2.1 Maximum Contracted Demand Contract

A MCD contract is an agreement between the consumers and the utilities on the maximum demand load that the consumer plans to use for a given time period [10]; if the consumers use more than the agreed load, they are charged a high penalty. This type of contract is advantageous in two ways: i) Knowledge of these MCD contracts allow the utilities a better estimate on demand, therefore the utilities can plan more effective electricity generation and transmission infrastructure. ii) The consumers reduce their electricity cost if they use their electricity more effectively under the agreed maximum demand load while not necessarily decreasing their overall electricity consumption, i.e., equivalent production.

2.2 Store Operation

A practical EMS should not be a system of only minimizing energy consumption or energy cost, but it should taken into account of the context in which the EMS is to be used. In a convenience store, the context can be defined by the store's SOP, where sale performance might be more valued than pure energy related performance. We focus on the part of the SOP related to equipment and appliance operation in our EMS, e.g., switching off the refrigerator would minimize energy consumption, but this course of action could lead to a decrease of cold drink sales in the hot summer day. Thus maybe the optimal point would be increasing refrigerator temperature a degree or two which would reduce the energy consumption by a bit, but retain the same number of sales. Similarly a home EMS should taken into account comfort and convenience of the residents. Thus it is important to be able to set different rules for different contexts.

3. RELATED WORK

There are increasing interests in improving software solutions using complex event processing in many different applications [4], e.g., logistics, operation monitoring, information dissemination, threat Detection, financial applications, health monitor, smart homes and cities, gaming etc. Klien and Jerzak applied their implementation framework in the context of a sustainable manufacturing plant automation, covering the whole end-to-end energy life cycle of products starting from production and ending with daily use [5]. Guerra et al. presented, based on the Intensive Care Unit environment of the University of Utah Health Sciences Center, a system that: i) integrates in one place historical data, events, rules, and data mining models; ii) is highly customizable letting users create or change rules; and iii) identifies possible future risks by performing data mining in soft-real-time [3]. Tóth implemented a proof of concept on real world data to extend their CEP with predictive capabilities in the context of conference prediction in a given space [11]. We implement our CEP in the context of store operation monitoring with energy-econ-awareness.

Klien and Jerzak proposed a GINSENG Data Processing Framework (DPF), which is composed of a stateless publish/subscribe system, traditional event stream processing system and business rule processing engine [5]. Their DPF

closes the gap between the devices and the business management systems. In order to infer high-level phenomena, Wun et al. proposed a semantic engine such that sensor data can be filtered, aggregated, correlated, and translated from many heterogeneous and dispersed sensor networks [13]. Ranganathan developed tools that allow domain experts to construct, parameterize and deploy specific flows that follow a certain pattern [9]. These 'functional' patterns help in codifying best practices in terms of event processing flows in different domains. In this paper, we focus on specific flows at the sensor-level data, i.e., forecasted events and classified events, such that domain experts can write down relevant rules to define events at management level. Our *preprocessed events* not only close the gap but the vocabulary of the devices is increased such that business rules can be applied to more applications. Our contribution includes new scope in semantics, thus more high-level phenomena can be inferred.

4. ARCHITECTURE OVERVIEW

In this section, we give a detailed description of our CEP architecture as seen in Fig. 1.

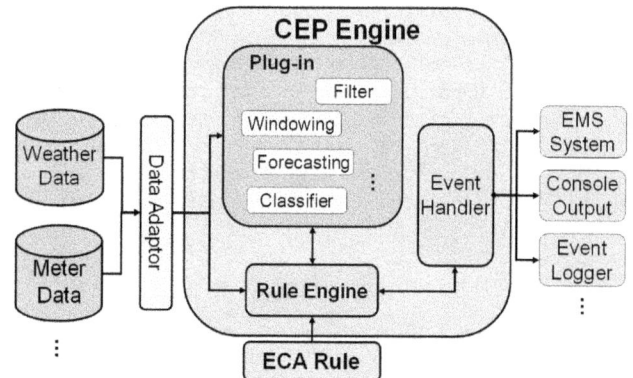

Figure 1: CEP platform for EMS system.

4.1 Raw Events

For flexible and scalable deployment of our sensor network (as can be seen in Fig. 2), we used power meters, iMeter equipped with our own developed Zigbee communication module, which is then connected to a gateway. This allows the server to control the iMeter via the internet. Each iMeter can measure 12 single-phase circuits and the voltage, current, power factor, real power, apparent power and energy can be recorded for the store and for each appliance. For the database server we use a push-pull strategy, where the database server send query to the iMeter circuits. These circuits have been monitored since 2010 July, with a total of 566 circuits available for query. Another source we use in our system is from Yahoo! Weather RSS Feed[1] which includes attributes such as, timestamp, temperature, wind direction, wind speed, humidity, visibility, air pressure, the time of sunrise and sunset, and weather condition.

4.2 Preprocessed Events

Many different processed event types are necessary for complex event processing, because it is intuitive to keep rule

---

[1] http://developer.yahoo.com/weather/

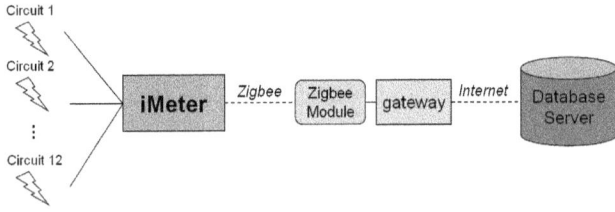

Figure 2: Sensor Network Deployment.

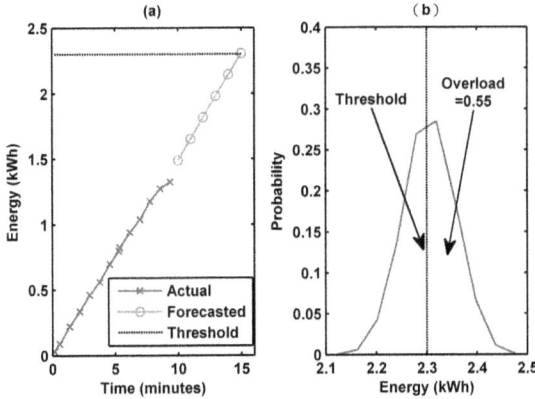

Figure 3: Load forecasting events; (a) time series forecast, (b) likelihood of event.

management simple for application users. We want system operators to deal with higher level business rules, we do not expect system operators to be writing rules to do complex computation of power signals. We discuss briefly two types of preprocessed events that were packaged as plug-ins used in our CEP in our EMS.

4.2.1 Forecasted Events

In our initial implementation, we use causal forecasting methods using time factor, i.e., a similar day of week and similar time of day approach [12]. We use 15 minute intervals, a good trade off between time resolution and sample size for consistent modelling. For each store we create a simple statistical model for each similar load profile. We then carry out numerical simulations over a large number of outcomes based on the likelihood of our load profile statistical models. Since the parameters of our application, power consumption, is dynamic by nature, we choose to implement this plug-in using the simulation approach instead of the online scoring approach [1]. The forecasted event for overload in the contract period can be attributed with a probability distribution of the load as can be seen in Fig. 3, which can be discretized into events based on the likelihood and used for higher level rule management.

4.2.2 Classified Events

We monitor each appliance, such as central air conditioner, different set of refrigerators, lighting, etc. Since the measurement is continuous, and needs to be classified into states for easier rule management. Although most events regarding appliances comprise of on-off states which can be classified using simple threshold classifiers, they can be implemented using ECA rules. We have some fault detection events for some appliances which require a domain-knowledge classifying algorithm. Preprocessed events from sensor signals, forecasted or classified can be used in the rule

manager for useful energy or operation management, i.e., SOPs can easily be defined in the rule manager in terms of derived events.

4.3 Rule-based Events

For the rule manager which comprise of the rule engine and event handler, we use a RIF-like[2] syntax to illustrate some of the basic SOP events expressed in ECA rules:

- *Raw event* only: if sensor data *dropout*, message for system maintenance appointment.

```
Forall ?S ?M ?R (
If And ( "op:time-now" ( ?TN )
        "Sensor:Data"( ?S ?TN ?D )
        "Data:TimeStamp"( ?D ?T )
        "op:time-after" ( ?TN "5m" ?T)
        "Event:Message" ("Event:DataLoss" ?M )
        "Event:Receiver" ("Receiver:Maintenance" ?R )
Then Do( Action(?M ?R "op:Send-Message") ) )
```

- *Preprocessed event-classified* only: if billboard is not *on* anytime from 5pm to 5am, alert store manager to switch the billboard on.

```
Forall ?B ?M ?R (
If And ( "op:time-now" ( ?T )
        "Billboard:PowerOn"( ?B ?OOn )
        "op:time-between"( ?T "17:00" "05:00" )
        "op:text_match"( ?OOn "Off" )
        "Event:Alert" ("Event:BBPowerOff" ?M )
        "Event:Receiver" ("Receiver:Manager" ?R )
Then Do( Action(?M ?R "op:Send-Alert") ) )
```

- *Preprocessed event-forecasted* only: If overload probability is high, alert store manager

```
"Event:OverLoad" (?Ev) :-
Exists ?S (
And ( "op:time-now" ( ?T )
      "LoadForcast:Shop"( ?S ?T, ?LA)
      "PowerConsumption:Contract" ( ?S ?PC )
      "op:greater-than"( ?LA ?PC ) ) )
Forall ?Ev ?R (
If And ( "Event:ReadBuffer"( ?Ev "Event:OverLoad" )
        "Event:Receiver" ("Receiver:Manager" ?R )
Then Do( Action(?Ev ?R "op:Send-Alert") ) )
```

We now show some examples that incorporate combination of different layers of event to create more powerful and richly described SOP events:

- If overload probability is high and oden[3] cooker is on and outdoor temperature is above 30°C, then alert to switch off the oden cooker.

```
"Event:OdenOff" (?Ev, ?T) :-
Exists ?Ev ?O (
And ( "Event:ReadBuffer"( ?Ev "Event:OverLoad" )
      "Electricity:ODenCooker"( ?O )
      "Electricity:PowerOn"( ?O, ?OOn )
      "Environment:Temperature"( ?TM )
      "op:greater-than"( ?TM "30" )
      "op:text_match"( ?OOn "On" )
      "op:time-now" ( ?T ) ) )

Forall ?Ev ?O (
If And ( "Event:OdenOff"( ?Ev ?T )
```

[2]http://www.w3.org/TR/2010/NOTE-rif-overview-20100622/
[3]http://en.wikipedia.org/wiki/Oden

```
        "op:time-now" ( ?TN )
        "Electricity:PowerOn"( ?O, ?OOn )
        "op:text_match"( ?OOn "On" )
        "op:time-after" ( ?TN "5m" ?T)
Then Do( Action(?O "op:power-off") ) )
```

5. DISCUSSIONS AND CONCLUSIONS

Etzion and Niblett suggested the future of CEP to be 'going from monolithic to diversified', 'going from stand-alone to embedded', 'intelligent event processing' [2]. We do not aim to build a general purpose CEP, but specific to EMS application and embedded in our EMS. We try to illustrate so called intelligent event processing by classifying raw sensor data which could cause uncertainty or inexactness, and by introducing forecasted events, our event processing is proactive rather than reactive.

Mednes et al. proposed a framework for benchmarking CEP engines [8], which include latency, throughout, accuracy, etc. Mendes et al. then evaluated micro-benchmarks on three CEP engines [7]. While in the context of high frequency trading, internet activity monitoring deal with events in seconds or milliseconds, evaluation metrics such as latency and throughput are key performance indices. Our application deals with time resolution in minutes, since sensor signal at a higher sampling rate would just include more noise and burden the computation. The events in our application comprise of human activity events, in which time resolution in minutes is more appropriate. Therefore we believe a more suitable benchmarks should include application specific performance: accuracy, electricity bills or potentially with the integration of point of sale systems, revenue analysis. These type of performances are harder to measure quantitatively and can be considered to be independent of the CEP engine. From the industry point of view, how enabling the CEP is in creating valued added solutions is the most important benchmark.

Experiments in six store locations show promising results and benefits of the proposed CEP architecture/platform for our proactive application scenario. We implemented simple data integration and developed and integrated intelligent algorithms into our application. These intelligent algorithms can be configured in the rule manager for rapid (re)development of high level energy and operation management. SOPs of the stores can then be enhanced and modified for better store KPI by monitoring event patterns with business objectives in mind.

6. ADDITIONAL AUTHORS

Additional authors: David Wu (Networks and Multimedia Institute, Institute for Information Industry, email: david.wu@nmi.iii.org.tw)

7. REFERENCES

[1] M. K. Chandy, O. Etzion, and R. von Ammon. Executive summary and manifesto – event processing. In K. M. Chandy, O. Etzion, and R. von Ammon, editors, *Event Processing*, number 10201 in Dagstuhl Seminar Proceedings, Dagstuhl, Germany, 2011. Schloss Dagstuhl - Leibniz-Zentrum fuer Informatik, Germany.

[2] O. Etzion and P. Niblett. *Event Processing in Action*. Manning Publications, 1 edition, 2010.

[3] D. Guerra, U. Gawlick, and P. Bizarro. An integrated data management approach to manage health care data. In *Proceedings of the Third ACM International Conference on Distributed Event-Based Systems*, DEBS '09, pages 40:1–40:2, New York, NY, USA, 2009. ACM.

[4] A. Hinze, K. Sachs, and A. Buchmann. Event-based applications and enabling technologies. In *Proceedings of the Third ACM International Conference on Distributed Event-Based Systems*, DEBS '09, pages 1:1–1:15, New York, NY, USA, 2009. ACM.

[5] A. Klein and Z. Jerzak. Ginseng for sustainable energy awareness: flexible energy monitoring using wireless sensor nodes. In *Proceedings of the Fourth ACM International Conference on Distributed Event-Based Systems*, DEBS '10, pages 109–110, New York, NY, USA, 2010. ACM.

[6] Y. Magid, G. Sharon, S. Arcushin, I. Ben-Harrush, and E. Rabinovich. Industry experience with the ibm active middleware technology (amit) complex event processing engine. In *Proceedings of the Fourth ACM International Conference on Distributed Event-Based Systems*, DEBS '10, pages 140–149, New York, NY, USA, 2010. ACM.

[7] M. R. Mendes, P. Bizarro, and P. Marques. Performance evaluation and benchmarking. chapter A Performance Study of Event Processing Systems, pages 221–236. Springer-Verlag, Berlin, Heidelberg, 2009.

[8] M. R. N. Mendes, P. Bizarro, and P. Marques. A framework for performance evaluation of complex event processing systems. In *Proceedings of the second international conference on Distributed event-based systems*, DEBS '08, pages 313–316, New York, NY, USA, 2008. ACM.

[9] A. Ranganathan. Experiences with codifying event processing function patterns. In *Proceedings of the Fourth ACM International Conference on Distributed Event-Based Systems*, DEBS '10, pages 206–215, New York, NY, USA, 2010. ACM.

[10] Taipower. Tariff book. Technical report, Taiwan Power Company, 2008.

[11] G. Tóth, L. J. Fülöp, L. Vidács, A. Beszédes, H. Demeter, and L. Farkas. Complex event processing synergies with predictive analytics. In *Proceedings of the Fourth ACM International Conference on Distributed Event-Based Systems*, DEBS '10, pages 95–96, New York, NY, USA, 2010. ACM.

[12] R. Weron. *Modeling and Forecasting Electricity Loads and Prices: A Statistical Approach*. Wiley, 2006.

[13] A. Wun, M. Petrovi, and H.-A. Jacobsen. A system for semantic data fusion in sensor networks. In *Proceedings of the 2007 inaugural international conference on Distributed event-based systems*, DEBS '07, pages 75–79, New York, NY, USA, 2007. ACM.

A Paradigm Comparison for Collecting TV Channel Statistics from High-volume Channel Zap Events

Pål Evensen[*]
paal.evensen@altibox.no
Hein Meling
hein.meling@uis.no
Department of Electrical Engineering and Computer Science
University of Stavanger, Norway

ABSTRACT

The current approach used to obtain official television channel statistics is based on polls combined with specialized reporting hardware. These are deployed only on a small scale and batch processed every 24 hours. With the enhanced capabilities of present-day IPTV set-top-boxes, network operators can track channel popularity and usage patterns with a degree of precision and sophistication not possible with existing methods. One such network operator, Altibox, is the largest provider of IPTV in Norway with a deployment of over 320,000 set-top-boxes. By tapping into the high-volume stream of channel zap events sent from these set-top-boxes, very accurate viewership can be obtained and presented in near real-time.

In this paper, we examine two programming paradigms for implementing applications to compute viewership based on channel zap events. One based on a general-purpose programming language (Java) and the other based on a highly specialized event stream processing language (EPL). An important characteristic of this application is stateful event processing. We are interested in exploring the trade-offs between these two implementations, to determine their suitability for such applications. Specifically, we are interested in the performance trade-off and the program complexity of each implementation.

Our results show that a pure Java implementation has a significant edge over EPL in terms of performance. Although, our numbers cannot be used to draw a general conclusion, it seems indicative that an event stream processing engine would suffer more than a general-purpose language as query complexity grows. We conjecture that this is because it is easier to construct custom data structures for the specific problem in a general-purpose language like Java. In terms of program complexity, EPL has a slight edge in all metrics, and a significant edge when event streams can be reused to perform more complex processing, indicating that less effort is necessary to extend functionality.

---

[*]Pål Evensen is also with Altibox.

Categories and Subject Descriptors

C.2.4 [**Computer Systems Organization**]: Computer-Communication Networks—*distributed systems, distributed applications*; D.2.8 [**Software Engineering**]: Metrics—*complexity measures, performance measures*

General Terms

Experimentation, Measurement, Performance

Keywords

TV viewership statistics, Stream processing

1. INTRODUCTION

Viewer statistics is the most important metric used by television broadcasters to plan their programming, and for many broadcasters, to rate their advertisement time slots. Gaining an improved understanding of viewer behavior and responses to the current programming is essential to a successful TV channel. The state-of-the-art approach to obtain the viewership of a program is to *sample* a very small *selected, but hopefully representative* portion of the population. In Norway, the sample size is 1,000 out of 2,000,000 television households (0.05 %) [11], while in the US, only 25,000 out of 114,500,000 households are sampled (0.02183 %) [18]. Such a small sample size is often criticized as being statistically insignificant [18], and may lead to incorrect conclusions about actual viewer interests in a specific program, and viewer exposure to advertisements.

With the enhanced capabilities of present-day IPTV set-top-boxes (STBs), network operators can track channel/program popularity and usage patterns with a degree of precision and sophistication not possible with existing methods. This can be done by recording or aggregating channel change events (also called *zap events*) from customer STBs. Hence, assuming that the network operator's customers represents a statistically significant portion of the population, collecting statistics based on zap events is likely to provide a much more accurate statistic compared to state-of-the-art.

There are generally two approaches to compute accurate viewership. One is to store every zap event for later bulk processing, e.g. using transactional databases or techniques based on Map-Reduce [8, 15], or aggregate statistics can be computed on-the-fly, based on in-memory state. We take the latter approach, as we are mainly interested in aggregate information from these events and want to avoid storing huge volumes of data. Only aggregate numbers are stored on disk or forwarded to interested parties.

In this paper, we describe the architecture in which STBs are deployed, and how channel zap events are propagated to an aggregation cluster for online incremental event processing. Based on this architecture, our goal is to analyze the capabilities and trade-offs between two programming paradigms for building our application to obtain viewership statistics. Hence, we have implemented two applications that compute two different statistics based on received zap events: (i) the number of viewers for all channels, and (ii) detecting 15 % rise/drop in the viewership for a channel. The first is used to generate a *top-ten* list of the most popular channels/programs in near real-time. The second application reveals useful information about which programs are luring people away from other channels. An important characteristic of both these applications is that they are stateful and demand significant computational resources to ensure timely processing. Although the applications that we cover here are fairly simple, we have already implemented several other interesting incremental statistical measures that network operators and broadcasters might find interesting, and we expect to publish those results in follow-up work.

The two applications have been implemented in two very different programming paradigms. One based on the general-purpose object-oriented programming language Java, and the other based on the Event Processing Language (EPL) [9, 17]. EPL is highly specialized declarative event stream processing language derived from SQL. We are interested in exploring the trade-offs between these two paradigms, to determine their suitability for our applications. Specifically, we are interested in the performance trade-off and the program complexity of each implementation.

Java is expected to have higher program complexity than EPL, since EPL is specifically designed for processing events. We compare our implementations using on several metrics for analyzing code complexity, including lines of code and Halstead's complexity measure [13, 6, 12], in addition to a more subjective discussion based on our experience developing these applications. The results indicate that EPL might yield easier reuse compared to Java.

Previous, but simple, benchmarks using EPL [19, 10], and running the EPL benchmark kit, have indicated that it would offer competitive performance. However, at the outset of this work it was not clear if EPL would offer competitive performance for our somewhat involved applications. Our performance evaluation involves data obtained from more than 250,000 STBs. We conduct both memory profiling and throughput analysis, and find that our implementations of these applications have very different performance characteristics in the two programming paradigms.

Paper organization: Section 2 introduce the problem of obtaining viewership statistics and surveys the state-of-the-art techniques used. In Section 3 we describe the architecture of our current deployment, and outline plans for improving the accuracy of statistics, and provide new services to customers. Focusing on the event processing logic, Section 4 describe the details of our applications, and their implementation in the two programming paradigms. In Section 5 we give a brief analysis of the viewer statistics obtained from our current deployment. Additionally, we evaluate our implementations in terms of throughput and memory usage, and program complexity. Section 6 surveys related work. Finally, Section 7 concludes the paper with an overall discussion of the merits of the two paradigms.

2. BACKGROUND

We begin by describing the current state-of-the-art in measuring viewership and program rating, focusing on the Norwegian television market. This is followed by an architectural overview of the network infrastructure used by an IPTV network operator in Norway.

TNS Gallup [23] is a Norwegian company that specializes in polls and ratings, and is the main provider of viewership to the official television networks in Norway. To measure the viewership, a device dubbed the *mediameter* is used to record and log inaudible sonic signatures emitted from the audio part of television and radio programs that the device is exposed to. The participants in this continuous poll are required to *carry the device with them*, and to keep the sound audible in order for the *mediameter* to record appropriately. The device must then be placed in a docking station overnight, to transmit the recorded data to TNS Gallup. In addition to *mediameter*, TNS Gallup also collect data from 1,000 selected households whom have a specialized logging device attached to their television, but still requires operating a special remote to record changes. The device records viewer data and transmits these every night. Viewership is computed from the collected data, where each household supposedly represents 2,000 households from the same district. This type of continuous polling represents the state-of-the-art in obtaining viewership, and similar systems are deployed in many other countries, including the US [18]. Anecdotally, non-technological approaches like *viewer diaries* are apparently also still being used [18].

Altibox [4] is the largest distributor of television over a pure IP-based network in Norway, with a deployment of over 320,000 STBs, distributed amongst approximately 300,000 households. Customers are connected to two main distribution centers by fiber-to-the-home, giving customers a unique bandwidth capacity to support a variety of services, including Internet, Voice over IP telephony, IPTV, Video-on-Demand (VoD), and Personal Video Recording (PVR). The STB is the host device for IPTV, VoD, and PVR services, and to simplify interacting with these services, an Electronic Program Guide (EPG) is also available to users. Technically, the EPG is essentially a database accessible through a web service interface that associate channel name to information about the programming of that channel. Currently, Altibox offers a total of 253 TV channels, accessible through the STB by way of IP multicast (through their fiber-based broadband network). The software on STB devices are regularly updated with new service offerings, bug fixes, and QoE monitoring and diagnostics applications [14, 1]. Moreover, since STBs also have two-way communication capabilities, network operators can update their functionality to track program popularity and usage patterns by recording zap events. This can take place without any changes to current user behavior, such as using a special remote or carrying a *mediameter*. Thus, data collection is transparent to the user, and the reported data is expected to be more accurate, since users cannot forget to record the change. Moreover, we also avoid the embarrassment factor sometimes present in surveys, where users report an idealized version of their habits due to embarrassment over their factual habits. It is not unthinkable that this factor can play a role when viewers decide whether to use the special remote when viewing programming that is perceived as of lesser quality. Finally, it also allows for a much more accurate understanding of viewer behavior than existing methods, as the sample size is more than 300 times larger, representing approximately 16 % of the Norwegian television population.

2.1 Event Processing Language

Here we briefly survey the capabilities of the EPL language and its runtime environment, referred to as the Esper processing engine. Esper [10] provides an open-source implementation of the EPL processing engine, and the necessary Java libraries for interacting with it. Our choice of Esper and EPL is primarily motivated by its focus on stream processing, and secondary its open-source licensing model.

EPL is a declarative query language derived from SQL; it shares much of its syntax and functionality with SQL, such as select, insert, update, and aggregation functions for summation, averaging, and join operators. However, instead of operating on relational database tables, EPL operates on streams of data. Using these operators, one can construct a wide variety online queries that can be used process data from event streams, such as the stream of channel zaps from customer STBs. An EPL query will process one or more event streams, looking for event patterns that match the query, and produce an output event. Moreover, since streams are continuous, i.e. not temporally restricted, EPL introduces a sliding window concept to be able to construct queries that operate over limited, but sliding, time intervals. This is used in our implementation of rise/drop detection.

Esper can handle events represented in a variety of ways, e.g., as Java or C# objects that provide getter and setter methods to access its attributes, and is the approach used in this paper.

Deploying an Esper server typically involves the following steps: (i) start the Esper processing engine, (ii) install EPL queries, (iii) establish subscriptions by registering listener objects with the Esper processing engine, and (iv) receive and parse events from the data stream, and construct Java objects to be passed to the processing engine to be processed by the installed queries. The subscriptions are connected with the installed queries, acting as handlers for output events generated by the queries.

3. ARCHITECTURE

In this section, we present the architecture of our current deployment, and discuss some changes that we are planning to implement in the near future. These changes will significantly improve the accuracy of our measurements, at the expense of more demanding processing and network overhead. We also outline a few applications that become possible with more accurate measurements.

3.1 Current Deployment

The STB devices deployed in customer residences for supporting IPTV, VoD, and PVR, are fully capable of two-way communication, and have been augmented with a software agent to keep track of and report zap events to a centralized server. We call these the ZAPREPORTER client and ZAP-COLLECTOR server, respectively. A simplified architecture is illustrated in Figure 1.

The ZAPREPORTER monitors channel changes performed by the user of the STB, and generates zap events containing the following information:

$$\langle \text{DATE, TIME, STB-IP, TOCHANNEL, FROMCHANNEL} \rangle$$

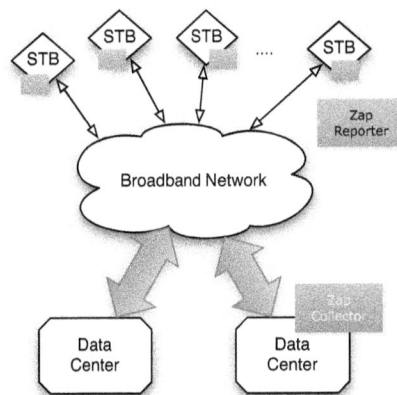

Figure 1: Network architecture illustrating STBs.

The event is encoded as text, and one event is typically less than 60 bytes, hence approximately 25 events can be sent in one 1500 byte message. The clocks on the STBs are synchronized using NTP, and thus provide more accuracy than what is needed for our purposes.

Events are generated according to Algorithm 1, and described informally as follows. When a user change channel, the ZAPREPORTER record this change event locally on the STB and starts a timer. If the user stay on the same channel longer than 60 seconds, the event is saved away in *unsent*. If the user change channel again before the 60 second timer expires, the event is overwritten (i.e. not recorded in *unsent*). Periodically, the events stored in *unsent* is sent off to the ZAPCOLLECTOR and emptied.

Algorithm 1 ZAPREPORTER pseudo code

1: **Initialization:**
2: $T \leftarrow 60$ {Timeout period (seconds)}
3: $S \leftarrow 1$ {Period of between sends (hours)}
4: $event \leftarrow \perp$ {Most recent event, not yet recorded in *unsent*}
5: $unsent \leftarrow \emptyset$ {Set of unsent zap events}
6: startPeriodicTimer($\langle \text{SENDTIMEOUT} \rangle, S$)

7: **on** $\langle \text{CHANNELCHANGE}, toCh, fromCh \rangle$
8:    $event \leftarrow$ preparEvent($toCh, fromCh$) {Update event}
9:    restartTimer($\langle \text{RECORDTIMEOUT} \rangle, T$)

10: **on** $\langle \text{RECORDTIMEOUT} \rangle$
11:    $unsent \leftarrow unsent \cup event$ {Record event}

12: **on** $\langle \text{SENDTIMEOUT} \rangle$
13:    $\forall e \in unsent :$ **send** $\langle \text{ZAPEVENT}, e \rangle$ to ZAPCOLLECTOR
14:    $unsent \leftarrow \emptyset$

This strategy ensure that the total number of messages sent are kept to approximately one message per hour per STB, and at most 60 events needs to be kept in STB memory. We expect that we would rarely see more than 25 events generated by the same STB in one hour, requiring more than one 1500 byte message to be sent. Hence, in the worst case, when all 320,000 STBs are active, we might see a total of 320,000 messages per hour, or just over 1 Mbps (on average). Moreover, if all messages contain 25 zap events, the processing rate would have to be about 2.2k events/second.

On the server side, the ZAPCOLLECTOR collect events

from all the STBs and store them in log files that are rotated daily. The events are stored in the order they are received from the STBs. However, since each message contains about one hour worth of zap events, the log files are not initially sorted by the timestamp. Therefore, the event logs must be sorted before they can be used to produce incremental statistics. Currently, there are no service offerings at Altibox that take advantage of these log files, but next we explain our plans for extending this to provide more accurate statistics and near real-time updates of these statistics.

3.2 Planned Deployment

There are several reasons why we are interested in increasing the accuracy of these statistics. First of all, we want to be able to provide a ranking (top-10 list) of programs in near real-time to both viewers and broadcasters. Also, we are interested in detecting flash crowds, i.e. when a large number of viewers change to or from the same channel within a short period of time. This might be expected either when a new (popular) program is beginning, or during commercial breaks. The former we have seen evidence of from our current datasets. However, to understand better the user behavior in commercial breaks, we need more accurate information from the ZAPREPORTER. Also to provide a real-time ranking, we must to revise the ZAPREPORTER.

Thus, in the planned deployment we are aiming to report channel changes (lasting 3 seconds or more) within a 10 second interval. Thus, in Algorithm 1, we set $S = 10$ seconds, and $T = 3$ seconds. Obviously, no message will be sent if there are no channel changes. To determine the worst case network resources necessary with this sampling frequency, assume all 320,000 STBs generate 3 events every 10 seconds. Assuming every event takes 60 bytes, the packet size should be roughly 180+70 bytes (including headers). Under these assumptions, the worst case network load would be 64 Mbps overall, and 96,000 events/second would have to be processed. These numbers are obviously above what is expected in the normal case, but we would like to be able to handle flash crowds that might reach towards such numbers.

Note that, the ZAPREPORTER functionality implemented in STBs is beyond the direct control of the authors of this work. However, we can influence and request implementation changes to the STBs. The reasons for this is corporate policies relating to accountability for changes that can potentially cause problems for customers. Moreover, the STB can only be updated two times a year, during a relatively short time window. Hence, this poses some challenges for us in implementing the desired functionality.

On the ZAPCOLLECTOR end, we instead introduce a ZAPPROCESSOR to process events incrementally to compute statistics for program ranking in near real-time, and for detecting flash crowds and other similar statistics. We have implemented these services and in Section 5 we evaluate our ZAPPROCESSOR implementations in both Java and EPL, based on real data obtained from our log files.

4. EVENT PROCESSING

In this section we present our two applications for obtaining viewership statistics and detecting sudden changes of viewership on a channel. We describe their implementation in both Java and EPL, specifically focusing on the event processing aspect.

4.1 Viewer Statistics in Java

Algorithm 2 gives an overview of the ZAPPROCESSOR implementation to obtain viewer statistics. Lines 10-13 of Algorithm 2 checks to see if the STB have been active in the past, and if so replaces the $fromCh$ field of the message with the last recorded previous channel. This is necessary because not all channel changes are propagated to the ZAPPROCESSOR, due to the 1 minute rule or even the 3 second rule imposed by the ZAPREPORTER. Otherwise, our counting in the last part would not be correct. In order to obtain statistics for the different channels, we simply count the occurrences of zap events changing to the different channels. We implement this using a multiset, where each entry (the channel) is associated with a count value representing the number viewers on that channel. Moreover, we also have to reduce the count for the channel the STB is moving away from (or the previously recorded channel of that STB). We do not reduce the count of any channel if the event originate at an STB from which we have no recorded events.

Algorithm 2 ZAPPROCESSOR pseudo code

1: **Initialization:**
2:   R {Subscribers of output events}
3:   EPG {Electronic Program Guide database}
4:   $S \leftarrow 10$ {Period of between output events (seconds)}
5:   $STBs \leftarrow \emptyset$ {Set of known STB-IP addresses}
6:   $viewers \leftarrow \emptyset$ {Multiset: viewer count for each channel}
7:   $prevCh \leftarrow \emptyset$ {Map from STB-IP to previous channel}
8:   startPeriodicTimer($\langle$OUTPUTTIMEOUT$\rangle$, S)

9: **on** $\langle$ZAPEVENT, $date, time, ip, toCh, fromCh\rangle$
10:   $prev \leftarrow prevCh$.get(ip)   {Get previous channel of ip}
11:   **if** $prev \neq$ **null then**
12:     $fromCh \leftarrow prev$
13:   $prevCh$.put($ip, toCh$)   {Update previous channel of ip}
14:   $viewers$.add($toCh$)   {Increase count of $toCh$}
15:   **if** $ip \in STBs$ **then**   {Have we seen STB before?}
16:     $viewers$.remove($fromCh$)   {Reduce count of ch.}
17:   **else**
18:     $STBs$.add(ip)   {New STB, record ip}

19: **on** $\langle$OUTPUTTIMEOUT$\rangle$
20:   $topCh \leftarrow viewers$.mostFrequent(10)   {Top-10 ch.}
21:   **for** $ch \in topCh$
22:     $prog \leftarrow EPG$.getProgram(ch)   {Query EPC}
23:     $topProgList$.add($prog$)   {Create top-10 program list}
24:   **send** $\langle$TOP10LIST, $topProgList\rangle$ to R

Periodically, output events are generated by first determining which channels have the most viewers, and for each channel query the EPG to determine which program is currently being broadcast on that channel. To avoid frequent database queries, we cache program information in memory. From this we construct the top-10 list of programs to be sent to interested subscribers, providing near real-time viewership information. One such subscriber that we have implemented is the EPG itself. In this case, we integrate the top-10 list within the program guide interface on the STB device, enabling users to viewer statistics and choose program from the list.

An important improvement that these real-time viewer statistics provide over batched statistics is that broadcasters could potentially adjust their advertisement programming

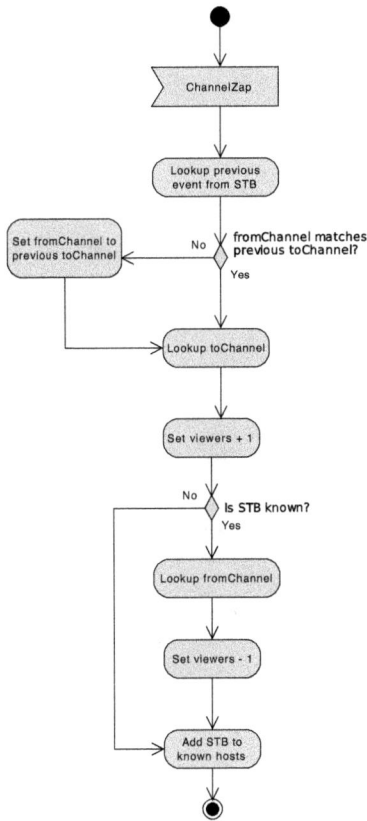

Figure 2: Viewer Statistics Activity Diagram

based on actual viewer numbers, as opposed to predicted number of viewers.

4.2 Viewer Statistics in EPL

Both implementations share a common overall logic in how events are handled (see Figure 2 and Algorithm 2). However, the EPL implementation requires a slightly different understanding of how events are related, and hence the following gives a more succinct description from the EPL perspective, while the algorithmic descriptions closely match the Java implementation.

As shown in Figure 2, incoming events are matched against the previous event received from the same STB, comparing its *fromChannel* field with the *toChannel* field of the STB's previous event. Different values might be observed at this stage, either due to packet loss, or more likely due to the way that ZAPREPORTER generate events (not all events are actually sent). To compensate for this, we set the *fromChannel* of the incoming event to the *toChannel* of the previous event. If no previous event exist, no action is taken.

The next step is updating the number of viewers by adding one to the channel matching the *toChannel* field and subtracting one from the channel matching *fromChannel*. If the event received is from a previously unknown STB, the *fromChannel* is not subtracted, as it is the first event received from this particular STB. Finally, the STB is added to the list of known devices.

The EPL queries contains all of the logic depicted in Figure 2, while the EPL implementation also requires some Java code to handle parsing and object creation for incom-

ing events. Also, listener objects must implement a callback interface in Java to receive output events generated by the Esper engine. We have not included the Java code.

Listing 1 EPL Viewer Statistics

```
create schema ChannelTotViewers
  as (channelName string, viewers int
create window ChannelWin.std:unique(channelName)
  as ChannelTotViewers
create window StbWin.std:firstunique(ip)
  as tv.ChannelZap
create window ZapWin.std:unique(ip)
  as tv.ChannelZap

insert into ZapWin
  select * from tv.ChannelZap

update istream tv.ChannelZap as zap
  set fromChannel =
    (select toChannel from ZapWin where ip = zap.ip)
  where fromChannel !=
    (select toChannel from ZapWin where ip = zap.ip)

on tv.ChannelZap zap merge ChannelWin cw
  where zap.toChannel = cw.channelName
  when matched
    then update set viewers = viewers + 1
  when not matched
    then insert
      select toChannel as channelName,
      1 as viewers

on tv.ChannelZap zap merge ChannelWin cw
  where zap.fromChannel = cw.channelName and
    exists (select * from StbWin where ip = zap.ip)
  when matched
    then update set viewers = viewers - 1

insert into StbWin select * from tv.ChannelZap

insert into ZapSnap
select *, percent(viewers, sum(viewers)) as activity
  from ChannelWin
  output snapshot every 15 sec
  order by viewers desc
```

Listing 1 shows the complete EPL code for generating viewer statistics. The **tv.ChannelZap** variable refers to the Java object created when parsing incoming events. The **update istream** query is necessary to compensate for any discrepancy in from/to channel values, as described above, and operates on the **tv.ChannelZap** event before it enters any stream. In addition, the code updates a **ChannelWin**, containing viewer numbers, as well as adding the STB to the **StbWin**, containing known STBs. The reason for using the whole **tv.ChannelZap** object most of the time, instead of extracting only the necessary values is that according to the Esper documentation [9], selecting individual properties from an underlying event object comes with a performance penalty, as the engine must then generate a new output event containing exactly the selected properties. Additionally, it simplifies the syntax. The final statement in Listing 1 outputs an ordered snapshot of the channel window every 15 seconds, decorating it with a percentage value, calculated by a custom method implemented in Java.

We ran both the Java and EPL implementations over the same datasets, and after a few rounds of debugging, we observed identical output for both implementations.

4.3 Annoyance Detection in Java

Next, we discuss our last application which is aimed at detecting if a particular ad is causing viewers to change channel. Broadcasters would most likely want to know about this, in order to remove or charge more for ads that annoy or upset viewers. To support such ad annoyance detection, we must detect changes in the viewership beyond some threshold, e.g. measured as a fraction, P, of the total number of viewers on that channel. Algorithm 3 shows the additional code necessary for such detection. To implement this, we again rely on a multiset to keep a count of the number of zap events seen in the current interval. The interval used in this case is 60 seconds, but this can easily be adjusted for more fine grained intervals. Note that $ival$ is an integer, and the + symbol represents concatenation. Hence, the element of the multiset is the concatenation of channel name and an integer representing an interval. To ensure that memory usage is kept low, we immediately expunge data from a previous interval, and if an output event is generated within one interval, we reset the counting for that interval. This allows multiple output events to be generated for the same interval, if the fraction of viewers changing channel in that interval is $\geq 2P$.

Algorithm 3 Annoyance detection pseudo code

1: **Initialization:**
2:   F {Multiset: count viewers moving from ch. in intervals}
3:   $M \leftarrow 2000$ {Minimal # of viewers to consider for detection}
4:   $P \leftarrow 0.15$ {Fraction of viewers moving from ch. in interval}
5:   $prevIval \leftarrow \perp$ {The previous interval}

6: **on** $\langle \textsc{ZapEvent}, date, time, ip, toCh, fromCh \rangle$
7:   $ival \leftarrow time/60$ {Get interval of this event (sec)}
8:   **if** $ival \neq prevIval$ **then**
9:     F.clear()   {New interval begun; expunge old entries}
10:     $prevIval \leftarrow ival$
11:   F.add($fromCh+ival$)
                        {Inc. count changing from ch. in ival}
12:   F.remove($toCh+ival$)
                        {Reduce count for ch. moved to in ival}
13:   $v \leftarrow viewers$.count($fromCh$)   {#Viewers on fromCh}
14:   **if** $v > M \wedge F$.count($fromCh+ival$) $\leq P \cdot v$ **then**
15:     Generate output
16:     F.setCount($fromCh+ival$, 0) {Reset count for ival}

4.4 Annoyance Detection in EPL

The annoyance detector in Listing 2 looks at the average viewer number over the last minute, constantly comparing the most recent number with the average. If the viewer number drops with 15 % compared with the last minute average, an output event is triggered.

Here, the power of sliding time windows are illustrated: It selects some properties from a sliding time window, operating on the `ZapSnap` stream of viewer statistics. `ZapSnap` refers to an event stream from the viewer statistics code in Listing 1, where a snapshot of each channel's viewers is published every 15 seconds. As in the Java implementation, channels having less than 2000 viewers are filtered out before they enter the window in order to prevent channels with only a few or no viewers from triggering drop events. The average is calculated from the events kept in the 1 minute window, while events older than this leave the window.

Listing 2 EPL Annoyance Detector

```
select channelName, viewers, avg(viewers)
  from ZapSnap(viewers > 2000).win:time(1 min)
  group by channelName
  having viewers < avg(viewers) * 0.85
```

5. EVALUATION

The main goal of this paper is to evaluate two paradigms for developing event-based systems, and specifically if it can be applied to our enhanced high-volume use case. Moreover, in this section we first give a brief analysis of the data obtained from the initial deployment of ZapReporter. This will be followed by a performance benchmark and software complexity evaluation.

5.1 Brief Data Analysis

To be able to predict the kind of traffic one might expect, when scaling up the number of events that will be generated, we examine the current trend of channel zapping. Hence, we selected a 15-day period (January 31 — February 14) from our logged datasets obtained using our current infrastructure, as described in Section 3.1. This period constitutes approximately 1.7G bytes of data, or 118M bytes per day. The sampled dataset contains events from 253,985 unique STBs, and 183 different channels were visited at least once during the period.

The number of events generated each day is shown in Figure 3, and the same data is also shown in Figure 4(a) sampled at hour intervals. An interesting observation from Figure 3 is that Wednesdays (5,12) and Thursdays (6,13) represent a significant deviation from average zapping activity. We speculate that this might be due to poor programming on these days across the board among broadcasters. In Figure 4(b), we show the distribution of zap events over a 24-hour period based on data from January 31. The plot confirms what is expected from habitual patterns, with a peak in zapping activity around 20:00. We leave it for future work, to provide an in-depth analysis of these data, when we have better accuracy.

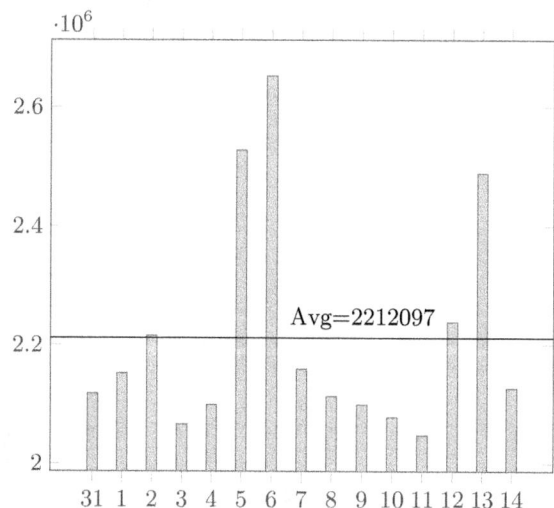

Figure 3: Number of zap events/day over a 15-day period.

(a) Number of zap events/hour over a 15-day period.

(b) Number of zap events over a 24-hour period.

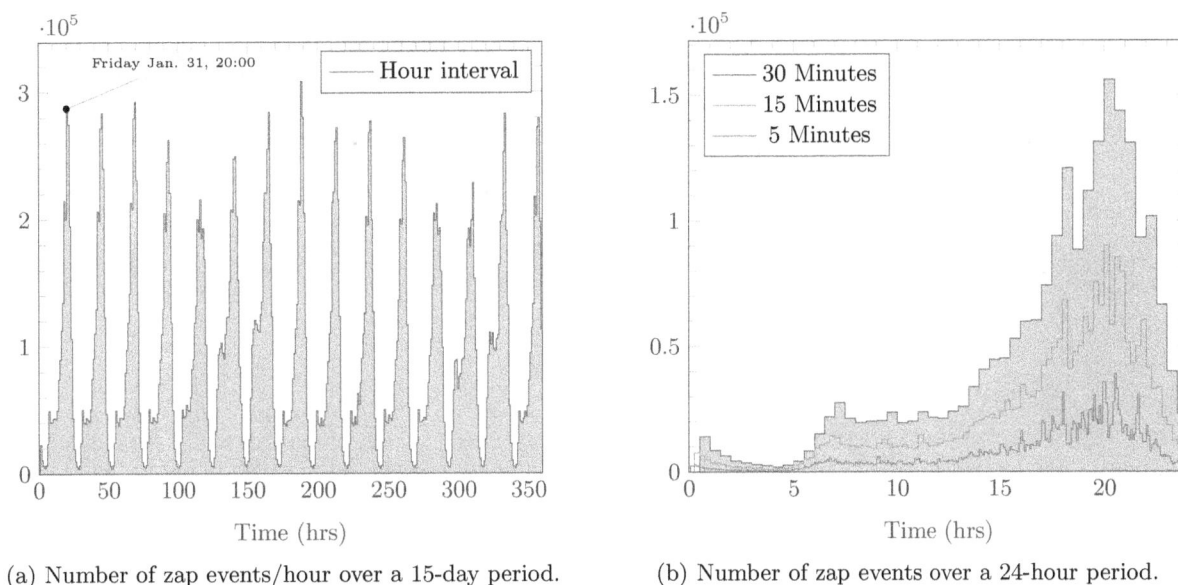

Figure 4: Zap events observed using different sampling intervals.

5.2 Performance Evaluation

Here we provide a brief performance evaluation of both our implementations for the viewer statistics application. The annoyance detector application was difficult to test with Esper due to lack of real data. We are working on ways to simulate this also for this application.

5.2.1 Environment and Experiment Setup

To benchmark our applications, we used a server with RedHat Enterprise Linux 6, 64-bit, 14GB RAM, and a single Intel Xeon E5530 (8MB cache) Quad Core 2.4GHz CPU.

Since the current ZAPREPORTER is not generating events at the desired rate, we wanted to verify if our implementations could sustain the expected traffic volume. Therefore, we built a test framework, in which we process a log file containing zap data from one day (January 31), carrying a total of 2,117,897 zap events. We measure the throughput obtained and memory usage while processing this file. The throughput is measured in four ways: (i) by reading the entire file into memory before processing it from memory, (ii) by reading the file line-by-line from disk, (iii) by receiving the events over UDP and (iv) by receiving the events via the HornetQ message bus. The reason for running both experiment (i) and (ii) was to reveal whether the performance bottleneck is I/O or CPU bound.

Each experiment was repeated 11 times, allowing one iteration for the Java hotspot compiler to optimize the code. The experiment results are presented as the average over ten iterations of each test, as shown in Figure 5. The results were validated by comparing the final state of both implementations, as they should end up with the exact same number of viewers per channel, and number of STBs observed after a completed run.

VisualVM v1.3.2 with a tracer plugin for collecting heap memory usage, was used to measure memory consumption. The sample rate was only 1 Hz, so the precision is limited, but nonetheless gives an overall impression of the memory consumption of the two implementations.

5.2.2 Results

As seen in Figure 5(a), the native Java implementation outperforms the EPL implementation by a very large margin, with an average throughput surpassing 700,000 events per second compared to an average of only 64,275 events for the EPL version with the in-memory tests. Similar results are observed for the from-disk tests. We believe this can be accredited to the flexibility offered by a general-purpose language like Java to express and optimize data structures for the specific problem at hand. Relying only on pure EPL code to express complicated queries seems to hurt performance in a significant way.

Another interesting observation is the negligible performance hit on both implementations introduced by reading the events from disk instead of memory, indicating that the performance bottleneck is CPU-bound. By looking at Figure 5(a), it is also clear that receiving events over UDP introduces a significant performance penalty, reducing throughput by approximately 90 % for the Java implementation, from an average of 641,112 events per second (from-disk) to 63,515 events per second (UDP). Using the HornetQ message bus for event passing, a further performance hit is observed, to 22,546 events per second, or only 3.5 % of the throughput compared to reading the events from disk. For the EPL version, the throughput drops from 62,846 to 34,146 events per second (46 % reduction) over UDP, and to 12,623 events per second when using HornetQ.

Although the performance hit on the Java application seems significant for the UDP and HornetQ cases, it still offers roughly 45 % higher throughput compared to the corresponding EPL versions. Moreover, the CPU load with the Java version is significantly lower.

The error bars in Figure 5(a) represent the standard deviation for each experiment. In the UDP experiments, the average packet drop for the Java version was 0.16 %, and 0.3 % for Esper. No packets were dropped by HornetQ.

Figure 5(b) once again shows the superior performance of the Java implementation. Average heap memory consump-

(a) Average throughput.

(b) Average heap memory consumption over 10 runs.

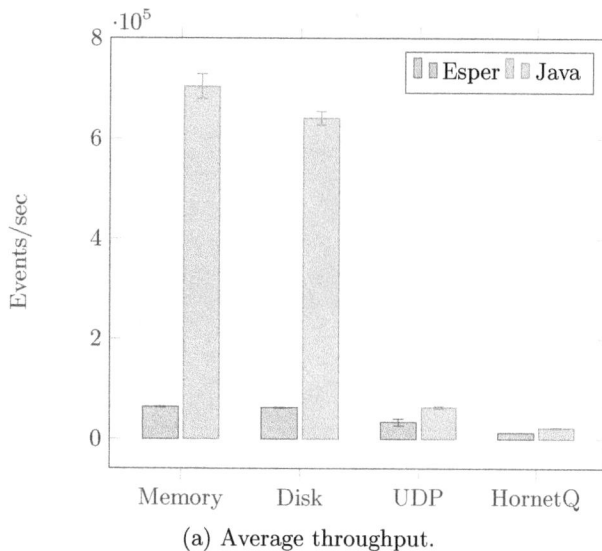

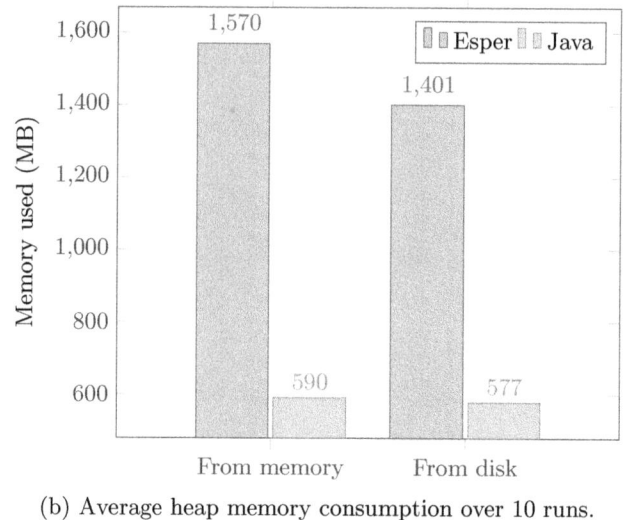

Figure 5: Throughput and memory performance.

tion of the Esper implementation is almost three times more than its Java counterpart, while it seems to confirm the negligible difference in performance between reading the events from disk versus loading them into RAM before processing.

5.3 Complexity

Software complexity is in general an equally important evaluation criteria to performance, when comparing the different approaches. Simpler code amounts to more robust and maintainable software [13], while the performance of hardware increases steadily. Therefore, we also evaluate our rather simple code examples using Halstead's software complexity metric along with a subjective discussion.

Complexity is measured using Halstead's formula [13, 21, 24, 2], that, when applied to the number of operators and operands in a program, is said to predict the following attributes:

- Length, volume, difficulty, and level of abstraction

- Effort and time required for development

- Number of faults

Predicting something that has already occurred is obviously self-contradictory, as the program must be developed before the number of operands and operators can be counted. The first two bullets are therefore in practice only used to validate the theory, and to give a metric of the complexity of a program, which is how it will be used in this evaluation.

There has been some dispute [12] regarding the usefulness and predictive powers of the Halstead metrics, and it could also be argued that the validity of these metrics are limited when applied to modern day object-oriented programming languages like Java, as they were conceptualized in an era of procedural languages. Nevertheless, we will include the non-predictive metrics, since these, together with total lines of source code, hopefully can give us some objective insight regarding the scope and complexity level of the implementations.

Originally, we used a software tool to automatically compute the Halstead metrics of the Java implementation. However, since we were unable find a tool that can compute the metrics for both Java and EPL, and because there are no universal consensus on the exact way of counting operators and operands in a given block of code [3], it was decided to calculate them manually instead, in order to ensure that the counting strategy is consistent between the two implementations.

Li *et al* [7] addresses some of the challenges involved in applying Halstead to object-oriented languages, and the essence of their findings is implemented in our own strategy for counting operators and operands. This includes ignoring import statements and package declarations, but counting everything that is necessary to express the program. Operators that are syntactical identical, but semantically different through context, are counted as different operators. Examples include the parenthesis '()' operator, which is counted as an operator in the case of grouping expressions, e.g. `(2+2)*4` and type casting, but not when used in methods. Furthermore, the dot operator '.' were ignored in package names when referring to objects, such as `tv.ChannelZap`, and included when delimiting an operator from an operand, as in `ZapWindow.std:unique()`. The colon operator ':' is also ignored in cases like this, when used to reference methods from package names, but included in statements like: `fields.hasNext() ? fields.next() : "OFF";`

Because Halstead's metric is designed to measure algorithms as opposed to complete programs [21], the metrics were calculated on class level in the Java implementation and subsequently summed together.

Figure 6 gives a break down per function for both EPL (upper bar) and Java (lower bar) implementations. It should be read as follows: The metric for the viewer statistics is shown to the left, followed by the metric for the annoyance detector application. In the case of Java, these are the only metrics necessary to represent both applications; event parsing is included in the code for the viewer statistics application. For the EPL implementation, we also include metrics for the additional Java code necessary for parsing,

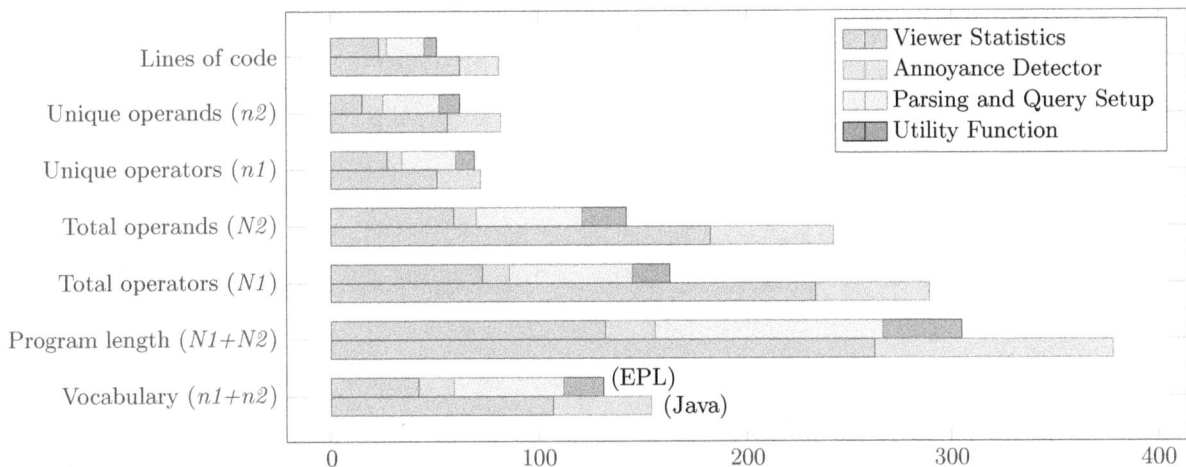

Figure 6: Complexity metrics break down per function for EPL (upper bar) and Java (lower bar).

Esper setup, and a custom utility function for calculating percentage. These are in addition to the query language itself. For both Java and EPL, the annoyance detector application builds upon the viewer statistics application, thus the numbers for the former includes the code from the latter.

On reading these metrics, it should be noted that the EPL implementation was done by a novice EPL programmer, and more efficient implementations might be possible.

The EPL implementation scores slightly better in all of the complexity metrics for the viewer statistics application, and significantly better for the annoyance detector. We do not find the difference in score between the two viewer statistics implementations wide enough to draw the conclusion that one is easier to develop than the other. However, upon expanding the basic viewer statistics application with annoyance detection capabilities, the additional programming effort required for expanding the Esper implementation (four lines of EPL) is significantly smaller than for the Java version (19 additional lines of code). The observed program length numbers points in the same direction, with an added program length of 116 versus only 24 for the EPL version.

One aspect of complexity, not covered by the software metrics, is the challenge of learning and understanding a new query language such as EPL. Although prior knowledge of SQL, possessed by many programmers, will be of great aid to this task. One concern in terms of using EPL for our applications is that we still had to write Java code to interface with other application code. Although, this interface code was minor in our case, it is easy to imagine having to write substantial amounts of wrapper/interface code outside of EPL for a variety reasons. Hence, it is obviously a disadvantage having to know and use two languages in order to develop an application. And another disadvantage with any declarative language is that we lose type-safety, an important software engineering principle for building robust applications.

Based on these observations, it is tempting to draw the conclusion that a general-purpose language is the most efficient tool for doing event stream processing. However, although it is the most effective implementation for the presented application in this case, there is reason to believe that dedicated event processing languages becomes more efficient

relative to general-purpose languages upon expansion of the processing tasks, as indicated by the lesser effort required to add annoyance detection capabilities. This however, assume that streams can be reused across applications.

6. RELATED WORK

In their 2008 study, Cha *et al* [5] captured the channel changes of 250,000 households over a period of six months. By thoroughly analyzing this massive data set, the authors were able to create more accurate statistics of user behavior than with traditional sampling methods like the ones utilized by Nielsen Media Research [18]. This work is closely related to ours, in that it analyzes channel changes from a large IPTV network, but is strictly a statistical analysis, and does not consider any real-time applications that use the data.

Sripanidkulchai *et al* [22] performed an analysis of the live workload of a large content delivery network by analyzing data collected over a three month period, containing over 70 million requests. Like in our paper, they also identified flash crowds and usage patterns, but on audio and video streams delivered over the Internet, and not in a residential IPTV setting. Like Cha *et al*, this work does not deal with real-time pattern detection either.

Commercial vendors like JDS Uniphase [20], Mariner [16] and Agama [1] delivers agent-based solutions for monitoring Quality of Service (QoS) that also provides channel usage statistics. However, the interaction model of these solutions are all pull-based, either trough a SOAP API, graphical view from within the application, or through export functions that allows users to export historical data to a file. For the purpose of computing channel statistics and presenting them in near real-time, none of the commercially available solutions today have interaction models that is suitable for incorporating their functionality into a larger event-driven architecture. Moreover, they cannot be used to develop specialized applications like annoyance detection. The reasons for this can probably be attributed to business protectionism, attempting to lock IPTV operators to their solutions as much as possible, coupled with limited knowledge of the push-based interaction model that is vital in developing event-driven architectures and real-time functionality.

What separates this work from previous work is that none of the aforementioned solutions leverage event stream processing ideas to compute online channel usage statistics, limiting their use to identifying historical usage patterns and trends. By performing the computations online in near real-time, we are able to provide the users and operators with the added value of having instant access to emerging trends and usage statistics.

The other contribution of this work is the direct comparison between different paradigms for performing this type of event stream processing, which, to the authors' knowledge is the first of its kind.

7. CONCLUSIONS

In this paper, we have demonstrated that we are able to get much more accurate viewer statistics than with traditional methods by capitalizing on the two-way communication capabilities of IP-enabled STBs. By operating on the stream of zap events from STBs, we have been able to generate viewer statistics in two very different programming paradigms. Furthermore, our results show that the general programming paradigm outperforms the query language approach by a surprisingly wide margin for this fairly simple application scenario, while at the same time being fairly similar to its counterpart in terms of total lines of code (taking the additional required lines of Java code into account).

The debate of which paradigm to choose for a specific implementation should be about choosing the right tool for the job. If the application complexity is modest and performance requirements are high, it is probably more efficient to use a general-purpose language in most cases. If however the processing task at hand is very complex, and performance requirements are met with a more specialized language, going the query language route opens up possibilities for more effortless maintenance and expansion of the application at a later stage. It is probably wise to keep a generous performance margin in such cases, as our tests indicated that added complexity hurts performance of the more specialized tool more than its Java counterpart in applications like this, because of the limited flexibility in selecting appropriate data structures.

8. ACKNOWLEDGEMENTS

The authors would like to thank Ronny Lorentzen, Dagfinn Wåge and the IPTV team at Altibox for their valuable ideas, encouragement and helpfulness, and Bjarne Helvik for his assistance concerning Halstead's metrics.

9. REFERENCES

[1] Agama web site. Web, 2011. http://www.agama.se.
[2] B. Agarwal, S. Tayal, and M. Gupta. *Software Engineering & Testing: an Introduction.* Jones & Bartlett Learning, 2010.
[3] R. Al Qutaish and A. Abran. An Analysis of the Design and Definitions of Halstead's Metrics. In *15th Int. Workshop on Software Measurement (IWSM'2005). Shaker-Verlag*, pages 337–352, 2005.
[4] Altibox web site. Web, 2011. http://www.altibox.no.
[5] M. Cha, P. Rodriguez, J. Crowcroft, S. Moon, and X. Amatriain. Watching Television over an IP Network. In *IMC*, 2008.
[6] B. Curtis, S. B. Sheppard, P. Milliman, M. A. Borst, and T. Love. Measuring the Psychological Complexity of Software Maintenance Tasks with the Halstead and McCabe Metrics. *IEEE Trans. Softw. Eng.*, 5:96–104, March 1979.
[7] V. Da Yu Li and O. Ormandjieva. Halstead's Software Science in Today's Object Oriented World. *Metrics News*, pages 33–41, 2004.
[8] J. Dean and S. Ghemawat. MapReduce: Simplified Data Processing on Large Clusters. *Commun. ACM*, 51:107–113, January 2008.
[9] Esper Documentation. Web, 2011. http://esper.codehaus.org/esper/documentation/documentation.html.
[10] Esper, Performance-Related Information. Web, 2011. http://esper.codehaus.org/esper/performance/performance.html.
[11] Hva er TNS Gallup TV-panel? (What is TNS Gallup TV-panel?). Web, 2011. http://www.tns-gallup.no/?aid=9072596.
[12] P. G. Hamer and G. D. Frewin. M.H. Halstead's Software Science - a critical examination. In *ICSE*, 1982.
[13] B. E. Helvik. *Dependable Computing Systems and Communication Networks - Design and Evaluation.* Tapir academic publisher, January 2009.
[14] Latens web site. Web, 2011. http://www.latens.tv.
[15] D. Logothetis, C. Olston, B. Reed, K. C. Webb, and K. Yocum. Stateful Bulk Processing for Incremental Analytics. In *SoCC*, 2010.
[16] Mariner Partners - IPTV Monitoring Software. Web, 2011. http://www.marinerpartners.com.
[17] A. Michlmayr, F. Rosenberg, P. Leitner, and S. Dustdar. Advanced Event Processing and Notifications in Service Runtime Environments. In *DEBS*, 2008.
[18] Nielsen Ratings. Web, 2011. http://en.wikipedia.org/wiki/Nielsen_ratings.
[19] D. Nyvik. CEP: Integrator and facilitator for pub/sub messaging. Technical report, December 2009.
[20] J. Schmitt. NetComplete Home Performance Management (PM). White paper, November 2009. http://www.jdsu.com/ProductLiterature/netcompletehomepm_WP_sas_TM_AE.pdf.
[21] V. Shen, S. Conte, and H. Dunsmore. Software Science Revisited: A Critical Analysis of the Theory and Its Empirical Support. *IEEE Trans. Softw. Eng.*, 9:155–165, 1983.
[22] K. Sripanidkulchai, B. Maggs, and H. Zhang. An Analysis of Live Streaming Workloads on the Internet. In *IMC*, 2004.
[23] TNS Gallup. Web, 2011. http://www.tns-gallup.no.
[24] H. Zuse. *A Framework of Software Measurement.* Walter de Gruyter & Co., Hawthorne, NJ, USA, 1997.

Securely Disseminating RFID Events

Florian Kerschbaum
SAP Research
Karlsruhe, Germany
florian.kerschbaum@sap.com

ABSTRACT

More and more companies are collecting data about each item of their supply chain using RFID tags in order to increase visibility across the supply chain and improve its performance. The data generated by reading an RFID tag is (also) called an event. These events are frequently distributed using event-based networks following the publish-subscribe pattern. This method of dissemination immediately raises security concerns, since supply chain operations' data is considered sensitive by companies.

Attribute-based encryption has proven successful in enforcing access control in publish-subscribe networks. Nevertheless, existing schemes do not support access control for RFID events. In this paper we present an encryption scheme that enables disseminating events that can only be decrypted by a selected set of parties that have been in possession of the RFID tag. Our scheme enables broadcasting event messages of constant ciphertext size to an entire network while enforcing access control policies via encryption. We prove our scheme secure under the Modified Bilinear Decisional Diffie-Hellman Assumption.

Categories and Subject Descriptors

D.4.6 [**Operating Systems**]: Security and Protection—*Cryptographic controls*; C.2.4 [**Computer-Communication Networks**]: Distributed Systems—*Distributed databases*

General Terms

Algorithms, Design, Security

Keywords

RFID, Supply Chain Management, Item Tracking, Attribute-Based Encryption, Publish-Subscribe Networks, Visibility Policies

1. INTRODUCTION

More and more companies are equipping their products with RFID tags [7]. Each RFID tag carries a unique identifier and allows tracking the item throughout the supply chain [21]. An RFID tag when read creates an event consisting of identifier, location and time.

When these events are shared among the companies of a supply chain they enable a whole new set of beneficial applications, such as anti-counterfeiting [13], targeted recalls [25] or supply chain benchmarking [14]. Nevertheless companies are very reluctant to do so. These events do not only reveal the information necessary to enable the applications, but also reveal additional information about the company's operation [16, 20]. They may, for example, reveal strategic supplier relationships, planned promotions or best practices.

In order to decrease these concerns, separate entangled supply chains and increase data sharing in [11] visibility policies have been proposed. These reciprocal policies are based on a simple and intuitive concept: Alice reveals to Bob all events about items that Bob also possessed. If Bob does the same the data sharing is fair in an information-theoretic sense, since both parties reveal information about the same set of items. This fairness should enable them to more easily enter into data sharing agreements.

RFID events are frequently distributed in event-based networks following the publish-subscribe pattern. Publish-subscribe networks [2, 17] are a novel data distribution mechanism. Publishers multicast events which have been enlisted by subscribers. These events – the same term has been coined by the RFID community – are a superset of the RFID events. Usually a publisher does not know all subscribers, since the routing of events is performed by the network [6].

Now, enforcing access control policies has become notoriously difficult, since there is no more policy enforcement point. Fortunately encryption may help. Particularly, attribute-based encryption (ABE) [1, 8, 10, 18] enables encrypting events, such that they can only be decrypted by parties that possess the corresponding attributes. This nicely corresponds to attribute-based access control (ABAC) [27] which allows access based on attributes of subject, object or environment. A clever adaptation to publish-subscribe networks has already been made in [24].

This would be excellent news, but ABE can only enforce subject attributes, i.e. attributes of the party accessing the data. In [11] it has already been noted that visibility policies rely on a combined subject-object attribute. The object is the data or item identifier on the RFID tag and a party may only access the event, if this party (subject) has been

327

in possession of this item (object). Therefore existing ABE cannot be straightforwardly applied to this problem.

In this paper we present an encryption scheme that enables a party to decrypt only if the party has received a (forwarded) message before and an authorization message. The forwarded message can, for example, be stored on the RFID tag and ensures that the party has been in possession of the item. The authorization message ensures, that the private key holder has enabled this party to decrypt any message it has received a forwarded message for.

Given this encryption scheme a sender in the publish-subscribe network can encrypt his events and be ensured that

a) they can be only read by parties that also had the item

b) they can be only read by parties that he explicitly authorized

These two conditions necessitate two proofs of security: one for the case a party has not received the item and one for the case a party has not been authorized. For both cases we prove ciphertext indistinguishability against a chosen plaintext attack under the (Modified) Decisional Diffie-Hellman Assumption.

In summary this paper contributes

- an *attribute-based encryption scheme* for enforcing visibility policies in publish-subscribe networks. To the best of our knowledge, this is the first ABE scheme that also involves object-related attributes.

- an IND-CPA style *proof* in case a party has not been authorized

- an IND-CPA style *proof* in case a party has not been forwarded the corresponding message

The remainder of the paper is structured as follows. In the next section, we review the visibility policy model. In Section 3 we describe the trivial construction and oppose the advantageous of our scheme. We also give the intuition behind our construction. In Section 4 we describe our encryption scheme in detail and in Section 5 we give its two security proofs. We review related work in Section 6, before we conclude the paper in Section 7.

2. BACKGROUND: VISIBILITY POLICIES

Visibility policies are an extension of attribute-based access control (ABAC). In ABAC the decision whether an access is granted is determined based on the attributes of subject, object and environment [27].

There are sets of attributes for subjects, objects and environment. For each subject, object or environment there is an assignment $ATTR()$ of a subset of these attributes. A policy rule is a Boolean function of the attributes of subject, object and environment of the request. If the function evaluates to true given the assignment of attributes, access is granted; otherwise it is denied.

Visibility policies do not fit the ABAC model of [27]. In RFID event distribution, subjects are companies and objects are items. A company (subject) is requesting access to data of a specific item (object). This access should be granted if, the item (object) has been in possession of the company (subject). Therefore visibility policies implement a combined subject, object attribute [11].

Let $ATTR(s, o)$ be the assignment function of combined subject, object attributes for subject s and object o. If o has been in possession of s, then $"vis" \in ATTR(s, o)$. One can now write policy rules implementing visibility policies, e.g., granting access to all supply chain partners for their items, but excluding a competitor "Charlie"

$$access(s, o) = "vis" \in ATTR(s, o) \land "Charlie" \notin ATTR(s)$$

3. TRIVIAL SOLUTION

There is a trivial solution to our problem described above. Simply store on each RFID tag the attribute token in the ABE scheme (or even more simple a password or symmetric key) that enables accessing events for this item. Every party that receives the RFID tag will store the token and can then access events.

Nevertheless this is a bad idea, because the token needs to be harshly safeguarded. It needs to be encrypted on the RFID tag to evade rogue readers and it needs to be stored securely in order to prevent theft. Even worse, the token is not traceable, i.e. if it is leaked, it cannot be determined by whom. As a consequence most parties may not be inclined to safeguard the password or even deliberately reveal it to outsiders.

Our construction avoids this problem by tying the information on the tag to its recipient. The stored information is always unique and can only be used in combination with private information by the recipient. We even include a special operation to authorize forwarding. Without this authorization a party must reveal its private information in order to enable decryption. This implements a strong form of traceability.

The intuition of our scheme is simple. We store a symmetric key on the RFID tag, but this key is not stored in plain. Instead it is encrypted by a key of the recipient. Nevertheless the recipient does not hold this key; it is held by a trusted third party. This trusted third party – we call her Trent – holds a key for each party and in order for Alice to forward Bob Trent has to issue Alice a proxy re-encryption key to Bob. Proxy re-encryption has been introduced in [4]. The basic idea is that a proxy can translate ciphertexts under Alice's key into ciphertexts under Bob's key without learning the plaintext, i.e. without decrypting. We somewhat reverse the scheme and make Alice the proxy while the trusted third party emulates all parties.

While this particular trusted third party is obviously not yet available in supply chains, there are a number of suitable candidates: the already successful PKI certificate authorities, the publish-subscribe network software vendor, the RFID standardization organization or even governmental bodies interested in securing IT infrastructure and supply chains.

We entangle the private keys held by Trent with the secret keys held by the parties and the password stored on the RFID tag, such that only all three pieces together are sufficient to decrypt a ciphertext. This entanglement clearly separates our work from previous ABE schemes. Loosely speaking, we present an ABE scheme where one attribute is encrypted and re-encryptable. The combination of both attributes enables enforcing visibility policies with an extension to the most commonly used subset of ABAC as proposed in [11].

4. ENCRYPTION SCHEME

Our encryption scheme consists of the following algorithms and protocols

- **Setup**$(k) \longrightarrow (prv, pbk)$ is an algorithm that on input of the security parameter k outputs a private key prv and a corresponding public key pbk.

- **Register**$((), ()) \longrightarrow ((sk_A), (ttk_A))$ is a protocol between Alice and Trent. The protocol has no input and Alice outputs a secret key sk_A and Trent outputs the corresponding trusted key ttk_A. We emphasize that in our use of proxy re-encryption the trusted key is not entirely public and contains secret information as well.

- **Trace**$((), (ttk_A, ttk_B)) \longrightarrow ((fwd_{AB}), ())$ is a protocol between Alice and Trent. Alice has no input and Trent inputs two trusted keys ttk_A and ttk_B. Alice outputs a forwarding key fwd_{AB} and Trent has no output. We emphasize that Trent is now aware that Alice can forward security tokens to Bob.

- **Forward**$(k_A, fwd_{AB}) \longrightarrow k_B$ is an algorithm that on input of a security token k_A and a forwarding key fwd_{AB} outputs a security token k_B. An initial security token can be created by random choice.

- **Authorize**$((sk_A), (), (prv, ttk_B)) \longrightarrow ((), (auth_{AB}), ())$ is a protocol between Alice, Bob and Trent. Alice inputs her secret key sk_A, Bob has no input and Trent inputs her private key prv and a trusted key ttk_B. Bob outputs an authorization key $auth_{AB}$ and the other parties have no output.

- **Encrypt**$(m, pbk, k_A, sk_A) \longrightarrow c$ is an algorithm that on input of a message m, a public key pbk, a security token k_A and secret key sk_A outputs a ciphertext c.

- **Decrypt**$(c, k_B, auth_{AB}) \longrightarrow m$ is an algorithm that on input of a ciphertext c, a security token k_B and an authorization key $auth_{AB}$ outputs a message plaintext m.

Let $Authorize_B((sk_A), (), (prv, ttk_B))$ denote Bob's output $auth_{AB}$ of the $Authorize$ protocol run on inputs $(sk_A), ()$, (prv, ttk_B). Let $Trace_A((), (ttk_A, ttk_B))$ denote Alice's output fwd_{AB} of the $Trace$ protocol run on inputs $(), (ttk_A, ttk_B)$. Our encryption is *consistent* if

$$\forall (prv, pbk) \longleftarrow Setup(k)$$
$$\forall ((sk_A), (ttk_A)) \longleftarrow Register((), ())$$
$$\forall ((sk_B), (ttk_B)) \longleftarrow Register((), ())$$
$$\forall k_A \xleftarrow{R} \mathbb{G}$$
$$\forall m \xleftarrow{R} \mathbb{G}$$

$$
\begin{aligned}
Decrypt(&\ Encrypt(m, pbk, k_A, sk_A), \\
&\ Forward(k_A, Trace_A((), (ttk_A, ttk_B))), \\
&\ Authorize_B((sk_A), (), (prv, ttk_B)) \\
=&\ m
\end{aligned}
$$

In an example scenario we envision the following use of the algorithms and protocols.

1. Trent executes *Setup* and publishes the public key pbk.

2. The parties Alice and Bob, each execute the protocol *Register* with Trent generating their secret keys sk_A and sk_B, respectively, and their trusted keys ttk_A and ttk_B, respectively, at Trent.

3. Alice executes the protocol *Trace* with Trent outputting forwarding key fwd_{AB}.

4. Alice may authorize Bob to receive messages by executing the protocol *Authorize* with him and Trent. Bob will then obtain authorization key $auth_{AB}$.

   Note that this step only needs to be performed once at setup time. In corporate publish-subcribe networks it is key to authorize your recipients, since the network may forward to site you do not intend to disclose your data.

5. Alice when preparing for a shipment of items to Bob, executes *Forward* generating security token k_B. The input security token k_A may either have been received by Alice with the items or randomly generated if Alice manufactured the items.

6. Alice sends the security k_B to Bob. Steps five and six may be repeated multiple times, once for each item. Items may also be forwarded along the entire supply chain by other parties and in this case the security token is passed through analogous *Forward* algorithms and send operations. The most elegant way to send the security tokens is to store them on the RFID tags, but our scheme is not tied to this way of transport. The security token could also be sent in an accompanying electronic message.

   Note that this step is transitive and only needs to be performed once for each item. The recipient may then forward the item to the next person in the supply chain. The ideal moment for this operation is when anyway shipping the item. There is no need to perform this operation per event sent in the publish-subscribe network.

7. Alice when preparing to send an event encrypts the message using the *Encrypt* algorithm.

8. Alice broadcasts the message in the publish-subscribe network. Steps seven and eight may also be repeated multiple times, once for each event.

   We emphasize that there is no need for authorization or otherwise communication besides sending the encrypted event. We maintain the communication pattern for publish-subscribe networks and create no additional overhead besides adding a (necessary) one-time authorization layer.

9. Bob – as an eligible receiver – decrypts the ciphertext and obtains the event message.

   Parties receiving the item at a later stage can store the events and decrypt them when receiving the item.

Our example scenario is somewhat restricted. It can be easily extended to more than two parties and multi-directional RFID forwarding and event publishing. In fact, in this scenario the use of our encryption scheme may seem strange, since Alice could simply decide to send or not send, but, of

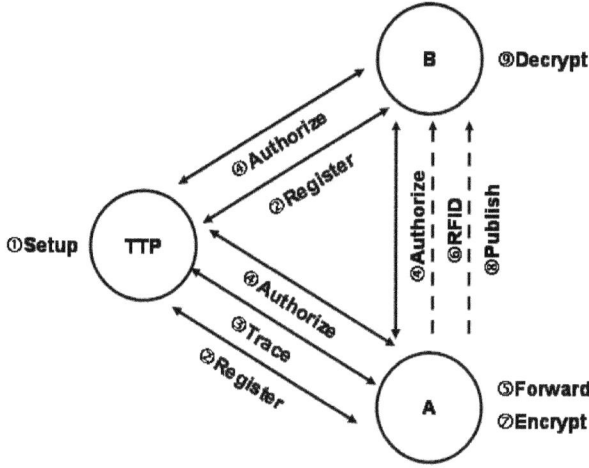

Figure 1: Use of Our Encryption Scheme in Supply Chain Scenario

course, our scheme is still able to enforce visibility policies, if Alice and Bob are several hops apart. However, for clarity and brevity we prefer this example scenario. Also, our security games and proofs follow this scenario, although they could be extended in the same way. Figure 1 depicts the interactions. We emphasize that all communication except, of course, the sending of the security token via RFID (step 6) and the publishing of events (step 8) should be done over secure and authenticated channels.

4.1 Security Definition

In order to assess the security of our encryption scheme, we define two games of ciphertext indistinguishability under chosen plaintext attack. Loosely speaking, in the first game WOAUTH-IND-CPA the adversary is excluded from executing the necessary *Authorize* protocol and in the second game WOFWD-IND-CPA the adversary is excluded from obtaining the necessary, forwarded security token. In each game the adversary operates as a party of the supply chain in a simulated environment. This environment consists of Trent, one more party Alice in the supply chain and infinitely many items.

4.1.1 Game WOAUTH-IND-CPA

Setup: The simulator hands a public key to the adversary. The adversary may register with Trent via *Register*. The adversary may request a forwarding key to Alice via *Trace*.

Phase I: The adversary may request Alice to generate (and send) security tokens k_B. The adversary may send security tokens k_A to Alice. The adversary may request Alice to encrypt (and publish) any plaintext m, even corresponding to a security token (item) k_A or k_B of his choice. This phase ends at the discretion of the adversary.

Challenge: The simulator chooses a security token $k_A^\star$ and gives the security token $Forward(k_A^\star, fwd_{AB})$ to the adversary. The adversary chooses two plaintexts $m_0^\star$ and $m_1^\star$ and gives them to the simulator. The simulator flips a random coin $f \in \{0, 1\}$, encrypts $m_f^\star$ under $k_A^\star$ and gives the ciphertext $c^\star$ to the adversary.

Phase II: The adversary may request the same operations from Alice as in Phase I. This phase also ends at the discretion of the adversary.

Guess: The adversary outputs a guess $f^\star$ of f.

We say that the adversary wins the game, if he correctly guesses $f^\star = f$.

DEFINITION 1. *The advantage of the adversary in winning game* WOAUTH-IND-CPA *is* $Adv^{WOAUTH}(1^k) = |Pr[f^\star = f] - \frac{1}{2}|$.

4.1.2 Game WOFWD-IND-CPA

Setup: The simulator hands a public key to the adversary. The adversary may register with Trent via *Register*. The adversary may request a forwarding key to Alice via *Trace*. And different to the previous game, the adversary may request to be authorized by Alice via *Authorize*.

Phase I: The adversary may request Alice to generate (and send) security tokens k_B. The adversary may send security tokens k_A to Alice. The adversary may request Alice to encrypt (and publish) any plaintext m, even corresponding to a security token (item) k_A or k_B of his choice. This phase ends at the discretion of the adversary.

Challenge: The simulator chooses a security token $k_A^\star$. Different to the previous game, this token is not given to the adversary. The adversary chooses two plaintexts $m_0^\star$ and $m_1^\star$ and gives them to the simulator. The simulator flips a random coin $f \in \{0, 1\}$, encrypts $m_f^\star$ under $k_A^\star$ and gives the ciphertext $c^\star$ to the adversary.

Phase II: The adversary may request the same operations from Alice as in Phase I except requests for the security token $k_A^\star$. This phase also ends at the discretion of the adversary.

Guess: The adversary outputs a guess $f^\star$ of f.

Again, the adversary wins the game, if he guesses correctly and his advantage is defined accordingly.

Our searchable encryption scheme operates on elliptic curves and uses bilinear maps. Let $\mathbb{G}$ and $\mathbb{G}_T$ be groups of order p for some large prime p where the bit-size of p is determined by the security parameter k. A bilinear map is a function $\hat{e} : \mathbb{G} \times \mathbb{G} \mapsto \mathbb{G}_T$ with the following properties:

- Bilinear: for $g \in \mathbb{G}$ and $a, b \in \mathbb{Z}_p^*$
$$\hat{e}(g^a, g^b) - \hat{e}(g, g)^{ab}$$

- Non-degenerate: $\hat{e}(g, g) \neq 1$ is a generator of $\mathbb{G}_T$

- Computable: there exists an efficient algorithm to compute $\hat{e}(g, g)$ for all $g \in \mathbb{G}$

Modified Weil or Tate pairings on supersingular elliptic curves are examples of such bilinear maps. Next, we define the assumption we use in order to prove our encryption scheme secure.

DEFINITION 2. *We say that the* Bilinear Decisional Diffie Hellman (BDDH) *assumption holds, if given values* $g, g^a, g^b, g^c \in \mathbb{G}$ *and* $\hat{e}(g, g)^d \in \mathbb{G}_T$ *it is not computationally feasible to decide if* $d = abc$.

Furthermore, we also use the Modified Bilinear Decisional Diffie Hellman assumption which includes the additional element $g^{c^{-1}}$. It has been introduced in [5] and clearly implies the BDDH assumption.

DEFINITION 3. *We say that the* Modified Bilinear Decisional Diffie Hellman *(MBDDH) assumption holds, if given values* $g, g^a, g^b, g^c, g^{c^{-1}} \in \mathbb{G}$ *and* $\hat{e}(g,g)^d \in \mathbb{G}_T$ *it is not computationally feasible to decide if* $d = abc$.

We propose (and later prove) the following theorems for the security of our encryption scheme

THEOREM 1. *If the BDDH assumption holds, the adversary's advantage*

$$Adv^{WOAUTH}(1^k) < \frac{1}{poly(k)}$$

is a negligible function of the security parameter k.

THEOREM 2. *If the MBDDH assumption holds, the adversary's advantage*

$$Adv^{WOFWD}(1^k) < \frac{1}{poly(k)}$$

is a negligible function of the security parameter k.

4.2 Algorithms and Protocols

We now describe how we implement the algorithms and protocols defined above.

Setup: Given the security parameter k Trent chooses groups $\mathbb{G}$ and $\mathbb{G}_T$ with bilinear map $\hat{e}$. Let g be a generator of $\mathbb{G}$. Trent also uniformly chooses a random number $\alpha \in \mathbb{Z}_p^*$. The public key is g, g^α. The private key is α.

Register: Alice contacts Trent with her desire to register – as in all protocols of our encryption scheme via a secure and authenticated channel. Trent uniformly chooses the trusted key $y_A \in \mathbb{Z}_p^*$. Trent sends $g^{y_A^{-1}}$ to Alice. Alice uniformly chooses a random number $z_A \in \mathbb{Z}_p^*$. Her secret key is $z_A, g^{y_A^{-1}}$.

$$
\begin{array}{rl}
A \longrightarrow T & A \\
T & y_A \xleftarrow{R} \mathbb{Z}_p^* \\
T \longrightarrow A & g^{y_A^{-1}} \\
A & z_A \xleftarrow{R} \mathbb{Z}_p^*
\end{array}
$$

Trace: Alice contacts Trent with her desire to forward to Bob. Trent looks up the trusted keys y_A and y_B for Alice and Bob, respectively. Trent sends the forwarding key $y_A^{-1} y_B$ to Alice.

$$
\begin{array}{rl}
A \longrightarrow T & B \\
T \longrightarrow A & y_A^{-1} y_B
\end{array}
$$

In case Alice requests forwarding keys for more than one party, these keys remain uniformly distributed. All keys are perfect secret shares of the same secret y_A^{-1}.

Forward: Given security token k^{y_A} and forwarding key $y_A^{-1} y_B$ Alice computes the security token k^{y_B}.

$$k^{y_B} = (k^{y_A})^{y_A^{-1} y_B}$$

She may forward this token to Bob, e.g. by storing it on the RFID tag for the associated item.

Authorize: Alice uniformly chooses a random number $r \in \mathbb{Z}_p^*$. She contacts Trent with her desire to authorize Bob and sends along with it r^{-1}. She then looks up her secret key z_A and sends $s = r z_A$ to Bob. Trent looks up his private key

α, Bob's trusted key y_B and sends $t = \alpha^{-1} y_B^{-1} r^{-1}$ to Bob. Bob computes the authorization key as $\alpha^{-1} y_B^{-1} z_A = st$.

$$
\begin{array}{rl}
T & r \xleftarrow{R} \mathbb{Z}_p^* \\
A \longrightarrow T & B, r^{-1} \\
A \longrightarrow B & s = r z_A \\
T \longrightarrow A & t = \alpha^{-1} y_B^{-1} r^{-1} \\
B & \alpha^{-1} y_B^{-1} z_A = st
\end{array}
$$

Encrypt: Alice (or Bob) may be ready to encrypt. She uniformly chooses a random number $r \in \mathbb{Z}_p^*$. She looks up the public key g^α, the security token k^{y_A} and her secret key $z_A, g^{y_A^{-1}}$. Given message m she computes the ciphertext $c = \langle C, D \rangle$

$$C = g^{\alpha r}, D = m \hat{e}(k^{y_A}, g^{y_A^{-1} z_A})^r$$

Decrypt: Bob (or Alice) may be ready to decrypt. He looks up the security token k^{y_B} and the authorization key $\alpha^{-1} y_B^{-1} z_A$. Given the ciphertext $c = \langle C, D \rangle$ he computes

$$m = D/\hat{e}(k^{y_B}, C)^{\alpha^{-1} y_B^{-1} z_A}$$

For consistency observe that

$$\hat{e}(k^{y_A}, g^{y_A^{-1} z_A})^r = \hat{e}(k, g)^{z_A r} = \hat{e}(k^{y_B}, g^{\alpha r})^{\alpha^{-1} y_B^{-1} z_A}$$

We will exploit this relation in our security proofs and simulate one side of the equation per proof.

5. SECURITY PROOFS

We prove Theorems 1 and 2 by reduction to the security assumptions. We give a simulator that given an instance of the assumed hard problem simulates the game $WOAUTH-IND-CPA$ or $WOFWD-IND-CPA$, respectively. The simulation is indistinguishable from the view in a real attack against our encryption scheme, if the given problem instance is a BDDH quadruple or MBDDH quintuple, respectively. If the problem instance is random, our simulation contains no information about the plaintexts. We can then exploit the advantage of an attacker in the simulated game to break the assumed hard problem.

PROOF. We proof Theorem 1 by constructing a simulator that given a BDDH problem instance, simulates the game WOAUTH-IND-CPA.

5.1 Game WOAUTH-IND-CPA

Outline: The simulator is given an instance g, g^a, g^b, g^c, $\hat{e}(g,g)^d$ of the BDDH problem. It will make its random choices, such that $\log_g k = a$, $r = b$ and $z_A = c$ in the challenge ciphertext. Note that k and r are unique to the challenge ciphertext and z_A is only used in its given form g^{z_A}.

Setup: The simulator is given an instance g, g^a, g^b, g^c, $\hat{e}(g,g)^d$ of the BDDH problem. It uniformly chooses a random number $\alpha \in \mathbb{Z}_p^*$. The public g, g^α is given to the adversary.

If the adversary queries to be registered, i.e. it invokes the *Register* protocol with the simulated Trent, the simulator uniformly chooses $y_B \in \mathbb{Z}_p^*$. It sends $g^{y_B^{-1}}$ to the adversary.

If the adversary queries to request a forwarding key to Alice, i.e. it invokes the *Trace* protocol with the simulated

Trent, the simulator uniformly chooses $y_A \in \mathbb{Z}_p^*$. It sends $y_B^{-1} y_A$ to the adversary.

The simulator uniformly chooses y_A and y_B, respectively, if the adversary does not query. The adversary may not query to be authorized in this game. A query to authorize Alice to receive messages from the adversary produces no output at the adversary.

Phase I: If the adversary queries to be sent a security token, the simulator uniformly chooses $k \in \mathbb{G}$. It sends k^{y_B} to the adversary.

The adversary may send security token k^{y_A} to the simulated Alice.

The adversary queries to encrypt m. If the adversary specifies security token k^{y_A}, the simulator may use this value unmodified in the subsequent computation. If the adversary specifies security token k^{y_B}, the simulator computes $k^{y_A} = (k^{y_B})^{y_B^{-1} y_A}$. If the adversary does not specify a security token, the simulator uniformly chooses $k^{y_A} \in \mathbb{G}$. The simulator now uniformly chooses $r \in \mathbb{Z}_p^*$. It computes

$$C = g^{\alpha r}, D = m\hat{e}(k^{y_A}, (g^c)^{y_A^{-1}})^r$$

If the adversary chooses to end this phase, the simulator proceeds.

Challenge: The simulator sends the security token $k_B^\star = (g^a)^{y_B}$ to the adversary. The adversary chooses two plaintexts $m_0^\star$ and $m_1^\star$ and gives them to the simulator. The simulator flips a random coin $f \in \{0, 1\}$. It computes

$$C^\star = (g^b)^\alpha, D^\star = m_f^\star \hat{e}(g, g)^d$$

It sends the challenge ciphertext $c^\star = \langle C^\star, D^\star \rangle$ to the adversary.

Phase II: The simulator responds to the queries as in phase I. If the adversary queries for an encryption under $k_B^\star$, the simulator uses $k = g^a$.

If the adversary chooses to end this phase, the simulator proceeds.

Guess: The adversary outputs a guess $f^\star$ of f. If $f^\star = f$, the simulator outputs $d = abc$ and otherwise $d = r$.

Claim: The view of the adversary is as in a real attack, if the problem instance is a BDDH quadruple. The simulated view is perfectly indistinguishable. In case $d = r$, the challenge ciphertext $c^\star$ contains no information about the plaintext $m_f^\star$. It is uniformly distributed. Therefore, if the adversary has advantage ϵ in breaking the game $WOAUTH-IND-CPA$, the simulator has advantage $\frac{\epsilon}{2}$ in solving the BDDH problem.

□

PROOF. We proof Theorem 2 by constructing a simulator that given a MBDDH problem instance, simulates the game WOFWD-IND-CPA.

5.2 Game WOFWD-IND-CPA

Outline: The simulator is given an instance $g, g^a, g^b, g^c, g^{c^{-1}}, \hat{e}(g, g)^d$ of the MBDDH problem. It will make its random choices, such that $\log_g k = a$, $r = b$ and $y_B = c$ in the challenge ciphertext. Note that k and r are unique to the challenge ciphertext. Nevertheless the simulator for this game is more sophisticated, since y_B is also used in the *Register*, *Trace* and *Authorize* protocols. We therefore need the additional element $g^{c^{-1}}$ for the *Register* protocol.

Due to the additional random elements the output of the other two protocols can be simulated independently. We give the details for the individual phases.

Setup: The simulator is given an instance $g, g^a, g^b, g^c, g^{c^{-1}}, \hat{e}(g, g)^d$ of the MBDDH problem. It uniformly chooses a random number $\alpha \in \mathbb{Z}_p^*$. The public g, g^α is given to the adversary.

If the adversary queries to be registered, i.e. it invokes the *Register* protocol with the simulated Trent, the simulator sends $g^{c^{-1}}$ to the adversary.

If the adversary queries to request a forwarding key to Alice, i.e. it invokes the *Trace* protocol with the simulated Trent, the simulator uniformly chooses $\beta \in \mathbb{Z}_p^*$ and sends it to the adversary. Note that the real element $y_B^{-1} y_A$ is uniformly distributed in $\mathbb{Z}_p^*$ as well, since y_A is uniformly distributed in $\mathbb{Z}_p^*$. Furthermore, this is the first query answer involving the random element y_A and therefore it can be chosen independently.

If the adversary queries to be authorized, i.e. it invokes the *Authorize* protocol with the simulated Alice and Trent, the simulator uniformly chooses two random numbers $\gamma \in \mathbb{Z}_p^*$ and $\delta \in \mathbb{Z}_p^*$. It sends γ as Alice to the adversary and δ as Trent. Note that the real element $s = rz_A$ is uniformly distributed in $\mathbb{Z}_p^*$, because z_A is uniformly distributed in $\mathbb{Z}_p^*$, and that the same holds for $t = \alpha^{-1} y_B^{-1} r^{-1}$ and r^{-1}. This is the first query answer involving the random choices r^{-1} and z_A. Therefore the random choices are independent. Any subsequent query answer in phases I and II will be consistent with the random choices.

As in game $WOAUTH-IND-CPA$ a query to authorize Alice to receive messages from the adversary produces no output at the adversary.

Phase I: If the adversary queries to be sent a security token, the simulator uniformly chooses $\kappa \in \mathbb{Z}_p^*$. It sends $k^{y_B} = (g^c)^\kappa$ to the adversary.

The adversary may send security token k^{y_A} to the simulated Alice.

The adversary queries to encrypt m. If the adversary specifies security token k^{y_B}, the simulator sets

$$k' = k^{y_B}$$

If the adversary specifies security token k^{y_A}, the simulator computes

$$k' = (k^{y_A})^{\beta^{-1}}$$

If the adversary does not specify a security token, the simulator uniformly chooses

$$\kappa \xleftarrow{R} \mathbb{Z}_p^*, k' = (g^c)^\kappa$$

The simulator uniformly chooses $r \in \mathbb{Z}_p^*$ and sends to the adversary

$$C = g^{\alpha r}, D = m\hat{e}(k', g^{\alpha r})^{\gamma \delta}$$

Note that the use of γ and δ does not contradict the independency claim for γ and δ, since we perfectly maintain the distributions of the encryption scheme. We simulate the reverse operation to game $WOAUTH-IND-CPA$ and use the bilinear map of the decryption function instead.

If the adversary chooses to end this phase, the simulator proceeds.

Challenge: There is no need to choose the security token $k_B^\star$ (or $k_A^\star$) yet, since no output is produced at the adversary, but assume $\kappa^\star = a$. The adversary chooses two plaintexts $m_0^\star$ and $m_1^\star$ and gives them to the simulator. The simulator flips a random coin $f \in \{0, 1\}$. It computes

$$C^\star = (g^b)^\alpha, D^\star = m_f^\star(\hat{e}(g, g)^d)^{\alpha\gamma\delta}$$

It sends the challenge ciphertext $c^\star = \langle C^\star, D^\star \rangle$ to the adversary.

Phase II: The simulator responds to the queries as in phase I. If the adversary queries for an encryption under $k_B^\star$, the simulator uniformly chooses $r \in \mathbb{Z}_p^*$ and computes

$$C = g^{\alpha r}, D = m\hat{e}(g^a, g^c)^{\alpha\gamma\delta r}$$

Note that the adversary does not know $k_B^\star$, but he might know the associated unique identifier of the RFID item.

If the adversary chooses to end this phase, the simulator proceeds.

Guess: The adversary outputs a guess $f^\star$ of f. If $f^\star = f$, the simulator outputs $d = abc$ and otherwise $d = r$.

Claim: The view of the adversary is as in a real attack, if the problem instance is an MBDDH quintuple. The simulated view is perfectly indistinguishable, even for the protocols involving the replaced random choice y_B. In case $d = r$, the challenge ciphertext $c^\star$ contains no information about the plaintext $m_f^\star$. It is uniformly distributed. Therefore, if the adversary has advantage ϵ in breaking the game $WOFWD - IND - CPA$, the simulator has advantage $\frac{\epsilon}{2}$ in solving the MBDDH problem.

$\square$

6. RELATED WORK

Our encryption scheme is an instance of attribute-based encryption (ABE). ABE is a special form of identity-based encryption (IBE). The concept of IBE has been proposed in [22] and the first practical implementation has been presented in [3].

IBE is an alternative to public-key cryptography. Instead of creating private/public-key pairs, one can use any string, i.e. the identity, to encrypt. Then there is an authoritative private key generator that can create the private key for an identity. As a result there is no need to distribute public keys before communication any longer.

The basic idea of ABE is now simple. Let the identity be an attribute, similar to an attribute in attribute-based access control. For example, let there be an attribute for being older than 18 years and one for possessing a driver's license. The challenge is to combine attributes, i.e. decryption should only be possible, if a set of attributes are available. This enables to specify complex policies.

This idea has been realized early and the first proposal has been made in [23]. It already allowed combining attributes by logical AND and OR combinations. It also noted the close relation to access control and the ability to enforce access on control on published data. The term attribute-based encryption has been first used in [10]. An implementation based on threshold combination of attributes has been introduced in [19]. Note that threshold allows to express logical AND combinations as $n - out - of - n$ threshold and logical OR combinations as $1 - out - of - n$ threshold. A generalization to AND and OR combinations has then been made again in [8]. This has been extended to also include negations, i.e. logical NOT, in [18].

A challenge of attribute-based encryption is that, if parties collude, they are able to decrypt the ciphertext of the union of their attributes. Collusion resistance has been built into ABE in [1].

ABE has also been combined with proxy re-encryption in [26]. They use it for revocation, but do not extend the policy model. ABE has been adapted to publish-subscribe networks in [24]. As we already mentioned, we furthermore extend the notion of ABE to also include object-related attributes, in particular our visibility policies. We are not aware of any ABE scheme that addresses this challenge.

IBE (not even ABE) has been used to protect item-level data in a shared setting before. In [9] a specialized access control enforcement for data from ubiquitous devices – like RFID – is proposed. It also does not yet include object-related policies or the more powerful visibility policies.

Enforcement of visibility policies in distributed databases can be achieved using the authentication protocol of [15]. Of course, one cannot authenticate each event in a publish-subscribe network.

7. CONCLUSION

In this paper we have studied an attribute-based encryption scheme tailored for the use in RFID-enabled supply chains. In such supply chains data exchange is sensitive and restrictive access-control policies are necessary. Nevertheless information is often distributed in publish-subscribe networks where there is no access control policy enforcement point and recipients might even be unknown. Our encryption scheme enables the publisher to selectively encrypt its messages, such that only recipients that have had possession of the same item are able to decrypt. We also enable a trusted third party to trace the forwarding of items, such that there is an incentive to keep security-relevant information secret. We prove our scheme secure in the standard model using common security assumptions.

Future work includes to extend the scheme to a cloud-based setting with a central, but encrypted database. In this case, there is a need to query the database about an item without compromising the confidentiality of events.

8. REFERENCES

[1] J. Bethencourt, A. Sahai, and B. Waters. Ciphertext-policy attribute-based encryption. *Proceedings of IEEE Symposium on Security and Privacy*, 2007.

[2] K. Birman, and T. Joseph. Exploiting virtual synchrony in distributed systems. *ACM SIGOPS Operating Systems Review 21(5)*, 1987.

[3] D. Boneh, and M. Franklin. Identity-based encryption from the Weil pairing. *Proceedings of CRYPTO*, 2001.

[4] M. Blaze, G. Bleumer, and M. Strauss. Divertible protocols and atomic proxy cryptography. *Proceedings of EUROCRYPT*, 1998.

[5] S. Chow, S. Yiu, L. Hui, and K. Chow. Efficient forward and provably secure ID-based signcryption scheme. *Proceedings of the 6th International Conference on Information Security and Cryptology*, 2003.

[6] P. Eugster, P. Felber, R. Guerraoui, and A. Kermarrec. The many faces of publish/subscribe. *ACM Computing Surveys 35(2)*, 2003.

[7] K. Finkenzeller. RFID handbook: fundamentals and applications in contactless smart cards and identification. *John Wiley & Sons*, 2003.

[8] V. Goyal, O. Pandey, A. Sahai, and B. Waters. Attribute based encryption for fine-grained access control of encrypted data. *Proceedings of the 13th ACM Conference on Computer and Communications Security*, 2006.

[9] U. Hengartner, and P. Steenkiste. Exploiting hierarchical identity-based encryption for access control to pervasive computing information. *Proceedings of the 1st International Conference on Security and Privacy for Emerging Areas in Communications Networks*, 2005.

[10] A. Juels, and M. Szydlo. Attribute-based encryption: using identity-based encryption for access control. *Manuscript*, 2004.

[11] F. Kerschbaum. An Access Control Model for Mobile Physical Objects. *Proceedings of the 15th ACM Symposium on Access Control Models and Technologies*, 2010.

[12] F. Kerschbaum, D. Dahlmeier, A. Schröpfer, and D. Biswas. On the Practical Importance of Communication Complexity for Secure Multi-Party Computation Protocols. *Proceedings of the 24th ACM Symposium on Applied Computing*, 2009.

[13] F. Kerschbaum, and N. Oertel. Privacy-preserving pattern matching for anomaly detection in RFID anti-counterfeiting. *Proceedings of the 6th Workshop on RFID Security*, 2010.

[14] F. Kerschbaum, N. Oertel, and L. Weiss Ferreira Chaves. Privacy-preserving computation of benchmarks on item-level data using RFID. *Proceedoings of the 3rd ACM Conference on Wireless Network Security*, 2010.

[15] F. Kerschbaum, and A. Sorniotti. RFID-based supply chain partner authentication and key agreement. *Proceedings of the 2nd ACM Conference on Wireless Network Security*, 2009.

[16] C. Kuerschner, F. Thiesse, and E. Fleisch. An analysis of data-on-tag concepts in manufacturing. *Proceedings of the 3rd Konferenz Ubiquitäre und Mobile Informationssysteme*, 2008.

[17] G. Mühl, L. Fiege, and P. Pietzuch. Distributed Event-Based Systems. *Springer*, 2006.

[18] R. Ostrovsky, A. Sahai, and B. Waters. Attribute-based encryption with non-monotonic access structures. *Proceedings of the 14th ACM Conference on Computer and Communications Security*, 2007.

[19] A. Sahai, and B.Waters. Fuzzy identity based encryption. *Proceedings of EUROCRYPT*, 2005.

[20] B. Santos, and L. Smith. RFID in the supply chain: panacea or pandora's box? *Communications of the ACM 51(10)*, 2008.

[21] S. Sarma, D. Brock, and D. Engels. Radio frequency identification and the electronic product code. *IEEE Micro 21(6)*, 2001.

[22] A. Shamir. Identity based cryptosystems and signature schemes. Proceedings of CRYPTO, 1984.

[23] N. Smart. Access control using pairing based cryptography. *Proceedings of the RSA Conference – Cryptographers' Track*, 2003.

[24] M. Tariq, B. Koldehofe, A. Altaweel, and K. Rothermel. Providing basic security mechanisms in broker-less publish/subscribe systems. *Proceedings of the 4th ACM International Conference on Distributed Event-Based Systems*, 2010.

[25] L. Weiss Ferreira Chaves, and F. Kerschbaum. Industrial privacy in RFID-based batch recalls. *Proceedings of the IEEE International Workshop on Security and Privacy in Enterprise Computing*, 2008.

[26] S. Yu, C. Wang, K. Ren, and W. Lou. Attribute based data sharing with attribute revocation. *Proceedings of the 5th ACM Symposium on Information, Computer and Communications Security*, 2010.

[27] E. Yuan, and J. Tong. Attributed based access control (ABAC) for web services. *Proceedings of the IEEE International Conference on Web Services*, 2005.

Distributed Middleware Reliability and Fault Tolerance Support in System S

Rohit Wagle
IBM T.J. Watson Research
Center
Hawthorne, NY, USA
rwagle@us.ibm.com

Henrique Andrade[*]
Goldman Sachs
New York, NY, USA
Henrique.Andrade@gs.com

Kirsten Hildrum
IBM T.J. Watson Research
Center
Hawthorne, NY, USA
hildrum@us.ibm.com

Chitra Venkatramani
IBM T.J. Watson Research
Center
Hawthorne, NY, USA
chitrav@us.ibm.com

Michael Spicer
IBM T.J. Watson Research
Center
Hawthorne, NY, USA
spicer@us.ibm.com

ABSTRACT

We describe a fault-tolerance technique for implementing operations in a large-scale distributed system that ensures that all the components will eventually have a consistent view of the system even in the face of component failures. To achieve this, we break the distributed operation into a series of smaller operations, each of which is local to a single component, carefully linked together. Thus, the effect of a component failure and restart in the middle of a multi-component operation is limited to that component and its immediate neighbors. This framework is used in SYSTEM S, a commercial grade stream processing platform. In that context we will show empirically that our approach is effective and imposes low overhead on distributed inter-component operations.

Categories and Subject Descriptors

D.4.5 [**Software**]: Operating Systems—*Reliability*

General Terms

Design,Performance,Reliability

1. INTRODUCTION

Reliable large-scale distributed systems are difficult to build because multiple components are employed and failure in any single component can have system-wide effects. This is particularly true for middleware that aims to simplify the process of constructing large-scale, distributed applications

---

[*]This work was conducted when the author was in IBM Research.

ranging from low-level infrastructure such as MPI [11] and PVM [8], to IBM's Websphere [17] middleware and other web-services based architectures.

Operations in a large distributed system usually trigger a chain of activity across several tiers of distributed components. For example, an online purchase can trigger actions in the web front-end, a database system and a credit card clearinghouse component. Furthermore, components may maintain an internal state. In traditional transaction-oriented systems, failures in one or more components require that all state changes related to the current operation be rolled back across components [23]. This approach is cumbersome and may be impossible to use in cases where components do not have the ability to roll back. Other approaches such as the ones advocated by Fault-Tolerant CORBA [9, 25] and architectures like DOORS [29, 30] and AQuA [24] rely heavily on the existence of reusable replicas which raise a set of complicated problems in terms of distributed state consistency.

We take a different approach, essentially converting a distributed operation into a set of component-local operations and link those operations together with fault-tolerant communication protocols.

The distributed operation is never rolled back once the first local operation is completed. Instead, the relevant local operations are completed in order. If a local operation fails (for example, because a component is down), only that operation is retried until it completes. To enable this, we ensure that communication between components is tolerant to failures and that the communication protocol implements a retry policy. Second, each component persists enough data so that when restarted after a failure, it continues pending requests where its predecessor left off. If the state of the system changes (for example, the system is being quiesced) we adjust the operation as appropriate. Implementing this policy across all the system components ensures that the whole system is resilient to failures and can autonomically recover from them once the component is restarted.

One key innovation is that the Remote Procedure Calls (RPCs) between the component-local operations are stored as work items in a queue and the state of the queue is saved as part of the local action in cases where an operation spans multiple components. In addition, each state-changing procedure call has an OPERATION TRANSACTION IDENTIFIER (oTid) associated with it. A component receiving an operation transaction identifier for a call that has already completed does not repeat the call, but instead returns the results of the last call (stored when the last call was completed) with that identifier.

Thus, we show that global, distributed fault tolerance can be achieved by ensuring that individual components adhere to two key design properties:

- The ability to persist internal state to a durable repository as an integral part of the process of executing a remote operation and

- Caching the result of recent state-changing operations, so that these operations are not repeated, even if the RPC is retried.

In the rest of the paper, we describe a framework that provides the following support:

- A reliable transport for handling incoming and outgoing remote operations;

- A definition of algorithmic operational transaction boundaries for multi-component chained remote operations;

- A mechanism for capturing the internal state of a pool of worker threads, which carry out chained remote operations.

As we will show, the reliability support we propose is agnostic as far as the underlying communication substrate and component-based technology. Our current implementation supports components written in Java and C++ in the context of the product-grade SYSTEM S stream processing middleware.

2. BACKGROUND

2.1 A System S Overview

SYSTEM S [1] comprises of a middleware runtime system and an application development framework [7], geared towards supporting the development of large-scale, scalable and fault-tolerant stream processing applications. An *application* is essentially a flowgraph in which operators carry out portions of the data processing analytics by consuming and producing new streams, leading to the extraction of relevant results [38]. Once an application is compiled, a set of runnable processing elements is created. A *processing element* (PE) is a runtime container for portions of the flowgraph, i.e., a collection of operators and their stream interconnections. PEs belonging to an application can be logically grouped together to form *jobs*. A SYSTEM S user can then start up the application by submitting it to the middleware runtime system, thereby creating one or more jobs. The jobs can then be monitored, moved and canceled using system management tooling.

SYSTEM S has been designed to make use of a flexible hardware runtime environment, from a single x86-based host to x86-based clusters. It includes fault tolerance mechanisms that span the system software infrastructure as described in the present work, allowing the runtime to survive host and management component crashes. The SYSTEM S runtime also includes support for fault tolerance at the application level [21, 22]. Interested readers can refer to prior

approaches that have been explored for achieving fault tolerance in older versions of the SYSTEM S runtime [19, 20].

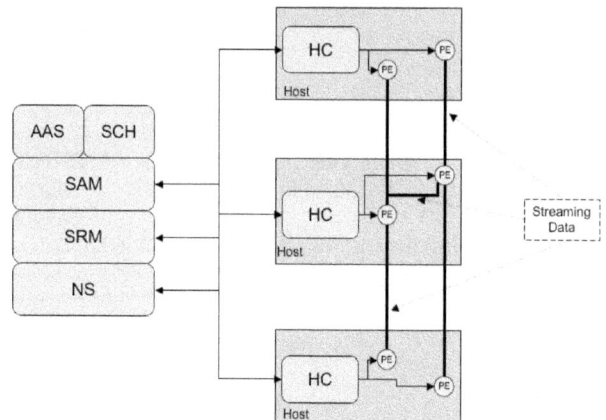

Figure 1: System S Runtime Architecture

The SYSTEM S middleware runtime architecture (Figure 1) separates the *logical* system view from the *physical* system view. The runtime contains two distinct sets of components – the centralized components are responsible for accepting job management and monitoring requests, deploying and tracking streaming applications on the runtime environment and the distributed components, which are responsible for managing application pieces deployed on individual hosts. Specifically, the Streams Application Manager (SAM) is the centralized gatekeeper for logical system information related to the applications running on SYSTEM S. SAM provides access to this information to the administration and visualization tooling. SAM also functions as the system entry point for job management tasks. The Streams Resource Manager (SRM) is the centralized gatekeeper for physical system information related to the software and hardware components that make up a SYSTEM S instance. SRM is the middleware bootstrapper, carrying out the system initialization upon an administrator request. In the steady-state, SRM is responsible for collecting and aggregating system-wide metrics, including the health of hosts that are part of a SYSTEM S instance and the health of the SYSTEM S componentry itself, as well as relevant performance metrics necessary for scheduling and system administration.

The runtime system also includes additional components, which we briefly describe here. The Scheduler (SCH) is the component responsible for computing placement decisions for applications to be deployed on the runtime system [36, 37]. The Name Service (NS) is the centralized component responsible for storing service references enabling inter-component communication by associating symbolic names with resource endpoints that can be registered, unregistered and remotely queried. The Authentication and Authorization Service (AAS) is the centralized component that provides user authentication as well as inter-component cross authentication, vetting interactions between the components.

The runtime system has two distributed management components. The Host Controller (HC) is the component running on every application host and is responsible for carrying out all local job management tasks including starting, stopping and monitoring processing elements on behalf of requests made by SAM. The HC is also responsible for acting as the distributed monitoring probe on behalf of SRM ensuring that the distributed pieces of applications remain healthy. Finally, a SYSTEM S runtime instance typically includes several instances of the Processing Element Container (PEC), which hosts the application user code embedded in a processing element. To ensure physical separation, there is one PEC per processing element running on the system.

Some SYSTEM S components (SAM, AAS, SRM and NS) maintain an internal state in order to carry out their operations. Each component's internal state reflects a partial view of the overall SYSTEM S instance state to which the component belongs. This internal state must be *durable* if the component is to recover from failure.

3. CHALLENGES

SYSTEM S was designed to deploy and manage streaming applications that can run for days, weeks or more at a time [33]. A single SYSTEM S instance can be used to manage multiple streaming applications. A SYSTEM S instance reacts to events from user (for example, a user submits a job, restarts a PE, etc) as well as the environment (for example, a PE dies, a streaming connection is broken, etc). The reaction to each event is different and depends on the state of the system and of the running applications at the time of the event. Events may occur at any time and can overlap on several occasions. The SYSTEM S component that handles a particular event is dependent on the type of event and the responsibilities of the component (Section 2.1).

An operation triggered by an external event may take a long time to complete. For example, the deployment of all PEs in a job and establishing stream connections, in response to a job submission request, may take anywhere from a few seconds to several minutes to complete, depending on the load in the system. The operation is not considered completed unless all PEs in the job are reported as *running*. If a failure (involving one or more components) occurs before the operation is complete, the system must be able to tolerate this failure and continue the deployment of PEs once the failed component (or components) are recovered.

Component failures can occur at any time whether a component is either idle or busy processing one or more operations. Some operations can possibly fail due to an abnormal situation (for example, a user submitting a job may get an exception and the job rejected from the system). However an operation triggered in response to a system event (for example, restarting a failed PE) is harder and in some cases impossible, to roll back. Such operations have to be processed to completion for the applications to function properly.

Completing an operation may require one or more components interacting with each other. Communication between components can happen in any order, depending on the type of operation and may involve calling a particular component one or more times. The state of a component may be updated more than once during the processing of a single distributed operation. Also, since the system may be handling more than one operation at any given point in time, a component's state may be updated several times making it increasingly difficult and time-consuming to rollback operations due to a failure.

4. ARCHITECTURE

In this section we describe how we obtain system-wide reliability in SYSTEM S by deploying locally and independently recoverable components. Two fundamental building blocks are required.

Building Block #1: The underlying inter-component communication infrastructure must be reliable, in the sense that remote procedure calls are either correctly carried out or failures are conveyed back to the caller. This assumption is satisfied by most communication libraries such as MPI, PVM and plain connection-oriented socket-based protocols. SYSTEM S uses CORBA[1] as the basic remote procedure call (RPC) mechanism.

Building Block #2: The data storage mechanism must be durable. Our implementation uses an IBM DB2 [15] database as the data store.

The central idea that permeates our reliability approach is to convert a distributed operation into component-local transactions connected with a communication protocol that can retry remote operations until they succeed. The operations are always retried in case of failure (component failure or communication failure) until either the operation is explicitly canceled by the user or until the system is shutdown. The retries can also be stopped in case of logical errors (for example, in SYSTEM S an operation requesting the termination of an application can be discarded if the application has already terminated). In other words, we ensure that a particular remote operation will *always* be executed eventually. Thus, all operations complete eventually and different operations can be interleaved. The component servicing the request may *temporarily* fail, but the request continues. In our design, all failures are seen as transient in nature under the assumption that failed components will be restarted quickly and primed with the state they held *before* the failure. The last part of our design relies on the client's ability to transparently retry or backout from pending remote operations, thereby ensuring that transitions caused in the remote component preserve the overall system state consistency. This design relies on a set of mechanisms that we describe next.

4.1 The Reliability Framework

In contrast with existing dependable distributed objects architectures (see Section 8), we devised our reliability architecture to be deployable as part of the component design, rather than baking it into a particular framework such as CORBA, which would be very challenging from an engineering perspective. Indeed, there are multiple additional reasons behind this approach. For example, many distributed systems grow organically and different components may choose to present a remote interface that relies on different communication substrates (e.g., web-services or CORBA). A simpler case, but still difficult to handle with existing models, is when the whole system relies on the same communication mechanism (e.g., CORBA), but different components rely on ORBs with different fault tolerance capabilities, which happened to be our own situation in SYSTEM S. Another reason is that component writers can pick

---

[1]The SYSTEM S inter-component communication mechanism is CORBA-based and employs two non-fault-tolerant ORBs: omniORB [10] for the C++ components and the internal IBM JDK CORBA implementation for the Java components.

different reliability levels for different components and even for different interfaces in a component.

Another aspect of our design is the management of a component's internal state, i.e., the information that is required to be maintained by the component for performing its operations. This information must be persisted and restored if a component is restarted after a failure. This information includes the components static state and the asynchronous work items used to carry out requests to external components. These work items are deleted on completion (Section 4.5).

4.2 Component State Management

For every component that maintains an internal state which needs to be restored after a failure, the following information must be persisted in the durable data store:

(a) The components in-core management data structures;

(b) The serialized asynchronous processing requests (i.e., the work items in the component work queue); and

(c) The repository of completed remote operations and their associated results.

Persisting a component's in-core data structures needs to be engineered in such a way that one is not tied to a particular durable storage solution. In our implementation, we employed the same paradigm made popular by Hibernate [2]. The top layer of our persistence model presents an object/relational interface that can be used to wrap traditional data structures, in particular, associative maps (e.g., hash maps, red-black trees). Associative maps store pairs of <key, object> tuples. The lower layer of the persistence model is used to hookup to the data storage converting entries in these maps into database records.

Persisting asynchronous work items (Section 4.5) is achieved by serializing the work items while maintaining their order of submission. Thus, while retrieving them from data store after a crash, the work items are scheduled to execute in the same sequence they would have before the crash. The deletion of the work items from the data store is done after the work item has completed its execution.

4.3 Component Operation Processing

In SYSTEM S, as is the case for other distributed systems, it is required that some remote operations be executed *at-most-once*. In other words, if for some reason, the same request is made multiple times, the reliability middleware must ensure that the multiple invocations of the same request are harmless or that the re-issue of the same request is flagged and correctly dealt with. For this reason, once a component's interface has been defined, each of the external operations is classified as one of the following types:

- *Idempotent*: Multiple operation invocations of the same request do not affect the remote component's internal state, but they might return different results (for example, an operation querying the state of a component may yield different results each time)

- *Non-Idempotent*: An operation invocation will yield an internal state change in the remote component.

In our framework, ensuring *at-most-once* semantics is a collaborative task between the component's client interface

and the component's server interface as we describe later. No special handling is required for idempotent operations as they can be safely retried in case of error without the fear of adversely affecting the component's state. We focus the rest of our discussion on handling non-idempotent operations.

For each non-idempotent operation, an OPERATION TRANSACTION IDENTIFIER (OTID) field is added to the arguments of the interface, to identify if a particular operation is being repeated. The OTID is guaranteed to be unique[2] and is sent from the client to the server along with the remote call parameters. On the server side, the function that implements the remote service works under the assumption that every operation may have failed.

Figure 2 shows the block diagram of a typical non-idempotent operation processing shown in the context of a SYSTEM S *submitJob* operation (see Section 5.1). The first step in processing a non-idempotent operation is to determine if the call has already been executed. If the operation has not been processed, it is executed and its results are logged in the component's internal log repository whose contents are persisted in durable storage. If the call has been processed, the results of the call are simply retrieved from the repository and returned to the caller. In this case, the actual processing of the call is skipped altogether.

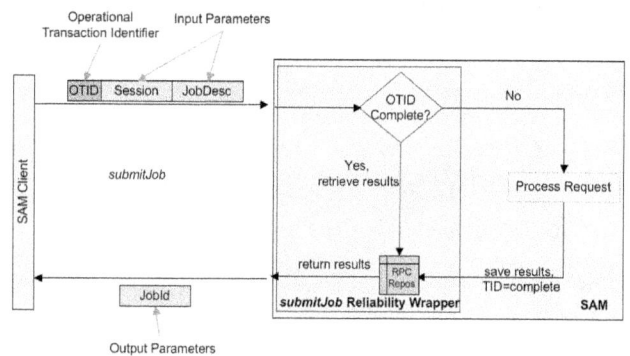

Figure 2: *submitJob* **Call Processing Block Diagram**

4.4 Integrating Database Transactions

Consider a simple non-idempotent operation processing scenario where the structure of code for handling network service requests is shown in Listing 1.

Listing 1: Simple Non-Idempotent Code Handling

```
1 Begin Network Service (oTid)
2    Non−Idempotent code
3    Log service request result (oTid, result)
4 End Network Service
```

"Non-Idempotent code" may change the internal state of the component, but *does not* initiate requests to external components or carry out additional asynchronous processing to complete the request. The non-idempotent code is implemented such that it is wrapped within a database transaction. As we mentioned before, in our case, the durable stor-

---

[2]Any GUID generator can be used. Our implementation uses a combination of the clients host name, process identifier, thread identifier and current timestamp to generate a unique OTID.

age component is a DB2 database and we make use of its C/C++ APIs for that purpose. Such APIs exist for most commercial grade DBMSs. Hence the operation code adheres to the pattern depicted by Listing 2.

Listing 2: Non-Idempotent Code handling with Database Transactions

```
1 Begin Network Service (oTid)
2   DB Transaction Begin
3     Non-idempotent code
4     Log service request result (oTid, result)
5   DB Transaction End (commit)
6 End Network Service
```

If a crash happens inside the DB transaction boundary (on or before step 5) then the state changes are not committed to durable storage and, hence, we maintain a consistent state (obviously, a component's in-core state is wiped out by the crash).

The client requesting the remote operation will continue retrying the request until completion. The operation will complete once the failed component is restarted (possibly in a new location) with its internal state fully recovered from durable storage.

If the crash happens after the transaction is committed (after step 5), but before the result is returned to the client, then the framework has already committed the log of the service request (which contains the service OTID and the response that needs to be sent back to the client). After a crash and restart, if the request comes back, the reliable protocol layer will just look at the log and reply back with the original result.

4.5 Processing Asynchronous Tasks

Consider a scenario in which one of the middleware components servicing an operation needs to perform additional operations, possibly by making use of other component's services. For example, in SYSTEM S, the launching of Processing Elements (see Section 5.1) is a time consuming operation. While the validation of certain pre-conditions as well as certain security checks must be performed synchronously, once the validity of the job is asserted, the dispatching of processing elements can be carried out asynchronously on the multiple hosts that will be employed by the user-written application. In the rest of this section, we will discuss how such dependent (or chained) remote operations are handled by our framework.

Our approach is to schedule the asynchronous processing of a task only after the database transaction under which the task was created has been logged to the durable repository. Consider an asynchronous PE deployment operation (*startPE*) that is delivered and which schedules and completes even while the original *submitJob* thread is still processing the request (details in Section 5.1). Now consider that the component (in this case SAM) crashes at this stage (before the *submitJob* thread logs its results). On a recover, since the *submitJob* operation did not complete, it will be re-executed and the asynchronous task items are reissued. This can lead to inconsistencies in the system. One way to solve this problem is to recognize that each execution of a new unit of work on each thread has to go through the reliability approach we discussed in Section 4.4 with similar semantics as previously discussed. This is usually complicated to im-

plement, let alone determining the in/out semantics for each function.

All this complexity can be avoided if we assume that the work units can be scheduled after a commit from the original request in which case we can guarantee that they are executed only once. Hence the structure for asynchronous request follows the pattern depicted by Figure 3.

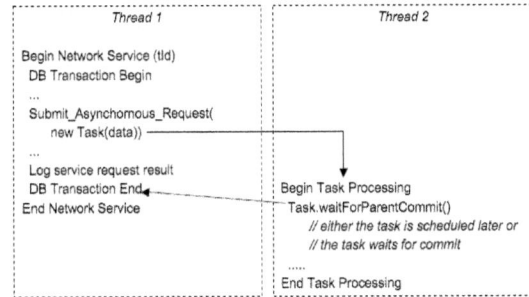

Figure 3: Asynchronous Request Processing

With this arrangement, worker threads can execute the asynchronous requests, which begin processing only after the task creation operation has completed and committed its results to durable storage. Requests are deleted from the storage after they complete.

5. PROCESSING INTER-COMPONENT OPERATIONS

As previously described, executing a remote operation in a component might involve interacting with other components as part of the process. We now discuss, in the context of two examples, what is needed to handle such interactions in our framework. The first example below describes a user-initiated distributed operation and the second example describes a system-initiated distributed operation. We close this section with a description of a general purpose technique.

5.1 The SubmitJob Operation

The SYSTEM S job submission process consists of six steps. The initial request from user is accepted and the overall operation is coordinated by the SAM component. The following steps describe the operations.

1. Accept Job Description from User.

2. Check Permissions. This is a query into the AAS server, but does not change AAS' local state.

3. Determine PE placement. This is a query into the SCH server determining scheduling placements of PEs. The SCH contacts the SRM for assessing node availability. The states of SCH and SRM remain unchanged during these calls.

4. Update local state. Insert the job into SAM's local tables.

5. Register the job with AAS. This does change AAS' local state. It is an error to register the same job twice.

6. Deploy the PEs. Though this operation changes the state of the system, the HCs do not maintain any persisted state, so this is essentially a stateless operation. (On restart, an HC searches for PEs on its current node and determines its state from that.)

A naive implementation would be to place all these actions within a single call. Suppose that is the implementation and while the state-changing *registerJob* call is being made from SAM to AAS, AAS crashes and the call appears to have failed. There are two possibilities: either AAS completed the *registerJob* operation or it did not. In the first case, it would be an error for SAM to re-register the job, as the job is already in the system. In the second case, SAM must register the job. As long as SAM continues to run, it can re-try the register harmlessly with the same operation transaction identifier.

But now consider the case where SAM fails during the *registerJob* operation. In this case, we may leave the distributed system in an inconsistent state. For SAM, it is as if the job had never existed. However, the *registerJob* operation on the AAS server may have succeeded. On restart, SAM may try the *submitJob* operation again (as its client will be retrying the operation while SAM is down), but it is an error to register the job if it has already been registered and a necessity to register the job if it has not been registered. This is the situation the fault-tolerance mechanism must prevent.

Note that the call to SCH and the AAS permission check call do not cause that same problem–both can be harmlessly repeated when SAM is restarted after a crash, whether or not they were executed, since they do not change the internal component state.

Our technique is to slightly change the operation flow as follows. The bold notation marks the new parts.

- Preparation, completed as a local transaction.

  1. Accept Job Description from User

  2. Check Permissions. This is a query into the AAS server, but does not change AAS' local state.

  3. Determine PE placement. This is a query into the SCH server determining scheduling placements of PEs. The SCH contacts the SRM for assessing node availability. The states of SAM, SCH and SRM remain unchanged during these calls.

  4. Update local state. Insert the job into SAM's local tables.

  5. **Generate oTid for AAS** *registerJob* **and queue registration work item with that id.**

  6. Commit current state (SAM's internal tables and work queue) to the database.

- Register and launch (the work item from the above flow)

  1. Register the job with AAS, **using the already generated oTid**.

  2. Start a local database transaction.

3. Deploy the PEs. Though this operation changes the state of the system, the HCs do not maintain any persisted state, so this is essentially a stateless operation. (On restart, an HC searches for PEs on its current node and determines its state from that.)

4. Commit current state to database.

The *Preparation* phase contains no calls that change any state. Likewise, the *Register and Launch* phase may be repeated as many times as necessary. If the SAM server fails before the database transaction begins, on retry, the *Register and Launch* is retried from the beginning. However, since it will use the same operation transaction identifier for the call to the AAS server, there is no danger of the job being registered twice.

There are two subtle points. First the operation transaction identifier must be generated and persisted in a completed transaction, before the call to AAS can be made. Generating and saving the operation transaction identifier without completing a transaction within SAM would result in problem of the naive implementation. Second, the launch of PEs requires queuing work into SAM's work queue and updates to SAMs internal tables containing PE state information. That is why the *Register and Launch* section is also a transaction.

5.2 Restarting a PE

Another common type of operation handled by SYSTEM S occurs in response to a failed PE event. In contrast to the job submission flow described in Section 5.1, which is user initiated, this operation is initiated by a system event. Such operations cannot be rejected or rolled-back.

When a processing element (PE) fails, it needs to be automatically restarted. The local Host Controller (HC) notices that the PE is down, it contacts SAM. Here is the stepwise description of what happens in SAM.

1. Begin SAM's local database transaction.

2. SAM updates its state to indicate that the PE is down.

3. SAM contacts SCH for alternate placement.

4. SAM launches PE and waits for confirmation that it is running.

5. Commit SAM's local database transaction.

Suppose that SAM fails during this operation. The local HC will try the request again (with the same operation transaction identifier). But suppose that in the first run, SAM had gotten as far as re-launching the PE, but had not yet committed. When the HC repeats the call, SAM will relaunch the PE.[3]

- Preparation

  1. Begin SAM's local database transaction.

  2. SAM updates its state to indicate that the PE is down.

---

[3]If it is relaunched on the same host, there is no problem, because the HC will not start the PE if it is already running. But if it is relaunched on a different host, then the HC on that host will start it.

340

3. SAM contacts SCH for alternate placement.

4. SAM places *startPE* work item on the queue

5. Commit SAM's local database transaction.

- *StartPE* work item

    1. SAM contacts HC with a request to launch PE.

Under this new scenario, the HC's repeated notification that a PE is down has the correct result: the transaction completes and SAM relaunches the PE or alternatively the transaction does not complete and no state is changed in SAM.

One key fact is that the work item completion triggers its removal from the database, so there is a state update and a database transaction implicit in that work item.

5.3 Generalizing

For concreteness, in the preceding sections, we discussed a specific SYSTEM S distributed operations. In general, the transformation we applied can be described by a straightforward algorithm.

- Divide the operation into a series of steps separated by state-changing remote procedure calls.

- Each step (except the first) corresponds to a separate work item. The work item is the preceding remote procedure call, followed by a transaction that includes the work in this state. Note that the remote procedure call itself is **not** part of the transaction.

- As the last task in each step, generate an operation transaction identifier for the next remote procedure call and enqueue the corresponding item into the work queue.

Using this technique and the system infrastructure we already mentioned, any distributed operation can be rewritten as a fault-tolerant operation.

6. TYING IT ALL TOGETHER

In this section, we show how techniques described in the previous sections are used along with communication retries to achieve system-wide fault tolerance.

6.1 Retry Policy

As mentioned in the previous sections, the interaction between components is governed by the component client interface. In our architecture, the retry behavior is managed by a *Retry Controller* that defines the nature of retries once failures are encountered. Retries can be *bounded* or *unbounded* in nature.

Bounded retries are used for operations where the request is directly initiated by a user. In our job submission example (Section 5.1), the SAM client handling the initial *submitJob* request (initiated by a user) will use *bounded* retries while trying to contact SAM. If the SAM component has failed, the client will eventually timeout and return an error back to the user. For such cases, the retries can be capped in terms of re-issue of remote requests and attempts to reconnect with the component.

Unbounded retries are typically used for inter-component requests. In our PE restart example (Section 5.2), if the SAM component has failed, the HC will use *unbounded* retries while communicating with SAM. Note that *unbounded* retries only indicate that the retry will not time out after a specific number of attempts. The retries may be abandoned in case of shutdown or error conditions (for example, if the component initiating the operation is shutdown, etc). The design of the Retry Controller borrowed a few ideas from the Iona ORB timeout policies [18].

6.2 Fault Detection and Recovery

During the normal operation of the SYSTEM S middleware, once failures are detected, the recovery process is automatically kick-started. In SYSTEM S, failure detection is the responsibility of the SRM component[4]. Failures are detected in two different ways. Central components are periodically contacted by SRM to ensure their liveness. This is done using an application-level *ping* operation that is built into all the components as a part of our framework. moreover, all distributed components communicate their liveness to SRM via a scalable heartbeat mechanism [26].

The recovery process is simple and involves only the restart of the failed component or components. Once a failed component is restarted, its state is rebuilt from information in durable storage before it starts processing any new or pending operations. First, the component in-core structures (Section 4.2) are read from storage. Next, the list of completed operations is retrieved followed by re-populating the work queue with any pending asynchronous operations. Once all the state is populated, the component starts accepting new external requests and the pending requests start being processed. Any components trying to contact the restarted component will be able to receive responses and the system will resume normal operation.

6.3 Handling Multiple Failures

The framework described in this paper is able to handle multiple component failures at the same time without any additional work or coordination. The failed components can be restarted in any order and will begin processing requests as and when they are restarted. The completion of a pending distributed operation depends on the availability of all components needed to service that operation. The failure of a component after it has completed its part of the distributed operation does not affect the completion of the operation.

7. EXPERIMENTAL EVALUATION

In this section, to show the breadth of our approach, we measure the effect of failures in three different mocked-up component-graph configurations. Then we assess the performance and suitability of our system in a high performance environment, by experimentally showcasing our fault tolerance approach in a realistic scenario. We look at the overhead of the reliability layer imposes on normal operations of SYSTEM S components. Finally, we also look at the time taken by the components to recover after a failure.

All experiments were conducted with SYSTEM S running on up to five Linux hosts. Each host contains 2 Intel Xeon 3.4 GHz CPUs with 16GB RAM[5]. As discussed before, we

---

[4]SRM itself is monitored and restarted by a Unix `cron` job.
[5]SYSTEM S was running in test mode with debugging enabled. Measurements do not indicate performance of system in a production environment.

use an IBM DB2 database as durable storage running on a separate dedicated host.

7.1 Operation Completion Time

We make use of mock components to show the impact component failures have on the completion time of a distributed operation. In order to determine what variables affect the completion times of an operation, we developed a mock component with a non-idempotent interface. Multiple instances of this mock component can be used to create a component graph emulating any distributed system configuration. The components can be configured to simulate a failure by abruptly exiting during the processing of a request. This way we are able to insert a failure anywhere in the component-graph. We are also able to vary the size of internal state being stored by each component while processing a operation and the delay[6] between the failure of a component and the time of its restart.

Figure 4 shows the component graph configurations we used in our experiment. We chose configurations typical of distributed system operations. The chain graph and the distributed graph both occur in SYSTEM S operations. The vertices denote components and the edges are non-idempotent RPCs. The numbers on top of each edge show the sequence of the calls in the distributed operation[7]. In the experiments, for each measurement, we induced a crash in all components serially (except the first component in the graph), restarted the component after a specified amount of delay and measured the time taken for the operation to complete. Figure 5 shows the range of completion times for the three configurations and five restart delays for (1KB state persisted by each component). Each bar represents the minimum, maximum and average completion times over 10 runs. All experiments were conducted on a single host. The average restart delay is denoted with a dot. While the distributed configuration takes slightly longer, the completion time is nearly the same for all three configurations.

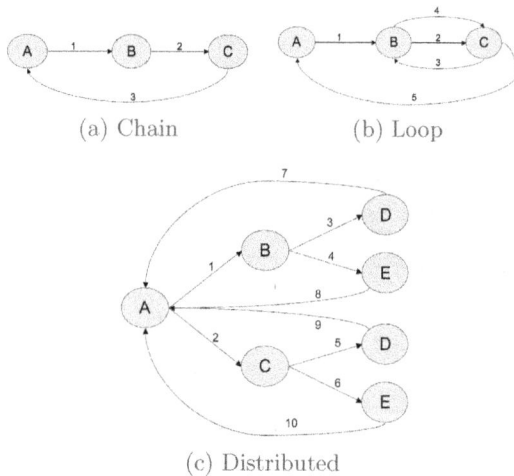

Figure 5: Operation Completion Times (1 KB State Size)

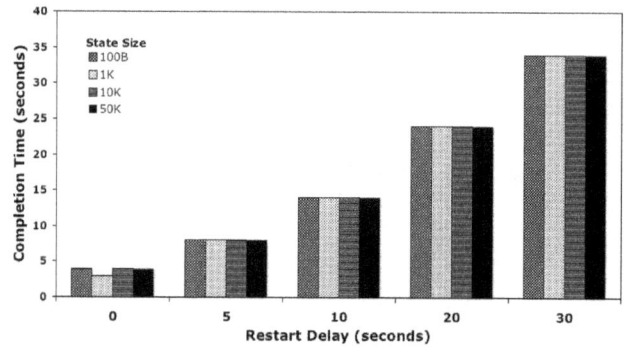

Figure 6: Operation Completion Times By State Size (Distributed Configuration)

As shown in Section 7.2, the Time To Recover (TTR) is fairly low (in the order of milliseconds) as compared to the operation completion times (in the order of seconds). The delay in restarting components (which is approximately 15 seconds in SYSTEM S) has the most effect on the completion times. Note that in all the configurations, for very low restart delays, there is a 3-4 second completion time for the operations. This is due to the time taken for detecting the failure, before a restart can be attempted. The type of component-graph seems to have little or no impact on the completion times.

We also looked at the impact of the size of the state being persisted in the data store on the completion time of the operation. To evaluate this, we repeated our experiment with different state sizes being stored by each component in the component-graph during the completion of the operation. The results for the distributed component-grap, depicted by Figure 4(c), are shown in Figure 6. As shown the state size seems to have little to no impact on the completion time of the operation. The results were similar for the Chain and Loop configurations, therefore the graphs have been omitted from this paper.

In the next set of experiments, two reference applications are used to impose load on the middleware:

(a) Chain   (b) Loop

(c) Distributed

Figure 4: Distributed Operation Configurations

---

[6]Does not include time to detect the failure, which could be between 1 and 3 seconds.

[7]Sequence depicted in Figure 4(c) is approximate, as the calls may be executed in parallel.

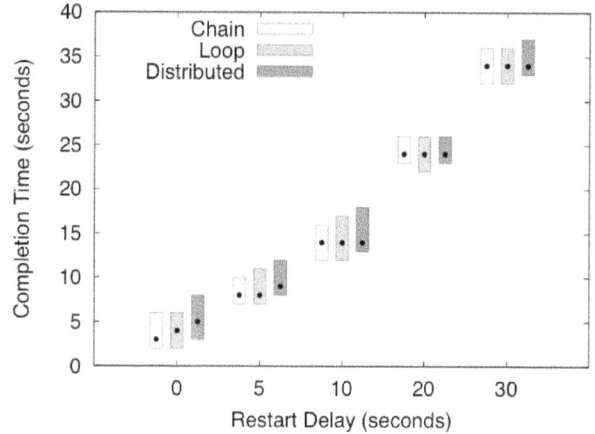

- *Source-Relay-Sink* (SRS): The first is a simple Source-Relay-Sink application. It consists of one job containing three PEs. The Source PE generates streaming data which is read by the Relay PE which in turn forwards it to the Sink PE.

- *Market Data Processing* (MDP): The second is a real-world application [39] where a high data rate stream of options trading transactions are processed. This application consists of 55 PEs.

Using these applications we evaluate our system with respect to two main middleware metrics:

- *Time To Recover*: This is the time taken for a component to rebuild its state and begin processing requests once it has been restarted after a crash (an induced crash, in our case).

- *Steady State Reliability Overhead*: This is the overhead imposed by the reliability layer in the course of carrying out remote operations required by other components or client user-interface utilities[8].

For obtaining the above metrics, we focus on the performance of the SAM component. We remind the reader that SAM is the component responsible for the deployment and management of PEs and is central to most operations in the SYSTEM S middleware. Qualitatively, SAM maintains a substantial amount of state that must be recovered post-failures. Spread across its several data structures, the following types of information are maintained:

- *Job Information*: Job related data structures capture job ownership and execution status.

- *PE Information*: PE related data structures capture information on individual PEs, including their runtime parameters and executable information.

- *Dataflow Information*: Dataflow related data structures capture the connections between PEs as well as routing information pertaining to stream connections, both static and dynamic, i.e., transient stream connections made as new applications get deployed [13].

7.2 Time To Recover

The Time to Recover (TTR) metric provides an indication of how long it takes to restore a component's state after a crash. For experimentally computing this metric, the SYSTEM S runtime is first started on a set of hosts. The test applications are submitted to the system and a crash is induced in the SAM component once all PEs have been deployed successfully. SAM is then restarted and the time taken for the restart is measured. This process is carried out multiple times and an average of the restart times is shown for each configuration. Since we are not considering the time taken for the user-written application to be deployed, the impact of number of hosts used by the application is not relevant to our analysis.

Figure 7 shows the average "Per PE TTR" (in milliseconds), over 10 runs, for SAM under various application loads.

---

[8]The reliability layer can be bypassed, turning it off in SYSTEM S.

The error bars denote the minimum and maximum over all the runs [9]. The SRS application was submitted multiple times (specifically, 1, 5, 10, 50 and 100 times), thus emulating the presence of several simultaneous applications sharing a single middleware instance. Note that we have subtracted the cost of restarting SAM with no jobs in the system from the TTR values.

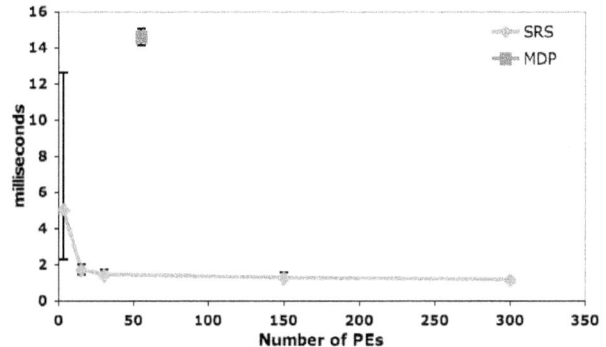

Figure 7: Time To Recover Per PE

The "Per PE TTR" is fairly high when the number of PEs in the system is small, indicating a relatively large fixed *startup* cost. The time spent with database communication dominates the cost of persisting the information about the PEs. We see a linear increase in the "Overall TTR" for the SRS application for higher number of PEs (30 to 300). The "Per PE TTR" reduces significantly as the number of PEs increases, as shown in Figure 7 and stabilizes for larger number of PEs.

Switching focus to the MDP application [39], the longer recovery time required for this application can be attributed to the large number of inter-PE connections and the corresponding information that needs to be persisted due to the nature of the application. Compared to the SRS application, the cost for de-serializing the large amount of data being stored per PE, is a lot higher in the MDP application. The time taken to retrieve this data from the database and reconstructing the in-memory structures in SAM, contributes to the higher recovery times for the MDP application.

We believe that these results demonstrate that the key SYSTEM S component can recover rather quickly after a failure, ensuring overall availability of the middleware.

7.3 Steady State Overhead

In the next set of experiments, we look at the overhead imposed by the reliability framework. Here, the test applications are submitted to the system and the PE launch time is measured. The actual PE startup process is short-circuited (i.e., PEs are considered to be launched as soon as the deployment order for the PE is issued by SAM to the HCs). That way, delays caused due to remote host communications as well as load on the remote hosts are avoided.

We repeated the same set of experiments with reliability mode *on* and *off* and measured the extra time required for the operation to complete when the reliability mode was

---

[9]Some of the minimum and maximum values may not be clearly seen in the figure as they are very close to the average value.

on. The experiments were repeated 10 times per data point and the average of the respective measurements were used. The calculated average "Overhead Per PE", along with the corresponding minimum and maximum values as indicated by the error bars, is shown in Figure 8.

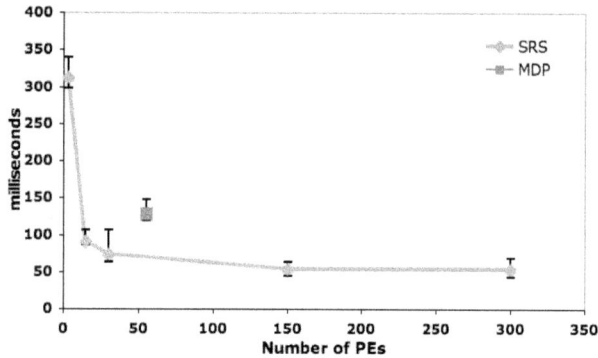

Figure 8: Overhead Per PE

The "Overhead Per PE" is high for smaller number of PEs. As is the case for the TTR metric, the database communication cost initially accounts for the lion's share of the total overhead. This reduces significantly for a larger number of PEs in the SRS application. Again, the overhead is relatively higher for the MDP application due to the larger amount of data (related to more complex dataflow-graph connections as compared to SRS) being persisted per PE.

As can be seen, the overhead can be substantial on a relative basis for small workloads. However, it is quite reasonable for realistic workloads, considering that ensuring durability of SAM's state implies persisting data by using a full blown relational database system (as opposed to a dedicated durable storage solution).

8. RELATED WORK

There have been a number of approaches and architectures dedicated to achieving reliability, fault tolerance and recovery in distributed systems. Most of these approaches can be summarized as one of three different types:

(a) *Replica and Consistency Management* [3, 24, 27, 29, 30, 35]: In these cases, reliability is achieved by supporting multiple replicas and assigning a failed request to another replica, once failure is detected. Most of the work in this area focused on how to physically set up the replicas, how to monitor them, how to switch to a different one and how to maintain consistency. Typically, the disadvantage of such approaches is in managing replicas and ensuring consistency in the presence of non-idempotent operations;

(b) *Flexible Consistency Models* [6, 32]: In these cases, failure is dealt with by relaxing ACID (Atomicity, Consistency, Isolation and Durability) semantics, by essentially allowing clients to temporarily face an inconsistent state. It has been shown [32] that many applications can actually work under such relaxed assumptions. These methods take advantage of the relaxed consistency requirement to achieve scalability.

(c) *Distributed Transaction Support* [23]: Many mechanisms have been provided to allow a distributed transaction to roll back in case of failures. While distributed transaction support addresses the requirements we have, it does so at the expense of central coordination as well as by relying on a global roll back mechanism.

We look into these categories in more details in the rest of this section.

As a general source of inspiration to the fault-tolerant mechanism discussed in this work, the Berkeley's Recovery Oriented Computing paradigm [31] states that faults are a fact of life and must be coped with – bug-free environments are simply not possible. It is stated that the focus should be on quick recovery, lowering the mean time to recover (MTTR) rather than increasing the mean time to failure (MTTF). The ROC project itself provides guidelines, but not mechanisms, which is the focus of this work.

Vaysburd [34] has addressed the problem of providing fault tolerance in an integrated fashion for a 3-tier application – client/server/database. This work provides an interesting characterization of the end-to-end reliability problem. It suggests that the client tier should tag requests. The server tier should offload state to a database and that the database tier alone should be concerned with reliability. Therefore, the focus of this work is in analyzing fault tolerance support when applications make use of commercial databases.

A replica-based approach to fault tolerance is explored by Beedubail et al [3]. Their approach relies on hot replicas where multiple copies of a service exist in standby. A fault tolerance layer, which is part of a general-purpose middleware, relays state changes from the primary replica to the secondary ones to maintain consistency.

In terms of fault-tolerant middleware support, the first standardization effort that occurred was on fault-tolerant CORBA – or FT-CORBA, for short. The standardization effort, started in 1998 by OMG [28], relies on service replication and strong consistency as the main mechanism for providing transparently reliable service when distributed non-idempotent requests are expected. A report on experiences and challenges in building fault-tolerant systems using CORBA is presented in [12].

Towards the refinement of the FT-CORBA standard, Vaysburd and Yajnik [35] described a mechanism for achieving *exactly-once* end-to-end semantics by using an FT request id, which is similar to the transaction identifiers we employ in our approach. However, the assumption is that in case of failures a replica will pick up the request and a multicast mechanism is used in order to ensure that all replicas are aware of the transaction. A survey of approaches for developing fault-tolerant applications using FT-CORBA has been written by Felber and Narasimhan [5].

DOORS [29, 30] is a Bell Labs-based effort to design a framework for end-to-end application fault tolerance. Like our approach, it uses an interception approach to capture the inter-component interactions. However, the central tenet for providing fault tolerance in DOORS was also replication.

AQuA [24] is a dependable, distributed, fault tolerance architecture designed at the University of Illinois. AQuA's design revolves around the concept of Quality Objects (QuO), which is used by applications to describe the level of availability to be be provided by an application. The key contribution of AQuA is in being tunable as far as the level of dependability that is desired.

In the realm of large-scale cluster-based network services, the prior art is mainly in identifying consistency models that are adequate to applications a typical Internet-based content provider will make available to customers. For example, Fox et al [6] proposes an architecture for scalable network services based on three fundamental requirements: incremental scalability, availability through fault masking and cost effectiveness. In their model, with weaker-than-ACID data semantics, availability is provided through massive replication. This model called BASE (Basically Available, Soft State, Eventual Consistency) is fine for many services, however, it does not handle situations where non-idempotent requests are carried out.

Another approach for providing reliability to Internet-based services is Neptune. Shen et al [32] propose a middleware for clustering support and replication management of network services. As in Fox's architecture, the key insight is to provide a flexible replication consistency support, again because weaker consistency models that lead to eventual consistency are acceptable for many applications.

Some of the more recent approaches, such as Chubby [4] and Zookeeper [14] provide a scalable and fault tolerant infrastructure for managing distributed applications. Zookeeper uses wait-free data objects while Chubby employs locking to provide synchronization guarantees. Both these approaches are useful in instances where group services are are required, such as when a set of nodes vote to elect a master. Zookeeper, a close clone of Chubby, employs replicated servers and databases to provide high availability. These approaches may not be ideal in systems such as ours where group services are not required. Moreover, our system is designed to run on installations which can have as few as one or two nodes. In such cases, replication will add an unnecessary high overhead.

9. CONCLUSION

We described a production-grade mechanism for achieving reliability and fault tolerance in large-scale distributed systems. Our framework is fully built and used in a real-world middleware [16].

Our approach avoids complex rollbacks procedures and the overhead of maintaining active replicas of components. More importantly, our architecture can be implemented as an extension to existing low-level distributed computing technologies (e.g., CORBA, DCOM, etc.) making it simple to adopt in the development of other distributed system middleware. The architecture is agnostic to the communication mechanism or durable storage solution, making it independent of the technologies we chose to use in SYSTEM S. It also provides support for both stateful and stateless components allowing the system to grow organically with different levels of reliability among components.

Our design is also able to incorporate other lower-cost alternatives for ensuring durability, for example, journaling file systems. As we have discussed, in SYSTEM S, this architecture is used by central and distributed components to provide fault tolerance and reliability while maintaining global state consistency.

Our experiments show that the reliability framework induces little overhead during normal operations and has very low recovery/restart times, providing high availability at a relatively low cost as we demonstrated experimentally. We have also shown that almost any distributed componentl-graph configuration can be implemented using our approach and that the system has the ability to tolerate and recover from one or more concurrent failures.

In the near future, we plan to experiment with other alternatives for the durable storage mechanism as well as the use of our reliability mechanism in other distributed middleware platforms.

10. REFERENCES

[1] L. Amini, H. Andrade, R. Bhagwan, F. Eskesen, R. King, P. Selo, Y. Park, and C. Venkatramani. SPC: A Distributed, Scalable Platform for Data Mining. In *DMSSP*, pages 27–37, New York, NY, USA, 2006. ACM.

[2] C. Bauer and G. King. *Hibernate in Action (In Action series)*. Manning Publications Co., Greenwich, CT, USA, 2004.

[3] G. Beedubail and U. W. Pooch. An Architecture for Object Replication in Distributed Systems. In *PDPTA*, pages 50–59, 1997.

[4] M. Burrows. The Chubby Lock Service for Loosely-Coupled Distributed Systems. In *OSDI*, pages 335–350. USENIX Association, 2006.

[5] P. Felber and P. Narasimhan. Experiences, Strategies, and Challenges in Building Fault-Tolerant CORBA Systems. *IEEE TOC*, 53:497–511, May 2004.

[6] A. Fox, S. D. Gribble, Y. Chawathe, E. A. Brewer, and P. Gauthier. Cluster-Based Scalable Network Services. In *SOSP*, pages 78–91, 1997.

[7] B. Gedik, H. Andrade, K.-L. Wu, P. S. Yu, and M. Doo. SPADE: The System S Declarative Stream Processing Engine. In *SIGMOD*, pages 1123–1134. ACM, 2008.

[8] A. Geist, A. Beguelin, J. Dongarra, W. Jiang, R. Mancheck, and V. Sunderam. *PVM: Parallel Virtual Machine. A Users' Guide and Tutorial for Networked Parallel Computing*. MIT Press, 1994.

[9] A. S. Gokhale, B. Natarajan, D. C. Schmidt, and J. K. Cross. Towards Real-Time Fault-Tolerant CORBA Middleware. *Cluster Computing*, 7(4):331–346, 2004.

[10] D. Grisby, S.-L. Lo, and D. Riddoch. The omniORB version 4.1 – User's Guide. Apasphere Ltd. and AT & T Laboratories Cambridge, 2009.

[11] W. Gropp, E. Lusk, and A. Skjellum. *Using MPI: Portable Parallel Programming with Message-Passing Interface*. MIT Press, 1999.

[12] R. Guerraoui, P. Eugster, P. Felber, B. Garbinato, and K. Mazouni. Experiences with Object Group Systems. *SPE*, 30:1375–1404, October 2000.

[13] M. Hirzel, H. Andrade, B. Gedik, V. Kumar, G. Rosa, M. Mendell, H. Nasgaard, R. Soule, and K.-L. Wu. SPL – Stream Processing Language Specification. Technical Report RC24897, IBM Research, 2009.

[14] P. Hunt, M. Konar, F. P. Junqueira, and B. Reed. ZooKeeper: Wait-free Coordination for Internet-scale Systems. In *In USENIX Annual Technical Conference*, pages 11–11, 2010.

[15] IBM. DB2. http://www-01.ibm.com/software/data/db2.

[16] IBM. IBM Infosphere Streams. `http://www-01.ibm.com/software/data/infosphere/streams/`.

[17] IBM. IBM WebSphere. `http://www-01.ibm.com/software/websphere`.

[18] IONA. Iona. `http://web.progress.com/en/index.html`.

[19] G. Jacques-Silva, J. Challenger, L. Degenaro, J. Giles, and R. Wagle. Towards Autonomic Fault Recovery in System S. In *ICAC*, page 31. IEEE Computer Society, 2007.

[20] G. Jacques-Silva, J. Challenger, L. Degenaro, J. Giles, and R. Wagle. Self healing in System S. *Cluster Computing*, 11(3):247–257, 2008.

[21] G. Jacques-Silva, B. Gedik, H. Andrade, and K.-L. Wu. Language Level Checkpointing Support for Stream Processing Applications. In *DSN*, pages 145–154. IEEE, 2009.

[22] G. Jacques-Silva, Z. Kalbarczyk, B. Gedik, H. Andrade, K.-L. Wu, and R. K. Iyer. Modeling stream processing applications for dependability evaluation. In *DSN*, 2011.

[23] R. Koo and S. Toueg. Checkpointing and Rollback-Recovery for Distributed Systems. *IEEE TSE*, 13(1):23–31, 1987.

[24] S. Krishnamurthy, W. H. Sanders, and M. Cukier. An Adaptive Quality of Service Aware Middleware for Replicated Services. *IEEE TPDS*, 14(11):1112–1125, 2003.

[25] S. Maffeis. Adding group communication and fault-tolerance to CORBA. In *COOTS*, pages 10–10, Berkeley, CA, USA, 1995. USENIX Association.

[26] S. Meng, S. R. Kashyap, C. Venkatramani, and L. Liu. REMO: Resource-Aware Application State Monitoring for Large-Scale Distributed Systems. In *ICDCS*, pages 248–255. IEEE Computer Society, 2009.

[27] A. P. A. V. Moorsel and S. Yajnik. Design of a Resource Manager for Fault-Tolerant CORBA. In *Proceedings of the International Workshop on Reliable Middleware Systems*, pages 1–6, 1999.

[28] L. E. Moser and R. J. Martin. Fault Tolerance for CORBA (Joint initial fault tolerance RFP submission by Eternal Systems and Sun Microsystems), 1998.

[29] B. Natarajan, A. S. Gokhale, S. Yajnik, and D. C. Schmidt. Applying Patterns to Improve the Performance of Fault Tolerant CORBA. In *HiPC*, pages 107–120, 2000.

[30] B. Natarajan, A. S. Gokhale, S. Yajnik, and D. C. Schmidt. DOORS: Towards High-Performance Fault Tolerant CORBA. In *DOA*, pages 39–48, 2000.

[31] D. Patterson, A. Brown, P. Broadwell, G. Candea, M. Chen, J. Cutler, P. Enriquez, A. Fox, E. Kiciman, M. Merzbacher, D. Oppenheimer, N. Sastry, W. Tetzlaff, J. Traupman, and N. Treuhaft. Recovery Oriented Computing (ROC): Motivation, Definition, Techniques, and Case Studies. Technical Report UCB/CSD-02-1175, EECS Department, University of California, Berkeley, Mar 2002.

[32] K. Shen, T. Yang, and L. Chu. Clustering Support and Replication Management for Scalable Network Services. *IEEE TPDS*, 14(11):1168–1179, 2003.

[33] D. S. Turaga, H. Andrade, B. Gedik, C. Venkatramani, O. Verscheure, J. D. Harris, J. Cox, W. Szewczyk, and P. Jones. Design Principles for Developing Stream Processing Applications. *SPE*, 40(12):1073–1104, 2010.

[34] A. Vaysburd. Fault Tolerance in Three-Tier Applications: Focusing on the Database Tier. In *SRDS*, pages 322–327, 1999.

[35] A. Vaysburd and S. Yajnik. Exactly-Once End-to-End Semantics in CORBA Invocations across Heterogeneous Fault-Tolerant ORBs. In *SRDS*, pages 296–297, 1999.

[36] J. Wolf, N. Bansal, K. Hildrum, S. Parekh, D. Rajan, R. Wagle, K.-L. Wu, and L. Fleischer. SODA: An Optimizing Scheduler for Large-Scale Stream-Based Distributed Computer Systems. In *Middleware*, pages 306–325, 2008.

[37] J. L. Wolf, N. Bansal, K. Hildrum, S. Parekh, D. Rajan, R. Wagle, and K.-L. Wu. Job Admission and Resource Allocation in Distributed Streaming Systems. In *JSSPP*, pages 169–189, 2009.

[38] K.-L. Wu, P. S. Yu, B. Gedik, K. Hildrum, C. C. Aggarwal, E. Bouillet, W. Fan, D. George, X. Gu, G. Luo, and H. Wang. Challenges and Experience in Prototyping a Multi-Modal Stream Analytic and Monitoring Application on System S. In *VLDB*, pages 1185–1196, 2007.

[39] X. J. Zhang, H. Andrade, B. Gedik, R. King, J. F. Morar, S. Nathan, Y. Park, R. Pavuluri, E. Pring, R. Schnier, P. Selo, M. Spicer, V. Uhlig, and C. Venkatramani. Implementing a high-volume, low-latency market data processing system on commodity hardware using IBM middleware. In *SC-WHPCF*. ACM, 2009.

Scheduling for Real-Time Mobile MapReduce Systems

Adam J. Dou
UC Riverside
Riverside, CA
jdou@cs.ucr.edu

Vana Kalogeraki
AUEB
Athens, Greece
vana@aueb.gr

Dimitrios Gunopulos
Univ. of Athens
Athens, Greece
dg@di.uoa.gr

Taneli Mielikäinen   Ville Tuulos
Nokia Research Center
Palo Alto, CA
{taneli.mielikainen,ville.h.tuulos}@nokia.com

ABSTRACT

The popularity of portable electronics such as smartphones, PDAs and mobile devices and their increasing processing capabilities has enabled the development of several real-time mobile applications that require low-latency, high-throughput response and scalability. Supporting real-time applications in mobile settings is especially challenging due to limited resources, mobile device failures and the significant quality fluctuations of the wireless medium. In this paper we address the problem of supporting distributed real-time applications in a mobile MapReduce framework under the presence of failures. We present Real-Time Mobile MapReduce (MiscoRT), our system aimed at supporting the execution of distributed applications with real-time response requirements. We propose a two level scheduling scheme, designed for the MapReduce programming model, that effectively predicts application execution times and dynamically schedules application tasks. We have performed extensive experiments on a testbed of Nokia N95 8GB smartphones. We demonstrate that our scheduling system is efficient, has low overhead and performs up to 32% faster than its competitors.

Categories and Subject Descriptors

C.2.4 [**Computer-Communication Networks**]: Distributed Systems

General Terms

Algorithms, Design, Experimentation, Reliability

Keywords

Distributed Systems, Mobile Systems, Real-Time, MapReduce

1. INTRODUCTION

In the last few years we have witnessed a significant growth of location-based systems where the physical location of the users is utilized to deliver information of interest, to encourage sharing of location-based information or to adapt the services in order to improve the level of service provided to the users. A number of location-based systems have emerged. Examples include traffic monitoring systems for real-time delay estimation and congestion detection [42], personalized weather information, location-based games or receiving spatial alarms upon the arrival to a reference time point [9], as well as social networking applications for sharing photos and personal data with family and friends [35]. In the search for economic power, companies are building these services over portable electronics such as smartphones, PDAs and mobile devices. These devices have significant processing and networking capabilities and are outfitted with a wide array of sensing capabilities such as GPS, WiFi, microphones, cameras and accelerometers, which have introduced new and more efficient ways of communication. However, this new application development brings new challenges to the design of system software. More specifically, providing real-time, low-latency and scalable execution for these applications presents three important challenges that need to be addressed:

1. we need to understand how the mobile setting affects the development of distributed applications over networks of smartphones and address the implications;

2. we need to provide a flexible and efficient way to program, develop and deploy the applications on the phones that is portability across multiple devices.

3. we need to be able to simplify programmability by hiding the difficult issues of distribution, real-time scheduling, device failures and connectivity issues from the application developer.

Application development over networks of smartphones. Several applications have been and are being developed for mobile platforms. Some applications focus on making the users daily lives easier by providing GPS guidance such as traffic congestion detection and delay estimates [42] and spacial alarm applications [9] which alert a user when they are a close by another user or a pre-designated area. Other applications help users stay connected. As people are expanding their use of social networking sites such as Facebook and Myspace, mobile applications are allowing them to view and modify their information in real-time from anywhere. The popularity of these real-time social sharing applications is evidenced by recent application compaigns [1] emphasizing these features. The usability of these systems is highly dependent on them running in a timely fashion when providing notifications and feedback. One challenge today is that there are still many problems which hinder the development of distributed applications on them. Mobile devices are not easy to develop for. There are many specialized languages and proprietary systems which have steep learning curves. With relatively limited resources compared to desktop and servers, memory management and application flow is different from traditional programming forcing new software paradigms, leading to many software defects. The main problem however is that distributed applications involving mobile devices exacerbate the problem by introducing several concurrency issues to consider. For example, because of user mobility and spotty connection coverage, network connectivity is often degraded or even lost.

Application Programmability. The second challenge is that several location-based applications, require the involvement of multiple users in the process of sensing and data processing, in order to achieve a task. These are deemed *participatory sensing* applications. For example, the Metro-Track system [3] is a mobile event tracking system capable of tracking mobile targets through collaboration among local sensing devices that track and predict the future location of a target. How to efficiently schedule work across a set of collaborating devices to accomplish a task is not an easy process. Recently, the MapReduce framework [14] was introduced to provide a highly scalable, distributed computing environment for conducting data processing computations. MapReduce has been successfully deployed in traditional server based environments [13] [43], specialized environments [25] [40], as well as in a variety of applications by many prominent companies such as Google, Yahoo, Facebook and IBM. The MapReduce framework's support for the weak connectivity model of computations across open networks, makes it very appropriate for a mobile network setting. It is important to note though, that, although we chose the MapReduce framework for our system, we do not target the same types of applications as traditional data warehouse based MapReduce systems, as the limited resources available on the mobile systems makes them unsuitable for any multi-petabyte data processing. Instead, our goal is to explore the use of the framework for participatory sensing applications such as monitoring and social networking applications and gain further insights into the possibilities of using the MapReduce framework for the next-generation of location-based applications over networks of smartphones.

Achieving Real-Time Response. The third challenge is how to support the execution of distributed applications with real-time response requirements on a network of smartphones. While the MapReduce framework provides the programming interfaces for developing mobile applications, all the low-level details of the real-time execution, fault tolerance and wireless network communication are not handled by the framework. Thus, the key question of how to provide support for applications with real-time response requirements, still remains. To date, most of the work on providing real-time application execution are either based on the deployment of static sensor networks (such as [33] and [26]), or are integrated within specific MAC or network layers [27] [18] to encapsulate application-specific tradeoffs in terms of resource constraints, shared wireless medium, lossy communication, and highly dynamic traffic or are restricted to a single node movement [30]. Supporting real-time mobile applications such as distributed mobile sensing is an important step for the wider adoption of the devices and to create opportunities for building new kinds of mobile application services. However, *timely execution* is a challenging problem in these settings due to highly dynamic topology, device unavailability and fluctuations in network quality and channel capacity. This makes it extremely difficult to estimate execution times and provide end-to-end real-time support to distributed applications. Unlike traditional cluster environments, mobile systems cannot rely on a static infrastructure and do not have control over the individual nodes. The problem is further exacerbated by *failures* of mobile devices. Permanent and transient failures such as battery depletion and user mobility can greatly affect the timeliness of distributed applications by reducing the processing power of the system, causing large delays and energy wastage.

In this paper we present *MiscoRT*, our system aimed at supporting the execution of real-time application tasks on mobile MapReduce systems. Our proposal follows a two-level approach to scheduling distributed real-time mobile applications. We first develop an analytical model to estimate the execution times of the applications in the presence of failures. Using this model, we determine the application urgencies based on our estimates of their execution times under failures and their timing constraints. Our goal is to maximize the probability that the end-to-end deadlines of the applications are met. By incorporating the expected failure model in the scheduling policy, we can adjust the fault-tolerance characteristics of the overall system. We see this as a major motivation for using the MapReduce model in mobile environments which are typically inherently unstable. Furthermore, we envision that methods developed for heterogeneous and unstable mobile environments of today can be useful in extremely loosely coupled computing environments of tomorrow which will not be confined to a single, well-controlled data center. We have built our approach on Misco [15], our MapReduce system that runs on mobile phones. We have implemented and tested our scheduling scheme on a testbed of Nokia's third generation NSeries phones [39]. We have built a mobile tourist application to evaluate our system. Our extensive experimental results demonstrate that our approach is efficient, has low overhead and completes applications up to 32% faster than its competitors.

2. OBJECTIVES

In this section we summarize the main objectives of our approach.

Supporting real-time applications: Our first objective is to support applications with real-time response requirements in the form of deadlines. In several applications such as traffic monitoring for real-time route suggestions and congestion detection, location-based notification of events or proximity notification for friends, users rely on the collaborative sensing of data from multiple phones and the timely collection and processing of the data, to generate outputs of interest and detect important events. However, mobile devices have limited computation and communication resources. Limited capacity, queuing and channel access delays can greatly affect the timeliness of the applications. Our approach is to provide real-time response to the applications, schedule the applications based on their relative urgencies and respond to changing conditions by dynamically scheduling the execution of application tasks to meet their deadlines. We have to note that the applications we develop on our system do not have hard real-time response requirements; rather, we target soft real-time applications where our goal is to maximize the number of deadlines met, and missing a deadline is not catastrophic for the system.

Accounting for device failures: We consider mobile node failures an integral part of mobile environments, thus our approach is to account for these failures when deriving an estimate of the execution times of the applications. Device failures have a major impact on the timeliness of our system. These failures are the results of hardware and software issues, user actions and user mobility. These errors can be classified as *permanent* and *transient* failures.

Permanent failures are failures where the device becomes unavailable for an extended period of time during which it is unable to participate in processing results for the system. Permanent failures can occur from software errors where critical software has crashed due to software or hardware faults or when users are shutting off their devices. A permanent device failure is equivalent to having less processing units or power in our system. This results in an overall slowing of the processing rate for our applications and can cause more deadline misses.

Transient failures are the more interesting failures we deal with as the device recovers from the failures and continues to operate normally after a period of downtime. In software errors, phone self shutdowns [12] and user actions such as removing the battery from a visually unresponsive device or manually resetting a device contribute a bit to the rate of transient errors, the largest factor for mobile devices would be user mobility [31]. Mobile devices make use of wireless access points when they are able to, and these APs have a typical range of less than 100 meters. When a user is outside of coverage range he/she is unable to communicate with the server, and during these times, if the device needs to send results, they are considered to have failed. When the device regains communication coverage, it resumes processing. We use these mobility and failure statistics to extract a failure distribution for our worker devices. [31] reports that the time spent at any AP or location follows a log-normal distribution, and that the movement speeds of the users also follow a log-normal distribution. Based on this result, in our experiments, we have set the failure rates for our devices to follow such a distribution.

Devices which display transient failures are still very useful in our system. In our work, we predict the failure rate of these devices due to their self-similar nature, a device which fails often is expected to fail often in the future. We can produce an expected time for different devices to perform tasks which helps us develop a better schedule for the applications to meet their deadlines. By selectively replicating tasks to less failure prone workers and profiling the execution times of the tasks, we can effectively meet the real-time constraints, even under failures. Our focus in this paper is on device failures; server failures can be addressed with the use of backup servers and checkpointing techniques that record the state of the server and transfer it to a backup server in the event of a failure[19]. In our previous work, we have studied the problem of fault tolerance for distributed object systems[34] [38]. However, the issue of server failures is a research area by itself, and is not considered in this paper.

3. BACKGROUND

In this section we first provide an introduction to the MapReduce framework. For the baseline MapReduce implementation we have used Misco [15], a distributed mobile MapReduce platform targeted at any device that supports Python and network connectivity. This is a porting of the MapReduce system to run on a network of smartphones. For completeness, in this section we give a brief description of the specific implementation of Mapreduce we have developed to run on the network of smartphones. In the next sections we describe the current work which is the real-time model and the scheduling strategy.

3.1 The MapReduce Framework

The MapReduce framework [14] is a flexible, distributed data processing framework designed as an abstract machine to automatically parallelize the processing of long running applications on petabyte sized data in clustered environments where nodes have high and stable connectivity, relatively low failure rates and a shared file system. The MapReduce programming model provides a simple way to split a large computation into a number of smaller tasks; these tasks are independent of each other and can be assigned on different worker nodes to process different pieces of the input data in parallel. The main insight of MapReduce is that the programming model is clean and simple to use, yet powerful enough to do sophisticated computations in parallel. Due to the independent nature of the tasks, replication of the tasks due to worker failure is simply a matter of reassigning the task at another worker if the server does not receive a response from the first worker.

MapReduce was inspired by two functional language primitives: *map* and *reduce*. The map function is applied on a set of input data and produces intermediary $< key, value >$ pairs, these pairs are then grouped into R partitions by applying some partitioning function (e.g. $hash(key)$ MOD R). All the pairs in the same partition are passed into a reduce function which produces the final results. The popularity of the MapReduce framework is attributed to its simplicity, portability and powerful functional abstractions. Application development is greatly simplified as the user is only responsible for implementing the map and reduce functions and the system handles the scheduling, data flow, failures and parallel execution of the applications.

3.2 The Misco System

The Misco system is a MapReduce implementation that runs on mobile phones. Misco comprises a *Master Server* and a number of *Worker Nodes*. The Master Server keeps track of user applications, while the Worker Nodes are responsible for performing the map and reduce operations. The Master server also maintains the input, intermediary and result data associated with the applications, keeps track of their progress and determines how application tasks should be assigned to workers. [15] provides in-depth design and implementation details of the system. The Misco system is publicly available at http://www.cs.ucr.edu/~ jdou/misco/.

The main responsibility of the *worker* is to process map and reduce tasks and return the results to the server. When a worker is free, it will contact the server and request a task. Each task is characterized by the name of the application which the task belongs to, the location of the module containing the map or reduce operations and the location of the input file. The worker stores locally: its input data, module and any results it has generated for each task. Finally, a logger component is used to maintain local statistics regarding the processing times of the tasks and progress.

The *Server* is in charge of keeping track of applications submitted by the user and assigning tasks to workers. The Server is multi-threaded, spawning a new thread to handle incoming worker connections. Applications are created and managed by the user using a browser interface. The server consists of an *Application Repository* component that keeps track of application input and output data, and an *HTTP Server* that serves as the main communication between the workers and the server. It is responsible for receiving requests, displaying application statuses to the user via the web UI and handling the downloading and uploading of data files. The *UDP Server* is used to listen for incoming worker logs, which it stores in *Worker Logs*.

The Server also gathers failure and computation time statistics for the workers in the *Client Information* component. The success rate of a worker is calculated as the number of successful results it has returned divided by the total number of tasks it has been assigned. In cases of transient failures, if the worker is unable to contact the server when it returns the results, it will abort the task and enter into idle mode and poll the server for new tasks.

We have extended the system with a *Scheduler* component that implements our scheduling approach (described in the next sections). We have developed the system in Python and run it on the Nokia N95 8GB smart-phones [39]. The reason we use Python is because the Nokia N95 smart-phones support a beta implementation of Python 2.5.4 called PyS60. Our design does not use any proprietary or any Python-specific features, and therefore can be run on any Python enabled phone or can be ported to different operating or programming environments.

4. MICRORT SYSTEM MODEL

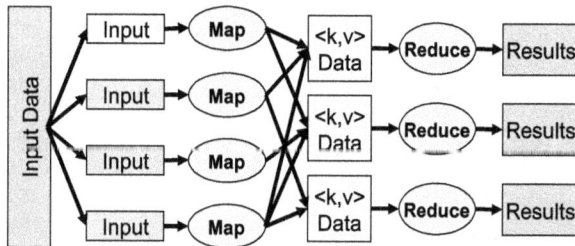

Figure 1: A simple visual representation of the map reduce model.

We consider a system that consists of a set of N distributed applications $A = A_1, A_2, ..., A_N$ running on a set of M worker nodes (mobile phones) $W = W_1, W_2, ..., W_M$. Each distributed application A_j is represented as a flow graph (shown in Figure 1) that consists of a number of *map tasks* (T_{map}^j) and a number of *reduce tasks* (T_{reduce}^j) executing in parallel on multiple worker nodes.

Distributed applications are triggered by the user, they are aperiodic and their arrival times are not known a priori. Each application A_j is associated with a number of parameters: We call *ready time* r_j the time the application becomes

available in the system. $Deadline_j$ is the time interval, starting at the ready time of the application, within which the application A_j should be completed. The *execution time*, $exec\_time_j$ of the application is the estimated amount of time required for the application to complete. This is estimated based on previous executions of the applications, by measuring the difference from the *ready time* of the application until all its map and reduce tasks complete. Thus, the $exec\_time_j$ of an application depends on (1) the number of T_{map}^j and T_{reduce}^j tasks, (2) the size of the application input data, and (3) the number of worker nodes available to run the tasks. This information is recorded and stored by the Server for each application run in the system. We associated with each application a laxity value, which represents a measure of urgency for the application and is used to order the execution of the application tasks on the worker nodes. $Laxity_j$ is computed as the difference between the Deadline of the application and its estimated execution time. The laxity value is adjusted dynamically based on failures and queuing delays experienced by the tasks. The advantage of using the laxity value is that it gives us an indication of whether the execution of the tasks has delayed and how close the task is to missing its deadline; the task with the smallest laxity value has the higher priority, while, when the laxity value becomes negative the task is estimated to miss its deadline and thus it can be dropped. Our work targets soft real-time systems, where missing a deadline is not catastrophic for the system. Thus, our goal is to maximize the number of applications that meet their deadlines.

For each task t of an application A_j we compute: the *processing time* $\tau_{t,k}^j$, the time required for the task to execute locally on worker W_k. This includes the time required to process input data, upload the results to the server and clean up any temporary files it generates. These times can be either provided by the user or obtained easily through profiling mechanisms with low overhead [29].

Our system schedules map and reduce tasks to execute in parallel on the worker nodes. Each worker node is able to run either a map or reduce task at any one time. Tasks cannot be preempted once they have been assigned to a worker, however, the execution of tasks from different applications can interleave. The worker is only responsible for executing the current task it is assigned, it does not keep track of the tasks (and from which applications) it has completed as the server maintains this information. This is possible because all tasks are independent of each other and the system is responsible for providing the proper input data for each task.

We are not concerned about the network topology of the system, similar to other cell phone based systems [36], we assume that if we have connection to the server, it is over a one-hop HTTP connection. Any networking overhead is implicitly accounted for by monitoring worker timings and gathering statistics.

5. OUR SCHEDULING SCHEME

The main responsibility for our MiscoRT scheduler is to assign tasks to workers when they make requests. We have developed a two-level scheduling scheme, as follows (the architecture of our system is shown in figure 2):

- The first-level scheduler, the *Application Scheduler*, determines the order of execution of the applications based on their urgencies and timing constraints. It estimates the execution times of the applications using an analytical model that also considers mobile node failures.

- The second-level scheduler, the *Task Scheduler*, dynamically schedules application tasks and uses the measured laxity values of the tasks to adjust their scheduling order to compensate for queuing delays and worker node failures.

5.1 Failure Model

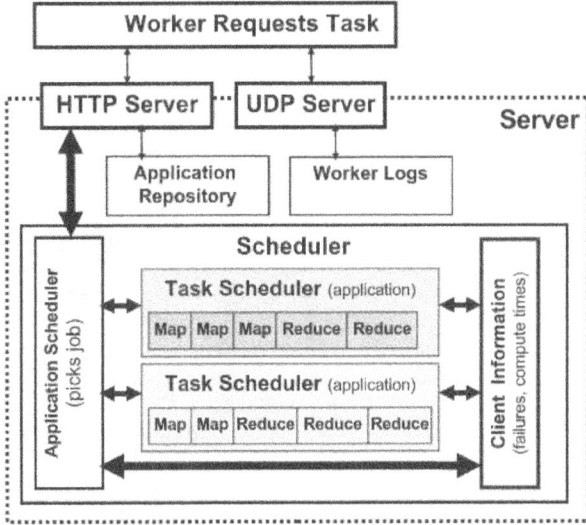

Figure 2: Our system architecture.

In this section we present our model to estimate the execution times of the applications under failures. We assume that the failures of the worker devices follow a Poisson distribution and that failures are transient. In cases where permanent failures occur, the total number of workers would be reduced as the failed workers cannot make any further requests for tasks and are, therefore, not assigned any additional tasks. It has been shown that the time to failure for systems can be accurately represented using a Poisson distribution [16]. Assume that λ_i is the failure arrival rate for a single worker W_i. When a worker fails, all progress on the task it was executing is lost, and the worker experiences a failure downtime following a general distribution with mean time for recovery μ_i.

For application A_j and worker W_i, we summarize these parameters as follows:

- λ_i - failure arrival rate for worker W_i

- τ_i^j - local processing time for task of application A_j on worker W_i

- μ_i - mean recovery time from a failure for worker W_i

- w_i^j - expected task processing time including failures

5.1.1 Single Task, Single Worker

Our basic unit of work is a single task executing on a single worker W_i with processing time, including failures, C (we omit superscripts and subscript where there is no ambiguity). The probability of failure during a task processing is $\tau\lambda$, the corresponding probability of success is $1 - \tau\lambda$. Let F be the number of failures before the first success, this is a geometric series, from probability theory [32], we can compute the expected number of failures using:

$$E[F] = \frac{\tau\lambda}{1 - \tau\lambda} \qquad (1)$$

We now calculate the amount of time to successfully complete a task. This is comprised of 3 parts: (1) a successful run, requiring τ time, (2) the sum of all the times wasted (W) processing a task before failures occur and (3) the sum of all the downtime (D) in order for the worker to recover from failures:

$$C = \tau + \sum W + \sum D \qquad (2)$$

Since failure arrival follows a Poisson distribution, failures occur at the workers with an exponential distribution and tasks are expected to fail halfway through processing, so the expected wasted processing time is given by:

$$E[W] = \frac{\tau}{2} \qquad (3)$$

Let $E[D] = \mu$ be the mean recovery time from a failure. Finally, we can compute the expected processing time for a task on a node, including failures, as:

$$w = E[C] = \tau + \frac{\tau}{2} * \frac{\tau\lambda}{1 - \tau\lambda} + \mu * \frac{\tau\lambda}{1 - \tau\lambda} \qquad (4)$$

5.1.2 Multiple Tasks, Multiple Nodes

We consider T tasks belonging to a single application A_j and M workers. Each worker W_i can be characterized by a different failure arrival rate parameter λ_i and mean failure downtime μ_i. The total execution time C^j for all T tasks of application A_j is the maximum of the individual processing times for each worker executing tasks for this application.

Since all workers are either processing a task or in a failure state, we can model this by considering a equal-time workload for each worker. The rate of work for worker W_i is the inverse of its expected processing time: $1/w_i$. For the workers to finish their tasks at the same time, the number of tasks ρ_i assigned to worker W_i ($1 \le i \le M$) is:

$$\rho_i = \left\lceil \frac{1/w_i}{\sum_{k \in M} 1/w_k} * T \right\rceil \qquad (5)$$

Then, we can compute the expected execution time for the application as:

$$exec\_time_j = E[C^j] = max_{i \in M}(\rho_i * w_i) \qquad (6)$$

5.2 MiscoRT Application Scheduler

Our application scheduler is based on the least-laxity scheduler and is used by the server to determine the order of execution for the applications in the system. The *Least Laxity First* (LLF) scheduling algorithm has been shown to be effective in distributed real-time systems [29]. In LLF scheduling, each application is associated with a laxity value which represents its urgency. We compute the laxity value $Laxity_j$ of an application A_j as the difference between its deadline

---
Pseudo Code 1 The MiscoRT Schedulers

MiscoRT Application Scheduler
  Input: Set of applications A in system
  for all Application A_j in A **do**
    calculate $Laxity_j$ of A_j
  Order A by $Laxity_j$
  Task $\leftarrow$ TaskScheduler(A_j with smallest $Laxity_j$)
  return Task

MiscoRT Task Scheduler
  Input: worker W_k requests a task, job A_j
  step 1. **if** unassigned task $T_i^j \in A_j$ **then return** T_i^j
  step 2. **if** failed task $T_i^j \in A_j$ **then return** T_i^j
  step 3. $T_i^j \leftarrow$ slowest task in A_j
    if T_i^j will complete after $deadline_j$
      and T_i^j will complete on W_k before $deadline_j$ **then**
        return T_i^j
---

and our estimate of the execution time of the application under failures:

$$Laxity_j = Deadline_j - current\_time - exec\_time_j \quad (7)$$

where the estimate of the application's execution time is computed using formula 6 to include worker node failures.

The laxity value for a distributed application is computed when the application first enters the system, this is denoted as the initial laxity. As an application executes, its laxity value is adjusted to compensate for variations in the processing speeds of the workers, worker node failures and queuing delays. As workers start to fail and their failure rates change, we use our analytical model to recalculate the expected execution time and laxity. To minimize computational overheads, the laxity value for each application is computed only when a worker makes a request. Applications with negative laxities are estimated to miss their deadlines and their tasks should not be scheduled ahead of applications which have positive laxities. Note that no applications are dropped and that all applications will complete eventually if at least one worker remains available.

The advantage of this scheduling scheme is that the schedule is driven by both the timing requirements of the applications and node failures, while it allows us to dynamically adapt to changes of resource availability or queuing delays. If the workers processing the tasks for a certain application is slower, or exhibit failures, the laxity value of the application will decrease and thus its priority will increase. For applications with the same laxity value, a simple tie breaking mechanism is used to decide which to schedule first; these applications are treated in a first-come-first-served order.

5.3 MiscoRT Task Scheduler

The goal of the task scheduler is two-fold: First, to ensure that all tasks of the application are scheduled for execution. Second, the task scheduler may dynamically change the number of workers allocated to the application to compensate for failures or queuing delays. If, however, the application completes more quickly than projected, the excess workers can be used by other applications. When a worker becomes available, the MiscoRT task scheduler decides which task to run next, following these steps:
Step 1: The application scheduler determines the application with the smallest laxity value (*i.e.,* this is the appli-

cation with the highest *priority* in the system). The task scheduler first checks whether any of the tasks of the application have not been assigned yet. The primary insight of this is that an application completes when all of its tasks complete, thus we need to ensure that all of the application tasks are scheduled for execution. During the execution of an application, mobile devices may fail or become unavailable due to spotty connectivity; this can affect the capability of an application to finish within its deadline. In these cases we need to reinstantiate the tasks (these are called *task replicas*) to other mobile devices. To minimize the number of task replicas, we reassign tasks only if we have speculated that the workers executing those tasks have failed or if the task is not progressing as fast as it was estimated, causing the application to miss its deadline.

Step 2: The next step is to check whether the task failed to complete because of worker failures. We term that a task has failed when all of the workers which it was assigned to, are estimated to have failed. When the task scheduler assigns a task t to a worker W_i, it records the $start\_time_{t,i}$ of the task and the $worker\_id$ processing the task, so that multiple workers can be tracked in the case that the same task is later assigned to other workers. When the task completes, the task scheduler records the $completion\_time_{t,i}$ of the task. It then computes the task processing time, $\tau_{t,i}^j$ and averages it over multiple runs of the task. Note that this time represents the time required for one successful execution of the task. Thus, the task scheduler can estimate that a worker has failed if the time to process the task is significantly higher than the *average processing time* τ_t^j computed from previous runs of the task. This information can be obtained at runtime with low overhead (as we show in our experimental section), or, in the absence of information about previous task executions, we can use a user-defined threshold that can be updated from the current runs.

Step 3: The last step is to check the progress of the assigned tasks. Using formula 4 we can estimate the amount of time required for each task t to complete, as $\epsilon_{t,i}^j = w_i^j - elapsed\_time_{t,i}$. (In the case that a task has been assigned to multiple workers, the minimum $\epsilon_{t,i}^j$ is used). We then consider the task t with the largest remaining execution time, $\epsilon_{t,i}^j$, this is considered as the slowest task and we check whether this task can complete before its deadline. The idea is, that, if the completion time of the slowest task is later than the application's deadline, then with high probability the application is estimated to miss its deadline. This is achieved by performing an execution time projection to examine whether the progress of the task will cause the application to miss its deadline. The task scheduler will also evaluate whether allocating the task to the worker will enable the task to complete within the application's deadline. If this is not possible, then the task scheduler can use the worker for executing other applications in the system.

Note, that, it is possible for the task scheduler to not assign any tasks to the worker even if some tasks are not yet complete. This occurs when tasks have already been assigned to workers and their estimated remaining completion times $\epsilon_{t,i}^j$ is smaller than the time it would take the new worker to complete the task. Assigning an already assigned task to the new worker will most likely lead to duplicated work with no benefit to the application's performance. In our experiments we show that our scheme manages to minimize the duplicate work. Furthermore, note that, under

Figure 3: Our testbed of Nokia N95 8GB phones and a Linksys Router.

high failure rates where multiple nodes have failed and applications have strict timing constraints, applications can still miss their deadline. In such unstable environments, it might not be possible to find enough resources to run all the applications.

6. EXPERIMENTAL RESULTS

6.1 Experimental Setup

We have conducted an extensive set of experiments to evaluate the efficiency and performance of our scheduling scheme using applications of different sizes and various worker node failure rates.

Our experimental platforms consists of a testbed of 30 Nokia N95 8GB smart-phones [39]. The Nokia N95 has ARM 11 dual CPUs at 332 Mhz, supports wireless 802.11b/g networks, bluetooth and cellular 3g networks, 90 MB of main memory and 8 GB of local storage. Our server is a commodity computer with a Pentium-4 2Ghz CPU and 640 MB of main memory. The server has a wired 100 MBit connection to a Linksys WRT54G2 802.11g router. All of our phones are connected via 802.11g to this router.

For the experiments, we used a set of 11 applications (mobile tourist application, described below), 8 with 100KB input data and 3 with 1MB input data. We set the deadlines for the applications such that 5 applications have tight deadlines, 2 have medium and 3 have loose deadlines. We derived these deadlines empirically by running the applications and observing their runtimes, the deadlines used were between 100 and 550s. The failure of worker nodes follows a Poisson distribution, as explained in section 5.1; to vary the failure rates of our workers, we adjust the failure arrival rate, λ. Each experiment is repeated 5 times.

To provide a fair comparison, we chose to compare our scheduling scheme with the *Earliest Deadline First (EDF)* scheduling policy, which is the most well known and effective real-time scheduler for single processor environments. In EDF, applications are ordered based on their deadlines, the application with the earliest deadline has the highest priority. We paired the EDF application scheduler with a sequential task scheduler. The same experimental parameters such as deadline and data input were used for the comparisons.

We measure the performance of our MiscoRT scheduling scheme using the following metrics: (1) *Miss Ratio* represents the fraction of applications that miss their deadlines and (2) *End-to-end time* measures the time the execution of the entire application set completes.

6.2 Mobile Tourist Application

We have built a mobile tourist application[4] [20], a location-based social networking application, to evaluate the performance of our approach. In the mobile tourist application, tourists seek pictures of other tourists and the places where these were taken in real-time, to identify popular locations in a given geographical area that they visit. Popular locations are identified through the number of pictures taken at these places.

To run the application we have compiled a dataset from the Flickr photo sharing system. Flickr is an example of a social application where users can keep photos of places they have visited. In Flickr each picture is tagged with the location (Latitude and Longitudes) where it was taken along with the corresponding dates and times. Our dataset consists of 50,000 image metadata (8.75 MB) taken from publicly available Flickr photos. We queried the initial seed photos from Santa Barbara and downloaded pictures from these users, the resulting image locations span the globe. This application operates on the user tags found in photo metadata. The application counts the occurrences of each tag and compiles a list of common tags to identify popular picture types.

The map function creates key-value pairs where the key is a tag and the value counts the instances of the key, the value is initially 1. When there are multiple duplicate keys from one map task input, they are grouped together and the values summed before being sent to the server. The reduce tasks add up all the values from the same key and arrive at the most popular tags for photos.

This mobile tourist application is an example of a mobile location-based social application that have recently seen wide adoption and fully exercises all aspects of the system and demonstrates the timeliness of our scheduler. More complex applications mainly differ in the functions performed in the map and reduce tasks and not in the system's execution sequence.

6.3 Performance of MiscoRT

For our first set of experiments, we have evaluated the performance of our MiscoRT by measuring the deadline misses and the end-to-end times of the applications. For this set of experiments, we have set all workers to the same failure rate and vary this failure rate. The reason we chose these metrics is because these are the standard performance metrics in real-time systems. To further establish our choice, we note here, that the reason for employing MapReduce is to satisfy our desiderata, specifically, have a system that offers ease of programmability and ease of adding and managing new resources. Our goal is not to use the additional resources (extra smartphones) to do the work faster and increase throughput, because it is difficult to send data around in a wireless environment, and there are also privacy constraints. Rather, the larger system can, easily and transparently to the programmer, be expanded to handle the additional data that come from the additional resources (smartphones).

Figure 4 shows the application **Miss ratio**. As the fig-

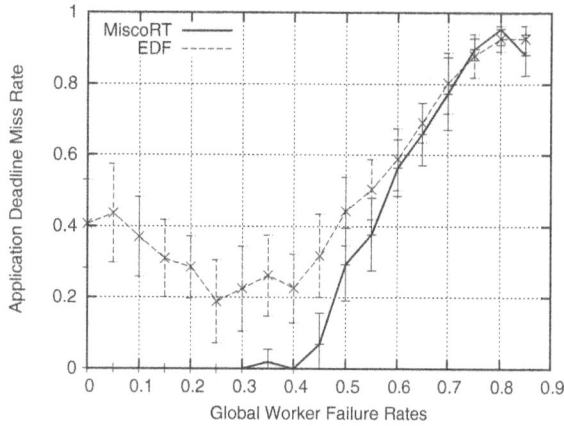

Figure 4: Application miss rate for MiscoRT compared to EDF with uniform distribution of worker failures.

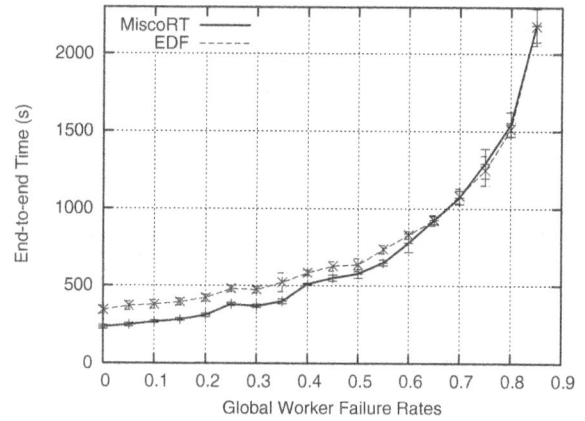

Figure 5: End-to-end times for MiscoRT compared to EDF with uniform distribution of worker failures.

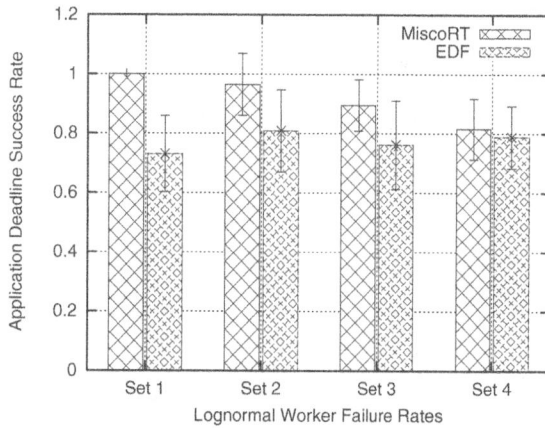

Figure 6: Application success rates for MiscoRT compared to EDF with lognormal distribution of worker failures.

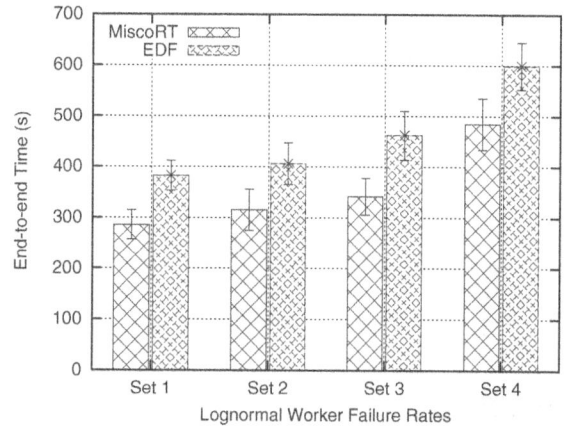

Figure 7: End-to-end times for MiscoRT compared to EDF with lognormal distribution of worker failures.

ure illustrates, for low worker failures, below 40% in this case, there is sufficient resources for MiscoRT to schedule all applications with only a few rare deadline misses. As the worker failures increase further, both schedulers perform very poorly, however, this is expected as very few devices are available to do useful work. The figure shows that at low failure rates the EDF algorithm causes some applications to miss their deadlines. The reason this happens even with small numbers of failures is that with EDF each task takes approximately 50our algorithm results in a much better performance.

The **End-to-end times** of the applications are shown in Figure 5. Our scheduling scheme consistently performs better than the EDF scheduler. At low failure rates, EDF applications complete 47% slower than MiscoRT and as failure rates increase, EDF continues to perform worse than MiscoRT, being 10% slower at 50% failure rates. The reason is that our task scheduler has the ability to adapt to failures by selectively providing redundancy even as failure rates become higher. As the failures increase, the end-to-end time for both schedulers increase exponentially.

In a second set of experiments, we use a log-normal failure distribution among the workers to simulate the failure characteristics from user mobility [31]. The 4 sets of failure rates are shown in table 1. From figures 6 and 7, we see that MiscoRT has a 30% higher success rate than EDF for lower levels of failures and maintains a higher success rate as more failures are introduced. MiscoRT also completes applications faster than EDF by approximately 20% for all our failure sets.

Comparison of MiscoRT with different Task Schedulers

To further illustrate the benefit of our MiscoRT task scheduler, we performed experiments to show our MiscoRT task scheduler's performance compared to alternative task schedulers. We use our MiscoRT application scheduler as the first level scheduler and use different task schedulers as the second level scheduler. We perform the same set of experiments as in section 6.2, but due to lack of space, we only show the results for log-normal worker failure rates. In particular, we used the following task schedulers for comparison:

The random task scheduler is a naive scheduler which

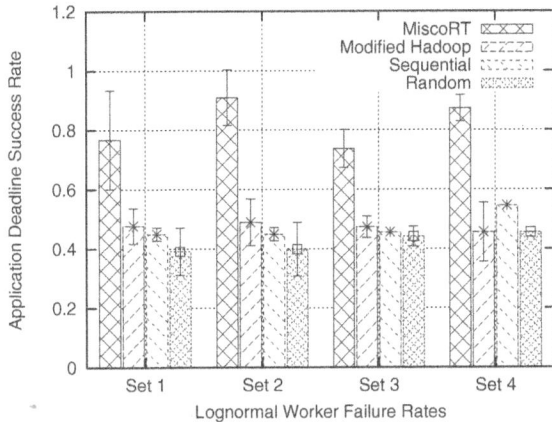

Figure 8: Application success rates for MiscoRT compared to other task schedulers. Each task scheduler was paired with the MiscoRT application scheduler

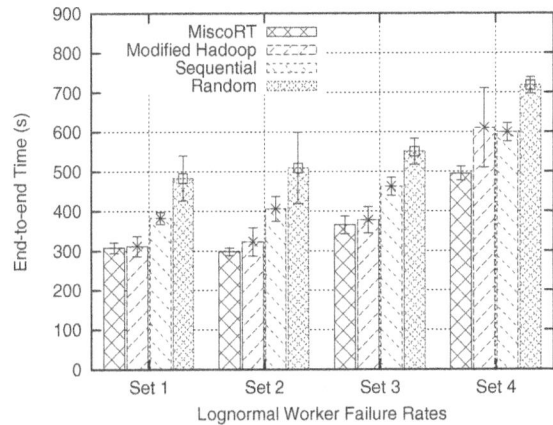

Figure 9: End-to-end times for MiscoRT compared to other task schedulers. Each task scheduler was paired with the MiscoRT application scheduler

Table 1: Log-normal Failure Rates for Workers

Worker	1	2	3	4	5	6	7	8	9	10
Set 1	0.0	0.0	0.0	0.0	0.0	0.0	0.0	0.1	0.2	0.5
Set 2	0.0	0.0	0.0	0.0	0.0	0.1	0.1	0.2	0.4	0.8
Set 3	0.0	0.0	0.0	0.1	0.1	0.1	0.2	0.4	0.8	0.9
Set 4	0.0	0.0	0.0	0.2	0.2	0.4	0.6	0.8	0.9	0.9

picks a random task from the application to execute. The advantage of the random task scheduler is that it has very low overhead, it does not have to store any information about workers, but it wastes computational resources.

The sequential task scheduler is a baseline scheduler which improves on the random task scheduler by reducing the number of duplicate task assignments. It picks tasks in sequential order until they successfully execute. This scheduler has low overhead as it does not keep track of statistics, however, it does not consider worker failures.

The Modified Hadoop task scheduler is based on the FIFO-based task scheduler used by the popular Hadoop MapReduce framework [13]. Hadoop is designed for cluster-based environments where there is constant feedback from the workers informing the scheduler of their progress on tasks. Our system, on the other hand, has limited resources and no fixed infrastructure, thus, implementing such progress tracking would be infeasible. To provide a fair comparison, we follow the spirit of the Hadoop scheduler, however, we attempt to speed up the execution time by re-assigning tasks only when the previous worker is taking more than the average amount of time to complete that task.

The **Miss Ratio** in figure 8 and **End-to-end times** in figure 9 demonstrates that our task scheduler consistently outperforms its competitors. MiscoRT has a 25% to 40% higher success rate than the other task schedulers. MiscoRT has comparable end-to-end application times with the modified Hadoop scheduler when the failure rates are lower, but performs better when failure rates are higher.

6.3.1 Model Validation

In our next experiment, we wanted to validate our model by comparing the predicted execution time for an applica-

tion (using the model described in section 5.1) with actual measured execution times of the application. For this experiment, we used a single application consisting of 73 tasks. We also assume that all worker nodes fail with the same rate, and we varied the failure rate of the nodes. As figure 10 shows, our model is very accurate, as it's predicted times are very close to the measured times observed from running the application in our system, even at high failure rates.

6.3.2 Scalability

We also wanted to measure the scalability on our system. For this set of experiments, we varied the number of applications in the system, while the failure rates of the phones were set to 0. Figure 11 shows the **End-to-end times**, it increases linearly with the number of applications, as we expected, this is due to us having a fixed processing power and linearly increase the amount of work.

6.3.3 Deadline Sensitivity

In this experiment, our goal was to test the sensitivity of deadline value on the application miss rate. We have varied the tightness of the deadlines by a constant factor, ranging from the original deadlines to 20% of their values, while leaving the other parameters the same. A tighter deadline means that the applications have less time to execute. We report the results when the global worker failure rate was set to 20%, but we have obtained similar results for other failure rates. Figure 12 shows that both schedulers perform worse as the deadlines tighten, but MiscoRT outperforms EDF consistently. When the deadlines are set very tight, at 0.2 of their original values, all applications miss their deadlines when using EDF while only 70% miss their deadline using MiscoRT.

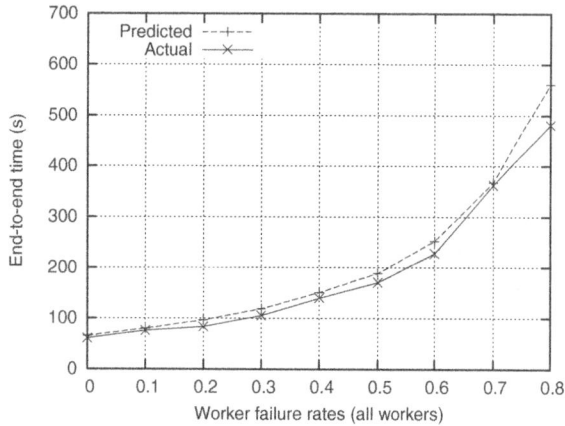

Figure 10: Model validation over various worker failure rates.

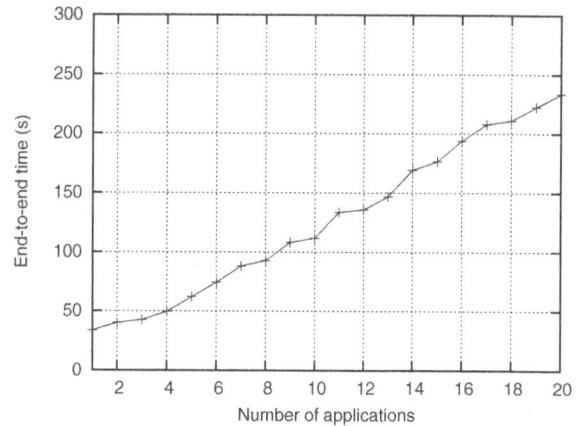

Figure 11: End-to-end time as number of applications are varied.

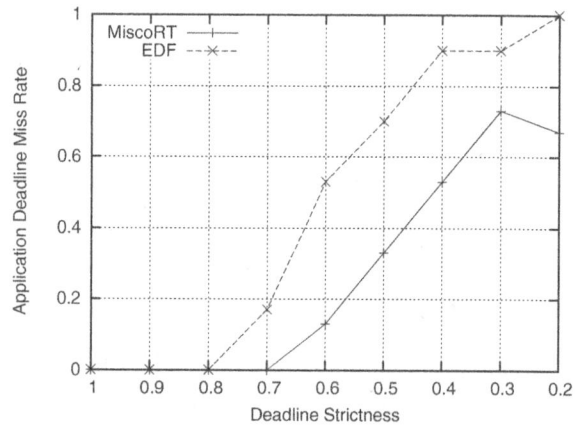

Figure 12: Application miss rates as a function of deadline strictness.

6.3.4 Overhead and Resource Usage

In this set of experiments, we measure the overhead and resource usage of our system. We monitor the CPU, memory and power consumption using the Nokia Energy Profiler [2]. The MiscoRT system only requires 800KB of memory and our scheduler does not introduce any additional overhead as it is very small, requiring only 150 lines of code. This memory usage is very small compared the 90MB of free RAM available.

As the application runs, the memory usage is dependent on the user's modules and how much of the data is stored into memory. For our applications, during the map tasks, we stored mapping key,value pairs in memory and required slightly more memory than our input data pieces, up to an additional 300KB. We use larger reduce partitions and our additional memory requirements there went up to 700KB.

We also monitored the power usage on the phones. We found that processing data requires 0.7 watts while network access requires more than twice that amount of power at 1.6 watts. It is much more energy efficient to process data locally than to send data over the network. The CPU utilization for tasks is dependent on the application and also on any other programs or program schedulers running on the phone. MiscoRT will gladly use any processing power available to it.

In the last experiment (figure 13) we also measured the overhead of the Master Server. Note, that, the Master Server is responsible to keep track of the user applications and maintain the input, intermediate and result data from each application submitted in the system. In this experiment, the workload we used was an application with 1MB input data; this was split to workers with 100 line pieces for each worker. The figure shows that the Server manages to keep its load below 6% at all times. We also measured the memory usage of the Server. Our measurements indicate that the MiscoRT Server uses 1,572,369 bytes on an Intel(R) Core(TM)2 Duo CPU E8200 (running at 2.66GHz) processor.

7. RELATED WORK

Recently, many MapReduce systems have been introduced [13] [43] [25] [40]. [25] targets graphics processors and [40] provides MapReduce for multi-core and multiprocessor sys-

tems while are concerned with mobile devices. Hadoop [13] is currently one of the most popular MapReduce frameworks, is targeted at a cluster environment with long running applications. It offers a *Capacity Scheduler* which is a fair scheduler that guarantees a predefined fraction of the computing capacity to each queue. Disco [43] is another framework, targeted at the same environment as Hadoop. Disco provides a single first-come-first-serve scheduler, any excess capacity in the system is then allocated to subsequent applications on the queue. Unlike these works, we consider the problem of meeting the end-to-end real-time requirements of the applications in resource restrictive environments (mobile systems) and under unstable conditions. [37] has implemented a MapReduce system on cell phones and showed that cell phones already provide a significant source of computational power. However, they do not consider any timing concerns.

In our previous work, we have introduced Misco [15], a MapReduce framework aimed at mobile phones, in this work, we have extended the Misco system with a scheduling system to provide support for applications with timing constraints in the form of deadlines.

The problem of scheduling in the presence of failures has

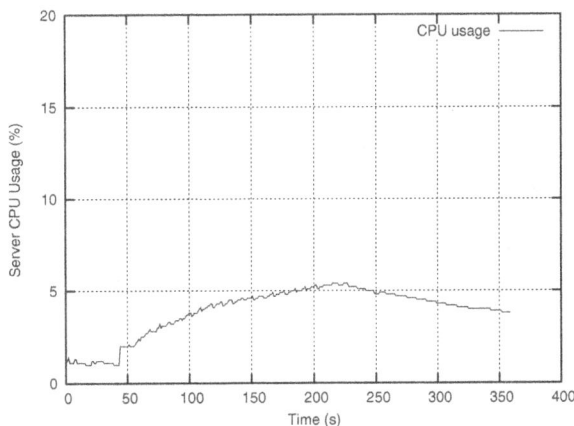

Figure 13: Master Server workload.

been studied in prior works, primarily in cluster-based and distributed system settings [7] [44]. The main methods of dealing with failures are *spatial redundancy*, *temporal redundancy* and *checkpointing*. Spatial redundancy replicates tasks on multiple nodes so that if any of the nodes fail, the execution of the task is not interrupted; however, this scheme requires extra nodes to run the replicas. Temporal redundancy re-executes tasks after they have failed, this has the disadvantage of requiring more time but does not require extra nodes. Checkpointing [19] is used to limit the amount of work lost when failures occur, but the frequency of checkpointing is an important consideration. Scheduling distributed applications in mobile settings with restrictive resources, frequent failures and network fluctuations, which is the problem we are dealing with in this work, is not trivial.

Fault tolerant real-time scheduling is explored in [21] [11] [6] [24] where the goal is to schedule applications to meet hard real-time deadlines. [11] replicates a task K times on homogeneous processors, while [24] considers heterogeneous processors. [21] tolerates one fault per time interval by reserving enough slack in the schedule and [6] uses an AI planner to generate feasible schedules for different possible faults. In these works, schedules are first constructed offline and are limited by the number of failures they can tolerate. Unlike their work, we place no restriction on the number of failures in our system and we are not considering hard real-time requirements. [44] mathematically determines the optimal replication factor for tasks. [17] explores the problem of placing replicas in a way so that the utility of the system degrades gracefully when failures do occur. Probabilistic reliability under failures is explored in [10] to provide the best reliability given a number of resources or find the minimum number of resources for a desired level of reliability. The imprecise computation model, proposed in [8] is based on tasks where precision can be exchanged for timeliness. Our work, on the other hand, provides results based on user supplied modules.

Middleware architectures for mobile users have also been proposed [41]. The primary focus is on concerns such as interoperability, context awareness, network connectivity and server/client APIs. A first come first server scheduling strategy for mobile devices has been proposed in [5]. However, these systems do not consider real-time or fault-tolerant issues. Fault-tolerant and real-time CORBA is explored in

[28] [23]; unlike our work they propose light weight replications for task groups on different nodes. [22] proposes a method to split an application across both servers and phones to improve its performance, but only deals with single phone, server pairings. Our work is to improve the performance of a distributed systems of phones.

Social applications [42] [9] [35] for phones have emerged recently, however these are built over specialized systems. Our objective is to make distributed mobile applications easier to develop in order to become widely accessible to users and application developers.

8. CONCLUSION

In this paper, we presented MiscoRT, a system for supporting the execution of real-time applications on networks of smartphones. We propose a scheduling system which considers both the timing requirements of the applications and the failure rates of the worker nodes when scheduling the tasks. This is the first system, that we know of, that proposes a real-time MapReduce scheduler for mobile environments. Through an extensive evaluation on our testbed of Nokia N95 smart-phones, we demonstrate that our system (1) performs effectively, even under failures, (2) has low overhead, and (3) consistently outperforms its competitors. For our future work, we plan to further explore data locality aspects and consider device heterogeneity issues.

Acknowledgment

This research has been supported by the European Union through the Marie-Curie RTD (IRG-231038) project, the SemsorGrid4Env project and the MODAP project, and by AUEB through a PEVE2 project.

9. REFERENCES

[1] Kin: Its nice to meet you. http://kin.com.
[2] Nokia energy profiler. http://www.forum.nokia.com/ main/ resources/ user experience/ powermanagement/ nokia energy profiler/.
[3] G.-S. Ahn, M. Musolesi, H. Lu, R. Olfati-Saber, and A. T. Campbell. Metrotrack: Predictive tracking of mobile events using mobile phones. In *IEEE DCOSS*, June 2010.
[4] G. Andrienko, N. Andrienko, P. Bak, S. Kisilevich, and D. Keim. Analysis of community-contributed space- and time-referenced data (example of flickr and panoramio photos). In *IEEE Symposium on Visual Analytics Science and Technology, Atlantic City, NJ, Oct*, 2009.
[5] H. K. Anna and J. Gerda. A robust decentralized job scheduling approach for mobile peers in ad-hoc grids. In *CCGrid. Rio de Janeiro, Brazil*, 5 May 2007.
[6] E. M. Atkins, T. F. Abdelzaher, K. G. Shin, and E. H. Durfee. Planning and resource allocation for hard real-time, fault-tolerant plan execution. *Autonomous Agents and Multi-Agent Systems*, 4(1-2):57–78, 2001.
[7] H. Aydin. On fault-sensitive feasibility analysis of real-time task sets. In *RTSS, Lisbon, Portugal*, pages 426–434, Dec 2004.
[8] H. Aydin, R. Melhem, and D. Mosse. Optimal scheduling of imprecise computation tasks in the presence of multiple faults. In *RTCSA, South Korea*, Dec 2000.

[9] B. Bamba, L. Liu, A. Iyengar, and P. S. Yu. Distributed processing of spatial alarms: A safe region-based approach. In *ICDCS*, pages 207–214, Washington, DC, USA, 2009.

[10] V. Berten, J. Goossens, and E. Jeannot. A probabilistic approach for fault tolerant multiprocessor real-time scheduling. *IPDPS, Greece*, 0:152, 2006.

[11] J.-J. Chen, C.-Y. Yang, T.-W. Kuo, and S.-Y. Tseng. Real-time task replication for fault tolerance in identical multiprocessor systems. In *RTAS, WA*, Apr 2007.

[12] M. Cinque, D. Cotroneo, Z. Kalbarczyk, and R. K. Iyer. How do mobile phones fail? a failure data analysis of symbian os smart phones. In *DSN*, pages 585–594, Washington, DC, USA, 2007.

[13] D. Cutting. Hadoop core. http://hadoop.apache.org/core/.

[14] J. Dean and S. Ghemawat. Mapreduce: Simplified data processing on large clusters. In *OSDI, San Francisco, CA, USA*, pages 137–150, Dec 2004.

[15] A. J. Dou, V. Kalogeraki, D. Gunopulos, T. Mielikainen, and V. H. Tuulos. Misco: A mapreduce framework for mobile systems. In *PETRA 2010*, Samos, Greece, June 2010.

[16] C. Ebeling. *An Introduction to Reliability and Maintainability Engineering*. McGraw-Hill, 1997.

[17] P. Emberson and I. Bate. Extending a task allocation algorithm for graceful degradation of real-time distributed embedded systems. In *RTSS, Barcelona, Spain*, Dec 2008.

[18] T. Facchinetti, L. Almeida, G. Buttazzo, and C. Marchini. Real-time resource reservation protocol for wireless mobile ad hoc networks. In *RTSS, Portugal*, Dec 2004.

[19] T. H. Feng and E. A. Lee. Real-time distributed discrete-event execution with fault tolerance. In *RTAS, St. Louis, MO*, Apr 2008.

[20] J. Freyne, A. Brennan, B. Smyth, D. Byrne, A. Smeaton, and G. Jones. Automated murmurns: The social mobile tourist application. In *SMW'09 - Social Mobile Web 2009*, 2009.

[21] S. Ghosh, R. Melhem, and D. Mosse. Enhancing real-time schedules to tolerate transient faults. In *RTSS, Pisa, Italy*, pages 120–129, Dec 1995.

[22] I. Giurgiu, O. Riva, D. Juric, I. Krivulev, and G. Alonso. Calling the cloud: Enabling mobile phones as interfaces to cloud applications. In *Middleware*, November 30 - December 4 2009.

[23] A. S. Gokhale, B. Natarajan, D. C. Schmidt, and J. K. Cross. Towards real-time fault-tolerant corba middleware. *Cluster Computing*, 7(4):331–346, 2004.

[24] S. Gopalakrishnan and M. Caccamo. Task partitioning with replication upon heterogeneous multiprocessor systems. *RTAS, San Jose, CA, USA*, 06.

[25] B. He, W. Fang, Q. Luo, N. K. Govindaraju, and T. Wang. Mars: a mapreduce framework on graphics processors. In *PACT, ON, Canada*, Oct 2008.

[26] T. He, J. A. Stankovic, C. Lu, and T. F. Abdelzaher. SPEED: A stateless protocol for real-time communication in sensor networks. In *ICDCS*, Tokyo , Japan, May May 2003.

[27] P. S. Huan Li and K. Ramamritham. Scheduling messages with deadlines in multi-hop real-time sensor networks. In *RTAS*, pages 415–425, 2005.

[28] H.-M. Huang and C. Gill. Design and performance of a fault-tolerant real-time corba event service. In *ECRTS, Dresden, Germany*, pages 33–42, Aug 2006.

[29] V. Kalogeraki, P. M. Melliar-Smith, and L. E. Moser. Dynamic scheduling of distributed method invocations. *RTSS, Orlando, Florida, USA*, Nov 2000.

[30] K. Karenos and V. Kalogeraki. Traffic management in sensor networks with a mobile sink. *IEEE TPDS*, 21(10):1515 – 1530, 2010.

[31] M. Kim and D. Kotz. Extracting a mobility model from real user traces. In *INFOCOM*, 2006.

[32] A. Leon-Garcia. *Probability and Random Processes for Electrical Engineering (2nd Edition)*. Prentice Hall, July 1993.

[33] C. Lu, B. M. Blum, T. F. Abdelzaher, J. A. Stankovic, and T. He. RAP: A real-time communication architecture for large-scale wireless sensor networks. In *IEEE RTAS*, pages 55–66, San Jose, CA, Sep. 2002.

[34] P. Melliar-Smith, L. Moser, V. Kalogeraki, and P. Narasimhan. The realize middleware for replication and resource management. In *Middleware'98*, The Lake District, England, September 1998.

[35] E. Miluzzo, C. Cornelius, A. Ramaswamy, T. Choudhury, Z. liu, and A. Campbell. Darwin phones: the evolution of sensing and inference on mobile phones. In *Mobisys 2010, June 15-18, 2010, San Fransisco, CA*, 2010.

[36] E. Miluzzo, N. D. Lane, K. Fodor, R. A. Peterson, H. Lu, M. Musolesi, S. B. Eisenman, X. Zheng, and A. T. Campbell. Sensing meets mobile social networks: the design, implementation and evaluation of the cenceme application. In *SenSys*, 2008.

[37] S. Mishra, P. Elespuru, and S. Shakya. Mapreduce system over heterogeneous mobile devices. In *SEUS, Newport Beach, CA, USA*, 2009.

[38] L. Moser, P. Melliar-Smith, P. Narasimhan, L. Tewksbury, and V. Kalogeraki. Eternal: Fault tolerance and live upgrades for distributed object systems. In *Proceedings of the IEEE Information Survivability Conference*, Hilton Head, SC, Jan 2000.

[39] Nokia. N95 8gb device details. http://www.forum.nokia.com/devices/N95_8GB.

[40] C. Ranger, R. Raghuraman, A. Penmetsa, G. Bradski, and C. Kozyrakis. Evaluating mapreduce for multi-core and multiprocessor systems. *HPCA*, 2007.

[41] T. Salminen and J. Riekki. Lightweight middleware architecture for mobile phones. In *PSC, Las Vegas, NV*, Jun 2005.

[42] A. Thiagarajan, L. Ravindranath, K. LaCurts, S. Madden, H. Balakrishnan, S. Toledo, and J. Eriksson. Vtrack: accurate, energy-aware road traffic delay estimation using mobile phones. In *SenSys*, USA, 2009. ACM.

[43] V. Tuulos. Disco. http://discoproject.org/.

[44] F. Wang, K. Ramamritham, and J. A. Stankovic. Determining redundancy levels for fault tolerant real-time systems. *IEEE Trans. Comput.*, 44(2):292–301, 1995.

Processing Flows of Information:
From Data Stream to Complex Event Processing

Alessandro Margara
Dip. di Elettronica e Informazione
Politecnico di Milano, Italy
margara@elet.polimi.it

Gianpaolo Cugola
Dip. di Elettronica e Informazione
Politecnico di Milano, Italy
cugola@elet.polimi.it

ABSTRACT

An increasing number of distributed applications requires processing continuously flowing data from geographically distributed sources at unpredictable rate to obtain timely responses to complex queries. Examples of such applications come from the most disparate fields: from wireless sensor networks to financial tickers, from traffic management to click-stream inspection.

These requirements led to the development of a number of systems specifically designed to process information as a flow according to a set of pre-deployed processing rules. We collectively call them *Information Flow Processing (IFP) Systems*. Despite having a common goal, IFP systems differ in a wide range of aspects, including architectures, data models, rule languages, and processing mechanisms.

In this tutorial we draw a general framework to analyze and compare the results achieved so far in the area of IFP systems. This allows us to offer a systematic overview of the topic, favoring the communication between different communities, and highlighting a number of open issue that still need to be addressed in research.

Categories and Subject Descriptors

H.4 [**Information Systems Applications**]: Miscellaneous; I.5 [**Pattern Recognition**]: Miscellaneous; H.2.4 [**Database Management**]: Systems—*Query Processing*; A.1 [**General**]: Introductory and Survey

General Terms

Documentation

Keywords

Survey, Complex Event Processing, Stream Processing

1. INTRO

An increasing number of distributed applications requires processing continuously flowing data from geographically distributed sources at unpredictable rate to obtain timely responses to complex queries. Examples of such applications come from the most disparate fields: from wireless sensor networks to financial tickers, from traffic management to click-stream inspection.

These requirements led to the development of a number of systems specifically designed to process information as a flow according to a set of pre-deployed processing rules. We collectively call them *Information Flow Processing (IFP) Systems*.

Despite having a common goal, IFP systems differ in a wide range of aspects, including architectures, data models, rule languages, and processing mechanisms. In part, this is due to the fact that they were the result of the research efforts of different communities, each one bringing its own view of the problem and its background for the definition of a solution, not to mention its own vocabulary. After several years of research and development we can say that two models emerged and are today competing: the *data stream processing* model [1] and the *complex event processing* model [3].

We claim that neither of the two aforementioned models may entirely satisfy the needs of applications, which often require features coming from both worlds.

In this tutorial, which is based upon our recently published work [2], we draw a general framework to compare the results coming from the different communities, and use it to provide a review of the state of the art in the area. In doing this, we have two main goals: on the one hand, we aim at favoring the communication between different communities, thus reducing the effort to merge the achievements reached so far; on the other hand, we highlight a number of open issue that still need to be addressed in research.

2. A MODELLING FRAMEWORK FOR IFP SYSTEMS

In this section we overview our modelling framework for IFP systems [2]. It includes severals models that focus on the different aspects relevant for an IFP system.

Functional Model. Defines an abstract architecture that describes the main functional component of an IFP system. This architecture brings two contributions: *i.* it allows a precise description of the functionalities offered by an IFP system; *ii.* it can be used to describe the differences among the existing IFP engines, providing a versatile tool for their comparison.

Processing Model. Isolates the relevant aspect that concur in determining the output of processing.

Deployment Model. Describes how the different components that implement the functional model can be distributed over multiple nodes to achieve scalability.

Interaction Model. Describes the characteristics of the

interaction among the main components that form an IFP application, more in particular among information sources and processors, among different processors, and among processors and information receivers or sinks.

Data Model. Describes the representation of single information items, and their organization into information flows.

Time Model. Describes the relationship between the information intems flowing into the IFP system and the passing of time. More in particular, defines the ability of an IFP system to associate some kind of *happen-before* relationship to information items.

Rule and Language Models. The rule model describes the different approaches used to define processing rules; the language model also presents and classifies the operators adopted in existing systems.

3. FUTURE RESEARCH DIRECTIONS

In [2] we adopted our modeling framework to analyze and compare a large number of existing IFP systems, coming both from the academia and from the industry. This allows us to identify a number of open issues that in our opinion should drive the research efforts in the near future. We present here the ones that in our opinion are more significant.

Language. Different kinds of languages have been proposed to define processing rules. Mainly, they belong to two classes: *transforming languages* specify a sequence of operations that transform one or more input flows into one or more output flows; *detecting languages* aim at detecting relevant patterns of information items inside the input flows.

Despite many systems are today offering features coming from both classes, this often leads to the definition of complex languages, difficult to write and understand.

This opens up a significant research direction: finding a proper formalism to compare the semantics of different operators and possibly extract a reasonable set of operators to offer a good trade-off between expressiveness and ease of use.

Support for uncertainty. Current systems hardly ever support data uncertainty (i.e., imprecise, or even incorrect data from sources). Moreover, they are usually not expressive enough to define rules that produce probabilistic results.

We think that the support for uncertainty deserves more investigation. It could increase the expressiveness and flexibility, and hence the diffusion of IPF systems.

Processing. Despite several processing algorithms have been proposed in existing IFP systems, we believe that processing still deserves further inverstigations, mainly to understand how to better exploit parallelism to speedup the most complex computations.

Distribution of processing. The distribuition of processing to meet the requirements of large scale scenarios has been addressed only marginally in existing systems. Mainly, the research so far has focused on optimizing the delay perceived by applications and the use of bandwidth by computing an optimal placement of operators on nodes according to abstract models.

We believe that distribution deserves more investigations. More in particular, research may focus on defining techniques to automatically adapt the system when the load changes, possibly thruogh protocols that do not assume a complete knowledge of the network, thus allowing autonomous decisions at each processing node.

Another major issue strictly related with the distribution of processing is the management of information items loss and out-of-order arrival. Future reseach may focus on finding a trade-off between correct and low latency processing, possibly allowing the users to specify the desired behavior of the system through predefined or customizable policies.

Definition of workloads. Currently, a major problem when it comes to evaluate and compare different systems is the lack of workloads. It would be useful to define generic benchmarks, that could capture (most of) the features present in existing systems. At the same time, it is necessary to identify real case studies to guide future research efforts, both to identify which operators are more relevant in a IFP systems, and to understand how to optimize processing algorithms and implementations accoring to the real requirements of applications.

4. CONCLUSIONS

In our tutorial we present a modeling framework to analyze and compare IFP systems. The framework allows us to fulfill three goals: *i.* provide a review of the state of the art in the area; *ii.* favor the communication between different communities, thus reducing the effort to merge the achievements reached so far; *iii.* highlight a number of open issue that still need to be addressed in research.

Acknowledgment

This work was partially supported by the European Commission, Programme IDEAS-ERC, Project 227977-SMScom; and by the Italian Gov. under the project PRIN D-ASAP.

5. REFERENCES

[1] B. Babcock, S. Babu, M. Datar, R. Motwani, and J. Widom. Models and issues in data stream systems. In *PODS '02: Proceedings of the twenty-first ACM SIGMOD-SIGACT-SIGART symposium on Principles of database systems*, pages 1–16, New York, NY, USA, 2002. ACM.

[2] G. Cugola and A. Margara. Processing flows of information: From data stream to complex event processing. *ACM Computing Surveys*, to appear.

[3] D. C. Luckham. *The Power of Events: An Introduction to Complex Event Processing in Distributed Enterprise Systems*. Addison-Wesley Longman Publishing Co., Inc., Boston, MA, USA, 2001.

Tutorial: Event Processing Grand Challenges

Pedro Bizarro
University of Coimbra
Portugal
pedro.bizarro@gmail.com

K. Mani Chandy
California Institute of Technology
U.S.A
mani@cs.caltech.edu

Nenad Stojanovic
Karlsruhe Institute of Technology
Germany
nstojano@fzi.de

ABSTRACT
This tutorial discusses grand challenges for the event processing community.

Categories and Subject Descriptors
G.3. [**Probability and Statistics**]: Experimental Design.

C.2.1 [**Computer-Communication Networks**]: Network architecture and Design

General Terms
Algorithms, Management, Performance, Design, Economics, Reliability, Experimentation, Security, Human Factors, Standardization, Languages, Theory,

Keywords
Real-time analytics, sense and respond, distributed systems, event processing, anomaly detection

1. Goal of the Tutorial
This tutorial discusses several grand challenges related to event processing and then suggests a single grand challenge to serve as a mechanism for coordinating research across the spectrum of people working on event processing.

2. Elements of a Grand Challenge for Event Processing
The challenge should exercise most of the components of the event processing architecture including:

- Data acquisition components such as sensors, software agents that poll Web sites, and human beings.
- Event processing agents that integrate data from multiple sources over time to estimate the states of the world relevant to the given application. These components may estimate the probabilities of different future trajectories of the state of the world and plan sequences of actions to deal these outcomes.
- Responders or actuators that execute actions.
- Communication networks for transmitting information between components. These networks may be implemented using publish/subscribe protocols.
- Management components that are used to specify, monitor, and control the entire system.
- People who participate in the overall system including those who provide data, carry out analytics, and help respond

3. Challenges in Event Processing
1. Build an infrastructure, built upon widely accepted open standards, that enables all the components of event processing architecture to be plugged into an event-processing "fabric" with minimal effort. The Internet grew rapidly because plugging into the network using IP was easy; our challenge is to develop an event-processing fabric into which components can plugged and unplugged almost as easily.
2. Demonstrate the use of the event-processing fabric for critical applications, such as the following:
   a. Extreme-scale disasters: use the fabric to help society respond to situations such as tsunamis, earthquakes, disasters in nuclear plants, and terrorist attacks. Data sources include sensors managed by government agencies (e.g., meteorological services tracking storms), companies (e.g., companies that monitor congestion in roads), and individuals (e.g., web sites that contain images or videos of situations such as forest fires and buildings after quakes).
   b. Critical societal applications such as managing the "smart" electric grid, the "smart city," and home healthcare for the aged. These systems are becoming increasingly event driven. For example, as the electric grid relies increasing on "green" sources of energy, such as wind and solar power, the energy sources become less dependable; thus predicting, detecting and responding to events, such as cloud cover over solar arrays or sudden drop in wind speeds, becomes more important.
   c. Personal applications such as determining the optimum commute using buses, trains, taxis based on sensing where resources are, when resources are likely to become available, and planning the best routes.
   d. Social "eventing," a step in the evolution of social networking: Data sources in social networks, such as Twitter and Facebook, are proliferating. Many organizations are working on mining this data. The challenge is to use an event-processing fabric to complete the loop from data acquisition, to information fusion, planning, and responding, so as to allow members of a social network to monitor their "friends" in the network and to respond to their actions easily.

4. Implementation Issues

A critical challenge is to develop a plug-and-play event processing fabric that helps in developing many (but not all) event-processing applications. For example, the fabric may be inappropriate for highly secure applications such as military or Homeland Security applications. Likewise, the fabric may be unsuitable for very high performance applications such as real-time stock trading. The goal is to emulate the Internet – it is extremely useful, but not the only way to connect components. Indeed, different plug-and-play fabrics may be appropriate for different types of applications.

One opportunity is to exploit cloud computing for implementing event-processing agents that manage the network, acquire data, detect and predict events, plan actions, and manage responses including data dissemination. Of course, this is merely one way among many; however, we now have an opportunity of demonstrating a prototype event-processing fabric that would have been very difficult a few years ago.

5. Research Issues

- Security: ensuring that hackers cannot attack the fabric.
- Performance requirements for extreme-scale disasters vary dramatically over time; the requirements are heaviest when disasters occur. The fabric must accommodate variable requirements.
- Plug-and-play standards are necessary for the fabric to be a fabric.

- User interfaces: research needs to be done to ensure that the broad public can tailor the fabric for their own needs.
- Integration of geographic information systems and event detection algorithms
- Integration of signal processing and machine learning with event detection.

6. Research Directions Explored

This tutorial investigates several research directions that can play a role in event processing grand challenges. These include advances in analytics and machine learning, the impact of widespread adoption of mobile phones including smart phones and tablets, use of cloud computing services across the world, decreasing costs of sensors including medical sensors, techniques for rapidly evaluating alternative responses by using high-performance parallel computers, and cheaper massive storage repositories.

7. REFERENCES

[1] The Event Processing Manifesto, http://www.dagstuhl.de/10201

[2] Etzion, O. and Niblett, P. 2011. *Event Processing in Action.* Manning Publications

[3] Chandy, K.M. and Schulte, R. 2010. *Event Processing: Designing IT Systems for Agile Companies*, McGraw-Hill

[4] Luckham, D. *The Power of Events*, Addison-Wesley, 2002

Architectural and Functional Design Patterns for Event Processing

Paul Vincent
Tibco Software Inc., UK
Business Optimization
Business Rules & CEP
+44 208 133 6228
pvincent@tibco.com

Alex Alves
Oracle Corp.
+16505153607
alex.alves@oracle.com

Catherine Moxey
IBM, UK
+16505153607
catherine_moxey@uk.ibm.com

Adrian Paschke
Freie Universität Berlin
Koenigin-Luisen-Str. 24/26,
Germany
+49 30 838 75225
paschke AT inf.fu-berlin.de

ABSTRACT

The tutorial introduces the EPTS Reference Architecture and its components, and covers some of the Reference Architecture subfunctions as design patterns against some implementation languages. The patterns are analysed and mapped to some of the current available system and languages (such as IBM, Oracle, TIBCO and Prova open source).

Categories and Subject Descriptors

D.2.11 [**Software Architectures**]

General Terms

Design, Standardization, Languages.

Keywords

Complex Event Processing, Design Patterns, Reference Architecture

1. INTRODUCTION

The Event Processing Technical Society (EPTS) Reference Architecture Working Group has developed a Functional Reference Architecture that describes the functions of event processing (EP) / complex event processing (CEP) operations. [1] [2] This includes design and administration as well as runtime considerations.

For the purposes of this tutorial we focus on the functions of the runtime aspect of EP/CEP, and drill down into some of them as design patterns [3][4] for some typical commercial and/or open source EP/CEP tools.

At runtime the EP/CEP that is carried out, between event production and event consumption, can include a number of event processing functions. These are classified loosely as Event Preparation, Event Analysis, Complex Event Detection and Event Reaction types. It should be noted that

- none or all of these types could be involved in any particular application,

- some might be carried out more than once

- the ordering of the functions is not mandated (although there is some degree of logical ordering).

These function types can be better described as:

- *Preparation* - Typically, the first processing is likely to be some form of selection from the events that have been received. The events may be Filtered on information in the event payload or in metadata, such that some subset is selected for further processing. Events could also be Enriched by adding additional information to them from other data sources or from other events.

- *Analysis* - some form of computation might be carried out on events. Examples include: Identification of events, and potential removal of duplicates; Transformation of events, which normally acts on the event payload, and might convert the event to a different format, or normalize the event; Analytic techniques, which can include predictive capabilities such as trend computations; Tracking of events passing through the system, in terms of their location and time attributes; Scoring and Rating of events by computing values of events and their associated data, and Classification by identifying event types and associations.

- *Detection* - this processing covers aspects of deriving different ("complex" or derived) events from individual events, where multiple events might be Aggregated or Consolidated into a smaller number of events. Functions include Consolidation, in which additional event data can be added into complex events, Composition in which new events are created based on preceding events, and Aggregation, where information across multiple events is combined to provide summarised data. A key aspect to event detection is Pattern Matching, which enables new events to be derived by detecting a particular pattern of events, often across time, and event Correlation which allows related events to be correlated.

- *Reaction* - Event Reaction is identifying actions to be taken as a result of events, usually events arising from previous processing. This can include Assessment of a change in situation that should be acted upon and Routing of events to appropriate destination(s). Event reaction can also involve advanced capabilities such as Prediction of future events or behaviours, using machine learning or predictive analytics, application of business rules to make decisions based on the events, and even the Discovery of new event types, event patterns and analyses.

Within each of the types of functionality there are multiple subfunctions, which form the basis for any discussion on design patterns for EP/CEP functions.

Note that there is no compulsory ordering of functions and subfunctions, and indeed some subfunctions may cross function types. For example, event identification could be handled in event preparation, but may in term require some analysis operations. Another example might be event filtering, or transformation of raw events, could occur at the event producer (in the context of a particular system) rather than being carried out within this event processor. From the latter one can understand how EP/CEP, or aspects of it, may be federated across a number of event processing systems.

For EP/CEP design patterns, the most appropriate level to apply to the Functional Reference Architecture is that of the subfunction: for example, event filtering.

Event filtering may take place in

- preparation (removing uninteresting events),

- analysis (looking at specific characteristics of subsets of events, or filtering as a part of classification),

- detection (detecting some subset of events), or

- reaction (applying a reaction to a specific subset of events).

These different function types for a filtering subfunction may of course have different characteristics:

- filtering in preparation involves removing an event (or not moving an incoming event onto an EP/CEP operation)

- filtering in analysis, detection and reaction involves defining some subset of events for other operations

We cover some of the Reference Architecture subfunctions in the tutorial as design patterns against some implementation languages; for example:

- Filtering

- Enrichment

- Aggregation

- Routing

We also investigate a more complex, monitoring pattern based on incoming events being counted over a period of time.

This tutorial targets those interested in EP/CEP functions and design patterns and how they map to some of the available EP/CEP languages and systems. Attendees will gain an initial familiarisation of these EP/CEP design patterns.

2. ACKNOWLEDGMENTS

This work has been conducted within the scope of the Event Processing Technical Society Reference Architecture working group.

3. REFERENCES

[1] Paschke, A. and Vincent, P.: A reference architecture for Event Processing. In *Proceedings of the Third ACM International Conference on Distributed Event-Based Systems* (DEBS '09). ACM, New York, NY, USA, 2009.

[2] Paschke, A., Vincent, P., and Catherine Moxey: Event Processing Architectures, *Fourth ACM International Conference on Distributed Event-Based Systems* (DEBS '10). ACM, Cambridge, UK, 2010.
http://www.slideshare.net/isvana/debs2010-tutorial-on-epts-reference-architecture-v11c

[3] Paschke, A.: Design Patterns for Complex Event Processing, 2nd International Conference on Distributed Event-Based Systems (DEBS'08), Rome, Italy, 2008.

[4] Opher E.: Tutorial Event Processing Architecture and Pattern, 2nd International Conference on Distributed Event-Based Systems (DEBS'08), Rome, Italy, 2008.
http://www.slideshare.net/opher.etzion/tutorial-in-debs-2008-presentation

Non Functional Properties of Event Processing

Opher Etzion
IBM Haifa Research Labs
Haifa 31905, Israel
opher@il.ibm.com

Ella Rabinovicn
IBM Haifa Research Labs
Haifa 31905, Israel
ellak@il.ibm.com

Inna Skarbovsky
IBM Haifa Research Labs
Haifa 31905, Israel
inna@il.ibm.com

ABSTRACT

An important aspect of any system is the non-functional aspect, which is not concerned with *what* a system does, but rather with *how well* a system works. Since event processing applications are not monolithic, there are various considerations which vary among these applications. In this tutorial we survey the various non-functional properties of event processing systems that in general relate to scalability and performance, availability, correctness and security. The tutorial is presented along three aspects for each topic: requirements, mapping of requirements to event processing application type and current state-of-the-art and research efforts to cope with the various requirements.

Categories and Subject Descriptors

H3.4. Systems and software (Performance evaluation), D4.5 (Reliability), D4.6 (Security and Protection), D4.8 (Performance)

General Terms

Event processing, non functional properties.

Keywords

Event processing- non functional properties, event processing – performance evaluation

1. Goal

The non-functional aspects of event processing gained a lot of attention due to the variability on one hand, and strict requirements in some applications on the other hand. The goal of this tutorial is to educate the community about the non-functional aspects of event processing, the challenges in the state-of-the-art and survey contemporary research in this area.

2. Tutorial topics

Table 1 shows the different topics covered by this tutorial, each of these topics is briefly explained.

2.1 Scalability and performance considerations

While the common scalability consideration in event processing is scalability in the volume of processed events, we discuss several additional dimensions of scalability: scalability in the quantity of agents, scalability in the quantity of consumers, scalability in the quantity of producers, scalability in the quantity of context partitions (e.g. windows), scalability in the size of internal state, scalability in the complexity of computation, and scalability in the processing environment.

Table 1: The main tutorial topics

#	Topic
I	Introduction to non functional properties of event processing
II	Scalability and performance considerations
III	Availability considerations
IV	Correctness considerations including validation and auditing
V	Security and privacy considerations
VI	Summary: Non-functional properties and the role of platforms, fabrics and clouds

The discussion is about techniques to scale-up, scale-down, scale-out and scale-in. The scalability techniques are driven by the performance metrics; we intend to survey various performance objectives that relate to latency and throughput, and discuss their applicability to various types of systems.

2.2 Availability considerations

We discuss the availability and recoverability aspects of event processing systems, discussing different assumptions, and trade-offs between availability and performance.

2.3 Correctness considerations

The temporal nature of event processing is manifested by the fact that the order of events may change the end result, both since some of the functions are order-related (sequence, trends, finding first or last), and the classification of events to time windows relate on the order relation between the event, and the window's initiator/terminator event. We discuss difficulties and fallacies that exist in current systems today along with existing solutions, existing work on explicit correctness schemes, and further research challenges. It also survey the use of verification techniques to ensure correctness and logical integrity.

2.4 Security and privacy considerations

Security and privacy considerations relate to who can produce event, process event, and consume events, protecting event processing systems from physical and logical threats, and privacy considerations and challenges in the current world.

The tutorial will summarize by describing the impact of non-functional properties, and classify event processing systems based on these roles.

REFERENCES

[1] Ron Ben-Natan: Implementing Database Security and Auditing: Includes Examples for Oracle, SQL Server, DB2 UDB, Sybase. Digital Press, 2005

[2] Philip A. Bernstein, Vassos Hadzilacos, and Nathan Goodman: \Concurrency Control and Recovery in Database Systems. Addison Wesley, 1987.

[3] K. M. Chandy and W. R. Schulte: Event Processing: Designing IT Systems for Agile Companies. McGraw-Hill Osborne Media, 2009.

[4] Opher Etzion, Peter Niblett: Event Processing in Action. Manning Publications Company 2010

[5] Leslie Lamport: *Time, Clocks, and the Ordering of Events in a Distributed System*, Communications of the ACM 21(7): 558-565 (1978)

[6] Geetika T. Lakshmanan, Yuri G. Rabinovich, and Opher Etzion. A stratified approach for supporting high throughput event processing applications. DEBS 2009. http://portal.acm.org/citation.cfm?doid=1619258.1619265.

[7] Ella Rabinovich, Opher Etzion, Sitvanit Ruah, Sarit Archushin: Analyzing the behavior of event processing applications. DEBS 2010: 223-234.

[8] Schmidt, Klaus:. High Availability and Disaster Recovery: Concepts, Design, Implementation. Springer., 2006

[9] Mudhakar Srivatsa, Ling Liu, *Securing Publish-Subscribe Overlay Services with EventGuard.* ACM Conference on Computer and Communications Security 2005: 289-298

Hybrid Programming Abstraction for e-Science Workflows and Event Processing

Chathura Herath

School of Informatics and Computing

Indiana University, Bloomington, USA

+1 (812) 855-8305

cherath@cs.indiana.edu

Beth Plale

School of Informatics and Computing

Indiana University, Bloomington, USA

+1 (812) 855-4373

plale@cs.indiana.edu

ABSTRACT

The scientific event processing for research and development adds extra dimension to the complexities associated with scientific computing. In achieving this, experience gained building scientific computing infrastructures that could span and scale into super computing resources can be reused in significant ways. But there are many unresolved issues relating to managing event streams in such an environment that require attention. Over the years the volumes of events generated in scientific disciplines have steadily grown. The limiting factor of many of these systems have become the time and attention of scientist and with expertise to derive insight out of the high volumes of events generated by the sensors. In this tutorial we propose to share the motivating use cases, research issues and outcomes and tools and frameworks used for event processing in science gateways in conjunction with complex event processing. We would provide hands on experience to the programming model, framework and tools that had evolved as a result of research over the years and relate how the scientific workflow based programming paradigm can provide a cleaner abstraction for query based Complex event processing systems.

Categories and Subject Descriptors

C.2.4 [**Computer-Communication Networks**]: Distributed Systems—Distributed applications, Distributed

General Terms

Management, Design

Keywords

Event processing, Complex Event Processing, Scientific Workflow, Control-flow, Composition tool

1. INTRODUCTION

The event processing systems in grid systems have grown in volume over the years and like to continue to grow because the events sensors become cheaper or event generating processes like social networks become more popular [4]. Whether it is processing weather radar events to detect tornedos or finding near earth object from astronomical data, the volume of data that need to be processed to find the actionable information is significant. Given the scale many event systems need to be processed real-time and yet the level of processing and the manageability of the

processing impose much harder requirements on the event processing middleware. In many cases event processing lead to providing some sort of insight into a particular domain which in most cases involve further analysis by expert domain users and [1] theorizes that time and attention of such users would become the scarce resource and event processing systems try to make the event volumes be manageable.

Scientific workflows have become an acceptable simple programming abstraction for e-sciences that allows domain scientist to setup their experiments. Most scientific workflows capture complex control-flows may it be short running or long running, although the amount of effort put to manage long running scientific workflows are significant. Most event processing systems work independently of suck workflow systems [5] and event processing systems lack a coherent programming model that would capture the entire spectrum of processing phases from downsampling, filtering, assimilation to high end scientific computation.

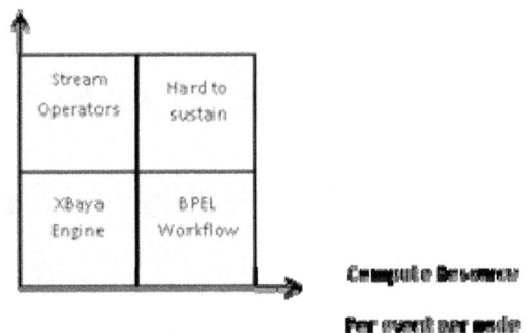

Figure 1

2. Diversity in Event Processing Systems

Lack of universal programming abstraction could be due to the diverse characteristics in the spectrum of problems the system is expected to solve. Consider the phase diagram for event processing systems shown in Figure 1 which identifies different event processing systems based on the event rates it is expected to handle and the compute resource requirements per event. There are systems that handle ultrahigh frequency event streams with limited computational capabilities [6]. There are systems that deal with high event rates that consume low resources there are many event processing systems that would handle this [8]. On the other hand there are many workflow systems capable of long running workflow applications low event rates [9]. There has always between these different system. It should be noted that the systems that need to sustain high event throughputs and requiring high resource requirements are hard to sustain. Example high resource requiring workflow would be a 36 hour WRF [2] weather forecast over 800kmx800km region with 5km resolution which would require approximately over 1 hour of computation time with 1024 nodes in Indiana university BigRed supercomputer.

3. Streamflow approach

In this tutorial we present a programming abstraction similar to scientific workflow programming model yet capable of capturing the three manageable quadrants in the phase diagram shown in Figure 1. The programming model lets the user define their application using Directed Acyclic Graph (DAG) based dataflow diagram.

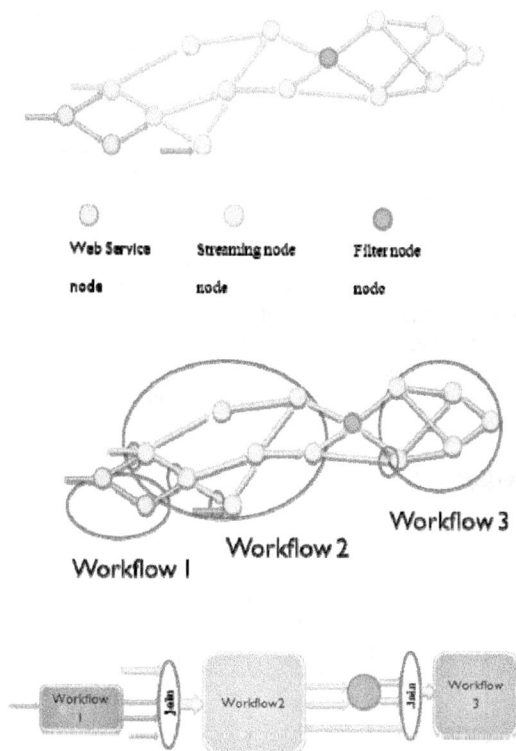

Web Service node   Streaming node node   Filter node node

Workflow 1   Workflow 2   Workflow 3

Figure 2

Streamflow framework [3] consist of graphical composition tool XBaya[7] and event processing runtime services. XBaya has means for users to compose DAG based stream processing applications and compilation, scheduling and deployment modules for such graphs. It would partition the user defined DAG based on the runtime characteristics like event rates the particular sub-graph need to sustain, resource requirements for the sub-graph and programming semantics the sub-graph consist of.

Figure 2 shows a partitioning of a DAG based on a preserving controlflow as well as runtime characteristics of the sub-graphs.

The edges are color coded to show different event rates in the edge. The idea behind the partitioning is that partitioned sub-graph's runtime characteristics would match the characteristics of one of the quadrants shown in Figure 1. In such case Streamflow framework would try to schedule the sub-graph to one of the three designated runtime i.e. Complex Event Processing engine, High throughput workflow engine or BPEL engine for long running applications.

Some of the nodes of the workflow can be CEP nodes that capture any give CEP query or other workflow nodes like web services, control structures. Some of the nodes produce will produce one output event per each input event, other like filter will not. So the edges of the graph represent some event flow and in certain nodes there will be mismatches in the event rate that its different input edges would produce. All such situations would prompt joins as shown in Figure2.

This tutorial covers a setting up of event processing application with diverse resource requirements using the Streamflow programming model and introduction to the underlying framework that would facilitate the programming abstraction.

4. REFERENCES

[1] K. Chandy, M. Charpentier, and A. Capponi. 2007. *Towards a theory of events*. In Proceedings of the 2007 inaugural international conference on Distributed event-based systems, pages 180-187. ACM.

[2] J. Done, C. Davis, and M. Weisman. 2004. *The next generation of nwp: Explicit forecasts of convection using the weather research and forecasting (wrf) model*. Atmospheric Science Letters, 5(6):110-117.

[3] C. Herath and B. Plale. 2010. *Streamflow-Programming Model for Data Streaming in Scientific Workflows*. In 2010 10th IEEE/ACM International Conference on Cluster, Cloud and Grid Computing, pages 302-311. IEEE.

[4] T. Hey and A. Trefethen. 2003. *The data deluge: An e-science perspective*. In Grid Computing (2003), pp. 809-824. doi:10.1002/0470867167.ch36

[5] Y. Liu, D. Hill, A. Rodriguez, L. Marini, R. Kooper, J. Myers, X. Wu, and B. Minsker.2009. *A new framework for on-demand virtualization, repurposing and fusion of heterogeneous sensors*. In International Symposium on Collaborative Technologies and Systems, CTS '09.

[6] D. Luckham. 2001. *The power of events: an introduction to complex event processing in distributed enterprise systems*. Addison-Wesley Longman Publishing Co., Inc. Boston, MA, USA.

[7] S. Perera, S. Marru, and C. Herath. 2008. *Workflow infrastructure for multi-scale science gateways*. In TeraGrid Conference.

[8] R. Stephens. 1997. *A survey of stream processing*. Acta Informatica, 34(7):491-541.

[9] I. Taylor. 2007. *Workflows for e-science: scientific workflows for grids*. Springer-Verlag New York Inc.

DEBS Challenge

Nenad Stojanovic

FZI, Research Center for Information Technology
Haid-und-Neu-Str. 10-14,
76131 Karlsruhe, Germany
Nenad.Stojanovic@fzi.de

Categories and Subject Descriptors

I.0 [**Computing Methodologies**]: General

General Terms

Experimentation, Performance

Keywords

Event Processing

1. INTRODUCTION

The overall objective of the DEBS Challenge is to promote the research and development in the Event Processing area by:

- Enabling R&D groups (research and industry ones) and software vendors to demonstrate the strength of their results and;

- Creating awareness in the broader community of the potential of the event-processing paradigm for developing various, challenging real-world applications.

Therefore, the Challenge is oriented toward developing new event-based solutions for a challenging problem, that will be evaluated properly and the results will be disseminated in the broader community.

This year the Challenge is related to the realization of a system the Trivia Geeks Club (described below) and optionally to providing some creative extensions of it. The Challenge consists of two competitive tracks and one non-competitive track. The competitive tracks are:

- Basic: satisfying the enclosed specification;

- Extended: extending the scenario with capabilities that demonstrate novel functional or non-functional capabilities selected by the competitors.

All competitors participate in the basic track; in addition a competitor can chose to participate in the extended track. The non competitive track has the same ground rules (should satisfy the basic scenario, and may include extensions) and is intended for those who wish to present their solutions in DEBS 2011, but not participate in the competition. The competition is completely open for both research and commercial solutions.

2. THE CHALLENGE: TRIVIA GEEKS CLUB: A SOCIAL GAME

This specification has to be fully implemented using event processing functions, without reading or writing from a database.

The *Trivia Geeks Club* is a game that is played within a social network group. A trivia question is being asked approximately every 30 seconds throughout the day (24 hours), one can answer the question until the next question is being asked. The question is a trivia question with four possible answers, a person may answer the question directly, or ask to receive the most frequent answer among the group so far and then answer.

The following rules apply for the game:

1. It is possible to do an annulment of the answer within ten sec of giving an answer, but only within 30sec that a question is valid in.

2. The official time is client time and the system should be able to process "late" answers (the players have to install client program that takes the time from a shared time server)

3. In order to make the game more interesting, the system should be able to change a predefined scoring rule (see later), this change is triggered by a control event.

As a part of the Extended Track, the presented system can be extended with additional functionalities that prove novel functional or non-functional capabilities. The system can be upgraded in an arbitrary way. An example is to enable reactivity of the system by supporting different types of monitoring alarms. Additionally, different supporting technologies can be introduced, e.g. semantics, NLP technologies (by extending, the list of questions), for dealing with probability or security issues.

Evaluation of the solution will be performed in both categories as follows:

Basic:

- Completeness and correctness of the functionalities

- Simplicity of expressions

- Usability of the solution

Extended:

The criteria will be based on the creativity and benefits of the solution

Evaluation will be performed by the Evaluation committee.

Scenario specification:

There are three event producers:

- Trivia question generator which generates the trivia question and emits an event with trivia question and answer, the question (without the correct answer – of course) is sent to all subscribers.

- Player which can generate events of three type: answer, answer annulment, and request for most frequent answer, in that case the system generates an answer to this request and sends it as an event to the player.

- The system that generates control events that trigger the changes in some scoring rules

The event consumers are:

- A scoreboard manager which displays points for all players on a scoreboard, the system sends each "point increase/decrease" event to that consumer.

- A Player, getting response to a most frequent answer request.

The system functions are:

- Get new questions

- Get answers – determine if the question is still valid, and if yes match against the answer, and create score event if applicable

- Get request for most frequent answer, calculate the most frequent answer and send the player

- Enable annulment of answers

The score is kept online and the scoreboard is constantly updated whenever a *point increase/decrease* event is derived.

The monthly bonus for most appearances is calculated once a month, at the end of the day of the last day of the month, after calculating the bonus the best player(s) of the month are selected and share a $1M prize; the scoring starts every month from zero (the bonus for best weekly score, when the week spans over months are counted in the month in which the week ends).

Control event injects a change in the number of points associated with one of the cases above.

The scoring system creates score event with points for player according to the following scoring table:

Case	Points
Correct answer	5
Correct answer after asking for the most frequent answer	1
First who answered	100
Incorrect answer	-1
Three answers incorrect without a correct answer in the middle	-50
Correct answers to 10 consecutive questions*	500
Correct answers to 10 questions within 30 minutes* during late night hours (1:00 – 5:00)	500
Best daily score (may apply to multiple players)	1000**
Most appearances in the daily top five within a month (may apply to multiple players)	1000**
Best weekly score, given every Sunday midnight (may apply to multiple players)	1000**

*: each correct answer is counted towards a single bonus of the same type and cannot be counted twice.

**: If there are several players that are tied in one of the "best" categories, each of them receives the bonus of 1000 points.

The Challenge is advised by a board of experts working at universities and in private industry. The advisory board also acts as an evaluation committee and award the best solutions at the DEBS Conference based on the advertised criteria.

For more information about DEBS Challenge see http://debschallenge.event-processing.org/

Credits: The basic idea of the game was created by Technion students Uri Fridland and Ivan Savchenko,

Demo: Distributed Event Processing For Activity Recognition

Visalakshmi Suresh, Paul Ezhilchelvan, Paul Watson, Cuong Pham, Dan Jackson,
Patrick Olivier
Newcastle University
School of Computing Science
Newcastle Upon Tyne,UK
firstname.lastname@ncl.ac.uk

ABSTRACT

Stream-processing systems inevitably face unpredictable variations in incoming event loads. One way of handling this without affecting end-to-end performance metrics, will be to dynamically distribute event-processing on multiple computers and thus avail compute power for optimal performance. More precisely, data streams are processed in part or in parallel on multiple computers connected by a high bandwidth network. The number of computers being used is to be varied dynamically to cope with input load fluctuations. This paper uses data from ambient kitchen to make a preliminary assessment of performance advantages by distribution of real-time data stream processing. The motivation is to leverage cloud computing for optimal realtime event processing.

Categories and Subject Descriptors

C.2.4 [**Distributed Systems**]: Distributed Applications; C.3 [**Special-purpose and application based systems**]: Real Time and Embedded Systems; C.4 [**Performance Of Systems**]: [Performance Attributes]

General Terms

Distributed Event Processing, CEP

1. INTRODUCTION

The ambient kitchen [2] is constructed in the university research laboratory, utilising RFID readers and tags on all movable non-metallic objects, IP cameras, wireless accelerometers, pressure sensitive floor sensors, projectors and speakers. The Ambient kitchen is designed to emulate a pervasive computing prototyping environment, particularly focusing on machine learning, activity recognition, distributed event processing and for research in social inclusion. Long term goal is to support people with cognitive impairments. An investigation of the food preparation actions with embedded three axis accelerometers in the kitchen utensils (such as knifes, spoon etc.) was carried out using lay subjects. The classification algorithms used in the activity recognition framework are Decision Tree C4.5, Bayesian Network and Naïve Bayes.

To address the event distribution issues [1], we pursue an approach to analyse an use case centric approach where splitting of the event stream is undertaken as an operation without involving evaluation of complex predicates from multiple attributes in an event tuple. We examine a few schemes for event distribution in terms of distribution operators that can be used to '*fix*' loss of accuracy in the final outcome and address non-functional aspects such as scalability and performance of event based systems. The latter is assessed on dimensions relevant to our given use case such as volume of events with varying number of input agents, producers, consumers, contexts, complexity of the computation and processing environment.

2. ARCHITECHTURE OVERVIEW

Figure 1 describes the overview of system architecture where the real time streaming events generated from the ambient kitchen are fed in to autonomous event processing networks (EPN). The EPN shown as a graph in figure 1, is composed of processing elements constituting the nodes of a graph. The nodes have input or output terminals for the flow of events between them.

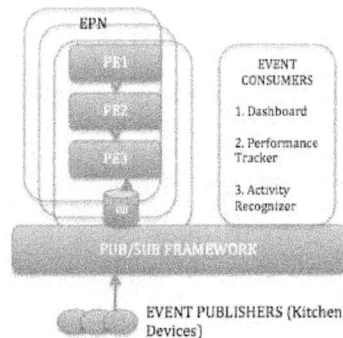

Figure 1: Architecture

2.1 EVENT PRODUCERS:

ADXL330 accelerometers are event producers and are embedded inside the kitchen devices to sense the acceleration along three axes to measure motion, shock or vibration. They are set to 40hz providing approximately 40 samples every second

2.2 EVENT CONSUMERS:

The event consumers are java messaging queue which collects the activity recognised by EPN. They would aggregate the recognised activities with temporal dimensions to create assistive prompting for the users in the kitchen who are likely to be dementia patients. The latter part of the experiment is not considered here. Rather, the focus will be on the effects on performance when EPN is distributed over multiple computers.

Two types of EPN distribution are possible: horizontal and vertical distribution. In the former, several computing nodes host a distinct EPN acting on inputs from a distinct subset of devices. In the vertical distribution, the processing elements(PEs) of a single EPN are hosted on distinct computing nodes. Our experiments indicate that the vertical distribution exhibits poor performance due to high communication costs between PEs.

2.3 PROCESSING ELEMENT 1 (PE1):

PE1 in the EPN acts as a filter and windows the incoming events based on the specified dimension (temporal or spatial) and sequence of arrival from message queue.

2.4 THE PROCESSING ELEMENT 2(PE2):

PE2 acts as a transformation operator, where each event instance is processed depending on other instances processed by the operators. They differ based on the kind of transformation it performs such as stateless or stateful. For this use case, mathematical aggregate functions such as mean, standard deviation, energy and entropy are used.

2.5 THE PROCESSING ELEMENT 3(PE3):

PE3 acts as a pattern detector operator emitting one or more derived events if it detects an occurrence of the specified pattern in the incoming stream. An exhaustive machine learned patterns for the activity recognition experiments run by Pham et.al. is used in this experiment.

3. DEMONSTRATION

1. We will demonstrate real time activity recognition of the low level food preparation activities such as chopping, coring, stirring, slicing, dicing, eating, peeling, spreading, scooping, scraping and shaving using continuous streaming data from accelerometers as in figure 2.

2. The performance in terms of latency and throughput measurements processed by a single EPN hosted in single computing node will be displayed in the live dashboard in relation to the raw data from the accelerometers.

3. Multiple devices will then be considered and the excessive throughput and latency fluctuations we have observed (as shown figure 3) will be demonstrated.

4. With the increases in arrival rates and number of devices, the effects of horizontal distribution of EPN will be demonstrated. Adding multiple EPN instances on additional computing nodes result in stable throughput and lower latencies. A real time performance tracker will illustrate the latency and throughput.

4. CONCLUSION

In the activity recognition scenario, performance at the current instance of time is critical. During cooking in an ambient kitchen, few seconds of processing delay would have

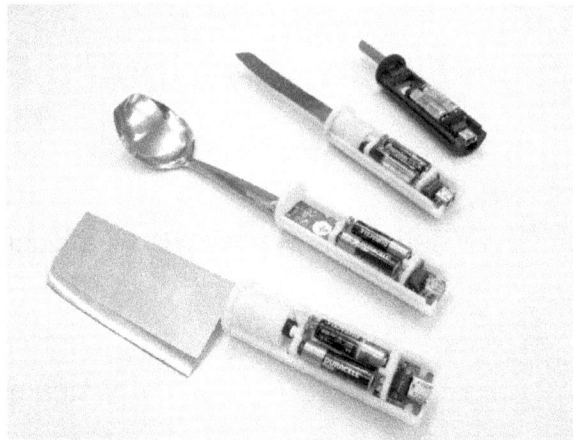

Figure 2: Devices

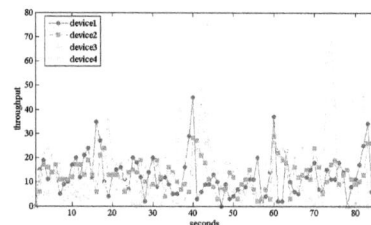

Figure 3: Throughput Fluctuations for Multiple Devices

resulted in the user moving from cutting to peeling and subsequently faulty inferences arise in situated prompting. Processing multiple devices in a single event processing network provides an average throughput. However, the instantaneous throughput is very critical. When considering individual instance of time, the fluctuation is huge. The processing elements need to be scaled to multiple computing nodes in order to meet the QoS. In horizontal distribution, the latency and throughput of multiple instances of event processing network serving individual devices provides a stable performance. Movement of tuples to cloud and round trip cost for communication introduces additional few milliseconds latency. Given the quality of service, this needs to be evaluated for each individual use case.

5. ACKNOWLEDGMENTS

Support for this project was provided by RCUK Digital Economy Research Hub EP/G066019/1 - SIDE: Social Inculsion through the Digital Economy.

6. REFERENCES

[1] M. Balazinska, H. Balakrishnan, and M. Stonebraker. Load management and high availability in the medusa distributed stream processing system. In *Proceedings of the 2004 ACM SIGMOD international conference on Management of data*, SIGMOD '04, pages 929–930, 2004.

[2] C. Pham, T. Plötz, and P. Olivier. A dynamic time warping approach to real-time activity recognition for food preparation. In *Proceedings of the First international joint conference on Ambient Intelligence*, AmI'10, pages 21–30, 2010.

Demo: fpga-ToPSS – Line-speed Event Processing on FPGAs

Mohammad Sadoghi, Harsh Singh, Hans-Arno Jacobsen
Middleware Systems Research Group
Department of Electrical and Computer Engineering
University of Toronto, Canada
mo@cs.toronto.edu,{harshvps,jacobsen}@eecg.toronto.edu

ABSTRACT

In this demo, we present *fpga-ToPSS* [1] (a member of Toronto Publish/Subscribe System Family), an efficient event processing platform for high-frequency and low-latency algorithmic trading. Our event processing platform is built over reconfigurable hardware—FPGAs—to achieve line-rate processing. Furthermore, our event processing engine supports Boolean expression matching with an expressive predicate language that models complex financial strategies to autonomously mimic the buying and the selling of stocks based on real-time financial data.

Categories and Subject Descriptors

H.3.3 [**Information Search and Retrieval**]: Information filtering

General Terms

Measurement, Experimentation, Performance

Keywords

FPGA, Publish/Subscribe, and Complex Event Processing

1. INTRODUCTION

Efficient event processing is an integral part of growing number of data management technologies such as algorithmic trading [ ], real-time data analysis [ ], intrusion detection system [ ], and (complex) event processing (e.g., [, ,]).

A prominent application for event processing is algorithmic trading; a computer-based approach to execute buy and sell orders on financial instruments (e.g., securities). Financial brokers exercise investment strategies (*subscriptions*) using autonomous high-frequency algorithmic trading fueled by real-time market *events*. Algorithmic trading is dominating financial markets and now accounts for over 70% of all trading in equities [ ]. Therefore, as the computer-based trading race among major brokerage firms continues, it is crucial to optimize execution of buy or sell orders at the microsecond level in response to market events, such as corporate news, recent stock price patterns, and fluctuations in currency exchange rates, because every microsecond translates into opportunities and ultimately profit [ ]. For instance, a classical arbitrage strategy has an estimated annual profit of over $21 billion according to TABB Group [ ]. Moreover, every 1-millisecond reduction in response-time is estimated to generate the staggering amount of

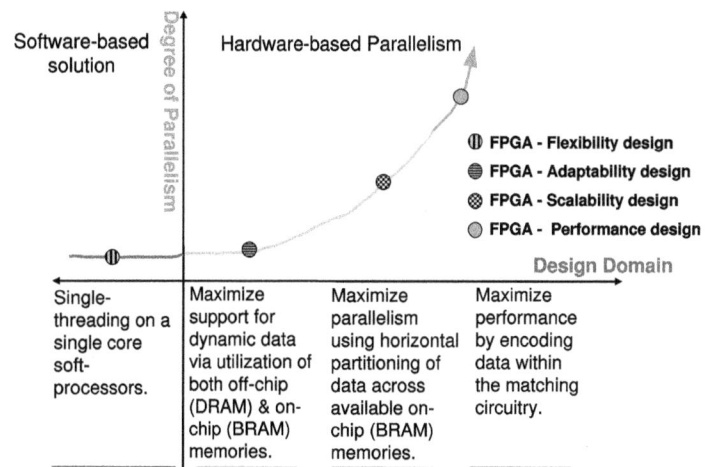

Figure 1: Various Degrees of Parallelism

over $100 million a year [ ]; such requirements greatly increases the burden placed on scaling the event processing platforms.

To achieve throughput at this scale, we demonstrate our novel FPGA-based event processing designs (Field Programmable Gate Array) [ ]. An FPGA is an integrated circuit designed to be reconfigurable to support custom-built applications in hardware. Potential application-level parallelism can be directly mapped to purpose-built processing units operating in parallel. Configuration is done through encoding the application in a programming language-style description language and synthesising a configuration uploaded on the FPGA chip.

Thus, in this demo, we demonstrate our solutions as a design trade-off between the degree of exploitable parallelism (cf. Fig. 1) versus the desired application-level requirements [ ]. Requirements considered are: the ease of the development and deployment cycle (*flexibility*), the ability of updating a large subscription workload in real-time (*adaptability*), the power of obtaining a remarkable degree of parallelism through horizontal data partitioning (*scalability*), and, finally, the power of achieving the highest level of throughput by eliminating the use of memory and by specialized encoding of subscriptions on FGPA (*Performance*) [ ].

The ability of an FPGA to be re-configured on-demand into a custom hardware circuit with a high degree of parallelism is key to its advantage over commodity CPUs for data and event processing. Using a powerful multi-core CPU system does not necessarily increase processing rate (Amdahl's Law) as it increases interprocessor signaling and message passing overhead, often requiring complex concurrency management techniques at the program and OS level. In contrast, FPGAs allow us to get around these limitations due to their intrinsic highly inter-connected architecture

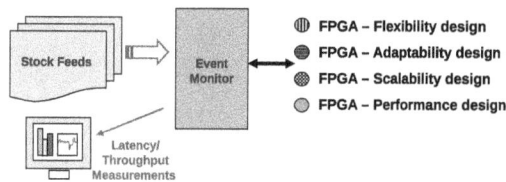

Figure 2: Demo Setup

and the ability to create custom logic on the fly to perform parallel tasks. In our design, we exploit parallelism, owing to the nature of the matching algorithm, by creating multiple matching units which work in parallel with multi-giga bit throughput rates, and we utilize reconfigurability by seamlessly adapting relevant components as subscriptions evolve.

2. DEMO METHODOLOGY

This section describes our demo setup including the hardware used to implement our FPGA-based algorithmic trading solution and the measurement infrastructure.

Demo Setup The input to our platform is a stream of events; events are encoded in the packets of the transport protocol that transmits event data to the FPGA board. In our implementation, we use UDP as transport over a directly connected 1 Gb/s Ethernet link (cf. Fig. 2). UDP simplifies the implementation, especially on our event processing platform side. Due to the direct, unshared Ethernet link, there are no severe transmission reliability issues to consider, except for the filling up of input/output buffers on the board. If no further events can be accepted by the board, packets are dropped and the maximal sustainable processing rate is achieved.

Our demonstration setup includes a laptop with a 1 Gb/s Ethernet interface (cf. Fig. 2). This machine drives the demo by generating the stock feeds, either based on our "event data stream generator," or from log-files of captured event traces. In practice, the online event data stream would be channeled to our platform in a similar manner so that the UDP data packets are transmitted to/from the Xilinx Virtex 5 LXT ML505 board, which is the employed FPGA board in our platform and for our demo. A USB-JTAG link is employed to program the FPGA board by a second laptop loaded with the Xilinx ISE10.1 EDK development tool suite for design synthesis and bit stream generation.

Demo Workload We generate a workload of tens of thousands of subscriptions derived from investment strategies such as arbitrage and buy-and-hold. In addition, we generate market events using the Financial Information eXchange (FIX) Protocol with FAST encoding (cf. `fixprotocol.org`). The generated workload is transmitted to FPGA through our workload replayer (cf. Fig. 3(a)).

Demo Measurements We characterize the system throughput as the maximum sustainable input packet rate obtained by determining, through a bisection search, the smallest fixed packet inter-arrival time where the system drops no packets when monitored for five seconds—a duration empirically found long enough to predict the absence of future packet drops at the given input rate. The latency of our solutions is the interval between the time an event packet leaves the Event Monitor output queue to the time the first forwarded version of the market event is received and is added to the output queue of the Event Monitor.

Demo Visualization As part of our demo, the latency information is continuously aggregated over a multitude of dimensions and presented visually in order to demonstrate the trade-offs and benefits of each solution (cf. Fig. 3(b)).

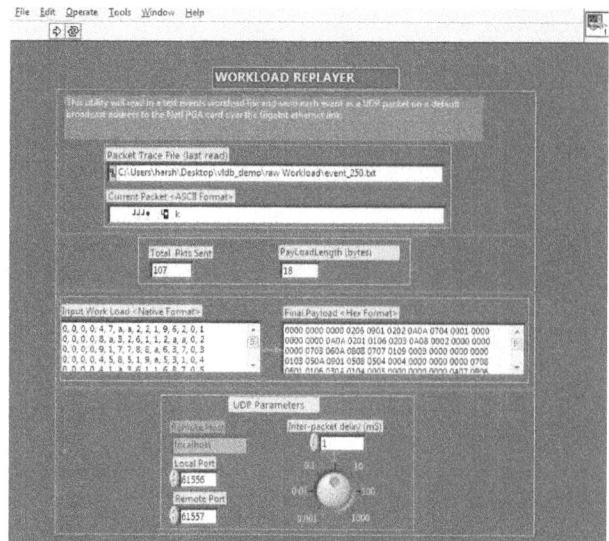

(a) Workload Replayer

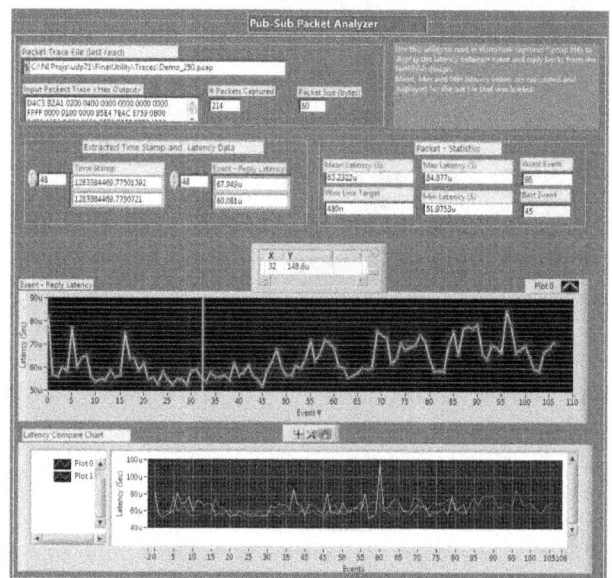

(b) Event Packet Analyzer

Figure 3: *fpga-ToPSS* Interface.

3. REFERENCES

[1] M. K. Aguilera, R. E. Strom, D. C. Sturman, M. Astley, and T. D. Chandra. Matching events in a content-based subscription system. In *PODC'99*.

[2] F. Fabret, H.-A. Jacobsen, F. Llirbat, J. Pereira, K. A. Ross, and D. Shasha. Filtering algorithms and implementation for fast pub/sub systems. *SIGMOD'01*.

[3] A. Farroukh, M. Sadoghi, and H.-A. Jacobsen. Towards vulnerability-based intrusion detection with event processing. In *DEBS'11*.

[4] K. Heires. Budgeting for latency: If I shave a microsecond, will I see a 10x profit? *Securities Industry, 1/11/10*.

[5] R. Iati. The real story of trading software espionage. *TABB Group Perspective, 10/07/09*.

[6] R. Martin. Wall street's quest to process data at the speed of light. *Information Week, 4/21/07*.

[7] M. Sadoghi and H.-A. Jacobsen. BE-Tree: An index structure to efficiently match boolean expressions over high-dimensional discrete space. In *SIGMOD'11*.

[8] M. Sadoghi, M. Labrecque, H. Singh, W. Shum, and H.-A. Jacobsen. Efficient event processing through reconfigurable hardware for algorithmic trading. In *VLDB '10*.

[9] M. Sadoghi, H. Singh, and H.-A. Jacobsen. Towards highly parallel event processing through reconfigurable hardware. In *DaMoN'11*.

[10] D. Srivastava, L. Golab, R. Greer, T. Johnson, J. Seidel, V. Shkapenyuk, O. Spatscheck, and J. Yates. Enabling real time data analysis. *PVLDB'10*.

Demo: Complex Event Pattern Evolution based on Real-Time Execution Statistics

Sinan Sen
FZI Research Center for
Information Technology
Haid-und-Neu-Strasse 10-14
Karlsruhe, Germany
sinan.sen@fzi.de

Ruofeng Lin
FZI Research Center for
Information Technology
Haid-und-Neu-Strasse 10-14
Karlsruhe, Germany
rlin@fzi.de

Bijan Fahimi Shemrani
FZI Research Center for
Information Technology
Haid-und-Neu-Strasse 10-14
Karlsruhe, Germany
fahimi@fzi.de

ABSTRACT

In this demo we present an approach for the evolution of complex event patterns based on real-time pattern execution statistics. Complex event patterns encode the knowledge about a situation of interest which must be detected and reported. Therefore complex event patterns are considered as one of the most valuable assets in Complex Event Processing.

The quality, meaning the accuracy of modelling with regard to the situation of interest, of the detection increases and decreases with the quality of the defined complex event patterns. In order to guarantee the quality of a complex event pattern we describe the importance of the transparent detection process, its necessity for the complex event pattern evolution and present an approach in order to support the evolution of complex event patterns.

Categories and Subject Descriptors

H.1 [**MODELS AND PRINCIPLES**]: Systems and Information Theory

General Terms

Management

Keywords

Statistics, Complex Event Pattern, Evolution, Management, Suggestions

1. INTRODUCTION

The detection of a complex event is the result of the matching process which takes place within the CEP engine based on the knowledge encoded in the complex event patterns (CEPATs) [1]. A CEPAT is an expression formed by using a set of events (simple or complex events) and a set of event operators. Current approaches in Complex Event Processing (CEP) are mainly focused on the extreme processing of a large number of events. This is without a doubt important but to turn the argument on its head, the need for more manageable CEP systems is neglected [2]: like the efficient generation, representation, deployment and evolution of CEPATs which is the main focus of this demo pa-

per. We assume that the next generation of CEP systems will deal with probabilities about the matching process instead of deterministic matching. Current CEP approaches are designed as a black-box where a CEP engine matches predefined CEPATs with incoming events.

However, we believe that this approach is not sufficient in order to detect anomalies in pattern execution in real-time and to generate suggestions to evolve a pattern that behaves unusual. The detection of these anomalies requires a paradigm shift towards a transparent CEP engine (see figure 3). In a transparent CEP engine the pattern execution statistics are processed in real-time to detect unusual behaviour of a CEPAT.

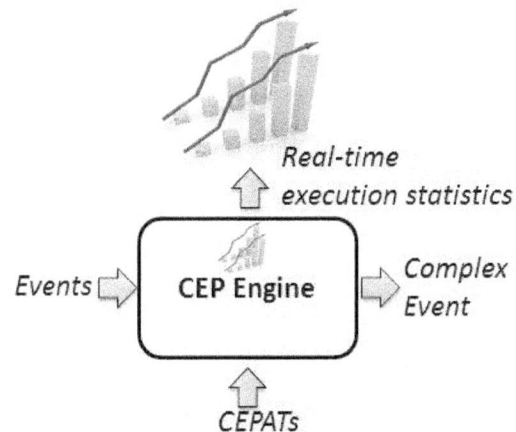

Figure 1: Transparent Complex Event Processing engine

Since CEPATs will change over time there is a need for methods of continually updating them in order to ensure their continued relevance for new situations. A continual improvement assists the preparation for change. It states that potential changes improving the CEPAT may be discovered semi-automatically from the analysis of the structure of CEPATs, through the analysis of their usage and their execution statistics. Since CEP systems are designed for real-time environments a delay in a pattern update may lead to increased downtime (possible ignorance of real problems).

2. EVOLUTION OF COMPLEX EVENT PATTERNS

We divide the evolution of CEPATs into three phases namely *Collecting Phase*, *Detection Phase* and *Suggestion Phase*. In the *Collection Phase* we receive the execution statistics (PES= pattern execution session) for a given pattern and prepare them for further processing. Every PES is a detailed execution path for a given CEPAT in a single execution step. PES contains information like the order of the pattern matching process, the number of incoming events before the pattern was fulfilled or discarded. The *Detection Phase* detects based on several metrics which CEPAT behave unusual compared to the average execution in the past. In the *Suggestion Phase* we detect the part of a CEPAT that causes the unusual behaviour and inform the user about this unusual behaviour. The user can decide whether a presented CEPAT needs to be updated or not which forms a feedback loop. The aim to detect an unusual behaviour followed by

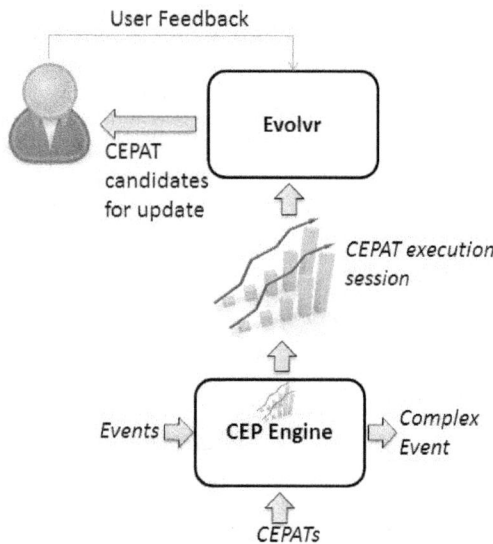

Figure 2: Transparent CEP with evolution related user feedback

a proper suggestion is based on two categories of statistics which are described below.

2.1 Context-free execution statistics

Context-free execution statistics contain the number of complete fulfilment of a CEPAT. In this case the PES contains the information that a pattern has been fulfilled without taking into account the order and details of the matching process. The context-free statistics are used in order to detect whether the execution of a CEPAT is for a given time-period unusual.

Unusualness is an often used synonym for anomaly in common language. Our definition is based on two features, *importance* and *unexpectedness*. The delimitation is necessary because an anomaly detection only refers to the problem of finding outliers that might not be necessarily important. A CEPAT CP is important if the the support is greater than a given minimum support threshold and the confidence is greater than a given minimum confidence threshold. A

CEPAT CP is unexpected if the unusualness factor is greater than the minimum unusualness threshold.

2.2 Context-sensitive execution statistics

Once a CEPAT is detected as unusual our goal is to detect possible reasons for this unusual behaviour and to generate suggestions in order to help the user to update this pattern. In order to do that we consider also the execution path of previous PES for a given CEPAT. The root-cause analysis is based on several pattern relations (subpattern, superpattern, overlapping, similar, etc.). Based on this root-cause analysis we generate suggestions. The user can determine whether the suggestion makes sense and if the evolution of a pattern is identified correctly.

2.3 Evolvr

The figure below presents the user interface of the *Evolvr* system. It shows the observed CEPATs, their unusualness factor, the probability and the degree of the unusualness.

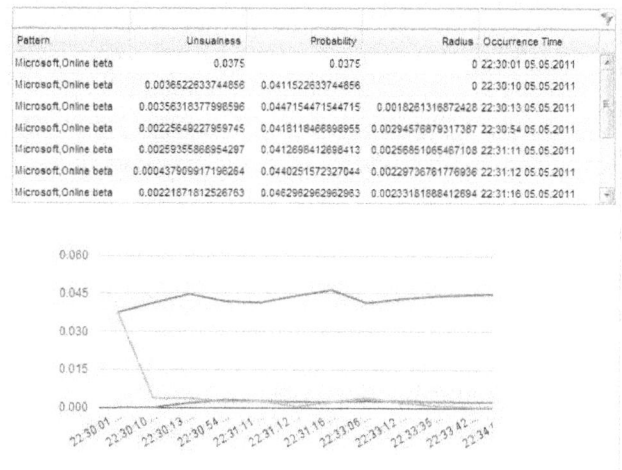

Figure 3: User interface of the Evolvr system.

3. CONCLUSION

In this demo paper we presented the importance of a transparent CEP matching process and its necessity for the complex event pattern evolution. The key contribution of our approach is to detect an unusual behaviour of a CEPAT in real-time and to provide a proper root-cause analysis in order to identify the part of a CEPAT that may behave unusual. We believe that such an approach would help the pattern engineer to keep the pattern base up-to-date. Since CEP systems are designed for real-time environments a delay in a pattern update may lead to increased downtime or possible ignorance of real problems.

4. REFERENCES

[1] D. C. Luckham. *The Power of Events: An Introduction to Complex Event Processing in Distributed Enterprise Systems.* Addison-Wesley Longman Publishing Co., Inc., Boston, MA, USA, 2001.

[2] S. Sen and N. Stojanovic. Gruve: A methodology for complex event pattern life cycle management. In B. Pernici, editor, *CAiSE*, volume 6051 of *Lecture Notes in Computer Science*, pages 209–223. Springer, 2010.

Demo: Altibase DSM: CTable for Pull-based Processing in SPE*

Jaemyung Kim, Vladimir Verjovkin, Sergey A. Fedorov,
Younghun Kim, Dae-Il Kim, Sungjin Kim
Altibase Corporation
182-13, Guro-dong, Guro-Gu
Seoul, 152-790, Korea
{ jmkim,verjovkin,fedorov,
yhkim,newdaily,sjkim }@altibase.com

Sang-Won Lee
School of Information & Communications Engr.
Sungkyunkwan University
Suwon, 440-746, Korea
swlee@skku.edu

ABSTRACT

We demonstrate streaming applications of the Altibase Data Stream Middleware (DSM), the distributed Stream Processing Engine using the Publish/Subscribe Communication Model. Altibase DSM has the Cached Table that is a key-value store supporting not only insert but also update and delete operations. The demos include the Sex-offender Tracking and Bus Arrival Information Systems.

Categories and Subject Descriptors

D.2.11 [**Software Architectures**]: Domain-specific architectures

General Terms

Design,Performance,Algorithm

1. INTRODUCTION

Recent advances in wireless technologies and mobile devices such as smartphones and tablet computers, and new applications including location-based and social network services generate a significant amount of data. These services involve online analytic processing, which requires a Stream Processing Engine (SPE) due to its performance benefits. Streaming applications are naturally distributed, and with increasing loads, the demand for distributed architecture [3, 5] has emerged. Advanced network infrastructures such as Gigabit Ethernet and InfiniBand (RDMA) also play a vital role in heavily loaded distributed systems.

While traditional DBMS uses pull-based processing, SPE uses push-based processing. Although SPE benefits from its push-based model, it often refers to static relational data from DBMS for meaningful analytic processing. Fetching data from DBMS can degrade the entire performance due to its frequent occurrence. Conversely, output stream events also need to be converted to relational tables or accessed through legacy applications designed for pull-based processing. Therefore, it entails additional implementation cost to connect two systems with different processing paradigm.

We implement the Altibase Data Stream Middleware (DSM), a distributed SPE with Publish/Subscribe Communication Model,

*This work was supported in part by MKE, Korea under ITRC (NIPA-2011-(C1090-1121-0008)) and also supported in part by Seoul Metropolitan Government 'Seoul R&BD Program (PA090903)'

because each distributed Event Processing Agent (EPA) can be loosely coupled. Altibase DSM includes the Cached Table (CTable) feature, a key-value store supporting not only insert but also update and delete operations. It can be solely used as a relational table and convert an event stream object into a CTable with a mapping function. For example, to minimize the latency in accessing a database table, CTable is able to replicate a table from the Altibase Hybrid Database (HDB). When DSM starts up, it transmits all HDB source table records. During operation, the HDB transaction log of DML can be captured and converted into DML operations of DSM. On the DSM side, to perform event processing, which refers to the DBMS table, the CTable replicated with a HDB's table can be joined with standard event streams and windows.

CTable can be regarded as a transition technology which reduces the introduction costs of SPEs to legacy systems. Unbounded streaming events are bound in the CTable with a unique up-to-date key constraint. DSM supports SQL-like languages with a DBC-style interface such as ODBC and JDBC. Furthermore, to facilitate integration with the legacy system, DSM additionally supports pull-based query in an open-fetch-close manner when the query includes only CTable(s) on the FROM clause. We explain the distributed architecture of the DSM and the Cached Table in Section 2 and demonstrate machine to machine (M2M) applications such as sex-offender tracking and bus arrival information in Section 3.

2. ALTIBASE DSM AND CTABLE

In this section, we describe the distributed architecture of Altibase DSM using the Publish/Subscribe communication model and Cached Table. This paper mainly describes the CTable and its applications, and briefly explains our distributed architecture.

The event-processing tasks of SPE can be represented as an Event Processing Network (EPN). EPN is an event flow, which is a collection of staged executions of Event Processing Agents (EPAs). Because Altibase DSM is designed to be distributed, it can have an EPN that spans multiple nodes (Figure 1).

While Borealis [1] tightly manages distributed nodes and uses the Medusa distribution logic, and TCP connections between EPAs and TCP multiplexing for optimization, we use the Publish/Subscribe Communication Model (Pub/Sub Model) for loosely coupled EPN programming, UDP, and multicast technology for scalability. EPAs are participants of the Pub/Sub Model that directs the flow of messages from senders to receivers based on receivers' data interests (Topic) [4]. To query distributed events, the event stream of the Altibase DSM is mapped on the Topic of the Pub/Sub Model. Using this mapping, physically separated stream queries (EPAs) can send and receive the events without socket programming.

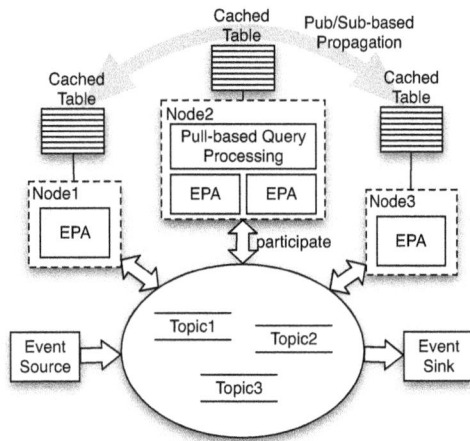

Figure 1: Publish/Subscribe-based Distribution

SPE converts streaming events into a window, which is a temporal relational table to perform online aggregation. The events from the window are then reconverted into streaming events. Bidirectional conversion between stream and relation is inevitably used for aggregation in SPE. Likewise, we believe that the manageability of relational tables in SPEs and transition between push-based to pull-based processing are required in use-cases mentioned.

As mentioned in [2], stream queries may join event streams and relational tables. Because tables are mostly stored in DBMS, many SPEs implement various input adapters like feeding data from DBMS and fetching tuples from DBMS using DBC interfaces. However, for this reason, the Altibase DSM support the relational table feature that can be updated from the DBMS tables. While a window for online aggregation is designed for append-only streaming events, the CTable can perform update and delete operations.

In addition, we found that legacy systems hardly change from pull-based to push-based processing architecture. Despite the benefits of SPE, customers and application developers complain about the difficulty in combining stream applications with legacy applications and prefer to use pull-based processing while minimizing the changes in legacy systems. To reduce this introduction cost, the CTable maintains the most recent record for each key to cache unbound streaming events, and, internally, it exploits the index structure, which is optimized for frequent update operations. CTable's recent values suit applications such as monitoring a dynamic dashboard containing stock market symbols [6]. For event-processing, DSM executes a set of queries before the events occur. Subsequently, when an event meets the query condition, DSM notifies a user (push-based processing). However, the queries containing only CTable(s) on the FROM clause are classified as 'CTable query' and are executed in pull-based processing (open-fetch-close method) through ODBC and JDBC interfaces.

3. DEMONSTRATION

We apply Altibase DSM to track sex offenders and as a bus arrival time information system.

Sex Offender Tracking System: Figure 2 is one of the machine-to-machine (M2M) communication service usages. Paroled sex offenders are obligated to stay in the district designated by law. For monitoring purposes, such individuals are obligated to wear an electronic anklet embedded with GPS and/or RFID for location tracking and a CDMA module for communication. Each offender has a

different designated district, jurisdiction, and related organizations (e.g., Police Agency, Public Prosecutors' Office). This information is scattered across different databases and is joined using the location data of the offender. Altibase DSM joins the location tracking events and CTables from the remote databases.

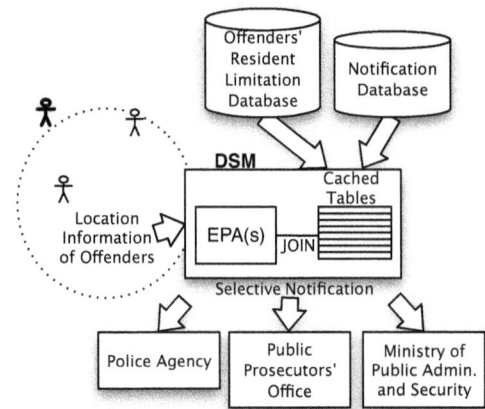

Figure 2: A Use Case for CTable

Bus Arrival Information System: In Seoul, South Korea, bus arrival information at each station and the current location of the buses for each route are provided online. Passengers are able to estimate the waiting time for a particular bus at the station. Possible implementations include 1) electric display at a bus station, 2) bus routes, and arrival information on a website, and 3) smartphone applications. The three abovementioned systems provide information to users in the pull-based processing mode, even though bus location events are processed in the push-based mode. To this end, the Altibase DSM and its CTable are applied.

4. ACKNOWLEDGMENTS

We would like to thank Dmitry Klimkin, Maxim Tomilov, and all other members of Altibase DSM Team for their efforts with development of this product. We are also grateful to Sungmin Kim, Sungil Bae, and Jae-Keoung Lim of Altibase for continuous supporting to our direction.

5. REFERENCES

[1] D. J. Abadi, Y. Ahmad, M. Balazinska, U. Cetintemel, M. Cherniack, J. Hwang, W. Lindner, A. S. Maskey, A. Rasin, E. Ryvkina, N. Tatbul, Y. Xing, and S. Zdonik. The design of the borealis stream processing engine. In *CIDR*, 2005.

[2] B. Babcock, S. Babu, M. Datar, R. Motwani, and J. Widom. Models and issues in data stream systems. In *In roceedings of the 21st ACM PODS*, pages 1–16, 2002.

[3] M. Cherniack, H. Balakrishnan, M. Balazinska, D. Carney, U. Çetintemel, Y. Xing, and S. B. Zdonik. Scalable distributed stream processing. In *CIDR*, 2003.

[4] Y. Diao and M. J. Franklin. Publish/subscribe over streams. In *Encyclopedia of Database Systems*, pages 2211–2216. 2009.

[5] J. M. Hellerstein and M. Stonebraker. *Readings in Database Systems: 4th Edition*, chapter 10. The MIT Press, 2005.

[6] A. Moga, I. Botan, and N. Tatbul. Upstream: Storage-centric load management for data streams with update semantics. Technical report, ETH Zurich, CS Dept., 2009.

Demo: Efficient Energy Consumption in a Smart Office Based on Intelligent Complex Event Processing

Yongchun Xu
FZI, Research Center
for Information
Technology
Haid-und-Neu-Str. 10-
14,
76131 Karlsruhe,
Germany
xu@fzi.de

Ljiljana Stojanovic
FZI, Research Center
for Information
Technology
Haid-und-Neu-Str. 10-
14,
76131 Karlsruhe,
Germany
stojanov@fzi.de

Jun Ma
FZI, Research Center
for Information
Technology
Haid-und-Neu-Str. 10-
14,
76131 Karlsruhe,
Germany
junma@fzi.de

Darko Anicic
FZI, Research Center
for Information
Technology
Haid-und-Neu-Str. 10-
14,
76131 Karlsruhe,
Germany
danicic@fzi.de

ABSTRACT

In this demo we present a scenario of an efficient energy consumption in a smart office based on the intelligent processing of events coming from the conventional ("cheap") sensors.

The results are very encouraging: smart decisions for the efficient usage of energy can be made by the intelligent processing of "cheap" sensor events.

Categories and Subject Descriptors

H.3.4 [Information Systems]: SYSTEMS AND SOFTWARE – information networks.

General Terms

Design, Management, Experimentation, Performance, Economics.

Keywords

Energy Efficiency, Intelligent Complex Event Processing, Smart Office

1. INTRODUCTION

This demo presents the results of our work towards a control system that intelligently processes signals from simple sensors in order to discover situations to be reacted on. Therefore, the main idea is to show that putting more intelligence in processing signals/events enables more efficient detection of the situation of interest, even in the case when signals are very simple. Therefore, the meaning of complex situations can be built based on simple events, if they are processed in a complex way.

We use the energy efficiency as the application domain. Moreover, we selected occupancy control in public office use case as a very promising one for demonstrating the advantages of our approach from two reasons:

- there are many situations of interests that can be defined in the context of the energy consumption

- these situations of interests will be evolving during the time.

These two requirements imply the necessity of more expressive patterns to be detected (complex situations) and the need for a more systematic approach for the management of patterns. In this demo we treat only the first requirement.

In the nutshell of this demo is the combination of the iCEP approach (www.icep.fzi.de) and a sensor system.

2. iCEP APPROACH FOR THE ENERGY EFFICIENCY

2.1. Architecture

Figure 1 shows the conceptual architecture of the combination of sensor system and iCEP system. On the left side is the sensor system containing sensors and actuators. On the right side is the iCEP system, which can process the sensor information in real time.

Figure 1: The conceptual architecture of the iCEP approach system for energy efficiency

Event adapter transforms the received sensing information to sensor events according to the event schema, which describes the event format that can be recognized by CEP engine. It has two sub components: event schema manager and event transformer. Event schema manager manages the event schema and sends the corresponding schema to event transformer, when the sensing information is received from sensors. Event transformer transforms the Sensing information to sensor events.

Knowledgebase service manages the all knowledgebase, which are used in our system, such as Domain Ontology. Domain ontology models the background knowledge of the use cases.

CEP engine (ETALIS) is the core of the iCEP system. ETALIS[1] is based on a declarative semantics, grounded in Logic Programming. Complex events are derived from simpler events by means of deductive rules. Due to its root in logic, ETALIS engine also supports reasoning about events, context, and real-time

---

[1] http://code.google.com/p/etalis/

379

complex situations. ETALIS loads the domain ontology and does reasoning in the domain ontology to achieve intelligent Complex Event Processing (iCEP).

ESB Bus is Enterprise Service Bus, such as Petals[2]. ESB uses publish/subscribe mechanism to transmit the data.

Pattern Editor UI provides a graphic editor environment to users. Pattern service manages all defined patterns and sends them to the CEP engine.

Interpretation service interprets the results of the complex event processing and then Procedure manager sends the commands to the actuators.

2.2. Modeling domain knowledge

By using complex event processing (CEP) in a sensor system users can define or change the event processing procedure through patterns without changing the hardware or software of the system. The only problem is the pattern definition is not so easy for most users, especially in the sensor system.

Our iCEP system uses domain ontology that models the background knowledge to solve the above problem. The information of sensors, actuators and associated real world entities are modeled in the Domain ontology.

In our iCEP system the events can be divided into two groups. The first event group is *sensor/actuator event* that is created by sensors or will be sent to actuators.

The second event group is *RWE Status event (real world entity event)*, which presents the status of the real world entities and can be easily understood by most users. Furthermore *RWE Status event* can also be used to describe the status of a kind of real world entities, which have the same character, in this way we call it *universal RWE Status event*.

The patterns used in iCEP system can also be categorized into two types. The first pattern type is called a *transformation pattern*. We use transformation patterns to transform *sensor/actuator event* to *RWE Status event* or reversely. The transformation pattern should be defined by the user, who knows not only the sensor system but also the association between the sensors (actuators) and the real world entities.

2.3. Modeling complex situations

Complex situation are modeled using so called procedure patterns These patterns are used to describe the workflows of the system, i.e. which status of the real world entity must be achieved when the conditions (the statuses of itself or other real world entities) are met. The procedure patterns consist of only RWE Status events.

The procedure pattern can be defined in two ways. Firstly users can use RWE Status events describing the status of certain real world entities to define the procedure patterns. Because the RWE Status events describing the status of certain real world entities are easy to understand, most users are able to create the patterns.

In the second way users can use universal RWE Status event in the patterns.

As already mentioned, one of the main advantages of our approach is the possibility to define the situations of interests in a

declarative way and reason about them based on the incoming sensor data.

3. Demo

In order to illustrate the abstractions introduced by our system, we will demonstrate a very illustrative example for the occupancy control based on the office context presented in Figure 3.

In the traditional approaches, the situation of interests:

"a person left the room and her/his desk lamp should be switched off within 5 sec"

must be described by using one rule for each possible situation. An example is illustrated in Figure 2: a person left the room by traversing from Region F, through Region D and B till the door.

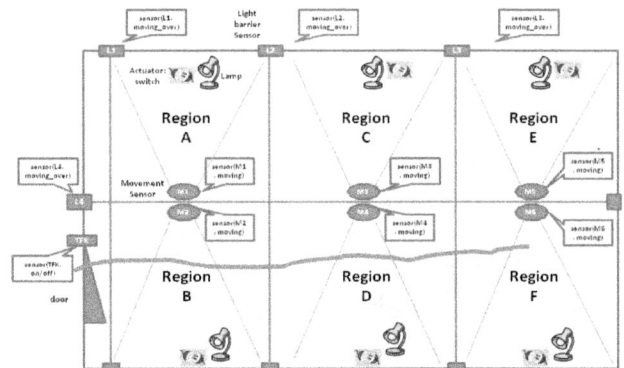

Figure 2: A possible path from the office desk to the door: a situation that can lead to switching off the lamp at the desk in the Region F

Therefore, traditional approaches must cover use all possible "evacuation" paths which is a tedious and error prone process. On the other hand, in our approach there is only one logic-based statement that covers all requested situations, by describing them declaratively.

This demo will show how flexible is our approach: we can very easily introduce new situations or evolve already existing situations.

The demo will present also a novel method for the visualization of complex events, sketched in Figure 3.

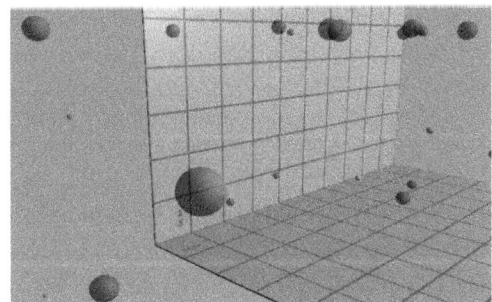

Figure 3: 3D Visualization of complex events

VISIO is a platform for the 3-D visualization of complex events. The innovative approach enables representation of different parameters related to the importance of an event, supporting a decision maker in better understanding of an emerging situation. The tool enables real-time decomposition of complex situations into more understandable visualization elements.

---

[2] http://petals.ow2.org/

Demo: eQoSystem – Supporting Fluid Distributed Service-Oriented Workflows

Vinod Muthusamy, Young Yoon, Mohammad Sadoghi, and Hans-Arno Jacobsen
Middleware Systems Research Group
University of Toronto
Toronto, Canada
{vinod, yoon, mo, jacobsen}@msrg.utoronto.ca

Categories and Subject Descriptors

H.4 [**Information Systems Applications**]: Miscellaneous

General Terms

Design, Management

1. INTRODUCTION

Many distributed applications have emerged as Web mashups [ ], as well as loosely-coupled decentralized services predominant in a business ecosystem [ ]. Many of these applications are implemented as service-oriented workflows and operated over cloud infrastructures. As a result, these applications demand agile development processes and low-touch maintenance life-cycles.

Furthermore, in the cloud environment, application developers must account for the complex multi-tiered ecosystem that includes the services and resources they depend on, but which none of the developers have much control over. Therefore, it is essential for application developers to have tools that proactively adapt the application to the changes of the underlying ecosystem. We meet this need through eQoSystem[1], a framework that provides distributed workflow processing, declarative modeling of service-level agreements (SLAs), event-driven resource selection, and mobility of distributed tasks.

In this demonstration, we focus on dynamically redeploying distributed workflows such that a whole or a part of the workflow is allocated to different execution engines that are possibly geographically dispersed. The redeployment of the workflow is enabled by a federated content-based publish/subscribe overlay that also serves as the basis for driving the autonomous and event-driven execution of workflows.

2. ARCHITECTURE

eQoSystem takes a novel architectural approach whereby individual process instances are executed in a distributed manner. As shown in Figure 1, a distributed execution engine decomposes a workflow, such as a BPEL process, into its individual tasks and deploys these tasks to any set of execution engines in the system. These tasks then coordinate by publishing and consuming events over the PADRES[2] distributed publish/subscribe broker overlay [ ]. For example, consider the execution of a task t_i that depends on

---

[1]Project website at http://eqosystem.msrg.org.
[2]Available for download at http://padres.msrg.org.

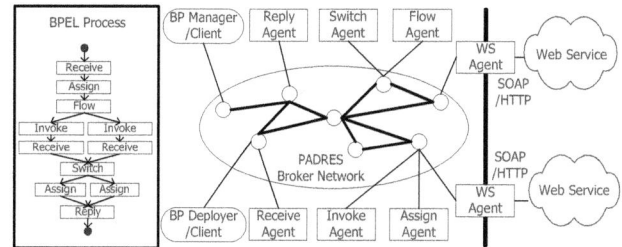

Figure 1: Distributed workflow execution platform

the completion of other tasks. To guarantee correctness, the task t_i must subscribe to the composite events that indicate the completion of all its dependent tasks [ ]. The brokers in our distributed model decouple tasks in space and time as publishers and subscribers, thus making the publish/subscribe paradigm particularly well-suited for large and dynamic distributed workflows.

The execution engines in this architecture can be light-weight as they only execute fine-grained tasks, as opposed to complete processes. Another benefit of such an architecture is the ability to deploy portions of processes close to the data they operate on, thereby minimizing bandwidth and latency costs of a process. For example, for data intensive workflows, it is possible to deploy only those portions of the process that require access to large data sets close to their respective data sources.

3. FEATURES

In this section, we review the key features of eQoSystem: declarative SLA modeling, event-driven resource discovery, and transactional mobility.

3.1 Declarative SLA modeling

eQoSystem offers an approach to simplify the development of workflows governed by SLAs [ ]. An SLA model, extended from the WSLA language, is used to precisely express the business goals of the process. Portions of the SLA are then mapped to a cost model that captures various relevant factors. For example, the distribution cost represents the overhead of distributing a process into fine-grained tasks, the engine cost captures the resource usage of a task on the engine it is executing at, and the service cost relates to the expense of calling external services.

The model is loosely coupled with the workflow that it is referencing. Developers can therefore evolve both the workflow and SLA model concurrently. In addition, the proposed model is highly modular, and makes it easy to construct complex SLA contracts by composing and extending elementary SLAs.

3.2 Event-driven resource discovery

eQoSystem supports three resource discovery models: static, dynamic, and continuous [ ]. The static model is used to discover resources with fixed attributes, the dynamic model is used for resources with attributes that may be updated, and the continuous model is used to allow for real-time notifications of newly registered resources. All three models can co-exist in one system and complement one another. In addition, a similarity-based optimization algorithm takes advantage of publish/subscribe covering techniques in order to reuse the discovery results among different concurrent discovery requests.

3.3 Transactional mobility

It is desirable for the movement of tasks in a publish/subscribe-based distributed workflow engine to be transparent to both the moving task and those it interacts with, such that an application consisting of stationary clients behaves the same as one where clients move. Among other things, this means that clients should not miss any notifications while moving, and their movement should not be visible to others. eQoSystem enables the guaranteed movement of tasks of the distributed workflow according to well-defined properties [ ]. The transactional concerns of the publish/subscribe system, client, and routing layers are outlined and atomicity, consistency, and isolation properties for these three layers are specified. Unlike protocols where client mobility is handled by the

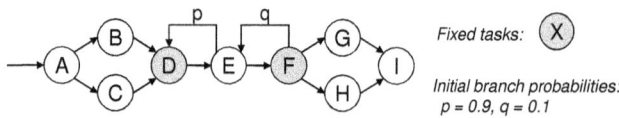

Figure 2: Evaluated sample workflow

4. USE CASES

Given the aforementioned features, eQoSystem can be utilized in many ways. For instance, workflows can be dynamically redeployed at runtime based on the automated SLA monitoring and periodic discovery of candidate resources that can better serve the tasks in the workflows.

The following experiment highlights the benefit of runtime redeployment of a simple workflow consisting of nine tasks as depicted in Figure 2. The tasks are mapped to nine execution engines, with each engine running on a machine with a 1.6 GHz Xeon processor and 4 GB of memory. The execution engines utilize an overlay of PADRES publish/subscribe brokers communicating over a 1 Gbps switch. The process is invoked every second, and each process instance traverses the process graph according to the branch probabilities p and q as indicated in Figure 2. Notice that with 90% probability task E transitions to task D (as opposed to task F) resulting in a process hotspot at tasks D and E. About halfway through the experiment, the transition probabilities of p and q are reversed, so that a hotspot now occurs at tasks E and F. Due to the initial tight loop around tasks D and E, the message overhead can be reduced if these tasks were deployed on the same engine. Hence, it is beneficial to first reconfigure the workflow deployment by moving tasks A, B, C, and E to the same engine as task D, and by redeploying tasks G, H, and

5. DEMONSTRATION

The demonstration is focused on the mobility of distributed workflows. We show how eQoSystem is developed on top of PADRES

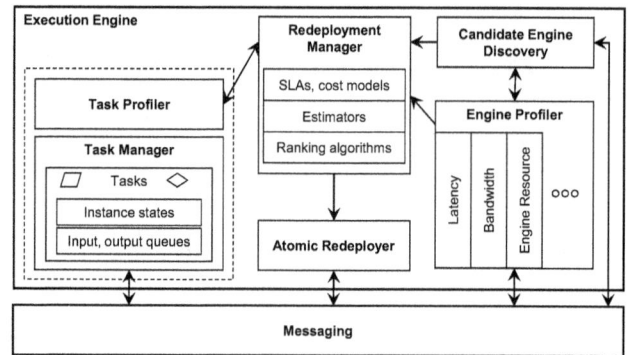

Figure 3: Architecture of autonomic execution engine

by presenting the usage of key publish/subscribe messaging APIs in-depth at a source level. Then, we illustrate the end-to-end scenario of using eQoSystem: (1) decomposition of a workflow; (2) deployment of decomposed tasks; (3) event-driven execution of the workflow; and (4) migration of tasks to different locations. This demonstration is accompanied by a workflow execution monitor that tracks messages traversing the PADRES broker overlay network.

6. CURRENT STATUS

More advanced components (as shown Figure 3) are being developed to automate the redeployment procedure. Specifically, a *Candidate Engine Discovery* component is used to find other execution engines in the system, and these candidates are periodically probed by the *Engine Profiler* to gather various statistics. The *Redeployment Manager* computes the cost function for each task executing in the engine, and determines if a more optimal placement of the task is available among the known candidate engines. Finally, tasks that are to be moved are redeployed using the *Atomic Redeployer* component which is responsible for ensuring that the movement of the task does not affect the execution of the workflow.

7. REFERENCES

[1] Yahoo Pipes. http://pipes.yahoo.com.

[2] E. Fidler, H.-A. Jacobsen, G. Li, and S. Mankovski. Distributed publish/subscribe for workflow management. In *ICFI*, 2005.

[3] S. Hu, V. Muthusamy, G. Li, and H.-A. Jacobsen. Distributed automatic service composition in large-scale systems. In *DEBS*, 2008.

[4] S. Hu, V. Muthusamy, G. Li, and H.-A. Jacobsen. Transactional mobility in distributed content-based publish/subscribe systems. In *ICDCS*, 2009.

[5] G. Li, V. Muthusamy, and H.-A. Jacobsen. A distributed service-oriented architecture for business process execution. *ACM Trans. Web*, 2010.

[6] V. Muthusamy, H.-A. Jacobsen, T. Chau, A. Chan, and P. Coulthard. SLA-driven business process management in soa. In *CASCON*, 2009.

[7] W. Yan, S. Hu, V. Muthusamy, H.-A. Jacobsen, and L. Zha. Efficient event-based resource discovery. In *DEBS*, 2009.

Demo: A Scenario and Design Pattern Based Tool for Modeling and Evaluating Implementations of Event-based Reactive Systems

Vojislav D. Radonjic
School of Computer
Science,
Carleton University
Ottawa, Canada
radonjic@acm.org

Soheila Bashardoust
School of Computer
Science,
Carleton University
Ottawa, Canada
sbtajali@scs.carleton.ca

Jean-Pierre Corriveau
School of Computer
Science,
Carleton University
Ottawa, Canada
jeanpier@scs.carleton.ca

Dave Arnold
School of Computer
Science,
Carleton University
Ottawa, Canada
davearnold@me.com

ABSTRACT

Scenarios are useful in modeling external behavior of a system, and design patterns are useful in bridging from what is required to how to build it in a given context. Together, scenarios and design patterns, can be a basis for an effective approach to modeling and evaluating alternative designs of event-driven reactive systems. However, both techniques are informal and imprecise for purposes of evaluating implementations. Here we demo a tool based on a precise model of scenarios and design patterns that allows for executing and evaluating a system's implementation relative to required scenarios and design alternatives.

Categories and Subject Descriptors

D.2.2 [**Software Engineering**]: Design Tools and Techniques – Computer-aided software engineering

General Terms

Measurement, Design, Experimentation.

Keywords

design patterns; scenarios; design variant selection;

1. INTRODUCTION

In this demo we will present an evaluation tool that brings together two widely used but rarely combined techniques – scenarios and design patterns. First, we will show how to model to a high degree of precision event-response requirements of a system using a particular executable form of scenarios (ACL scenarios [2]). Second, we describe a novel pattern-based model for design and evaluation of event-based reactive systems.[1] And, third, we present an end-to-end walk through on the example of an event-driven control system.

2. PRECISION MODELING OF SCENARIOS AND DESIGN PATTERNS: A NECESSARY CHALLENGE

Precise models are more complex and harder to use, but are necessary if we are to make them useful in evaluating implementations.

Use-cases [11] are the most widespread form of scenarios. They are a well established, understood and standard technique for modeling, however, they lack precision necessary for use in executable forms of system evaluation. Corriveau and Arnold have addressed this in ACL [2], an executable requirements modeling language. Arnold has developed a corresponding tool, Validation Framework (VF) for evaluating .NET executables relative to ACL specified requirements models [2].

Design Patterns and their use are challenging to represent with existing modeling techniques [1]. In particular, it is not clear how we can evaluate a decision made in selecting a given pattern and a given variant of that pattern. The first step is making visible the space of choices and the criteria for selection by modeling the content of a pattern description. The second step is building a tool that allows us to represent that model, the choices, the selection criteria and the ability to evaluate and differentiate these choices.

Helm et al. [5] present the 'root' modeling attempt at representing reusable and implementation-independent object-oriented designs. They chose precision over ease of use of the model by the target audience, the day to day developer: the result was few users. A few years on, with the lesson learnt, a more accessible and informal, template based model was used to represent the GoF design pattern catalogue [3]: the biggest selling software engineering book to date [9]. Our approach, in essence, aims to achieve the precision of the contract model, with the ease of use of the GoF model. We present an implementation of that model in ACL and VF [2].

Design Patterns and their use is challenging to model because of the following:

- Traceability [12] from use cases to variations and their implementations,
- Variability modeling [13] in analysis, design, and implementation,
- Interaction between traceability and variability, and
- Evaluation of selected variants relative to intents and detailed design properties, and corresponding implementations.

The model we have developed [1] to address the above challenges is based on generative modeling and programming techniques [8], combined with modeling-by-contract [2][4][5][6].

3. IMPLEMENTING THE MODEL USING ACL AND VF

We present several GoF [3] design patterns modeled in ACL [2] with corresponding implementations. In particular, we show how the selection forces are represented through metrics, and how the implementations are evaluated both in terms of their functional and non-functional design requirements.

The Validation Framework, Fig. 1, allows us to evaluate candidate implementations of ACL specified design patterns and their variants. In particular, it allows us to implement a model of traceability from designs to implementations; specifically, from detailed design properties, i.e. consequences, to candidate implementations.

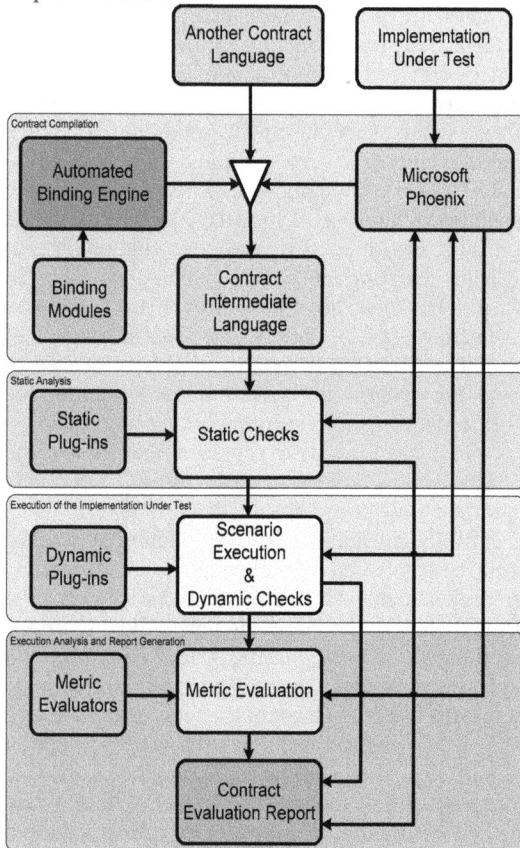

Figure 1: Validation Framework [2]

We additionally contrast our approach to that of Jezequel et al. [6], Antkiewicz et al. [10], and Pattern-Based Engineering of Ackerman and Gonzalez [7].

4. DEMO: A SIMPLE EVENT-DRIVEN CONTROL SYSTEM

First, we will show how to model to a high degree of precision event-response requirements of the system using ACL scenarios [2]. Second, we will show several pattern-based design alternatives, and, third we will show how to evaluate the corresponding alternative implementations relative to the requirements model and the design alternatives.

5. REFERENCES

[1] V. D. Radonjic, *An Open Pattern-based Framework for Evaluating Software Systems*, PhD. Thesis (in preparation) Carleton University, School of Computer Science.

[2] D. Arnold and J.-P. Corriveau, *Validation Framework and Another Contract Language, http://vf.davearnold.ca/*

[3] E. Gamma, R. Helm, R. Johnson, & J. Vlissides, *Design Patterns-Elements of Reusable Object-Oriented Software* (Reading, MA: Addison-Wesley, 1994).

[4] B. Meyer, "Design by Contract," IEEE Computer, vol. 25, no. 10, pp. 40-51, October 1992.

[5] Helm, R., Holland, I., Gangopadhyay, D.: *Contracts: Specifying Behavioral Compositions in Object-Oriented Systems*. In proceedings of the Object-Oriented Programming Systems, Languages and Applications Conference (OOPSLA'90), pp. 169-180, October 1990.

[6] J.-M. Jezequel, M. Train, and C. Mingins, *Design Patterns and Contracts*, Addison-Wesley, 2000.

[7] L. Ackerman and C. Gonzalez, Pattern-Based Engineering, Successfully Delivering Solutions via Patterns, Addison-Wesley, 2011.

[8] K. Czarnecki and U. Eisenecker: *Generative Programming: Methods, Tools, and Applications*, Addison-Wesley, June 2000.

[9] http://en.wikipedia.org/wiki/Design_Patterns

[10] M. Antkiewicz, K. Czarnecki, and M. Stephan, *Engineering of Framework-Specific Modeling Languages*, IEEE Trans. Software Eng., vol. 35, no. 6, pp. 795-824, Nov/Dec 2009.

[11] I. Jacobson, M. Christerson, P. Jonsson and G. Overgaard: *Object-Oriented Software Engineering: A Use Case Driven Approach*, Addison-Wesley, 1992.

[12] J.-P. Corriveau, *Traceability Process for Large OO Projects*, IEEE Computer, pp. 63-68, Sep 1996.

[13] S. Bashardoust, V.D. Radonjic and J.-P. Corriveau and D. Arnold, *Challenges of Variability in Model-Driven and Transformational Approaches: A Systematic Survey*, Workshop on Variability in Software Architecture, WICSA2011, Boulder, Colorado, USA, 2011.

Poster: Cost Analysis for Complex In-Network Event Processing in Heterogeneous Wireless Sensor Networks

Mumraiz Khan Kasi
Department of Computer Science
University of Waikato, New Zealand
mk218@waikato.ac.nz

Annika Hinze
Department of Computer Science
University of Waikato, New Zealand
a.hinze@waikato.ac.nz

ABSTRACT

Complex event processing requires events to be integrated from multiple sources. In *heterogeneous* Wireless Sensor Networks, this integration is performed at powerful gateway nodes, requiring continuous communication among sensor nodes and with gateway nodes. We propose to use semantic context-aware in-network processing for heterogeneous WSN. Our energy-based cost model shows under which circumstances in-network processing is advantageous for heterogenous networks. Reduced energy consumption will lead to extended network lifetime.

Categories and Subject Descriptors

C.2.1 [**Network Architecture**]: Wireless Sensor Networks

General Terms

Theory, Design, Performance

1. INTRODUCTION

A Wireless Sensor Network (WSN) consists of small sensor nodes capturing event data of environmental phenomena. Traditional (homogeneous) WSN support sensors of one type only; with recent developments having lead to availability of *heterogenous* WSN supporting a variety of node types [2, 6]. So far, complex event detection in heterogeneous WSN has to be done at central gateway nodes (e.g. [6]). In-network processing has only been implemented for homogeneous WSN (e.g. [1]).

In centralized aggregation (see Fig. 1), sensor nodes have no knowledge of the significance of the events at their own level; it causes unnecessary energy consumption. WSN are often employed in remote areas; minimizing energy consumption is of critical importance.

We propose to perform data integration at the sensor node level for maximum energy benefits. Due to the heterogeneity of the network, each node now needs to be aware of the neighboring sensor types to make routing decisions (i.e, the node's context). Note that mobile WSNs have changing node contacts. Moreover, semantic information [6] may need to be encoded in each node to support complex event processing. Employment of such semantic context-aware in-network processing in heterogeneous WSN [3] has the potential to reduce the energy consumption for event communication but may incur additional processing costs (see Fig. 2). This

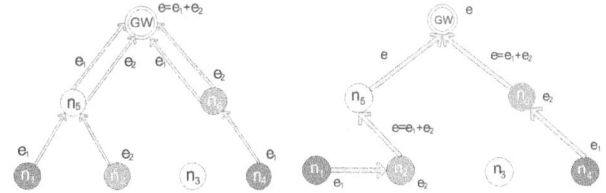

Figure 1: Centralized　　　　**Figure 2: In-network**

paper develops an energy-based cost model to explore under which circumstances in-network processing is advantageous for heterogenous networks.

Cost models for in-network data processing have been proposed considering hardware parameters [2, 7] and for routing in homogeneous WSN[4, 5]. To the best of our knowledge, no cost model has been proposed for processing and routing in heterogeneous WSN.

2. COMPARATIVE COST MODEL

Costs are measured as energy consumed at sensor nodes for sensing, processing and communicating events to the gateway node. The total energy consumption of a WSN depends on the set of events E available to the network and the set of filters F for simple and complex events:

$$C_{wsn}(E, F) = C_{sense}(E) + C_{proc}(E, F) + C_{comm}(E, F)$$
$$= \sum_{e \in E} C_{sense}(e) + \sum_{\substack{e \in E \\ f \in F}} C_{proc}(e, f) + \sum_{e \in E_F} C_{comm}(e)$$

where E_F refers to the set of events being communicated within the network (i.e. the events $e \in E$ that are matched by filters $f \in F$). Note that $\varnothing \subseteq E_F \subseteq E$ if F contains only simple event filters ($E_F = E_F^{sim}$). For complex events, E_F may be larger or smaller than E when using in-network processing ($E_F = E_F^{sim} + E_F^{com}$). For centralized processing it always holds $E_F = E_F^{sim}$.

To compare the costs of in-network processing $C_{wsn}^{I}(E, F)$ to centralized processing $C_{wsn}^{C}(E, F)$, we need to evaluate each of the three cost components. Naturally, the costs of sensing events are equal $C_{sense}^{I}(E) = C_{sense}^{C}(E)$ (equal node sets and sensors).

Processing cost. In the centralized setup, the processing cost at each sensor node $n_i \in N$ (set of all nodes N, $i \in \mathbb{N}$) is twofold: simple event filtering at the source node $n(e) \in N$ of an event e (F^{sim} being the set of simple event filters) and routing table looking-up to identify the direction of communication towards the gateway node GW:

$$C_{proc}^{c}(E, F) = \sum_{\substack{e \in E \\ f \in F^{sim}}} C_{filter}(e, f) + \sum_{\substack{n_i \in N \\ e \in E_F^{sim}}} C_{rlup}(e, n_i) * \chi(n_i, n(e), GW)$$

with $\chi(n_i, n(e), GW) = \begin{cases} 1 & n_i \text{ part of route from } n(e) \text{ to GW} \\ 0 & otherwise \end{cases}$

Note that any calculations at the gateway node do not need to be factored in for energy consumption.

In our complex in-network processing, a source node $n(e)$ consumes energy by filtering the sensed event data for simple events and processing the matching events for semantic annotation. Source nodes and other nodes en-route to the gateway additionally perform filtering of complex events, semantic annotation of complex events and routing. The complex event detection may require several sensor nodes to recognize an event; nodes that identify complex events are called rendezvous nodes. There may be several rendezvous nodes identifying parts of complex events ($r(e)$ refers to the number of nodes for event e). The overall processing costs are:

$$C^I_{proc}(E, F) = \sum_{\substack{e \in E \\ f \in F^{sim}}} C_{filter}(e, f) + \sum_{e \in E^{sim}_F} C_{semantic}(e)$$
$$+ \sum_{\substack{e \in E^{com}_F \\ f \in F^{com}}} C_{filter}(e, f) * r(e) + \sum_{e \in E^{com}_F} C_{semantic}(e)$$
$$+ \sum_{\substack{n_i \in N \\ e \in E_F}} C_{rlup}(e, n_i) * \bar{\chi}(n_i, n(e), GW)$$

with $\bar{\chi}(n_i, n(e), GW) = \begin{cases} 1 & n_i \text{ part of the context-dependent} \\ & \text{route from } n(e) \text{ to GW} \\ 0 & otherwise \end{cases}$

The different routing paths of χ and $\bar{\chi}$ are illustrated in Figures 1 and 2, respectively. By comparing the above equations we see that $C^C_{proc}(E, F) \le C^I_{proc}(E, F)$.

Communication cost. In the centralized setup, all sensor nodes forward their matching simple events $e \in E^{sim}_F$ to the gateway node according to their sampling frequency $f(e)$ traversing along a multi-hop network. Each hop within the network is assumed to incur a base energy cost of C^{hop}, which may vary for different WSN. Complex events are detected at the gateway node. Their contributing simple events need to be communicated to the gateway. For a complex event e^c, the set of all contributing simple events is denoted by $E^{sim}_F(e^c)$.

$$C^C_{comm}(E, F) = \sum_{\substack{n_i \in N \\ e \in E^{sim}_F}} f(e) * \chi(n_i, n(e), GW) * C^{hop}$$
$$+ \sum_{\substack{n_i \in N \\ e^c \in E^{com}_F \\ e \in E^{sim}_F(e^c)}} (f(e, n_i) \times \chi(n_i, n(e), GW)) * C^{hop}$$

Simple event detection in in-network processing is identical. For complex event detection, let R be the set of all rendezvous nodes and $S(n_r, e^c)$ the set of all sensor nodes that collaborate to form a complex event e^c at node n_r. Overall communication costs are:

$$C^I_{comm}(E, F) = C^I_{comm}(E^{sim}_F) + C^I_{comm}(E^{com}_F)$$
$$= \sum_{\substack{n_i \in N \\ e \in E^{sim}_F}} f(e) * \bar{\chi}(n_i, n(e), GW) * C^{hop}$$
$$+ \sum_{\substack{n_r \in R \\ n_i \in N \\ e^c \in E^{com}_F}} \left(f(e^c, n_r) \times \bar{\chi}(n_i, n_r, GW) \right.$$
$$+ \sum_{\substack{n_j \in S(n_r, e^c) \\ e \in E^{sim}_F(e^c)}} \left. (f(e, n_j) \times \bar{\chi}(n_j, n(e), n_r)) \right) * C^{hop}$$

For both centralized and in-network communication, we omitted the cost-reduction factor caused by overlaps between simple events and events contributing to complex events.

3. TRADE-OFF ANALYSIS

We now analyse the conditions for in-network processing to be advantageous for energy consumption, i.e., $C^I_{wsn}(E, F) \le C^C_{wsn}(E, F)$. For this to be true, we require the following condition while using the equations of Section 2:

$$\sum_{e \in E_F} C_{semantic}(e) + \sum_{\substack{e \in E^{com}_F \\ f \in F^{com}}} C_{filter}(e, f) * r(e) +$$
$$\sum_{\substack{n_i \in \Delta N \\ e \in E_F}} C_{rlup}(e, n_i) \le C^C_{comm}(E, F) - C^I_{comm}(E, F)$$

with ΔN being the set of nodes that may additionally have to be traversed using the context-aware routing. Thus the condition states that the costs for semantic annotation, complex filtering and routing-table lookup in additional nodes have to be less or equal to the improvements in communication cost.

Communication costs will decrease if the frequency of simple events contributing to complex events is higher than that of the complex events. This has been argued in [4, 5]. However, this depends on both the set of filter definitions F and the WSN layout.

4. CONCLUSION

The limited energy resources necessitate energy-efficient processing and communication of events in WSN. Cost models for in-network processing in homogenous WSN report a trade-off for communication cost that depends on the application domain [4, 5]. No calculations for the expected higher processing load had been proposed, as previous work focussed on cost of transmission [5].

This paper analysed the energy costs for complex event processing in heterogenous environments. The costs of a centralized approach for complex events (simple events are processed in the distributed WSN) were compared with the fully-distributed approach of semantic context-aware in-network processing. We identified a trade-off between lower communication cost and higher processing cost due to sematic annotation, context analysis for routing and processing of complex events. Any algorithms for context-based routing and semantic analysis of complex events need to be under our identified threshold for the increase in energy consumption.

In our model, by processing event data locally, the sensor nodes will make decisions quickly and remotely without the need for instructions from gateway nodes. This makes our model particularly appropriate for mobile environments and situations in which a stable WSN cannot be guaranteed.

5. REFERENCES

[1] Y. Chen, H. V. Leong, M. Xu, J. Cao, K. C. C. Chan, and A. T. S. Chan. In-network data processing for wireless sensor networks. In *Proc. Int. Conf. on Mobile Data Management (MDM '06)*, 2006.

[2] D. Jung, T. Teixeira, and A. Savvides. Sensor node lifetime analysis: Models and tools. *ACM Trans. Sen. Netw.*, 5:3:1–3:33, February 2009.

[3] M. Kasi and A. Hinze. In-network semantic data integration for energy efficient wireless sensor networks. In *NZCSRSC'11 workshop*, 2011.

[4] K. Terfloth, K. Hahn, and A. Voisard. On the cost of shifting event processing within wireless environments. In *Event Processing*, number 07191 in Dagstuhl Seminar Proceedings, 2007.

[5] A. Voisard and H. Ziekow. Designing sensor-based event processing infrastructures. In *Proc. IEEE Hawaii Int. Conf. on System Sciences (HICSS'10)*, pages 1–10, 2010.

[6] A. Wun, M. Petrovi, and H.-A. Jacobsen. A system for semantic data fusion in sensor networks. In *Proc. of International Conference on Distributed Event-Based Systems*, DEBS '07, pages 75–79, 2007.

[7] L. Yuan, X. Wang, J. Gan, and Y. Zhao. A data gathering algorithm based on mobile agent and emergent event-driven in cluster-based wsn. *Journal of Networks*, 5(10), 2010.

Poster: Collaboration Pattern Assistant, an Event-driven Tool for Supporting Pattern-based Collaborations

Nikos Papageorgiou
National Technical
University of Athens
Iroon Polytechniou 9,

15780 Zografos, Greece
+302107721227

npapag@mail.ntua.gr

Yiannis Verginadis
National Technical
University of Athens
Iroon Polytechniou 9,

15780 Zografos, Greece
+302107721227

jverg@mail.ntua.gr

Dimitris Apostolou
University of Piraeus
Karaoli & Dimitriou 80
18534 Piraeus, Greece
+302104142476

dapost@unipi.gr

Gregoris Mentzas
National Technical University
of Athens
Iroon Polytechniou 9,

15780 Zografos, Greece
+302107722415

gmentzas@mail.ntua.gr

ABSTRACT

Modern enterprises collaborate intensively in order to operate effectively in a convoluted, dynamic business environment. To facilitate collaborations, patterns have been exploited as models for repeatable collaboration processes for recurring high-value collaborative tasks. We present Collaboration Patterns Assistant, a software tool for supporting pattern-based collaboration by exploiting the advantages of Event-Driven Architecture.

Categories and Subject Descriptors

H.5.3 [**Information Interfaces and Presentation**]: Group and Organization Interfaces – *Computer-supported cooperative work.*

General Terms

Design

Keywords

Collaboration Patterns, Event Driven Architecture, Semantics

1. INTRODUCTION

Collaboration is essential for value creation in the modern business environment. Collaboration may span across organizational and geographical boundaries and is often used for mission critical tasks [1]. Over the last two decades, many organizations and individuals have relied on electronic collaboration between distributed teams to achieve higher productivity and produce joint products. Technology has evolved from standalone tools, to open systems supporting collaboration in both intra- [2] and inter-organizational settings [3], and from general purpose platforms to specialized collaboration tools. Even for carefully planned processes with human participation however, ad-hoc adaptation and intervention is required due to the complexity of human tasks, people's individual understanding and unpredictable events. This limits the applicability of existing tools. Collaborative environments are subject to continuous changes because participation is dynamic and business goals may be evolving. In such dynamic environments there is a need for adapting the ways of collaboration to reflect the current conditions.

By focusing on collaboration in dynamic environments, we explore Collaboration Patterns (CPats) as models for recurring high-value collaborative tasks [4], which can be intelligently identified, retrieved and enacted when needed. CPats can be a means to capture best practices about solutions to recurring collaborative problems. In this poster we present Collaboration Pattern Assistant (CPA), a collaborative software tool which is built on the concept of CPats and is based on an innovative coupling of semantic technologies with Event-Driven Architecture to enable collaboration support which can respond and adapt to continuously changing circumstances.

Research in patterns has focused on various areas related to collaboration, such as workflow patterns which formalize recurrent problems and proven solutions related to the development of workflow applications [5] or service interaction patterns which focus on collaborative business processes and apply to the service composition layer and to lower layers dealing with message handling and protocols [4]. Other important efforts introduce activity patterns which model recurring human activities performed in the context of collaborative work [6] and task patterns as templates aiming at supporting users in executing either personal or collaborative work [7]. Moreover, there are works targeting the analysis of patterns in collaborative environments, e.g., offline pattern mining, runtime analysis of ad-hoc collaboration processes [8]. To our knowledge, no prior work takes advantage of the concept of collaboration patterns for adapting collaborations to reflect changing conditions as these are triggered by events.

2. EVENT-DRIVEN COLLABORATION PATTERN ASSISTANT

CPats describe collaborative problems and related solutions within a specific context and under specific conditions. We tackle collaboration adaptation by recommending dynamically CPats in response to changing collaboration conditions. To support reactive, context-based triggering of CPat recommendations, a mechanism for detecting and appropriately responding to changing conditions is needed. Event-Driven Architecture (EDA) provides such a mechanism. By being deployed on EDA, CPats can be triggered proactively based on event triggers and conditions describing the current context. We represent CPat conditions and triggers [9] using OWL-DL (www.w3.org/2007/OWL/). The starting point for recommending a CPat is the arrival of a (complex) event. Following the arrival of an event, all CPat triggers are examined. For each CPat whose trigger, i.e., the class that is related to the CPat with the hasTrigger property, has some instance, the corresponding CPat Condition class is examined. If the condition is true, i.e., has at least one instance, then a CPat recommendation is generated.

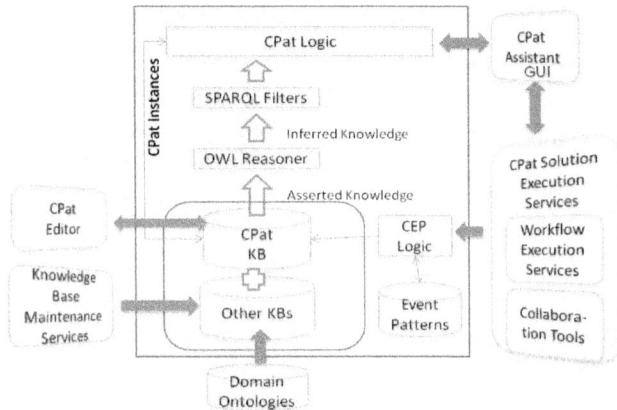

Figure 1. CPA Architecture

The conceptual architecture of CPA is shown in figure 1. The CPA user interface assists users in collaborating by e.g., providing information about their assigned tasks and tools to use. CPat specifications are inserted into the system by a dedicated CPat Editor. CPats are stored in OWL-DL in the CPat Knowledge Base (KB). Knowledge about the ongoing collaborations is maintained in other KBs. Information about events that occur during collaboration arrives through the Complex Event Processing (CEP) component and its associated event patterns store.

The CPat Logic component implements the CPat triggering and execution logic using an OWL-DL reasoner and drives the recommendation of the CPat. In order to provide more fine-grained results, besides the OWL-DL property restrictions which are being executed automatically by the reasoner, we have implemented a SPARQL filter evaluation mechanism. The classes which define CPat conditions, triggers, or recommenders may be associated also with SPARQL filters. The system automatically adds the filter to the instance retrieval SPARQL queries.

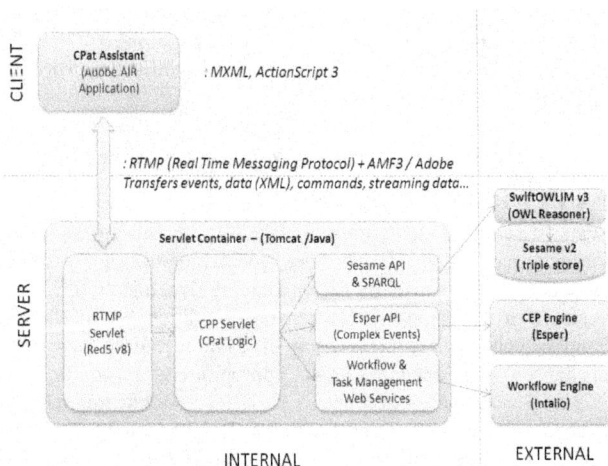

Figure 2. CPA Technical Implementation

CPA has been implemented using the Adobe Flex/AIR framework for the client and the open source Flash server Red5 (figure 2). The Red5 server is written in Java and runs inside the Tomcat servlet container allowing easy integration with a plethora of open-source tools and services. The business logic of CPats is written in Java in the form of a servlet that plugs in the Red5 RTMP servlet. Complex Event Processing is implemented using ESPER while CPat solutions including workflows are managed by Intalio. The CEP engine is used in order to process simple events, combine them and produce complex constructs of events that may trigger CPats. An event service bus, implemented using PETALS, acts as a lightweight, ubiquitous integration backbone through which events flow through intelligent routing mechanisms.

The preliminary evaluation of CPA showed positive but not conclusive findings regarding the system ability to adapt collaborations based on events. We plan to conduct more user evaluations of the system in order to determine which aspects of a CPat-based system are most important to users and how we should grow the system to best meet users' needs.

3. ACKNOWLEDGMENT

This work has been partly funded by the European Commission within the FP7 projects SYNERGY (216089) and PLAY (258659).

4. REFERENCES

[1] Hlupic, V. and Qureshi, S., 2003. A research model for collaborative value creation from intellectual capital. In *Proceedings of the Twentififth International Conference of Information Technology Interfaces,* Cavtat, Croatia.

[2] Dennis, A.R., George, J.F., Jessup, L., Nunamaker J.F. and Vogel, D.R. 1988. Information Technology to Support Electronic Meetings. *MIS Quartery*, 12(4), 591-624.

[3] Roth, A.V. 1996. Neo-operations strategy: linking capabilities-based competition to technology. In: Gaynor, G. (Ed.), *Handbook of Technology Management*. McGraw-Hill, New York, NY, 38.1–38.44.

[4] Barros, A.P., Dumas, M., ter Hofstede, A.H.M., 2005. Service interaction patterns. In *Proceeding of the BPM, LNCS*, vol. 3649, pp. 302–318.

[5] van der Aalst, W., M., P., ter Hofstede, A., H., M., Kiepuszewski, B. and Barros A., P., 2003. Workflow Patterns. *Distributed and Parallel Databases*, 14(3):5–51.

[6] Moody, P., Gruen, D., Muller, M. J., Tang, J. and Moran, T. P., 2006. Business Activity Patterns: A New Model for Collaborative Business Applications. In *IBM Systems Journal*, 45(4), 2006, pp. 683 – 694.

[7] Hu, B., Du, Y., Chen, L., Riss, U., V. and Witschel, H. F., 2009. Utilising Task-Patterns in Organisational Process Knowledge Sharing. In *Proceedings of the ASWC*, 216-230.

[8] Truong H.L. and Dustdar, S., 2009. Online Interaction Analysis Framework for Ad-Hoc Collaborative Processes. In *Proceedings of the ToPNoC II, LNCS*, 5460, pp. 260–277.

[9] Papageorgiou, N., Verginadis, Y., Apostolou, D. and Mentzas, G., 2010. Ontology Based Patterns for Collaborative Process Management. In *Proceedings of the 5th International Workshop on Semantic Business Process Management, ESWC 2011.*

Poster: SIP-based QoS Support and Session Management for DDS-based Distributed Real-time and Embedded Systems*

Akram Hakiri, Pascal Berthou , and
Thierry Gayraud
Université de Toulouse; UPS, INSA, INP, ISAE;
LAAS; F-31077 Toulouse, France
{Hakiri, Berthou, Gayraud}@laas.fr

Aniruddha Gokhale, Joe Hoffert, and
Douglas C. Schmidt
ISIS, Dept of EECS, Vanderbilt University
Nashville, TN 37212, USA
{gokhale,jhoffert,schmidt}@dre.vanderbilt.edu

ABSTRACT

End-to-end quality-of-service (QoS) support in middleware is critical to achieve publish/subscribe (pub/sub)-based distributed real-time and embedded (DRE) systems. This poster describes ongoing work on supporting QoS properties over wide area networks within the OMG's Data Distribution Service (DDS) by leveraging the Session Initiation Protocol (SIP) and Session Description Protocol (SDP).

Categories and Subject Descriptors

D:Software [**2:Software Engineering**]: 2:Design Tools and Techniques

General Terms

Design, Performance

Keywords

DDS over WANs, SIP, QoS

1. INTRODUCTION

Many publish/subscribe (pub/sub)-based distributed real-time and embedded (DRE) systems operate in heterogeneous environments that receive data from a large number of sensors and multimedia sources and stream it in real-time to remote entities. A key requirement of these DRE systems is to optimize the performance and scalability of applications and provision/control key network resources [1]. The Object Management Group (OMG)'s Data Distribution Service (DDS) [2] is a data-centric pub/sub middleware that simplifies application development, deployment, and evolution for DRE systems. Contemporary DDS implementations, however, do not currently support key QoS properties of pub/sub DRE systems over wide area networks (WANs) because the DDS middleware inherently resides on end-systems and thus defines only mechanisms that control end-system

*This research is supported in part by NSF CAREER #CNS 0845789. Any opinions, findings, and conclusions or recommendations expressed in this material are those of the author(s) and do not necessarily reflect the views of the National Science Foundation.

properties, such as OS-level parameters and tuning network parameters for the connecting link. In particular, DDS provides no mechanisms for provisioning/controlling end-to-end QoS over WANS, which complicates the assurance of QoS for large-scale DRE systems.

A promising approach to address these challenges is to integrate DDS with the Session Initiation Protocol (SIP) [3] and the Session Description Protocol (SDP) [4]. SIP/SDP are powerful mechanisms available over WANs to convey new enhanced services including information about the end-systems, identification of the originator of a session, identification of the multimedia content in the session initiation request which might contain pictures, signals from sensors, and a personalized ring-tone.

Despite the promise of SIP/SDP, the integration with DDS is not straightforward since the level of abstraction of SIP/SDP makes them agnostic to account for the application QoS needs of pub/sub DRE systems. The rest of this paper outlines our solution approach to close the gap between SIP/SDP and DDS so that DDS and its QoS support can be realized over WANs.

2. SUPPORTING OMG DDS OVER WANS

This section briefly outlines our approach to supporting OMG DDS over WANs. The solution requires addressing two primary challenges discussed below.

2.1 End-to-End QoS Provisioning

Context: Recent work [5] describes how applications are increasingly being distributed over multiple machines in WANs to ensure scalability and availability. Not only is the amount of data exchanged becoming large, but the exchanged flows are becoming more diverse. DiffServ flows have different priorities, delays, and bandwidth requirements, which must obtain the required network resources to fulfill application requirements [6].

Problem: An important property for WAN-based pub/sub DRE systems is that the right answer delivered too late becomes the wrong answer, *e.g.,* small delays can incur substantial damage or losses. As Next Generation Networks (NGNs) [7] become increasingly reliant on IP, providing end-to-end network QoS assurance becomes hard. To ensure that end-to-end QoS is met, developers of DRE systems must define traffic profiles for each application and ensure this service specification is never exceeded.

Solution Approach: To provision WAN-level resources to

support end-to-end QoS, we define a new SIP Signaling Class of Service (S-CoS) for transferring signaling messages. To provision this new S-CoS, we leverage DDS latency, transport priority, and bandwidth QoS settings. Using appropriate S-CoS dimensioning enables control of transfer packet setup latency in the access and core network for resource provisioning. Moreover, to support the DDS QoS policies, SDP is used to describe the session characteristics, such as which media streams are included in the session, and the codec used for data streaming. We define a new QoS support for SIP-based network architecture to integrate DDS application (SIP Client), QoS-enabled SIP (Q-SIP) Server, and policy based network management. We also define new SDP extensions to integrate DDS QoS policies in SIP/SDP packet headers. Our approach requires no modifications to applications, which can continue to use standard DDS QoS policy and programming interfaces.

2.2 Autonomic Adaptation and Robustness in Dynamic Environment

Context: A multimedia application for, say, a UAV video distribution using multi-layer resource management mechanisms, is often coordinated via middleware to ensure video flows can meet their mission QoS requirements by adapting both the computer and the network resources. The architecture adaptively controls the video transmission captured from cameras (publishers) subsequently sending them to middleware based distributed processing units. The information is then distributed over QoS-aware networks to one or more remote receivers (subscribers) including displayers and image processing software. UAVs should provide high data rate and ultra-low latency and involve data dissemination to multiple operators that cooperate in the operation in ground station.

Problem: There are many challenges associated with providing reliable and low latency communication with ground stations, including consistency, configurable reliability, and reliable delivery atop any type of reliable or unreliable transport. With the advent of wireless sensors networks, minimizing the amount of data transmission across is crucial [8]. Moreover, various QoS properties are essential to provide to each operator with only the necessary data at the right time. The network infrastructure should therefore be flexible enough to support varying workloads at different times during operations, while also maintaining highly predictable and dependable behavior. Meeting these challenges requires a high level of structural and temporal decoupling for the control, adaptation of resources, and to maintain real-time performance. Such a capability should seamlessly interoperate at both the end-systems and the network.

Solution Approach: SIP/SDP allows the usage of static and dynamic media payload description (which exists as a well-known id associated to it) that can be used by the transport protocol. The dynamic media payload description should, however, include more information that characterizes the format to ensure the robustness and the automatic adaptation in dynamic environment. The dynamic mechanism is that the DDS QoS policies mapped into SIP messages are used by the SIP proxy (Q-SIP). Thus, when the host changes its QoS requirements, the SIP message is intercepted by the proxy SIP to be redirected to the destination for notification (offer/response contract).

Subsequently, the receiver node adapts its DDS QoS poli-

cies with those notification (here just changeable QoS setting are applied) and sends a response to its Q-SIP which notifies an underlying Bandwidth broker with the new QoS requirements to adapt its class of Service (to change from, say, real-time CoS to non real-time CoS, and vice versa). For interoperability, this mean that the SIP messages including DDS QoS settings are used for non DDS application, because they are just text messages (like HTTP). Any SIP compliant terminal should interpret SIP messages and ignore SIP DDS attributes in the messages. Thus, it is possible to distribute thousands of messages per second, while maintaining the scalability, an ultra-low predictable latency, controlling a tradeoff between latency and throughput, and stability under low resource conditions.

3. CONCLUDING REMARKS

This paper describes our approach to supporting OMG DDS and its QoS policies over WANs. Our solution comprises two artifacts: (1) At the service plane, DDS applications use SIP signaling messages that allow senders to contact receivers to obtain their IP addresses and to agree the media description and "qos-dds" attributes; (2) At the control plane, the network QoS provisioning mechanism encodes application QoS requirements within SDP messages supplied to the network elements to (a) negotiate QoS, (b) coordinate the data path and signaling path management, and (c) enforce the end-to-end network resource reservation. Our ongoing work is focused on conducting experiments to validate the end-to-end QoS expected by DDS-based DRE systems operating over WANs.

4. REFERENCES

[1] D.C. Schmidt et al, *Middleware R&D Challenges for Distributed Real-time and Embedded Systems*, ACM SIGBED, Volume 1 Issue 1, April 2004
[2] OMG-DDS, "*Data Distribution Service for Real-Time Systems Specification*". DDSv1.2, http://www.omg.org/spec/DDS/1.2/
[3] Rosenberg, J., Schulzrinne, H., Camarillo, G., Johnston, A., Peterson, J., Sparks, R., Handley, M., and E. Schooler, "*SIP: Session Initiation Protocol*", RFC 3261, June 2002.
[4] Rosenberg, J. and H. Schulzrinne, "*An Offer/Answer Model with Session Description Protocol (SDP)*", RFC 3264, June 2002.
[5] J. Hoffert, et. al. *Adapting Distributed Real-time and Embedded Pub/Sub Middleware for Cloud Computing Environments*, ACM/IFIP/USENIX Middleware Conf, Bangalore, India, Springer/LNCS 6452, Nov 2010.
[6] L. Veltri, et. al. "*SIP Extensions for QoS support in DiffServ Networks*," IETF Draft, April 2002.
[7] TISPAN. Defining the Next Generation Network, http://www.etsi.org/tispan/
[8] E.D. Jong, *End-to-End UAV Messaging over Unreliable Data Links*, COTS Journal, April 2009.

Poster: Representing Events in a Clinical Environment A Case Study

Leendert W. M. Wienhofen
Department of Computer and
Information Science, Norwegian
University of Science and Technology
Sem Sælandsv 7-9
NO-7489 Trondheim, Norway

leendert.wienhofen@idi.ntnu.no

Andreas D. Landmark
Department of Computer and
Information Science, Norwegian
University of Science and Technology
Sem Sælandsv 7-9
NO-7489 Trondheim, Norway

andreala@idi.ntnu.no

ABSTRACT
Through observations of a specific workflow in a Norwegian University Hospital, we found that the clinical environment offers a number of challenges that seem under-addressed in current event-related literature. In this paper we attempt to highlight some challenges raised in the dynamic world of healthcare and discuss the implications for event quality.

Categories and Subject Descriptors
H.4 [**Information Systems Applications**]: Miscellaneous; J.3 [**Life and Medical Sciences**]: Medical information systems

General Terms
Design, Theory

1. INTRODUCTION
Healthcare is a domain where changes, updates and exceptions to the plan are more common than not. All these exceptions make it inherently difficult, if not impossible, to create and design detailed and robust models for software attempting contain representations of clinical reality. If one accepts "changes of significance"[1] as a fair description of an event, one could say that work in healthcare is also very much event driven. By organising their work in this event-based manner, healthcare professionals can react to unforeseen circumstances and complete work that would be difficult or almost impossible to plan ahead of time. However, this also creates a t ension between proactive and planned work. Planned work that has to be performed is constantly pre-empted by unplanned/unforeseen acute work, which by nature is highly reactive and initiated by certain events or in special circumstances.

Due to this apparent non-deterministic nature of healthcare work, regular Complex Event Processing (CEP) mechanisms can only solve parts of our problem. More regular business processes can be modelled into Business Process Models (BPM) following pre-determined paths that generally are not deviated from. In the medical domain however, one can only successfully create high-level abstract patient trajectories[2], rather than detailed process

models. While it is possible to detect patterns, due to the non-deterministic nature we can never be sure that these patterns or predictions will be followed. This makes event processing, and especially event enriching, a challenging task.

1.1 Purpose
Our research is driven by real world problems and real world data. The methodology (design science [3]) behind this is firm in applied science, but there are still many research challenges related to CEP that remain to be solved both theoretically and proven practically.

The purpose of this poster is to describe the problem domain very briefly and highlight some of the peculiarities we identified through observations in an actual hospital and interviews with stakeholders. Based on these actual observation, we, unlike many others in the event-based systems community, do not focus on performance of event communication or inference engines, but rather on the quality of the inferred events, as seen from an end-user perspective.

2. USE CASE DESCRIPTION
The use case observed was a set of pre-operative preparatory tests, for workflow reasons, compressed into a single day. This involves a single day of seven or eight diagnostic procedures. For the patient this means fewer visits to the hospital and a more streamlined visit, whilst for the hospital this places strict demands on coordination of their effort due to several interdependencies where the results from one procedure is input to another and can dictate changes to the workflow.

The procedures involves simple procedures such as blood work and radiologic examinations, which are highly automated and follow a fairly rigid plan – but also procedures involving human judgment where the plan is highly dependent on t he diagnosis, physical state and even anatomy of the patient.

The event-processing application described here, is part of an awareness application to help describe the processes unfolding in the hospital to support and facilitate oversight and self-coordination amongst healthcare professionals.

2.1 Event Sources
Typical sources of events in this scenario would be the information systems in use by the healthcare professionals. This involves various documentation systems such as electronic patient journal, laboratory systems and radiological information systems.

Additionally a lot of the medical equipment used in the procedures is networked and is able to report about their own state and progress of their internal protocols. Each of these systems provide *digital events* that, when aggregated, up to a certain level describe a *real life event* (in our case, one of these events would be one of the procedures)

2.2 Event behaviour

Through observations in the field and various discussions and interviews with medical stakeholders, we elicited the following key concerns:

1   Non-deterministic occurrence of events: With some systems operating in isolation, every significant event in the real world is not represented by a digital event. The order of events is indeterminate, and human reporting of events in a high paced environment even more so.

2   Context-dependent meaning of events: Two equal events produced by the same system can have a totally different meaning. Their interpretation is subject to the current context, the events that have already occurred and those that are about to occur.

3   Quality awareness in events: The inference of complex events should account for the quality of information of its constituents. The quality of an event (probability of occurrence, reliability, relevance, etc.) may vary over time and influence the confidence in the value of an encompassing complex event.

3. DISCUSSION

The crux of the problem of event-based human-oriented decision support systems lies in the volatility and massiveness of the different event streams[4] being produced for each stakeholder in every patient flow. To properly interpret events and detect complex event patterns, we need sufficient expressive power to correlate events when attempting to reliably recognize a situation of interest. As mentioned before, based on observations, it is not performance which is the main issue, but the quality of the representation of the events which is the most important element in our use case. Stakeholders claim that precision on the level of minutes is sufficient, as long as the quality is acceptable (though the exact definition of "acceptable" is subjective, posing yet another challenge).

Relating to the event behaviour addressed in the section above, we identify the following aspects to be critical for measuring the relevance of events and the quality of the inferred knowledge.
•   Temporal locality: Aggregating events implicitly introduces a notion of time, since the most common operators to relate events to one another explicitly deal with the order in which they occur [5]. The relevance of events may also be limited in time. When a particular combination of events does not occur within a given time period, the events may be safely discarded [6].

•   Spatial locality: In addition to temporal locality, events can also be correlated in the space domain. For example, body sensors may produce events to notify about an increased heart rate. These values would not be alarming if the person is working out for a physiotherapy assessment. Spatial correlations between event producers (e.g. location sensors and body sensors) may determine the outcome of making a correct decision.

•   Non-deterministic ordering and causality: The event-condition-action (ECA) paradigm is often used to model causality between on the one hand events that occurred and on the other hand actions that have to be carried out or decisions that have be taken. Non-determinism is caused by (E) the indirect observations of real life events, (C) an incomplete representation of the situation due to some real life events not having a digital counterpart, and (A) the contextual dependency on any action or decision to be pursued.

•   Ambiguity and incompleteness: Events can be periodic, stochastic or sporadic in nature. This complicates the process of defining and interpreting relevant event patterns as some situations of interest become very hard to represent as a single series of events. When listing all possible variations of event sequences becomes infeasible, then partial orderings may be more appropriate to capture relevant event patterns.

To address these quality concerns, our goal is to contextualize events in order to improve their quality and to make sure that event streams are correctly interpreted.

4. FURTHER WORK

We have implemented a lab setting with the possibility to manually trigger events that represent the real events that can be captured at the university hospital. In addition, we have set up near real-time ultrasound positioning equipment, which generates an event stream with position information. In the hospital we do not yet have such a system, but we are interested in evaluating the impact adding location information to the context pool.

We have built an initial framework for handling these events using Esper. The next step is to attempt to incorporate simple quality metrics and evaluate the effect of taking into account simple quantifications of information quality into the inference engine both with and without location information. This step may lead to a change in direction with regards to the choice of the event handling software.

5. ACKNOWLEDGMENTS

This work was supported by the VerdIKT-programme of the Research Council of Norway (grant no. 187854/S10).

6. REFERENCES

[1] Chandy, K. M., Charpentier, M. and Capponi, A. Towards a theory of events. *Proceedings of the 2007 inaugural international conference on Distributed event-based systems*2007), 180-187.

[2] Strauss, A. and Fagerhaugh, S. *Social organization of medical work*. Transaction Pub, 1997.

[3] Hevner, A. R., March, S. T., Park, J. and Ram, S. Design science in Information Systems research. *Mis Quart*, 28, 1 (Mar 2004), 75-105.

[4] Banavar, G., Kaplan, M., Shaw, K., Strom, R. E., Sturman, D. C. and Wei, T. *Information flow based event distribution middleware*. City, 1999.

[5] Mühl, G., Fiege, L. and Pietzuch, P. *Distributed event-based systems*. Springer-Verlag, Berlin, 2006.

[6] Bruno, B. *Extending the RETE Algorithm for Event Management*. City, 2002.

Poster: Efficient and Cost-aware Operator Placement in Heterogeneous Stream-Processing Environments

Michael Daum   Frank Lauterwald   Philipp Baumgärtel
          Niko Pollner   Klaus Meyer-Wegener

Dept. of Computer Science, Friedrich-Alexander University of Erlangen-Nürnberg, Germany
{md,frank.lauterwald,philipp.baumgaertel,niko.pollner,kmw}@cs.fau.de

ABSTRACT

Operator placement for distributed stream-processing systems is still a challenging problem that can be modeled as a *Task Assignment Problem* (TAP). Multiple objectives are relevant for the optimization in heterogeneous stream-processing systems as there are different capabilities of the underlying networks and stream-processing nodes. We present an approach based on linear programming relaxation and iterative deterministic rounding. It uses an efficient linearization approach for the quadratic objective function that results from the TAP.

Categories and Subject Descriptors: C.2.4 COMPUTER-COMMUNICATION NETWORKS: Distributed Systems, D.2.8 SOFTWARE ENGINEERING: Metrics[complexity measures, performance measures]

General Terms: Algorithms, Performance

Keywords: optimization techniques, (self-)management, federated event-based systems, performance modeling, operator distribution

1. INTRODUCTION

In order to apply in-network query processing, stream processing must be distributed in a way that operators like filter and aggregation can reduce communication already in the vicinity of the stream sources. Our project *Data Stream Application Manager* (DSAM) provides a framework for such a placement of operators in heterogeneous distributed stream-processing systems. The appropriate placement decision must take many constraints into account, e.g. node capacities and energy consumption. Different approaches to this problem have been published, which cannot be presented here in detail due to space limitations. Some handle only a limited set of operators or make other restricting assumptions. That allows them to find a globally optimal solution, or they focus on local performance improvements. Others consider finding a globally optimal solution to be an unsolvable problem once a certain complexity is reached. We follow this valuation and strive to provide good results for a certain range of complexity that suffices for most scenarios.

As our approach comprises cost-based operator distribution, only costs and capacities are relevant. Given appropriate cost models, this approach can be used with models of stream and complex-event processing other than DSAM, too. It regards operator placement as a *Task Assignment Problem* (TAP) with an operator taken to be a task and a processor seen as a node. This leads to a quadratic program:

$$\min \sum_{t \in T} \sum_{p \in P} c_{tp} x_{tp} + \sum_{t_1 \in T} \sum_{p_1 \in P} \sum_{t_2 \in T} \sum_{p_2 \in P} k_{p_1 p_2} r_{t_1 t_2} x_{t_1 p_1} x_{t_2 p_2} \quad (1)$$

with constraints: $\sum_{t \in T} c_{tp} x_{tp} \leq b_{ip}, \forall p \in P$;
$\sum_{p \in P} x_{tp} = 1, \forall t \in T$; $x_{tp} \in \{0,1\}, \forall p \in P, \forall t \in T$.

The variable x_{tp} equals 1 if task t is to be deployed on processor p and $x_{tp} = 0$ otherwise. Equation (1) is the objective function consisting of the processing costs c_{tp}, communication costs $k_{p_1 p_2}$ and rates $r_{t_1 t_2}$. The only quadratic term are the communication costs in the objective function. The constraints ensure that no capacity is exceeded and guarantee that every task is distributed on exactly one processor. An optimization algorithm is needed to find values for the x_{tp} minimizing the objective function. These values for the x_{tp} represent the optimal distribution.

2. APPROXIMATELY SOLVING THE TAP

Finding an optimal solution for the TAP is NP-hard. Therefore, an approximation is more feasible. Iterative rounding [2] is a well-known approach to construct approximation algorithms for linear programs. To our knowledge, it has not been applied to quadratic programs like the TAP yet.

We relax the TAP by ignoring the integer constraints. Then efficient algorithms, like interior point methods, exist to find optimal or near-optimal solutions for the relaxed problem. These solutions however are possibly invalid distributions, because an operator could be partially distributed over multiple nodes.

The following iterative rounding algorithm constructs a valid integer solution to the original TAP.

```
tap ← RELAXTAP(tap)
x̃_tp ← SOLVE(tap)
for i = 1 to |T| do
    loop
        (t_max, p_max) =    argmax      x̃_tp
                         (t,p) ∈ T × P
        tap ← (x_{t_max p} = 0), ∀p ∈ P
        tap ← (x_{t_max Pmax} = 1)
        if SOLVABLE(tap) then
            x̃_tp ← SOLVE(tap)
            break
        else
            x̃_{t_max Pmax} ← 0
            tap ← (x_{t_max P} = undefined), ∀p ∈ P
        end if
        if x̃_tp = 0, ∀p ∈ P, ∀t ∈ T then
            FALLBACK(tap)
            break
        end if
    end loop
end for
return x̃_tp
```

In the first step, the algorithm tries to distribute the task with the highest affinity to a processor. If that is not feasible, it proceeds with the next highest affinity and so on. The algorithm then reduces the TAP by excluding the distributed task and solves the remaining relaxed problem. These steps are repeated until every task is distributed to exactly one processor. In the reduction step, the

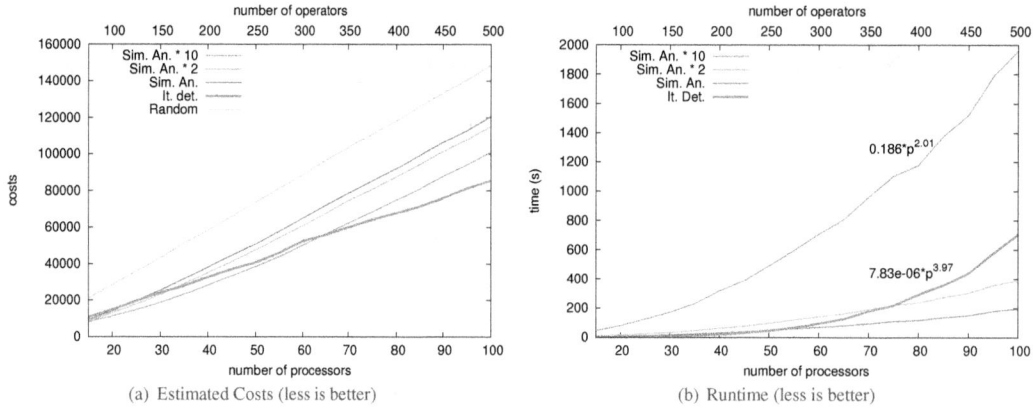

Figure 1: Comparison between the estimated costs and runtime of the iterative rounding method and simulated annealing

distribution problem is just slightly altered. The fallback strategy is to distribute one operator randomly with constraint checking.

Solving quadratic problems appeared to be too inefficient for our purposes. Linear programming algorithms tend to be more efficient than nonlinear programming techniques.

Chang [1] introduced an efficient linearization method for integer programs. This method can be used to transform the original TAP to a *Mixed Integer Linear Program* (MILP) by reformulating the objective function and introducing additional variables. To achieve linearization of this quadratic problem, the property of the x_{tp} being binary variables is utilized.

Replacing the quadratic terms in (1) by additional variables $h_{t_1 p_1}$ provides a linear version of the TAP's objective function:

$$\min \sum_{t \in T} \sum_{p \in P} c_{tp} x_{tp} + \sum_{t_1 \in T} \sum_{p_1 \in P} h_{t_1 p_1}$$

with additional constraints

$$h_{t_1 p_1} \geq 0 \qquad \forall t_1 \in T, p_1 \in P$$

$$h_{t_1 p_1} \geq B_{t_1 p_1}(x_{t_1 p_1} - 1) + \sum_{t_2 \in T} r_{t_1 t_2} \sum_{p_2 \in P} k_{p_1 p_2} x_{t_2 p_2} \, \forall t_1 \in T, p_1 \in P$$

This linearization approach needs $|T| \cdot |P|$ additional variables and $2 \cdot |T| \cdot |P|$ additional constraints. The new variables $h_{t_1 p_1}$ are no longer integer variables. Therefore the TAP is not an *Integer Linear Program* (ILP) but a MILP.

However, our iterative rounding algorithm does not depend on a particular method to find the optimal solution of the relaxed TAP. Hence, the MILP approach shown above could be replaced with other linearization methods, and even the original quadratic programming methods could be used.

3. FIRST RESULTS

We implemented a modular distributor interface to compare different distribution algorithms to our approximation approach. A distributor based on the simulated annealing algorithm from the GNU Scientific Library serves as comparison to our approach. We evaluated different parameter settings for the simulated annealing technique and chose the parameters with the best results. Three different settings for simulated annealing leading to good results were used in this evaluation. These simulated annealing versions use a different amount of runtime and therefore, they find solutions with different quality. We chose a fast version offering quick optimization results, a version being 2 times slower finding better solutions and a version being 10 times slower finding very good solutions.

To evaluate our approximation approach, we constructed synthetic operator graphs consisting of an arbitrary number of operators. The operator graphs used in our evaluation are balanced binary trees with each node being an abstract binary operator followed by an abstract unary operator. Each leaf is an abstract unary

operator. This kind of operator-graph structure is typical for data stream applications. However, our techniques are not limited to tree-structured operator graphs. Operator semantics are not relevant for the distribution algorithm as they are handled by the cost estimator.

In our experiments, we used random cost values for the cost constants. The ranges for the values are: Capacity (b_p) [500, 1000]; Cost (c_{tp}) [50, 100]; Communication costs ($k_{p_1 p_2}$) [10, 20]; Rate ($r_{t_1 t_2}$) [10, 20]

To be able to depict our results, we chose the number of operators to be linearly dependent on the number of processors. Therefore, we conducted each experiment with 5 times as many operators than processors. Each algorithm gets the same cost values and problem structure from the random cost estimator.

We compared our approximation algorithm combined with the efficient linearization technique to simulated annealing.

Figure 1(a) shows the solution quality of three different Simulated Annealing versions, our iterative rounding technique and a valid random distribution. In this figure, each value is the mean of 25 experiments with random cost values.

Our approach turned out to perform much better than the two fast simulated annealing variants and even better than the slow version of simulated annealing for problems with more than about 70 processors and 350 operators.

Figure 1(b) shows the measured runtime of the different algorithms. The estimated time complexity is also depicted in Figure 1(b).

For problems up to 250 operators, our approach turned out to be much faster than each version of simulated annealing, we evaluated. For problems with 100 processors and 500 operators our approach is a bit slower than the fast simulated annealing variants, but still much faster than the slow simulated annealing variant.

Our solution can also be used to create the initial solution for simulated annealing. Since the time for continuous optimization of distributions is very limited, only the fast versions of simulated annealing could be applied here.

4. REFERENCES

[1] C.-T. Chang. An efficient linearization approach for mixed-integer problems. *European Journal of Operational Research*, 123(3):652 – 659, 2000.

[2] K. Jain. A Factor 2 Approximation Algorithm for the Generalized Steiner Network Problem. In *39th Annual Symposium on Foundations of Computer Science (FOCS)*, page 448, Washington, DC, USA, 1998.

Poster: A Capacity Planning Framework for Event Brokers in Intelligent Transportation Cyber Physical Systems

Laura K. Poff
Vanderbilt University,
Dept of CEE
VU Station B #351831
Nashville, TN 37212
laura.k.poff@vanderbilt.edu

Mark P. McDonald
Vanderbilt University,
Dept of CEE
VU Station B #351831
Nashville, TN 37212
mark.p.mcdonald@vanderbilt.edu

Aniruddha Gokhale
Vanderbilt University,
Dept of EECS
1025 16th Ave South
Nashville, TN 37212
a.gokhale@vanderbilt.edu

ABSTRACT

Transportation engineering is a mature discipline of engineering that provides effective and efficient methods and tools for traffic modeling and capacity planning, however, these artifacts incur limitations in the context of intelligent transportation systems (ITS) because they seldom incorporate cyber issues in their design. Conversely, Computer Science provides many sophisticated solutions for resource management in the cyber world but often overlook physical issues inherent in ITS. Consequently, neither discipline prepares designers and planners to implement a fully functional ITS. Capacity planning solutions for ITS require solutions that can holistically integrate physical artifacts, such as traffic modeling, with cyber artifacts, such as solutions for real-time information dissemination over wireless networks. To address these challenges, this paper presents preliminary ideas on the design of a framework based on the principles of surrogate modeling wherein small-scale, micro-simulations of the ITS cyber-physical system are used to develop training points, which in turn are used to train a surrogate model. The surrogate model is subsequently used to make planning decisions for ITS.

Categories and Subject Descriptors

I.6.5 [**Computing Methodologies**]: Simulation and Modeling – *model development, analysis and validation,*
J.2 [**Computer Applications**]: Physical Sciences and Engineering.

General Terms

Algorithms, Design, Experimentation.

Keywords

Capacity planning, event dissemination, cyber-physical, modeling, design methodology, interdisciplinary.

1. INTRODUCTION

Intelligent Transportation Systems (ITS) are envisioned to address the numerous challenges faced by the transportation sector [7]. One category of solutions envisioned in ITS, pertains to the real-time and reliable delivery of traffic-related information to drivers

both for safety-critical applications (such as blind spot warnings during lane changing) and for applications that improve driving experience and help the environment (such as notification of congestion and rerouting advise that can help to alleviate traffic congestion and lost productivity). The dissemination of information for these services is facilitated by brokers, such as road side units (RSUs) and even cellular towers. For the timely and scalable dissemination of information, there is a need for effective capacity planning for the RSUs or equivalent infrastructure.

Capacity planning for ITS is a hard problem because it must account for both the transportation-related challenges, *i.e.,* the physical dimension, and the information technology challenges, *i.e.,* the cyber dimension. Deploying real infrastructure elements and testing different hypotheses is unrealistic due to high capital costs. What is required is a design-time solution that can accurately model the ITS CPS, which in turn can help resolve the capacity planning challenges. However, for a design-time solution an approach based on detailed simulations is infeasible due to scalability issues arising from the computationally intensive properties of such simulations.

In this paper we present preliminary ideas on a framework that provides a way in which decisions regarding the system can be made quickly and inexpensively, moving the design of the cyber-physical system closer to its real-world goal. To address the problems with scalability of simulations, we rely on using a surrogate model, which is trained using a relatively small number of training points obtained from a small set of microsimulations. The chosen surrogate model is then used to make decisions regarding the system. We believe that the strength of this framework is that once the system is characterized using a surrogate model, subsequently the model can be used in both the planning stages (*e.g.,* infrastructure decisions like placement of the RSUs) and at runtime once the system is built (*e.g.,* for information dissemination such as how to reroute vehicles and when to send out the rerouting information). Our research is seeking to validate these claims.

2. RELATED RESEARCH

Since the inception of ITS, simulation has been used in order to envision potential implementations. Microsimulation in particular is suggested as the appropriate method for testing ITS, over both Highway Capacity Manual (HCM) procedures and macroscopic simulation in [3]. Both [3] and [1] provide suggestions on how best to build and validate realistic microscopic models for transportation systems. An actual ITS deployment is validated against microsimulation models in [5], although the system is for adaptive traffic control systems and not for information dissemination in vehicular adhoc networks (VANETs).

The use of optimization techniques for infrastructure deployment and system planning is also already in use within the field of ITS. There are various optimization statements and goals that are being utilized: maximizing coverage while guaranteeing a minimum amount of coverage time [9]; maximizing the reliability of information dissemination [8]; bandwidth minimization as well as travel-time minimization [6]; and maximizing the utility that comes from hardware distribution and information gathering [2].

Our research proposes extending current decision-making practices in ITS development and deployment to include surrogate models in order to characterize the system more efficiently than just microsimulation and optimization can do alone.

3. A METHODOLOGY AND FRAMEWORK FOR CAPACITY PLANNING IN ITS

Our proposed methodology shown in Figure 1 comprises the following four steps:

1. **Collecting training points** – A small number of microsimulations involving the CPS properties of ITS are conducted to collect training points needed to develop the surrogate models of ITS CPS.
2. **Building surrogate models** – the second step is to develop the surrogate models using the training points for the system under study. We use the Gaussian Process (GP) modeling approach [4].
3. **Validating the surrogate models** – once the surrogate models are developed, they must be validated for accuracy and correctness, which forms our third step.
4. **Optimizing the decisions** – once the models are validated, we use optimization techniques to make optimized engineering decisions.

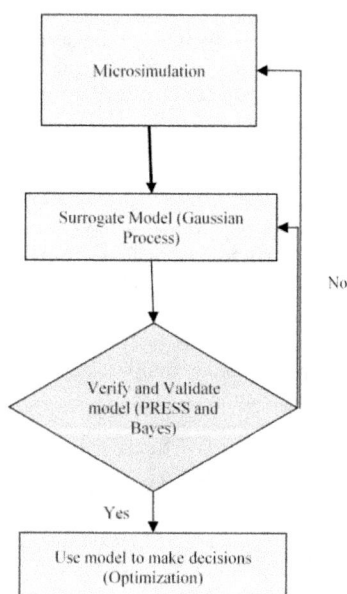

Figure 1. Methodology

Surrogate modeling provides an inexpensive but highly accurate design-time solution for designing complex systems. We believe

that such a methodology has not been exploited in ITS, which illustrate complex event processing and event dissemination properties.

The proposed methodology has thus far been applied by using a simulation involving one vehicle passing an RSU. The speed of the vehicle and power of the RSU beacon are varied as inputs and the communication window is measured as an output. Training points are used in order to train a GP model. The model is verified and used in order to create a Pareto front that demonstrates the speed and power trade off inherent in this physical system.

In the future, this methodology will be applied to more complex, realistic systems. The ability to model such complex systems using a surrogate model will make it feasible to examine the full range of trade-offs prior to deployment (in the design phase) and will greatly increase the likelihood of being able to make run-time decisions during the ITS deployment.

4. ACKNOWLEDGMENTS

This research was made possible in part by grants from the US National Science Foundation CAREER CNS 0845789 and CNS/SHF 0915976 Awards, and Vanderbilt University Discovery Grant. The opinions and finding expressed in this paper are those of the authors only.

5. REFERENCES

[1] Brockfeld, E. et al. 2003. Toward benchmarking of microscopic traffic flow models. *Transportation Research Record: Journal of the Transportation Research Board.* 1852, -1 (2003), 124-129.

[2] Crainic, T.G. et al. 2009. Intelligent freight-transportation systems: Assessment and the contribution of operations research. *Transportation Research Part C: Emerging Technologies.* 17, 6 (2009), 541-557.

[3] Dowling, R. et al. 2004. *Traffic Analysis Toolbox Volume III: Guidelines for Applying Traffic Microsimulation Modeling Software.* Technical Report #FHWA-HRT-04-040. FHWA, U.S. Deparment of Transportation.

[4] Forrester, A.I.J. et al. 2008. *Engineering design via surrogate modelling: a practical guide.* Wiley.

[5] Kergaye, C. et al. 2010. Comparative Evaluation of Adaptive Traffic Control System Assessments Through Field and Microsimulation. *Journal of Intelligent Transportation Systems.* 14, 2 (2010), 109-124.

[6] Lochert, C. et al. 2008. Data aggregation and roadside unit placement for a vanet traffic information system. *Proceedings of the fifth ACM international workshop on VehiculAr Inter-NETworking* (2008), 58-65.

[7] Maccubbin, R.P. et al. 2008. *Intelligent transportation systems benefits, costs, deployment, and lessons learned: 2008 update.*

[8] Sardari, M. et al. 2009. Infocast: a new paradigm for collaborative content distribution from roadside units to vehicular networks. *Sensor, Mesh and Ad Hoc Communications and Networks, 2009. SECON'09. 6th Annual IEEE Communications Society Conference on* (2009), 1-9.

[9] Trullols, O. et al. 2010. Planning roadside infrastructure for information dissemination in intelligent transportation systems. *Computer Communications.* 33, 4 (2010), 432-442.

Poster: Towards An Adaptive Event Dissemination Middleware For MMVEs

Thomas Fischer, Johannes Held, Frank Lauterwald, Richard Lenz
University of Erlangen-Nuremberg
Department of Computer Science 6 (Data Management)
Martensstrasse 3, D-91058 Erlangen
{thomas.fischer,johannes.held,frank.lauterwald,richard.lenz}@cs.fau.de

ABSTRACT

The *Massive Multiuser Event InfraStructure* (M^2etis) project is aimed at a generic middleware that supports the optimization of event dissemination based on a multidimensional semantic classification of event types. In this paper, we introduce the M^2etis system architecture with its core concepts.

Categories and Subject Descriptors

C.2.4 [**COMMUNICATION NETWORKS**]: Distributed Systems

General Terms

Management, Performance

Keywords

Event Semantics, Publish Subscribe, MMVE

1. INTRODUCTION

Massive Multiplayer Online Games (MMOGs) require enormous server clusters to enable thousands of players to interact within a common area of some virtual world, while maintaining the illusion of a fluent real-time game. In contrast, classical multiplayer games like Quake 3 Arena, which require only one server, have shown that without any major optimizations, the limit for a reasonable simulation rate of 30-60 fps is reached with about 64 clients. To scale beyond this limit specialized event dissemination architectures and optimization strategies are used to exploit application-specific event semantics. Based on current research and existing industrial *Massive Multiuser Virtual Environments* (MMVEs), we assume a homogenous distributed system with identical software running on all nodes. The event types required for a particular MMOG are well-known at design-time. Therefore, the general strategy for optimized event dissemination may be made at compile-time as there exists a suitable patching mechanism to update all nodes in the system with new content and system upgrades.

M^2etis is a generic middleware for optimized event dissemination. New MMOGs can be developed based on M^2etis without the need to develop application-specific event dissemination algorithms. Instead, event types are seman-

tically categorized using a multidimensional classification schema. The middleware can then choose readily implemented dissemination strategies that fit to the specified requirements.

2. THE M^2ETIS APPROACH

Events occur between entities in the world, an entity and an avatar or between two avatars. We abstract the system to an underlying network and to channels. Therefore M^2etis may be seen as a distributed channel-based publish subscribe system, as this is a suitable paradigm in the domain of MMVEs. The developer is able to configure each channel's behavior to optimize it regarding the semantic properties of the event type it is representing. This requires the developer to describe the semantic properties of each event type at design time and an optimizer generates an optimal channel by composing it of different strategies. Afterwards the generated channels are compiled and deployed. Figure 1 shows

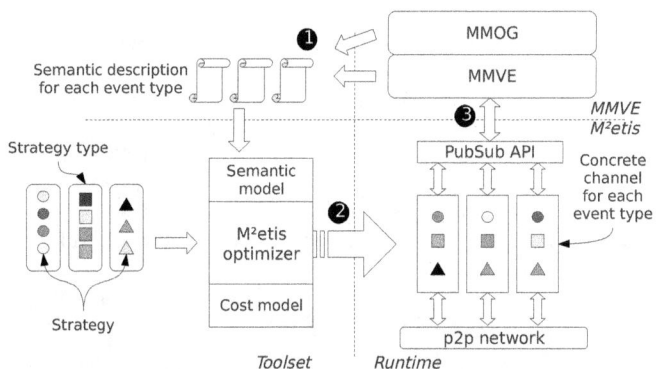

Figure 1: Architecture of M^2etis

different aspects of M^2etis. The lower left part shows the toolset of M^2etis. The toolset contains a semantic model, a cost model and the M^2etis optimizer, as well as a repository of strategy types with associated strategies. The semantic model defines the means of describing event types. In order to exploit the semantics of events, the M^2etis approach proposes a multidimensional event classification. The classification is refined from [2] to five dimensions in the context of MMVEs. The context dimension defines the set of context classes, each describing the set of nodes affected by a certain event. The Synchronization dimension describes the degree of order a certain channel provides for its context. Persistency means, each event of an persistent channel has an effect on the state of the application. Security is currently not considered in this research and therefore not described. In contrast to [2], we redefine validity as a mapping, defining all messages relayed to the application. Each dimension has a certain number of classes each defining a different semantical behavior along the dimension. An event type has exactly one class along each dimension. The cost model defines the actual rules and heuristics to rate each fitting strategy for the optimizer, taking all semantic requirements and non functional parameters into account.

M^2etis provides different implementations for each strategy type, which defines the interface of event processing for each implementation, named strategy. Strategy types are therefore sets of strategies, implementing the same functionality, only differing in their non-functional properties. Strategy types and their association with the dimensions is the step from the semantic description to the actual publish/subscribe channel. To generate a channel, an optimizer configures a channel with different strategies, one of each strategy type. The optimizer's task is to estimate the costs for each available strategy and select the best one for a certain scenario, while making sure that only strategies with the appropriate semantic characteristics are chosen. Each strategy is annotated with cost information that is used together to choose the best strategy of each type in the optimization step.

The lower right part of Figure 1 shows how M^2etis is seen at runtime. M^2etis provides a network layer for the MMVE, hiding the used *Peer-to-peer* (P2P) network with a channel-based publish/subscribe system. Every channel corresponds to an event type and is highly optimized for that event type.

The workflow for application development using M^2etis requires that the MMVEs' engineer identifies all event types which need to be distributed among the nodes of the MMVE and describes each according to the semantic model in step 1 of Figure 1. These semantic annotations are processed via the M^2etis optimizer according to the semantic model and the cost model. The optimizer assembles a communication channel for each event type using the best matching strategy for every strategy type leading to an optimized distribution for every event type (step 2). At runtime, the MMVE uses the provided publish/subscribe API to publish and receive its events (step 3) without any further knowledge of the optimizations.

3. PROOF OF CONCEPT

As a proof of applicability of the M^2etis approach, we implemented a prototypic game called *tri6*. This game is a fast-paced racing game in which each player is able to perform different actions. As discussed in the context of the architecture and usage of M^2etis, the framework is used as the networking component of this game.

The M^2etis prototype itself currently consists of the prototypic implementation of the publish/subscribe component. We chose C++ and *key-based routing* (KBR)-overlays as possible underlying networks. In order to minimize the overhead introduced by the flexibility of such a framework e.g. regarding message size or stack depth caused by function calls, we use *template metaprogramming* (TMP) and *policy based*-design to create the optimized channels at compile-time. The different optimization strategies for each dimension are implemented as policies. With TMP, it is possible to derive custom-tailored message headers, depending on the

chosen strategies. This ensures small message sizes with a high payload ratio. All described design decisions ensure a small footprint at runtime.

4. DISCUSSION

M^2etis addresses a gap in existing publish/subscribe architectures as there exist no middleware architectures using semantic classification of event types to optimize their dissemination. Existing solutions like [1, 3] use a uniform treatment of all event types. By the support of different MMVE-specific and generic strategies and the extensible architecture M^2etis tries to close this gap. One constraint of the proposed approach is the focus on simple event processing without the possibility to process complex events. As the performance requirements in the domain of MMVE are very demanding the question is whether it is desirable to process complex events. In our studies, we did not encounter any application requirements which made it absolutely necessary. The publish/subscribe paradigm also states a controversial interaction scheme, as some MMVE use a request/reply paradigm. Which paradigm is the best-fitting model, depends on the rate of subscriptions and unsubscriptions, as these form the overhead of the communication. Another point of discussion is the P2P based approach of M^2etis. In times of cloud computing one may also argue, that MMVE clusters may be extended by the usage of cloud resources. This argumentation is valid and in our opinion a field, which should be analyzed in the context of MMVEs, but our approach is theoretically applicable in cloud environments, especially enabled by its flexibility gained by the underlying network abstraction. The idea of the exploitation of the different event semantics on the other hand promises to be an approach to optimized event dissemination architectures not only fitting for MMVEs.

Based on the existing prototype, further work must be done. Currently we are adapting different existing optimization algorithms. Based on this variety of algorithms, measurements will be taken by suitable simulation. As a foundation for the planned evaluation and performance measurements, a simulator is currently under development. Another part of our ongoing research is the extension of the M^2etis system model to support stateful channels and persistence. We understand the current prototype as the first step towards an adaptive middleware for MMVEs.

5. REFERENCES

[1] A. Bharambe, J. R. Douceur, J. R. Lorch, T. Moscibroda, J. Pang, S. Seshan, and X. Zhuang. Donnybrook: Enabling Large-Scale, High-Speed, Peer-to-Peer Games. *SIGCOMM Comput. Commun. Rev. (CCR)*, 38(4):389–400, 2008.

[2] T. Fischer, M. Daum, F. Irmert, N. C. P., and R. Lenz. Exploitation of Event-Semantics for Distributed Publish/Subscribe Systems in Massively Multiuser Virtual Environments. In *IDEAS '10*, Montreal, QC, Canada, 2010.

[3] S.-Y. Hu, J.-F. Chen, and T.-H. Chen. VON: A Scalable Peer-to-Peer Network for Virtual Environments. *IEEE Network*, 20(4):22–31, July 2006.

Poster: DejaVu – A Complex Event Processing System for Pattern Matching over Live and Historical Data Streams

Nihal Dindar, Peter M. Fischer, Nesime Tatbul
Systems Group, ETH Zurich, Switzerland
{dindarn, peter.fischer, tatbul}@inf.ethz.ch

ABSTRACT

This short paper provides an overview of the *DejaVu complex event processing (CEP) system*, with an emphasis on its novel architecture and query optimization techniques for correlating patterns across live and historical data streams.

Categories and Subject Descriptors

H.2.4 [**Database Management**]: Systems - Query Processing

General Terms

Performance, Languages, Theory

1. INTRODUCTION

CEP has proven to be an important technology for analyzing complex relationships over high volumes of data in many application domains. High-performance pattern matching over live event streams has been a central focus in CEP research to date. Though a less explored research direction, archiving streams and integrating them into the live stream processing pipeline offers many new key capabilities for CEP systems. In particular, longer-term data analysis, such as making predictions about future event occurrences or identifying causal relationships among complex events across multiple time scales is beyond the scope of existing CEP systems.

In this paper, we provide an overview of the DejaVu system developed at ETH Zurich, which provides declarative pattern matching capability over live and archived streams of events. DejaVu proposes a novel integrated CEP architecture and focuses on scalable data management techniques for processing various forms of pattern matching queries over event streams. We summarize the fundamental concepts behind DejaVu's architectural design, as well as its approach to optimized processing of a useful class of hybrid pattern matching queries, namely *pattern correlation queries (PCQ)*.

2. DEJAVU SYSTEM OVERVIEW

DejaVu is a CEP system that integrates declarative pattern matching over live and archived streams of events [4]. We have built DejaVu on top of the MySQL relational database system [1]. As such, we follow the basic architecture of MySQL, while making new extensions for supporting pattern matching queries. Figure 1 illustrates a high-level architecture of DejaVu. One of the key architectural features of MySQL that we exploit in our design is its pluggable storage engine API, introducing two new types of stores:

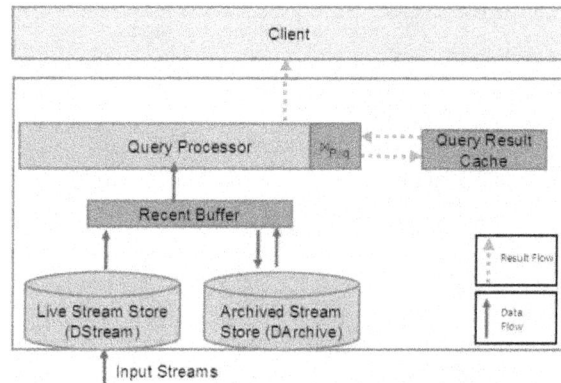

Figure 1: Architectural overview of the DejaVu CEP system

- **Live Stream Store (DStream)** is an in-memory store that accepts push-based inputs. It essentially acts like a tuple queue, providing live events into the Query Processor (QP) as they arrive. It supports both pull and push access by the QP.

- **Archived Stream Store (DArchive)** is a persistent stream store to materialize live events for long-term access. Given the predefined order of the events, it only support append updates.

Recent Buffer, an in-memory cache, mediates between the DStream, the DArchive, and the QP to provide efficient access to recent input tuples as well as handling bulk inserts into the DArchive.

Furthermore, we have extended the QP of MySQL with a finite state machine (FSM) implementation for pattern evaluation. More specifically, patterns are expressed with regular expressions and are represented with FSM operators, which are then integrated into the relevant parts of the MySQL query plan. New join algorithms are also implemented for handling pattern correlation queries. As a relational database system, MySQL is designed to work on one-time queries only. Thus, we have added query life-cycle management and continuous result reporting into the MySQL QP.

The last key component in our architecture is the **Query Result Cache**. Like materialized views in databases, it provides novel data structures to store previous pattern matches that can be reused later.

DejaVu follows a data model where streams are totally ordered sequences of relational tuples with start and end timestamps. Ensuring the total order for all streams provides DejaVu queries to be fully composable. As for the query model, in DejaVu, complex event patterns are expressed through an SQL-like declarative language that is based on a standard proposal for pattern matching over row sequences [5]. This proposal extends the FROM part of SQL with a new MATCH_RECOGNIZE clause that enables pattern specifications over the listed data sources. As an addition to the original proposal, we also allow streaming sources in the FROM part along with regular tables (see [3] or [4] for query examples). In

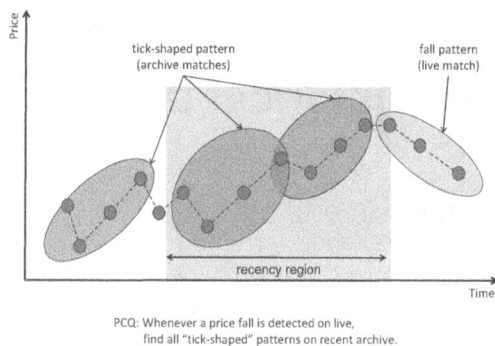

(a) Pattern correlation query

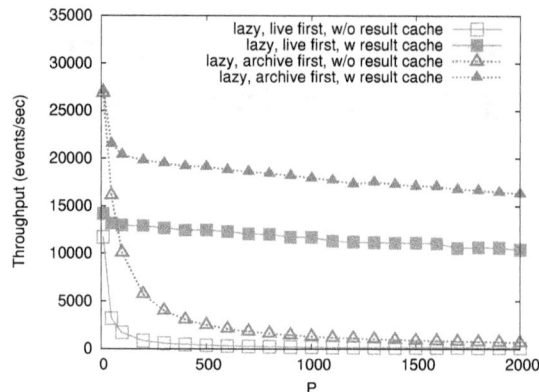

(b) Results with the NYSE TAQ dataset [2]

Figure 2: Financial use case

this case, the `MATCH_RECOGNIZE` clause in effect defines a "semantic window" over the live stream. This way, DejaVu's extended language can express a wider range of queries including hybrid pattern matching queries, such as pattern correlation queries.

3. PATTERN CORRELATION QUERIES

Correlating live and historical complex events for identifying causal dependencies between them or for predicting the reoccurrence of similar past events is a critical capability needed in many application domains such as medical diagnosis, algorithmic trading, travel time estimation for route planning. In DejaVu, we provide this capability via *Pattern Correlation Queries (PCQs)* [3].

Figure 2(a) illustrates a typical use case for PCQs from the algorithmic trading domain, where a trader would like to predict the stocks that could bring profits in the near future based on a query posed over market data events which does the following: Upon detecting a fall in the current price of stock X on the live data stream, look for a tick-shaped pattern for X within *recent* archive, where a fall in price was followed by a rise in price that went higher up than the beginning price of the fall. This use case requires evaluating complex events over live (falling) and archived streams (tick-shaped), and correlating them based on a recency criteria. The high-rate live stream and the high-volume archived stream, as well as the need for low-latency results for catching momentary trading opportunities render this use case a highly challenging one.

In current CEP systems, the only way to correlate two streams is using a join operator with time- or tuple-based windows. While PCQs can be implemented using such windows (forming all possible recency windows on live and archived streams, joining them, performing pattern processing on each joined result, and then joining the matched patterns), this approach would obviously be very costly. A better alternative would be to first apply pattern matching on both sources and then join the matched patterns using the recency window using a regular join. This *eager* pattern processing approach would be significantly cheaper, however, would still lead to processing some redundant patterns that will never contribute to the final result. In DejaVu, we instead propose a *lazy* pattern processing approach, where a pattern on one source (live or archive) is only computed if a corresponding pattern that falls in the recency window is found on the other one (archive or live). Moreover, on top of this lazy approach, we introduce three further optimizations:

- **Recent input buffering** enables the caching of the most recent stream tuples in memory for efficient access for both live and historical pattern matching.

- **Query result caching** avoids the redundant recomputation of patterns on one source that are correlated with multiple patterns on the other one.

- **Join source ordering** ensures that the source with the more selective pattern is used as the outer source to the hybrid nested loops join algorithm that implements our lazy approach, thus further reducing the total number of pattern computations.

We have implemented all the algorithms and optimization techniques summarized above in the DejaVu system and studied their performance through detailed experiments. Here, we provide a selected result for the financial PCQ illustrated above, run over a real stock market dataset from NYSE [2]. Figure 2(b) shows how throughput (i.e., input events consumed per second) changes with increasing recency window size (P). There are two important observations to make: (i) Since the historical pattern is more selective on this dataset, archive-first outperforms live-first (thus, also showing that join source ordering can yield significant performance gains); (ii) For both live-first and archive-first, using a query result cache leads an improve by more than order of magnitude.

A detailed description and evaluation of DejaVu's PCQ processing and optimization techniques is provided in a recent paper [3].

4. FUTURE DIRECTIONS

DejaVu presents a rich platform for exploring further research problems. Short-term directions include studying other forms of PCQs with correlation criteria based on, e.g., context similarity or other spatio-temporal relationships across complex event patterns, as well as providing suitable storage management techniques for efficient archive access (e.g., indexing). In the longer term, we would like to explore query rewrite-based optimizations for `MATCH_RECOGNIZE`.

5. REFERENCES

[1] MySQL. http://www.mysql.com/.
[2] NYSE Data Solutions. http://www.nyxdata.com/nysedata.
[3] N. Dindar, P. M. Fischer, M. Soner, and N. Tatbul. Efficiently Correlating Complex Events over Live and Archived Data Streams. In *ACM DEBS Conference*, New York, NY, July 2011.
[4] N. Dindar, B. Güç, P. Lau, A. Özal, M. Soner, and N. Tatbul. DejaVu: Declarative Pattern Matching over Live and Archived Streams of Events (Demo). In *ACM SIGMOD Conference*, Providence, RI, June 2009.
[5] F. Zemke, A. Witkowski, M. Cherniack, and L. Colby. Pattern Matching in Sequences of Rows. Technical Report ANSI Standard Proposal, July 2007.

Poster: Towards an Inexact Semantic Complex Event Processing Framework

Qunzhi Zhou
Department of Computer
Science
University of Southern
California
qunzhizh@usc.edu

Yogesh Simmhan
Ming Hsieh Department of
Electrical Engineering
University of Southern
California
simmhan@usc.edu

Viktor Prasanna
Ming Hsieh Department of
Electrical Engineering
University of Southern
California
prasanna@usc.edu

ABSTRACT

Complex event processing (CEP) deals with detecting real-time situations, represented as event patterns, from among an event cloud. The state-of-the-art CEP systems process events as plain data tuples and are limited to detect precisely defined patterns. Emerging application areas like optimization in smart power grids require CEP to incorporate semantic knowledge of the domain for easier pattern specification, and detect inexact patterns in the presence of uncertainties. In this paper, we present motivating use cases, discuss limitations of existing CEP systems and describe our work towards an Inexact Semantic Complex Event Processing (InSCEP) framework.

Categories and Subject Descriptors

H.4 [**Information Systems Applications**]: Miscellaneous

General Terms

Design, Languages

Keywords

Complex event processing, Semantic Web, demand response

1. INTRODUCTION

Complex event processing deals with detecting real-time situations, represented as event patterns, from among an event cloud. In recent years, research into CEP has received much attention in the research community motivated by applications in domains like financial services [2] and RFID data management [4]. Many research prototypes, and several commercial systems such as ruleCore [1] and Esper [2] have been developed.

Demand response optimization (DR) in Smart Grid is an emerging application area for CEP [5]. Smart Grid is the modernization of power grid by integrating digital and information technologies, with the deployment of millions of sensors and smart meters to monitor energy use activities.

[1] http://www.rulecore.com
[2] http://esper.codehaus.org

DR, a cornerstone application of Smart Grid, deals with curtailing power load when a peak load is encountered. Continuous data relevant to DR emanating from various sources can be abstracted as events. These may be from smart appliances (*ThermostatChange* event), smart meters (*MeterUpdate* event), weather phenomena (*HeatWave* event) or consumer activity (*ClassSchedule* event). CEP can correlate these heterogeneous events to detect patterns that predict peak load occurrences or identify load curtailment opportunities for DR in a timely manner.

Limitations of existing CEP systems limit their uses in diverse information space like Smart Grid. Existing systems process events as relational data tuples. As such, event patterns can only be defined as a combination of attributes presented in event data. In addition, most CEP systems only support precise pattern matching, without any leeway to relax pattern constraints. However, uncertainty is an intrinsic feature of real world cyber-physical applications, where potentially incomplete and even incorrect information exist, yet need to be matched within certain bounds.

An effective CEP solution for DR optimization needs to extend traditional CEP systems in two aspects. First, it must be extensible to meet the organic growth of the Smart Grid information diversity with the provision to easily model and identify new events and event patterns by both domain experts and non-domain users. Second, it should capture uncertainties of events, and relax deterministic event patterns for inexact pattern detection.

2. USE CASES

We present example DR event patterns for load prediction, curtailment and monitoring, and use them to illustrate key features that our proposed Inexact Semantic Complex Event Processing (InSCEP) framework should provide. Consider in a campus micro grid, the DR application processes information coming from sensors and equipments that report their measurements or operations. We have the following patterns,

i. *Load Prediction:* A teaching building consumes 90% of its peak load, more than 5 classrooms have high probabilities of increasing from base load according to meter readings, class schedules and weather conditions.

ii. *Load Curtailment:* The thermostat in one office room is tuned 5 degrees lower than the average set point of thermostats in the same type of rooms which were tuned in the last 30 minutes.

iii. *Load Monitoring:* Conservative curtailment patterns were applied, followed by a sequence of meter readings that indicate power load remains steady or increases.

Traditional CEP systems define patterns by specifying precise constraints of event data. However, the above examples illustrate the need to incorporate semantics and flexibility in pattern specification. The background knowledge of events from multiple domains (e.g. electrical systems, appliances, room scheduling, etc) need to be captured. In addition, flexibility has to exist to allow a limited number of errors or mismatches to still detect a relevant pattern. The need for specify such inexact patterns lies in two reasons, (1) component events can be probabilistic due to imprecise or incomplete observations, and (2) event pattern itself is uncertain and may have infinite acceptable equivalences. For instance, in the third example the sequence of meter readings need not strictly remain constant or monotonically increase. A small fraction of outsider readings should be tolerated.

3. INSCEP: SYSTEM DESCRIPTION

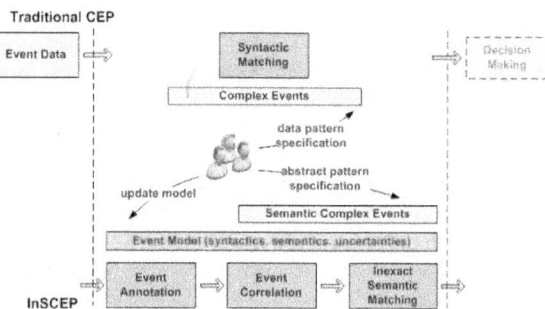

Figure 1: CEP (top) and InSCEP (bottom)

The proposed InSCEP framework for demand response optimization extends traditional CEP with Semantic Web technologies and uncertain pattern detection. As shown in Figure 1, our approach allows users to specify inexact event patterns based on a domain-specific event model at high level. As the system processes events, it *annotates source data* using the semantic event model, correlates events to *derive unobserved events* and then *performs inexact and semantic matching* to detect pattern occurrences.

Semantic and Uncertain Event Model

We develop an event model that captures semantics and uncertainties. Events are modeled using Semantic Web ontologies and represented using the Web Ontology Language (OWL). The event ontology is modular, for easy extension with new domain ontologies. The top level, core event ontology captures concepts and relationships between events. The notion of an event is classified into domain specific classes, like *ThermostatChange* event and *MeterUpdate* event. The second layer of the model are the subjective domain ontologies, which capture the Smart Grid domain entities, including grid networks, meters and appliances. The lowest level of the model captures entities in other relevant domains such as weather and transportation. Event correlations are modeled using rules represented using Semantic Web Rule Language (SWRL). We capture uncertainties of events by annotating probabilities to events and assigning confidences to correlation rules.

A formal event algebra is defined for specifying complex events that incorporate semantic and inexact query features. Some of the algebraic operators such as *Selection, Aggregation, Projection* and *Renaming* originate from relational algebra and are supported in existing CEP systems [1, 3]. The added expressive power of our algebra lies in the *Semantic* and *Inexact Selection* operators. *Semantic Selection* evaluates pattern constraints based on the semantic equivalence of attribute meanings captured by the event ontology instead of syntactic identical attribute values. *Inexact Selection* selects events and allows a limited number of mismatches to detect relevant patterns. A similarity function is associated with *Inexact Selection* to evaluate relevances between matching patterns and target patterns.

Inexact and Semantic Pattern Detection

Events in InSCEP are represented as RDF triples, accompanied with timestamps and probabilities. Algebraic expressions of complex events are mapped onto an extended version SPARQL query language.

We propose to extend existing automata and tree based matching algorithms to detect different types of inexact patterns. In particular, we generalize the NFA model proposed in [1] to match inexact sequential patterns: (1) state transitions are controlled by using both semantic predicates and similarity evaluations. A transition edge can be traversed *iff* the predicate evaluation is true and the accumulative mismatch is less than a predefined threshold; (2) it allows to skip intermediate states and transit to indirectly connected matching states.

4. DISCUSSION AND FUTURE WORK

CEP is a promising solution for demand response optimization in Smart Grid. Ease of use, expressive pattern definition and scalable pattern matching are key issues to address. We propose to enhance CEP by incorporating semantic and inexact query features to suite DR application needs. Currently we are implementing semantic and inexact pattern matching algorithm into an existing open source CEP system. Future work includes extending the simplified event uncertainty model, and combining CEP with pattern mining to assist automatic pattern discovery. The second problem is interesting because identifying meaningful event patterns manually in an diverse information space like Smart Grid is difficult. In addition, event patterns that correspond to certain interests such as predicting peak demand of a building may constantly change over time, for example, due to changes of owners and weather conditions.

5. REFERENCES

[1] A. Demers et al. Cayuga: A general purpose event monitoring system. In *CIDR*, 2007.

[2] A. Adi, D. Botzer, G. Nechushtai, and G. Sharon. Complex event processing for financial services. In *IEEE Services Computing Workshops*, 2006.

[3] Y. Diao, N. Immerman, and D. Gyllstrom. SASE+: An agile language for Kleene closure over event streams. Technical report, UMass, 2007.

[4] D. O'Keeffe and J. Bacon. Reliable complex event detection for pervasive computing. In *DEBS*, 2010.

[5] Y. Simmhan et al. An informatics approach to demand response optimization in Smart Grids. Technical report, USC, 2011.

Poster: Large-scale, Situation-driven and Quality-aware Event Marketplace: The Concept, Challenges and Opportunities[1]

Roland Stühmer
FZI Forschungszentrum Informatik
Haid-und-Neu-Str. 10-14
76131 Karlsruhe

Nenad Stojanovic
FZI Forschungszentrum Informatik
Haid-und-Neu-Str. 10-14
76131 Karlsruhe

ABSTRACT

This poster presents a novel approach for large scale, context-driven and quality-aware distributed event processing. We present the conceptual architecture of the system and mapping in an ongoing use-case deployment. In particular we give examples of the usage of the platform in this use-case. Additionally, we present the challenges and opportunities of such an architecture, namely logic-based CEP, combined with historic events and background knowledge, elastic run-time configuration in the cloud for CEP as a Service, maintenance of QoS for events, a unified language for reasoning and querying current and historic events. The approach leads to an Event Marketplace, a platform for mediating between event providers and (complex) event consumers in very large and heterogeneous environments.

Categories and Subject Descriptors

H.2.4 [**Information Systems**]: DATABASE MANAGEMENT – *Systems.*

Keywords

Complex Event Processing, Event Marketplace, Distributed Systems, Web-scale CEP.

1. INTRODUCTION

Due to a very progressive globalization (geographical, social) the context in which a service (and more generally, an actor in a process) co-exists becomes very broad. The notion of context is going beyond the local time and space into global and virtual "everything". For example, offering a customer in a restaurant something that two of her/his Facebook friends found very tasty recently in the same restaurant chain in China is an interesting opportunity for having a satisfied customer. Note that we are talking about proactive information exchange/delivery: not the customer alone, but the service she/he was involved in discovered an opportunity.

In this poster we present the concept and the architecture of a platform that can satisfy these requirements. We argue that the proposed solution can scale regarding the distribution of services (sources) and the throughput of interesting information that can be exchanged and can be easily extended with new services (openness). In addition, the platform uses its cloud-computing nature to be "elastic" and operate in the "pay as you go" mode. It

[1] This work was in part supported by the European Commission (PLAY, Grant 258659).

has governance that can enforce different non-functional quality criteria (e.g. that a *critical* event cannot be lost in this huge distributed processing environment) and we have introduced the notion of Event Level Agreement (ELA) that formalize these principles.

We can consider the platform as an Event Marketplace (similar to the notion of the service marketplace) where events coming from different producers can be arbitrary combined by different event consumers. This research has been performed in the scope of a research project the vision of which is to develop and validate an elastic and reliable architecture for dynamic and complex, event-driven interaction in large highly distributed and heterogeneous service systems. Such architecture will enable ubiquitous exchange of information between heterogeneous services, providing the possibilities to adapt and personalize their execution, resulting in the so-called situational-driven adaptivity.

In this poster we focus on deriving requirements for such an Event Marketplace and on describing its main conceptual elements. We elaborate in main details about the main advantages of the platform, its large scale distributed nature, cloud-based elasticity in processing, situational-orientation and quality-awareness, as described above

2. MOTIVATING EXAMPLE

Let us consider the following scenario as an example of ubiquitous interaction between services resulting in a more personalized service execution:

"Paul is a businessman who has been flying from Paris to New York. He used the entertainment service on board, but hasn't finished watching the movie before the landing. Two hours later he is entering his room in the downtown hotel he booked earlier and wow: the room entertainment service is ready to PLAY the movie Paul was watching in the plane – of course only the unfinished part."

Figure 1 illustrates the realization of this scenario on the example of Air France and Sheraton. Very shortly: ESB represents Enterprise Service Bus where event sources are connected to the platform, Event Cloud resolves subscriptions / notifications brokering of events in a robust, scalable & efficient way, Complex Event Processing enables the detection of complex events, Subscription Recommender suggest relevant subscriptions and Service Adaptor supports personalization of the service execution.

However, there are many challenges in the realization of this scenario. Figure 1 illustrates the most important challenges:

1. The event that Paul watched in the plane a movie is a private one and cannot be shared with everyone, but only with the parties that has a kind of partnership with Air France

2. The event that Paul entered the room must be transported for processing since it is critical for the contextualization of the situation in which a service should be personalized / adapted. Note that loss of an event is one of the problems inherent in the distributed processing.

3. The detection of the complex event that the movie in Paul's room should be continued must be performed very fast in order to enable wow effect – that Paul after entering the room immediately sees the message about the continuation of the movie.

4. From the reason of having wow effect, the complex event that indicates continuation of the movie must be transported with a higher priority through the distributed environment. Note that distributed environment introduces a priori delays in the transport.

5. The complex event pattern that combines watching the movie in the plane and entering a hotel room can be an expensive one and shouldn't be deployed all the time, but only if the context indicates that such a relevant situation appears

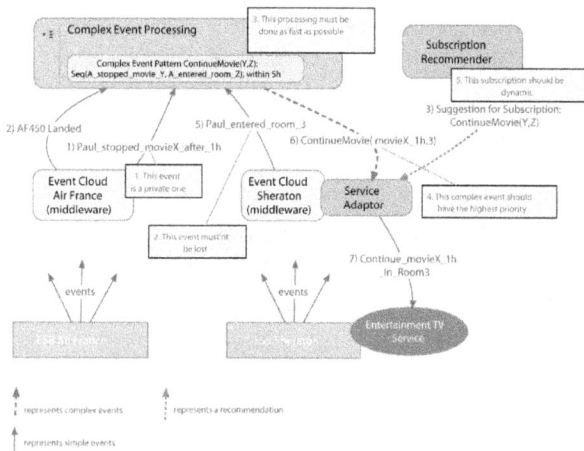

Figure 1: Critical challenges for the event interaction of our motivating scenario

3. OUR APPROACH: CONCEPTUAL ARCHITECTURE

We briefly introduce the components of our architecture:

The **Distributed Service Bus (DSB)** provides the SOA and EDA infrastructure for components and end user services. It acts as the basis for service deployments, and processes (BPEL, BPMN), routing synchronous and asynchronous messages from services consumers to service providers. Based on the principles of the system integration paradigm of Enterprise Service Bus the DSB is distributed by nature.

The **Governance** component allows users to get information about services and events, as well as specifying QoS requirements as SLA contracts using the WS-Agreement standard. The Governance component extends a standard Service-based governance tool (OW2 Petals Master) by adding governance mechanisms for event-based systems. It provides standards-based APIs and a graphical user interface.

The **Event Cloud** provides storage and forwarding of events. The role of the Event Cloud is a unified API for events, real-time or

historic. To that end, it contains a peer-to-peer network to store histories of events durably in a distributed fashion. In the same way the list of subscribers is distributed across the peers to notify subscribers if a given new event is stored at any node and a corresponding matching subscription exists in the system. Subscriptions may use a simple set of operators such as conjunctive queries which can be evaluated efficiently on a single peer. More complex queries are executed in the DCEP component.

The **DCEP** component (Distributed Complex Event Processing) has the role of detecting complex events and reasoning over events by means of event patterns defined in logic rules. To detect complex events, DCEP subscribes to the Event Cloud for any simple event defined in the event patterns at a given point in time. DCEP supports event operators such as sequence, concurrent conjunction, disjunction, negation etc., all operators from Allen's interval algebra (e.g., *during, meets, starts, finishes* etc.), window operators, filtering, enrichment, projection, translation, and multiplication. Out-of-order event processing is supported (e.g. events that are delayed due to different circumstances such as network anomalies).

4. ADVANTAGES

The main advantages of the platform will be listed here are as follows:

Semantic event format: While designing an event-based system at Internet-scale, we decided to employ widely available Semantic Web technologies to model events. RDF and its schema language RDFS are well suited for distributed Web-scale exchange of data (in our case events) between inhomogeneous systems.

Unified language for reasoning and querying: As a pattern language we are building on the language from previous and ongoing work on the ETALIS system called EP-SPARQL. It works based on logic rules and as such is well suited to reason with semantic data such as RDF.

Elastic Event processing as a service in cloud: Our platform should be able to deal with a high throughput of events utilizing computing resources in a cloud. Moreover, since events are created asynchronously by distributed sources they happen spontaneously and can dynamically alter their rate of occurrence. Therefore, reorganisation might be required at run-time. Each node has dynamic properties which will be monitored to decide when to reorganise the nodes.

5. CONCLUSION

This poster presents a novel approach for large scale, context-driven and quality-aware distributed event processing. We presented the conceptual architecture of the system. We are working on the realization of the platform and it might be that some of the challenges will evolve in our future work. In parallel we are working on sustainable business models for operating such a platform once it would be available.

6. ACKNOWLEDGMENTS

We would like to thank the whole consortium of project PLAY for their contributions to the challenges and the software architecture. Special thanks goes to Laurent Pellegrino, Francesco Bongiovanni, Aurelie Charles, Yiannis Verginadis, Louis Plissonneau and Christophe Hamerling.

Author Index

Alves, Alexandre de Castro 1
Alves, Alexandre 363
Andrade, Henrique 231, 335
Anicic, Darko 303, 379
Apostolou, Dimitris 387
Arnold, Dave 383
Artikis, Alexander 11
Bacon, Jean 159
Bashardoust, Soheila 383
Baumgärtel, Philipp 393
Berthou, Pascal 389
Bizarro, Pedro 361
Blondia, Chris 63
Buys, Jonas 63
C. Schmidt, Douglas 389
Candan, K. Selçuk 279
Candan, Kasim Selçuk 137
Carzaniga, Antonio 207
Chandrashekar, Jaideep 255
Chandy, K. Mani 89, 361
Corriveau, Jean-Pierre 383
Cugola, Gianpaolo 183, 359
Damaggio, Elio 51
Daum, Michael 393
De Florio, Vincenzo 63
De Masellis, Riccardo 51
Dehors, Sylvain 149
Dindar, Nihal 243, 399
Dou, Adam J. 347
Engel, Yagil 125
Etzion, Opher 101, 125, 365
Eugster, Patrick 113
Evensen, Pål 317
Eyers, David M. 159
Ezhilchelvan, Paul 371
Farroukh, Amer 171
Faulkner, Matthew 89
Fedorov, Sergey A. 377
Feng, Ming Whei 313
Ferguson, Donald Francis 49
Fischer, Peter M. 243, 399
Fischer, Thomas 397
Fournier, Fabiana 51, 149
Gal, Avigdor 101
Ganesan, Siddarth 195
Gayraud, Thierry 389
Gedik, Buğra 231, 267
Gehrke, Johannes 87
Gokhale, Aniruddha S. 389, 395

Grummt, Eberhard 219
Gunopulos, Dimitrios 347
Gupta, Manmohan 51
Hakiri, Akram 389
Heath, III, Fenno (Terry) 51
Held, Johannes 397
Herath, Chathura 367
Hildrum, Kirsten 335
Hinze, Annika 385
Hobson, Stacy 51
Hoffert, Joe 389
Hull, Richard 51
Iyer, Ravishankar K. 231
Jackson, Dan 371
Jacobsen, Hans-Arno 171, 195, 373, 381
Jacques-Silva, Gabriela 231
Jayaram, K. R. 113
Kaarela, Pekka 11
Kalogeraki, Vana 347
Kasi, Mumraiz Khan 385
Kepplinger, Peter 39
Kerschbaum, Florian 327
Kim, Byoungjip 137
Kim, Dae-Il 377
Kim, Jaemyung 377
Kim, Sungjin 377
Kim, Younghun 377
Klein, Rüdiger 29
Kulkarni, Ashish A. 23
Lahiri, Bibudh 255
Lakshmanan, Geetika T. 75
Landmark, Andreas D. 391
Lauterwald, Frank 393, 397
Lee, SangJeong 137
Lee, Sang-Won 377
Lee, Youngki 137
Lenz, Richard 397
Li, Ming 291
Liang, Minsiong 313
Lin, Gu Yuan 313
Lin, Ruofeng 375
Lin, Tao 291
Linehan, Mark H. 51, 149
Liu, Annie 89
Ma, Jun 379
Malekpour, Amirhossein 207
Mani, Murali 291
Maradugu, Sridhar 51
Margara, Alessandro 183, 359

McDonald, Mark P. 395
Meling, Hein 317
Mentzas, Gregoris 387
Meyer-Wegener, Klaus 393
Mielikäinen, Taneli 347
Milenovic, Dejan 303
Mishkin, Nathaniel 15
Moxey, Catherine 363
Muthusamy, Vinod 381
Nigam, Anil 51
Noldus, Lucas P. J. J. 11
Obweger, Hannes 39
Olivier, Patrick 371
Olson, Michael 89
Papageorgiou, Nikos 387
Paschke, Adrian 363
Pedone, Fernando 207
Pham, Cuong 371
Plale, Beth 367
Poff, Laura K. 395
Pollner, Niko 393
Prasanna, Viktor 401
Pu, Calton 229
Rabinovich, Ella 101, 149, 365
Radonjic, Vojislav D. 383
Rhee, Yunseok 137
Rozsnyai, Szabolcs 39, 75
Rundensteiner, Elke A. 291
Sadoghi, Mohammad 171, 373, 381
Schiefer, Josef 39
Sen, Sinan 375
Seyfer, Naomi 15
Shemrani, Bijan Fahimi 375
Simmhan, Yogesh 401
Singh, Harsh 373
Singh, Jatinder 159
Skarbovsky, Inna 365
Slominski, Aleksander 75

Soner, Merve 243
Song, Junehwa 137, 279
Spicer, Michael 335
Stojanovic, Ljiljana 303, 379
Stojanovic, Nenad 303, 361, 369, 403
Studer, Rudi 303
Stühmer, Roland 403
Sukaviriya, Piwadee (Noi) 51
Sung, Today 313
Suntinger, Martin 39
Suresh, Visalakshmi 371
Tatbul, Nesime 243, 399
Tibbetts, Richard 15
Tirthapura, Srikanta 255
Toffetti Carughi, Giovanni 207
Tsai, Gary 313
Tuulos, Ville 347
Usov, Andrij 29
Vaculin, Roman 51
Varjola, Mika 11
Venkatramani, Chitra 335
Verginadis, Yiannis 387
Verjovkin, Vladimir 377
Vincent, Paul 363
Wagle, Rohit 335
Wang, Kun 267
Wang, Xinxin 279
Watson, Paul 371
Wen, Jimi Y. C. 313
Wienhofen, Leendert W. M. 391
Wu, Chien Ming 313
Wu, Kun-Lung 231
Xie, Jingquan 29
Xu, Yongchun 303, 379
Yoon, Young 195, 381
Zhou, Qunzhi 401
Zou, Qiong 267